RO

THE R

Turkey

written and researched by

Marc Dubin and Terry Richardson

with additional contributions by

Darren Humphreys, Zoe Smith and Martin

740006434863

roughguides.com

Contents

Introduction to
Turkey

A mesmerizing mix of the exotic and the familiar, Turkey is much more than its clichéd image of a "bridge between East and West". Invaded and settled from every direction since the start of recorded history, it combines influences from the Middle East and the Mediterranean, the Balkans and Central Asia. Mosques coexist with churches, Roman theatres and temples crumble near ancient Hittite cities, and dervish ceremonies and gypsy festivals are as much a part of the social landscape as classical music concerts or football matches.

The friendliness of the **Turkish people** makes visiting a pleasure; indeed you risk causing offence by declining invitations, and find yourself making friends through the simplest of transactions. At the big resorts and tourist spots, of course, this can merely be an excuse to sell you something, but elsewhere, despite a history in which outsiders have so often brought trouble, the warmth and generosity are genuine.

Politically, modern Turkey was a grand experiment, largely the creation of one man – **Kemal Atatürk**. With superhuman energy, he salvaged the Turkish state from the wreckage of the Ottoman Empire and defined it as a modern, secular nation. Following 2011's record-breaking third successive election victory by the **AKP** (Justice and Development Party), largely supported by conservative Muslims, some secular Turks fear an Iranian-style Islamic theocracy. This seems most unlikely, however, in a country that has been a multi-party democracy for over sixty years, and successfully blended secularism, parliamentary democracy and global capitalism with Islam.

Despite official efforts to enforce a uniform Turkish identity, the population is remarkably **heterogeneous**. When the Ottoman Empire imploded, refugees streamed into Anatolia, including Muslim Slavs, Greeks, Albanians, Crimean Tatars, Daghestanlis, Abkhazians and Circassians. There they joined an already mixed population that included a very sizeable minority of Kurds. Thanks to recent arrivals from former Soviet or Eastern Bloc territories, that diversity endures. Another surprise may be Turkey's sheer **youthfulness**: more than half the population is under thirty, with legions of young

ABOVE GÖREME

FACT FILE

- Turkey covers a vast 814,578 sq km (97 percent in Asia, 3 percent in Europe). Four seas lap its 8333-km **coastline**: the Mediterranean, the Aegean, the Marmara and the Black Sea. Numerous **peaks** exceed 3000m, the highest being Ararat (Ağrı Dağı; 5165m). Turkey's three longest **rivers** – the Kızılırmak, Yeşilırmak and Sakarya – flow into the Black Sea, while its largest lakes is Lake Van (3713 sq km).

- The population of over 70 million is 98 percent **Muslim** (Sunni or Alevi), with dwindling **minorities** of the Armenian Apostolic or Catholic, Greek Orthodox, Syrian Orthodox and Jewish faiths. Besides standard Turkish, two dialects of Kurdish are widely spoken; other **languages** include Arabic, Laz, Circassian, Albanian, Macedonian, Bulgarian, Romany and Greek. Well over half the inhabitants live in cities; the four largest are İstanbul, Ankara (the capital), İzmir and Adana.

- Turkey's **economy**, rated sixteenth in the world in 2011, has undergone sustained growth in recent years. Inflation has fallen to single digits, inward investment rocketed, major infrastructure projects have been realised at an astonishing rate, and the Turkish lira has more than held its own with the major currencies.

- Since 1922 Turkey has been a **republic**. The single-chamber Grand National Assembly (Büyük Meclis) in Ankara has 550 seats, and elects the president.

people working in coastal resorts, and shoals of schoolkids surging through the city streets.

A huge part of Turkey's appeal lies in its **archeological sites**, a legacy of the bewildering succession of states – Hittite, Urartian, Phrygian, Greek, Hellenistic, Roman, Byzantine, Armeno-Georgian – that held sway here before the twelfth century. From grand Classical cities to hilltop fortresses and remote churches, some still produce exciting new finds today. In addition, Turkey holds a vast number of graceful **Islamic monuments**, as well as intriguing **city bazaars**, still hanging on amid the chain stores and shopping malls. Sadly, ugly modern architecture spoils most coastal resorts, where it's often hard to find a beach that matches the tourist-board hype. **Inland Turkey**, with its Asiatic expanses of mountain, steppe, lake, and even cloud-forest, may leave a more vivid memory, especially when accented by some crumbling *kervansaray*, mosque or castle.

Where to go

Western Turkey is the most economically developed, and most visited, part of the country. It would take weeks even to scratch the surface of the old imperial capital, **İstanbul**, straddling the straits linking the Black and Marmara seas, and still Turkey's cultural and commercial hub. Flanking it on opposite sides of the Sea of Marmara, the two prior seats of the Ottoman Empire, **Bursa** and **Edirne**, abound in monumental attractions and regal atmosphere. Beyond the Dardanelles and its World War I battlefields lie Turkey's two **Aegean islands**, Gökçeada and Bozcaada, popular for their excellent beaches, lingering Greek-ethnic identity and (except in midsummer) tranquillity.

Further south, the olive-swathed landscapes around Bergama and Ayvalık epitomize the Classical character of the **North Aegean**. Ancient Sardis, and the old Ottoman princely training-ground of Manisa, also make a fine pair, although İzmir serves merely as a functional introduction to the **central and southern**

Aegean. Celebrated Ephesus tends to overshadow the equally deserving ancient Ionian sites of Priene and Didyma, or the intriguing ruins of Aphrodisias and Labranda – and don't overlook evocative hill towns like Şirince or Birgi. Also inland are tranquil, islet-dotted Bafa Gölü, the architectural showcase town of Muğla, and the compelling geological oddity of Pamukkale, where travertine formations abut Roman Hierapolis. While the coast itself is heavily developed, its star resorts – Datça is the quietest, Bodrum the most characterful – make comfortable bases.

Beyond the huge natural harbour at Marmaris, the Aegean gradually becomes the Mediterranean. Coastal cruises make popular pastimes in brazen Marmaris or more manageable Fethiye, the principal town of the **Turquoise Coast**, while fine beaches stretch at Dalyan and Patara, near eerie ancient Lycian tombs. Further east, Kaş and Kalkan are busy resorts, good for resting up between explorations of the mountainous hinterland. Beyond relatively untouched Çıralı beach, at ancient Olympos, fast-growing Antalya sprawls at the start of the **Mediterranean Coast** proper. This is graced by extensive sands and archeological sites – most notably Termessos, Perge, Side and Aspendos – though its western parts get swamped in season. Beyond castle-topped Alanya, however, tourist numbers diminish; points of interest between Silifke and Adana include Roman Uzuncaburç and the romantic offshore fortress at Kızkalesi. Further east, Arab-influenced Antakya is the heart of the **Hatay**, culturally part of Syria.

Inland in **South Central Anatolia**, the rock-hewn churches, subterranean cities and tuff-pinnacle landscapes of **Cappadocia** await you. The dry, salubrious climate, excellent wine, artistic and architectural treasures, plus horseriding or hot-air ballooning could occupy you for ten days, including a stop in Kayseri on the way north. You might also pause at the historic lakefront towns of Eğirdir or Beyşehir, or in Konya, renowned for its Selçuk architecture and associations with the Mevlevi dervishes.

Author picks

Our authors traversed every corner of Turkey, from the bazaars of İstanbul to the resorts of the Turquoise Coast and the summit of Mount Nemrut. Here are some of their favourite experiences:

A night on the town İstanbul's Beyoğlu district (p.105) is renowned for its vibrant nightlife, at its hedonistic best on Friday and Saturday evenings.

Trails and peaks Head for the hills on a wonderful waymarked hiking trail, like the Lycian Way (p.304) or St Paul Trail (p.421), or scale alpine Mount Kaçkar (p.556) or biblical Mount Ararat (p.644).

The open range Cappadocia's big skies, rolling grasslands, plunging valleys and bizarre rock formations make superb horseriding country (p.430).

The heart of Ionia Hire a car in the pretty Aegean resort of Kuşadası (p.246), and explore three captivating Graeco-Roman sites in a single day – Priene (p.251), Miletus (p.254) and Didyma (p.255).

Best beaches Iztuzu (p.310) and Patara (p.321) are vast enough to escape the crowds; bohemian Kabak is an out-of-the-way retreat (p.304); and Phaselis is backed by a fabulous ancient site (p.350).

Ruins with a view The mountaintop sanctuary of Nemrut Dağı looks down over the Euphrates valley (p.595); the majestic Doric temple at Assos soars above the Aegean (p.203); and the ghost town of Ani stares across a dramatic gorge to Armenia (p.568).

Lakeland pleasures Famed for its coastline, Turkey also holds some beautiful lakes. Head for the relaxed resort of Eğirdir (p.416) or, more adventurously, for distant, high-altitude Lake Van (p.622).

> Our author recommendations don't end here. We've flagged up our favourite places – a perfectly sited hotel, an atmospheric café, a special restaurant – throughout the guide, highlighted with the ★ symbol.

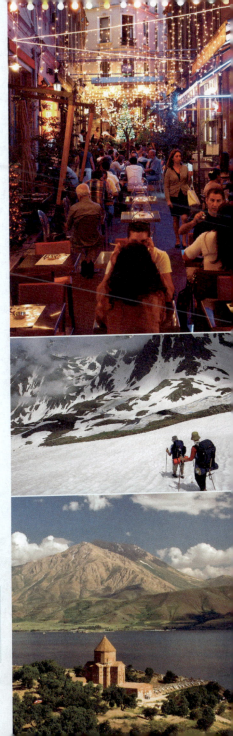

OPPOSITE EGYPTIAN BAZAAR, İSTANBUL **RIGHT FROM TOP** BEYOĞLU DISTRICT, İSTANBUL; HIKING ON MT KAÇKAR; LAKE VAN

Ankara, Turkey's capital, is a planned city whose contrived Western feel indicates the priorities of the Turkish Republic; it also features the outstanding Museum of Anatolian Civilizations. Highlights of surrounding **North Central Anatolia** include the bizarre temple of Aezani, near Kütahya; the Ottoman museum-town of Safranbolu; exquisitely decorated early Turkish monuments in Divriği; and remarkable Hittite sites at Hattuşaş and Alacahöyük. As you travel north, pause in the Yeşilırmak valley towns of Sivas, Tokat and Amasya. The lush shoreline of the Black Sea beyond holds little more than a chain of Byzantine-Genoese castles; the oldest, most interesting towns are Sinop, Anatolia's northernmost point, and Amasra. Fabled Trabzon, east of Sinop and once the seat of a Byzantine sub-empire, is now convenient for Aya Sofya and Sumela monasteries.

The Ankara–Sivas route positions you to head along the Euphrates River into the "back half" of Turkey. First stop in **Northeastern Anatolia** is likely to be Erzurum, Turkey's highest and bleakest major city, a base for visits to the temperate, church-studded valleys of southern medieval Georgia, or treks in the Kaçkar mountains. Kars is mainly visited for the sake of nearby Ani, the ruined medieval Armenian capital.

The **Euphrates and Tigris basin** have a real Middle Eastern flavour. Booming Gaziantep, offers world-class Roman mosaics, an atmospheric old quarter and Turkey's spiciest cuisine. Further east, biblical Urfa is distinguished by its colourful bazaar and sacred pool,

CAMELS

Most **camels** in Turkey are simply tourist attractions, used for pleasure rides or as photo props in places like Pamukkale and Side. It wasn't always so, however. Camel caravans once crisscrossed Anatolia, transporting gemstones, spices and woven finery. Before the Balkan Wars of 1912–13, they extended northwest as far as Bosnia, beyond which the beasts fell ill due to the damp central European climate.

In Muslim folklore the perceived haughty demeanour of the animals is attributed to their knowledge of the hundredth, mystical epithet of Allah – humans only know the conventional ninety-nine.

The sport of **camel wrestling** is a quintessentially Turkish spectacle. The bizarre sight of male camels in rut, butting and leaning on each other (their mouths are bound to prevent biting) draws vast crowds across the western Aegean region; there's even a camel wrestling league.

OPPOSITE FROM TOP TURQUOISE COAST; BLUE MOSQUE, İSTANBUL

WHO ARE THE TURKS?

Today's Turks are descended from nomadic pastoralist Turkic tribal groups that originated in Siberia, China and Central Asia, went on to conquer the Anatolian landmass, and have subsequently intermarried on a large scale with the region's already extremely heterogeneous population. Although historical records can trace them as a readily identifiable people as far back as the sixth century BC, only during the sixth century AD were they first recorded (by the Chinese) as "Tu-keh" or, to the west, **Turks**.

From around 1000 AD onwards, the Turks gradually migrated southwards and westwards. By the time they reached Anatolia, which would eventually become the heartland of the mighty Ottoman Turkish empire, most had converted to **Islam**. Turks still maintain ethnic, linguistic and cultural links with Turkic peoples in Central Asia, the Caucasus, northwest Iran, northern Iraq, southern Russia, and Xinjiang in western China.

Turkish, the official language of the modern Republic of Turkey, is neither Indo-European nor Semitic in origin, but **Altaic**, a language group that includes Japanese, Korean and Mongolian as well as the Turkic languages. Turkish Turks can still communicate with their ethnic and linguistic cousins in places like Azerbaijan, Turkmenistan and Uzbekistan, even if centuries of isolation from them, and the language reforms instituted by Atatürk in the early years of the Turkish Republic, make the task difficult. Nonetheless, Turks today still feel an affinity with their Turkic kin, and the Turkish government is the first to kick up a fuss at, for example, Chinese mistreatment of its Uigur Turkish minority.

while cosmopolitan Mardin overlooks the vast Mesopotamian Plain. The major attraction, however, is a dawn or sunset trip to Nemrut Dağı's colossal ancient statues. Between Mardin and Nemrut Dağı, teeming, ethnically Kurdish Diyarbakır nestles inside medieval basalt walls. The terrain becomes increasingly mountainous towards the Iranian frontier, an area dominated by the unearthly blue, alkaline expanse of Lake Van. Urartian, Selçuk and Armenian monuments abound within sight of the water, in particular the exquisite, restored Armenian church on Akdamar islet. The east-shore city of Van is notable for its massive camel-shaped rock punctured with ancient tombs. Beyond Van looms the

STORKS

Between April and September, **storks** are a common sight across Turkey, which forms a stopover between the birds' winter quarters in Africa and their summer habitat in the Balkans and central Europe. The clattering of their beaks is an equally common sound. Storks mate for life, and around thirty thousand breeding pairs are believed to visit Turkey, often returning to the same nest year after year to raise new chicks.

Considered lucky in both Christian and Islamic belief, and dubbed "pilgrim birds" in Turkish, they are rarely harmed. Some municipalities even build special platforms to augment the storks' favourite nesting perches, which range from chimneys and minarets to utility poles.

fairy-tale Kurdish castle of Hoşap, while just outside Doğubeyazıt, another isolated folly, the İshak Paşa Sarayı, stands in the shadow of Mount Ararat at the very end of Turkey.

When to go

Among coastal areas, İstanbul and the Sea of Marmara shores have a relatively damp, Balkan climate, with muggy summers and cool, rainy (though seldom snowy) winters. These areas get crowded between late June and early September. The popular Aegean and Mediterranean coasts can be uncomfortably hot during July and August, especially between İzmir and Antakya; in spring or autumn, the weather here is gentler and the crowds thinner, while late October and early November see the idyllic *pastırma yazı* or "Indian summer". Even during winter, the Turquoise and Mediterranean coasts are – except for rainy periods in January and February – still fairly pleasant. The Black Sea is an anomaly, with exceptionally mild winters for so far north, and rain likely during the nine coolest months, lingering as mist and subtropical humidity during summer.

Cut off from the coast by mountains, Central Anatolia is mostly semi-arid steppe, with a bracing climate – warm but not unpleasant in summer, cool and fairly dry in winter, from late November to late March. Cappadocia makes a colourful, quiet treat during spring and autumn – or even December, when its rock formations are dusted with snow. As you travel east, into Northeast Anatolia and around Lake Van, the altitude increases and conditions become deeply snowy between October and April, making late spring and summer by far the best time to visit. In the lower Euphrates and Tigris basin, a pronounced Middle Eastern influence exerts itself, with winters no worse than in Central Anatolia but torrid summers, without the compensation of a nearby beach.

CLIMATE
Average midday temperatures in °C & °F and monthly rainfall in mm

	Jan	Feb	Mar	Apr	May	Jun	Jul	Aug	Sep	Oct	Nov	Dec
İSTANBUL												
Temp (°C)/(°F)	6/43	6/43	7/45	12/54	17/63	21/70	24/75	24/75	20/68	16/61	12/54	8/47
Rainfall in mm	57.6	69.5	61.8	48.5	39.6	24.6	31	37	43.7	100.1	85.7	102
ANTALYA												
Temp (°C)/(°F)	11/52	12/54	13/56	17/63	21/70	23/77	29/84	29/84	25/77	21/70	16/61	12/54
Rainfall in mm	178	110.4	111.6	75.7	33	3	1	1	2	89.3	174.9	277.5
ANKARA												
Temp (°C)/(°F)	1/34	1/34	5/41	12/54	17/63	20/68	24/75	24/75	19/66	13/56	8/47	3/37
Rainfall in mm	14	15	20.5	25.1	24.9	16.5	22.3	7.1	25.2	19.1	26.1	30.9
TRABZON												
Temp (°C)/(°F)	8/47	8/47	9/48	12/54	16/61	20/68	23/73	24/75	20/68	17/63	14/57	10/50
Rainfall in mm	76	65.7	62.7	60.4	65	44.7	45.6	60.7	111.1	153.2	108.1	82.6
DIYARBAKIR												
Temp (°C)/(°F)	2/35	4/39	9/48	14/57	20/68	26/79	31/88	31/88	25/77	18/65	10/50	5/41
Rainfall in mm	57.3	72.5	62.4	52.4	42.6	20.2	1	5.4	2	48.5	55.4	67.4

27

things not to miss

It's not possible to see everything Turkey has to offer in one trip – and we don't suggest you try. What follows is a selective and subjective taste of the country's highlights: outstanding buildings and historic sites, natural wonders and exciting activities. Each entry has a page reference to take you straight into the Guide, where you can find out more.

1 HOT-AIR BALLOONING OVER CAPPADOCIA
Page 440
A lighter-than-air float gives an unrivalled perspective on the "fairy chimneys" and other features of the landscape.

2 İSHAK PAŞA SARAYI
Page 642
Strategically set astride the Silk Route, this architecturally eclectic seventeenth-century palace is one of eastern Turkey's most emblematic sites.

3 ORTHODOX MONASTERY OF SUMELA
Page 529
Dramatically built into the side of the Pontic mountains, this Byzantine monastery harbours excellent, if damaged, frescoes.

4 WHIRLING DERVISHES
Page 426
Members of a sect founded by the Konya-based Sufi mystic Celaleddin Rumi conduct "turning" ceremonies to effect union with God.

5 ANCIENT EPHESUS
This ancient city, addressed by Saint Paul in one of his epistles, is the best preserved of its kind in the Eastern Mediterranean.

6 LAKE VAN
The cobalt blue expanse of Turkey's largest lake is at its most scenic in late spring or early summer.

7 LYCIAN WAY
This well-marked path, suited to all abilities, follows some of the most scenic portions of the Turquoise Coast.

8 NEMRUT DAĞI
Extraordinary mountain-top temple-tomb complex that's the outlandish legacy of an obscure, ancient kingdom.

9 BYZANTINE FRESCOES, CAPPADOCIA
Cappadocia's many rock-hewn churches contain superb early Christian frescoes.

10 SHOPPING IN A BAZAAR
You may not get a bargain, but you can't beat the ba nter, especially at İstanbul's Grand Bazaar.

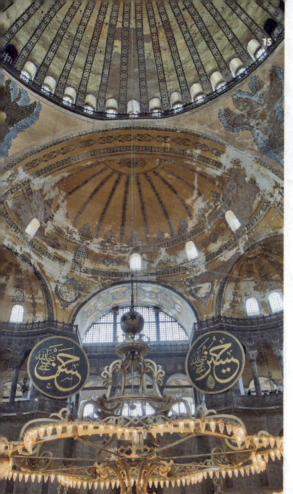

15

11 MUSEUM OF ANATOLIAN CIVILIZATIONS, ANKARA
Page 472
Home to finds of native cultures from the Stone Age onwards, this superb museum is the capital's one must-see attraction.

12 ANI RUINS
Page 568
Medieval Armenian capital in a superb setting at the Turkish border, scattered with fine churches.

13 ROMAN THEATRE AT ASPENDOS
Page 370
Anatolia's largest and best preserved Classical theatre hosts an opera and ballet festival in summer.

14 MARDİN
Page 607
Medieval houses, historic mosques and churches, and boutique hotels mingle in this hilltop eyrie, high above the Mesopotamian plain.

15 AYA SOFYA, İSTANBUL
Page 72
The seemingly unsupported dome of Aya Sofya is one of the architectural marvels of the world.

16 HITTITE CAPITAL OF HATTUŞA
Page 492
The ancient capital of the Hittites still impresses, with its extensive perimeter walls.

16

18

19

20

21

26

22 CHURCHES OF THE GEORGIAN VALLEYS

Page 546

The medieval churches northeast of Erzurum are among northeastern Anatolia's most striking monuments.

23 KARIYE MUSEUM, İSTANBUL

Page 99

The finest collection of Byzantine mosaics and frescoes in Turkey, adorning an attractive church near the city's land walls.

24 BAKLAVA

Page 40

The favourite dessert of the sweet-toothed Turks, rich, buttery *baklava*, in which thin layers of filo pastry are stuffed with pistachio or walnuts, is best enjoyed with a strong, black Turkish coffee.

25 GALLIPOLI CEMETERIES AND MEMORIALS

Page 188

Moving and unexpectedly beautiful legacy of one of the fiercest campaigns of World War I.

26 CRUISING THE SOUTHWEST COAST

Page 296

The deeply indented coastline between Bodrum and Finike is the venue for multi-day cruises on a *gulet*, or traditional wooden motor-schooner.

27 ACROPOLIS OF ANCIENT PERGAMON

Page 212

Pergamon was one of the chief Roman cities of Anatolia, and extensive ruins remain; shown here is the sanctuary of the restored Trajan temple.

27

Itineraries

By European standards, Turkey is a huge country, the size of the UK and France combined; it's impossible to see it all in a single trip. Lovers of the beach, mountains and Graeco-Roman sites will be attracted to the beautiful southwest Mediterranean coast. With a little longer you can combine vibrant İstanbul with Cappadocia's fairy-tale landscape, while adventurers with more time to spare will be drawn to the spectacular "wild east".

THE TURQUOISE COAST

Allow a minimum of ten days to enjoy the best of Turkey's Mediterranean coast.

❶ **Dalyan** This small resort, well served by Dalaman international airport, is unusually but beautifully situated on a reed-fringed river, opposite a superb ancient site and handy for the turtle-nesting beach at İztuzu. **See p.306**

❷ **Patara** A superb coastal retreat, with low-key accommodation in the village of Gelemiş, a Roman site peeking from the dunes, and Turkey's longest beach. **See p.321**

❸ **Kaş** Turkey's self-styled adventure capital, located at the feet of towering mountains, makes an excellent base to try scuba diving, sea kayaking, paragliding, canyoning or hiking the Lycian Way – or just chill. **See p.326**

❹ **Çıralı** A relaxed resort hidden in citrus groves, backed by mountains and home to the romantic Roman ruins at adjoining Olympos, the eternal flames of the Chimaera, and a great sweep of shingle beach. **See p.346**

❺ **Antalya** This bustling city is home to a superb archeological museum as well as the old walled quarter of Kaleiçi, which offers characterful accommodation, great nightlife and a tiny but pretty beach. **See p.356**

INTO ANATOLIA

With fifteen days at your disposal, you can get to know İstanbul; explore the wonders of Cappadocia; and visit the ancient treasures of the Mediterranean coast.

❶ **İstanbul** Truly one of the world's great cities, straddling Europe and Asia, İstanbul is blessed with fascinating Byzantine churches, curvaceous Ottoman mosques and bustling bazaars. It even boasts a buzzing nightlife scene. **See p.105**

❷ **Cappadocia** A unique landscape of weird rock pinnacles and deep valleys is enhanced by rock-cut, frescoed churches and entire underground cities. Two full days is an absolute minimum. **See p.430**

❸ **Konya** Once home to the founder of the mystical "whirling dervish" order, the city captivates the spiritually inclined. **See p.423**

❹ **Eğirdir** A welcome respite from a surfeit of sightseeing; most visitors to lakeside Eğirdir stay on the tiny island and simply admire the mountains, swim and eat. **See p.416**

❺ **Pamukkale** Glistening white travertine basins and hot springs form a geological wonder to match Cappadocia. The Greeks and Romans would agree; their ruined spa-city, Hierapolis, remains integral to the experience. **See p.280**

ABOVE PAMUKKALE

❻ Bodrum This former Greek fishing town is now an all-white architectural treat of a resort. Famed in ancient times for the Mausoleum of Halikarnassos, today it's better known for its club of (nearly) the same name, *Halikarnas*. **See p.261**

❼ Selçuk Charming little town with welcoming places to stay, a good museum, the Basilica of St John and the remnants of the Temple of Artemis. It's also handy for both iconic Ephesus and İzmir international airport. **See p.238**

WAY OUT EAST

To do justice to Turkey's stunning "wild east", you'll need at least three weeks.

❶ Gaziantep The perfect gateway to Turkey's east. Explore Gaziantep's Arab-like bazaars, taste some of the country's finest cuisine, and admire the fantastic Roman mosaics at the state-of-the-art Zeugma Mosaic Museum. **See p.579**

❷ Nemrut Dağı The colossal Hellenistic statues that dominate this remote mountaintop fully reward the effort it takes to reach them. **See p.595**

❸ Şanlıurfa Famed for its pool of sacred carp, this traditional bazaar city makes the perfect base to visit the unique Neolithic temple sanctuary of Göbeklitepe, and the beehive houses at Harran. **See p.585**

❹ Yuvacalı For a real understanding of what makes eastern Turkey tick head to the impoverished but fascinating village of Yuvacalı to "homestay" with a local Kurdish family, and sleep beneath a star-washed sky on the flat roof of their simple abode. **See p.591**

❺ Mardin Honey-coloured medieval houses cluster beneath an ancient citadel, looking out over the checkerboard fields of the impossibly flat Mesopotamian plain. **See p.607**

❻ Hasankeyf Going but not yet gone, this incredible medieval ruined city, perched above the Tigris, will disappear beneath the waters of a controversial dam. **See p.615**

❼ Van Explore the vivid blue-soda Lake Van and its high-mountain hinterland, studded with unique Urartian sites and atmospheric Armenian churches – notably on Akdamar island. **See p.622**

❽ Doğbeyazıt This scruffy town, close to Iran, is the base for assaults on nearby Mt Ararat, and more sedate visits to the fairy-tale palace of a Kurdish chieftain, İshak Paşa Sarayı. **See p.642**

❾ Kars Set in vast, rolling tablelands, this city was brought to life in Orhan Pamuk's *Snow*. Take a day-trip to the long-abandoned Armenian city of Ani. **See p.563**

❿ Erzurum An upland city that holds fascinating Islamic monuments and is the gateway to Turkey's best ski resort, Palandöken. **See p.546**

⓫ Kaçkar Mountains This beautiful, green alpine range, dominated by Mt Kaçkar, spangled with *yaylas* (alpine pastures), glacier lakes and flowers, is perfect for trekking. **See p.556**

⓬ Trabzon Ancient Trebizond, a fiercely proud Black Sea port, has a superbly frescoed Byzantine church, the Aya Sofya, and is the base for day trips to the spectacular cliff-hanging monastery of Sumela. **See p.520**

EMİNÖNÜ DISTRICT, İSTANBUL

Basics

Getting there

The wide range of flights to Turkey from the UK (fewer from Ireland) take between 3hr 30min and 5hr, depending on your start and end point. Only two carriers fly direct to Turkey from North America, so most North Americans reach Turkey via a European gateway airport. Many travellers from Australia and New Zealand use a Round-the-World (RTW) ticket that includes İstanbul; there are direct flights from South Africa to İstanbul.

Airfares from Europe and North America are at their highest during Easter week and from June to early September. They're lower in April and May, and from late September into October, while you'll get the best prices of all between November and March (excluding Christmas and New Year, when seats are at a premium). Australian and New Zealand fares are lowest from mid-January to the end of February and October/November; peak season is mid-May to August, plus December to mid-January. Flight comparison sites like Ⓦskyscanner.net are a good way to search for the cheapest option.

Flights from the UK and Ireland

You can **fly direct from the UK** to İstanbul (both airports), Ankara, İzmir, Bodrum, Dalaman and Antalya. Reaching any other destination in Turkey involves a change in İstanbul.

Direct, **scheduled flights** are provided by Turkish Airlines (THY; Ⓦturkishairlines.com) and British Airways (Ⓦba.com). THY links London (Stansted or Heathrow) with İstanbul (Atatürk or Sabiha Gökçen) year-round, with less frequent flights from Edinburgh, Manchester and Birmingham. Return flight prices range from £200 in winter to as much as £550 in summer, with London Heathrow and Stansted generally the cheapest departure airports. BA has three daily services from Heathrow (from around £350 return in July & Aug). Information on onward domestic flights with either THY or competitors such as Sunexpress can be found on p.35.

Budget and charter flights

Among **budget airlines**, **easyJet** (Ⓦeasyjet.com) flies from London Luton to İstanbul Sahiba Gökçen all year; from Gatwick to Antalya, Bodrum, İzmir and Dalaman (these four destinations are April to early Nov only); from Stansted to Bodrum or Dalaman; and from Manchester or Edinburgh to Dalaman (April–Oct). Advance low-season fares can be under £40 each way, though this can rise to £250 for late, summer-period bookings.

Pegasus (Ⓦflypgs.com) links Stansted to İstanbul Sabiha Gökçen daily all year, with fares likely to be a bit higher than easyJet. **Jet2** (Ⓦjet2.com) serves Dalaman and Bodrum from Leeds-Bradford, Manchester, East Midlands and Newcastle (summer only, from about £100 each way). **Atlasjet** (Ⓦatlasjet.com) also fly from Stansted to İstanbul all year, and to Antalya and İzmir in the summer.

The widest choice of **charter flights** to Turkish coastal resorts is offered by Thomas Cook (Ⓦthomascookairlines.com) and Thomson (Ⓦthomsonfly.com). With Thomas Cook, you can choose different departure and return airports and book one-way tickets. There are year-round charters to Antalya and Dalaman, while services to İzmir and Bodrum usually operate from late April/early May to late October. Peak-season prices can be as high as scheduled flights, but in winter they may drop as low as £100 return.

Flights from Ireland

From Belfast, British Airways offer year-round daily scheduled services, involving a stop in London or Manchester, but prices are high (in excess of £300 in July & Aug). From Dublin, Turkish Airlines have a direct daily flight, starting at €350. Probably the cheapest option is to use a budget carrier from either Dublin or Belfast into Gatwick, then continue with easyJet, Atlasjet or Pegasus on to İstanbul.

Flights from the US and Canada

The cheapest way to reach Turkey from North America is to buy a bargain transatlantic fare to Europe, and arrange your onward flight separately.

Turkish Airlines (THY; @turkishairlines.com) and Delta Airlines (@delta.com) are the only carriers who fly direct year-round **from the US**. THY operate twice daily flights (once daily in winter) from New York (JFK); several weekly from Los Angeles and Washington DC; and once daily out of Chicago, while Delta fly out of JFK daily in summer, and several times weekly in winter. United Airlines (@united.com) generally has the cheapest stopping fares, via Frankfurt. European carriers, such as British Airways (@ba.com), Air France (@airfrance.com), KLM (@klm.com), Alitalia (@alitalia.com) and Swiss (@swiss.com), route through **hubs** such as London, Paris, Milan and Zürich; the best choice is probably Lufthansa (@lufthansa.com) via Frankfurt.

One-month **fares** out of New York start from US$675 in winter and up to US$1800 in peak season for a direct flight with THY, $650–2500 with Delta. From LA prices range $1000–2400.

There is only one direct flight **from Canada** to Turkey: THY fly between Toronto and İstanbul several times a week, with fares from CAN$1000. Otherwise, several airlines fly to İstanbul via major European hubs. Winter fares from Montréal start at CAN$1100 and summer ones at CAN$1380, on British Airways via London.

Flights from Australia, New Zealand and South Africa

There are no direct flights **from Australia or New Zealand** to Turkey. However, several weekly scheduled flights will get you there after either a plane change or short layover in the airline's hub city – typically Bahrain, Bangkok, Singapore or Milan – before the final leg of the journey. A marginally less expensive but far more time-consuming strategy would involve taking a flight to London and then proceeding from there with, say, easyJet.

Two-stop itineraries from Sydney are around AUS$1850 in low season to AUS$2700 high season, with Malaysian or Singapore airlines. **From Auckland**, Lufthansa (@lufthansa.com), Singapore Airlines (@singaporeair.com) and Emirates (@emirates.com) fly to İstanbul from NZ$2300 year-round.

Round-the-World (RTW) tickets including Turkey use combinations of airlines, and could be worth considering for a long trip taking in many destinations; generally, some free stopovers are allowed, with fares starting at AUS$2500.

From South Africa, Turkish Airlines (@turkish airlines.com) flies five times a week **from Johannesburg** to İstanbul with starting prices around R7300 – early booking rather than time of year is the most important criterion for bagging a cheap seat. Several airlines also fly **from Cape Town**. South Africa Airways (@flysaa.com) flies daily via Frankfurt or Munich, but these are longer and more expensive.

Trains

Travelling to Turkey **by train** is slow and expensive. It only makes sense if you are a rail buff or wish to visit several other countries en route. The best route **from the UK** begins with the Eurostar (@eurostar .com) service from London Waterloo to Paris, then an overnight sleeper to Munich, followed by a daytime Euro-City departure to Budapest, and finally two more nights aboard a sleeper to İstanbul (including a change of engine in Bucharest), making a total journey of five days and four nights. At the time of writing the final leg, between the Bulgarian-Turkish border and İstanbul, was closed for line maintenance, with a replacement bus service in operation. Check the excellent @seat61 .com for more information. As each leg is booked separately, you can stop off in any of the cities where you change trains, but the cost, a minimum of £350 one-way, makes the purchase of an InterRail pass (see p.28) mandatory.

InterRail passes

The best train deal is provided by an **InterRail pass** (@interrailnet.com), which offers unlimited travel (except for express train supplements and reservation fees) on a zonal basis within thirty European rail networks. These passes are only available to European residents, and you must provide proof of residency to purchase one. To reach Turkey via the route described above, you need a Global Pass. For under-26s, a pass valid for one month's second-class travel covering thirty countries, including Turkey, costs €409 (£360); the price for over-26s is €619 (£545). A cheaper alternative is their five-days-travel-within-ten-days option – €169 (£149) for under-26s, or €259 (£228) for over-26s. It's possible to travel first class on an over-26s' pass at a considerably higher cost.

InterRail passes do not allow free travel between Britain and the Continent, although InterRail pass holders are eligible for discounts on rail travel in Britain and Northern Ireland, the cross-Channel ferries, and the London to Paris Eurostar service.

By car from Europe

You can **drive from the UK** to Turkey in three to four days. However, this allows little time for stopping and sleeping, and most travellers prefer to do it more slowly, taking in a few places en route. For customs formalities and car insurance cover once in Turkey, see "Getting around", p.30.

The all-land itinerary goes via Belgium, Germany, Austria, Hungary, Romania and Bulgaria, though a more relaxing if less direct route is through France, Italy and Greece.

Ferries

Ferries no longer run from Italy direct to Turkey, but it's possible to take a ferry from either Ancona, Brindisi or Bari to Patras in Greece, and make your way by road or rail to Athens (Piraeus). Regular ferries sail from there to several Greek islands that are linked by further ferries to Turkey (see p.29). Useful websites for information on Italy–Greece services include ⓦ feribot.net and ⓦ directferries.co.uk.

Ferries and catamarans from Greece

Many travellers take the short-hop ferries or catamarans over from the Greek islands of Lésvos, Híos, Sámos, Kós, Kastellorizo/Meis, Sými and Rhodes to the respective Turkish ports of Ayvalık, Foça, Çeşme, Kuşadası, Datça, Bodrum, Kaş, Marmaris and Fethiye. Services are daily in season (early May to early Oct) and, except for the Fethiye- Foça- and Datça-based services, still run after a fashion in winter, though you may have to wait five to seven days between departures. Although fares have dipped slightly in recent years, they're still overpriced for the distances involved; full details of every service are given at the relevant points in this book. At the time of writing **car-shuttle services** serve all the above Turkish ports except Foça, Fethiye, Kaş and to a degree Kuşadası, which only has one semi-reliable service weekly.

AGENTS AND OPERATORS

Alternative Travel UK ☎ 0207 249 9800, ⓦ www.alternativeturkey .com. Specialist Turkish travel agency, good for Cyprus Turkish Airlines flights to coastal resorts.

Avro UK ☎ 0161 209 4259, ⓦ avro.co.uk. Seat-only sales of charter flights to Antalya and Dalaman from various regional airports.

North South Travel UK ☎ 01245 608291, ⓦ northsouthtravel .co.uk. Friendly, competitive flight agency, offering discounted fares – profits are used to support projects in the developing world.

Turkish Tursan Travel US ☎ 212 888 1180. Turkish specialist consolidator, based in New York.

Package tours and special-interest holidays

Scores of companies in the UK offer Turkish **package deals**. Most of these target İstanbul and

the coast between Çeşme and Alanya, but most outfits also feature fly-drive plans. Coastal yachting (*gulet*) packages are available from May to October, while winter breaks are increasing in popularity. Inland holidays concentrate on Cappadocia, while special-interest programmes include trekking, bird-spotting, yoga retreats, whitewater rafting and battlefield tours.

Three- or four-night İstanbul city breaks start at around £130 off season for three-star bed-and-breakfast accommodation (including flights and transfers), £700-plus for boutique or five-star hotels.

Prices for a cheap-and-cheerful two-week **beach package** start at around £250 per person (double occupancy) in low season, including flights; using a four-star hotel will set you back £500–800. Quality self-catering villas tend to cost £700–1100 per person for one/two week(s), flight included, increasing to £1100–1800 at peak periods.

A seven-day **yachting or cruising** holiday will cost £650–850 per person (double occupancy basis) depending on season, booked in the UK through an agent, less if arranged in Turkey directly with skippers. **Cycling/hiking** trips vary from £300–350 for 7 to 8 days along the Lycian Coast arranged locally, to £650–750 for a higher-quality adventure booked in the UK.

Specialist holidays, relying on the services of expert natural history/archeological guides, are priciest of all, from £1200 (1 week) to over £2000 (2 weeks). All these figures exclude flights.

The best of the US-based cultural or adventure tours don't come cheap either – expect to pay at least US$5100 for a 13-day land-and-sea combo (inevitably with a couple of days in İstanbul at the start and end). The price will include all meals (excluding drinks), guides and ground transport, but not flights.

GENERAL TOUR OPERATORS

Anatolian Sky ☎ 0121 764 350, ⓦ anatoliansky.co.uk. Mid-range to upmarket hotels and apartments on the southwest coast (particularly Kalkan, Dalyan, Akyaka, the Loryma peninsula, Antalya and Ölüdeniz), classic hotels in İstanbul, and a tailor-made programme.

Cachet Travel ☎ 0208 847 8700, ⓦ cachet-travel.co.uk. Small selection of villas and hotels along the Turquoise Coast, plus guided, low-season special-interest tours, and select İstanbul/Cappadocia hotels.

Exclusive Escapes ☎ 0208 605 3500, ⓦ www.exclusiveescapes .co.uk. Perhaps the best portfolio of properties (both boutique hotels and villas) along the Turquoise Coast, as well as points west to Datça, Cappadocia and İstanbul. Noted for a high level of customer service, which extends to dedicated check-in counters at airports.

Tapestry Holidays ☎ 0208 995 7787, ⓦ www.tapestryholidays .com. Limited but carefully selected portfolio of hotels and villas along the Turquoise Coast, as well as boutique hotels in Cappadocia and İstanbul.

Turkish Collection (Ilios Travel) ☏ 01444 225633, ⊛ iliostravel .com. Top-quality (and thus pricey) villas-with-pool on the Bodrum and Datça peninsulas, plus rather more conventional accommodation at Akyaka, Kalkan and Kaş.

SAILING AND YACHTING

Cavurali ☏ 0090 542 595 7377, ⊛ cavurali.com. Turkish-American guide Enver Lucas and his father-in-law Tosun Sezen, both with years of local experience, offer bespoke sailing (and scuba) itineraries along the Turquoise Coast in a *gulet*-dive boat.

Day Dreams ☏ 01884 849200, ⊛ turkishcruises.co.uk. Large fleet of *gulets* or schooners hosting "house parties" for singles and couples; also makes on-land arrangements in unusual areas like Kazdağı.

Nautilus Yachting ☏ 01732 867445, ⊛ nautilus-yachting.co.uk. Bare-boat charters out of Marmaris, Bodrum, Fethiye and Göcek, plus set flotilla itineraries from Bodrum or Fethiye.

Setsail ☏ 01787 310445, ⊛ setsail.co.uk. Flotilla holidays from Göcek and Marmaris; also bare-boat charter.

Sunsail ☏ 0844 463 6495, ⊛ sunsail.co.uk. Flotilla holidays out of Göcek, Orhaniye and Turgutreis, taking in the Turquoise Coast and the peninsulas between Bodrum and Marmaris.

SCIC ☏ 0208 510 9292, ⊛ tussockcruising.com. Bodrum-area-based fleet of three wooden *gulets* specially adapted so that you actually travel under sail power rather than (as normally on such craft) with merely decorative rigging.

TREKKING AND ADVENTURE OPERATORS

Adrift ☏ 01488 71152, ⊛ adrift.co.uk. Whitewater rafting on the Çoruh River from late May to late July; one-week programme.

Exodus Travel ☏ 0208 675 5550, ⊛ exodus.co.uk. Strong on mountain biking and hiking along the Lycian Coast; also more conventional itineraries, staying in small hotels and village houses.

Explore Worldwide ☏ 01252 760 000, ⊛ explore.co.uk. Selection of 8- or 15-day trips, mostly in Cappadocia, the east and Lycia (including a cruising section).

The Imaginative Traveller ☏ 01473 667337, ⊛ imaginative -traveller.com. Vast assortment of 7- to 19-day tours, many pitched at families, taking in all the Turkish highlights plus some lesser known spots, makes this about the best overland group-tour operator for Turkey.

SPECIAL-INTEREST HOLIDAYS

Andante Travels UK ☏ 01722 713 800, ⊛ andantetravels.co.uk. Very comprehensive selection of itineraries covering most of this archeologically fascinating country, covering all the major (and many minor) sites, led by experts in their fields.

Cultural Folk Tours US ☏ 1800 935 8875, ⊛ culturalfolktours .com. US-based company offering up to nine annual tours (accompanied by company founder and Turkish musician Bora Ozkok) that give a real insight into seldom-visited regions of the country.

Geographic Expeditions US ☏ 1800 777 8183, ⊛ geoex.com. Offers Aegean Odyssey (taking in some Greek islands as well), or 16-day

walk-plus-*gulet*-cruises off the Turquoise Coast; four-day Cappadocia add-on available.

Gölköy Centre UK ☏ 0208 699 1900, ⊛ yogaturkey.co.uk. Yoga retreat on Bodrum peninsula offering week-long courses, also encompassing shiatsu and assorted "personal growth" themes, from May to October; budget £415–495 per person per week, including full board and activities but not flights.

Greentours UK ☏ 01298 83563, ⊛ greentours.co.uk. Three annual, one- or two-week natural-history holidays (emphasis on wildflowers), typically inland from the Turquoise or Mediterranean coasts. Enthusiastic English or Turkish guides know their subjects in incredible depth.

Holt's Battlefield Tours UK ☏ 01293 865000, ⊛ holts.co.uk. One-week tour of Gallipoli and the Dardanelles, in autumn (thus avoiding Anzac Day mayhem).

Huzur Vadisi ⊛ huzurvadisi.com. One-week yoga programmes from May to October at a secluded complex with felt yurts or nomad dwellings set around a renovated farmhouse and pool, 10km inland from Göcek. From £450 a week, including full board and activities but not flights.

Mythic Travel US ☏ 831 688 6550, ⊛ mythic-travel.com. Distinctly New Age company offering "Magic Carpets" as opposed to tours, with themed tags like "Mary and the Divine Feminine", "Jewish Life" and "Sufi Solstice".

Wilderness Travel US ☏ 1800 368 2794, ⊛ wildernesstravel .com. Three tours in western Turkey, including a 16-dayer incorporating an 11-day cruise using the same personnel and itinerary as Geographic Expeditions.

World Expeditions Australia, five city branches; New Zealand ☏ 0800 350354, ⊛ worldexpeditions.com.au. Probably the most interesting Antipodean adventure operator for Turkey: its 20-day "Turkey Panorama", including five days' trekking and three days' cruising, is one of half a dozen itineraries.

Getting around

Virtually the whole of Turkey is well covered by public transport, including long-distance buses, domestic flights, minibuses and ferries. The aged train network is being overhauled, with new high-speed lines linking the capital Ankara with İstanbul, Konya and Sivas. Late booking is the norm for public transport users in Turkey, but reserve well in advance for major public holidays – especially for flights and trains. Car rental rates are reasonable if you look around, and low-season rentals usually considerably cheaper than in high season.

By train

Turkey's train network is run by **Turkish State Railways** (TCDD; ⊛ tcdd.gov.tr). Unfortunately, a major overhaul of the network means there is much current uncertainty as to which trains are operational. As an example, until work is completed on the new high-speed line between İstanbul and Ankara, scheduled for 2015, the only option for rail travellers is to take the bus to Eskişehir and then the high-speed train onto Ankara (and vice versa). The service between İstanbul and Konya has been cancelled, though it is still possible to reach İzmir by rail by taking the high-speed ferry (see p.35) from Yenikapı and the 6 Eylül Ekspres onto İzmir from Bandırma. A useful new high-speed service also links Ankara with Konya.

Until the situation becomes clearer, in general trains are probably best used to reach provincial centres such as Adana, Kayseri, Erzerum, Kars and Diyarbakır from Ankara. These trains are slow because the mountainous terrain has resulted in circuitous routes. As a result, journeys can sometimes take double the time by road. The advantages are the chance to stretch your legs, unwind and watch the scenery unfold at leisure. To get accurate schedule **information**, especially with the plethora of delays and re-schedulings caused by the network overhaul, go to the station in person, scan the placards and then confirm departures with staff. Several choices of **seats** are available on most routes, including first-class, reclining Pullman seats; first-class standard seats (usually in a six-seater compartment) and second-class seats (generally in an eight-seater compartment). For long distances, though, it's advisable to get a **sleeper**. Cheapest are küşetli (couchettes), with either four or six bunks in a compartment depending on the route, and two-bedded yataklı (sleeping-cars) with a basin, soap, towel and air conditioning. All yataklı beds come with sheets, pillows and blankets provided, as do örtülü küşetli beds; for standard küşetli beds you'll need to bring your own bedding. For maximum privacy, and for women travelling without male companions, it's probably best to book a yataklı berth to avoid having to share. There are always (usually helpful but tip expected) porters on hand to make up beds. Note that all beds fold away in the day to convert the compartment into a seating area.

All long-distance services should have a licensed büfe wagon, offering simple meals at surprisingly reasonable prices, but it's as well to check in advance (note that most wayside stations offer some sort of snacks). On major train routes it's essential to **reserve ahead**, but unfortunately this cannot be done earlier than two weeks in advance – and it's almost impossible to arrange sleeper facilities from a station that's not your start point. It's theoretically possible to book online, but the English version of TCDD's website is so hard to use that you'd be brave to risk it (rail site Ⓦseat61.com has a step-by-step guide on this). Probably the best option for most travellers, especially for long-distance train travel, is to buy tickets from a reputable travel agency, though that incurs a small supplement.

Fares and passes

To give some idea of **prices**, a pullman seat for the lengthy 28hr, 1076km journey from Ankara to Kars (close to the Armenian border) costs ₺35.5, while a bed in a two-berth yataklı compartment costs ₺82.5. An economy seat on the Yüksek Hızlı Tren (High-Speed Train) for the 233km journey between İstanbul and Eskişehir costs ₺25, and a pullman seat on the Bandırma to İzmir (334km) train is ₺20. Buying a return ticket brings the fare down by twenty percent, while foreign **students** (with appropriate ID) and children also get twenty percent off. InterRail passes (see p.28) are valid, though a better bet for Turkey-only travel is the one-month **TrenTur** card (available at major stations) which costs ₺175 a month for unlimited second-class travel, or ₺550 for any class of sleeping car.

By long-distance bus

Long-distance buses are a key part of the Turkish travel experience and, despite keen competition from domestic flights and relatively high road accident rates, look set to remain so. Major otogars (bus stations) are veritable hives of activity, with dozens of separate companies vying for business and a plethora of places to eat, drink, souvenir shop or have your shoes shined.

The vehicles used by many companies are luxurious coaches, complete with air conditioning, though without on-board toilets. Journeys are sometimes accompanied by loud Turkish music or film soundtracks, though increasingly the better (and more expensive) companies use coaches with aeroplane-style screens set in the back of the seat in front, along with headsets. There's a choice of TV channels and films, though very seldom in English. Several companies also have free wi-fi aboard, which is of far more use to the non-Turkish-speaking traveller. Traditional services remain, however, with attendants dishing out free drinking water and cologne for freshening up. In addition, most companies serve free coffee/tea/soft drinks and cakes on board. Every couple of hours or so there will be a fifteen-minute **rest stop** (*mola*) for tea, as well as less frequent half-hour pauses for meals at purpose-built roadside cafeterias.

Bus companies are private concerns and there's no comprehensive national bus **timetable**, although individual companies often provide their own. **Prices** vary considerably between top- and bottom-drawer companies, though convenience of departure and on-board service are equally important criteria. If in doubt, inspect the vehicle out in the loading bay (*peron* in Turkish) and ask at the ticket office how long the trip will take.

Bear in mind that long-haul journeys (over 10hr) generally take place at night, and that because of rest stops buses never cover more than 60km per hour on average. As a broad example of fares, İstanbul–Antalya (a 450km trip) costs around ₺45 with a standard bus company, ₺60 with a premium company. The 1240km journey from İstanbul to Hopa, on the Black Sea near the Georgia border, costs ₺85 with a premium company.

Buying tickets

Most bus companies have ticket booths both at the **otogars** (bus terminals) and in the city centre. One of the big advantages of coach over plane travel is that, national holidays apart, you can usually just turn up at the bus station and find a seat. If you do this it's worth checking out various companies to see which offers the best price and most convenient departure – touts that work for particular companies will not necessarily take you to the office of the company that has the cheapest or soonest departure.

Unacquainted women and men are not usually allowed to sit next to each other, and you may be asked to switch your assigned seat to accommodate this convention. If you buy your ticket at a sales office in the centre of town, ask about free *servis* (service) **transfer buses** to the *otogar*, especially if (as most now are) it's located a few kilometres out. These buses will often also take passengers from *otogars* into town centres, but that system is more erratic. Of the country's two **premium coach companies**, Ulusoy (Ⓦulusoy.com.tr) and Varan (Ⓦvaran.com.tr), Ulusoy offer by far the most comprehensive network. Their seats are more comfortable than most and they don't segregate single passengers by sex. Both have online booking systems in English. Kamil Koç (Ⓦkamilkoc.com.tr) and Pamukkale (Ⓦpamukkaleturizm.com.tr) are two of the best standard outfits, though neither has online systems in English.

By dolmuş

A **dolmuş** (literally "stuffed") refers to a car or small van (*minibüs* in Turkish) that runs along set routes, picking passengers up (give a normal taxi hand signal) and dropping them off along the way (just say *inecek var* or *müsait bir yerde* to be set down). Few cities have car-type dolmuşes left – these include Bursa and Trabzon. On busy **urban routes** it's better to take the dolmuş from the start of its run, at a stand marked by a blue sign with a black-on-white-field "D", sometimes with the destination indicated – though usually you'll have to ask to learn the eventual destination, or look at the dolmuş' windscreen placard. The **fare** is invariably a flat rate (usually ₺2), making it very good value for cross-city journeys, not so great for a one-stop hop. In some cities (eg Antalya) dolmuşes have been banned because pulling in at random is both dangerous and slows traffic. Locals, confusingly, still refer to the midibuses that replaced them, and stop only at fixed points, as dolmuşes.

Inter-town and village services are always provided by twelve- or fifteen- seater minibuses, and in these instances the term "*dolmuş*" is seldom used. For the remotest villages there will only be two services a day: to the nearest large town in the morning and back to the village in mid-afternoon. Generally, though, minibuses run constantly between 7am or 8am and 7pm in summer, stopping at sunset in winter or extending until 10pm or 11pm (or even later) near popular resorts.

By city bus and taxi

In larger towns, the main means of transport are **city buses**, which usually accept only pre-purchased tickets available from kiosks near the

---

SEATING PLAN TIPS

When buying tickets, ask to see the **seating plan** so that you can choose window or aisle, a front seat (better views) or avoid certain less comfortable seats, such as those above the wheels and immediately behind the central door, which have less legroom. Even more important, if you're making a daytime trip in the heat of summer, work out the general direction of travel and try to get a seat on the shady side of the bus – a powerful sun beating down on the windows of even an air-conditioned bus makes quite a difference.

main terminals, newsagents, or from kerbside touts (at slightly inflated prices). This is certainly the case in İstanbul, where you have to use a pre-purchased token (*jeton*) or a smart travel card (İstanbul Kart). In some cities, such as Antalya, it's still possible to pay on the bus.

Yellow city **taxis** are everywhere, with ranks at appropriate places. Hailing one in the street is the best way to get a cab, but in suburban areas you can call them from useful street-corner telephones; sometimes you just press a buzzer and wait for a cab to turn up. City cabs all have working, digital-display meters and **fares** are reasonable. Each town sets its own rates, which includes the minimum charge and a unit charge for the distance covered. The main problem with using a cab is that few drivers – even in tourist areas – speak much English, so you may have to write down your destination on a piece of paper. Overcharging of foreigners is, unfortunately, not uncommon – in İstanbul and major resorts – make sure that the driver turns his meter on and (trickier) that he doesn't take you all around the houses to reach your destination.

By car

While the excellent intercity bus network makes travel between major centres easy, having a **car** allows you to visit off-the-beaten-track sites. But be warned – the standard of driving in Turkey is often both poor and aggressive and the enforcement of traffic rules arbitrary, all factors that have led to the high **road accident rate** with over four thousand fatalities per year. Driving during public holidays, especially the religious Şeker and Kurban *bayram*s, and an hour or so prior to the *iftar* (fast-breaking meal) during Ramadan, is especially dangerous.

Rules of the road

You **drive on the right**, and yield to those approaching from the right. **Speed limits** are 50km/h within towns (40km/h if towing a trailer or caravan); open road limits are 90km/h for cars, 80km/h for vans (70km/h if towing something); motorways (*otoyol* in Turkish), 120km/h for cars, 100km/h for vans and small trucks. **Drink-driving laws** are in line with those of the European Union – 50mg of alcohol per 100ml of blood – and drink-driving carries a fine of ₺590. Even so, drink-driving is a major problem; in 2010, almost 140,000 Turkish drivers had their licences seized for the offence. Front seat belts are mandatory and it's a fineable (₺66) offence not to buckle up – though few drivers do.

Traffic control points at the approaches to major cities are common. You'll probably be waved through simply upon showing your foreign ID, especially if it's a rental car. Make sure the rental company provides the insurance certificate, the pollution compliance certificate (*eksoz muayene tasdiknamesi*), and the vehicle registration, or certified copies thereof.

Speeding fines, levied on a sliding scale according to how far above the limit you were, are heavy, with penalties of up to ₺300 (though there's a considerable "discount" if the fine is paid within ten days). Usually you'll be given a ticket, which you take to a designated bank to pay. Jumping a red light carries a fine of ₺140.

If you have an accident serious enough to immobilize you and/or cause major damage to other people's property, the traffic police will appear and administer alcohol tests to all drivers, results of which must also be submitted along with an official **accident report** (*kaza raporu*) in order to claim insurance cover. It used to be an offence to move a vehicle involved in a car crash before the police showed up, but if there is only minor damage it is now OK to do so providing you have exchanged details with the other driver.

Heed the signposted **no-parking zones**, especially in resorts, as towing is common and although the fines are not too heavy the hassle of finding the pound and negotiating language barriers is considerable. Generally, it's wisest to patronize the covered (*katlı*) or open *otoparks*. In open car parks you may well be required to leave your keys so the attendant can move your car. If you leave your car in the street in some towns and cities, you may return to find a chit on your windscreen (typically ₺5), to be paid to the roving attendant.

Road conditions

Road conditions have improved enormously over the last few years, with better surfaces and more and more dual carriageways. On both single and dual carriageways there's usually a hard-shoulder area to the right of the driving lane, and often slower-moving vehicles pull into this to allow impatient drivers to overtake. Be very wary of doing this, especially at night, as you might find yourself ploughing into pedestrians or parked/broken-down vehicles. With continual road improvements being made countrywide, roadworks are often a (sometimes dangerous) nuisance – especially in the southeast. Sizeable archeological sites are usually marked by large white-on-brown-field signs, but side roads to minor sites or villages are often poorly signposted.

ROAD SIGNS

Dur	Stop
Tek yön	One way
Çıkmaz sokak	Dead end/cul-de-sac
Yol kapalı	Road closed
Yol boyunca	Road narrows
Tırmanma şeridi	Overtaking lane
Araç çıkabılır	Vehicles exiting
Yaya geçidi	Pedestrian crossing
Yol yapımı	Roadworks
Bozuk satıh	Rough surface
Düşük banket	Abrupt verge/shoulder
Şehir merkezi	City centre
Park yapılmaz/ edilmez	No parking
Araç giremez	No entry
Araçınız çekilir	Your car will be towed
Giremez	No entry
Askeri bölge	Military zone
Heyelan bölgesi, heyelanlı bölge	Landslide zone

Typical **hazards** include drivers overtaking right, left and centre, failure to signal and huge trucks. Small-town driving hazards include suicidal pedestrians, horse-carts, speeding scooters and motorcycles (often with the entire family astride one vehicle) and tractors.

Toll highways, marked with white-on-green signs, are well worth the modest fees but to use them you'll need to buy a KGS (*Kartlı Geçis Sistemi*) smart card, as many toll booths will not accept cash. They are available from some rental outlets, several banks including Halkbank, İşbankası, Garanti Bankası and Ziraat Bankası, and some toll booths, and can be topped up at "*KGS dolum noktası*" machines at many motorway service stations.

Main toll roads include İstanbul–Ankara, İstanbul–Edirne; Adana–Gaziantep; Adana–Pozanti through the Cilician Gates; İzmir–Çeşme; and İzmir–Denizli.

Night driving is best not attempted by beginners – be prepared for unlit vehicles, glare from undipped lights, speeding intercity coaches and trucks and, in rural areas, flocks of sheep and goats and unlit tractors. Warning triangles are obligatory; make sure you put it on the road behind your vehicle following a flat, breakdown or accident, and ensure your rental car has one.

Fuel and repairs

Filling stations are commonplace and open long hours, so it's difficult to run out of fuel. Fuel costs are very high owing to high taxes, and even diesel (*mazot or dizel*) is ₺4.1 per litre. Petrol (*benzin*),

available in four-star (*süper*) and lead-free (*kurşunsuz*) grades, goes for around ₺4.6 per litre. Rental cars generally use unleaded, but in some remote eastern areas it may be difficult to find.

In western Turkey, roadside **rest-stop culture** conforming to Italian or French notions is the norm. You can eat, pray, patch a tyre, phone home, shop at mini-marts and, sometimes, even sleep at what amount to small hamlets (essentially the descendants of the medieval *kervansarays*) in the middle of nowhere. In the east you'll find more basic amenities.

Credit and debit cards (Visa Electron, Visa and MasterCard but also American Express) are widely honoured for fuel purchases in much of Turkey (chip-and-PIN protocol is the norm), but carry cash in more remote rural areas and the east.

Car **repair workshops** are located in industrial zones called *sanayis* at town outskirts. To repair a punctured tyre (a common event in Turkey) head to a *lastıkçı* (tyre workshop); new tyres for small cars start from ₺95. Always check that the spare and toolkit are sound and complete before leaving the rental agency.

Car rental

To rent a car you need to be at least 21 with a **driving licence** held for at least one year. Your home country licence should be enough, but it is very helpful, especially at traffic-control points, to be able to show an international driver's permit (IDP). A compact car rented from a major chain on the Aegean and Mediterranean coast will cost around €75 per day or €395 per week in high season (April–Oct), less in low season. Rent a car from a local firm in low season and you may be able to find something for around €30 a day, €40 in high season. Diesel-fuelled rental cars are becoming more widely available at a premium but are well worth considering if you intend doing a lot of kilometres. If you pick up a car at one of İstanbul's two airports (and think carefully before you do so, the city traffic is horrendous, parking and route-finding difficult and accidents commonplace), you will be required to buy a KGS card for ₺35, otherwise you won't be able to leave the motorway at the exit booth – most do not accept cash!

Some rental companies allow rental in one town and drop-off in another – at a premium. The international players like Hertz have outlets at many of Turkey's airports as well as downtown/resort offices; local outfits (some of which also offer advance, online booking services) may not have an office in the airport but with advance booking will bring the car to the airport and have someone meet you outside arrivals. Be warned: tanks are sometimes near empty so you need to fill up right away.

When checking any car out, agency staff should make a thorough note of any **blemishes** on the vehicle – go around the vehicle with them when they do this as you may be liable for scratches and dents not noted at the time of rental. Basic **insurance** is usually included, but CDW (Collision Damage Waiver) is not, and given typical driving conditions taking this out is virtually mandatory. Along with KDV (Value Added Tax), all these extras can push up the final total considerably. Rental insurance never covers smashed windscreens or ripped tyres.

By bicycle and motorcycle

Touring Turkey by **bicycle** is perfectly possible for experienced cyclists, so long as you avoid the hottest months, the busiest roads and don't expect any kind of deference from motorists. Be prepared to do your own repairs as local mechanics experienced in working on state-of-the-art bikes are thin on the ground and confined to big cities such as Ankara, Antalya, İstanbul and İzmir. There is a well-developed home-grown mountain bike industry, and spares by such as Shimano are readily found in the big cities. Indeed, unless you're passing through Turkey or are a real bicycle freak, it's worth considering buying a home-grown model here, as that way the spares and repairs will be less problematic. Reasonable bikes start from ₺350, though imported models are likely to be far more expensive than you could buy at home. In cities, lock your bike; in rural areas theft is not likely to be a problem, even if the curious stares of incredulous locals could be. **Bikes-rental facilities** are few and far between in Turkey; a notable exception is Cappadocia, particularly Göreme (see p.440), and there are outlets in bigger resorts such as Antalya.

Given Turkey's road conditions, only confident, experienced **motorcyclists** should consider driving here. Plenty of visitors risk a day or two on a **scooter** in resort areas. In larger resorts and big cities there will be at least one motorbike **rental agency**, or a car-rental company that also rents out motor-scooters and mopeds (*mobilet*). You'll need an appropriate driving licence, and most companies insist that it has been held for at least a year. As with cars, always check the bike for scratches and dents before renting it. Helmets are mandatory, despite the endless numbers of helmet-less riders you'll see.

By ferry

Turkey's domestic **ferry network** is confined to İstanbul and the Sea of Marmara. Şehir Hatları (Ⓦsehirhatlari.com) operates ferries along the Bosphorus, between the European and Asian sides of the same strait, and to the Princess Islands. Longer runs across the Sea of Marmara to Yalova (for Termal & İznik), Mudanya (for Bursa) and Bandırma (for the Aegean coast) are the preserve of İstanbul Deniz Ötobüsleri (Ⓦido.com.tr) sea-buses. Any of the trans-Marmara car-ferry links save time compared to the dreary, circuitous road journey, but are relatively expensive with a vehicle.

Private companies offer services from the Mediterranean town of Taşucu to Girne in Northern Cyprus year-round, and catamarans run from the resort of Alanya in the summer months.

By plane

Travel by air is becoming the norm in what is a very big country, and makes sense for those on a tight schedule or who wish to visit far-flung places like Van or Erzurum. **Turkish Airways** (Türk Hava Yolları or THY; ☎0212 225 0566, Ⓦthy.com) offers the most comprehensive domestic flight network, though most flights from the west of the country are routed through either İstanbul or Ankara. THY faces stiff competition from private airlines, and has set up its own budget wing, **Anadolujet** (☎444 2538, Ⓦanadolujet.com.tr), which covers many of the same domestic routes as its parent, with Ankara as the hub.

Sunexpress (☎444 0797, Ⓦwww.sunexpress .com), which has direct flights from the Mediterranean gateway resort of Antalya to Adana, Ankara, Bodrum, Dalaman, Diyarbakir, Erzurum, Gaziantep, Hatay (Antakya), İstanbul, İzmir, Kars, Kayseri, Malatya, Mardin, Samsun, Trabzon and Van, was set up jointly by THY and Lufthansa.

Of the private airlines, **Onur Air** (☎0212 663 2300, Ⓦonurair.com.tr) offers direct flights from İstanbul to the following destinations: Adana, Antalya, Diyarbakır, Erzurum, Gaziantep, İzmir, Kayseri, Kars, Malatya, Samsun and Trabzon.

Atlasjet (☎444 0387, Ⓦatlasjet.com) covers the same destinations plus Nevşehir, Sivas and Van, while **Pegasus** (☎444 0737, Ⓦflypgs.com) covers Adana, Ankara, Antalya, Bodrum, Gaziantep, İzmir, Kayseri, Trabzon and Van.

Fares with THY are reasonable – for example, promotional one-way fares from İstanbul to Antalya (tax inclusive) are ₺94, though more usual prices are from ₺124. THY also offers variable student, youth and family discounts. Fares with Atlas, Onur, Pegasus and Sunexpress also start from as low as ₺59 one way (occasionally less if there's a special offer), and are very good value.

The key to finding cheap economy fares is early booking – generally six weeks to a month prior to departure, except at peak holiday periods when earlier booking is advised. These fares are often comparable to, if not cheaper than, inter-city bus fares, though getting to and from some airports by cab adds to the cost considerably.

Beware, last-minute cancellations (by text message in Turkish) are not unknown, particularly with Sunexpress. You're told to appear at the airport 1hr 30min before your departure, but an hour is usually adequate leeway for completing security procedures. Baggage allowances vary between companies – usually it's either 15 or 20kg, but make sure you check to avoid unwanted extra baggage charges.

Be sure to remember that İstanbul has two airports (see p.112), one on the Asian and one on the European side. Some carriers use both airports, Sunexpress only Sabiha Gökçen on the Asian side of the city.

Accommodation

Simply turning up and finding a bed for the night is generally not a problem in Turkey, except in high season at the busier coastal resorts and larger cities such as İstanbul. Many places have internet booking services so you can reserve a room ahead if you want to be sure. Despite Turkey's buoyant economy, prices remain good value by most Western European standards, though İstanbul can be very expensive. In most of the larger coastal resorts, the big cities and well-touristed inland areas such as Cappadocia, a wide range of accommodation is available, from humble pansiyons (guesthouses) to five-star hotels. In relatively untouristed towns of the interior, however, there's often little choice between fleapits or four-star luxury.

Rooms are generally on the small side by European standards, with dim lighting and rarely enough power points. In the newer, three- to five-star establishments **single rooms** generally go for just over half the price of a double, since proprietors are well used to lone (male) business travellers. Rooms with **en-suite bathrooms** generally cost about 25 percent more than unplumbed ones; triples are also usually available, costing about thirty percent more than a double.

To avoid **noise**, pick a room away from main thoroughfares and/or an adjacent mosque. You won't cause offence by asking to see another room, and never agree on a price for a room without seeing it first. Though break-ins aren't the norm in Turkey, **security** should be at least a token consideration.

Hot water (*sıcak su*) is not always reliable, even in starred hotels, as the solar-powered systems ubiquitous in coastal resorts struggle to cope with demand – check to see if there's an electric back-up. Plumbers quite frequently pipe the taps up the wrong way round, so check that the tap that should be hot is not the cold! Bathtubs and sinks seldom have plugs, so bring a universal plug from home. Especially on the south and southwest coast, **air conditioning** (a/c) is found in most accommodation, even *pansiyons*, though some charge extra for this as electricity prices are so high. **Double beds** for couples are becoming more popular; the magic words are *Fransiz yatak* ("French" bed). Incidentally, in some conservative rural areas, hotel management may refuse to let a heterosexual couple share a room unless there is documentary evidence that they are married. A law exists to this effect, so it's no use arguing the toss.

Touts can be a nuisance in places on the backpacker trail (for example Cappadocia, Selçuk and Eğirdir), greeting weary travellers off the long-distance bus with offers of accommodation. It's best to ignore them and use the recommendations in this guide. If you do decide to check out the accommodation offered by a tout, make sure it's up to standard before accepting – there will be plenty more choice available.

Lift/elevator buttons can be a source of potential confusion. "Ç" stands for "call", a lit-up "K" means the car is already on your floor; an illuminated "M" means "in use"; "Z" stands for ground floor; and "A" means the mezzanine floor.

Hotels

Turkish hotels are graded on a scale of one to five stars by the Ministry of Tourism; there is also a lower tier of unstarred establishments rated by municipalities. At the **four- and five-star** establishments expect to pay from €110–180 at the lower end of the scale to €200–500 for restored palaces or very upmarket boutique hotels. **Two- or three-star** outfits (€50–90) are more basic; no tubs in bathrooms and more spartan breakfasts, though in resort areas they may have a small pool, terrace and bar. The walk-in price of three-star and up hotels is always much higher than if it is pre-booked, but if the hotel is slack you may be able to negotiate a much better deal.

Boutique hotels are popping up all over the place, especially in restored old mansions in such places as Amasya, Cappadocia, Gaziantep, İstanbul, Mardin, Safranbolu and Urfa. However, the term is overused to market any accommodation that has been done up in a minimalist or modernist style, and prices vary widely accordingly.

The **unrated hotels** licensed by municipalities can be virtually as good as the lower end of the one-star class, and most have en-suite bathrooms, televisions and phones (€35–45). Others though, at the very bottom end of the market, will have a basin in the room but shared showers and (squat) toilet down the hall, with prices ranging between €20 and €30. Most solo female travellers will feel uncomfortable in unstarred and even many one- and two-star hotels, especially in less touristed parts of the interior.

Pansiyons and apartments

Often the most pleasant places to stay are **pansiyons** (pensions), small guesthouses common in touristy areas. These usually have en-suite facilities, and many feature common gardens or terraces where breakfast (usually, but not always, included in the price) is served. Rooms tend to be spartan but clean, furnished in one-star hotel mode and always with two sheets (*çarşaf*s) on the bed. Hot water is always available, though with solar-powered systems not always when you want it. Many have air conditioning, often for a supplement.

Particularly when it comes to family-run pensions, you may well find that the proprietor has links with similar establishments in other towns; often he/she will offer to call ahead to arrange both a stay and a transfer from the *otogar* for you. This informal network is a good way of avoiding the hassle with touts and a late-night search for a comfy bed.

Self-catering apartments are widespread in coastal resorts, and are mostly pitched at vacationing Turks or foreigners arriving on pre-arranged packages. Some are available to walk-in trade – local tourist offices maintain lists.

Apart from the weekly price the major (negotiable) outlay will be for the large gas bottle feeding the stove. Ensure, too, that kitchens are equipped well enough to make them truly self-catering.

Hostels, lodges and treehouses

While there are only a handful of internationally affiliated, foreigner-pitched hostels in the country, this gap has been amply filled by **backpackers' hostels**, found most notably in İstanbul, Çanakkale, Selçuk, Köyceğiz and Fethiye. Often 1970s *pansiyon*s that have been adapted to feature multi-bedded rooms, laundry and internet facilities, self-catering kitchen, tours and lively bars, they can be fair value – costs vary €10–18 per head in a large dorm, considerably more for a double room.

In recent years, a large number of **trekkers' lodges** have sprung up in the foothills of the Kaçkar mountains, especially on the south slope, and along the Lycian Way. These generally offer a choice between communal sleeping on mattresses arrayed on a wooden terrace, or more enclosed double to quadruple rooms without en-suite facilities – strangely, cooking facilities may often also be absent. Costs are generally comparable to the backpackers' hostels, though some are far more expensive.

So-called **"treehouses"**, usually just elevated shacks, are found principally on the southwest coast between Antalya and Fethiye. Some have dorm rooms while an increasing number are designed for two people and have doors, windows, electricity, air conditioning and, rarely, en-suite facilities.

Campsites

In areas frequently visited by independent travellers, *pansiyon*s and hostels with gardens will often allow **camping**. Charges run from a couple of euros to €7 per head in a well-appointed site at a major resort; you may also be charged to park your vehicle. The most appealing campsites are those run by the **Ministry of Forestry**, open April to October inclusive; look for brown wooden signs with yellow lettering. Twenty of them are sited in shady groves at strategic locations (mostly coastal) across the west of the country, and they make an ideal choice if you have your own transport, especially a combi-van or car and caravan.

Camping rough is not illegal, but hardly anybody does it except when trekking in the mountains, and, since you can expect a visit from curious police or even nosier villagers, it's not really a choice for those who like privacy.

Food and drink

Turkish food is among the best in the world and is sometimes ranked alongside French and Chinese as one of the world's three great cuisines. Many venerable dishes are descended from Ottoman palace cuisine. The quality of produce is exceptional, with most ingredients available locally. Eating out is often very good value and many locals do so frequently. The cheapest sit-down meals are to be found in establishments which do not serve alcohol (içkisiz), where it's possible to find a hearty three-course meal for ₺18 (€9). However, you'll often pay considerably more in resorts not so frequented by Turkish tourists. It's easy to get stuck in the kebab rut, but show a little adventure and there are plenty of dishes available – more than enough to satisfy all but the strictest vegetarians.

Places to eat and specialities are summarized below, but for a full **menu reader**, turn to p.705. Generic "Mediterranean" restaurants and burger/pizza/coffee chains, needing no translation, are almost everywhere.

Breakfast

The standard "Turkish" **breakfast** (kahvaltı) served at modest hotels and pansiyons usually comprises a basket of soft white bread, a pat of butter, a slice or two of feta-style cheese and salami, a dab of pre-packed jam, a scattering of black olives, a boiled egg and a few slices of tomato and cucumber. Only tea is likely to be available in quantity, and extras such as omelette will probably be charged for.

Things are far more exciting in the better hotels, where you can expect a range of breads and pastries, fresh fruit slices, a choice of olive and cheese types, delicious fresh yoghurt, dried fruits and nuts, and an array of cold and hot meats, plus eggs in various styles, though freshly squeezed orange or pomegranate juice will be extra. Turks are very fond of their breakfast, and often on a Sunday invite friends or family round for a big spread. Alternatively, they head out en masse to cafés that offer a full Turkish-style breakfast deal for as little as ₺10.

Street food

Unlike in Britain, **kebabs** (kebap in Turkish) are not generally considered takeaway food unless wrapped in dürüm, a tortilla wrap-like bread; more often you'll find döner or köfte in takeaway stalls, served on a baguette. A **sandwich** (sandviç) is a baguette chunk with various fillings (often kokoreç – stuffed lamb offal – or fish). In coastal cities deep-fried **mussels** (midye tava) are often available, as are midye dolması (mussels stuffed with rice, pine nuts and allspice) – best avoided during summer because of the risk of food poisoning. In İstanbul and some other cities, look out for vendors (often street-carts) selling nohutlu pilav (pilau rice with chickpeas) and roast chestnuts.

A flat, pizza-like bread stuffed with various toppings, **pide** is served to diners in a pideci or pide salonu from 11am onwards. Its big advantage is that this dish is always made to order: typical styles are kaşarlı or peynirli (with cheese), yumurtalı (with egg), kıymalı (with mince) and sucuklu (with sausage).

Other specialities worth seeking out include **mantı** – the traditional Central Asian, meat-filled ravioli, served drenched in yoghurt and spice-reddened oil – and **gözleme**, a stuffed-paratha-like delicacy cooked on an upturned-wok-style dish.

Restaurants

A "**restoran**", denoting anything from a motorway-bus pit stop to a white-tablecloth affair, will provide ızgara yemek or meat dishes grilled to order. **Kebapçıs** traditionally specialize in kebabs and at their most basic offer only limited side dishes – sometimes just salad, yoghurt and a few desserts. Many today, however, are veritable palaces, where you'll get a free flat-bread to tear, share and mop up a few simple dips, then choose from a menu

---

BARGAIN BREAKFAST BITES

The classic budget breakfast is the national dish of **simit**, a bread ring coated in sesame seeds. These are usually sold by street vendors for ₺1 or less, and can be enlivened by a processed cheese triangle – a surprisingly good combo. Another favourite is **börek**, a rich, flaky, layered pastry containing bits of mince or cheese, often available from specialist büfes (snack-cafés) for ₺2 and up. Bakers (fırıncı) are a great source of **poğça** (soft rolls usually filled with either cheese, olive spread or a spicy potato mixture) for ₺1 and up. A winter warmer favourite is a bowl of **çorba** (soup), invariably lentil with a lemon wedge, for around ₺4.

including soups, all kinds of kebabs, *köfte* (meatballs), *lahmacun* (a flat-bread "pizza" topped with spicy mincemeat) and *pide*. A **lokanta** is a restaurant emphasizing *hazır yemek*, pre-cooked dishes kept warm in a steam-tray. Here also can be found *sulu yemek*, "watery food" – hearty meat or vegetable stews. Despite their often clinical appearance, the best *lokanta*s may well provide your most memorable taste of Turkish cooking. **İskembe salonus** are aimed at revellers emerging from clubs or taverns in the early hours, and open until 5am or 6am. Their stock-in-trade is tripe soup laced liberally with garlic oil, vinegar and red pepper flakes, an effective hangover cure. A **çorbacı** is a soup kitchen.

Another kind of place that has become very popular over the last few years is **Ev Yemekleri** (home-cooked foods) cafés. Typically these are run by women and dish up good-value meals more typical of those you'd find in a Turkish home rather than a standard restaurant, with *hazır* and *sulu yemek*, *börek*, *dolma* (stuffed vegetables) and *mantı* all usually figuring. Many feature excellent-value three-course lunches for as little as ₺6.

At an **ocakbaşı**, the grill and its hood occupy centre-stage, as diners watch their meat being prepared. Even more interactive is the **kendin pişir kendin ye** (cook-it-and-eat-it-yourself) establishment, where a *mangal* (barbecue with coals), a specified quantity of raw meat, plus *kekik* (oregano) and *kimyon* (cumin) are brought to your outdoor/indoor table.

Meyhanes are taverns where eating is on a barely equal footing to tippling. Once almost solely the preserve of men, the fancier İstanbul ones, as well as some in the bigger cities and resort towns of Western Turkey, are frequented by "respectable" Turkish (and foreign) women. They can be great fun as well as dishing up excellent food. Plenty of *meyhanes* are not really suitable for foreign couples or female travellers, however, so examine the place before making your choice. **Balık Restoran** (fish restaurants) are ubiquitous in Western Turkey, made viable by the fish-farming industry, which produces an endless supply of sea bass and sea bream.

Prices vary widely according to the type of establishment. Expect to pay from ₺7 for a hearty *pide* in a *pideci*, ₺10 and up for a kebab or *köfte*. A simple grill or kebab in a licensed restaurant is likely to be twenty percent more expensive than in an unlicensed *kebabcı*. A *meyhane* meal is likely to set you back ₺25–30 for the food, plus whatever you drink. Many have set deals, typically involving an array of cold and hot *meze*, a grilled-fish main and fruit dessert for around ₺80 – which includes as many local drinks as you desire. A main course in a *hazır yemek* joint usually costs around ₺5 for a vegetable dish, ₺8 and up for meat. A meal in a flashy fish restaurant serving wild-caught rather than farmed fish may set you back well over ₺100 without drinks.

Dishes and specialities

The most common **soups** (*çorbas*) are *mercimek* (lentil), *ezo gelin* (a thick rice and vegetable broth – an appetizing breakfast) and *işkembe* (tripe). *Çoban* (shepherd's) *salatası* means the ubiquitous, micro-chopped cucumber, tomato, onion, pepper and parsley **salad** (approach the peppers with caution); *yeşil* (green) salad, usually just some *marul* (lettuce), is less often available. The more European *mevsim salatası* ("seasonal" salad) – perhaps tomato slices, watercress, red cabbage and lettuce hearts sprinkled with cheese and drenched in dressing – makes a welcome change from "shepherd's" salad.

Meze and vegetable dishes

Turkey is justly famous for its **meze** (appetizers). Found in any *içkili restoran* or *meyhane* (and some unlicensed places as well), they are the best dishes for vegetarians, since many are meat-free.

Common platters include *patlıcan salatası* (aubergine mash), *piyaz* (white haricot vinaigrette), *semizotu* (purslane weed, usually in yoghurt), *mücver* (courgette croquettes), *sigara böreği* (tightly rolled cheese pastries), *imam bayıldı* (cold baked aubergine with onion and tomato) and *dolma* (any stuffed vegetable, but typically peppers or tomatoes).

WAITER TRICKS

Fancy, and not so fancy, restaurants sometimes levy both a *küver* (cover charge) *and* either a *garsoniye* ("waiter" charge) or *servis ücreti* (service charge, typically ten percent), though if it's not documented in writing on the menu, technically you don't have to pay this. At places without **menus** (common), you'll need to ascertain prices beforehand and review bills carefully when finished. Waiting staff are adept at bringing you items (pickles, garlic bread, *çiğ börek*, mini-*meze*, bottled water, etc) that you haven't specifically ordered – but which you will definitely pay for unless announced by the magic words *ıkramızdır* (with our compliments).

In *hazır yemek* restaurants, *kuru fasulye* (haricot bean soup), *taze fasulye* (French beans), *sebze turlu* (vegetable stew) and *nohut* (chickpeas) are the principal **vegetable dishes**. Although no meat may be visible, they're almost always made with lamb or chicken broth; even bulgur and rice may be cooked in meat stock. Vegetarians might ask *İçinde et suyu var mı?* (Does it contain meat stock?).

Bread and cheese

The standard Turkish loaf is delicious hot out of the oven, but soon becomes stale. Flat, unadorned *pide* is served with soup, during Ramadan and at *kebapçıs,* as is delicious *lavaş,* a flat bread brought hot to the table puffed-up like a balloon. *Kepekli* (wholemeal) or *çavdar* (rye bread; only from a *fırın* or bakery) afford relief in larger towns. In villages, cooked *yufka* – the basis of *börek* pastry – makes a welcome respite, as does *bazlama* (similar to an Indian *paratha*).

Beyaz peynir (like Greek feta) is the commonest Turkish **cheese**, but there are many others. *Dil peynir* ("tongue" cheese), a hard, salty cheese comprised of mozzarella-like filaments, and the plaited *oğru peynir,* can both be grilled or fried like Cypriot halloúmi. *Tulum peynir* is a strong goat's cheese cured in a goatskin; it is used as *börek* stuffing, although together with walnuts, it makes a very popular *meze*. *Otlu peynir* from the Van area is cured with herbs; cow's-milk *kaşar,* especially *eski* (aged) *kaşar* from the Kars region, is also highly esteemed.

Meat dishes

Grilled meat dishes – normally served simply with a few *pide* slices and raw vegetable garnish – include several variations on the kebab. *Adana kebap* is spicy, with sprinkled purple sumac herb betraying Arab influence; *İskender kebap,* best sampled in Bursa, is heavy on the flat bread, tomato sauce and yoghurt; *sarmı beyti* is a ground-beef kebab wrapped in durum bread and baked in the oven. Chicken kebab (*tavuk* or *piliç şiş*) is ubiquitous, and chicken is also served as *şiş, pırzola* (grilled breast) or *kanat* (grilled wings). Offal is popular, particularly *böbrek* (kidney), *yürek* (heart), *ciğer* (liver), and *koç yumurtası* (ram's egg) or *billur* (crystal) – the last two euphemisms for testicle.

More elaborate **meat-and-veg combinations** include *mussaka* (inferior to the Greek rendition), *karnıyarık* (a much better Turkish variation), *güveç* (clay-pot fricassee), *tas kebap* (stew), *hunkar beğendi* (lamb, puréed aubergine and cheese), *saray kebap* (beef stew topped with béchamel sauce and oven-browned), *macar kebap* (fine veal chunks in a spicy sauce with tomatoes and wine) and *saç kavurma,*

an Anatolian speciality of meat, vegetables and spices fried up in a *saç* (the Turkish wok). *Şalgam,* a fiery drink made from fermented turnip and carrot, is an acquired taste that makes the best accompaniment to *Adana kebab*.

Fish and seafood

Fish and seafood is good. Usually sold by weight (₺40–45 per kilo in remote spots, more than double that in flash resorts), though per-portion prices of about ₺15–20 prevail for less bijoux and fish-farmed species. Choose with an eye to what's in season (as opposed to farmed, frozen and imported), and don't turn your nose up at humbler varieties, which will likely be fresher. Budget mainstays include *sardalya* (grilled sardines), *palamut* (autumn tuna), *akya* (liche in French; no English name) and *sarıgöz* (black bream). *Çipura* (gilt-head bream) and *levrek* (sea bass) are usually farmed. Fish is invariably served simply, with just a garnish of spring onion (*soğan*) and rocket (*roka*).

Desserts and sweets

Turkish chefs pander shamelessly to the sweet-toothed, who will find a huge range of sugary treats at a **pastane** (sweet shop).

Turkish Delight and baklava

The best-known Turkish sweet, *lokum* or "**Turkish Delight**", is basically solidified sugar and pectin, flavoured (most commonly) with rosewater, often stuffed with pistachios or other nuts and finally sprinkled with powdered sugar. There are also numerous kinds of **helva**, including the tahini-paste chew synonymous with the concoction in the West. *Yaz halvası* (summer helva) is made from semolina flour – the chocolate and nut-stuffed version is delicious.

Of the syrup-soaked **baklava**-type items – all permutations of a sugar, flour, nut and butter mix – the best is *antep fıstıklı sarması* (pistachio-filled *baklava*), though it's pricey at ₺5–8 per serving. Other *baklava* tend to be *cevizli* (walnut-filled), and slightly cheaper. *Künefe* – the "shredded wheat" filaments of *kadayif* perched atop white cheese, baked and then soaked in syrup – has become a ubiquitous dessert in kebab and *lahmacun* places; both *baklava* and *künefe* are often served with large dollops of glutinous Maraş ice cream.

Puddings, ice cream and fruit

Less sweet and healthier are the **milk-based** dishes, popular everywhere. *Süpangile* ("süp" for short, a corruption of *soupe d'Anglais*) is an incredibly dense, rich chocolate pudding with sponge or a biscuit embedded inside. More modest are *keşkül* (vanilla and nut-crumble custard) and *sütlaç* (rice pudding) – one dessert that's consistently available in ordinary restaurants. The most complicated dish is *tavukgöğsü*, a cinnamon-topped morsel made from hyper-boiled and strained chicken breast, semolina starch and milk. *Kazandibi* (literally "bottom of the pot") is *tavukgöğsü* residue with a dark crust on the bottom – not to be confused with *fırın sütlaç*, which is actually *sütlaç* pudding with a scorched top baked in a clay dish.

Aşure is a sort of rosewater jelly laced with pulses, wheat berries, raisins and nuts. It supposedly contains forty ingredients, after a legend which claims that after the Ark's forty-day sail on the Flood, and the first sighting of dry land, Noah commanded that a stew be made of the forty remaining kinds of food on board.

Traditional Turkish ice cream (*dondurma*) is an excellent summer treat, provided it's genuine *Maraşlı döşme* (whipped in the Kahraman Maraş tradition – a bit like Italian gelato). The outlandishly costumed *dondurma* street-sellers of yore have been overtaken by upmarket parlours selling every conceivable flavour; the best chain of these is Mado, with high prices but equally high quality.

Summer fruit (*meyve*) generally means *kavun* (Persian melon, honeydew) or *karpuz* (watermelon). Autumn choices include *kabak tatlısı* (candied squash with walnut chunks and *kaymak*, or clotted cream) or *ayva tatlısı* (stewed quince served with nuts or dried fruit, topped with *kaymak* and dusted with grated pistachio).

Slightly more healthy options include *cezeriye*, a sweetmeat made of carrot juice, honey and nuts; the east Anatolian snack of **peştil** (dried fruit), most commonly apricot and peach, pressed into sheets; and **tatlı sucuk**, a fruit, nut and molasses roll.

Coffee and tea

The Ottomans introduced **coffee** – and the notion of the coffee house – to the West during the seventeenth century. Intermittently banned as hotbeds of sedition and vice by the religious authorities, coffee houses had nonetheless become fixtures of İstanbul society by the mid-sixteenth century. The coffee was prepared, as it still is today, using finely ground coffee brewed up in a small pan and served, in tiny cups, *sade* (without sugar), *orta şekerli* (medium sweet) or *çok şekerli* (very sweet). Coffee fell out of favour during the early Republican period

as, following the loss of the coffee-producing Arab territories, it had to be imported. But after decades of being both exorbitantly expensive and hard to find, coffee is making a major comeback. Traditional Turkish coffee is widely available today, and in the big cities and resorts there are plenty of cafés serving filter, latte and other types of coffee, though in more remote areas the usual standby is (invariably over-strong) instant coffee.

Tea has, however, become the national drink, especially in rural areas and among the less well off, as it's still much cheaper than coffee. Home-grown in the eastern Black Sea region since the 1920s, it's an essential social lubricant. It's prepared in the *çaydanlık* or *demlik*, a double-boiler apparatus, with a larger water chamber underneath the smaller receptacle containing dry leaves, to which a small quantity of hot water is added. After a suitable (or unsuitably long) wait, the tea is decanted into tulip-shaped glasses, then diluted with more water to taste: *açık* is weak, *demli* or *koyu* steeped. Sugar comes as cubes on the side; milk is never added.

Herbal **teas** are also popular, particularly *ıhlamur* (linden flower), *kuşburnu* (rose hip), *papatya* (camomile) and *ada çay* ("island" tea), an infusion of a sage common in coastal areas. The much-touted **apple tea** (*elma çay*) contains chemicals and not a trace of real apple essence.

Soft drinks

Fruit juices (*meyva suyu*) nowadays usually come in cardboard cartons or cans, and are refreshing but high in added sugar. Flavours include *kayısı* (apricot), *şeftali* (peach) and *vişne* (sour cherry). Fresh orange juice is widely available in tourist areas and big cities, as is *nar suyu* (pomegranate juice).

Bottled **spring water** (*memba suyu*) or fizzy **mineral water** (*maden suyu or soda*) are restaurant staples, but cheaper establishments usually offer free potable tap water in a glass bottle or a jug. *Meşrubat* is the generic term for all types of carbonated **soft drinks**.

Certain beverages accompany particular kinds of food or appear at set seasons. *Sıcak süt* (hot milk) is the traditional complement to *börek*, though in winter it's fortified with *salep*, made from the ground tubers of a phenomenally expensive wild orchid (*Orchis mascula*) gathered in coastal hills near İzmir. **Salep** is a good safeguard against colds (and also reputedly an aphrodisiac), though most packages sold are heavily adulterated with powdered milk, starch and sugar. **Ayran** (chilled, watered-down yoghurt) is always on offer at *pidecis* and *kebapcı*s, an excellent accompaniment to spicy meat. In autumn and winter, stalls sell **boza**, a delicious, mildly fermented millet drink.

Alcoholic drinks

Since the accession of the nominally Islamist AK Party in 2002, the price of **alcoholic drinks** has risen sharply – mainly because of the eighty percent tax levied. Alcoholic beverages are still widely available, however, especially in the big cities of western Turkey and all resort areas. You'll have more trouble finding a place serving alcohol in provincial and conservative towns in central and eastern Anatolia, such as Afyon, Konya, Erzerum or Diyarbakır.

Wine

Wine (*şarap*) comes from vineyards scattered across western Anatolia between Cappadocia, the Euphrates Valley, Thrace and the Aegean. Fine wine now has a local audience, with expensive imported labels available in most upmarket town-centre or hotel restaurants and the bigger supermarkets. Local wines are also now better distributed, resulting in a huge variety in trendy resorts, though quality remains inconsistent. Red wine is *kırmızı*, white *beyaz*, rose *roze*. In shops, count on paying ₺12–30 per bottle of basic to mid-range wine. In restaurants, a standard table wine will set you back a minimum of ₺30, but more usually ₺40–50. Most places sell wine by the glass for ₺8–12.

The market is dominated by two large vintners: Doluca (try their Antik premium labels, or Moskado Sek) and Kavaklıdere (whose Çankaya white, Angora red and Lâl rose are commendable). Kavaklıdere also produces a sparkling white, İnci Damalası, the closest thing to local champagne. Other smaller, regional brands to watch for include Turasan, Narbağ, and Peribacası (Cappadocia). Feyzi Kutman red in particular is superb, though rarely found outside the largest centres; another affordable Aegean producer worth sampling is Sevilen, which makes organic reds – Merlot and Cabernet – at premium prices, good whites and a palatable, MOR label, Tellibağ. Similarly confined to their areas of production are Majestik red, available only around İzmir, cheap-and-cheerful wines from Şirince, plus the vintners of Bozcaada, covered in detail on p.198.

Rakı and other spirits

The Turkish national aperitif is **rakı**, not unlike Greek ouzo but stronger (45–48 percent alcohol), usually drunk over ice and topped up with bottled water. The *meyhane* routine of an evening is for a group to order a big bottle of rakı, a bucket of ice and a few bottles of water, and then slowly drink themselves under the table between bites of seafood *meze* or nibbles of *çerez* – the generic term for pumpkin seeds, roasted chickpeas, almonds etc, served on tiny plates. The best brand is reckoned to be Efe, particularly its green-label line. However, Burgaz brand is often better value and nearly as good (again in green-label variety). Tekirdağ, especially its "gold series", is also recommendable. Yeni is the most widely available at most establishments, with a double rakı in a *meyhane* running ₺8–12. A 70cl bottle of Yeni Rakı in a Turkish shop costs around ₺70, and all brands are much cheaper bought duty-free.

Stronger **spirits** – *cin* (gin), *votka* (vodka) and *kanyak* (cognac) – exist as imported labels or cheaper but often nastier *yerli* (locally produced) variants. Avoid drinking spirits that are suspiciously cheap; several tourists have died in recent years from drinking bootleg liquor made from deadly methyl alcohol.

TURKISH BEER

Local brewery Efes Pilsen has a stranglehold on the Turkish beer (*bira*) market, sponsoring everything from a blues festival to one of the country's leading basketball teams. Luckily they produce a generally well-regarded pilsner-type brew, which comes in either 33cl or 50cl bottles or cans. From a supermarket or *bakkal* (small grocery store) expect to pay around ₺4 a bottle, slightly more for a can. **Efes Dark** is a sweeter, stronger stout-style beer, while **Efes-Xtra** is eight percent proof, though neither is widely available in bars or restaurants. **Tuborg**, of Danish origins, is the other major home-grown beer. It is less widely available than Efes, though some people swear by it. Their red label beer is stronger than the standard green. **Carlsberg** is also brewed locally, while Gusta is a decent, dark, home-produced wheat beer.

Prices in bars and restaurants vary widely, with the cheaper places selling a 50cl beer for ₺5, trendier places for ₺12 and up. If the bar has draught (*fıçı*) beer, it's usually a little cheaper. If it's available, you'll pay at least a third more for the dubious privilege of drinking Corona, Fosters, Heineken or Becks.

Health

No special inoculations are required for Turkey, although cautious travellers might want typhoid and tetanus jabs, particularly for eastern Anatolia. Some visitors also get injections against hepatitis A, for which the risk is possibly greater in İstanbul than in rural areas. Malaria is theoretically a seasonal (April–July) problem between Adana and Mardin, especially in areas irrigated by the Southeastern Anatolia Project. However, for brief visits you shouldn't need prophylactic drugs. For up-to-date advice, consult a travel clinic.

Stomach upsets and drinking water

Many visitors experience bouts of **diarrhoea**, especially on longer stays. If you do get struck down, note that Lomotil or Imodium (trade names for diphenoxylate) are easily available in Turkey. They allow you to travel without constantly running to the bathroom, but do not kill the bug that ails you. Buscopan, also sold locally, is particularly good for stomach cramps, while Ge-Oral powder dissolved in pure water is an effective rehydration remedy. **Turkish tap water** is heavily chlorinated and usually drinkable, but it's probably best to stick to bottled water, especially in İstanbul. **Rural springs** are labelled içilir, içilebilir or içme suyu (all meaning "potable"), or içilmez (not drinkable).

Particularly during the hot summer months, serious **food poisoning** is a possibility – even in the biggest cities and resorts, and especially in south-eastern Turkey. In restaurants, avoid dishes that look as if they have been standing around, and make sure meat and fish are well grilled. Don't, whatever you do, eat stuffed mussels in summer. If you're struck down, try to let the bug run its course and drink lots of fluids; eating plain white rice and yoghurt also helps. Stubborn cases will need a course of antibiotics or Flagyl (metronidazole), the latter effective against giardia and protozoans as well as certain bacteria; pharmacists are trained to recognize symptoms and you don't need a prescription.

Bites and stings

Mosquitoes are sometimes a problem, and since no good topical repellents are available locally, you should bring your own. At night mozzies are dispatched with locally sold incense coils (spiral tütsü) or an Esem Mat, a small, electrified tray that slowly vaporizes an odourless disc. Hotels and pansiyons in heavily infested areas often have mosquito screens on the windows.

Jellyfish are an occasional hazard along the Aegean shore. **Sea urchins**, whose spines easily detach if trodden on, are more ubiquitous; the splinters must be removed to prevent infection. **Snakes** and **scorpions** can lurk among the stones at archeological sites, and in nooks and crannies of ground-floor accommodation. There are two kinds of vipers (engerek in Turkish): the deadly, metre-long Ottoman viper, fortunately rare, and the smaller, more common and less dangerous asp viper. Neither is particularly aggressive unless disturbed; both are most commonly seen during mild spring days.

Certain **ticks** in Turkey carry the Crimean-Congo haemorrhagic fever (**CCHF**) virus, with hundreds of cases (and fatalities in two figures) annually, though the danger seems confined to rural areas of several provinces between Ankara and the Black Sea.

Although rare (one to two cases per year), **rabies** is another potential danger. Be wary of any animal that bites, scratches or licks you, particularly if it's behaving erratically. If you do suspect you have been bitten by a rabid animal, wash the wound thoroughly (preferably with iodine) and seek medical attention immediately. Turkish cities are full of stray cats and dogs; dogs with a tag in their ear have been inoculated against rabies and other diseases and put back on the street with the blessing of the local authority.

Medical treatment

Minor complaints can be dealt with at a **pharmacy** (eczane); even the smallest town will have one. Turkish pharmacists may speak some English or German, and dispense medicines that would ordinarily require a prescription abroad. Prices for locally produced medicines are low, but it may be difficult to find exact equivalents to your home prescription. Pharmacies close on Sundays and (usually) 7pm–7am weekdays, but take turns to be a Nöbet(ci) (Duty) pharmacy. Each town or city will have one or more chemists open at night and on a Sunday; a duty roster is posted in Turkish in every chemist's front window. Note that there are usually several pharmacies near major hospitals, one of which is often the nöbet(ci) pharmacy.

For more serious conditions, go to one of the **public clinics** (sağlık ocağı), or a **hospital** (hastane), indicated by a blue street sign with a large white "H" on it. Hospitals are either public (*Devlet Hastane* or *SSK Hastanesi*) or private (*Özel Hastane*). In terms of cutting bureaucracy and speed of treatment it is far better to use a private hospital, especially as many of the major ones have an English- (and often other languages) speaking assistant whose job is to deal with foreigners. Fees are lower than in northern Europe and North America but still substantial enough to make insurance cover essential (there are no reciprocal healthcare arrangements between Turkey and the EU). Expect to pay €35 and up to see a general doctor in a hospital, €90 and up to see a specialist consultant. The medical faculties of major universities – eg İstanbul, İzmir, Edirne, Antalya and Bursa – also have teaching hospitals, which are infinitely better than the state hospitals, but usually less expensive than the private ones. Summoning a doctor to your hotel room will cost about €50, plus medication delivered from a local pharmacy. If you're on a **package tour**, the better companies will have arrangements with competent, English-speaking doctors and dentists in or near the resort. In a medical **emergency**, summon an ambulance by dialling ☎112.

Contraception and female hygiene

International brands of **birth control** pills (*doğum kontrol hapıları*) are sold at pharmacies. **Condoms** (*preservatif*) are sold in most pharmacies and also supermarkets like Migros; don't buy off street-carts, where stock may be tampered with or expired. **Tampons** are available from pharmacies and supermarkets at UK prices; Orkid is the adequate domestic brand of "sanitary towel".

Culture and etiquette

Many Turks, even in remote areas, have lived and worked abroad (mainly in Germany) or at tourist resorts in Turkey, and are used to foreign ways. But traditional customs matter, and although you're unlikely to cause offence through a social gaffe, it's best to be aware of prevailing customs. Also, many Turks are devout (or at least conservative) Muslims, so you should adhere to local dress codes – particularly away from resorts and when visiting mosques.

Invitations and meals

Hospitality (*misafirperverlik*) is a pillar of rural Turkish culture, so you're unlikely to leave the country without at least one invitation to **drink tea**, either in a *çayhane* (teahouse) or someone's home. If you really can't spare the time, mime "thanks" by placing one hand on your chest and pointing with the other to your watch and then in the direction you're headed. If you do stop, remember that drinking only one glass may be interpreted as casting aspersions on their tea. If offered a full meal, decline the first offer – if it's sincere it will be repeated at least twice and custom demands that you accept the third offer.

Being **invited for a meal** at a Turkish home is both an honour and an obligation. Always remove your shoes at the door. In urban, middle-class homes you'll sit at a table and eat with cutlery. In village houses, however, the meal is usually served at a low table with cushions on the floor; hide your feet under the table or a dropcloth provided for the purpose. (Feet, shod or not, are considered unclean and should never be pointed at anyone.) When scooping food with bread sections from a communal bowl, **use your right hand** – the left is reserved for bodily hygiene. If you use toothpicks provided at restaurants, cover your mouth while doing so.

Dress and body language

What is acceptable dress-wise depends very much on which part of the country – or even which part of a city – you are visiting. Overall, though, Turkey is conservative concerning dress. **Beachwear** should be confined to the beach, while strolling shirtless around resort streets is offensive (though plenty of foreign men do it). Revealing clothing like miniskirts and skimpy shorts should be avoided away from heavily touristed areas. **Nude sunbathing** is not acceptable anywhere, though at any major Mediterranean/Aegean resort discreet topless sunning takes place.

If you venture much off the tourist track, accept that being **stared at** is part of the experience and not considered rude. In some parts of the southeast, you may be mobbed by small children wishing to guide you around the local ruins and/or begging for pens, sweets or money.

Turks employ a variety of not immediately obvious **body language**. Clicking the tongue against the roof of the mouth and simultaneously raising the eyebrows and chin means "no" or "there isn't any"; those economical of movement will rely on their eyebrows alone. By contrast, wagging the head rapidly from side to side means "Explain, I don't understand", while a single, obliquely inclined nod means "yes".

Black and Asian travellers

In remoter areas, **black and Asian people** may find themselves something of a curiosity, and may receive unsolicited comments – ranging from *Arap!* (a Black!) to the notionally more appreciative *çok güzel* (very pretty!). Turkey is in fact one of the least racist countries around the Mediterranean. Many black footballers from Africa and South America play in Turkish teams and you may also notice the country's black minority group, termed "Afro Turks", particularly around İzmir.

Female travellers

While many **female travellers** encounter little more than some flirtatious banter while travelling in Turkey, a minority experience unwanted attention and more serious harassment in both resorts and rural areas. The key to avoiding trouble is to be aware of your surroundings, dress and behaviour and how it might be interpreted. If travelling alone, it's best to stick to mid-range hotels (particularly in the interior) and schedule transport to arrive during daylight hours. That said, the backstreets of most Turkish towns are a lot safer at night than those of many Western cities. This is partly due to a heavy police presence; do not hesitate to ask them for help. Away from the main resorts, **unaccompanied women** are a rare sight at night; when heading out for an evening, try to go as part of a group, preferably mixed-sex, otherwise as an all-female group, which may, however, get some unwelcome attention. In restaurants, unaccompanied women may be directed to the *aile salonu* (family parlour), usually upstairs, rather than be served with other diners. While **public drunkenness** is unacceptable for both genders, this is especially true for women.

Turkish women have over the years devised successful tactics to protect themselves from **harassment** – specifically, avoiding eye contact with men and looking as confident and purposeful as possible. When all else fails, the best way to neutralize harassment is to make a public scene. The words *Ayıp* ("Shame!") or *Beni rahatsız ediyorsun* ("You're disturbing me"), spoken very loudly, generally have the desired effect – passers-by or fellow passengers will deal with the situation for you. *Defol* ("Piss off!") and *Bırak beni* ("Leave me alone") are stronger retorts. In general, Turkish men back down when confronted, and cases of violent sexual harassment are very rare.

Prostitution

Prostitution is thriving in Turkey, both in legal, state-controlled brothels and, illegally, on the

---

WOMEN IN TURKEY

Acceptable behaviour and roles for **women** vary widely by class and region. In İstanbul and along the heavily touristed coastline, social freedom approximates that in Western Europe; in more traditional areas females act conservatively, with headscarves in abundance.

Turkish women have long held **jobs** in the professions and civil service as well as in the tourist sector in hotels and for airlines. There are female police, and an increasing number of women can be found working in restaurants and bars – though only in resorts and some of the more westernized cities such as Antalya, Ankara, İstanbul and İzmir. Recently, fast-food chains and supermarkets have offered more job opportunities. In rural areas, women rarely have access to formal employment and work the land. **Literacy rates** for girls are also significantly lower in rural areas despite compulsory education up to the age of fifteen.

In villages parents still choose wives for their sons; in cities more Western attitudes prevail and couples even live together unmarried. Despite the current AKP government openly calling for a ban, abortion is still available on demand; contraceptives are readily obtainable; and a baby can be registered to unmarried parents. The average number of children per family is two, though there's a huge disparity between eastern and western Turkey, with families of up to twelve not uncommon in poorer southeastern (ethnically Kurdish) parts of the country. The law gives men considerable say over their children, though divorce law is fairly equitable.

Sadly Turkey is also known for hundreds of annual **"honour" killings**, particularly in Kurdish areas. These occur for actual or suspected adultery, pregnancy out of wedlock or dating someone disapproved of by the family. While in the past this crime was carried out by a male relative, lately women have been forced to commit suicide instead.

streets and in certain bars and dubious hotels. Many prostitutes who work illegally come from Russia and former Soviet-bloc countries such as Moldova or Ukraine, and are known locally as "Natashas". Female travellers may be mistaken for prostitutes by local men assuming that any foreign woman out unaccompanied at night must be on the game. If you wander through **seedy districts** such as Aksaray in İstanbul, or stumble across known pick-up points on major highways, expect to be followed by kerb-crawlers; it's usually enough to explain that you're not a *natasha*. This Guide doesn't recommend hotels used for prostitution, but management and clientele can change, so keep your antennae primed.

Gay and lesbian travellers

Turkish society has always been deeply ambivalent about male **homosexuality**, since the days of a rampantly bisexual Ottoman culture, when transvestite dancers and entertainers were the norm. That said, public attitudes are generally intolerant or closeted. The only place with a recognized gay scene is İstanbul, though the more liberal towns of Antalya and İzmir and the resorts of Bodrum, Marmaris and Alanya are considered gay-friendly.

Homosexual acts between adults over 18 are legal, but existing laws against "spreading homosexual information" in print – ie advocating

---

HAMAMS (TURKISH BATHS)

The **hamam** (Turkish bath) once played a pivotal role in hygiene, social discourse and religious life (they were often part of a mosque complex) in Turkey, but as the standard of living has increased, its importance has diminished. As an exercise in nostalgia, however, it's well worth visiting one – İstanbul in particular boasts many historic hamams (see p.88, p.91, p.92, p.93) worth experiencing for their architecture alone – and, of course, they make for a very relaxing end to a day of slogging around the sights.

Most Turkish towns have at least one hamam, usually signposted; otherwise look for the distinctive external profile of the roof domes. Ordinary hamams **charge** ₺10–12 basic admission, the price normally indicated by the front desk; hamams in coastal tourist resorts and İstanbul can be far more expensive (₺15–180), with an optional scrub and/or massage adding to the cost. Baths are either for men or women, or **sexually segregated** on a schedule, with women usually allotted more restricted hours, usually midweek during the day.

HAMAM ETIQUETTE

On entering, leave your **valuables** in a small locking drawer, keeping the key (usually on a wrist thong) with you for the duration. Bring soap and shampoo as it's not always sold in the foyer. Men are supplied with a *peştamal*, a thin, wraparound sarong, women generally enter in knickers but not bra; both sexes get *takunya*, awkward wooden clogs, and later a *havlu* (towel). Leave your clothes in the changing cubicle (*camekan* in Turkish).

The *hararet* or **main bath chamber** ranges from plain to ornate, though any decent hamam will be marble-clad at least up to chest height. Two or more *halvets*, semi-private corner rooms with two or three *kurnas* (basins) each, lead off from the main chamber. The internal temperature varies from tryingly hot to barely lukewarm, depending on how well run the baths are. Unless with a friend, it's one customer to a set of taps and basin; refrain from making a big soapy mess in the basin, which is meant for mixing pure water to ideal temperature. Use the scoop-dishes provided to sluice yourself. It's considered good etiquette to clean your marble slab with a few scoopfuls of water before leaving.

At the heart of the hamam is the *göbek taşı* or "navel stone", a raised platform positioned over the furnaces that heat the premises. The *göbek taşı* will be piping hot and covered with prostrate figures absorbing the heat. It's also the venue for (very) vigorous massages from the *tellâk* or masseur/masseuse. A *kese* (abrasive mitt) session from the same person, in which dead skin and grime are scrubbed away, will probably suit more people. Terms for the *tellâks*' services should be displayed in the foyer. Few hamams have a masseuse, so female visitors will have to think very carefully before accepting a massage from a masseur – though this is far from unknown. Scrubs and massages are charged extra, so make sure you know what you'll be paying. Upon return to your cubicle with its reclining couch(es) you'll be offered tea, soft drinks or mineral water – charged extra as per a posted price placard. Except in heavily touristed establishments, **tips** apart from the listed fees are not required or expected.

MOSQUE MANNERS

As you stroll around the tourist-thronged sites of İstanbul's Sultanahmet or the promenade of an Aegean or Mediterranean resort, it can at times be hard to remember that you are in a predominantly Muslim country – though even here the call to prayer echoes out five times daily: sunrise, midday, late afternoon, sunset and after dark.

Many of Turkey's inhabitants are, however, both conservative and devout. Bear this in mind particularly when visiting a mosque. All those likely to be of interest to a foreign visitor (and many more besides) display some kind of "conduct" notice at the door outlining the **entry rules** – which are simple:

- Cover your head (women) and shoulders/upper arms (both sexes)
- No shorts or miniskirts
- Take off your shoes before entering. (Many mosques now provide a plastic bag for this – before entering, slip your shoes in to the bag and carry them around with you. Alternatively, place your footwear on the shelves provided.)

Especially if you are in a very conservative part of the country (which includes most of inland Anatolia as well as conservative districts within the big cities, like İstanbul's Fatih) try to avoid your visit coinciding with **noon prayers** – particularly those on a Friday, the most important prayer session of the week. Once inside the mosque, you're free to wander around, take photographs and admire the interior – but keep your voice down (there are often people praying or reciting the Koran outside of the five daily prayer times) and don't take pictures of worshippers unless they give their permission. Although the imam is a state-paid official, upkeep of the building is down to charity, so you may want to put a **donation** in the collection box.

---

the lifestyle – are sporadically enforced, "Gay Pride" festivals have been forcibly cancelled and cruising is an offence. Advocating a gay lifestyle remains an offence, though on a more positive note in 2011 a major Gay Pride Week march down İstiklal Caddesi in İstanbul attracted over ten thousand participants and passed without incident.

Lambda (W lambdaistanbul.org) is a domestic gay activist group, as is **Kaos** (W kaosgl.com), but both websites are Turkish only and frequently inaccessible. More reliable and useful to visitors for information on İstanbul's gay scene are W istanbulgay.com and W absolutesultans.com.

Smoking

With over forty percent of the adult population (around 25 million) indulging in the nicotine habit, the old saying "smokes like a Turk" is a fairly accurate assessment. Yet things have changed dramatically in recent years. Smoking was **banned** on public transport and in airports, bus terminals and train stations back in 1997, and then further prohibited in 2009 in all public buildings, and all enclosed public spaces including bars, cafés, restaurants and clubs – including nargile (hookah) cafés. There was of course a major outcry, largely from the owners of *kahvehane*s (the basic, invariably all-male,

tea-and-coffee dens) and bars and restaurants. The ban is widely flouted despite the steep fines for proprietors, many of whom have muddied the waters by erecting tent-like awnings at the front or rear of their establishment, warmed in winter by outdoor heaters.

Toilets

Western-style toilets are now common in many hotels, restaurants, cafés and bars. The only difference you're likely to notice is a small pipe fitted at the rear rim of the basin – which serves the same purpose as a bidet. The tap to turn it on is usually located on the wall behind the loo. The waste bins provided are for used toilet paper – blockages are not uncommon.

In rural areas (and less touristed parts of major cities), however, traditional **squat toilets** are still the norm, especially those attached to service stations, basic eateries and mosques. Mosque loos are often the only "public" toilet you'll be able to find in remote parts of big cities or in smaller towns. There's always a tap and plastic jug next to the toilet for washing the unmentionables, but few provide paper, so carry some around with you. An attendant at the entrance will divest you of a lira or so on your way out and, in return, give you a tissue and splash of cologne on your hands.

Festivals

Celebrations in Turkey include religious festivals, observed throughout the Islamic world on dates determined by the Muslim Hijra calendar, as well as annual cultural or harvest extravaganzas held in various cities and resorts across the country.

Religious festivals

The most important religious festival is **Ramadan** (*Ramazan* in Turkish), the Muslim month of daylight abstention from food, water, tobacco and sexual relations. Otherwise, life carries on as normal during Ramadan, despite the fact that half the population is fasting from sunrise to sunset. Some restaurants close for the duration or severely curtail their menus, others discreetly hide their salons behind curtains, but at most establishments you will be served with surprisingly good grace. The Koran allows pregnant and nursing mothers, the infirm and travellers to be excused from obligatory fasting; immediately after dark there's an orgy of eating (the *iftar yemeği*) by the famished in places public and private, and restaurants sell out of everything within an hour of sunset.

Kadir Gecesi (The Eve of Power), when Mohammed received the Koran from Allah, takes place between the 27th and 28th days of the month of Ramadan. Mosques – brilliantly illuminated for the whole month – are full all night, as it's believed that prayers at this time have special efficacy. On **Arife**, the last day of Ramadan, it is customary to go to the cemeteries and pay respects to departed ancestors; many rural restaurants close that evening.

The three-day **Şeker Bayramı** (Sugar Holiday) immediately follows Ramadan, celebrated by family reunions and the giving of presents and sweets to children, and restrained general partying in restaurants; on *Arife* eve, the night after **Kadir Gecesi**, you will have to book well in advance for tables at better establishments.

The four-day **Kurban Bayramı** (Festival of the Sacrifice), in which the sacrificial offering of a sheep represents Abraham's son Ishmael (a Koranic version of the Old Testament story), is marked by the massive slaughter of sheep and goats. Only wealthy families can afford to buy a whole animal, so part of the meat is distributed to the poor of the neighbourhood.

During the *Şeker* and *Kurban festivals* **travel** becomes difficult – reserve well in advance for a seat on any long-distance coach, train or plane. If you travel by road in national holiday periods, note that the already high traffic accident rate soars. Many shops and all banks, museums and government offices close during these periods (although corner grocery stores and most resort shops stay open) and when the festivals occur close to a national secular holiday, the whole country effectively grinds to a halt for up to a week.

Religious festival dates

As the Islamic calendar is lunar, the **dates** of the four important religious festivals drift backwards eleven days each year (twelve in a leap year) relative to the Gregorian calendar. Future dates of festivals given on Islamic websites are provisional, owing to factors such as when the moon is sighted and the international date line.

2013 Şeker Aug 8–10; **Kurban** Oct 14–20
2014 Şeker July 28–30; **Kurban** Oct 3–7
2015 Şeker July 17–19; **Kurban** Sept 22–28
2016 Şeker July 6–9; **Kurban** Sept 11–18

Cultural festivals

Cultural festivals are most interesting in cities and resorts that have the resources to attract internationally renowned acts. Almost every town has some yearly bash, though many are of limited interest to outsiders. We've highlighted the best below, with fuller descriptions in the Guide.

Folk-dance festivals provide an opportunity to see Turkey's best dance troupes perform a sample of the varied repertoire of Turkish dances in traditional costumes. There's a full festival calendar for İstanbul on p.131, in addition to the summary below.

January

Camel wrestling Selçuk. The festival itself takes place on the last two weekends, though bouts occur throughout Aydın province from December onwards.

April

İstanbul International Film Festival İstanbul ⓦ film.iksv.org /en. Full-length features and documentaries.

May

Conquest Celebrations İstanbul ⓦ ibb.gov.tr. Week-long celebration of the Ottoman conquest of old Constantinople – concerts by the Ottoman Mehter military band, fancy-dress processions and fireworks.

Ephesus Festival Ephesus. The ancient theatre hosts folk dancing plus more conventional acts.

International Puppet Festival İstanbul ⓣ 0212 232 0224. A celebration of Turkish Shadow Theatre, or *karagöz* – silent puppets tell their tale behind a two-dimensional screen.

İstanbul International Theatre Festival İstanbul ⓦ iksv.org. Even-numbered years only; dance and workshops as well as theatre performances.

Hıdırellez Gypsy festival Edirne. Celebration of the coming of spring, with gypsy bands performing, dancing in the street and jumping over bonfires. May 5–6.

Takava Gypsy Festival Kırklareli. The same celebrations as at the Hıdırellez festival in Edirne. May 5–6.

June–July

Oil wrestling Yağlı Güreş, near Edirne. Competitors from all over the country tangle with each other in the country's major, week-long oil wrestling event, plus lots of music and dance events. Late June or early July.

Kafkasör Festival Artvin. Bullfighting between young beasts in a beautiful alpine setting, plus performances from folk-dance troupes and musical events – and lots of drinking. Late June.

Pir Abdal Musa Tekke village near Elmalı. Rites honouring the second most important Alevî saint after Hacı Bektaş Veli; early June.

İstanbul International Classical Music Festival İstanbul ⓦ iksv.org. Performances by top soloists and orchestras, often in historic venues.

Efes Pilsen One Love İstanbul ⓦ efespilsenonelove.com. Moderately alternative city-centre weekend-long festival generally held at trendy Santralistanbul, with plenty of DJ-led dance sets and performances from international bands and local bands.

Rock N' Coke Near İstanbul ⓦ rockncoke.com. A weekend of Western and Turkish rock held on an airfield 50km to the west of the city; buses run from Taksim. Headliners in recent years have included Franz Ferdinand and The Cure.

International İzmir Festival İzmir ⓦ iksev.org. Month-long classical music, pop, ballet and jazz festival with many international names performing at Ephesus theatre and Çeşme castle.

Aspendos Opera and Ballet Festival Near Side, Antalya province ⓦ aspendosfestival.gov.tr. The Mediterranean coast's big highbrow event, now expanded to run from mid-June through mid-September.

İstanbul Jazz Festival İstanbul ⓦ iksv.org. Jazz as well as rock acts (see p.131); early July.

August

Chef's Contest Mengen, Bolu province. The region purportedly produces the country's best cooks.

Hacı Bektaş Veli Commemoration Hacıbektaş village, Cappadocia. Bektaşis and their affiliates, the Alevîs, meet for a weekend of ritual singing and dancing; second half of Aug.

September–October

Bodrum Festival Bodrum. Centred on the castle, and emphasizing ballet and opera; early Sept.

İstanbul Biennial İstanbul ⓦ bienal.iksv.org.tr. Art exhibition, held odd-numbered years, with dozens of projects; lasts into Nov.

Akbank Jazz Festival İstanbul ⓦ akbanksanat.com. A more traditional programme than İstanbul's other jazz festival, in July.

Altın Portakal ("Golden Orange") Film Festival Antalya ⓦ altinportakal.org.tr) A major fixture on the international festival circuit.

Grape Harvest/Wine Festival Ürgüp, Cappadocia. Featuring some of the better local winery products.

Watermelon Festival Diyarbakır. A showcase for the region's most outsized fruit. Mid- to late Sept.

Tourism and Handicrafts Festival Avanos. A celebration of the town's distinctive pottery.

December

Mevlâna Festival Konya. Whirling dervish performances at the home of the order. Dec 10–17.

The media

Newspapers and magazines were forbidden in Turkey until the mid-nineteenth century; now there are dozens of titles, representing the full gamut of public tastes. The airwaves were government-controlled until the late 1980s, but the advent of satellite dishes and cable has seen a huge growth in TV and radio stations of variable quality.

Turkish-language publications

Three titles – *Sabah*, *Hürriyet* and *Milliyet* – dominate the **newspaper** market. Politically left of these stands *Radikal*, although another title, *Taraf*, is far more radical than *Radikal* and frequently incurs establishment ire. *Cumhuriyet*, founded as the mouthpiece of the Turkish republic in 1924, mixes conservative nationalism with old-style socialism. Turkey's liberal-Islamist papers, *Yeni Şafak* and *Zaman*, give generally intelligent and thoughtful coverage. Satirical weekly **comic strips** have a long history in Turkey. Look out for the distinctive artwork of L-Manyak, Le Man, Penguen and Uykusuz.

Television

Turkish channels include several **state-owned TRT** (Turkish Radio and Television) channels, with a mix of films, panel discussions, classical Turkish music shows and soaps. TRT-6, launched in 2009, broke a long-held Republican taboo by broadcasting in Kurdish. The most watched **private channels** include Show, Star, ATV and Kanal D. For Turkish pop the MTV-style Kral, Kral Pop and Power Turk lead the way.

The nation's leading digital company, Digiturk, has a number of English-language channels including CNBC-e and E2, both of which concentrate on re-runs of US TV shows and films. BBC Entertainment offers a mix of BBC comedies, dramas and soaps, while CNN, BBC World and Al Jazeera offer 24-hour news. Most high-end hotels subscribe to the Digiturk package screening these channels.

Digiturk also shows Turkish Premier League **football** on its Lig TV channel. English Premier League matches are shown on Premier League TV. Many bars and cafés subscribe to these and often have big screens showing Turkish matches. Bars in tourist areas usually have English and other European football games on.

Radio

Frequency-crowding means even popular channels are almost impossible to pick up without interference. Of the four **public radio stations**, Radyo Üç (the Third Programme or TRT-3), most commonly found at 88.2, 94 and 99MHz, broadcasts the highest proportion of Western music. NTV Radiyo (102.8) has the news in English at 6pm daily.

For Western music try Açık Radyo (FM 94.9) for rock, jazz and soul. Alternatively, search out FM (99.5), Kiss FM (90.3) and Metro FM (97.2). Radyo Blue (94.5FM) specializes in dance, electronica and blues. For Turkish music, the best stations are Kral (92.0) and Best FM (98.4).

Cinema

With the exception of İstanbul's Beyoğlu district, where some period pieces date back to the 1920s, most cinemas are in shopping malls. **Films** are shown in the original language with Turkish subtitles, though kids' films are dubbed into Turkish. The volume is often excessively high, making the obligatory fifteen-minute interval a relief. There are often five screenings daily, generally at 11.30am or noon, then at around 3pm, 6pm, 9pm and sometimes midnight. **Tickets** in provincial cities cost ₺7–12, with reduced prices (₺6) one or more days midweek; plusher cinemas charge ₺15 and up.

Shopping

Few visitors return from Turkey without some kind of souvenir; whether it's a cheap-and-cheerful pack of local herbs and spices or an expensive carpet depends on the budget of the traveller and the skill of the salesman. The best selection of good-quality wares is to be found in the major tourist centres: İstanbul, Cappadocia, Bursa and the coastal resorts. You won't find a bargain at the production centres themselves; wholesalers and collectors have been there long before you.

How to bargain

Bargaining is a way of life in Turkey; whether you love it or hate it depends on your character. In general it's acceptable to haggle over the price of souvenirs, which often lack price tags, so the vendor is able to adjust his asking price according to what he thinks you can or will pay. This applies to everything from expensive items such as carpets or kilims through to cheaper items like *lokum* (Turkish Delight) and spices. As a guideline, begin at a figure lower than whatever you are prepared to pay, say half the shopkeeper's starting price. Once a price has been agreed, you are ethically committed to buy, so don't commence haggling unless you are reasonably sure you want the item.

"Assistance" from **touts**, whether in İstanbul, major resorts or even provincial towns, will automatically bump up the price thirty to fifty percent, as they will be getting a commission. Also, be prepared to hand over between three and seven percent extra if paying by credit card; your bargaining position is strongest with crisp, bunched notes, either foreign or **t**.

Don't bargain for bus, rail or air tickets, or for fruit or vegetables at street markets.

Bazaars, shops and markets

Several types of traditional bazaar continue to coexist in Turkey with the modern American/European-style shopping malls that increasingly dominate the wealthier districts of large cities.

Covered bazaars are found in larger towns like İstanbul, Bursa and Şanlıurfa. Essentially medieval Ottoman shopping malls, they comprised several *bedesten*s at which particular types of goods were sold, linked by covered arcades also originally assigned to a particular trade – though strict segregation has long since broken down.

Surrounding these covered bazaars are large areas of **small shops**, open-air extensions of the covered areas and governed by the same rules: each shop is a separate unit with an owner and apprentices, and successful businesses are not allowed to expand or merge.

Street markets are held in most towns and all cities, similar to those in northern Europe and selling cheap clothes, household utensils and most importantly fruit, vegetables, cheese, yoghurt, olives, nuts and the like. More exotic are the semi-permanent **flea markets** (*bit pazarı*, literally "louse markets"), ranging in quality from street stalls where old clothes are sold and resold among the homeless, to lanes of shops where you can buy antiques and bric-a-brac.

In many cities, particularly in İstanbul, everyday shopping is increasingly done in Western-style department stores, shopping malls and supermarkets.

Carpets and kilims

Turkish carpets and **kilims** (flat-weave rugs) are renowned for their quality and have a very long history (the designs on many kilims have their origins in the Neolitihic period). Be warned, though, that they are no longer necessarily cheaper in Turkey than overseas, and some dealers reckon there are now more old kilims and carpets outside the country than in it.

Most visitors will find themselves in a carpet shop at some point in their visit – willingly or unwillingly. It's very easy to be drawn into buying something you don't really want at a price you can barely afford once you've been smooth-talked and drip-fed with copious quantities of apple tea. However, it's still possible to get a good deal and enjoy the process; see our tips below.

Carpets

Turkish carpets are single-sided, and knotted with a pile. They are either all-wool, wool pile on cotton warps and wefts, all-silk or – easily mistaken for silk – a glossy mercerized cotton pile on cotton warps and wefts. Needless to say, the higher the silk content, the more expensive the rug, with new, hand-woven wool carpets starting from around €150 per square metre, and pure silk ones starting

---

CARPET AND KILIM BUYING TIPS

- Do some research, preferably before you leave home (check out some of the books reviewed on p.694).
- Avoid buying in the first shop you visit, and look around several. You can always go back – preferably the next day, when you've had time to think about it.
- Don't be embarrassed at how many carpets the dealer is laying out for you – that's his (or usually his lowly assistant's) job.
- Ask as many questions as you can – this will test the dealer's worth, and could give you some interesting historical background should you make a purchase.
- Check the pieces for flaws, marks and the density of weave – hand-woven wool is preferable to machine as it is stronger and the rug will last for longer.
- Natural dyes such as tobacco and saffron are the most highly prized and less likely to fade. You should be able to tell by opening up a section of the pile with your fingers. If the tint at the bottom of the pile is different to that at the top it is a chemical dye.
- Even in the most reputable shop bargaining is essential. Whatever you do, don't engage in the process if you've no intention of buying.
- You'll probably get a better deal for cash – this will also help overcome the temptation to credit-card splurge.
- Most important of all, only buy the piece if you really like it and are sure it'll look the part back home – any other considerations such as future appreciation are mere distractions.

at €550. Turkish carpets are made using the double-knot technique, making them more durable than their single-knot Persian counterparts. The most famous Turkish carpets are Hereke, named after their town of origin. Pure silk, they have an extremely high knot density. Larger Hereke take up to four years to weave and cost around €1010 per square metre, with prime examples going for tens of thousands of euros. Silk carpets woven in the central Anatolian province of Kayseri are usually a third cheaper. Other key carpet maufacturing areas are Bergama, Uşak and Milas – all near the Aegean coast. Be warned – any carpets that seem suspiciously cheap, especially silk ones, are almost certainly Chinese, not Turkish.

Kilims

A **kilim** is a pile-less, flat-woven wool rug. The better ones are double-sided (that is, the pattern should look much the same top or bottom). A *cicim* is a kilim with additional, raised designs stitched onto it. Traditionally woven by nomadic Anatolian tribal groupings such as the Turcomans and Kurds, kilims are generally much more affordable than carpets. Prices for newly woven examples (invariably woven by women and sold by men) start from around €30 per square metre, whereas a rare antique kilim can fetch thousands of euros. The vast majority of kilims are heavily patterned with geometric motifs – invariably stylized birds, animals, flowers or other images from the natural world that formed the backdrop to the nomads' lives. Originally they served as floor coverings, tent partitions and blankets or, stitched together, as storage/saddlebags and bolsters.

Clothes

Turkish designs are beginning to match the quality of local fabrics such as Bursa silk and Angora wool. Nowadays you will pay near-Western prices for genuine locally designed items at reputable shops – local brands are aggressively protected from counterfeiting, if necessary by police raids.

However, many visitors find it hard to resist the allure of the cheap **fake designer clothing** available everywhere, with all the usual suspects (Armani, Diesel, Louis Vuitton et al) the victims. Genuine international designer wear is priced little differently to elsewhere.

Jewellery

Both in terms of design, quality and price, Turkey is a great country to buy **jewellery**, though gold prices in particular have rocketed in recent years. Gold and silver jewellery are sold by weight, with little regard for the disparate level of craftsmanship involved – at the time of writing silver was ₺1.9 per gram, gold ₺94 – and so too are semi-precious stones. One particularly intricate method is *telkâri* or wire filigree, most of which comes from eastern Turkey, particularly Diyarbakır and Mardin. Gold in particular can be very good value and is so pure (22 carat) that *telkâri* bangles bend easily. Also remember that sterling silver items should bear a hallmark.

Leather goods

Leather is still big business in Turkey. The industry was originally based in western Anatolia, where alum deposits and acorn-derived tannin aided the tanning process. Today, İzmir and İstanbul still have the largest workshops, though the retail business also booms on the Mediterranean coast, particularly in Antalya and Alanya. Jackets are the most obvious purchase, the prices of which vary from around €75 from a downmarket outlet to well over €350 from a branded "designer" shop such as Matraş, Desa or Derimod. Shoes are less good value and women's sizes rarely go over 40.

Miscellaneous souvenirs

A *tavla takimi* or **backgammon** set makes a good souvenir of Turkish popular culture. Mother-of-pearl inlaid sets are the most expensive, but fakes abound so if in doubt go for one of the plain, wood-inlay sets. **Copperware** is still spun and hammered in the traditional way in some Turkish towns, notably Gaziantep in the southeast. The most popular items are lidded jugs, large serving trays and bowls. *Mavi boncuk* (blue bead) key rings, lintel ornaments and animal collars are sold all over the place to ward off *nazar* (the evil eye).

Meerschaum **pipes**, carved from *lületaşı* stone quarried near Eskişehir, are available in all tourist areas. Less common are Karagöz puppets, representing the popular folk characters Karagöz and Hacıvat, preferably made from camel skin in Bursa. Towelling and silk goods, the best of which come from Bursa, are also good buys, as are the pure cotton *peştamal*s (the usually striped cotton wraps used in Turkish baths), bathrobes and tablecloths woven in Denizli. Kütahya **ceramics** may not be the finest ever produced in Turkey, but the vases, bowls, plates and, in particular, tiles, churned out in this western Anatolian town, are attractive enough and reasonable value as decorative items. Revived İznik ware is a cut above, and discussed fully on p.164. For more contemporary ceramics try the nationwide store Paşabahçe.

Musical instruments

Traditional Turkish **musical instruments** are sold all over the country. The most easily portable are the *ney*, the Mevlevî flute made from a length of calamus reed; the *davul* or drum; and the *saz/bağlama*, the long-necked Turkish lute. Rock and jazz musicians might like to score, a bit cheaper than abroad, a set of cymbals from one of two world-famous brands – İstanbul and Zildjian – both made by İstanbul-based or İstanbul-origin Armenian companies.

If you've any interest in local recordings it's worth listening to a cross section of Turkish styles and making a purchase (CDs go for ₺15 and up) or two. See p.691 for a discography of recommended items.

Spices and foodstuffs

Acknowledging the slight risk of having certain goods confiscated on return to the European Union or North America, locally produced **spices, condiments and foodstuffs** make for a compact, lightweight souvenir purchase. Low-grade saffron (*zafran*), the stamen of a particular kind of crocus, is still gathered in northern Anatolia. Sumac (*sumak*) is a ground-up purple leaf for sprinkling on barbecued meats and salad onions. Pine nuts (*çam fıstığı*), gathered in the coastal mountains, are excellent and, especially if purchased in northwest Turkey, are considerably cheaper than in Europe. *Pekmez* (molasses of grape, mulberry or carob pods) is nutritious and makes a splendid ice cream, muesli or yoghurt topping. Olive oil, most famously from Gemlik, is a worthwhile purchase, as are the olives it's made from. Olive-oil soaps are also popular, especially Defne Sabunı, a laurel-scented soap from Antakya. Both hot and sweet peppers are made into concentrated pastes (*salçalar*), while dried aubergine/eggplant and pepper shells are convenient for stuffing. *Nar eksisi* is a sour-sweet pomegranate syrup widely used as a salad dressing or meat marinade. Turkish Delight (*lokum*) is a perennial favourite and comes in a bewildering variety of flavours.

Sports and outdoor activities

Whether you want to stand alongside some of the most passionate football fans in the world, hike a long-distance trail, climb up or ski down a mighty peak, raft the rapids of a mountain torrent, or paraglide over/dive beneath the warm waters of the Mediterranean, Turkey is the place to do it.

Football

Football is hugely popular in Turkey. Most Turks, no matter where they are from, profess allegiance to one of the "Big Three" İstanbul sides – Galatasaray, Beşiktaş or Fenerbahçe (see p.108). The one exception is the Black Sea coastal town of Trabzon, whose citizens support their local team, Trabzonspor, which ranks up there with the İstanbul big boys.

Turkey has produced plenty of home-grown footballing talent (some now play in England, Germany and Spain), and many Turkish teams include international players, particularly from Africa and South America. The managers of the İstanbul giants are often recruited from abroad (with mixed results; Spain's successful national coach Arragones lasted only a year at Fenerbahçe). Although the teams qualifying for the Champions League usually fall at the first hurdle, Galatasaray became the first Turkish team to win the UEFA Cup (in 2000; beating Arsenal 4–1 on penalties).

ANTIQUES AND SMUGGLING: A WARNING

Under Turkish law it is an offence to buy, sell, export or even possess genuine antiquities (which includes fossils). Exact age limits are not specified, suggesting that decisions by customs officials are subjective, though a principal measure of antiquity is rarity. At popular archeological sites like Ephesus, you may be offered "antiques" by hawkers, which are invariably fake.

In the case of **carpets** handled by established dealers, you run a very slight risk of investing a lot of money in a supposed "collector's item" that turns out to be collectable only by the Turkish Republic. If you're apprehensive about a proposed purchase, ask the dealer to prepare both a *fatura* (invoice) recording the exact purchase price – also necessary to satisfy customs – and a declaration stating that the item is not an antiquity. Expect a heavy fine and possibly imprisonment if you transgress these laws.

Matches are played between September and May. There's usually a match on Friday evening, then more on Saturday afternoons/evenings and Sunday afternoon. Obtaining **tickets** for provincial teams is usually both cheap and easy, with tickets available at the ground on match day for as little as ₺10, but prices can rise tenfold when one of the İstanbul "giants" is in town. Many bars show games on big screens, and can be very atmospheric, especially for derby games.

Football violence is not uncommon (in 2000, two English Leeds United fans were stabbed to death in İstanbul during running street-fighting with Galatasaray fans), though the average foreigner is unlikely to get caught up in trouble. Turkish football was scarred by a big match-fixing scandal in 2012, which delayed the start of the new season and resulted in Fenerbahçe's chairman being jailed. After big games, especially those involving the "Big Three", expect delirious celebrations, with flag-waving fans leaning on the horns of cruising cars embroiled in massive traffic jams.

Hiking and mountaineering

Turkey's wild mountain ranges are a treat for experienced hikers prepared to carry their own tents and food and cope with few facilities. The lack of decent maps makes mountain exploration a real adventure, but the unspoiled countryside, the hospitality of rural Turks, the fascination of the *yayla*s (summer pastures), and the friendliness of other mountaineers more than compensate.

The alpine **Kaçkar Dağları**, paralleling the Black Sea, are the most rewarding mountains in Turkey for trekking, and several companies organize expeditions there. Next up in interest are the limestone **Toros (Taurus) ranges**, especially the lofty Aladağlar mountains south of Cappadocia.

Aside from this, high-altitude **mountaineering** in Turkey consists mostly of climbing the volcanoes of the central plateau. All offer superb views from their summits. Most famous is 5137m **Ağrı Dağ**, or Ararat (see p.644) on the eastern borders of Turkey, though this requires a special permit because of its sensitive location. By contrast, 3916m **Erciyes Dağı** (see p.462) offers exhilarating climbing without any of the expense or bureaucracy prevalent at Ararat. **Süphan Dağı** (see p.628) Turkey's second-highest volcanic peak (4058m), stands in splendid isolation north of Lake Van. Unfortunately the magnificent Cilo–Sat mountains south of Lake Van are sometimes a battleground between the Kurdish separatists and Turkish security forces so are currently closed to outsiders.

Hiking equipment and safety

Alpine huts are nonexistent, so you'll need to carry full camping gear to trek in the mountains. It's best to bring your own as only İstanbul and Ankara have European-standard mountaineering shops. **Water** can be a problem in the limestone strata of the Toros, while on the volcanoes, detailed **maps** are very difficult to obtain and **trails** (when present) are seldom marked.

Rescue services are no match for those in more developed mountain areas in Europe and the US, but things are improving. The local *jandarma* (see p.57) will turn out in an emergency, and AKUT (Search and Rescue Association; ⓦ akut.org.tr) have established eight centres across western, southern and central Turkey (though not yet in the popular Kaçkar range).

You'll find details on specific hiking routes through the Kaçkar Dağları, and a selection of walks on Bursa's Uludağ and along the Turquoise Coast, in the Guide, but if you're daunted at the prospect of going alone, contact one of the adventure-travel companies listed on p.30.

WAYMARKED TRAILS

The exhilarating **Lycian Way** long-distance trail (see p.304) weaves its way through the westernmost reaches of the Toros, while the more challenging **St Paul Trail** (see p.421) crosses the range from south to north. Both trails are marked with red-and-white paint flashes and take in some stunning mountain and gorge scenery, remote ancient sites and timeless villages. Each has its own guidebook and map (see p.700), with more information on ⓦ trekkinginturkey.com.

A number of other trails have recently sprung up. These include the **Evliya Çelebi Way** in northwest Turkey, a trail suitable for horseriders and walkers; **Abraham's Path**, linking Yuvacalı village (see p.591) with Harran and the Syrian border; the **Carian Way** on the southwest Aegean coast; and the **Phrygian Way**. You can find more information on those routes, and several others, at ⓦ cultureroutesinturkey.com.

Except for the long-distance trails and the Kaçkar mountains (see p.556), it's virtually impossible to obtain large-scale **topographical maps** of specific areas for **trekking** (though usable enough maps for the most popular trekking areas can be found in *Trekking in Turkey*, an unfortunately out-of-print guide that's still available secondhand).

Skiing

While few foreigners come to Turkey specifically to **ski**, the sport is growing in popularity, and if you're visiting between December and April it's well worth considering a day or more on the piste. If you're willing to forego doorstep skiing, it's surprisingly easy and cheap to ski while based in towns like Erzurum or Bursa that are near to resorts. The Turkish State Meteorological Service gives information on snow heights at the various resorts (ⓦmgm.gov.tr).

Turkey's best-known ski resort is **Uludağ**, above Bursa, with easy and intermediate runs, but the slopes are prone to melt and snow turns slushy after February. The **Saklıkent** complex in the Beydağları near Antalya would seem potentially ideal for an early spring sea-cum-ski holiday, but snow cover tends to be thin and the runs are limited. Close by is much better **Davraz**, near İsparta, where snow conditions are more reliable and there's plentiful accommodation in the nearby lakeside town of Eğirdir as well as at the resort. Roughly midway between İstanbul and Ankara, near Bolu, **Kartalkaya** is better than any of the foregoing, despite a modest top altitude of 2223m; facilities now nearly match those of Uludağ, plus there are several red and black runs and, most importantly, in recent years there has been plentiful snow. The longest season and best snow conditions are usually at **Palandöken**, near Erzurum, where the top lift goes over 3000m and the Turkish Olympic team trains; there are three chairlifts, one T-bar and a 3km gondola car to service a mix of blue and red runs. At **Tekir Yaylası** on Erciyes Dağı near Kayseri, the season is nearly as long, the snow almost as powdery, and the top lift is 2770m (one to 3100m is planned), though thus far runs are only green and red grade, served by two chairlifts and two T-bars. **Sarıkamış**, near Kars, has two chairlifts and one T-bar to service a handful of runs (mostly red and blue grade); top lift is 2634m.

Watersports

Most medium to large resorts offer **waterskiing** and its offspring, **parasailing**; the even more exciting thrill of **kite-surfing** is centred on Alaçatı,

---

> ### BIRDWATCHING
>
> Turkey stands astride several major bird migration routes and possesses some very bird-friendly habitat. Well-known birdwatching sites include the Göksu delta near Silifke (see p.384), the Belen Pass en-route to Antakya (see p.400), and Lake Van (see p.629). On an active birdwatching holiday you could expect to tick off nearly three hundred different species. For a database of bird species and distribution in Turkey, as reported by local and foreign birdwatchers, see ⓦkusbank.org.

near Çeşme, while **windsurfers** head for the Bodrum peninsula. **Sea kayaking** makes a great way to explore the indented coastline, islets and shallow, clear waters in the environs of the southwest Mediterranean resort of Kaş.

For more thrills and spills but less skill (you just sit there unless you happen to be thrown – or pushed – into the torrent), there's also **whitewater rafting**. This is very popular on the Köprülü River near Antalya and the Dalaman River close to Fethiye, though for more serious outings the dam-threatened Çoruh in northeast Turkey is a world-class rafting river. Another freshwater-based activity of a very different nature is **canyoning**, which involves abseiling down waterfalls, leaping into plunge pools and generally exploring precipitous gorges – trips are organized by outfits in Kaş.

Scuba diving is one of the most popular water-based activities; outfits in Kaş, Kalkan and, further west, in Bodrum, Marmaris and Fethiye offer instruction and gear. There are underwater reefs and fish, wrecks and caves to explore, all in the (usually) clear, calm and warm waters of the Aegean/Mediterranean.

Other activities

With cheap flights, countless rock faces and ample winter sun, it's only a matter of time before Turkey begins to rival Spain on the itineraries of **climbers**. The best place to start is Geyikbayırı, conveniently located just 25km from the gateway Mediterranean resort of Antalya. Five hundred bolted routes track their way up an imposing limestone cliff, and there are several camping/wooden chalet-style places to stay in the forest below. There's more climbing from beach level at the beautiful resort of nearby Olympos. For more information check out ⓦclimb -europe.com.

Cappadocia's bizarrely sculpted rock pinnacles and plunging valleys rank among the world's most striking landscapes. The best way to see this geological wonderland is to drift over it in an expertly piloted **hot-air balloon**. For more of an adrenaline rush, try paragliding (in tandem with a qualified pilot) from the mountains behind the bustling resorts of Kaş or Ölüdeniz.

Travelling with children

Turks adore children, and Turkish families tend to take their children with them wherever they go, thinking nothing of letting them run around restaurants until the early hours. In this sense, the country is a great place to visit with kids. And, of course, the coastal resorts offer a generally calm, warm sea and have pools, beaches (and sometimes water-parks) aplenty. On the down side, the number of play areas and children's attractions lags far behind Western Europe.

Turks have an uninhibited Mediterranean attitude toward children. Don't be surprised to find your child receive an affectionate pinch on the cheek by a passer-by, often accompanied by the word *maşallah*, which serves both to praise your offspring and ward off the evil eye, while waiters will sometimes unselfconsciously pick a kid up and waltz them off into the kitchen to show their workmates, often accompanied by cries all around of "how sweet" ("*çok tatlı*").

With a few honourable exceptions (eg Miniatürk and the Rahmi M. Koç Industrial Museum in İstanbul, and minicity in Antalya), there are few **attractions** aimed specifically at younger children, and few museums have kid-friendly displays or activities. And for buggy-pushing parents, the uneven surfaces and metre-high kerbs of the average Turkish pavement (where there is one) are a nightmare. For older kids there are plenty of outdoor activities on offer – kayaking and windsurfing at some coastal resorts, for example, and whitewater rafting, mountain biking and canyoning in the hinterland.

Turkish **food** should appeal to most kids – what's *köfte* but a (very) tasty burger, *pide* a pizza without the tomato paste, and *gözleme* a stuffed pancake? Maraş ice cream is just as delicious as Italian gelato and comes in myriad flavours. In general, restaurants are very welcoming to families – just don't expect highchairs. Disposable nappies are widely available from supermarkets and the larger *bakkals*.

Travel essentials

Archeological sites

Most **archeological sites** open daily between either 8am, 8.30am or 9pm and 6.30pm or 7pm in summer; the exact times are listed in the Guide. Winter opening hours are usually shorter. Some smaller archeological sites are only guarded during the day and left unfenced, permitting (in theory) a free wander around in the evening, though, in the wake of antiquities theft (see p.53), this could feasibly result in you being picked up by the *jandarma*.

Don't pay **entrance fees** unless the wardens can produce a ticket, and keep it with you for the duration of your visit. Sites like Patara and Olympos straddle the route to a good beach. If you are staying nearby and want to visit the beach on several occasions, Smart PlajKarts are available, allowing multiple site/beach entries. One card can be shared but they are only valid for ten days.

Beaches

Except near major cities, where seawater is sometimes polluted, Turkish **beaches** are safe to swim at, though be prepared for occasional mountains of rubbish piled at the back of the beach. Tar can also be a problem on south-coast beaches that face Mediterranean shipping lanes; if you get tar on your feet scrub it off with olive oil rather than chemical solvents. All beaches are free in theory, though luxury compounds that straddle routes to the sand will control access in various ways, and you'll pay for the use of beach-loungers and umbrellas.

Costs

Turkey is no longer the cheap destination it used to be; **prices** in the heavily touristed areas are comparable to many places in Europe. Exercise a little restraint, however, be prepared to live life at least occasionally at the local level (many Turks somehow survive on ₺700 a month) and you can still enjoy a great-value trip here.

Stay in a "treehouse" or backpackers' inn, eat in local workers' cafés or restaurants, travel around by train or bus, avoid alcohol and the most expensive sites, and you could get by on ₺60–75 (€30–37.50) a day. If that doesn't sound like much fun, double that and you could stay in a modest hotel, see the sights and have a beer or two with your evening meal. Equally, a night out on the town in İstanbul or one of the flasher coastal resorts could easily set you back over ₺100 (€50), and if you intend to see a lot of what is a very big country, transport costs could be a considerable drain on your budget – though taking night buses saves accommodation costs.

The more expensive tourist sites such as Ephesus, the Tokapı Palace and Aya Sofya cost ₺25 (€12.50), but there are many more sites varying between ₺3 and ₺15. There are no student discounts, and the *Müze Kart* (Museum Card), which gives admission to all state-run museums for ₺30 per annum, is for Turkish citizens only.

Crime and personal safety

Turkey's **crime rate** remains lower than most of Europe and North America, although pickpocketing and purse-snatching are becoming more common in İstanbul (see p.72) and other major cities. Violent street crime is fortunately rare. Keep your wits about you and an eye on your belongings just as you would anywhere else, and make sure your passport is secure at all times, and you shouldn't have any problems. Except for well-known "red-light" districts, and some eastern towns, female travellers (see p.45 for more) are probably safer on their own than in other European countries.

As well as the usual warnings on drugs, note that exporting antiquities (see p.53) is illegal. It is also an offence to **insult Atatürk or Turkey**, which can result in a prison sentence. Never deface, degrade or tear up currency or the flag; drunkenness will likely be considered an aggravating, not a mitigating, factor. Also, do not take **photographs** near the numerous, well-marked military zones.

The police, army and gendarmerie

Turkey's police service is split into several groups. The blue-uniformed **Polis** are the everyday security force in cities and towns with populations over two thousand; the white-capped **Trafik Polis** (traffic police) are a branch of this service. İstanbul and several other large towns have a rapid-response squad of red-and-black-uniformed motorbike police known as the *yunus* (dolphin) *polis*; they are generally courteous and helpful to tourists and may speak some English. The dark-blue-uniformed **Çevik Kuvvet Polis** are a rapid response team most likely seen at demonstrations, football matches and other events where large crowds are expected. In towns **Belediye Zabıtası**, the navy-clad market police, patrol the markets and bazaars to ensure that tradesmen aren't ripping off customers – approach them directly if you have reason for complaint. You're unlikely to come across plain-clothes police unless you wander off the beaten track in the ethnically Kurdish southeast (see p.57).

In most rural areas, law enforcement is in the hands of the **jandarma** or gendarmerie, a division of the regular army charged with law-enforcement duties. Gendarmes are usually kitted out in well-tailored green fatigues; most are conscripts who will be courteous and helpful if approached.

Note that it is obligatory to **carry ID** at all times – for locals and foreigners alike – so if you are concerned about having your passport stolen (or losing it) while out and about, at least carry a photocopy of the pages with your details and Turkish entry stamp on your person.

Security and restricted areas

There is a noticeable security presence in the Kurdish-dominated southeast of the country, with firefights between Turkish security forces and the autonomy-minded **PKK** (Kurdish Workers Party) continuing at the time of writing. Security is tightest along the Iraqi and Iranian borders, particularly south and east of Hakkari and around Şırnak in the mountains south of Lake Van, in the rural

---

KDV: TURKISH VAT

The Turkish variety of VAT (*Katma Değer Vergisi* or **KDV**), ranging from eight to 23 percent depending on the commodity, is included in the price of virtually all goods and services (except car rental, where the 18 percent figure is usually quoted separately). Look for the notice *Fiyatlarımız KDV Dahildir* (VAT included in our prices) if you think someone's trying to do you for it twice. There's a VAT refund scheme for large souvenir purchases made by those living outside Turkey, but it's such a rigmarole to get that it's probably not worth pursuing; if you insist, ask the shop to provide a *KDV İade Özel Fatura* (Special VAT Refund Invoice), assuming that it participates – very few do, and they tend to be the most expensive shops.

hinterland of Diyarbakır and in the mountainous region of Tunceli (the last not covered in this Guide). PKK attacks are invariably made in remote rural areas, often targeting military vehicles with remotely detonated bombs, though occasional fully-fledged assaults on military outposts are made – inevitably followed by major reprisals by Turkish security forces.

Kidnappings of Turkish military personnel and civilians have also become increasingly common, and in spring 2012 a British traveller was briefly detained by the PKK having been kidnapped from an inter-city bus in Diyarbakir province. Given the civil war that was raging in Syria at the time of writing, the 800km Turkish/Syrian border could also become problematic, especially as Turkey's biggest nightmare, a proto-Kurdish state run by Syria's Kurdish minority, appeared to be developing across the frontier.

But what does this mean to the average traveller hoping to visit this beautiful region? The British Foreign and Commonwealth Office, for example, posts the following on its website (ⓦfco.gov.uk) "Due to the high risk of terrorism we advise against all but essential travel to the provinces of Hakkari, Şırnak, Siirt and Tunceli. Visitors should remain vigilant when travelling in other provinces in south-eastern Turkey". The official line, then, is to avoid the mountains south of Lake Van that border the de facto Kurdish state in northern Iraq – but then places like Tunceli are a long, long way from the border, and the FCO in any case also writes "There is a high risk of terrorism in Turkey" full stop. The problem is compounded by the ever-fluctuating state of relations between the state and the PKK, with long ceasefires interrupted by violent flare-ups. Although at the time of writing (2012) PKK attacks were fairly numerous, it's quite possible the situation may have calmed down dramatically by the time you read this. In other words, read about what is happening in the press and on travellers' forums, and use your common sense and judgement before you travel.

Although there are fewer checkpoints on main roads than there were, you may be stopped if you attempt to travel to off-the-beaten-track sites and/or villages, and your presence may attract the attention of the *jandarma* (and quite possibly the plain-clothes secret police, who generally stand out a mile from the locals). This may involve, at most, a rather tedious, though polite, interrogation. Lone males especially may find themselves suspected of being journalists and/or having Kurdish/Armenian sympathies. Avoid talking politics with anyone unless you are absolutely sure you can trust them, and, if you are questioned, keep calm, smile a lot, and emphasize wherever possible that you are a *turist* (tourist). Of more concern to the average visitor are the violent pro-Kurdish street demonstrations that break out from time to time in south-eastern cities such as Diyarbakır and Van – though major cities in the west of the country are not immune, especially İstanbul, Adana and Mersin, which have large and sometimes volatile Kurdish communities. One traditional spark for demonstrations is the Kurdish New Year or Nevruz (Newroz), on or around March 21. For more information on the Kurdish problem see Contexts.

Electricity

Turkey operates on 220 volts, 50 Hz. Most European appliances should work so long as you have an adaptor for European-style two-pin plugs. American appliances will need a transformer as well as an adaptor.

Entry requirements

Early in 2012 Turkey changed its **tourist visa** rules. Prior to this amendment it was possible to enter the country on a 90-day visa, then at the end of that period slip across the border to a Greek island, Bulgaria or even North Cyprus, re-enter immediately and get a new three-month stamp. Mainly in order to stop people living and working (illegally) in the country for an indefinite period, the new visa is valid for 90 days within 180 days. In other words, stay for 90 days consecutively, and you cannot re-enter for another 90 days. Alternatively, you can make multiple trips to Turkey within the 180-day validity period of the visa so long as the total stay does not exceed 90 days.

The **tourist visas** (available at ports of entry for a fee) are issued to citizens of the UK ($20, €15 or £10), Ireland ($20, €10 or £10), the US (($20 or €15), Canada ($60 or €45) and Australia (($20 or €15). South Africans should be able to get a 30-day visa at the point of entry, but would be wise to enquire at a Turkish consulate before travelling. New Zealanders do not currently require visas. Everyone, regardless of nationality, should have at least six months' validity on their passport. For the latest information on visas, check with the Turkish Ministry of Foreign Affairs at ⓦmfa.gov.tr.

If you want to stay in the country longer than a tourist visa allows, the best option is to apply for a six-month **residence permit** from the Security

Division (*Emniyet Müdürlüğü*), preferably in a provincial capital that's well used to foreigners. Do this well before your time expires, as it takes at least two weeks to process. You will need to complete an "Ikamet izni beyanname formu" application form and supply four passport-sized photographs, along with photocopies from your passport of the photo-page and the page showing your last entry into Turkey. The rub is that you also need to show that you have changed $500 for each of the six months – showing change receipts from a bank or *döviz* will suffice. Residence permit rates vary according to nationality – UK citizens for example pay $80 (payable in ₺ on the day, according to the exchange rate on the day you apply), but the cost of the "blue book" containing the permit is a steep ₺172. This is a one-off payment, however, as once you have the book you can keep renewing your permit for periods of between six months and ten years.

Turkish embassies and consulates abroad

Australia 60 Mugga Way, Red Hill, Canberra ACT 2603 ☎ 02 6295 0227.
Canada 197 Wurtemburg St, Ottawa, ON K1N 8L9 ☎ 613 789 4044.
Ireland 11 Clyde Rd, Ballsbridge, Dublin 4 ☎ 01 668 5240.
New Zealand 15–17 Murphy St, Level 8, Wellington ☎ 04 472 1290.
South Africa 1067 Church St, Hatfield 0181, Pretoria ☎ 012 342 5063.
UK 43 Belgrave Square, London SW1X 8PA ☎ 0207 393 0202.
US 2525 Massachusetts Ave NW, Washington, DC 20008 ☎ 202 612 6700.

Customs and border inspections

As Turkey is not yet an EU member, **duty-free limits** – and sales – for alcohol and tobacco are still prevalent. Limits are posted clearly at İstanbul's airports, and apply for all frontiers.

Few people get stopped departing Turkey, but the guards may be on the lookout for **antiquities** and **fossils**. Penalties for trying to smuggle these out include long jail sentences, plus a large fine. What actually constitutes an antiquity is rather vague (see p.53), but it's best not to take any chances.

Insurance

It is essential to take out an **insurance policy** before you travel, to cover against illness or injury, as well as theft or loss. Some all-risks homeowners' or renters' insurance policies may cover your possessions when overseas, and many private medical schemes (such as BUPA and WPA) offer coverage extensions for abroad.

Rough Guides offers its own insurance policy, detailed in the box below. Most policies exclude so-called **dangerous sports** unless an extra premium is paid: in Turkey this can mean scuba diving, whitewater rafting, paragliding, windsurfing and trekking, though probably not kayaking or jeep safaris. Travel agents and package operators may require travel insurance when you book a holiday – you're not obliged to take theirs, though you have to sign a declaration saying that you already have another policy. Similarly, many no-frills airlines make a tidy sum from selling unnecessary insurance at the time of booking – beware, and opt out.

Internet

Many hotels, pensions and hostels have **internet access** – often both terminals and wi-fi signal – as do an ever-increasing number of cafés. Access is usually free except in the more expensive international chain hotels. In more remote places in the interior, and the east of the country, only the more expensive hotels have wi-fi. Rates in internet cafés tend to be ₺2 per hour. The Turkish-character keyboard you'll probably be faced with may cause some confusion. The "@" sign is made by simultaneously pressing the "ALT" and "q" keys. More frustrating is the dotless "ı" (confusingly enough found right where you'll be expecting the conventional "i") – the Western "i" is located second key from right, middle row.

Mail

Post offices are easily spotted by their bold black-on-yellow **PTT** (Posta, Telegraf, Telefon) signs. Stamps are only available from the PTT, whose website (W ptt .gov.tr) has a (not necessarily up-to-date) English-language listing of services and prices. Post offices are generally open Monday to Friday 8.30am to 5.30pm and until noon on Saturday. Airmail (*uçakla*) rates to Europe are ₺1.10 for postcards, ₺2 for letters up to 20g, ₺19 for 2kg, the maximum weight for letters. Delivery to Europe or North America can take seven to ten days. A pricier express (*acele*) service cuts delivery times to the EU to about three days. When sending airmail, it's best to give your stamped letter/card to the clerk behind the counter, who will ensure it gets put in the right place; otherwise, place it in the relevant slot if one is available (*yurtdışı* for abroad; *yurtiçi* for elsewhere in Turkey).

Maps

Maps of Turkey are notoriously poor quality owing to the lack of survey-based cartography. The best **foreign-produced touring maps**, accurately showing many smaller villages, are those published by Kartographischer Verlag Reinhard Ryborsch (1:500,000; Frankfurt, Germany), which cover the entire country in seven maps. They are usually available online, but both original and pirated versions are sold at better bookshops in İstanbul, Ankara and big resorts. Reasonable second choices, easier to obtain, include Insight's *Turkey West* and Insight *Turkey* (both 1:800,000), both of which are easy to read and reasonably accurate, and the equally reliable Turkey Geocentre Euro map (1:750,000).

In terms of **Turkish-produced touring maps**, the 1:400,000 atlas produced by *Atlas* magazine is highly accurate but difficult to read owing to murky printing. The best regional touring maps are Sabri Aydal's 1:250,000 products for Cappadocia, Lycia, Pamphylia and Pisidia, available from local bookshops and museums.

İstanbul, Ankara, Antalya, Bursa and İzmir (as well as overseas) tourist offices stock reasonable, free **city street plans**. Sketch plans from provincial tourist offices vary widely in quality.

Among **Turkish-produced city maps**, Net's "All of İstanbul" 1:9000 is more comprehensive than Keskin

Colour's 1:8500 "İstanbul Street Plan", and includes useful maps of the Prince's islands. The most detailed A–Z-style atlas for the European side, ideal for out-of-the-way monuments, is Mepmedya's 1:7500 "İstanbul Avrupa Yakası", though it's pricey (₺50) and heavy. All these are sold in town and (Mepmedya excepted) cheaper than anything produced abroad.

For **trekking maps** see p.54.

Money

Turkey's currency is the Turkish Lira (Türk Lirası) or ₺ for short, divided into smaller units known as kuruş. Coins come in denominations of 1, 5, 10, 25, 50 kuruş and ₺1, with notes in denominations of ₺5, ₺10, ₺20, ₺50, ₺100 and ₺200. The symbol ₺, introduced in 2012 to reflect the growing confidence in the stability and value of the currency, is slowly phasing out the old system, where the price was suffixed by the letters TL, as in 10TL.

At the time of writing the **exchange rate** was around ₺2.10 to the euro, ₺2.70 to the pound and ₺1.70 to the US dollar. As recently as 2004 hyperinflation meant that millions of lira were needed to purchase the smallest everyday item. and many Turks still talk in millions, which can be confusing when you are asked "bir milyon" or one million lira for a ₺1 glass of tea.

Rates for foreign currency are always better inside Turkey, so try not to buy much lira at home. Conversely, don't leave Turkey with unspent lira, as you won't get a decent exchange rate for them outside the country. It's wise to bring a fair wad of **hard currency** with you (euros are best, though dollars and sterling are often accepted), as you can often use it to pay directly for souvenirs or accommodation (prices for both are frequently quoted in euros). **Travellers' cheques** are, frankly, not worth the bother, as exchange offices (see p.60) and some banks refuse them.

Changing money

While most banks, such as İşbank and Yapıkredi, change money, the best exchange rate is usually given by the **state-owned banks** Ziraat Bankası, which has dedicated *döviz* (exchange) counters – but despite the automated ticket/queuing system queues can be long. **Döviz**, or exchange houses, are common in Turkey's cities and resorts. They buy and sell foreign currency of most sorts instantly, and have the convenience of long opening hours (usually 9/10am–8/10pm) and short or nonexistent queues. Most do not charge commission, but give a lower rate than the banks.

Remember to keep all foreign-exchange slips with you until departure, if only to prove the value of purchases made in case of queries by customs.

Credit/debit cards and ATMs

Credit cards are widely used in hotels, shops, restaurants, travel agencies and entertainment venues and with no commission (though many hotels and shops offer discounts for cash rather than credit-card payments). Don't expect, however, to use your card in basic eating places or small corner shops. Swipe readers plus **chip-and-PIN** protocol are now the norm in most of Turkey.

The simplest way to get hold of money in Turkey is to use the widespread **ATM** network. Most bank ATMs will accept any debit cards that are part of the Cirrus, Maestro or Visa/Plus systems. Screen prompts are given in English on request. You can also normally get cash advances at any bank displaying the appropriate sign, and in major cities and resorts some ATMs will give euros and dollars. It's safest to use ATMs attached to banks during normal working hours, so help can be summoned if your card is eaten (not uncommon). Turkish ATMs sometimes "time out" without disgorging cash, while your home bank may still debit your account – leaving you to argue the toss with them. ATM fraud is rife in Turkey – make sure you are not overlooked when keying in your PIN. You can also use Visa or MasterCard to get cash from ATMs.

Opening hours and public holidays

Office workers keep conventional Monday to Friday 9am to 6pm schedules, with a full lunch hour. Civil servants, including tourist offices and museum staff, in theory work 8.30am to 5.30pm, but in practice hours can be much more erratic – don't expect to get official business attended to the same day after 2.30pm. Most state **banks** are open Monday to Friday, 8.30am to noon and 1.30pm to 5pm. Private banks such as Garanti Bankası and Koç operate throughout the day.

Ordinary **shops**, including large department stores and mall outlets, are open continuously from 8.30am or 9am until 7pm or 8pm (sometimes even later in many major cities and resorts). Craftsmen and bazaar stallholders often work from 9am to 8pm or 9pm, Monday to Saturday, with only short breaks for meals, tea or prayers. Even on Sunday the tradesmen's area may not be completely shut down – though don't count on this.

Museums are generally open from 8.30am or 9am until 4.30pm or 5pm in winter, later in the summer. Virtually all state, and some private, museums are closed on Monday, though in İstanbul closing days are staggered so make sure you check the individual listings. All tourist sites and museums are closed on the mornings of public holidays (see p.61). Mosques are theoretically open all the time, but many of the less visited ones are kept locked outside of prayer times, and many do not encourage visitors at prayer times!

Public holidays

Secular **public holidays** are generally marked by processions of schoolchildren or the military, or by some demonstration of national strength and dignity, such as a sports display. Banks and government offices will normally be closed on these days (exceptions given below). See p.48 for religious holidays.

Jan 1 *Yılbaşı* – New Year's Day.

April 23 *Ulusal Egemenlik ve Çocuk Bayramı* – Independence Day, celebrating the first meeting of the new Republican parliament in Ankara, and Children's Day.

May 19 *Gençlik ve Spor Günü* – Youth and Sports Day, also Atatürk's birthday.

May 29 İstanbul's capture by Mehmet the Conqueror in 1453 (İstanbul only).

July 1 *Denizcilik Günü* – Navy Day (banks and offices open).

Aug 26 *Silahlı Kuvvetler Günü* – Armed Forces Day (banks and offices open).

Aug 30 *Zafer Bayramı* – Celebration of the Turkish victory over the Greek forces at Dumlupınar in 1922.

Sept 9 *Kurtuluş Günü* – Liberation Day, with parades and speeches marking the end of the Independence War (İzmir only).

Oct 29 *Cumhuriyet Bayramı* – commemorates the proclamation of the Republic by Atatürk in 1923.

Nov 10 *Anniversary of Atatürk's death in 1938*. Observed at 9.05am (the time of his demise), when the whole country stops whatever it's doing and maintains a respectful silence for a minute. It's worth being on a Bosphorus ferry then, when all the engines are turned off, and the boats drift and sound their foghorns mournfully.

Phones

Most fixed-line **telecom services** are provided by TT (Türk Telekom); its website (🌐 turktelekom.com .tr) has an English-language page listing all services and tariffs. The best place to make phone calls is from either a PTT (post office) or a TT (Türk Telekom) centre. Inside, or just adjacent, there is usually a row of card (*kontürlü* or *smartkart*) call boxes (TTs are blue and turquoise), and/or a *kontürlü* (metered, clerk-attended) phone, the latter sometimes in a

USEFUL TELEPHONE NUMBERS

EMERGENCY NUMBERS

Ambulance ☎112
Fire ☎110
Police ☎155
Tourist Police ☎0212 527 4503

ASSISTANCE

Directory assistance ☎118
International operator (reverse charges) ☎115
Intercity operator ☎131

INTERNATIONAL DIALLING CODES

Australia ☎61
Ireland ☎353
New Zealand ☎64
South Africa ☎27
UK ☎44
US & Canada ☎1

---

closed booth. **Public phones** are to be found in squares and parks, outside many public buildings and at train stations and ferry terminals. The standard Turkish phone replies are the Frenchified *Allo* or the more local *Buyurun* (literally, "Avail yourself/at your service").

"Smart" **phonecards** are available from PTT or TT centres; when using these, wait for the number of units remaining to appear on the screen before you dial, and be aware that you will have little warning of being cut off. They are bought in units of 50 (₺3.75), 100 (₺7.50), 200 (₺15) and 350 (₺19). A steadily increasing number of phones have also been adapted to accept foreign **credit cards**. **Metered booths** inside PTTs or TTs, or at street kiosks or shops (look for signs reading *kontürlü telefon bulunur*), work out more expensive than cards, but are certainly far cheaper than hotels, and also tend to be quieter (plus you won't be cut off). Their disadvantage is that you can't see the meter ticking over, and instances of overcharging are not unknown.

Overseas calls

Overseas call rates are ₺0.25 per minute to Europe or North America. Try not to make anything other than local calls from a hotel room – there's usually a minimum 100 percent surcharge on phonecard rates. For extended chat overseas, it's best to buy an international phonecard. Best is the Alocard, available from PTT branches and usable in public phones. Reveal the 12-digit PIN by scratching; then call the domestic access number, followed by the destination number. Rates are low – for example, a ₺10 card allows 104 minutes to the UK or US. The cards can also be used for domestic calls, giving 140 minutes of calling time.

Turkey uses a system of eleven-digit **phone numbers** nationwide, consisting of four-digit area or mobile-provider codes (all starting with "0") plus a seven-digit subscriber number.

To call a number in Turkey **from overseas**, dial your country's international access code, then 90 for Turkey, then the area or mobile code minus the initial zero, and finally the subscriber number. To call home **from Turkey**, dial ☎00 followed by the

GETTING MOBILE

Given the Turkish penchant for chatting, **mobile phones** are essential accessories here. Assuming that you have a roaming facility, your home mobile will connect with one of the local network providers – however, US mobiles won't work here. Charges, though, are high (up to £1.30/min to the UK), and you pay for incoming calls as well. Purchasing a **local SIM card** and pay-as-you-go package may be worth considering if you intend to make a lot of calls. Turkcell SIM cards (which can take up to 24hr to activate) cost ₺35, including ₺5 calling credit, or ₺45 will get you the card and ₺20 credit. Typically, calls cost 80 kuruş per min to Europe and North America, an SMS message to the UK the same. To purchase a SIM card, you'll need to sign an agreement form and present your passport for photocopying at a major Turkcell, Avea or Vodafone outlet where they'll fit the new card. All three companies have stands at arrivals in Istanbul's Atatürk and Sabiha Gökçen airports; Turkcell has the widest coverage. Note that the rules on bringing in mobiles from overseas and using them with a Turkish SIM card change regularly. This is because mobiles are much cheaper when bought outside the country, so the government keeps introducing ever more stringent conditions in the hope of preventing people bringing them in and selling them on. At the time of writing, a mobile registered at a legitimate outlet can be used with a Turkish SIM for one month, after which it will be blocked. If you buy from one of the many smaller mobile phone stores and don't sign an agreement you run the risk of your phone not being registered for use in Turkey, and it will be blocked within a matter of days.

relevant international dialling code (see p.62), then the area code (without the initial zero if there is one) then the number.

Time

Turkey is two hours ahead of GMT in winter. As in Europe, daylight saving is observed between March and October – clocks change at 2am on the last Sunday in each month – so effectively Turkey remains two hours ahead of the UK year-round.

Tourist information

Most Turkish towns of any size will have a *Turizm Danışma Bürosu* or **tourist office** of some sort, often lodged inside the *Belediye* (city hall) in the smaller places. However, outside the larger cities and obvious tourist destinations there's often little hard information to be had, and world-weary staff may dismiss you with useless brochures. Lists of accommodation are sometimes kept at the busier offices; personnel, however, will generally not make bookings. On the other hand, staff in out-of-the-way places can be embarrassingly helpful. It's best to have a specific question – about bus schedules, festival ticket availability or museum opening hours – although in remote regions there is no guarantee that there will be anyone who can speak English.

Tourist offices generally adhere to a standard opening schedule of 8.30am to 12.30pm and 1.30pm to 5.30pm, Monday to Friday. Between May and September in big-name resorts and large cities, these hours extend well into the evening and through much of the weekend. In winter, by contrast, many tourist offices in out-of-the-way spots will be shut most of the time.

Turkish information offices abroad

Overseas Turkish tourist offices (often the embassy's Information Office) will provide a few very basic maps and glossy brochures. For more information check Ⓦ goturkey.com.

UK 29–30 St James's St, London SW1A 1HB ☎ 0207 8397778, Ⓦ gototurkey.co.uk.

US 821 United Nations Plaza, New York, NY 10017 ☎ 212 687 2194; 2525 Massachusetts Ave NW, Washington, DC 20008 ☎ 202 612 6800; 5055 Wilshire Blvd, Suite 850, Los Angeles CA 90036 ☎ 323 937 8066, Ⓦ tourismturkey.org.

Useful websites

Ⓦ **biletix.com** An online booking service for arts, cultural, music and sports events (mainly in İstanbul and Ankara), in both English and Turkish.

Ⓦ **cultureroutesinturkey.com** Umbrella site for all the country's hiking and horseriding trails.

Ⓦ **goturkey.com** Turkey's official tourist information site.

Ⓦ **muze.gov.tr** Government website with information on the country's state-run museums, including the latest opening hours and admission fees.

Ⓦ **mymerhaba.com** Intended for long-term residents, and strongest on İstanbul, but nonetheless an authoritative, wide-ranging site with news of upcoming events and ticket-booking functions.

Ⓦ **trekkinginturkey.com** Well-researched information on major trekking areas and long-distance routes, with links to relevant outdoor-activity-type sites.

Ⓦ **turkeycentral.com** Useful information portal with links to huge range of sites from scuba-diving operators to estate agents.

Ⓦ **turkishculture.org** Not terribly innovative – but it does give a useful rundown on everything from architecture to ceramics, literature to music and lifestyles to cuisine – with plenty of photographs and illustrations.

Ⓦ **turkeytravelplanner.com** This very useful site has loads of practical tips for journey planning, plus many links to vetted service providers.

İstanbul and around

AYA SOFYA

1

İstanbul and around

Uniquely among the world's cities, İstanbul stands astride two continents, Europe and Asia. As if its spectacular geographical location were not enough, it can also boast of being the only city to have played capital to consecutive Christian and Islamic empires, a role that has shaped the region's history for more than 2500 years and bequeathed to İstanbul a staggering wealth of attractions; these range from the masterpiece Byzantine church of Aya Sofya to the formidable city walls, and the domes and minarets of the Ottoman mosques and palaces that dominate the city skyline. Although no longer its capital, the city remains the vibrant economic, cultural and intellectual heart of modern Turkey, a bustling, go-ahead city where east really does meet west.

In conservative districts such as Fatih, bearded men sporting skullcaps and baggy *shalwar*-style trousers devoutly heed the call to prayer, while women wouldn't dream of leaving the house with their heads uncovered. Yet across the water, the tidal wave of humanity sweeping down İstiklal Caddesi (Independence Street) holds young Turkish men and women in designer jeans and trainers who have never been to the mosque in their lives. In business districts such as Şişli, commuters arrive via the metro to work in high-rise office blocks, shop in state-of-the-art malls, and at weekends can be out clubbing until 6am.

Whether yours is the İstanbul of the Blue Mosque and the Topkapı Palace, or the Beyoğlu nightclubs and swish rooftop cocktail bars, the city takes time to get to know. Three to four days is enough to see the major historical sights in **Sultanahmet** and take a ferry trip on the **Bosphorus**. But plan on staying a week, or even two, if you want to explore fully the backstreets of the **Old City** and the outlying suburbs and islands.

Brief history

In 2008, while digging the Yenikapı metro station, archeologists uncovered a Neolithic settlement dating back to circa 6500 BC. In popular tradition, however, the city was founded in the seventh century BC by **Byzas**, from Megara in Greece – hence the original name of **Byzantium**. Over the next thousand years, Byzantium became an important centre of trade and commerce, though not until the early fourth century AD did it reach the pinnacle of its wealth, power and prestige. For more than 350 years, it had been part of the Roman province of Asia. On Diocletian's retirement in 305, Licinius and **Constantine** fought for control of the empire. Constantine finally defeated his rival on the hills above Chrysopolis (Üsküdar) and chose Byzantium as the site for the new **capital of the Roman Empire** in 330 BC. The hilly promontory, commanding the Bosphorus and

TOPKAPI PALACE

Highlights

❶ **Aya Sofya** The monumental Church of the Divine Wisdom is the ultimate expression of Byzantine architecture. **See p.72**

❷ **Topkapı Palace** Contemplate the majesty of the Ottoman sultanate in the fine buildings, gilded pavilions and immaculate gardens of this beautiful palace complex. **See p.76**

❸ **Kariye Museum** Mosaics and frescoes portraying the life of Christ are among İstanbul's most evocative Byzantine treasures. **See p.99**

❹ **Galata Bridge** Spanning the bustling waters of the Golden Horn, this landmark bridge, packed with simple fish restaurants and bars, is wonderful at sunset. **See p.101**

❺ **İstiklal Caddesi** Lined with attractive nineteenth-century apartments, this lively street is the spine of the pulsating entertainment quarter of Beyoğlu. **See p.105**

❻ **İstanbul Modern** This bold contemporary art gallery enjoys stunning views over the Bosphorus from a converted warehouse. **See p.107**

❼ **Cruise the Bosphorus** Float past sumptuous villas, imposing fortresses, timeworn villages and two intercontinental bridges. **See p.117**

❽ **Princes' Islands** One of the world's cheapest cruises takes you from the city's heaving streets to these tranquil, historic islands, in the sparkling Sea of Marmara. **See p.140**

HIGHLIGHTS ARE MARKED ON THE MAP ON P.68 AND PP.70–71

1

easily defensible on its landward side, was a superb choice. It was also well placed for access to the troublesome frontiers of both Europe and the Persian Empire.

In 395, the **division of the Roman Empire** between the two sons of Theodosius I left what was now named **Constantinople** as capital of the eastern part of the empire. It rapidly developed its own distinctive character, dissociating itself from Rome and adopting the Greek language and **Christianity**. Long and successful government was interrupted briefly, in Justinian's reign, by the Nika riots in 532. Half a century later, however, the dissolution of the Byzantine Empire had begun, as waves of Persians, Avars and Slavs attacked from the east and north. The empire was overrun by Arab invaders in the seventh and eighth centuries, and by Bulgars in the ninth and tenth. Only the city walls saved Constantinople, and even these could not keep out the **Crusaders**, who breached the sea walls in 1204 and sacked the city.

The Ottoman conquest

As the Byzantine Empire declined, the **Ottoman Empire** expanded. The Ottomans established first Bursa, then Edirne, as their capital, and Ottoman territory effectively surrounded the city long before it was taken. In 1453, **Mehmet II (the Conqueror)** – also known as Fatih Sultan Mehmet – besieged the city, which fell after seven weeks. Following the capture and subsequent pillage, Mehmet II began to rebuild the city, starting with a new palace and continuing with the Mosque of the Conqueror (Fatih Camii) and many smaller complexes. Tolerant of other religions, Mehmet actively encouraged Greek and Armenian Christians to take up residence in the city. His

ISTANBUL AND AROUND

İSTANBUL ORIENTATION

İstanbul is divided in two by the **Bosphorus**, the narrow 30km strait that separates Europe from Asia and links the Black Sea and the Sea of Marmara. Feeding into the southern end of the strait from the European side, the **Golden Horn** is a 7km-long inlet of water that empties into the mouth of the Bosphorus. The European side of the city effectively has two **centres**, separated by the Golden Horn. The old city, centred on the **Sultanahmet district**, is İstanbul's historical core and home to the main sights, while **Beyoğlu/Taksim** across the Horn form the fulcrum of the modern city. The two can easily be made out from the water, distinguished respectively by the landmarks of the Topkapı Palace and the Genoese Galata Tower.

A little way west of Sultanahmet, the massive Grand Bazaar (**Kapalı Çarşı**) is the focal point of a disparate area stretching from the shores of the Sea of Marmara in the south up to the hill overlooking the Golden Horn to the north. Above is the commanding presence of the impressive **Süleymaniye Camii**. Some 6km west of the old city, stretching between the Sea of Marmara and the Golden Horn, are the remarkably intact Byzantine **land walls**.

From Sultanahmet and Eminönü, you're most likely to cross the Golden Horn by the Galata Bridge, entering the port area of **Karaköy**, then heading up the steep hill through the ancient **Galata** district. Near the northern end of Galata bridge, the **Tünel**, the French-built underground funicular railway, chugs up to **Beyoğlu**, the city's elegant nineteenth-century European quarter. From the upper Tünel station, an antique tram runs the length of Beyoğlu's pedestrianized boulevard, **İstiklal Caddesi**, to **Taksim Square**, the twin focal points of the modern city's best hotels, bars, clubs and restaurants.

North of Taksim, on the M2 metro line, the city's newest business districts of Harbiye, Etiler, Nişantaşi and Şişli hold many airline offices and embassies. Downhill from Taksim, on the Bosphorus shore, lie Tophane, **Beşiktaş** and **Ortaköy**, inner-city districts with scenic waterside locations and a number of historic palaces and parks. Across the straits, in Asia, the main centres of **Üsküdar**, **Haydarpaşa and Kadıköy** form part of İstanbul's commuter belt, but also have a few architectural attractions and decent shops, restaurants and clubs.

successor Beyazit II continued this policy, settling Jewish refugees from Spain into the city in an attempt to improve the economy.

In the century following the Conquest, the victory was reinforced by the great military achievements of **Selim the Grim** and by the reign of **Süleyman the Magnificent** (1520–66), "the Lawgiver" and greatest of all Ottoman leaders. His attempted conquest of Europe was only thwarted at the gates of Vienna, and the wealth gained in his military conquests funded the work of **Mimar Sinan**, the finest Ottoman architect.

From Ottoman Empire to Turkish Republic

A century after the death of Süleyman, the empire began to show signs of **decay**. Territorial losses abroad combined with corruption at home, which insinuated its way into the very heart of the empire, Topkapı Palace itself. Newly crowned sultans emerged, often insane, from the institution known as the Cage (see p.76), while others spent time in the harem rather than on the battlefield, consorting with women who increasingly became involved in grand-scale political intrigue.

As Ottoman territory was lost to the West, succeeding sultans became interested in Western institutional models. A short-lived parliament of 1876 was dissolved after a year by Abdülhamid II, but the **forces of reform** led to his deposition in 1909. The end of World War I saw İstanbul occupied by Allied troops as the victors procrastinated over how best to manage the rump of the once-great empire. After the War of Independence, Atatürk's declaration of the **Republic** in 1923 and the creation of a new capital in Ankara effectively solved the problem.

İstanbul today

The **population** of Greater İstanbul has increased twelvefold since the establishment of the Turkish Republic, and stands today at around 15 million. This rapid urban growth has

1

HIGHLIGHTS

1. Aya Sofya
2. Topkapı Palace
3. Kariye Museum
4. Galata Bridge
5. İstiklal Caddesi
6. İstanbul Modern
7. Cruise the Bosphorus

İSTANBUL

1

> ### CITY CRIMEWATCH
>
> İstanbul is undoubtedly far safer than most European or North American cities, and cases of mugging and assault against tourists are rare. Having said this, the crime rate is soaring, due in part to the increasing disparity between rich and poor.
>
> For the average visitor, pickpocketing is the main cause for concern: be particularly careful around Sirkeci station, the Eminönü waterfront, the Galata Bridge, and around Taksim (especially at night). Also avoid being on or around the Byzantine land walls at dusk/night. Be very careful, too, on **public transport**, particularly when it is crowded. If you feel anyone is harassing or attempting to pickpocket you, try calling out *imdat!*, 'meaning "help!", and contact the tourist police (see p.136).

left the city with more than its fair share of problems, from horrendous traffic congestion to housing and water shortages and rising crime rates. A UNESCO threat to revoke the city's "World Heritage" status and place it on the "In Danger" list focused the minds of the government and local authorities on preserving the city's glorious heritage, and İstanbul emerged from its year as a **European Capital of Culture** in 2010 with great credit.

Much else has been done to improve the infrastructure of one of the world's leading cities. A government-backed housing scheme offers quality, affordable housing to low-income families in order, eventually, to replace the shanty-dwellings that have long ringed the suburbs. The gigantic **Marmaray transport project** will see the European and Asian sides of the city linked by a rail tunnel under the Bosphorus by 2015, and the metro systems either side of the Golden Horn should be linked by a (controversial) bridge around the same time. The Horn itself, once heavily polluted, has been cleaned up, and both anglers and cormorants can now be seen successfully fishing in its waters.

Sultanahmet

Most short-stay visitors spend all their time in **Sultanahmet**, home to İstanbul's main sightseeing attractions: the church of **Aya Sofya**, the greatest legacy of the Byzantine Empire; the **Topkapı Palace**, heart of the Ottoman Empire; and the massive **Sultanahmet Camii** (Blue Mosque). Here also are the ancient **Hippodrome**, the **Museum of Turkish and Islamic Art** (housed in the former Palace of İbrahim Paşa), the eerily lit **Yerebatan Sarnıcı**, a fascinating Byzantine underground cistern, and the **Grand Bazaar** (Kapalı Çarşı), the largest covered bazaar in the world. The monumental architecture, attractive parks and gardens, street-side cafés, and the benefits of a relatively traffic-free main road combine to make this area pleasant for both sightseeing and staying – but beware of **hustlers**, particularly the carpet-selling variety.

Aya Sofya

Tues–Sun: April–Sept 9am–7pm, last entry at 6pm, upper galleries close at 6.30pm; Oct–March 9am–4.30pm • ₺25; audioguide ₺10 • ⓦ www.ayasofyamuzesi.gov.tr

For almost a thousand years **Aya Sofya**, or Haghia Sophia, was the largest enclosed space in the world, designed to impress the strength and wealth of the Byzantine emperors upon their own subjects and visiting foreign dignitaries alike. Superbly located between the Topkapı Palace and Sultanahmet Camii on the ancient acropolis, the first hill of İstanbul, the church dominated the city skyline for a millennium, until the domes and minarets of the city's mosques began to challenge its eminence in the sixteenth century.

Brief history

Aya Sofya, "the Church of the Divine Wisdom", is the third church of this name to stand on the site. Commissioned in the sixth century by Emperor Justinian after its

---

predecessor had been razed to the ground in 532, its architects were **Anthemius of Tralles** and **Isidore of Miletus**. Prior to their pioneering design, most churches followed the pattern of the rectangular, pitch-roofed Roman basilica or meeting hall. Anthemius and Isidore were to create a building of a type and scale hitherto unknown to the Byzantine world. The mighty 30m-plus diameter **dome** was unprecedented, and no imitation was attempted until the sixteenth century. Constructed in five years, the building survived several earthquakes before, some twenty years later, the central dome collapsed. During reconstruction the height of the external buttresses and the dome was increased, and some of the windows blocked, resulting in an interior much

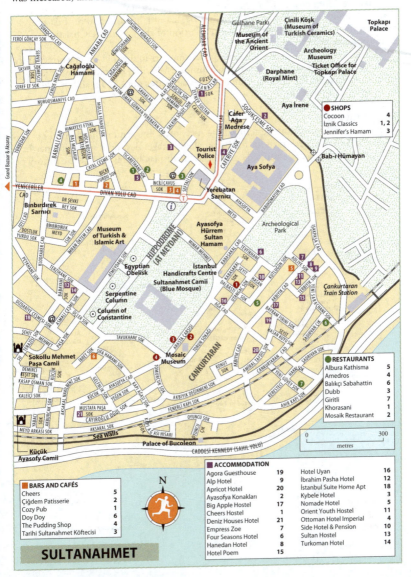

SHOPS
Cocoon 4
İznik Classics 1, 2
Jennifer's Hamam 3

RESTAURANTS
Albura Kathisma 5
Amedros 4
Balıkçı Sabahattin 6
Dubb 3
Giritli 7
Khorasani 1
Mosaik Restaurant 2

BARS AND CAFÉS
Cheers 5
Çiğdem Patisserie 2
Cozy Pub 6
Doy Doy 4
The Pudding Shop 1
Tarihi Sultanahmet Köftecisi 3

ACCOMMODATION
Agora Guesthouse 19
Alp Hotel 9
Apricot Hotel 20
Ayasofya Konakları 2
Big Apple Hostel 17
Cheers Hostel 1
Deniz Houses Hotel 21
Empress Zoe 7
Four Seasons Hotel 6
Hanedan Hotel 8
Hotel Poem 15
Hotel Uyan 16
İbrahim Pasha Hotel 12
İstanbul Suite Home Apt 18
Kybele Hotel 3
Nomade Hotel 5
Orient Youth Hostel 11
Ottoman Hotel Imperial 4
Side Hotel & Pension 10
Sultan Hostel 13
Turkoman Hotel 14

SULTANAHMET

1

gloomier than originally intended. The dome collapsed again in 989 and was rebuilt in its final form by an Armenian architect, Tridat.

In 1204, Aya Sofya was ransacked by Catholic soldiers during the **Fourth Crusade**. Mules were brought in to help carry off silver and gilt carvings, and a prostitute was seated on the throne of the patriarch. In 1452, far too late, the Byzantine Church reluctantly accepted union with the Catholics in the hope that Western powers would come to the aid of Constantinople against the Turks. On May 29, 1453, those who had said they would rather see the turban of a Turk than the hat of a cardinal in the streets of Constantinople got their way when the city was captured. **Mehmet the Conqueror** rode to the church of Aya Sofya and stopped the looting that was taking place. He had the building cleared of relics and said his first prayer there on the following Friday; this former bastion of the Byzantine Christian Empire was now a mosque.

Extensive restorations were carried out on the mosaics in the mid-nineteenth century by the Swiss **Fossati brothers**, but due to Muslim sensitivities the mosaics were later covered over again. The building functioned as a **mosque** until 1932, and in 1934 it was opened as a **museum**.

The narthexes

Five large portals pierce the western wall of Aya Sofya. The central **Orea Porta** or "Beautiful Gate" was reserved for the imperial entourage. Beyond it, the **outer narthex** or vestibule is a long cross-vaulted corridor where display boards outline the history of the site.

Five further doors lead through into the **inner narthex**, with a vaulted ceiling covered in gold mosaic and walls embellished with beautiful marble panels. The central portal to the nave is the **Imperial Gate**, above which a superb mosaic depicts a seated **Christ Pantocrator** (the All Powerful) holding an open book showing a Greek inscription that reads "Peace be upon you, I am the light of the world". Grovelling to Christ's right, Emperor Leo IV begs forgiveness for having married more times than was permitted under Church law.

The nave

The nave awes by the sheer sense of space created by the heavenly dome, some 32m in diameter and 55m above floor level. Pierced by forty windows, its scale is cleverly exaggerated by the addition of half-domes to west and east. The tympanum walls to the south and north also emphasize the height of the building, especially as they are studded with rows of large, arched windows. At each corner of the nave are semicircular niches (*exedrae*). The galleries, which follow the line of these *exedrae* around the building, are supported by rows of columns and by four massive piers, which provide the main support for the dome.

In the northwest corner of the aisle is the **weeping column**. A legend dating from at least 1200 tells how St Gregory the Miracle-worker appeared here – the moisture subsequently seeping from the column has been believed to cure a wide range of conditions. Diagonally opposite, to the right of the apse, the circular marble-inlay panel in the floor is the **omphalos**, marking the spot where Byzantine emperors were crowned. The huge half-dome of the apse itself contains a ninth-century **mosaic of the Virgin Mary**, Christ seated on her lap. What remains of the **abstract mosaics**, and of the large areas of plain gold that covered the underside of the dome and other large expanses of wall and ceiling, dates from the sixth century.

When the building became a mosque, several new features were added to suit its new purpose. Still visible today are the *mihrab*, slightly offset in the apse, a *mimber* (pulpit), a sultan's loge, and the enormous wooden plaques that bear sacred Islamic names of God, the Prophet Mohammed, the first four caliphs and the Prophet's grandchildren Hasan and Hussein.

The upper galleries

To reach the **upper galleries** of Aya Sofya, head up the sloping ramp at the northern end of the inner narthex. Proceed across the western gallery, past the circle of green Thessalian marble that marked the **throne of the empress**, then turn left and pass through the gap in a marble screen into the south gallery. All the **figurative mosaics** in Aya Sofya date from after the Iconoclastic era (726–843). Among the finest is a **Deisis** scene to the right of the marble screen, depicting Christ, the Virgin and St John the Baptist. Opposite this, scratched into the balustrade running around the inside of the gallery, is some Viking **runic graffiti**.

The east wall of the south gallery holds a **mosaic of Christ flanked by an emperor and empress**. The inscriptions over their heads read "Zoë, the most pious Augusta" and "Constantine in Christ, the Lord Autocrat, faithful Emperor of the Romans, Monomachus". It is believed that the two figures are Constantine IX Monomachus and Empress Zoë. The other mosaic in the south gallery, dating from 1118, depicts the **Virgin and Child between Emperor John II Comnenus and Empress Irene**, and their son Prince Alexius, added later.

Caferağa Medresesi

Caferiye Sok, just west of Aya Sofya • Daily 9am–6pm • ☎ 0212 528 0089

Built by the great Ottoman architect Sinan in the sixteenth century, the **Caferağa Medresesi** is a beautiful courtyard *medrese* that's now an artists' workshop-cum-traditional

1

handicrafts shopping centre. It's a charitable foundation and a rare low-key shopping opportunity in Sultanahmet, with traditional wares for sale, plus workshops where visitors can join in and learn about painting miniatures.

Topkapı Palace

Mon & Wed–Sun: April–Sept 9am–7pm, last entry 6pm; Oct–March 9am–5pm • ₺25, free to enter the first court; ₺15 for Harem; audioguides ₺10 • ⓦ www.topkapisarayi.gov.tr

The **Topkapı Palace**, the symbolic and political centre of the Ottoman Empire for nearly four centuries, stands commandingly on the very tip of the promontory on which the old city of İstanbul is set. Its sheer opulence defies its origins in the tented encampments of nomadic Turkic warriors. Similar to the Alhambra of Granada, and every bit as unmissable, the palace consists of a collection of buildings arranged around a series of courtyards and attractive gardens.

The first courtyard and Aya Irene

The **first courtyard** of the Topkapı Palace, its service area, was always open to the general public. It's entered from the street through Mehmet the Conqueror's **Bab-ı Hümayün**, the great defensive imperial gate opposite the fountain of Ahmet III. The **palace bakeries** lie behind a wall to the right of the courtyard, while the buildings of the **imperial mint and outer treasury** are behind the wall north of the church of Aya Irene. In front of Aya Irene stood the quarters of the straw-weavers and carriers of silver pitchers, around a central courtyard in which the palace firewood was stored.

Today, **Aya Irene**, "the Church of the Divine Peace", is generally only opened for large groups by special request at the Directorate of Aya Sofya, located at the entrance of Aya Sofya. It does however also open for concerts, especially during the summer İstanbul music festival. The original church was one of the oldest in the city, but it was rebuilt along with Aya Sofya after being burnt down in the Nika riots of 532.

Ortakapı and the second courtyard

To reach the **second courtyard** of the Topkapı Palace, you pass through the **Bab-üs Selam**, "the Gate of Salutations", otherwise known as the **Ortakapı**, or middle gate (where the entry fee is collected). Entering through Ortakapı, with the gateway to the third courtyard straight ahead of you, the Privy Stables of Mehmet II (closed to the public) are on your immediate left, while beyond them are the buildings of the Divan and the Inner Treasury and the entrance to the Harem. Opposite the Divan, on the right side of the courtyard, is the kitchen area.

The gardens between the paths that radiate from the Ortakapı are planted with ancient cypresses and plane trees, rose bushes and lawns. Originally they would also have been resplendent with peacocks, gazelles and fountains. Running water, considered to have almost mystical properties by Muslims, was supplied in great quantity to the palace from

---

THE CAGE

The Cage or *Kafes* was the suite of rooms of the Harem where possible successors to the throne were kept incarcerated. The practice was adopted by Ahmet I as an alternative to the fratricide that had been institutionalized in the Ottoman Empire since the rule of Beyazit II. After the death of their father, the younger princes would be kept under house arrest along with deaf mutes and a harem of concubines, while their eldest brother acceded to the throne. They remained here until such time as they were called upon to take power themselves. The concubines never left the Cage unless they became pregnant, in which case they were immediately drowned. The decline of the Ottoman Empire has been attributed in part to the institution of the Cage, as sultans who spent any length of time there emerged crazed, avaricious and debauched. The most infamous victim was "İbrahim the Mad" (see p.80).

the Byzantine cistern of Yerebatan Sarnıcı (see p.84). This **second courtyard** would have been the scene of pageantry during state ceremonies, when the sultan would occupy his throne beneath the Bab-üs Saadet, "the Gate of Felicity".

The Divan

As you enter the buildings of the **Divan**, to the left of the second courtyard, you'll see a metal grille in the Council Chamber (the first room on the left), called "the Eye of the Sultan". Through this he could observe the proceedings of the Divan, where the eminent imperial councillors sat in session, and which took its name from the couch that ran around the room's three walls. The building dates essentially from the reign of Mehmet the Conqueror, while the Council Chamber was restored to its sixteenth-century appearance in 1945, with some of the original İznik tiles and arabesque painting.

The armoury museum

Next to the Divan stands another building from Mehmet the Conqueror's original palace, the **Inner Treasury**, a six-domed hall that holds displays of Ottoman and European **armour**. Look out for Mehmet's curved sword, inscribed with the words "may the necks of the enemies of Sheriat become the scabbards of this sword", and all the usual paraphernalia of late medieval warfare, from maces and axes to bows and shields. Kids may be intrigued by the hologram room, with flickering 3-D representations of Ottoman janissaries and cavalry.

The kitchens

The **palace kitchens and cooks' quarters**, with their magnificent rows of chimneys, stand across the courtyard from the Armoury and Divan. Each of the ten kitchens, which had a staff of 1500, served a different purpose, including two just to make sweets and *helva*. Unfortunately they have been closed to visitors for some years due to ongoing restoration work.

The third courtyard

Pass through the **Bab-üs Saadet**, "the Gate of Felicity", and the **Throne Room** is immediately in front of you. This building, mainly dating from the reign of Selim I, was where the sultan awaited the outcome of sessions of the Divan in order to give his assent or otherwise to their proposals. The restrained grey marble building at the centre of the third courtyard is the **Ahmet III Library**.

The room to the right of the gate and throne room and library, southwest of the courtyard, is the **Hall of the Expeditionary Force**, sometimes referred to as the Hall of the Campaign Pages (*Seferli Koğuşu*). It houses a collection of embroidery and a very small assortment of imperial costumes.

The Treasury

The two-storey **Imperial Treasury** is housed in the rooms that once functioned as the Pavilion of Mehmet II, which takes up most of the southeast side of the third courtyard, to the right of the entrance. This two-storey building, with its colonnaded terrace, boasts the shell-shaped niches, stalactite capitals and pointed window arches so typical of the fifteenth century.

The first room contains a number of highly wrought and extremely beautiful objects, including a delicate silver model of a palace complete with tiny birds in the trees, a present to Abdül Hamid II from Japan. The big crowd-puller in room two is the **Topkapı Dagger**, which starred alongside Peter Ustinov in the Sunday-matinée classic *Topkapi*. A present from Mahmut I to Nadir Shah that was waylaid and brought back when news of the shah's death reached Topkapı, the dagger is decorated with three enormous emeralds, one of which conceals a watch. The third room holds the **Spoonmaker's Diamond**, the fifth-largest diamond in the world.

1

TOPKAPI PALACE

1	Ortakapı or Middle Gate	**16**	Room of the Robe of the Prophet
2	Kitchens and Cooks' Quarters	**17**	Rooms of the Relics of the Prophet
	(Porcelain & Glass Collection)	**18**	Hall of the Treasury (Closed)
3	Reconstructed Kitchen		(Sultans' Portraits & Miniature Collection)
4	Stables and Harness Rooms	**19**	Hall of the Pantry (Museum Directorate)
5	Barrack of the Halberdiers of	**20**	Imperial Treasury (Pavilion of Mehmet II)
	the Long Tresses	**21**	Disrobing Chamber of Selim II Hamam
6	Hall of the Divan	**22**	Site of Selim II Hamam
7	Offices of the Divan	**23**	Site of Selim II Hamam Boilers
8	Inner Treasury (Arms & armour collection)	**24**	Hall of the Expeditionary Force
9	Gate of Felicity (Bab-üs Saadet)	**25**	Circumcision Köşkü
10	Quarters of the White Eunuchs	**26**	Terrace and Bower
	(Costume collection)	**27**	Pool
11	Throne Room	**28**	Baghdad Köşkü
12	Ahmet III Library	**29**	Pool
13	Library (Mosque of the School)	**30**	Revan Köşkü
14	Harem Mosque	**31**	Tulip Gardens of Ahmet III
15	Court of the Room of the Robe	**32**	Mustafa Paşa Köşkü

33	Physician's Tower	**51**	Apartments of Senior women
34	Mecidiye Köşkü	**52**	Court of Women's hospital
35	Third Gate	**53**	Hospital Hamam
36	Entry to the Harem (Carriage Gate)	**54**	Hospital Kitchen Quarters
37	Mosque of the Black Eunuchs	**55**	Sultan Ahmet Kiosk
38	Court of the Black Eunuchs	**56**	Harem Garden
39	Barrack of the Black Eunuchs	**57**	Valide Sultan's Court
40	Princes' School	**58**	Valide Sultan's Dining Room
41	Quarters of the Chief Black Eunuchs	**59**	Valide Sultan's Bedroom
42	Quarters of the Treasurer	**60**	Valide Sultan's Hamam
43	Quarters of the Chamberlain	**61**	Kadin's Quarters
44	Aviary Gate (Kuşhane Kapisi)	**62**	Golden Road
45	Courtyard of the Women of the Harem	**63**	Ahmet III Dining Room
46	Kitchen of the Women	**64**	Throne Room Within
47	Hamam of the Women	**65**	The Sultan's Hamam
48	Stairs to Bedrooms	**66**	Osman III Terrace
49	Laundry	**67**	Terrace of Selâmlik Garden
50	Women's Dormitory	**68**	Apartment of the Selamlik (Sultan's Rooms)

1

The fourth room boasts a bejewelled throne, and the hand and part of the skull of John the Baptist, but otherwise it's a relative haven of restraint and good taste. Ivory and sandalwood objects predominate, refreshingly simple materials whose comparative worth is determined by craftsmanship rather than quantity.

The Pavilion of the Holy Mantle

Across the courtyard from the Treasury, the **Pavilion of the Holy Mantle** houses the **Rooms of the Relics of the Prophet**, holy relics brought home by Selim the Grim after his conquest of Egypt in 1517. The relics were originally viewed only by the sultan, his family and his immediate entourage on days of special religious significance. They include a footprint, hair and a tooth of the Prophet Mohammed, as well as his mantle and standard, swords of the first four caliphs, and a letter from the Prophet to the leader of the Coptic tribe. This section is often incredibly busy, with dishearteningly long queues.

The fourth courtyard

The **fourth courtyard** of the Topkapı Palace is entered through a passageway that runs between the Hall of the Treasury and the display of clocks and watches in the Silahdar Treasury. It consists of several gardens, each graced with pavilions, the most attractive of which are located around a wide marble terrace beyond the tulip gardens of Ahmet III.

The **Baghdad Köşkü**, the cruciform building north of the terrace, is the only pavilion currently open to the public. It was built by Murat IV to celebrate the conquest of Baghdad in 1638. The exterior and cool, dark interior are tiled in blue, turquoise and white, while the shutters and cupboard doors are inlaid with tortoiseshell and mother-of-pearl. The attractive pool and marble fountain on the terrace were the scene of debauched revels among İbrahim I and the women of his harem. Deli İbrahim, or **İbrahim the Mad**, emerged dangerously insane from 22 years in the Cage; his reign culminated in a fit of sexual jealousy when he ordered death by drowning in the Bosphorus for the 280 concubines of his harem.

The **Circumcision Köşkü**, in the Portico of Columns above the terrace, also dates from the reign of İbrahim the Mad. The exterior is covered in prime-period İznik tiles of the sixteenth and early seventeenth centuries. At the other end of the Portico of Columns, the **Revan Köşkü** was built to commemorate the capture of Erivan in the Caucasus by Mehmet IV.

The **Mecidiye Köşkü** – the last building to be erected at Topkapı – commands the finest view of any of the pavilions. It's been opened as the *Konyali Café*, which has fine views across the Bosphorus but expensive, mediocre food.

The Harem

Mon & Wed–Sun 10am–4pm • ₺15

The **Harem** is usually relatively uncrowded because of the extra admission fee. The word "harem" means "forbidden" in Arabic; in Turkish it refers to a suite of apartments in a palace or private residence where the head of the household lived with his wives, odalisques (female slaves) and children. Situated on the north side of the Second Court, it consisted of over four hundred rooms, centred on the suites of the sultan and his mother, the Valide Sultan.

The Carriage Gate

The Harem was connected to the outside world by means of the **Carriage Gate**, so called because the odalisques would have entered their carriages here when they went on outings. To the left of the Carriage Gate as you enter the Harem is the Barracks of the Halberdiers of the Long Tresses, who carried logs and other loads into the Harem. The Halberdiers, who also served as imperial guardsmen, were only employed at certain hours, and even then they were blinkered. Both the Carriage Gate and the Aviary Gate were guarded by black eunuchs, who were responsible for running the Harem.

THE WOMEN OF THE HAREM

The **women of the harem** were so shrouded in mystery that they became a source of great fascination for the world in general. Many were imported from Georgia and Caucasia for their looks, or were prisoners of war, captured in Hungary, Poland or Venice. Upon entering the harem, they would become the charges of the *haznedar usta*, who would teach them how to behave towards the sultan and the other palace inhabitants. The conditions in which most of these women lived were dangerously unhygienic, and many died of disease, or from the cold of an İstanbul winter. Those women who were chosen to enter the bedchamber of the sultan, however, were promoted to the rank of imperial odalisque, given slaves to serve them, and pleasant accommodation. If they bore a child, they would be promoted again, to become a favourite or wife, and given their own apartments. If the sultan subsequently lost affection for one of these women, he could give her in marriage to one of his courtiers.

The most renowned of the harem women was Haseki Hürrem, or **Roxelana** as she was known in the West, wife of Süleyman the Magnificent. Prior to their marriage, it was unusual for a sultan to marry at all, let alone to choose a wife from among his concubines. This was the beginning of a new age of harem intrigue, in which women began to take more control over affairs of state, often referred to as the "Rule of the Harem".

The rooms of the Harem

The **Court of the Black Eunuchs** dates mainly from a rebuilding programme that started after the great fire of 1665 damaged most of the Harem, as well as the Divan. The tiles in the eunuchs' quarters date from the seventeenth century, suggesting that the originals were destroyed in the fire. The *Altın Yol* or **Golden Road** ran the entire length of the Harem, from the quarters of the Black Eunuchs to the fourth courtyard. Strategically located at the start of the Golden Road, the **apartments of the Valide Sultan** were also rebuilt after 1665. They include a particularly lovely domed dining room.

The apartments and reception rooms of the *selâmlik*, the sultan's own rooms, lie beyond the Valide Sultan's apartments. In the largest and grandest, the **Hünkar Sofrası** or Imperial Hall, the sultan would entertain visitors. Another important room in this section is a masterwork of the architect Sinan: the **bedchamber of Murat III**, covered in sixteenth-century İznik tiles.

The northernmost rooms of the Harem are supported by immense piers and vaults, creating capacious basements that were used as dormitories and storerooms. Below the bedchamber is a large indoor **swimming pool**, with taps for hot and cold water, where Murat is supposed to have thrown gold to women who pleased him. The light and airy **library of Ahmet I**, next to the bedchamber, has windows overlooking both the Bosphorus and the Golden Horn. Beyond it, the walls of the **dining room of Ahmet III** are covered in wood panelling painted with bowls of fruit and flowers, typical of the extravagant tulip-loving sultan.

Visitors leave the Harem by way of the **Aviary Gate**, or Kuşhane Kapısı, into the Third Court.

Gülhane Parkı

Surrounding Topkapı Palace on all sides, **Gülhane Parkı** was once the extended gardens of the sultans. It is now a public park with a relaxed atmosphere – the nesting heron colony in spring apart – that's primarily noteworthy as home to the three museums that form the **Archeology Museum complex**, and the separate İstanbul History of Science and Technology in Islam Museum. The park also holds a modest array of kids' play equipment, and is home to a decent tea garden, the Set Üstü, down the slope towards the northeast corner of the park, which gives fine views across the Bosphorus.

1

The Archeology Museum complex

Osman Hamdi Bey Yokuşu, Gülhane Parkı

The **Archeology Museum complex,** entered either through Gülhane Parkı or from the first courtyard of the Topkapı Palace, is one of the most underrated attractions in the city. A moderately thorough exploration of its three separate buildings will take at least half a day. By far the largest is the impressive Neoclassical **Archeology Museum** (Arkeoloji Müzesi), while the much smaller **Museum of the Ancient Orient** lies just beyond the ticket barrier, and the **Çinili Köşk** (Tiled Pavilion) is opposite the Archeology Museum itself.

The Archeology Museum

Osman Hamdi Bey Yokuşu, Gülhane Parkı • Tues–Sun: April–Sept 9am–7pm; Oct–April 9am–5pm • Combined entry with Museum of the Ancient Orient and Çinili Köşk ₺10, audioguides ₺10 • ⓦ istanbularkeoloji.gov.tr

Built by a French architect in 1891, the impressive Neoclassical **Archeology Museum** (Arkeoloji Müzesi) centres on a marvellous collection of sarcophagi from Sidon, housed in two rooms to the left of the entrance on the ground floor. The most famous is the so-called **Alexander Sarcophagus** from the late fourth century. Covered with scenes of what is presumed to be Alexander the Great hunting and in battle, it cannot be Alexander's own tomb; he's known to have been buried in Alexandria. Instead it's ascribed variously to a ruler of the Seleucid dynasty, or to the Phoenician Prince Abdolonyme.

Rooms 13 to 20, to the right of the entrance, contain a comprehensive collection of statuary dating from the Archaic through to the Roman period, much of it of superb quality. Room 16 exhibits a vivid statue of the young Alexander the Great, carved in the stylized manner popular at Pergamon, on Turkey's Aegean coast, in the second century BC.

On the first floor, the **İstanbul through the Ages** exhibition is well worth visiting. Tracing the history of the city from archaic to Ottoman times, it includes the chain used by the Byzantines to block entry to the strategically crucial Golden Horn. The next level up exhibits some of the fascinating finds made by Schliemann and Dorpfeld at **Troy**, including beautiful gold jewellery. Down in the basement, but beautifully presented, are finds from the oft-neglected **Byzantine period**, with some lavishly carved capitals among the pick of the exhibits.

The Museum of the Ancient Orient

Osman Hamdi Bey Yokuşu, Gülhane Parkı • Tues–Sun: April–Sept 9am–7pm; Oct–April 9am–5pm • Combined entry with Archeology Museum and Çinili Köşk ₺10, audioguides ₺10 • ⓦ istanbularkeoloji.gov.tr

The **Museum of the Ancient Orient** contains a small but dazzling collection of Anatolian, Egyptian and Mesopotamian artefacts. These include the oldest peace treaty known to mankind, the **Treaty of Kadesh** (1280–1269 BC), which was signed after a battle fought between Pharaoh Ramses II and the Hittite king Muvatellish ended in a stalemate. Uncovered during excavations at the site of the Hittite capital of Hattuşa (see p.492), the version of the treaty displayed here includes a ceasefire agreement and pledges of a mutual exchange of political refugees. A copy decorates the entrance to the UN building in New York.

The blue-and-yellow **animal relief** in the corridor beyond the first room dates from the reign of Nebuchadnezzar (604–562 BC), the last hero-king of Babylonia, where it would have lined the processional way in Babylon. Other exhibits were taken from the palace-museum of Nebuchadnezzar, located at the Ishtar Gate. Another massive relief, in Room 8, depicts the **Hittite king Urpalla** presenting gifts of grapes and grain to a vegetation god, who is three times his own size. This is a plaster copy of a relief found at İvriz Kaya near Konya, dating from the eighth century BC.

FROM TOP YEREBATAN SARNICI (P.84); GRAND BAZAAR (P.89)>

1

Çinili Köşk

Osman Hamdi Bey Yokuşu, Gülhane Parkı • Tues–Sun: April–Sept 9am–7pm; Oct–April 9am–5pm • Combined entry with Archeology Museum and Museum of the Ancient Orient ₺10, audioguides ₺10 • ⓦ istanbularkeoloji.gov.tr

The graceful **Çinili Köşk**, or Tiled Pavilion, was built in 1472 as a kind of grandstand, from which the sultan could watch sporting activities such as wrestling or polo. It now houses the **Museum of Turkish Ceramics**, displaying tiles of a quality equal to those in Topkapı Palace and İstanbul's older mosques, along with well-written explanations of the different periods in the history of Turkish ceramics.

İstanbul History of Science and Technology in Islam Museum

Gülhane Parkı • Mon & Wed–Sun 9am–4.30pm • ₺5

Housed in former stables, within Gülhane Parkı, the **İstanbul History of Science and Technology in Islam Museum** is a generally successful attempt to show the contribution made by scientists and inventors from the Islamic world to civilization between the eighth and sixteenth centuries. Carefully constructed replicas illustrate everything from astronomical observatories to medical equipment. Highlights include a model of a planetarium based on the tenth-century works of the Islamic astronomer as-Siğzi, and a re-creation of a twelfth-century water-powered clock, shaped like an elephant.

Yerebatan Sarnıcı

Yerebatan Cad 13 • Daily: April–Sept 9am–6.30pm; Oct–March 9am–5.30pm • ₺10, audioguide ₺10 • ⓦ yerebatan.com

The **Yerebatan Sarnıcı**, the "Sunken Palace" – also known as the Basilica Cistern – once formed an integral part of the Old City's water supply. Buried beneath the very core of Sultanahmet, it's first of several such underground cisterns to have been extensively excavated.

Probably built by the Emperor Constantine in the fourth century, and enlarged by Justinian in the sixth, the cistern was supplied by aqueducts with water from the Belgrade Forest. It in turn supplied the Great Palace and later Topkapı Palace. Having fallen into disuse after the Ottoman conquest, the cistern was rediscovered in 1545 by the Frenchman **Petrus Gyllius**. His interest was aroused when he found fresh fish being sold in the streets nearby, and he enquired at local houses. The residents let him in on their "secret" – wells sunk through into the cistern, and boats kept on the water from which they could fish its depths.

Restored in 1987, the cistern is now **beautifully lit** and access is made easier by specially constructed walkways. The largest covered cistern in the city, at 140m by 70m, Yerebatan held eighty thousand cubic metres of water. The small brick **domes** are supported by 336 columns, many of which have Corinthian capitals. Two of the columns are supported by **Medusa heads**, clearly relics of an earlier building.

The Hippodrome

The arena of the **Hippodrome**, formerly the cultural focus of the Byzantine Empire, is now a long paved municipal park known as At Meydanı, or Square of Horses. An **Egyptian Obelisk** adorns what was once the *spina* or central barrier of the chariot-racing track, at the centre of the park. It originally stood 60m tall, but only the upper third survived shipment from Egypt in the fourth century. It was commissioned to commemorate the campaigns of Thutmose III in Egypt during the sixteenth century BC, but the scenes on its base commemorate its erection in Constantinople under the direction of Theodosius I. Among the figures depicted are dancing maidens with musicians, Theodosius and his family watching a chariot race (south side), and a group of captives kneeling to pay homage to Theodosius (west side).

The **Serpentine Column**, also on the line of the *spina*, came from the Temple of Apollo at Delphi, where it was dedicated to the god by the 31 Greek cities that defeated the Persians at Plataea in 479 BC. It was brought to Constantinople by Constantine the Great. Each of the three intertwining bronze serpents originally had a head; the sole survivor is on display in the Archeology Museum (see p.82).

The third ancient monument on the *spina* is a huge lump of masonry, a 32m-high column of little or no decorative or practical worth. The origins of this so-called **Column of Constantine** are uncertain, but an inscription records that it was already decayed when Constantine restored it.

The Blue Mosque

Sultanahmet Camii • Mon–Thurs, Sat & Sun from 9am until one hour before dusk prayer call; Fri until midday prayers

The monumental **Blue Mosque**, more properly known as the **Sultanahmet Camii**, dominates the southeastern side of the Hippodrome. With its six minarets, imposing bulk and commanding position on the skyline of old İstanbul, it is one of the most famous and visited monuments in the city. Viewed from the all-important approach from the Topkapı Palace, it forms a striking mass of shallow domes, half-domes and domed turrets, but its most striking profile is from the Sea of Marmara where, elevated above the hillside, it totally dominates its surroundings.

Before construction began under architect Mehmet Ağa, in 1609, there were objections that planning a mosque with six minarets would be an unholy attempt to rival the six minarets of the mosque at Mecca. More importantly, it would drain state resources, already in a parlous state following wars with Austria and Persia. But Sultanahmet I, after whom the mosque is named, was determined to outdo his predecessors, even if it meant bankrupting his empire – he even helped dig the foundations himself.

Visiting the mosque

The mosque is best approached from the attractive and graceful northwest, Hippodrome-facing side, from where an eleborate portal leads into the beautiful **courtyard.** Surrounded by a portico of thirty small domes, this has the same dimensions as the mosque itself. It's also possible to enter the courtyard from the Aya Sofya side of the mosque, through the northeast portal.

Only practising Muslims are permitted to enter the prayer-hall itself via the main southwest-facing door. If you are not a Muslim, and wish to go inside, exit the courtyard of the mosque via the southwest portal, then bear left along the outside of the mosque to reach a side door, where there is often a sizeable queue. Here you must remove your shoes and put them in a plastic bag (provided).

Inside, four "**elephant foot**" **pillars**, so called because of their 5m diameter, impose their disproportionate dimensions on the interior – particularly the dome, which is smaller and shallower than that of Ottoman master architect Sinan's İstanbul masterpiece, the nearby Süleymaniye Camii. The name "Blue Mosque" derives from the mass (over twenty thousand) of predominantly **blue İznik tiles** that adorn the interior, though much of the "blue" is, in fact, stencilled paintwork. Most of the glass in the numerous arched windows was originally coloured Venetian bottle glass, but this has now been replaced by poor-quality modern windows.

The richly decorated **royal pavilion**, approached by ramp at the northeast corner of the complex, gives access to the sultan's loge inside the mosque. The ramp enabled the sultan to ride his horse right up to the door of his chambers.

Tomb of Sultan Ahmet

Tues–Sat 9am–4pm • Free

Outside the precinct wall to the northwest of the mosque, the *türbe* or **tomb of Sultan Ahmet** is decorated, like the mosque, with seventeenth-century İznik tiles. Buried here along with the sultan are his wife and three of his sons, two of whom (Osman II and Murat IV) ruled in their turn.

Rahmi M. Koç Industrial Museum, Miniatürk, Santral İstanbul, Kasımpaşa & Golden Horn

Kadir Has University

ATATÜRK BRIDGE

GOLDEN
HORN

Eski İmaret
Camii

FATİH

Zeyrek
Camii

Fatih
Camii

ZEYREK

Rüstem
Paşa Camii

SÜLEYMANİYE

Tomb of
Mimar Sinan

Aquaduct
of Valens

Süleymaniye
Library

Süleymaniye
Camii

Arkeoloji
Park

Saraçhane
Parkı

İstanbul
University

Şehzade
Camii

İstanbul
Municipal
Building

Horhor
Antique
Market

Kalenderhane
Camii

Beyazit
Kulesi

SEE 'GRAND
BAZAAR' MAP

Valide
Camii

Laleli
Camii

İstanbul
University
(Faculty of
Science &
Literature)

Beyazit
Camii

Grand Bazaar
(Kapalı Çarşı)

ORDU CAD

Aksaray

Laleli/Üniversite

ORDU CAD

ORDU CAD

Beyazit

Column of
Constantine

YENİÇERİLER CAD

Mesıpaşa
Camii

Havaş Airport
Bus Stop

Yenikapı
Station

Surp
Asdvadzaszin

Yenikapı
Parkı

Kumkapı
Station

KENNEDY CADDESİ

KUMKAPI

0   250
metres

Yenikapı
Ferry Terminal

Kumkapı
Harbour

Yalova (Termal & İznik) & Güzelyalı (for Bursa)

THE OLD CITY

1

Bosphorus Tour

Kadıköy

Üsküdar

Harem & Haydarpaşa

Kabataş, Dolmabahçe & Tophane

Arap Camii

BAKALAR CAD

TERSANE CAD

KEMANKEŞ CAD

TERSANE CAD

KARAKÖY

Yeraltı Camii

Karaköy / Galata

RIHTIM CAD

Karaköy Ferry Terminal

Bus Station

KENNEDY CAD

KENNEDY CAD

KENNEDY CAD

Eminönü

Yeni Camii

Sarayburnu Parkı

Atatürk Monument

KENNEDY CADDESİ

Mısır Çarşısı (Spice Bazaar)

HAMİDİYE CAD

BÜYÜK POSTAHANE CAD

ANKARA CAD

İSTASYON YOLU

Sirkeci Station

Hodja Pasha Cultural Centre

AŞİREFENDİ CAD

EMİNÖNÜ

Vilayet Binası

EBUSUUD CAD

History of Science & Technology in Islam Museum

Gülhane Parkı

Goth's Column

Museum of Turkish Ceramics

Nuruosmaniye Camii

Çemberlitaş Hamam

Press Museum

Çağaloğlu Hamamı

Gülhane

Museum of the Ancient Orient

Museum of Turkish Ceramics

Topkapı Palace

Archeology Museum

Darphane

Aya İrene

Ahirkapi Lighthouse

Nuruosmaniye Cad

Yareba Camii

Caferağa Medresesi

Aya Sofya

Tomb of Sultan Mahmut II

Yerebatan Sarnıcı

Ahmet III. Fountain

Çemberlitaş

Sultanahmet

Museum of Turkish & Islamic Art

CANKURTARAN

HIPPODROME (ATMEYDANI)

Archeological Park

Sultanahmet Camii (Blue Mosque)

Cankurtaran Station

Sokollu Mehmet Paşa Camii

SEA OF MARMARA

Mosaic Museum

Küçük Ayasofya Camii

KENNEDY CADDESİ (SAHİL YOLU)

Palace of Bucoleon

SEE 'SULTANAHMET' MAP

■ BARS & CAFÉS	
Erenler Çay Bahçesi	3
Konyalı Cafe (Topkapı)	1
North Shield Pub	2

● RESTAURANTS	
Ağa Kapısı	2
Hamdi Et Lokantası	1
Kör Agop	8
Paşazade	6
Siirt Şeref Büryan	3
Subaşı Lokantası	7
Tarihi Kuru Fasuliye Süleymaniye Erzincanlı Ali Baba	4
Vefa Bozacısı	5

1

The Ayasofya Hürrem Sultan Hamamı

Bab ı Humayan Cad 1 • Daily 7am–midnight • Bath packages €86–180; separate men and women's sections • ☎ 0212 517 3535, Ⓦ ayasofyahurremsultanhamami.com

Built in 1556 by Mimar Sinan in honour of Süleyman the Magnificent's wife Roxelana (known to Turks as Haseki Hürrem), the opulent **Ayasofya Hürrem Sultan Hamamı** reopened in 2011 after a lengthy restoration process. Virtually all its historical features – down to the marble squat toilets – have been preserved intact. It's the most expensive hamam experience in the city, but arguably worth it for the skill of the masseurs and the sheer loveliness of the interior.

The Museum of Turkish and Islamic Art

Atmeydan Sok 6 • Tues–Sun: April–Sept 9am–7pm; Oct–March 9am–5pm • ₺10 • ☎ 0212 518 1805

The attractive **İbrahim Paşa Sarayı** (Palace of İbrahim Paşa) now holds the **Museum of Turkish and Islamic Art** (Türk ve İslam Eserleri Müzesi), containing one of the best-exhibited collections of Islamic artefacts in the world. The main concentration of exhibits deals with Selçuk, Mamluk and Ottoman Turkish art, though several important Timurid and Persian works are also on display. The **Selçuk Turks**, precursors of the Ottomans, are represented by some beautiful wall tiles and fine woodcarvings. Other impressive exhibits include sixteenth-century Persian miniatures and the tiny Sancak Korans, intended to be hung on the standard of the Ottoman imperial army in a *jihad* (holy war), so that the word of God would precede the troops into battle.

The **Great Hall** of the palace houses a wonderful collection of **Turkish carpets**. These range from tattered thirteenth-century remains to carpets that once adorned İstanbul's palaces, some weighing in at thousands of kilograms. On the basement floor, an ethnography section holds everything from the black goat-hair tents of the *Yörük* tribes of Anatolia, to a re-creation of the interior of a late-Ottoman wooden house in Bursa.

Sokollu Mehmet Paşa Camii

Usually open; the *imam* should be around to unlock it during the day if not

The little-visited **Sokollu Mehmet Paşa Camii** ranks among the most attractive mosques in the city. A short walk downhill from the Hippodrome, it's one of Mimar Sinan's later buildings (1571), and was commissioned by Sokollu Mehmet Paşa, the last grand vizier of Süleyman the Magnificent.

The **interior** of the mosque is distinguished by the height of its dome and the impressive display of **İznik tiles** on its east wall. These date from the best period of Turkish ceramics: the white is pure, the green vivid, and the red intense. Calligraphic inscriptions are set against a jungle of enormous carnations and tulips, and the designs and colours are echoed all around the mosque and in the conical cap of the *mimber*, the tiling of which is unique in İstanbul.

Küçük Ayasofya Camii

500m below the Blue Mosque, downhill on Küçük Ayasofya Cad • Daily 7am–dusk • Donations expected

The often overlooked, recently restored **Küçük Ayasofya Camii**, the "small mosque of Aya Sofya", was before its conversion to a mosque known as the "Church of St Sergius and Bacchus". Built between 527 and 536, it's actually older than Aya Sofya up the hill. It was originally named after two Roman soldiers, **Sergius** and **Bacchus**, who were martyred for their faith and later became the patron saints of Christians in the Roman army, but was renamed because of its resemblance to Aya Sofya. The church was converted into a mosque early in the sixteenth century, during the reign of Beyazit II.

Like most Byzantine churches of this era, its **exterior** is austere brick, and only inside can the satisfying proportions be properly appreciated. It is basically an octagon with semicircular niches at its diagonals, inscribed in a rectangle, but both these shapes are extremely irregular. A delicately carved frieze, honouring Justinian, Theodora and St Sergius, runs around the architrave under the gallery, and numerous columns sport ornate Byzantine captials.

Mosaic Museum

Torun Sok, Sultanahmet • Tues–Sun: April–Sept 9am–7pm; Oct–March 9am–5pm; last entry 1hr before closing • ₺8

The mosaics displayed in the **Mosaic Museum** (Büyüksaray Mozaik Müzesi) were originally a part of the Byzantine Great Palace, which stood on and around this area for many centuries. It is reached by running the gauntlet of salespeople in the **Arasta Çarşısı** – a renovated street-bazaar selling tourist gifts, whose seventeeth-century shops were originally built to pay for the upkeep of the nearby Sultanahmet Camii.

The building has been constructed to allow some of the mosaics, probably dating from Justinian's rebuilding programme of the sixth century, to be viewed from a catwalk as well as at floor level. Among them are portrayals of animals in their natural habitats, and domestic scenes. These include a vivid illustration of an elephant locking a lion in a deadly embrace with its trunk, and two children being led on the back of a camel. The museum was being upgraded at the time of writing, so the display layout may have changed.

Divan Yolu

The main approach from Sultanahmet to Beyazit (see p.92) is **Divan Yolu**, a major thoroughfare that gained its name because it was the principal approach to the Divan from the Topkapı Gate. Hordes of people would pour along it three times a week to make their petitions to the court. In Roman and Byzantine times, this street was the Mese or "Middleway". It ran from a triumphal arch known as the **Milion**, a marked fragment of which remains at the eastern end of Divan Yolu, westwards through the city, and eventually linked in with the great Roman road system to reach as far as the Adriatic. It remains a crucial part of the city's transport network, though it is now given over to the trams that rattle their way from Zeytinburnu, through old İstanbul and over the Golden Horn to Kabataş.

Binbirdirek Sarnıcı

İmran Ökten Sok, off a narrow street running south from Divan Yolu Cad • Hours vary • ₺10

At 64m by 56m, the **Binbirdirek Sarnıcı** (Cistern of a Thousand and One Columns) is the second-largest cistern in the city. It's accessible via an entrance in its impressively thick retaining wall. The structure, now bone dry and half its former height due to a false floor, charges visitors for entry when it's not being used as a function room for weddings, circumcision ceremonies and the like.

The Grand Bazaar and around

İstanbul's Ottoman-era **Grand Bazaar** gets more than its fair share of souvenir-hungry visitors. The area around it, however, is relatively little explored, which is a shame as it holds some very worthwhile attractions, from the historic **Cembirlitaş Hamamı**, one of the best Turkish baths in the country, to the city's very best mosque, the hilltop **Süleymaniye Camii**. Throw in the ornate Baroque **Laleli Camii**, and it's easy to see how you can spend a day in this area alone. To get here from Sultanahmet, either walk or take the T1 tram.

1

The Grand Bazaar: Kapalı Çarşı

Kapalı Çarşı • Mon–Sat 9am–7pm

With 66 streets and alleys, more than four thousand shops, numerous storehouses, moneychangers and banks, a mosque, post office, police station, private security guards and its own health centre, İstanbul's **Grand Bazaar** is said to be the largest **covered bazaar** in the world. In Ottoman times it was based around two *bedesten*s (domed buildings where foreign trade took place and valuable goods were stored): the İç Bedesten probably dates from the time of the Conquest, while the Sandal Bedesten was added in the sixteenth century. The bazaar sprawls further, into the streets that lead down to the Golden Horn. This whole area was once controlled by strict laws laid down by the trade guilds, thus reducing competition between traders. Each shop could support just one owner and his apprentice, and successful merchants were not allowed to expand their businesses.

Visiting the bazaar

The best time to visit the bazaar is during the week, as it's very crowded with local shoppers on Saturday. Expect to get lost as most streets are either poorly marked, or their signs are hidden beneath goods hung on display. However, try finding Kavaflar Sok for **shoes**, Terlikçiler Sok for **slippers**, Kalpakçılar Başı and Kuyumcular *caddesi*s for **gold**, and Tavuk Pazarı Sok, Kürkçüler Sok, Perdahçılar Caddesi and Bodrum Han for **leather**

● RESTAURANTS		■ BAR AND CAFÉ		● SHOPS					
Havuzlu	1	Bedesten Cafe	1	Abdulla	3	Ethnicon	5	Şişko Osman	2
Subaşı	2			Abdullah Şalabi	6	Koç Deri	8	Tradition	7
				Adnan & Hasan	4	Necdet Danış	1	Yörük	9

Map labels:

GRAND BAZAAR (KAPALI ÇARŞI)

Mercan Ali Paşa Han

BAZAAR GATES
1 Nuruosmaniye Kapısı
2 Kürkcüler Kapısı
3 Merdivenli Kapısı
5 Çarşıkapı Kapısı
7 Beyazit Kapısı
8 Haci Hüsünü Kapısı
9 Fesciler Kapısı
11 Yorgancılar Kapısı
12 Lütfullah Kapısı
14 Örücüler Kapısı
15 Tacirler Kapısı
18 Mahmut Paşa Kapısı
20 Kılıçlar Kapısı

Mercan Ağa Mescidi
TİCGİLAR SOK
TARAKÇILAR CAD
MERCAN HAN
ÇUKAR HAN
YAĞLIKÇILAR CAD
İÇ CEBECİ HANI
Mercan Kapısı
KALCILAR HAN
ZİNCİRLİ HAN
MAHMUT PAŞA YOKUŞU
Menekşe Döviz
PERDAHÇILAR CAD
TERLİKÇİLER SOK
KAVAFLAR SOK
ACICESME SOK
AYNACILAR SOK
Police Station
VARAKÇI SOK
KUYUMCULAR CAD
AĞA SOK
KILIÇLAR SOK
MUHAFAZACILAR SOK
YORGANCILAR CAD
GANİ ÇELEBİ SOK
EVLİYA HANI
Çakır Ağa Camii
Havuzlu
Toilets
Zabita (Market Police)
HALICILAR ÇARŞISI CAD
RESSAM BASMACILAR
ORTA CAD
TAKKECİLER SOK
ZENNECİLER SOK
CEVAHİR BEDESTENİ
KESECİLER CAD
SANDAL BEDESTEN SOK
ATM
SANDAL BEDESTENİ
BODRUM HANI
CADIRCILAR CAD
Sahaflar Çarşısı
FESCILER CAD
KAVUNCULAR SOK
ÇARŞIS SOK
Marble Fountain
KESEÇLER CAD
DİVRİKLİ SOK
KOLANCILAR KAPISI SOK
TERZİLER SOK
Nuruosmaniye Camii
KALPAKÇILAR BAŞI CAD
NURUOSMANIYE KAPISI SOK
HACI HÜSÜN SOK
TERPUSCULAR SOKAĞI
KAZASLAR SOK
KALPAKÇILAR BAŞI CAD
RUBİYE HAN (W.C./INSIDE)
KÜRKÇÜLER CADDESİ
TAVUK PAZARI SOK

clothing. Carpet-sellers are just about everywhere, with more expensive collector's pieces on sale on Halıcılar Çarşısı, Takkeciler and Keseciler *caddesi*s, and cheaper ones in the tiny Rubiye Han or İç Cebeci Han. **Ceramics** and leather and kilim **bags** can be found along Yağlıkçılar Caddesi, just off it in Çukur Han, and also along Keseciler Caddesi.

The old bazaar (or İç Bedesten), located at the centre of the maze, was traditionally reserved for the most precious wares because it could be locked at night. These days, however, it's indistinguishable from the rest of the complex.

A number of decent cafés in the bazaar (see p.122) enable shoppers to unwind and avoid the constant importuning of traders.

East of the Grand Bazaar

The landmark **Çembirlitaş** ("the hooped stone"), a burnt column of masonry also known as the **Column of Constantine**, stands on the north side of the tramline on the approach to the Grand Bazaar. Erected by Constantine the Great in 330 AD, it commemorated the city's dedication as capital of the Roman Empire. The column and baths opposite it to the east, the **Çemberlitaş Hamamı** (see below), mark the southern end of Vezirhanı Caddesi.

Turn north up here to reach the **Nuruosmaniye Camii**, just outside the bazaar to the east. Begun by Mahmut I in 1748 and finished seven years later by Osman III, this was the first and most impressive of the city's Baroque mosques.

Back on Yeniceriler Caddesi, and just west of the Column of Constantine, the **Gazi Atik Ali Paşa Camii** is one of İstanbul's oldest mosques. It was built in 1496 by the eunuch Atik âli Paşa, who rose to the rank of grand vizier under Sultan Beyazit II.

Çemberlitaş Hamamı
Vezirhan Cad 8 • Daily 6am–midnight • ₺29, ₺46 with massage; separate men's and women's baths • ☎ 0212 522 7974, ⓦ www.cemberlitashamami.com.tr

The four-hundred-year-old **Çemberlitaş Hamamı**, across Vezirhan Caddesi from the Column of Constantine, was founded in the sixteenth century by Nur Banu, one of the most powerful Valide Sultans. Architecturally it's among the finest Ottoman hamams in İstanbul, and well used to dealing with novice visitors.

The Süleymaniye Külliyesi

Northwest of the Grand Bazaar, on the third hill of the Old City, the **Sülemaniye Külliyesi** is a complex of buildings that includes theological schools, a hospital, library, soup kitchen, caravanserai, shops and tombs. The centrepiece of the entire complex is a magnificent mosque, the **Süleymaniye Camii**. Built by the renowned architect **Mimar Sinan** (see p.93), in honour of his most illustrious patron, Süleyman the Magnificent, the complex is arguably his greatest achievement.

Süleymaniye Camii
Daily except for prayer times • Free

The beautifully restored **Süleymaniye Camii** is entered via the southwest portal, where plastic bags are provided for footwear. Once inside the mosque, the overwhelming impression is of light and uncluttered space, with a central dome 53m high (twice its diameter), surmounting a perfect square of 26.5m. The sense of space is further emphasized by the addition of supporting semi-domes to the northwest and southeast, while the monumental arched spaces to the southwest and northeast are filled with great tympana walls, pierced by windows through which the light pours. The four great rectangular piers that support the dome have been cleverly masked on two sides by linking them in with the arched colonnade walls. All in all, the mosque is a very successful take on the much earlier Aya Sofya (see p.72).

1

A rope prevents non-worshippers from entering the main part of the prayer-hall, but it's easy enough to admire the restrained arabesques and Koranic calligraphy that adorn the interior, along with the simple Proconnesian marble *mihrab*. The tiles here, used sparingly for effect, are top-notch İznik-ware, fired with flower motifs in blue, red and turquoise on a white ground.

The **Türbe (tomb) of Mimar Sinan** himself is located on the north side of the Sülemaniye Külliyesi complex, on Mimar Sinan Caddesi. Otherwise, the buildings of the complex served the usual functions. Despite its ornate design, the *imaret* (soup kitchen; today the *Darüzziyafe* restaurant) on Şifahane Sokak was constructed as a public kitchen to supply food for the local poor. There's also a *kervansaray* (hotel), a *mektep* (primary school) and a library.

Tombs of Süleyman and Roxelana

Both closed at time of writing; normal hours daily 5.30am–8pm • Free

The **cemetery** outside the southeast prayer-wall of Süleymaniye Camii holds the **tombs** of Süleyman the Magnificent and Haseki Hürrem, better known to the West as his powerful wife Roxelana. Süleyman's tomb is particularly impressive: its doors are inlaid with ebony, ivory, silver and jade, and his turban is huge. The spectacular inner dome has been faithfully restored in red, black and gold, inlaid with glittering ceramic stars.

Süleymaniye Hamamı

Mimar Sinan Cad 20 • Daily 10am–midnight, last entry 10pm • €35 for bath, scrub and massage • ☎ 0212 519 5569, ⓦ suleymaniyehamamı.com

The **Süleymaniye Hamamı** was built by Mimar Sinan in 1557, and legend has it that the great architect took all his baths here from 1557 to 1588. Today, however, it doesn't accept single males or females, only couples and families, and the bathing is mixed sex. It has been beautifully restored and is very atmospheric.

The Aqueduct of Valens

The magnificent **Aqueduct of Valens** spans Atatürk Bulvarı around 300m southwest of the Süleymaniye complex, here reaching a height of 18.5m. Originally built during the late fourth century, as part of a waterworks programme carried out by the Emperor Valens, the aqueduct belonged to a distribution network that included reservoirs in the Belgrade Forest and various cisterns located around the city centre. It was used right up to the end of the nineteenth century, having been kept in good repair by successive rulers, who maintained a constant supply of water to the city in the face of both drought and siege.

Beyazit Meydanı

Beyazit Meydanı, just west of the Grand Bazaar, is the main square of Beyazit. On the north side of the square, the principal approach to İstanbul University is marked by a magnificent portal, while a monumental nineteenth-century fire-tower, Beyazit Kulesi, stands behind it in the university grounds.

On the east of the square, **Beyazit Camii**, completed in 1506, is the oldest surviving imperial mosque in the city. Its sombre courtyard is full of richly coloured marble, including twenty columns of verd antique, red granite and porphyry. Inside, the building is a perfect square of exactly the same proportions as the courtyard (although the aisles make it feel elongated). Just behind the mosque, on the approach to the Grand Bazaar, the famous **Sahaflar Çarşısı** is a secondhand booksellers' market that dates back to the Byzantine era.

On the south side of the T1 tram line, opposite the southwest corner of the *meydan*, a jumble of fallen marble columns is decorated with curious teardrop patterns. These formed part of the famed triumphal **Arch of Theodosius**, erected in 393.

MIMAR SINAN, MASTER BUILDER

Many of the finest works of Ottoman civil and religious architecture throughout Turkey can be traced to **Mimar Sinan** (1489–1588), who served as court architect to three sultans – Süleyman the Magnificent, Selim II and Murat III. Probably born to Greek or Armenian Christian parents, he was conscripted into the janissaries in 1513. As a military engineer, he travelled the length and breadth of southeastern Europe and the Middle East, giving him the opportunity to become familiar with the finest Islamic – and Christian – monumental architecture there. His bridges, siegeworks, harbours, and even ships, earned him the admiration of his superiors.

Sultan Süleyman appointed Sinan court architect in April 1536, and he completed his first major religious commission, İstanbul's Şehzade Camii, in 1548. Shortly thereafter, he embarked on a rapid succession of ambitious projects in and around the capital, including the waterworks leading from the Belgrade Forest and the Süleymaniye Camii. Competing with the Süleymaniye as his masterpiece was the Selimiye Camii, constructed between 1569 and 1575 in the former imperial capital of Edirne (see p.149). Despite temptations to luxury, he lived and died modestly, being buried in a simple tomb he made for himself in his garden in the grounds of the Süleymaniye Camii – the last of more than five hundred constructions by Sinan, large and small, throughout the empire.

Laleli Camii

Ordu Cad, 1min walk from the Laleli/Üniversite tram stop

Perching above busy Ordu Caddesi, the attractive **Laleli Camii** was built in the Ottoman Baroque tradition. The main Baroque elements in the mosque complex are the use of ramps (including one that the reigning sultan would have used to ride up to his loge), the grand staircases, and the exquisite detail, noticeable in the window grilles of the tomb and in the carved eaves of the *sebil* (drinking fountain).

Eminönü

Heading north from Sultanahmet brings you to the waterfront district of **Eminönü**. Once the maritime gateway to the city, it remains a large and convenient transport hub, where buses, ferries, trams and trains converge. The latter arrive at the grand **Sirkeci station**, once the last stop on the famed Orient Express. Sights within this district include the **Cağaloğlu Hamamı** and the landmark **Yeni Cami** complex, which includes the ornate Ottoman-era **Spice Bazaar**.

Cağaloğlu Hamamı

Kazım Ismail Gürkan Cad 34 • Daily: men 8am–10pm; women 8am–8.30pm • ₺24 for self-service bath, ₺54 for bath and scrub, ₺72 for bath, scrub and massage • ☎ 0212 522 2424, ⊛ www.cagalogluhamami.com.tr

The very popular **Cağaloğlu Hamamı** is famous for its beautiful *hararet*s or steam rooms – open cruciform chambers with windowed domes, supported on a circle of columns. The baths were built in 1741 by Mahmut I to pay for the upkeep of his library in Aya Sofya, and the arches, basins and taps of the hot room, and also the entries to the private cubicles, are all magnificently Baroque. Florence Nightingale is said to have bathed here, and the hamam has appeared in several films, including *Indiana Jones and the Temple of Doom*.

Yeni Cami

The **Yeni Cami**, or "new mosque", is a familiar city landmark, sited across the busy road from Eminönü's bustling waterfront. Completed in 1663, it was the last of İstanbul's imperial mosques to be built, erected for the powerful Valide Sultan, Safiye, mother of Mehmet III.

1

THE GOLDEN HORN

The **Golden Horn** (*Halic* or "estuary" in Turkish) is one of the finest natural harbours in the world. Its fortunes have been closely entwined with those of İstanbul. On two separate occasions, capture of the Horn proved to be the turning point of crucial military campaigns. The first time, in 1203–04, was when the Crusaders took the Horn and proceeded to besiege the city for ten months, until they breached the walls separating the inlet from the city. The second was a spectacular *tour de force* by Mehmet the Conqueror, who was prevented from entering the Horn by a chain fastened across it and so carried his ships overland at night and launched them into the inlet from its northern shore. Mehmet then constructed a pontoon across the top of the Horn, over which he transported his army and cannons in preparation for the siege of the land walls, which were finally breached in 1453. For the Ottoman Empire, the Horn was a vital harbour, supplying the Genoese, Venetian and Jewish trading colonies on its northern shore.

Spice Bazaar

Daily 9am–7pm

The most intriguing part of the Yeni Cami mosque complex is the **Spice Bazaar**, known in Turkish as the **Mısır Çarşısı** or "Egyptian Bazaar". Completed a few years before Yeni Cami, the L-shaped bazaar has been the city's premier spice outlet for several centuries. Endowed with customs duties from Cairo – hence its name – it has 88 vaulted rooms and chambers above the entryways at the ends of the halls. Far more manageable than the Grand Bazaar, it sells a wide range of herbs, spices and Turkish Delight. It's very touristy and expensive, however; the shops that line the exterior of the Spice Bazaar, and in the narrow streets between it and the **Rüstem Paşa Camii** (see p.94), sell the same goods at cheaper prices.

Rüstem Paşa Camii

A short walk west of the spice bazaar

Rüstem Paşa Camii is one of the most attractive smaller mosques in İstanbul. Built for Süleyman the Magnificent's grand vizier Rüstem Paşa in 1561, it's decorated inside and out by some of the finest İznik **tiles** in Turkey. Designs covering the walls, piers and pillars, and decorating the *mihrab* and *mimber*, include famous panels of tulips and carnations and geometric patterns. Built by Sinan on an awkward site, the mosque is easy to miss as you wander the streets below. At ground level on the Golden Horn side, an arcade of shops occupies the vaults, from where a flight of steps leads up to the mosque's terrace. Through an attractive entrance portal is a wide courtyard and a tiled double portico along the west wall.

The northwest quarter

Catch #99 bus from Eminönü to the Atatürk Bridge, and walk up to Zeyrek and Fatih, or stay on the bus to Fener and Balat; you can also walk up from the Aksaray stop on the T1 tramline, or take a ferry from Eminönü or Karaköy to Ayvansaray

One of the least visited but most fascinating areas of the old city, the **northwest quarter** is bounded on the west by the major thoroughfare of Fevzi Paşa Caddesi, to the north by the land walls of Theodosius, to the east by the Golden Horn, and on the south by traffic-choked Atatürk Bulvarı. Once home to a cosmopolitan population of Muslims, Christians and Jews, it's now a devoutly Muslim area, particularly in the district of **Fatih**, where you'll notice many women in chadors and bearded men in *şalvar* pants, long baggy shirts and skullcaps (dress appropriately).

The most notable sights are a former Byzantine church, now the **Zeyrek Camii**; two notable Ottoman mosques, the **Fatih** and **Yavuz Selim**; the magnificent Byzantine mosaics in the **Fethiye Museum**, the spiritual centre of the Orthodox Christian world; the **Greek Orthodox Patriarchate**; and the curious cast-iron church of **St Stephen of the**

Bulgars. A spiritual centre of a different order awaits a couple of kilometres up the Golden Horn from the Patriarchate, the **Eyüp** area, sacred to Muslims worldwide as it boasts the tomb of Eyüp Ensari, standard-bearer of the Prophet Mohammed.

Zeyrek Camii

Nestling in the heart of Zeyrek, **Zeyrek Camii**, the former Church of the Pantocrator, was built in the twelfth century and converted into a mosque at the time of the conquest. The building was under restoration at the time of writing; once the work is complete, it will hopefully be more readily accessible than previously. It originally consisted of two churches and a connecting chapel, built between 1118 and 1136 by John II Comnenus and Empress Irene.

Fatih Camii

Just over 300m east of Zeyrek Camii

Work on the **Fatih Camii**, or "Mosque of the Conqueror", started in 1463 on the site of the famous Byzantine Church of the Holy Apostles, but was not completed until 1470. Much rebuilt following a devastating earthquake in 1766, the **inner courtyard** contains green antique marble and highly polished porphyry columns supporting a domed portico, while an eighteenth-century fountain is surrounded by four enormous poplar trees. The architect was supposedly executed because the dome wasn't as large as that of Aya Sofya. The whole complex has recently been restored to its former glory.

Yavuz Selim Camii

Yavuz Selim Cad, Fatih

Also called the Selimiye Camii, the **Yavuz Selim Camii** ranks among İstanbul's most attractive mosques. Recently beautifully restored, it's built on a terrace on the crest of one of the city's seven hills (the fifth, counting from Topkapı). The mosque of Yavuz Selim, or Selim the Grim, was probably begun in the reign of Selim and completed by Süleyman the Magnificent. It is much more basic than the other imperial mosques, with just a single large dome atop a square room with a walled courtyard in front of it. The *avlu* (courtyard) in front of the prayer hall is quite beautiful, with a central fountain surrounded by tall cypress trees. The floor of the portico is paved with a floral design, while the columns are a mix of marbles and granites.

The interior of the mosque is stunning in its simplicity, its shallower than usual dome emphasizing the sense of space. Light floods in through a series of windows in the tympanum arches and from the 24 stained-glass windows that pierce the dome. The interior of the mosque falls well short of the austere, though; gorgeous blue and white İznik tiles fill the lunettes above the lower windows, and gilt-work highlights the beautiful geometry of the stalactite carving above the *mihrab*.

The **tomb of Selim the Grim** (daily except Tues 9.30am–4.30pm; ₺1), beside the mosque, has lost its original interior decoration but retains two beautiful tiled panels on either side of the door.

Fethiye Museum

Fethiye Cad, Katip Mustehattın Mah, Fatih • Mon, Tues & Thurs–Sun 9am–4.30pm • ₺5

A major, but little-visited, Byzantine gem, the **Fethiye Camii** was once the **Church of Theotokos Pammakaristos**. This medium-sized church, attractively set on a terrace overlooking the Golden Horn, was built during the twelfth century and conforms to the usual cross-in-a-square design, its large central dome enhanced by four smaller, subsidiary domes. Despite the Ottoman conquest of Constantinople in 1453, it

1

remained a Christian place of worship. Indeed, between 1456 and 1587 it served as the seat of the **Greek Orthodox Patriarch** (now situated nearby, in the district of Fener). It finally became a mosque in 1573, when it was renamed the Fethiye Camii or "Mosque of the Conquest". The main body of the building continues to function as a mosque and is usually only unlocked around prayer times. The southwest wing – originally a side chapel or *parecclesion* of the main church, added in 1310 – now serves as a **museum**. Helpful display boards in the entry to the chapel locate and give information on each of the mosaics, superb examples of the renaissance of Byzantine art, including, in the dome, Christ Pantocrator, encircled by the twelve prophets of the Old Testament. Other notable scenes show Christ with the Virgin Mary, the baptism of Christ and St John the Baptist.

The Greek Orthodox Patriarchate

Sadrazam Ali Paşa Cad 35, Fener • Daily 9am–5pm • Free

The **Greek Orthodox Patriarchate**, north of the Yavuz Selim Camii almost on the shores of the Golden Horn, has been the spiritual centre of the Orthodox world since 1599. It remains so today – despite the fact that the Greek Orthodox community in the city is now so meagre (around 2500), and that a Turkish court controversially ruled that the authority of the Patriarch (currently Bartholomew I) was confined solely to Turkey's remaining Greek Orthodox Christians, rather than to the Orthodox Christian community worldwide.

St Stephen of the Bulgars

Mürsel Paşa Cad 85–8, Fener • Daily 8am–5pm • Free

St Stephen of the Bulgars is a curious, neo-Gothic white-painted church, stranded on a massive traffic-island-cum-park area. Built in 1896, it is made entirely from iron, cast in Vienna and carted all the way to İstanbul. Signs of rust betray the chosen building material, and the church was undergoing restoration at the time of writing.

The land walls

To reach the north end of the walls take the ferry from Eminönü or Karaköy to Ayvansaray İskelesi on the Golden Horn, just before the Haliç bridge, or bus #99 from Eminönü; for the southern end of the walls take the suburban (*banliyo*) train to Yedikule, bus #80/T from Taksim, or bus #80 from Eminönü to Yedikule

Theodosius II's **land walls** are among the most fascinating Byzantine remains in Turkey. Well-preserved remnants can still be found along the whole of their 6.5km length, though purists (and UNESCO) decry the fact that much of the recent work done on the walls looks like new-build rather than restoration.

The land walls were named after Theodosius II, and construction started in 413 AD. Stretching from the Marmara to Tekfur Saray, 2km further out than the previous walls of Constantine, they were built to accommodate the city's expanding population. All citizens, regardless of rank, were required to help in the rebuilding following their collapse in the earthquake of 447 AD, in the light of the imminent threat of attack by Attila the Hun. The completed construction consisted of the original wall, 5m thick and 12m high, plus an outer wall of 2m by 8.5m, and a 20m-wide moat, all of which proved sufficient to repel Atilla's assault.

Walking along the walls takes a little over two hours, though a full day allows time to enjoy it, and the adjacent sites, fully. Most of the outer wall and its 96 towers are still standing; access is restricted on some of the restored sections, though elsewhere there's the chance to scramble along the crumbling edifice. As there are still plenty of run-down **slums** in this area, it's best avoided at night (especially Topkapı).

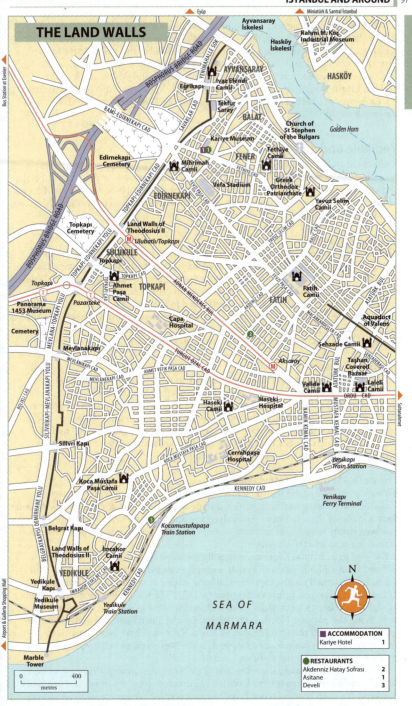

THE LAND WALLS

▲ Eyüp
▲ Miniatürk & Santral İstanbul

Ayvansaray
İskelesi

Rahmi M. Koç
Industrial Museum

HASKÖY

Bus Station at Esenler

BOSPHORUS BRIDGE ROAD

YENİMAHALLE SOK

Haşköy
İskelesi

AYVANSARAY

İvaz Efendi
Camii

Eğrikapı

RAMİ-EDİRNEKAPI CAD

SAVAKLAR CAD

Tekfur
Saray

BALAT

Church of
St Stephen
of the Bulgars

Golden Horn

Edirnekapı
Cemetery

TOPKAPI-EDİRNEKAPI CAD

Kariye Museum

Mihrimah
Camii

FENER

Fethiye
Camii

FETHİYE CAD

Greek
Orthodox
Patriarchate

Vefa Stadium

EDİRNEKAPI

Yavuz Selim
Camii

BOSPHORUS BRIDGE ROAD

Topkapı
Cemetery

TOPKAPI-EDİRNEKAPI CAD

Land Walls of
Theodosius II

Ⓜ Ulubatlı/Topkapı

SULUKULE

Topkapı

ⓉTopkapı

MEVLANA-TOPKAPI YOLU

TOPKAPI YOLU

Ahmet
Paşa
Camii

TOPKAPI CAD

TOPKAPI

ADNAN MENDERES BUL

MÜ

Fatih
Camii

FEVZİ PAŞA CAD

FATİH

Şehzade Camii

HALİÇ CAD

Aqueduct
of Valens

Panorama
1453 Müseum

Ⓣ

Pazarteke

Cemetery

Mevlanakapı

Çapa
Hospital

TURGUT ÖZAL CAD

AKDENİZ CAD

Aksaray
Ⓜ

ATATÜRK BUL

Taşhan
Covered
Bazaar

MEVLANAKAPI CAD

AHMET VEFİK PAŞA CAD

Valide
Camii

MACARKARDEŞLER CAD

Laleli
Camii

ORDU CAD

SİLİVRİKAPI-MEVLANAKAPI YOLU

Haseki
Camii

Haseki
Hospital

MUSTAFA KEMAL CAD

Sultanahmet

Silivri Kapı

NAMIK KEMAL CAD

Cerrahpaşa
Hospital

Yenikapı
Train Station

BELGRATKAPISI DEMİRHANE YOLU

KOCA MUSTAFA PAŞA CAD

Koca Mustafa
Paşa Camii

KENNEDY CAD

Yenikapı
Ferry Terminal

Belgrat Kapı

Kocamustafapaşa
Train Station

İmrahor
Camii

Land Walls of
Theodosius II

VEDİKULE

Yedikule
Kapı

Yedikule
Museum

İMRAHOR ANKAYBEY CAD

KENNEDY CAD

Yedikule
Train Station

N

Airport & Galleria Shopping Mall

SEA OF
MARMARA

Marble
Tower

0   400
metres

■ ACCOMMODATION
Kariye Hotel   1

● RESTAURANTS
Akdeniz Hatay Sofrası   2
Asitane   1
Develi   3

1

The three principal sights can also be visited independently. The **Yedikule fortifications**, towards the southern terminus of the walls, are best reached by walking up from the suburban train station at Yedikule. The **Kariye Museum**, a former Byzantine church containing some of the best-preserved mosaics and frescoes in the world, just in from Edirnekapı and around 750m north of the Golden Horn, is easily accessed from the Ulubatlı M1 metro stop or the Pazartekke T1 tramstop, the **Mihrimah Camii** likewise – or take #28, #38E or #336E bus from Eminönü to Edirnekapı.

Yedikule and around

The run-down but attractive old quarter of **Yedikule** (Seven Towers), around 5km from the west of Sultanahmet, is ripe for gentrification. Its most impressive sight is the **Yedikule Museum** (Yedikule Müzesi; Tues–Sun 9am–6pm; ₺10), a massive fortification astride the line of the walls, situated southwest of İmrahor Camii on Yedikule Meydanı Sokak, Yedikule Caddesi.

The Golden Gate

The so-called **Golden Gate**, constructed by Theodosius I in 390, is actually made of stone, and was used by important visitors of state, as well as conquering emperors, to enter the city. Four of Yedikule's towers once formed part of the land walls, while the other three were added by Mehmet the Conqueror. These three "new" towers were linked together by curtain walls, which extended to the line of the land walls, and thus created the enclave that can be seen today. Despite its design, this was never actually used as a castle; two of the towers served as prisons, and others as treasuries and offices for the collection of revenue of the *Vakıf* or pious foundation.

The prison towers

Yedikule's two **prison towers** stand immediately to the left of the entrance: the "tower with inscriptions", and the tower on the north side of the Golden Gate. The inscriptions around the outside of the former were carved into the walls by prisoners, many of whom were foreign ambassadors on some hapless errand. The prison in the second tower doubled as an execution chamber; the wooden gallows and "well of blood", into which heads would roll, can still be seen, and the odd instrument of torture remains laying about outside in the courtyard.

The walls – Yedikule to Mevlanakapı

To walk along one of the best-preserved sections of the land walls, start by exiting Yedikule and heading north, then turn sharply west to a gate in the land walls, **Yedikule Kapı**. Go out of that, and head north along the outside of the walls, which here have not been overly restored (as are some sections further north), though the former moat is now in use as market gardens.

The next gate, **Belgrat Kapı**, was originally intended for military use only, and differed from a public gateway in that no bridge crossed the moat beyond the outer walls. It was named for the captives who were settled in this area by Süleyman the Magnificent after his capture of Belgrade in 1521. The walls here, which are floodlit at night, have been substantially renovated, and it's now one of the best places to walk along the parapet. North from Belgrat Kapı to **Silivri Kapı**, the walls are largely untouched, though the sections around Silivri Kapı itself have been extensively renovated. There is more restoration work at the **Mevlanakapı**, where the outer wall holds some interesting inscriptions.

A road system dominates the outer side of the 1km Mevlanakapı–Topkapı section of wall, and a pleasant pavement has been constructed along the moat. Just south of Topkapı, the walls have been destroyed to make way for the enormous thoroughfare of Turgut Özal Caddesi, complete with its central tram track. Beyond it is the **Topkapı** (the "Gate of the Cannonball"), named after the most powerful cannon of Mehmet the Conqueror (see below), the famed **Orban**, which was trained on this part of the walls during the siege of 1453.

Panorama 1453 History Museum

Topkapı/Edirnekapı Cad • Daily 9am–6.30pm • ₺10, audioguide ₺5 • ⓦ panoramikmuze.com • T1 tram from Sultanahmet to the Topkapı stop

Set in a pleasant park on the west side of horrendously busy Topkapı/Edirnekapı Caddesi, the small **Panorama 1453 History Museum** pays homage to a landmark date in Turkish history, the siege and capture of Constantinople by Mehmet the Conqueror. Its centrepiece is a scene depicting the Ottoman army besieging the walls, painted in a 360-degree sweep around the drum and shallow dome of the building, and viewed from a circular central platform. Between the viewing platform and the painted scene, the battlefield has been re-created with a realistic tableau of models and mannequins. It's all the more powerful for being set in the shadow of the walls themselves, close to the point the Ottomans first breached them on May 29, 1453.

The walls – Topkapı to Edirnekapı

Between Topkapı and Edirnekapı, Vatan Caddesi follows a pronounced valley that was once the course of the Lycus River. At this point the walls are at their least defensible, since the higher ground outside gives the advantage to attackers. It was here that the besiegers finally breached the walls and entered the city.

The gate of **Edirnekapı** takes its name from the route to modern Edirne. Close by, the beautifully restored sixteenth-century **Mihrimah Camii** stands on the highest of İstanbul's seven hills. It was named after Mihrimah, the favourite daughter of Süleyman the Magnificent, whose passion for architecture was as great as that of her husband Rüstem Paşa.

Kariye Museum

Kariye Cami Sok 26 • Mon, Tues & Thurs–Sun 9am–6pm • ₺15 • ⓦ choramuseum.com • Take M1 metro to Topkapı/Ulubatlı and walk, or catch a bus to Edirnekapı: #28 from Beşikta, #36/V and #37/Y from Vezneciler, #38 from Beyazit, #38/E from Eminönü, or #55/EB from Beyazit

Formerly the church of St Saviour in Chora, the **Kariye Museum** (Kariye Müzesi) is decorated with a superbly preserved series of **frescoes and mosaics** portraying the life and miracles of Christ. Arguably the most evocative of all the city's Byzantine treasures, it's thought to have been built in the early twelfth century on the site of a much older church far from the centre: hence "in Chora", meaning "in the country". Between 1316 and 1321, the statesman and scholar Theodore Metochites rebuilt the central dome and added the narthexes and mortuary chapel.

The mosaics

Inside the church, the most prominent of the mosaics is that of **Christ Pantocrator**, bearing the inscription "Jesus Christ, the Land of the Living". Opposite is a depiction of the Virgin and angels, with the inscription "Mother of God, the Dwelling Place of the Uncontainable". The third in the series, located in the inner narthex, shows Metochites offering a model of the building to a seated Christ. Saints Peter and Paul are portrayed on either side of the door leading to the nave, and to the right of the door are Christ with his Mother and two benefactors, Isaac (who built the original church), and the figure of a nun.

The two domes of the inner narthex hold medallions of **Christ Pantocrator** and the Virgin and Child, while in the fluting of the domes there's a series of notable figures –

1

starting with Adam – from the **Genealogy of Christ**. The **Cycle of the Blessed Virgin** is located in the first three bays of the inner narthex. Episodes depicted here include the first seven steps of the Virgin; the Virgin caressed by her parents, with two beautiful peacocks in the background; the Virgin presented as an attendant at the temple, the Virgin receiving a skein of purple wool, as proof of her royal blood; Joseph taking the Virgin to his house, in which is also depicted one of Joseph's sons by his first wife; and Joseph returning from a trip to find his wife pregnant.

The next cycle, found in the arched apertures of the outer narthex, depicts the **Infancy of Christ**. The mosaics can be followed clockwise, starting with Joseph dreaming, the Virgin and two companions, and the journey to Bethlehem. Apart from well-known scenes such as the Journey of the Magi and the Nativity, there are depictions in the seventh bay of the Flight into Egypt. In the sixth bay is the Slaughter of the Innocents, complete with babies impaled on spikes.

The **Cycle of Christ's Ministry** fills the vaults of the outer narthex and parts of the south bay of the inner narthex. It includes wonderful scenes of the Temptation of Christ, with dramatic dialogue (Matthew 4: 3–10) that could almost be in speech bubbles, beginning "Devil: If thou be the Son of God, command that these stones be made bread. Christ: It is written, Man shall not live by bread alone, but by every word that proceedeth out of the mouth of God."

The frescoes

The main frescoes in the nave of St Saviour echo the mosaics, featuring the death of the Virgin over the door and, to the right, a depiction of Christ. The best known of all the works in the church, however, are the frescoes in the **funerary chapel** to the south of the nave.

The most spectacular of these is the **Resurrection**, also known as the Harrowing of Hell. It depicts Christ trampling the gates of Hell underfoot, and forcibly dragging Adam and Eve from their tombs. A black Satan lies among the broken fetters at his feet, bound at the ankles, wrists and neck. To the left, animated onlookers include John the Baptist, David and Solomon, while to the right Abel is standing in his mother's tomb; behind him is another group of the righteous.

Other frescoes in the chapel, in the vault of the east bay, depict the **Second Coming**, while in the east half of the domical vault Christ sits in judgement.

Eyüp

Coming from Eminönü, the conservative district of **Eyüp** is most easily reached by boat – it's the last ferry stop before the Golden Horn peters out into two small streams. The main sights here are **Eyüp mosque**, the tombs of various Muslim notables, and the hilltop cemetery.

The hills above the mosque are covered in plain modern stones interspersed with beautiful Ottoman tombs. This is the **Eyüp cemetery**, most beautiful at sunset with an arresting view of the Golden Horn. A twenty-minute walk from Eyüp Camii will bring you to the romantic *Pierre Loti Café* (daily 8am–midnight) overlooking the Horn, or take the new cable car (₺2) from the shores of the Golden Horn.

Eyüp Camii

Camii Kebir Cad • 10min walk from ferry terminal, or catch bus #39/A or #99

Eyüp owes its status as one of the holiest places in Islam to the fact that its mosque, **Eyüp Camii**, is the site of the tomb of **Eyüp Ensari** (674–678), the Prophet Mohammed's standard-bearer who was killed in the first Arab siege of Constantinople. Muslims come here from all over the Islamic world on pilgrimage. Try not to visit on Fridays, out of respect for conservative worshippers.

Originally built by Mehmet the Conqueror in honour of Eyüp Ensari, the mosque was destroyed by an earthquake in the eighteenth century. Its Baroque replacement, filled with light, gold, pale stone and white marble, was completed in 1800 and later used in the investiture ceremonies of the Ottoman sultans.

The adjoining **tomb of Eyüp Ensari** (Tues–Sun 9.30am–4.30pm), with its tile panels from many different periods, is more compelling than the mosque.

Tombs of Sokollu Mehmet Paşa and Siyavus Paşa

Camii Kebir Cad, 5min walk from Eyüp Camii towards the Golden Horn • Tues–Sun 9.30am–4.30pm

In addition to the tomb of Eyüp Ensari, the Eyüp district holds several other important tombs. The **tombs of Sokollu Mehmet Paşa and Siyavus Paşa**, facing each other across Camii Kebir Caddesi, were both designed by master architect Mimar Sinan. The former is especially notable for its stained glass, some of which is original.

Galata and around

Immediately across the **Galata bridge** from Eminönü and the old city, the gritty port area of **Karaköy** is now swamped with cruise liners. Further inland is **Galata** proper, once a Genoese city-state within İstanbul and now an up-and-coming district full of bars and restaurants.

The Galata bridge

The first bridge to span the Golden Horn was completed in 1845. It was rebuilt three times before its most recent incarnation, the **Galata Köprüsü** (Galata bridge), was erected in the late 1980s. While this latest version may lack grace, its stunning location and supreme importance in linking the old and new İstanbuls more than make up for its lack of architectural merit. A walkway follows either side of the bridge close to water level, backed by a myriad of lively cafés, bars and restaurants. The tram rumbles across the upper level, and the bridge's guardrails are invisible behind a solid wall of expectant anglers. To discover more about this landmark bridge and the people whose lives revolve around it, read Geert Mak's *The Bridge* (see p.699).

Karaköy

From the rough-and-ready port area of **Karaköy**, at the northern end of the Galata bridge, you can either walk up to Galata/Beyoğlu on the steep Yüksek Kaldırım Caddesi, past the Galata Tower, or take the **Tünel** underground train/funicular (daily 7am–10pm; ₺4). Karaköy's port and Ottoman shipyard was once enclosed within the walls of the Castle of Galata. In 1446 the Byzantines stretched a great chain across the mouth of the Horn to prevent enemy ships from entering. Originally constructed around 580 AD, the subterranean keep of the castle is thought to be preserved as the **Yeraltı Cami**, or "Underground Mosque", on Kemankeş Caddesi. At the far end of the port area is another mosque, the **Kılıç Ali Paşa Camii**, constructed in 1580 by Sinan, and essentially a smaller copy of Aya Sofya.

Jewish Museum

Meydanı Perçemli Sok • Mon & Thurs 10am–4pm, Fri & Sun 10am–2pm • ₺10 • muze500.com

The Zülfaris Synagogue, west of the Galata bridge, is home to İstanbul's **Jewish Museum**. Its small but fascinating display includes documents and photographs donated by local Jewish families, chronicling Turkish Jews since they first came to the country over seven hundred years ago.

1

GALATA, BEYOĞLU & TAKSIM

RESTAURANTS

Cezayir	7
Ficcin	6
Galata House	8
Hacı Abdullah	3
Imroz	5
Kenan Usta	2
Mardin Kaburga Sofrası	1
Nature & Peace	4

SHOPS

By Retro	9
Crash	11
Felt in Love	13
Gülüoğlu	14
Homer	6
Lale Plak	10
Leyla	7
Mavi	3
Mudo	8
Mustamel Esya Evi	5
Naturel Müzik	12
Pandora	1
Roll	4
Vakko	2

Kabataş & Beşiktaş

Military Museum & Nişantaşı

TAKSIM CADDESI

Atatürk Cultural Centre

Taksim Parkı

Bus Station

Taksim

TAKSIM SQUARE

Cumhuriyet Anıtı

French Consulate

CIHANGIR

German Hospital

Aya Triada

Taksim Hospital

Akbank Culture & Arts Centre (Akbank Sanat)
Cinemaximum Cinema

Ağa Camii

Surp Asdvadzadzin

Emek Cinema

ÇUKURCUMA

Atlas Pasajı & Cinema

Galatasaray Hamamı

Galatasaray Meydanı

Galatasaray Lycée

Garajistanbul (arts centre)

Italian Consulate

Çiçek Pasajı

Galatasaray

Yapı Kredi Cultural Centre

St Antoine

French Palace

Palais de Hollande

St Mary Draperis

Borusan Arts & Cultural Centre

Mudo

Pera Museum

Terkoz Çıkmaz

British Consulate

Kasımpaşa Stadium

Haşanpaşa Parkı

BOSPHORUS

N

TOPHANE

BEYOĞLU

GALATA

KARAKÖY

GOLDEN HORN

İstanbul Modern

Nusretiye Camii

Nargile Cafés

Tophane

Kılıç Ali Paşa Camii

Turkish Orthodox Church of Panghia

Cruise Ship Terminal

Crimean Memorial Church

Galata Mevlevihanesi

Botter House

Galata Tower

Yüksek Kaldıram C

Ottoman Bank Museum

Jewish Museum

Kamondo Steps

British Prison

Yeraltı Camii

Karaköy/Galata

Karaköy Ferry Terminal

Haydarpaşa & Kadıköy

Tünel (İstiklal)

Tünel (Karaköy)

Church of St Peter and St Paul

Arap Camii

Eminönü & Sultanahmet

GALATA BRIDGE

250
metres
0

BARS & CAFÉS	
Galata Konak Pattisserie	28
Kafe Ara	18
Nizam Pide	6,9
Ramiz Köfteci	7
Rocinante	4
Saray	13
Sugar Cafe	21

CLUBS	
Andon	16
Arpa Bar	25
Babylon	24
Dogzstar	17
Ghetto	14
Indigo	19
James Joyce Irish Pub	11
Jazz Stop	15
Leb-i-Derya	23
Love Dance Point	1
Mektup	5
Munzur	10
Nardis Jazz Club	26
Pano Saraphanesi	12
Pasific	22
Peyote	8
Prive	3
Ritim Galata	27
Sultana's	2
X-Large	20

ACCOMMODATION	
Büyük Londra Oteli	4
Divan Taksim Suites (apt)	1
Galata Residence	10
Hotel Devman	6
Pera Palace Hotel	5
Richmond Hotel	7
Suite Home İstiklal Apt	2
Sumo Cat Hostel	9
Triada Residence	3
World House Hostel	8

1

Ottoman Bank Museum

Bankalar Cad 35 • Tues–Sun noon–8pm • Free • ⓦ saltonline.com

Karaköy's Bankalar Caddesi (Street of Banks) is home to the former head office of the Ottoman Bank, designed by the renowned French architect Alexander Vallaury in 1890. In late 2011, the building became a part of the Garanti Bank's SALT contemporary arts project, complete with a public library, rooms dedicated to research, and exhibition space. It also contains the fascinating **Ottoman Bank Museum**, which relates the story of the bank's history through to the 1930s.

Kamondo Steps

The sculptural **Kamondo Steps** run up from Bankalar Caddesi towards the Galata Tower, from close to the Ottoman Bank Museum. Gracefully curving twin staircases, they were commissioned and paid for by the wealthy Jewish Kamondo family, and photographed by Henri Cartier-Bresson in the 1960s.

The Galata Tower and around

Galata Tower daily 9am–8pm • ₺12

In 1261, the Byzantine emperor Michael Paleologus granted the area of **Galata**, north of Karaköy, to the **Genoese**, as a reward for supporting his attempts to drive out the Crusaders. Built by the Genoese in 1349, the **Galata Tower** (Galata Kulesi) sits on the site of a former tower constructed by Justinian in 528. Originally known as the Tower of Christ, it stood at the apex of the several sets of fortifications that surrounded the Genoese city-state. It has had a number of functions over the centuries, including turns as a jail, fire tower and even a springboard for early adventurers attempting to fly. Nowadays, there's a restaurant on the top floor. At 61m high, the tower's **viewing gallery** – reached by elevator – offers magnificent panoramas of the city and views across the Sea of Marmara and Golden Horn.

A short walk south of the tower, at Galata Kulesi Sok 61, is the **British prison**. Under the capitulations granted by the Ottomans, Western powers had the right to try their citizens under their own law, so consulates possessed their own courthouses and prisons. The court originated in the 1600s, but the current building dates from 1904 and today houses the *Galata House* restaurant-café (see p.126).

The only remaining Genoese **city gate** stands around 300m further south on Yanık Kapı (or "Burned Gate") Sokak. Somewhat the worse for wear, it still boasts a marble slab bearing the Cross of St George. Nearby, the recently restored bulk of the **Arap Camii** boasts a tall square tower and pyramidal roof. Under the Genoese this was the largest church in Galata, but it became a mosque for Moors expelled from Spain in the early Ottoman period.

The Galata Mevlevihanesi

Galipdede Cad • Daily except Tues 9am–4.30pm; whirling dervishes perform *sema* dances to Sufi music daily at 7.30pm • ₺5 • ⓦ rumimevlevi.com

An unassuming doorway on Galipdede Caddesi, on the right if you're heading up from the Galata Tower, leads to the tranquil courtyard of the **Galata Mevlevihanesi**, reopened in 2012 following restoration. A former *tekke* (monastery) containing a *semahane* (ceremonial hall) of the **whirling dervishes**, the building now serves as a museum to the Mevlevi Sufi sect.

Constructed in the late fifteenth century, this is the oldest surviving dervish monastery in İstanbul, though it has been rebuilt several times. The downstairs rooms, which you should go around clockwise, hold well-signed displays dealing with the dervish life, and covering everything from musical instruments to traditional dress, and from utensils used in the lodge's kitchen to the begging bowls of wandering dervishes.

1

Upstairs is the star of the show, the *semahane*, a beautifully restored, high-ceilinged room complete with wooden dancefloor where the dervishes whirl.

The **Mevlevi Sufi order** is one of the many mystical sects of Islam, once rife across Anatolia, that were banned by Atatürk because of their supposed political affiliations and religious conservatism. The founder of the sect, Mevlana, was an iconoclast who, in the thirteenth century, repudiated the strictures and hypocrisy of mainstream Sunni Islam. Preaching love, charity and tolerance, he believed that union with God was possible through contemplation, meditation, dance and music (hence the "whirling" ceremonies in which the disciples engage).

Beyoğlu

North and uphill from the sprawl of Galata and Karaköy, the district of **Beyoğlu** is the beating heart of modern İstanbul. Locals head in droves to İstiklal Caddesi in particular, to shop, wine and dine, take in a film, club, gig or gallery – or simply promenade. So, too, do an ever-increasing number of visitors, who base themselves here to take advantage of the nightlife.

Beyoğlu's pedestrianized main boulevard, **İstiklal Caddesi**, boasts a cute antique tramway (see p.116), and bustles with life virtually twenty-four hours a day. Massive **Taksim Square**, at its northern end, is regarded as a symbol of the secular Turkish Republic, and holds numerous hotels as well as convenient bus and metro terminals. Side streets hereabouts are host to scores of lively bars, clubs and restaurants, many of which stay open until six in the morning.

Brief history

What's now **Beyoğlu** used to be known as **Pera** (Greek for "beyond" or "across"). By the mid-nineteenth century, Pera was where the main European powers chose to build their ambassadorial palaces, and this imported **architecture** still dominates today. The completion of the Orient Express Railway in 1889 encouraged an influx of tourists, catered for in luxurious hotels like the splendid *Pera Palas*.

The **nightlife** of the quarter was notoriously riotous even in the seventeenth century. By the nineteenth and early twentieth centuries, the area had become fashionable for its operettas, music halls, inns, cinemas and restaurants. Only after the gradual exodus of the Greek population from İstanbul following the establishment of the Turkish Republic in 1923 did Galata and Pera begin to lose their cosmopolitan flavour.

Along İstiklal Caddesi

The exit from the upper **Tünel station** in Beyoğlu is fronted by a small square from which **İstiklal Caddesi** (known as the "Grand Rue de Pera" prior to Independence) heads 1.5km north towards Taksim Square.

Not far up İstiklal Caddesi on the right, the **Botter House**, a fine Art Nouveau apartment building with a carved stone facade and wrought-iron balcony designed by the Italian architect Raimondo D'Aronco, was under renovation (it will be a hotel) at the time of writing. Further up on the right is the **Palais de Hollande**. Built in 1858 on the site of the home of Cornelis Haga, the first Dutch diplomat in Constantinople during the fifteenth century, it now houses the Consulate to the Netherlands.

The oldest church in the area is **St Mary Draperis** at no. 429, which dates from 1789, although the Franciscans built their first church on the site in the early fifteenth century. Better known is the Franciscan **church of St Antoine** at no. 325, a fine example of red-brick neo-Gothic architecture. Originally founded in 1725, it was demolished to make way for a tramway at the start of the twentieth century, and rebuilt in 1913.

1

Just off İstiklal Caddesi, on Nuru Ziya Sokak, is the imposing **French Palace**, with its large central courtyard and formal gardens, the residence of ambassadors and consuls from 1831 until the present day. Below the Palace, on Tom Tom Kaptan Sokak, the **Italian Consulate** was originally the Palazzo di Venezia, built in the seventeenth century, and host to Casanova in 1744. Turning left off İstiklal Caddesi, Hamalbaşı Sok leads in 100m to the **British Consulate**, an impressive Renaissance-style structure, designed by Charles Barry, architect of the British Houses of Parliament.

The famous **Çiçek Pasajı** (Flower Passage) enjoyed its heyday in the 1930s, when the music and entertainment was supplied courtesy of anti-Bolshevik Russian émigrés. These days it's home to an assortment of attractive but rather overpriced and touristy restaurants. Far better are **Nevizade Sokak**, a street dedicated to fish restaurants (all with outside tables) and incredibly lively bars and clubs and, further south near the Tünel entrance, the similar but trendier streets around **Asmalımescit Sokak**.

Pera Museum

Meşrütiyet Cad 25, 200m south of the British Consulate • Tues–Sat 10am–7pm, Sun noon–7pm • ₺10 • ⓦ peramuzesi.org.tr

Housed in an artfully restored nineteenth-century building that was formerly the prestigious *Bristol Hotel*, the wonderful **Pera Museum** (Pera Müzesi) is home to an impressive collection of European Orientalist works, painted between the seventeenth and nineteenth centuries, as well as ceramics from Küthaya and an interesting collection of historic weights and measures. It's also the most convenient place in the city to see temporary exhibitions of works by major international artists.

Taksim Square and around

Taksim in Turkish means "distribution"; **Taksim Square** takes its name from the low **stone reservoir** on its south side. The reservoir was constructed in 1732 to distribute water brought from the Belgrade Forest by aqueduct. Steps on the north side of the square, above the main bus terminal, lead up to the pleasant **Taksim Parkı**, with its bench-lined paths and open-air tea gardens.

Atatürk Cultural Centre

Closed at the time of writing, pending controversial redevelopment plans, the **Atatürk Cultural Centre** (Atatürk Kültür Merkezi or AKM), east of Taksim Square, has long been a leading venue for İstanbul's international festivals. It's also home to the State Opera and Ballet, the Symphony Orchestra and the State Theatre Company.

Military Museum

1.5km north of Taksim • Wed–Sun 9am–5pm • ₺4 • Walk or catch a bus north along Cumhuriyet Cad to the İstanbul Radyoevi (radio building), or take the M2 metro to Osmanbey

İstanbul's **Military Museum** (Askeri Müzesi) is housed in the military academy where Atatürk received some of his training. Its comprehensive collection of memorabilia is proudly displayed and labelled in English. The most striking exhibits are the cotton- and silk-embroidered tents used by campaigning sultans, and a rich collection of Ottoman armour and weaponry. A traditional Ottoman military band known as the Mehter performs daily between 3pm and 4pm.

Tophane

The mixed dockland area of **Tophane** is named after the Imperial Armoury – now housing a university – that churned out cannonballs for the Ottoman war machine. It's dotted with venerable Ottoman buildings, most notably the **Kılıç Paşa Camii**, dating from 1780, and the more recent **Nusretiye Camii** (1822), both recently restored. It's also well known for its large congregation of nargile (water-pipe) cafés.

İstanbul Modern

Meclis-i Mebusan Cad • Tues, Wed & Fri–Sun 10am–6pm, Thurs 10am–8pm • ₺14; audioguide ₺4 • ⓦ www.istanbulmodern.org • From Sultanahmet, take the T1 tramway to the Tophane stop just west of Nusretiye Camii, then walk 3min

Turkey's leading contemporary arts gallery, **İstanbul Modern**, is housed in a revamped warehouse on the edge of the Bosphorus, just in front of the Nusretiye Camii. The interior is all big, blank white walls and exposed ventilation pipes, with picture windows giving views across the Bosphorus to the Topkapı Palace. The collection includes the best of modern Turkish art, as well as some intriguing video installations from foreign artists. There's a reference library, a cinema showing arts and independent movies, and a trendy café with a terrace overlooking the Bosphorus.

Beşiktaş

Bus #25/T or #40 from Taksim or #28 or #28/T from Eminönü

Most visitors to the district of **Beşiktaş** are here to see the **Dolmabahçe Palace**, successor to Topkapı as the residence of the Ottoman sultans. However, it's worth aiming to spend a few more hours in the neighbourhood if you can, to visit the city's excellent **Naval Museum**, as well as **Yıldız Parkı** and palace. It's also home to one of İstanbul's three major football teams (see p.108).

Concrete shopping centres and a sprawling fruit and vegetable market cluster around the main shore road and **ferry terminal**, in front of which stands the **bus station**.

Dolmabahçe Palace

Dolmabahçe Cad • Tues, Wed & Fri–Sun: Nov–March 8.30am–4pm; April–Oct 8.30am–5pm; no cameras allowed inside • Selamlik/ Administrative section ₺15; Harem ₺10; combined ticket ₺20 (sold until 3pm only)

The **Dolmabahçe Palace** is the largest and most extravagant of all the palaces on the Bosphorus, with an impressive 600m waterside frontage. Flanked by symmetrical flower-lined gardens, with a magnificent clover-shaped pond and fountain at its heart, the exterior of the palace is arguably more beautiful than the interior. It was built in the mid-nineteenth century by Armenian architect Karabet Balian and his son Nikoğos, and its brazen riches suggest that good taste suffered along with the fortunes of the Ottoman Empire. The modern European stylings opt for flamboyance over flair, with crystal-lined staircases and chandeliers, dazzling upholstery and such profuse lashings of gold that the effect is a virtual assault on the senses.

With groups of up to fifty people ushered through at a rapid pace, the tour experience (see p.36) is more akin to herding cattle; the friendly, multilingual guides spend more time dealing with crowd control than dealing out choice snippets of information about the key rooms.

The first half of the tour consists of shuffling down corridors, peeking into the cordoned-off rooms and trundling single-file through exhibition rooms that display semi-interesting collections of delicate tea cups and ornate household items. The second floor holds a few more impressive highlights – the **Sultan's reception room** is a Venetian-style boudoir with an outrageously decadent gold-plated ceiling; the antiquated **Abdul Medjid Library** offers an intriguing glimpse into the past; and the hamam and bathing quarters feature possibly the world's most luxurious squat toilet, made of exquisite marble. In the dining hall, the handmade parquet floors – an intricate puzzle design carved from ebony, rosewood and mahogany – are an incongruously delicate masterpiece.

1

FEVER PITCH

İstanbul's three leading football teams **Beşiktaş**, **Fenerbahçe** and **Galatasaray** receive fanatical support – match times remain one of the few occasions when the city streets fall silent – and dominate the Turkish league. While there are sporadic outbreaks of football violence, the chances of a foreigner getting caught up in it are slim. There are two Turkish daily newspapers, *Fotomaç* and *Fanatik*, devoted almost entirely to the three İstanbul heavyweights, while matches (Aug–May) are staggered over each weekend in season so television coverage of the three doesn't clash.

Beşiktaş (☎0212 236 7202, ⓦ www.bjk.com.tr) play at the most convenient and attractive ground of the three, İnönü Stadium on Kadırgalar Cad, between Taksim and Beşiktaş, opposite the Dolmabahçe Palace; walk down the hill, or take bus #23/B from Taksim Square or #30 from Sultanahmet or Eminönü.

Fenerbahçe, the wealthiest club (☎0216 449 5667, ⓦ www.fenerbahce.org), play at the 52,000-capacity Şükrü Saracoğlu Stadyium on Bağdat Cad in Kızıltoprak on the Asian side of the Bosphorus; take a ferry to Kadıköy, then a dolmuş marked "Cadde Bostan".

Galatasaray (☎0212 251 5707, ⓦ www.galatasaray.org.com) play at the Türkcell Arena Stadyumu in Aslantepe (Şişli); catch the M2 metro from Taksim to Sanayı then the branch line to Seyrentepe.

Tickets are sold at the stadiums two days before a match. Regular fixtures cost from ₺25. Tickets are also available online from Biletix (ⓦ www.biletix.com) and Biletix outlets. For information in English see ⓦ www.budgetairlinefootball.co.uk.

The masterful 36m-high **ceremonial hall** (double the height of the rest of the rooms), held up by 56 elaborate columns, is the crown jewel of the tour. Its centrepiece, a 4.5tonne crystal chandelier glittering with 664 bulbs, is among the largest ever made – a lavish present from Queen Victoria.

The harem section provides little stylistic deviation from the main building; its main attraction is Atatürk's bedroom, where the founder of the Turkish Republic died in 1938. The room itself, with its enormous Turkish flag adorning the bed, is a little disappointing except for Atatürk-loving Turkish visitors. The clock in the room is still set at 9.05 – the hour of his death.

The Naval Museum

Barbaros Hayrettin Paşa İskelesı Sok, off Beşiktaş Cad • Wed, Thurs & Fri 9am–5pm, Sat & Sun 11am–7pm • ₺4

The collection at the **Naval Museum** is divided between two buildings. One, facing the water, houses seagoing craft; the other covers the maritime history of the Ottoman Empire and the Turkish Republic. Although most of the labels are in Turkish, the best exhibits – such as the enormous wooden figureheads depicting tigers and swans, and the display of items from Atatürk's yacht, the *Savarona* – need little explanation. In the building nearest the Bosphorus, the exhibition includes a collection of caïques, which were used to row the sultans to and from their homes along the Bosphorus. The oarsmen – the *Bostanci* – reputedly barked like dogs as they rowed, so as not to overhear the sultans talking.

Yıldız Parkı

Public entrance opposite the Çırağan Sarayı on Çırağan Cad • Daily 8am–11pm • Free

Yıldız Parkı is a vast wooded area, dotted with mansions, pavilions, lakes and gardens, which was the centre of the Ottoman Empire for thirty years during the reign of Abdülhamid II. Its superb hillside location makes this one of the most popular places in İstanbul for city-dwellers. Of the many buildings in the park, only the Yıldız Palace Museum and the Şale Köşkü are open to the public, though it's easy enough to wander around the outside of the other pavilions, each with marvellous terraces and panoramic views of the Bosphorus.

Şale Köşkü

Yıldız Parkı • Tues, Wed & Fri–Sun: March–Sept 9.30am–5pm; Oct–Feb 9.30am–4pm • Obligatory guided tours ₺4, camera ₺6

The most important surviving building in Yıldız Parkı is the **Şale Köşkü**. The first of the pavilion's three separate sections was modelled on a Swiss chalet, while the second and third sections were built to receive Kaiser Wilhelm II on his first and second state visits, in 1889 and 1898. The most impressive room, the Ceremonial Hall, takes up the greater part of the third section, with a Hereke carpet so big (approximately 400 square metres) that part of a wall had to be knocked down to install it.

Yıldız Palace Museum

Yıldız Parkı • Daily except Mon 9.30am–6pm • ₺5

The **Yıldız Palace Museum** (Yıldız Sarayı Müzesi), in the same complex as the Şale Köşkü, is housed in Abdülhamid's converted carpentry workshop, and exhibits items and furniture from throughout the palace. While not in their original grand settings in the pavilions, there are some exquisite porcelain pieces, giant vases and more of the joinery produced by the sultan himself.

Ortaköy

1km northeast of Beşiktaş, beyond Yıldız Parkı and the Çırağan Palace • Bus #40 or #42T from Taksim or #30 from Eminönü; or T1 tram from the old city to Kabataş, then bus #22 or #25/E to Ortaköy; or take a bus or ferry to Beşiktaş and walk 15min

The former Bosphorus backwater of **Ortaköy** was traditionally an area of tolerance – a mosque, church and synagogue have existed side by side for centuries. While it remains cosmopolitan, its erstwhile character has been hijacked by flash nightclubs, trendy eateries, and the overwhelming presence of the first Bosphorus suspension bridge, completed in 1973, just to the north.

When Ortaköy was just a tiny fishing village, university students and teachers used to gather here to sip tea and discuss weighty topics. That time is remembered in the name of the Sunday *entel*, or "intellectual", **market**, a crowded affair held on the waterfront square, which sells all kinds of arts and crafts. Daily market stalls also sell trendy silver jewellery and sunglasses on the waterfront. That's also the location of the attractive, Baroque **Büyük Mecidiye Camii**, built in 1855 and much photographed in juxtaposition with the suspension bridge towering behind.

The Golden Horn

Northwest of Beyoğlu, along the newly spruced-up north shore of the once heavily polluted **Golden Horn**, three sights are well worth a look, especially if you're fed up with historic buildings and/or have kids in tow: the **Rahmi M. Koç Industrial Museum**, Turkey's landmark buildings done to scale at **Miniatürk**, and the trendy exhibition centre of **Santralistanbul**, in a refurbished power station.

The Rahmi M. Koç Industrial Museum

Hasköy Cad 27 • April–Sept Tues–Fri 10am–5pm, Sat & Sun 10am–8pm; Oct–March Tues–Fri 10am–5pm, Sat & Sun 10am–6pm • ₺12.5
• ⓦ www.rmk-museum.org.tr • Catch bus #47 from Eminönü, on the opposite side of the Horn, or the #54/HT from Taksim; or it's a short walk from Hasköy ferry terminal, a stop for ferries between Eminönü and Eyüp

Formerly home to a substantial Jewish community, **Hasköy**, a couple of kilometres up the Golden Horn from Karaköy, was also the location of an Ottoman naval shipyard and royal park. Today it's noted for the excellent **Rahmi M. Koç Industrial Museum**, an old factory restored by Rahmi M. Koç, one of Turkey's most famous – and wealthiest – industrialists, to house his private collection of models, machines,

1

vehicles and toys. Upstairs, the starboard main engine of the *Kalender* steam ferry, made in Newcastle-upon-Tyne in 1911, is the main exhibit. Downstairs holds a number of old bikes, from penny-farthings to an early Royal Enfield motorbike, and much else besides.

Miniatürk

İmrahor Cad • May–Oct Mon–Fri 9am–7pm, Sat & Sun 9am–9pm; Nov–April daily 9am–9pm • ₺10, under-9s free • ⓦ www.miniaturk .com • Bus #47/A from Eminönü, or #54/H from Taksim

Upstream of Hasköy in dull Sütlüce, on the north side of the monumental Haliç Bridge, **Miniatürk** is one of those attractions you'll either love or hate. It displays over a hundred 1:25 scale models of Turkey's most impressive sights, spaced out along a 1.8km signed route. İstanbul itself is home to 45 of the attractions – from mundane Sirkeci Post Office through to the Blue Mosque – while another 45 cover sights in Anatolia. Not all the well-detailed models are buildings – if you've ever wanted to see Cappadocia's fairy chimneys or the travertine cascades of Pamukkale in miniature, then this is the place to see them.

Santralistanbul

Museum of Energy Kazımkarabekir Cad 2 • Tues–Fri 10am–6pm, Sat & Sun 10am–8pm • ₺10 combined entry • ⓦ www .santralistanbul.org • A free, 20min shuttle-bus runs to and from the AKM building on Taksim Square (daily every 30min, 8am–8.30pm), while the #47 runs between Eminönü and Santralistanbul; after 9.30pm you'll be reliant on a taxi

Set in the attractively landscaped campus of Bilgi University, built on reclaimed industrial land at the head of the Golden Horn, **Santralistanbul** is a striking symbol of the new İstanbul. The major point of interest is the **Museum of Energy**, housed, appropriately enough, in an old power station. Between 1914 and its closure in 1983, this plant, the Silahtarağa, was the only electricity generating station in İstanbul. The interior is now a successful mix of the carefully preserved innards of the power plant and hi-tech wizardry. Events in the impressive exhibition space to the left of the entrance range from retrospectives of contemporary Turkish art to displays on the headscarf issue. The campus also holds a couple of trendy bars/venues, *Otto Santral* and *Tamirhane*, and hosts the annual "One Love" alt-music festival (see p.131).

Asian İstanbul

The best single reason to head across to the **Asian shore** of the city is to experience the ferry ride. The views from the Bosphorus are superb, with domes and minarets dominating the skyline of the Old City, and skyscrapers the business districts beyond Beyoğlu – and where else in the world can you cruise from one continent to another for just over a euro? The three Asian neighbourhoods, **Üsküdar**, **Haydarpaşa** and **Kadıköy**, all hold some interesting sites, including fine Ottoman mosques and a British war cemetery – not to mention a handful of eating places of some repute.

Üsküdar

Üsküdar's main square is due, in 2015, to become the exit point of the Marmaray rail tunnel; until then, catch a ferry from Eminönü; buses run from in front of İskele Camii on Paşa Liman Cad in Üsküdar up the Bosphorus, as far as Anadolu Kavağı

Üsküdar holds some notable Islamic monuments. Its most obvious mosque, **İskele** or **Mihrimah Camii**, sits on a high platform, fronted by an immense covered porch, opposite the ferry landing on İskele Meydanı. Designed by Mimar Sinan and built in 1547–48, it's the only Ottoman mosque with three semi-domes (as opposed to two or four), thanks to the requirements of a difficult site against the hillside behind.

Directly across the square, the **Yeni Valide Camii** was built between 1708 and 1710 by Ahmet III in honour of his mother. It's most readily identified by the Valide Sultan's green, birdcage-like tomb, whose meshed roof was designed to keep birds out while allowing rain in to water the garden tomb below.

Kız Kulesi

Tues–Sun noon–7pm • Free • ⓦ kizkulesi.com.tr • Boats from Salacak (on main coast road between Üsküdar and Harem) daily 9am–6.45pm (₺5); private boat service for restaurant customers, daily 8.30pm–12.30am

South of Üsküdar, on an island in the Bosphorus, the small white **Kız Kulesi** (Maiden's Tower) is also known as Leander's Tower. Many myths are associated with it: in one a princess, who was prophesied to die from a snake bite, came here to escape her fate, only to succumb to it when a serpent was delivered to her retreat in a basket of fruit. The tower also featured in the 1999 James Bond film, *The World Is Not Enough*. Now open to visitors, it doubles as an expensive restaurant in the evening (daily 7.30pm–1am).

Haydarpaşa

Ferries to Haydarpaşa depart regularly from Eminönü and Karaköy; all continue the short way to terminate at Kadıköy (see p.111)

South of Üsküdar and across the bay from Kadıköy, the serried ranks of enormous nineteenth- and early twentieth-century buildings in **Haydarpaşa** make quite an impact as you approach by ferry. The palace-like mainline **Haydarpaşa train station**, jutting into the Bosphorus, was completed in 1908 by a German architect as part of Germany's grandiose plans for a Berlin-to-Baghdad railway. It was presented to Sultan Abdülhamid II by Kaiser Wilhelm II; its stained glass is particularly impressive. The station is likely to be sidelined by the giant Marmaray transport infrastructure project (see p.113), and was only open for suburban services at the time of writing.

Directly north of the station, between the sea and Tıbbiye Caddesiare, is the Marmara University and the **British War Cemetery** (daily 7am–7pm), a beautifully kept spot sheltering the dead of the Crimean War and the two world wars.

The Florence Nightingale Museum

Kavak Iskele Cad • By appointment only, Mon–Fri 9am–5pm; fax a photocopy of the identity page of your passport – plus desired visiting date and time – and phone number to the museum's military guardians, at least 24hr before your intended visit • Free • ☎ 0216 553 8000 or ☎ 0216 3107929

The imposing **Selimiye Barracks**, whose northwest wing was used as a hospital by the British during the Crimean War (1854–56), today houses the **Florence Nightingale Museum**. Florence Nightingale lived and worked in the northern tower, where she reduced the death toll among patients from twenty percent to two percent, and established universally accepted principles of modern nursing. The museum contains two of her famous lamps, and you can see the rooms where she lived and worked. Whether you decide it's worth the effort involved to gain access depends on your level of interest in the great woman.

Kadıköy

The suburb of **Kadıköy** makes for a surprisingly enjoyable outing from the European side of the city. It's a lively place, with some great shops, restaurants, bars and cinemas. One of the area's charms is its local feel – which is hardly surprising, as unlike in Sultanahmet or Beyoulu, most of the people out and about here are residents. Towards the end of the nineteenth century, when the introduction of steam-driven ferries made it feasible to commute across the Bosphorus, Kadıköy became a popular residential area

1

for foreign businesspeople and wealthy Greeks and Armenians. Their most visible legacy is the **churches** southeast of the ferry terminal. There's a scattering of older constructions amid the concrete: look out for the tall, narrow curves of the cream Art Deco-style **Kuru Kahveci Mehmet Efendi building**, home to the famous purveyor of Turkish Coffee, and the beautifully restored **Süreyya Opera House** on Bahariye Caddesi (see p.130); dating back to 1927, its ornate Neoclassical facade is adorned with relief-work pilasters, cherubs and classical-style theatre masks.

Most sites of interest in Kadıköy are located between the waterfront **Sahil Yolu** (coast road) and **Bahariye Caddesi**, a right turn off Söğütlüçeşme Caddesi, the steep, wide street that leads uphill from the ferry terminal. The two latter streets have their own tram, a grittier version of İstiklal Caddesi; indeed, the area bounded by Söğütlüçeşme Caddesi to the north, Bahariye and Emin Bey caddesis to the east and south and the Bosphorus waterfront to the west is becoming a mini-Beyoğlu, with a similar mix of alternative-clothing outlets, bookstores and bric-a-brac shops dotted among the cafés and restaurants that spill out onto jam-packed pedestrianized streets. It's also a great area for shopping, especially for spices, coffee, olives, dried fruit, nuts, Turkish delight and other goodies, in the colourful permanent market centred on **Guneşlibahçe Sokak**.

ARRIVAL AND DEPARTURE
İSTANBUL

İstanbul's main points of arrival by air are **Atatürk airport** on the European side of the Bosphorus, and **Sabiha Gökçen airport** across the strait in Asia. Most buses come into **Esenler bus station**, in the suburbs on the European side, and trains into the centrally located **Sirkeci station**. Taxis and public transport run from all these transport hubs to the main accommodation areas, in Sultanahmet and Taksim/Beyoğlu.

BY AIR
Atatürk airport 24km west of the centre at Yeşilköy, near the Sea of Marmara (Atatürk Hava Limanı; ☎0212 465 5555, ⓦ www.atatürkairport.com). The international (*dışhatları*) and domestic (*içhatları*) terminals are in linked buildings.
Sabiha Gökçen airport Near Pendik on the Asian side of the city (☎0216 585 5000, ⓦ www.sgairport.com).
Destinations Adana (at least 17 daily; 1hr 30min); Ankara (at least 25 daily; 1hr 5min); Antalya (at least 22 daily; 1hr 5min); Bodrum (at least 11 daily; 1hr); Dalaman (at least 6 daily; 1hr 10min); Denizli (2 daily; 1hr 10min); Diyarbakır (at least 10 daily; 1hr 45min); Erzurum (at least 4 daily; 1hr 50min); Gaziantep (at least 6 daily; 1hr 40min); İzmir (at least 18 daily; 1hr); Kars (direct 2 daily; 2hr; via Ankara 3 daily; at least 3hr 25min); Kayseri (at least 4 daily; 1hr 25min); Konya (at least 7 daily; 1hr 15min); Malatya (at least 4 daily; 1hr 30min); Mardin (at least 3 daily direct; 2hr; 3 daily via Ankara; at least 4hr 10min); Samsun (at least 6 daily; 1hr 15min); Şanlıurfa (at least 3 daily; 1hr 50min); Trabzon (at least 10 daily; 1hr 35min); Van (at least 4 daily; 2hr 5min).

TRANSFERS FROM ATATÜRK
By bus The Havaş bus service (☎0212 465 4700, ⓦ havas .net) runs from both the international and the domestic terminals to the THY (Turkish Airlines) office on Cumhuriyet Caddesi on the north side of Taksim Square (every 30min, daily 4am–1am; 30–40min; ₺10). Drops are at Aksaray, 200m from Yenikapı train station, where you can catch a

municipal train to Cankurtaran station (for Sultanahmet) or walk up the hill to the Aksaray T1 tram stop for trams into Sultanahmet or Eminönü, and at Tepebaşı (for Galata/Beyoğlu). To return to Atatürk airport, Havaş buses depart from Cumhuriyet Caddesi, Taksim, picking up at Tepebaşı and Aksaray (every 30min, daily 4am–1am; ₺10).
By metro Cheaper than the bus, the M1 metro (*hafif metro*; see p.113) runs from the airport to the city centre (every 10min, daily 6am–12.30am. To catch it, follow signs for "Hafif Metro/Rapid Transit", and buy two tokens or *jetons* (₺3 each) from the kiosk. Get off at Zeytinburnu and follow the signs a short distance to the Zeytinburnu T1 tram stop, which is where you need the second *jeton*. The T1 tram runs to Sultanahmet and across the Golden Horn, via the Galata bridge, to Kabataş. To reach Beyoğlu, get off at the Karaköy stop just over the Galata bridge, and either walk or take the Tünel funicular train up to the southern end of İstiklal Caddesi.
By taxi A taxi from Atatürk airport to Sultanahmet or Taksim should cost ₺40–50. Many hotels, and several travel agents on Divan Yolu Cad, can arrange airport taxi collections and drop-offs (on request) for around ₺35.

TRANSFERS FROM SABIHA GÖKÇEN
By bus Havaş shuttle buses run into Taksim Square (every 30min, daily 5am–midnight; journey time 1hr 30min; ₺12); return trips from Taksim run longer hours (every 30min, daily 3.30am–1am). You can also buy an İstanbulkart (see p.115) from the kiosk outside the airport, and catch the green #E10

bus to Kadıköy (journey time 45min; ₺3). The bus terminates opposite the Turyol ferry, which will whisk you across the Bosphorus to either Eminönü (for Sultanahmet) or Karaköy (for Beyoğlu) for ₺3 – note that the Turyol service only operates 6.45am–8.30pm. Alternatively there's an IDO ferry a short walk south, with the last ferry to Eminönü at 8.30pm, and a useful later ferry to Karaköy at 11pm.

By taxi A taxi into town from Sabiha Gökçen will cost at least ₺60.

AIRLINES

Most airlines have their offices around Taksim Square, Elmadağ and the business districts of Şişli/Levent further north. Major world player THY (Turkish Airlines; ☎444 0849, ⊛turkishairlines.com) offers the widest range of domestic and international flights; its subsidiary Anadolujet (☎444 2538, ⊛anadolujet.com.tr) offers budget flights throughout Turkey but all are routed via Ankara. Other budget carriers, which also offer a limited number of international flights, include Atlas Jet (☎444 3387, ⊛atlasjet.com), Pegasus Airlines (☎444 0737, ⊛flypgs.com), Onur Air (☎0212 233 3800, ⊛onurair.com.tr) and Sunexpress (☎444 0797, ⊛sunexpresss.com). For more comprehensive international services, contact: Air France (☎0212 310 1919, ⊛airfrance.com); Alitalia (☎0212 315 1900, ⊛alitalia.com); British Airways (☎0212 317 6600, ⊛britishairways.com); El-Al (☎0212 246 5303, ⊛elal.co.il); Emirates Airlines (☎0212 315 4545, ⊛emirates.com); KLM (☎0212 310 1900, ⊛klm .com); Lufthansa (☎0212 315 3434, ⊛lufthansa.com); Olympic Airways (☎0212 247 3701, ⊛olympicair.com); Qantas (☎0212 240 3532, ⊛quantas.com.au); Singapore Airlines (☎0212 232 3706, ⊛singaporeair.com); Swiss (☎0212 349 9900, ⊛swiss.com).

BY TRAIN

For the time being, attempting to start or finish a rail journey in İstanbul is more trouble than it's worth. The city's two main-line train stations – one in Europe at Sirkeci, the other in Asia, at Haydarpaşa, across the Bosphorus – are very likely to be sidelined because of massive transport infrastructure projects both within İstanbul and Anatolia. Haydarpaşa train station, 1km north of Kadıköy, used to be the hub of Anatolian train travel, but in 2012 it was closed to inter-city trains to allow work on the new high-speed İstanbul–Ankara line and on the Marmaray project (see p.113), and may well not re-open as a working station.

For the foreseeable future – until at least 2015 – would-be rail passengers have to head 150km to Arifiye for links to the high-speed train from Eskişehir to Ankara and the İç Anadolu Express to Konya. Works on the line to the west, linking İstanbul with Europe, mean passsengers are ferried out by bus to the Turkish/Bulgarian border, where they board the train for Bucharest (Bosfor Ekspresi; daily departures). Keep an eye out for any improvements on ⊛seat61.com.

BY BUS

İstanbul has two major otogars (bus stations): Esenler, 10km northwest of the centre, and Harem, on the Asian side between Üsküdar and Kadıköy. Most national bus services stop at both, regardless of destination, and both are open 24hr.

ESENLAR OTOGAR

Esenler bus station is well organized. Some 150 companies have numbered ticket stands. Most run free service buses to and from Taksim, or can arrange for you to travel with another company. To get to Sultanahmet from Esenler, take the M1 metro (every 15min, daily 6am–midnight) from the station in the centre of the *otogar* to Aksaray, and switch to the T1 tram to Sultanahmet. After midnight, your only option is to take a taxi into town (around ₺25). Travelling from the city centre to Esenler by metro, remember to get off at Otogar, not Esenler station. For tickets booked through a travel agent or bus company's city offices, a (free) shuttle service runs from Taksim or Sultanahmet to Esenler (usually an hour before departure).

HAREM OTOGAR

Arriving in İstanbul by bus from Asia, it's worth disembarking at Harem, thus saving a tedious journey to

THE MARMARAY PROJECT

In the autumn of 2008, the laying of sections of tubing to form a tunnel under the Bosphorus was completed, and an **underwater link** between European and Asian İstanbul – an idea that first hit the drawing board back in the Ottoman period – finally became a reality.

The much-delayed opening of the so-called **Marmaray Project** was scheduled, at the time of writing, for 2015 – but don't be surprised if it's delayed further. The tunnel will form part of a line stretching some 76km, and will link the city's two international airports, Atatürk and Sabiha Gökçen. The section from Yenikapı to Sirkeci will be underground, as will the new Sirkeci station and its counterpart across the Bosphorus in Üsküdar. Work has been delayed by the unearthing of many important archeological finds, notably a massive Byzantine harbour, complete with more than thirty ships, at Yenikapı.

1

İSTANBUL BUS COMPANIES

The following reputable bus companies are based at Esenler *otogar*.

Adıyaman Ünal (bay 29; ☎0146 216 1112, ⓦadiyamanunalturizm.com.tr) for Nemrut Dağı.

Göreme Turizm (bay 18; ☎0212 658 1213) for Cappadocia.

Has Diyarbakir (☎444 1121) for southeast Anatolia.

Kamil Koç (bays 144–146; ☎0212 658 2000, ⓦwww.kamilkoc.com.tr) to Ankara and Aegean and Mediterranean resorts.

Mersin (bay 8; ☎0212 658 3535) for the east.

Metro (bays 51–52; ☎444 3455, ⓦwww.metroturizm.com.tr) for the Black Sea coast.

Nevtur (bay 24; ☎444 5050) for Cappadocia.

Nevşehir Seyahat (☎444 5050, ⓦnevsehirliletseyahat.com.tr) for Cappadocia.

Özdiyarbakır (bay 152; ☎0212 658 0475, ⓦwww.ozkaymak.com.tr) for southeast Turkey, Konya and the southwest Mediterranean.

Pamukkale (bays 41–42; ☎0212 658 2222, ⓦwww.pammukkaleturizm.com.tr) to the west and southern coasts.

Ulusoy (bay 127; ☎444 1818, ⓦwww.ulusoy.com.tr) to major cities and the Black Sea coast.

Vangölü (bays 47–48; ☎0432 2231545, ⓦvangoluturizm.com.tr) to Van and eastern Turkey.

Varan (bays 1–2; ☎444 8999, ⓦwww.varan.com.tr) for western and southern destinations including nonstop luxury services to Ankara, İzmir and south-coast resorts.

Yeşil Artvin Ekspres (bays 71–72; ☎0466 2126161, ⓦyesilartvinekspres.com.tr) to Black Sea and northeast Turkey.

Esenler through terrible traffic snarl-ups. From Harem, regular (car) ferries cross the Bosphorus to Eminönü (every hour, daily 7.30am–9.30pm), while private boats run to Beşiktaş and Kabataş. *Dolmuşes* run every few minutes to Kadıköy and to Üsküdar, leaving from the south side of the complex, beyond the ticket offices. From either of these suburbs, ferries cross to Eminönü (daily 7am–8.40pm), or from Üsküdar to Beşiktaş (daily 7am–8.30pm) for Taksim.

DOMESTIC BUS SERVICES

Although distances are long, bus travel in Turkey is generally very comfortable, and still usually works out cheaper than taking an internal flight (see p.35).

Black Sea coast Artvin (1 daily; 22hr); Hopa (3 daily; 19hr); Rize (4 daily; 19hr); Samsun (4 daily; 9hr); Trabzon (9 daily; 18hr).

Cappadocia Avanos (5 daily; 11hr); Göreme (5 daily; 11hr); Nevşehir (5 daily; 11hr); Ürgüp (5 daily; 11hr 30min).

Eastern Turkey Antakya: (2 daily; 17hr); Antep (4 daily; 20hr); Diyarbakır (3 daily; 19hr); Doğubeyazit (1 daily; 24hr); Erzurum (3 daily; 24hr); Gaziantep (several daily; 16hr); Konya (7 daily; 10hr); Mardin (1 daily; 22hr); Urfa (1 daily; 21hr).

Mediterranean and Aegean coasts Adana (several daily; 13.5hr); Alanya (12 daily; 15hr); Antakya (2 daily; 17hr); Antalya (several in the evening from 6pm; 12hr); Ayvalık (hourly; 8hr); Bodrum (hourly; 12hr); Datça (1 daily; 17hr); Fethiye (3 daily in the evening; 14hr); İzmir (hourly; 10hr); Kuşadası (5 daily; 9hr); Marmaris (4 daily; 13hr); Side (several in the evening from 6pm; 14hr).

Western Turkey Ankara (several hourly; 5–6hr); Bandırma (hourly; 5hr); Bursa (hourly; 3hr); Çanakkale

(hourly; 5hr 30min); Denizli (3 daily; 10hr); Edirne (hourly; 2hr 30min); Kütahya (6 daily; 5hr 30min).

INTERNATIONAL BUS SERVICES

Onward travel by bus to neighbouring countries can make sense – especially if you want to be flexible and not commit to buying an early (and therefore affordable) plane ticket. Buses depart from the Esenler *otogar*.

Bulgaria With Alpar and Metro: Sofya (several daily; 12hr).

Georgia With Mahmudoğlu: Tiflis (2 daily; 30hr).

Greece With Ulusoy and Varan: Athens (2 weekly; 22hr 30min); Thessaloniki (2 weekly; 12hr 30min).

Russia With Ortadoğu: Moscow (2 weekly; 36hr).

BY FERRY

Passenger-only sea-bus (*deniz otobüsleri*) and high-speed car/passenger ferries (*hızlı feribotları*) operated by IDO (İstanbul Deniz Otobüsleri; ☎0212 444 4436, ⓦwww.ido.com.tr), run from Yalova and Bandırma (on the İzmir–İstanbul route), arriving at the Yenikapı ferry terminal, off Kennedy Caddesi in Kumkapı, just south of Aksaray. From here, catch the suburban (*banliyö*) train from Yenikapı station across the road from the ferry terminal; it's two stops to Sultanahmet (Cankurtaran station), or three to Sirkeci. Frequent buses depart Yenikapı for Taksim via Aksaray. There are also IDO car ferries across the Bosphorus from Harem to Eminönü (daily 7.30am–9.30pm).

Destinations Bandırma (*hızlı feribotları* 3 daily, more at weekends; 2hr; many connect with the train to İzmir; *deniz otobüsleri* 2 weekly); Güzelyalı (for Bursa) (*hızlı feribotları* at least 4 daily; *deniz otobüsleri* 6 weekly mid-June to end

Aug); Yalova (*hızlı feribotları* at least 7 daily; 1hr; *deniz otobüsleri* 1 daily).

CRUISE SHIPS

Passengers arriving on cruise ships go through customs and immigration procedures at Karaköy International Maritime Passenger Terminal, across the Galata bridge from Eminönü. From here, you can either take the T1 tram to Sultanahmet; the Tünel up to Beyoğlu; the funicular from Kabataş to Taksim Square; or a taxi.

GETTING AROUND

İstanbul has a wide range of transport, from ferry to high-speed tram. Traffic jams are unavoidable, so where possible either walk or travel by tram, metro, suburban train or ferry, though all can be jam-packed at peak times. The newly extended metro and tramway links most parts of the city that you're likely to want to visit, while the bus system is daunting, but manageable on certain routes. The municipal trains are ramshackle but efficient, dolmuşes (shared taxis) occasionally useful and cheap and taxis very reasonably priced (assuming you're not over-charged!). A great way to explore a city that, historically, has put its best face towards the water, is by ferry.

BY BUS

İstanbul's buses (*otobus* in Turkish) are usually the red-and-cream, green and green/blue municipality buses, all with "IETTT" (İstanbul Elektrik Tramvay ve Tünel) written on them. For information on bus routes and numbers (which change regularly) see ⓦ www.iett.gov.tr/en. There are also some private buses, usually pale blue. Most buses run daily 6.30am–11.30pm. For all municipal buses, either use an *İstanbulkart* (see p.115) or buy a *jeton* (₺3; see p.116) in advance from a Jetonmatik machine. On privately run buses, the conductor will usually accept cash, a *jeton* or the *İstanbulkart*.

BUS TERMINALS

The old city holds useful bus terminals at Beyazit, Eminönü and Vezneciler, across the Golden Horn in Taksim Square, Beşiktaş and Kabataş and, on the Asian side, at Üsküdar and Kadıköy.

Eminönü From Eminönü bus station, three tram stops down the hill from Sultanahmet, buses run to Taksim; westbound to Aksaray and Topkapı; and to the Bosphorus shore through Beşiktaş, Ortaköy and Arnavutköy to Bebek, where you can change to continue through the suburbs as far as the village of Rumeli Kavaği.

Taksim Square Buses from Taksim Square head through Mecidiyeköy to the northern suburbs; down along the Bosphorus through Beşiktaş, Ortaköy and Aranvutköy; and across the Horn to Topkapı and Aksaray.

USEFUL ROUTES

#12 and #12/A Kadıköy to Üsküdar

#15 Üsküdar along the Bosphorus to Beylerbeyi, Kanlıca and Beykoz

#22 Kabataş up the Bosphorus to Beşiktaş, Ortaköy, Kuruçeşme, Arnavutköy, Bebek, Emirgan and İstinye

#25/A Levent Metro, Maslak, Sariyer and Rumeli Kavaği

#28T Topkapı to Beşiktaş via Fatih, Eminönü, Karaköy, Tophane and Kabataş

#36/V and #37/Y Vezneciler to Edirenkapı

#38 Beyazit to Edirnekapı (city land walls)

#38/E Eminönü to Edirne Kapı via Unkapanı/Atatürk Bridge and Fatih

#40 Taksim up the Bosphorus including Beşiktaş, Kuruçeşme, Bebek, Emirgan, İstinye, Tarabya and Sariyer

#54HT Taksim to upper Golden Horn (for Miniatürk, Rami Koç Museum and Santralistanbul).

İSTANBULKART – THE SMARTCARD WAY TO TRAVEL

An **İstanbulkart** is a must for anyone staying in İstanbul for a few days who wants to explore the city on public transport. A credit-card-sized smartcard, it can be purchased for a one-off fee of ₺6 from kiosks at Sabiha Gökçen (though not, at the time of writing, Atatürk) airport on arrival, in Eminönü, Sultanahmet, Sirkeci, Beyazit/Grand Bazaar, Aksaray and many other major transport stops, and be "charged" to whatever value you require at the same places – or from machines labelled "Elektronik bilet ve dolum cihazı" (electronic ticket top-up machine), located close to major transport stops. These provide touch-screen instructions in English and German as well as Turkish. The passes are accepted on all municipal and some private buses, sea buses, ferries, trains (for local journeys only), the metro and the tram. Convenience aside, you also make a sizeable saving on each journey (1.05 kuruş) by using your card rather than a *jeton*, and bigger savings on Princes' Islands ferries, the antique tram and Tünel.

The entrances to tram, metro, train and ferry transport stops hold turnstiles; place the *İstanbulkart* against the receptor, and the journey cost (₺1.95) is deducted.

1

JETONS

If you don't want to buy the *İstanbulkart* (see p.115), you'll have to buy plastic tokens (*jetons*), which work on city buses, trams, metro, light rail, rail and ferries, from a *Jetonmatik* machine. Located next to many stops – including Eminönü, Sultanahmet and Sirkeci – the machines accept 5, 10 and ₺20 notes as well as 25 kuruş, 50 kuruş and ₺1 coins. You insert the *jetons* into the turnstiles at the entrance to tram, metro, train and ferry stops. Buy a handful of *jetons* before you set off on city explorations, as some *Jetonmatik* machines may be out of order.

BY TRAIN

The most useful suburban (*banliyö*) line runs from Sirkeci (☎0212 527 0051) to Halkalı daily 6am–midnight, running along the shores of the Sea of Marmara, and stopping at Kumkapı (known for its fish restaurants), Yenkapı (for the sea-bus ferry terminal) and Yedikule fortress (for the land walls). All journeys cost the same flat fare (₺3), and the *İstanbulkart* is accepted. When the Marmaray project is completed, the most useful section of line, between Sirkeci and Yenikapı, will disappear underground.

FUNICULARS AND THE CABLE CAR

Tünel Known as the Tünel, the antique funicular between Karaköy and İstiklal Caddesi in Beyoğlu connects with the antique tram (see p.105) on İstiklal Caddesi.
F1 A modern funicular, F1 links Kabata, at the northern end of the tramline, with Taksim Square (and the M2 metro).
Cable car The cable car that links the southern shore of the Golden Horn in Eyüp with the *Pierre Loti* café and Eyüp cemetery may not connect with the rail or tram systems, but it does save your legs. Use your *İstanbulkart* or buy a *jeton* for all of these.

BY TRAM

T1 tram The main T1 tram service runs from Zeytinburnu via Topkapı Gate to Aksaray, Laleli, Beyazit, Cemberlitaş, Sultanahmet, downhill to Eminönü, and across the Galata bridge to Karaköy (for Beyoğlu/Galata), Tophane, Fındıklı and Kabataş (where it connects with the funicular to Taksim Square and the ferry terminal for boats to the Princes' Islands). Trams are frequent and operate 6am–midnight. Approaching trams signal their arrival with a bell, and passengers must wait on the concrete platforms, placed at regular intervals along the tracks. Note that the tram stops are marked, confusingly, by the same "M" sign as the metro (*hafif metro*). *Jetons* (₺3) can be bought at machines next to the platforms, and are put in turnstiles on entry, or you can use the *İstanbulkart*.

Antique tram The antique tram (with ticket collectors in appropriately antiquated uniforms) runs between the Tünel station, at the Beyoğlu end of İstiklal Caddesi, for 1.5km to Taksim Square (every 15min, daily 9am–9pm; ₺3). *Jetons* can be purchased from kiosks at either end of the route or at the one fixed stop halfway at Galatasaray School; *İstanbulkart* also accepted.

BY METRO

Once the building of a controversial bridge across the Golden Horn has been completed, the metro system will connect the whole of the European side of İstanbul. There are several metro lines, but only two are of interest to the vast majority of visitors. Trains leave every fifteen minutes (Mon–Thurs 6am–12.30am, Fri & Sat 6.30am–1am, Sun 6.30am–12.30am); *jetons* (₺3) are inserted in turnstiles on entry, or use the *İstanbulkart*.

M1 The southern M1 metro line runs west from Aksaray via the intercity *otogar* near Esenler, to Atatürk airport. Although it's called a metro, only short sections run underground.

M2 On the northern side of the Golden Horn, the M2 metro runs from Şişhane (at the southern end of İstiklal Caddesi) all the way out to Haciosman via Taksim Square, Osmanbey, Şişli, Gayrettepe Levent and Levent 4.

BY DOLMUŞES AND MINIBUSES

Dolmuşes are shared taxis – either cabs or, more usually, minibuses – that run on fixed routes, departing only when full ("dolmuş" means "full"). Vehicles display their destination in the window, and charge a flat fare fixed by the municipality: watch what Turkish passengers are paying – usually a little more than a municipality bus – shout your destination to the driver and pay accordingly, passing the money via other passengers. *Dolmuş* and minibus stands at points of origin are denoted with a signposted "D".
Routes The only dolmuş routes of interest to most visitors are the yellow minibuses departing from the northern end of Tarlabaşı Bulvarı, just below Taksim Square, which run across into the old town and along the Sea of Marmara to the city land walls near Yedikule, or those running up the Asian side of the Bosphorus between Kadıköy and Üsküdar and beyond.

BY TAXI

Taxis are ubiquitous, with over 19,000 legal *taksici* (taxi drivers) in İstanbul. They are invariably painted yellow. Fares are reasonable: an official rate of ₺1.7 per km plus a flat starting rate of ₺2.7, with an extra toll when crossing either of the Bosphorus bridges. All taxis are equipped with meters, but check that the driver switches it on to avoid arguments later. It's also worth noting that there are upward of ten thousand unregistered cabs in the city – be wary.

BY FERRY AND SEA BUS

ŞEHIR HATLARI

The main ferry company is the efficient Şehir Hatları (City Lines; ☎ 444 1851, ⓦ sehirhatlari.com.tr). Timings change seasonally; it's essential to get hold of the current timetable, available from the ferry terminals and from tourist offices as well as their website, so that you can be sure when the last ferry back departs. The busiest routes, such as Karaköy to Haydarpaşa and Kadıköy, generally have three to five ferries per hour, 6am–11pm; all charge a flat fare of ₺3 each way. For both ferries and the faster sea buses (see p.117), buy a *jeton* and deposit it at the turnstile on entry, or use your *İstanbulkart*.

TURYOL

The busiest routes are also served by several other small, privately run ferries, many under the umbrella of the cooperative Turyol. Most Turyol boats leave from a terminal just west of the Galata Bridge in Eminönü, or over the water in Karaköy, again just west of the Galata Bridge, the destinations being Haydarpaşa and Kadıköy, respectively; tickets are sold at kiosks on the quayside.

CITY FERRY TERMINAL

The main City Ferry Terminal at Eminönü – between Sirkeci station and the Galata Bridge – holds a line of ferry quays or terminals (*iskelesi* in Turkish), which are listed below, from west to east. Be wary, however: at the time of writing, they were being reorganized, and the authorities may change the destinations from the new departure terminals.

Yemiş İskelesi On the west side of the Galata Bridge; Haliç Hattı (Golden Horn Lines) ferries up the Golden Horn to Eyüp via Kasımpaşa, Hasköy, Ayvansaray and Sütlüce (roughly hourly, daily 7am–8pm). The ferry actually originates across the Bosphorus in Üsküdar, so on the return journey make sure you get off at Eminönü.

Boğaz İskelesi The nearest terminal to the east side of the Galata Bridge; ferries run up the Bosphorus to Rumeli Kavağı (see p.139).

Hezarfen Ahmet Çelebi Ferries to Üsküdar (daily 6.35am–11pm).

Evliya Çelebi İskelesi Ferries across the Bosphorus to Kadıköy (daily 7.30am–9pm).

Katib Çelebi İskelesi At the time of writing, this newly constructed terminal was not yet in operation.

IDO terminal Car ferries to Harem (daily 8am–9.30pm).

OTHER FERRY TERMINALS

Karaköy On the north side of the Galata Bridge; regular Şehir Hatları ferries to Haydarpaşa and Kadıköy (daily 6.30am–11pm).

Kabataş The last east-bound stop on the T1 tram, northeast of Galata/Beyoğlu. Ferries cross the Bosphorus to Kadıköy (Mon–Fri 7am–8pm), with a daily service

---

THE BOSPHORUS CRUISE

Taking a **boat trip** up the Bosphorus, from the bustling quays of Eminönü to the quiet fishing village of Anadolu Kavağı, is a highlight of any visit to İstanbul. The long **Bosphorus Cruise**, run by the Şehir Hatları company (☎ 444 1851, ⓦ sehirhatlari.com.tr), leaves from the Boğaz Ferry Terminal just east of the Galata Bridge in Eminönü (daily: May–Oct 10.35am & 1.35pm, Nov–April 10.35am; one-way ₺15, round-trip ₺25).

In summer, especially at weekends, the queues to buy **tickets** can be very long, so allow at least half an hour, or, preferably, buy your ticket a day or two in advance. There are also often long queues to board, so late-comers end up sitting in the worst seats. The ferries are rather antiquated but comfortable enough, and you can buy snacks, sandwiches and drinks on board. The round trip, including a 2hr 30min **lunch** stop at Anadolu Kavağı, takes about seven hours.

The boat **stops** at Beşiktaş, Kanlıca (Asia), Yeniköy, Sariyer and Rumeli Kavağı (all Europe) and, finally, Anadolu Kavağı (Asia); the only stop on the return is Beşiktaş. You can leave the boat at any of the landings to explore the waterfront or hinterland, but most passengers do the return cruise. A shorter version is also available for ₺10, departing from the same ferry terminal and covering the same distance with no stops (other than to pick up more passengers at Üsküdar). The tour takes around two hours, departing Eminönü at 2.30pm (April–Oct daily; Nov–March Sun & public holidays).

On Saturday nights only, between early June and mid-September, a **night-time Mehtaplı cruise** (₺20) makes an attractive alternative, with the great suspension bridges lit up like Christmas trees, and the lights of Asia and Europe twinkling on either side. The boat departs Eminönü at 7pm, reaching Anadolu Kavağı at 8.30pm, where it moors for dinner, before arriving back in Eminönü around midnight.

The private Turyol company (see p.117) also runs tours up the Bosphorus, as far as the Fatih bridge. Boats depart every hour on the hour on weekdays, more frequently at weekends, and the 1hr 30min round trip costs ₺12.

1

(6.45am–9pm) from Beşiktaş to Kadıköy and Üsküdar. Also regular ferries to the Princes' Islands, as well as faster sea buses (deniz otobüsleri) run by İDO (İstanbul Deniz Otobüsleri; ☎ 0212 444 4436, ⓦ ido.com.tr; see p.117).

BY SEA TAXI

Water taxis (deniz taksi) are massively over-subscribed, so unless the fleet has considerably increased don't bank on being able to whizz up and down the Bosphorus in one. Theoretically, you call ☎ 444 4498, give your name and your pick-up and drop-off points, and a water taxi will collect you from one of the 27 designated docks, which include the Prince's Islands as well as numerous stops on both sides of the Bosphorus as far up as Rumeli Kavağı.

Unless you are a Turkish-speaker, the ⓦ www.deniztaksi .com website is of little use, so use your hotel to book one.

BY CAR

If you're determined to drive in this traffic-choked, accident-waiting-to-happen metropolis, the agencies below have pick-up points at Atatürk International Airport and (bar Europcar) Sabiha Gökçen, and offices elsewhere in İstanbul – check their websites for working hours. Expect to pay ₺70–190 a day for a week's rental (ten percent more for daily rental), depending on the car. Many of the major arteries around İstanbul are toll roads; they don't accept cash, so you have to buy a KGS toll card for €20 or ₺35 from the rental agency.

INFORMATION

Tourist offices İstanbul's most helpful tourist office is on Divan Yolu Caddesi, in Sultanahmet, near the Hippodrome (daily 9am–5pm; ☎ 0212 518 8754). Others can be found in the international arrivals area of Atatürk airport (daily 24hr; ☎ 0212 573 4136); Sirkeci train station (daily 9am–5pm; ☎ 0212 511 5888); Karaköy International

Maritime Passenger Terminal (Mon–Sat 9am–5pm; ☎ 0212 249 5776); and the Hilton Hotel arcade on Cumhuriyet Caddesi (Mon–Sat 9am–5pm; ☎ 0212 233 0592). Each hands out abundant city maps and leaflets and the staff have an excellent working knowledge of most European languages.

ACCOMMODATION

New hotels open in İstanbul on a seemingly daily basis, so it's nearly always possible to find a decent room with a modicum of advance planning – but bear in mind that spring and autumn are the busiest and most expensive times. For nightlife stay across the Golden Horn in Beyoğlu, while to be on the doorstep of the major historical sites base yourself in or around Sultanahmet. Virtually all but the most basic hotels have free wi-fi. Note that walk-in rack rates can often be unrealistically high, having been fixed in a busy season or for the benefit of tour companies, and many hotels will be happy to bargain. High season is mid-March to mid-November, and Christmas and New Year. Some establishments are a little cheaper in July and August, and most places offer discounts during the main low season, usually around fifteen to twenty percent.

SULTANAHMET

Some of İstanbul's best small hotels, pansiyons and hostels are in Sultanahmet, the historic heart of touristic İstanbul, within a few minutes' walk of the Blue Mosque, Topkapı Palace and Aya Sofya. Those around the Hippodrome are particularly well placed to offer a sense of history. Accommodation is especially concentrated in and around Akbıyık Caddesi and Cankurtaran, while the hotels off Divan Yolu Caddesi have the advantage of being handy for the tram.

AROUND THE HIPPODROME

Deniz Houses Çayıroğlu Sok 14 ☎ 0212 518 9595, ⓦ denizkonakhotel.com; map p.73. This very friendly establishment consists of a couple of adjacent townhouses on a characterful side street. The front rooms in A Blok have sea views but some noise from the railway, while all of the smallish rooms have funky kilims and wooden floors. Rooms in B Blok are plusher and more spacious, but lack sea views. **€60**

★ **İbrahim Pasha** Terzihane Sok 5 Adliye Yani ☎ 0212 518 0394, ⓦ ibrahimpasha.com; map p.73. This lovingly converted pair of early twentieth-century townhouses

forms arguably the most tasteful boutique hotel in Sultanahmet, successfully blending a stylish modern interior with Ottoman antiques. Views from the recently expanded roof terrace across the domes and minarets of Sultanahmet and down to the Sea of Marmara are superb, and the freshly prepared breakfast in the cosy and charming downstairs breakfast room is a delight. Ten percent discount for cash. **€99**

Turkoman Hotel Asmalı Çeşme Sok, Adliye Yanı 2 ☎ 0212 516 2956, ⓦ www.turkomanhotel.com; map p.73. Converted house in nineteenth-century Turkish style, right on the Hippodrome and opposite the Egyptian obelisk, with fine views of the Blue Mosque from the roof terrace. Each attractive room is named after one of the old Turkoman tribes, and has a brass bed and wooden floors. Free airport transfers. **€129**

AROUND TOPKAPI PALACE

Ayasofya Konakları Soğukçeşme Sok ☎ 0212 513 3660, ⓦ ayasofyakonaklari.com; map p.73. Created from a series of ten nineteenth-century wooden houses on a cobbled street squeezed between the walls of the Topkapı

Palace and the Aya Sofya, this is one of the most atmospheric hotels in the city. Taking a room in the imposing Konuk Evi, a detached wooden mansion in its own garden opposite the main hotel, is about as close to period living as you can get, with original brass beds, parquet flooring adorned with Turkish carpets, and painted wooden ceilings. €136

AROUND DIVAN YOLU CADDESI

★ **Cheers** Zeynepsultan Cami Sok 21 ☎0212 526 0200, ⊛cheershostel.com; map p.73. Set in an old house on a quiet side street just off the tram line below the Aya Sofya, this hostel makes a refreshing change from the Old City options clustered around Akbıyık Caddesi. In addition to four- and ten-bed dorms, a/c doubles and twins are also available. Apart from the peaceful location, a real draw is the terrace bar, which looks over mature plane trees onto the west face of the Aya Sofya, a view few visitors ever see. Dorm €15, double €60

Kybele Hotel Yerebatan Cad 35 ☎0212 511 7766, ⊛www.kybelehotel.com; map p.73. Atmospheric, unusual, late nineteenth-century rendered brick building, colourfully painted. Inside are over three thousand multi-hued antique-style light fittings and some great original Bakelite radios. The sixteen spacious rooms sport marbled wallpaper and old wood flooring. Breakfast is served in a courtyard full of candelabras, cushions, empty bottles and other knick-knacks. Friendly staff. €110

★ **Nomade Hotel** Ticarethane Sok 15 ☎0212 511 1296, ⊛www.hotelnomade.com; map p.73. Described as "ethnic trendy" by the French designer responsible for its chic interior, this hotel has white-floored rooms finished in bold colours, with rich coordinating fabrics and blonde-wood modernist furniture. The charming and sophisticated twin sisters who run it ensure excellent service. There's a great roof terrace, too, with stunning views across Sultanahmet. €110

Ottoman Hotel Imperial Caferiye Sok 6/1 ☎0212 513 6151, ⊛www.ottomanhotelimperial.com; map p.73. Hard to believe this well-positioned, tastefully refurbished hotel was once the *Yücelt Hostel*, mainstay of the young and impecunious heading out to India in the 1970s (and some apparently came back). The best rooms, at a premium, have views over the Cafer Ağa Medresesi, big tubs, plasma TVs – all have tea- and coffee-making facilities and wi-fi. €129

Sirkeci Konak Taya Hatun Cad 5 ☎0212 528 4344, ⊛sirkecikonak.com; map pp.86–87. Good old-fashioned comfort in a former nineteenth-century Ottoman *konak* (mansion), right next to the walls of Gülhane Parkı, with tea- and coffee-making facilities in the rooms, palatial en-suite bathrooms and comfy beds. There's a fitness centre and small pool in the basement, and free afternoon tea for guests. €170

SULTANAHMET (CANKURTARAN)

Agora Guest House and Hostel Amiral Tafdil Sok 6 ☎0212 458 5547, ⊛agoraguesthouse.com; map p.73. Blurring the lines between hotel and guesthouse, this excellent budget choice is right in the heart of the Old City. The tastefully furnished communal breakfast/lounge area has a massive flat-screen TV, a funky terrace and a great atmosphere. There are ten well-appointed doubles, and dorms range from four to ten beds. Dorm €15, double €80

Alp Hotel Akbıyık Cad, Adliye Sok 4 ☎0212 517 9570, ⊛www.alpguesthouse.com; map p.73. This fine establishment, with a dark-wood exterior, is situated down a quiet lane. Its smallish rooms (some with sea views) are immaculately furnished, some with four-poster beds, and have a/c, wooden floors and tidy bathrooms. The pretty breakfast terrace commands views of palaces, mosques and the sea. €80

Apricot Amiral Tafdil Sok 18 ☎0212 638 1658, ⊛apricothotel.com; map p.73. Set in a quiet backstreet running parallel to busy Akbıyık Cad, and run by a Turkish/American business partnership, this small hotel has an intimate atmosphere. Rooms vary in size and are painted in soothing apricot tones; some have balconies. Bathrooms either have big baths, fancy showers or jacuzzis. They also have three stylish townhouse apartments nearby, with sea views. €69

Big Apple Bayram Fırını Sok 12 ☎0212 517 7931, ⊛hostelbigapple.com; map p.73. Dorms have laminate floors and metal bunk beds and there are shared, clean, separate toilets and showers on each floor. For a substantial price hike, double, triple and family rooms are available – though a couple of these are windowless. The covered terrace and small roof terrace both boast good views over the Sea of Marmara and Princes' Islands, and are the venue for the reasonable Turkish-style breakfast and cheap night-time drinking. Dorm €13, double €55

★ **Empress Zoe** Akbıyık Cad, Adliye Sok 10 ☎0212 518 2504, ⊛www.emzoe.com; map p.73. Owned by American Ann Nevans, who has decorated throughout with her personal touch – the nineteen rooms are in dark wood with richly coloured textiles, accessed by a narrow spiral staircase. Parts of the basement walls belong to the remains of the Byzantine Palace, and the sun terrace has panoramic views of the Blue Mosque and Aya Sofya. Ten percent discount for cash. €120

Four Seasons Hotel Tevfikhane Sok 1 ☎0212 638 8200, ⊛www.fourseasons.com; map p.73. Until it was completely renovated as a five-star hotel in the early 1980s, this formidable building served as the Sultanahmet Prison. The watchtowers and exercise court are still evident beneath the flowers and vines, but the 54 beautiful high-ceilinged rooms are unrecognizable as former cells. Excellent, attentive service, as you'd expect. €490

1

★**Hanedan** Akbıyık Cad, Adliye Sok 3 ☎0212 516 4869/418 1564, ⓦhanedanhotel.com; map p.73. Tucked away on a quiet side street off Akbıyık Cad, this friendly hotel, run by four friends, is great value for the quality of accommodation and service. The dark-wood floors in the rooms are offset by the pale plain walls, and the overall feel is of unfussy comfort. A roof terrace offers stunning views over the Aya Sofya and the Sea of Marmara, while the great breakfast includes filter coffee. Discount for long stays. €65

★**Poem** Terbıyık Sok 12 ☎0212 638 9744, ⓦhotelpoem.com; map p.73. This friendly and immaculately run establishment has been created from two adjoining nineteenth-century wooden mansion houses, and rooms are named after famous Turkish poets or their poems. There's a twenty percent winter discount, and a further five percent off for cash. Rooms with sea views and/or balconies are more expensive. The roof terrace has panoramic views of the Aya Sofya and the sea. €55

Sultan Hostel Akbıyık Cad 21 ☎0212 516 9260, ⓦsultanhostel.com; map p.73. This 160-bed hostel is very popular because of its convenient location, spotless rooms, comfy beds sporting gleaming white linen, and regularly cleaned shared bathrooms. Dorm prices vary according to the number of beds per room; some have en-suite showers and toilets. The doubles are not such good value. Dorm €15, double €60

Side Hotel & Pension Utangaç Sok 20 ☎0212 517 2282, ⓦwww.sidehotel.com; map p.73. Owned by three charismatic brothers, this place is bright, spacious and friendly, and resists the pressure to go all modern or faux-Ottoman. Pricier en-suite rooms (a/c) on the hotel side, cheaper ones (some with shared bathroom) in the pension, both sharing the extensive breakfast terraces, which have great views of the Princes' Islands. Pension €40, hotel €70

★**Uyan** Utangaç Sok 25 ☎0212 518 9255, ⓦuyanhotel.com; map p.73. Atmospheric 29-room hotel set in a beautifully renovated 1920s corner-plot building in the heart of the old city. The ground-floor rooms are a little gloomy, but the rest are light and airy, with light wood floors scattered with oriental rugs, white walls and white bed linen. Different-sized rooms range from small doubles to a honeymoon suite. "Blue Mosque", room 405, has great views over the Blue Mosque and Aya Sofya, as well as Scandinavian-style furniture and a jacuzzi. An added bonus is the breathtaking view from the roof terrace. €70

THE GRAND BAZAAR AND AROUND

A stay in this workaday quarter makes a refreshing change from the heavily touristed streets of Cankurtaran, but the main sites are still within easily walking distance, and the Beyazit and Çemberlitaş tram stops are very convenient.

★**Niles** Dibekli Cami Sok 13 ☎0212 517 3239, ⓦhotelniles.com; map pp.86–87. Well-established hotel, offering better value than most of its competitors in nearby Sultanahmet. The standard rooms are well appointed, with small but immaculately finished shower-bathrooms, while the suites, at just under twice the price, are more elaborately furnished and decorated in faux-Ottoman style, and boast marble, Turkish-bath-style bathrooms. There's a pretty ground-floor courtyard garden and a roof terrace with panoramic views over busy Yenikapı Harbour. Excellent value. €70

THE NORTHWEST QUARTER

★**Kariye** Kariye Camii Sok 6, Erdirne Kapı ☎0212 534 8414, ⓦkariyeotel.com; map p.97. Situated right next door to the Kariye Museum, arguably the finest Byzantine site in the city (see p.99), this nineteenth-century mansion has been restored with style and restraint. The rooms are kitted out in soft pastel colours, much of the furniture is ornate late nineteenth-century in style, and the polished honey-coloured parquet floor is enlivened by the odd tasteful kilim. The reasonable prices reflect the rather small, shower-only bathrooms and fans rather than a/c. €85

BEYOĞLU, TAKSIM AND THE WATERFRONT

The heart of Beyoğlu, the former European quarter, is undoubtedly İstiklal Caddesi – lined with gorgeous nineteenth-century townhouses and arcades, it's İstanbul's premier entertainment area, home to the city's densest concentration of restaurants, bars and clubs. Tepebaşı, a mixed commercial/tourist district just west of İstiklal Caddesi's southern end, gives easy access to İstiklal but has charms of its own, from trendy rooftop bars and restaurants to the impressive Pera Museum. There are also a couple of options close to the Galata Tower. At the northeastern end of İstiklal Caddesi, the business district of Taksim has a wide range of hotels aimed largely at business travellers and tour groups. Rates here are usually higher than in other areas, but bargains can be found.

TEPEBAŞI, İSTIKLAL CADDESI AND GALATA

Büyük Londra Oteli Meşrutiyet Cad 117, Tepebaşı ☎0212 249 1025, ⓦwww.londrahotel.net; map pp.102–103. Palatial, mid-nineteenth-century townhouse. Many of the rooms are timeworn and cluttered with battered period furniture, which gives the hotel its retro-bohemian charm. Others that have been modernized have inevitably lost their raffishness. Ernest Hemingway stayed here in 1922, as a journalist covering the Turkish War of Independence, as did Alexander Hacke when shooting the definitive film of the city's music scene, *İstanbul: Crossing the Bridge*. €50

★ **Hotel Devman** Asmalımescit Sok 52 ☎ 0212 245 6212, ⓦ devmanhotel.com; map pp.102–103. Modern hotel in the arty nineteenth-century backstreets off İstiklal Cad, with spotless blue-tiled bathrooms with power shower, firm beds and a (meagre) open-buffet breakfast. Good value for the location and right next to the nightlife – try to bag a room at the rear to avoid the worst of the noise of carousing diners and music from the bars. **€60**

Pera Palas Meşrutiyet Cad 52, Tepebaşı ☎ 0212 377 4000, ⓦ perapalace.com; map pp.102–103. A contender for the most atmospheric hotel in İstanbul (see p.105), the *Pera* was built in the nineteenth century to accommodate Orient Express passengers – its rooms are marked with the names of famous occupants such as Agatha Christie and Graham Greene. It reopened in 2010 following a lengthy restoration, and has managed to maintain much of its character. **€200**

Richmond Hotel İstiiklal Cad 445 ☎ 0212 252 5460, ⓦ richmondhotels.com.tr; map pp.102–103. Nowhere near as trendy as you might think, given its central location on buzzing İstiklal Cad and the presence of one of Beyoğlu's coolest roof-bars, *Leb-i-Derya Richmond* (see p.128). The standard rooms are plain, with white walls and muted brown soft furnishings, but do come with music systems. It's perennially popular with businessmen and travellers alike – and if you can stretch to a suite, they're considerably more stylish (and expensive). Top-floor rooms on the back have Bosphorus views and a hefty €40 supplement. **€139**

★ **Sumo Cat** Ali Hoca Arkası, off Kalsıran Cad. Galata ☎ 0212 292 7866, ⓦ sumocathostel.com; map pp.102–103. A labour of love by its laidback and welcoming English-speaking owners, this excellent conversion of a nineteenth-century Galata townhouse offers homely yet stylish accommodation in three dorms (all en-suite) and two en-suite doubles – all with a/c. Rooms are individually decorated with funky murals, and beds new and comfy. Space is at a premium in the dorms, but with the buzzing nightlife of the quarter on your doorstep nobody cares. There's a small downstairs kitchen and a ground-floor garden area. Dorm **€14**, double **€60**

Triada Residence İstıklal Cad, Meşelik Sok 4 ☎ 0212 251 0101, ⓦ triada.com.tr; map pp.102–103. Small but very stylish rooms in a lovely early twentieth-century townhouse on a quiet side street. All rooms have boldly grained wood laminate floors, an American-style kitchen including a coffee-making machine and fridge, and there's a shared sauna. One of the few genuine boutique-style hotels in this part of town, with fabulous views from the roof terrace over the domes of the Greek Orthodox Aya Triada church. **€120**

World House Hostel Galipdede Cad 85 ☎ 0212 293 5520, ⓦ worldhouseistanbul.com; map pp.102–103. This colourful ninety-bed hostel ticks all the boxes for a budget traveller – clean, modern and in a great location. Despite the nearby 24hr entertainment, it's quiet too, bar the prayer call from the adjacent mosque. The hostel also has a sister hostel *Liberta*, just off Istiklal Cad, as well as short/long-term apartments – check the website for details. Dorm **€12**, double **€50**

APARTMENTS

Booked on a night-by-night basis, the price of a small apartment is often similar to that of a hotel, making them increasingly popular with visitors – and for stays of a week or more, the cost can drop substantially. The prices quoted here are for a one-night stay. New apartments are coming onto the market all the time, and the following websites are worth checking out: ⓦ istanbul-flats.com, ⓦ thehouseapart.com and ⓦ perfectplaces.com.

THE OLD CITY

★ **İstanbul Suite Home** Dizdariye Çeşmesi Sok 51 ☎ 0212 458 5255, ⓦ istanbulsuitehome.com; map p.73. Situated in a tall, narrow townhouse on a quiet backstreet south of Divan Yolu, the five apartments here are extremely stylish and very good value. Three of them have two bedrooms, two just one bedroom; they're modish without being minimalist, all pale wood and white. All have a spacious dining area with attached kitchen. **€155**

GALATA, BEYOĞLU AND TAKSIM

Divan Taksim Suites Cumhuriyet Cad 49 ☎ 0212 254 7777, ⓦ divan.com.tr; map pp.102–103. White blinds, white rugs, white furnishings, blonde-wood floors: this is Scandinavian-style minimalism in the heart of Taksim. The suites all work on an open-plan scheme, with nicely kitted-out kitchens off a spacious sleeping/dining/sitting area. All suites have large workstations and wi-fi, plus a music system and TV. **€210**

★ **Galata Residence** Bankalar Cad, Felek Sok 2, Galata ☎ 0212 292 4841, ⓦ galataresidence.com; map pp.102–103. A range of apartments of varying sizes for short- and long-term stays, housed in three beautifully restored late nineteenth-century buildings in close proximity. While not as designer-flash as some of the newer places around, the apartments are extremely comfortable, well located, and fitted with a/c. **€81**

Suite Home İstiklal İstiklal Cad 45 ☎ 0212 245 0772, ⓦ istanbulsuite.com; map pp.102–103. In the heart of the action, near the Taksim end of buzzing İstiklal Cad, offering three standards of room: business class; business roof room, where you pay more for the view; and spacious family suites. Decor is simple and modern without being too minimalist, and the kitchens are well equipped and functional. **€99**

EATING

İstanbul is home to Turkey's best restaurants, including several that lavish time and skill on old Ottoman cuisine, and, thanks to the lengthy coastline, fish is a firm menu favourite. Snacks are ubiquitous, with kebab stands, pastry shops, fast-food outlets and cafés across the city catering to locals, workers and tourists alike. Restaurants around tourist honey-pot Sultanahmet tend to be of poorer quality, and are more expensive than elsewhere in the city.

ESSENTIALS

Opening hours Workers' cafés and *lokantas* open as early as 6am and serve until 4pm; other cafés generally open daily between 9am and 9pm. Restaurants open for lunch and dinner, with last orders at 10pm or 11pm, with those in more popular areas (such as Nevizade Sokak) and live music venues staying open until the early hours. In the more commercial districts, restaurants follow the shops and close on a Sunday.

Costs Prices vary depending on the establishment and location, but range from ₺1 for a *simit* to ₺3 or so for a takeaway chicken *durum* (slivers of döner chicken and salad in a flat-bread wrap); a café latte or similar, by contrast, will likely set you back at least ₺6. Main courses start from ₺7 at a cheap restaurant frequented by locals, and run up to ₺100 or more at a swish restaurant with all the trimmings. Some places serve set meals at ₺60–90, with a wide choice of *mezes* followed by a substantial main course, Turkish desserts and, usually, half a bottle of wine or rakı. Credit cards are widely accepted in all but the smallest restaurants.

CAFÉS AND BUDGET EATING

Today's İstanbul holds a wide range of cafés, ranging from sophisticated continental cafés serving trendy coffees and imported alcoholic drinks to simple *lokantas* dishing up cheap-and-cheerful stews from *bains-maries*. Budget options include *lokanta*-style buffets (where what you see is what you get), and *pide* or *kebap salonu* for cheap and filling meat- and bread-based staples. Barrow-boys all over the city offer *simits* and other bread-type snacks, and fishermen in Karaköy and Eminönü serve fish sandwiches off their boats, while booths and pushcarts in the more salubrious areas sell sizzling tangles of sheep innards (*kokoreç*), stuffed mussels (*midye dolması*), corn-on-the-cob, roast chestnuts and *pilaf* rice.

SULTANAHMET

Çiğdem Patisserie Divan Yolu Cad 62 ☎0212 526 8859; map p.73. For more than forty years, the *Çiğdem* has been offering a good selection of both Turkish and non-Turkish pastries and sweets – plus fresh juices, coffee (including latte) and tea. The *baklava* and *sutlaç* (rice pudding) are both reliable. Daily 8am–11pm.

★ **Doy Doy** Sıfa Hamamı Sok 13 ☎0212 517 1588; map p.73. A backpackers' favourite with a well-deserved reputation for cheap and well-prepared kebabs, *pide* and *sulu yemek*. Try the unusual *fıstıklı fırın beyti* (oven-cooked kebab with pistachios). Dining is on four floors, including a

roof terrace with great views of the harbour and a night-time light show over the Blue Mosque. No alcohol. Daily 8am–11pm.

The Pudding Shop (Lale Restaurant) Divan You Cad 6 ☎0212 522 2970, ⊛puddingshop.com; map p.73. This Sultanahmet institution first opened its doors in 1957, and in the late 1960s became the meeting place for hippies and other travellers overlanding to India. Times have changed but the *Pudding Shop* is still dishing up its signature rice pudding along with a wide array of traditional Turkish dishes. The food's not outstanding, but it's well located right on Divan Yolu, serves alcohol and has a unique place in the history of baby-boom-generation travel. Daily 7am–11pm.

★ **Tarihi Sultanahmet Köftecisi** Divan Yolu 4 ☎0212 511 3960; map p.73. Longest established of the three *köfte* specialists at this end of Divan Yolu, and well frequented by Turkish celebrities (check out the framed newspaper clippings and thank-you letters on the tiled walls). A plate of tasty meatballs, haricot-bean salad, pickled peppers, fresh bread and a spicy tomato-sauce dip will set you back ₺16. Daily 11am–11pm.

GRAND BAZAAR AND AROUND

★ **Ağa Kapısı** Nazir Izzet Efendi Sok 11 ☎0212 519 5176; map pp.86–87. Tucked away on a dead-end street just below the Süleymaniye Camii and frequented mainly by local traders, young headscarved women students and their lecturers, the *Ağa Kapısı* boasts the picture window beyond compare, giving a stunning panoramic view down over the Galata Bridge, the mouth of the Golden Horn and the Bosphorus beyond. Try the *gözleme* (a kind of paratha stuffed with goat's cheese) and a glass of tea, traditional Turkish style, or splash out on Ottoman-style sherbet drinks. Daily 8am–midnight.

★ **Bedesten Café** Cevahir Bedesteni 143–151, Kapalı Çarşı ☎0212 520 2250; map p.90. The best café in the Grand Bazaar, an oasis of peace and tranquillity away from the main thoroughfares (look out for the two giant *alem* – the crescent- and star-topped finials that adorn mosque domes and minarets – and an even bigger portrait of Atatürk). The food is quality, with delicacies such as scrambled omelette *menemen* and Turkish ravioli (*manti*) in garlic and yoghurt sauce (₺17). There's also a great selection of cakes. Mon–Sat 9am–6.30pm.

Erenler Çay Bahçesi Ali Baba Türbe Sok Medressi, Yeniçeriler Cad 36/38; pp.86–87. In the courtyard of a

1

three-hundred-year-old *medrese* (religious school), this cheap-and-cheerful worker-oriented nargile café has waterpipes for ₺12, tea for a lira and snacks like toasted sandwiches. No alcohol. Daily 7am–midnight.

★ **Subaşı Lokantası** Nuruosmaniye Cad 48, Çarşı Kapı ☎0212 522 4762; map pp.86–87. Behind Nuruosmaniye Camii, just inside the main entrance of the Grand Bazaar, this spit-and-sawdust place serves excellent lunchtime food to the market traders. Go early (noon–1pm), as it gets packed and food may run out. Mains cost ₺8–14 per portion, depending how much meat they contain – try the stuffed peppers or delicious *karnı yarık* (mince-topped aubergine). Mon–Sat 9am–6pm.

Tarihi Kuru Fasuliye Süleymaniye Erzincanlı Ali Baba Siddik Sami Onar Cad 11 ☎0212 513 6219; map pp.86–87. In the gorgeous Süleymaniye Camii complex, with tables set out on the precinct between the mosque and *medrese* behind, this simple place serves up some of the tastiest beans in town for a bargain ₺5 – though beware of the hot chilli pepper draped innocently atop your steaming bowl of buttery, tomato-sauce-drenched pulses. Daily 9am–7pm.

Vefa Bozacısı Katip Çelebi Cad 104/1 ☎0212 519 4922, ⊕vefa.com.tr; map pp.86–87. Worth a look just to see the interior: old tiled floor, dark-wood shelves, ornate Victorian-style mirrors, 1920s light fittings, and bottles of vinegar with label designs unchanged for decades (Atatürk was here in 1937). The *boza* (₺3), a cloudy, viscous drink made by fermenting millet with sugar and water that's best drunk in winter, is an acquired taste but very healthy. Daily 7am–midnight.

BEYOĞLU

Galata Konak Patisserie Haci Ali Sok 2 ☎0212 252 5346, ⊕galatakonakcafe.com; map pp.102–103. Just down from the Galata Tower, this stylish café dishes up delicious lattes (with amaretti biscuits) and tempting cakes and desserts from ₺6. For something a little more substantial, head up the lantern-lit stairwell or take the antique lift to the rooftop terrace restaurant for a mix of Turkish and European fare and an expansive view over the Golden Horn. Popular with locals and tourists alike, it always seems to be packed. No alcohol. Daily 9am–9pm.

★ **Kafe Ara** Tosbağa Sok8/A, off Yeniçarşı Cad, Beyoğlu ☎0212 245 4105; map pp.102–103. Great place tucked away just off Galatasaray Meydani, with a raft of tables out in the alley and a lovely dark-wood bistro-style interior lined with black-and-white photography by Ara Güler. A large, tulip-shaped glass of Turkish tea costs a reasonable ₺3, big bowls of salad ₺12–18. Mon–Thurs 8am–11pm, Fri 8am–midnight, Sat & Sun 10am–11pm.

Nizam Pide İstiklal Cad, Büyükparmakkapı Sok ☎0212 249 7918; map pp.102–103. Offers excellent

pides (₺8 and up). A second branch on Kalyoncu Kulluğu Cad, behind Nevizade Sok in the fish market, has framed articles from Turkish newspapers proclaiming it to be one of the top ten *pide* outlets in Turkey. Daily 24hr.

Ramiz Köfteci İstiklal Cad ⊕kofteciramiz.com; map pp.102–103. Now a modish chain, the original outlet opened in provincial Akşehir back in 1928. It mixes the traditional (delicious *köfte*) with the contemporary (a serve-yourself salad bar). Salad plates cost ₺6 (40 varieties), *köfte* ₺8. Daily 10am–10pm.

Saray İstiklal Cad 102–104, Beyoğlu ☎0212 292 3434, ⊕saraymuhallebicisi.com; map pp.102–103. Established in 1935, the emphasis is on classic Turkish desserts such as *fırın sütlaç* (baked rice pudding), *irmik helvası* (semolina with nuts) and *baklava*-type sweets, including wonderful *fıstık sarma* (pistachios packed in a syrup-drenched pastry roll) – cakes cost ₺5 and up – though it also serves soups and grills. Daily 8am–11pm.

ASIAN İSTANBUL

Baylan Muvakkithane Cad 19, Kadiköy ☎0216 346 6350. This famous patisserie is a must for nostalgia freaks, with its 1950s dark-wood and chrome frontage. The trellis-shaded garden area is popular with mums and their offspring, many of whom tuck into traditional ice creams or plates of pastel-coloured macaroons. The liqueur chocolates demonstrate the café's Christian Armenian origins. Daily 10am–10pm.

RESTAURANTS

Generally the Old City, including Sultanahmet, can't compare with the city's Beyoğlu entertainment hub for variety or quality, but there are a few exceptions. Kumkapı, south of Laleli, off the coast road, Kennedy Caddesi, boasts more than fifty fish restaurants. It's a popular spot on a balmy summer evening, with candlelit tables spilling out on to the narrow, traffic-free streets. Restaurants in Beyoğlu, Galata and Taksim cater for theatre- and cinema-goers and young people filling up before a night out, as well as for those who want to linger all evening over a meal and a bottle of rakı. The liveliest spot is undoubtedly Nevizade Sokak, where restaurants serve *mezes*, kebabs and fish, accompanied by the sound of serenading street musicians. Otherwise you can try your luck in the cobbled streets around the ferry terminal in Ortaköy, where numerous trendy options rub shoulders with older, more traditional places, or across the Bosphorus in Üsküdar or Kadıköy.

SULTANAHMET

Albura Kathisma Akbıyık Cad 26 ☎0212 517 9031, ⊕alburakathisma.com; map p.73. Quite a few restaurants hereabouts now serve regional Anatolian-style dishes, but *Albura* was among the first and remains one of the best. Try the special *Kathisma Palace*, a lamb casserole with figs and almonds (₺50 for two). Angora wine is priced at a reasonable (for İstanbul) ₺50 per bottle. The dining room is a cavernous but stylish bare-brick affair, and there are plenty of outside tables on this bustling tourist street. Daily 10am–11pm.

Amedros Hoca Rüstem Sok 7, Divan Yolu ☏0212 522 8356, ⊛amedroscafe.com; map p.73. A sophisticated café-restaurant with an interior that manages to be both stylish and homely. The food is good, too – a mixture of European (try the Flame Marmer steak) and traditional Anatolian (the *testi* kebab, a succulent lamb and vegetable stew slow-cooked in a sealed clay pot, is a good bet). The service is attentive without being obsequious, and the whole place is very professionally run. Mains from ₺20. Daily 11am–1am.

★ **Balıkçı Sabahattin** Seyit Hasan Koyu Sok 1, Cankurtan ☏0212 458 1824, ⊛balikcisabahattin.com; map p.73. Fish restaurant by Cankurtan station, five minutes' walk but a world away from the tourist joints up the hill. While not cheap (it's *the* in place for moneyed locals), it's about as atmospheric as you can get, with vine-shaded tables set out in a narrow alley in summer, and a wood-floored dining room in an old wooden house in winter. Starters begin at ₺10, mains ₺30 and up, with every kind of locally caught fish on the menu. Daily 11am–1am.

★ **Dubb** İncili Çavuş Sok ☏0212 513 7308, ⊛dubbindian.com; map p.73. A funky spot with one Indian and two Turkish chefs serving up authentic dishes from the Subcontinent in a chic yet ethnic setting. Spread over several floors, the rooms are small, and there's a roof terrace and tables on the street. Delicious samosa and pakora, vegetable curries from ₺15. Owner Mehmet and his Japanese wife also run *Dubb Ethnic* on Mimar Ağa Cad 25, just off Akbıyık Cad, with ethnic cuisine from Turkey to Japan. Daily noon–midnight.

★ **Giritli** Keresteci Hakkı Sok, Ahırkapı ☏0212 458 2270, ⊛giritlirestoran.com; map p.73. Atmospheric fish restaurant set in a historic building near the *Armada Hotel*, specializing in Cretan dishes. For a no-holds-barred evening out, go for the fixed menu at ₺95, and enjoy a sea-food pilaf, 23 *meze* morsels, and three hot starters, followed by a choice of four or five fish – and as much beer, wine or rakı as you can drink. Daily noon–midnight.

Khorasani Ticarethane Sok 39/41, Divan Yolu ☏0212 519 5959, ⊛khorasanirestaurant.com; map p.73. If you are staying in Sultanahmet, this is the nearest place to sample authentic southeastern Turkish cuisine, including hummus and the spicy walnut and pepper dip, *muhamara* (₺8 a portion). The wonderful kebabs, prepared *ocakbaşı* style over a charcoal grill, range ₺19–26. There are tables on the cobbled pedestrian street, and a stylish mezzanine-floored dining room for colder weather. Watch out for the ten percent service charge. Daily noon–1am.

Mozaik Restaurant Divan Yolu Cad, İncili Çavuş Sok 1 ☏0212 512 4177, ⊛mozaikrestaurant.com; map p.73. A well-established restaurant in a nicely restored, late nineteenth-century house, all wooden floors, kilims and subdued lighting. The tables out in the quiet side street are great in the warmer months, and there's a cosy downstairs bar (with small beers at ₺7). Serves a range of less common Turkish dishes, including Armenian, Greek and Kurdish specialities. Daily 9am–midnight.

GRAND BAZAAR AND AROUND

★ **Akdeniz Hatay Sofrası** Ahmediye Cad 44/A, Aksaray ☏0212 531 3333, ⊛hataysofrasi.com; map p.90. This spotless emporium serves up the best southeastern Turkish cuisine in the city. The hummus is served warm and liberally sprinkled with pistachios, and the dip *muhamara* (a spicy mix of breadcrumbs, walnuts, tomato and hot pepper) is delicious; the whole chicken roasted in salt (*tuzda tavuk*) has to be ordered a couple of hours ahead. To get here take the T1 tram to the Aksaray stop, then walk 500m along Vatan Cad; it's next to the Historia mall. Mon–Sat 9am–midnight, Sun 8am–1pm.

Havuzlu Gani Çelebi Sok 3, Kapalı Çarşı ☏0212 520 2250; map p.90. Appealing Grand Bazaar restaurant, with Ottoman-style decor and white tablecloths on dark-wood tables laid out beneath a barrel-vaulted ceiling. A good range of kebabs (the İskender is recommended) and *hazır yemek* (steam-tray food) dishes. Brisk service, tasty food and reasonable prices (kebabs around ₺12). No alcohol. Mon–Sat 10am–5pm.

Kör Agop Ördekli Bakkal 7–9 ☏0212 517 2334; map pp.86–87. Third-generation Armenian-owned fish restaurant, one of the oldest in town (since 1938) and hugely popular. A standard selection of seasonal fish, *mezes* and salads, accompanied by a *fasil* band in the evening. Not cheap, at about ₺50 a head, but a reliable night out. Daily noon–2am.

Siirt Şeref Büryan Kebap Salonu, İtfaye Cad 4, Fatih ☏0212 635 8085; map pp.86–87. Located in the shadow of the towering late Roman Aqueduct of Valens, this great establishment has been dishing up regional dishes from the Arab/Kurdish southeast of Turkey for decades. Best is the *perde pilaf*, a tasty concoction of rice, shredded chicken, almonds, pine-nuts and various herbs cooked in a pot until the outside "burns" to a tasty crust (₺10). *Büryan* is spring lamb cooked in a deep clay *tandır* (tandoori) oven and served chopped on a bed of soft *pide* bread. Daily 11am–11pm.

NORTH OF SULTANAHMET

Hamdi Et Lokantası Kalçin Sok 17 Tahmis Cad, Eminönü ☏0212 528 0390; map pp.86–87. The uninspiring facade of this five-floor joint, fronting the square in Eminönü, belies the quality of the food on offer inside. Tender, charcoal-grilled kebabs of various kinds

1

form the mainstay of the menu, but it's also a good place to try *lahmacun*, a thin, chapati-type bread smeared with spicy mincemeat. The clientele is a mix of local shopkeepers, businessmen and tourists – try to get a seat at the terrace, which offers great views over the Golden Horn. Mains from ₺19. No alcohol. Daily 11am–midnight.

Paşazade Sirkeci İbn-I Kemal Cad 13 ☎0212 513 3757; map pp.86–87. Well-run faux-Ottoman place. Though the interior may verge on twee, the service is good and the food (try the lamb blanquette with quince) tasty and good value (mains from ₺15). It's traditional Turkish cuisine with a twist, there's plenty of choice for vegetarians, and in warm weather the outside tables make for great people-watching. Daily noon–1am.

THE LAND WALLS AND AROUND

★ **Asitane** Kariye Hotel, Kariye Camii Sok 18 ☎0212 534 8414, ⓦasitanerestaurant.com; map p.97. Garden-restaurant next door to the Kariye Museum. It's expensive, but you may feel like splashing out for good service and food in such a peaceful (if far-flung) location. The menu is described as nouvelle Ottoman cuisine – plenty of meat- and fruit-based stews from ₺26–40, or try the *hükar beğendi* (tender lamb with aubergine purée). Meals served on a lovely terrace swamped by roses, accompanied by classical Turkish music. Daily 11.30am–11pm.

★ **Develi** Gümüş Yüzük Sok 7, Samatya ☎0212 529 0833, ⓦdevelikebap.com; map p.97. This posh (and unusually, licensed) joint, serving up the best food from Gaziantep in Turkey's southeast, is out of the way but easy enough to reach on the suburban train line from either Sirkeci or Cankurtaran – get off at the Kocamustafapaşa stop. Great kebabs from ₺19–25, but best are the starters (hummus with pastrami) and *baklava*-type desserts. Nice roof terrace overlooking a quaint square, with the Sea of Marmara beyond. Daily noon–midnight.

BEYOĞLU, GALATA AND TAKSIM

Cezayir Hayriye Cad 16 ☎0212 245 9980, ⓦcezayir -istanbul.com; map pp.102–103. This stylish restaurant sprang up before the boom in minimalist chic, and is no worse for that. Set in a beautifully restored early twentieth-century townhouse, it is soothingly atmospheric, with stripped-pine doors, space-enhancing mirrors, chandeliers and other refreshingly anti-modernist features. The food (modern Mediterranean/Turkish) is generally good, too. Best bet for a reasonable night out is one of the fixed menus – the cheapest option, with two drinks included, is ₺45. Daily 9am–2am.

Ficcin İstiklal Cad, Kallavi Sok 13 ☎0212 293 3786, ⓦficcin.com; map pp.102–103. Unpretentious and great-value place on this quiet (by Beyoğlu standards) side street, offering some unusual and substantial dishes. Try the eponymous *ficcin*, a kind of hearty, Caucasian meat pie,

or the *çerkez mantası*, a ravioli-style dish in which the pasta is stuffed with tomato and served in a yoghurt sauce (mains from ₺7). Soups include a tasty rocket-based one, wine and beer are both reasonably priced, and there's plenty of choice for vegetarians. Tues–Sat 8am–10pm.

Galata House Galata Külesi Sok 61 ☎0212 245 1861, ⓦthegalatahouse.com; map pp.102–103. This restaurant offers all the comfort of eating in your own living room, with small, cosy rooms, an outdoor terrace lit by fairy lights, and a menu of hearty Georgian cuisine (mains around ₺20) – try the house speciality *hindali* (meat-filled dumplings in a tomato sauce). History buffs can ogle the original prison fittings and try to decipher graffiti etched into the wall by prisoners. With only fifty seats, it's best to book ahead. Tues–Sun 3pm–midnight.

Hacı Abdullah İstiklal Cad, Sakızağacı Cad 17 ☎0212 293 8051, ⓦhaciabdullah.com.tr; map pp.102–103. One of the best traditional restaurants in town, sporting a high-ceilinged atrium salon at the back. Main courses from ₺12 – try the *hunkar beğendili kebap* (beef stew on a bed of aubergine and cheese purée) and the *ayva tatlı* (stewed quince with clotted cream). Strictly no alcohol served. Daily 11am–10pm.

★ **İmroz** Nevizade Sok 24 ☎0212 249 9073, ⓦkrependekiimroz.com.tr; map pp.102–103. This Greek-owned İstanbul institution has been dishing up reasonably priced fish dishes (mains around ₺16) since 1942. Spread over three floors, it's perhaps the liveliest of the fish restaurants in the Balık Pazarı area. Daily 11am–2am.

★ **Kenan Üsta Ocakbaşı** Kurabiye Sok 18 ☎0212 293 5619; map pp.102–103. Watch master grillsman Kenan cook *lavaş* (tortilla-style bread) over his basement charcoal grill, smear it with olive oil, sprinkle it with pepper flakes, thyme and salt, then pop it back on the grill to finish. This bread is used as the "plate" to serve an astonishing array of kebabs and grilled meat to a loyal and virtually one hundred percent Turkish clientele. Mains from ₺20; licensed. Daily 10am–2am.

Mardin Kaburga Sofrası Şehit Muhtar Cad 9, Taksim ☎0212 225 9595; map pp.102–103. Unassuming little place specializing in the cuisine of the Mardin region, right on the Syrian border in Turkey's southeast. The *kaburga* is the main attraction – tender rib of lamb stuffed with delicately spiced *pilaf* rice (₺50 for two people). For *meze*, there's *içli köfte*, spiced meatballs wrapped in a bulgur-wheat casing, steamed to a mouth-watering tenderness (₺3). No alcohol. Daily noon–2am.

Nature and Peace İstiklal Cad, Büyükparmakkapı Sok 21 ☎0212 252 8609, ⓦnatureandpeace.com; map pp.102–103. Earthy vegetarian restaurant on a lively street, where specialities include green lentil balls, falafels and nettle soup, from around ₺9 a dish. Some chicken dishes served, too; the only alcohol available is wine. Daily 10am–11pm.

ORTAKÖY

Banyan Salhane Sok 3, off Muallim Naci Cad ☎0212 259 9060, ⓦbanyanrestaurant.com. Asian cuisine is the theme here, everything from Indian to Vietnamese, which makes it stand out from most café-restaurants in the city. The views of Ortaköy mosque and the Bosphorus Bridge from the pretty terrace are stunning, but you pay for them, with mains at ₺39–75. Daily noon–2am.

House Café Salhane Sok 1, off Muallim Naci Cad ⓦ0212 227 2699, ⓦthehousecafe.com. The food is largely aimed at young, affluent and Westernized Turks, with (admittedly upmarket) burgers and pizza a couple of menu staples – along with an expensive (₺40) Sunday brunch. Outdoor eating here has its charms, though, especially if you can grab one of the tables right on the edge of the Bosphorus. Now has branches near Tünel and on İstiklal Cad. Daily 8am–2am.

ASIAN İSTANBUL

★ **Çiya Sofrası & Kebapçi** Güneşlibahçe Sok 43 ☎0216 349 1902, ⓦciyasofrasi.com. "Çiya" means "mountain" in Kurdish, though the inspiration for the food here comes from many different corners of this vast country – and beyond to the Middle East and Balkans. There are actually three restaurants; the two on the right as you approach along pedestrianized Güneşlibahçe street are kebab-orientated, the one on the left focuses on salads, *meze* and stews. Choose your own selection of *meze* and salads and have your plate weighed to learn the price (around ₺10 for a substantial lunch). Daily 10am–midnight.

Kanaat Selmanipak Cad 25, Üsküdar ☎0216 341 5444, ⓦkanaatlokantasi.com.tr. One of the city's more famous *lokantas*, established in 1933, featuring copies of İznik-tile panels from the Selimiye Camii in Edirne and a copper chimney-piece. Meals are reasonably cheap at about ₺12 a head; no alcohol served. Daily 6am–11pm.

Yanyalı Fehmi Lokantası Yağlıka İsmail Sok 1, off Soğütlüçeşme Cad, Kadıköy ☎0216 336 3333. Established back in 1919 by refugees from Greece, this well-run place serves up some of the best food on the Asian side of the Bosphorus – and there's an incredible variety to choose from, with twenty types of soup alone, including non-standards such as okra or spinach. The *çömlek* kebab – meat, aubergine, beans, peppers, onion and garlic oven-cooked in a clay pot – is delicious (₺12). Desserts include *kabak tatlısı* (candied courgette), delicious when, as here, it's done well. No alcohol. Daily 9.30am–10.30pm.

NIGHTLIFE

With such a youthful population, a booming economy and relentless Westernization, it is not surprising that İstanbul is establishing a major reputation for **clubbing**. The best **bars** and **clubs** are in Beyoğlu, Taksim, Ortaköy and the richer Bosphorus suburbs such as Kadıköy. For a more traditional night out, head to a **meyhane** (tavern), where a *fasil* band might accompany your food and bottle of rakı. Alternatively, try a **Türkü bar**, where you can drink and listen to the plaintive sounds of Anatolian folk music. Both *meyhanes* and Türkü bars are enjoying something of a revival of late, but if you want something more familiar there are countless café-bars and modern nightclubs as well.

BARS

Away from conservative Islamic areas like Fatih and Eyüp, İstanbul takes drinkers in its stride, and you'll find bars ranging from the dangerously seedy to the chic and overpriced. Sultanahmet's bars are dull in comparison to buzzing Beyoğlu, where drinking goes on well into the early hours. There's a wide range of bars along the lively streets leading off İstiklal Caddesi, at the Taksim Square end – from jazz joints to student-bars, sophisticated rooftop cafés to throbbing basement rock-bars. At the time of writing, the number of tables set out in many streets had been severely restricted by order of the local municipality, reducing both congestion and atmosphere, but this may well ease in the future.Kadıköy on the Asian side of the Bosphorus boasts several drinking haunts. To reach Kadıköy's studenty/arty Kadife Sokak, walk or take a taxi from the Kadıköy ferry terminal south down Moda Caddesi, until it turns into Doktor Esat Işik Caddesi – Kadife Sokak is on the left. The line between İstanbul's bars and cafés tends to blur, with most open during the day to serve food and coffee, becoming more alcoholic as the evening progresses. A cover charge is often introduced between 10pm and 2am if there is live music.

İSTANBUL LISTINGS

The monthly magazine *Time Out İstanbul* (ensure you buy the English-language version) is available from newsstands all over the city for ₺6. It is the best source of listings and features on what to do and see in the city. Other English-language publications include the bimonthly *İstanbul: The Guide*, available in hotel lobbies or bookshops for ₺6, also with listings and city features. *Cornucopia*, a glossy bimonthly covering the Ottoman arts scene, auctions, galleries and exhibitions, is available from bookshops that stock foreign newspapers and publications.

1

SULTANAHMET

Cheers Akbıyık Cad 20; map p.73. It's been around on busy Akbıyık Cad long enough to know what it's doing – knocking out reasonably priced beer to a mix of impecunious backpackers and strays from the street's posher establishments. It often gets lively, particularly when there's big-screen sport to be watched. Daily 10am–2am.

Cozy Pub Divan Yolu Cad 66 ☎0212 520 0990; map p.73. Situated on a prominent corner plot, this pleasant dark-wood bar has tables out on the street in the warmer months – great for people-watching on hectic Divan Yolu. Beers a reasonable ₺8. Daily 10am–2am.

North Shield Pub Ebusuud Cad 2 ☎0212 527 0931; map pp.86–87. Situated right opposite the Gülhane tram stop and just a short step downhill from the Aya Sofya, this mock-English pub, part of a chain, is usually packed with sports addicts taking in big-screen football, rugby and cricket matches from around the world. Beers ₺10. Daily 11.30am–1.30am.

BEYOĞLU

Arpa General Yazgan Sok 5 ☎0212 249 0550; map pp.102–103. If you're not in the big-money, rooftop-drinking league, this is one of the best places in Beyoğlu. Small and cosy in winter, its summer scene has been curtailed by the outdoor table ban. Crowded with students and alternative types, it serves cheap beer; people-watching and occasional live bands (usually winter only) provide the entertainment. Daily 9am–2am.

James Joyce Irish Pub Irish Centre, Balo Sok 26 ☎0212 224 2013; map pp.102–103. Housed in a wonderfully ornate and rambling nineteenth-century apartment block, the Irish Centre's focal point is this lively pub. There's also a games bar with big-screen sports TV that gets very crowded for big occasions, and live bands play most nights of the week. Daily 1pm–2am.

★ **Leb-i-Derya** Kumbaracı Yokuşu 115/7 ☎0212 293 4989; map pp.102–103. A great place for an early-evening (or early-morning) drink, with fabulous Bosphorus views and chilled-out sounds. It's not cheap, though, at ₺12 for a small beer, and you may be turned away if you look scruffy. There's also a decent food menu if you're peckish. Daily 11am–4am.

Pano Şaraphanesi Kamiriye Sok 9, near Nevizade Sok ☎0212 292 6664; map pp.102–103. Beautifully restored century-old Greek wine bar. Beer, local wine and good-value – if not particularly exciting – food available (*meze* from ₺6, pasta dishes from ₺13 and steaks ₺28 and up). Packed to the rafters on Thurs, Fri and Sat evenings – get here early if you want a seat. Daily 11am–1am.

Pasific Sofyalı Sok ☎0212 292 7642; map pp.102–103. Small, friendly bar with a good selection of rock music and well-priced beer (₺6 for draught). Also shots for ₺5, if that's your thing. It's a struggle to find a seat on the alleyway tables in summer, though the *Kino Garden* next door is run jointly with *Pasific* and has a garden out back. Daily 10am–2am.

Ritim Galata Galata Kulesi Sok 3/C ☎0212 249 0252; map pp.102–103. Just down from the Galata Tower, this mellow bar attracts a more sophisticated crowd than many of the places up in Beyoğlu. In summer a few tables spill out onto the street, and the cosy interior, with a mezzanine floor and exposed brickwork, is great. Large beers cost ₺10, not bad considering the soothing sounds from the DJ, and Turkish-fusion food menu. Daily 10am–2am.

ASIAN İSTANBUL

Isis Kadife Sok 26, Caferağa Mah ☎0216 349 7381. Kadıköy three-storey townhouse that's a café by day and bar-disco at night. Cutting-edge music and good food, plus a garden open during the summer months. Daily 11am–2am.

Karga Kadife Sok 16, Kadıköy ☎0216 449 1725. A self-consciously cool venue on the trendiest street in Asian İstanbul, this grungy/arty place is set in a tall, narrow nineteenth-century townhouse. Part pub (the lower floors) and part art gallery (top floor), it also has a large, pleasant garden out back. Daily 11am–2am.

CLUBS AND LIVE MUSIC

İstanbul's best clubs are bang up to date in terms of design, lighting and atmosphere, while live music – jazz, rock, alternative, blues, R&B and even reggae – is plentiful around the backstreets of Beyoğlu. Expect to spend no less than you would in London, New York or Sydney on a night out. Most places have entry charges at weekends (anything from ₺10 to ₺60), and tend to be open from around 9pm until 2am or 4am. Local and visiting foreign bands also play at a welter of annual festivals – including two jazz festivals, a couple of rock festivals, an international music festival, plus separate dance and techno and blues events.

BEYOĞLU AND AROUND

Babylon Şehbender Sok 3, Asmalımescit ⊕babylon .com.tr; map pp.102–103. Set in a modest-sized but atmospheric bare-brick vault, this is İstanbul's premier live music club with a regular programme of local and foreign groups playing jazz, world, indie and electronica. Ticket prices vary wildly according to the act (booking office across the street daily noon–6pm, or from Biletix); performances usually start around 10pm. Adjoining and part of the setup is *Nublu Babylon*, a smaller venue to showcase new artists. In summer, the action moves to the Aegean coast near İzmir and the venue closes its doors; see website for details. Tues–Thurs 9.30pm–2am, Fri & Sat 10pm–3am; closed in summer.

Dogzstar Kartal Sok 3, İstiklal Cad ⊕dogzstar.com; map pp.102–103. Run by dedicated alternative-music fanatic Taylan, who aims to support Turkish bands of all kinds, from psychobilly to electro-punk. You can see the results at the regular live gigs; the venue itself is spread over three floors, with great views from the terrace. Entry prices vary according to the act. Daily 6pm–5am.

Ghetto Kamer Hatun Cad10, Ⓦghettoist.com; map pp.102–103. A great venue offering an eclectic mix of contemporary music styles, from funk and indie to dance and jazz. A real bonus is the beautifully restored nineteenth-century Greek house in which it is set – complete with original frescoes on a long, barrel-vaulted ceiling. It also boasts a cool terrace, which is free if you are not interested in the act on offer. Entry price varies. Daily 9pm–4am.

Indigo Akarsu Sok 1/2, off İstiklal Cad Ⓦlivingindigo .com; map pp.102–103. This remains the venue of choice for electronica lovers, though it has now embraced a more inclusive policy, and offers a wider range of musical styles. Bigger-name DJs and acts, many international, tend to play Fri and Sat. Mon–Thurs & Sun 10pm–4am, Fri & Sat 11pm–5am.

Jazz Stop Tel Sok 2, off Büyükparmakkapı Sok Ⓦjazzstop .com; map pp.102–103. Stylish bare-brick basement club with steep cover charge – one of İstanbul's leading venues for jazz and flamenco. Owned by the band members of the local jazz group Moğollar, who perform regularly. Performances start about 11pm. Mon–Sat 4.30pm–4am.

★ **Nardis Jazz Club** Galata Kulesi Sok 14, Galata Ⓦnardisjazz.com; map pp.102–103. Run by a couple of enthusiasts, this small, intimate venue is a great introduction to the city's jazz scene, with performances by both local and international artists. The emphasis is on the mainstream, but modern, fusion and ethnic get an airing from time to time. Advance booking recommended. Mon–Thurs sets 9.30pm & 12.30am, Fri & Sat 8pm–2am.

Peyote Kameriye Sok 4, Balık Pazarı Ⓦpeyote.com; map pp.102–103. The city's best place for alternative/ indie types looking for an "underground" scene. In a band themselves, the owners give stage space to upcoming rivals from across the metropolis. There's a lively roof terrace with an eclectic mix of music, live bands play on the second floor, while the first floor is given over to electronica. Beers are a reasonable ₺7 and the (variable) entry charge is not too steep. Daily 10pm–4am.

ORTAKÖY

Q Jazz at Les Ottomans Muallim Naci Cad 163 Ⓦlesottomans.com. If you're not intimidated (or appalled) by the thought of listening to jazz in one of the city's most expensive hotels, this could be for you. The 200-seat Bosphorus-front venue helps to compensate for the incongruity, along with an ever-changing line-up of international jazz artists. Live music starts at 11pm and there's a ₺30 entrance fee. Mon, Tues & Thurs–Sun 7pm–3am.

Reina Muallim Naci Cad 120 Ⓦreina.com.tr. Summer drinking outside until dawn for the bright young things who manage to get through the door. There are dancefloors, video screens and bars all directly overlooking the Bosphorus, and overpriced sushi – early birds get thirty percent off drinks between 6pm and 8pm. June–Sept only, daily 6pm–4am.

GAY BARS AND CLUBS

İstanbul is Turkey's gay capital, with the scene centred on Taksim and Beyoğlu. For information on the gay scene check out Ⓦistanbulgay.com, which gives a rundown of the best gay bars and clubs (including guided cruises of the best venues) and gay-friendly hotels, reviews the sauna cruising scene, and has a section on lesbian İstanbul. Otherwise try Ⓦabsolutesultans.com or the weekly *Time Out İstanbul* reviews of gay and lesbian venues.

CAFÉS

Sugar Café Sakalsalim Çıkmazı 3/A, off İstiklal Cad, Beyoğlu; map pp.102–103. Low-key meeting and hangout joint off the busy main drag, somewhere to decide what you're going to do later on. Daily 11am–1am.

BARS AND CLUBS

Love Dance Point Cumhuriyet Cad 349, Harbiye ☎0212 296 3358; map pp.102–103. Glitzy, hi-tech and spacious club opposite the Military Museum with free admission Wed, ₺25 cover Fri & Sat including one drink. DJs spin a wide range of sounds, from techno to Turkish pop. A proper club rather than a glorified café/bar, it also holds regular parties. Wed 11.30pm–4am, Fri & Sat 11.30pm–5am.

Prive Tarlabasi Bul 28, Taksim ☎0212 235 7999; map pp.102–103. Gay-only dance club, with a devoted following due to its reputation as a pick-up place. The mix of electro and Turkish music will appeal to most punters. Entry Fri & Sat only (₺20 including a drink). This street has a bad reputation in the city – and not just among straights – so take care if you decide to venture out here. Daily 11pm–5am.

Rocinante Cafe Bar Oğut Sok 6/2, Sakızağcı Sok Cad, Beyoğlu ☎0212 244 8219; map pp.102–103. Behind the prominent Ağa Camii (mosque) on İstiklal Caddesi is this popular lesbian-friendly (the owner and many of her friends are lesbian) café-cum-meeting point. Daily 2pm–2am.

X-Large Kallavi Sok 12, off Meşrutiyet Cad, Tepebaşı ☎0212 788 737; map pp.102–103. Housed in a long-defunct historic Beyoğlu cinema, this mainstream but atmospheric venue features a popular drag revue and a massive bar. Locals consider it the most European-style of İstanbul's gay clubs. Wed–Sat 11pm–5am.

1

ARTS, ENTERTAINMENT AND FESTIVALS

İstanbul hosts a decent range of annual cultural **festivals**, and matches other European cities for the breadth of its **arts scene**. State-subsidized theatre, opera and ballet make performances affordable for all, and there's something going on almost every night at venues around the city. Music features heavily over the summer months, when international festivals draw musicians from all over the world.

Tickets Tickets for many cultural events, as well as sporting events, can be purchased online from Biletix (ⓦ biletix.com) or ⓦ pozitif-ist.com. There is also a useful Biletix outlet in D & R books on İstiklal Caddesi.

FILM

Hundreds of cinemas (*sinema*) all over İstanbul show mainly Hollywood releases with Turkish subtitles. Many of the modern complexes are situated in large shopping malls, with the best old-style cinemas in Beyoğlu, once the centre of domestic film production. Most still have a fifteen-minute coffee and cigarette interval. Tickets cost from ₺10, but most cinemas have one or more day(s) midweek where tickets are discounted. The annual International Film Festival (mid-April to May) takes place mainly at cinemas in Beyoğlu.

Cinemaximum İstiklal Cad 24–26, Beyoğlu ☎0212 292 1111, ⓦ afm.com.tr; map pp.102–103. Popular ten-screen cinema not far from Taksim Square, showing the newest films. It's the smartest cinema in Beyoğlu, but lacks character.

City Life City's Mall, Teşvikiye Cad 162, Nişantaşı ☎0212 373 3535, ⓦ citylifecinema.com. Seven-screen, state-of-the-art cinema housed in the retro-style City's Mall shopping centre in upmarket Nişantaşı, with trendy (and expensive) café-bars attached.

Kanyon, Mars Kanyon Mall, Büyukdere Cad 185, Levent ☎0212 353 0814, ⓦ marssinema.com. Not surprisingly, given its location in this ultra-modern shopping mall, the ticket prices are above average, but probably worth it if you want the comfiest seats and best picture and sound quality in town.

Şafak Yeniçeriler Cad, Çemberlitaş ☎0212 516 2660, ⓦ ozenfilm.com.tr. The closest cinema to Sultanahmet lies buried deep within the bowels of a shopping centre, with seven screens showing the latest Western and Turkish releases.

THEATRES AND CONCERT HALLS

There are regular classical music, ballet and opera performances in İstanbul. The main annual event is the International Music Festival during June and July, which includes jazz, classical and world music concerts, as well as performances by the İstanbul State Symphony Orchestra. Theatre is popular, but it's mostly Turkish plays that are performed on the thirty or so stages in the city. One of the main venues for state-funded companies, Atatürk Cultural Centre in Taksim, was closed at the time of writing for major repairs. Information on all music and

theatre events, and on the various cultural festivals, is available from the İstanbul Foundation for Culture and Arts (IKSV, ⓦ iksv.org).

Akbank Culture and Arts Centre (Akbanksanat) İstiklal Cad 8/A, Beyoğlu ☎0212 252 3500, ⓦ akbanksanat.com; map pp.102–103. Multi-purpose centre including a café, art gallery, dance studio, music room, library and theatre. The centre also hosts film festivals and organizes the annual Akbank Jazz Festival (see p.111). Tues–Sat 11am–7pm.

Borusan Arts and Cultural Centre İstiklal Cad 421, Tünel, Beyoğlu ☎0212 292 0655, ⓦ borusansanat .com; map pp.102–103. Home to the Borusan Philharmonic Orchestra, one of Turkey's most successful private orchestras, which performs two monthly concerts (tickets ₺16–24). Also boasts one of the country's most extensive CD libraries.

Cemal Reşit Rey (CRR) Darulbedayi Cad 1, Harbiye ☎0212 231 5497, ⓦ crrks.org. Chamber music, classical, jazz and Turkish music, plus regular performances by visiting international orchestras. Venue for the International Music Festival in June and the CRR Piano Festival in December. The season runs Oct–May, with ticket prices at ₺8–16; no credit cards. Oct–May daily 8pm.

Garajistanbul Kaymakan Reşit Bey Sok 11, off Yeniciler Cad, Beyoğlu ☎0212 244 4499, ⓦ www .garajistanbul.com; map pp.102–103. Trendy, stripped-down performing-arts venue in a former underground car park just off Galatasaray Meydanı. This is as cutting-edge as it gets in İstanbul, with workshops, films and art projects, modern dance, theatre and other performances. With seating limited to 250, it's worth booking for most things. Performances Sept–June only.

Süreyya Opera Bahariye Cad 29, Kadıköy ☎0216 346 1531, ⓦ www.sureyyaoperasi.org; tickets ⓦ dobgm .gov.tr. Set in a gorgeous, beautifully restored opera house built in 1924, this is a delightfully intimate place to watch opera, ballet and classical music, and a rare oasis of culture on the Asian side of the Bosphorus. Performances Oct–May only.

TURKISH MUSIC AND CABARET

A night of traditional Turkish music in a friendly bar-restaurant is not to be missed. Most venues offer either a kind of Türkü (folk) music, usually played on a *bağlama* (long-necked stringed lute), or *fasil*, generally played by gypsy bands and heavy on the violin with *ud* (lute), *darabuka* (drum) and maybe a *zurna* (clarinet). As well as

İSTANBUL FESTIVALS

The annual festival calendar is pretty full, especially between April and October. The most important modern art event is the **International İstanbul Biennial**, held on odd-numbered years. Organized by IKSV, the İstanbul Foundation for Culture and Arts (Ⓦ iksv.org), it uses venues ranging from historic buildings like the Topkapı Palace to urban-chic warehouses.

APRIL

International Film Festival Ⓦ film.iksv.org/en. Turkish, European and Hollywood movies premiere at İstanbul's cinemas, mainly in Beyoğlu, plus the best of the non-English-speaking world's releases from the previous year.

Tulip Festival Week-long festival honouring the national flower, including concerts, arts events and competitions at different locations around the city. Over three million bulbs flower across the city, planted by the municipality.

MAY

Chill Out Ⓦ chilloutfest.com. Dance and electronica festival held in the incongruous surroundings of ultra-posh Kemer Golf and Country Club in Belgrade Forest.

Conquest Celebrations Ⓦ ibb.gov.tr. Week-long celebration of the Ottoman conquest of old Constantinople (May 29, 1453) – concerts by the Ottoman Mehter military band, fancy-dress processions and fireworks.

Freshtival Ⓦ millerfreshtival.com. Held in Maçka's Kücükçiftlik Parkı, this festival mixes indie, dance and rock sounds, with both international and local acts and DJs.

International Puppet Festival ☎ 0212 232 0224. A celebration of Turkish Shadow Theatre, or *karağoz* – silent puppets perform behind a two-dimensional screen.

International Theatre Festival Ⓦ iksv.org. The year's best Turkish plays (both local avant-garde and established theatre groups), and performances by visiting foreign theatres.

JUNE/JULY

Efes Pilsen One Love Ⓦ efespilsenonelove.com. Moderately alternative city-centre weekend-long festival, usually held at Santralistanbul, with plenty of DJ-led dance sets and performances from international bands such as Röyksopp and Klaxons, plus assorted home-grown acts.

The International Music Festival Ⓦ iksv.org. This hugely successful festival was launched in 1973 to celebrate Turkey's fifty years of independence and brings top-notch orchestras and soloists from all over the world to perform in such atmospheric venues as the church of Aya Irene.

Sonisphere Ⓦ sonispherefestivals.com. Two-day head-banging event for (mainly Turkish) heavy-metal lovers.

JULY/AUGUST

International Jazz Festival Ⓦ iksv.org. Two weeks of gigs and jamming sessions from world-class performers (with the definition of jazz stretched to include rock artists such as Lou Reed and Marianne Faithful).

Rumeli Hisarı Fortress Concerts Nightly summer concerts within the walls of this Ottoman fortification overlooking the Bosphorus – a varied programme from classical to rock.

Rock N' Coke Ⓦ rockncoke.com. Attracts major international acts – often a little past their prime – to the (defunct) Grand Prix track on the Asian side of the city.

SEPTEMBER

İstanbul Arts Fair Ⓦ tuyap.com. A week-long fair selling the work of some fifty or so İstanbul galleries and visiting foreign artists – paintings, sculptures, pottery and fabrics.

International İstanbul Biennial Ⓦ iksv.org. Multimedia contemporary arts festival that usually runs mid-September to the first week in November. Held odd years: 2013, 2015, etc.

OCTOBER/NOVEMBER

Akbank International Jazz Festival Ⓦ akbanksanat.com. Two-week festival concentrating on traditional jazz, with performers such as Dave Holland and Henry Threadgill. Events include film screenings, informal jamming sessions and drum workshops. Varied venues include the Byzantine church of Aya Irene and the Babylon Performance Centre in Beyoğlu.

Efes Pilsen Blues Festival Two-day late-night blues festival – a showcase of new local talent and famous foreign bands.

1

the places around Beyoğlu listed below, most of the fish restaurants in Kumkapı have live *fasil* music in the evenings. Expect to pay ₺50–90 per head for a meal and a couple of drinks (sometimes included in the charge) in a restaurant that provides traditional live music. Cabaret is probably the most expensive and least authentic way to develop a feel for the Orient. Stick to the more established venues, some of the best of which are reviewed below, otherwise you may be overcharged for anything you eat or drink. Notre also that belly dancers expect to be given generous amounts of money by foreign tourists. Unless otherwise stated, the cabaret venues have daily performances, with dinner served at 7.45pm, and the show running from 8.30pm to around midnight.

FASIL AND TÜRKÜ VENUES

Andon Sıraselviler Cad 89 ☎ 0212 251 0222; map pp.102–103. Popular with İstanbul's fashionable set, with five overwhelming floors, each with their own personality: the first-floor Pera bar has music mixed by the city's top DJs; the second floor has a *Wine House* with local and imported wines and cheese; live Turkish music and belly dancing features in the third-floor *Müdavim Bar*; and the fourth-floor *meyhane* features 101 types of *meze* accompanied by *fasil* music. Capping it all off are the stunning views from the fifth-floor roof-terrace restaurant. A fixed-price menu of ₺70 includes unlimited local alcoholic drinks; booking advised. Daily noon–2am.

Mektup Imam Adnan Sok 20, off İstiklal Cad ⓦmektup .com; map pp.102–103. The food on offer here is limited in range but perfectly passable. More importantly, the *Türkü* music is of a very high standard – it has seen sets by notable artists such as Ebru Destan and Tuğbay Özay. Voted the best *Türkü* bar in the country by the *Hüriyet* newspaper, so

booking is advisable, especially at weekends. Daily noon–4am.

Munzur Hasnün Galip Sok 9, off İstiklal Cad ☎ 0212 245 4669; map pp.102–103. The Munzur mountains, away to the east in the heartland of Turkey's Kurdish Alevî population (the Alevî have spawned the nation's best *bağlama* players), are the inspiration for this no-frills but lively Türkü bar. The food is OK, the drinks not too pricey, and when things get going there are plenty of linked bodies dancing around the tables. Daily 6pm–4am.

CABARET VENUES

Hodja Paşa Culture Centre Hodjapaşa Hamam Sok 3/B, Sirkeci ⓦhodjapasha.com; map pp.86–87. Housed in a beautifully restored Ottoman hamam, with the dance area and seats atmospherically set beneath an exposed brick dome. A 70min show introduces the visitor to music and dances from all parts of the Ottoman Empire for ₺50, including an interval drink. There's also a more specialist whirling dervish ceremony put on by sufis from the Galata Mevlevihanesi. Whirling dervish ceremony Mon, Wed & Fri–Sun 7.30pm; regular show Tues & Thurs 8pm, Sat & Sun 9pm.

Orient House President Hotel, Tiyatro Cad 27, Beyazit ⓦorienthouseistanbul.com; map pp.86–87. Traditional Turkish and folk music, plus belly dancing. A four-course meal with wine and show is ₺120 a head (without food ₺80). Daily 8pm–midnight.

Sultana's Cumhuriyet Cad 40/D, Harbiye ⓦsultanas -nights.com; map pp.102–103. Belly dancing and folklore show, costing €70 with dinner, unlimited local drinks plus free transport from any hotel (cheaper rates can be negotiated if you just turn up at the door). A deal without dinner but including one drink costs €40. Daily 8pm–midnight.

SHOPPING

Shopping in İstanbul is an experience. Whether or not it's a pleasant one depends on your ability to ignore the hustlers when you're not in the mood, and to bargain hard when you are. Don't miss the **Grand Bazaar** (see p.89), a hive of over four thousand little shops. Equally interesting shopping districts scattered around the city include **İstiklal Caddesi** for clothes, **Nişantaşı** for upmarket international fashion; and the **Spice Bazaar** (Mısır Çarşısı) and its environs for spices and sweets. Out of the centre, **shopping malls** have taken off in a big way, good for homeware and clothes. The covered bazaar is credit-card friendly, as are all shops except the smallest of grocers (*bakals*) or kiosks.

ANTIQUES AND BRIC-A-BRAC

If you're expecting to find bargain antiques, you'll probably be disappointed. The average İstanbullu may care little for the old and worn, but a city of over 15 million holds enough who do to ensure buoyant prices. Bear in mind that you're supposed to have clearance from the Museums Directorate to take anything out of the country that's over one hundred years old (see pp.78–79). The best places to find twentieth-century items, up to 1980s retro stuff, are the streets leading down from İstiklal Caddesi in Çukurcuma, or the Horohor Antiques market in Aksaray.

Abdullah Sandal Bedestan 6, Kapılı Çarşısı; map p.90. Established in 1880 and run by the fluent English-speaking Pol Şalabi, this small shop stocks a treasure trove of icons, jewellery from 1800 to the 1950s, and much else besides. Mon–Sat 9am–7pm.

Horhor Antique Market Yorum Kırık Tulumba Sok 13/22, Aksaray; map pp.86–87. Over two hundred bric-a-brac and antique shops in a multi-storey building in the drab suburb of Aksaray, a 15min walk from the Aksaray metro station. Daily 10am–8pm.

Kadıköy Antika Çarşısı Tellalzade Sok, Çakıroğlu İş

Han, Kadıköy. Tellalzade Sokak has a number of small shops selling all kinds of retro and bric-a-brac items, plus some genuine antiques. An excursion here fits in well with food souvenir shopping and the wonderful *Çiya* restaurant. Daily 10am–7pm.

Levant Corner of Ağa Hamam Cad & Turnacıbaşı Cad, off İstiklal Cad, Beyoğlu; map pp.102–103. Eclectic range of wares in a funky shop, from Greek Orthodox icons to 1950s tin toys, and from Erickson phones to kitsch figurines. Mon–Sat 10am–7pm.

Leyla Altıpatlar Sok 10, Çukurcuma; map pp.102–103. This well-established shop stocks all manner of antique clothing, from the late nineteenth century to the 1960s, plus all sorts of cloth-related items – including embroidered cushions and throws – collected by enthusiast Leyla Seyhanlı. Mon–Sat 10am–7pm.

Müstamel Eşya Evi Turnacıbaşı Cad 38/1, off İstiklal Cad, Beyoğlu; map pp.102–103. Spread over two floors, this retro-orientated shop is run by friendly, architect-trained Aslıhan Kendiroğlu, and concentrates on the 1950s to the 1970s, from bakelite phones to chrome light-fixtures, and from furniture to clothes. Mon–Sat 9am–7pm.

BOOKS, MAPS AND PRINTS

The most traditional place to buy books in the city is Sahaflar Çarşısı (old book market) at Beyazit, between the Grand Bazaar and Beyazit Camii, which stocks numerous new titles on both İstanbul and Turkey in general – in English – as well as some secondhand books. For the widest range of books, Beyoğlu is the best bet, either on or just off İstiklal Caddesi; there are also several secondhand booksellers around here.

Galeri Kayseri Divan Yolu Cad 58, Sultanahmet w galerikayseri.com; map p.73. The biggest distributor of English-language books in Turkey, with a vast range of books on Ottoman history and all other imaginable Turkish topics. Daily 9am–8.30pm.

Greenhouse Bookshop Café Moda Cad 28, Kadıköy. The best bookshop on the Asian shore, managed by an English woman and stocking an excellent range of books in English, including an extensive children's department. Mon & Wed–Sat 10am–6.30pm.

Homer Yeni Çarşısı Cad 28, Beyoğlu; map pp.102–103. A wonderful selection of anything archeological, historical and cultural written on Turkey, plus the odd *Rough Guide*. Mon–Sat 10am–7.30pm.

Pandora İstiklal Cad, Büyükparmakkapı Sok 3, Beyoğlu; map pp.102–103. Excellent selection of foreign-language books on three storeys; carries some gay literature and will order books on request. Mon–Thurs 10am–8pm, Fri & Sat 10am–9pm, Sun 1–8pm.

Robinson Crusoe İstiklal Cad 389, Tünel, Beyoğlu; map pp.102–103. Extensive, reasonably priced collection of English-, French- and German-language books, as well as guides and maps. Mon–Sat 10am–9pm.

CLOTHES

Many Western high-street stores produce their clothes in Turkey, and outlets across the city specialize in seconds and production overruns at bargain prices. Fakes abound, so check thoroughly before purchasing. The best places to look are the arcades off İstiklal Caddesi. Turkish stores (with multiple branches) to watch out for include: Beymen, Damat Tween, Homestore, Karaca, La Luna, Mudo City, Mudo, and Yargıcı. Vakko is one of the most reputable fashion chains in İstanbul; Vakkorama is its youth-market offshoot.

RETRO AND BARGAIN CLOTHES

Atlas Pasajı Off İstiklal Cad 209, Beyoğlu; map pp.102–103. This trendy and historic arcade behind the Atlas Cinema has bargain clothing – plus alternative/street-style clothes outlets, funky jewellery shops, piercing places and CD/DVD shops, and an amazing array of original film posters in a couple of the basement stores. Daily 9.30am–11pm.

Beyoğlu İş Merkezi İstiklal Cad 331–369; map pp.102–103. Three floors of bargain end-of-line and seconds clothing, with the odd genuine bargain for the persistent. Daily 10am–10pm.

Terkoz Çıkmaz Off İstiklal Cad, Beyoğlu; map pp.102–103. This side street off İstiklal Cad – next to the Paşabahçe glass store, down towards Tünel – is crammed with stalls selling overruns that bear British, French and German high-street names. Daily 10am–10pm.

By Retro Suriye Pasajı, İstiklal Cad, Beyoğlu ☎0212 245 6420, w byretro.com; map pp.102–103. Set in the basement of this historic arcade is what claims to be Europe's largest secondhand clothing shop. Owner Hakan Vardar scours Europe for vintage clothes and there are rails and rails of the results here. Daily 10am–10.30pm.

HIGH-STREET AND DESIGNER CLOTHES

Beyman Akmerkez Shopping Mall, Etiler. Quality chain store for tailored men and women's suits, dress shirts, silk ties and scarves and other accessories for the well-turned-out executive. Daily 10am–10pm.

Crash Galip Dede Cad 35, Galata; map pp.102–103. A small, alternative outlet in up-and-coming Galata, with a good range of individually designed T-shirts, hoodies and shorts – plus some secondhand retro stuff. Mon–Sat 10am–9pm.

Mavi İstiklal Cad 117, Beyoğlu; map pp.102–103; and in all shopping malls. Gap-inspired jeans label, good-quality denimwear, T-shirts (including a good range of "cool" İstanbul designs), sweat tops and funky bags. Daily 10am–10pm.

Roll Turnacıbaşı Sok 13/1, off İstiklal Cad, Beyoğlu; map pp.102–103. The outlet of choice for indie types who want cutting-edge street fashion. Much of their output is generic, but look out for the range of tongue-in-cheek T's

1

emblazoned with "legendary" Turkish cars such as the Murat 124 and the Anadol. Also stocks secondhand retro-style clothing. Daily 10am–10pm.

Vakko İstiklal Cad 123–125, Beyoğlu; map pp.102–103; Akmerkez Shopping Mall, Etiler, and other branches; ⓦ www.vakko.com.tr. Classy fifty-year-old Turkish fashion label renowned for its sense of style and use of fine fabrics. Vakkorama is the younger version aimed at wealthy teenagers. At the *Vakko Sales Store*, at Seylülislam Hayri Cad in Eminönü, items can be picked up for a quarter of the regular price. Daily 10am–10pm.

Yargıcı Akmerkez Shopping Mall, Etiler and other branches. Turkey's answer to Marks & Spencer – well-made and reasonably priced clothing from work suits to sportswear and underwear. Daily 10am–10pm.

CARPETS AND KILIMS

Adnan & Hasan Halıcılar Cad 89–92, Grand Bazaar ⓦ adnanandhasan.com; map p.90. A wide range of modern and antique kilims and carpets from a reputable dealership, established in 1978, with Ushak and Hereke carpets vying for shop space with Anatolian and Caucasian kilims. Mon–Sat 9am–7pm.

Ethnicon Takkeciler Sok 58–60, Grand Bazaar ⓦ ethnicon.com; map p.90. Fixed prices for kilims made in the traditional way (with natural dyes and no child labour) but with contemporary (often large, geometric blocks of colour) styling. Mon–Sat 9am–7pm.

Şişko Osman Zincirli Han, Grand Bazaar ☎0212 528 3548, ⓦ siskoosman.com; map p.90. Arguably the most knowledgeable dealer in the Grand Bazaar, reputable Şişko ("Fat") Osman's family origins are in the east of Turkey, but he has been flogging top-quality rugs to all-comers (including the rich and famous) here for many years. Over sixty percent of his clients are Turks, which gives some idea of the quality of the (mainly) dowry pieces on offer here. His kilims range from €400 to €2500 and carpets €500 to €2500 – excluding the more expensive genuine period pieces, some dating back to the eighteenth century, stocked in one of his four adjacent shops. Mon–Sat 9am–7pm.

Tradition Rubiye Han 11/12, Kürkçüler Sok, Grand Bazaar ☎0212 520 7907; map p.90. Opened in 1988 and co-run by French woman Florence Heilbron, this fine establishment has a very good reputation, lots of repeat customers (including a coterie of French diplomats and politicians) and sells pieces from €50 to €10,000. Mon–Sat 9am–7pm.

Yörük Kürkçüler Cad 17, Grand Bazaar; map p.90. Run by Ersoy, whose family came to the city from the Caucasus in 1864 via the Central Anatolian town of Kayseri. The stock runs from chemical-dyed pieces for as little as €80 to vintage dowry pieces up to €5000. Very reliable. Mon–Sat 9am–7pm.

FOOD AND SPICES

İstanbul is a great place to stock up on herbs and spices, most obviously in the Mısır Çarşısı (Spice Bazaar), though the streets roundabout it, and Güneşlibahçe Sokak in Kadıköy, are far better value. Dried fruits are also great value and delicious. Two specialities to look out for are *nar ekşisi*, the viscous pomegranate syrup used so liberally in many Turkish salads, sold in small bottles, and *pekmez*, a sweet topping for yoghurt, usually made from either grapes or mulberries. Turkish coffee (*Türk kahvesi*) is about as traditional a Turkish product as you can get, though you'll need to buy a small pan known as a *kahve tenceresi* if you want to make it properly back home. Then, of course, there is *lokum*, known in the West as Turkish delight.

Ali Muhidin Hacı Bekir Hamidiye Cad 83, Eminönü; map pp.86–87. Founded in 1777, this is the best place in the city to buy Turkish delight – choose from over twenty varieties – and more unusual delicacies such as *fındıklı ezmesi* (hazelnut marzipan). The interior is wonderful, with an eye-catching array of sugary treats displayed on period wooden shelves and in glass-fronted cabinets. Daily 9am–9pm.

Güllüoğlu Mumhane Cad 171, Karaköy; map pp.102–103. Arguably the best *baklava* in the city, delicious, buttery and nut-filled. If you're looking to take some home, this is the place to buy it – not only is it the best, but it's not so syrupy as other brands and therefore less likely to leak over your hand luggage. Daily 10am–midnight.

Kurukahveci Mehmet Efendi Tahmis Sok 66, Eminönü; map pp.86–87. There are always big queues outside this wonderful paean to the aromatic coffee bean. Started in 1871, it's now housed in a rare (for this city) and impressive Art Deco building west of the Spice Bazaar. Sells beans and powder for Turkish and filter coffees, plus *sahlep*, the ground-orchid-root drink so popular in İstanbul in the winter. Mon–Sat 9am–7pm.

Mısır Çarşısı Eminönü; map pp.86–87. To choose between the myriad purveyors of different spices, herbs, herbal teas, Turkish delight, nuts and dried-fruits in the historic Spice Bazaar would be meaningless – don't be afraid to try a taste before you buy. Daily 9am–7pm.

GIFTS AND HANDICRAFTS

In their own way just as authentic as the traditional Ottoman crafts are the modern twists on old designs sold in upmarket household goods stores such as Paşabahçe – especially glassware.

Abdulla Halıcılar Cad 53, Kapalı Çarşı; map p.90. Restrained design is the key to this chic store selling handmade olive-oil-based soaps, bath wraps (*peştemal*), bed linen, fluffy towels and the like – it tweaks traditional products to fit the tastes of the city's new elite and Western visitors alike. Mon–Sat 9am–7pm.

Cocoon Küçük Aya Sofya Cad 13; map p.73. Four floors showcasing gorgeously hued and patterned felt hats, bags, animals and even jewellery, plus a wide range of traditional Central Asian textiles, carpets and kilims. It's all very tastefully done and the prices are not too unreasonable. There's a smaller shop in the Arasta Bazaar. Daily 9am–7pm.

Felt in Love Camekan Sok 2, Galata; map pp.102–103. Adorable handmade figurines made entirely out of felt. The whirling dervish statuettes are obvious eye-catchers, while everyone from Santa Claus to Jesus has been immortalized in hand-sewn felt. Daily 9.30am–7pm.

İstanbul Handicrafts Centre Kabasakal Cad 5, Sultanahmet; map p.73. Restored *medrese* – an extension to the *Yeşil Ev Hotel* – where artists and craftsmen keep alive traditional skills such as ebru marbling, calligraphy, lace-making and embroidery. Daily 10am–7pm.

İznik Classics Arasta Çarşısı 67, Sultanahmet; map p.73. Some of the best examples of İznik tiles you'll see anywhere, beautifully displayed in this small shop in the Arasta Bazaar (there are other outlets in the Grand Bazaar and on nearby Utangaç Sokak). The tiles are hand-made by different artists, and all reflect the high quality of the finest period of İznik pottery and are consequently expensive, with prices from ₺120 and up. Daily: summer 9am–9pm, winter 9am–7pm.

Jennifer's Hamam Arasta Bazaar, Sultanahmet; map p.73. All the textiles here are made from organic cotton, linen or silk, and woven by hand on traditional looms. Prices are a little above average because of this, but the product is top-notch, with a fabulous range of *pestemals*, fluffy towels and scarves on offer. The owner is a knowledgeable Canadian. Daily 9am–8pm.

Mudo Pera İstiklal 401, Beyoğlu; map pp.102–103. Worth entering just to see its gorgeous Art Nouveau interior, this long-established outlet sells a range of upmarket giftware as well as quality clothing. Mon–Sat 10am–7.30pm.

Necdat Danış Yağlıkçılar Sok, Kapalı Çarşısı; map p.90. This place has been selling hand-woven textiles for over forty years, and has an excellent reputation for its keen prices and wide range of scarves, peştemals, tablecloths and reams of gorgeous fabrics. They supplied the textiles used in the Hollywood film, *Troy*. Mon–Sat 9am–7pm.

LEATHER

Note that you run less chance of getting ripped off if you shop at one of the classier outlets listed below, rather than in the Grand Bazaar.

Derimod Akmerkez Mall, Nisbetiye Cad, Etiler. Excellent-quality leather goods – coats, jackets, bags, shoes and other accessories. Classic rather than cutting-edge, but then most people don't want to make a short-lived fashion mistake at these prices. Daily 10am–10pm.

Koç Deri Kürkçüler Cad 22/46, Kapalı Çarşı; map p.90. Established in 1960, this specialist leather shop in the Grand Bazaar runs up stuff for the likes of Armani and Dolce&Gabbana. Needless to say, it's not cheap, but it does have a good reputation – your wallet may be considerably lighter after a purchase, but you won't have been "done". Mon–Sat 9am–7pm.

Matraş Akmerkez Mall, Nisbetiye Cad, Etiler. Everything in leather from this quality Turkish store, including wallets, handbags, belts and briefcases. Daily 10am–8pm.

MUSIC AND MUSICAL INSTRUMENTS

Turkish music aside, you'll find a good general selection of world music, classical, pop and jazz in the music shops listed below, and in the many outlets on İstiklal Caddesi and in the shopping malls. Traditional musical instruments are on sale in the Grand Bazaar, though prices are much better at any one of the myriad instrument shops on and around Galipdede Caddesi, near the upper Tünel station in Beyoğlu.

D & R Kanyon Mall. Chain that stocks a decent range of traditional and contemporary Turkish sounds, as well as foreign CDs, DVDs, computer accessories, books, magazines and games. Other branches across the city. Daily 10am–10pm.

Dore Müzik Şahdeğirmeni Sok 3/B, just off Galipdede Cad, Galata; map pp.102–103. One of several shops selling İstanbul-made cymbals alongside various major drum brands and some traditional Turkish percussion items. Daily 10am–7pm.

Lale Plak Galipdede Cad 1, Tünel, Beyoğlu; map pp.102–103. Funky old-style music store, the best place for traditional Turkish music CDs but even more so for jazz. The staff know their stuff – aided, no doubt, by the continuity of a business that's been going for nigh on fifty years. Daily 10am–7pm.

Naturel Müzik Galipdede Cad 103/B, Beyoğlu; map pp.102–103. A good choice on "music alley", stocked with reasonably priced quality guitars, *bağlama*, *saz*, *ud*, *darasbuka* and other traditional Turkish instruments. Daily 10am–7pm.

SHOPPING MALLS

Looked at in a positive way, an American-style mall is just a modern version of a bazaar – and while their food courts may boast a *McDonald's* or *Burger King*, they hold far more outlets knocking out traditional Turkish fare such as *pide*, *lahmacun* and *köfte*.

Cevahir Büyükdere Cad 22, Şişli ⓦ istanbulcevahir .com. Conveniently located close to Levent metro, this is said to be the largest mall in Europe. Set over six storeys, it's very popular with İstanbullus, and boasts the inevitable multiplex. Daily 10am–10pm.

City's Mall Teşvikiye Cad 162, Nişantaşı ⓦ citysnisantasi .com. Upmarket addition to the city's mall scene, well

1

designed, with sleek Art Deco lines. It's exclusive and mainly fashion-orientated – think Louis Vuitton, Dolce&Gabbana, Jean-Paul Gaultier and the like. There's an attached luxury multi-screen cinema and a few posh eateries. Daily 10am–10pm.

Kanyon Büyükdere Cad 185, Levent ⓦ kanyon.com.tr. Take the metro to Levent for this "open-air" canyon-shaped, four-storey, state-of-the-art shopping mall. It features the most popular Western consumer chains and has an extremely plush cinema. Daily 10am–10pm.

STREET MARKETS

For a lively atmosphere it's worth heading out to one of the city's famous street markets. Most now concentrate

on fresh fruit, vegetables, olives, cheese and other foodstuffs –along with cheap (often fake designer-ware) clothing and household essentials.

Beşiktaş Pazarı Beşiktaş. Saturday bazaar held in a warren of streets to either side of Şair Nedim Cad (about 10min from the ferry terminal). It's pot luck what you'll find, as just about any kind of clothing can turn up here. Sat 9am–dusk.

Çarşamba Pazarı Fatih; map p.97. Held every Wednesday and occupying the narrow streets close to Fatih Cami, this is the most authentic of the city's markets, but better for fruit, vegetables and the like than bargain clothing. Wed 8am–dusk.

DIRECTORY

Banks and exchange Exchange offices (*döviz*) around Eminönü, Sultanahmet and Taksim, and on most main city thoroughfares, change cash. Most don't charge commission, but check first to confirm; daily 9am–8pm (sometimes later in peak season). There are also exchange offices at the airport (24hr), Esenler *otogar* (daily 8.30am–11pm) and Sirkeci station (daily 9am–5pm). Opening hours for banks are Mon–Fri 9am–12.30pm and 1.30–5pm, though the larger branches of Garanti Bankası stay open through lunch; major banks have ATMs, some of which also dispense euros. Bank rates are generally better than *döviz*, especially at the Ziraat Bankası.

Consulates Australia, Asker Ocağı Cad 15, Elmadağ, Şişli (☎ 0212 243 1333); Canada, Tekfen Tower, 209 Büyükdere Cad, Levent 4 (☎ 0212 385 9700); New Zealand, İnönü Cad 48/3, Taksim (☎ 0212 244 0272); South Africa (Honorary Consul), Alarko Centre, Musallim Naci Cad 113–115, Ortaköy (☎ 0212 260 378); UK, Meşrutiyet Cad 34, Tepebaşı, Beyoğlu (☎ 0212 334 6400); US, Kaplıcalar Mevkii Sok 2, İstinye (☎ 0212 335 9000).

Dentists The main alternatives to the practices in the German and American hospitals (see below), both with English-speaking staff, are Prodent-Can Ergene, Valikonağı Cad 109/5, Nişantaşı (☎ 0212 230 4635), and Reha Sezgin, Halaskargazi Cad 48/9, Harbiye (☎ 0212 240 3322).

Emergencies Ambulance ☎ 112; Fire ☎ 110; Police ☎ 155.

Hospitals The Taksim First Aid Hospital (Taksim İlkyardim Hastanesi) at Sıraselviler Cad 112, Taksim (☎ 0212 252 4300), is state-run and deals with emergencies only; patients are often referred on to one of the hospitals listed below. For emergencies, as well as regular doctor's appointments, private foreign hospitals are better, though more expensive than the state hospitals, which are understaffed and overcrowded. One of the city's best equipped is the American Hospital (Amerikan Hastanesi), Güzelbahçe Sok 20, Nişantaşı (☎ 0212 311 2000, ⓦ www .amerikanhastanesi.org). The German Hospital, at

Sıraselviler Cad 119, Taksim (☎ 0212 293 2150, ⓦ www .almanhastanesi.com.tr; map pp.102–103), also has a dental and eye clinic.

Internet access Almost all İstanbul hotels and hostels have wi-fi and/or an internet terminal for guests to use. Many cafés also have wi-fi, and there are internet cafés all over town.

Left luggage Left-luggage offices (*Emanet* in Turkish) can be found at Atatürk airport (open 24hr, ₺15 standard-size bags, ₺20 large bags). Esenler and Harem *otogars* and Sirkeci and Haydarpaşa train stations also have left-luggage facilities.

Pharmacies Pharmacies (*Eczane*) are found everywhere and Turkish pharmacists are qualified to give injections, take blood pressure and treat minor wounds. In each İstanbul neighbourhood they take turns in providing a 24hr service called *Nöbetçi*. At night, the *Nöbetçi* rota is posted on the window of the other pharmacies.

Police Reports of theft or loss should be made to the Tourist Police, in a prominent blue wooden building at Yerebatan Cad 6, Sultanahmet (☎ 0212 527 4503); there are English-speaking officers on the premises 24hr daily. Any commercial misdealings should be reported to the *Zabita* (market police) offices found all over town, including a handy one in Sultanahmet, at the far end of the Hippodrome.

Post offices The main post office (PTT) is on Büyük Posthane Cad in Sirkeci, not far from the train station (daily 8.30am–5.30pm for full postal services, 24hr section for stamps and phonecalls). Other branch offices, including that at Cumhuriyet Cad in Taksim Square, are open daily 8.30am–12.30pm & 1.30–5pm. Smaller branch offices are usually open Mon–Fri 8am–3pm.

Swimming pools For a substantial fee (₺50 up to well over ₺100 at weekends) visitors can use the pools in major hotels including *Ceylan Intercontinental*, Asker Ocağı Cad 1, Taksim, which has the great advantage of being centrally located in Taksim, with a large, heated outdoor pool and pool bar. The expensive *Cirağan Palace Hotel Kempinski*, Ciragan Cad 32, Beşiktaş, has indoor and outdoor pools; the *Hilton* on Cumhuriyet Cad, Harbiye, has a fitness centre as well; and the monstrous *Ritz Carlton* on Asker Ocağı Cad in Elmadağ has indoor and outdoor lap pools, plus stunning views over the Bosphorus and the rest of the city.

Telephones İstanbul has two phone-number prefixes, one for Europe, one for Asia, which must be used when calling the opposite shore; Europe ☎0212, Asia ☎0216. Local and international calls can be made from any public booth, at the PTTs (post offices) or TT (Türk Telekom) centres. Useful clusters of booths can be found in Sultanahmet, Taksim Square and Sirkeci train station. Most accept "Smart" phonecards, which can be bought at PTT counters, newsagent kiosks and shops.

Travel agents Travel agents are concentrated along Divan Yolu Cad in Sultanahmet and Cumhuriyet Cad in Taksim. Most can book destinations anywhere in Turkey, and arrange hotel stays, car rental and transfers to the airport or bus station: try the reliable Turista Travel, Divan Yolu Cad 16 (☎0212 518 6570, ⓦturistatravel.com). For budget tours, bus tickets and backpacker travel, contact Backpackers Travel, Yeni Akbiyik Cad 22, Sultanahmet (☎0212 638 6343, ⓦbackpackerstravel.com).

Along the Bosphorus

The 30km strait known as the **Bosphorus** divides Europe and Asia and connects the Marmara and Black seas, its width varying from 660m to 4.5km. Its name derives from the Greek myth of Io, lover of Zeus, whom the god transformed into a cow to conceal her from his jealous wife Hera. She plunged into the straits to escape a gadfly, hence Bosphorus, or "Ford of the Cow".

Around eighty thousand cargo ships, oil tankers and ocean liners pass through the strait each year, while for residents and visitors alike the Bosphorus remains İstanbul's most important transport artery. The passenger ferries and sea buses that weave their way up and down from shore to shore provide one of the city's real highlights: along the way are imperial palaces and ancient fortresses interspersed with small fishing villages and wooden *yalıs* (waterside mansions). Despite its pollution the Bosphorus is also full of fish – from swordfish to *hamsi* (a small fish belonging to the anchovy family).

The European shore

The **European shore** is very built up, as far as the second Bosphorus bridge. The villages turned suburbs of **Arnavutköy** and **Bebek**, popular haunts of the rich, are pretty enough when viewed from a boat. Further north, the fish restaurants in the villages of **Sariyer** and **Rumeli Kavağı** make pleasant destinations for lunch or dinner. West of Sariyer, the **Belgrade Forest** is İstanbul's nearest tract of woodland, offering quiet, rural surroundings.

Arnavutköy

North of Ortaköy, the coast road runs under the 1km-long **Atatürk bridge**, completed in 1973. A couple of kilometres beyond, **ARNAVUTKÖY** is famous for its line of *yalıs*, wooden waterfront mansions with their boat moorings carved out beneath them. It's home to several trendy restaurants, while in the backstreets behind the waterfront, a sizeable Greek Orthodox church and the remains of a synagogue testify to the settlement's cosmopolitan past.

Bebek

Affluent **BEBEK** lies a fifteen-minute walk up the strait from Arnavutköy. If you arrive by boat, Bebek's most famous building stands to the left of the jetty: the beautifully restored waterfront **Hıdıv Sarayı** (Khedive's Palace), an Art Nouveau-style mansion belonging to the Egyptian consulate.

The impressive **fortress of Rumeli Hisarı** is another fifteen-minute walk along the promenade north of Bebek (Tues–Sun 9am–6pm; ₺3). Grander than its counterpart, Anadolu Hisarı, across the strait, this Ottoman fortress was constructed in four months in 1452, before the Ottoman conquest of the city. It houses a small open-air theatre,

1

THE BOSPHORUS

providing a summer-evening venue for concerts and plays, particularly during the International Music Festival (see p.131). Like Arnavutköy, Bebek holds a number of upscale restaurants.

Fatih Sultan Mehmet bridge

The second Bosphorus bridge, the **Fatih Sultan Mehmet bridge**, looms high above the fortress of Rumeli Hisarı. Completed in 1988, it's among the world's longest suspension bridges, at 1090m, and spans the Bosphorus at the point where King Darius of Persia crossed the straits by pontoon bridge in 512 BC.

Emirgan

EMIRGAN is home to the excellent **Sakip Sabancı Museum** (Sakip Sabancı Müzesi; Tues, Fri, Sat & Sun 10am–6pm, Wed 10am–8pm; ₺10; ⓦmuze.sabanciuniv.edu). Located in a beautifully restored 1920s villa just behind the waterfront, the museum boasts exquisite examples of Ottoman calligraphy, and hosts varied and prestigious temporary exhibitions; past subjects have included Picasso and Dalí.

A short walk north from the museum, **Emirgan Park** is the most attractive park in the city, with delightfully landscaped gardens and some quaint, pastel-hued *köşks* (pavilions).

Yeniköy

Swanky **YENİKÖY**, a couple of kilometres north along the Bosphorus from Emirgan, is the most expensive place on the İstanbul Monopoly board. Just north of it is **TARABYA**, just as posh as its neighbour and home to the Sait Halim Paşa *yalı*, a fine Art-Nouveau waterfront mansion guarded by a pair of stone lions.

Sariyer

SARIYER, a stop on the Bosphorus Cruise, is around 5km north of Yeniköy. The main reason to visit is its **Sadberk Hanım Museum** (Sadberk Hanım Müzesi), Büyükdere Cad 27–29, which holds a beautifully displayed assortment of archeological items, the vast majority found in Anatolia (Mon, Tues & Thurs–Sun 10am–5pm; ₺7; ⓦsadberkhanimmuzesi.org.tr). Finds range from the Neolithic through to the Byzantine period, and there's also a splendid display of Ottoman-era ethnographical objects, collected by one of the nation's wealthiest families, Koç, displayed over three floors.

Rumeli Kavağı

The last village on the European Bosphorus shore is **RUMELI KAVAĞİ**, a 2km *dolmuş* or short ferry ride from Sariyer. Nicer than Sariyer, with more of a village feel, it's no more than a string of houses, with some simple **fish restaurants** clustered around its ferry terminal. A local ferry connects Rumeli Kavağı with Anadolu Kavağı on the opposite Asian shore, and with Sariyer.

The Asian shore

The **Asian side** of the Bosphorus holds vast suburbs and small villages, all virtually unknown to tourists. The Bosphorus Tour (see p.117) calls in at the suburb of Kanlıca on the way to its final stop Anadolu Kavağı, the last village on the Asian side.

Beylerbeyi Palace

Tues, Wed, & Fri–Sun 9.30am–6pm • ₺5

Just 500m north of the first (Atatürk) Bosphorus bridge, the **Beylerbeyi Palace** is a nineteenth-century white marble summer residence and guesthouse of the Ottoman sultans. The interior decoration was designed by Sultan Abdülaziz himself, while some of the furniture, including the matching dining chairs in the harem and the *selâmlik*, was carved by Sultan Abdülhamid II during his six years of imprisonment here up to his death in 1918.

Anadolu Kavaği

The last call on the Bosphorus Tour from Eminönü is **ANADOLU KAVAĞİ**, where the boat stops for a couple of hours. The village has a distinct, if dilapidated, charm – balconied houses with boat-mooring stations overlook the Bosphorus. The waterfront and main street have some decent **fish restaurants** and food stands, which is just as well

1

as this is the longest stop on the Bosphorus Cruise. The Byzantine **fortress** from which the village takes its name sprawls across an overgrown hilltop above Anadolu Kavaği. Closed for restoration at the time of writing, it affords excellent views of the Bosphorus. Approaching from above, you'll see various Greek inscriptions.

ARRIVAL AND DEPARTURE
ALONG THE BOSPHORUS

Bosphorus Tour Most visitors prefer the ease of the Bosphorus Tour (see p.117). To ensure a good outside seat in summer, arrive at least half an hour before departure.

By ferry and bus While it's possible to explore the Bosphorus by ferry and bus, using the crowded and unfamiliar local buses is hard work. Make sure you have Şehir Hatları and IDO ferry timetables to hand, and buy plenty of *jetons* (or better, a topped-up *İstanbulkart*) for the ferries and buses in advance.

Along the European shore The #25/E bus runs from the Kabataş tram terminal along the coast to Rumeli Kavağı, the last stop on the European shore of the Bosphorus Cruise. Alternatively, take a #25/T or #40 from Taksim to

Sariyer, then a dolmüş or the #25/A on to Rumeli Kavağı. Another option is the Boğaz Hattı sea bus from Kabataş for İstiniye then Sariyer (Sat & Sun only, departs 8.15am, returns from Sariyer at 6pm). The #22 and #22/RE from Kabataş are both useful for reaching Arnavutköy, Bebek and Emirgan (for the Sakip Sabancı Museum). Şehir Hatları ferries run reasonably regularly from Sariyer up to both Rumeli and (more frequently) Anadolu Kavağı.

Along the Asian shore From the best starting point, Üsküdar, bus #15 runs as far as Beykoz, the #15/A on to Anadolu Kavağı. A Şehir Hatları ferry zigzags between Cegelköy (Asia) and İstiniye (Europe), taking in Bebek, Kanlıca and Emirgan.

The Princes' Islands

With their charming waterfront villages, *fin-de-siècle* architecture, wooded hills and rocky coves, the romantic **Princes' Islands** have always been a favourite retreat from the mainland. Set in the Sea of Marmara between 15km and 30km southeast of the city, the islands are easily accessible by ferry from İstanbul, and can get very crowded in summer, especially at weekends. Cars are banned on the islands, so **transport** is either by foot, phaeton (horse-drawn carriage), hired bike or donkey. Their proximity to the city makes them an easy, enjoyable and very cheap day-trip, but accommodation is surprisingly expensive, and, on summer weekends, hard to come by.

Brief history

The copper mines of Chalkitis (**Heybeliada**), famed in antiquity, are long since exhausted, but they remain visible near Çam Limanı. During the Byzantine era, numerous convents and monasteries were built on the islands, which soon became luxurious prisons for banished emperors, empresses and princes (often after they had been blinded). The islands were neglected by the conquering Ottoman Turks and became a place of refuge for Greek, Armenian and Jewish communities.

In 1846 a ferry service was established and the islands grew popular with Pera's wealthy merchants and bankers, becoming İstanbul's favourite summer resort after the establishment of the Republic in 1923. Mosques began to appear in the villages, and hotels and apartment buildings soon followed. A Turkish naval college was established on Heybeliada and Atatürk's private yacht was moored here as a training ship.

Sivriada, uninhabited and unvisitable, gained public notoriety in 1911 when all the stray dogs in İstanbul were rounded up, shipped out there and left to starve, while **Yassıada** is best known as a prison island, used for the detention of political prisoners.

Kınalıada

Kınalıada, "Henna Island", takes its name from the red colouring of its eastern cliffs; in Greek it was known as *Proti*, as it's the nearest of the islands to the mainland. Like Heybeliada, Kınalıada's history is notable for exiles, including Romanus IV Diogenes, deposed after his disastrous defeat at the Battle of Manzikert by the Selçuk Turks. Today, its population is seventy percent Armenian, and their nineteenth-century **Surp Krikor Lusovoric** church, in the bustling village clustered around the ferry quay, is the one notable site. The island is popular for swimming (there's a free Halk Plajı or "People's Beach" on the southeast shore), and bikes can be rented in the village for ₺15 per day.

Burgazada

Rising in tiers from the waterfront and ferry quay, the sleepy village of **BURGAZADA** is pretty enough, with a number of fine nineteenth- and early twentieth-century villas slumbering beneath fig, bay and oleander trees. Its most prominent landmark is the dome of its church of St John the Baptist. Across the square on which it stands, there's a small **museum**, at Burgaz Çayırı Sok 15 (Tues–Fri 10am–noon & 2–5pm, Sat 10am–noon; free), dedicated to the novelist **Sait Faik**, who's often described as the Turkish Mark Twain. Most people come here, however, to swim. The Alpazankaya area (₺2.5 weekdays, ₺5 weekends) on the west side of the island (₺20 in a phaeton, or rent a bike for ₺15 a day) is a good bet, and has a nice restaurant attached.

Heybeliada

Most visitors come to **Heybeliada** to cycle around its charming hilly terrain – Heybeliada means "Island of the Saddlebag", a reference to its two hills, separated by a low saddle – or swim and/or sunbathe at one of the beach clubs.

Strolling around the island, you might, in addition to the School of Theology described below, come across the **Heybeliada Sanatorium**, a private home for TB sufferers located off Çam Limanı Yolu on the south side of the island. The **Naval High School** (Deniz Harp Okulu), on the east shore, along the coast road from the main jetty, was originally the Naval War Academy, situated here since 1852. There is also a further Orthodox church, that of **Aya Nikola**, a prominent red-and-cream building with a curious clocktower, just behind the waterfront in the town centre.

Greek Orthodox School of Theology

Entry by appointment only, Mon–Sat 10am–noon & 2–4pm • Free • ☎ 0216 351 8563

The nineteenth-century, hill-top **Greek Orthodox School of Theology**, the Aya Triada Manastiri, is a pleasant fifteen-minute walk through pine forest from the port, though you can also take a phaeton. The building is set in beautiful grounds, and encloses a

THE BEACHES OF THE PRINCES' ISLANDS

While beaches are by no means the only reason to visit the Princes' Islands, the most popular strands attract multitudes of visitors from the city in summer. In several instances, the best way to reach a particular beach is by catching a small boat from the island's ferry port.

HEYBELIADA

Değirmen Burnu Plajı Northwest Heybeliada. This small, shingly curve of beach is set in pretty pine forest, at the foot of some small cliffs, on the south shore of a peninsula that projects from the northwest corner of the island. Mon–Fri ₺10.25, Sat & Sun ₺13.25. Daily 9am–dusk.

Green Beach Club On the opposite side of Heybeliada from the ferry terminal ⓦ green beachclub.com. A free service boat ferries customers to the beach, departing from just north of the quay. Mon–Fri ₺25, Sat & Sun ₺35. Late April to Sept daily 8am–sunset.

BÜYÜKADA

Halik Köyü Plajı Further south down the coast from the Yörükali Plajı. Although stony, this beach, looking across to the green, southern shores of the Sea of Marmara, has an Aegean island feel. Reached via a free boat from the ferry terminal, or a 20min bike ride. ₺10. Daily 8am–dusk.

Yörükali Plajı Halfway along the west coast of the island ⓦ yorukali.com. Sunbathing is accompanied by loud Turkish pop, but the beach is sandy and good for kids. Free boat transfers from the ferry terminal. ₺20 including lounger and umbrella. Mid-April to Sept daily 8am–sunset.

1

pretty, eight-hundred-year-old church, with a stunning gilt iconostasis. Getting inside the compound is by appointment only, however, and permission is hard to obtain.

Büyükada

Büyükada (the "Great Island", the original *Prinkipo*, or "Prince's Island", in Greek) is the largest and by far the busiest of the islands, and has long been inhabited by minorities. Leon Trotsky lived here from 1929 to 1933, spending most of his time at **İzzet Paşa Köşkü**, a currently derelict mansion awaiting restoration on Çankaya Caddesi, just below the very impressive and newly restored Con Paşa Köşkü. Many of the island's mansions have beautiful gardens, filled with magnolia, mimosa and jasmine, and myrtle, lilac and rock roses grow wild in the surrounding forests.

The island consists of two hills, both surmounted by monasteries. The southernmost, **Yüce Tepe**, is home to the **Monastery of St George**, probably on the site of a twelfth-century building. To reach the monastery, take a phaeton to the small park on the main road that goes over the hill, from where a steep path leads up several hundred metres to the monastery. Alternatively, take a donkey from the stables at the bottom of this path.

The monastery on the northern hill, **İsa Tepe**, is a nineteenth-century building, formerly a Greek orphanage. Over on the east side of the island, the **Aya Nikola Hangar** (₺5; Tues–Sun 9am–5pm) holds a permanent exhibition focusing on the island's writers and poets, and hosts temporary exhibitions.

ARRIVAL AND DEPARTURE

THE PRINCES' ISLANDS

Sea buses The fastest way to reach the islands, IDO sea buses (*deniz otobüs*) sail from the Adalar terminal in Kabata, at the end of the T1 tramline run to Kınalıada. They go to Burgazada (9 daily), Heybeliada (12 daily) and Büyükada (12 daily); services are much less frequent in winter. Journeys take 25–45min; ₺9 each way, ₺7.10 with an *İstanbulkart*. Arrive early, as queues can be massive.

Şehir Hatları ferries Slower, cheaper Şehir Hatları ferries sail to the four larger islands – Büyükada, Heybeliada, Burgazada and Kınalıada – from both the Adalar terminal in Kabataş and from Kadıköy (summer 15 daily Mon–Sat from 6.50am, Sunday from 7.30am; less frequently in winter; ₺5 each way, ₺3.5 *İstanbulkart*). The journey time to Büyükada is around 1hr 30min.

Island-hopping among the islands is easy, but check ferry times at the dock as the service is notoriously changeable. An *İstanbulkart* or a handful of *jetons* makes island-hopping easier.

HEYBELIADA

Ferries and sea buses arrive at Heybeliada ferry terminal on the main quayside of Rıhtım Caddesi.

BÜYÜKADA

Ferries and sea buses dock at two adjacent terminals on Büyük İskele Caddesi in Büyükada's main town, from where the main square and most of the hotels, restaurants and shops are just a short walk away.

GETTING AROUND

HEYBELIADA

Walking and cycling are good ways to enjoy Heybeliada, its pine forests and hills making for scenic rides and rambles.

Bike rental Imralı Sok 3, near the quayside; ₺5 an hour, ₺15 a day.

Phaeton tours Horse-and-carriage tours (for up to four people; short tour ₺50, long tour ₺60) leave from the phaeton park off the main square on Isa Çelebi Sokak, 50m above the ferry terminal.

Donkey rides Donkey rides (about ₺10 per ride) up the hills start from a little park just up Kadayoran Caddesi from the centre of town.

ACCOMMODATION

HEYBELIADA

Heybeliada is lower-key, and offers cheaper accommodation, than neighbouring Büyükada, though booking in advance is recommended, particularly at weekends.

Özdemir Pansiyon Ayyıldız Cad 41 ☎0216 351 1866, ⓦadalar-ozdemirpansiyon.com. The cheapest option on

the island, with tiny chalet-type en-suite rooms with a shower over squat loos, plus larger rooms in the main block. Both are comfortable enough. Prices rise by fifty percent on Fri and Sat. No breakfast. ₺50

Prenset Pansiyon Ayyıldız Cad 74 ☎216 351 9388, ⓦhalkiprenset.com. This converted apartment building with wood-trimmed exterior offers reasonable value, though most rooms don't have views. Friendly management, comfortable rooms with immaculate modern bathrooms, and central heating in winter. Prices, which include breakfast, rise fifty percent at weekends. ₺100

BÜYÜKADA

Accommodation on Büyükada is uniformly expensive, though the chance to stay in a grand restored mansion or boutique sea-front hotel may be appealing. Rates rise at weekends.

Ayanikola Butik Aya Nikola Mevki 104 ☎ 0126 382 4143, ⓦ ayanikolabutikpansiyon.com. This eleven-room boutique hotel is a gem. Each room has a sea view and is individually furnished with antique furniture and fittings, which contrast wonderfully with the plain white walls,

stripped floors and exposed brickwork. The "special" rooms have a bed right next to a picture window giving stunning views over to Asia. €105

Naya Retreat Maden, Yılmaz Türk Cad 96 ☎ 0216 382 4598, ⓦ nayaistanbul.com. A fine 105-year-old wooden mansion set in lush gardens on the island's east coast, the unusual *Naya* is a hybrid yoga/alternative therapy/meditation centre-cum-semi-rural retreat offering rooms furnished in upmarket ethnic-hippie style, in the house, or tents in the rambling garden. €80

Splendid Palas Nisan Cad 23 ☎ 0216 382 6950, ⓦ splendidhotel.net. A few minutes west of the ferry terminal, the *Splendid Palas*, dating from 1908, once played host to Edward VIII and Mrs Simpson. It has serious *fin-de-siècle* grandeur, with cupolas, balconies and a swimming pool out back. Closed Nov–March. €120

EATING AND DRINKING

HEYBELIADA

Heybeliada's restaurants cater to locals all year round, so there are plenty to choose from – generally good, simple and cheap, offering standard *lokanta*, kebab and *pide*; most are situated on Ayyıldız Caddesi.

BÜYÜKADA

There are lots of good fish restaurants along the shore to the left of the ferry terminal. One street back from the shore road, İskele Caddesi holds a selection of cheaper cafés, selling all the usual Turkish dishes.

Alibaba Restaurant Gülistan Cad 20. Period waterfront

restaurant to the left of the jetty, frequented by Atatürk in the 1930s. It's a friendly place with white tablecloths. Farmed-fish meals from ₺18, sea-caught fish from ₺70 per kilo, and the usual selection of *meze*. Alcohol served. Daily noon–midnight.

Yücetepe Kır Gazino Aya Yorgi, Yüce Tepe. Excellent restaurant with beautiful views from its location atop Yüce Tepe. The food is freshly prepared and hearty, with deep-fried, cheese-filled *börek* as a highlight. The home-made chips are delicious. A satisfying lunch with a beer will set you back ₺18–24. Daily 10am–10pm.

Around the Sea of Marmara

SELIMIYE CAMII

Around the Sea of Marmara

2

Despite their proximity to İstanbul, the shores and hinterland of the Sea of Marmara are neglected by most foreign travellers. While this may not be altogether surprising – Turkey here is at its most Balkan and, at first glance, least exotic – there are good reasons to visit. Above all, the exquisite early Ottoman centres of Edirne and Bursa are the real highlights. If those whet your appetite, historic Lüleburgaz and İznik make good postscripts to the former imperial capitals. While most of the Thracian coast is disappointing, and the scrappy beaches of the Marmara islands hold little interest, two bright spots stand out – the beach-and-fortress town of Kıyıköy on the Black Sea, and the Saros Gulf resort of Erikli. To cross the Sea of Marmara, the port of Tekirdağ has potentially useful ferries to the southern shore, while Gelibolu, on the eponymous peninsula, is linked by ro-ro craft to Lapseki opposite.

For evocative inland scenery in the southern Marmara, two shallow lakes, **Uluabat Gölü** and **Manyas Gölü**, support a dwindling fishing community and a bird sanctuary respectively. The **Uludağ** range above Bursa attracts skiers in winter and hikers in summer, while **Cumalıkızık** at the base of the mountain is a showcase village.

Before the wars and population exchanges of the early twentieth century, much of the local population was Greek (or Bulgarian) Orthodox, though all the larger towns held substantial Jewish and Armenian communities. After the Turkish Republic was established, massive immigration – both internal and from abroad – changed the mix. The resultant ethnic stew includes people of Çerkez (Circassian), Artvinli and Greek Muslim descent, as well as a large settled Romany population, but consists predominantly of **Pomak**, **Bosnian** and **Macedonian Muslims**, plus **Bulgarian Turks**. All these groups had, in fact, been trickling in for decades before 1923, as Austro-Hungarian or Orthodox nationalist victories in the Balkans made their previous homes inhospitable to Turks or Slavic Muslims.

Thrace

Thrace (Trakya in Turkish), the historic territory bounded by the rivers Danube and Nestos and the Aegean, Marmara and Black seas, is today divided roughly equally among Turkey, Greece and Bulgaria. In ancient times it was home to warlike tribes, whose bizarre religions and unruly habits presented a continual headache for rulers bent on subduing them. Contemporary life is decidedly less colourful. Until the late 1960s, nearly all of Thrace was a military security zone, off-limits to foreigners. Most of the area is now unrestricted, though the towns remain heavily garrisoned.

The flatter terrain of southern Thrace has long since been denuded of trees, while much of the coast has fallen prey to estates of concrete holiday homes – seasonal barbecue pads for İstanbul's workers. Inland is staunchly agricultural; in summer a

OIL-WRESTLING

Highlights

❶ **Selimiye Camii** The masterpiece of architect Mimar Sinan, considered to be the finest mosque in Turkey. **See p.152**

❷ **Kırkpınar festival** Wrestlers slicked down head-to-toe in olive oil battle it out every July in a 650-year-old tournament at Edirne. **See p.153**

❸ **Termal** Get steamy at Termal's near-scalding hot springs, where people have taken the waters since Roman times. **See p.161**

❹ **İznik** Sleepy lakeside town nestled in an olive-mantled valley, famous for its sixteenth-century tile craft, now revived. **See p.162**

❺ **Bursa's Koza Hanı** Centrepiece of Bursa's covered bazaar, occupied by silk-breeders at the early summer auction. **See p.170**

❻ **Muradiye Külliyesi and the Royal Tombs** Shaded by centuries-old trees, this tranquil complex houses an impressive mosque and the finely decorated tombs of various Ottoman royal family members. **See p.172**

❼ **Cumalıkızık** A finely preserved Ottoman village, its cobbled streets full of classic Ottoman houses. **See p.177**

HIGHLIGHTS ARE MARKED ON THE MAP ON P.148

AROUND THE SEA OF MARMARA

HIGHLIGHTS

1. Selimiye Camii
2. Kırkpınar festival
3. Termal
4. İznik
5. Bursa's Koza Hanı
6. Muradiye Külliyesi and the Royal Tombs
7. Cumalıkızık

BLACK SEA

kilometres
0   50

N

SEA OF MARMARA

THRACE

ISTRANCA

GREECE

Istanbul

Edirne

İznik

Bursa

Uludağ (2543m)

Çanakkale

The Dardanelles

Gelibolu (Gallipoli) Peninsula

Saros Gulf

BIRD PARADISE/ KUŞ CENNETİ

Kapıdağı Peninsula

Marmara Adası

Avşa Adası

Paşalimanı Adası

sea of yellow sunflowers, grown for oil, spreads for many kilometres. Further west, in the wetter lands around Üzünköprü, rice is predominant; to the north, the rolling Istranca hills with their dense forests of oak and conifers hide itinerant charcoal burners and myriad fish farms raising rainbow trout. Across the whole region opencast mines extract sand and gravel from the prehistoric sea bed.

The E80 motorway from İstanbul to the main Thracian town of **Edirne** runs parallel to the route of the Roman and Byzantine **Via Egnatia**, which later became the medieval route to the Ottoman holdings in Europe, and is now the D100 highway. Many towns along this road began life as Roman staging posts, a role continued under the Ottomans who endowed each with a civic monument or two. Few spots have much to detain you, though keep an eye out for fine **old bridges**, which like the road itself may be Ottoman reworkings of Roman or Byzantine originals. The best of these is the quadruple Büyükçekmece span, crossing the neck of an estuary west of İstanbul and built by the great architect Mimar Sinan in 1563.

Edirne

More than just the quintessential border town, **EDİRNE** – 230km northwest of İstanbul – is one of the best-preserved Ottoman cities, and makes an impressive, easily digestible introduction to Turkey. A lively, attractive place of almost 140,000 people, it occupies a rise overlooking the mingling of the Tunca, Arda and Meriç rivers, very near the Greek and Bulgarian frontiers. Its life derives from day-tripping foreign shoppers, discerning tourists and students from the University of Thrace.

Downtown, teeming bazaars and elegant domestic architecture vie for attention with a clutch of striking **Ottoman monuments**. The best of these, crowning the town's central hillock and sufficient reason alone for a visit, is the **Selimiye Camii**, masterpiece of the imperial architect Mimar Sinan.

To explore all Edirne's main sights on foot, you'll need a full day. Many of its Ottoman monuments lie north and west of town, deliberately rusticated by the early sultans to provide a nucleus for future suburbs. Because of depopulation since the 1700s, urban growth never caught up with some of them, which have a rather forlorn atmosphere. Still, if the weather's fine, walking there is a pleasure, especially since you'll follow the willow-shaded banks of the **Tunca River** for some distance.

Brief history

The strategic point now occupied by Edirne has always held a settlement of some kind, destined to be repeatedly captured – and sometimes sacked for good measure – over the centuries. Thracian Uscudama became Hellenistic Orestia, but the city really entered history as **Hadrianopolis**, designated the capital of Roman Thrace by Emperor Hadrian. Under the Byzantines it retained its significance, not least as a forward base en route to the Balkans – or, more ominously from the Byzantine point of view, first stop on the way to attempts on the imperial capital itself. Unsuccessful besiegers of Constantinople habitually vented their frustration on Hadrianopolis as they retreated, and a handful of emperors met their end here in pitched battles with Thracian "barbarians" of one sort or another.

In 1361, after Hadrianopolis surrendered to the besieging Murat I, the provisional **Ottoman capital** was effectively transferred here from Bursa. A century later, Mehmet the Conqueror trained his troops and tested his artillery here in preparation for the march on Constantinople; indeed, the Ottoman court was not completely moved to the Bosphorus until 1458. Because of its excellent opportunities for hunting and falconry, Edirne, as the Turks renamed it, remained a favourite haunt of sultans for three more centuries, earning the title *Der-I Saadet* or "Gate of Contentment" – during which it saw enough victory celebrations, circumcision ceremonies and marriages to rival Constantinople.

2

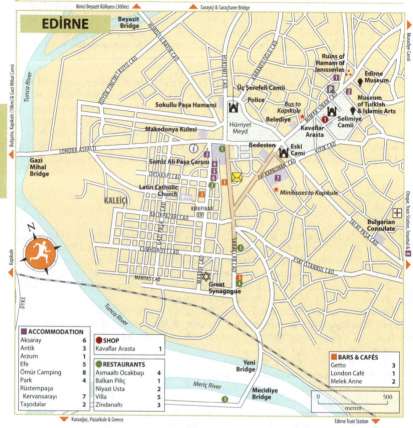

EDİRNE

ACCOMMODATION
Aksaray	6
Antik	3
Arzum	1
Efe	5
Ömür Camping	8
Park	4
Rüstempaşa Kervansarayı	7
Taşodalar	2

SHOP
Kavaflar Arasta	1

RESTAURANTS
Asmaaltı Ocakbaşı	4
Balkan Piliç	1
Niyazi Usta	2
Villa	5
Zindanaltı	3

BARS & CAFÉS
Getto	3
London Café	1
Melek Anne	2

Decline set in after a 1751 **earthquake**, while Tsarist troops occupied and pillaged the city during each of the **Russo-Turkish wars** of 1829 and 1878–79. Worse followed, when the Bulgarians (with Serbian aid) besieged Odrin – as they called, and still call, the city – for 143 days from November 3, 1912 before taking it, thus ending the First Balkan War. The Greeks, as one of the victorious World War I Allies, annexed "**Adrianópoli**" along with the rest of Turkish Thrace from 1920 to 1922, and Turkish sovereignty over the city was only confirmed by the 1923 **Treaty of Lausanne**. Bulgarian, Latin Catholic and Greek Orthodox churches remain, along with elegant houses and a ruined synagogue in the former Jewish quarter, as evidence of the pre-1912, multicultural city, of which half the population was Turkish, and the remainder Greek, Bulgarian, Armenian and Jewish.

Eski Cami
Corner of Mimar Sinan and Talat Paşa cads

The logical starting point for explorations of Edirne is the boxy **Eski Cami**, the oldest mosque in town, with recycled Roman columns out front and some celebrated giant calligraphic inscriptions inside. Topped by nine vaults arranged three-square, and supported by four square pillars, it's a more elaborate version of Bursa's Ulu Cami. Emir Süleyman, son of the luckless Beyazit I, began it in 1403, but it was his younger brother Mehmet I – the only one of three brothers left alive after a bloody succession struggle – who dedicated it eleven years later.

The Bedesten
Muaffiklarhane Sok

The fifteenth-century **Bedesten** was Edirne's first covered market, a portion of whose rents helped maintain the nearby Eski Cami mosque. Constructed by Mehmet I, the barn-like structure with its fourteen vaulted chambers – indebted to a Bursa prototype – was restored in the 1980s, but shops with tatty wares and cheap tiles underfoot let the interior down.

Semiz Ali Paşa Çarşısı
At the top of Saraçlar Cad

The six-gated, multi-domed covered bazaar of **Semiz Ali Paşa Çarşısı** was constructed by Mimar Sinan in 1568 at the behest of Semiz Ali, one of the most able and congenial grand viziers. Located at the top of Edirne's liveliest, mostly pedestrianized modern commercial street, a massive 1992 fire gutted many of its 130 shops, but renovations were administered with care – and the building far outshines the mostly dull merchandise sold inside.

Makedonya Kulesi
Opposite the north entrance of Semiz Ali Paşa Çarşısı

The **Makedonya Kulesi** (Macedonia Tower) is the sole remnant of the town's extensive Roman/Byzantine city walls; the Ottomans, in a burst of confidence after expanding the limits of empire far beyond Edirne, demolished the rest. The tower was partially restored around the millennium, and you pass through the ground floor to a viewing platform overlooking some of Roman Hadrianopolis, excavated in 2003 (no entry).

Kaleiçi

The **Kaleiçi** district, a rectangular grid of streets dating from Byzantine times and lined with much-interrupted terraces of ornate eighteenth- and nineteenth-century townhouses, sprawls west and south of the Semiz Ali market. The best streets for strolling are Maarif Caddesi, the parallel Gazi Paşa Caddesi, and their linking perpendicular Cumhuriyet Caddesi, once the heart of the **Jewish quarter**, where house dedication dates (in the Hebraic calendar) go up to 1912. When built in 1906 to replace thirteen others destroyed by fire, the derelict synagogue at the bottom of Maarif Caddesi was the largest in the Balkans – an indication of how huge the community then was. Within a few decades, however, the new frontiers, populist pogroms (unusual in Turkey) and official harassment had compelled local Jews to flee to Europe, İstanbul or Israel.

Üç Şerefeli Cami
North of Semiz Ali and Hürriyet Meyd

The **Üç Şerefeli Cami** replaced the Eski Cami as Edirne's Friday mosque in 1447. Ten years in the making, its conceptual daring represented the pinnacle of Ottoman religious architecture until overshadowed by the Selimiye Camii a short time later. Its name – "three-balconied" – derives from the three galleries for the muezzin on the tallest of its four whimsically idiosyncratic **minarets**; the second highest has two balconies, the others one, and each of the multiple balconies is reached by a separate stairway within the minaret. The **courtyard**, too, was an innovation, centred on a *sadırvan* and ringed by porphyry and marble columns pilfered from Roman buildings. The mosque's experimental nature is further confirmed by its **interior**, much wider than it is deep and covered by a main dome 24m in diameter, with four flanking domes. It was the largest that the Turks had built at the time; to impart a sense of space, the architect relied on just two freestanding columns, with the other four recessed into front and back walls to form a hexagon.

Sokullu Paşa Hamamı

Opposite the Üç Şerefeli Cami • Daily 7am–10pm (men); 10am–5pm (women) • Wash and massage ₺30

The sixteenth-century **Sokullu Paşa Hamamı** was built by master architect Mimar Sinan for Grand Vizier Sokullu Mehmet. An entrance of ornate columns and a triple-vaulted portico mirrors the Üç Şerefeli Cami across the road. One of Turkey's largest hamams, it is traveller friendly and has separate wings for men and women.

Selimiye Camii

Between Kiyik and Mimar Sinan cads

Designed by the eighty-year-old **Mimar Sinan** (see box, p.93) in 1569, at the command of Selim II, the masterly **Selimiye Camii** is one of Turkey's finest mosques. The work of a confident craftsman at the height of his powers, it's visible from some distance away on the Thracian plain.

You can approach the Selimiye across the central park, Dilaver Bey, then through the **Kavaflar Arasta** (Cobbler's Arcade), built by Sinan's pupil Davut and still used as a covered market, full of household goods, souvenirs and cheap clothing. Every day, beneath the market's prayer dome, the shopkeepers promise to conduct their business honestly.

The mosque **courtyard**, approached from the *arasta* up a flight of stone steps, is surrounded by a colonnaded portico with arches in alternating red and white stone, ancient columns, and domes of varying size above the arcades. Its delicately fashioned *şadırvan* (ablutions fountain) is the finest in the city. In a nod to his predecessors, Sinan gave each of the four identical, slender **minarets** three balconies. At 71m, they're the second tallest in the world after those in Mecca. The detailed carved portal once graced the Ulu Cami in Birgi and was transported here in pieces, then reassembled.

It's the celestial **interior**, however, and specifically the dome, which impresses most (no photos). Planned expressly to surpass that of Aya Sofya in İstanbul, it succeeds, at 31.5m in diameter, by a bare few centimetres, thus achieving Sinan's lifetime ambition. Held aloft by eight mammoth but surprisingly unobtrusive twelve-sided pillars, the cupola floats 44m above the floor, covered in calligraphy proclaiming the glory of Allah. Immediately below the dome, the muezzin's platform, supported on twelve columns, is an ideal place from which to contemplate the proportions of the mosque. The water of the small marble drinking fountain beneath symbolizes life, under the dome of eternity. The most ornate stone carving is reserved for the *mihrab* and *mimber*, backed by fine İznik faïence illuminated by sunlight streaming in through the many windows.

Museum of Turkish and Islamic Arts

Eastern corner of Selimiye Camii mosque precinct • Tues–Sun 9am–5pm • ₺3 • ☎ 0284 225 1625

A former *medrese* of the Selimiye Camii, the recently renovated **Museum of Turkish and Islamic Arts** (*Türk İslam Eserleri Müzesi*) consists of fifteen rooms around a central courtyard. Originally used to house and educate Koranic pupils, they display assorted wooden, ceramic and martial knick-knacks from the province, including one gallery dedicated to oil-wrestling and another to artefacts decorated by Dervish calligraphers.

Edirne Museum

Northeast of Selimiye Camii • Tues–Sun 9am–5pm • ₺3 • ☎ 0284 225 1120

The good archeological section at the main **Edirne Museum** holds bronze, glass and ceramic relics from ancient Aenos at the mouth of the Meriç as well as from Hadrianopolis, partly labelled in English. There's also a Turkish-only ethnographic section featuring carpet-weaving and colourful village bridal-wear, the rule at weddings before bland white concoctions were adopted from the West.

Muradiye Camii

Mimar Sinan Cad, 10min easy walk from Selimiye Camii • Admission at prayer times only

According to legend, Celaleddin Rumi, founder of the Mevlevî dervish order, appeared in a dream to the pious Murat II at some date between 1426 and 1435, urging him to build a sanctuary for the Mevlevîs in Edirne. The result is the pleasing, T-shaped **Muradiye Camii**, a *zaviye* or dervish convent crouched on a hill looking north over vegetable patches and the Tunca River; the grassy entry court lends a final bucolic touch. The interior is distinguished by the best İznik tiles outside Bursa, which cover the *mihrab* and walls up to eye level. The calligraphic frescoes that once adorned the higher surfaces have probably been missing since the catastrophic earthquake of 1751. The dervishes initially congregated in the *eyvans*, the ends of the T's cross-stroke; Murat later housed them in a separate *tekke* in the garden.

Along the Tunca River

Only one bridge crosses the bigger of Edirne's two rivers, the **Meriç** – the graceful **Mecidiye**, completed in 1847, which is now effectively Edirne's municipal logo. The narrower **Tunca River**, on the other hand, is spanned by a half-dozen fifteenth- or sixteenth-century bridges, better suited to pedestrians and horse-carts than the motor vehicles that trundle across them. The best way to see the spans is to stroll along the east (city-side) bank, parallel to the dykes and water meadows.

The pair furthest upstream, the fifteenth-century **Saray (Kanûni)** and **Fatih bridges**, join the left and right banks of the Tunca to the river-island of **Sarayiçi**. The island takes

OIL-WRESTLING IN EDİRNE: THE KIRKPINAR FESTIVAL

Oil-wrestling (*yağlı güreş*) is popular throughout Turkey, but reaches the pinnacle of acclaim at the doyenne of tournaments, the three-day annual **Kırkpınar festival**, staged early each summer on Sarayiçi islet outside Edirne (Ⓦkirkpinar.com or Ⓦturkishwrestling.com). The preferred date is the first week of July, but the event is moved back into June if it conflicts with Ramadan or either of the two major *bayrams* that follow it.

The wrestling matches have been held annually, except during war or Edirne's occupation, for over six centuries. Despite the less than atmospheric environment of the modern stadium where it now takes place, tradition still permeates the event. The contestants – up to a thousand – dress only in leather knickers called *kisbet* and are slicked down head-to-toe in diluted olive oil. Wrestlers are classed by height and ability, not by weight, from toddlers up to the *pehlivan* (full-size) category. Warm-up exercises, the *peşrev*, are highly stereotyped and accompanied by the *davul* (deep-toned drum) and *zurna* (single-reed Islamic oboe). The competitors and the actual matches are solemnly introduced by the *cazgır* (master of ceremonies), usually a former champion.

Several bouts take place simultaneously. Each lasts anything from a few minutes to nearly an hour, until one competitor collapses or has his back pinned to the grass. Referees keep a lookout for the limited number of illegal moves or holds, and victors advance more or less immediately to the next round until only the *başpehlivan* (champion) remains. Despite the small prize purse donated by the *Kırkpınar ağaları* – the local worthies who put on the whole show – a champion should derive ample benefit from appearance and endorsement fees, plus the furious on- and off-site betting. Gladiators tend mainly to be villagers from across Turkey who have won regional titles, starry-eyed with the prospect of fame and escape from the rut of rural poverty.

In addition to providing the music of the *peşrev*, the local Romany population descends in force during Kırkpınar, setting up a combination circus-carnival on the outskirts of town. They also observe the ancient pan-Balkan **spring festival** (**Hıdırellez**) in the fields around the stadium during the first week of May. The Romany King lights a bonfire on the evening of May 5, a torch relays the flame to other nearby bonfires, and a dish of meat and rice is given to the gathered picnickers. The next morning, young Romany girls are paraded through the streets on horseback around the Muradiye Camii (focus of a Romany *mahalle*) to the accompaniment of *davul* and *zurna*, wearing their own or their mothers' wedding dresses.

its name from the *saray* or royal palace that formerly stood here, which was blown up by the Ottomans in 1877 to prevent munitions from falling into Russian hands. The concrete stadium that hosts the Kırkpınar wrestling matches stands beside the ruins.

Following the riverbank west and downstream, past the **Saraçhane bridge**, brings you, after twenty minutes, to the double-staged **Beyazit bridge**, across another small island in the Tunca, and its extension **Yalnızgöz** ("one-eyed" after its single hump) **bridge**.

İkinci Beyazit Külliyesi

Sağlık Müzesi, Yenimaret, across the Beyazit and Yalnızgöz bridges • Daily 9am–6pm • ₺10

The vast **İkinci Beyazit Külliyesi** was built in 1488 by Hayrettin, court architect to Beyazit II. Within a single irregular boundary wall, beneath a hundred domes, are assembled a mosque, food storehouse, bakery, *imaret*, dervish hostel, medical school and insane asylum. Unfortunately, most of the buildings are closed to the public these days, though the *imam* or his son may give you a short tour (essentially peering through windows and gates).

Apart from its handsome courtyard and the sultan's loge inside, the **mosque** itself is disappointing; more interesting is the **medical school** in the furthest northwest corner of the complex. This was conveniently linked to the *timarhane*, or madhouse, built around an open garden, which in turn leads to the magnificent **darüşşifa** (therapy centre). This hexagonal, domed structure consists of a circular central space onto which six *eyvans* open; the inmates were brought here regularly, so that musicians could play to soothe the more intractable cases. Strange five-sided rooms with fireplaces open off three of the *eyvans*. The *darüşşifa* now houses the **Sağlık Müzesi**, or Health Museum, in which interesting displays chronicle Ottoman medical history.

Gazi Mihal bridge

Londra Asfaltı

The western entrance to Edirne crosses the Tunca River via the **Gazi Mihal bridge**, an Ottoman refurbishment of a thirteenth-century Byzantine span. Gazi Mihal was a Christian nobleman who became an enthusiastic convert to Islam – hence the epithet *Gazi*, "Warrior for the Faith".

ARRIVAL AND DEPARTURE   EDİRNE

By bus Edirne's *otogar* is just over 8km southeast of the centre on the access road to the E80; minibuses or urban bus #5 will drop you in the centre near the tourist office.
Destinations Çanakkale (5 daily; 4hr); İstanbul (every 30min; 2hr 30min); Keşan (every 20min; 2hr 30min); Kapıkule (every 30min; 25min); Lüleburgaz (every 30min; 1hr).

By train Edirne's train station, the most likely entry point from abroad, is 4km southeast of the centre; infrequent city buses (#3), private minibuses or taxis connect it with the centre.
Destinations İstanbul (2–3 daily; 5–6hr). For international services out of Edirne, see p.155.

By car Drivers will find most of Edirne patrolled by wardens selling parking chits, with some of the few free spaces in the far west of the old quarter, Kaleiçi. Street spaces have a notional limit of three hours, so you may have to use off-street car parks.

INFORMATION

Tourist office Londra Asfaltı 76 (Mon–Fri 8.30am–noon & 1–5.30pm, may close later in summer; ☎0284 225 5260); there's also a booth at the Bulgarian (Kapıkule) frontier gate (daily 8.30am–5pm; ☎0284 238 2019). Both supply an excellent map of Edirne.

ACCOMMODATION

Accommodation can be tight in Edirne, with most places demanding rack rates at or near coastal-resort prices. Book at least a month in advance during the main Turkish holidays and the Kırkpınar festival. At slow times, however, bargaining usually achieves discounts of about a third. The cheaper central options line **Maarif Caddesi**, though a few serious dives here are worth avoiding, and all are beset by **traffic noise** – get a rear-facing room if possible. **Parking** here is heavily controlled – hoteliers may have a few private spaces or be willing to intercede for you with the parking wardens.

THRACE BORDER CROSSINGS

The Turkish–Greek and Turkish–Bulgarian frontier posts nearest Edirne are **open 24 hours**. For EU nationals and citizens of the US, Canada, Australia and New Zealand, there are no restrictions on travel between Greece and Turkey, or Bulgaria and Turkey, and no advance visas are necessary. South Africans do not need an advance visa to enter Turkey; however, they do to enter Greece and Bulgaria. The Bulgarian consulate at Talat Paşa Cad 31 (Mon–Fri 9am–noon; ☎0284 214 0617) in Edirne can issue tourist visas, though the Greek consulate in Edirne, Kocasinan Mahallesi, İkinci Sok 13 (☎0284 235 5804), is unlikely to be able to help. South African nationals should apply for a Schengen Zone visa for Greece in their home country before travelling.

TURKEY–BULGARIA

The vast **Bulgarian–Turkish border** complex straddles the busy E80 expressway at **Kapıkule**, 18km northwest of Edirne (and 320km south of Sofia, Bulgaria's capital).

Minibuses from Edirne to Kapıkule (every 30min, daily 6.30am–9pm; ₺5) leave from stops along Londra Asfaltı near the tourist office; a taxi will set you back ₺30. There are no facilities in the nearest Bulgarian village, Kapitan Andreevo, but two reasonable hotels in **Svilengrad**, the first proper town 9km beyond. **Balkan Express trains** depart daily at 3am from Edirne, 4am from Kapıkule for Svilengrad, Sofia and Belgrade. The **Bosphor Express** (same train, different wagons) leaves Edirne and Kapıkule at the same time, bound for Veliko Tûrnovo, Bucharest and (with a change) Budapest. Expect an hour's delay near the frontier while Bulgarian customs officials comb the train.

TURKEY–GREECE

The Turkish frontier post of **Pazarkule**, separated from the Greek one at Kastaniés by a kilometre-wide no-man's-land, is 8km west of Edirne and 2km beyond the last Turkish village of **Karaağaç**.

Minibuses **to Karaağaç** (₺1.50) depart regularly from behind the Rüstempaşa Kervansarayı, but you must walk the final 2km from Karaağaç to Pazarkule. If heavily laden, it's easier to take a taxi (€10/₺20) directly from Edirne **to Pazarkule**. Once through the Turkish post, you may have to take a Greek taxi to the **Kastaniés** post, as you're not usually allowed to walk across; this applies coming from Greece too – budget €4/₺8 per car for the 1km gap. From Kastaniés, on the Greek side, three trains daily (5.58am, 11.40am, 5.56pm), and about as many buses, make the 2hr 30min run down to Alexandhroúpoli, the first major Greek city.

The main, far busier Turkish–Greek road crossing between İpsala and Kípi in Greece lies just off the E90/110 highway, 31km west of Keşan, itself 115km south of Edirne. The two posts here are open 24 hours, but as at Pazarkule–Kastaniés, there's a 500m-wide military zone that you're forbidden to cross on foot. During daylight hours at least, it's fairly easy to arrange a ride over in either direction with a truck, though drivers will routinely refuse to take you further. From Kípi, 1500m beyond the actual frontier, several buses daily run further into Greece; at the Turkish immigration post only taxis are available for the 8km run to İpsala. You might very well forego all this, as there's a through Greek bus service between Keşan's *otogar* and Alexandhroúpoli in each direction run by the KTEL (Greek bus co-op) of Évrou province.

The sole **Turkey–Greece rail link** goes from **Uzunköprü** (whose station is 6km north of town at the end of the new bridge) to **Pýthio** just over the border formed by the **Meriç/Évros River** and its wetlands. The high-standard, sleeper-only **Dostluk/Filia (Friendship) Express** leaves İstanbul at 9pm, passing through Uzunköprü station at 1.40am (where passports are stamped), continuing to Pýthio where there's a brief halt for passport controls before continuing to Alexandhroúpoli and Thessaloníki. An evening/midnight express in the reverse direction passes through Pýthio and Uzunköprü (passengers disembark to buy visas) just before 4am. The slower daytime train runs unreliably; when it does, it passes through Uzunköprü bound for Greece at about 2pm, and in the opposite direction at 4.40pm.

HOTELS AND PANSIYONS

Aksaray Alipaşa Ortakapı Cad 9, corner of Maarif Cad ☎0284 212 6035. The compact rooms in this good-value, well-located *pansiyon* – a converted old mansion – are basic but modern, clean and have central heating; some offer tiny en-suite bathrooms, while the cheaper rooms share facilities. ₺85

★ **Antik** Maarif Cad 6 ☎0284 225 1555,

2

w edirneantikhotel.com. Popular boutique hotel in a convenient location, with three creaky floors' worth of large, plush en-suite rooms, and slightly kitsch antique decor. There's a pleasant courtyard garden restaurant and the staff are friendly and well managed. Rates include breakfast. **₺170**

Arzum Hamam Sok 9 ☏ 0284 213 1334. Cheap and cheerful *pansiyon* on a quiet side street opposite Selimiye Camii, with small but modern and spotlessly clean en-suite rooms. Mosque-facing rooms come with balconies while those at the rear are quieter, and both street and guarded parking is available. **₺75**

Efe Maarif Cad 13 ☏ 0284 213 6166, w efehotel.com. Salubrious, if somewhat overpriced hotel where the cheerful, well-appointed rooms vary – those at the back are almost suite-sized, with double beds and fridges. There's also an English-style, street-side winter pub, and a very pleasant garden restaurant at the rear. **₺150**

Park Maarif Cad 7 ☏ 0284 213 5276. With its well-worn 1980s common areas, this business-class hotel is not quite as spruce as the *Efe*, though the ground-floor restaurant is more contemporary. The bland but spacious rooms are good value if you can bargain them down a category. **₺90**

Rüstempaşa Kervansarayı İki Kapılı Han Cad 57 ☏ 0284 212 6119, w edirnekervansarayhotel.com. A sympathetic

restoration retained much of the exotic atmosphere of this sixteenth-century *kervansaray*, including a romantic, peaceful courtyard and thick walls that buffer most of the noise from the busy street outside. The cell-like rooms have original vaulted ceilings and the smallest of exterior windows, and can disappoint with their cheap, spartan decor. **₺140**

Taşodalar Hamam Sok 3, behind Selimiye Camii ☏ 0284 213 1404, w tasodalar.com. One of Edirne's better hotels, this restored fifteenth-century building is much the best choice for families (there's a quad room) and for drivers (with its private, secure car park). The nine rooms have dark-wood floors and trim throughout, though the decor – a mix of genuine antiques and kitsch – is in variable taste, to say the least. The upstairs rooms look towards the mosque – the best, no. 109, has a bay window – and there's a peaceful tea garden/restaurant (no alcohol served) at the back. Discounts of up to 30 percent possible. **₺230**

CAMPSITES

Ömür Camping Just off the D100 on the D020 towards Kırklareli ☏ 0284 226 0037. Large campsite in a nice rural spot that unfortunately suffers at times from overly officious, German-run management. There's space for fifty caravans, as well as a large swimming pool (₺10 extra), clean ablutions and laundry facilities (₺10 extra). **₺35**

EATING AND DRINKING

Most of Edirne's **restaurants** are undistinguished, and licensed places are scarce in the centre – we've indicated all known options. The local speciality is **ciğer tava**, deep-fried slivers of calf's liver with tomato, onion and hot chilli garnish. Despite the large student contingent, **nightlife** is limited to a few venues along Saraçlar Caddesi, especially towards the old Jewish bazaar at the south end, and the area along Karaağaç Yolu between the two river bridges, known as *Bülbül Adası* – "Nightingale Island".

RESTAURANTS

Asmaaltı Ocakbaşı Saraçlar Cad 149 ☏ 0284 212 8712. Occupying two floors of an attractively restored old industrial building, this is the only licensed meat-grill downtown, thus a bit bumped up in price – allow ₺20 minimum a head. Daily noon–3pm & 7–11pm.

Balkan Piliç Saraçlar Cad 14 ☏ 0284 225 2155. Popular *lokantası* with tables both inside and on the pavement of the busy pedestrian-only street. A helpful picture menu offers plenty of wholesome *lokanta* fare – not just chicken but enticing vegetable dishes and good roast lamb – served by efficient, and fast, waiters. Soups ₺4, mains ₺6–12. Daily 9am–10pm.

★ **Niyazi Usta** Alipaşa Ortaköy Cad 9 ☏ 0284 213 3372, w www.cigerciniyaziusta.com.tr. The best regarded of several *ciğercis* (liver purveyors) in this area, worth a slight price premium for their expert rendition of *ciğer tava* (₺10). The salubrious surroundings stretch over two floors, festooned with photos of founder Niyazi and various celebrities. There's also an annexe a few doors up at no. 5. Daily 9am–9pm.

Villa 1.5km south of town along Karaağaç Yolu, on the Meriç River ☏ 0284 223 4077, w www.edirnevilla.com. Licensed restaurant specializing in meat and *meze*, plus sometimes *yayın* (catfish). While open all year, their *raison d'être* is a summer outdoor terrace overlooking the river and its elegant, honey-coloured bridge. You pay premium prices, of course, for the view – typically around ₺23 a head. Daily 11am–11pm.

Zindanaltı Meyhanesi Saraçlar Cad 127 ☏ 0284 212 2149. About the only central *meyhane*, arrayed over three floors in an atmospheric stone- and- wood building. The ground floor and pavement are more for drinking, while the top floors and a roof terrace serve the usual *mezes* and grills for around ₺5–9. Daily 11am–11pm.

BARS & CAFÉS

Getto Saraçlar Cad 143 ☏ 0284 214 6050. Straightforward booze-and-music bar – one of only a few downtown – whose name recalls the area's Jewish history. There's a neon-lit smoky interior or pleasant shaded tables overlooking the pedestrian street. Beers ₺3. Tues–Sat noon–11pm.

London Café Saraçlar Cad 74 ☎ 0284 213 8052. This two-storey affair serves proper European coffees, imported alcoholic drinks, and Western snack food like pasta, burgers and sandwiches, indoors or out at pavement tables. Salads ₺10–19, mains ₺12.50–22. Daily 9am–11pm.

Melek Anne Maarif Cad 18 ☎ 0284 213 3263. The walled, tree-studded courtyard is the highlight at this snack-café, which operates out of an old house. Dishes include *mantı, menemen, gözleme, katmer* and the like. Free wi-fi. Mains ₺6–9. Daily 9am–10pm.

South of Edirne

There's little reason to stop at any point along the E87 highway as it heads south from **Havsa**, the junction 27km southeast of Edirne. This road does, however, connect two transit towns en route to and from Greece, **Uzunköprü** and **Keşan**.

Uzunköprü

Formerly called Plotinopolis, **UZUNKÖPRÜ**, 64km south of Edirne, gets its current name, meaning "Long Bridge", from the 1400m-long, 174-arched **Ottoman bridge** that spans the Ergene River's water meadows at the north end of town. A remarkable feat of engineering, completed in 1443, the bridge remains entirely intact despite its location in an earthquake zone. For many years it was a notorious traffic bottleneck, clogged with heavy lorries and buses, but most drivers now use a new, four-lane bridge, which ends just south of the train station 2km east.

Keşan

KEŞAN, 53km south of Uzunköprü, is a nondescript place that most travellers don't even enter, as its *otogar* – with frequent connections to İstanbul, Edirne and Çanakkale, as well as İpsala for the Greece-bound – is on the ring road at the northwest outskirts. It's also a jump-off point for Turkey's northernmost Aegean resorts, on the Gulf of Saros.

İbrice Limanı

Although the port of **İBRİCE LİMANI**, on the **Saros Körfezi** (Saros Gulf) 40km south of Keşan, amounts to little more than one fish **restaurant** and a few **scuba-dive** boats, it's home to four seasonal diving schools. As well as being a popular spot for beginners, the gulf provides experienced divers with access to a dozen nearby sites. The best beach for non-divers is at **Bakirkoyu**, 3km east of the harbour.

Erikli

ERİKLİ, the only developed resort on the Saros Gulf coast, stands roughly 7km west of İbrice Limanı. With transport, it makes an excellent first or last stop en route from or to Greece.

While Erikli is a bit tatty at the inland edges, which border a small inland lake frequented by flamingoes, its glorious broad **beach**, over 1.5km long, compensates. Only in July and August do things get really busy.

ARRIVAL AND DEPARTURE   SOUTH OF EDİRNE

ERİKLİ

By bus Services to Erikli's dusty bus park, two blocks north of the beach in the middle of the village, are generally scarce, but frequent minibuses arrive from Keşan in summer, especially over weekends.

DIVE SCHOOLS

İBRICE LIMANI

İbrice Dalış Merkezi ☎ 0536 466 6690, ⊛ idm.gen.tr. A well established PADI- and CMAS-certified set-up based in Edirne, offering accompanied night dives as well as multi-day beginner courses.

Mavi Tutku Dalış Merkezi ☎ 0555 995 2322. Very professional PADI-certified dive school with an impressive twin-level boat, offering dives for all levels as well as first-aid certifications.

2

2

ACCOMMODATION

İBRICE LIMANI

★ **Sığınak** Off the road to Mecidiye, 3km north of the port ☎0284 783 4310, ⊕siginak.com. The closest accommodation to the coast, in a pleasant though isolated rural setting. Ten rustic wood-and-stone bungalows and rooms are tucked away in the Thracian maquis, with a welcoming fireplace-lounge and fish restaurant in the main building. Half board only June–Sept. B&B ₺400, half board ₺600

ERIKLI

Erikli Far western end of the beach, 400m from village centre ☎0284 737 3565, ⊕eriklihotel.com. Low-rise beachfront hotel with modern, airy en-suite rooms; most face the sea, not all are a/c. There's a good restaurant with both indoor and outdoor tables, as well as a large outdoor beach bar-cum-lounge area that's very popular in summer. ₺140

İşçimen Right in the middle of the beach ☎0284 737 3148, ⊕iscimenhotel.com.tr. The less salubrious of Erikli's two beachfront hotels, family-owned since the 1970s. The ageing rooms are relatively small but nonetheless comfortable; all have a/c and most have sea views. The fish restaurant is highly regarded, with plenty of tables both inside and under shade on the beach. The beach club (and its associated noise) here can last well into the night during summer. ₺125

EATING AND DRINKING

ERIKLI

Keyif Beach Far western end of the beach, 400m from village centre, opposite Erikli Hotel. This all-wood beach-shack café and bar serves a pretty good menu of snack food, including omelettes, hamburgers and fajitas as well as nice salads. The tables are mostly indoors but there's some seating outside in summer, perfect for a sunset beer. Mains ₺3–9. July–Sept daily 9am–11pm; Oct–June Fri–Sun 11am–10pm.

Saros Balık In the middle of the beach, next to İşçimen Hotel ☎0284 737 3399. The menu at Erikli's best restaurant is obviously biased towards seafood, some of which is bought to order from fishermen selling their catch in the adjacent car park. They also serve a good breakfast *kahvaltı*. A/c tables inside, plus outdoor tables on the beach. Daily 9am–11pm.

Kıyıköy

The sleepy, walled citadel of **KIYIKÖY**, 80km northwest of İstanbul, occupies an idyllic location overlooking the Black Sea. Flanked on both sides by slow-moving rivers, and backing onto lushly forested spurs of the Istranca hills, the village was fortified by the Byzantines around the sixth century, though most of what remains dates from the thirteenth and fourteenth centuries. While Kıyıköy's pre-1923 Greek population was replaced by Balkan Muslims, many inhabitants still use the former name, "Midye" – a corruption of Medea – after the locally harvested mussels. Today, the village meanders quietly from one day to the next, and offers visitors a photogenic palette of gently crumbling half-timbered houses and quiet backstreets festooned with fishing nets – the small harbour here is the only deep-water anchorage on this part of the coast. The main approach into the walled citadel is via the narrow south gate, sadly painted in an almost-pink shade of ochre. Within the citadel is a central, leafy square, where there is an ATM, and from where all accommodation and restaurants are within walking distance.

Aya Nikola Manastırı

800m southwest of the village, signposted from the road to Kazandere River • Daily 24hr; unenclosed • Free

Kıyıköy's most conspicuous ancient monument is the Byzantine **Aya Nikola Manastırı** (St Nicholas Monastery). This extraordinary complex is carved into the rock of the hillside, deep inside which a rock-cut church – complete with colonnaded aisles, barrel vaulting and a semicircular apse of tiered seats where the clergy used to sit – remained in use until 1923. You can also see the remains of a sacred pool, where the ailing and diseased bathed in the hope of a cure; hundreds of tiny crosses etched into the walls near the entrance are a reminder of their visits.

Beaches

Alongside the river mouth of the Kazandere River, 1.5km west of Kıyıköy's south gate, **Belediye Plaji** is a long stretch of sandy beach that's backed by low cliffs oozing fossils.

Sadly, during summer, the landscape here can be blighted by campers' rubbish and semi-permanent tents. With your own transport, however, several more almost-empty beaches – indeed, some of the most beautiful and undeveloped in Turkey – lie within reach roughly 5km north of Kıyıköy, near where the Pabuçdere meets the sea.

ARRIVAL AND DEPARTURE	KIYIKÖY

By bus Direct buses from İstanbul (summer 2 daily, winter 1 daily; 3hr) stop outside the citadel's south gate. More frequent buses run from İstanbul to sleepy Saray, 29km southwest, served by regular buses to Kıyıköy (every 2–3hr, daytime only).

ACCOMMODATION

★ **Endorfina** West of the citadel, signposted from the road to Vize ☎ 0288 388 6364, ⓦ hotelendorfina .com. Comfortable and professionally managed hotel with distant views of the beach and river. The contemporary, minimalist-styled rooms (no a/c) all have sea-view balconies, overlooking a large garden and wood-decked pool, and there's an excellent restaurant. Istanbul/Saray pick-ups and boat trips available, as well as discounted rates Oct–May. Half board only, ₺280

Genç Cumhuriyet Cad, 50m west of square ☎ 0288 388 6568. Central hotel with two floors of ageing, sterile en-suite rooms that are nonetheless large and clean. Restaurants and supermarket across the road, and a quiet bar on the ground floor. ₺70

Koç On the village's western fringe ☎ 0537 324 7252. Friendly hotel, overlooking open fields to the sea. Five basic but clean en-suite rooms with a/c and balconies, above an indoor/outdoor restaurant that is rarely busy or noisy. ₺85

EATING AND DRINKING

Endorfina Restaurant West of the citadel, off the road to Vize ☎ 0288 388 6364, ⓦ hotelendorfina.com. While the house speciality at this well-run hotel restaurant is freshly grilled turbot, the menu also includes *meze*, chicken and grilled meat. Eat inside or on a shaded terrace looking out to the distant beach. Mains ₺13–25. Daily noon–3pm & 7–10pm.

Köşk 50m south of square, signposted from square ☎ 0536 475 8169. Cosy, all-wood restaurant run by a father-and-son team, with just ten tables and a fireplace inside, and a few outdoor tables on a shaded verandah with harbour views through the trees. As well as the daily

and seasonal seafood menu, they also offer a delicious *meze* and a few grilled meat dishes. Mains ₺5–16. Daily 9am–10pm.

Köşk 1 Cumhuriyet Cad ☎ 0546 760 5769. Modern restaurant, built from natural stone and overlooking the sea, at the far end of the main road within the citadel. Clean and classy, the dining is all indoors, with mainly seafood dishes but also *koftë* and grilled chicken. The outdoor wooden benches in the somewhat scruffy garden below are good for a relaxed drink. Mains ₺7–16. Daily noon–4pm & 7–11pm.

The North Marmara coast

West of İstanbul, the city's straggling suburbs slowly dissipate into small, unattractive settlements squeezed between the main highway and the north Marmara coast. Roughly halfway between İstanbul and the Gelibolu Peninsula, **Tekirdağ** is the largest port on this coastline and makes a decent lunch stop en route to **Gelibolu**, the last port before the Dardanelles.

Tekirdağ

Enjoying a hilly setting at the head of a gently curving bay, **TEKİRDAĞ** – the ancient and medieval Rodosto – is a fairly pleasant town, with a few remaining, dilapidated wooden houses and a ferry service across the Sea of Marmara that can be a real boon for self-drivers.

Gelibolu

Strategically sited at the northwestern entrance of the Dardanelles, **GELİBOLU** is a moderately inviting, if often windy, medium-sized town. Founded by the ancient Greeks as Kallipolis, it served as the Anglo-French headquarters during the Crimean War, and still holds an important naval base. As the Gallipoli battlefields (see p.188)

2

are another 50km further southwest, the town is usually too far to be a practical base unless you have your own transport or if there's no closer accommodation available, as can occur on Anzac Day (April 25).

The colourful, square **fishing harbour** at the heart of town is ringed by cafés and restaurants. Only a conspicuous tower remains of the fortifications of Byzantine Kallipolis. Held by an army of rebellious Catalan mercenaries for seven years in the early fourteenth century, the fortress later fell to the Ottomans (1354), who rebuilt and expanded it.

The only other points of interest in Gelibolu are a few sturdy but otherwise unremarkable Ottoman tombs, inland from the port and around **Hamzaköy**, the resort district in the north of town, with its long, coarse-sand beach.

Piri Reis Museum

In Gelibolu's tower • Mon–Wed & Fri–Sun 8.30am–noon & 1–5pm • Free

The broad stone **tower** that separates the two pools of Gelibolu's harbour now holds the **Piri Reis Museum** (Piri Reis Müzesi). Intriguing displays trace the story of the legendary sixteenth-century Turkish cartographer, who prepared navigation charts of the Mediterranean and was the first man to accurately map the American coastline.

ARRIVAL AND DEPARTURE   THE NORTH MARMARA COAST

TEKİRDAĞ

By ferry From the *eski iskele* (old jetty) on the shorefront boulevard, afternoon ferries ply to Erdek on the far side of the Sea of Marmara, via some of its inhabited islands; the evening ferry leaves from the *yeni liman* (new port) just over 1km west. These ro-ro craft are not meant for foot passengers, but can save drivers a long and pricey journey. Destinations Bandırma (April–Oct, daily 7pm; 4hr 30min); Erdek (April–Oct, daily 3pm & 5pm, via Marmara islands; ₺90 car; 5hr 30min).

GELİBOLU

By ferry The ferry jetty is at the inner harbour entrance. Destinations Lapseki, car ferry (hourly 8am–1am, less often at night; ₺24 cars, ₺2 foot passengers; 30min).
By bus Gelibolu's *otogar* is 600m out on the Eceabat road, though a few minibuses to Eceabat or Çanakkale may pass by the harbour. Destinations Eceabat (hourly; 40min); Kilitbahir (hourly; 50min).

ACCOMMODATION

TEKİRDAĞ

Rodosto Iskele Cad 34 ☎ 0282 263 3701, ⊛ rodosto hotel.com.tr. Tekirdağ's best-value hotel, slightly set back from the noisy boulevard on a hillside, holds assorted tired but clean rooms. The higher you go, the larger and more expensive they become. Street noise is minimal, and the sea views are impressive. ₺150

GELİBOLU

Butik Hotel Gelibolu Across from the harbour ☎ 0286 566 6600, ⊛ butikhotelgelibolu.com. The newest hotel in town, elegantly furnished throughout, makes a welcome contrast with Gelibolu's other tired accommodation options. While the rooms hold all the latest facilities, they're remarkably small. The in-house restaurant is OK for breakfast, but eat dinner elsewhere. ₺170

EATING AND DRINKING

TEKİRDAĞ

Restaurants immediately below the old jetty specialize in savoury, pellet-shaped meatballs known as *Tekirdağ köfteleri*. None is licensed, so you can't sample the renowned local wine or rakı, said to be Turkey's best, thanks to the good local water.

Güverte In the eski iskele ☎ 0282 262 3058. One of the better fish restaurants within the *eski iskele*, though it also offers a decent-sized plate of *köfteleri*. Mains ₺7–18. Daily 7pm–midnight.

GELİBOLU

Be sure to try the locally caught fish, particularly *mezgit* (whitebait), *kanat* (baby bluefish) and mackerel, as well as grilled *sardalya* (sardines), the canned variety being the town's main commerce. The harbour pool is surrounded by half a dozen restaurants suitable for lunch.

Yelkenci Corner of the harbour ☎ 0286 566 4600. Reliable licensed restaurant, with indoor and outdoor tables. Fair-sized portions of seasonal fish, including grilled sardines and sea bass, plus other seafood. Mains ₺7–19. Daily 11am–11pm.

Southern Marmara

The **southern shoreline** of the Sea of Marmara is sparsely populated west of Erdek, while polluted dormitory communities for İstanbul sprawl to the east. Many of these were devastated by the **earthquake** of August, 1999, which killed an estimated 30,000 people – victims of rogue builders who ignored building regulations yet miraculously managed to pass official inspections.

Fortunately, **İznik**, historically the most interesting town, suffered little damage. To the south, **Bursa**, once one of Turkey's most attractive cities, has succumbed to rapid growth since the 1980s, bringing greater wealth but destroying much of its colourful provincial atmosphere.

The best way to explore the region is to use the fast car and foot-passenger **ferries** to Yalova, Mudanya and Bandırma from İstanbul's Yenikapı terminal; book ahead in summer. Using buses to İznik and Bursa, or your own vehicle, you could see all the sights in three to four days. Buses, which follow a congested five-hour route along the gulf shore via İzmit, are not recommended.

Southern Marmara ports and resorts

While the coastal ports of **Yalova** and **Zeytindağı** like to call themselves resorts, they hold few compelling attractions. The coastline here is mostly rocky, with inland contours softened by the ubiquitous olive groves and conifer forest.

Yalova

Little more than an hour's ferry ride from İstanbul, **Yalova** is the main transport hub for the Southern Marmara. Few visitors hang around any longer than it takes to catch a dolmuş from the ferry terminal to the new *otogar* at the southern edge of town, where onward services leave at least hourly for Termal, Bursa and İznik.

Termal

Although patronized by Byzantine and Roman emperors, the hot springs at **TERMAL** only became fashionable again in the 1890s, and most of the spa's Ottoman *belle époque* buildings date from that era. The village itself, 12km southwest of Yalova, has unfortunately sprawled in recent years, and now holds several so-called luxury hotels, all offering spa treatments and wellness sessions. You can also get here on a short dolmuş ride inland from Çınarcık, served by a summer sea-bus service from İstanbul.

Kurşunlu Banyo

In the central park • Mon–Wed, Fri & Sat 8am–10.30pm, Thurs & Sun 8am–8.30pm • ₺20 for 1hr 30min in pool

The most popular of Termal's many bathing centres is the **Kurşunlu Banyo**. The water is supposedly beneficial for rheumatism and skin diseases, but temperatures reach 65°C, so the best time to take the plunge is in winter. Otherwise, there's an **open-air pool** nearby at a more manageable 38°C.

Mudanya

Although it's the closest port to Bursa, **MUDANYA** receives fewer ferries from İstanbul than Yalova. Now rather unappealing, the town's major moment in history was when the provisional armistice between Turkey and the Allies was signed on October 11, 1922, in a wooden waterside mansion that's now a small (missable) museum.

ARRIVAL AND DEPARTURE	SOUTHERN MARMARA PORTS AND RESORTS

YALOVA

By ferry IDO ferries (⑩ido.com.tr) connect Yalova with İstanbul (May–Oct 5 ferries & 1 sea-bus daily, Nov–April 2–3 daily; foot passenger ₺13, car ₺65; 1hr 10min) and Pendik (11 ferries & 2 sea-buses daily; ₺6 foot passenger, ₺50 car; 45min).

MUDANYA

By ferry IDO ferries from İstanbul: at least 2 daily early morning and early evening; foot passenger ₺20, car ₺80; 1hr 45min (ⓦido.com.tr). Minibuses to Bursa and Çanakkale connect with arriving boats.

ACCOMMODATION

TERMAL

Dinana Üvezpınar ☎0226 675 7668. A much cheaper alternative to the luxury hotels in Termal proper, in the idyllic village of Üvezpınar, 2km southeast of Termal, and reached by hiking up the road from the *jandarma* station to the left of the entrance to Termal, or up steps from within the resort itself. Family-run and clean, it holds pleasant balconied rooms overlooking the forested mountains, and a restaurant serving simple meals. ₺85

Limak Thermal Adnan Kahveci Cad ☎0226 675 7800 ⓦlimakhotels.com. Once a summer residence for Atatürk and restored in 2010 to its former 1930s glory. As you'd expect for the price, the rooms are palatial in size and furnishings, with individual jacuzzis fed by thermal waters. The service is usually very good, as is the in-house spa. ₺700

MUDANYA

Montania Eski İstasyon Cad ☎0224 544 6000, ⓦmontaniahotel.com. Mudanya's best hotel, in a renovated 150-year-old train station and customs house on the seaside esplanade. Spread over two buildings – be sure to request the sea-view rooms – it has indoor and outdoor pools, a hamam and well-equipped rooms, though management and maintenance levels have dropped lately. ₺230

İznik

It's hard to believe that **İZNİK** (ancient Nicaea), today a backwater among fruit orchards and olive groves at the east end of the eponymous lake, was once a seat of empire and scene of desperate battles. As you look around this fertile valley, however, you can understand its attraction for imperial powers needing a fortified base near the sea lanes of the Marmara. With its regular street plan, İznik's walled centre is easy to navigate on foot, and most people visit as a long day out of İstanbul or Bursa, staying a night at most. That's enough time to sample the monuments, and pick up souvenirs from the local ceramics workshops. During its sixteenth-century heyday, İznik produced Turkey's finest **tiles**, and the tradition has recently been revived.

Brief history

Founded by Alexander's general Antigonos in 316 BC, İznik was seized and enlarged fifteen years later by his rival Lysimakhos, who named it **Nicaea** after his late wife. He also gave Nicaea its first set of walls and the grid plan typical of Hellenistic towns; both are still evident. When the Bithynian kingdom succeeded Lysimakhos, Nicaea alternated with nearby Nicomedia as its capital until bequeathed to Rome in 74 BC. After prospering as capital of the Roman province, the city continued to flourish during the Byzantine era.

Nicaea played a pivotal role in early Christianity, hosting two important **ecumenical councils**. The first, convened by Constantine the Great in 325 AD, resulted in the condemnation of the Arian heresy – which maintained that Christ's nature was inferior to God the Father's – and the promulgation of the **Nicene Creed**, affirming Christ's divine nature, which remains central to Christian belief. Empress Irene presided over the second council to be held here (the seventh in all) in 787 AD, in which the Iconoclast controversy was settled by the pronouncement, widely misunderstood in the West, that icons had their proper place in the church so long as they were revered and not worshipped.

Nicaea's much-mended walls seldom repelled invaders. The Selçuks took the city in 1081, only to be evicted by a combined force of Byzantines and Crusaders sixteen years later. The fall of Constantinople to the Fourth Crusade in 1204 propelled Nicaea into the spotlight once more, for the Byzantine heir to the throne Theodore Laskaris retreated here, and made it the base of the improbably successful **Nicaean Empire**. The Laskarid dynasty added a second circuit of walls before returning to

FROM TOP CUMALIKIZIK (P.177); TILES FROM İZNİK (P.164) >

2

Constantinople in 1261, but these again failed to deter the besieging Ottomans, who, led by Orhan Gazi, the victor of Bursa, broke through in March 1331. Renamed İznik, the city embarked on a golden age of sorts, interrupted briefly by the pillaging of Tamerlane in 1402.

While virtually all the surviving monuments predate the Mongol sacking, the most enduring contribution to art and architecture – the celebrated **İznik tiles and pottery** – first appeared after Çelebi Mehmet I brought skilled potters from Persia to begin the local industry. This received another boost in 1514 when Selim the Grim took Tabriz and sent more craftsmen west as war booty. By the end of the sixteenth century, ceramic production was at its height, with more than three hundred functioning kilns. The flowering was brief; within a hundred years war and politics had scattered most of the artisans. By the mid-eighteenth century the local industry had packed up completely. İznik began a long, steady decline, hastened by near-total devastation during the 1920–22 war.

Aya Sofya Camii
On İznik's central roundabout

Originally the Byzantine Church of Holy Wisdom, the **Aya Sofya Camii** (Aya Sofya Müzesi) was founded by Justinian I. The present building was built after an earthquake in 1065. As the cathedral of the provisional Byzantine capital, it hosted the coronations of the four Nicaean emperors. The Ottomans converted it into a mosque directly upon taking the city, and Mimar Sinan restored it, but the premises were half ruined when razed to the ground in 1922. Recent restoration raised the walls to their former height and added a roof, and it has now reverted from a museum back to a mosque. Inside there's little to see except some damaged floor mosaics and a faint **fresco** of Christ, John the Baptist and Mary, at ground level behind a glass panel to the left as you enter.

Yeşil Cami
Yeşil Cami Cad

The **Yeşil Cami** or Green Mosque, erected toward the end of the fourteenth century, is a small gem of a building, where the highlight is the fantastic marble relief on the portico. The mosque takes its name from the green İznik tiles that once adorned its stubby minaret, which looks back to Selçuk models. Sadly, though, the tiles have long since been replaced by mediocre, tri-coloured work.

İZNİK TILES

To watch **İznik tiles** being made, visit the **İznik Vafkı**, or İznik Foundation, at Vakıf Sok 13, near Saray Kapisi (◍iznik.com), which was established in 1993 to restart production using traditional methods. It sells tiles of extremely high quality, and correspondingly high price – around ₺100 for a 20cm x 10cm border piece. However, numerous other local **workshops** (atölyes) offer bulk discounts, which bring the price down to a more affordable ₺20 for a 10cm x 10cm tile. Be aware, however, that most workshops primarily take orders for domestic customers, and are likely to have only one or two items of each particular design – anyone showing up on spec hoping to decorate an entire kitchen or bathroom is apt to be disappointed.

The best, reasonably priced, one-stop shop is **Adil Can Nursan Sanat Atölyesi**, just inside the İstanbul Kapısı. Other quality (as opposed to kitsch) shops cluster along Demircan Sokağı and inside the Süleyman Paşa Medresesi, the oldest (1332) Ottoman medrese in Turkey and the first one with an open courtyard, surrounded by eleven chambers and nineteen domes.

The toughest, best, most waterproof – and most expensive – tiles are not ceramic-based but made primarily from locally quarried, finely ground **quartz**. Quartz-rich tiles are air-porous, have good acoustic qualities (hence their use in mosques), and make good insulators, as they contract slightly in winter and expand in summer.

IZNIK

N

Iznik Gölü

2

Nilüfer Hatun İmareti

İznik Museum, Müze Cad • Tues–Sun 9am–noon & 1–5pm • ₺3

The sprawling, T-form **Nilüfer Hatun İmareti**, with a huge main dome flanked by two smaller ones, is more accurately called a *zaviye* than a mere soup kitchen (*imaret*), and is one of the few that never doubled as a mosque. It was commissioned by Murat I in 1388 in honour of his mother, Nilüfer Hatun, the daughter of a Byzantine noble who was married off to Orhan Gazi to consolidate a Byzantine–Ottoman alliance. Her ability was soon recognized by Orhan, who appointed her regent during his frequent absences.

The *imaret* was originally the meeting place of the Ahi brotherhood, a guild drawn from the ranks of skilled craftsmen that also acted as a community welfare and benevolent society. It now contains the **İznik Museum**, where you can see genuine İznik pottery, including fourteenth-century tile fragments excavated from the town's kilns. Other exhibits include a bronze dancing Roman-era Pan, some Byzantine gold jewellery and, standing out amid the nondescript marble clutter, a sarcophagus in near-mint condition.

2

The walls

While only enthusiasts will want to walk the entire perimeter of İznik's double walls, now missing most of their hundred original watchtowers, two of the seven portals are worth some time. Heavy traffic has been rerouted through modern breaches in the fortifications to prevent vibration damage to the original openings, now restricted to tractors and pedestrians.

The closest gate to the Yeşil Cami, the eastern **Lefke Kapısı**, is a three-ply affair incorporating two towers erected by Emperor Hadrian between the two courses of walls. You can get up on the ramparts here for a stroll, as it is at the northerly **İstanbul Kapısı**, the best-preserved gate. It too is triple-layered, with the middle section a triumphal arch celebrating Hadrian's visit in 123 AD. The innermost gate is decorated by two stone-carved **masks**, probably taken from the city's Roman theatre.

Other traces of Roman Nicaea are evident in the southwestern quarter, including the so-called **Senatus Court** by the lakeshore, outside the **Saray Kapısı**, and the all-but-vanished **Roman theatre**, just inside the gate.

Abdülvahap hill

2.5km east of the Lefke Kapısı

If time permits, you might walk or drive past a Roman aqueduct to the obvious **Abdülvahap hill** for comprehensive views over İznik and its surroundings – a popular summer excursion for locals at sunset. The less compelling tomb on top is that of Abdülvahap, a semi-legendary figure in the eighth-century Arab raids.

From the hill you can also see the vast **İznik Gölü** (lake), which provides decent swimming in summer, though the shoreline near the town is uninviting. In order to reach the best beaches, located at its far western end between Gölyaka and Orhangazi, you really need a car.

ARRIVAL AND DEPARTURE   İZNİK

By bus İznik's tiny *otogar* is on Çelebi Sokağı, in the southeast quarter.
Destinations Bursa (every 30min; 1hr 30min); Yalova (hourly; 1hr).

By car or bike Drivers and cyclists should note that the northern-shore road from Orhangazi is far wider, faster and safer than the narrow, twisty southern-shore one.

INFORMATION

Tourist office Unlabelled, on the ground floor of the *Belediye* on Kılıçaslan Caddesi (Mon–Fri 8.30am–noon & 1–5.30pm; ☎0224 757 1933). There's also a seasonal wooden information booth by Aya Sofya.

ACCOMMODATION

★ **Belekoma** Göl Sahili Yolu 8 ☎0224 757 1407, ✆iznikbelekomahotel.com. The newest and best lakeside accommodation, reopened in 2012 after extensive renovation. The standard rooms are very comfortable with excellent facilities and modern bathrooms, and a few larger suites are perfect for families. There's also a decent restaurant, large pool and off-street parking. ₺110

Çamlık Göl Sahili Yolu 11 ☎0224 757 1362, ✆iznik-camlikmotel.com. Lakeside motel with rooms of varying sizes, decorated in bland 1980s style, though there are good orthopedic beds and decent bathrooms. Rooms with lake-view balconies suffer more road noise. ₺100

Cem Göl Sahili Yolu 34 ☎0224 757 1687, ✆cemotel.com. Well-run lakeside hotel, with cheery tan-and-earth-tone decor, modern though small bathrooms, mosaic-paved stairs and a competent ground-floor restaurant, the

Antik. Set back a bit in a gap of the walls, so quieter than the nearby *Çamlık*. ₺100

İznik Vakfı Konukevi Vakıf Sok 13 ☎0224 757 6025, ✆iznik.com. The upstairs guesthouse of the tile foundation (see p.164) is, not surprisingly, adorned with colourful, intricate tiles. Rooms are simple but comfortable and quiet, but are sometimes booked out by special-interest groups. ₺70

Kaynarca Gündem Sok 1 ☎0224 757 1753, ✆kaynarca.net. İznik's best budget option, run by English-speaking Ali and his charming family, with dorm beds, as well as en-suite rooms with satellite TV; breakfast (₺7.50 extra) is served on the rooftop terrace and there's a guest kitchen with a gas cooker. Dorms ₺25, rooms ₺70

EATING AND DRINKING

Maple-canopied Kılıçaslan Caddesi holds a few unlicensed restaurants of the *pide*-and-*köfte* variety, but most visitors choose to eat at licensed places by the lakeshore, which may serve the excellent local grilled or fried *yayın* (catfish). Tea gardens and *dondurma* parlours overlook the lake too, as does the town's only central bar.

Arti Göl Sahili Yolu. Small garden/lake-view bar serving affordable beers – the only place in town to get a drink outside the licensed restaurants. Beers ₺4. Tues–Sun noon–10pm.

Çamlık Restaurant Göl Sahili Yolu 11 ☏0224 757 1362, ⊕iznik-camlikmotel.com. The nicest setting of the waterside restaurants, though staff can be rather brusque. Expect to pay a minimum of ₺20 a head for a main course, *mezes* and a beer. Daily noon–3pm & 6–10pm.

Karadeniz Pide Salon Kılıçaslan Cad. Popular local restaurant located on the ground floor of an atmospheric 1935 building, serving fresh and cheap *pides* and pizzas washed down with *ayran*. Mains ₺5–8. Daily 11am–11pm.

★ **Köfteci Yusuf** Atatürk Cad 75 ☏0224 757 3597. Main branch of a small local chain that's a quick-serving, friendly (though unlicensed) carnivore heaven – not just *köfte* on offer but chicken wings, kidneys, *şiş* and the like. A limited range of salads (such as *piyaz*) and desserts rounds off the menu; seating on two levels, with an open terrace. *Köfte* portions ₺7. Daily 11am–3pm & 6–10pm.

Bursa

Draped like a ribbon along the leafy lower slopes of Uludağ, which towers more than 2000m higher, and overlooking a fertile plain, **BURSA** does more justice to its setting than any other Turkish city apart from İstanbul. Gathered here are some of the country's finest early Ottoman monuments, set within neighbourhoods that, despite being increasingly hemmed in by concrete tower blocks, remain appealing.

Straggling for some 20km either side of the E90 highway, and home to a population of over two million, Bursa is no longer exactly elegant. Silk and textile manufacture, plus the local thermal spas, were for centuries its most important enterprises; they're now outstripped by automobile manufacture (both Renault and Tofaş have plants), plus canneries and bottlers that process the rich harvest of the plain. Vast numbers of settlers from Artvin province have been attracted by factory jobs, while the students of Uludağ University provide a necessary leavening in what might otherwise be a uniformly conservative community. Some of this atmosphere derives from Bursa's role as first capital of the Ottoman Empire and burial place of the first six sultans, their piety as well as authority emanating from the mosques, social-welfare foundations and tombs built at their command.

Although Bursa is sometimes touted as a long day out from İstanbul, it really merits a one- and preferably two-night stay. The compact city centre, defined by the River Gök Dere and the Hisar plateau, is particularly good for exploring on foot, whether through the hive of the bazaars, the linear parks of the Hisar district or the anachronistic peace of the Muradiye quarter.

Brief history

Although the area had been settled at least a millennium previously, the first city on the site of modern Bursa was founded early in the second century BC by King Prusias I of Bithynia, who in typical Hellenistic fashion named the town **Proussa** after himself. Legend claims that Hannibal helped him pick the location of the acropolis, today's Hisar.

Overshadowed by nearby Nicomedia (modern İzmit) and Nicaea (İznik), the city stagnated until the **Romans**, attracted by its natural hot springs, spent lavish amounts on public baths and made it capital of their province of Mysia. Justinian introduced silkworm culture, and Byzantine Proussa flourished until Arab raids of the seventh and eighth centuries, and the subsequent tug-of-war for sovereignty between the Selçuks and Greeks, precipitated its decline.

The dawn of the fourteenth century saw a small band of nomadic Turks, led by **Osman Gazi**, camped outside the walls of Proussa. After more than a decade of siege,

BURSA

N

Çanakkale & Mudanya

Yeni
Kaplıca

Archeological
Museum

Kültür Parki

Atatürk
Stadium

İkinci Murat
Hamamı

Hüsnü Züber Evi

Muradiye
Külliyesi &
The Royal Tombs

MURADIYE

HWY E-90/200 ANKARA CAD

HİSAR
(TOPHANE)

Geyve

Devlet (State)
Hastanesi

Alâeddin
Camii

Zindan
Kapısı

Pinarbaşı
Kapısı

Çılımboz Deresi

BARS & CAFÉS

| Mahfel | 4 |
| Set Café | 3 |

ACCOMMODATION

Artıç	3
Atlas	5
Çeşmeli	2
Efehan	1
Gold Butik	6
Gönlüferah City	7
Güneş	4
Kitap Evi	9
Safran	8

RESTAURANTS

Arap Şükrü	7
Çiçek İzgara	2
Hacibey İskender	4
Kebapçı İskender	3, 5
Safran Restaurant	6
Üç Köfte	1

SHOPS

Adım (Haşet) Kitapçılık	6
Bedesten	1
Covered bazaar	2
Eski Aynalı Çarşı	3
Irgandı Sanat Köprüsü	5
Koza Hanı	4

LIVE MUSIC VENUES

| Kültür Merkezi (Cultural Centre) | 1 |
| Kültür Parkı's open-air theatre | 2 |

0 — 250
metres

the city capitulated in 1326 to Osman's son, Orhan, and the **Ottomans** ceased to be
a wandering tribe of marauders. Orhan marked the acquisition of a capital and the
organization of an infant state by styling himself sultan and giving the city its present
name. Bursa then embarked on a second golden age: the silk industry was expanded
and the city, outgrowing the confines of the citadel, was graced with monuments.

Following Orhan's death in 1362, the imperial capital was gradually relocated to Edirne, but Bursa's place in history, and in the hearts of the Ottomans, was ensured; succeeding sultans continued to add buildings, and to be laid to rest here, for another hundred years. Disastrous fires and earthquakes in the nineteenth century, and the 1919–22 War of Independence, only slightly diminished the city's splendour.

Orhan Gazi Camii
Orhan Gazi Meydani Sok, across from the main tourist office

Founded in 1336, the **Orhan Gazi Camii** is Bursa's second-oldest mosque, even if it has twice been destroyed and rebuilt since. Originally built as a *zaviye* for dervishes, it's the earliest example of the T-form mosque with *eyvans* flanking the main prayer hall. **Karagöz puppets**, the painted camel-leather props used in the Turkish national shadow-play, supposedly represent workers who were involved in building the Orhan Gazi Camii. According to legend, the antics of Karagöz and his sidekick Hacıvat so entertained their fellow workmen that Orhan had them beheaded to end the distraction. Later, missing the comedians and repenting of his deed, he arranged to immortalize the pair in the art form that now bears the name of Karagöz.

Ulu Cami
Corner of Atatürk and Ulu Cami cads, west of Orhan Gazi

The compact **Koza Parkı**, with its fountains, benches, strolling crowds and street-level cafés, is the real heart of Bursa. On its far side looms the tawny limestone **Ulu Cami**, built between 1396 and 1399 by Yıldırım Beyazit I, using booty won from the Crusaders at Macedonian Nikopolis. Before the battle, Yıldırım (Thunderbolt) had vowed if granted victory to construct twenty mosques. Consisting of twenty domes supported by twelve free-standing pillars, the present building was his rather loose interpretation of this promise, but was still the largest and most ambitious Ottoman mosque of its time. The interior is dominated by a huge *şadırvan* pool in the centre, whose dome oculus (now glassed over) once stood open to the elements, as well as an impressive collection of exquisite calligraphy and an intricate walnut pulpit pieced together, it's claimed, without nails or glue. From the north porch you can descend to the two-storey **Emir (Bey) Hanı**, originally a dependency of the Orhan Gazi Camii and now home to offices and shops. A fountain plays next to teahouse tables under the trees in the courtyard.

The bazaar district
Around Uzun Çarşı Cad, directly north of Orhan Gazi Camii and Ulu Cami

Bursa's **covered bazaars**, assorted galleries and lesser *hans* sell clothes, silk goods, towels, bolts of cloth as well as clothing, and furniture, all provincial specialities. The nearby **bedesten** is given over to the sale and warehousing of jewellery and precious metals.

The centrepiece of the bazaar, the **Koza Hanı**, or "Silk-Cocoon Hall", flanks Koza Parkı. Built in 1490, when Bursa was the final stop on the Silk Route from China, it's still filled with silk and brocade merchants, as well as a few jewellery stores. On the lower level, in the middle of a cobbled courtyard, a minuscule **mescit** (small mosque) perches directly over its *şadırvan*, while a subsidiary court bulges asymmetrically to the east; both hold teahouses.

Abutting the Koza Hanı to the west, though lacking access from it, the **Eski Aynalı Çarşı**, formerly the **Bey Hamamı** of the Orhan Gazi complex (note the domes and skylights), sells more tourist-orientated goods than the surrounding bazaars.

The **Demirciler Çarşısı**, or ironmongers' market – just the other side of İnönü Caddesi, best crossed by the pedestrian underpass at Okçular Caddesi – has also kept its traditions intact despite quakes and blazes. Stall upon stall of blacksmiths and braziers attract photographers; some expect a few lira for posing.

Irgandı Sanat Köprüsü
Between Atatürk Cad and Demirciler Çarşısı

The pedestrianized **Irgandı Sanat Köprüsü** (Irgandı Artisanry Bridge) spans the **Gök Dere**, one of two streams that tumble through Bursa, and forms an eastern boundary for the centre. Built in 1442, the bridge has received numerous facelifts over the centuries. The latest was in 2004, when the municipality made a feeble bid to ape Florence's Ponte Vecchio bridge; it now holds rows of faux-Ottoman cafés and tourist shops.

BURSA SILK AND THE COCOON AUCTION

The annual highlight in Bursa's bazaar is the **cocoon auction** of late June and early July, when silk-breeders gather to hawk their valuable produce. The courtyard floor of the Koza Hanı becomes a lake of white torpedoes the size of a songbird's egg; the moth, when it hatches, is a beautiful creature with giant onyx eyes and feathery antennae, though this rarely happens, as the cocoons are boiled to kill the grub inside, and the fibre is then spun. You can watch the melee from the upper arcades, but, if you're careful, the merchants don't mind you walking the floor.

Bursa's silk trade declined due to French and Italian competition during the eighteenth century, but has since experienced a tentative revival. However, the quality of contemporary fabric cannot compare to museum pieces from the early Ottoman heyday, and most of the better designs use imported material, better quality than the Turkish. If you're buying silk, make sure the label says *ipek* (silk) and not *ithal ipek* (artificial silk).

2

Yeşil

Yeşil, Bursa's eastern neighbourhood around the eponymous mosque and tomb, is only a few minutes' walk up from the far side of the Gök Dere. The immediate environs of the two monuments swarm with tour groups; competition has restrained prices at most of the nearby cafés, but also ensured that a clutch of garishly repainted old houses are glutted with souvenir dross. For genuine antique dealers, head over to the lane (İkinci Müze Sokağı) that flanks the *medrese* downhill.

Yeşil Cami
Yeşil Cad

Designed by architect Hacı İvaz atop a slight rise, the **Yeşil Cami** was started in 1413 by Çelebi Mehmet I, who won the civil war caused by the death of Beyazit I. Although unfinished – work ceased in 1424, three years after Mehmet's death – and despite catastrophic damage from two nineteenth-century earth tremors, it's the most spectacular of Bursa's imperial mosques. The incomplete entrance, faced in a light marble, lacks a portico, and, beside the stalactite vaulting and relief calligraphy, you can see the supports for arches never built.

Pass through a foyer supported by pilfered Byzantine columns to reach the **interior**, a variation on the T-plan usually reserved for dervish *zaviyes*. A fine *şadırvan* occupies the centre of the "T", but your eye is monopolized by the hundreds of mostly blue and green **tiles** that line not just the dazzling *mihrab* but every available vertical surface up to 5m in height, particularly two recesses flanking the entryway. Tucked above the foyer, and only accessible with permission from the imam, the **imperial loge** is the most extravagantly decorated chamber of all. Several artisans from Tabriz participated in the tiling of Yeşil Cami but the loge is attributed to a certain Al-Majnun, which means "madman" (due to the effects of excessive hashish-smoking) in Arabic.

Yeşil Türbe
Yeşil Cad, on the same knoll as the mosque, across the pedestrian precinct • Daily 9am–1pm & 2–6pm • Free

The **Yeşil Türbe** contains the sarcophagus of Çelebi Mehmet I and his assorted offspring. Inside, the walls and Mehmet's tomb glisten with the glorious original Tabriz material, while the battered exterior is currently being restored with new İznik tiles.

Museum of Turkish and Islamic Arts
Yeşil Cad • Tues–Sun 9am–1pm & 2–6pm • Free

Originally the fifteenth-century *medrese* for the Yeşil Cami, Bursa's **Museum of Turkish and Islamic Arts** (Türk ve İslam Eserleri Müzesi) is set around a pleasant courtyard with fountain, trees and picnic tables. Its collection includes poorly labelled İznik ware, dervish paraphernalia, Beykoz glass and antiquarian manuscripts. Rooms may be closed if the museum is short-staffed.

Emir Sultan Camii

Doyuran Cad, 300m east of Yeşil Cami

The **Emir Sultan Camii** lies amid extensive graveyards where every religious Bursan hopes to be buried. Endowed by a Bokharan dervish and trusted adviser to three sultans beginning with Beyazit I, the mosque was rebuilt from earthquake ruins in the Ottoman Baroque style during the early nineteenth century. Further restoration in 1990 left little of its original essence. The pious, however, continue to worship in strength at the tombs of the saint and his family.

2

Yıldırım Beyazit Camii

3km northeast of the centre • It's a substantial hike, but dolmuşes (marked "Heykel–Fakülte" or "Heykel–Beyazit Yıldırım"), pass 200m below

The **Yıldırım Beyazit Camii**, perched on a small hillock at the northeastern edge of Bursa's city centre, can be reached on foot from Emir Sultan Camii's graveyard, by climbing down steps and crossing the urban lowlands. Completed by Beyazit I between 1390 and 1395, the mosque features a handsome, five-arched portico defined by square columns. Its interior is unremarkable except for a gravity-defying arch that bisects the prayer hall, its lower supports apparently tapering away to end in stalactite moulding. The only other note of whimsy in this spare building is the use of elaborate niches out on the porch.

The associated **medrese**, exceptionally long and narrow because of its sloping site, huddles just downhill; today it houses a medical clinic. The **türbe** (tomb) of the luckless Beyazit, supposedly kept in an iron cage by the rampaging Tamerlane until his death in 1403, is usually locked. Perhaps the mosque custodians fear a revival of the Ottoman inclination to abuse the tomb of the most ignominiously defeated sultan.

Hisar (Tophane)

Bursa's original fortified nucleus, **Hisar**, also known as Tophane, looks over modern-day Bursa from atop a plateau on the western edge of the centre. The atmospheric old city retains clusters of dilapidated Ottoman housing within its warren of narrow lanes, and some courses of medieval wall along its perimeter, including the Sultanat Gate on the east. From the point where Atatürk Caddesi becomes Cemal Nadir Caddesi, just before the modern **Zafer Plaza** shopping mall with its landmark glass pyramid, you can climb up to Hisar's plateau via pedestrian ramps that negotiate the ancient walls. Alternatively, Orhangazi Caddesi allows access to vehicles.

Where Orhangazi Caddesi stops climbing, the **Osman and Orhan Gazi Türbeleri** stand at the edge of the fortified acropolis which Osman besieged and Orhan conquered. The tombs – post-earthquake restorations in gaudy late Ottoman style – are on the site of a long-vanished Byzantine church. More impressive is the view from the cliff-top **park** that sprawls around the tombs and adjacent clocktower. Reasonable cafés stand at the head of walkways down to Cemal Nadir and Altıparmak caddesis, the latter of which is home to posh shops and cinemas.

Near the southernmost extreme of the citadel, exit at the **Pınarbaşı Kapısı**, lowest point in the circuit of walls and the spot where Orhan's forces finally entered the city in 1326. Head west from here, parallel to the walls, re-entering at the **Zindan Kapısı**, inside of which the simple, box-like **Alâeddin Camii** was erected within a decade of the conquest and is thus the earliest mosque in Bursa.

Muradiye

The streets of **Muradiye**, best described as Bursa's uptown neighbourhood, house the city's best-preserved medieval dwellings and exudes a refined, cultured air. Things liven up a bit during Tuesday's vibrant **street market**.

Muradiye Külliyesi

The easy-to-find **Muradiye Külliyesi** is definitely the place to capture Bursa's early Ottoman spirit – it holds a few low-key trinket-sellers, but there's little pressure to buy and no coachloads shatter the calm. Begun in 1424 by Murat II, the complex was the last imperial foundation in Bursa. The **mosque** itself is similar in plan to Orhan Gazi, but more impressive with its profuse tiling low on the walls, calligraphy higher up and two domes.

Royal Tombs

Muradiye Külliyesi complex, Sedat Sok • Daily 8.30am–noon & 1–5.30pm, may close earlier in winter • Free

The ten **royal tombs** for which Muradiye is famous are mostly the final resting places of Ottoman crown princes who fell victim to stronger, or smarter, relatives hell bent on power by any means. Added piecemeal during the century or so after the mosque was founded in 1424, the tombs are set in lovingly tended and fragrant gardens whose serenity belies the tragic stories of those entombed.

The first tomb you come to holds **Şehzade Ahmet** and his brother Şehinşah, both murdered in 1513 by their cousin Selim I. The luxury of the two-tone blue İznik tiles within contrasts sharply with the adjacent austerity of **Murat II's tomb**, where Roman columns inside and a wooden canopy out front are the only superfluities. As much contemplative mystic as warrior-sultan, Murat was the only Ottoman ruler ever to abdicate voluntarily, though pressures of state forced him to leave his dervish order and return to the throne after just two years. The last sultan to be interred at Bursa, he's one of the few here who died in his bed; both the coffin and dome were originally open to the sky "so that the rain of heaven might wash my face like any pauper's".

Next along is the tomb of **Şehzade Mustafa**, Süleyman the Magnificent's unjustly murdered heir; perhaps indicative of his father's remorse, the tomb is done up in extravagantly floral İznik tiles, with a top border of calligraphy. Nearby, the tomb of **Cem Sultan**, his brother Mustafa and two of Beyazit II's sons is decorated with a riot of abstract, botanical and calligraphic paint strokes up to the dome, with turquoise tiles below. Cem, the cultured favourite son of Mehmet the Conqueror, was an interesting might-have-been. Following Mehmet's death in 1481, he lost a brief dynastic struggle with the successful claimant, brother Beyazit II, and fled abroad. For fourteen years he wandered, seeking sponsorship from Christian benefactors who in all cases became his jailers: first the Knights of St John at Bodrum and Rhodes, later the papacy. At one point it seemed he would command a Crusader army to retake İstanbul, but all such plans came to nothing for the simple reason that Beyazit anticipated his opponents' moves and each time bribed them handsomely to desist, making Cem a lucrative prisoner indeed. His usefulness as a pawn exhausted, Cem was probably poisoned in Italy by Pope Alexander VI in 1495, leaving reams of poems aching with nostalgia and homesickness.

Hüsnü Züber Evi

Uzunyol Sok 3, 1min walk uphill from Muradiye Külliyesi • Tues–Sun 10am–noon & 1–5pm • ₺3

A former Ottoman guesthouse, built in 1836, the **Hüsnü Züber Evi** sports a typical overhanging upper storey, wooden roof and garden courtyard. It now houses a collection of carved wooden musical instruments, spoons and farming utensils, many made by former owner Hüsnü Züber. The main exhibit, however, is the house itself, one of the few of its era to have been well restored and opened to the public.

Kültür Parkı

Çekirge Cad • Token admission charge when entry booths are staffed; parking ₺3

An oasis of green within Bursa's busy centre, the city's largest and most popular park, the expansive **Kültür Parkı**, was cleaned up and landscaped in 2006. The maturing trees and plants are already providing welcome shade and a sense of seclusion from the surrounding streets. Courting couples stroll along broad driveways dotted with park benches, while young families enjoy play areas and a small funfair with rides. There's also a popular tea garden, a small boating lake and a few overpriced, licensed restaurants, while an open-air theatre hosts summer concerts.

2

Archeological Museum

Kültür Parkı • Tues–Sun 8.30am–12.30pm & 1.30–5pm • ₺5

Bursa's mildly diverting **Archeological Museum** (Arkeoloji Müzesi) stands near the centre of the Kültür Parkı. Sadly lacking in labelled explanations, the exhibits in its right-hand gallery vary from the macabre (a Byzantine ossuary with a skull peeking out) to the homely (a Roman cavalryman figurine), but the adjacent hall featuring metal jewellery from all over Anatolia – watch chains, breastplates, belts, buckles, bracelets, anklets, chokers – steals the show. The left wing houses miscellaneous small antiquities, including fine Roman glass items and Byzantine and Roman bronzes.

Çekirge

20min walk along Çekirge Cad from southwest side of Kültür Parkı • Buses, including #2/A, and dolmuşes shuttle to and from stops on Atatürk Cad

The main incentive to visit the thermal centre of **Çekirge** – "Grasshopper", presumably a reference to the natural soundtrack of a summer evening – is to enjoy a dip in its **hot springs**.

Yeni Kaplıca

Kurkurtlu Cad, just west of Kültür Parkı • Daily 6am–10pm • ₺8 • ☎ 0224 236 6968

The water at the **Yeni Kaplıca** (New Spa) usually flows out at a whopping 84°C. The spa itself dates from the mid-sixteenth century and has a women's section, though it is nothing like as splendid as the men's with its huge, deep central pool. According to legend, Süleyman the Magnificent was cured of gout after a dip in the Byzantine baths here and had his vizier Rüstem Paşa overhaul them. Fragments of mosaic paving stud the floor and the walls are lined with once-exquisite, now blurred, İznik tiles. Within the same complex are two other spas, the rather grim **Kaynarca baths** for women only and the **Karamustafa spa** (54°C at source) for families. It's mainly frequented by locals, but the odd tourist turns up, and the friendly staff is very accommodating.

Eski Kaplıca (Old Baths)

Eski Kaplica Sok, off Çekirge Cad, next to Kervansaray Termal Hotel • Daily 7am–10.30pm • ₺26 • ☎ 0224 233 9300

Bursa's most ancient baths, the **Eski Kaplıca** (Old Baths), is much the nicest public bath for women. Byzantine rulers Justinian and Theodora improved a Roman spa on this site, and Murat I had a go at the structure in the late fourteenth century. Huge but shallow keyhole-shaped pools dominate the *hararetler* (hot rooms) of the men's and women's sections, whose domes are supported by eight Byzantine columns. The baths are now managed by the hotel next door, hence the high admission cost.

Hüdavendigar (Birinci) Murat Camii

Junction of Çekirge and Murat cads

With its five-arched portico and alternating bands of brick and stone, the **Hüdavendigar (Birinci) Murat Camii** resembles a Byzantine church from Ravenna or Macedonia. Indeed, tradition asserts that the architect and builders were Christians, who dallied twenty years at the task because Murat I, whose pompous epithet literally means "Creator of the Universe", was continually off at war and unable to supervise the work. The interior plan, consisting of a first-floor *medrese* above a highly modified, T-type *zaviye* at ground level, is unique in Islam. Unfortunately, the upper storey is rarely open for visits.

Murat's türbe

Junction of Çekirge and Murat cads, across the street from the Hüdavendigar (Birinci) Murat Camii

The body of Murat I, brought back from Serbia in 1389, lies in a much-modified **türbe**. In June of that year Murat was about to win his greatest triumph, over the Serbian king Lazar and his allies at the **Battle of Kosovo**, when he was stabbed to death in his tent by Miloš Obilić, a Serbian noble who had feigned desertion. Murat's son Beyazit, later styled as Yıldırım, immediately had his brother Yakub strangled and, once in sole command, crushed the Christian armies. Beyazit's acts had two far-reaching consequences: the Balkans remained under Ottoman control until early in the twentieth century, and a gruesome precedent of fratricide was established for subsequent Ottoman coronations.

ARRIVAL AND DEPARTURE   BURSA

By plane Bursa's airport, near Yenişehir 43km east, is only served by flights from Ankara with Borajet, is served by taxis but not buses, and has car rental outlets.

By bus From the *otogar*, 10km north of town on the Yalova road, bus #38 serves the centre, #96 serves Çekirge suburb, and service buses run straight to Heykel (also known as Cumhuriyet Alanı), the focal point of the city. There's a 24hr left-luggage service.

Destinations Ankara (hourly; 6hr); Çanakkale (hourly;

5hr 15min); Gölyazı (10 Mon–Sat, 6 Sun; 40min); İstanbul, with ferry transfer (hourly; 3hr); İzmir via Balıkesir and often Ayvalık (hourly; 7hr); Kütahya (4 daily; 3hr); Mudanya (every 30min; 30min); Yalova (every 30min; 1hr).

By car International rental chains based in Çekirge include Avis, Çekirge Cad 139 (☎0224 236 5133), and Europcar, Kürkütlü Cad 39. Local operators at the city end of Çekirge Cad include the recommended Liberty Rent-A-Car, Çekirge Cad 25 (☎0224 222 9011).

GETTING AROUND

Buses and dolmuşes The two most useful city bus routes are #2/A (connecting Emir Sultan in the east with Çekirge to the west) and #3/A (linking Heykel with the Uludağ *teleferik*); tickets (₺2) must be pre-purchased at kiosks or shops displaying the BuKart logo. More useful are Bursa's multicoloured dolmuşes, with major terminals near Koza Parkı and Heykel, plus other pick-up/set-down points

marked with a large "D" sign; fares start from ₺1.25.

Metro Few visitors use the single-line, east–west metro, which links various remote suburbs with points well north of the centre.

Driving Parking is a nightmare – there are never enough central street spaces to be had, and car parks are expensive. Park some way out, and walk to the sights.

INFORMATION

Tourist office In a row of shops under the north side of Atatürk Caddesi, opposite Orhan Gazi Camii, 200m from

Heykel (daily 8am–noon & 1–5.30pm, closed Sat & Sun except in summer; ☎0224 220 1848).

ACCOMMODATION

There's usually no shortage of reasonably priced **hotel** beds in Bursa. Wealthier foreigners gravitate towards the luxurious spa-hotels at **Çekirge**, which also has a cluster of modest establishments, around the Birinci Murat Camii. If your prime interest is monumental Bursa, staying in the bazaar or Hisar districts makes more sense.

BAZAAR DISTRICT

Artıç Atatürk Cad, Ulu Cami Karşısı 95 ☎0224 223 5505, ⚟artichotel.com. Set slightly back from the boulevard, this standard business hotel has bland, carpeted rooms with all the usual amenities, though very small bathrooms; a few larger suites come with views. The staff are friendly, and the breakfast (included) plentiful. ₺180

Çeşmeli Gümüşçeken Cad 6 ☎0224 224 1511. Welcoming hotel with female-only staff, offering spacious, comfortable rooms (if a little dated), with double-glazing to buffer the noise. A very good buffet breakfast is included, and parking is available. ₺110

Efehan Gümüşçeken Cad 34 ☎0224 225 2260, ⚟efehan.com.tr. Despite its grim exterior, this three-star hotel has tasteful rooms that are very good value, with modern bathrooms and some mountain views. The top-floor restaurant offers sweeping city panoramas, and there's parking nearby. ₺120

Güneş İnebey Cad 75 ☎0224 224 1404. One of Bursa's very few budget options; a clean and friendly family-run

pansiyon in a converted Ottoman house. The laminate-floor rooms are small but heated, though the (shared) bathrooms are separate. ₺55

HISAR

★ **Kitap Evi** Burç Üstü 21, in from Saltanat Kapısı ☎0224 225 4160, ⚟kitapevi.com.tr. Bursa's only true boutique hotel was originally an avant garde bookstore. Eclectically decorated throughout, there's a range of themed rooms (some old-fashioned, some contemporary in design) and suites with dark-wood floors and (often) free-standing baths. The front rooms (and roof suite) have glorious city views but some noise; quieter units face the rear-garden breakfast café/restaurant. Limited street parking, and free pick-ups from Bursa *otogar* or Mudanya ferry. Rates include breakfast. ₺270

Safran Ortapazar Cad, Arka Sok 4, inside Saltanat Kapısı ☎0224 224 7216, ⚟safranotel.com. Converted wooden-house hotel with atmospheric common areas. The a/c rooms themselves are blandly modern and a bit overpriced, but there's a very good in-house restaurant (see p.176), ample breakfasts and friendly, helpful staff. Limited parking. Rates include breakfast. ₺160

ÇEKIRGE

Atlas Hamamlar Cad 29 ☎0224 234 4100, ⓦatlasotel .com. Reproduction Art Nouveau common areas complement the well-kept rooms with flat-screen TVs, designer bathrooms and modern furnishings; the best ones face the garden courtyard. There's also a marble basement hamam, open June–Sept only. ₺130

Gold Butik Brinici Murat Cami Arkasi 17 ☎0224 232 1964, ⓦhotelgold.com.tr. Also known as *Gold 2*, this much-altered eighteenth-century building is one of Bursa's quietest hotels, with lavender wallpaper and laminate floors throughout, a creaky lift, pleasant breakfast/bar area, and some parking out front. Some top-floor rooms have balconies; no. 401 has a view of the mosque domes. ₺150

Gönlüferah City Murat Cad 20 ☎0224 233 9500, ⓦgonluferahcity.com. Four-star hotel whose plain rooms have medium-dark veneer trim and marble sinks, some with great views over the city. There's an adjoining *hamam* and spa, as well as a decent terrace restaurant, and secure parking. ₺210

EATING AND DRINKING

Bursa's **cuisine** is solidly meat-oriented and served in a largely alcohol-free environment. The most famous local recipes are *İskender kebabı* (essentially *döner kebap* soaked in a rich butter, tomato and yoghurt sauce) and *İnegöl köftesi* (rich little pellets of mince sometimes laced with cheese, when they're known as *kaşarlı köfte*). The city is also famous for its *kestane şekeri* (candied chestnuts), sold ubiquitously within a 50km radius. If you're sick of Turkish sponge-bread, look out for Bursan *kepekli* (whole bran) loaves at any bakery. For licensed restaurants, head to the pedestrianized **Sakarya Caddesi** between Altıparmak Caddesi and the walls of Hisar above – the former fish market and main commercial street of the **Jewish quarter** now make an atmospheric venue for an outdoor fish dinner on a summer's evening.

RESTAURANTS

Arap Şükrü Sakarya Cad 6 & 27, Tophane. This cobblestoned lane is known locally as Arap Şükrü Sokağı, after the owner of the first restaurant here. The lane now offers a dozen restaurants all owned by members of Arap Şükrü's extended family and all named the same as the original. Two sons run identical restaurants straddling the lane's east end, *Arap Şükrü Ahmet* and *Arap Şükrü Çetin*, offering near-identical menus of good fish dishes (starting from ₺20 a portion), *mezes* (₺4–6) displayed on trays, and beer, wine or rakı to wash it down, served at tables on both sides of the pedestrianized lane or indoors. Daily noon–11pm.

Çiçek İzgara Belediye Cad 15. Part of a Bursa chain, this popular mid-town venue overlooks a leafy square and is known for its signature meatball dish *kaşarlı köfte* (₺10), as well as *sütlü kadayıf*, a pudding of shredded wheat in a milk sorbet (₺7). Mon–Sat noon–3pm & 7–10pm.

Hacıbey İskender Taşkapı Sok 4, off Atatürk Cad. This tiny, two-storey establishment near Heykel claims to be the original *İskender* salon, with decor of old wood, fake Ottoman tiles and photos of Olde Bursa. Indeed, their *İskender* is excellent, though you pay extra for the ambience. Mains ₺18. Daily noon–11pm.

Kebapçı İskender Unlu Cad 7A, Heykel. This fake Ottoman building is one of many local claimants to be the inventor of the namesake dish – and that's all they serve, not even salads. Always packed, even though it's moderately expensive (₺17 and up for smallish portions). There's an annexe on Atatürk Cad, near the Kültür Merkezi. Daily noon–10.30pm.

★ **Safran Restaurant** Safran Hotel, Ortapazar Cad, Arka Sok 4, Hisar. Chic little restaurant offering cold and hot *mezes*, meat and mushroom stews, good salads, and heavenly sweets such as *kaymaklı ayva tatlısı* (quince with clotted cream). Expect to pay ₺25–30 for a three-course meal, drinks extra. Daily 7–11pm.

Üç Köfte Hacı İvaz Paşa Çarşısı 3. The name of this long-established spot, in the north of the covered bazaar, means "three (*İnegöl*-style) meatballs", and that's what you get, served up three times so the food on your plate is always piping hot. Mains ₺12. Mon–Sat 11am–3pm.

BARS AND CAFÉS

Mahfel Namazgah Cad 2, southeast side of Setbaşı bridge. Supposedly Bursa's oldest café, serving slightly pricey Western snacks but lovely, reasonably priced, puddings (₺6). Some evenings, there's live music on its riverside terrace. Daily 11am–10pm.

Set Café Setbaşı bridge, Namazgah Cad, Heykel. Reasonably priced café-bar on a recessed terrace below street level, which attracts a lively student crowd. Enjoy a ₺4 beer looking downstream to the next bridge, or on one of the four levels indoors. Daily noon–10pm.

ENTERTAINMENT

Kültür Merkezi (Cultural Centre) Atatürk Cad ☎0224 223 4461. Regular (and free) evening dervish displays, along with temporary art exhibitions and occasional concerts.

Open-air theatre Kültür Parkı. The main venue (tickets ₺15–25) for musical performances of the annual Uluslararası Bursa Festival (June–July; ⓦbursafestivali.org), mostly showcasing popular Turkish acts but also with a token roster of foreign performers.

DIRECTORY

Books Adım (Haşet) Kitapçılık, at Altıparmak Cad 50, stocks some English-language titles and foreign magazines.
Consulate UK (honorary consulate), Resam Şefik Bursalı Sok, Başak Cad (☎ 0224 220 0436).
Hamams See p.174, or try the central, historic Çakır Ağa, located just below Hisar on Cemal Nadir Cad (men and women; 6am–midnight); or İkinci Murat, next to the Muradiye tomb complex (daily 10am–6pm; Fri & Sun men only, Mon–Thurs & Sat women only).
Hospitals Devlet (State) Hastanesi, Hasta Yurdu Cad, Hisar (☎ 0224 220 0020), and Üniversite Hastanesi, P. Tezok Cad, Hastane Sok, Çekirge (☎ 0224 442 8400).

Around Bursa

A couple of worthwhile targets for half-day or even overnight outings are located immediately around Bursa. The picturesque rural Ottoman village of **Cumalıkızık** served as the setting for a popular Turkish TV serial several years ago, which greatly enhanced its tourism potential, while the mountain resort of **Uludağ** is a year-round attraction.

Further afield, the 120km route west from Bursa towards Bandırma port is enlivened by two large but shallow lakes, the largest inland bodies of water in the historical region of Mysia. The first, 36km from central Bursa, is **Uluabat Gölü**, home to the appealing village of **Gölyazı** built atop the ancient settlement of Apollonia, while the second lake, **Manyas Gölü**, southeast, supports a bird sanctuary.

Cumalıkızık

The showcase village of **CUMALIKIZIK**, set on the lower slopes of Uludağ, 17km from Bursa on the Ankara road – head east, then south – is the most attractive of several such *kızık* (valley) villages in the region. While the earliest records of the village mosque and hamam date from 1685, it's thought to be at least three centuries older. Cumalıkızık's cobbled streets are full of traditional dwellings, some restored and painted, others leaning brokenly into each other.

The narrow alleys that radiate from the village square, dominated by two enormous plane trees, are often only wide enough for pedestrians and pack animals. The ground and first floors of the village houses traditionally harboured the storerooms and stables, while the living quarters with their latticed bay windows were upstairs under tiled eaves. Many of the surviving double-front doors sport large-headed nails, wrought-iron strips and massive handles.

Uludağ

The dramatic, often cloud-cloaked massif of 2543m-high **Uludağ** (or "Great Mountain") presides over Bursa, its northern reaches dropping precipitously into the city. In ancient times it was known as the Mount Olympos of Mysia, one of nearly twenty peaks around the Aegean so named (Olympos was possibly a generic Phoenician or Doric word for "mountain"). Locals insist this was the seat from which the gods watched the battle of Troy. Early in the Christian era the range became a refuge for monks and hermits, replaced after the Ottoman conquest by Muslim dervishes.

These days the scent of grilling meat has displaced the odour of sanctity, since Bursans cram the alpine campsites and picnic grounds to the gills on any holiday or weekend. Getting there has always been half the fun, especially if you opt for the **cable car** (*teleferik*), which links the Teleferüç borough of Bursa with the **Sarıalan** picnic grounds at 1635m, where a cluster of *et mangals* and *kendin pişin kendin ye* (cook-it-yourself establishments) await your custom. At the time of writing, however, a new cable-car line was being built and the entire *teleferik* service was shut down, pending its completion.

Much of the dense middle-altitude forest has been designated a **national park**, though only a few kilometres are marked hiking trails. In fact, the best part of the mountain lies outside the park to the east, where a few hours' walking brings you to glacial **lakes** in a wild, rocky setting just below the highest summit. The best months to visit are May and June, with wildflowers in bloom, or September and October, when the mist is less dense.

2

HIKING AROUND ULUDAĞ

From the top of Oteller, a 90min walk along a jeep track will bring you to a **tungsten mine**. An obvious path slips up behind the mine's guardhouse onto the broad, barren watershed ridge, just below the secondary summit of **Zirve** (2496m); follow this trail for a further 90min to a fork. The right-hand path leads to the **main peak** (2543m), though the cairned left-hand choice is more rewarding, descending slightly to overlook the first of Uludağ's lakes, **Aynalıgöl**, reachable by its own side trail 30min beyond the junction.

While Aynalıgöl holds campsites, there are none at **Karagöl**, the second and most famous lake, 15min southeast, sunk in a deep chasm and speckled with ice floes. **Kilimligöl**, the third substantial lake, is tucked away on a plateau southeast of Karagöl and offers more good high-altitude camping. The crags above Aynalıgöl conceal two smaller, nameless tarns.

As long as the weather is good, when you return to Oteller you can stay with the ridge rather than revisiting the tungsten works, passing below the ruined hut on Zirve to meet a faint trail. This soon vanishes and thereafter it's cross-country downhill along the watershed as far as **Cennetkaya**, a knoll above the hotels, served by a marked trail. High above the trees, crowds and jeep tracks, you just might glimpse patches of the distant Sea of Marmara to the north.

However, thanks to the nearby Sea of Marmara, the high ridges trap moist marine air, and whiteouts or violent storms can blow up during most of the year. **Skiing** is possible from December to March, though it's better earlier in the season than later. At around 1800m, there's a dense cluster of hotels known as **Oteller**, most with their own ski lift (day-passes ₺15), and you can rent skis and ski clothes on the spot.

Gölyazı

Minibus #5/G links Gölyazı with Bursa's Küçük Sanayı metro station; if driving, look for an inconspicuous sign, 31km west of Bursa, that indicates the 5km side road to the village

Largely constructed on an island that's now lashed by a causeway to the shore of **Uluabat Gölü**, **GÖLYAZİ** is an atmospheric community of storks' nests and a few surviving half-timbered houses daubed with rust-tint or ochre paint. Bits of Roman and Byzantine **Apollonia** have unconcernedly been pressed into domestic service, with extensive courses of wall ringing the island's shoreline.

In the smaller mainland neighbourhood, the huge **Ayos Yorgos** Greek church, large enough for a few hundred parishioners, is slowly being restored. The lake itself, speckled with nine islets, is only 2m deep, murky and not suitable for swimming, though it does attract water birds. There's a daily (11am) **fish auction** at the island end of the causeway, while women mending nets and rowing boats are much in evidence.

Gölyazı holds no reliable **accommodation**, but there are various **tea houses** on either side of the causeway.

Bandırma

Bandırma, the largest port on the Southern Marmara, 95km west of Bursa, makes an easy route between İstanbul and the North Aegean. Having been all but flattened during battles in 1922, however, it lacks any atmospheric old quarter or architectural heritage, and in the absence of decent accommodation, it's best to avoid staying here if at all possible. Most services offered by the adjacent ferry and train terminals connect with relatively short waiting times, while the edge-of-town *otogar* offers abundant departures to the major regional centres.

Bird Paradise National Park

Northeast corner of Manyas Gölü, 19km southeast of Bandırma • Daily 7am–5.30pm • ₺3 • No public transport

The **Bird Paradise National Park** (Kuş Cenneti Milli Parkı) spreads for 160 acres across a stream delta and swamps at the northeast corner of the **Manyas Gölü** lake. Its small visitor centre is filled with dioramas, labelled in Turkish, and stocked with stuffed geese, orioles, spoonbills, herons, pelicans, ducks, egrets and owls. More interesting, though, is the wooden **observation tower** (bring your own binoculars), from where you can view pelicans (white and Dalmatian, nesting in May), smews, spoonbills, spotted eagles and night herons, with cormorants and grey herons also common. The best months to visit are October – during the first rains, and various species' southward migrations – and April and May, when the swamps are at their fullest and the birds are flying north. During these migrations, up to three million birds of some 239 species stop by.

While there are no facilities in the park grounds, **Eski Sığırcı** village, 1.5km before the gate, holds a simple roadside restaurant with a couple of *pansiyon* rooms.

ARRIVAL AND DEPARTURE

CUMALIKIZIK

By bus Buses stop in the village square; catch city bus #22 (every 90min) from Atatürk Caddesi in Bursa.
By car Park at the village entrance (₺2).

ULUDAĞ

By teleferik The cable car to Sarıalan was being rebuilt as this book went to press. Assuming it's once more operative, you can reach the lower cable-car terminus, in Teleferüç in Bursa, via dolmuş from the corner of Resam Şefik Bursalı and Atatürk caddesis. Hours and prices may well have changed, but previously the *teleferik* left every 45min, and took 30min (daily: summer 8am–9.30pm, winter 8am–4.30pm; ₺8 return). Try to avoid travelling mid-afternoon, when students make the ascent after school, or at weekends when hour-long queues are the norm. A fleet of dolmuşes waits at Sarıalan to take visitors to Oteller.
By dolmuş Dolmuşes from Bursa's Orhangazi Caddesi go all the way to Oteller, along 32km of paved, twisty road (min 6 passengers; ₺7 per person).
By car The 32km road to Oteller veers off above Çekirge and climbs rapidly through successive vegetation zones. Staff at the Karabelen national park gate, 20km into the

AROUND BURSA

park, charge ₺5 per car and sometimes hand out information. The final stretch of road, from just below the gate to Oteller, is very rough cobble, designed to prevent drivers from skidding – or speeding – so allow nearly an hour for the trip. In bad weather, you may not be allowed to make the journey unless you have chains on your wheels.

BANDIRMA

By ferry From the port, in the heart of town, all roads lead upwards and inland.
Destinations İstanbul (summer 4–5 daily, winter 2–3 daily; mix of fast car ferries and sea-buses; ₺30 foot passenger, ₺120 car; 2hr; w ido.com.tr).
By train The station adjoins the ferry port.
Destinations İzmir (1–2 daily; 5hr 30min). Morning ferries from İstanbul dovetail well (30min layover) with onward trains; midday ferries entail a longer wait (up to 2hr).
By bus and dolmuş The main *otogar* is on the southern outskirts of town, 1800m inland and uphill from the ferry terminal. Catch a taxi, or a city bus labelled "Garaj/600 Evler", from a marquee 200m east of the ferry terminal.
Destinations Bursa (approx hourly; 2hr); Çanakkale (hourly; 3hr); İzmir (7 daily; 6hr).

ACCOMMODATION AND EATING

CUMALIKIZIK

★ **Mavi Boncuk** Saldede Sok ☎ 0224 373 0955, w cumalikizik-maviboncuk.com. A pair of old village houses owner/managed by a delightful retired couple, this guesthouse exudes a welcoming, rustic charm, with creaky floorboards, granny-style embroidered pillows and home-made jams. The small but comfortable and private rooms sit upstairs, while downstairs is a quaint, lush garden and an open-sided verandah. They serve an excellent breakfast and lunch (open to the public) full of fresh herbs, good olive oil and home-made bread. ₺140

ULUDAĞ

The many resorts at the road's end in Oteller hold around 7500 hotel beds. There's little to distinguish each resort

from the next; all are listed on w turkeyskihotels.com. Summer rates can dip as low as ₺160, but expect to pay up to ₺500 (full board) in ski season. Camping is not recommended; the national park campsites are squalid and always full in summer.

GÖLYAZI

Pehlivan İkizce Yolu ☎ 0535 395 3297. This atmospheric restaurant is within a wooden cabin overhanging the lake's edge, with tables both inside (heated by a wooden stove) and under a covered balcony. The menu includes reasonably priced *yayın* (catfish) and *turna* (pike), plus decent mixed-*meze* platters. *Meze* ₺6, mains ₺7–16. Licensed. Tues–Sun noon–3pm & 7–10pm.

The North Aegean

SARDIS

The North Aegean

In antiquity, Turkey's North Aegean was known as Aeolia, and provided the setting for the Trojan war. Civilization first bloomed here under the Phrygians, who arrived in Anatolia during the thirteenth century BC. Later, Greek colonists established coastal settlements, leaving the region rich in Classical and Hellenistic remains. These days, however, it sees far fewer visitors than the coastline further south. While there are some excellent sandy beaches, the lower sea temperature and lack of a major airport have protected the region from widespread development. Most summer visitors are Turks, and even in August visitor numbers are relatively low. Away from the few resorts, farming, fishing and heavy industry (near İzmir) provide the main livelihoods.

While the sparse ruins of **Troy** don't quite live up to their literary and legendary reputation, ancient **Assos** and **Pergamon** (modern **Bergama**) display more tangible reminders of the power and wealth of the greater Greek cultural sphere. Less visited are the recently excavated ruins of **Alexandria Troas**, and the isolated Lydian city of **Sardis**, ancient capital of King Croesus, huddled at the foot of impressive mountains.

Coming from İstanbul or anywhere else in northwest Turkey, the most obvious entry point is **Çanakkale** – useful as a base for both the ruins at Troy and the World War I battlefields on the **Gelibolu** (Gallipoli) peninsula. Offshore, the fine Turkish Aegean islands of **Gökçeada** and **Bozcaada** provide an easy escape. The road south from Çanakkale is justifiably marked as scenic on most maps; much of the route is wooded and gently hilly, giving way to a coastal strip backed by the mountains of the Kazdağı range that conceal idyllic villages like **Yeşilyurt** and **Adatepe**. Further south, the best stretches of beach lie near the long-established resort of **Ayvalık-Cunda**, but there are also pleasant sands north of **Foça**.

In general there's less to see **inland**, with a mountainous landscape and a few predominantly industrial cities. However, the **İzmir–Bandırma railway** provides an alternative approach to the region, passing through unremarkable Balıkesir (from where frequent buses run to Ayvalık), Soma (a short bus ride from Bergama), and **Manisa** – the only town worthy of prolonged attention.

Çanakkale

Blessed with a superb setting on the Dardanelles straits, **ÇANAKKALE** is a vibrant harbour town with a multicultural past that can be found in its compact old quarter, and a busy seafront that's home to a replica of the **Trojan horse** used in the 2004 film

BOZCAADA

Highlights

❶ Battlefield sites and cemeteries The Gelibolu (Gallipoli) peninsula was the scene of a major Allied defeat during World War I, commemorated each April on Anzac Day. **See p.193**

❷ Gökçeada Turkey's largest island is a scenic, rugged place, with idyllic beaches and a lingering ethnic-Greek presence. **See p.195**

❸ Bozcaada (Tenedos) Small, popular island with an elegant harbour town, fine wines and decent beaches. **See p.198**

❹ Assos The ancient site offers stunning views of Lésvos island: the hilltop medieval village and

picturesque harbour are built of the same volcanic stone. **See p.203**

❺ Ayvalık and Cunda Relax in these adjacent, former Greek olive-oil-processing ports, with their intriguing mix of derelict and restored Greek and Ottoman houses. **See p.207**

❻ Ancient Pergamon Both the acropolis, with its sweeping views and restored temple, and the Asklepion downhill rank among the finest Roman ruins in the Aegean. **See p.212**

❼ Sardis With an evocative Artemis temple and restored baths, these remote ruins reward a detour inland. **See p.220**

HIGHLIGHTS ARE MARKED ON THE MAP ON P.184

THE NORTH AEGEAN

HIGHLIGHTS
1. Battlefield sites and cemeteries
2. Gökçeada
3. Bozcaada (Tenedos)
4. Assos
5. Ayvalık and Cunda
6. Ancient Pergamon
7. Sardis

AEGEAN SEA

N

0   50
kilometres

THE WEARY WATERS OF THE DARDANELLES

The **Dardanelles** – in Turkish, Çanakkale Boğazı – have defined Çanakkale's history and its place in myth. The area's Classical name, **Hellespont**, derives from Helle, who, escaping from her wicked stepmother on the back of a winged ram, fell into the swift-moving channel and drowned. From Abydos on the Asian side, the youth **Leander** used to swim to Sestos on the European shore for trysts with his lover **Hero**, until one night he too perished in the currents; in despair, Hero drowned herself as well. In 1810, enthusiastic swimmer **Lord Byron** succeeded in crossing the channel only on his second attempt – a feat he often claimed as his greatest-ever achievement.

Persian hordes under **Xerxes** crossed these waters on their way to Greece in 480 BC, and in 411 and 405 BC the last two naval battles of the Peloponnesian War took place in the straits; the latter engagement ended in decisive defeat for the Athenian fleet. Twenty centuries later, **Mehmet the Conqueror** constructed the elaborate fortresses of Kilitbahir and Çimenlik Kale, across from each other, to tighten the stranglehold being applied to doomed Constantinople.

In March 1915, an Allied fleet attempting to force the Dardanelles and attack İstanbul was repulsed by Turkish shore batteries, with severe losses, prompting the even bloodier land campaign usually known as **Gallipoli**. These days the straits are still militarized, and modern Çanakkale is very much a navy town.

Troy. While the town undeniably makes a convenient base for the World War I battlefields at Gallipoli, on the European side of the Dardanelles, as well as the ruins of Troy, Çanakkale itself deserves at least an overnight stop, with a couple of interesting sights and a nightlife scene that positively hums in the summer. It's also the starting point for sea buses to the Turkish Aegean islands of Gökçeada and Bozcaada.

Çimenlik Park

Naval Museum Çimenlik Sok • Tues, Wed & Fri–Sun 9am–noon & 1.30–5pm • ₺5 • ☎ 0286 217 1707

Çimenlik Park, beyond the bazaar, contains Sultan Mehmet II's castle, **Çimenlik Kale**, and an assortment of torpedoes and artillery from various countries. It's also home to the **Naval Museum** (Deniz Müzesi), which holds more military paraphernalia, as well as photos of Seddülbahir in ruins after Allied shelling, and of Atatürk's funeral.

Also within the park, there's a moored replica of the minelayer **Nusrat**, which stymied the Allied fleet in March 1915 by re-mining at night zones that the French and British had swept clean by day.

Archeological Museum

Barbaros Mahalessi, 100-Yil Cad; almost 2km south of the town centre along Atatürk Cad • Tues–Sun 9am–5pm • ₺5 • ☎ 0286 217 6565 • Served by any Atatürk Cad dolmuş labelled "Kepez" or "Güzelyalı"

The poorly labelled collection in Çanakkale's **Archeological Museum** (Arkeoloji Müzesi) is strong on brass implements, delicate glass and glazed pottery, gold and jewellery, unfired lamps, and Hellenistic figurines from the nearby Bozcaada and Dardanos tumuli. The highlights, however, are two exquisite **sarcophagi**: the late Archaic "Polyxena", in perfect condition, with a procession on one side and the sacrifice (in grisly detail) of Priam's daughter on the other, and the fourth-century BC "Altıkulaç", more damaged but showing a finely detailed boar hunt and battle scene with a mounted warrior spearing a victim.

ARRIVAL AND DEPARTURE   ÇANAKKALE

By ferry Ferries from Eceabat on the Gelibolu peninsula or from Gökçeada dock at the base of Cumhuriyet Bulvarı; those from Kilitbahir dock a block southwest. Tickets for the

Çanakkale–Eceabat car ferry are valid to continue the same day from Kabatepe to Gökçeada, and vice versa.

Destinations Bozcaada (1 sailing on Wed, Sat & Sun;

CANAKKALE

RESTAURANTS	
Adana Sofrası	6
Cafe du Port	5
Cafeka	3
Sardunya	4
Seaside	2
Şehir Kulübü	1

BARS AND CAFÉS	
Benzin	1
Han Kahvesi	2
Kahveci	3

ACCOMMODATION	
Akol	1
Anzac	4
Artur	3
Cetinkaya	2
Helen	5
Kervansaray	6

6, Archeological Museum, Troy & Airport

55min; sea bus, no cars); Eceabat (June–Sept on the hour; Oct–May on the hour 7am–1am, plus 3am & 5am; 30min); Gökçeada (June–Sept 1 sailing on Mon, Tues, Thurs & Sun; Oct–May 1 sailing on Mon, Thurs & Fri; 1hr; sea bus, no cars); Kilitbahir (every 30min 6.30am–9.30pm, then according to traffic up to 1.30am; 8min).

By air The airport is 2km southeast of town (✆0286 212 1849); shuttle buses (₺7) or taxis usually await incoming flights.

Destinations Ankara (daily; 1hr 30min); İstanbul (2–3 weekly, June–Sept only; 1hr).

By bus or dolmuş Çanakkale's *otogar*, with buses to Bursa, Edirne and all north Aegean destinations, is 1km out on Atatürk Caddesi, a 15min walk from the central seafront, and served by free shuttle from bus-company offices near the tourist office. However, many buses pass straight through town to cross the straits, and you can also board at the ferry docks. Dolmuşes to Troy run from a riverside terminal adjacent to the northern end of the bridge over the Sarı Çay, 1km southeast of the town centre.

Destinations Ayvalık (hourly; 3hr 30min); Bursa (hourly; 4hr 30min); Edirne (5 daily; 4hr 30min); İzmir (hourly via Thrace; 5hr 30min); Lapseki (hourly; 5hr 30min); Yükyeri İskelesi via Geyikli (timed to meet Bozcaada ferry; 1hr).

INFORMATION

Tourist office Cumhuriyet Mey, next to the main dock (June–Sept daily 8am–noon & 1–7pm, Oct–May Mon–Fri 8am–noon & 1–5pm; ✆0286 217 1187). Bus and ferry timetables, plus an excellent, free, pocket-sized city guide.

Consulate The Australian Embassy has an honorary consul at the *Kolin Hotel*, south of the town centre on Atatürk Cad ✆0286 218 1721.

ÇANAKKALE POTTERY

The name **Çanakkale** means "Pottery Castle", after the unique local ceramics that find their way into the ethnographic section of every Turkish museum. Dating from the nineteenth century, the style favours brown, green and yellow glazes – a statue-sized model of a popular design looks over Cumhuriyet Bulvarı – and was once considered crude and garish. Tastes seem to have changed, however. Genuine antique Çanakkale pottery is back in fashion, and fetches high prices in the fashionable decor shops of İstanbul.

A good place to poke around for a hidden bargain is the well-restored old **bazaar** beyond the clocktower. With its ornate shops – especially the 1889-built **Yalı Hanı** – and houses, it testifies to the town's pre-1923 polyglot profile. Until Cretan Muslims arrived as part of the population exchanges, Çanakkale (like İzmir) held significant Greek, Jewish and Armenian populations, and even foreign consuls – the Italian one donated the clocktower in 1897.

ACCOMMODATION

Akol Kayserili Ahmet Paşa Cad ☎0286 217 9456, ⓦhotelakol.com. Located right on the waterfront, close to the town centre, this multistorey four-star hotel offers a decent level of luxury – albeit rather impersonal – in good-sized, carpeted rooms with large bathrooms and small balconies (some with sea views). The two restaurants serve mostly bland buffets, but the rooftop bar is a good spot for a sunset drink. ₺230

★ **Anzac Hotel** Saat Kulesi Meyd 8, opposite the clocktower ☎0286 217 7777, ⓦanzachotel.com. A very friendly and welcoming mid-range hotel whose rather grim exterior belies cheerful, good-value earth-tone rooms with LCD TVs and big bathrooms. There's also an on-site restaurant and separate café decorated with mirror art, and private parking. Sister hotel to the more upmarket *Kervansaray*. ₺120

Artur Hotel Cumhuriyet Meyd 28 ☎0286 213 2000, ⓦhotelartur.com. The brown, cream and ochre decor of the rooms at this three-star hotel don't quite match the lobby for splendour, but the bathrooms are modern and fair-sized, and there are some superior suites (without balcony, however). Recommended ground-floor restaurant (see p.188). ₺130

Cetinkaya Kızılay Sok 18 ☎0286 217 1069. Well located with secure parking close by, this is one of the best-value but least-known hotels in town. The simply furnished rooms have wooden floors and modern bathrooms with walk-in showers, accessed by a winding staircase (the one drawback). Not to be confused with *Cetinkaya 2 Hotel*, next door. ₺115

Helen Hotel Cumhuriyet Meyd 57 ☎0286 212 1818, ⓦhelenhotel.com. A good-value, well-located mid-range hotel. The clean and comfortable rooms have wood-panelled floors and modern bathrooms, but no balconies. Pleasant breakfast mezzanine and off-street parking, and friendly, helpful management. ₺130

Kervansaray Fetvane Sok 13 ☎0286 217 8192, ⓦotelkervansaray.com. Justifiably popular hotel in a 1903 judge's mansion with a later rear annexe, co-managed with the *Anzac*. The mansion rooms are boutique-style, with mock *belle époque* furnishings, though the front ones suffer from street noise – ask for 206 or 207 facing the lovely central garden. Other than their parquet floors, the annexe rooms are less distinguished, perched over the area where the above-average breakfast is served. There's also a rather nautical garden suite. ₺150

EATING, DRINKING AND NIGHTLIFE

Restaurants and **cafés** line the quayside both north and south of the main ferry terminal, with seafood, unsurprisingly, prominent. Touting is common, and heading a few steps inland will get you better value. A major university town, Çanakkale has a lively student **nightlife**, especially along Fetvane Sokağı running south from the clocktower. Bars there change regularly – choose according to the soundtrack and the crowd, and whether you mind smoky interiors or not. In summer, many restaurants and bars set up outdoor tables along the waterfront esplanade. The AFM **cinema** in the Carrefour shopping centre by the *otogar* shows mainstream releases in English; there's also a Friday-night cinematheque in the Belediye İş Merkezi, behind the Atatürk statue.

RESTAURANTS

Adana Sofrası Barış Kordonu, corner Yeni Kordon 1 ☎0286 213 9168. That rare beast: an upmarket, licensed *kebap* place in a quiet spot with sea views. A good lunch option after taking in the nearby archeological museum,

with a free shuttle from the town centre on request. Mains ₺9–20. Daily noon–10.30pm.

Cafe du Port Limani Hotel, Yali Cad 12 ☎0286 217 2908. This friendly restaurant, across from the harbour, offers elegant surroundings and an affordable, varied menu as well as a very good breakfast buffet. It's licensed, with a wine list including very good local vintages. Breakfast ₺11, mains ₺7–21. Daily 8am–10.30pm.

★ **Cafeka** Cumhuriyet Meyd 28 ☎0286 217 4900. A welcoming dining space beneath the *Artur Hotel*, with a happy ambience and attentive service. The affordable Mediterranean bistro-style menu is a definite departure from local cuisine, with dishes such as salmon fettuccine and a chicken and cheese crêpe, and alcohol is available. Mains ₺8–19. Daily noon–11pm.

Sardunya Fetvane Sok 11 ☎0286 213 9899. The most popular of several similar *ev yemekleri* (home-style cooking) places on this lane, where for a set price of ₺10 (including a non-alcoholic drink) you fill your own salad plate and staff top up a bigger platter with stews of the day. Sit on the narrow, vine-shaded patio out back, or in the funky old house in cooler weather. Daily noon–9pm.

Seaside Eski Balikhane Sok 3 ☎0286 214 2726. Popular with locals and travellers alike, with designer interior, hovering waiters, sculpted vegetables and a Western soundtrack. Choose from covered outdoor tables or more comfortable seating inside, and a Med-bistro menu that's better for pizza, pasta and salads than seafood. Breakfast and alcohol also available. Breakfast buffet ₺10, mains ₺9–19. Daily 9am–11pm.

Şehir Kulübü Kayserili Ahmet Paşa Cad, opposite yacht marina ☎0286 214 1632. The "City Club" offers a refined dining area across from the waterfront, with a reasonably inexpensive menu heavy on seafood, such as line fish, calamari, and a seafood-grill *meze*. The "live music" often consists of a crooning violinist. Mains ₺8–21. Daily noon–11pm.

BARS AND CAFÉS

Benzin Eski Balikhane Sok 11 ☎0286 212 2237. Consistently among the liveliest bar-cafés along the waterfront. A few tables outside on the busy pavement, and plenty of tables and comfortable chairs and lounges in the cosy, wooden interior. Popular with locals and travellers, the beer is always cold and there's also a good menu of light meals and comfort food. Beer ₺3, light meals ₺2–9. Daily noon–late.

★ **Han Kahvesi** Fetvane Sok 28. The courtyard of the historic Yalı Hanı is the place for a well-priced tea, coffee, soft drink, beer or nargile (hookah) at any hour. There's DJ or live music a few nights a week in the upstairs bar, when prices climb slightly and the student contingent attends in force. Coffee costs ₺2, and beer ₺3. Daily 10.30am–midnight.

Kahveci Çarşı Cad 14, opposite the Yalı Camii. An inviting café with a small, rustic interior of wooden floors and exposed brick walls, and a few tables out on the pavement. The young staff serve proper European cappuccinos and espressos – at European prices. Coffee ₺4–7. Daily 9am–9pm.

The Gelibolu peninsula

Burdened with a grim military history, but nonetheless endowed with fine scenery and beaches, the slender **Gelibolu (Gallipoli) peninsula** – roughly 60km long and from 4km to 18km wide – forms the northwest side of the **Dardanelles**, the straits that connect the Aegean with the Sea of Marmara. Site of the 1915 **Gallipoli landings**, the peninsula is scattered with memorials, both Allied and Turkish.

The **World War I battlefields and cemeteries** are a moving sight, the past violence made all the more poignant by the present beauty of the landscape, which consists of fertile rolling country interspersed with thick scrub and pine forest that's alive with birds. Much of the flatter land is farmed, and every year ploughing still turns up rusting equipment, fragments of shrapnel, human bones and even unexploded munitions.

The entire area southwest of Eceabat and Kabatepe is a **national historical park**, which means no camping, picnicking, fire-lighting, foliage-plucking or second-home development beyond the few existing villages. The Allied cemeteries and memorials, built in the early 1920s and mostly designed by Scottish architect Sir John Burnet, replaced and consolidated the makeshift graveyards of 1915. Over half the deceased were never found or identified, however – hence the massive cenotaphs.

The battlefields and cemeteries are also popular with Turkish visitors – up to two million annually – who arrive on massive pilgrimages often organized by municipalities run by the nationalistic-leaning AK Party, especially in May and late September. These religious tourists venerate the Turkish fallen as *şehitler*, or martyrs for Islam – in

Beşyol

Kemikli Burnu
(Cape Suvla)

✝1
✝2

Suvla
Bay

Salt
Lake

✝3

Küçük Anafarta

✝4

Büyük Anafarta

Hill 60
NZ Memorial

Hill 971 ▲

✝5

✝6

Çonkbayırı (Chunuk Bair)

✝7 ✝8

Bigalı

✝9 ✝10

Arıburnu &
Anzac Cove

57th Turkish Regiment Cemetery

✝11

Johnston's Jolly

✝12 ✝13

Kemalyeri

✝14

✝15

✝16 ✝17

Kocadere

ℹ Statue

Mehmetçik
Memorial

Kabatepe
Information
Centre

Kabatepe

CEMETERIES ✝	
Azmak	1
Baby 700	10
Beach	16
Canterbury	12
Embarkation Pier	7
Green Hill	4
Hill 10	2
Lala Baba	3
Lancashire Landing	22
Lone Pine	15
The Nek	6
New Zealand	
No 2 Outpost	8
No 2 Outpost	11
Pink Farm	20
Quinn's Post	13
Redoubt	19
Shell Green	14
Shrapnel Valley	17
Skew Bridge	21
Twelve Tree Copse	18
Walker's Ridge	9
7th Field Ambulance	5

Eceabat

Kum
Limanı

Kilitbahir

Çanakkale

Behramlı

✝18 Alçıtepe

✝19

✝20

✝21 French
Cemetery

22

Cape
Helles
Memorial

Morto Bay

Seddülbahir
'V' Beach

Çanakkale
Şehitler Anıtı
(Abide)

Çanakkale Boğazı (Dardanelles)

Güzelyalı

N

Kumkale

Military Zone

0   5
kilometres

Gelibolu

Gelibolu

Lapseki & Bursa

3

Troy & Assos

THE GELİBOLU (GALLIPOLI) PENINSULA

pointed contrast to the secularist narrative spun around the eight-month Gallipoli campaign, which made famous a previously unknown lieutenant-colonel, Mustapha Kemal, later Atatürk.

Eceabat

ECEABAT, 40km south of Gelibolu and diagonally opposite Çanakkale, is a scruffy, quiet place. Without your own transport, however, it makes the most convenient base for touring the battlefields. There's a **PTT** on the street leading north from the jetty, and ATMs on the jetty plaza, or *meydan*.

3

THE GALLIPOLI CAMPAIGN

Soon after World War I began, the Allies realized that Russia could not be supplied by sea, nor a Balkan front opened against the Central Powers, unless Ottoman Turkey was eliminated. **Winston Churchill**, then the British First Lord of the Admiralty, decided that the quickest way to accomplish this would be to force the Dardanelles with a fleet and bombard İstanbul into submission. A combined **Anglo-French armada** made several, repulsed attempts on the straits during November 1914, before returning in earnest on March 18, 1915, when they reached 10km up the waterway before striking numerous Turkish mines, losing several vessels and hundreds of crew.

The Allied fleet retreated and regrouped on the Greek island of Límnos to prepare an amphibious assault on Turkish positions along the peninsula. The plan involved an Anglo-French landing at Cape Helles, Seddülbahir and Morto Bay at the mouth of the straits, and a simultaneous **Anzac** (Australia-New Zealand Army Corps) assault at Kabatepe beach, 13km north. The Australians landed first at dawn on April 25, 1915, with the British and French landing an hour afterwards, followed by the New Zealanders later in the day.

This hare-brained scheme ran into trouble immediately. Anglo-French brigades at the southernmost cape were pinned down by Turkish fire, and the French contingent virtually annihilated; after two days they had only penetrated 6.5km inland, just before Krithia (Alçıtepe) village, and never got any further. The fate of the Anzac landing was even more horrific: owing to a drifting signal buoy, the Aussies and Kiwis disembarked not on the broad sands of Kabatepe, with gentle terrain inland, but at a cramped cove by Arıburnu, 2km north, overlooked by Turkish-held cliffs. Despite heavy casualties (around 2000 on the first day alone), the Australians advanced inland, as the Turks initially retreated. The next day, they threatened the Turkish stronghold of Çonkbayırı, where lieutenant-colonel **Mustafa Kemal** told his poorly equipped, illiterate troops: "I am not ordering you to attack, I am ordering you to die." Turkish reinforcements soon arrived, and the Anzac force never made it further than 800m inland.

A supplementary British landing at northerly Cape Suvla was followed by ferocious assaults on the summit in the middle of August, which the Turks repulsed. Otherwise the confrontation consisted of stagnant trench warfare; neither side had sufficient artillery to gain a decisive advantage. Finally, in November 1915, the Allies gave up. The last troops left Seddülbahir on January 9, 1916. Churchill's career went into temporary eclipse, while that of Mustafa Kemal was only just beginning.

The reasons for the **Allied defeat** are many. In addition to the chanciness of the basic strategy, the incompetence of the Allied commanders – who often countermanded each other's orders or failed to press advantages with reinforcements – was significant. Much credit for the successful **Turkish resistance** goes to Mustafa Kemal, later known as **Atatürk**, whose role in the two Turkish victories at Çonkbayırı is legendary (countrywide, he's depicted hunched over in silhouette, patrolling that ridge). Enjoying a charmed life, he narrowly escaped death on several occasions and, aside from his tactical skills, succeeded – by threats, persuasion or example – in rekindling morale among often outgunned and outnumbered Ottoman infantrymen.

At various times, half a million men were deployed at Gallipoli; over fifty percent were killed, wounded or missing. Allied deaths totalled around 46,000, while the Turkish dead are estimated at 86,000. Fatal **casualties** among the Anzacs in particular – around 11,500 – were severe compared to the island-nations' populations, but would be dwarfed by the 48,000 or so Anzacs killed on the western front later in the war. Claims that the Allied top brass regarded Anzac "colonials" as expendable cannon fodder – a major thesis of Peter Weir's *Gallipoli* – don't bear scrutiny; two Irish battalions suffered over fifty percent casualties on the first day, and the 42nd Manchester Division was almost completely wiped out. However, this baptism by blood had several long-term effects: a sense that Australia and New Zealand had come of age as sovereign countries; the designation of April 25 as Anzac Day, a solemn holiday in Australia and New Zealand; and a healthy antipodean scepticism about joining international adventures – though both countries were press-ganged by the US into sending troops to Vietnam.

Kilitbahir

The tiny fishing village of **KILITBAHIR**, 5km south of Eceabat and accessible by ferry from Çanakkale, makes a peaceful, if slightly underwhelming, entry into "Europe" from "Asia". While there are a few teahouses along the shoreline, the nearest accommodation is in Eceabat, accessible by dolmuş.

Kilitbahir Kale

Yalı Cad • Tues–Sun 8.30am–noon & 1.30–5pm • ₺3

Kilitbahir is dwarfed by Sultan Mehmet the Conqueror's massive, irregularly shaped **castle**. Constructed in 1452, **Kilitbahir Kale** was built in conjunction with Çimenlik Kale across the strait in Çanakkale, to strengthen the siege on doomed Constantinople. It features a lobed, triangular keep and six steep stairways leading up to the curtain walls; lacking any safety railings, ascending the stairs, especially on a windy day, requires confidence and good balance. The imposing seven-storey tower within the walls was built a century later, by Süleyman the Magnificent.

Namazgah Tabyası

Yalı Cad, on the seaward side of Kilitbahir Kale • Tues–Sun 8.30am–noon & 1.30–5pm • ₺1

The **Namazgah Tabyası**, a series of half-subterranean bunkers and shore batteries built in the 1890s, formed part of the Ottoman defence system against the Allied fleet during February and March 1915. A large statue of an Ottoman soldier, bare-chested and carrying a massive artillery shell, pays tribute to the Turkish gunners who stood firm against shelling from Allied warships. A small museum houses interesting photographs from World War I.

The west-coast sites

The logical first stop on a tour of the west coast's Gelibolu sites, the **Kabatepe Information Centre and Museum**, 9km northwest of Eceabat (daily 9am–1pm & 2–6pm; ₺3), contains archive photos, maps, weapons, trenching tools, uniforms, mess-kits, personal effects – like touching letters home – and a few human remains, including a Turkish skull with a bullet lodged in it.

The first sites along the coast road north of the Centre are the **Beach**, **Shrapnel Valley** and **Shell Green** cemeteries – the latter 300m inland up a steep track, suitable only for 4WD vehicles. Shrapnel Valley was the one perilous supply line up-valley from what's now the Beach Cemetery to the trenches.

These are followed by **Anzac Cove** and **Arıburnu**, site of the first, bungled Anzac landing and location of the dawn service on Anzac Day. At both, memorials bear Atatürk's famous conciliatory quotation concerning the Allied dead, which begins: "Heroes who shed their blood and lost their lives! You are now lying in the soil of a friendly country. Therefore rest in peace." Looking inland, you'll see the murderous badlands – including the eroded pinnacle overhead nicknamed "The Sphinx" by the hapless Australians – that gave the defenders such an advantage. Beyond Anzac Cove, the terrain flattens out and the four other cemeteries (Canterbury, No. 2 Outpost, New Zealand No. 2 Outpost and Embarkation Pier) are more dispersed.

Good dirt tracks lead north from Arıburnu to the beaches and salt lake at **Cape Suvla**, today renamed Kemikli Burnu ("bone-strewn headland"), location of four more cemeteries of August casualties, mostly English, Scottish, Welsh and Irish.

Central inland sites

A one-way road, roughly following what was the front line, leads uphill from the Kabatepe Information Centre to the former strongholds (now cemeteries) scattered around **Çonkbayırı** hill.

3

Beside the road, a massive **statue** depicts a purported incident from the first day of landings – a Turk carrying a wounded Australian officer back to his lines – supposedly witnessed by another officer who later, as Lord Casey, became Governor-General of Australia. However, Casey didn't mention the incident in his memoirs, and wasn't even at that sector of the lines, so the statue is best viewed as an allegory of the chivalry that (sometimes) prevailed in the campaign.

Just beyond is **Lone Pine** (Kanlı Sırt), lowest strategic position on the ridge and the largest graveyard-cum-memorial to those buried unmarked or at sea. Action here was considered a sideshow to the main August 6–9 offensive further up Çonkbayırı; 28,000 men died in four days at the two points. Just up from Lone Pine is the **Mehmetcik memorial** to the Turkish soldiers who perished, while at **Johnston's Jolly** (named after an artillery officer who liked to "jolly the Turks up" with his gun) there's a heavily eroded section of **trench** beneath the pine trees. Most of the trenches on display are reconstructions; the originals are hidden and little visited. British/Anzac ones followed a zigzag course, while the Turks adopted the German dogtooth pattern. All along the ridge, opposing trenches lay within a few metres of each other; the modern road corresponds to the no-man's-land in between.

Further along, on the right, is the **57th Turkish Regiment cemetery**, whose men Mustafa Kemal ordered to their deaths, thus buying time for reinforcements to arrive. Here the religious aspect of the campaign for contemporary Turks is made clear, with an inscription eulogizing martyrdom and a small open-air prayer area. Just beyond, a left fork leads to **The Nek** – the scene of the futile charge and massacre of the Australian Light Horse Brigade at the conclusion of Peter Weir's 1981 film *Gallipoli*.

To the right, the main road continues uphill past **Baby 700** cemetery – marking the furthest Allied advance on April 25 – and to the massive New Zealand memorial obelisk and the five-monolith Turkish memorial atop **Çonkbayırı** hill (Chunuk Bair). An inscription chronicles Kemal's organization of successful resistance to the August Allied attacks, and marks the spot where Atatürk's pocket-watch stopped a fragment of shrapnel, thus saving his life.

Kabatepe

KABATEPE port, the boarding point for the car ferry to the Turkish Aegean island of Gökçeada (see p.195), lies 1km southwest of the Kabatepe Information Centre. There's a fair **beach** north of the harbour – intended site of the Anzac landing – and another just south at a forestry picnic ground (₺3 admission). A third beach, 5km south at **Kum Limanı**, is the best of the lot, with warm, clean, calm sea, but access is straddled by the grounds of the large *Kum Hotel*.

Southern peninsula sites

Beyond the rural hamlet of **Alçitepe**, at the entrance to the southern section of the peninsula, assorted cemeteries, consequences of the landing at Cape Helles, and the huge British **Cape Helles Memorial**, lie scattered towards Seddülbahir. The views are magnificent, with abundant **Ottoman fortifications** hinting at the age-old importance of the place. Tucked between the medieval bulwarks is the **V Beach** of the Allied expedition, behind which lies the biggest of the local British cemeteries.

Alçitepe

There's not much to **ALÇITEPE**, other than a museum and a few souvenir stands. War graves in the immediate vicinity, however, include the British **Pink Farm** cemetery, named after the reddish soil on which the site lies, and the Turkish **Sargı Yeri** cemetery.

3

VISITING THE BATTLEFIELDS AND CEMETERIES

Whether you visit the battlefields independently or on a tour, **Çanakkale**, and **Eceabat** in the south of the peninsula, make the best bases; modern Gelibolu town (see p.159) at the northern end of the peninsula is too far away.

The numerous open-air sites have **no admission fees** or fixed opening hours. Even with your own transport, you'll need a day – two for enthusiasts – to see the major cemeteries and cenotaphs. You'll also want time to wander a little, take in the natural beauty and, in season, swim. Outside the villages of Eceabat and Seddülbahir there are few amenities, so lunch stops must be carefully planned.

It's also possible to visit the sites using a combination of minibus rides and walking. **Minibuses** run from Eceabat to Kabatepe dock, via the Kabatepe Information Centre/Museum, and from Eceabat to Kilitbahir. From the information centre, you can walk around the main sites just north within a couple of hours. At Kilitbahir, minibuses meet the Çanakkale car ferries in summer and take passengers to Seddülbahir via Alçitepe, from where you can tour the surrounding cemeteries and memorials on foot. It's also usually possible to **rent mountain bikes** in Eceabat, but some roads are steep, and secondary tracks can be rough and muddy in winter.

GUIDED TOURS

There's little to choose between the many mainstream companies that offer **guided tours** of the battlefields – all are supposed to have licensed, English-speaking guides with a thorough knowledge of the sites. All tours from Çanakkale or Ecebat tend to cost the same (around ₺90 per head), be the same length (5hr; in the afternoon), and visit identical sites, usually including lunch. Itineraries, with a strong Anzac emphasis, don't stray much from a core area just north of the park boundary and visit – in this order – the Kabatepe Museum, several beach cemeteries nearby, the Lone Pine cemetery, Johnston's Jolly, the Turkish 57th Regiment cemetery, The Nek and Çonkbayırı hill.

Crowded House Huseyin Avni Sok 4, Eceabat ☎0286 814 1565, ⓦcrowdedhousegallipoli.com. By far the best of the conventional tours. For an additional ₺35, they offer a morning's add-on of snorkelling over the *Milo*, an Allied ship scuttled in Suvla Bay.
Hassle Free Travel Agency Çanakkale ☎0286 213 5969, ⓦanzachouse.com. This recommended operator offers the standard tours from Çanakkale, and offers return tours from İstanbul.
Kenan Çelik Çanakkale ☎0532 738 6675, ⓦkcelik .com. If you have your own transport, consider hiring the best private guide to the battlefields. An instructor at Çanakkale's university, Kenan leads full- and multi-day tours as well as the usual itineraries.

Salim Mutlu War Museum

Just north of the main intersection in Alçıtepe • Daily 8am–5pm • ₺1

The small **Salim Mutlu War Museum** houses the private collection of the late Salim Mutlu, a local farmer who turned his house into a museum to display objects found in the battlefields by fellow farmers. While slightly amateurish and a bit rustic, the collection affords an insight into the sheer amount of artillery that was let loose during the 1915 battle.

Seddülbahir

The sleepy village of **SEDDÜLBAHİR**, at the far southern tip of the peninsula, consists of a few basic *pansiyons* and restaurants, and an Ottoman-era fortress overlooking a quaint harbour. A fine specimen of Ottoman military architecture from the early modern era, the fortress – like its sister fortress, Kumkale, across the Dardanelles on the opposite shore – was built in 1658 by the mother of Sultan Mehmed IV, Hadice Turhan Sultan.

A southeast turning just before Seddülbahir leads to the striking **French Cemetery**, above the sandy Morto Bay, with its massive ossuaries, rows of black metal crosses (with North and West African troops disproportionately represented), and memorial to the sailors of the *Bouvet*, sunk on March 18, 1915. At the end of this road, the 41.7m-high Çanakkale Şehitler Anıtı, or **Çanakkale Martyrs' Memorial**, which resembles a stark, four-legged footstool, commemorates all the Ottoman dead.

ARRIVAL AND DEPARTURE

THE GELİBOLU PENINSULA

ECEABAT

By bus Most buses arrive at the relevant ticket offices behind the jetty.

By ferry Regular car ferries from Çanakkale arrive at the jetty.

Destinations Çanakkale (June–Sept 24hr on the hour; Oct–May on the hour 6am–midnight, then 2am & 4am; 30min).

KILITBAHIR

By ferry The fastest and, for drivers, cheapest ferry trip

over the Dardanelles crosses its narrowest point, at 1300m, to Çanakkale.

Destinations Çanakkale (every 30min, 6am–9.30pm, then according to traffic up to 1am; 8min).

KABATEPE

By ferry Tickets on the Çanakkale–Eceabat car ferry are valid to continue the same day from Kabatepe to Gökçeada, and vice versa.

Destinations Gökçeada (June–Sept 6 daily 8am–9pm; rest of year 3 daily 10am, 3pm & 7pm; 1hr 20min).

ACCOMMODATION

ECEABAT

Boss Cumhuriyet Cad 14, on ferry plaza ☎0286 814 2458, ⓦheyboss.com. One of several "boss" hotels in town, this one overlooks the ferry plaza and offers very good-value, modern en-suite rooms, with either wooden or newly carpeted floors; the cheaper singles are exceptionally small, but other rooms sleep up to five adults. Free parking. **₺75**

Crowded House Huseyin Avni Sok 4, one block inland from ferry plaza ☎0286 814 1565, ⓦcrowded housegallipoli.com. This friendly, well-managed hotel is the best budget option by far. The small en-suite rooms and six-bunk dorms are modern and clean. Meals and drinks are available from a very pleasant mezzanine-level beer garden, and they offer very good battlefields tours. Dorm **₺18**, double **₺70**

★ **Gallipoli Houses** Kocadere village, 7km northwest of Eceabat, just off the Kabatepe road ☎0286 814 2650,

ⓦthegallipolihouses.com. State-of-the-art rooms in this Belgian/Turkish-run place are distributed over a restored main house (with roof terrace) and newer garden units: all have terraces or balconies, wood cabinets, insect screens, rain showers and terracotta tiles for under-floor heating. The evening meals are a highlight, marrying Turkish *mezes* with continental mains and an excellent regional wine-and-rakı cellar; advance booking is essential, especially in May and autumn. There's no public transport to the village. Rates shown are for B&B; half board, compulsory Mon–Fri, costs ₺70 extra. **₺250**

TJs Hostel Cumhuriyet Cad 5, just north of ferry plaza ☎0286 814 2458, ⓦanzacgallipolitours.com. Owned by a Turkish–Australian couple and renovated in 2012, with spacious, modern hotel-standard rooms that come with a/c and flat-screen TVs, and dorms with a new lick of paint. Helpful ground-floor tour desk, and a popular roof bar. Dorm **₺18**, double **₺70**

KABATEPE

Kum Hotel Kum Limanı ☎ 0286 814 1455, ⓦ hotelkum
.com. A large resort-style hotel with modern but bland
rooms in two-storey concrete blocks, plus various bars and
swimming pools, and a restaurant that serves up
wholesome if repetitive buffet meals; room rates include
half board. The private beach is a short walk away, and
there's also a grassed campsite for caravans and camper
vans. Closed Nov–March. Caravan ₺35, rooms ₺190

SEDDÜLBAHIR

Helles Panorama Cape Helles road, at the northern
edge of the village ☎ 0286 862 0035. The pleasant
Panorama has simple but clean rooms with shared
bathrooms, accessed through lovely gardens and with
panoramic views of both the Çanakkale Martyrs' and Cape
Helles memorials. ₺60

EATING AND DRINKING

ECEABAT

Boomerang Bar Cumhuriyet Cad 102, on the water's
edge at the town's northern entrance ☎ 0286 814
2144. Scruffy, very welcoming, and legendary among
Antipodeans for its Anzac Day "celebrations", the
Boomerang is a relaxed place to enjoy a beer and Western
(read: Aussie and Kiwi) music. If you fancy staying, they'll
offer you a mattress or you can pitch a tent on the beach.

Beer ₺3. Daily 11am–late.
Yavus Zübeyde Hanım Cad 5 ☎ 0286 814 2005. One of
several *lokantasis* just south of the ferry plaza, the family-
run *Yavus* has been here since 1950. Typical *lokanta*-style
food, with plenty of steam-heated trays to choose from, as
well as *kebap*, salads and soups. The service is usually
quick, even during the tour-group rush at lunchtime. Mains
₺5–11. Daily 9am–10pm.

3

The Turkish Aegean islands

Strategically straddling the Dardanelles, **Gökçeada** and **Bozcaada** were the only Aegean
islands to revert to Turkey after the 1923 Treaty of Lausanne concluded the Greek-
Turkish war. While the islands' Greek Orthodox inhabitants were exempt from that
year's population exchange, both islands were re-militarized after 1937, and the
Turkish authorities began to assert their sovereignty more forcefully. Although a formal
population exchange was never instigated, most of the islands' Greek population had
left by 1974, to be replaced by Turkish settlers.

Both islands have **good beaches**: the smaller Bozcaada is fashionable with weekenders
from İstanbul, thus expensive, while larger Gökçeada is cheaper and more dramatic,
with less tourism.

Gökçeada (İmbroz)

Turkey's largest island, just northwest of the Dardanelles, **GÖKÇEADA** makes a blissful
escape from the often overdeveloped mainland Aegean coast. Unpretentious and for
the most part unchanged, it's scenic, fertile and volcanic, with healthy pine and kermes
oak forests, fields of oleander and wild thyme, sandy beaches with mountain
backdrops, and springs pure enough to drink from.

Known as İmbroz until 1970, the island was taken by Greece in the 1912–13 Balkan
Wars. During the Gallipoli campaign, it served as British commander Sir Ian Hamilton's
HQ, and an important way-station between Límnos and the battlefields. Handed over
to Turkey in 1923, it remains an important military base, though its main claim to fame
is its superb organic produce, especially olive oil, tomato jam, honey and cheese. Its
summer tourist trade comprises some Romanians and Bulgarians, but mostly consists of
thousands of returned Greek islanders and their descendants, especially around the main
Orthodox *panayır* (festival) of August 14–16, when beds are at a premium.

Gökçeada Merkez

Gökçeada's small inland capital is known as **GÖKÇEADA MERKEZ** (Panayiá). A modern
settlement with little character, it is the island's business hub as well as a transit point
for travel elsewhere.

Northeast Gökçeada

Gökçeada's **northeast coast** is home to the island's small ferry harbour, at **Kuzu Limani**, and the seaside village of **Kaleköy. Gökçeada Su Altı Milli Parkı**, stretching between the two, is a national marine park where Turkish marine biologists are trying to revitalize the endangered black mussel population, which grow as much as 5cm wide.

Kaleköy

5km north of Gökçeada Merkez

KALEKÖY consists of two separate areas. At the end of the road on the north shore, **Kaleköy Limani** is a modern seafront settlement with a small, unattractive beach – an off-limits military zone – and a new quay dotted with fishing boats. Much of the island's **accommodation** overlooks the quay, which also holds a few bars and restaurants.

The settlement reaches uphill to **Kaleköy Yukarı** (Kástro), the atmospheric original Greek village with a ruined Byzantine-Genoese castle, a renovated church, Agios Nikolaos, and the island's former cathedral, **Ayía Marína**, now derelict, but also set for renovation.

Western hill villages

West of Gökçeada Merkez, scenic hilltop villages hold rustic stone houses dotted among shrubs of pink oleander and shady fig trees. Historically, their elevated locations above the central valley saved them from sea raiders, but they were also close to the island's natural springs. New villages have since been built in the lowlands.

Zeytinliköy

3km west of Gökçeada Merkez

ZEYTINLIKÖY (Áyii Theodhóri) takes its name from the Turkish word for olive; its oil is considered the country's best. Most of the island's remaining Greek Orthodox population lives here, and the spiritual leader of the world's 300 million Orthodox Christians, the Ecumenical Patriarch Bartholomew I, was born and raised in the village. A Turkish citizen, he returns regularly. Many of the village's central **cafés** are Greek-run and specialize in *dibek kahvesi* – coffee ground in a giant mortar and pestle.

Tepeköy

10km west of Gökçeada Merkez

Exclusively Orthodox-inhabited, and said to be the only settlement in Turkey without a mosque, hilltop **TEPEKÖY** (Agrídhia) is a pretty village with a myriad of stone houses, many restored by their summer-holidaying Greek owners. The village's Orthodox church is the focus of the mid-August *panayır* (festival), observed with a fervour now lacking in much of metropolitan Greece.

Dereköy

15km west of Gökçeada Merkez

DEREKÖY (Skhinoúdhi) was once the island's largest village, with 1900 houses, shops, craftsmen and even a cinema. A vast communal laundry-hall by the main church hints at its former population of 5500, but today it's only home to fifty full-time inhabitants. A track leads 7km north from its western edge, to **Marmaros** pebble cove, where there's a 38m **waterfall** 1km inland.

The south-coast beaches

Arguably the best (and closest) of several south-coast **beaches**, just 10km from Gökçeada Merkez, is **Aydıncık**, 1500m of sugary blonde sand lapped by warm, pristine water. The salt lake just inland is a major habitat for migratory birds, especially flamingos, and the entire area is supposedly a protected reserve – though this has neither prevented tourist development nor deterred Balkan tourists from wallowing in the shoreline's black mud, said to have healing properties. Windsurfing conditions are the best in the north Aegean, so windsurfing schools cluster on the beach.

A paved road heads west from here, mostly hugging the coast, for 15km to the long, unsigned **Kapıkaya** beach (no amenities); another 5km leads to the marked (1km) side road to **Lazköyü** (Ayía Káli), a 400m, scenic, protected sandy bay with just a summer snack-shack.

There's no public access to any beyond before **Yuvalı**, a further 9km, and even there you must patronize the beach restaurants of the sprawling *Mavi Su Resort* (see p.198). The final beach, 3km west of little **Uğurlu** (Livoúnia) fishing port, is **Gizli Liman**, with no facilities but fine sand and a pine-grove backdrop. From Uğurlu a paved road leads back to the western hill villages.

ARRIVAL AND DEPARTURE
GÖKÇEADA

By bus Truva Turism (wtruvaturism.com) offers a direct service to Gökçeada from İstanbul's Esenler Otogar, travelling by road to Kabatepe and then ferry to the island. The 7hr journey leaves İstanbul daily at 2pm, and Gökçeada Merkez at 7am.

By ferry Gökçeada is easily accessible by car ferry from Kabatepe and sea bus (passenger only) from Çanakkale. All services are run by Gestaş (t0286 444 0752, wgdu.com .tr). In August, or any summer weekend, car-space must be booked hours in advance, and south winds may cancel services. Boats dock at Kuzu Limani (Áyios Kírykos), 6km from Gökçeada Merkez. Tickets for the Çanakkale–Eceabat

car ferry are valid to continue the same day from Kabatepe to Gökçeada, and vice versa.
Destinations Çanakkale (June–Sept Mon, Tues, Thurs, Sun; Oct–May Mon, Thurs & Fri; 1hr); Kabatepe (June–Sept 6 daily, 7am–9pm; Oct–May 3 daily 7.15am, noon & 5pm; 1hr 20min).

By plane Borajet (wborajet.com.tr) usually flies in summer from İstanbul's Sabiha Gökçen Airport to the tiny Çanakkale-Gökçeada Airport, 6km west of Gökçeada Merkez.
Destinations İstanbul (June–Sept, Thurs & Sat only).

GETTING AROUND

By car The easiest way to explore Gökçeada is by car. Gökçeada Rent A Car, Soğuk Hava Deposu Yanı in Gökçeada Merkez (t0536 377 5602), is the sole rental agency; small sedans cost around ₺300 per day. The only petrol station, between Kuzu Limani and Gökçeada Merkez, can run dry in the summer.

By bus and dolmuş Public transport between Kuzu Limani, Gökçeada Merkez and Kaleköy only runs irregularly, in daytime.
By taxi Private taxis from Kuzu Limani to Gökçeada Merkez cost up to ₺15, and a further ₺15 to continue to Uğurlu.

INFORMATION

Tourist office Seasonal information booth on the central roundabout in Gökçeada Merkez (daily June–Sept, 10.30am–7pm).

Banks and money The various ATMs in Gökçeada Merkez can run dry in summer, so come prepared.

ACCOMMODATION

GÖKÇEADA MERKEZ

Taşkin Çınarlı, Zeytinli Cad 3, 300m southwest of the main intersection t0286 887 3266, wtaskinotel.com. While the *Taşkin* won't win any beauty awards, the rooms are perfectly spacious and comfortable, with big modern bathrooms and small balconies; those at the rear face open countryside. ₺65

KALEKÖY

★ **Anemos** Kaleköy Yukarı, 15min uphill walk from Kaleköy Limani waterfront t0554 541 4737, wanemos.com.tr. Opened in 2011, set in peaceful, semi-rural surroundings and offering the quintessential getaway. 24 rooms of varying sizes and prices, in six

two-storey villas made from local stone; the best have balconies with either valley or sea views. Activity centres around the sizeable pool, where sunset cocktails are the norm. Discreet and exemplary service, plus rental bikes and a free shuttle bus. Rates include breakfast. ₺285

Imbros Eski Bademli Köyü, 3km inland from Kaleköy Limani t0286 887 4840. Set up high, with simply stunning Aegean views from its wide terrace, this stone-and-wood hotel offers comfortable and spacious rooms. Some have balconies, all have large, modern bathrooms. Owner-managed and family-friendly, the hotel's restaurant is open to non-guests, and serves up healthy Mediterranean cuisine and delicious buffet breakfasts. You'll need your own transport or an expensive taxi to go anywhere. ₺135

3

Kale Motel Barbaros Cad 34, Kaleköy Limani ☎ 0286 887 4404, ⓦ kalemotel.com. One of several waterfront hotels and *pansiyons*. The smallish upstairs rooms come with a/c and en-suite bathrooms. The downstairs restaurant is a great spot for people- and sunset-watching. ₺75

ZEYTINLIKÖY

Zeytindali Zeytinliköy 168, 200m from the main square ☎ 0286 887 3707, ⓦ zeytindali.com. The village's only accommodation, a superbly restored old inn that's accessed on foot by a narrow, cobbled lane, makes a great base. Two connecting stone buildings in the traditional Greek style house sixteen individually decorated rooms that are simple without being spartan, with a few conveniences and large bathrooms. Most have distant sea views or overlook the village. ₺200

TEPEKÖY

Barba Yorgo Tepeköy ☎ 0286 887 4247, ⓦ barbayorgo .com. Accommodation in this idyllic village is available in rustic, 3-bedroomed houses and family-friendly 2-bedroomed villas, with en-suite or shared bathrooms and fitted kitchens, all restored and owner-managed by larger-than-life local Yorgos (George) Zarbuzanis. Closed early Sept to Easter. ₺100

AYDINCIK

Gökçeada Windsurf Club On the beach ☎ 0286 898 1022, ⓦ surfgokceada.com. The stone-clad bungalows of the beach's most luxurious option have contemporary earth-tone decor, a/c, fridge and big bathrooms. Those facing the lake catch the stiff breeze, those facing the sea suffer slightly from noise coming from the very good licensed restaurant and nearby beach bar. Rates include breakfast. Closed Nov–March. ₺200

Şen Campsite Beachfront ☎ 0286 898 1020. Sandy, unshaded campsites for both tents and camper vans, plus a few ramshackle wooden bungalows, and a small shop selling basic provisions and snacks. Camping ₺8, bungalows ₺60

YUVALI

Mavi Su Resort Yuvalı Plaj ☎ 0286 897 6090, ⓦ mavisuresort.com. This family-friendly resort has its own private beach, all-inclusive buffet restaurant, overpriced bars, and well-appointed though ageing doubles and quad bungalows. Although it suffers from a slightly institutional 1980s feel, it nonetheless offers long stretches of sandy beach and an almost exotic sense of isolation. Closed Nov–March. Doubles ₺180, bungalows ₺250

EATING AND DRINKING

KALEKÖY

★ **Meyhane Son Vapur** Barbaros Cad 34, Kaleköy Limani ☎ 0538 415 5700. Professional and welcoming restaurant on the waterfront, with a large covered terrace and a few alfresco pavement tables. The interesting menu includes good-quality *mezes*, seafood and a "village" breakfast with local cheese, all at moderate prices given the location. Licensed. Mains ₺7–18. Daily 8am–11pm.

ZEYTINLIKÖY

Zeytindali Restaurant Zeytinliköy 168, Zeytinliköy ☎ 0286 887 3707, ⓦ zeytindali.com. The ground-floor restaurant of this atmospheric hotel opens onto a cobbled alleyway, and is a perfect spot for a lazy brunch or lingering sunset dinner. Efficient staff preside over a menu big on

local organic produce; the mainly vegetarian *meze* is a house speciality, as is the thyme-flavoured honey offered at breakfast. Daily 8–11am & 7–11pm.

TEPEKÖY

Barba Yorgo Taverna Tepeköy ☎ 0286 887 4247, ⓦ barbayorgo.com. Gökçeada's most authentic Greek taverna is run by the man himself, Barba Yorgo (Papa George). The menu features good *mezes* and well-priced mains, including goat and wild boar. More a vintner than a restaurateur, George makes most of the island's (rather rough-and-ready) wine from *kundúra* or *kalambáki* grapes, available in copious amounts at the taverna or a separate restaurant, on the edge of the village opposite the old primary school, which serves the same menu. Mains ₺6–23. Closed early Sept to Easter. Daily 11am–11pm.

Bozcaada (Tenedos)

Only seven nautical miles from the Turkish mainland, and a mere forty square kilometres in size, the island of **BOZCAADA** (Tenedos) is less militarized and more architecturally homogeneous than neighbouring Gökçeada. Its gently undulating countryside, covered in vineyards, leads to near-deserted sandy beaches and pebbly coves. Lacking great sights as well as the pretensions of other Aegean and Mediterranean islands, it's a place to wander and absorb, as well as eat and drink.

That idyllic picture tempts Turkish holiday-makers and second-home buyers alike, and the island can be quite overrun in summer, when you'll need to book accommodation in advance. Bozcaada's popularity may also prove to be its downfall, however. The little island is struggling with energy and waste issues, and there's talk of dredging the quay to accommodate cruise ships. Meanwhile, Turkish customs opened an office in Bozcaada town in 2012, perhaps preparing for access from nearby Greek islands.

Bozcaada Merkez

The only real settlement on the island, **BOZCAADA MERKEZ**, centres on a single, slightly scruffy square, just inland from the taverna-lined quay and its neighbouring castle. A surprisingly elegant town, built on a grid plan along a slight slope, it holds an atmospheric Greek quarter of cobbled streets and old houses shaded by leafy vines.

The castle

Daily 10am–1pm & 2–6pm • ₺2

Among the largest citadels in the Aegean, the enormous **castle** that dominates the little fishing port and ferry jetty was successively expanded by Byzantine, Genoese, Venetian and Turkish occupiers, and most recently restored in the 1970s.

There's not a lot to see inside its double walls, apart from remnants of two mosques and some Roman pillars, as well as various tombstones and an old army barracks. For anyone interested in geocaching, there's a cache tucked away in a hole within the inner walls.

The beaches

Bozcaada's most developed beach, **Ayazma**, 6km southwest of town, offers watersports and sunbeds, plus four restaurants just inland. The next bay west, **Sulubahçe**, has good broad sand but no parking or facilities, other than a **campsite** well inland. Beyond, **Habbelle** is more cramped, with a single snack bar/sunbed franchise.

Inland from Ayazma and its abandoned monastery, another paved road leads southeast past secluded, sandy **Beylik** cove, and then above small **Aqvaryum** bay, tucked scenically to one side of the **Mermer Burnu** cape. Once past **Tuzburnu** with its lighthouse and sandy if exposed bay, the road swings north on its way back to the port.

ARRIVAL AND DEPARTURE

BOZCAADA

By ferry Gestaş (wgdu.com.tr, ☎0286 444 0752) run ferries to Bozcaada Merkez from both Çanakkale and Geyikli (Yükyeri) İskelesi, a tiny port 70km southwest of Çanakkale that's served by direct dolmuşes from Çanakkale's *otogar*. If you're approaching from the south, head first to Ezine, then Geyikli. Book ahead to bring a car in high season.

Destinations Çanakkale (Wed, Sat, Sun; 55min; ₺10, sea bus, no cars); Geyikli (June–Sept 7 daily 9am–9pm, plus midnight service Fri–Sun; return 7 daily 7.30am–8pm plus weekends at midnight; Oct–May 3 daily 10am–7pm; 30min).

BOZCAADA WINES

Thanks to its breezy climate and volcanic soil, **Bozcaada** has been famed for its wine ever since the days of Homer – a two-thousand-year-old silver coin struck here bears a bunch of grapes. Around eighty percent of the island's arable land is currently under vine, much of it the traditional grape varieties found only here and on Gökçeada, such as the whites Vasilaki and Çavuş, and the reds Karalahna, Kuntra and Karasakız. The white grapes are extremely sweet, so need to be fermented to almost thirteen percent alcohol. Local red wines tend to be rather tannic; the entire grape is left in the vats throughout the fermentation process.

Of the island's six vintners, Talay, Corvus and Çamlıbağ have the best reputation; all have well-signed **tasting boutiques** in the Greek quarter. Corvus (wcorvus.com.tr) is the most prestigious, but also overpriced; at the other outlets you can buy decent wines from ₺10 a bottle. The Talay tastery has its own wine bar upstairs, with cheese and charcuterie platters accompanying wine by the glass.

GETTING AROUND

By car The two petrol stations in Bozcaada Merkez can run empty in high season. The only free car parks in Bozcaada Merkez are behind the castle, and between the *Ege* and *Kale* hotels.

By minibus Bozcaada is small enough to get around using the summer-only minibuses that loop around the island from the quayside, passing some fine south-coast beaches.

By scooter or mountain bike İskele Sancak Café, Alaybey Mahalessi 38 (📞 0286 697 8791), offers rentals.

INFORMATION

Tourist information Two friendly cafés in Bozcaada Merkez, Ada – whose managers run the helpful website ⓦ bozcaada.info – and Lisa's, serve as unofficial tourist centres-cum-gossip posts.

Banks and money The ATMs, on the main square in Bozcaada Merkez, can run out in high season, so come prepared.

ACCOMMODATION

Ege Mektep Sok, behind castle 📞 0286 697 8189, ⓦ egehotel.com. In the nineteenth-century Greek school, this hotel has well-appointed rooms over three floors – the smaller top-floor ones have balconies facing the castle. There's a pleasant garden bar, which serves a tasty breakfast with local jams. Open all year; some private parking. ₺190

Güler Pansiyon Tuzburnu Yolu Üzeri, Tuzburnu 📞 0286 697 8454. Elegant stone-clad farmhouse, beautifully sited behind a small, sandy beach, with only vines –the owners make their own wine – between it and the sea. Some of the simple and clean rooms have very basic cooking facilities, and you're only 2km from the restaurants in Bozcaada town. ₺75

Kaikias Duvarlıkuyu Sok 1, on the north shore behind the castle 📞 0286 697 0250, ⓦ kaikias.com. Masonry fragments, nautical Greek antiques, faded hall frescoes and distressed wood floors make this rambling boutique hotel seem older than its 2001 origins. Rooms are large, with vaulted ceilings and marble-clad bathrooms, and the upstairs front rooms catch the sea breeze. ₺240

Kale Alsancak Sok 9 📞 0286 697 8617, ⓦ kalepansiyon .net. One of the few professionally run *pansiyons*, at the top of the Greek quarter a steep walk from the ferry landing. Lacking balconies or a/c but with sea-breeze views of the castle, the clean, wooden-floor, en-suite rooms are comfortable enough but only just manage to match the high-season price. Proprietress Pakize sells home-made jam and serves breakfast at a shaded terrace opposite. ₺195

★ **Katina** Eylül Cad, Kısa Sok 1, 300m south of the ferry landing 📞 0286 697 0242, ⓦ katinaas.com. One of the better boutique hotels, occupying two old houses. The warm and inviting designer-style rooms are all individually decorated, with large modern bathrooms. In-room tea and coffee, while drinks and meals, including an ample breakfast, are served in the lane under the vines, or in the ground-floor café. ₺285

Panorama Değirmenler Sok 24, on the southern ridge overlooking town 📞 0286 697 0217, ⓦ panoramaotel .com. A very welcoming family runs this quiet, luxurious inn. All six rooms benefit from a classy feminine touch, and blend antique furniture with modern finishes. The large ground-floor terrace, with leather sofas around a fireplace, doubles as a very good café and offers stunning views. ₺290

Rengigül İstiklal Sok 12, below the church 📞 0286 697 8171, ⓦ rengigul.net. This upmarket *pansiyon*, in a 1876-vintage townhouse, has different-sized guestrooms (only one en-suite), all decorated with antiques, artwork and curios by its charming and attentive female owner. An impressive breakfast is served within a conservatory in the walled rear garden, shaded by a pomegranate tree. ₺170

EATING, DRINKING AND NIGHTLIFE

★ **Ada** Çınalı Çarşı Cad 35, between the central square and the quay 📞 0286 697 8795. This friendly café is known for its red-poppy-based drinks and desserts, but also serves up a very good breakfast, tasty *mezes*, and traditional dishes like grilled calamari. Alcohol served. Mains ₺9–20. Daily 8.30am–11pm.

Café at Lisa's Cami Sok 1, just inland from the middle of the harbour 📞 0286 697 0182. Charming little café, run by a former Aussie and now long-time Bozcaada resident. Comfort food, such as breakfasts with muesli, home-cooked cakes, mini-pizzas, pasta and (alcoholic) drinks. A good spot to catch up on island gossip, it hosts occasional exhibits by island-resident artists. Mains ₺12–15. Daily 9am–9pm.

Polente Yali Sok 41, between the town square and the quay 📞 0286 789 5012. Bozcaada's most durable nightspot; motto: "Life is a Cabernet". Its youngish clientele, both local and foreign, enjoy jazz during the day, cutting-edge Greek and Latino at night. Beer ₺3. Daily 8pm–2am.

Salkım Çınarçarşı Lale Sok 16, across from the museum 📞 0286 697 0540. This unassuming ten-table courtyard bistro impresses even hard-nosed *İstanbullus* with local dishes like sardines wrapped in vine leaves, octopus stew with fennel and olives, and fried goat's cheese. Alcohol

served. Mains ₺7–19. Daily noon–3pm & 7–11pm.
Şehir Kurtuluş Cad 31 ☎ 0286 697 8017. This year-round waterfront restaurant offers a decent if at times overpriced

menu of fish dishes, plus hot and cold *mezes* and grilled *koftë*. Alcohol served. Mains ₺9–25. Daily 11am–11pm.

Troy to İzmir

Squeezed between the azure blue waters of the North Aegean and a succession of largely untouched mountain ranges, the coastline and immediate hinterland between **Troy** and **İzmir** rewards the inquisitive traveller with an enticing palette of ancient ruins, historical towns, lively coastal villages and sleepy mountain hamlets.

Troy

While by no means Turkey's most spectacular archeological site, **Troy** – thanks to Homer – is probably the most celebrated. Known as Truva or Troia in Turkish, the remains of the ancient city lie 30km south of Çanakkale, 5km west of the main road. If you show up without expectations and use your imagination, you may well be impressed. An English-speaking guide also helps to bring the ruins alive, but modern excavation work has greatly clarified the site, making it easier for non-specialists to grasp the basic layout and different settlement periods.

Brief history

Troy was long believed to have existed in legend only. The Troad plain, where the ruins lie, was known to be associated with the Troy that Homer celebrated in the *Iliad*, but all traces of the city had vanished. Then, in 1871, **Heinrich Schliemann**, a German/American businessman turned amateur archeologist, obtained permission from the Ottoman government to start digging on a hill called **Hisarlık**, where earlier excavators had already found the remains of a Classical temple and signs of further, older ruins.

Schliemann's sloppy trenching work caused considerable damage to the site, only rectified by the first professional archeologist to work at Troy, Carl Blegen, who began excavations in 1932. Schliemann was also responsible for removing the so-called **Treasure of Priam**, a large cache of copper, silver and gold vessels, plus some fine jewellery, which he smuggled to Berlin where it was displayed until 1941. The hoard disappeared when the Red Army sacked the city in May 1945, but resurfaced in Moscow in 1993, and is now exhibited in the Pushkin Museum there. Germany and the Russian Federation continue to wrangle over legal ownership, and Turkey has put in a claim too.

Whatever Schliemann's shortcomings, his unsystematic excavations did uncover nine distinct layers of consecutive urban developments, spanning four millennia. The oldest, **Troy I**, dates to about 3600 BC and was followed by four similar settlements. Either

---

ALEXANDRIA TROAS

The ruins of **Alexandria Troas**, an ancient city founded by Alexander the Great's general Antigonos I in 300 BC, lie 30km south of Troy, and 2km south of Dalyan village. Excavated since 2000 by archeologists from the University of Münster, the site (unenclosed; free) consists of mostly Roman ruins surrounded by 8km of **city wall**. A sacred way linked it to Smintheion (see p.203), while another avenue lined with shops (now uncovered) served the ancient harbour at Dalyan. The modern road roughly bisects the city; just west of this are the site's most obvious features, including the **agora temple**, its columns and reliefs set aside for restoration; a huge structure of unknown function; and a partly dug-up **odeion** with two massive arched entrances. On the other side of the road are a **basilica** and one of several **baths**, with clay piping exposed. If the warden is present and you can understand Turkish, a free guided tour is available: if not, you can wander the site at will.

3

Troy VI or **VII** is thought to have been the city described by Homer: the former is known to have been destroyed by an earthquake in about 1275 BC, while the latter shows signs of having been wiped out by fire a quarter of a century later, around the time when historians estimate the Trojan War took place. **Troy VIII**, which thrived from 700 to 300 BC, was a Greek foundation, while much of the final layer of development, **Troy IX** (300 BC to 300 AD), was built during the heyday of the Roman Empire.

Although there's no way to prove the **Trojan War** did take place, circumstantial evidence suggests that the city was the scene of some kind of armed conflict, even if it wasn't the ten-year struggle described in the *Iliad*. Homer's epic may have been based on a number of wars fought between Mycenaean Greeks and the inhabitants of Troy, who were by turns trading partners and commercial rivals.

The site

Daily: May–Sept 8am–7pm; Oct–April 8am–5pm • ₺15 admission, ₺4 parking

A 1970s reconstruction of the Homeric **wooden horse** stands immediately beyond the entrance to the site of Troy. You can climb a ladder up into the horse's belly and look out of windows cut into its flanks (which presumably didn't feature in the original design). A few paces west, the city ruins cloak an outcrop overlooking the Troad plain, which extends about 8km to the sea. A circular trail takes you around the site, with twelve explanatory panels that go some way towards bringing the ruins to life. Standing on what's left of the ramparts and looking across the plain, it's not too hard to imagine a besieging army camped below.

The most impressive remains are the **east wall and gate** from Troy VI (1700–1275 BC), of which 330m survive, curving around the eastern and southern flanks of the city. Angled inwards, the walls, 6m high and over 4m thick, would have been surmounted by an additional brick section. A ramp paved with flat stones from Troy II (2500–2300 BC), which would have led to the citadel entrance, also stands out, as does the nearby partially reconstructed **Megaron Building** (protected beneath a giant canvas roof) from the same era, the bricks of which were turned a bright red when Troy II was destroyed by fire. Schliemann erroneously used the evidence of this fire to conclude that this had been Homer's Troy and that the hoard he discovered here made up "Priam's treasure".

The most important monument of Greco-Roman Troy VIII–IX, or Ilium, is the Doric **temple of Athena**, rebuilt by Alexander the Great's general, Lysimakhos, after Alexander himself had visited the temple and left his armour as a gift. The most famous relief from the temple, depicting Apollo astride four pawing stallions, is now in Berlin. Troy was an important religious centre during Greek and Roman times, and another **sanctuary to the Samothracian deities** can be seen near the westernmost point of the site, outside the walls. East of this are a Greco-Roman odeion and bouleuterion (council hall).

ARRIVAL AND DEPARTURE

TROY

By bus or dolmuş Dolmuşes run from the open-air terminal beside the river bridge in Çanakkale, the most sensible base for seeing Troy, to Tevfikiye village just outside the site entrance. If you're moving on further south, catch the Troy–Çanakkale minibus to the main road, then flag down a long-haul bus.

Destinations Çanakkale (hourly: winter 9.30am–5pm; longer hours in summer; 30min).

INFORMATION

Tourist information The on-site gift shop, and souvenir shops on the approach road, sell the map/guide *A Tour of Troia*, written by Dr Manfred Korfmann, the archeologist who between 1988 and his death in 2005 oversaw the site's excavation.

Tours Most travel agencies in Çanakkale and Eceabat offer morning tours of Troy (around ₺70 per person), usually connecting with their afternoon Gallipoli tours.

Guides English-speaking guides are sometimes available at the site entrance for guided tours, costing around €50 for 1–2hr.

ACCOMMODATION

Staying in the small village of Tevfikiye, 1km from the entrance to Troy, gives you both a head start on the crowds, and the chance to experience a little slice of rural Turkey.

Hisarlık Hotel Tevfikiye, near the minibus stop 500m from Troy ☎0286 283 0026. Veteran establishment, owned by a local Troy guide. The downstairs restaurant serves up a decent, rather than great, menu of Turkish standards that manage to at least refuel the body after a morning's exploration. The upstairs rooms, however, are very basic and overpriced. ₺120

Varol Pansiyon Tevfikiye Merkez, in the village centre ☎0286 283 0828. Tucked away from the busy road to Troy, this friendly family-run *pansiyon* has large, simply furnished rooms with clean bathrooms. There's a large living room and guests are welcome to use the kitchen. There's a grocery store next door, but breakfast is included. ₺80

Smintheion

62km south of Troy, at the western edge of Gülpınar village • **Ionic temple** • Daily 8am–5pm • ₺5 includes museum entrance • **Museum** • Daily 8am–2pm (Aug–Sept) or open on request • With only scanty dolmuş service from Ezine, or Ayvacık via Behramkale (Assos), it's best to visit by bike or car

Within the ancient Greek and Roman settlement of **Smintheion** is a shrine dedicated to one of the more bizarre manifestations of the god, as Slayer of Mice. When the original Cretan colonists here were besieged by mice, they remembered an oracle advising them to settle where they were overrun by the "sons of earth". This they took to mean the rodents, so founded the ancient town of Khryse nearby. Coins excavated from the site depict Apollo treading on a mouse.

The surviving Hellenistic, Ionic **temple** has been partly restored and some columns re-erected, though its southwest corner has been re-clad in garish new stone. The Efes beer brewery has funded the renovation as well as the ongoing excavations at adjacent **Khryse**, which have so far exposed a square **reservoir** in the sacred precinct, an arcaded **baths** complex just below, and part of the **Sacred Way** from Alexandria Troas.

A one-roomed **museum** at the site entrance displays **temple pediment reliefs** depicting scenes from the *Iliad*, including an early episode where Achilles kidnaps the priestess of the temple here, only to have Agamemnon appropriate her. Apollo duly inflicts a plague on the Greeks for this outrage, alleviated only upon the return of the girl to her father, the temple priest. Apart from the mourning of Patroklos, however, the reliefs are unfortunately damaged.

Assos

Situated on and around the eponymous ancient Greek city, the modern-day settlement of **ASSOS**, 25km south of Ayvacık, encompasses the charming late-medieval village of **Behramkale**; the **Assos acropolis**, perched above it; and a tiny, attractive **harbour** below, known as İskele or Assos Liman.

Exploring the ruins and the village aside, Assos is simply a place to unwind and gaze out over a perfectly blue sea. Most visitors to Assos rush up to Behramkale to see the temple before heading down to enjoy the eating and drinking pleasures of the harbour.

The journey from Ayvacık in particular is very pleasant, as the road threads through hilly countryside covered with olive trees and valonia oak, whose acorns yield tannin, used to make leather – the main business of Assos until the early twentieth century. The final approach passes a fourteenth-century, humpback Ottoman bridge, built with ancient masonry during the same period as the Hüdavendigar Camii, in Behramkale.

Brief history

Assos dates from about 950 BC, when Greek colonists from Mithymna on neighbouring Lesbos (modern Lésvos) established a settlement. Hermias, a eunuch disciple of Plato, ruled here during the fourth century BC, attempting to put Plato's theories of the ideal city-state into practice. Between 348 and 345 BC, **Aristotle** lived in Assos as Hermias' guest before crossing to Lesbos, just before the Persians arrived and put Hermias to death. **St Paul** also passed through en route to Lesbos during his third evangelical journey (c.55 AD; Acts 20:13–14). The site was rediscovered and initially excavated in 1880–83 by a 25-year-old American, Francis Bacon.

Assos Acropolis

Behramkale • Open daylight hours • ₺5

The enclosed acropolis site contains the iconic **Temple of Athena** dating back to 530 BC, with sweeping views across the straits to Greek Lésvos. In an attempt to give visitors an idea of what it would have looked like in its heyday, the temple's Doric columns were re-erected during the 1980s using inappropriate concrete, but remedial work is now under way to replace this with stone from the original quarries. To reach the temple, simply follow the string of tourist stalls that line the road up from Behramkale's village square. While it is the most familiar relic of ancient Assos, other ruins (unenclosed) are scattered down the hillside towards the harbour, including a second-century BC theatre with another spectacular straits view, the sarcophagi of the necropolis and the remains of a Byzantine basilica, as well as a stretch of Roman road on the landward side of the road shortly after it starts its descent from Behramkale village.

Behramkale

The hilltop village of **Behramkale**, just below the Temple of Athena, has a central core of attractive old houses built in the same local volcanic stone (andesite) as the temple.

The single-domed **Hüdavendigar Camii** (closed), beside the temple entrance, is often overlooked in the rush to get to the temple. Built during the reign of Murat I Hüdavendigar (1359–89), it's an austere, square-plan fourteenth-century mosque that incorporates masonry taken from a sixth-century Byzantine church in its walls.

Assos Liman (İskele)

Assos's few hundred metres of waterfront, stretching two hundred steep metres below Behramkale, is very picturesque. Summer weekends see it overflowing with busloads of tour groups, but it can be idyllic out of season. The cluster of old stone buildings along the water's edge, which originally served as warehouses to store locally tanned leather, now hold sea-view hotels.

ARRIVAL AND DEPARTURE   ASSOS

By dolmuş Regular dolmuşes connect Assos with Ayvacık to the north and Küçükkuyu to the southeast. They don't usually leave Ayvacık with fewer than eight passengers, but at quiet times you can pay extra to avoid a long wait. Dolmuşes from Ayvacık usually continue to Assos Liman (İskele), where they wait for return custom. In summer, a shuttle bus usually connects the two all day, or it's a 30min walk.
Destinations Ayvacık (several daily; 20min; ₺3); Küçükkuyu (several daily; 1hr).

By car Turn left, uphill, at the road junction as you approach from Ayvacık or Gülpınar to reach Behramkale, with the Assos acropolis above. Keep straight on and downhill instead, and you'll come to Assos Liman (İskele); there's almost no parking at the bottom, so you have to park on the final curve before the descent, a 5min walk from the sea.
By ferry Despite the tempting anchorage at Assos harbour, there's little yacht traffic here and crossing to Greece is illegal – something enforced by the quayside *jandarma* post.

ACCOMMODATION

Popular with the İstanbul literati, Assos is anything but cheap. On summer weekends advance bookings are essential, though midweek, and in May or September, you can still find rooms at realistic prices. While it attracts numerous coach tours, few stay in Assos overnight. Accommodation in Behramkale is far more relaxed and personal than down in the harbour, where most hotels insist on half board, and have decks crammed with loungers and swimming platforms to make up for the lack of a beach.

BEHRAMKALE

★ **Assos Alarga** Behramkale Köyü 88, east of the square ☎ 0286 721 7260, ⓦ assosalarga.com. This family home turned designer *pansiyon* is as good as they come. Exquisitely and sympathetically restored throughout, the house offers three large, elegantly furnished rooms with modern bathrooms and gloriously large windows looking out over the pool and onto the valley. The impeccable service accommodates all-comers, including late brunches and home-style dinners, plus free access into the kitchen for those with babies and small children. B&B ₺230

Assosyal Ozel Alan Meyd 8, at the east end of the village ☎ 0286 721 7046, ⓔ assosyalotel@gmail.com. A modern boutique hotel, whose room interiors contrast sharply with the stone exterior of the three wings. Eclectically decorated throughout, the rooms and accompanying en-suites are on the small side, but most have balconies with sweeping valley views. Breakfast is taken on the north-facing conservatory-terrace, also a licensed restaurant. Half board available. ₺310

Biber Evi Behramkale Köyü 46, signposted just before the end of the road to the temple ☎ 0286 721 7410, ⓦ biberevi.com. Offering some of Behramkale's best lodgings, *Biber Evi* is named for the twenty species of peppers (*biber*) growing in its garden. There are three rooms in the main house (built in 1860) – the best has a fireplace – and three more modest ones in the annexe; rates include breakfast. Outside is a popular winter fireplace-lounge-bar with terrace. Annexe ₺300, house ₺340

Eris Pansiyon Behramkale Köyü 6, at the east end of the village ☎ 0286 721 7080. This charming *pansiyon*, owner-managed by a very hospitable American, offers plain but tasteful en-suite B&B rooms with valley views. More a house than a hotel, *Eris*'s common areas, including a book-swap library, are very communal and sociable places, especially the garden terrace where a 5pm "high tea" is served. ₺130

Tekin Pansiyon Behramkale Köyü 8, at the east end of the village ☎ 0286 721 7099. The friendly *Tekin*, at the entrance to Behramkale, is the village's best budget option, with simple but serviceable en-suite rooms, some with a terrace. There's also an on-site restaurant and a communal balcony upstairs, overlooking the village. ₺110

ASSOS LIMAN (İSKELE)

Assos Kervansaray Assos İskele 3 ☎ 0286 721 7093, ⓦ assoskervansary.com. One of the converted warehouses in the small harbour, this large hotel has disappointingly small rooms that are nonetheless clean, modern and comfortable, some with sea views. There's indoor and outdoor pools, a restaurant on the water and private parking. Half board ₺170

Nazlıhan Assos İskele 6 ☎ 0286 721 7385, ⓦ assosnazlihan.com. Ageing hotel, set in a converted warehouse. Three grades of boutique-style room, though only eight face the sea and all have exceptionally small bathrooms. The waterside restaurant is popular. Half board ₺160

EATING, DRINKING AND NIGHTLIFE

All the hotels down in the harbour boast licensed restaurants, although the quality of their cuisine tends to reflect a captive market and can be expensive; ask for a menu with prices before ordering. Up in Behramkale, the options are more limited and laidback.

BEHRAMKALE

Biber Evi Restaurant Behramkale Köyü 46, signposted just before the end of the road towards the temple ☎ 0286 721 7410, ⓦ biberevi.com. Lütfi, the gregarious host of this upmarket *pansiyon*, is a fount of local lore and offers excellent meals, including roasted lamb or goat accompanied by fresh greens and herbs from the kitchen garden. Licensed, and also serving proper European coffee; best to book ahead. Mains ₺19–31. Daily 7–10.30pm.

Börek Evi Behramkale Köyü 19, in the village centre ☎ 0286 721 7050. Popular with locals, *Börek* offers standard *lokantasi* fare, pre-prepared and kept warm in steam trays. Choose between mainly chicken and lamb dishes, though there's usually a good selection of hot and cold *mezes*. One of very few licensed restaurants in the village. Mains ₺7–9. Daily 9am–7pm.

ASSOS LIMAN (İSKELE)

Uzun Ev Assos İskele 3 ☎ 0286 721 7007. One of the better fish restaurants in the harbour; *Uzun Ev*'s steamed sea bass dish is a local speciality, best enjoyed at their waterfront tables though they also have a terrace across the road. In summer, it turns into the local nightspot, hosting live acoustic Turkish music some evenings. Mains ₺11–23. Daily 11am–11pm.

Yıldız Saray Assos İskele 6 ☎ 0286 721 7025, ⓦ assosyildizsarayotel.com. The restaurant of this waterfront hotel, a converted warehouse, far outranks the accommodation. Diners can choose from atmospheric tables surrounding a fireplace within the hotel's stone building, or on a shaded floating pontoon on the water's edge. The menu offers a good selection of mainly fish dishes at reasonable prices, plus a fine array of mainly local wines. Mains ₺9–27. Daily 11am–11pm.

3

Along the Gulf of Edremit

The E87/550 Çanakkale–İzmir road descends beyond Ayvacık in curves through pine-forested hills, allowing occasional glimpses over the **Gulf of Edremit**. The highway straightens out at **Küçükkuyu**, the only real coastal town and gateway to the two traditional villages of **Yeşilyurt** and **Adatepe** in the foothills of the Kazdağı range (the ancient Mount Ida). Beyond here, the road leads past a dreary succession of Turkish-dominated resorts and second-home complexes to the inland county town of **Edremit**. At Burhaniye, 18km south, a side road leads 5km west to the old-fashioned resort of **Ören**, with an excellent, long, west-facing sandy beach.

Küçükkuyu

29km southeast of Ayvacık

An attractive small fleet still lies at anchor in the small fishing and olive-oil town of **KÜÇÜKKUYU** ("Little Well"). It's joined by dozens of fancy leisure craft during the summer, when the town swells with holidaying Turks. There are some atmospheric backstreets to wander, dotted with shops selling all manner of olive-oil products, but few visitors stay longer than it takes to have a seafood **meal** on the port quay.

Yeşilyurt

3km west of Küçükkuyu on the E87/550, then 1km inland

The attractive village of **YEŞİLYURT** huddles around a picturesque main square, then continues down tree-lined cobbled streets to the river and uphill again, peeking at the sea from their pirate-proof location. Most of the houses are built in honey-coloured stone and many are being converted into boutique *pansiyons* for well-to-do *İstanbullus*.

Adatepe

Just over 4km northeast of Küçükkuyu

The exquisitely preserved village of **ADATEPE** is most noteworthy for its "**Zeus Altarı**", a 15min marked walk from the approach road. This is merely a carved rock platform with a cistern, from where Zeus was believed to have watched the fighting at Troy on the plains below; the views from the top of the steps are superb.

Adatepe's architecture, unlike Yeşilyurt, enjoys statutory protection; some stone houses all but sprout from volcanic boulders. Again unlike Yeşilyurt, it was ethnically mixed from the 1850s, when, in the wake of a killing frost, cash-strapped olive-oil magnates paid their Greek workers with a grant of fields and building plots in the lower quarter, though the Orthodox church on the plane-tree plaza was destroyed after 1923.

ACCOMMODATION AND EATING
ALONG THE GULF OF EDREMIT

KÜÇÜKKUYU

Alp Balık Evi Suleyman Sakalli Cad 49 ☎ 0286 752 5304. The most popular and well known of a number of quayside restaurants, the *Alp* is obviously big on fresh fish, with its own supplier sticking the fridges daily with sardines, whiting and sea bass. The food is good, but the service sometimes wanes. No alcohol. Mains ₺11–27. Daily 11.30am–10.30pm.

YEŞİLYURT

Manici Kasrı Yeşilyurt Köyü 16 ☎ 0286 752 1731, ⊛ manicikasri.com. An all-stone villa with 11 elegant rooms, in warm, colourful tones and stylishly furnished with antiques and large beds. The olde-worlde common areas include a fireplace, beamed ceilings and a terrace swimming pool and restaurant. Half board only. ₺350

★ **Taş Teras Otel** Yeşilyurt Köyü 18 ☎ 0286 752 6666,

⊛ tasteras.com. A classy and design-conscious villa of stone and red brick, owner-managed by a well-travelled Turkish couple. The rustic-chic rooms all offer individual fireplaces and modern bathrooms, some with private terraces. The common areas include a large dining terrace, offering a menu that's big on local and traditional produce. ₺280

ADATEPE

Hünnap Han Adatepe Köyü 34 ☎ 0286 752 6581, ⊛ hunnaphan.com. Adatepe's best accommodation, this welcoming owner-managed place is named after the jujube tree in its serene walled main garden. Stone and wood-trim rooms occupy a rambling, main *konak*, dating from 1750, with the *Taş Ev* annexe (sleeping 8) for groups, and a second annexe (*Palmiye*) downhill with a swimming pool. Half board only. ₺250

Ayvalık and around

Thanks to its charming old quarter of picturesque Greek houses, **Ayvalık**, 56km south of Edremit, has long been popular with Turkish and European visitors. The closest good beaches are at the mainstream resort of **Sarımsaklı** (see p.208), with some remoter, rockier ones on **Cunda island** (see p.211), both easily reached from town. Ayvalık is also convenient for day-trips to ancient Pergamon, and the Greek island of Lésvos opposite, served by regular ferry.

Brief history

Due to its excellent anchorages, the area has been inhabited since ancient times, but today's Ayvalık began as the **Ottoman Greek** settlement of Kydoníes during the early eighteenth century. Both Turkish and Greek names refer to the local quince orchards, now vanished.

In the 1790s, the town was effectively granted autonomy by Grand Vizier Cezayırlı Hasan Paşa, who, as an Ottoman admiral, had been rescued in 1771 by the Greeks of Ayvalık following a disastrous defeat by the Russian navy. This soon became the most prosperous and imposing town on the Aegean coast after İzmir, boasting an academy, a publishing house and around twenty Orthodox churches, many of which still remain,

3

AYVALIK

AEGEAN SEA

N

Otogar, Ferry Terminal, Edremit & Cunda

ACCOMMODATION	
Annette's House	7
Ayvalık Palas	6
Bonjour	3
Kaptan	4
Şato	2
Sızma Han	1
Taksiyarhis	5

Ex-Customs

Taksiyarhis Kilisesi

GÜMRÜK MEYD

Saatlı Cami

TALATPAŞA CADDESI

HÖRSECART MEYDAN

CUMHURIYET MEYD

BAZAAR

Çınarlı Cami

Island Tour Boats

İSKELE MEYD

Dive Boats

Cunda (Alibey)

0   100
metres

Sarımsaklı & Faneroméni

BAR AND CAFÉ	
Bar Dak	1

RESTAURANTS	
Balıkçı	1
Caramel Café	4
Hüsnü Baba'nin Yeri	2
Şehir Kulübü	3
Tostcular Çarşı	5

albeit converted into mosques after 1923. Ironically, most of the people resettled here were Greek-speaking Muslims from Crete and Mytilini (Lésvos), and many of Ayvalık's older inhabitants still speak Greek.

Ayvalık

Unlike resorts to the south that are dominated by the holiday trade, **AYVALIK** is relatively free of touts, and has retained a fishing fleet and olive-based commerce (including oil and green soap), as well as a prestigious classical music academy and some lively markets – Thursday is the special market day for produce from the surrounding villages, with its epicentre at two *meydans* either side of *Annette's House pansiyon*.

Almost uniquely for the Aegean, central Ayvalık is pretty much a perfectly preserved Ottoman market town, though few of the traditional trades are left. Riotously painted horse-carts still clatter through the cobbled **bazaar** (home to a colourful, regional produce market every Sunday), emanating from a *meydan* to the south where the animals and their drivers wait for commissions.

While few specific sights other than converted nineteenth-century churches punctuate the warren of inland streets, use the minarets as landmarks and surrender to the pleasure of wandering under numerous wrought-iron window grilles and past ornately carved doorways.

A few soaring brick chimneys are all that survive of the factories that once churned out olive oil by the vat-load. Nowadays the work has moved into modern factories on the outskirts.

Sarimsaklı

7km south of Ayvalık • Frequent dolmuşes from just south of İskele Meydanı

SARIMSAKLI ("Garlic Beach"), a mainly Turkish resort, is home to the longest local **beach**. Its 3km or so of sand is at its most attractive at the western end, where development is set back some distance from the water. There are all the resort trappings you'd expect, but with a slightly downmarket flavour, and few would choose to stay overnight.

ARRIVAL AND DEPARTURE

AYVALIK

By plane Borajet (ⓦborajet.com.tr) operates a few weekly flights from İstanbul's Sabiha Gökçen Airport to the small Balıkesir Koca Seyit Airport, 5km south of Edremit and 37km north of Ayvalık.

By bus Most southbound buses drop passengers at the Ayvalık highway junction, 5km northeast of town, and served by taxis. The *otogar* is 1.5km north of the town centre, but any city bus labelled "Çamlık", and most major-company *servis* vehicles, will take you into town. Buses from İzmir usually pass through the central seafront İskele Meydanı, while those for Bergama collect from the main square on their way to/from the *otogar*.

Destinations Balıkesir (hourly; 2hr); Bergama, some via Dikili (11 daily; 1hr 45min); Bursa (10 daily; 4hr 30min); Çanakkale (6 daily; 3hr 30min); Edremit (hourly; 1hr); İstanbul (10 daily; 8hr); İzmir (hourly; 3hr).

By boat or ferry The morning ferry to Lésvos departs from a modern passenger terminal 1800m north of the centre, opposite the lone ticket agency, Jale (ⓣ0266 331 3170, ⓦjaletour.com); remember to take your passport. Boats to Cunda leave from the main quay.

Destinations Cunda (June–Sept, 2–3 hourly; 15min); Lésvos, Greece (May–Oct Mon–Fri & Sun 6pm, Sat 9am & 6pm, Nov–April 3 weekly at 5pm, & 1 weekly at 9am; 1hr 30min).

By car Parking is very limited in the old quarter, where the network of narrow one-way lanes makes navigation especially difficult. There are car parks along the waterfront, or drivers can also stay on Cunda (see p.211) and take the shuttle-ferry or bus into town.

Car rental Central agencies include Avis, Talatpaşa Cad 61/B (ⓣ0266 312 2456); Duke, İskele Meydanc (ⓣ0266 312 3794); and Europcar, Atatürk Bul 186/A (ⓣ0266 312 3446).

INFORMATION AND TOURS

Tourist office Atatürk Cad, just south of the marina (Mon–Fri 8am–noon & 1–5pm; ⓣ0266 312 2122). In summer, there's also an information kiosk on the waterfront.

3

Boat trips Day-trips around local islets leave from the main quay, stopping off for swimming, sunbathing and a bit of island exploring. The trips run May–Oct, departing at 10am, returning at 4.30pm, and include lunch. **Körfez** Atatürk Bul Özeral Pasaji 617A ☎ 0266 312 4966, ⍟ korfezdiving.com. The Ayvalık area is noted for deep-growing red coral, submerged archeological artefacts and caves. This well-established scuba-diving outfitter, one of several along the main quay, pioneered many local dive sites off Ayvalık, and offers CMAS- and PADI-affiliated courses, as well as night dives.

ACCOMMODATION

OLD QUARTER

Annette's House Neşe Sok 12 ☎ 0542 663 3193, ⍟ annetteshouse.com. This Turkish version of a British B&B is owner-managed by gentle German Annette, and comprises two linked houses in the maze-like old quarter. The rooms are slightly "granny-like" but perfectly comfortable, with a top-floor quad suite and a good ratio of bathrooms to the other rooms. Delicious home-cooked breakfasts (₺10) are served in a plant-filled garden, and parking is possible except on Thurs, market day. **₺100**

Bonjour Mareşal Çakmak Cad, Çeşme Sok 5 ☎ 0266 312 8085, ⍟ bonjourpansiyon.com. Occupying a grand mansion with painted ceilings and antiques throughout, this former French embassy (hence the name) offers rooms and bathrooms in the main house, plus one en-suite behind the courtyard where breakfast (₺20) is served. **₺110**

Şato İsmet Paşa Mahalessi 100 ☎ 0266 312 2351. Hard to find, but wonderfully ensconced high in the old quarter, with antique- and art-filled rooms (some en-suite) in two houses on the same street. The original century-old house has a Lésvos-view terrace and guest-friendly kitchen, and is also where super-friendly hosts Cemal and Fatma serve a large breakfast in the shaded garden. **₺120**

★ **Taksiyarhis** İsmet Paşa Mahalessi 71, directly west of Taksiyarhis Kilisesi church ☎ 0266 312 1494, ⍟ taksiyarhispension.com. One of the most characterful pensions on the Aegean coast, occupying two knocked-together Greek houses, eclectically decorated with antiques and curios from owner Yasemin's travels. Comfortable a/c rooms spaced out over a number of floors, sharing spotless bathrooms. There are also two terraces – breakfast (₺15) on the top one is a major highlight – and a kitchen for guest use. **₺110**

THE WATERFRONT

Ayvalık Palas Gümrük Meyd ☎ 0266 312 1064. While definitely not a "palace", this serviceable waterfront hotel has decent if slightly bland, carpeted rooms, some with balconies offering exceptional sea views. The large on-site restaurant is only recommended for the buffet breakfast. **₺145**

Kaptan Balıkhane Sok 7 ☎ 0266 312 8834, ⍟ kaptanotelayvalik.com. Set in a restored waterfront olive-oil warehouse; rooms are starting to age but still offer a few comforts and large windows, some with wonderful sea views. Breakfast is served on a seaside terrace. **₺135**

★ **Sızma Han** Gümrük Cad, İkinci Sok 49 ☎ 0266 312 7700, ⍟ butiksizmahan.com. Beautifully renovated olive-oil factory from 1908, enthusiastically managed by owner Mustafa; the competent, seafood-strong seaside terrace restaurant features Sevilen wines. The compact rooms with original small windows are low-key modern with veneer floors and furniture, and exposed stone pointing. The lounge-with-fireplace is a focal point, and there's safe but limited street parking. Heavily discounted off-season rates. **₺180**

EATING, DRINKING AND NIGHTLIFE

Bar Dak Balıkhane Sok ☎ 0530 582 4062. Ayvalık's main nightlife option, within a cavernous brick-and-stone building near the waterfront, attracts a young crowd of both locals and travellers, with a Western–Turkish music mix (both DJ and live) and reasonably priced drinks. Beer ₺3.50. Tues–Sat 8pm–late.

Balıkçı Balıkhane Sok 7 ☎ 0266 312 9099. Something of a local legend, *Balıkçı* offers the waterfront's best-value seafood. Friendly waiters will explain the catches of the day, and you can dine on an outside terrace or indoors, often to the accompaniment of live *fasıl* music. Mains ₺15–25. Daily 7–11pm.

Caramel Café Barbaros Cad 37/A ☎ 0266 312 8520. This tiny pink-and-mauve café offers a refreshingly inventive, home-cooked menu of Turkish standards and Mediterranean classics, such as seafood pasta, pesto penne, Turkish ravioli, and an excellent chocolate mousse. Owner-chef Yasemin is both a welcoming host and impressive chef, and the service is always friendly. Mains ₺6–11. Daily noon–10pm.

Hüsnü Baba'nin Yeri Tenekeçiler Sok 16, inland from Bellona Furniture ☎ 0266 312 8714. One of very few remaining restaurants in the bazaar, this welcoming *meyhane* specializes in *mezes* and seafood, including *papalina* (fried sprat) and *deniz kestanesi* (sea urchin) in season, cooked in oil from gregarious owner/chef Hüsnü's own olive grove. Tables inside and out on the cobbled lane, but no written menu; confirm all prices in advance. Mains ₺4–11. Daily 7–11pm.

Tostcular Çarşı Nisan Sok 16. Next door to Tansaş supermarket, the popular "Toast-makers Market" is a huddle of small cafés serving *Ayvalık Tostu*, a toasted sandwich packed solid with salami, pickles, tomatoes and pepper, and coated with liberal doses of mayonnaise and tomato sauce (₺0.50–2). Daily 8am–8pm.

Şehir Kulübü Gazinolar Cad ☎ 0266 312 3676. Often busy with local office workers devouring seafood lunches, and a notch in presentation and price above most along the waterfront. Their *papalina* (fried sprat) is usually not too greasy, and the wonderful sea views can be appreciated inside or outside. Mains ₺11–23. Daily 11am–11pm.

Cunda

Across the bay from Ayvalık, the island of **CUNDA** – known as Yonda in Ottoman times, and now officially **Alibey Adası**, and also accessible via causeway – constitutes either a good day-trip destination or an overnight halt. It's a marginally quieter, less grand version of Ayvalık old town, with a lively main harbour and cobbled backstreets lined by restored stone houses – remnants of life before 1923, when Cunda was known as Moskhonísi to its Greek Orthodox inhabitants. After the Christians were sent to Greece, the island was resettled with Cretan Muslims from around Haniá, and most older people speak Cretan Greek as a matter of course. Cunda has become popular with affluent İstanbulites bent on owning an Aegean retreat, though the dense ranks of tatty trinket and ice-cream stalls along the quay clash somewhat with its twee image.

Halfway up the slope from the waterfront, the Orthodox **Taksiyarhis Cathedral**, heavily damaged by a 1944 earthquake, is undergoing a welcome restoration. At the top of the hill, a chapel and adjacent windmill have been converted by the Koç Foundation into a worthwhile café with stunning views.

Northern Cunda, known as **Patriça**, is supposedly a protected nature reserve – not that villa construction has completely stopped – and holds some relatively deserted beaches. A dirt road goes to them, while boat tours from Ayvalık harbour visit two derelict **Greek monasteries**, Áyios Yórgis and Áyios Dhimítrios tou Sélina, accessible only by sea.

ARRIVAL AND DEPARTURE
CUNDA

By boat Small bus-boats leave for Cunda from Ayvalık's main quay (June–Sept, at least hourly; 15min).

By bus Hourly city buses from Ayvalık's İskele Meydanı cross the causeway that links Cunda to the mainland.

ACCOMMODATION

Ada 3km southwest of town ☎ 0266 327 1211, ⓦ www .adacamping.com. Good facilities at this large campsite include an on-site restaurant and self-catering kitchen. The grassed sites have a little shade, and a number of a/c wooden bungalows overlook the sandy beach. Closed Dec–March. Camping ₺34, bungalow ₺150

Altay Pansiyon Ayvalık Cad 18 ☎ 0266 327 1024, ⓦ altaypansion.com. Cunda's oldest pension, in the cobbled streets behind the waterfront, is a friendly family-run affair. Decorated throughout in a quirky mix of dated/retro objects, the simple, tiled en-suite rooms are set round a central shaded courtyard. ₺140

Zehra Teyze'nin Evi Şeref Sok 7 ☎ 0266 327 2285, ⓦ cundaevi.com. In the grounds of Taksiyarhis Cathedral, "Aunt Zehra's House" is the former priest's residence. Homely and cheerful rather than particularly smart, its comfortable en-suite rooms are accessed via a pleasant shaded garden. ₺155

EATING AND DRINKING

The cheap local **seafood speciality** is *papalina* (fried sprat, a kind of whitebait) and fried mussels in a garlic, olive oil and white-wine sauce. Half a dozen restaurants directly overlook the quay.

Cunda Deniz Sahil Yolu 15 ☎ 0266 327 1685. One of the island's original fish restaurants, and still among the best. Popular with locals and tourists, the waterfront *Deniz* offers excellent, seasonal *mezes* to accompany a wide range of fresh fish and other seafood, including mussels in white wine. Mains ₺11–15. Daily 11.30am–11pm.

Lal Girit Mutfağı *Altay Pansiyon*, Ayvalık Cad 18 ☎ 0266 327 1024. Run by a welcoming Cretan (*Girit*) couple, this small restaurant is renowned for its excellent home-cooked food, especially the hot and cold *mezes* and seasonal stuffed courgette. Mains ₺8–17. Daily noon–3.30pm & 8–11pm.

Taş Kahve Sahil Böyu 20 ☎ 0266 327 1166. Cunda's most atmospheric café, where old men play cards on rickety wooden chairs in a church-like stone-walled hall with high wooden ceilings and large stained-glass windows. Good breakfasts and *mezes* accompany piping hot coffee and tea. Meze ₺7. Daily 8am–10pm.

Bergama

Although possible as a day-trip destination from Ayvalık, **BERGAMA**, site of the ancient city of **Pergamon**, rates an overnight stop in its own right. Towering over modern Bergama, the stunning acropolis of the Pergamene dynasty is the main attraction, but two lesser sights, the **Asklepion** and **Kızıl Avlu**, as well as the town's medieval quarter, are well worth exploring. Bear in mind that the two parts of ancient Pergamon, unshaded and extremely hot at midday in summer, are some distance from each other.

Brief history

Pergamon rose to prominence as the base of Lysimakhos, a successor to Alexander the Great who died in 281 BC. He left considerable treasure to his eunuch-steward Philetaeros who passed it on to his nephew Eumenes I, founder of the Pergamene dynasty. The city only achieved true greatness under **Eumenes II** (197–159 BC), who built its gymnasium, the Altar of Zeus, library, theatre and acropolis wall. Eumenes' brother Attalos II ruled until 138 BC, followed by the five-year reign of the cruel but scholarly **Attalos III**, who perversely left the kingdom to the **Romans**. Under them Pergamon became an artistic and commercial centre of 150,000 people, but after the arrival of the Goths in 262 AD, it declined and fell into ruin.

The German engineer **Carl Humann** rediscovered ancient Pergamon in 1871, when some locals showed him a strange mosaic that turned out to be part of the relief from the Altar of Zeus. Humann bought the mosaic, and began excavating the acropolis. Work was completed by 1886, but unfortunately most of the finds were carted off to Germany, including the Altar of Zeus reliefs, now in the Pergamon Museum in Berlin.

In 1998 a second significant archeological site, the Roman spa and asklepion of **Allianoi**, was discovered 19km east of Pergamon. However, it had only been partly excavated before the Yortanlı irrigation dam flooded the site in 2011 despite domestic and international protest (see ⓦallianoi.org). The site was first "re-buried" under a protective layer of clay so that future generations may be able to excavate it once the dam's tenure (only 50 years say some experts) is complete.

The acropolis

Akropol Cad • Daily: July–Aug 8.30am–6.30pm; Sept–June 8.30am–5.30pm • ₺20, ₺4 parking • The lower cable-car station – ₺10 each way – is 200m east of Kızıl Avlu, and the upper station at the site's car park and ticket booth, which is also where taxis drop visitors; the footpath up starts on the far side of the second bridge upstream from the Kızıl Avlu, angling obliquely up to the road; cross here and follow a steep incline into the lower agora

Once you enter the site of Pergamon's **Acropolis**, an uphill path from the former city gate leads southwest to the huge, square **Altar of Zeus**, standing in the shade of two large stone pines. Built by Eumenes II to commemorate his father's victory over the Gauls, the altar was decorated with reliefs depicting the battle between the Titans and the gods, symbolizing the triumph of order over chaos (and, presumably, that of Attalos I over the Gauls). Even today its former splendour is apparent, if much

---

EXPLORING PERGAMON

Bergama's various archeological sites are so widely spread out that only the most ardent (and thrifty) of walkers would insist on walking to them.

The entrance to the **Acropolis** is accessible on foot from the old town, but the most direct route is an uphill path that can be hard to find, while the main road, which is also steep, is not particularly direct, doubling back on itself for about 5km. Most visitors choose to ride up to the ticket booth by **cable car** and then walk down through the ruins.

The **Asklepion** is also an uphill hike from the town centre, either on a steep track or along a winding road. Both pass through a large, clearly marked military zone (no photos), closed to all traffic at dusk. More walker-friendly are the **Archeological Museum** and **Kızıl Avlu**, around 1500m apart and at the southern and northern ends of Bergama's main road respectively.

3

BERGAMA

Kale Yolu

Ayvalık ve Kozak

Bergama Çayı

ACROPOLIS

Temple of Trajan

Theatre

Temple of Dionysos

Library

Royal Palaces

City Gate

Ticket Booth

Upper Cable Car Station

Heroön

Temple of Athena

Path

Altar of Zeus

Upper Agora

Wall Course

Gymnasium

Temple of Demeter

Lower Agora

OLD TOWN

Ulu Cami

IMAM ÇIKMAZI

İSTIKLAL MEYDANI

Path

Lower Cable Car Station

Kızıl Avlu (Red Basilica)

Kınık Caddesi

Bergama Çayı

Allibeyi (20km)

Soma & Rail line

Roman Amphitheatre

Roman Theatre

Bankalar Caddesi

Çarşı Hamamı

Taxi Rank

Kurşunlu Cami

ATATÜRK MEYDANI

Archeological Museum

Cumhuriyet Caddesi

ASCLEPION

Sacred Fountain

Theatre

Library

Propylon

Sacred Way

Underground Passage

Temple of Asklepios

Temple of Telesphoros

TRACK

Old Otogar

Army Camp

Böblingen Caddesi

Tanpınar Sok

Asklepion Caddesi

Atatürk Bulvarı

Football Stadium

Army Camp

Kaymakam Kemal Bey Caddesi

N

0 — 500
metres

Otogar (6km), İzmir & Ayvalık

■ ACCOMMODATION	
Akropolis	2
Anıl	3
Gobi	4
Odyssey	1

■ BAR AND CAFÉ	
Sofa Café	1

● RESTAURANTS	
Bergama Sofrası	2
Bergama Ticaret Odası Sosyal Tesisleri	1

diminished by the removal of the reliefs to Berlin. The main approach stairway was on the west, now the most deteriorated side.

Directly northeast of, and exactly parallel to, the Altar of Zeus, on the next terrace up, lie the sparse remains of the third-century BC **Temple of Athena**. Only some of its stepped foundations survive *in situ*, although the entrance gate, with its inscribed dedication "King Eumenes to Athena the Bearer of Victories", has been reconstructed in Berlin. The scanty north stoa of the temple once housed Pergamon's famous **Library**, which at its peak rivalled Alexandria's (see p.201).

A narrow staircase leads down from the Temple of Athena to the spectacular Hellenistic **theatre**, cut into the hillside and with capacity for ten thousand spectators. The wooden stage was removed after each performance – the holes into which the supporting posts were driven can still be seen on the stage terrace – to allow free access to the **Temple of Dionysos**, on the same terrace.

Still further north and uphill looms the Corinthian **Temple of Trajan**, where both Trajan and Hadrian were revered during Roman times – their busts were also taken to Berlin. German archeologists have re-erected some of the temple columns, plus much of the stoa that surrounded the shrine on three sides. The north architrave is lined with Medusa heads, two of them modern recastings.

Behind the temple are the remains of barracks and the highest reaches of the city's **perimeter wall**. Nearby yawns a cistern once fed by an **aqueduct**, traces of which are still visible running parallel to a modern one on the hillside to the northwest. Finally, as you begin your descent back down towards the main entrance, you'll pass – east of the library and Athena temple – the extensive but jumbled ruins of the **royal palaces**.

The terrace south of the Altar of Zeus now holds little more than Carl Humann's grave, though as the **upper agora** it was once the commercial and social focus of Pergamon. An ancient street descends past the **Temple of Demeter**, where the local variant of the Eleusinian Mysteries was enacted. Across the way lies the **gymnasium**, where the city's youth were educated. Its upper level, with its palaestra and lecture hall, was for young men, the middle was used by the adolescents, and the lower served as a playground for small boys. From the **lower agora**, the path back down to town is indicated by blue waymarks.

The Asklepion

Asklepion Cad • Daily: July–Aug 8.30am–6.30pm; Sept–June 8.30am–5.30pm • ₺15, plus ₺4 parking fee

Perched upon a hilltop at the southern end of modern-day Bergama, the ancient, sacred therapeutic centre of **Asklepion** is named after Asklepios, the god of healing, and was the world's first psychiatric hospital.

Healing methods at all *asklepia* combined the ritualistic and the practical. Patients were required to sleep in the temple so that Asklepios, semi-divine son of Apollo and god of healing, might appear in their dreams to suggest diagnosis and treatment. However, special diets, bathing in hot or cold water and exercise also figured in the

PERGAMON'S LIBRARY AND THE BIRTH OF THE MODERN BOOK

Founded by Eumenes II and enlarged by Attalos II, both fanatical collectors of books, Pergamon's **Library** grew to contain 200,000 titles – volumes by Aristotle and Theophrastos were paid for with their weight in gold. Eventually the Egyptian Ptolemies, alarmed at this growing rival to their own library in Alexandria, banned the export of papyrus, on which all scrolls were written, and of which they were sole producers.

In response to this bid to stem the library's expansion, the Pergamene dynasty revived the old practice of writing on specially treated animal skins, **parchment**. That led quickly to the invention of the **codex** or paged book, since parchment couldn't be rolled up like papyrus. The words "parchment" and the more archaic "pergamene" both derive from "Pergamon". The library was appropriated by Mark Antony, who gave it to Cleopatra as a gift, and many of its works survived in Alexandria until destroyed by the Arabs in the seventh century.

therapeutic regimes. **Galen** (129–202 AD), the greatest physician of antiquity, whose theories dominated medicine until the sixteenth century, was born in Pergamon, and worked here as well as in Rome.

Much of what survives dates from the reign of **Hadrian** (117–38 AD), when the Asklepion functioned much like a spa. Some came for specific cures, but for the wealthy and leisured a prolonged visit was part of their social life.

The site

A long, colonnaded **sacred way**, originally lined with shops, leads from the site entrance to the **propylon**, or monumental entrance gate, rebuilt in the third century AD, after an earthquake seriously damaged it in the previous century. North of the propylon, the square **library** housed the statue of Hadrian that's now in the local museum.

South of the propylon, the circular **Temple of Asklepios** (150 AD) was modelled on Rome's Pantheon. Although only foundations remain today, when intact its graceful dome was 24m across, with an oculus for light and air to penetrate. The broad, open area to the west was originally enclosed by colonnaded stoas. At the western end of the re-erected, mostly Ionic northern colonnade, an over-restored **theatre** seated 3500 and entertained townspeople as well as patients. At the centre of the open area, the **sacred fountain** still trickles weakly radioactive water. Nearby, an 80m underground passage leads to the **Temple of Telesphoros** (the lesser deity of Accomplishment), where patients slept while awaiting dream diagnoses. Only its lower, vaulted level survives in good repair.

Archeological Museum

Cumhuriyet Cad • Tues–Sun 8.30am–noon & 1–5.30pm • ₺5 • ☎ 0232 631 2884

Bergama's **Archeological Museum** (Arkeoloji Müzesi) holds a large collection of locally unearthed relics, including a statue of Hadrian from the Asklepion. Assorted fourth-century BC statues also display the naturalistic technique that was first developed in Pergamon, and later influenced European Baroque art. Incorporating accentuated body shape and muscle tone, the technique allowed a wider range of expressions to be shown than the traditional, more abstract and grotesque style. Also of interest is an impressively complete Roman mosaic of Medusa, and a large figurine of Aphrodite holding an oyster shell, found at Allianoi (see p.212).

Kızıl Avlu

Kınık Cad • Daily 8.30am–5.30pm • ₺5

Bergama's foremost attraction, the huge red-brick **Kızıl Avlu** or "Red Basilica", is on the river below the acropolis. Originally built in the second century AD as a temple to the Egyptian gods Serapis, Harpokrates and Isis, it was used as a basilica by the Byzantines – who merely built a smaller church within the confines.

It was also one of the Seven Churches of the Apocalypse addressed by St John the Divine, who referred to it in Revelation 2:13 as "the throne of Satan", perhaps a nod to the still-extant Egyptian cult. Now an attractive though crumbling ruin, with some sections roped or fenced off, it's in dire need of restoration.

Inside the walls, one of the towers holds the Kurtuluş Cami (mosque), while the ancient **Selinos River** (today the Bergama Çayı) passes beneath the basilica via two tunnels. Just downstream you'll see a handsome Ottoman bridge, built in 1384, with two equally well-preserved Roman bridges upstream.

The Old Quarter

Bergama's **old quarter**, north of the river uphill from Kızıl Avlu, is a jumble of Ottoman buildings, antique and carpet shops, mosques and maze-like streets. The antique stalls are full of very beautiful, overpriced copperware – too many coach tours have had their effect. Similarly, the reputation of Bergama carpets has been besmirched by too much synthetic dye and machine-weaving.

ARRIVAL AND DEPARTURE

By bus The new *otogar*, inconveniently located 6km south near the junction of the E87/550 highway, is linked to the old *otogar*, 500m south of the Archeological Museum, by dolmuşes and a free *servis* shuttle (every 30min, 6am–7pm only). The last direct minibus to Ayvalık leaves the *otogar* at 5pm, but indirect services via Dikili run until 8pm. By far the easiest and cheapest way to get to İstanbul from Bergama is to take a bus to Soma, 45km northeast, then take a short taxi ride to Soma's train station, to catch a train to Bandırma and the fast ferry to İstanbul. So-called "direct" night buses tend to be slow and expensive.

Destinations İstanbul (2 daily; 11hr); İzmir (every 45min; 1hr 45min); Soma (hourly; 1hr).

GETTING AROUND

By dolmuş During the day, dolmuşes travel along the main road through town, between the old *otogar* and Kızıl Avlu.

By taxi Taxi drivers offer to ferry passengers arriving at Bergama's *otogar* around the ruins for the extortionate sum of ₺50–60, or slightly less in low season. This might make sense if you're in a group, or in a hurry, but it's a bit of a racket, limiting you to one hour at the acropolis (you really need two), 10min at the Red Basilica and 30min at the Asklepion. The main taxi stand in central Bergama is beside two mosques and the Çarşı Hamamı.

INFORMATION

Tourist office Cumhuriyet Cad, near the Archeological Museum (Mon–Fri 8.30am–noon & 1–5.30pm; ☎0232 631 2851).

ACCOMMODATION

Akropolis Guest House Kayalık Sok 3, base of the road up to the ancient city ☎0232 631 2621, �🌐akropolisguesthouse.com. The rooms of these two adjoining stone buildings, close to the cable car and Kızıl Avlu, look inward to a pleasant courtyard with a welcoming (in summer) pool. Standard rooms are a little dark while the airier deluxe rooms, costing ₺20 extra, offer better views and more light. There's also parking, and a well-priced restaurant. ₺115

Anıl Hatuniye Cad 4 ☎0232 633 2153, �🌐anilhotelbergama.com. Well located in the town centre, the *Anıl* had a complete makeover in 2012. While the futuristic, neon-lit theme won't be to everybody's taste, the rooms are nonetheless very comfortable with conveniences including fancy walk-in showers. The management is super-helpful, and will organize parking. ₺195

Gobi Pension Atatürk Bul 18 ☎0232 633 2518, �🌐gobipension.com. Run by a friendly father and English-speaking son team, the simple, good-value rooms here are a mix of new and old, some en-suite. Street noise is generally minimal despite the main-street location, and a shady garden makes a pleasant setting for a home-cooked breakfast. ₺75

★ **Odyssey Guesthouse** Abacıhan Sok 13 ☎0232 631 3501, �🌐odysseyguesthouse.com. Very traveller-friendly with a guaranteed warm welcome from the English-speaking managers, this guesthouse consists of two linked century-old Greek houses. With wooden floorboards and stairs, both offer delightful views from roof terraces-cum-reading rooms, heated in winter, and a guest kitchen. All rooms are high-ceilinged and very comfortable, but only some, costing ₺10 more, are en-suite. ₺50

EATING AND DRINKING

Bergama Sofrası Bankalar Cad 44 ☎0232 631 5131. Easy to find on the edge of the old quarter, this simple *lokanta* is the best in Bergama. Walk through the brightly lit café to the rear, and choose from the likes of beef stew, lamb shanks in bechamel, and *köfte* in tomato sauce, as well as rice, spinach, beans and aubergine dishes. Although not licensed, they can usually offer a glass of wine. Mains ₺5–8. Daily 10am–8pm.

Bergama Ticaret Odası Sosyal Tesisleri Uckemer Cad, 150m uphill from the Ulu Cami ☎0232 632 9641. One of the very few licensed restaurants in town, family-run and set in a former Greek school. While the menu doesn't quite match the fantastic views (from inside and out), the moderately priced grills (lamb, veal, chicken) and *mezes* are still very good. Mains ₺10–16. Daily 11am–10pm.

★ **Sofa Café** Kınık Cad 77/B ☎0232 632 7601. In the shadow of Kızıl Avlu, this new bistro-café is a welcome surprise in Bergama. Choose from pavement tables offering excellent people-watching, or an a/c interior with walls adorned with local art. The vibe is relaxed and easy-going, and staff ready to talk you through the menu, which ranges from an organic, locally sourced breakfast to home-cooked cakes, crunchy salads and heartier meat dishes. Alcohol available. Breakfast ₺8, mains ₺7–14. Daily 9am–late.

Foça

The small coastal resort of **FOÇA**, 86km north of İzmir, is an attractive and welcoming place, where the charming cobbled backstreets are lined with Greek fishermen's cottages and a few more opulent Ottoman mansions. A very worthwhile and relaxing stopover, it's sometimes called Eski (Old) Foça to distinguish it from its smaller and less interesting neighbour 25km further north, **Yeni Foça**, which is unlikely to appeal to international visitors.

Derived from the ancient Greek for "seal", the name "Phokaia" refers either to the suggestively shaped islets offshore, or to the handful of Mediterranean **monk seals** that still live in the local waters. They're monitored and protected by the Turkish Underwater Research Foundation, but you're most unlikely to see any on a boat tour. Frankly you'd need to *be* a seal to really enjoy the sea here which, thanks to strong currents and a sharp drop-off, is notoriously chilly for much of the year.

Thanks to a pervasive military presence, much of the nearby coast is in any case out of bounds to visitors. Foça's naval base houses the Turkish Amphibious Brigade, and is the only location in the country where marines are trained.

Ancient Phokaia

Foça stands on the site of **Phokaia**, founded around 1000 BC by Ionian colonists. Great seafarers, the Phokaians plied the Mediterranean as far as the Straits of Gibraltar, founding numerous colonies, including (around 600 BC) Massalia, now Marseilles.

Little now remains of the ancient town. The most striking remnant, 8km east of modern Foça, is the **Taş Ev**, an unusual tomb cut from the rock in the eighth century BC, squatting beside an Ottoman bridge and a modern cemetery. A small, much later **ancient theatre** marks the east entry to Foça, while some mosaic pavements from a Roman villa, including a portrayal of four Bacchus heads and birds, have been unearthed about 150m southwest.

Beşkapılar fortress

The oldest intact structure in Foça itself is the waterfront **Beşkapılar fortress** (open for art exhibitions). Originally Byzantine, it was much modified by successive occupiers, including the Genoese, who occupied the castle until the Ottomans seized it in the fifteenth century. Two interesting mosques from that era bracket Beşkapılar: the unheralded but beautiful **Fatih Camii**, and the **Kayalar Camii**, at the summit of the castle enclosure, sporting a distinctly lighthouse-like minaret.

The harbours

Foça's castle headland splits the bay into two smaller harbours. The northerly, more picturesque **Küçükdeniz** is where most of the action takes place, along seafront Reha Midilli Caddesi, while bleak, southerly **Büyükdeniz** is of interest only as the point where ferries from Lésvos dock and the fishing fleet is anchored. Neither bay has a decent beach, though that doesn't stop bathers from establishing themselves on the slightly grubby shingle or launching themselves from platforms at rocky Küçükdeniz.

Beaches

Some excellent **beaches** are dotted along the scenic 20km of road that separates Foça from Yeni Foça. However, they're either only accessible on foot, or by paying fees of up to ₺15 to the **campsites** that own them, such as *People*, 5km out, and *Kosova*, 2km beyond. The best sand is at *Acar Kamping* (after 10km), but 700m before that, paths from the roadside lead down beneath some high-voltage power lines to a succession of idyllic coves opposite an islet. Alternatively, *Mambo Beach Club*, 5km short of Yeni Foça, usually allows free access to the beach if you patronize their snack bar.

Kozbeyli

11km southeast of Yeni Foça • served by Menemen–Yenifoça bus #45

The peaceful fourteenth-century village of **Kozbeyli** makes a pleasant day-trip from Foça. Flocks of sheep and goats graze the surrounding green pastures, while towering oak and pine trees surround the village itself. Enriched by runoff from Şaphane Dağı as well as underground springs, the fertile soil also fosters the growth of olive trees; some in the village are said to be three hundred years old. Old stone houses cluster around a much-prized fountain and central *meydan*, the setting for a vibrant Sunday market as well as a vine-shaded coffee house that's famous for its stone-ground *dibek kahvesi*.

ARRIVAL AND DEPARTURE FOÇA

By bus or dolmuş Direct buses from İzmir arrive just south of the seafront main square behind Büyükdeniz. Long-haul buses on the E87/550 highway drop passengers at Buruncuk, 26km east of Foça, served by regular connecting dolmuşes.

Destinations İzmir (hourly; 1hr 15min).
By ferry Ferries dock in Büyükdeniz harbour.
Destinations Karaburun (June–Sept 2 daily on Tues, Wed, Sat, Sun; 1hr); Lésvos (Mytilini), Greece (June–Sept Tues, Wed, Fri, Sun 6pm; 2hr).

INFORMATION AND TOURS

Tourist office Cumhuriyet Meyd (May–Sept Mon–Fri 8.30am–noon & 1.30–5.30pm, Sat 10am–5.30pm; Oct–April Mon–Fri 8.30am–5.30pm; ☏ 0232 812 5534).
Boat trips Most excursions from Küçükdeniz to the small

islets northwest of Foça follow similar itineraries, with three stops for swimming, and a grilled lunch included (May–Sept daily 10.30am–6pm; ₺30).

ACCOMMODATION

Foçantique Reha Midilli Cad 154 ☏ 0232 812 4313, ⊛ focantiquehotel.com. Owned by two former tour guides, Foça's first boutique hotel is a restored old garden-house whose small rooms have exposed stonework and rather average bathrooms (except for one with a converted hamam). A modern extension at the front holds a sea-view bar/breakfast area and an apartment to rent. ₺250
Huzur 139 Sok 5, at the north end of Küçükdeniz ☏ 0232 812 1203, ⊛ huzurpansiyon.com. Family-run *pansiyon*, with direct sea frontage. The simple, tiled rooms are all en-suite, some pricier ones have sea views. There's a delightful, shaded breakfast terrace at pavement level. ₺100
★ **İyon Pansiyon** Ismetpaşa Mahallesi, 198 Sok 8 ☏ 0232 812 1415, ⊛ iyonpansiyon.com. Welcoming, family-run *pansiyon* with a choice of more basic rooms in a restored Greek house at the front, or more spacious, comfortable ones in the rear garden annexe. Breakfast and drinks are served on the raised front deck, and the common

lobby has a wood-burning stove and book swap. Located close to the action but on a quiet side street, with parking nearby. ₺110
★ **Lola 38** Reha Midilli Cad 140, corner of 149 Sok ☏ 0232 812 3826, ⊛ lola38.com. Foça's best boutique hotel, in a 120-year-old mansion and former Orthodox priest's residence. With attentive hosts, sea frontage and a perfect blend of antique and contemporary decor throughout, the rooms are spread over the main house and quaint stone buildings in the back garden with its lawn-bar and small spa-pool. ₺245
Sempatik Hotel Güneş Ismetpaşa Mahallesi, 163 Sok 10 ☏ 0232 812 1915, ⊛ sempatikhotelgunes.com. One of many family-run hotels in Foça, the "Sun Hotel" is 50m from the shore, with parking nearby. The attractive exterior belies spacious but somewhat bland rooms, all with balconies (some with partial sea views) and decent bathrooms with walk-in showers. ₺120

EATING, DRINKING AND NIGHTLIFE

The pedestrianized plaza at the head of Küçükdeniz harbour is crammed with seafood restaurants, none that exciting but packed on weekends. Adjacent to *Foça Meyhane*, noisy music bars provide the town's **nightlife**.

Çarşı Lokantası 187 Sok 43 ☏ 0232 812 2377. Around the corner from *Foça Meyhane*, down a shaded cobbled lane, the cheerful and busy *Çarşı* serves typical, well-priced *lokanta* home-cooked dishes, including a few vegetable-only options and pasta as well as the usual rice. Eat indoors or on pleasant (and popular) pavement tables. Mains ₺4–11. Daily noon–8pm.

Foça Meyhane 187 Sok 14 ☏ 0232 812 1108. In the warren of bazaar lanes east of the seafront esplanade, this popular *meyhane* attracts the locals with its diverse and affordable menu of *mezes*, such as istifnos (a type of leafy green vegetable) and tongue. The wine list is also pretty good, including locally grown Chardonnay. Daily noon–11pm.

★ **Fokai** 121 Sok 8, behind the castle overlooking Büyükdeniz ☎ 0232 812 2186, ⊕ fokaibalik.com. At this excellent licensed fish restaurant, the daily catch is the best and most reasonably priced in town, with fresh and farmed fish clearly distinguished. The menu also includes *mezes*, pizzas and meat, plus a delicious chocolate cake. Mains ₺9–18. Daily 11.30am–3pm & 7–11pm.

Nazmi Usta Girit Dondurmaları Reha Midilli Cad 82 ☎ 0232 812 5471. This small *dondurma* outlet on the Küçükdeniz seafront esplanade is easily the best in Foça, attracting long queues in summer. Fabulous ice cream in dozens of flavours, including mastic gum, best slurped at a pavement table while watching the world go by. *Dondurma* ₺2. Daily 11am–late.

Manisa

Spilling out from the foothills of the Manisa Dağı range, the sprawling city of **MANISA** lies 38km east of Menemen along the E87/550 highway, and is easily reached from there or from İzmir, also 38km away. While most of its historic centre was torched by the Greek army during its 1922 retreat, a few fine Selçuk and Ottoman monuments survive, and it's now home to more than over 280,000 people.

Brief history

The area was settled early in the first millennium BC, by veterans of the Trojan War according to legend, and the ancient town of Magnesia ad Sipylus was an important Roman centre. For a short time during the thirteenth century, after the Fourth Crusade sacked Constantinople, Manisa was capital of the Byzantine Empire. In 1313 it was captured by Selçuk chieftain Saruhan Bey, responsible for the earliest of the surviving local monuments. Later, the Ottomans sent heirs to the throne here to serve an apprenticeship as local governors, to prepare them for the rigours of İstanbul palace life.

Sultan Camii

Sultan Meyd, corner of İzmir Cad and İbrahim Gökçen Bul

Dominating the well-signed Sultan Meydanı, the **Sultan Camii** was built in 1522 for Ayşe Hafize, mother of Süleyman the Magnificent, who lived here with her son while he was serving as governor. It's a rectangular mosque, much wider than it is deep, with a single central dome that's flanked by two pairs of satellite domes. Late Ottoman Baroque paint decoration and a tiny wood-railed pulpit on the west enliven the porch – actually a *son cemaat yeri* (latecomers' praying place). Of the surrounding complex, which included a *medrese* and mental hospital, only the hamam continues in its original function.

Every year around the spring equinox, the *Mesir Macunu Şenlikleri*, or **Power-Gum Festival** – now well into its fifth century – takes place around the Sultan Camii, to commemorate local doctor Merkez Efendi's concoction of a special resin to cure Ayşe Hafize of an unspecified ailment. Re-created each year, the gum, or *mesir macunu*, containing 41 herbs and spices, is scattered from the minaret by the muezzin to crowds who use the paste as a remedy against aches, pains and snake or insect bites.

Muradiye Camii

Murat Cad, 100m east of Sultan Meyd

Designed by the great imperial architect Mimar Sinan, the **Muradiye Camii** was eventually built by Mehmet Ağa (famed builder of İstanbul's Sultanahmet Camii) for the future Murat III, while he was governor here in 1583–85. The interior, with its stained-glass windows and walls decorated with exquisite İznik tiles, is impressive: the carved wooden *mimber*, or pulpit, and the sultan's loge are particularly fine. Unusually, a large women's gallery runs the full length of the cross-stroke of the reverse-T ground plan.

Manisa Museum

Murat Cad, next door to Muradiye Camii • Tues–Sun 9am–noon & 1–5pm • ₺3 • ☎ 0236 231 3685

The Muradiye Camii was originally part of a larger complex that included a *medrese* (theological school) and *imaret* (soup kitchen), the latter of which now holds the

3

3

Manisa Museum. Inside is an interesting collection of archeological and ethnological exhibits, including items retrieved from Sardis and fossilized footprints dating back to 20,000–25,000 BC, found in the nearby region of Salihli.

Ulu Cami

On a natural, landscaped terrace 250m above Manisa Museum, accessed by steps

Manisa's oldest surviving mosque, the Ulu Cami, was built atop a Byzantine church in 1366 by Işak Çelebi, Saruhan Bey's grandson. The spectacular view north over town rewards the steep climb up. Entering the open-roofed courtyard via the ornate portal, you confront the glory of the place, a forest of **antique columns**, some "double" and others carrying Byzantine capitals, presumably recycled from the church that once stood here.

ARRIVAL AND DEPARTURE

MANISA

By bus Manisa's *otogar* is on İbrahim Gökçen Bulvarı, 2km north of Sultan Meydanı. Dolmuşes marked "Ulu Parkı" ply the route between the *otogar* and Sultan Meydanı along İbrahim Gökçen Bulvarı, otherwise it's a 15min walk.
Destinations İzmir (every 10min; 1hr); Salihli via Sart/

Sardis (every 30min; 1hr 20min).
By train The station is 2km northwest of Sultan Meydanı, along Atatürk Bulvarı.
Destinations Balıkesir (2 daily; 2hr 30min); İzmir (6 daily; 1hr 45min).

ACCOMMODATION

Arma Sekiz Eylül Cad 14, 700m from Manisa Museum ☎ 0236 231 1980, ⊕ hotelarma.com.tr. This central hotel holds no surprises. Its carpeted business-class rooms are starting to age but remain spacious and clean, with

thick windows buffering any noise from the busy street below. The in-house restaurant serves a decent buffet breakfast, and the reception staff are both friendly and professional. ₺170

EATING AND DRINKING

MANISA

Gediz Kebap Peker Cad 42, opposite Sultan Meyd ☎ 0236 231 9924. This popular restaurant serves up a carnivore's delight of *döner*, *pide* and *kebap*, including the local sausage-like version. Dessert offerings include the chicken-and-milk pudding *tavuk göğsü*, or less adventurous chocolate profiteroles. Mains ₺3–12. Daily 10am–10pm.
Hankafe Yenihan, corner of Dr Sadik Ahmet &

Dumlupınar cads ☎ 0236 231 4343. This much-loved local restaurant is one of several located in the open courtyard of a restored nineteenth-century *han* (inn). The menu includes pasta and stir-fry dishes, home-baked cakes, *tostlarımızı* (toasted sandwiches), and teas. The courtyard sometimes hosts live music and events, and there are craft shops upstairs. Mains ₺3.50–11. Daily 8am–10pm.

Sardis

Ancient **Sardis** (Sart in Turkish) stands in the small village of Sartmustafa, 65km east of Manisa. The surrounding countryside, on the lower slopes of the Bozdağ range, is dominated by sultana-producing vineyards. Capital of the ancient kingdom of Lydia, Sardis also saw Persian, Greek, Roman and Christian rule, and housed a prosperous Jewish community. While not as impressive as Ephesus – whose Temple of Artemis was paid for by Croesus – the partially restored ruins are pleasantly free of crowds and touts. Both its clusters of ruins are easily reached on foot from the main road in Sartmustafa village, though the uphill one is a hot walk in summer.

Brief history

Sardis became incredibly wealthy thanks to the gold flecks that were washed down from Mount Tmolos (now Bozdağ) and caught in sheepskins by the locals. According to legend, the source of this wealth was the eighth-century BC Phrygian king **Midas**, whose touch turned everything to gold. Unable to eat, his curse was lifted when the gods bid him wash his hands in the River Paktolos, which flowed down to Sardis from the south.

Not surprisingly, perhaps, the Lydians invented coinage under Sardis's most celebrated king, Croesus (560–546 BC). When his wealth attracted the attention of the

Persians under Cyrus, the Delphic oracle ambiguously advised a worried Croesus that should he attack first, a great empire would be destroyed. Croesus went to war and was defeated, and after a two-week siege Sardis fell; taken prisoner by Cyrus, Croesus was burned alive, though some accounts have him rescued from the pyre by a rainstorm.

As a Persian city, Sardis was sacked during the Ionian revolt of 499 BC. It revived under Alexander the Great, but was destroyed by an earthquake in 17 AD, and rebuilt by the Romans. Although Sardis ranked as one of the Seven Churches of Asia addressed by St John in Revelation 3:1–6, that didn't spare Byzantine Sardis from conquest by Saruhan and destruction at the hands of Tamerlane in 1401. The city only came to light again when American archeologists excavated here between 1904 and 1914.

The Gymnasium and synagogue

Daily: summer 8am–6pm; winter 8am–5pm • ₺3, same ticket as temple of Artemis

The first of Sardis's two sites lies just north of the road on the eastern edge of Sartmustafa. Entry is via a partially revealed, marble-paved **Roman avenue**, which passes various shops, though low walls with discernible doorways are all that remain.

A break in the shopping mall leads into the restored **synagogue**. The walls are covered with copies of the original coloured stonework, now housed in the Manisa Museum; the extensive floor mosaics are, however, original.

Adjacent to the synagogue, the **gymnasium and bath complex** was once the city's most prominent building. Its **Marble Court**, the entry from the palaestra to the baths, has been spectacularly restored to its appearance when first built in 211 AD. The walls behind the columns would have had marble revetments and the podia would have supported statues, forming a splendid multistorey facade implying association with some imperial cult. Behind the court are the remains of a plunge-pool and rest area.

The temple of Artemis

Daily: summer 8am–7pm; winter 8am–5pm • ₺3, same ticket as Gymnasium and synagogue • Reached along a paved lane that leads 1200m south from the Sartmustafa village teahouses

The **Temple of Artemis**, once among the four largest temples in Asia Minor, was built by Croesus, destroyed by Greek raiders during the Ionian revolt, and rebuilt by Alexander the Great. Today fifteen massive Ionic columns remain standing, though only two are intact. However, enough of the foundations remains to suggest just how large the building, constructed to rival the temples of Ephesus, Samos and Didyma, used to be. The remains of a small Byzantine church huddle beside the two complete columns. More than anything, it's the beauty of the setting, enclosed by wooded and vine-covered hills and accented by weird Cappadocia-like pinnacles, that leaves a lasting impression.

ARRIVAL AND DEPARTURE

SARDIS

By bus or dolmuş Salihli-bound dolmuşes from Manisa, and buses from İzmir, drop passengers on the main highway, 1km north of Sartmustafa.

By train Only one daily combination of trains – the early-afternoon Manisa–Alaşehir service, and the evening

Uşak–İzmir service – allows enough time to visit Sardis by train. The run-down, unmanned station at Sartmahmut is inconveniently located 1500m north of the site; make sure you buy a return or through ticket from wherever you start your journey.

ACCOMMODATION

Hotel Lidya Sardes Kursunlu Kaplicalari Yolu 107, Salihli ☎ 0236 715 5555, ⓦ lidyatermalotel.com. The nearest accommodation to Sardis, overlooking the mountainside town of Salihli, 8km east on the İzmir–Afyon road, this enormous hotel caters to tour buses, but also offers good-value rooms for independent travellers.

Apartment-style suites have loads of space, and kitchens, but are an uphill walk from the main hotel, where the carpeted rooms are also spacious, with subtle, Sardis-like decor. Various dining and drinking options, plus a swimming pool-thermal complex that offers good spa treatments. Rooms ₺225, suites ₺310

The central and southern Aegean

PAMUKKALE

The central and southern Aegean

The central and southern Aegean coast and its hinterland have seen foreign tourism longer than any other part of Turkey. The territory between modern İzmir and Marmaris corresponds to the bulk of ancient Ionia, and just about all of old Caria, and contains a concentration of Classical Greek, Hellenistic and Roman antiquities unrivalled in Turkey. Ephesus is usually first on everyone's list, but the understated charms of exquisitely positioned sites such as Priene and Labranda hold at least as much appeal. Of course, most of the visitors who come here are drawn especially by the beaches – Kuşadası, Bodrum and Marmaris are among the largest resorts in the whole of Turkey. Bursting with cruise passengers and package tourists they may be, but they remain nonetheless rather likeable places. Independent travellers may prefer to seek more secluded sections of coast: the resort of Çeşme is certainly not overblown, the Datça peninsula is unspoiled and quite spectacular, while the towns and villages on the Çeşme, Bodrum and Hisarönü peninsulas are highly popular with moneyed locals.

There's plenty to see once you get away from the coast, too. Sprawling **İzmir**, the third-largest city in Turkey, is an earthy city that attracts almost no foreign visitors, while little **Selçuk**, though it's most famed as the jumping-off point for Ephesus, is a delightful place in its own right. The even smaller settlements of **Muğla** and **Birgi** are unselfconscious Ottoman museum-towns, while both **Alaçatı** and **Şirince** are well-preserved former Greek villages that remain just the right side of tweeness. For much of the time in this region, it's the extraordinary quality of the landscape itself that provides the attraction, and often it can be utterly compelling – take a look at the eerie lake of **Bafa Gölü**, or the otherworldly travertine terraces that surround the hot springs of **Pamukkale**.

If you've been travelling in other parts of Turkey, the Aegean area's high **accommodation prices** may come as an unpleasant surprise – rates at the coastal resorts go through the roof in summer, though inland (including İzmir, Selçuk and Pamukkale) you can find budget rooms at any time of year. As for **Aegean cuisine**, it's unusual in placing far less emphasis on meat, and far more on fresh herbs and vegetables.

EPHESUS

Highlights

❶ Alaçatı This marvellous little village has become one of the best places in which to sample the Aegean area's unique cuisine. **See p.236**

❷ Ephesus Hot, crowded and exhausting it may be, but you simply can't miss Turkey's best-preserved ancient city – a magnificent monument to the wealth of Rome. **See p.240**

❸ Şirince A beautiful hillside village surrounded by vineyards a short drive from Selçuk. **See p.244**

❹ Priene Scramble over the ruins of a superbly preserved Hellenistic town and gaze out over the Meander basin. **See p.251**

❺ Heracleia ad Latmos Former monastic village on Lake Bafa, which had a compelling hold on the imaginations of the Romantic poets. **See p.257**

❻ Bodrum Spend a few days sampling the nightlife at Turkey's most fashionable and sophisticated beach-resort. **See p.261**

❼ Pamukkale Visit the geological oddity that has found its way onto every Turkish tourism poster. **See p.280**

❽ Aphrodisias New excavations at this beautifully sited Roman city are revealing a site to rival Ephesus in grandeur and importance. **See p.284**

HIGHLIGHTS ARE MARKED ON THE MAP ON PP.226–227

THE CENTRAL AND SOUTHERN AEGEAN

Gediz River
Afyon
0   25
kilometres
Kula
Salihli
utlu
Alaşehir
Gölcük
Baz Dağı
(2137m)
Ödemiş
Birgi
ır
Kiraz
Küçük Menderes River
Hierapolis
Karahayıt
Tire
Pamukkale
7
Nyssa
Nazilli
Sultanhisar
Büyük Menderes River
Denizli
Aydın
Karacasu
Geyre
550
Aphrodisias
8
Çine
Tavas
nda
Karpuzlu
Kale
Labranda
omos
Milas
Peçin Kale
Yatağan
330
330
ıru
Muğla
Ula

HIGHLIGHTS
① Alaçatı
② Ephesus
③ Şirince
④ Priene
⑤ Heracleia ad Latmos
⑥ Bodrum
⑦ Pamukkale
⑧ Aphrodisias

Ören
Akyaka
Köyceğiz
Gulf of Gökova
Şedir Adası
Karacasöğüt
Dalyan
Ortaca
Marmaris
Turunç
Dalaman
İçmeler
Limanı
Orhaniye
Kumlubükü
Datça
Selimiye
Bozburun
Bayır
Söğüt
Sími
(Greece)
Taşlıca
Loryma
Rhodes
Fethiye

Afyon & Isparta
Salda Gölü & Burdur

İzmir

The city of **İzmir**, the third largest in the land, is now home to well over three million people. Many travellers give it a wide berth, but it certainly has some merit, not least its enviable position straddling the head of a 50km-long gulf. Surrounded on all sides by mountains, it's arrayed like a gigantic amphitheatre, with the **Ionian Sea** functioning as a sort of never-ending show.

Site of ancient **Smyrna**, İzmir has a long and illustrious history (see p.228). Its current incarnation is rather more modern, particularly in the swanky, bar-filled **Alsancak** area just north of the centre, the **Konak** shopping area to the south, and the coastal road that binds them together. However, a bustling bazaar district, parks and a clutch of grand old buildings are remnants of a glorious past. One negative point is that the weather, though mild for much of the year, gets stinking hot in the summer – there are no city beaches to escape to, but the Çeşme peninsula (see p.234) is not too far away.

Brief history

The site of modern İzmir was settled by aboriginal **Anatolians** as long ago as the third millennium BC. Around 600 BC, Lydian raids sent the area into a long decline; it was recovering tentatively when **Alexander the Great** appeared in 334 BC. Spurred by a timely dream corroborated by the oracle of Apollo at Claros, Alexander decreed the foundation of a new, better-fortified settlement on Mount Pagos, the flat-topped hill today adorned with the Kadifekale. His generals, Antigonus and Lysimachus, carried out Alexander's plan after his death, by which time the city bore the name – **Smyrna** – familiar to the West for centuries after.

Roman rule endowed the city with impressive buildings, but **Arab** raids in the seventh century AD triggered several centuries of turbulence. **Selçuk** Turks held the city for two decades prior to 1097, when the **Byzantines** recaptured it. The thirteenth-century Latin tenure in Constantinople provoked another era of disruption at Smyrna, with Crusaders, Genoese, Tamerlane's Mongols and minor Turkish emirs jockeying for position. Order was re-established in 1415 by Mehmet I, who finally incorporated the town into the **Ottoman Empire**, his successors repulsing repeated Venetian efforts to retake it.

Following **World War I**, Greece was given an indefinite mandate over İzmir and its hinterland. Foolishly, a huge Greek expeditionary force pressed inland, inciting the resistance of the Turkish nationalists under Atatürk. The climactic defeat in the two-year struggle against Greece and her nominal French and Italian allies was the entry into Smyrna of the Turkish army on September 9, 1922. The secular republic not having yet been proclaimed, the **reconquest of the city** took on the character of a successfully concluded jihad, or holy Muslim war, with three days of murder and plunder. Almost seventy percent of the city burned to the ground and thousands of non-Muslims died. A quarter of a million refugees huddled at the quayside while British, American, French and Italian vessels stood idly by, refusing to grant them safe passage until the third day.

AFRO-TURKS

Many travellers to western Turkey, and İzmir in particular, are surprised by the sight of **Africans** who are obviously not visitors. Often termed *Arap* or "Arabs" by other Turks, they are in fact descendants of the large numbers of Sudanese, Somalis, Algerians and Egyptians who were brought to Anatolia during the Ottoman Empire. Many arrived as slaves, forced to work in the tobacco and cotton fields or as household servants, particularly wet-nurses.

Today there are about 20,000 **Afro-Turks** (as they prefer to be known) in the western Aegean provinces, most of whom live in the mountains between İzmir and Mersin. Speaking fluent Turkish and devoutly Muslim, they are often proud of their Turkish heritage, though intermarriage is rare with other Turks.

İZMİR

■ ACCOMMODATION

Antik Han	8
Beyond	1
Güzel İzmir	5
Key	4
Mövenpick	2
Myhotel	3
Ömerim	7
Park	6

■ RESTAURANTS

Adabeyi	4
Alisa Vitamin	5
Altınkapı	1
Asansör	7
Café La Cigale	2
Deniz	3
Ezo	5
Orkide	6

■ BARS AND CAFÉS

Acı Kahve	5
Eko	2
Hayalbaz	1
Karnaval	3
Mennan	4

0 ___ 200
metres

İzmir Bay
(İzmir Körfezi)

Asansör

Off Mithatpaşa Cad, 15min walk southwest of Konak • Daily 6am–midnight • Free

Offering views across most of the city, the old-fashioned **Asansör** (lift) makes an ideal place to start a visit to İzmir. Constructed in 1907 in a 50m-high brick tower, it originally served as a quick route to and from the mansions perched on the hill above. The elevator has since been completely refurbished; from the highly recommended

Asansör Restaurant & Café (see p.232) at the top, you can look down on narrow streets of crumbling houses and out over the bay.

Archeological Museum

Turgutreis Parkı in Konak, just above Konak bus terminal and metro station and alongside the Ethnographic Museum • Tues–Sun 8am–5.30pm • ₺8

The **Archeological Museum** features an excellent collection of finds from all over İzmir province and beyond. The ground floor is largely given over to statuary and friezes of all eras, while the top floor focuses on smaller objects, with an emphasis on Bronze Age and archaic pottery – more exciting than it sounds.

Ethnographic Museum

Turgutreis Parkı in Konak, just above Konak bus terminal and metro station and alongside the Archeological Museum • Tues–Sun 8am–5.30pm • Free

Built in 1831 and originally functioning as a hospital, the **Ethnographic Museum** feels somewhat neglected. Exhibits on its lower floor concentrate on the two types of traditional İzmir house, the wooden Turkish residence and the more substantial "Levantine" (Christian and Jewish merchants) house; up the spiral staircase you'll find weaponry and woven ware.

4

The agora

Off Eşrefpaşa Cad • Daily 8.30am–noon & 1–5.30pm • ₺3

The only surviving pre-Ottoman monument in the flatlands, the **agora** is İzmir's most accessible ancient site. It probably dates back to the early second century BC, but what you see now are the remains of a later reconstruction, financed during the reign of the Roman Emperor Marcus Aurelius, after the catastrophic earthquake of 178 AD. It's an impressive site, with water still coursing through ancient ducts and channels. Principal structures include a **colonnade** of fourteen Corinthian columns on the west side and the remains of reputedly the second-largest basilica in the Roman world.

Way up above the agora, the **Kadifekale**, or "Velvet Castle" – visible by night as well as by day thanks to skilful floodlighting – is only worth visiting for the views over the city.

ARRIVAL AND DEPARTURE

İZMİR

BY PLANE

Adnan Menderes airport (domestic ☎0232 274 2626, international ☎0232 455 0000; ⊛adnanmenderesairport.com) is just 18km southeast of the city, linked by both train and metro to Basmane station in central İzmir; trains also head directly to Selçuk (see p.238). Havaş airport buses (hourly; ₺10; 50–60min) will deposit you in front of the *Swissôtel Grand Efes* on Gaziosmanpaşa Bulvarı. The hourly city bus #202 (₺4) follows a similar route from the airport, terminating in Cumhuriyet Meydanı. Taxis are around ₺45 to downtown İzmir.

Destinations Adana (4 daily); Ankara (every 30min);

A BOAT TRIP ACROSS İZMİR BAY

One of İzmir's best sights is the city itself, seen from the bay it surrounds – at ₺6.50 for a return trip, these are by far the Aegean's cheapest **boat trips**. Boats head from three docks – Konak, Pasaport and Alsancak – to the best destination, **Karşıyaka**. Leaving from Pasaport provides the most spectacular trip, crawling past İzmir's 1970s' tricolore of white-yellow-brown buildings to Alsancak, before heading across the bay.

Karşıyaka itself is a pleasant part of İzmir, its pedestrianized central street – **Kemalpaşa Cad** – sporting a clutch of shops, restaurants and cafés. Try eating at *Alesta*, a small restaurant facing the local mosque, selling cheap seafood sandwiches, and sandwiched itself by two fishmongers.

Antalya (hourly); Dalaman (hourly); Gaziantep (2 daily); Hatay (daily); İstanbul (every 30min); Kayseri (daily); Kars (daily); Samsun (daily); Trabzon (daily); Van (daily).

BY BUS

The main bus station, known as the *büyük otogar*, is 8km northeast of the centre. Many bus companies offer free servis buses to their offices in 9 Eylül Meydanı, just north of Basmane; otherwise, it's best to take a taxi (₺35) into the centre. Getting to and from the Çeşme peninsula by bus is tough: no servis buses go to the main *otogar*, so make your own way to the coastal suburb of Üçkuyular, 6km southwest of downtown (₺25 by taxi, or hunt down one of numerous buses), from which there are hourly buses.

Destinations Afyon (5 daily; 5hr); Ankara (hourly; 8hr 30min); Antalya (hourly; 7hr); Aydın (every 30min; 2hr);

Bodrum (hourly; 3hr 30min); Bursa (hourly; 7hr); Çanakkale (5 daily; 6hr); Çeşme (every 20min; 1hr); Datça (6 daily; 5hr 15min); Denizli (hourly; 4hr); Edirne (6 daily; 12hr); Fethiye (15 daily; 6hr); İstanbul (hourly; 9hr); Kuşadası (every 30min; 2hr); Marmaris (hourly; 3hr 30min); Selçuk (every 20min; 1hr).

BY TRAIN

Long-distance trains pull in at Basmane station, right in the centre of town. To get to or from İstanbul it's best to use a train-ferry combination; Bandırma has ferries to the capital.

Destinations Afyon (1 daily; 13hr); Denizli (4 daily, via Aydın & Nazilli; 5hr); Bandırma (2 daily; 5hr 30min); Ankara (3 daily; 11–13hr); Ödemiş (5 daily; 2hr); Selçuk (4 daily; 1hr); Söke (1 daily; 2hr 45min).

GETTING AROUND

On foot Walking is much the quickest and easiest way to explore the city. The level of city traffic means you're rarely better off taking a bus.

By Metro The underground Metro line (daily 6am–midnight; ₺1.70) provides a fast, useful transport link between Basmane Station and the Konak district, as well as the airport. Further extensions are planned.

By bus Most of the municipality's numbered bus routes start from Konak Bus Terminal at Konak Meydanı.

Tickets Buses, metro and ferries run on prepaid card systems – you'll even need one to board a bus, as none will accept cash. At the time of writing the whole system was due for an overhaul; for now, your best bet is to buy a Kent Card with ₺5–10 of value, or more if you're staying longer than a day or two.

INFORMATION

Tourist office There's a tourist office in the airport arrivals hall (daily: Nov–March 8am–5pm; April–Oct 8.30am–8.30pm; ☎0232 274 2214), and a central bureau at 1344 Sok 2, Pasaport district, across from the Borsa

(Mon–Sat 8.30am–5.30pm; ☎0232 483 5117). The offices don't book, only suggest, accommodation (mid-range and up), and often run out of their very useful, free, city plan.

ACCOMMODATION

It's normally easy to find somewhere to stay, though street noise (particularly from car horns) is a nearly universal problem. The main area for budget hotels is immediately in front of **Basmane** train station; single travellers will be able to find something for ₺30 or under. For more salubrious digs, head for the streets around the seafront **Cumhuriyet Meydanı**.

BASMANE AND AROUND

Antik Han Anafartalar Cad 600 ☎0232 489 2750, ⓦotelantikhan.com. Curious little place, tucked away in the bazaar area, whose (unintentionally) retro lobby leads onto rooms that, though carpetless, feature all mod cons. Breakfast can be taken by a lemon tree in the charming courtyard. ₺160

Güzel İzmir 1368 Sok 8 ☎0232 483 5069, ⓦguzelizmirhotel.com. Far more traveller-friendly than other budget hotels nearby, with friendly staff, wi-fi throughout and a cute café-cum-"fitness room" (ie, two machines) downstairs. It's a little overpriced, though, and single rooms are tiny. ₺100

★ **Ömerim Hotel** 1368 Sok 6 ☎0232 445 9898. Nicest of four large hotels under the same management, with friendly (if confused) staff, and rooms that can be

incredible value – see a few, as they vary wildly in size and style. Single travellers can usually knock rates down to ₺35. ₺60

★ **Park Hotel** 1366 Sok 6 ☎0232 425 3333, ⓦparkhotelizmir.com. The Basmane area's token boutique hotel, and it's not half bad. Even after walking through the semi-swanky, Orient Express-style lobby, the rooms do not disappoint – large and well appointed, with pleasing flourishes. The price is right, too. ₺150

CUMHURIYET MEYDANI AND AROUND

Beyond Hotel 1376 Sok 5 ☎0232 463 0585, ⓦhotelbeyond.com. Contemporary boutique choice that's great for couples – think mood lighting, dangling lamps and elaborate bedheads. Rooms come in six colours: you're encouraged to choose your mood. ₺230

★ **Key** 1379 Sok 55, Sevgi Yolu ☎0232 489 1940, ⓦkeyhotel.com. Formerly the city's central bank, this brazenly modern affair is now its most appealing hotel. Even the smallest of its 31 rooms is huge – get one on the waterfront and you may wake to find your ceiling ashimmer with reflected sunlight. Service is impeccable, and staff have a few tricks up their sleeve: you can, for example, be picked up from the airport in the hotel's own Silver Ghost Rolls-Royce. ₺380

Mövenpick Cumhuriyet Bul 138 ☎0232 488 1414, ⓦmoevenpick-hotels.com. The city's newest and best designed five-star, offering all you'd expect of the chain. The 185 rooms share a chocolate colour scheme, and some have a partial view of the sea; facilities are excellent, especially the pleasing indoor pool. ₺800

Myhotel Cumhuriyet Bul 132 ☎0232 445 3837, ⓦmyhotel.com.tr. İzmir's original boutique hotel, opened in 2006. All 30 rooms have a/c, wi-fi and huge TVs, with neat features such as fluffy rugs, and free fruit and raisins. Bathrooms can be pokey, but this makes for larger bedrooms. Rates include a very tasty buffet breakfast. ₺220

EATING

The budget options within sight of Basmane station have tables on the street and offer the usual range of kebabs, *pide* and stews. The **bazaar** holds another selection of inexpensive outfits, although its warren of streets can be confusing. **Alsancak** and the Birinci Kordon **waterfront** offer a definite step up in quality and price.

ALSANCAK AND BIRINCI KORDON

Altınkapı 1444 Sok 14/A ☎0232 422 5687. Good *döner* and *tavuk* (chicken) grills at this long-established restaurant, which sports popular outdoor seating on a pedestrianized street. They also have a good lokanta opposite. Daily 10am–11pm.

★ **Café La Cigale** Fransız Kültür Merkezi, Cumhuriyet Bul 152 ☎0232 421 4780. The French Cultural Institute's leafy gardens are the place to be on a sunny afternoon, with various dishes from kebabs to pizza and crepes served up on chequered tablecloths. It's hard to say no to their lemon cheesecake (₺6.5). Mains from ₺12. Daily 8.30am–10.30pm.

★ **Deniz Restaurant** İzmir Palas Hotel, Atatürk Bul ☎0232 422 0601. Somewhat pricey local favourite offering a sophisticated range of seafood dishes, including stuffed squid (₺9) or mixed *Deniz* appetizers (₺25). Reservations are absolutely essential at weekends. Daily 11am–11pm.

BASMANE AND AROUND

★ **Alisa Vitamin** 1369 Sok. Small snackbar, where you can get a small meal for ₺3.50: it's ₺2.50 for a tasty *çiğ köfte*, and ₺1 for *ayran* or a glass of freshly squeezed carrot, grapefruit, orange or pomegranate juice. Daily 7am–11pm.

Ezo 1366 Sok. The best of the area's kebab restaurants – popular enough, in any case, to have two outlets facing each other. Kebabs cost from ₺10 per portion, and there's good *pide* available, too. Daily 10am–11pm.

KONAK AND THE BAZAAR

Acı Kahve Bazaar. The main part of this café is on the second floor of the bazaar, but bustle on up to the second floor and you'll be able to take your take tea or lemonade (both ₺1) with a mosque view. Daily 8am–8pm.

Adabeyi Konak Pier. Perfectly poised on a swish terrace at the tip of Konak Pier, this restaurant offers the best possible views of the bay. The menu has Turkish staples livened up with some intriguing additions; the stuffed sardines (₺18) are superb, as is the semolina helva with ice cream (₺10). If there are a few of you, try the full cold starter set. Daily noon–11pm.

Asansör Off Mithatpaşa Cad. At the top of this old elevator (see p.229) you'll find a café and restaurant; the former serves light snacks and (occasionally atrocious) coffee, while the latter offers good ₺16 set menus featuring fish, meat, salad and a glass of wine. Café daily 8am–midnight; restaurant daily 7–10pm.

Mennan Bazaar. If you find yourself in the bazaar, hunt down this little ice-cream vendor, selling little scoops of heaven for ₺2 and up. Daily 8am–8pm.

Orkide Bazaar. The pick of the bazaar's restaurants, specializing in *kokoreç* – a Turkish dish somewhat similar to haggis (₺12). Non-offal meats also available. Daily 8am–9pm.

DRINKING AND NIGHTLIFE

Upper **Alsancak** has blossomed as the district for trendy **nightlife**, with assorted bars and clubs tucked inland along pedestrianized side streets invisible from **Birinci Kordon**. As ownership and themes of each establishment tend to roll over on a two-year cycle, specific recommendations are subject to change, but each street has its own distinct atmosphere. Starting from the south, narrow **Sokak 1448** is a vine-shaded street with an upbeat, indie air. One street north, **Can Yucel** has a slightly older crowd and a more refined atmosphere. North again, **Sokak 1453** is a wider affair, boasting proper pubs and clubs in restored old houses. All the pricey bars on **Konak Pier** offer good sea views.

THE INTERNATIONAL İZMİR FESTIVAL

The Linchpin of İzmir's summer season is the **International İzmir Festival**, running from mid-June to early July. It's a bit of a misnomer since many events take place at various restored venues at Ephesus or Çeşme castle. Tickets run to ₺20–100 a head, but 50 percent student discounts are available and the acts featured are often world-class – past names have included the Moscow Ballet, Paco Peña and Ravi Shankar. Get this year's programme at ⓦiksev.org; ticket vendors are also listed online.

Eko Corner of Pilevne Bul and Cumhuriyet Cad. Pub-style place that's popular with expats, as well as İzmir's young and trendy. Daily 10am–late.

Hayalbaz 1448 Sok. The most popular and reliable place on this trendy road, its young crowd amusing themselves with beer, backgammon boards and raucous (though not overloud) conversation. Daily 11am–late.

Karnaval South of Cumhuriyet Meyd. This round-the-clock seafront bar may be old-fashioned, but it's fun nonetheless. Drink a 2.5-litre "tower beer" (₺25) outside by the sea, then buzz inside when the bar area morphs into a disco later on. Daily 24hr.

ENTERTAINMENT

Atatürk Cultural Centre Mithatpaşa Cad 92 ☎0232 483 8520. Home to the local symphony orchestra, which plays regularly on Fridays and Saturdays and hosts occasional concerts by soloists.

State Opera and Ballet Milli Kütüphane Cad ☎0232 489 0474, ⓦdobgm.gov.tr. The pleasingly varied programme at this wonderful Ottoman Art Deco venue ranges from chamber music to pop and jazz.

SHOPPING

The shops that fill the narrow lanes of İzmir's wonderfully atmospheric **Kemeraltı bazaar** sell all sorts, from spices to Chinese-made socks. If you've a purchase in mind, however, head straight to the **Kızlarağası Hanı** section, a restored *kervansaray* with dozens of places to buy waterpipes, jewellery, knives and musical instruments.

Bağdat Saz Evi Kızlarağası Hanı. The best place in town for traditional Turkish instruments. Daily 9am–9pm.

Dösim Next to the PTT at Cumhuriyet Bul 115/A. Turkish Ministry of Culture shop selling high-quality reproductions of Turkish and Ottoman crafts: kilims, silver jewellery and copperware. Daily 9am–6pm.

İlhan Etike Kızlarağası Hanı. One of the best places to buy nargiles (waterpipes) on the Aegean. Daily 9am–9pm.

DIRECTORY

Books Remzi Kitabevi, Konak Pier; D&R, 175 Cumhuriyet Bul (sells English magazines).

Consulates UK, 1442 Sok 49 ☎0232 463 5151, ⓦukinturkey.fco.gov.uk; US, 1387 Sok, Mustafa Bey Cad ☎0232 464 8755, ⓦturkey.usembassy.gov.

Hamam The cleanest and most secure is Hoşgör, on an alley inland from Mithatpaşa Cad 10, opposite Karataş Lisesi (daily: men 8–11am & 5pm–midnight; women 11am–5pm; ₺15).

Hospitals The most central state hospitals are Alsancak Devlet Hastanesi on Ali Çetinkaya Bul (☎0232 463 6465), and the Konak Hospital (with dental section), across from the ethnographic and archeological museums (☎0232 483 2191). Much better are the American Hospital, 1375 Sok (☎0212 444 3777) and the Özel Sağlık Hastanesi on 1399 Sok (☎0232 463 7700).

Pharmacies Merkez Eczane, near Basmane at 9 Eylül Meyd 5 ☎0232 483 2467; also try Kent Eczane, Fevzi Paşa Bul 174/C ☎0232 484 2149.

Police 1207 Sok, Basmane ☎0232 446 1456; Konak ☎0232 489 0500.

Post office Main PTT office is at Cumhuriyet Meyd (Mon–Sat 8am–8pm, Sun 8.30am–5pm); for less bureaucracy, UPS, Akdeniz Cad 8/K (office hours), also provides cost-effective air delivery to North America and the UK.

The Çeşme peninsula

The claw-like mass of land that extends west from İzmir, the **Çeşme peninsula**, terminates near **Çeşme** itself, the least touristed and most relaxing of the central Aegean's main coastal resorts. A one-hour bus ride from İzmir, it makes a decent base for the few attractions within shouting distance of town – most notably **ancient Erythrae** (see p.235), the hip town of **Alaçatı** (see p.236) and **Altınkum** beach (see p.235).

The immediate environs of Çeşme are green and hilly, with added colour from the deeply aquamarine sea and the white of the wind turbines on the approach to the peninsula. The **climate** here is noticeably drier, cooler and healthier than anywhere nearby on the Turkish coast, especially in comparison with occasionally hellish İzmir or muggy Kuşadası. These conditions, combined with the presence of several thermal springs, have made the peninsula a popular resort for over a century.

Çeşme

A picturesque, often sleepy town of old Greek houses wrapped around a Genoese castle, **ÇEŞME** ("drinking fountain" in Turkish) doubtless takes its name from the many Ottoman fountains, some still functioning, scattered around its streets.

RESTAURANTS	
Fatih	2
No Problem	3
Rıhtım	1

ÇEŞME

BARS AND CAFÉS	
Mado	2
Rumeli	1

ACCOMMODATION	
7800	2
Alim Pansiyon	5
Çeşme Marin	3
Kanuni Kervansaray	4
Pasifik	1

Getting around is easy. You'll soon find yourself on the main bazaar thoroughfare, **İnkilap Cad**, which ends at the sea; head left for the castle, and right to stroll the town's **esplanade**, which itself ends at a small crescent-shaped beach.

Çeşme Castle

Tues–Sun 9am–6.30pm • ₺5

Visitors are free to clamber about every perilous centimetre of Çeşme's **castle**. Much repaired by the Ottomans, it's now home to a small museum containing an interesting collection of archeological finds from nearby Erythrae, as well as a permanent exhibition detailing a sea battle fought in the straits here in 1770, in which the Russian fleet annihilated the Ottoman navy. The castle's crumbling open-air theatre also hosts performances during the **International İzmir Festival** (see p.233).

Altınkum

9km southwest of Çeşme • Dolmuşes from Çeşme (every 45min) stop at the first cove, and continue 1km to the central, even better, cove in summer (June–Sept)

The best local beaches on the Çeşme peninsula lie along **ALTINKUM**, a series of sunbaked coves, beyond the seaside township of Çiftlik. In fact, with multi-hued water lapping hundreds of metres of sand and dunes, this is probably the best beach between Bozcaada and the Turquoise Coast.

ARRIVAL AND DEPARTURE

By bus or dolmuş Çeşme's small *otogar* is 1km south of the town centre, although local buses and dolmuşes serving most nearby destinations, including İzmir, Dalyan, Ilıca and Alaçatı, stop at the eastern end of İnkilap Cad.
Car rental Uzun Rent-a-car, 16 Eylül Mah, 3010 Sok 3 (☎0232 712 0928), is about the cheapest; they also rent motorbikes, perfectly adequate for exploring the peninsula.

By ferry Çeşme has ferry connections to Hios in Greece, which is known as Chios in Turkish (Mon & Thurs 7pm, Tues, Wed & Fri–Sun 9.30am & 7pm; 1hr; €20 return), to and from a ferry dock just across the bay. Three different operators have ticket booths below the castle. To take a day-trip, you have to book the day before.

INFORMATION AND ACTIVITIES

Tourist office There's a helpful tourist office by the Customs Office near the quayside (Mon–Fri 8.30am–5.30pm, Sat & Sun 9am–noon & 1–5pm; ☎0232 712 6653).
Boat trips Daily boat trips leave from just north of Cumhuriyet Meydanı, heading along the coast to local

beauty spots and nearby Donkey Island. They usually set off at 10.30am, returning at 5.30pm, and cost around ₺35, including lunch.
Hamam Belediye Hamamı on Çarşi Cad, 200m down from the *kervansaray*.

ACCOMMODATION

Çeşme's popularity as a summer bolt hole for İzmiris means there's a plethora of accommodation, though prices go berserk in July and August. The most desirable places to stay line the waterfront; alternatively, drop by the kiosk (☎0232 712 6176) by the bus stop on İnkilap Cad, where staff will help you book a *pansiyon* or home stay (around ₺120 for a double in the summer, far less at other times).

ÇEŞME

★ **7800** Boyalık, 5km northeast of Çeşme ☎0232 712 0087, ⊕7800cesme.com. Ultra-modern spa hotel, on the bus route between Çeşme and Alaçatı, with luxurious, spacious rooms right on the beach. Outside the peak summer season, you can get a double for under ₺300. ₺750
Alim Pansiyon 1021 Sok ☎0232 712 6971. The cheapest place in town, near a mosque with overloud speakers. The rooms are spartan but just about acceptable. Try to get the rooftop double – great views, and a floor entirely to yourself. ₺70

Çeşme Marin Otel By the harbour ☎0232 712 7580. Relatively new hotel where many of the spick-and-span rooms have balconies and wonderful sea views. There's a bar on the ground floor, though this can make things a little noisy. Prices halve out of season. ₺270
★ **Kanuni Kervansaray** 1015 Sok ☎0232 712 0630. Dating back to the days of Süleyman the Magnificent, this restored *kervansaray* is now a suitably plush hotel, with a swimming pool and a couple of date palms in its courtyard. Its cave-style rooms are small but atmospheric (opt for the upper level), and there are great views from the rooftop

4

seating area. ₺300

Pasifik Otel 16 Eylül Mah, Tekke Plajı Mevkii 16 ☎0232 712 2700, ⓦpasifikotel.com. Adjacent to Çeşme's most popular beach, with an excellent fish restaurant on the ground floor. Half-board rates available. ₺250

ALTINKUM

EATING AND DRINKING

Fatih Behind Ayios Haralambos, off İnkilap Cad. The town's *pide* specialists, doling out crispy meals from ₺6. Daily 9am–11pm.

Mado On the harbour. Branches of this dessert chain are all over Turkey, but few are so magnificently located – right on the new harbour, the view all sea and sail-masts. Good *baklava* and ice cream, as well as savoury brunch meals. Daily 9am–midnight.

No Problem Off 1015 Sok. One of those restaurants that ropes in tourists (mostly British), and confuses the hell out

Okan's Place ☎0532 394 0131, ⓦokansplace.com. Rents out very basic bungalows that can attract the odd bug during the summer. The attached beach club and restaurant are popular at weekends, the latter serving assorted fish (₺15 and up), spicy *menemen* and veggies from the on-site organic garden. Summer only. ₺250

of locals. Still, if you're really in the mood for a fried breakfast or some beans on toast, this is the place to go; there's a good book-exchange too. Daily 24hr.

Rıhtım Overlooking the fishing port. Simple affair that's the best place in town for fish, with good-value set menus including sea bream and bass. Daily 10am–10pm.

Rumeli Pastanesi İnkilap Cad 44. A local legend, with some of the best ice cream on the Aegean (₺1.5 per scoop); try the *sakızlı* (mastic resin). They also sell home-made fruit preserves (*reçel*). Daily 10am–midnight.

Alaçatı

The architecturally stunning old Greek village of **ALAÇATI** is one of the most upmarket locales on the Aegean coast. With an undeniably Mediterranean air, it's one of those places that makes you question whether you're still in Turkey at all – the lone call to prayer is heeded by next to no one, while cafés, shops and wine bars run a brisk trade. However, this is no Brit-packed beach resort. Most of it is manifestly inland, for a start, while the overwhelming majority of visitors are Turkish – mainly cosmopolitan, moneyed sorts from İstanbul and İzmir, who pop by on weekend trips.

Things have changed considerably since 2001, when Alaçatı was just another charming peninsular village. Then one of the town's old stone houses opened up as a swish designer hotel. Within a few years it had spawned a dozen tasteful imitators, and a similar number of gourmet restaurants. There are now something like 150 hotels and 50 restaurants, and numbers are still growing; however, strict building regulations have ensured the rapid growth has had little effect on Alaçatı's architectural character. Its old lanes and cobbled streets, particularly on the main thoroughfare, Kemalpaşa Caddesi, are dotted with antique shops, art galleries and snazzy boutiques selling designer goods.

Most visitors head to the town's 300m-long sandy **beach**, 4km south, to take advantage of unique **windsurfing** and **kiteboarding** conditions. The strong, reliable "Meltemi" wind, combined with shallow water and lack of waves, makes the bay ideal for learners.

ARRIVAL AND DEPARTURE
ALAÇATI

By bus or dolmuş Most buses between Çeşme and İzmir stop in Alaçatı; the centre is a short walk south of the bus stop.

Destinations Çeşme (every 45min; 20min).

ACTIVITIES

Bicycle rental The *Naciye Teyze* hotel rents out bikes from ₺10 per hour, or ₺30 per day.

Kite surfing Kite Turkey (ⓦwww.kite-turkey.com) work

with all levels, and can supply all gear needed. Ten-hour courses from €300.

ACCOMMODATION

Though landlocked, Alaçatı's accommodation follows a coastal pattern: wildly expensive in summer, often full on weekends, and far cheaper out of season. Surfers generally camp out of town on the beach.

Naciye Teyze Cemaliye Cad 6 ☎0232 716 8970, ⓦnaciyeteyze.com. One of the town's cheaper options (which isn't saying much), with a pleasant garden and perfectly adequate rooms, most equipped with balconies. ₺200

Sailors Otel 3005 Sok 5 ☎0232 716 8765, ⓦsailorsotel .com. The best *pansiyon* in town, with spacious wooden-floored, white-and-blue-painted doubles. The owners have also opened up another, quieter, place on a backstreet. ₺250

★ **Taş Otel** Kemalpaşa Cad 132 ☎0232 716 7772, ⓦtasotel.com. The hotel that kick-started the town's regeneration (see p.236) is, despite the copycats, still the best in town. Set in a lovingly restored 1890s building, it

has eight large, stylish rooms, all with balconies and a/c. Service is professional yet relaxed, and just wait until you see breakfast – best enjoyed by the pool. ₺370

Ümit Ev Otel Yeni Mecidiye Mah, 3058 Sok 24 ☎0232 716 8133, ⓦumitevotel.com. Simple rooms surrounding an organic garden (used to supply ingredients for breakfast), located on a backstreet. Single rooms are significantly cheaper. ₺180

Vintage Boutique 3046 Sok 2 ☎0232 716 0716, ⓦvintagealacati.com. Relatively new boutique hotel, with modern decoration and a huge garden for breakfast or coffee. The huge mirrors dotted about the place further enhance the feel of space. ₺350

EATING AND DRINKING

★ **Asma Yaprağı** 1005 Sok 50. Quaint little place on a side street by the mosque, serving simple – but utterly delicious – home cooking. This is Aegean cuisine at its finest: a blend of seasonal (almost entirely vegetarian) family recipes, all made with local ingredients. You'll find most of the day's dishes laid out before you on entry – the artichoke, stuffed vine leaves and samphire are highly recommended. Daily noon–midnight.

Avrasya Uğur Mumcu Cad 22. Bored with the town's slightly snobby air? Head to this place by the main road for tasty, traditional Turkish cooking at regular Turkish prices. Daily 9am–11pm.

Ferdi Baba Şifne waterfront ☎0232 717 2145. For a fabulous fish blowout, grab a cab south out of town to Şifne's stretch of seafront terraces. Though pricey, the seafood is as exquisite as the location – try the stuffed squid or the octopus kebabs. Daily noon–1am.

Köşe Kahve 1005 Sok 2. Small but highly trendy café that's good for coffee by day or cocktails in the evening – try one of their house sangrias. Daily 9am–late.

Roka Bahçe Kemalpaşa Cad 107a. Smart-looking restaurant serving delectable fusion dishes – Aegean specialities with a twist, best eaten under the trellises outside. It's pricey, for sure, but worth it. Daily noon–11pm.

Ancient Ionia

The territory of **Ancient Ionia** begins south of İzmir. Its undoubted highlight is the ensemble of ruins that span numerous eras: most notably at **Ephesus** and **Priene** – perhaps the most dramatic site of all the Ionian cities; at sprawling **Miletus**, further south; and at **Didyma**, with its gargantuan temple. **Kuşadası** is an unabashedly utilitarian resort that serves well for excursions to the major antiquities and the nearby national park around ancient Mount Mycale. Nearby **Selçuk** is a prettier, more relaxed, base.

ANCIENT IONIA

The **Ionian coast** was first colonized by Greek-speakers in the twelfth century BC. The culture reached its zenith during the seventh and sixth centuries BC, when it was at the forefront of the newly emergent sciences, philosophy and the arts. Enormous advantages accrued to those who settled here: an amenable climate, fertile, well-watered terrain, and a strategic location between the Aegean – with its many fine harbours – and inland Anatolia. Partly thanks to the silting up of local rivers, the coastline soon began to recede; and by mid-Byzantine times virtually all of the Ionian cities had been abandoned; with the declaration of Christianity as the state religion, religious centres and oracles met a similar fate.

Today's inhabitants have found the silver lining to the cloud of the advancing deltas, cashing in on the rich soil brought down from the hills. Vast tracts of cotton, tobacco, sesame and grain benefit from irrigation works, while groves of pine, olive and cypress, which need no such encouragement, adorn the hills and wilder reaches. And with the sea, though more distant than in former times, still beckoning when tramping the ruins palls, tourism is now threatening to outstrip agriculture.

Selçuk

One has to admire little **SELÇUK**. No more than a farming town only a generation ago, it has been catapulted into the limelight of premier-league tourism by its proximity to the ruins of **Ephesus** (p.240), the second most visited site in the whole of Turkey. Despite this, and its status as the burial place of **St John the Evangelist**, Selçuk remains an incredibly relaxed, easy-going place – swallows squeal and wheel from eave to eave, storks build nests atop Roman columns, and life dawdles by at a snail's pace.

Selçuk has maintained its relaxed air largely because Ephesus is also very close to the coast – the overwhelming majority of visitors to the ruins base themselves in nearby Kuşadası (p.246). Unless you absolutely need to be by the sea (which, in any case, is less than half an hour away), Selçuk is an excellent travel base, with super-cheap accommodation, good restaurants and a pleasing, backpackery feel.

As far as sightseeing goes, Ephesus is not the end of the story – stay a couple of days here (or in Kuşadası) and you'll be able to see the hill village of **Şirince**, the shrine at **Meryemana**, and Selçuk's own array of antiquities, most pertinently those in its excellent **museum**.

Alasoluk Hill

Daily 8am–6.30pm • ₺8

The obvious first spot to head for, **Ayasoluk Hill**, has been the focal point of settlement in every era. It's famed as the burial place of **St John the Evangelist**, who came to Ephesus in the middle of the first century and died there around 100 AD. Indeed, the hill's name is thought to be a corruption of Ayios Theologos, or "Divine Theologian". The sixth-century Byzantine emperor Justinian decided to replace two earlier churches sheltering John's tomb with a basilica worthy of the saint's reputation. Until its destruction by Tamerlane's Mongols in 1402, it was among the largest and most ornate of all Byzantine churches.

You'll enter the site through the **Gate of Persecution**, so called by the Byzantines because it was once adorned by a relief of Achilles in combat, mistakenly thought to depict Christians being martyred in the amphitheatre of Ephesus. Then come the re-erected colonnades and walls of the **Basilica of St John**; the purported tomb of the evangelist is marked by a slab on the former site of the altar. Beside the nave is the **Baptistry**, where tourists pose in the act of dunking for friends' cameras. A restored **Byzantine castle** stands atop the hill.

Ephesus Museum

Daily 8.30am–6.30pm • ₺8 • ☎ 0232 892 6010

Always packed, the **Ephesus Museum** is well worth visiting. Arranged thematically rather than chronologically, its galleries present the ancient city as a living space rather than being just a repository of artefacts. Celebrated bronze and ceramic objects in the first three halls include effigies of the phallic god Priapus; a bust of the Greek dramatist Menander; Eros riding a dolphin; and excellent miniatures from the Roman terrace houses at Ephesus. A large courtyard holds sarcophagi, column capitals and stelae.

Continuing through the main galleries, and a hall devoted to tomb finds and mortuary practices, you reach the famous **Artemis room**. This holds two renditions of the goddess studded with multiple bull's testicles (not breasts, as is commonly believed) and tiny figurines of real and mythical beasts, honouring her role as mistress of animals.

The Artemision

300m west of the centre, off the Ephesus road • Daily 8.30am–5.30pm • Free

The scanty remains of the **Artemision**, or sanctuary of Artemis, lie on the outskirts of town. The archaic temple here replaced three predecessors dedicated to Cybele, and was itself burned down in 356 BC by Herostratus, a lunatic who (correctly) reckoned his name would be immortalized by the act. The massive Hellenistic replacement was considered to be one of the **Seven Wonders of the Ancient World**, though that's hard to believe today. After the Goths sacked it in 263 AD, the Byzantines carted off most of the remaining masonry to Ayasoluk and Constantinople, leaving just a lone column (re-erected in modern times) amid battered foundation blocks.

İsa Bey Camii

Off 1054 Sok • Free

The **İsa Bey Camii** is the most distinguished of the Selçuk monuments that gave the town its name. A late fourteenth-century Aydınoğlu mosque, it represents a transition between Selçuk and Ottoman styles, with its innovative courtyard – where most of the congregation would worship – and stalactite vaulting over the entrance. Inside the main hall, you'll see a high, gabled roof supported by Roman columns and some fine tile-work in the south dome.

ARRIVAL AND DEPARTURE SELÇUK

By train Selçuk's cute train station, just east of the centre, has (incredibly cheap) connections to İzmir, Denizli (for Pamukkale) and Söke (for Priene).
Destinations Denizli (2 daily, via Aydın; 4hr); İzmir (4 daily; 1hr).

By bus The simple *otogar* is conveniently located at the southern end of Atatürk Cad.
Destinations İstanbul (5 daily; 10hr); Kuşadası (every 20min; 30min); Şirince (every 20min; 20min).

INFORMATION

Tourist office On the corner of the central park and Uğur Mumcu Cad, or "Love Street" as the sign proclaims (Mon–Fri 8.30am–noon & 1–5.30pm, Sat 8.30am–noon & 1–5pm; ☎ 0232 892 6328).
Tours Agencies all over town offer guided tours to Ephesus,

but independent travellers can easily make their own way. Day-tours of Priene, Miletus and Didyma go for around ₺100 per person; operators only tend to have one such trip each per week, so you'll have to ask around.

ACCOMMODATION

Most **hotels** offer free transport to Ephesus, as well as collection from the ferry in Kuşadası. Prices, already low, plummet further off season. **Camping** is possible on Pamucak beach, a short bus ride away.

Hotel Akay 1054 Sok 3 ☎0232 892 3172, ⓦhotelakay .com. Affordable boutique-style two-star choice spread over two properties, with standard and superior rooms. You'll be able to relax on deckchairs by the swimming pool – who needs the beach? ₺120

ANZ Guesthouse 1064 Sok 12 ☎0232 892 6050, ⓦanzguesthouse.com. Run by a returned Turkish-Australian, this *pansiyon* has basic rooms but a nice rooftop bar, where occasional barbecues are served. Dorm beds available. Rates for doubles include breakfast. Dorms ₺7.5, doubles ₺60

★ **Barım Pansiyon** 1045 Sok 34 ☎0232 892 6923, ⓦbarimpension.com. One of the cheapest places in a uniformly cheap town, set in a restored, rambling old house complete with lush courtyard/garden. Rooms have traditional Turkish decor and stone-clad walls, with modern fixtures and fittings. ₺60

★ **Hotel Bella** St John Cad 7 ☎0232 892 3944, ⓦhotelbella.com. Opposite the basilica gate, this veteran option is still Selçuk's best, and phenomenal value for the price. Service is friendly and informative, rooms are beautifully decorated, and there's a great restaurant – open to non-guests, too (see p.240). ₺100

Boomerang Guesthouse 1047 Sok 10 ☎0232 892 4879, ⓦboomerangguesthouse.com. A relative newbie, this spick-and-span little guesthouse enjoys a quiet yet wonderfully central location. An extra ₺20 will get you a balcony, or a mini garden area if you're on the ground floor. ₺70

Jimmy's Place Atatürk Mah 1016 Sok 19 ☎0232 892 1982, ⓦjimmysplaceephesus.com. Near the central market and run by an irrepressible, well-travelled Turk, this cheapie offers standard, superior and luxury en-suite rooms, plus a hotel pool down the road. ₺60

Nilya 1051 Sok 7 ☎0232 892 9081, ⓦnilya.com. Owned by the same team as the *Bella* up the road, this hotel has an even quieter setting behind high walls, with charmingly cluttered kilim-strewn rooms (all en-suite) laid out around a peaceful, tree-lined courtyard. Excellent breakfasts. ₺170

EATING AND DRINKING

Selçuk's **restaurants** tend to much the same as each other, though they're usually good value. Several hotels also operate decent dining rooms that are open to the public. Alcohol is easy to track down; many restaurants are licensed, and there are several noisy **bars** in the warren of streets around the train station.

Amazon Prof A Kaluncur Cad 24. On the western fringe of town, this restaurant has views of a Wonder of the Ancient World from its outdoor tables, set in a niche across the road. The food's OK, a mix of foreign meals including pasta, schnitzel and the like. Mains from ₺7.50. Daily 10am–10pm.

Hotel Bella St John Cad 7. The best of the hotel restaurants, plonked up on the rooftop with views of the basilica, castle, surrounding countryside and – if you're in luck – stork nests. It's ₺15 for a kebab, ₺5 per *meze*, and ₺25 for a full meal including some fish and soup. Daily 6–11pm.

★ **Café Carpouza** On the north side of the aqueduct. Set in a glorious building dating back to 1875, this is the most atmospheric place for coffee, set at tables dotted around a garden so large it's basically a park. They also serve good desserts, and cocktails in the evening. Daily 8am–1am.

Efes Köftecisi Cengiz Topel Cad. Lokanta serving up good, simple and cheap steam-tray specials. You should eat for under ₺10, bar the grilled meats, which are a little more expensive. Daily 8am–11pm.

Garden Restaurant 1047 Sok. Relatively elegant, and great value, offering good Turkish home cooking in a leafy courtyard. It's a particularly good spot for lunch – a mixed *meze* for one will set you back ₺10 – or an evening nargile. Daily 9am–10pm.

Pink Bistro Siegburg Cad 26. Café-bar with tables spilling out onto the street. Good for coffee by day or carousing by night. Daily 10am–11pm.

Ephesus

3km southwest of Selçuk • Daily 8am–6pm • ₺25, audioguides ₺15 • Selçuk hotels offer free drop-offs and pick-ups, while regular minibuses from Selçuk and Kuşadası drop passengers near the lower entrance, and taxis cost ₺15 from Selçuk, ₺80 from Kuşadası

Of Turkey's superb array of ancient cities, **Ephesus** (known as Efes in Turkish) is by far the best preserved. In fact, with the possible exception of Pompeii, one could argue that it's the world's finest surviving example of a Greco-Roman **classical city**. A big claim, but with so much to back it up – the ruins here are not merely rocks on the ground, but near-fully-fledged incarnations of what life must have been like in ancient times.

The tantalizing prospect of delving back so many centuries in architectural time makes Ephesus a cast-iron must-see if you're in, or anywhere near, the area. As one would expect, the ruins are mobbed for much of the year, particularly with summer

EPHESUS

Selçuk & Magnesia Gate

Selçuk

Meryemana (5km)

Kuşadası

MOUNT PION (PANAYIR DAĞI)

MOUNT KORESSOS (BÜLBÜLDAĞI)

Cave of the Seven Sleepers

Magnesia Gate

East Gymnasium

Upper Entrance & Ticket Office

Varius Baths

Odeon

Upper Agora

Trajan's Fountain

Vedius Gymnasium

Stadium

Paved Access Road

Lower Entrance & Ticket Office

Car & Coach Park

St Mary's Church

Theatre

MARBLE STREET

Wide Walk

Path

Arcadian Way

Harbour Baths & Gymnasium

Old Port

Tower of St Paul

CURETES STREET

STEPS

PATH

Lower Agora

Serapis Temple

Library of Celsus

Terrace Houses

Domitian Temple Museum of Inscriptions

Hellenistic Wall

N

1 Scholastica Baths
2 Temple of Hadrian
3 Brothel
4 Latrines
5 Byzantine Fountain
6 Gate of Hercules
7 Prytaneum

0   100
metres

cruise-ship arrivals from nearby Kuşadası – after the Sultanahmet district of İstanbul, this is the most visited tourist attraction in Turkey. However, with a little planning and initiative it's possible to tour the site in relative peace.

There are **two entrances** to Ephesus, both surrounded by stands selling souvenirs and overpriced snacks. The prevailing current of people heads downhill from the upper entrance – a particularly good idea in summer – which is the route followed in this guide. You'll need two to three hours to see Ephesus, and in summer you'll need a **hat** – there's next to no shade, meaning that the acres of stone act as a grill in the heat of the day. Whatever the season, you'll probably need to carry **water** too; this is only sold at the entrances, from which multilingual **audioguides** are also available.

Brief history

Legends relate that Ephesus was founded by **Androclus**, son of King Kodrus of Athens, who was advised by an oracle to settle at a place indicated by a fish and a wild boar. Androclus and his entourage arrived here to find natives roasting fish by the sea; embers from the fire set a bush ablaze, out of which charged a pig, and the city was on its way. The imported worship of Artemis melded easily with that of the indigenous **Cybele**, and the Ephesus of 1000 BC was built on the north slope of Mount Pion (Panayır Dağı), very close to the temple of the goddess.

Alexander the Great, on his visit in 334 BC, offered to fund the completion of the latest version of the Artemis shrine, but the city fathers tactfully demurred, saying that one deity should not support another. Following Alexander's death, his lieutenant **Lysimachus** moved the city to its present location – necessary because the sea had already receded considerably – and provided it with its first **walls**, traces of which are still visible on Panayır Dağı and Mount Koressos (Bülbül Dağı) to the south.

In subsequent centuries, Ephesus changed allegiance frequently and backed various revolts against Roman rule. Yet it never suffered for this lack of principle: during the Roman imperial period it was designated the **capital of Asia** and ornamented with magnificent public buildings – those on view today – by successive emperors. Ephesus's quarter-million population was swollen substantially at times by the right of sanctuary linked to the sacred precinct of Artemis, allowing shelter to large numbers of criminals. Of a somewhat less lurid cast was the more stable, mixed population of Jews, Romans, and Egyptian and Anatolian cultists.

The Christians arrive

Christianity took root early and quickly at Ephesus. St John the Evangelist arrived in the mid-first century, and **St Paul** spent the years 51–53 AD in the city, proselytizing foremost among the Jewish community. As usual, Paul managed to foment controversy even in this cosmopolitan environment, apparently being imprisoned for some time – in a tower bearing his name near the west end of the walls – and later provoking the famous silversmiths' riot, described in Acts 19:23–20:1.

Under the Byzantines, Ephesus was the venue for two **councils of the Church**, including one in 431 AD at which the Nestorian heresy (see p.639) was anathematized. However, the general tenor of the Byzantine era was one of decline, owing to the abandonment of Artemis-worship, Arab raids and (worst of all) the final silting up of the harbour. The population began to siphon off to the nearby hill crowned by the tomb and church of St John, future nucleus of the town of Selçuk, and by the time the Selçuks themselves appeared the process was virtually complete.

The upper agora and around

Approaching from the **upper entrance**, you'll almost immediately find yourself in the large, overgrown **upper agora**, which lies opposite the civic heart of the Roman community – the **prytaneum**. This housed the inextinguishable sacred flame of Ephesus and two of the Artemis statues in the Selçuk museum (see p.239), even though Hestia (also known as **Vesta**) was the presiding goddess; it also served as the reception area for official guests. The adjacent **odeon**, once the local parliament, has been as insensitively restored as the main theatre.

You'll soon find yourself heading down **Curetes Street**, which starts at the **Gate of Hercules**, where a remaining column relief depicts the hero wrapped in the skin of the Nemean lion. A little further down is **Trajan's Fountain**, whose ornamentation has been removed to the museum.

The Temple of Hadrian

The so-called **Temple of Hadrian** was donated in 118 AD by a wealthy citizen in honour of Hadrian, Artemis and the city in general. Most of the relief works here are plaster copies of the originals, which reside in the Selçuk museum. The two small heads on the arches spanning the four columns out front are of Tyche and possibly Medusa, respectively installed for luck and to ward off evil influences.

The public **latrines**, a little lower, provide evidence that ancient humans were human too, and understandably are a favourite photo opportunity with visitors.

Scholastica Baths

The first-century **Scholastica baths**, sprawling behind and above the Temple of Hadrian, are named after the fifth-century Byzantine lady whose headless statue adorns the entrance, and who restored the complex. There was direct access from here to the latrines and thence the brothel, though it seems from graffiti that the baths, too, were at one stage used as a bawdy house. As at many points in Ephesus, clay drainage pipes remain visibly lodged in the floor.

The terrace houses

West side of Curetes Street • Daily: summer 8am–6pm; winter 8am–5pm • ₺15

The 62 rooms of Ephesus' famous **terrace houses**, housed in a protective shelter, form one of the world's best-preserved Roman domestic environments. Oddly, many tour groups skip this incredible site – all the better for you to enjoy it unobstructed.

Broken down into seven dwellings, Terrace House 2 was buried, and thus very well preserved, by earthquakes during the third century AD. Excavation teams continue to work as visitors are channelled through the complex via transparent glass walkways. At the time of writing, highlights include a basilica "wall-papered" with thin sheets of marble in Dwelling 6, underfloor heating in Dwelling 5, and the mosaics and murals in the Room of the Nine Muses in Dwelling 3.

The Library of Celsus

Looming directly across the intersection of Ephesus' two major streets, the awe-inspiring **Library of Celsus** was erected by the consul Gaius Julius Aquila between 110 and 135 AD as a memorial to his father Celsus Polemaeanus, who is still entombed under its west wall. The elegant, two-storey facade is the classic image of Ephesus. It was fitted with niches for statues of the four personified intellectual virtues, today filled with plaster copies (the originals are in Vienna). Inside, twelve thousand scrolls were stored in galleries designed to forestall damp – the Goths burned them all when they sacked the area in 262 AD. Abutting the library, and designed to provide entry to the lower agora, stands the restored triple **gate of Mazaeus and Mithridates**.

Marble Street

The so-called **Marble Street** begins at the **lower agora** and ends near the base of the theatre; wheel-ruts in the road and the slightly elevated colonnade remnant to the right indicate that pedestrians and vehicles were kept neatly separated. Adjoining the agora is the **Serapis Temple**, where the city's many Egyptian merchants would have worshipped.

4

Across the road, metal stanchions protect alleged "signposting" – a footprint and a female head etched into the rock – for a **brothel**.

The Arcadian Way

Downhill from Marble Street, the ancient **theatre** has been somewhat brutally restored, although it's worth the climb for the views over the surrounding countryside. It faces the splendid **Arcadian Way**, named after the fifth-century Byzantine emperor Arcadius who renovated it. Currently roped off and the site of regular faux-gladiator performances, it was originally lined with hundreds of shops and illuminated at night. Its northern side is fringed by the **harbour baths** and **gymnasium**, though these are overgrown and difficult to explore.

St Mary's church

From the fenced-off end of the Arcadian Way, a small, little-trodden trail (signed "Meryem Kilisesi") leads to **St Mary's church**, an absurdly elongated hotchpotch constructed between the second and fourth centuries AD. The building, originally a Roman warehouse, was the venue of the ecumenical council in 431 AD; its baptistry is in good condition. Lastly – or your first view of the city if coming from the lower entrance – are the remains of the **Vedius gymnasium**, and a large **stadium** funded by Nero.

Meryemana

8km southwest of Selçuk, beyond Ephesus • Daily, dawn–dusk • ₺10 • No public transport; come by private car or taxi

Meryemana is a monument to piety and faith. Though most Orthodox theologians maintain that the Virgin Mary died and was buried in Jerusalem, another school of thought holds that the mother of Jesus accompanied St John the Evangelist when he left Palestine in the middle of the first century on his way to Ephesus.

Bar its Biblical history, however, Meryemana is not a particularly diverting place. Enclosed within a municipal park, the site is heavily commercialized. The **house** itself, now a chapel aligned unusually southwest to northeast, probably dates from early Byzantine times, though its foundations may indeed be first-century. It overlooks a beautiful wooded valley and two terraces where a spring gushes forth; nearby, tree branches are festooned with the votive rag-scraps left by Muslim pilgrims, for whom *Meryemana* (Mother Mary) is also a saint.

The Cave of the Seven Sleepers

En route to Meryemana from Selçuk, between the upper and lower Ephesus entrances • Daily dawn–dusk • Free • Walkable from Ephesus, but best seen as part of a taxi-trip that includes Ephesus

Seven persecuted Christians are said to have fled to the **Cave of the Seven Sleepers**, en route to Meryemana, then been sealed inside by their pursuers; exposed once more by an earthquake two hundred years later, they sidled into town for a bite to eat. More prosaically, it's the site of a **Byzantine necropolis** whose tombs were cut into the surrounding rock. It's a beautiful place, and most visitors munch on *gözleme* from one of the shacks outside.

Şirince

The evocative, well-preserved **hill village** of **ŞİRİNCE**, 8km east of Selçuk, was originally built by Greeks. It's surrounded by lush orchards and vineyards – you can taste the wines, and buy bottles at many shops. Laden with pesky hawkers in season, it's much more pleasant and relaxed outside summer and genuinely lives up to its reputation as one of the region's most idyllic villages – this despite being a cab-ride from Selçuk.

FROM TOP ŞİRİNCE (P.244); BODRUM (P.262)>

The late nineteenth-century **church** at the edge of Şirince has a pebble-mosaic floor, plaster-relief work on the ceiling, and wooden vaulting, while the larger stone **basilica** nearer the centre dates from 1839. The main reason to visit, though, is the idyllic scenery and the handsome domestic architecture, which these days attracts wealthy urban Turks in search of characterful vacation homes.

ARRIVAL AND DEPARTURE
ŞİRİNCE

By dolmuş and taxi Regular dolmuşes (₺3; 20min) leave from Selçuk's *otogar*; taxis cost more like ₺35.

ACCOMMODATION AND EATING

Just before dusk, Şirince morphs from outdoor shopping mall to simple mountain village – locals pack up their goods, sit on the roadsides and chat until bedtime, making it tempting to **stay overnight**.

Artemis Restaurant At the western edge of town. Enjoying a spectacular setting in a former school overlooking the valley, this offers an excellent Turkish menu (mains ₺15 and up), as well as a wide range of local wines. Daily 9am–11pm.

Güllü Konakları Up from the main square ☎ 0232 898 3131. Şirince's fanciest hotel, its gorgeous rooms spread out over a wide, flower-filled swathe of hillside. There's an excellent restaurant, as well as an outdoor jacuzzi, and all manner of places to unwind. ₺240

Mystic Konak Downhill from the basilica ☎ 0232 898 3163. A cheap, characterful option, this *pansiyon* has pleasingly decorated rooms and a tranquil setting. The owners also have a cheaper place down the road. ₺100

Nişanyan Evleri High above the town ☎ 0232 898 3208, ⓦ nisanyan.com. Run by a local writer, this restored mansion has serene views and superb singles and doubles. It's easily visible from Şirince, but unless you want to lug your bags uphill (really, you don't), drop into their café at the entrance to the village, or just call on arrival, for a pick-up. ₺120

★ **Ocakbaşı** Just uphill from the basilica. This is where the locals come to dine out. Everything's phenomenal value, and the *mezes* – starting at ₺3 and all made with local ingredients – are simply out of this world. Try the samphire (*deniz börülce*), the stuffed pumpkin flowers (*kabak ciceği dolma*) or some of the tasty *köfte* (₺10). Daily 8.30am–11pm.

Kuşadası

Brash and mercenary it may be, but **KUŞADASI** holds a perennial charm for groups of mostly boozy Brits, Irish and Australians. In just three decades its population has swollen tenfold, and the scrappy, bustling conurbation now extends several kilometres along the coast and inland. The town is many people's first taste of Turkey: efficient ferry services link it with the Greek island of Sámos, while the resort is an obligatory port of call for Aegean **cruise ships**. These disgorge vast crowds in summer, who delight the local souvenir merchants both before and after a visit to the ruins of **Ephesus** just inland.

Despite its noisy nightlife, there are plenty of good reasons to stay in Kuşadası. It's an attractive place, with hundreds of good bars, restaurants and shops, as well as excellent connections to nearby attractions and **beaches**. There's not too much actually to see in town, though themed "Turkish Nights" concerts are held in its most beautiful building – the sixteenth-century **Öküz Mehmet Paşa Kervansaray**, now restored as a luxury hotel (see p.249). This backs on to a pleasing pedestrian precinct, within which you'll find a little **stone tower** and other remnants of the town's medieval walls. Out across the causeway, **Güvercin Adası** (daily 8am–8pm) presents a series of landscaped terraces within its fortifications – a leafy respite from the bustle of town.

ARRIVAL AND DEPARTURE
KUŞADASI

By plane The closest major airport is in İzmir. Taxis from both Kuşadası and the airport will be extremely keen to make the trip – €50 is the going rate. Otherwise, most long-distance buses bound for İzmir pass within 700m of the terminal proper; ask to be let off at *havalimanı kavşağı* ("airport junction"), and allow 1hr 30min for the trip. Taxis to Bodrum airport cost in the region of €85.

By bus or dolmuş The long-distance *otogar*, where arrivals from the south are dropped, is 2km south of the old town, just past the end of Kahramanlar Cad. Local dolmuşes, labelled "Şehir İçi", connect with the centre of town, stopping at the corner of Atatürk and İnönü buls. You

KUŞADASI

Selçuk & İzmir

Tusan & Pamucak

Samos (Greece)

Otogar & Dolmuş Terminal (350m)

Kadınlar Denizi (2km)

4

AEGEAN
SEA

Yacht
Marina

Halk Plaj

ATATÜRK BUL

Bus stop
for Tusan &
Pamucak

Main
Harbour

SEE INSET FOR DETAIL

Excursion
Boats

Güvercin Adası
(Pigeon Island)

Taxi Rank

KALE

Friday
Market
Area

Covered
Car Park

Minibuses to
Ladies' Beach,
Long Beach, Ephesus,
Milli Porkı & Selçuk

KAHRAMANLAR CAD

ZAFER SOK

YILDIRIM CAD

GÜVERCINADA CAD

Yılancı Burnu
Beach

Yılancı Burnu

N

**Customs &
Immigration**

Taxi
Rank

KALE

Kervansaray

Bank
Mailbox

Kale Camii

Barbaros

THY

İSMET

Covered
Car Park

Medieval
Wall

Tower

Hanım
Camii

Belediye
Hamam

Kale Hamamı

KAHRAMANLAR CAD

BARLAR SOK

ZAFER SOK

YILDIRIM CAD

KIBRIS CAD

ANIT SOK

GÜZEL SOK

BEZFRGAN SOK

ACCOMMODATION	
Anzac Golden Bed	4
Caravanseraii	2
Cennet	8
Efe Boutique	7
Liman	1
Önder	6
Sezgin	3
Villa Konak	9
Yat Kamping	5

RESTAURANTS	
Avlu	2
Castle	3
Kazım Usta	1
Komagene	5
Planet Yucca	4

BARS AND CAFÉS	
Another Bar	2
Jimmy's Irish Bar	3
Keremağa	1
Tuğba	4

CLUB AND MUSIC VENUE	
Jade Beach Club	5

WATERY FUN IN KUŞADASI

The main appeal of Kuşadası is that the sea is right next to it. Besides the posse of **beaches** that fringe the city, two huge **water parks** lie just to the north, and it's also possible to organize short **boat trips** around the bay.

BEACHES

Halk Plaj In the town centre itself, though not terribly appealing.

Yılancı Burnu The closest "real" beach to town, and quite a pleasing one too. It's within walking distance of the centre, though you'll have to navigate a small hill; failing that, jump on any minibus heading that way.

Ladies' Beach Kuşadası's most famous stretch of sand, 3km southwest of town, is a rather scrappy affair, but very popular in summer. Regular dolmuşes from town.

Paradise Beach One cove further along from Ladies' Beach, and accessible on the same minibuses, this is smaller and quieter with fewer bars.

Tusan Beach A nice, long stretch of hard-packed sand, 5km north of town, that's famed for its adjacent water parks (see p.248).

Pamucak Beach The best beach in the whole area, 15km north of town, and also easily accessible from Selçuk, though the sea can be rough on windy days. Regular minibuses from both Kuşadası and Selçuk.

BOAT TRIPS

A clutch of boats lies in wait just off Pigeon Island, their skippers eagerly drumming up custom in the morning, then again in the evening for the next day's venture. Most offer a similar itinerary, leaving at 9.30am, visiting three isolated beaches and returning by 4.30pm. The price hovers around ₺25 including lunch; chat with the skippers before you make your choice.

WATER PARKS

Both the large water parks off Tusan Beach run regular shuttle buses from Kuşadası, and are also accessible on Selçuk-bound minibuses. Both offer discounts for minors.

Adaland Off Tusan Beach ☎0256 618 1252, �🌐adaland.com. Packed with watery features, with loop slides and a "water coaster" as the most recent additions. Park entry costs ₺50, the dolphin section an extra ₺30 (₺200 extra if you want to swim with them), and it's ₺80 for the sea park, a fascinating aquarium in which you get to swim with the fishes. Daily 9am–dusk.

Aquafantasy Off Tusan Beach ☎0232 893 1111, �🌐aquafantasy.com. Also a hotel, this water park boasts a mind-boggling array of zany rides. Entry ₺50, ten percent discount for online bookings. Daily 9am–dusk.

can pick up minibuses to all nearby destinations, including Ephesus, the Milli Parkı and Söke, at the junction of Adnan Menderes and Candan Tahran buls, 600m southeast of the old town.

Destinations Aydın (hourly; 1hr 30min); Antalya (2 daily); 8hr); Bodrum (4 daily; 2hr); İstanbul (12 daily; 9hr); İzmir (every 30min; 2hr); Selçuk (every 20min; 30min).

By ferry Arriving by ferry from the Greek island of Sámos, you'll exit customs directly onto Liman Cad. Tickets to Sámos (1hr 30min) are available from any travel agent in town, with two alternative services: the Turkish boat (one-way €30, day-return €40, open return €55) leaves at 9am daily, and a Greek one (one-way €40, open return €60) at 5pm daily, bar Mon & Fri. For the Turkish boat, you have to buy tickets and register your passport the day before.

By car Car parks in the centre of town cost around ₺4 for up to three hours, ₺8 for the entire day.

Car rental Offices (including Avis and Europcar) cluster along İnönü and Atatürk buls; standard walk-in rates of around €60 a day can be bargained down to under €40 at slack times.

INFORMATION AND TOURS

Tourist office Liman Cad 13, opposite the ferry terminal (Mon–Fri 8am–12.30pm & 1.30–5pm; ☎0256 614 1103). They can offer maps and general advice, but can't book hotels.

Tours and travel agencies The *Sezgin* (see p.249) and several backpacker places offer day-tours to Ephesus, Pamukkale and combined trips to Didyma, Miletus and Priene, for around €35 per person. Recommended travel agents include Anker Travel, İsmet İnönü Bul 14 (☎0256 612 4598, �🌐ankertravel.com). Akdeniz Travel, Atatürk Bul 26, next to the Avis office, is good for plane tickets.

ACCOMMODATION

There are hotels and *pansiyons* all over Kuşadası, particularly along the seafront, but note that accommodation can get pricey in summer – if this bothers you, or pink-faced, beer-guzzling holiday-makers leave you cold, you might prefer Selçuk as a base from which to explore the fascinating hinterland. If you're set on Kuşadası, you should be able to find a room quite easily at all times of the year. The major out-of-town beach resorts are aimed squarely at package tourists, and not good value if you try to book independently.

Anzac Golden Bed Aslanlar Cad, Uğurlu Sok 1 ☎0256 614 8708, ⓦanzacgoldenbed.com. Signposted from Yıldırım Cad, this quiet, laidback *pansiyon* is nicely decorated with kilims and home furnishings, plus a well-used barbecue area. There are good views from the rooftop breakfast terrace. Book ahead. ₺95

Caravanserail Hotel Kale ☎0256 614 4115, ⓦkusadasihotelcaravanserail.com. Occupying much of the *Öküz Mehmet Paşa Kervansaray*, this show-stopper is built around an elegant courtyard-cum-restaurant. Rooms boast period furniture, parquet floors and lofty ceilings. ₺150

Cennet Pansiyon Yıldırım Cad 69 ☎0256 614 4893, ⓦcennetpension.com. A haven of peace with a garden containing 200-plus pot plants. Ably run for two decades by the kindly Ahmed, this *pansiyon* also boasts a sea-view roof terrace. ₺90

Efe Boutique Güvercinada Cad 37, ⓦefeboutique hotel.com. Among Kuşadası's more modern options, this attempt at a boutique hotel is a little rough around the edges, but not bad by any means – perhaps a good option for young couples. ₺250

★ **Liman Otel** Kıbrıs Cad, Buyral Sok 4 ☎0256 614 7770, ⓦlimanhotel.com. Exceptionally friendly service, fair-sized rooms with a/c and tiled bathrooms, in a small, modern building. Central but relatively calm; ask for a sea-facing room, or simply head on up to the rooftop bar-restaurant for the great view. ₺100

Sezgin Hotel Aslanlar Cad 68 ☎0256 614 4225, ⓦsezginhotel.com. This well-run backpacker favourite has a leafy garden, large pool, satellite TV, internet, basic double rooms and a wide range of other services including airport pick-up and discounts for the Turkish baths. ₺80

★ **Villa Konak** Yıldırım Cad 55 ☎0256 614 6318, ⓦvillakonakhotel.com. Lovely converted old house with delightful rambling gardens, thick with magnolia and citrus trees. The large, stylish bedrooms are decorated with antiques. Entertainment includes a sturdy old pool table and a hammock. ₺110

CAMPSITES

Önder Atatürk Bul 74 ☎0256 618 1590. Popular, tree-dappled place with good facilities, including tennis courts, kids' play park, swimming pool and restaurant. Open all year. Simple chalet-style double rooms also available. Camping ₺30 for two, doubles ₺60

Yat Kamping Atatürk Bul 76 ☎0256 618 1516. Just north of the similar *Önder* campsite, with tents for rent, a caravan area, a swimming pool, simple double rooms, a restaurant and laundry service. Camping ₺30 for two, doubles ₺60

EATING

Although the vast majority of **restaurants** in Kuşadası are indifferent, aimed squarely at the package holiday/cruise-liner crowd, authentic local cuisine can be found, and usually at cheaper prices. Almost all places are licensed. A fair few **cafés** strung along the promenade serve juice, coffee and desserts by day, then cocktails at night. Lastly, be sure to try the **mussels**, stuffed with rice and with a squeeze of lemon juice, sold by hawkers along the seafront – large ones cost ₺1 each, the runts ₺0.50.

Avlu Cephane Sok 15a. You'll do no better for traditional Turkish food than this ever-popular place with rear-courtyard seating. It serves low-priced grilled lamb, as well as steam-tray specialities for around ₺5. Daily 8am–midnight.

Castle Kaleiçi Camikebir Mahallesi Tuna Sok 35. A touch touristy, but a divine location underneath a leafy trellis in the middle of the Kale. The seemingly endless menu is strong on soups and meats, with a long list of beers, wines and *rakı* to accompany. Daily 9am–1am.

Kazım Usta Overlooking customs port. Seafood restaurant where you can make sure your meal is fresh – they'll happily cook up anything that you buy at the small fish market a stone's throw away. Sit and wait for it, or anything off the menu (whole fish ₺20–80), overlooking the harbour, supping rakı. Daily 8am–1am.

Keremağa Barbaros H Bul. In the middle of the main pedestrian drag, and selling sumptuous ice cream for ₺1 a scoop. Try the *karadut* (black mulberry). Daily 8am–late.

Komagene İsmet İnönü Bul 8. If you've never tried *çiğ köfte* before, this is your chance – ₺3 for a large wrap filled with fresh greens and a delicious spicy paste, a perfect summertime snack. Daily 8am–late.

Planet Yucca Sağlik Sok 65. A planet with five nations – Turkish, Chinese, Italian, Mexican and Indian food; for local food you're best off going elsewhere, but the others are all

VILLAGE FOOD IN CHERRY VALLEY

One of the Aegean's most interesting restaurants lies just a short drive from Kuşadası, beautifully set amid the orchards in the village of **Kirazlı Köy** in "Cherry Valley", and readily accessible by minibus from Kuşadası. While it remains all but unknown to foreign travellers, it has become hugely popular with Turkish visitors.

Riding the crest of the home-cooking wave that's washing over western Turkey, **Köy Sofrası** translates as "village feast", and that's exactly what you'll find if you make your way out here. Diners are treated to round after round of superb food, using the freshest ingredients from the surrounding countryside. This is the Aegean, so a mixed meze plate will best showcase the area's wonderful herbs, pulses and veggies; otherwise the breakfasts are phenomenal, if you can get here early enough in the morning.

surprisingly well done. It's highly popular with visiting cruise groups, though that doesn't detract from the quality of the food. There's usually a bit of live music – and a lot of drink – in the evenings. Daily 8am–2am.

Tuğba İsmet İnönü Bul 24a. Not a restaurant, but the city's best shop for Turkish delight and other sweeties. Cheery staff won't mind giving you a few samples of their delectable tidbits. Daily 8am–late.

DRINKING AND NIGHTLIFE

After-dark activity in Kuşadası is distributed over dozens of **bars**, which can be clumped into distinct groups: the arty, genteel bars of the Kale district; their more energetic neighbours, featuring live music that may be sung in either Turkish or English; and Irish/British pubs that come complete with karaoke gear and house music. The latter proliferate along **Barlar Sokak** ("Bar Street"), a side street where the list of establishments reads like an Irish phonebook. As well as bars full of cheap booze and pelvic-thrusting westerners, you'll find snack-shacks doling out English-style kebabs... and, somewhat worryingly perhaps, a fair few tattoo parlours.

Another Bar Tuna Sok 10. You've got to give them credit for the name, but in reality this is actually a cut above the rest of its ilk, set around a large palm tree and with happy hours that seem to last all night. Daily noon–late.

Jade Beach Club Yılancı Burnu. Just out of town on the beach of the same name (see p.247), this gigantic complex offers plenty to enjoy – a swimming pool, volleyball nets,

tune-spinning DJs and beachside deckchairs are all lined up for your pleasure. Daily 3pm–late.

Jimmy's Irish Bar Barlar Sok 8. The most raucous (usually) of a glut of bars on Bar Street. If it's quiet, expect the bar staff to start a line-dance in the hope that others will join in. Also the place to head if you've a burning desire to watch your football team in action. Daily 2pm–late.

DIRECTORY

Books English-language newspapers and magazines – including the likes of *OK!*, the *Mirror* and the *Daily Mail* – can be found around town. Eser Kitabevi off Hacivat Sok sells secondhand books.

Hamams Kale Hamamı, behind the Kale Camii, is very touristy, Belediye Hamam on Yıldırım Cad slightly less so. Both open daily 9am–8pm and cost ₺25.

Hospital The state hospital is at Atatürk Bul 32 (☏0256 613 1616), near the park; the new all-private Universal Hospital Kuşadası is on İstiklâl Cad.

Laundry Öven Laundry, Yıldırım Cad 29 opposite the Belediye Hamam.

Post office Barbaros Hayrettin Bul (Mon–Sat 8am–5pm).

WHEN IN TURKEY... HANGOVER CURES, LOCAL STYLE

As westerners around the world can tell you, at the end of a night on the booze the best way to say sorry to your body is by throwing a kebab into it. A handy Turkish (and, of course, Greek) cure to an international malady, but what do Turks themselves do? One answer is **işkembe çorba**, a soup made with cow offal, often with a dash of lemon juice to cut straight through the offending alcohol. Its success as a hangover remedy may be behind the fact that, for many Turks, it's the first meal of the year, consumed just after midnight on New Year's Day. A few soup kitchens around the back of the Hanım Camii sell *işkembe çorba*; some stay open all night long.

Dilek National Park

28km south of Kuşadası • Spring & autumn daily 7am–5pm; summer daily 8am–6.30pm; winter closed • ₺5, cars ₺10 • Served by minibuses from Kuşadası – signed for the Milli Parkı, and continuing as far as Karasu beach (every 30min; 45min; ₺7) – and Söke

Looming from the sea like a giant crocodile, the imposing outline of **Samsun Dağı** dominates the skyline south of Kuşadası. It's the central feature of **Dilek National Park** (Dilek Yarımadası Milli Parkı), a peninsular tract set aside in 1966 for, among other reasons, the protection of its thick forest and diverse **fauna**, said to include rare lynx, jackal and wild cats. However, you're unlikely to see any of those species, as much of the 28,000-acre park is an off-limits military zone; indeed, most visitors go no further than the pleasant **beaches** on the north side of the peninsula. The park has no facilities for overnight stays, but the village of **Güzelçamlı**, 1km from its main entrance, holds several **pansiyons**, including the wonderfully named *Moustache Pansiyon*.

The beaches

The most visited portion of the unrestricted zone of Dilek National Park consists of a 10km stretch of mostly paved road beyond the entrance and four good, but often windswept, beaches along it. Just beyond the gate, **İçmeler** is a popular hard-sand beach shaded by plane trees. Next come the pebble beaches of **Aydınlık** and **Kavaklı**, but it's best to continue to the last and prettiest one, **Karasu**, where the minibuses stop. This 700m-long stretch of gravel is perfect for swimming; stand in the sea for long enough and fish will nibble at your toes. Each beach has its own small snack bar or drinks kiosk operating in high season, as well as toilets, barbecue areas and a small café.

The cave of Zeus

A short walk back down the road from the park entrance, the **Cave of Zeus** is a water-filled grotto in which it's possible to swim in summer (though the water is still freezing cold). Though beautiful, the cave is highly popular with local visitors and often fills with cigarette smoke.

The summit ridge

The best access to the **summit ridge** east of 1237m Samsun Dağı is via a trail from **ESKİDOĞANBEY**, a village to the south. It's an all-day outing, best done in spring or autumn to avoid the heat. Chances of spotting wildlife, particularly badgers, jackals and birds of prey, are higher here than within the confines of the national park on the other side of the mountain. Since the closure of most short-term accommodation in Eskidoğanbey, walkers tend to take an early dolmuş to one or other of the trailheads, hike over the mountain, and take an evening dolmuş back to Söke or Kuşadası from the walk's end point.

Priene

The ancient Greek city of **Priene** represents the best-preserved Hellenistic townscape in Ionia, without any of the usual Roman or Byzantine additions. It also occupies perhaps the finest location of any such city. Perched on a series of pine terraces graded into the south flank of Samsun Dağı, this compact but exquisite site enjoys a situation to bear comparison with that of Delphi in Greece. Despite all this, and the fact that it's just 35km south of Kuşadası, Priene remains far less visited than Ephesus – even in summer, you'll largely have this wonderful place to yourself.

Brief history

The original settlement of Priene lay elsewhere in the Meander basin. Following the receding shoreline, however – now just visible to the west – its inhabitants re-founded

VISITING PRIENE, MILETUS AND DIDYMA

The absorbing ruins of **Priene**, **Miletus** and **Didyma** can all be visited on public transport. Infrequent minibuses head to all three from the town of **Söke**, itself very well connected to other parts of western Turkey.

Most visitors, however, find it far easier to take a **tour**, which is the only realistic option if you want to see all three sites in a single day. Travel agencies in Selçuk (see p.238) or Kuşadası (see p.246) will be happy to arrange these; in general, a seat on a group **minibus** will cost ₺70–100 from either.

If you're in a small group, chartering a **taxi** for the day can actually work out cheaper, at around €80–100 for the vehicle from either Selçuk or Kuşadası.

the city on its present site during the fourth century BC, just in time for **Alexander** to stop in and finance the cost of the principal temple of Athena. However, the city enjoyed little patronage from Roman or Byzantine emperors – which, of course, adds to its modern-day appeal.

The site

Daily: summer 9am–7pm; winter 9am–5.30pm • ₺5

Visitors to Priene who are dropped by dolmuş at the western edge of the strung-out village of **Güllübahçe** face an uphill walk to the site ticket office, and then another good steep walk up the hill to the northeast gate into the city itself. Beyond that, the ruins are strewn over a wide area, and all major points of interest have English-language information boards.

The town was set up along a grid pattern made up of various *insulae* (rectangular units), each measuring roughly 42m by 35m. Within each rectangle stood four private dwellings; a public building had its own *insula*, sometimes two.

The bouleuterion and around
Take the uphill path from the ticket office and the first civic monument you're likely to come across is the square **bouleuterion**, a former council chamber that's more or less in the centre of the site. The most intact such monument in Turkey, it consists of seats on three sides enclosing the speakers' area, together with a sacrificial altar. Beside the bouleuterion lie the scantier remains of the **prytaneion**, or town administration offices, with traces of a dining area for the highest municipal officials.

The sacred stoa, agora and Temple of Zeus
On the terrace immediately below the bouleuterion, the **sacred stoa** was originally graced by outer and inner series of Doric and Ionic columns. One step further down and you'll find the **agora** and the **Temple of Zeus** (still known as such, though it's actually the sanctuary of Asclepios, the god of healing). Little is left of these, but the commanding views suggest that this was the heart of public life in the city.

The gymnasium and stadium
Clearly visible below the Temple of Zeus, reached by way of a stairway from the agora, are the **gymnasium** and **stadium**, with nearby **bathing basins**, complete with gutters and lion-head spouts, for use after athletics. On the west side of the stadium there are a few sets of **starting blocks** for foot races; spectators watched from the north side of the 190m-by-20m area, where some seats are still discernible.

The residential district
Priene's densest surviving **residential district** lies west of the central street, down a gentle slope. Its thick walls stand up to 1.5m in some places. Just west are the remains of what was once a **fish and meat market**. West again, the city's **west gate** marks the end of the main street; a wonderful walking trail lies beyond.

Temple of Athena Polias
The most conspicuous monument in Priene, the **Temple of Athena Polias**, stands two terraces above the main residential street, its fallen columns strewn around like gigantic cogs. The temple took more than two centuries to complete and, in its time, was considered the epitome of Ionic perfection; a manual written by its designer Pytheos was still considered standard reading in Roman times.

The theatre and the Byzantine basilica
Priene's old **theatre** remains in an excellent state of preservation, its layout and seating (for five thousand, the entire population) unchanged from the Hellenistic original. Most prominent are five larger-than-average marble thrones for the municipal dignitaries. The stage buildings were extensively modified during the second century AD – virtually the only Roman tampering with Priene's public buildings. Just behind them are the remains of a **Byzantine basilica**, its entrance and columns clearly visible.

The acropolis
If you're keen on scrambling and the weather is not too hot, take the path beginning above the theatre to the **acropolis**; allow an extra hour and a half for the round trip.

ACCOMMODATION AND EATING
PRIENE

Priene Pansiyon 📞 0256 547 1725. Just a hop, skip and jump from the dolmuş rank – follow the signs – this charming *pansiyon* has friendly ownership and a swimming pool. It offers reasonable en-suite rooms, as well as camping space. ₺**70**

Vila Sultan Immediately adjacent to the dolmuş rank. The easiest and best place to eat, serving up *köfte*, kebabs and sandwiches at shady tables near a small fountain. Daily 8am–7pm.

Miletus

Daily: summer 8.30am–7pm; winter 8.30am–5.30pm • ₺5

Perched on an eminently defendable promontory, the ancient city of **Miletus** (Milet in Turkish) once outshone Priene. However, its modern setting, marooned in the seasonal marshes of the Büyük Menderes, leaves little to bear witness to the town's long and colourful past, although the massive theatre, visible from afar, testifies to its former glories. Up close, the site is a confusing juxtaposition of widely scattered relics from different eras, often disguised by weeds, mud or water, depending on the season. Note that following the theft of various artefacts, the **museum**, 1km south of the main ticket booth, is no longer open; ask about the current situation when you buy your ticket.

Brief history

Miletus is at least as old as Ephesus and far older than Priene; German archeologists have uncovered remnants of a **Creto-Mycenaean** settlement from the sixteenth century BC. **Ionian** invaders made their first appearance during the eleventh century, and by the seventh century BC Miletus was in the first flush of a heyday that lasted more than two hundred years.

While not strong enough completely to avoid Persian domination, Miletus did manage to secure favourable terms as an equal, and even took the opportunity to appropriate the nearby oracle of Didyma. But with Athenian instigation, the city was unwisely persuaded to take command of the abortive **Ionian revolt** against the Persians between 500 and 494 BC, which led to large-scale destruction. Within fifty years Miletus was rebuilt some way northeast of its original site, but it was never again as great – or as independent. **Alexander** saw fit to "liberate" the city from a new, short-lived occupation by the Persians and their allies. Later it was bequeathed to the **Romans**, under whose rule it enjoyed a brief renaissance – most of what you see today is a legacy of various emperors' largesse. The Byzantine town stubbornly clung to life, producing Isidorus, architect of İstanbul's Aya Sofya. In the ninth century Miletus was already dwindling, and by the time the Menteşe emirs, and then the Ottomans, took control, there was little left to prize.

The theatre

Miletus' most obvious attraction lies just behind the site entrance: a **theatre**, whose Hellenistic base was modified and enlarged during the second century AD to hold fifteen thousand spectators. A stone block on the orchestra floor bears two griffins carved in relief, while the centre front row sports two pillars that once supported the emperor's canopy. Further up, the vaulted exit passageways are enormous and virtually intact.

An eighth-century **Byzantine castle** and some contemporaneous ramparts surmount the theatre, giving a marvellous 360-degree view over the flood plain, as well as the site itself.

Around the old bay

Though the waters have long since retreated, the old "Lion Bay" is one of the best sections of the site in which to get your bearings. It was so called for the two **stone lions** that guarded the entrance, now mostly embedded into the marsh silt. Easier to spot is a round base marking the remains of the **naval monument**, commemorating an unknown victory of the first century BC.

The Sacred Way

In its time, the handsomely paved **Sacred Way** linked Miletus with Didyma. Standing at its north end is the sixth-century **Delphinion**, dedicated to Apollo Delphinius, patron of sailors, ships and ports. Not surprisingly in such a maritime community, this was the most important religious establishment in town, and you'll still be able to see the foundations of altars or semicircular benches, and the enclosing colonnade. On the same side of the pavement as you walk south stands a first-century AD **Ionic stoa**, which partly shields the enormous **Capito baths** and a **gymnasium** of the same era.

The most satisfying monument east of the Sacred Way is the **nymphaeum**, the largest public fountain of Miletus, once extremely ornate but now standing at barely half its original height. Just to the south are the ruins of a sixth-century **Byzantine church**, while the Roman **Baths of Faustina** (Marcus Aurelius's wife), west of here at the foot of the theatre hill, are distinctive for their good state of repair.

Didyma: the sanctuary of Apollo

Jutting incongruously from a dry, dusty, suburban area just north of **Altınkum** beach, the ancient Ionian sanctuary of **Didyma** (Didim in Turkish) is a real treat. Though half-ruined, its oracular **sanctuary of Apollo** rarely fails to impress, even when besieged by the tour groups that rock up throughout the day. The best time to visit is late afternoon or early evening, when the site is relatively calm, and its masonry glows in the sunset.

Brief history

While an oracle and shrine of some sort apparently existed at Didyma long before Ionian settlers arrived in the eleventh century BC – the name itself is an ancient Anatolian word – the imported **cult of Apollo** quickly appropriated whatever previous oracle, centred on a sacred well and laurel tree, had worked here. Didyma remained a sacred precinct, under the jurisdiction of a clan of priests originally from Delphi, and was never a town as such, though it eventually became a dependency of nearby Miletus. Every four years the sanctuary was also the venue for the Didymeia, a festival of music and drama as well as athletics.

CONSULTING THE ORACLE OF APOLLO

Pilgrims visiting the sanctuary of Apollo would first **purify** themselves at a well below the resting place of the Medusa head, then approach the still-prominent circular **altar** to offer a sacrifice before proceeding to the steps of the **shrine** itself. As at Delphi, prophecies were formulated by proxy – suppliants would first deliver their queries to the priest of Apollo, who would disappear to consult the **priestess**, who (accounts disagree) either drank from, bathed in, or inhaled potent vapours from, the waters. Her subsequent ravings were rephrased more delicately to those waiting out front; the priest would reappear after a suitable interval on a terrace some 2m higher to deliver the oracular pronouncement. Questions ranged from the personal to matters of state; prophecies were recorded and stored for posterity.

The archaic shrine, started during the eighth century BC, was finished within two hundred years. Though similar in design to the current structure, it was half the size. After their defeat of the Ionian revolt in 494 BC, the **Persians** destroyed this first temple and plundered its treasures, including the cult statue of Apollo. The oracle puttered along until Alexander appeared on the scene, when the cult statue was retrieved from Persia and a new temple (the one existing today) commissioned.

Despite continuing subsidy from the **Romans**, work continued at a snail's pace for more than five centuries and the building was never actually completed – not entirely surprising when you consider the formidable engineering problems it presented.

In the end Christianity put paid to the oracle, and when the edict of Theodosius in 385 AD proscribed all pagan practices, construction ceased for good, after which a medieval earthquake toppled most of the columns. At its zenith Didyma was approached not only from Miletus but also from Panormos, a cove 6km west, via a sacred way whose final stretches were lined with statuary. Neither pavement nor statues are visible today; the latter were spirited away to the British Museum in 1858.

The site
Daily 8.30am–6.30pm • ₺5

Didyma's best-known feature is the **Medusa head** that lies at the foot of the steps as you enter the site. Fallen from a Roman-era architrave, it's now the unofficial logo of the place, repeated ad infinitum on posters and cards all over Turkey.

Even in ruins, the **shrine** itself, which stands beyond the nearby **circular altar**, is still intimidatingly large. The surviving column stumps alone are considerably taller than a man, and in its nearly complete state it must have inspired reverence. The effect was accentuated by its position on a steep, stepped base and enclosure in a virtual forest of 108 Ionic **columns** – only three of which now stand to their original height. The remaining twelve stumps supported the roof of the entry porch, reached by a steep flight of steps, where suppliants would deliver their queries to the priest of Apollo (see box, p.256).

Only traces remain of the miniature shrine that formerly enclosed the cult statue of Apollo, his sacred laurel and the **sacred well**, but the well itself is still obvious.

Altınkum
5km south of Didyma

Many visitors combine a visit to the ruins at Didyma with hitting the nearby beach at **Altınkum** (not to be confused with the resort of the same name near İzmir). A gently sloping beach with no surf, it's ideal for children, although the packed-out sand and large British package presence means it's definitely not for everyone.

ARRIVAL AND DEPARTURE   DIDYMA

By bus or dolmuş Services between Söke and Altınkum beach run almost directly past the ruins. These are located in Didim village, the modern name for Didyma, though confusingly the whole beach resort is often referred to as Didim too – ask to get off at Didim Köyü. To head back out to Söke or Bodrum, there's no need to make the 2km trek into Altınkum (there are regular dolmuşes, or it's a 50min walk); simply wait in the car park where you were dropped off.

By ferry Ferries head to the Greek island of Kós (1hr) on Wed & Sat, June–Sept; the journey costs €40 one way or day return.

ACCOMMODATION AND EATING

Although there are a few **guesthouses** near the ruins, for actual hotels it's best to head for the beach at nearby Altınkum. The **restaurants** around the ruins are overpriced and serve poor food, so if you're staying the night, the beach is also the best place to eat, with umpteen places serving *pide*, kebabs, English breakfast and even Chinese food. Prices escalate the closer you approach the sand.

Medusa House Overlooking Didyma ☎0256 811 0063, ⓦ medusahouse.com. The best of the limited accommodation near Didyma, this comfortable, characterful place, run by a German–Turkish couple, features rustic rooms in a restored old building with a lovely rambling garden. ₺85

The southern Aegean

South of the main Ionian sites the southern Aegean begins with reminders of another ancient civilization, the **Carians**, a purportedly barbarous people indigenous to the area (a rarity in Anatolia) who spoke a language distantly related to Greek. **Bafa Gölü** (or Lake Bafa) and ancient **Heracleia ad Latmos** on its northeast shore make a suitably dramatic introduction to this once isolated and mysterious region. From the nearest substantial town, **Milas**, the ancient sites of **Euromos**, **Labranda** and **Iassos** provide tempting excursions.

South of Milas, on the Gulf of Gökova, **Ören** is a rare treat: an attractive coastal resort not yet steamrollered by tourism. Most visitors bypass Ören in favour of **Bodrum** and its peninsula, very much the big event on this coast. While the tentacles of development creep over the surrounding land, in places what first attracted outsiders to the area still shines through on occasion.

Further south, **Marmaris** is another big – and rather overblown – resort, from which the **Loryma (Hisarönü) peninsula** beyond, bereft of a sandy shoreline but blessed with magnificent scenery, offers the closest escape. As a compromise, **Datça** and its surroundings might fit the bill, with remote beaches nearby more rewarding than the much-touted ruins of ancient **Knidos**.

Bafa Gölü

Surrounded by jagged mountains and more than 100 sq km in size, Lake Bafa – in Turkish, **Bafa Gölü** – is an entrancing spectacle. Created when silt sealed off the Büyük Menderes River's passage to the sea, it's now most famed as the site of **Heracleia ad Latmos**, a spectacularly located set of lakeside ruins.

As for Bafa itself, the water is faintly brackish and fish species include *levrek* (bass), *kefal* (grey mullet), *yayın* (catfish) and *yılan balığı* (eel). Although levels are depleting, stocks are still high enough to support the arrival throughout the year of more than two hundred species of migratory wildfowl, including the endangered **crested pelican**, of which there are believed to be fewer than two thousand left in the world.

Heracleia ad Latmos

Look across Lake Bafa from its southern shore and you'll spy a patch of irregular shoreline, and the modern village of **Kapıkırı**, whose lights twinkle at the base of **Mount Latmos** by night. Strewn higgledy-piggledy around the village are the ruins of **Heracleia ad Latmos** (Heraklia in Turkish), one of the most evocatively situated ancient cities in all Turkey.

ENDYMION: DEMIGOD OF THE WET DREAM

Heracleia owes its fame, and an enduring hold on the romantic imagination, to a legend associated not with the town itself but with **Mount Latmos** behind. **Endymion** was a handsome shepherd who, while asleep in a cave on the mountain, was noticed by Selene, the moon goddess. She made love with him as he slept, and in time, so the story goes, bore Endymion fifty daughters without their sire ever waking. Endymion was reluctant for all this to stop and begged Zeus, who was also fond of him, to be allowed to dream forever; his wish was granted and, as a character in Mary Lee Settle's *Blood Ties* flippantly observed, thus became the only known demigod of the wet dream.

A settlement of **Carian** origin had existed here long before the arrival of the **Ionians**, though Latmos – as it was then known – had far better geographical communication with Ionia than with the rest of Caria. Late in the Hellenistic period the city's location was moved a kilometre or so west, and the name changed to Heracleia, but despite its numerous monuments and enormous wall it was never a place of great importance. Miletus, at the head of the gulf, monopolized most trade and already the inlet was starting to close up.

The site

Only the retaining wall and some rows of benches survive of the second-century BC **bouleuterion** that lies 100m east of the first parking area. The **Roman baths** visible in the valley below, and a crumbled but appealing **Roman theatre** off in the olives beyond, can be reached via an unmarked trail starting between the first and second parking areas. The path up to the **hermits' caves** on Mount Latmos begins at the rear of the second parking area; stout boots are advisable. Similar cautions apply for those who want to trace the course of the **Hellenistic walls**, the city's most imposing and conspicuous relics, supposedly built by Lysimachus in the late third century BC.

The restaurant of the *Agora Pansiyon* (see p.259) looks south over the **Hellenistic agora**, now an open, grassy square; the downhill side of its south edge stands intact to two storeys, complete with windows. The grounds offer a fine view west over the lake and assorted castle-crowned promontories. A box-like Hellenistic **Temple of Athena** perches on a hill west of the agora; less conspicuous is an inscription to Athena, left of the entrance.

From the agora a wide, walled-in path descends toward the shore and Heracleia's final quota of recognizable monuments. Most obvious is the peninsula – or, in wet years, island – studded with **Byzantine walls** and a **church**. A stone causeway half-buried in the beach here allowed entrance in (drier) medieval times. Follow the shore southwest, and across the way you should be able to spot the tentatively identified Hellenistic **Sanctuary of Endymion**, oriented unusually northeast to southwest. Five column stumps front the structure, which has a rounded rear wall – a ready-made apse for later Christians – with sections of rock incorporated into the masonry.

ARRIVAL AND DEPARTURE

BAFA GÖLÜ

By bus Frequent buses along the southern shore make the lake easy to see. If you'd like to get off, Söke–Milas dolmuşes (every 30min) are more flexible than the big coaches in terms of stopping. Getting to Kapıkırı and the ruins is the hard bit; if you have your own wheels, take a north turn at Çamiçi village, from where it's a juddering 8km. If you're on foot, you may find a taxi, but it's best to arrange pick-up with one of the hotels listed on p.259.

ACCOMMODATION

At the time of writing, the highway lining the **southern shore** of Bafa was being widened, and the whole stretch was a bit of a mess. Its slew of guesthouses and fish restaurants will surely return, but in any case basing yourself in the village of **Kapıkırı** provides a far more relaxing stay.

THE SOUTHERN SHORE

Club Natura Oliva ☎0252 519 1073, ⓦclubnatura .com. This German-owned establishment has thirty large, albeit undeniably somewhat spartan rooms, spread through nine houses, all of which have lake-view balconies. The associated restaurant serves a very broad range of dishes (all of them doused in their own home-pressed olive oil), and guided hikes of the local area are also offered. ₺110

KAPIKIRI

Agora Pansiyon ☎0252 543 5445, ⓦagorapansiyon .com. Doubles, bungalows and a rooftop restaurant, around an organic garden: they also organize boat trips, and guided hikes to cave paintings. Half-board obligatory. ₺225

★ **Karia Pansiyon** ☎0252 543 5490, ⓦkariapension .com. Smart guesthouse with a fern-filled garden, splendidly rustic rooms and superlative lake views from the roof. The food's simply wonderful, too. Half-board obligatory. ₺150

Milas and around

A small, initially nondescript town of some 35,000 people, **MİLAS** – or **Mylasa**, as it was formerly known – was an important **Carian** centre (its original location was at the nearby hill of Peçin Kale; see p.259). Few foreigners stay the night, but there are a few sights of interest here, and plenty within day-trip distance – the fantastic castle of **Peçin Kale**, the Carian ruins of **Euromos** and **Labranda**, and the beach resort of **Ören**.

Milas's lively tradesmen's **bazaar** covers the western slopes of Hisarbaşı hill, which has been the focus of settlement in every era. Once past the warren of alleys perpendicular to the main street, Cumhuriyet Caddesi, veer up to the summit and the late Ottoman **Belen Camii**. Immediately to its right stands the eighteenth-century **Çöllühanı**, one of the last semi-functioning, unrestored *kervansaray*s in western Turkey.

West of town, along Kadıağa Caddesi, an elaborate early Roman tomb known as the **Gümüşkesen** (literally "cuts-silver") lies in a slight depression south of Hıdırlık hill. This landscaped site is the most impressive relic of ancient Mylasa.

Peçin Kale

5km east of Milas · **Castle** Mon–Wed & Fri–Sun 8.30am–5.30pm · ₺3 · Take any Ören-bound dolmuş (every 45min)

Ancient Mylasa originally stood atop the hill of **Peçin Kale** (*Beçin Kale* in local dialect and signposting). Mylasa's shift to its current position during the fourth century BC means that the hill is actually more interesting for its **castle**, an unmistakable fortified bluff, originally Byzantine but adapted by the Menteşe emirs during the fourteenth century.

Clearly marked 400m south of the castle, the main Menteşe buildings include the unusual two-storey **Kızıl Han**, and the fourteenth-century **Orhan Bey Camii**. Bearing right takes you to the **medrese and türbe of Ahmet Gazi**, from the same era – tombs of a Menteşe governor and his wife that are venerated as those of minor Islamic saints, with coloured rags and candles.

Labranda

15km north of Milas · Daily 8.30am–5.30pm · ₺8 · Only accessible with your own vehicle, or by taxi (₺40 including waiting time)

While it's a bit of a haul to the isolated ruins of **Labranda**, they're a real treat for ancient-history enthusiasts. Set into a steep, pine-lined hillside, the **sanctuary of Zeus** is arguably the most beautifully located, and least visited, archeological zone of ancient Caria.

Euromos

200m from the highway, 12km northwest of Milas and 1km from Selimiye village · Daily 8.30am–5.30pm · ₺8 · Accessible on any Selimiye dolmuş or Milas–Söke bus

The impressive Carian ruins of **Euromos** boast a **Corinthian Temple of Zeus**, supposedly requisitioned by Hadrian. Only a few columns remain standing, and it's thought that the structure was never completed.

4

Iassos

15km west of Milas • Mon, Tues & Thurs–Sun, hours vary • ₺4• Served by hourly dolmuş

Set on a headland almost completely surrounded by the Gulf of Asim, ancient **Iassos** certainly has a dramatic location. Its ruins, however, dating mostly from the Roman Imperial period of the second century AD, are only mildly diverting. The real reason to come here is the delicious **seafood** caught nearby and served in the restaurants of the modern village of **Kıyıkızlacık**; *çipura* (gilthead bream) is the local speciality.

On entering Kıyıkızlacık, you first pass a Roman mausoleum, arguably more interesting than anything within the city walls and now in service as the site **museum**. Inside, the star exhibit is a Corinthian temple-tomb resting on a stepped platform.

The main highlights of the site itself are the well-preserved Roman **bouleuterion**, with four rows of seats, and a Roman **villa** with murals and mosaics. The meagre hillside **theatre**, of which only the cavea walls and stumps of the stage building remain, offers fine views over the northeast harbour. The hilltop **castle** was a medieval foundation of the Knights of St John, and after the Turkish conquest the place was known as Asimkalesi (Asim's Castle), Asim being a local *ağa* (feudal lord).

Ören

45km south of Milas • Dolmuşes from Milas (1hr) pass through the upper village then drop off at the beach

ÖREN is an endangered Turkish species – a coastal resort that's not completely overdeveloped. One of the few sizeable villages on the north coast of the Gulf of Gökova, it owes its pre-tourism history to the narrow, fertile, alluvial plain adjacent, and the lignite deposits in the mountains behind.

The **upper village**, an appealingly homogeneous settlement on the east bank of a canyon mouth exiting the hills, is scattered among the ruins of **ancient Keramos**. You can easily make out sections of wall, arches and a boat slip, dating from when the sea (now 1km distant) lapped the edge of town. The resort area down on the coast holds little in the way of relics, save for sections of column carted off from the main site by *pansiyon* owners for use as decoration. The **beach** is a more than acceptable kilometre of coarse sand, gravel and pebbles, backed by handsome pine-tufted cliffs; in clear weather you can spy the Datça peninsula opposite. A working harbour once stood at the east end of town, but what's left of the jetty now serves a few fishing boats and the occasional wandering yacht.

ARRIVAL AND DEPARTURE   MİLAS AND AROUND

By plane The Havaş bus to Milas–Bodrum airport stops at the roundabout at the end of Atatürk Bulvarı, and is geared to the times of THY internal flights.

By bus or dolmuş Milas's *otogar* is way out on the northern edge of town. You'll be left here unless you've come from Iassos or Ören, whose dolmuşes use a small terminal close to the town centre. To get into the centre from the *otogar*, take either a cab, a dolmuş marked "Şehir İçi" or the complimentary shuttle run by the big companies.

ACTIVITIES

Paragliding In the morning and late afternoon there are great thermals on the coast near Ören. The 640m-high Mount Koçatepe, looming above, makes an ideal jump-off point. Trips can be organized through the *Alnata* (see p.260).

ACCOMMODATION AND EATING

MİLAS

Sürücü Otel Atatürk Bul, opposite the Atatürk statue ☎0252 512 4001. A few hundred metres south of the centre, but surprisingly large and also good value, if a little lacking in character; students from the nearby university frequent its restaurant and café. ₺85

Yazar Otel Kadıağa Cad 50, close to the bazaar and Halk bank ☎0252 512 4203. The only central, savoury budget accommodation, sporting comfortable rooms with TV and minibar. They put on good buffet breakfasts, and there are also plenty of places to eat on the road outside. ₺50

ÖREN

Hotel Alnata Western edge of the beach ☎0252 532 2813, ⊛alnata.com.tr. The best mid-range option on this stretch of coast, with large, stylish rooms, a garden and pool. ₺120

Kerme Down on the shore ⓣ 0252 532 2065. With a rudimentary campsite, simple wooden cottages and attached seafood and kebab restaurant, this is a good choice. ₺120

Bodrum

It's fair to say that the coastal resort of **BODRUM** has a certain reputation. To many travellers, the very name conjures up images of drunken debauchery, full English breakfasts, and belly-out Europeans turning slowly pink on a Mediterranean beach. While there's an element of truth to that stereotype, the reality is somewhat different – with its low-rise whitewashed houses and subtropical gardens, Bodrum is the most attractive of the major Aegean resorts, given a more cosmopolitan air by the increasing number of Turkish visitors.

Bodrum is neatly divided into two contrasting halves by its castle, and a largely pedestrianized **bazaar** area that sits immediately to its north. To the west is the more genteel area that surrounds a spruced-up yacht marina, with its upmarket hotels and restaurants, while to the east the town's party zone holds its highest concentration of bars and restaurants. The eastern zone also features a thin, scrubby strip of beach, packed with sunbathers during the day and shoreside diners in the evening.

Lastly, mention must also be made of the delightful **peninsula** that Bodrum calls home; a tranquil and highly characterful place with beaches galore, it has recently become immensely popular with moneyed locals.

Brief history

Originally known as **Halikarnassos**, Bodrum was colonized by Dorians from the Peloponnese during the eleventh century BC. They mingled with the existing Carian population, settling on the small island of Zephysia, which later became a peninsula and the location of the medieval castle. During the fifth century BC, **Halikarnassos**' most famous son **Herodotus** chronicled the city's fortunes in his acclaimed *Histories*.

Mausolus (377–353 BC), leader of the **Hecatomnid satraps** dynasty, increased the power and wealth of what had already become a semi-independent principality. An admirer of Greek civilization, Mausolus spared no effort to Hellenize his cities, and was working on a suitably self-aggrandizing tomb at the time of his death – thereby giving us the word "mausoleum". **Artemisia II**, his sister and wife, completed the massive structure, which came to be regarded as one of the Seven Wonders of the Ancient World. She distinguished herself in warfare, inflicting a humiliating defeat on the Rhodians, who were tricked into allowing her entire fleet into their port.

After a period of little importance under the Roman and Byzantine empires, and brief shuffling among Selçuk, Menteşe and Ottoman occupiers, the **Knights of St John** slipped over from Rhodes in 1402 and erected the castle that is now Bodrum's most prominent landmark – indeed, the name *bodrum*, meaning "cellar" or "dungeon" in Turkish, probably pays tribute to the stronghold's subterranean defences.

The Castle of St Peter

Tues–Sun 8.30am–6.30pm • ₺10, plus additional fees for certain sections

Bodrum's main landmark, the **Castle of St Peter**, is now home to the excellent **Museum of Underwater Archeology**, with its array of towers, courtyards and dungeons, as well as separate museums displaying underwater finds from various wrecks.

The castle was built by the Knights of St John in 1406, over a small Selçuk fortress. Urgently needing to replace the fortress at Smyrna destroyed by the Mongols, the Knights engaged the era's finest military engineers to construct their new stronghold. More walls and moats were added over succeeding decades, along with water cisterns to guarantee self-sufficiency in the event of siege. The finishing touches had just been

4

BODRUM

ACCOMMODATION

Aegean Gate	9
Bodrum Backpackers	6
Bodrum Blu	5
Gözen Butik	7
Mars	1
Menekşe	4
Merhaba	8
Su	2
Yenilmez	3

BARS AND CAFÉS

Ebou	2
Red Lion	5
Shadow	1

CLUBS

Club Catamaran	3
Hadi Gari	4
Halikarnas	6

RESTAURANTS

Ceylan	5
Marina Köftecisi	1
Marina Yacht Club	3
Orfoz	7
Otantik Ocakbaşı	4
Sünger Pizza	2
Yeni Bodrum Ocakbaşı	6

AEGEAN SEA

applied in 1522 when Süleyman's capture of the Knights' headquarters on Rhodes made their position here untenable. Bodrum's castle was subsequently neglected until the nineteenth century, when the chapel was converted to a mosque, the keep to a prison, and a hamam installed.

Initial entrance is through the **west gate**, looking on to the water. Once inside the west moat, you'll notice bits of ancient masonry from the mausoleum incorporated into the walls, as well as some of the 249 Christian coats of arms.

The chapel and Italian tower

Stairs from the main entrance lead up to the seaward fortifications, and then into the **lower courtyard**. To the right, the **chapel** houses a fascinating reconstruction of a seventh-century Byzantine ship, whose remains were excavated off Yassıada. The display, incorporating the salvaged hull, shows how such ships were loaded with cargoes of amphorae. A building at the base of the **Italian Tower** holds a small glass collection, mostly Roman and early Islamic work.

Glass Wreck Hall

Tues–Fri 10am–noon & 2–4pm • ₺5 separate admission

The so-called **Glass Wreck Hall** houses well-labelled, climate-controlled displays on a **Byzantine shipwreck** and cargo found 33m down at Serçe Limanı in 1973. Dating from 1025, this was a peacetime trading vessel, tubby and flat-bottomed to permit entry to the Mediterranean's many shallow straits, plying between Fatimid and Byzantine territories. Only twenty percent of the original timbers are preserved. The rest is a mock-up, loaded with a fraction of the cargo: two tonnes of raw coloured glass. The personal effects of the passengers and crew include gaming pieces, tools and grooming items.

Uluburun Wreck Hall

Tues–Sun 9am–noon & 2–6.30pm • ₺5

On the east side of the castle precinct, the **Uluburun Wreck Hall** holds the local Bronze Age and Mycenaean collection. It features artefacts recovered from three Aegean wrecks, including finds from the Uluburun site near Kaş.

Carian Princess Hall

Tues–Fri 10am–noon & 2–4pm • ₺5

The **Carian Princess Hall** contains artefacts from an ancient tomb found miraculously unlooted during hotel construction in 1989. The sarcophagus, with its skeleton of a Carian noblewoman who died in the fourth century BC, is on view along with a few gold tomb finds – almost certainly imported, since the metal is not found locally.

The English Tower

Although financed and built by English Knights during the fifteenth century, the **English Tower** now appears a bald attempt to pander to Bodrum's major foreign constituency. Around the themed cafeteria inside, assorted standards of the Order of St John and their Muslim adversaries compete for wall space with an incongruous array of medieval armour and weapons. Many visitors attempt to decipher extensive swathes of Latin graffiti incised into the window jambs by bored Knights.

The dungeon

It's certainly worth making the long, dead-end detour to the Knights' former **dungeon**, adorned with dangling chains and bathed in lurid red light. In case you missed the point, an original Latin inscription over the door reads "Here God does not exist".

The Mausoleum

Turgutreis Cad, 10min walk northwest of the castle • Tues–Sun 8am–7pm • ₺8

Designed by Pytheos, architect of the Athena temple at Priene, the ancient **Mausoleum** was once a whacking great structure, measuring 39m by 33m at its base and standing nearly 60m high. A colonnade surmounted the burial vault and supported a stepped pyramidal roof bearing a chariot (now in the British Museum) with effigies of **Mausolus** himself and his sister-wife Artemisia. Despite diligent work by archeologists, little is left of the original mausoleum. Visitors can examine the precinct wall, assorted column fragments and some subterranean vaults probably belonging to an earlier burial chamber. A shed east of the foundation cavity exhibits plans and models, plus copies of the original friezes.

The ancient theatre

Off the Ring Road • Tues–Sun 8.30am–5.30pm • ₺8

Bodrum's **ancient theatre** has been almost overzealously restored, though if you've been to the mausoleum it's worth the extra five-minute walk uphill. Begun by Mausolus, it was modified in the Roman era and originally seated 13,000, though its current capacity is half that.

ARRIVAL AND DEPARTURE

BODRUM

BY FERRY

There are regular services to the Greek islands of Kós and Rhodes, as well as the Datça peninsula; domestic services to Marmaris and Dalyan have been in flux for some time and cannot be relied upon. For the latest information, check the websites of the two main operators, Bodrum Express (wbodrumexpresslines.com) and Bodrum Ferryboat Association (wbodrumferryboat.com).

To Kós Between May and October, daily services (one-way or day-trip €12, open return €20; 1hr) depart at 9.30am from the dock by the castle, and return at 4.30pm; buy your ticket the day before travel at the ticket booths by the pier.

To Datça Year-round services (one-way ₺30, return ₺50; 1hr 45min) depart daily at 9.30am and 5.30pm from a pier in the west harbour; pay at the booth.

To Rhodes In July and August only, services to Rhodes (one-way or day-trip €33, open return €50; 2hr 20min) depart at 9am Sat & Mon from the east pier, returning at 5.30pm; buy your ticket the day before travel.

BY BUS

Otogar The pleasingly central *otogar*, off Cevat Şakir Cad, is an easy walk from anywhere in the city centre. Destinations Ankara (4 daily; 11hr); Denizli (5 daily; 5hr); Fethiye (6 daily; 5hr); İstanbul (20 daily; 12hr); İzmir (hourly; 3hr 30min); Marmaris (hourly; 3hr 15min); Muğla (hourly; 2hr 30min); Ortakent (every 30min; 20min).

BY PLANE

Airport Milas-Bodrum airport (wbodrum-airport.com) is 35km northeast of town. Havaş buses (whavas.net) to and from Bodrum's *otogar* (₺15; 45min) are timed to correspond with flights. The only other option is taking a taxi, for around ₺90.

Airlines THY (Turkish Airlines), Kıbrıs Şehitleri Cad 82/2/22 (☎0252 317 1203). THY ticket-holders can book here for the shuttle bus to the airport.

BY CAR

Driving is difficult in Bodrum, made all the more so by a strict one-way system, and a lack of good parking; if you do find some, it's generally ₺4 per hour or ₺18 per day. Many hotels have their own spaces.

INFORMATION AND ACTIVITIES

Tourist office Barış Meyd, Mon–Sat 9am–5.30pm; ☎0252 316 1091. For a place with so many tourists, the information office is surprisingly unhelpful. They'll be able to give you maps of the city, and perhaps a little advice on accommodation or onward transport.

BOAT TRIPS, CRUISES AND DIVING AROUND BODRUM

Most of Bodrum's wide array of boat trips – well worth taking if you don't plan to tour the area by land – leave from the west harbour. A typical day out starts around 10.30am and finishes at 4pm, costing roughly ₺25 per person (including lunch).

Itineraries These vary little. First stop for most boats is the Akvaryum, a snorkellers' venue in the Ada Boğazı (Island Strait): the fish, however, have been frightened off, and are now seldom seen. Next halt is usually Kara Ada, a sizeable island southeast of town, where you bathe in hot springs issuing from a cave at the island's margin. The final moorings are often Kızıl Burnu (Red Bay) and Tavşan Burnu (Rabbit Bay).

Boats Boats range from sleepy 15-person *gulets* to wild party barges squeezing in 70 passengers: choose wisely. If you fancy something a little more upscale, hire your own (fully staffed) boat. Most set cruises hug the scenic Gökova gulf coast en route to Marmaris, though individual itineraries are catered for.

Diving There's good diving around Bodrum. Several operators offer courses and tours; hunt around the west harbour, where dive boats offer a full day out, usually including gear rental and lunch, for €45.

Aquapro ⓦ aquapro-turkey.com. One of Bodrum's longest-established dive operators.

Travel Is On ⓦ travelison.com. A long-running outfit offering personalized yacht tours.

S&J Travel & Yachting ⓦ sjyachting.com. Specializes in custom-itinerary tours.

ACCOMMODATION

To the **west** of the castle, things are quiet but the side streets not particularly pedestrian-friendly – a good place for families and anyone spending a lot of time in their hotel. To the **east**, there's a distinction between places with a sea view (often very noisy outside), and the quieter places burrowed into the backstreets. **Prices** tend to be higher than elsewhere in Turkey, particularly in July and August, when advance reservations are recommended. Beware the touts at the *otogar*, who often ply substandard accommodation to travellers fresh from an overnight bus ride. Out of season most hotels (except those with central heating) are closed. Air conditioning is a necessity in midsummer; all but the most humble *pansiyons* have it.

WEST OF THE CASTLE

Mars Turgutreis Cad, İmbat Çıkmazı 20 ☎ 0252 316 6559, ⓦ marsotel.com. A tranquil hotel surrounded by some splendid old buildings, in various states of disrepair. Rooms are simple, yet occasionally quite large, and there's also a small pool, Turkish bath and lively poolside bar. ₺150

Menekşe Çıkmazı Sok ☎ 0252 316 5890. Good-value rooms set in peaceful gardens, a world away from the noisy seafront. There's limited parking, and stroking the numerous pets is free. ₺100

★ **Su Hotel** 1201 Sok off Turgutreis Cad ☎ 0252 316 6906, ⓦ bodrumsuhotel.com. Large, well-equipped complex laid out around one of the biggest pools in town. The cheery multicoloured rooms all have balconies overlooking the central courtyard, where there's a cute bar. The hotel is inaccessible to cars (which helps to keep the noise levels down), but has its own parking around the corner; follow the river-mosaic down a side alley. ₺200

Yenilmez Çıkmazı Sok 30 ☎ 0252 316 2520. Central, quiet, modern *pansiyon* with a nice garden; a good option if the *Menekşe* next door is full. Breakfast in the shady courtyard is a delight. ₺100

EAST OF THE CASTLE

Aegean Gate Hotel Güvercin Sok 2 ☎ 0252 313 7853, ⓦ aegeangatehotel.com. A wildly popular and highly recommended option, 1km past the *Halikarnas* nightclub, boasting stupendous views over Bodrum bay. It's centred around an enchanting swimming pool, and has a minimum two-night stay. ₺230

★ **Baç Pansiyon** Cumhuriyet Cad 14 ☎ 0252 313 1602. This luxurious, but surprisingly affordable, decade-old boutique hotel is right in the heart of the action. All the stylish rooms are double-glazed, cutting out much of the noise, and those at the rear have castle-view balconies. ₺180

Bodrum Backpackers Atatürk Cad 31 ☎ 0252 313 2762, ⓦ bodrumbackpackers.net. Noisy place for partying backpackers, offering clean, well-kept dorms, a few poor-value private doubles, a roof terrace, internet access and laundry service. The bar downstairs is a great place to meet other travellers. Dorms ₺30, doubles ₺80

Bodrum Blu Atatürk Cad, Adliye Sok 44 ☎ 0252 316 6830, ⓦ bodrumblu.com. Splendid-value hotel, tucked into the backstreets. Rooms are small and plain, but the pool is a great place to chill out; in addition, owners will rustle up evening meals for an extra ₺10 per person. ₺80

Merhaba Hotel Akasya Sok 44 ☎ 0252 316 3978, ⓦ merhabaotel.com. Probably as cheap as you're going to want to get in Bodrum – rooms are simple, but, thanks to a quiet location, you'll get a good night's rest. The switched-on staff are another bonus. ₺60

EATING

Eating out in Bodrum can be pricey, especially if you're close to the water. Dismal fast-food joints offering British food are, slowly, being replaced by Turkish eateries. Small restaurants in the vine-covered **Meyhanelar Caddesi** in the bazaar vie to offer the traditional Turkish experience. Anywhere else, expect a jump up in price, especially overlooking either bay and at the upmarket restaurants around the harbour.

Ceylan Cumhuriyet Cad 112 ☎0252 313 3637. Elegantly understated waterside restaurant with glitzy tableware, an exciting array of *mezeler* and a solid wine list. Daily noon–midnight.

Marina Köftecisi Neyzen Tevfik Cad 158. Lively kebab joint with heaps of outdoor seating and bargain prices for its location – think *köfte* for ₺10. Splendid. Daily 9am–1am.

Marina Yacht Club Neyzen Tevfik Cad ☎0252 316 1228. Now here's a place to show off – eating on a rooftop, gazing down on the harbour's forest of masts. Meals range from the Turkish to the international – the mixed *meze* (₺28) will fill a hole, ₺10 more will get you a succulent salmon kebab, while elsewhere on the menu you'll find beef carpaccio, cheese platters and more. Daily noon–late.

★ **Orfoz** Cumhuriyet Cad 177B ☎0252 316 4285. This simple-looking restaurant enjoys by far the best reputation in town – you'll almost certainly need to reserve. There's no menu as such – most come for the superbly prepared set meals, starting with *mezes* made with shellfish, proceeding through soups, mixed salads, grilled fish and more before you're finally ready to pop. Reckon on ₺70–80 per head, excluding drinks. Daily. 6pm–late.

Otantik Ocakbaşı Atatürk Cad 12/B ☎0252 313 0058. Excellent *meze*, wood-fired *pide* and grilled meats dished up on a breezy outdoor terrace. Licensed. Daily 10am–midnight.

Sünger Pizza Neyzen Tevfik Cad 162. Cheap, cheerful and enduringly popular pizza restaurant, with excellent views from its rooftop; justifiably packed with yachties and locals most evenings. Pizzas from ₺18; delivery service available. Daily 10am–1am.

★ **Yeni Bodrum Ocakbaşı** Atatürk Cad 90 ☎0252 316 4319. Though it's in central Bodrum, this restaurant is far more proximate to "regular" Turkey as regards its prices, and the size of the meals. The *beyti sarma* (₺15) may be the pick of their authentic range of kebabs, and the *köfte* are great too. They also deliver. Daily 24hr.

NIGHTLIFE AND ENTERTAINMENT

Bodrum holds dozens of places to **drink and dance**, most of them lining **Dr Alim Bey Caddesi** (where many of the bars on the seaward side lead straight through to a waterfront area) and its continuation, Cumhuriyet Caddesi. All get packed and sweaty on a summer night, with the busiest hours from 11pm to 3am; places west of the castle tend to be more refined. Few bars have cover charges, though drink prices are high. Visitors seeking evening entertainment outside the clubbing scene would do well to plan a visit during April, when Bodrum hosts its annual **Rocks Fest**, or during August for the town's yearly **Ballet Festival** (ⓦbodrumballetfestival.gov.tr).

BARS

Ebou Uslu Sok 54. The most appealing café-bar on the strip, boasting candlelit tables on the beach so that you can drink while your feet are lapped. The inside's gorgeous too, and often hosts live music. Daily 11am–late.

Red Lion Cumhuriyet Cad 139. Pub-style place with a clutch of outdoor seats, offering long happy hours and last season's chart hits. Daily 9am–late.

Shadow Banka Sok. Live rock bar inside the bazaar's maze of side-alleys. If it looks too empty (or, of course, too full), there are plenty of others in the immediate area. Daily 3pm–late.

CLUBS

Club Catamaran ☎0252 316 3600, ⓦclubcatamaran .com. Bodrum's prime piece of partyware: a disco-boat that leaves port at 10pm and glams it up on the ocean waves until dawn. Regular shuttles to and fro ensure that you're not stranded out there. Daily 10am–dawn.

Hadi Gari Western end of Alim Bey ☎0252 316 0048, ⓦhadigari.com.tr. Though past its prime, there are still fantastic nights to be had at this disco-club, which boasts a truly spectacular location, four different bars and space for 2000 revellers. Entry sometimes free, can be up to ₺35 depending on who's DJ-ing. Daily 7pm–late.

Halikarnas Eastern end of Cumhuriyet Cad ☎0252 316 8000, ⓦhalikarnas.com.tr. Megaclub with room for over 5000 people. Under renovation at the time of research.

DIRECTORY

Books and newspapers English-language newspapers can be purchased at the kiosk at the eastern end of Şehir Meydanı. Books are harder to come by, but Kitabevi on Uçkuyular 5 sells an excellent selection of second-hand tomes.

Consulate Honorary British Consulate, Cafer Paşa Cad 2. Emsan Evleri 7 ☎0252 313 0021, ⓦukinturkey.fco.gov.uk.

Hamam Bodrum Hamam (ⓦbodrumhamami.com.tr) on Cevat Şakir Cad opposite the *otogar* (daily segregated bathing 6am–midnight), and Bardakçi Hamam on Dere Umurca Sok (daily 8am–8pm; later in summer according to demand).

Hospitals The English-speaking Karia Medical Centre, Kıbrıs Şehitler Cad 97 (☎0252 313 6233), and Medicare, Hamam Sok 4 (☎0252 316 7051), both promise 24hr,

seven-day attention. The City Hospital (Devlet Hastanesi; ☎0252 313 1420) is on Elmadağ Cad.
Laundry Mavi, Turgutreis Cad, Davutlar Sok 3.
Pharmacy Eczane Oasis, Oasis Alışveriş Merkezi ☎0252 317 0507.

Police Dr Alim Bey Cad ☎0252 316 1216; Emergency ☎0252 316 1004.
Post office PTT at Cevat Şakir Cad.
Supermarkets Migros, near the turning for Gümbet; Tansaş, by the *otogar*.

The Bodrum peninsula

For anyone staying in Bodrum, it's worth making at least one day- or half-day trip across the **peninsula** it calls home. You might even consider basing yourself in one of its many relaxed villages, such as **Gümüşlük** or **Akyarlar**, rather than in hectic Bodrum. The peninsular population was largely Greek Orthodox before 1923 and villages often still have a vaguely Hellenic feel, with ruined churches, windmills and old **stone houses**. However, the area has become immensely popular with moneyed Turks of late, and whitewashed cube-buildings have proliferated – some now appealing **boutique hotels**, others eerily empty, where building projects have gone belly-up. Luxury hotels, on the other hand, are proliferating – every major world chain either has, or is about to have, a hotel open here.

The peninsula still exudes a unique charm. Its **north side**, greener and cooler, holds patches of pine forest; the **south**, studded with tall crags, is more arid, with a sandier coast. There are also plenty of serviceable **beaches**, with Bitez, Ortakent, Yalıkavak and Türkbükü, among others, currently holding Blue Flag status for cleanliness.

Note that most of the peninsula's hotels and restaurants only open from **May to October**. Travel at other times is certainly possible, though, and it's blissfully relaxing.

GETTING AROUND

By dolmuş Frequent dolmuşes (6am–midnight) head from Bodrum's *otogar* to all the peninsula's towns. Journeys to anywhere bar Torba take 30–50min, and typically cost ₺5–9. Getting from A to B without doubling back to

Bodrum is often possible too, with hourly services between Yalıkavak and Turguturreis, and a few shorter-range hops. Services are heavily curtailed Nov–April.

The south coast

The south coast of the Bodrum peninsula is markedly dry, but holds some fantastic beaches. The first you'll reach from Bodrum – indeed, it's practically a suburb of the city – is **Gümbet**, 2km away. Its 600m-long, tamarisk-lined, gritty beach is usually packed, with parasailing, ringo-ing and waterskiing taking place offshore. Development here is exclusively package-oriented, and the (mainly young and English) clientele rather rowdy. However, the nightlife rivals that of Bodrum.

Bitez, the next cove west, is a little more upmarket, and seems to have adopted Gümbet's former role as a watersports and windsurfing centre. Reasonable watering holes cater to the yachties sailing or cruising through, but the beach is tiny, even after artificial supplementing.

Beyond Yahşi, a turning flanked with hotel signs at Gürece leads high above **Kargı**. The beach and bay are sandy and gently sloping, overlooked by the ubiquitous villas and a handful of fish restaurants. The next cove on, **Bağla**, seems initially off-putting – persevere and you'll find the softest sand on the peninsula.

Karaincir, the next bay with public access, is nearly as good – 600m of sand guarded by a pair of headlands. Canoes and windsurfing boards can be rented, and while mid-beach is completely crowded out by sunbeds and umbrellas, the south end of the strand inexplicably remains in its wild, natural state.

Nearby **Akyarlar** is more of an actual village – albeit surrounded by estates of concrete villas. Its often breezy conditions make it cooler and more comfortable in summer than sweaty Bodrum. Akyarlar's beach is small and hard-packed, mostly given over to windsurfing, but with both Karaincir and (in the opposite direction) the sandy cove at **Simin** within walking distance, this is no great loss.

ACCOMMODATION AND EATING

Accommodation on this stretch of coast is plentiful, particularly in the package-tourism resort of Gümbet. Bitez has some nice places to stay and eat, while Akyarlar has some of the cheapest *pansiyons* on the peninsula, as well as some great local restaurants.

BİTEZ

⭐ **Bitez Bağarası** Bitez ☎0252 363 7693. The best place on the peninsula to sample Aegean cuisine, serving hearty platefuls of fish and the region's famously tasty veggies. Aegean food centres on *mezes*, so order a nice mixed platter – freshly plucked samphire, stuffed pumpkin and zucchini flowers, and so, so much more. Reservations recommended. Daily 9am–11pm.

Okaliptüs Bitez ☎0252 363 7780, ⓦokaliptus.com.tr. This well-designed four-star, nestled in a grove of tangerine trees, is the pick of **Bitez**'s thirty-plus hotels, with its own pool and a small, private stretch of beach. Its restaurant is a winner, too. **₺250**

Şah Hotel Bitez ☎0252 363 7721, ⓦsahhotel.com.

One of the cheaper options in town, with slightly basic rooms arranged around a delightful, palm-fringed pool. **₺230**

BARBAROS BAY

Kempinski Barbaros Bay Barbaros Bay ☎0212 311 0303, ⓦkempinski.com. A great place to get away from it all, occupying a bay all to itself a 20min ride east of Bodrum. Once you're in, there's precious little reason to leave, with amenities strung down the cliffside – the pool is up there with the largest on the Med, there's a private stretch of secluded beach, the three restaurants (seafood, Asian and Italian) are all superb and differ greatly in style, and the on-site Six Senses spa fulfils all pampering needs. Blissful. **₺500**

The west coast

Less appealing than either the north or south, the Bodrum peninsula's windswept **west coast** nevertheless has a few fine beaches. The furthest south is at **Turgutreis**, the peninsula's second-largest town, though as a primarily all-inclusive resort it's not the best place to experience authentic local culture. The side road starting by its *otogar* leads north to better things, through a fertile landscape of the tangerine groves for which the region is famous. After 4km you reach **Kadıkalesı**, with its long, partly protected sand beach, and unbeatable views over to assorted islets.

If you've had a bellyful of villa complexes, then sleepy **Gümüşlük** (2km past Kadıkalesi) is a refreshing change. Easily the nicest spot on the peninsula, it partly occupies the site of **ancient Myndos**, so most new development has been prohibited. Yachties are drawn here by the excellent deep anchorage between the headland and Tavşan Adası (Rabbit Island), the latter surrounded by mosaics that snorkellers should check out. The half-kilometre-long sand-and-gravel **beach** extending south of the island is less protected but still attractive, with watersports gear for rent.

Lastly, there's unappealing **Yalıkavak** on the northwest corner of the peninsula. As with Turgutreis, this is a functional town year-round, and is most notable for its brand-new, Azeri-funded **marina** – already attracting yachties in droves, it's open to visitors and makes for a lovely walk.

ACCOMMODATION AND EATING
THE WEST COAST

Gümüşlük is by far the best place to **sleep** on the west coast – Turgutreis is full of package tourists and retired Europeans, and Yalıkavak's few decent *pansiyons* are frustratingly hard to track down (though there are some excellent upscale places in the hills above town). For **food**, Gümüşlük wins again, though Yalıkavak has some good restaurants leading up to the marina, which itself has a few cafés and bars.

GÜMÜŞLÜK

Balıkcı On the beach. Fish about as fresh as fish gets – staffed by fishermen, this beachside restaurant has its own private boat to supply the daily catch. Given this added luxury, prices are reasonable. Daily 10am–11pm.

Club Hotel Zemda On the beach ☎0252 394 3151, ⓦclubhotelzemda.com. Beachside hotel that has become the default go-to place for watersports – they offer special week-long accommodation-plus-lesson deals from €365 (windsurfing) or €385 (katamaran) per person. As should almost go without saying with such a place, there's a lively on-site bar. ₺200

Otel Gümüşlük Just back from the beach ☎0252 394 4828, ⓦotelgumusluk.com. This good-value hotel has large, modern rooms, and a pool surrounded by grass and deckchairs. They also rent out nearby apartments – good for long-termers. ₺140

Limon Above Gümüşlük town ⓦlimongumusluk.com. Café serving up home-grown produce in a bucolic, ruin-strewn garden setting that's up with the best on the peninsula; the same goes for the breakfasts. It's a bit far from the beach – one for those with their own transport. Daily 8am–6pm.

★ **Mimoza** On the beach. Beachside restaurant with a reputation that extends across the peninsula. Their seafood is divine, and their Aegean *mezes* beyond reproach. It's a particularly beautiful place at sundown, when the flowers dangling over the tables fade into darkness, their eye-candy role replaced by hanging lanterns. Daily noon–11pm.

YALIKAVAK

4 Reasons On the hillside above Yalıkavak ☎0212 385 3212, ⓦ4reasonshotel.com. Far removed from the near-eponymous international chain (which will make its own appearance on the peninsula in due course), this is a small, friendly establishment with a secluded location overlooking Yalıkavak. It's all very informal, though certainly no slouch as far as the rooms go – some sport wood fires and gigantic balconies. ₺400

Ali Baba Facing the marina on the edge of the harbour. A long-standing Yalıkavak fixture, this restaurant is renowned for its delectable seafood and kebabs; figure on ₺20 per head, excluding drinks. Daily 9am–11pm.

Club Billionaire On the end of the marina. This open-air bar has an interesting back story. During the marina's construction, word went out that it was to become a millionaires' hangout with a €1000 cover charge – utterly false, but a canny piece of marketing. In reality, any old schmuck can pop by for a coffee or cocktail. Bar the jacuzzi and crisply dressed waiters, it's not even that luxurious. Daily 9am–11pm.

The north coast

The heavily indented **north coast** of the Bodrum peninsula hides a few picturesque bays, which would have made great pirate coves in days of yore. Starting from the west, **Gündoğan** (also known as **Farilya**) is surrounded by pine forest; villas barely impinging upon its long, narrow beach, divided by a small harbour, while high winds make it a prime **windsurfing** spot. For a taste of the local Ottoman heritage, walk 1km inland to **Gündoğan village** proper, then climb to a ruined monastery.

Once-sleepy **Türkbükü**, one cove east, has become the St Tropez of the peninsula, losing most of its beach in the process. It's now a bit too trendy for its own good, though a good place to go Turkish star-spotting (if you know any); if you need to come by public transport you're just not posh enough, but dolmuşes run to the nearby village of Göltürkbükü.

Lastly, there's **Torba**, by far the closest north-coast town to Bodrum. It's a little like a budget Türkbükü, with added yachts and a decent stretch of beach.

ACCOMMODATION AND EATING   THE NORTH COAST

Much of the **accommodation** along the north coast is unashamedly luxurious and expensive, particularly in Türkbükü, though you'll find *pansiyons* on the fringes of all three villages. **Restaurants** also tend to be swanky, though in a neat reversal of global norms the cheapest options in Türkbükü are on the beach.

GÜNDOĞAN

Aspava Across from Migros on the main road. Along the way to Gündoğan village, stop to eat at this tiny place where three generations of the Başkan family serve up excellent home-made *gözleme*. Hours vary.

Butik Han Sahil Seridi Emek Sok ☎0252 387 9465, ⓦbutikhanotel.com. The actual rooms at this hotel are unquestionably a little uninspired, which is all the more reason to get out and enjoy the swimming pool, or slurp a cocktail with superlative bay views from the beach bar. ₺250

Gürkaya On the beach ☎0252 387 8352. Motel offering the most reasonably priced accommodation in the area – nothing special, but adequate nonetheless, and right on the beach. ₺100

Reana Yalı Mevki Cad ☎0252 387 7117. Beautifully decorated fish restaurant with a stellar reputation – such that you may have to book ahead, particularly for a dinnertime slot. The Aegean-style *mezes* are also out of this world, and the prices surprisingly affordable. Daily 11am–10pm.

Café Sail Loft Yalı Mevki Cad 39 ⓦgravity.com.tr. Waterfront café, particularly notable for the fact that it rents out windsurfing boards. Daily 8am–10pm.

TÜRKBÜKÜ

Bodrum Mantı & Café Liman Cad. An interesting concept – dumplings and coffee, around the clock. This being Türkbükü, it's wildly overpriced, but the *mantı* (from ₺17) are delicious and come in several quirky varieties. Daily 24hr.

Kaktüş Çiçeği Atatürk Cad 119 ☎0252 377 5254, ⓦkaktuscicegi.com.tr. About as cheap as you're going to find in this part of the peninsula, but still swanky enough – 18 lovely rooms, a small stretch of shoreline and an on-site restaurant that serves tasty Aegean specialities.

Note that prices plummet outside the mid-July to mid-August window. ₺250

Kuum Atatürk Cad 150 ☎0252 311 0060, ⓦkuumhotel .com. Architecturally adventurous? You bet. This space-age spa-hotel enjoys a premium spot in the middle of things at Türkbükü, though thanks to a stretch of private shoreline (not actually beach in this area), you'd never know it. Comfy lounge booths gaze out to sea, as do many of the snappy rooms. ₺400

Maça Kızı North of Türkbükü ☎0212 377 6262, ⓦmacakizi.com. Sitting in divine solitude north of Türkbükü, the "Queen of Spades" has been the talk of the peninsula – and many a Turkish celebrity – for some time. Their on-site restaurant has an equally lofty reputation – a mix of local and Mediterranean flavours, using local ingredients wherever possible. ₺800

TORBA

Casa Dell'Arte Torba ☎0212 367 1848, ⓦcasadellartebodrum.com. Oh-so-trendy hotel sitting pretty in not-trendy-at-all Torba. As you infer from the name, art plays a large role in proceedings; the owners are two of Turkey's most prominent collectors, and rooms and common areas alike are swathed with paintings and sculptures. The rooms themselves are highly picturesque – anything from the lighting to the bed shapes can come as a surprise. ₺700

Dalli On the coast road ☎0252 367 1076. Nice little cheapie towards the end of the stretch – basic rooms, though at this price you shouldn't expect too much. The friendly owners speak English, and whip up nice meals in the on-site restaurant. ₺120

Gonca Balık By the beach. Acclaimed seafood restaurant by the Casa Dell'Arte, with an array of cute blue and orange seats arranged along the beach. Fishy mains go for ₺25 and up. Hours vary.

APHRODISIAS (P.284) >

Marmaris

Along with Kuşadası and Bodrum, **MARMARİS** is the third of Turkey's less-than-holy trinity of hugely overdeveloped Aegean resorts. Little is left of the sleepy fishing village it used to be, a mere three decades ago. Development has dwarfed the old core of shops and *lokanta*s lining narrow, bazaar-like streets, an intricate warren contrasting strongly with the European-style marina and waterfront.

According to legend, Marmaris was named when Süleyman the Magnificent, not finding the **castle** here to his liking, was heard to mutter "*Mimarı as*" ("hang the architect") – a command that ought perhaps still to apply to the designers of the seemingly endless apartments and hotels. The castle itself holds a museum of local finds (daily 8.30am–noon & 1–6.30pm; ₺3), and serves as a venue during the May festival. The **bazaar**, including its diminutive *kervansaray*, now rivals that at Kuşadası for its array of glitzy kitsch, and only the **Kaleiçi** district, the warren of streets at the base of the tiny castle, offers a pleasant wander.

Tucked away at the far end of town, the large **Netsel Yacht Marina** is the main base for yacht charter organizations operating on the Turquoise Coast. Proximity to Dalaman airport also means that both foreign and domestic tourists pour in nonstop during the warmer months, and – the marina aside – Marmaris remains very much a package resort.

MARMARİS

Datça & State Hospital (200m)

ACCOMMODATION

Karadeniz	3
Ketenci	2
Nadir	5
Otel 47	4
Royal Maris	1

Muğla & Otogar (500m)

MUHARREM ELGİN BUL

RECAİ GÜREL BUL

ULUSAL EGEMENLİK CAD

YENİYOL

ALİ ESİN SOK

MUSTAFA MUĞLALI CAD

HASAN IŞIK CAD

HAMDİ YÜZAK SOK

Fountain Park

ATATÜRK CAD

ATATÜRK (KORDON) CAD

Abdi İpekçi Park

Dolmuşes

Football Stadium

MUSTAFA KEMAL CAD

ATATÜRK MEYD

Atatürk Statue

VENEDİK KEMAL KEMER SOK

19 MAYIS SOK

Excursion Boats

KORDON

Police

BAZAAR

TERSANE YOLU

Indoor Sports Centre

İSKELE MEYD

HACI MUSTAFA (BARLAR) SOK

Mosque

Excursion Boats

Hamam

Castle

BARBAROS CAD

Harbour

MUSTAFA MÜNİR ELGİN BUL

Netsel Yacht Marina

Rhodes

Uzunyalı, İçmeler & Turunç

RESTAURANTS

Birgül Ney	3
Gürbüz Lokantası	1
La Fortune	2
Pineapple	5
Rest...	4

BARS AND CAFÉS

Back Street	3
Bedesten Café	1
Sunshine Cafe Bar	2

0   200
metres

Cennet (Nimara) Adası, Aktaş & Ada Ağzı

Brief history

Marmaris' **history** has been determined above all by its stunning setting, in a deep, fjord-like inlet surrounded by pine-cloaked hills. This did not seem to spur ancient Physcus, the original Dorian colony, to any growth or importance, but Süleyman comfortably assembled a force of 200,000 here in 1522, when launching the successful siege of the Knights of St John's base in Rhodes. Shortly after this campaign Süleyman endowed the old town nucleus with the tiny castle and a *han*. In 1798 Nelson's entire fleet sheltered here before setting out to defeat Napoleon's armada at the Battle of Aboukir Bay in Egypt.

Beaches

You don't come to Marmaris for cultural edification, and you swim off the polluted **Kordon beach** at your peril – though this doesn't seem to deter the hundreds of bathers who use it daily.

It's far better to head out to **İçmeler**, 9km west of Marmaris by road and considerably less along the coastal footpath, and also served by regular dolmuşes and boat taxis. The sand is coarse but cleaner than at Kordon, as is the sea, while **İçmeler's** old village core survives precariously at the far edge of the recently developed resort.

ARRIVAL AND DEPARTURE
MARMARİS

By plane From Dalaman airport, a full 90km east of town, Havaş airport buses (90min; ₺15; 🖥 havas.net) run every hour or two to Marmaris *otogar*, from which a regular dolmuş service runs into town. The same buses pick up at Marmaris *otogar* 3hr before flights.

By bus Marmaris' *otogar* is set in a beautiful area 2km northeast of the centre on the Muğla road; most main bus companies run courtesy buses to the *otogar* to connect with their major routes. Tickets can be bought, and servis buses picked up, at said companies' offices at the Kordon Cad end of Ulusal Egemenlik Bul. Alternatively, there are regular dolmuşes (₺3).

Destinations Akyaka (every 30min; 30min); Ankara (14 daily; 11hr); Antalya (5 daily; 6hr); Bodrum (hourly; 3hr 15min); Bozburun (3–6 daily; 1hr); Datça (9 daily; 2hr); Denizli (8 daily; 3hr 30min); Fethiye (hourly; 3hr); İstanbul (9 daily; 13hr); İzmir (hourly; 3hr 30min).

By car No parking is allowed anywhere along the Kordon, but you can park at places strewn around town for ₺4 an hour, or ₺18 per day.

By ferry Daily services to Rhodes in Greece leave Marmaris at 9am and return at 5pm (€40 one-way, €42 day return, €58 open return; 1hr). Buy tickets from any travel agent in town.

Boat taxis Boat taxis to İçmeler and Turunç leave from in front of the tourist office (₺9 per person one-way, or ₺18 and ₺24 per boat, respectively).

INFORMATION

Tourist office By the excursion boat harbour on İskele Meydanı (Mon–Fri 8am–noon & 1–7pm, Sat & Sun 10am–noon & 1–5pm; ☎ 0252 412 1035). Though not terribly useful, they're able to dispense town plans, as well as information about bus schedules and accommodation.

ACTIVITIES

Bike/jeep rental and tours Best Motor, Kemal Elgin Bul opposite the *Balim Otel* (☎ 0252 412 9436), rents bikes, mopeds, motorbikes and jeeps.

Rafting Alternatif Turizm, Çamlık Sok 10/1 (☎ 0252 417 2720, 🖥 alternatifraft.com), offers regular springtime whitewater-rafting trips on the Dalaman River, plus river and sea kayaking, and tailor-made Turkey-wide outdoor-sports packages.

Yachting An annual yachting and arts festival (🖥 marmarisfestival.com) takes place mid-May. There's also a large yacht race during late October or early November, organized by the Marmaris Yacht Club (🖥 miyc.org).

ACCOMMODATION

Although there are very few *pansiyons* or small hotels in Marmaris, some apartment-hotels have sprung up in the area inland from the marina, while a handful of basic establishments survive in the **town centre**. Good value for money can be had out at the west end of the Kordon, close to where **Kemal Seyfettin Elgin Bulvarı** splits away to run parallel to **Uzunyalı** beach. Further west, some three hundred hotels line the 5km-long, palm-fringed strip, with the luxury, all-inclusive complexes clustering at the far end.

COASTAL CHARTERS AND BOAT EXCURSIONS AROUND MARMARİS

Chartering either a **motor schooner** (*gulet*) or a smaller **yacht** out of Marmaris will allow you to explore the convoluted coast from Bodrum as far as Kaş. Especially out of high season, the daily cost isn't necessarily prohibitive – no more than renting a medium-sized car, for example – and in the case of a *gulet*, a knowledgeable crew will be included. Virtually all the shore is accessible by boat, with abundant hidden anchorages.

You can pre-book a **yacht charter** through specialist holiday operators (see p.29), or make arrangements on the spot. Prices are always quoted in euros or US dollars, but it's possible to pay in Turkish lira. Substantial deposits are required – usually fifty percent of the total price.

The best option for individual travellers or small groups is a **cabin charter**. Several companies set aside one schooner whose berths are let out individually. The craft departs on a particular day of the week with a fixed itinerary of three to seven days. Typical prices, including all food and watersports equipment, range from €390 per person per week in April, May and October, to over €470 between June and September.

If you can assemble a large group, and have more time, consider a standard charter of a 20m **motor schooner**. A group of twelve, for example, will pay around €35 each daily during May or October, not including food or sporting equipment, and around €45 from June to September. Companies often offer to supply food from about €30 per person per day, though the best strategy is to dine in restaurants at your evening mooring and to keep the galley stocked for breakfast and snacks. If you tip the crew appropriately they're usually happy to shop for you. Old and reliable charter agencies in Marmaris include Yeşil Marmaris, Barbaros Cad 118 (☏0252 412 6486, ⊛yesilmarmaris.com).

For greater independence, so-called "**bareboat yacht**" charter is the answer. Prices range from under €1000 for the smallest boat in off season, to €5800 for the largest in high season. This assumes that at least one of your party is a certified skipper; otherwise count on at least €140 a day extra (plus food costs) to engage one. For bareboat yachts, a large local operator is Offshore Sailing at the Albatros Marina, 3km east of Netsel Marina (☏0252 412 8889, ⊛offshore-sailing.net).

BOAT TRIPS FROM MARMARİS

Day excursions aboard a *gulet* depart from the southern end of Kordon Cad and the castle peninsula. Trips usually visit highlights of the inner bay, heading to a fish farm on the north side of Cennet Adası, caves on its south shore, then completing the day with a visit to Kumlubükü or Turunç coves (see p.276). In summer, boats leave around 10.30am and return between 5pm and 6pm, and charge around ₺20 per person, including lunch (no drinks).

You'll also see signs in Marmaris offering trips to **Cleopatra's Isle**. These actually refer to the islet of Sedir Adası (Cedar Island), near the head of the Gulf of Gökova, and said to have served as a trysting place for Cleopatra and Mark Antony. The sand on its beach was supposedly brought from Africa at Mark Antony's behest, and indeed analysis has shown that the grains are not from local strata. The tours leave between 10 and 11am from Çamli İskelesı, and return at 4 or 5pm. The departure point is 6km down a side road that starts 12km north of Marmaris; most passengers get there on tour operators' shuttle buses, but hourly dolmuşes leave from the *otogar*.

TOWN CENTRE

Club Sultan Maris Yunus Nadi Cad ☏0252 417 2826, ⊛clubsultanmaris.com. A good resort-style hotel in the centre of town – sure, the beach is a little further away, but here you're guaranteed a more Turkish experience, and lower prices. They offer both studio rooms and one-room apartments, set around a small pool. ₺**120**

Otel 47 Atatürk Cad 10 ☏0252 412 4747. A huge seafront establishment bristling with balconies and communal sun terraces. It caters for Turks, not foreigners, hence the wonderful (and completely non-English) breakfasts and modest room rates. ₺**140**

★ **Otel & Pansiyon Nadir** Kemerati Mahalesi ☏0252 412 1167, ⊛nadirhotel.com. Forget the unfortunate name – this is as friendly and as cheap as the town's accommodation gets, with clean rooms, en-suite bathrooms, a/c and TV, many with balconies. For bargain hunters, their *pansiyon* rooms next door are cheaper still. There's also a cool café attached. Hotel ₺**80**, pansiyon ₺**50**

WEST OF THE CENTRE

Hotel Karadeniz Atatürk Cad (Kordon) 68 ☏0252 412 3614, ⊛karadenizhotel.com. Comfortable, well-run hotel (200m west off our map) offering all the usual amenities. Rooms are large and bright, but the best aspect is its convenient location, just across from the beach. ₺160

Ketenci Hotel Kemal Seyettin Elgin Bul ☎0252 412 6395. Its 1980s style may be faded – read piano bar, kidney-shaped pool and gloriously dated rooms – but the *Ketenci* still offers a touch of sea-view luxury at affordable prices. ₺130

Royal Maris Hotel Kenan Evren Bul ☎0252 412 8383, ⓦroyalmarishotel.com. Extremely slick beachside option (400m west off our map) with sumptuous rooftop pool and bar, hamam and indoor pool, plus ultra-modern guestrooms. ₺240

EATING

The most popular **restaurants** with tourists are along the harbour. These change names, management and cuisine frequently and are more or less identical; a meal with wine will run to around ₺35 a head. For cheaper eats, head into the bazaar. At the weekly **Thursday market**, west of Atatürk Meydanı near Anadolu Lisesi (and marked Açık Pazar on city maps), women from surrounding villages sell home-made goodies, including delicious jams.

★ **Bedesten Café** Below the mosque in the bazaar. A little cheesy, perhaps, but this greenery-filled courtyard is a relaxing, traditionally styled place for coffee, tea, or even a beer (oddly, since it adjoins a mosque). It's especially atmospheric at night, when the air is thick with nargile (waterpipe) smoke. Daily 8am–3am.

★ **Birgül Ney** Below the castle. One of several restaurants on the alleys heading up to the castle, this charming place is not yet a rip-off – unlike most of its neighbours. It serves up good Turkish home cooking, with mains from ₺10. Daily 9am–11pm.

Gürbüz Lokantası Bazaar. Duck into the bazaar from the excursion boat area, and you'll soon find yourself among the cheapest restaurants in town. This is the cheapest of the lot, selling *tavuk* (chicken) döner on rice for ₺2.50, and

tasty *pide* from just ₺3.50. Some of the outdoor seats have minaret views. Hours vary.

La Fortune Netsel Yacht Marina ☎0252 413 2955. Elegant restaurant with a good mix of Turkish and international dishes. The latter are probably the best – try the pastas, or splash out on something special such as sea bass in rakı sauce (₺35). Daily 9am–2am.

Pineapple Netsel Yacht Marina ☎0252 412 0976. Ever-popular dressy Turkish/English restaurant, famous for its oven-roasted lamb (₺32). With an attached English pub upstairs, things can get a bit noisy. Daily 10am–11pm.

Rest... Barbaros Cad 60. With some of the best views on the strip, this restaurant is worth tracking down for its English or Turkish breakfasts (both ₺9). It's also good for pasta, kebabs, or evening drinks. Daily 9am–late.

DRINKING AND NIGHTLIFE

Most of the town's **drinking** takes place along "Bar Street" (Barlar Sok), a zany place with dozens of bars and clubs. Again, names change on a very regular basis; you'll usually find the same old deals, such as three tequilas for ₺10.

Back Street Barlar Sok 123. The most enduring bar along Bar Street, this huge place consists of two levels surrounding a pretty courtyard. Daily 6pm–late.

Sunshine Cafe Bar Barbaros Cad. For something a little

different to the Bar Street bars, head to this sea-facing establishment, next to the octopus on the waterfront (you'll see). Drinks at good prices, including double rakı for ₺10, or big bottles of Efes for ₺5. Daily 10am–late.

DIRECTORY

Books Arkadaş Kitap, in front of the Sabaci High School on Kordon, has books in English; Sahaf, 33 Sok opposite the *Star Restaurant*, stocks secondhand English novels by the hundreds. Most kiosks, including the one in front of Tansaş, sell English daily newspapers.

Consulate Honorary British Consulate, c/o Yeşil Marmaris Tourism & Yachting, Barbaros Cad 118, near the marina ☎0252 412 6486, ⓦukinturkey.fco.gov.uk.

Hamam The old hamam is in the bazaar at Eski Cami Arkası 3 (daily 8am–11pm, both sexes; entrance, scrub & massage ₺30); the newer Armutalan Hamam is off the Datça road, 1km north (ⓦhamamcilarltd.com; daily 9am–10pm; packages €12–28).

Hospitals The state hospital is at the junction of Yunus Nadı Cad and the Datça road ☎0252 413 1029; Ahu Hetman private hospital is in Hatipirimi suburb, 167 Sok ☎0252 413 1415.

Laundry Marin laundry is located in the street behind the Netsel Yacht Marina.

Pharmacies The most central ones are: Fulya Eczanesi, Kemaltı Mah 53/3 ☎0252 412 9314; and Galenos Eczanesi, Ulusal Egemenlik Cad 81, Sok 3 ☎0252 413 0419.

Police On Kordon Cad, next to the government house ☎0252 412 2813.

Post office PTT is within the bazaar on 49 Sok (mail services until 6pm, outdoor phones 24hr).

4

Turunç

The mini-resort of **TURUNÇ**, 10km south of Marmaris, is easily accessible by water-taxi, or by dolmuş on a twisty-turny road. Little more than a few farms and a couple of restaurants in the late 1980s, it's now an exclusive package-holiday venue – no surprise since it's stunningly beautiful, boasting a 500m beach of coarse sand, backed by impressive, pine-tufted cliffs. These are dotted with hotels and villas, some of whose residents commute to sea level using cogwheel chairlifts.

A spur road heads south of Turunç, past ancient **Amos** (only Hellenistic walls and theatre remain) to **Kumlubükü**, another large bay with decent amenities. Along with Çiftlik bay, 4km southwest of here by rough tracks or paths, it's the only really big patch of sand on the whole peninsula.

ACCOMMODATION   TURUNÇ

Most hotels on the seafront stretch are package only, but two solid options are listed below. A handful of cheaper pensions lie back from the beach.

Diplomat Hotel ☎0252 476 7145, ⓦdiplomathotel .com.tr. Large, cliff-backed hotel complete with beach frontage and swimming pool. They also run a few cheaper self-catering apartments just off-site. **₺145**

Zeybek Hotel ☎0252 476 7014, ⓦzeybekhotel.com. This sizeable option boasts beach frontage, and tremendous bay views from its elevated swimming pool. Rooms are simple but perfectly adequate. **₺130**

The Hisarönü peninsula

In ancient times the peninsula that extends from the head of the Gulf of Gökova to a promontory between the Greek islands of Sími and Rhodes was known as the **Rhodian Peraea**. This was the mainland territory of the three united city-states of Rhodes, which controlled the area for eight centuries. Despite this, there is little evidence of the long tenure. The peninsula was (and still is) something of a backwater, today known as the **Hisarönü peninsula**. Up to now, yachts have been the principal means of getting around this irregular landmass. A proper road was completed in 1989, but the difficulty of access has so far kept development to a minimum.

Orhaniye
9km off the main highway

ORHANIYE is visited mostly for its yacht anchorage. The beach here is confined to muddy, sumpy shallows, though further out in the bay lurks a celebrated curiosity: a long, narrow, submerged sandspit known as **Kızkumu** (Maiden's Sand) extends halfway across the bay and gives anyone who walks on it the appearance of walking on water. There are a few hotels and *pansiyons* in Orhaniye, but most find it preferable to stay down the road in Selimiye or Bozburun.

Selimiye
9km south of Orhaniye

SELİMİYE village enjoys a truly spectacular location, at the edge of the large, mountain-lined Delikyol bay – which, from this angle, looks rather more like a lake. The clientele here has become notably more diverse since the improvement of the road – no longer just yachties, but retired expats, affluent locals, and a fair few independent travellers too, all mixed into a native population that remains surprisingly, and pleasingly, rural in nature.

Bozburun and beyond
7km from Selimiye

BOZBURUN slumbers in dusty heat six months of the year, but its setting, on a convoluted gulf with a fat islet astride its mouth and the Greek island of Sími beyond, is startling. The place is unlikely to go the way of Datça (see p.278), since there is precious little level land for villas, even less fresh water and absolutely no sand beaches. Nonetheless Bozburun has long been an "in" resort for various eccentrics – ex-journalists turned bartenders, recording executives turned restaurant proprietors, diehard Turkish hippies – who collect in this most isolated corner of coastal Turkey.

In cool weather you could walk east one valley to **SÖĞÜT**, essentially a farming oasis with a minimal shore settlement boasting a few restaurants and a couple of *pansiyon*s. The dolmuş serving Söğüt terminates at **TAŞLICA**, a hilltop village girded by almonds and olives sprouting from what's otherwise a stone desert. From the square where the dolmuş leaves you, a three- to four-hour trail leads south to ancient **Loryma**, where a Rhodian-built fort overlooks the magnificent harbour of **Bozukkale**, which in turn holds several restaurants. If you don't want to walk back the same way, you just might be able to hitch a boat ride out from here.

GETTING AROUND THE HISARÖNÜ PENINSULA

Overland access to the bulk of the peninsula is by way of a paved road, which branches south from the main Datça-bound highway, 21km west of Marmaris, then hits Orhaniye and Selimiye before continuing to Bozburun. Dolmuşes plough this route from Marmaris, every couple of hours. Having your own transport will avoid a lot of waiting around; you'll also be able to take a different route to or from Marmaris, via Bayar, Turunç and İçmeler.

ACCOMMODATION

SELİMİYE

Girit Hanım Pınarı Mevkii Yalı Cad 53 ☎0252 446 4250, ⓦgiritpansiyon.com. Both a restaurant and a *pansiyon*, and recommended as a cheap alternative for either need. Rooms are basic, but the meals are superb – try the *girit kalamar* (calamari rings; ₺15) with some of the freshly made *mezeler* (from ₺5). It's at the west end of the boardwalk stretch. ₺120

Jenny's House Just off the main road ☎0252 446 4289, ⓦjennyshouse.co.uk. The URL gives it away – this guesthouse is aimed squarely at the British market. However, it's an utterly charming place, with a delightful garden, a lovely pool, and rooms decorated in a faux-Ottoman style. Rooms are rented by the week; rates including a transfer from Dalaman airport. Weekly ₺600

★ **Les Terrasses de Selimiye** Up above town ☎0252 446 4367, ⓦselimiyepension.com. Classy, French-owned place boasting stupendous views from its beautifully designed infinity pool. The staff are highly friendly, and the sumptuous breakfasts something to behold. Then there are the prices, far lower than you'd normally expect for such a place. ₺150

BOZBURUN

Hotel Aphrodite 100m along a coastal path from the south end of the quay ☎0252 456 2268, ⓦhotelaphrodite.net. This vine-shaded, upmarket hotel is the nicest in town, with rooms that – while not quite plush – are a cut above the competition. One-week minimum, half-board obligatory. Weekly €800

Otel Mete At the south end of the quay ☎0252 456 2099, ⓦotelmete.com. An inexpensive family-friendly spot, complete with hammocks and a sunlounger-covered sea terrace. Half-board obligatory. ₺140

Pembe Yunus A few minutes south of the centre ☎0252 456 2154, ⓦbozburunpembeyunus.net. The "Pink Dolphin" is a buzzy alternative with a superb fish restaurant overlooking the sea – ever popular with Istanbul-based couples. Half-board obligatory. ₺170

Yılmaz On the seafront road ☎0252 456 2167. Rose-scented garden? Check. Sea views over breakfast? Check. Luxurious rooms? Not quite ... but they're air-conditioned, and about as cheap as you'll get in Bozburun. ₺100

EATING

BOZBURUN

Fisherman's House On the main quayside. A fun place, serving good sea bream and sea bass from ₺15 per portion. *Mezes* are cheap at around ₺5 each. Hours vary.

Möwe Just inland from the quayside. Though apparently twice frequented by Bill Gates, this restaurant looks nothing special – their seafood, however, is pretty darn good. It also turns into a bar of sorts of an evening. Daily noon–11pm.

The Datça peninsula

Slithering into the Aegean like a long, skinny snake, the elongated **Datça peninsula** is talked about in hushed tones by those from elsewhere along the coast. This is one part of the Aegean that has stubbornly refused to morph into a package-holiday destination:

once you're past little **Datça town**, itself quite cute in an urban way, the road is narrow and twisting, and probably not a good idea to drive on at night. Daylight will, in any case, allow you to see more of the wonderful view – naught but pine-speckled mountains, groves of almond and olive trees, flowers, and a sea occasionally thrusting in at little **coves**. Other than these, there's little to actually see on Datça, but at the very western end of the cape is **Knidos**, an ancient site best viewed on a **boat tour** from Datça town.

Datça

Too built-up and commercialized to be the backpackers' haven it used to be, **DATÇA** is still infinitely calmer than either Bodrum or Marmaris. Partly due to the basic accommodation on offer, as well as the difficulty of access, prices are noticeably lower than in Bodrum or Marmaris.

Life in and around Datça mostly boils down to a matter of picking your swimming or sunbathing spot. The **east beach** of hard-packed sand, known locally as Kumluk, is oversubscribed but has some shade. The less crowded **west beach**, mixed pebble and sand and called Taşlık, is acceptable and gets better the further you are from the anchored yachts.

ARRIVAL AND DEPARTURE · DATÇA

By bus Buses stop at, and depart from, the Pamukkale office on the main drag, more or less opposite the post office. In high season, services go to a few cities around western Turkey, but even at these times you might be best off taking a short-hop dolmuş to Marmaris, which offers more frequent onward departures.
Destinations Ankara (2 daily; 12hr); İstanbul (3 daily; 16hr); Marmaris (hourly; 2hr).
By ferry Ferries to and from Bodrum (one-way ₺30,

return ₺50; 1hr 45min) use a pier in Körmen Limani, 9km north of Datça town. Arriving, you'll be plopped onto a free shuttle bus to Datça town; going back out, the same bus will pick you up if you arrange this when buying your ticket (from any travel agency in Datça town). It's worth taking the boat in at least one direction to avoid duplicating the long bus journey in from the east. Small charter boats in Datça also offer trips to Knidos (see p.280).

INFORMATION

Tourist office Hidden away in a large, cream-coloured government building on the high street (Mon–Sat 8.30am–7pm; ☎0252 712 3163). It can supply maps and

lists of accommodation for the whole peninsula. From June–Oct, there's another tourist office at the far end of the beach (Mon–Fri, 9am–12noon & 1–5pm).

ACCOMMODATION AND EATING

Unlike most of the Aegean coast, Datça town holds a fair few budget **places to stay**. There are a few campsites in the area too, and a smattering of higher-end choices. However, unless you're in luxury mode it has to be said that if you've come this far, there's precious little point staying in town – press on that little bit further to one of the coves (see p.279). A clutch of near-identical **café-restaurants** overlooks the harbour, with near-identical menus – examples include Turkish breakfast for ₺10, and calamari for ₺18. They're also the best places to head for a **drink** – bottles of Efes cost a uniform ₺7.

HOTELS AND PANSIYONS
Datça Turk Evi Iskele Mah 36 ☎0252 712 9212, ⓦdatcaturkevi.com. A four-roomed boutique hideaway; stay here for a touch of Ottoman style in homely

surroundings. ₺250
★ **Mehmet Ali Aga Mansion** Kavak Meydani 1 ☎0252 712 9257, ⓦkocaev.com. Top-of-the-range boutique hotel. In the eighteenth century, this was the

---

BOAT TRIPS AROUND THE DATÇA PENINSULA
Local boat trips, as advertised on Datça's west harbour, make a good day out. Groups generally depart between 9am and 9.30am, returning between 5pm and 6pm. Standard stops include Palamut Bükü, Domuz Çukuru, Mesudiye Bükü and ancient Knidos. The going price per person, excluding lunch (usually in a restaurant at Palamut Bükü) and allowing three swim stops, is around ₺35 as far as Knidos, and ₺25 as far as Mesudiye Bükü – cheaper than taking a taxi, in any case.

home of the influential Tuhfezade family; Ottoman classics all, the buildings were left derelict for generations, but now that they're smartened up the rooms are up with the best in the land. ₺350

Tunç Pansion Iskele Mah ☎0252 712 3036. The cheapest option in town, yet surprisingly nice – on entry, it feels almost like a 1970s hotel with its lobby bar and breakfast tables. Rooms are a little Spartan, but their worn charm somehow seems to suit the town itself. ₺50

Villa Tokur Up on the hill ☎0252 712 8728, �🌐hoteltokur.com. Possibly the smartest choice in town,

with unparalleled views of the beach, run by a Turkish–German family, with pool and nicely tended garden. ₺190

CAMPSITE

Ilıca Kamping At the far end of the beach ☎0252 712 3400, �🌐ilicakamping.com. This small, friendly and perfectly located campsite is an ideal spot to relax, with a good restaurant, bar, and serene views, plus simple and upmarket bungalows and room for several dozen tents. Open all year. ₺70

Eskidatça

2km from Datça, back on the road towards Marmaris

If you think Datça is sleepy, take a look at the original hamlet, some 2km back up the road. **ESKIDATÇA**'s sleepy maze of alleys – used mainly by cows – and ancient stone-built farmhouses have lately become a haven for artists and writers, who have renovated many of the dilapidated country homes. A fair few **hotels** have opened up; for some they make tranquil places to stay, while other guests end up walking to and from Datça town in search of some life.

The south-coast coves

Okay, *this* is where Datça's at – the peninsula's ultra-relaxed south-coast coves were once accessible only by boat, but even now there's a road they remain dreamily quiet places to stay. Bar a spot of swimming in the sea, there's nothing much going on, and that's precisely the point of a visit.

Heading from east to west, the first cove you'll hit is the pretty shore hamlet of **HAYİT BÜKÜ**. It doesn't have such a great beach, but the bay itself is well protected by a scenic, claw-like headland to the west. Accordingly, it sees lots of boat traffic and there's a large dock, a few restaurants and some relatively upmarket **guesthouses**. Within walking distance west, **MESUDIYE BÜKÜ**, also known as Ova Bükü, has a far better beach and is more geared towards camping.

The 9km of rough coast road that link Mesudiye with **PALAMUT BÜKÜ** make a fairly tricky prospect without your own transport. The stark setting is balanced by a kilometre-long beach of tiny pebbles lapped by brisk, clear water, with an islet offshore.

If you're headed this way, stock up on **cash** before you leave Datça town – there are no banks or ATMs elsewhere on the peninsula.

ARRIVAL AND DEPARTURE

THE SOUTH-COAST COVES

By dolmuş Occasional services, scaled down heavily outside summer, run from Datça town to the main coves. Destinations Hayit Bükü (5 daily); Mesudiye Bükü (5 daily); Palamat Bükü (7 daily).

By taxi From Datça town, expect to pay ₺80–95 to any of the main coves.

ACCOMMODATION AND EATING

There's no real luxury accommodation around the coves, and prices at the **pansiyons** are pretty standard, with doubles varying ₺100–150. Many places, especially those on Mesudiye, allow **campers** to pitch tents, though pitches vary from well-tended grass to spaces between cars on the car parks (not an exaggeration). Most places shut down over the winter. As regards **eating**, each cove has a shop and snack-shack, though most *pansiyons* double as restaurants.

HAYİT BÜKÜ

★**Ogün's Place** Hayit Bükü ☎0252 728 0023, �🌐ogunplace.com. Relatively upmarket guesthouse with large rooms – some sea-facing – and an absolutely

fantastic on-site restaurant. A real favourite with yachties, so it may be necessary to book ahead. ₺140

★**Ortam** Hayit Bükü ☎0252 728 0228, �🌐ortamdatca .com. The cheapest rooms in this cove, especially if you've a group large enough to fill their ₺250 room, which sleeps five. Some rooms are a mere 10m from the beach – literally a hop, skip and jump, if you're nearing Olympic standard – and their on-site restaurant is superb. **₺110**

MESUDIYE BÜKÜ

Ova Pansiyon ☎0252 728 0105, �🌐ovapansiyon.com .tr. Relatively new hotel set in a pleasantly green complex,

with a couple of hammocks to swing on. Their restaurant is also the best on the strip, with food served from a surprisingly swish kitchen. **₺150**

PALAMUT BÜKÜ

Bük At the far eastern end of the bay ☎0252 725 5136. The most appealing *pansiyon* on the strip, with lovingly decorated rooms and a good on-site restaurant. **₺150**

Knidos

40km west of Datça • Daily 8.30am–7pm • ₺8 • Come on a boat tour from Datça town; catch a dolmuş along the awful road (daily 10.30am & noon); or take a ₺160 taxi

Out on wind-lashed Tekir Burnu, **Knidos** was one of the most fabled and prosperous cities of antiquity. With its strategic location astride the main shipping lanes of the Mediterranean, it was a cosmopolitan city, and many illustrious personalities hailed from here. However, the city was most notorious for an inanimate object – the **cult statue of Aphrodite** by Praxiteles, the first large-scale, freestanding nude of a woman. Modelled by the famous Athenian courtesan, Phryne, this adorned the new city from its earliest days and became Knidos's chief source of revenue; it's long gone, of course. In fact, very little at all remains of this former greatness, and it's probably not worth punishing any vehicle for the full distance from Datça to see it.

Hellenistic Knidos was laid out in a grid pattern, and most of its public buildings were on the mainland side. The **Hellenistic theatre**, overlooking the south anchorage, is the best preserved, while two **Byzantine basilicas**, one huge with extensive mosaics, overlook the north harbour.

Pamukkale

As you approach the UNESCO World Heritage Site of **PAMUKKALE** from Denizli, 20km south, a long white smudge along the hills to the north suggests a landslide or mine. Getting closer, this clarifies into the edge of a plateau, more than 100m above the valley and edged in white **travertine terraces**. The Turks have dubbed this geological fairyland *Pamukkale*, or "Cotton Castle". This incredible natural phenomenon was created by the hot spring waters that gush up at the centre of the ancient city of **Hierapolis**, whose blissfully located ruins would merit a stop even if they weren't coupled with the stunning terraces.

Only a fraction of the huge number of daily visitors to Pamukkale stay the night. Most foreign travellers who do so stay in **PAMUKKALE KÖYÜ**, a sleepy village at the base of the cliff that's still, by and large, a rural settlement – you'll see more tractors than cars on its outskirts, and its main "drag" holds only a small concentration of shops, restaurants and travel agencies. Accommodation is cheap, and almost all hotels feature spring-water swimming pools. Despite the incredible draw of Hierapolis and the travertines, it's one of western Turkey's best places to chill out for a few days.

Brief history

The therapeutic properties and bizarre appearance of the hot springs were known for thousands of years before an actual town, **Hierapolis**, was founded here by a Pergamene king during the second century BC. After incorporation into the Roman Empire in 129 BC, Hierapolis enjoyed considerable imperial favour, especially after catastrophic earthquakes in 17 AD and 60 AD – no fewer than three emperors paid personal visits, stimulating local emperor-worship alongside the veneration of Apollo and his mother Leto, who was venerated in the guise of Cybele.

BATHING IN PAMUKKALE'S SPRINGS

Pamukkale's spring waters have seduced vistors for thousands of years – including certain Roman emperors (see p.280). You can follow in their imperial footsteps by bathing in the waters today. Three different options are available. For the first, you don't even have to leave town: just off the main road, the **Natural Park** (24hr; free) is a new complex set around a lake. Natural attractions here include piped music and swan-shaped pedalos whose LEDs glow at night, as well as a couple of fake travertine terraces – whatever, the water is real enough, and the park is actually a nice place to spend the evening. The second option is also free, once you've bought your ticket to Hierapolis (see p.281) – as you head up the **travertine paths**, you can wade in the pools on the way.

However, if you want to take a proper bath in the springs, visit the **Pamukkale Thermal Baths** up on the plateau (daily 8am–7.30pm; ₺30), which encloses the sacred pool of the ancients, with mineral water bubbling from its bottom at 36°C. Changing rooms are available, as are drinks and snacks – many visitors choose to relax by the pool, coffee in hand, for an hour or more.

The presence of a flourishing Jewish community aided the rapid and early establishment of **Christianity**. Hierapolis is mentioned in Paul's Epistle to the (neighbouring) Colossians, and Philip the Apostle was martyred here, along with his seven sons. However, as at Aphrodisias, paganism lingered well into the sixth century, until a zealous bishop supervised the destruction of the remaining ancient worship sites and the establishment of nearly one hundred churches, several of which are still visible.

Hierapolis slid into obscurity in late Byzantine times, nudged along by Arab and Turcoman raids. After the Selçuks arrived in the twelfth century, the city was abandoned, not to figure much in the Western imagination until Italian excavations began in 1957.

Hierapolis and the travertines

Daily 24hr • ₺20 • ⓦ pamukkale.org.tr

The combined site of ancient Hierapolis and the travertines has three entrances. The first, the signposted "Güney Kapısı" or **South Gate**, is at the end of a 2km road describing a lazy loop up from the village. Here you'll find the visitor centre, plus a ticket booth and car park, followed by a long, shadeless walk to the ruins and terraces. Most tour buses use the **North Gate** (where there's another ticket booth and visitor centre) for access to the central car parks next to the museum; if you park at the North Gate, regular shuttle buses (₺2) will drop you outside the Thermal Baths. However, most recommended is the **travertine path** up from the village itself – a fifteen-minute hike, more if you fancy a quick splash in one of the pools.

4

Be sure to bring a **hat**, as the site is largely shadeless; once up on top, you'll be able to buy food or drink from stalls. As for **when to visit**, if you enter before sunrise you'll be more or less alone, and will see the travertines at their most beautiful. By 7am or so, crowds are already beating up the path.

The travertines

A 500m-long section of calcium deposits heads up from the village to the plateau. It takes you through a collection of **thermal pools**, where visitors are welcome to wallow. If you do plan to do so, wear appropriate clothing, and bring a small **towel** or flannel. Shoes are forbidden along the entire tract, so a **bag** in which to put your shoes would also come in handy. For the most part, the calcium surface makes for smooth and pleasant navigation. Pamukkale's hotels once siphoned off the precious mineral waters for their own heated pools; the waterflow is now strictly rotated in order to preserve the site and allow more diminished deposits to "regrow".

Deriving from a bubbling spring at the foot of Çal Dağı, this stunning natural wonder has been created over millennia. As thermal water surges over the edge of the plateau and cools, carbon dioxide is given off and hard chalk – also known as **travertine** – accumulates as a solidified waterfall, slowly advancing southwest. At sunrise or sunset, subtle hues of ochre, purple and pink are reflected in the water, replacing the dazzling white of midday.

The museum

Tues–Sun 9am–5.15pm • ₺3

One of the first things you'll see if you come up the travertine path is the **museum**, housed in restored second-century AD baths. Its gardens, visible without a ticket, are beautifully laid out. Indoors, the collection consists primarily of statuary, sarcophagi, masonry fragments and smaller knick-knacks recovered during excavations at Hierapolis.

The Temple of Apollo and Plutonium

Besides the museum and baths, a few ruins are worth tracking down in the area bounded by the city walls. The **Temple of Apollo** in its present, scanty form dates from the third century AD, though built on a second-century BC foundation. The adjacent **Plutonium** is of more interest – dedicated to the god of the underworld, this grotto is today a small, partly paved cavity beyond which you can hear rushing water and an ominous hissing: the emission of a highly toxic gas, probably a mixture of sulphurous compounds and carbon dioxide. In ancient times the eunuch priests of Cybele were reputedly able to descend into the chasm with no ill effect; today, a formidable metal cage-grille keeps daredevils out. Before this was installed, two Germans died attempting to brave the cave.

■ ACCOMMODATION			
Alida	1	Kervansaray	4
Artemis Yörük	3	Koray	5
Hal-Tur	2	Melrose	6

● RESTAURANTS	
Kayaş	2
Ünal	1

Nearby you'll also be able to find the **nymphaeum**, or fountain-house, and a large sixth-century **basilica** – probably the Byzantine-era cathedral, with two aisles sandwiching the nave. On the other side of the Temple of Apollo is a well-preserved **Roman theatre**, dating from the second century AD. Performances are held here during the **International Pamukkale Song Festival** (W turkcevizyon.com; late June): the 46 rows of seats are still capable of accommodating up to seven thousand spectators comfortably, which compares surprisingly well to its original capacity of ten thousand.

The colonnaded street

Arguably the most interesting part of Hierapolis, the **colonnaded street** once extended for almost 1km from a gate 400m southeast of the sacred pool to another breach in the north wall. This thoroughfare, parallel to the plateau's edge, unevenly bisected the grid plan of the Hellenistic city and terminated at each end in monumental portals a few paces outside the walls. Only the northerly one, a **triple arch** flanked by towers and dedicated to the Emperor Domitian in 84 AD, still stands.

The basilica and necropolis

The squat bulk of some second-century AD baths, which were converted 200 years later into a **basilica**, is easily distinguishable from the colonnaded street. Closer to the archway, west of the asphalt, stands the elaborate **Tomb of Flavius Zeuxis**, a prominent Hierapolitan merchant. This counts as the first of more than a thousand tombs of all shapes and sizes which together constitute the **necropolis**, the largest in Asia Minor. The entire complex extends for nearly 2km along the road. Many of the most sumptuous tombs bear epitaphs or inscriptions that warn transgressing grave-robbers of the dire fate that awaits them, while forecourts hold benches that were used for visits by the deceased's relatives.

4

ARRIVAL AND DEPARTURE

PAMUKKALE

To get to Pamukkale by public transport, you're likely to have to head first to the major city of **Denizli**, 20km south – an ugly place where you won't want to linger. If you've booked in advance, many of the recommended *pansiyons* are able to fetch you for free.

By plane Few travellers use Denizli Çardak airport, a full 70km east of Denizli, but it does have a few daily services to and from İstanbul and Ankara.

By train Four daily trains ply the route from İzmir, stopping at Selçuk along the way.
Destinations İzmir Basmane (4 daily, 5hr); Selçuk (4 daily, 3hr 30min).

By bus or dolmuş The Denizli *otogar*, under reconstruction at the time of writing, is well served by long-distance buses. If you've booked to Pamukkale, most companies will lay on a free servis to the town; going back, you'll be picked up outside your company's office at an appointed time. Otherwise, from Denizli you'll have to track down a dolmuş labelled "Pamukkale/Karahayıt" (7am–11.30pm; ₺2).
Destinations Antalya (14 daily; 5hr); Bodrum (6 daily; 4hr 30min); Konya (several daily; 7hr 15min); İstanbul (15 daily; 10hr); İzmir (hourly; 4hr); Marmaris (8 daily; 3hr 30min).

By taxi A taxi from Denizli costs around ₺35 per car-load.

ACCOMMODATION

Although Pamukkale is one of Turkey's most visited sights, few visitors stay the night, and fewer still stay longer. That's a great pity – not only is the town a rural charmer, but its accommodation stock is excellent value, particularly since most lodgings (even the real cheapies) boast a natural mineral water **swimming pool**.

Alida Off Mehmet Akif Ersoy Bul ☎0258 272 2602. This lemon-coloured hotel is a great budget option, its rooms arrayed around a courtyard in the style of a *kervansaray*. It's very close to the main road and therefore good for the travertines, but still quiet enough to get a good night's sleep. ₺60

Artemis Yörük Hotel Atatürk Cad ☎0258 272 2674, W artemisyorukhotel.com. Large option in the very centre of town. Rooms sleep up to five and surround a central pool, though this courtyard area can get noisy when it's barbecue night – which is seemingly every night. It's surprisingly cheap, and they even have a few dorms. Dorms ₺20, doubles ₺80

Hotel Hal-Tur Mehmet Akif Ersoy Bul 45 ☎0258 272 2723, ⓦwww.haltur.net. One of the most prestigious hotels in the village, directly opposite the terraces, with immaculate a/c rooms – some face the travertines, though you'll pay a fair bit extra. All have satellite TV and wi-fi, and there's also a swimming pool and good restaurant. ₺150

Hotel Kervansaray İnönü Cad ☎0258 272 2209, ⓦkervansaraypension.com. A long-standing favourite, owned by the welcoming Kaya family. Many of the centrally heated rooms overlook creek greenery, and there's a pool and a rooftop café-restaurant (though this is closed in winter). ₺70

Koray Hotel Fevzi Çakmak, Pamuk Mah 27 ☎0258 272 2222, ⓦotelkoray.com. Popular, small hotel built around a pool and leafy garden, with a good restaurant; half-board available. ₺80

★ **Melrose Hotel** Vali Vekfi Ertürk Cad 8 ☎0258 272 2250, ⓦmelrosehousehotel.com. A short walk south of the action, this is a truly wonderful place – plush rooms, a nice pool, excellent food from a real wood oven, and the friendliest owners in town. No wonder so many people come back year after year. ₺90

EATING

Eating out in Pamukkale is almost uniformly mediocre – you'll usually get better value from your *pansiyon*, almost all of which have an on-site restaurant. You'll find a few restaurants on the main drag; thanks to Pamukkale's popularity with Asian tourists, many offer their own takes on Japanese and Korean dishes. Give the *bibimbap* a try – greens, spices and a fried egg on top of rice.

Kayaş Atatürk Cad. Popular with backpacker types, this is a café, bar and restaurant all rolled into one. Meals include grills, cheap omelettes and a few Korean dishes (*bibimbap* ₺10). For drinks, a Turkish coffee will set you back ₺4, a beer ₺6 and a cocktail ₺15 – all are best enjoyed over a puff on a nargile (₺15). Daily 8am–8pm.

Ünal Menderes Cad 12. One of the few "real" restaurants in town – in other words, it's popular enough with villagers not to need to chase foreign customers. Most come for the cheap grills, but don't miss the delectable *mantı* (₺12). It's licensed, too. Daily 9am–late.

Laodicea

Daily 8am–6pm • ₺10 • 1km from Pamukkale–Denizli dolmuş route

A short bus ride from Pamukkale lies a great site in the making. This is **Laodicea**, whose ruins are almost visibly in the process of rising from the ground – just a few years ago, there was little of interest to see, but it's now a real feast for the eyes, even if some ruins have been somewhat crudely restored.

While Pamukkale up the road catered for pleasure, Laodicea was an important trading centre, thanks to its position at the junction of two major trade routes. Originally hosting a large Jewish community, in time it became a highly important Christian base – in fact, it was one of the **Seven Churches of Asia** mentioned in the Book of Revelation.

Most of the sights, including **temples**, a **nymphaeum** and an unusually square **agora**, are arrayed off a colonnaded thoroughfare now known as Syria Street – religious tours make a bee line for a cross near its far end. Also of interest are the two fantastic **theatres** north of the site, each vaguely facing Pamukkale – one had room for eight thousand people, the other twelve thousand.

Aphrodisias

Daily: summer 8am–6.30pm; winter 8am–5.30pm • ₺10 • Almost all visitors arrive on tour buses from Pamukkale, which generally depart at 9.30am and cost ₺30; public transport – in a taxi from Karacasu, the nearest sizeable town, 13km east – takes forever and saves no money at all

Situated on a high plateau over 600m above sea level, ringed by mountains and watered by a tributary of the Büyük Menderes, **Aphrodisias** is one of Turkey's most isolated and beautifully set archeological sites. Acres of marble peek out from among the poplars and other vegetation that cloaks the remains of one of imperial Rome's most cultured Asian cities. Late afternoon visits have the bonus of often dramatic cloud formations, spawned by the elevation, and the attendant dappled lighting.

APHRODISIAS

N

Geyre

Stadium

Path

City Walls

School of
Philosophy

Temple of
Aphrodite

Tetrapylon

Museum

P
Car Park

Bishops Palace

Odeion

COURTYARD

Ticket Office

Sebasteion

Double
Agora

Agora
Gate

Baths of Hadrian

City Walls

Path

Portico of Tiberius

Theatre

Tetrastoön

Theatre
Baths

City Walls

0   100
metres

4

It's quite easy to find your way around – most of the site's main features are accessible on a path that loops around the complex, maps are dotted around, and all signage is in English as well as Turkish. In general, it's best to follow a **clockwise** route, which will allow you to finish your visit in the air-conditioned cool of the museum, What's more, that route means that the short climb to the theatre will come when you're fresh, at the start, rather than adding to the sweat at the end.

Brief history

Aphrodisias was one of the earliest occupied sites in Anatolia. Neolithic and Bronze Age mounds have been found here, and there has been some sort of **fertility cult** here for just as long. The Assyrian goddess of love and war, Nin, became meshed with the Semitic Ishtar, with the Hellenic Aphrodite eventually assuming the goddesses' combined attributes.

Despite a strategic position near the meeting point of ancient Caria, Lydia and Phrygia, and its proximity to major trade routes, for many centuries Aphrodisias remained only a shrine. However, during the second century BC, its citizens were rewarded for their support of the Romans during the Mithridatic revolt. Imperial favour bestowed, various emperors patronized the burgeoning city. Aphrodisias became particularly renowned for its school of sculpture, sourcing high-grade marble from nearby quarries, and local works soon adorned every corner of the empire, including Rome itself.

Perhaps because of this fixation with graven images, paganism lingered here for almost two centuries after Theodosius banned the old religions. The reputation of its Aphrodite love cult had served to protect Aphrodisias since its inception, but by the fourth century AD, two earthquakes and sundry raids began to take their toll, and decline was the dominant theme of Byzantine times. The town was abandoned completely during the thirteenth century, its former glories recalled only by the Ottoman village of Geyre – a corruption of "Caria" – among the ruins.

Only since 1961 has work by a New York University team permitted a fuller understanding of the site. The intention is to render Aphrodisias on a par with Ephesus and the eventual results will certainly be spectacular, though for now some of the more interesting areas remain off-limits.

The Sebasteion, theatre and agora

The ornate **Sebasteion**, the first stop for many Aphrodisias visitors, consists of two parallel porticoes erected in the first century AD to honour the deified Roman emperors. From here is a pant up to the large, and virtually intact, **theatre**. Founded in the first century BC, it was extensively modified by the Romans for their blood sports three centuries later. At the rear of the stage building is a large square, the **tetrastoön**, originally surrounded by colonnades on all sides, while a large **baths complex** lies to the south.

Heading back downhill you'll pass the **double agora**, consisting of two squares ringed by Ionic and Corinthian stoas, though these are filled with vegetation, and fenced off. The **Portico of Tiberius** separates the agora from the fine **Baths of Hadrian**, preserved right down to the floor tiles and the odd mosaic; it is, however, expected to be under renovation until 2016 at the earliest.

The Bishop's Palace and Odeion

North of the baths, several blue-marble columns sprout from a multi-roomed structure commonly known as the **Bishop's Palace**, from its presumed use during Byzantine times. East of here huddles the Roman **odeion**, with nine rows of seats.

The Temple of Aphrodite

Only fourteen columns survive of the city's principal sanctuary, the **Temple of Aphrodite**. The Byzantines converted it to a basilica during the fifth century, so considerable detective work was required to re-establish the first-century BC foundations. Even these were laid atop at least two older structures, with evidence of mother-goddess worship extending back to the seventh century BC. The Hellenistic/Roman sanctuary had forty Ionic columns arranged eight by thirteen, with the cult image erected in the main hall. The Byzantines removed the columns at each end of the temple, fashioning an apse to the east, an atrium and baptistry on the west, and it's this architectural pastiche you see today. Immediately north is the so-called **School of Philosophy**, tentatively identified (like the bishop's palace) on the basis of resemblance to other such structures elsewhere.

The stadium and tetrapylon

The northernmost feature of the site is the 30,000-seat **stadium**, among the largest and best preserved in Anatolia. A version of Delphi's Pythian Games was held here, featuring sporting, musical and dramatic events.

Returning to the main loop trail, the last thing you'll notice before exiting onto the museum square is the re-erected **tetrapylon**, a monumental gateway with two double rows of four columns, half of them fluted, supporting pediments with intricate reliefs. This second-century AD edifice is thought to mark the intersection of a major north–south street with a sacred way heading toward the Aphrodite shrine.

The museum

Daily: summer 8am–6.30pm; winter 8am–5.30pm • ₺10, same ticket as site

Aphrodisias's wonderful (not to mention wonderfully air-conditioned) **museum** houses a wide array of sculpture recovered from the ruins. Given that Aphrodisias met most of the demand for effigies under the empire, even what remains after the loss of originals and the spiriting away of works to city museums is considerable. Highlights here include the "Aphrodite Hall", containing statuary related to the cult, with a rendition of the goddess, much defaced by Christian zealots, occupying the position of honour. There's also the "Imperial Hall", its walls lined with superb reliefs.

4

The Turquoise Coast

KAŞ THEATRE

5

The Turquoise Coast

Noted for its fine beaches and stunning mountainous scenery, Turkey's southwesternmost shore has long been dubbed "the Turquoise Coast", thanks to the hues of its horizons and the sea. It's dominated by the Baba, Akdağ and Bey mountains, which drop precipitously to the main coastal highway that often skims just above the water. In ancient times, known as Lycia, the region was home to an independent people whose most obvious legacy is the distinctive rock tombs that litter the landscape. Despite much recent development, many attractive coves and islets remain inaccessible to vehicles, so yachting and *gulet* trips are popular. As the impact of ever-increasing visitor numbers has, moreover, been minimized by restrictions on construction height, and special protection for archeological sites and wildlife habitats, much of the region has remained relatively unspoiled.

The usually excellent **Highway 400** between Marmaris and Antalya offers intermittent views, and connects several major sites along the way. The coast is best approached via **Dalaman airport**, busy with direct international flights most of the year, as well as domestic flights from İstanbul.

At the far west of the region, **Dalyan** is an attractive small resort that's also noted for its languid river, sandy beach – a sea-turtle nesting ground – and the ruins of **Kaunos**. East of here, **Fethiye**, despite its paucity of beaches, is the Turquoise Coast's oldest resort and largest town; along with **Ölüdeniz** lagoon, it's handy for spectacularly sited Lycian ruins such as **Oenoanda**, **Kadyanda** and **Tlos**, in dramatic mountainous locations. Further southeast, **Patara** abuts one of Turkey's best beaches, making it easy to combine sea and sun with cultural forays to the **Letoön** sanctuary, **Pınara**, **Sidyma** and **Xanthos**. Other convenient bases include the nearby resorts of **Kalkan** and **Kaş**, smaller than Fethiye and pitched at rather different clienteles.

The spectacular mountainous hinterland is also well worth exploring, especially with your own wheels, with dramatic ancient **Arykanda** the most obvious target. Also worth considering is the stunning drive from Kaş or Kalkan to **Gömbe**, in the shadow of a 3000m-plus peak.

Beyond the yacht-harbour-dominated town of Finike, east of Demre, the scenery becomes increasingly impressive as you enter conifer forests on the slopes of **Tahtalı Dağ**, officially designated a national park, before passing ancient **Olympos** – plus more good beaches at **Adrasan** and **Çıralı** – and ancient **Phaselis**. Thereafter a string of characterless purpose-built resorts dominated by German and Russian holiday-makers lines the approach to Antalya.

THE LYCIAN WAY

Highlights

❶ Kaya Köyü Abandoned Greek Orthodox village near Fethiye, an emotive relic of the 1923 population exchange. **See p.299**

❷ The Lycian Way This waymarked long-distance trail – linking coves, ruins and mountains – is ideal in low season. **See p.304**

❸ Dalyan river life Whether watching the waters slide by or being ferried downstream to a glorious beach, the river makes Dalyan the resort it is. **See p.306**

❹ Tlos Perhaps the most dramatically sited of Lycia's numerous ancient cities. **See p.312**

❺ Patara Roman ruins behind a great sweep of sandy beach that's among the longest strands in the entire Mediterranean. **See p.321**

❻ Kaş Set opposite the Greek islet of Kastellórizo, this is one of the most congenial resorts on this coast. **See p.326**

❼ Kekova Eerie seascapes and submerged ruins make these inlets an ideal arena for sea-kayakers. **See p.334**

❽ Çıralı A paradise for nature lovers, with a turtle-nesting beach and an ancient city, backed by the spectacular foothills of Mount Tahtalı. **See p.346**

HIGHLIGHTS ARE MARKED ON THE MAP ON P.292

Brief history

Mountainous, rugged **Lycia** (*Likya* in Turkish) lies south of a line drawn roughly between Antalya and Köyceğiz Gölü. At the core of the territory, the Bey Dağları and Akdağ, each exceeding 3000m elevation, isolate it from the rest of Anatolia. Relatively secure in their mountain fastness, the fiercely independent ancient Lycians – probably an indigenous, pre-Hittite people – organized their main cities and conurbations of smaller towns as the democratic **Lycian Federation**, with 23 voting units. This elected municipal and federal officials and, until imperial Rome assumed control, made decisions of state. Homer's *Iliad* mentions the Lycians as allies of the Trojans; later, in the sixth century BC, the region was subdued by the Persian general Harpagos, but then largely left to govern itself.

From 454 BC, after the Athenian general Kimon had expelled the Persians from the Mediterranean coast, the Lycians became members of the Athens-dominated Delian League. The League ceased to exist after the Peloponnesian War and Lycia again fell under Persian domination. Alexander the Great arrived in 333 BC and, after conquering Halikarnassos, easily secured the region's surrender; following his death, Lycia was ruled by his general, Ptolemy, also king of Egypt. During the third century BC, under Ptolemaic rule, Greek displaced the native Lycian language and Lycian cities adopted Greek constitutions. The Ptolemies were defeated by Antiokhos III in 197 BC, himself bested in 189 BC by the Romans, who handed the kingdom over to the Rhodians. The Lycians bitterly resented Rhodian control and succeeded in 167 BC in having this administrative relegation revoked.

Thereafter, the Lycians enjoyed over two centuries of semi-independence under a revived federation. After they resisted the Pontic king Mithridates in 88 BC, they were rewarded by Rome for their loyalty. During the Roman civil wars, Lycian reluctance to assist Brutus caused the destruction of Xanthos, and in 43 AD it was joined to Pamphylia in a larger Roman province. **Roman imperial rule** saw Lycia reach its maximum ancient population of 200,000, a figure not again equalled until the twentieth century, and the cities were graced by the Roman civic architecture that constitutes most of the ruins on view today.

During the fourth century the province was divided by Diocletian. A period of Byzantine-supervised decline followed, abetted by Arab raids in the seventh and eighth centuries. From then on, the area's history resembled that of the rest of western Anatolia, where, after Selçuk Turk sovereignty during the eleventh and twelfth centuries, and an interlude of minor emirates, the **Ottomans** installed a more durable Anatolian Muslim state. They continued a pattern of moving nomadic Turkic tribes into the Lycian uplands, leaving the coast to pirates and local chieftains, until in the eighteenth century the sultan ordered its settlement by more tractable, productive Greek Orthodox colonists from the offshore islands.

Fethiye

FETHİYE is the fulcrum of the Turquoise Coast, and a hub of its property industry. It remains, however, a lively market town of 80,000-plus souls, sprawling north along the coastal plain, and the transport and marketing of oranges and tomatoes is still important to its economy. Fethiye occupies the site of ancient **Telmessos**, and some impressive rock tombs are an easy stroll from the centre. It also makes a convenient base for the nearby **beaches** of Ölüdeniz and Kıdrak, while a short drive or long walk out of Fethiye brings you to the atmospheric ghost village of **Kaya Köyü**. Much of the nearby coastline is accessible only by sea, and with the **Gulf of Fethiye** speckled with twelve islands, one- to four-day boat tours from Fethiye harbour are popular, aiming for secluded coves in which to swim, fish and anchor for the night.

5

Brief history

Little is known about the early years of ancient **Telmessos**, except that the city wasn't originally part of the Lycian Federation, and, in the fourth century BC, actually resisted it. A Lycian ruler later subdued the Telmessans, and during the Roman imperial era it formed part of the Federation, albeit unique in maintaining good relations with Rhodes.

During the eighth century, the city's name was changed to **Anastasiopolis** in honour of a Byzantine emperor. This became **Makri** in the following century (*Meğri* in Turkish). Finally, a thousand years later, and following the expulsion of the predominantly Greek Orthodox population, it was changed once again during the 1930s to Fethiye, in honour of Fethi Bey, a pioneering pilot who was killed during World War I.

That little now remains of the medieval town is largely due to two immense **earthquakes**, in 1857 and 1957, which toppled most of its buildings; the rubble lies compacted beneath the present quay and shoreline boulevard. Another, lesser quake in the spring of 2012 did little damage, but nonetheless had a significant impact on domestic tourism to the town and its environs.

The Amyntas tomb

115 Sokağı • Daily 8.30am–sunset • ₺8

The remains of ancient **Telmessos** are obvious as soon as you arrive. Several **Lycian rock tombs** are located above the bazaar, strikingly close to town. Most notable is the **Amyntas Tomb**, so called because of the Greek inscription *Amyntou tou Ermagiou* (Amyntas son of Hermagios) on its wall. To get there, take any of the lanes leading south from Kaya Caddesi (also negotiable by car). These give on to 115 Sokağı, which runs along the base of the fenced-in archeological area.

The tomb porch consists of two Ionic columns surmounted by a triangular pediment. Carved in imitation of a temple facade – right down to the bronze nails on the doorframes – it gives an excellent impression of how wooden temple porches would have looked. The tomb itself would have been entered through the bottom right-hand panel of the doorway, which was broken by grave-robbers long ago.

FETHİYE

ACCOMMODATION	
Atapark	5
Duygu	6
Ece Saray	1
Ferah	7
Tan Pansiyon	3
Villa Daffodil	8
Yacht Classic	4
Yıldırım	2

Hellenistic theatre

Fethiye's conspicuous Hellenistic **theatre**, sprawling behind the main quay, has only been excavated since 1994. Much of its masonry was carted away after the 1957 earthquake for construction material, so it's rather frayed at the edges. Benefit concerts are sometimes staged to raise funds for further restoration, though the process is stalled at present.

Knight's Castle

On the hillside behind the bazaar • Daily 24hr • Free

The path up to Fethiye's so-called **Knight's Castle** leads through the backstreets from Çarşı Caddesi, affording good views of the town on the way. Although the fortress is attributed to the Knights of St John, its wide range of architectural styles suggests handiwork on the part of Lycians, Greeks, Romans, Byzantines and Turks.

Fethiye museum

Okul Sok • Daily: June–Sept 8am–7pm; Oct–May 8am–5pm • ₺3

Compact it may be, but **Fethiye museum** is well worth seeing if you want to flesh out your knowledge of the nearby sites. Its most compelling exhibit is a stele found at the Letoön (see p.317), dating from 358 BC; the trilingual text, in Lycian, Greek and Aramaic, was vital in deciphering the Lycian language. It's now located in a room to the left of the ticket desk, along with Bronze, Archaic and Classical age pottery, as well as some fine Roman-era statuary from Tlos (see p.312) and Kaunos (see p.309).

The room to the right of the entrance holds more finds from Kaunos, including a fascinating statuette of Kybele complete with symbolic scorpion and deer motifs, and incredibly detailed, larger-than-life statues of the Roman emperors Hadrian and Antoninus Pius, both from Tlos. The garden is also worth a look, with its fine collection of sarcophagi lids and a Roman-era olive pressing stone, whose cut-channels look remarkably like a peace symbol.

5

BOAT TOURS AND CRUISES FROM FETHİYE

Standard-issue, multi-island, one-day **boat tours** from Fethiye cost about ₺30 per person; just turn up at the quayside for daily departures between May and October, usually leaving at around 10am and returning at 6pm. Tours with Kardeşler, a reliable outfit (☎0252 612 4241, ⓦkardesler.com), depart daily 10.30am, and return at 6.30pm.

However, these one-day trips take in a set repertoire of relatively spoiled islands, with little time at each; it's far better to charter your own crewed boat to stop at just one or two selected islands. If you've more time, sign on for one of the **cabin cruises** that depart at least five days per week in season. A typical four-day, three-night itinerary heads east, overnighting near or at Gemiler Adası, Kalkan and Kekova before a final minibus shuttle from Andriake to the backpacker lodges at Olympos. Shorter cruises take in Aya Nikola, Ölüdeniz and Butterfly Valley. Paying a bit over the cheapest option, and boarding only owner-operated craft, is recommended to ensure quality; also make sure you check the vessel carefully before paying, and talk to returning clients – complaints about everything from blocked toilets to abusive, non-English-speaking crew to hidden extra charges are common.

Before Lunch ☎0535 636 0076, ⓦbeforelunch .com. A well-established, Australian/Turkish-run Fethiye outfitter that generates consistently positive feedback. Noted for good food, they're at the high end of the price spectrum, and run a new 25m-long boat that has six double cabins, and one family-sized one. A leisurely four-day, three-night Fethiye-to-Fethiye cruise taking in the twelve islands costs €250 per person in low season, €275 in high season.

Big Backpackers ☎0252 614 1981 or ☎0532 235 2978, ⓦbigbackpackers.com. This reliable Fethiye outfitter offers a four-day, three-night Blue Cruise, from Fethiye to Olympos, for €165 per person in low season, €195 in high season.

ARRIVAL AND DEPARTURE

By air Havaş shuttle buses run to the *otogar* in Fethiye from Dalaman airport (12–15 daily, 2.30am–9.30pm; ₺10). Tickets Labranda Tourism, Atatürk Cad opposite Belediye (☎0252 614 7500, ⓦlabrandatour.com), handles tickets for all airlines.

By bus Short-haul dolmuşes run almost constantly from Fethiye's *otogar*, over 2km east of the town centre at the junction with the Ölüdeniz road, to the accommodation district of Karagözler. Other dolmuşes to Ölüdeniz, Göcek, Faralya, Saklıkent and Kaya use the minibus garage, on 136 Sokağı south of Çarşı Caddesi, 500m east of the central market area. In season, the Patara Ko-op runs a 24-seat minibus service along the coast between Fethiye and Finike. **Destinations** Antalya (12 daily; 3hr inland, 6hr 30min by coast); Bodrum (6 daily; 4hr 30min); Denizli (6 daily; 4hr express, 6hr normal); Kabak (8 daily; 1hr 20min); İstanbul (5 daily; express 12hr, 15hr normal); İzmir (twice hourly; 7hr); Kaş (15 daily; 2hr); Marmaris (hourly; 3hr); Ölüdeniz (27 daily; 45min); Pamukkale (several daily; 5hr); Patara (15 daily; 1hr 30min).

By car Parking can be a nightmare in the town centre: park near the museum, buy a ticket either from a parking warden or pay-and-display machines, or use one of the handful of fee-paying *otoparks*.

By hydrofoil Between late May and early October, hydrofoils run almost daily from the main jetty to Rhodes in Greece. Yeşil Dalyan, facing the jetty at Fevzi Çakmak Cad 168, is the sole ticket outlet (☎0252 612 4015, ⓦyesildalyantravel.com).

Destinations Rhodes (June–Sept, daily except Wed & Sun at 9am; late May & Oct Tues, Thurs, Fri; 1hr 30min; €85 return).

GETTING AROUND

By taxi The main taxi ranks are near the PTT, and in front of the ancient amphitheatre.

Car rental Levent, Fevzi Çakmak Cad, Yat Limanı Gümrük Karşısı no. 37/B (☎0252 614 8096, ⓦleventrentacar.net).

Motorbike rental Abalı, just behind the theatre roundabout (☎0252 612 8812).

INFORMATION AND ACTIVITIES

Tourist office İskele Meydanı 1, near the harbour, but pretty useless (May–Sept Mon–Fri 8am–noon & 1–7pm, Sat & Sun 10am–noon & 1–5pm; Oct–April Mon–Fri 8am–noon & 1–5pm; ☎0252 614 1527).

Scuba diving Though lacking fish, the gulf offers reasonable visibility, coral and caves plus submerged ruins.

Outfits include Dolphin Diving Centre, its boat moored behind the post office (☎0535 717 3130, ⓦdolphindiving .com.tr), and Diver's Delight, Dispanser Sok 25/B, Cumhuriyet Mahallesi, near the memorial obelisk (☎0252 612 1099, ⓦdiversdelight.com). One-day introductory courses cost around £55, PADI four-day courses £265.

ACCOMMODATION

Fethiye has lodging for all tastes and budgets; unlike other coastal resorts, you should find something even in high summer. Unless otherwise stated, recommended accommodation is open (or claims to be open) year-round. Divided into Birinci (First) and İkinci (Second), the quiet, desirable **Karagözler** neighbourhood supports the oldest cluster of hotels and *pansiyons*, with most premises enjoying a bay view. The only drawback is remoteness from transport terminals and restaurants, but parking is easier than in the centre. Fethiye's **bazaar area**, extending two blocks to either side of Çarşı Caddesi, can be noisy even at night, and now holds very few accommodation options.

Atapark Hotel Shore road, İkinci Karagözler ☎ 0252 612 8899, ⓦ atapark hotel.com. Well located on the waterfront in a quiet part of town, with a hamam, good restaurant and small pool. Only the larger, pastel-coloured sea-view rooms are really worth the money, though all have flat-screen TVs and tea- and coffee-making facilities. **₺70**

Duygu Pension Karagözler Ortayol 54 ☎ 0252 614 3563, ⓦ duygupension.com. Situated on a pleasant residential street just behind the waterfront, the *Duygu* is the only Fethiye pension to have its own pool. All 11 en-suite rooms have a/c, and a nice roof terrace enjoys sea views. **₺60**

Ece Saray Marina quay, Birinci Karagözler ☎ 0252 612 5005, ⓦ ecesaray.net. Indisputably the top lodging in central Fethiye, this mock-traditional low-rise hotel occupies impeccably landscaped grounds in a quiet corner of the shore esplanade. All the plush rooms enjoy sea views, while common facilities include a spa, fitness centre, infinity pool, two bar/restaurants and a private marina. Good value for the facilities on offer. **₺380**

Ferah Pansiyon (Monica's Place) 16 Sok 21, İkinci Karagözler ☎ 0252 614 2816, ⓦ ferahpension.com. Part of a chain of Turkish backpackers' hostels, with dorm beds or basic but en-suite doubles, pick-up service from the *otogars*, internet access and optional evening meals. Some sea views, despite the location one block inland. Dorms **€14**, doubles **€35**

Tan Pansiyon Eski Karagözler Cad 41, Birinci Karagözler ☎ 0252 614 1584, ⓔ tanpansiyon@hotmail .com. Good budget option run by a friendly Turkish family. The bathrooms are on the small and eccentric side. The four roof-terrace units are the best, though the hottest in summer. The view across the bay from said terrace is wonderful. **₺70**

Villa Daffodil Fevzi Çakmak Cad 115, İkinci Karagözler ☎ 0252 614 9595, ⓦ villadaffodil.com. Overtly yellow, mock-Ottoman structure in one of the quieter shoreline corners, with a pool, on-site restaurant, hamam and landscaped grounds, as well as fair-sized pine- and white-tile rooms, making it a prime mid-range option. **₺125**

★ **Yacht Classic Hotel** Opposite the yacht marina, Birinci Karagözler ☎ 0252 614 1530, ⓦ yacht classichotel.com. A self-contained seaside resort, with private jetty, lush bayside breakfast garden and fair-sized pool. Rooms have recently been given a revamp in the neo-modernist style. Think clean white lines and a stylish lack of clutter. **₺220**

Yıldırım Guesthouse Fevzi Çakmak Cad 53, ☎ 0252 614 4627, ⓦ yildirimguesthouse.com. Backpackers' favourite run by the friendly Ömer, who takes guests on free guided walks from Ovacık to Faralya on request. Plain but tidy carpeted rooms are enhanced by the opportunity to make free tea or coffee all day. Dorms **₺25**, doubles **₺8**

EATING AND DRINKING

One of the best options for eating in Fethiye is to head for the central courtyard of the **fish and produce market**, and buy the fish of your choice (best selection before 7pm) from the central stalls, then take it to be cooked at one of several *meyhanes* around the perimeter (€2.50/₺5 basic fee); however, exorbitantly priced drinks and accompanying *meze* are the norm here, so maybe carry on into the vegetable section and eat your fish at the *Öztoklu* diner there. Otherwise the eating scene largely consists of basic Turkish with an admixture of British/Turkish crossover joints. Most of Fethiye's drinking bars are in the old bazaar, which also holds a smattering of live Turkish music venues (open Fri & Sat only).

RESTAURANTS AND CAFÉS

İslam Usta Belediye Cad 12 ☎ 0252 612 9487. This friendly, long-running, female-run *börek* place has a few outside tables, and is recommended for its tender *poğaça* (₺1), with a variety of savoury fillings, and cheesy *talaş* (puff-pastry) triangles – all best washed down with a glass of fresh black tea. Daily 7am–10pm.

Meğri Çarşı Cad 30 ☎ 0252 614 4047, ⓦ megrirestaurant.com. The doyenne of local restaurants, *Meğri* is equally popular with locals and

tourists alike for home-style Turkish. Pleasantly located on a lively corner in the backstreets. Mains around ₺20. Daily 8am–2am.

★ **Mozaik** Sok 2/A (behind Domino's Pizza) ☎ 0252 614 4653. This Turkish–English place brings the spicy taste of southeast Turkey to Fethiye. Try the mixed *meze* platter for two (₺16), which includes dips such as *cevizli biber* (spicy walnut, pepper and bread paste) and hummus. Kebabs and casseroles from ₺20, a good-value bottle of wine ₺30. Daily 10am–2am.

5

Nefis Pide Eski Cami Sok 9 ☎0252 614 5504. One of the best-value options in town, with *pides* ₺6–9 and kebabs from ₺10. There are a few tables out on the street, and unusually for a *pide* place, it's licensed. Daily 9.30am–midnight.

Öztoklu Meyve Pazarı (fruit market). Buy fresh fish from the adjacent fish market and bring it here to be cooked for a mere ₺5, which includes salad, bread or garlic bread and a special sauce. Drinks extra. Daily noon–midnight.

Paşa Kebap Çarşı Cad 42 ☎0252 614 9807, ⓦpasakebap.com. The *Paşa* may be a typical kebab restaurant, but it's a notch up on most of its rivals. Try the *soslu beyti* (spiced mincemeat baked in a wrap and served with tomato sauce and yoghurt; ₺15). They also serve *pides* from ₺6 and pizzas from ₺12.5, as well as *meze*. Daily 9am–1am.

Şamdan 96 Sok 7 ☎0252 614 2808. Cheap and cheerful unlicensed restaurant with soups (₺4), pizzas (₺10) and kebabs (from ₺12). It's not a place for a romantic supper, so best frequented at lunchtime. Daily 9am–midnight.

BARS

Car Cemetery Bar Hamam Sok 25 ☎0252 618 7872. A well-established favourite at the south end of Hamam Sokağı, which puts on live rock music most weekends. You can toke on a nargile if you're in the mood to relax. Daily 10am–4am.

Deep Blue Hamam Sok 23 ☎0252 612 1008. Almost adjacent to the *Car Cemetery Bar* on this narrow street; watch the world go by from a comfortable couch, cool beer in hand (₺7). Daily 10am–3am.

Val's Cocktail Bar Uğur Mumcu Parkı Yanı ☎0252 6142 2363. Popular with expats and well situated by the waterside, this is the place to enjoy a coffee, beer or something a little stronger, and settle down to read one of the 2000-plus books on the shelves. Daily 9am–1am.

DIRECTORY

Books Natur-el, near the Hayal Cinema and PTT, has a limited stock of foreign-language books.

Hamam Hamam Sok 2 (daily 7am–midnight, mixed-sex); usually lukewarm and touristy, not a particularly good introduction to Turkish baths despite the building's purported sixteenth-century vintage. Bath, soap and scrub ₺35.

Post office Atatürk Cad (Mon–Sat 8am–midnight, Sun 9am–7pm).

Shopping Fethiye's central food market is between Cumhuriyet Cad and Tütün Sok. The adjacent district offers plenty of fake (plus a few real) designer clothes and perfume; safflower marketed as saffron and adulterated honey (plus the odd pickpocket) abound too. Main market day is Tuesday, when local villagers flood into town with their produce; peak hours 10.30am–1pm. The place to hunt for carpets, leather goods and jewellery is Paspatur district, especially to either side of Hamam Sok.

Around Fethiye

Despite the overdevelopment that has taken place in the hills south of Fethiye, notably the mass-market British-orientated resorts of Ovacık and Hisarönü, there are still some notable attractions set in beautifully unspoiled locations. The best of these are the appealingly remote ancient city of **Kadyanda**, and the abandoned Greek village of **Kaya Köyü**, which is set in a pretty valley and holds plenty of accommodation options suited to those seeking a peaceful retreat.

Kadyanda

Around 25km north of Fethiye • Daily 24hr; unfenced • ₺8 when warden present • Frequent public transport to Üzümlü, from where you can either take a taxi or walk the direct path (1hr 30min up, 1hr down); if driving, turn left at Üzümlü onto a narrow 3.5km paved road that crosses a mountain pass, then turn right and follow 5km of improved dirt track

The ruined mountain-top city of **Kadyanda**, less than an hour's drive north of Fethiye, dates back at least 2500 years. The attractive village of **Üzümlü**, 16km north of Fethiye along a broad, well-marked road, makes little of its proximity to the site, other than a basic restaurant opposite the mosque and a low-key trade in its fine *dastar* cloth.

At the site itself, 9km further by road, an arrow points towards a self-guided loop walking trail. First bear south, past the vaulted tombs of the **necropolis**, then keep close to bits of the **city wall** on the left, followed by a climb to a false summit with a long, partly preserved **agora**, and views of Fethiye. The site's highlight is at the true highest point: a long, narrow **stadium**, with seven rows of seats surviving. Steps in the seats

Gölhisar & Denizli

Üzümlü

Kadyanda

Günlüklü

Yanıklar

Kargı

Katrancık

Çalış

Çamköy

Katrancık Adası

Şövalye Adası

Günlükbaşı

Kızıl Ada

Fethiye

HWY 400

MEDITERRANEAN SEA

Ocakköy

Mendos Dağı (1758m)

Keçiler

Patara, Kaş & Antalya

Kınalı

Kaya Köyü

Af Kule

Ovacık

Soğuk Su

Hisarönü

Gemiler Beach

Belceğiz

Kozağaçı

Lydian Way

Baba Dağı (1976m)

Aya Nikola (Gemiler Adası)

Ölüdeniz

Kıdrak Beach

Minare

Pınara

Faralya

Kirme

"Butterfly Valley"

Belen

Gemile Liman

Kabak

Karaağaç

AROUND FETHİYE

Alınca, Gey & Sidyma

climb to a huge jumble of masonry, all that's left of a **temple** to an unknown deity. On the opposite side of the stadium stand substantial **Roman baths**, with their polygonal masonry and entry archway. At the northeast edge of the stadium, a flat expanse is pierced by the mouth of a deep cistern that supplied the city with water – one of many, so beware holes in the ground.

Finally the path angles south to the best-preserved stretch of **city wall**, punctuated by windows and affording fine views of distant ridges and forested valleys in between. Crossing the top of a square bastion, you look down into the **theatre**, which retains its rear-facing and stage wall, plus many of its seats – though like most of Kadyanda it's only partly excavated. The descent to the road completes a leisurely 45-minute walk through superb mountain scenery – good reason enough for a visit.

Kaya Köyü

The atmospheric ghost village of **KAYA KÖYÜ**, whose Greek Orthodox Christian inhabitants were forced to leave their homes in the compulsory exchange of populations between the newly created Republic of Turkey and Greece in 1923 (see p.663), stands roughly 9km southwest of Fethiye. The roofless remains of the six hundred or so houses that comprised this community of some three thousand souls are arrayed in tiers up a pine-scented hillside. They stand above a pastoral idyll of a valley which has, so far, escaped the excesses of tourist development that have swamped nearby Ovacık and Hisarönü.

While the population of Kaya Köyü, or Levissi as it was known to Greek inhabitants, was being shipped west, Macedonian Muslims were sent to occupy the abandoned buildings. Most choose to emigrate rather than stay, considering the land too poor. Today the local population lives in a couple of hamlets, Keçiler and Kınalı, set in the valley below the ruins.

Although this is fertile farming land, tourism has become increasingly important to the inhabitants of this tranquil spot, and there are a number of attractive places to stay and eat. Clearly the ghost village of Kaya Köyü is the main attraction for most visitors, but there's plenty to keep you occupied for several days, including a superb half-day walk to Ölüdeniz, horseriding and kayaking. Or you could just relax and read Louis de Bernières' epic novel *Birds Without Wings* (see p.701), much of which is set in Eskibahçe, a thinly disguised Kaya Köyü. Beware, however, as a controversial plan to "restore" some of the village houses, and turn them into holiday homes, resurfaced in 2012.

The site

Daily 8.30am–6.30pm • ₺5

If you visit Kaya Köyü in high season – July and August – it's best to start your explorations of this unique place early, both because of the heat and to avoid the tour groups who arrive later in the day from nearby resorts. To get a flavour of the place, it's enough simply to wander the lichen-crusted cobbled pathways that cut between the derelict houses – most still with their fireplaces, earth-closets and cisterns still intact – and try to imagine the place as it might have been a hundred years ago, with workers on their way home from the fields, or dressing up in their Sunday best, ready for church.

If you want more of a focus, a small, barrel-roofed and whitewashed chapel, clearly visible on a hilltop just above the town, affords splendid views back over the settlement and, in the opposite direction, over the sea.

A more sizeable church dating to 1888, that of **Panayia Pyrgiotissa**, stands a couple of hundred metres above the road in the west of the village. Its red roof tiles, like those of many other buildings here, were imported from Marseille, a testament to the prosperity of the place prior to the expulsion of its inhabitants. The **Taksiarhis** church, in the east of the village, was restored in 1910, with a pretty courtyard floored with a black-and-white pebble mosaic.

ARRIVAL AND DEPARTURE | KAYA KÖYÜ

By dolmuş Dolmuşes run to Kaya from Fethiye (daily 7am–10pm, every 30min in summer, hourly in winter; ₺4).

On foot A paved 9km road – complemented by a largely intact cobbled path that makes a significant short cut – climbs to Kaya Köyü from behind the castle in Fethiye. The walk takes about 2hr, but don't underestimate it; many visitors get lost after leaving too late in the day.

ACTIVITIES

Horseriding The English-run Perma Ranch, on the eastern outskirts, offers horse rides (☎0252 618 0182, ⓦpermaranch.co.uk).

Sea kayaking Seven Capes Sea Kayaking, which has its HQ in Kınalı hamlet (☎0252 618 0390, ⓦsevencapes .com), offers well-priced sea-kayaking tours along the coast, as far south as the eponymous Seven Capes (Yedi Burunlar).

ACCOMMODATION

Kaya's satellite hamlets offer various accommodation options. In Kınalı, 2km west of Kaya, a trio of exquisitely refurbished old houses sleeping four can be booked through Exclusive Escapes (see p.29).

Keçiler Villas Keçiler ☎0044 118 932 1866, ⓦturkeyvillas.com. Four high-standard two-bedroom villas, arrayed around a pool, in the same hamlet as *Misafir Evi*; help finding flights and rental cars is available. Weekly rate £855

Misafir Evi Keçiler ☎0252 618 0162, ⓦkayamisafirevi .com. An excellent upmarket choice in Keçiler, on the valley's north slope, this boutique hotel offers nine tasteful, wood-trimmed rooms; a well-regarded restaurant, open all year; and a large pool. Rates include breakfast, half board costs ₺20 extra per person. ₺140

★ **Village Garden** East edge of Kınalı hamlet ☎0252 618 0259. One of the best-value establishments, comprising four tidy studios, 1.5km from Kaya's central teahouse. The fair-priced on-site restaurant balances meat, seafood and their own vegetables on its menu. ₺80

Villa Rhapsody Kınalı ☎0252 618 0042, ⓦvilla rhapsody.com. Substantial white house with dark wood trim set in a pretty garden with pool. Well run by fluent English-speaker Attilla and his wife for 25 years, it has simple but comfortable carpeted rooms. Closed Dec–March. ₺105

EATING

Bülent'in Yeri On the through-road near the colonnaded cistern. Good for a quick snack of budget-priced *saç böreği* or *gözleme*. Daily 9am–10pm.

★ **Cin Bal** Kayaköy ☎0252 618 0066. This popular year-round barbecue joint has pleasant tables under the trees in summer and a welcoming, open-fire warmed stone dining room for winter. Buy a kilo of lamb for ₺45–55 and grill to your taste over charcoal. *Meze* ₺5, beer ₺5, glass of wine ₺10. Daily noon–midnight.

Levissi Garden Kaya Köyü ☎0252 618 0173, ⓦlevissigarden.com. Atmospheric eating place in an old

Greek house at the edge of the ghost town. Try the local cheese platter with Turkish wine followed by a lamb sauté main for ₺22. A log fire provides warmth in the chilly winter months, while the breezy terrace is cool in the summer. Daily 11am–midnight.

Sarnıç Kaya Köyü. The best of the more ambitious local restaurants, open most of the year, with quality live music some nights and an informal museum of local finds inside what was once a prominent merchant's house. Daily 11am–midnight.

Ölüdeniz

Ölüdeniz, the "Dead Sea", lies 12km south of Fethiye, below the sprawling resorts of Ovacık and Hisarönü. This azure lagoon, now part of a nature park, features on countless Turkish travel posters and is one of Turkey's iconic sights. The area southeast of the lagoon, fronting onto an attractive sandy beach, has developed into the popular resort village of **Belceğiz** – though it is far more commonly referred to, even by locals, as Ölüdeniz. Belceğiz holds sufficient accommodation, cafés and bars to attract one- and two-week holidaymakers, and is also a world-ranking spot for paragliding

THE WALK FROM KAYA KÖYÜ TO ÖLÜDENIZ

A popular walk from Kaya Köyü leads along a spectacular coastal path, affording great views out to sea and, eventually, down onto Turkey's most photographed beach, Ölüdeniz. Mostly downhill, it takes between ninety minutes and two hours to reach the northwest shore of the lagoon, and another half-hour or so to the main dolmuş stop.

The route begins in Kaya at the easterly Taksiarhis church (aka Yukarı Kilise). Although it's fairly well marked by red-and-yellow blazes, it's essential to take care, as you could easily wander off-trail into potentially hazardous gully and cliff terrain. Ignore blue or rust-red paint blobs that would lead you over the pass with a windmill, chapel and Turkish flag. The proper path climbs somewhat faintly to a plateau within 15min, then levels out through pine woods for another 20min, before reaching fine overviews of Aya Nikola and Soğuk Su, and a stretch of well-engineered, cobbled, descending path. This ends at some charcoal-burners' flats, with a less distinct path to a large rectangular cistern just beyond, before the head of a ravine. Here the trail appears to split; the left-hand option is easier going. Just under an hour along, both routes converge before you reach an obvious pass with some pine-studded rocks on the right, affording the first eyeful of the lagoon. From here you've an uncomplicated, if sharp, drop to the first sunbed concession on the shore.

5

(see p.56). It's also handily located near the start of the waymarked **Lycian Way** walking trail (see p.304).

Ölüdeniz Nature Park

Daily dawn–dusk • ₺5 per person, ₺17 per car (or park on road outside for ₺5 and walk in)

Offically known as the **Ölüdeniz Nature Park** (Ölüdeniz Tabiat Parkı), the lagoon of Ölüdeniz lies just west of the resort of Belceğiz, a few minutes' walk along the road paralleling the sea, passing the PTT (Post Office) en route. Its warm, if occasionally turbid, waters make for pleasant swimming even in April or May, while in the height of summer the waters off the sand spit fronting the sea proper are more appealing. There are cafés, showers and toilets, and the views up to the dramatic pine-cloaked mountainsides are wonderful.

Kıdrak Beach

3km east of Belceğiz • May–Oct daily 8.30am–7.30pm • ₺4.5, sunbed and umbrella ₺10

The sands at **Kıdrak Beach** (Kıdrak Plajı), beside the all-inclusive *Club Lykia World* east of Belceğiz, belong to the forestry department. Cleaner and far less commercialized than Belceğiz itself, they hold no more than a small snack bar and seasonal sunbed/umbrella concession; there's also natural shade in the pines.

ARRIVAL AND DEPARTURE ÖLÜDENIZ

By dolmuş Dolmuşes run to Ölüdeniz from Fethiye (summer daily 7.30am–9pm, every 30min; half-hourly in summer; ₺4).

ACTIVITIES

Paragliding Ölüdeniz is among the very best paragliding spots in the world. The season lasts April–Nov, with the best visibility in autumn. Both Belceğiz and Kıdrak serve as landing venues for paragliders, kitted out by several beachfront outfits for a hefty ₺200 or thereabouts and taken to a point near the summit of 1976m Baba Dağı for launching. Sky Sports (☎0252 617 0511, ⓦ skysports-turkey.com) is the most heavily publicized and longest-established outfit, while Reaction Paragliding is also recommended (☎0252 617 0501, ⓦ reaction.com.tr).

ACCOMMODATION

Most accommodation clusters behind Belceğiz beach with its broad, landscaped pedestrian promenade. None of the rough-and-ready **bungalow-campsites** that welcomed the hippie vanguard here during the late 1970s survives; such clientele is now obliged to patronize four **tent/bungalow/caravan sites** along the north shore of the lagoon. The former orchards behind Belceğiz and on the slopes flanking the road in are now home to perhaps forty **hotels**, mostly in thrall to package companies, though worthwhile exceptions do exist.

BOAT TRIPS FROM ÖLÜDENIZ

A wide range of **boat trips** operate from Belceğiz, to some beautiful and fascinating destinations including remote coves, islets such as Gemiler, and Byzantine ruins. Among the potential pitfalls are limp lunches, bored guides and stops that are either rushed or missed out altogether.

The cheapest and most popular destination is the so-called **Butterfly Valley** (Kelebek Vadisi), a beach backed by a limestone canyon just inland (3 dolmuş boats, daily mid-May to Oct 11am–6pm; ₺15 return). Named after the many species that flutter about during the right seasons, it also holds a waterfall, 20min inland (₺5 admission). The beach itself is frequented by an uneasy mix of day-trippers sipping overpriced beers at the café, and New Age patrons attending regular yoga, Indian dance and healing seminars while staying in basic tent-or-bungalow accommodation (ⓦ thebutterflyvalley.blogspot.com).

5

Jade Residence Mid-promenade, Belceğiz ☎0252 617 0690, ⓦjade-residence.com. Two pleasant, mock-colonial-style stone buildings with wooden shutters and wrought-iron grilles, set in beautifully lush landscaped gardens. There's also a nice pool complete with decking, and a good buffet breakfast. €150

★ **Oyster Residences** Mid-promenade, Belceğiz ☎0252 617 0765, ⓦoysterresidences.com. 26 large, wooden-floored rooms done up in neo-colonial style, arranged around a fair-sized pool with wooden decking; also direct beach access. €110

Paradise Garden Ölüdeniz Yolu, halfway back to Ovacık ☎0252 617 0545, ⓦparadisegardenhotel.com. Best of the hillside hotels, set in vast grounds, with variably sized if low-ceilinged and balcony-less rooms. It's a longish walk through fifteen acres of garden to the main pool, but it's quite stunning when you get there. €96

Sugar Beach Club Ölüdeniz Cad 20 ☎0252 617 0048, ⓦthesugarbeachclub.com. The best of the campsites fronting the east shore of the lagoon, with three grades of wooden bungalows. Tents are available to rent if you don't have your own. Tents ₺24, doubles ₺80

Sultan Motel Kırancağıl Mahallesi ☎0252 616 6139, ⓦsultanmotel.com. High above the beach on the fringes of the resort of Ovacık, this slightly ramshackle motel is nevertheless great value, and conveniently located at the official start of the Lycian Way. The en-suite bungalow rooms are light and bright with decent balconies and LCD TVs. Great pool, too. €70

EATING, DRINKING AND NIGHTLIFE

Bronze Cafe In a backstreet just behind the Oyster Residences. This female-run *Ev Yemekleri* (home-cooking) café is good value for Ölüdeniz, with Turkish-style *moussaka* at ₺7, *köfte* ₺10 and *gözleme* ₺5. It even serves alcohol. Daily 10am–10pm.

★ **Kumsal Pide** Seyir Beach Hotel Yanı. This popular place is open year-round and dishes up *mezes* of above average in quality and size; a large *pide* (₺9–12) easily feeds two. There's even a bowling alley in the basement. Daily 9am–midnight.

Secret Garden In the back lanes of Belceğiz ☎0252 617 0231. Hidden away like the name suggests, with a lovely quiet garden location and good service that make it a great choice for a romantic dinner. The menu features slightly unusual dishes like *tandır kebap* and sea bass baked in a salt crust. Daily noon–2am.

Beyond Ölüdeniz: hamlets along the Lycian Way

South of Kıdrak, the **Yediburun** (Seven Capes) headlands constitute some of the most beautiful and least exploited coastline in Turkey, with several isolated villages lying just inland. The mountains, which reach close to 2000m in height, plunge dramatically into the sea, making road construction, and therefore tourist development, extremely difficult. What tourism there is remains low-key, with the majority of visitors either hanging out in bohemian "Butterfly Valley" or Kabak, or making the very most of the wild and picturesque seafront by walking the waymarked **Lycian Way** trail (see box, p.304).

Faralya

The cliff-side hamlet of **FARALYA** (officially Uzunyurt), set magnificently partway up the slopes of Baba Dağı, enjoys views across to Rhodes on clear days. Unless you're hiking the Lycian Way, there's little to do in Faralya, but a steady stream of walkers spend the night here.

Most of the accommodation options, including the three listed below, are perched just above "Butterfly Valley" (see p.302). A difficult trail, entirely distinct from the Lycian Way, drops to the eponymous beach in 45 minutes. Allow an hour to climb back up again, and take great care, using the rope and pegs provided for safety at the scrambly bits; the *jandarma* regularly have to be called out to rescue hapless bathers/explorers.

5

THE LYCIAN WAY

Inaugurated in 2000, the **Lycian Way** is a long-distance trail that runs parallel to much of the Turquoise Coast, In theory, it takes five weeks to complete the entire trail, but most walkers sample it in stages rather than tackling it all in one go.

Starting above Ölüdeniz and ending just shy of Antalya, the trail takes in choice mountain landscapes and seascapes en route, with many optional detours to Roman or Byzantine ruins not found in conventional guidebooks. Some of the wildest sections lie between Kabak and Gavurağili, above the Yediburun coast, and between Kaş and Üçağiz. Elevation en route varies from sea level to 1800m on the saddle of Tahtalı Dağ. The best walking seasons along most of the way are October (pleasantly warm) or April and May (when water is plentiful and the days long); except in the highest mountain stages, summer is out of the question.

The route itself ranges from rough boulder-strewn trails to brief stretches of asphalt, by way of forested paths, cobbled or revetted Byzantine/Ottoman roads and tractor tracks. While the entire distance is marked with the conventional red-and-white blazes used in Europe, plus occasional metal signs giving distances to the next key destination, waymarks can be absent when you need them most. Continual bulldozing of existing footpath stretches into jeep tracks is such a major problem that the notional initial section between Hisarönü and Kirme has now ceased to exist, with most hikers starting at Faralya, while periodic maintenance (and where necessary re-routing) barely keeps pace with fast-growing scrub and rockfalls.

An unofficial "add-on" route, the *Likya Yollari*, runs from Hisarönü to Fethiye via Kaya, while loop side trails and alternative routes are being marked in different colour schemes. Kate Clow, who marked the original Lycian Way, adapted the Turkish military's ordnance survey 1:50,000 maps for her *The Lycian Way*, a **guide-booklet-with-map**, which indicates points for water, camping and (often obsoletely) overnighting indoors. The English-language version is sold at select bookshops, newsstands and travel agencies all along the coast as well as from online book retailers. Hard-wearing and waterproof, the map often saves the day, as trail descriptions can be frustratingly vague. It's also important to be aware that timings in *The Lycian Way* apply to those carrying a full pack; deduct about a quarter when doing sections as day-hikes.

A website, 🌐 lycianway.com, offers updates on route conditions and a user forum.

ACCOMMODATION AND EATING
FARALYA

★ **Değirmen/Die Wassermühle** Faralya Köyü Hisar Mah 4 ☎ 0252 642 1245, 🌐 natur-reisen.de. In the area's most prestigious accommodation, you'll be lulled to sleep by the sound of mill-race water. Seven comfortable apartments and two conventional rooms are grouped around a restaurant (meals usually for guests only), the restored mill and a stone-crafted swimming pool; minimum one-week stays are preferred. Closed late Oct to March. ₺55

George House 500m northwest of Faralya centre ☎ 0252 642 1102, 🌐 georgehouse.net.tc. At the end of a dirt track, this well-regarded place has a small pool and great views down over Butterfly Valley. All rates are for two people, half board. Camping ₺70, treehouses ₺80, bungalows ₺90, en-suite rooms ₺100

Melisa Pansiyon 400m northwest of Faralya centre ☎ 0252 642 1012, 🌐 melisapension.com. Four simple yet comfortable en-suite B&B rooms with verandahs overlooking fruit orchards and the valley; you can also sleep on the flat roof or camp in the orchard, and use the kitchen and cosy lounge in cool weather. Tents ₺10, roof per person ₺25, doubles ₺80

Kabak

The village of **KABAK**, usually reached by bus from Fethiye, or on foot along the Lycian Way, straggles down a beautiful wooded valley from the narrow coastal road to the sea at **Gemile Liman**. While several pensions and eating options are strung along the main road, most visitors come here to chill out in one of the wooden huts/bungalows, set in the pine-forested valley behind the sand-and-pebble beach.

Whether you like Kabak or not is very personal. Some will find its ramshackle New Age hippy vibe a delight, others will baulk at the steep prices to stay in what is essentially a wooden hut. Either way, mosquito repellent is strongly recommended in summer.

ARRIVAL AND DEPARTURE

KABAK

By minibus and truck Minibuses run to Kabak, on the main coast road, from Fethiye, via Farlaya and Ölüdeniz (up to 8 daily; around 1hr; ₺6.5). From there, a 4WD truck ferries visitors down a horrendously dusty and steep track to the beach, stopping on request at the various accommodation options in the woods en route (₺5–7.5 depending on number of customers).

On foot To walk to the beach from the main road, follow the east-bound Lycian Way (around 40min) from the *Olive Garden* pension/restaurant.

ACCOMMODATION AND EATING

Full Moon At the end of the road ☏0252 642 1081, ⓦfullmooncamp.com. Thirteen hillside chalets, without en-suite facilities, and a proprietor who looks after trekkers and the local trails. There's a large hillside pool if you're not up for the drop to the beach, while meals are served at the popular bar area. Open all year. Half board only. **₺70**

Olive Garden Kabak Köyü ☏0252 642 1083. Seven bungalows with the best views and congenial locally born management. Half board only. **₺60**

Reflections Camp Kabak Köyü ☏0252 642 1020, ⓦreflectionscamp.com. Run by American Chris since its inception in 2001, this camp has a high ratio of toilets to accommodation and recycles its trash and grey water. Very chilled. Half board only, closed Nov–April. Tents **₺80**, bungalows **₺130**, en-suite rooms **₺180**

Sea Valley Kabak Köyü ☏0252 642 1236, ⓦseavalleybungalow.com. Opened in 2011, this large and luxurious bungalow complex is set in landscaped gardens just above the beach. Old Kabak hands may decry its attempts to take the "community" upmarket, but its spruce en-suite bungalows are very popular despite the very high prices. Open all year. Rates include breakfast. **₺220**

Turan's Camp Kabak Köyü ☏0252 642 1227, ⓦturancamping.com. Established back in 1987, one of the first in the valley, with seven bungalows in grades from basic to balcony en-suite, for twice the price. Relatively elaborate cooking, yoga programmes and a small plunge-pool. All rates include half board. Basic **₺80**, en-suite **₺160**

Göcek

In a stunning location at the northwest corner of the Gulf of Fethiye, **GÖCEK** is, thanks to its four marinas and busy boat-repair yard, an obligatory stop on yacht or *gulet* tours. Among both foreigners and Turks, it has become very trendy. The late President Özal vacationed here more than once – the main street is now named after him – and some very high-end apartment complexes front the bay. While there's no beach to speak of, the passing boat trade means an astonishing concentration of facilities for such a small place: supermarkets, laundries, yacht chandleries and posh souvenir shops along, or just off, the main inland commercial street, largely pedestrianized. The meticulously landscaped, lawn-fringed shore esplanade is car-free too, and the venue for a hugely popular evening promenade. For the average traveller, however, the main reason to stay here is the proximity to Dalaman airport.

ARRIVAL AND DEPARTURE

GÖCEK

By dolmuş Regular dolmuşes link Fethiye with Göcek, dropping passengers at the main car park just off the inland shopping street (hourly 8am–10pm; 45min; ₺5.25).

ACCOMMODATION

Tufan's Çarşı Yolu ☏0252 645 1334. Handily located just 50m behind the beach and right in the heart of the village, this small pension, with eight basic rooms, each kitted out with pine beds, is very good value for this upmarket resort. **₺60**

Ünlü Çarşı Yolu ☏0252 645 1170, ⓦgocekunluotel.com. Set in the village centre, just behind the seafront, the plain, old-fashioned rooms in this bog-standard mid-range hotel don't excite for their style, but it's comfortable enough and all rooms have sea views. **₺145**

Yonca Resort Gonca Sok, off Atatürk Bul ☏0252 645 2255, ✉info@yoncaresort.com. Set amid a grid of villas, well back from the waterfront in a pleasantly green suburb, the eight rooms of this guesthouse are all tastefully furnished in a dark-wood antique style. There's a small pool, and if you don't want to eat out food can be delivered from nearby restaurants. **₺150**

5

EATING AND DRINKING

Many local **restaurants**, and especially those closer to the Port Göcek Marina, cater exclusively for the trendy set with obligatory service charges and tiny portions. Plenty of simple cafés, however, dish up standard Turkish food at prices lower than, for example, Dalyan.

★ **Antep Sofrası (aka Kebab Hospital)** Turgut Özal Cad ☎ 0252 645 1873. Just inland in the pedestrian zone, this place specializes in quality kebabs (from ₺16) and *lahmacun* at affordable prices — they've now seaside seating as well. Daily 9am–midnight.

Café Bunka Turgut Özal Cad, at the far west end of the esplanade. This branch of İstanbul's Japanese Culture Centre is one of the few sushi bars on the Turkish coast, and thus predictably expensive. Daily 10am–midnight.

Café West Turgut Özal Cad. International cuisine dished up in a laidback café-bar-bistro, not far from the marina. Full English breakfast, smoothies and a wide range of coffees. Daily 9am–midnight.

Mercan Pizza Turgut Özal Cad ☎ 0252 645 2856. Simple café fronting the street parallel to the waterfront, with a few outside tables. It's good for lentil soup (₺4) and reasonable attempts at pizza (from ₺10). Daily 7am–midnight.

Dalaman

The first real town west of Fethiye is dull, bleak and grid-planned **DALAMAN**. As home to the Turquoise Coast's main airport, it provides many visitors with their introduction to the region. There's absolutely no reason to stay here, however, with both Göcek (see p.305) and Dalyan (see p.306) so close at hand, and Fethiye/Ölüdeniz not much further away. For that reason, we have only supplied information on how to arrive and depart.

ARRIVAL AND DEPARTURE

DALAMAN

By plane Dalaman airport, 6km south from town (☎ 0252 792 5291), is not linked with the town centre by public transport; a taxi to the central *otogar* costs at least ₺30. Domestic and international flights arrive at separate terminals. Havaş run regular coaches from the domestic terminal to both Fethiye (daily 1.40am–11.45pm; 1hr; ₺10) and Marmaris (daily 1.40am–11.45pm; 1hr 30min; ₺15). The airport has round-the-clock banking facilities, as well as three car rental booths: Avis (☎ 0252 792 5118), Budget (☎ 0252 792 5150) and Europcar (☎ 0252 792 5117).

Destinations Atlasjet, Onur Air, Pegasus and Turkish Airlines fly to İstanbul (Sabiha Gökçen or Atatürk) at least daily, while AnadoluJet fly to Ankara daily.

By bus The *otogar* is in the town centre, just east of the D555 highway.

Destinations Antalya (2 daily in summer; 6hr inland route); Bodrum (5 daily; 3hr 30min); Denizli (2 daily; 4hr 30min); Fethiye (every 30min; 1hr); İstanbul (2 daily; 14hr); İzmir (14 daily; 5hr); Kaş (4 daily; 3hr); Marmaris (12 daily; 1.5hr); Muğla (18 daily; 2hr); Ortaca (every 30min; 20min).

Dalyan and around

The growing but still beautiful riverside resort of **Dalyan**, 24km west of Dalaman, is home to around five thousand people. It makes a good base for visiting nearby attractions like the ancient site of **Kaunos** across the river, **İztuzu beach** at the river mouth, and the beautiful freshwater lake of **Köyceğiz** with its shoreline hot springs.

Dalyan first came to prominence in 1986, when controversy erupted over a proposed luxury hotel on nearby İztuzu beach, a hatching ground for **loggerhead turtles**. Conservationists succeeded in halting the scheme, and now the beach is statutorily protected between May and October, when eggs are laid. In the wake of this campaign, the town styled itself as ecologically correct, but with its mess of identikit restaurants, trinket shops, T-shirt vendors and loud bars, it's now, riverside location apart, little different from other mainstream resorts. You'll notice the turtle motif everywhere, from the turtle statue in the main square to restaurants and *pansiyon*s being named after the creatures.

Life in Dalyan revolves around the **Dalyan Çayı**, which flows past the village between Köyceğiz lake and the sea. Many choice *pansiyon*s line the river's east bank, and the

BIKE RIDES FROM DALYAN

Renting a **mountain bike** in Dalyan is an appealing option in the cooler months; they're available at better hotels and certain travel agents for around ₺15 a day, or from the *Lindos Pansiyon* (see p.308) at ₺25 for a quality machine.

The best local ride is to **İztuzu beach**: there's one nasty hill en route, with *ayran* and *gözleme* stalls to pause at for refreshment in the village of Gökbel. This land route is recommended at least once, as you loop around the Sulungur lake and get glimpses of marsh and mountain not possible amid the claustrophobic reed beds of the Dalyan Çayı. Alternatively, bikes can be rented on the far bank, with various attractions accessible on both paved and dirt roads.

boats that put-put up and down it are the preferred means of transport to the major local sites. Craft heading downstream pass a series of spectacular fourth-century BC "temple" tombs in the west-bank cliffs.

ARRIVAL AND DEPARTURE   DALYAN AND AROUND

By bus and dolmuş Dalyan's minibus yard is near the mosque, close to the centre.

Destinations from Dalyan Fethiye (2 daily; 1hr); Göcek (2 daily; 30min); Ortaca (frequent; 20min).

Destinations from Ortaca From the town of Ortaca, on Highway 400 13km north of Dalyan, buses run to: Antalya (2 daily; 7hr coastal route); Bodrum (5 daily; 4hr); Dalaman (every 30min; 20min); İzmir (10 daily; 5hr 30min); Kaş (5 daily; 3hr 30min); and Köyceğiz (every 30min; 30min).

By boat Dolmuş boats to the river end of İztuzu beach (₺10 return; 40min) depart from Kordon Boyu, opposite

the mosque. They leave as soon as they are full (almost constantly in the summer season), returning from 2pm or so until sunset. Otherwise, peak-season minibuses ply every 30min along the 13km road to the east end of the strand. Many of the riverside *pansiyons* and hotels also have their own small motorboats providing morning service to the beach for a nominal fee. To reach Kaunos (see p.309) take the little-publicized (most operators want you to take a tour) rowboat ferry; ₺4 round trip from the jetty inside the Kral Bahçesi.

INFORMATION AND TOURS

Tourist office On Cumhuriyet Meydan, but only open sporadically, and of little use; use ⓦ dalyanonline.net instead.

Adventure tours Kaunos Tours (☎0252 284 2816, ⓦ kaunostours.com) rents cars and organizes adventure trips – canyoning, scuba diving, horseriding, mountain biking, sea-kayaking and rafting on the Dalaman Çayı (aka Akköpru Çayı). Excursion days range £12–30, while rafting costs £50, including lunch and transfers.

Boat tours The most popular local outing is the day-tour offered by the quayside motorboat co-op. These excursions – usually departing by 10.30am – take in thermal springs on Köyceğiz lake, Kaunos ruins and the beach, and are passable value at about ₺30 per person. Custom-renting is considerably dearer but worthwhile if you have a large group. Riverside *pansiyons* may take you on evening boat trips to spy water snakes, and freshwater terrapins surfacing for air.

ACCOMMODATION

The most desirable *pansiyons* line or overlook the river; book well in advance in high season. Maraş Caddesi, which heads from the town centre to a dead end nearly 2km south, passes the junction with Kaunos Sokağı, home to several garden-set *pansiyons* and hotels, which serve breakfast at waterside terraces. The dolmuş boats to İztuzu beach will collect passengers from riverside accommodation. Drivers should take the signposted İztuzu road from the centre, then bear right at the second junction, to get around a one-way system and nocturnal street closures. Mosquitoes are a major plague, though repellents or vaporization mats are widely sold. Most establishments close between November and Easter.

RIVER-VIEW ESTABLISHMENTS

Asur Otel/Assyrian Hotel South end of Maraş Cad ☎0252 284 3232, ⓦ asurotel.com. Nicely landscaped complex, with a lawn/garden down to the river, that's popular with tour companies – especially Thomas Cook. Pleasant, if small and slightly dark hexagonal rooms, all with a/c and tidy en-suite bathrooms, ranged around a beautiful

pool. Double rooms £60, apartments per person £120

Caria Hotel Yalı Sok 9, off Maraş Cad ☎0252 284 2075, ⓦ hotelcaria.com. This has Dalyan's best roof terrace, with great views across to the tombs. Rooms are simple but very comfortable and many have river views. Nocturnal boat trips, barbecues, airport pickup on request, limited parking. Open all year. €35

Çınar Sahil Pansiyon Yalı Sok 14 ☎0252 284 2117. Set in a small citrus grove abutting a busy part of the waterfront, and perfectly located to make the most of the bustling town centre. The rather dated but clean and airy one-, two- or three-bed rooms are nonetheless adequate and there's a rooftop breakfast terrace. ₺100

KAUNOS SOKAĞI

Dalyan Resort Kaunos Sok 50 ☎0252 284 5499, ⒲dalyanresort.com. This self-contained complex, set in lovely gardens that roll down to the riverside, offers tasteful rooms, with travertine tiles much in evidence, an airy domed restaurant, rental canoes and a hamam with mud therapy offered. Popular with package operators, it remains open all year. Suites cost €30 extra. €110

Happy Caretta Hotel Kaunos Sok ☎0252 284 2109, ⒲happycaretta.com. Rustic, whitewashed stone building

nestling beneath a canopy of pines and palms. There's decking fronting the river, and all the ten standard and four deluxe rooms (₺50 extra) are immaculately kitted out. ₺170

Kilim Hotel Kaunos Sok 11 ☎0252 284 2253, ⒲kilimhotel.com. Anglo (Becky)-Turkish (Emrah)-managed, nicely overhauled 1980s' hotel. Half its stall-showered rooms have balconies and/or a/c, while breakfast is served in a new six-room riverside annexe opposite. There's a poolside lawn under palm trees, regular barbecues and snacks on request. ₺110

Lindos Pansiyon Kaunos Sok 28 ☎0252 284 2005, ⒲lindospension.com. Well-appointed bungalow rooms with both twin and double beds plus two family rooms and one four-bed studio. Pleasant library-lounge for cool weather, free canoes available, and genial management by English-speaking Levent Sünger. A keen mountain biker, he rents out quality bikes for ₺25 and knows all the best routes. Late March to end Oct. Doubles **€45**, family rooms **€65**

★ **Midas Pansiyon** Kaunos Sok 32 ☎0252 284 2195, ⓦ midasdalyan.com. Delightful setting right on the river, with decking and a ladder allowing patrons to bathe. Rooms are on the small side and plain, but spotlessly clean and easy to cool with the a/c. The hearty breakfast is served under the graceful branches of an ancient fig tree next to the river. **₺100**

DALYAN OUTSKIRTS
Kemaliye House 7km east towards Ortaca ☎0252 692 3613, ⓦyabanci.com/house.html. Sympathetically

renovated rural house sleeping six set in large gardens, with a pool. Run by local travel agent Alison Hawkes, who can also arrange flights. Open all year; minimum 3-night stay, week-long rentals preferred. **£90**

Manzara Villas Eastern edge of town off İztuzu road, 1km from centre ☎0252 284 4465, in UK ☎01304 375093, ⓦmanzara.co.uk. Three well-designed six-person villas, set around a pool-garden, with a view of the "Sleeping Giant" mountain, make an excellent self-catering choice for families, though good breakfasts are available. Genial owner Clare Baker's UK office can provide help in securing flights and car rental. As you arrive, call Döndü for directions on ☎0543 322 9800. Weekly rentals only. Weekly **£500**

EATING AND DRINKING

While Dalyan's **restaurants** tend to be bland, anglicized and a little overpriced, several establishments offer no-nonsense Turkish cuisine at sensible prices. Restaurants line the waterfront between the jetty and Cumhûriyet Meydan, with generally cheaper options inland northeast of the square. **Nightlife** is concentrated along the upper pedestrianized reaches of Maraş Caddesi.

Atay Dostlar Sofrası Gülpınar Cad ☎0252 284 2156. Opposite the central mosque, this inexpensive, licensed place serves a wide range of dishes, from pizzas (₺10) to grilled fish (₺15) as well as *meze* and *hazır yemek*. The quality isn't great, but portions and prices are. Open all year. Daily 7am–11pm.

Brothers Maraş Cad. Sit on comfy red sofas on busy Maraş Street and watch your fellow visitors promenade by, as you suck on a mellow nargile (₺12.5) or chug a cool beer (₺7). Daily 10am–1am.

★ **Çağrı Pide** Atatürk Bul ☎0252 284 3427. Inauspiciously located near the entrance to the minibus square, hidden behind ATMs and palm trees. There are a few tables set out in the street where you can enjoy *pides* (₺5–7), pizzas from ₺9 plus a range of *meze* and grills. Beers cost a bargain ₺5. Open all year. Daily 8am–midnight.

Gel-Gör Maraş Mah Dalko Karşısı ☎0252 284 5009. It's

well worth the 1km stroll from the town centre to this quietly located waterfront restaurant, with a great terrace overlooking the river and a rustic white and blue wooden shack for cooler evenings. Fifty types of *meze* (₺6 and up), farmed sea bass and sea bream (₺14), and wild-caught red mullet (₺70 per kilo). Open all year. Daily 9am–1am.

Saki Geçit Sok ☎0252 284 5212. Right on the river near the rowboat jetty, this small, no-menu place has some of the best traditional Turkish *meze* in town, specializing in vegetarian recipes as well as meat-based dishes. Mains from ₺15, *meze* from ₺5. Closed Nov–March. Daily 10am–11pm.

Sunray Maraş Cad. This long-established café-bar is the most sophisticated in Dalyan, with coffees, fresh juices and shakes as well as alcoholic drinks. Gaze across river to the illuminated rock tombs and chill to jazz and world music. Daily 1pm–1am.

Kaunos

1.5km southwest of Dalyan • Take a tour boat; drive from Köyceğiz via the Sultaniye baths and Çandır village, though the road beyond Sultaniye is potholed and indirect, with no parking by the upper site entrance; or cross the river from Dalyan on the rowboat-ferry (see p.307), and walk 15min

Excavations at ancient **Kaunos** began in 1967 and still take place each summer under the aegis of Başkent University. While the ruins are far from spectacular, they're well labelled with CGI reconstructions, and the site is among the least deservedly overlooked archeological sites on the Mediterranean coast. It's alive with herons and storks in summer, flamingos in winter, plus terrapins, tortoises, snakes and lizards in all seasons.

Passengers arriving by **tour boat** disembark either at the fish weir (*dalyan* means weir) or at another jetty at the base of the outcrop supporting Kaunos's acropolis. The fish caught are mostly grey mullet and bass, and a Kaunos ancient inscription suggests they've been part of the local diet since ancient times. From either landing point it's a seven-minute walk up to the fenced **site**.

5

Brief history

Although Kaunos was a ninth-century BC Carian foundation, it exhibited Lycian cultural traits, not least the compulsion to adorn nearby cliffs with rock tombs. Kaunos was also closely allied to the principal Lycian city of Xanthos; when the Persian Harpagos attempted to conquer the region in the sixth century BC, these two cities were the only ones to resist. Kaunos began to acquire a Greek character under the Hellenizing Carian ruler Mausolus. Subsequently, the city passed to the Ptolemies; then to the Rhodians; and finally, after fierce resistance to Rhodes, it came under indirect Roman imperial administration.

Besides its fish, Kaunos was noted both for its figs, and the prevalence of malaria; excessive fig consumption was erroneously deemed the cause, rather than the anopheles mosquitoes which, until 1948, infested the surrounding swamps. Another insidious problem was the silting up of its harbour, which continually threatened the city's commerce. The Mediterranean originally came right up to the foot of the acropolis hill, surrounding Kaunos on all sides apart from an isthmus of land to the north. But the Dalyan Çayı has since deposited over 5km of silt, leaving an expanse of marshy delta in its wake.

The site

Daily: April–Oct 8.30am–7pm; Nov–March 8.30am–5pm • ₺8

Much of Kaunos has yet to be unearthed, despite the long-running excavations. Well-preserved stretches of **defensive wall** extend north of the city, some constructed by Mausolus early in the fourth century BC. Just below the **acropolis** with its medieval and Hellenistic fortified area, the second-century BC **theatre** is the most impressive building. Resting against the hillside to the southeast, in the Greek fashion it's greater than a semicircle and retains two of its original arched entrances; in 2008 a **nymphaeum** was uncovered next to one archway. Between here and the Byzantine church, a **temple to Apollo** has been identified.

Northwest of the theatre and Apollo temple, closer to the upper ticket booth, the **Byzantine basilica** and the city's **Roman baths** are also in excellent condition. A cobbled street leads downhill from the baths to an ancient **Doric temple**, consisting most obviously of an attractive circular structure, possibly an altar, sacred pool or podium, flanked by bits of re-erected colonnade. A path continues to the **agora**, on the lowest level, graced by a restored **fountain-house** at the end of a long **stoa**. The ancient **harbour** below is now the Sülüklü Gölü, or "Lake of the Leeches"; the entrance could be barred by a chain in times of danger.

İztuzu beach

Extending for 4.5km southeast from the mouth of the Dalyan Çayı • Summer daily 8am–8pm, winter open 24hr • Dolmuşes serve the south end of the beach in season (every 30min; ₺8); drivers face a ₺5 parking charge (May–Oct)

Tourism and turtles have been made to coexist uneasily on the beautiful hard-packed sand of **İztuzu beach**. Be sure to look out for **turtle nests**, which can all too easily be trampled on. Turtle tracks – scrapings where the creatures have hauled themselves up onto the beach to lay their eggs – are visible in the sand during June and July. The marshes immediately behind are often alive with other wildlife too, while the approach road is lined with flowering oleander bushes, as well as trees deformed by high winter winds.

Lack of shade is a problem, though at the river end of the beach you can rent a couple of sunbeds and an umbrella for ₺9. The two identical and expensive snack kiosks, at either end of the beach, only sell crisps, ice cream, *gözleme* and *sandviç*, so it's best to bring some food. Umbrellas, whose masts damage the turtle nests, are not permitted from a line of squat marker-stakes down to the sea, and all access to the beach is banned at night in summer. Thanks to wind exposure, the water can be choppy and murky, but the gently shelving sea bed makes İztuzu excellent for children.

You can also be ferried across the river mouth (don't swim, there are dangerous currents) to a smaller, more peaceful beach, shaded by some pines.

Ilıca

10min by boat upriver from Dalyan, towards Köyceğiz • ₺5

The **Ilıca thermal baths** (40°C), a series of open-air mud pools, are located not far upstream from Dalyan. However, the total area is small, and in season gets packed with tour groups – best go at an odd hour, or have your skipper take you to the Köyceğiz Sultaniye Kaplıcaları hot springs, further upstream on the lakeshore itself.

Köyceğiz Sultaniye Kaplıcaları

7km by boat upriver from Dalyan, or 18km southwest of Köyceğiz on a paved road • Daily 6am–10pm • ₺5 • Driving, head west following signs for Ekincik, then veer left following signs for Çandır

Housed in a conspicuous white-domed structure right on the lakeshore, the **main baths** at the remote hot springs known as the **Köyceğiz Sultaniye Kaplıcaları** are claimed to be open around the clock, despite the nominal posted hours. However, 10.30am to 8pm is set aside for *tur* (ie mixed bathing), while at other times there are roughly alternating hours for men and women.

The dome shelters a large round pool with a naturally rocky, uneven bottom, from which the water wells up at 39–41°C; it's best appreciated at night or during the cooler months. Ancient masonry at the pool rim is evidence that the baths have been present in some form at least since Roman times. Three **open-air pools** are scattered around the domed structure: one hot (beside the bar), one cold, and one muddy-bottomed (beside the snack-café).

Köyceğiz

KÖYCEĞIZ, 23km north of Dalyan, is a laidback market town that has been eclipsed touristically by its rival across the lake. Its economy is based largely on cotton, olives, lake fishing, logging and citrus cultivation, though its position on the scenic **Köyceğiz Gölü** – once a bay open to the sea – allows it to function as a resort. The centre has a certain charm, with scattered buildings from the 1920s and 1930s, an atmospheric bazaar lane lined by *pide salonları* and *hazır yemek* kitchens – some open long hours – plus a well-attended lakeshore promenade on warm nights. As well as cheaper prices than Dalyan, Köyceğiz has better **transport** connections.

ARRIVAL AND DEPARTURE   KÖYCEĞIZ

By bus Dolmuşes shuttle regularly into town from the *otogar*, out towards the main highway, 2km north of the lakeshore.

Destinations Dalaman (hourly; 30min); Fethiye (8 daily; 1hr 30min); and Ortaca, for Dalyan (half-hourly; 30min).

TOURS

Boat tours Trips to the Sultaniye Kaplıcaları and Kaunos usually leave at 10am and return at 7pm (₺20, including lunch).

ACCOMMODATION

All the hotels and pensions that dot the waterfront and streets just west of the centre are pitched more at Turks than foreign visitors, but plenty of backpackers and independent travellers do make it out here.

Alila Emeksiz Cad ☎ 0252 262 1150, ✉ omeroflaz38 @mynet.com. The welcoming *Alila* has plain but serviceable rooms in varied sizes (including family suites sleeping five) with small balconies that mostly face the

lake, plus an outstanding ground-floor restaurant (see p.312). ₺70

★ **Flora Hotel** Cengiz Topel Cad 110 ☎ 0252 262 4976, 🌐 florahotel.info. Set at right angles to the lakefront, most of the simple but comfortable a/c rooms have water views. It's a notch up on the pensions and worth the extra money, especially as free bikes and a couple of canoes are available. Course anglers may be tempted by summer-resident Belgian Franky Wauters' carp fishing tours. ₺80

Fulya Pansiyon Ali İhsan Kalmaz Cad ☏ 0252 262 2301. On the second road in from the lakefront around 600m from the town centre, the basic but very clean sixteen-room *Fulya Pansiyon* boasts a fine roof terrace and has free bikes for guests. ₺70

Kaunos Cengiz Topel Cad ☏ 0252 262 4870. Renovated

in 2011, this is a basic concrete block, but has a great lakeshore position. Most of the 75 sparsely furnished but comfortable rooms (think bright walls and tiled floors) have sizeable balconies to take advantage of the views. Bathrooms are tidy with chrome shower stalls, and there's a big pool to one side. ₺130

Tango Pension Ali İhsan Kalmaz Cad ☏ 0252 262 2501, ⊚ tangopension.com. This somewhat institutionalized backpackers' favourite (cornflakes for breakfast), one block back from the water, has minimalist en-suite rooms or six-bed dorms, garden bar and roof terrace. Open all year. Dorms ₺35, doubles ₺60

EATING AND DRINKING

Alila Restaurant Emeksiz Cad. Much the best lakeshore restaurant is attached to the *Alila hotel*; owner Ömer's kitchen produces unusual *mezes* to die for, like stewed artichokes, yoghurt with coriander greens and caper shoots marinated in sour pomegranate syrup, while mains are

generous. Daily 10am–midnight.

Thera Cengiz Topel Cad ☏ 0541 833 6154. Reasonable fish restaurant with a fine location, separated from the lake by a narrow park. Assorted farmed (from ₺15 a portion) and wild-caught fish are on offer. Daily 9am–midnight.

The Xanthos valley

The heart of Lycia, east of Fethiye, is home to several archeological sites, including the ancient citadel-cities of **Tlos** and **Pınara**, on opposite sides of the **Xanthos valley**. Tlos had the geographical advantage, lying above a rich, open flood plain and sheltered to the east by the Massikytos range (today's Akdağ); Pınara's surrounding hilly terrain was difficult to cultivate. Even more remote and less fertile is mysterious **Sidyma**, up on the ridge separating the valley from the Mediterranean. All these cities were unearthed by the English traveller Charles Fellows between 1838 and 1842, contemporaneous with his work – or rather pillaging – at **Xanthos**, though he seems to have left the nearby religious sanctuary of **Letoön** and the naval fortress of **Pydnae** unmolested.

Mostly following the valley of the ancient Xanthos River (now the Eşen Çayı), the road between Fethiye and Kalkan threads through an immensely fertile area that's known for its cotton, tomatoes and other market-garden crops. The fact that plans for a local airport have never materialized, in tandem with archeological restrictions, means that has growth at **Patara**, the main resort, has remained modest by Turkish coastal standards. Between Tlos and Patara, the magnificent river gorge of **Saklıkent** is easily reached by dolmuş or with your own vehicle, though it's become something of a tourist circus. Fans of isolated ruins can instead visit the unpromoted, unspoiled Lycian city of **Oenoanda**, high in the mountains north of Tlos.

Tlos

Among the most ancient and important Lycian cities, **TLOS** stands beside modern Asarkale village. Hittite records from the fourteenth century BC refer to it as "Dalawa in the Lukka lands", and the local discovery of a bronze hatchet dating from the second millennium BC confirms the long heritage of the place. However, little else is known about its history.

The ruins themselves, while reasonably abundant, are often densely overgrown or even farmed, so precise identification of buildings is debatable. The setting is undeniably impressive, a high rocky promontory giving excellent views of the Xanthos valley. The acropolis bluff is dominated by an Ottoman Turkish fortress, home during the nineteenth century to the brigand and local chieftain, Kanlı ("Bloody") Ali Ağa, who killed his own wayward daughter to uphold the family's honour. Now used as a football pitch and pasture, it has obliterated all earlier remains on the summit. On its northeast side, the acropolis ends in almost sheer cliffs; the eastern slope bears traces of the Lycian city wall.

The site

Daily 8.30am–dusk • ₺8 when staff present

Entry to the **main site** at Tlos is via the still intact northeastern city gate, next to the guard's portakabin. Cobbled stairs climb to the main **necropolis** with its freestanding sarcophagi and complex of rock-cut house-tombs, one of which was discovered intact in 2005 yielding treasure kept at the Fethiye museum. If, however, you walk along a lower, level path from the gate, outside the city walls, you reach a second group of rock tombs. Dip below and right of these along a zigzagging trail to reach the temple-style **Tomb of Bellerophon**, at the hill's northern base. Its facade was hewn with columns supporting a pediment, and three carved doors. A relief on the left wall of the porch represents the mythical hero Bellerophon (from whom one of Tlos' ancient ruling families claimed descent), riding Pegasus, while facing them over the door a lion symbolically stands guard. It's a fifteen-minute scramble down requiring good shoes, with a ladder ascent at the end, and both figures have been worn down by vandals and the elements.

Between the east slope of the acropolis hill and the curving onward road, a large, seasonally cultivated open space is thought to be the **agora**. Close to the base of the hill are traces of seats, part of a stadium which lay parallel to the marketplace. The opposite side of the agora is flanked by a long, arcaded building identified as the **market hall**.

Well beyond this, reached by a broad path off the eastbound road, lie the **baths**, where the sound of running water in nearby ditches lends credence to its identification. This atmospheric vantage point is perhaps the best bit of Tlos: three complete **chambers**, one with an apsidal projection known as **Yedi Kapı** (Seven Gates), after its seven intact windows, which provide a romantic view of the Xanthos valley. Sadly, it's closed indefinitely for excavations that aim to uncover the fine marble floor and have also revealed a large, possibly Christian, cemetery.

Just north of the modern through-road, 34 rows of seats remain intact in a magnificent second-century AD **theatre**. The stage building holds several finely carved blocks – including one with an eagle beside a garlanded youth – and its northern section still stands to nearly full height, vying with the backdrop of mountains.

ARRIVAL AND DEPARTURE
TLOS

By minibus Patchy public transport to Tlos is provided by Saklıkent-bound minibuses from Fethiye, which occasionally detour to the site. As Tlos is firmly established on the organized-excursion circuit, however, you shouldn't need to hire a private taxi.

By car from Fethiye Head east on the main coast road, Highway 400, and veer left (east) after 22km onto Highway 350, the Korkuteli/Antalya road. Once across the Koca Çayı bridge, bear immediately right onto the marked side road to both Tlos and Saklıkent. After 8.5km, turn left (east) onto a

paved minor road festooned with signposting for restaurants and inns; the base of the acropolis hill is 4km along. In spring the route up, with snow-streaked Akdağ as a backdrop for the purple of flowering Judas trees, is memorably beautiful.

By car from Patara At Alaçat take the eastbound road marked "Saklıkent 15km"; at a T-junction in Kadıköy, with "Saklıkent" signposted opposite a mini-market for the right turning, bear left (north) instead, following a "Tloss" sign, for just over 2km until another "Tloss" sign points up the final 4km.

ACCOMMODATION AND EATING

★ **Mountain Lodge** Just under 2km down the road from the entrance to the ruins ☎0252 638 2515, ⊛themountainlodge.co.uk. Choose between nicely appointed, carpeted, beam-ceilinged en-suites in the garden annexe, or luxury units in the wing overlooking the pool and bar. Engaging owner Melahat prepares fine set evening meals

in an area thin on non-trout-based cuisine, served in the wood-beamed and stone pub-restaurant. She also organizes treks in the area, and is knowledgeable about local flora. All rates are for two people, including breakfast; a/c costs *20TL extra. Half board available for ₺30 extra per person. Closed mid-Nov to mid-Dec & mid-Jan to mid-Feb. **₺90**

5

Oenoanda

50km northeast of Tlos • Unrestricted access, daily 24hr • Free • No public transport; turn off Highway 400 onto Highway 350 at the Kemer river bridge, and head for Korkuteli; after 34km, bear east on a side road marked for Seki and Elmalı; after 1.1km turn south onto a more minor road; 800m down this, veer right at an unmarked fork to proceed 1.5km further to İncealiler village; then turn right at the phone box and park by the coffee house – do not follow the river further upstream

Ancient **Oenoanda** was among the northernmost and highest (1350–1450m elevation) of the Lycian cities. Set in wild, forested countryside, it's almost unpublicized. As an example of how all local sites used to be before tourism, however, it thoroughly rewards the effort that's required to reach it (own transport essential).

Oenoanda was the birthplace of Diogenes, the second-century AD Epicurean philosopher; to him is attributed antiquity's longest inscriptionary discourse, scattered in fragments across the site. First surveyed by British archeologists in 1996, Oenoanda is set for more vigorous future excavations. With luck, these will reassemble Diogenes' text to its full estimated length of 60m, and firmly identify structures. Until then, the site remains a romantic, overgrown maze of tumbled lintels, statue bases, columns, cistern mouths and buried arches, frequented only by squirrels and the occasional hunter or shepherd.

The site

From the coffee-house parking in İncealiler, head up the main pedestrian thoroughfare among village houses, then near the top of the grade bear right at heaped boulders onto a narrower track which soon dwindles to a path. Continue west towards the escarpment in front of you, where the first freestanding **tombs** poke up. The path describes a broad arc south around the top of a stream valley, forging through low scrub.

Some 45 minutes from the coffee-house, the trail fizzles out at polygonal masonry of the massive south-to-north **aqueduct** that supplied the city, whose site-bluff inclines gently to the south but is quite sheer on all other sides. Slip through a gap in the aqueduct, with necropolis tombs flung about on every side, and veer right along the ridge towards Oenoanda's massive Hellenistic **city wall**, with an arched window; the way through is left of this, by a strong hexagonal **tower** with archers' loopholes. Some fifteen minutes' walk north from here, keeping just east of the ridge line, brings you to the large flat paved **agora**; tentatively identified **baths** stand just beyond, with a surviving apse and dividing arch. Just northeast, a gate in the **Roman wall**, longer but much lower than the Hellenistic one, opens onto a vast flat area, provisionally dubbed an "esplanade", flanked by traces of stoas. Northwest of the presumed baths, a **nymphaeum** or small **palace** with a three-arched facade precedes the partly preserved **theatre**, its fifteen or so rows of seats taking in fine views of Akdağ.

Saklıkent

The hugely popular **Saklıkent gorge**, 44km from Fethiye, is the most dramatic geological formation in the Xanthos valley, and at 20km the second-longest gorge in Europe. Its mouth is deceptively modest; to reach it leave the road bridge for a 150m pedestrian **walkway** (open during daylight hours; ₺8) spiked into the canyon walls, ending at the **Gökçesu/Ulupınar springs**, which erupt at great pressure from the base of towering cliffs, exiting the narrows to mingle eventually with the Eşen Çayı. It's a magical place, seemingly channelling all the water this side of Akdağ, though less impressive if you coincide with the many tour groups that come, primarily, to eat trout at several restaurants that are built on wooden platforms suspended over the water.

The water-sculpted chasm extends 18km upstream, though further progress for all except rock-climbers is blocked after about 2km by a boulder slide. If you want to explore up to that point, it's initially a **wading** exercise – take submersible shoes, or rent a pair here. The entire length of the gorge was first descended in 1993 by a **canyoning** expedition that took eighteen hours, bivouacking halfway and abseiling down several dry waterfalls. This trip is now offered on a custom basis, during summer only, by BT in Kaş (see p.330).

ARRIVAL AND DEPARTURE

SAKLIKENT

By minibus Vehicles marked "Kayadibi/Saklıkent" operate a regular minibus service in season, from Fethiye's dolmuş *otogar*.
By car Drive east of Fethiye on Highway 400, and veer left (east) onto Highway 350 after 22km. Cross the Koca Çayı bridge and bear immediately right onto the marked side road to both Tlos and Saklıkent. After driving 17.5km south, bear left for just over 3km to the (signed) gorge mouth.

ACCOMMODATION

Saklıkent Gorge Club Saklıkent ☎ 0252 659 0074, ⓦ saklikentgorge.com. Set at the mouth of the gorge, near the car park, this backpacker-oriented tree-house place makes a great base if you want to explore the gorge and enjoy the ambience once the tour groups have gone. Tents €9, dorms €15, treehouse doubles €35

Pınara

46km southeast of Fethiye • Turn right off on Highway 400 and continue just over 3km to the village of Minare, from where the ruins are a 2.2km walk along a steep signposted track

Almost nothing is known about the ancient city of **PINARA** except that it may have been founded as an annexe of Xanthos. Later, however, Pınara – meaning "something round" in Lycian, presumably because of the shape of the original, upper acropolis – became one of the region's larger cities, minting its own coins and earning three votes in the Federation.

Approaching the site, the **cliff** on which the city was first founded all but blocks out the horizon – indeed it's worth the trip up just to see this towering mass, its east face covered in rectangular openings, either tombs or food-storage cubicles. These can now only be reached by experienced rock-climbers and it's hard to imagine how they were originally cut.

The site

Daily 8.30am–dusk • ₺8 when guard present

Most of the ruins of Pınara are on the lower acropolis hill, east of the cliff, where the city was relocated after defence became less critical. The access track reaches a point almost level with the **lower acropolis** itself, but it's densely overgrown with pines, and most of the buildings are unidentifiable.

The Royal Tomb

Pınara's **tombs** are its most interesting feature, especially a group on the west bank of the seasonal stream that passes the site. On the east side of the lower acropolis hill (follow arrows on metal signs), the so-called **Royal Tomb** sports detailed if well-worn carvings on its porch of walled cities with battlements, gates, houses and tombs; a frieze survives above, showing people and animals in a peaceable scene – perhaps a religious festival. Inside is a single bench set high off the ground, suggesting that this was the tomb of just one, probably royal, person.

The lower acropolis

The jumbled remains of the **lower acropolis** area sprawl across the hillside below the Royal and other tombs. Reached by a direct path north from the Royal Tomb, a house-tomb with an arched roof is topped by a pair of stone **ox horns** for warding off evil spirits. This stands near the summit of the **lower acropolis**, at the eastern edge of the presumed **agora**. Just north of the horned tomb, the massive foundations of a **temple** to an unknown god overlook the theatre. Hairpinning back south, a level path threads between the pigeonholed cliff and the lower acropolis, first past a ruinous but engaging **odeon**, then through a chaos of walls, uprights, heart-shaped column sections and tombs that clog the flattish heart of the city.

5

The theatre

Pınara's well-preserved **theatre**, signed northeast of the lower acropolis, is well worth seeking out. Small but handsome, it was never modified by the Romans (on-site signage to the contrary) and retains its classic Greek horseshoe shape. Its compact size gives a fair idea of just how modest the population of Pınara was.

Sidyma

Sited halfway up the ancient Mount Kragos – the modern coastal peak of Avlankara Tepesi – **Sidyma** is the remotest of the Xanthos valley's ancient cities. Indeed, it's scarcely in the valley at all. Set in a striking landscape astride the Lycian Way, it's a rewarding, understated site that was only "rediscovered" by Europeans during the mid-nineteenth century, and has never been properly excavated.

The site

Unrestricted access, daily dawn to dusk

Sidyma is one of many ancient sites in this part of the world to have been reoccupied at a much later date by local people, who have used the remains as a handy depository of ready-hewn stone blocks to build their own homes. Today's settlement is known as **Dudurga**, and the village mosque not only occupies the site of the baths but reuses pillars from the agora's stoa. Indeed the principal charm of Sidyma is how ancient masonry crops up everywhere: incorporated into house corners, used as livestock troughs, sprouting incongruously in courtyards next to satellite dishes. An exceedingly ruined **castle**, garrisoned in Byzantine times, sits on a hill to the north; scattered in the fields to the east, and requiring some scrambling over walls to reach, the **necropolis** holds various tomb types, though most have angular gabled roofs rather than the "Gothic" vaulted ones seen elsewhere.

Near the centre of the agricultural plain is a group of remarkable, contiguous tombs: one has ceiling panels carved with rosettes and human faces, while the adjacent tomb sports a relief of Eros on its lid and Medusas at the ends (a motif repeated elsewhere). Another spectacular cluster, including one tomb with two storeys, covers the low ridge beyond the fields.

The enormous, fairly intact, square structure in the middle of the necropolis is probably a Roman imperial **heroön** or temple-tomb. There's a walled-up doorway on its north side.

ARRIVAL AND DEPARTURE
                                                                SİDYMA

By car From Highway 400 take the turning marked for Eşen and "Sidyma, 13km", just north of a side road for Kumlova and Letoön. Turn left (south) at a junction 6km on, and it's just over 2km to the first buildings of Dodurga village, and another 3km to the road's end in Dodurga's

Asar Mahallesi, where two mulberry trees flank the ruins of the agora and a Lycian Way metal signpost.
On foot Trekking southeast on the Lycian Way, Sidyma is a day and a half's march from Kabak, via Alınca.

ACCOMMODATION AND EATING

In the absence of facilities in Dodurga, most visitors stay at either nearby **Alınca**, a pretty village astride the Lycian Way, or head up to remote **Karaağaç**.

ALINCA
Dervish Lodge Just off the Lycian Way at the top of Alınca village ☎ 0252 679 1142, ⓦ dervishlodge.com. Accommodation ranging from wooden bungalows (rates include half board) to log-house self-catering apartments (same rates, but without food), with views to die for. Non-trekkers can reach the lodge by dolmuş from Fethiye to

Eşen village (30min), and also, for ₺20, be collected from it. **₺150**

KARAAĞAÇ
Black Tree Farm Karaağaç, 3.5km beyond Alınca ☎ 0252 617 0045, ⓦ blacktree.net. Located in extensive grounds, 1100m up and well off the trail, with rare

Baba Dağı cedars nearby and a zoo's worth of animals on site. Accommodation comprises a restored trekkers' lodge with 16 dorm beds, and nine newer one- and three-bedroom cottages built in local stone and pine. There's a swimming pool, tennis courts and restaurant-bar serving simple lunches. A marked, non-Lycian Way trail links Karaağaç with Kirme, allowing the completion of circular hikes from Faralya (see p.303). Closed Nov–March. Dorm beds €12, one-bedroom cottages €54, three-bedroom cottages €72

The Letoön

16km south of Pınara • Dolmuşes run from Fethiye to Kumluova village, 500m from the site; if driving, take a turning marked "Kumluova, Karadere, Letoön 10", turn right after 4km at another Letoön sign, and then left again after 4km more

The Letoön, shrine of the goddess **Leto**, was the official religious sanctuary, oracle and festival venue of the Lycian Federation, and extensive remaining ruins attest its importance. Christianized following the demise of the federation, it was only abandoned after the Arab raids of the seventh century. The Letoön was initially rediscovered by Charles Fellows in 1840, although French-conducted digs didn't begin until 1962, since when it has been systematically uncovered and labelled.

The site

Daily: summer 8.30am–8.30pm; winter 8.30am–5pm • ₺8

Excavations of the Letoön have uncovered the remains of three temples and a nymphaeum, as well as various **inscriptions**. One stipulates conditions of entry to the sanctuary, including a strict dress code prohibiting rich jewellery, ostentatious clothing or elaborate hairstyles.

The temples

The low ruins of three **temples** occupy the centre of the site, beyond the relatively uninteresting (and waterlogged) agora. The westernmost temple, straight ahead as you approach from the site gate, bears a dedication to Leto. Once surrounded by a single Doric colonnade with decorative half-columns around the interior walls, it dates from the third century BC. Three columns on the north side of the structure plus the *cella* (inner chamber) walls have been reconstructed; though the masonry seems jarringly garish, it was, in fact, sourced from the original marble quarry near modern Finike.

The central temple, partly carved out of the rock, is from the fourth century BC, identified by a dedication to Artemis. The easternmost temple was similar to the Leto temple. The reproduction **mosaic** on the floor – the original is now in the Fethiye museum – depicts a lyre, bow and quiver with a stylized flower in the centre. This suggests a joint dedication to Artemis and Apollo, the region's most revered deities, since the bow and quiver symbolized Artemis, and the lyre Apollo. The architecture and mosaic technique date the temple to the second and first centuries BC.

THE LEGEND OF THE LETOÖN

In legend, the nymph **Leto** was loved by Zeus and thus jealously pursued by his wife Hera. Wandering in search of a place to give birth to her divine twins Apollo and Artemis, Leto approached a fountain to slake her thirst, only to be driven away by local herdsmen. Leto was then led by wolves to drink at the Xanthos River, and so changed the name of the country to Lycia, *lykos* being Greek for wolf. After giving birth, she returned to the spring – on the site of the existing **Letoön**, and forever after sacred to the goddess – to punish the insolent herdsmen by transforming them into frogs.

The name Leto may derive from the Lycian *lada* (woman), and the Anatolian mother-goddess, Cybele, may have been worshipped at this same site previously. Another similarity between the two goddesses is a link with incestuous mother-son unions, thought to have been common in Lycian society. The most famous of all the prophecies supposedly delivered at the Letoön predicted that Alexander the Great would destroy the Persian Empire.

The nymphaeum and theatre

A rectangular **nymphaeum**, flanked by two semicircular recesses with statue niches, extends southwest beyond the temples. This is abutted by a semicircular paved basin 27m in diameter, now permanently flooded by the high local water table and full of ducks, terrapins and Leto's croaking victims (see p.317). A **church** was built over the nymphaeum in the fourth century, but destroyed by Arab invaders in the seventh, so only its foundations and apse are now discernible. The notable stork mosaic on its floor is, alas, headless, though currently exposed to view.

Returning towards the car park, you'll reach a large, well-preserved Hellenistic **theatre**, entered through a vaulted passage. Sixteen plaques, adorned by comic and tragic relief **masks**, decorate the perilously collapsing northeast entrance to this passage. Nearby sits an interesting Roman **tomb**, with a carved representation of its toga-clad occupant.

Pydnae

Pydnae was a small, third-century BC port on the larger, deeper bay that existed here before the Özlen stream silted it up. It was in fact the only safe anchorage for Xanthos and Letoön, since even in ancient times the coast between here and Patara was marshland.

The irregularly shaped precinct of its ancient acropolis is built of almost perfectly preserved **polygonal masonry**, with steps leading up to the walls at various points and, every so often, square towers with loopholes for archers. The most recent structure inside is a Byzantine **church**, its arched apsidal window overlooking the reedy marshes where fleets once anchored.

ARRIVAL AND DEPARTURE
PYDNAE

By bus Dolmuşes from Kumluova village (labelled "Kumluova–Karadere") run 8km southwest to the end of the paved road, where the fortress of Pydnae is obvious on the right, on the far bank of the Özlen Çayı. To reach it, continue to the end of the onward mud-and-sand track (and final dolmuş stop) that leads to the good beach (grass-roofed snack-shack) at the stream mouth. Cross the rickety footbridge here, and then follow a sand-, then jeep-track around greenhouses to pick up Lycian Way markers from the first curve, from which a path leads to – and through – the fortress gate within 20min.

Xanthos

The remains of hilltop **Xanthos**, with their breathtaking views of the Xanthos River – now the Eşen Çayı – and its valley, are among the most fascinating in Lycia. The city was first made familiar in 1842, when Charles Fellows carried off the majority of its art works, just four decades after the Elgin marbles had been similarly pillaged. It took two months to strip the site and load the loot onto the HMS *Beacon* for shipment to London. The most important artefact, the fourth-century **Nereid Monument**, a beautifully decorated Ionic temple on a high podium, is one of several items now in the British Museum. However, enough was left behind here to still require a two-hour visit. Afternoons are scorchingly hot even by Lycian standards – go earlier or later in the day.

Brief history

Xanthos is linked in legend with Bellerophon and Pegasus (see p.348). King Iobates – who initially set impossible tasks for Bellerophon and later offered him a share in his kingdom – ruled here, and Xanthos was the birthplace of Bellerophon's grandson, Glaukos, cited in the *Iliad* as "from the whirling waters of the Xanthos".

While the earliest archeological finds date to the eighth century BC, the city enters history in 540 BC during the conquest of Lycia by the Persian Harpagos, who besieged Xanthos. The Xanthians' response was the first local holocaust, making a funeral pyre of their families with their household goods. The women and children died in the flames while the men perished fighting, the only survivors being out of town at the time.

XANTHOS

New Highway, Saklıkent & Tlos

N

Walls

NECROPOLIS

Byzantine
Monastery

ROMAN ACROPOLIS

Pillar Tomb

Site of
Lion Tomb

Walls

MODERN ROAD

Eşen Çay (Ancient River Xanthos)

Xanthian
Obelisk

Café

P

Roman
Agora

House Tomb

Late
Agora

Sarcophagus

Harpy Tomb
Lycian Sarcophagus

Roman Theatre

Byzantine
Basilica

Roman Tomb

Cistern

Lycian
Acropolis

Byzantine
building

Church

Royal
Terrace

Palace

Hellenistic
wall

LATE STREET

Walls

MODERN ROAD

Site of Nereid
Monument

0   100

metres

Arch of Vespasian &
Hellenistic Gateway

Kınık

Xanthos subsequently shared the fate of all Lycia, with Alexander following the Persians, in turn succeeded by his general Antigonos and then by Antiokhos III. After Antiokhos's defeat, Xanthos was given to Rhodes along with the rest of Lycia. The second Xanthian holocaust occurred in 42 BC during the Roman civil war, when Brutus's forces surrounded the city, prompting the citizens again to make funeral pyres of their possessions and immolate themselves. Xanthos prospered anew in Roman imperial times, and under Byzantine rule the city walls were renovated and a monastery built.

The site

Officially open daily: summer 8am–7.30pm, winter 8.30am–5pm; however, apart from the theatre area, the site is unfenced • ₺6 admission, plus parking fees

The monumental **Arch of Vespasian** and an adjoining **Hellenistic gateway**, which bears an inscription of Antiokhos III dedicating the city to Leto, Apollo and Artemis, stand alongside the access road from Kınık. East of the road, the former location of the **Nereid Monument** is marked by a plaque.

Theatre and acropolis

Xanthos's **Roman theatre**, near the summit of the access road, was built on the site of an earlier Greek structure and is pretty complete, missing only the upper seats, which were incorporated into the Byzantine city wall. Behind the theatre, overlooking the valley, lies the **Lycian acropolis**, in whose far southeastern corner are the square remains of what's probably an early Xanthian royal palace destroyed by Harpagos. Beneath protective sand, patches of sophisticated mosaic indicate Roman or Byzantine use of the acropolis. Water channels everywhere underfoot, and a huge cistern, suggest an advanced plumbing system and a preoccupation with outlasting sieges.

Pillar tombs

The **Harpy Tomb**, in front of the theatre to the north, was originally topped with a marble chamber that was removed by Fellows, and now replaced by a cement-cast reproduction. The paired bird-women figures on its north and south sides are identified as harpies, or – more likely – sirens, carrying the souls of the dead (represented as children) to the Isles of the Blessed. Other reliefs portray unidentified seated figures receiving gifts, except for the west face where they are regarding opium poppies. Beside the Harpy Tomb a third-century BC **Lycian sarcophagus** stands on a pillar. Traces of a corpse and pottery were found inside, along with a sixth-century BC relief – brought from elsewhere – depicting funeral games.

Just northeast of the Roman agora, the so-called **Xanthian Obelisk** is in fact another pillar tomb, labelled as the "Inscribed Pillar" and covered on all four sides by the longest-known Lycian inscription, 250 lines including twelve lines of Greek verse. Since the Lycian language hasn't been completely deciphered, interpretation of the inscription is based on this verse, which glorifies a champion local wrestler.

The basilica

East of the car park, then south through the "**late**" **agora**, lies a **Byzantine basilica**, fenced off but easy enough to enter – beware unauthorized guides offering incomprehensible and overpriced "tours". The basilica features extensive abstract **mosaics** – the best in western Turkey – and a synthronon in the semicircular apse. On the **Roman acropolis** to the north are various freestanding **sarcophagi**, and above, cut into the hillside, picturesque **tombs** mainly of the Lycian house (as opposed to temple) type. A well-preserved early **Byzantine monastery**, with washbasins along one side of its courtyard, stands further north.

ARRIVAL AND DEPARTURE
XANTHOS

By bus Dolmuşes between Fethiye and Patara drop passengers at Kınık, less than 2km beyond the southerly Letoön turn-off, from where the site is a 20min uphill walk.

By organized tour Xanthos features on many organized excursions, usually in tandem with the Letoön.

Gelemiş

The laidback village of **GELEMIŞ**, around 75km southeast of Fethiye and 15km northwest of the resort of Kalkan, serves as the base for visitors to explore the remarkable beachfront ruins of ancient **Patara** (see p.321) and enjoy its eponymous **beach**, the longest in Turkey. Set back a couple of kilometres from the beach, the village itself consists of a busy T-junction, with a main, crescent-shaped neighbourhood threaded by a single twisting high street extending west, and then uphill. Before 1950, the entire area was malarial – a municipal truck still sprays pesticide on spring nights – and the nomadic *Yörüks* who wintered here spent the hottest months up in the healthier mountain village of İslamlar, near Gömbe.

Over the last few years, Gelemiş has smartened itself up considerably. A decent crop of cafés, restaurants and even bars now makes it perfectly possible to enjoy a little low-key nightlife around the T-junction centre.

ARRIVAL AND DEPARTURE
GELEMIŞ

By bus and dolmuş Regular minibuses from Kalkan and Kaş stop in the centre near the PTT. Dolmuşes from Fethiye,

long-haul buses and all inter-city buses drop passengers on the roundabout on Highway 400, 3.5km from the centre,

connected by dolmuş to the village every 45min.
Destinations Antalya (8 daily; 5hr); Fethiye (8 daily; 1hr 15min); Kalkan (9 daily; 30min); Kaş (9 daily; 1hr).
Tours Agencies in the village offer activities that take advantage of Patara's natural beauty, including

horseriding, canoeing on the Eşen Çayı, scuba diving, and walking on the Lycian Way. Reputable operators include Gelemiş Turizm (w pataraviewpoint.com/gelemis-tours .html), Patara Canoeing (w pataracanoeing.com) and St Nicholas Travel (w patarabeachadventure.com).

ACCOMMODATION

Accommodation is a buyers' market, as Gelemiş has excess capacity, with package allotments absent. The most desirable premises are either on the ridge east of the T-junction, though sadly a 2008 fire removed all its forest, or on the western hillside.

★ **Akay** On the right of the main road as you approach the village from Highway 400 ☎ 0242 843 5055, w pataraakaypension.com. Kazim and Ayşe provide keen management and good cooking. Rooms – best facing away from the approach road – are plain but brand new, with orthopedic mattresses and mosquito nets. ₺60

Dardanos Hotel North edge of village centre ☎ 0242 843 5151, w pataradardanoshotel.com. A decent stab at a boutique hotel; the eighteen rooms are simply but tastefully furnished – think neutral walls and floors, white bed linen and traditional Turkish hanging lamps – with smart en-suite bathrooms, a/c and tidy balconies overlooking citrus groves. €50

Flower Pension On approach to village from Highway 400 ☎ 0242 843 5164, w pataraflowerpension.com. The first noteworthy *pansiyon* as you approach the village, with tidy bathrooms. Ayşe cooks up mean meals (and breakfast) on the terrace overlooking a lush garden. Very popular with Lycian Way walkers. ₺60

Golden Lighthouse Hotel North edge of village centre, above the mosque ☎ 0242 843 5107, w pataragoldenlighthouse.com. Quiet yet central, this hotel has large airy rooms with plain white decor, a/c and

new baths and an unusually large pool. Doubles ₺100, four-bed family rooms ₺180

Golden Pansiyon Near the crossroads in the village centre ☎ 0242 843 5162, w pataragoldenpension.com. Mayor Arif Otlu caters to budget travellers with fairly large rooms (some balconied, all double-glazed and a/c). The dead-central restaurant here is consistently reliable, and sometimes has trout or ocean fish on the menu. Open all year. ₺60

Patara Delfin Partway down the east ridge ☎ 0242 843 5120, w pataradelfinhotel.com. A mix of doubles, triples and a few pricier apartments, with a large pool, limited parking and half board available at *St Nicholas* restaurant. Free beach transfers and late-afternoon tea and cake. Doubles ₺90, two-bed apartments ₺100

★ **Patara View Point Hotel** ☎ 0242 843 5184, w pataraviewpoint.com. Muzaffer Otlu's and Anne-Louise Thomson's hotel enjoys an unbeatable setting on the easterly ridge. The tastefully decorated and furnished rooms have mosquito nets, balconies and heating with a/c. There's a shuttle to the beach, a pool-bar where breakfast is served, a Turkish-style night-time terrace with fireplace – and even a replica Lycian stone beehive out front. Good-value weekly rates. Closed Dec–Feb. ₺40

EATING AND DRINKING

Esra's Pancake House In the village centre. The best of several simple central places, specializing in *gözleme* (₺4), eaten either at small tables or nomad-style on cushions on the floor. As well as the standard flavours, there are 11 sweet pancakes plus *menemen* and *mantı* and, bizarrely, smoothies. The home-made *ayran* is tangy and delicious. Daily 8am–10pm.

Gypsy Just south of the village centre. This funky, rustic place is constructed from dark wood and has a pleasant upstairs terrace and mock ships'-wheel light fittings. Beers ₺6. Daily 9am–2am.

Medusa Just south of the village centre. Alongside

Gypsy, this place has occasional live Turkish music, best enjoyed lounging on one of the *kilim*-cushioned benches. Beers ₺6. Daily 9am–2am.

Sim Bar In the centre, next to the post office. The new kid on the block, this bar is located in a colonial-style bungalow, with an outdoor area for summer, and has special evenings such as reggae nights. Beers ₺6. Daily 9am–2am.

Tlos Right in the village centre. One of the longest established and still the best of the stand-alone restaurants in Gelemiş, this place serves big platters of hearty food such as *pide* (₺7) and *güveç* (₺15). Daily 8am–midnight.

Patara

Patara was the principal port of Lycia, famed for its oracle of Apollo, and as the birthplace in the fourth century AD of St Nicholas, Bishop of Myra (aka Santa Claus). Today, however, the area is better known for its huge sandy **beach**, a turtle-nesting area in summer that's off-limits after dark (May–Oct), while in winter the lagoon behind attracts considerable birdlife. Conservationists backed by the Ministry of the Environment have managed to exclude villas from the cape at the southeast end of the strand, while the area's protected archeological status has halted most new building at Gelemiş.

Brief history

Legend ascribes Greek origins to Patara, but in fact the city was originally Lycian, borne out by coins and inscriptions sporting an un-Hellenic PTTRA. The city was famous for its temple and oracle of Apollo, which supposedly rivalled Delphi's for accuracy, because Apollo was said to winter in the Xanthos valley. However, no verifiable traces of this temple have ever been found.

Patara served as a naval base during the wars between Alexander's successors. Later, in 42 BC, Brutus threatened the Patarans with a similar fate to the Xanthians (see p.318) if they didn't submit, giving them a day to decide. He released the women hostages in the hope that they would lessen the resolve of their menfolk. When this didn't work, Brutus freed all the remaining hostages, thereby endearing himself to the Patarans, who subsequently surrendered. Whatever his tactics, his chief motive was suggested by the fact that he exacted no other punishments, but merely confiscated the city's gold and silver.

The site

2km south of Gelemiş village • Daily: May–Oct 7.30am–7.30pm; Nov–April 8am–5pm • ₺5; smart PlajKarts, valid for ten days, allow multiple entry to the site, for multiple users; 10 entries ₺7.5, 25 entries ₺15 • Served by local dolmuşes from Gelemiş in summer

A gate and ticket booth controls vehicle access to both the beach at Patara and the **archeological site** beyond. Although the ruins are unfenced, visitors are not allowed in outside the official opening times.

Despite ongoing digs, much of Patara remains unexcavated, and only a few paths link the individual ruins. There are no facilities or shade – bring water, stout shoes and a head covering during summer.

The city's entrance is marked by a triple-arched, first-century AD **Roman gateway**, almost completely intact. A head of Apollo has been found on a little hill just west, prompting speculation that his temple was nearby. Outside the gate, a **necropolis** is being excavated by a team from Antalya's Akdeniz University.

The Roman baths

South of the hill near the entrance to Patara, there's a **baths complex**, similar to Yedi Kapı at Tlos, with arches and five rectangular apsidal windows. An exotic touch is lent to nearby foundations of either a **basilica** or an extension of the baths by a palm grove that sprouts from the floor and almost totally obscures it. West of these, tacked onto the longest surviving stretch of **city walls** – and difficult to reach – is an attractive second-century **temple**. While too modest to be the famous local Apollo shrine, it has a richly decorated 7m-high doorframe – its lintel on the point of collapse – leading into a single chamber.

Further south, reached by a different track, are more **baths** built by Emperor Vespasian (69–79 AD), impressing mainly by their squat bulk. Just west of these lies a large paved main agora or a processional street, with its north end submerged by the high local water table, and a growing number of re-erected columns.

The theatre and council chamber

Patara's **theatre**, under the brow of the acropolis hill southwest of the baths, is best reached by a track that heads off the main road, just before the beach car park. The cavea has been cleaned of sand to reveal eighteen rows of seats up to the diazoma (dividing walkway), and a dozen more beyond. The stage building is slowly being reassembled; a Greek inscription outside ascribes its erection to a woman, Vilia Prokla, and her father, both citizens of Patara. Funding for it was approved by the Lycian Federation's assembly, which apparently met in the **bouleuterion**, between the theatre and the agora, with a horseshoe array of seating. The restoration – critics would say, rebuilding – of this fine council chamber building, which held over 1400 citizens, was completed in 2012, and it's now arguably the finest example of its kind in Turkey.

The acropolis area

A reasonable path climbs uphill, south of the theatre, to reach the city's **acropolis**. At the top lurks an unusual rectangular pit, 10m across, with a pillar (for measuring water level) rearing out of the bottom and badly damaged stairs down its side. This was almost certainly a **cistern**, and not the **lighthouse** as originally supposed; that is the square, arched tower, its top collapsed, on the west side of the hill, which still has a fine view over the sea, beach and brackish swamp that was once the **harbour**. After gradually silting up in the Middle Ages, the harbour was abandoned, and is now separated from the beach by 300m-wide dunes. On the far side of the swamp, across the dunes, stand the bulky remains of **Hadrian's granary**.

The beach

Patara's fine white-sand **beach** ranks as one of the longest continuous strands in the Mediterranean: it measures 9km from the access road to the mouth of the Eşen Çayı, and then another 6km to the end. Rather than making the hot, half-hour stroll out from the centre of Gelemiş in summer, most visitors take a **beach dolmuş** or transport laid on by the hotels. Parking (free) at the road's end is limited, as the archeological authorities have refused permission to expand the space. The sole café is run by the owner (and local mayor) of the *Golden Lighthouse* and *Golden Pension* and is no more expensive than the places in the village. Local youth are employed and all proceeds go into the village community chest.

In season the immediate vicinity of the beach entrance gets crowded, but walking northwest past the dunes brings you to plenty of solitary spots – and a few unharassed colonies of nudists. Spring and autumn swimming is delightful, but in summer the exposed shoreline can be battered by body-surfable waves.

Kalkan and around

The former Greek fishing village of **Kalkan** is today a very popular and slightly upmarket resort. Its population of four thousand includes some 1500 expats, two-thirds of whom are British, and most of the small boutique hotels that used to be Kalkan's lifeblood have been converted into apartments and second homes. The surviving package-holiday trade dominates the remaining short-stay accommodation, and ensures that Kalkan remains more exclusive than nearby Kaş. Once you accept the resort's pervasive social profile, lack of a sandy beach and the fact that restaurants, though good, are uniformly overpriced, Kalkan makes a good base for exploring Patara and the Xanthos valley, while **excursions** east or inland might occupy another day or so.

Kalkan

Once the Greek Orthodox village of Kalamaki, **KALKAN**, 15km southeast of Patara, tumbles down a steep slope to a smart marina. Despite the rash of new villas and apartments spreading over the hillsides around, the compact centre has retained many of its nineteenth-century Greek houses, many now serving as restaurants and bars, and thus at least some of its charm. Tourism and property sales, now the town's *raison d'être*, are fairly new phenomena: until the late 1970s both Kalkan and neighbouring Kaş eked out a living from charcoal burning and olives. It's hard today to imagine it as it was in the 1980s, when its rather bohemian atmosphere contrasted starkly with the often oppressive conditions prevailing in Turkish cities after the 1980 coup.

5

SCUBA DIVING NEAR KALKAN

Most of the twenty-odd **dive sites** near Kalkan are 25–40min away by boat, with many located around the islets at the mouth of the bay. Of these, beginners dive the shallows at the north tip of **Yılan Adası** (Snake Island), and almost the entire perimeter of the remoter Heybeli; another excellent novice or second-dive-of-day venue is **Frank Wall** on the east side of the bay, with spectacular rock pinnacles and plenty of fish. More advanced divers are taken to an even more dramatic wall between 20m and 50m at the south tip of "Snake", alive with barracuda, grouper and myriad smaller fish; to reefs off Heybeli and Öksüz; or to sand-bottom **caves** on the mainland with their entrances at 25m.

The most spectacular calm-weather dive site, for intermediate and advanced divers, is **Sakarya Reef**, southeast of Kalkan off İnce Burun. Here, the mangled remains of the *Duchess of York*, a North Sea trawler built in Hull in 1893 and apparently scuttled for an insurance payout sometime after 1930, lie in 15m of water. However, more interesting is the newer, larger Turkish-built *Sakarya* nearby, wrecked in the 1940s, broken into three sections at depths of 35–60m, retaining teak-plank decking, intact winches and a vast cargo of lead ballast.

Except in the caves, fed by chilly fresh water, **water temperatures** are a comfortable 18–30°C; the sea warms up abruptly in late May or early June with a current change, and stays warm into November. **Visibility** is typically 25–30m.

The two local dive operators are **Dolphin Scuba Team**, working off its boat in Kalkan's main port (☎0242 844 2242 or ☎0542 627 9757, ⓦdolphinscubateam.com), and **Kalkan Diving/ Aquasports**, at the Kalamar Beach Club (☎0242 844 2361 or ☎0532 553 2006, ⓦkalkandiving .com). **Prices** are competitive, with two-dive mornings from £35/€43, and a PADI Open Water course from £180/€260.

Town beaches

The artificially supplemented **pebble beach** called **Kömürlük**, at the east edge of Kalkan, is pleasant enough, with reasonably clean water that's chilled by freshwater seeps. Although larger than it looks from afar, it still gets hopelessly full in summer, when the sunbeds (₺7 for two beds and an umbrella) are at a premium.

One alternative is to use the swimming platforms or **lidos** that flank the bay, accessible on well-priced shuttle boats. The only other bona fide beach within walking distance is a coarse-pebble one well southwest on the coast, visited by the Lycian Way on its way to Gelemiş.

İslamlar

Dramatically set, high in the mountains 8km north of Kalkan, **İSLAMLAR** has long provided a summer refuge from the steamy heat of the coast. The village's old name of Bodamya – Ottoman Greek for "rivers" – remains in use, and it is indeed alive to the sound of falling water, used to power mills and nurture various trout-farm **restaurants**. Local accommodation is largely the preserve of the more upmarket package companies.

Bezirgan

The attractive upland pasture village of **BEZİRGAN** lies 17km northeast of Kalkan. Famous in the past for its horses, but today devoted to barley, sesame, chickpeas and orchard crops, this fertile plain was a prehistoric lake, drained finally by an ingenious Roman tunnel. The hillside holds a sprinkling of Lycian rock tombs and an ancient citadel.

By studying the Lycian Way map, you can fashion a **loop walk** with the *ova* as pivot; only 1.6km separates the two intersections of the path with the ascending road from Kalkan, and indeed this circular walk is offered as an organized outing. On your own, take a minibus from Kalkan's top roundabout to Bezirgan – there are two daily from Kınık bound for Gömbe – and then walk back to Kalkan in about three hours.

Kaputaş beach

The deep canyon known as **Kaputaş Gorge** slashes back into the cliffs on the beautiful coastal road to Kaş, just under 6km out of Kalkan. Steps from the roadside parking area – where there's a *jandarma* post, and signs warning you not to leave valuables in cars (break-ins are rife when the *jandarma* aren't patrolling) – take you down to **Kaputaş beach**. This 150m expanse of pebble and blonde sand is normally pretty packed, given the mediocre quality of beaches closer to Kalkan or Kaş. Kaputaş has served as the backdrop for innumerable TV advert shoots, and unless there's been a southerly storm the water is crystalline.

ARRIVAL AND DEPARTURE
KALKAN AND AROUND

KALKAN

By bus Kalkan's *otogar* is at the very top of town, by the roundabout on the bypass road.
Destinations Antalya (7 daily; 4hr 30min); Bodrum (1 daily; 6hr); Fethiye (every 30min; 1hr 20min); İstanbul (1 daily; 15hr); İzmir (2 daily; 8hr); Kaş (every 30min; 30min); Marmaris (2 daily; 4hr 30min); Patara/Gelemiş (9 daily; 30min).

İSLAMLAR

By car Take the Sütlüğen/Elmalı road from the town-edge roundabout, then the first unsigned left, and then turn right at the top of the grade.

BEZIRGAN

By car Drive north from Kalkan to join Highway 400, then follow the sign for Elmalı. Follow another sign 1km along, towards Sütleğen/Elmalı, then turn left for Bezirgan after another 10km.

ACCOMMODATION

KALKAN

A handful of surviving *pansiyons* occupy converted old buildings lining the central grid of lanes – Yalıboyu district – that drops from Hasan Altan Sokağı down to the harbour, and merges east into Dereboyu towards the ravine. There's also a district of newer, purpose-built hotels extending 1.5km west along Kalamar Yolu, towards Kalamar Bay. Most such establishments are block-booked by tour operators; larger rooms, and swimming pools, offset the disadvantage of a hefty walk into town.
Caretta Boutique Hotel İskele Sok 3, 1.5km west of town ☎0242 844 3435, ⓦcarettaboutiquehotel.com. Housed in the last building on the west bay shore, this cult *pansiyon*-restaurant, suffused with the character of owner-chef Gönül Kocabaş, has a loyal Turkish and UK following. Rooms have quirky decor in cheerful pastels, with stone floors and terraces – best is the rooftop "penthouse". There's a swimming pool with stunning views. Closed early Nov to Easter. **€69**
Çelik Pansiyon Süleyman Yılmaz Cad 9 ☎0242 844 2126, ⓦcelikpansiyon.com. The cheapest place in town has eight no-frills but immaculately kept rooms with tiled floors and white walls. There's a fine breakfast/roof terrace with sea views. Closed early Nov to Easter. **₺60**
Gül Pansiyon Şehitler Cad, Sok 7 ☎0242 844 3099, ⓦkalkangulpansiyon.com. Perched 300m above the waterfront, and enjoying expansive views from the roof terrace, this long-standing family-run pension is very good value for Kalkan. There's a mix of six a/c doubles, all with balconies, and three slightly more expensive apartments with kitchens. Open all year. **₺80**

Meldi Hotel 800m along Kalamar Yolu on the seaward side ☎0242 844 2541, ⓦmeldihotel.com. Fair-sized rooms, all with up-to-date bathrooms and small balconies, either with garden or mountain views; breakfast is served next to the decent-sized pool. Airport transfer from Dalaman included for stays of a week or longer. Closed Nov–April. **€55**
★ **Türk Evi (Eski Ev)** Şehitler Cad 19 ☎0242 844 3129, ⓦkalkanturkevi.com. Near the top of a lane heading up from Süleyman Yılmaz Cad, Yalıboyu, this wonderfully refurbished old house features welcoming common areas and rooms with kilims and, in some cases, fireplaces. Open in winter by arrangement (there's no other heating). **₺60**
Viewpoint Villas Halfway along Kalamar Yolu, on the uphill side ☎0242 844 3642, ⓦviewpointvillaskalkan.com. Six villas arranged around a pool and equipped to a very high standard – jacuzzi, full kitchen, fireplace in sitting room, etc – each sleeping 4–5. Weekly rate **£600**
★ **Villa Mahal** Mahal Yolu, 1.5km east of town on the east bay shore ☎0242 844 3268, ⓦvillamahal.com. Kalkan's most exclusive lodging has road access, but the best way to approach is on a free boat shuttle from the harbour. A segmented veranda wraps itself around ten irregularly shaped standard rooms, some with huge bathrooms and private massage rooms. Steps descend past an infinity pool to the sea and lido – one of the few in Kalkan directly linked to accommodation, though open to the public for the sake of its popular restaurant. There's also a pool suite and two detached cottages furnished in the same designer-minimalist decor, with the multi-terrace setting among olive trees guaranteeing privacy. Friday-evening barbecue. Closed Nov–April. **€220**

5

★ **White House/Courtyard** 5 Nolu Sok ☎ 0242 844 3738 or ☎ 0532 443 0012, ⊛ kalkanwhitehouse.co.uk. Very welcoming Turkish–English-run *pansiyon* with large, airy, pine- and white-tile rooms ranging from singles to quads. Although only four of the ten have balconies, the roof terrace is one of the best in town, with superb sea views. Three adjoining, lovingly renovated 1920s properties, known as the *Courtyard at Whitehouse*, comprise six beautiful a/c rooms ranged around said courtyard, which boasts pretty black-and-white pebble mosaic flooring. Closed early Nov to Easter. *White House* £50, *Courtyard* £120

EATING AND DRINKING

KALKAN

Restaurants are scattered fairly evenly across town, though bars tend to cluster either just above the seafront or along Hasan Altan Sokağı, which after dark becomes the main pedestrianized drag into the village centre. Meal prices, however, are very high for Turkey; the usual resort trick of heading inland for better deals doesn't always apply.

Ali Baba Hasan Altan Cad ☎ 0242 844 3627. Pretty much the cheapest place in town, this simple *lokanta* serves generous portions of standard Turkish food such as *pide* and kebabs. Daily 24hr in season.

Aubergine İskele Sok ☎ 0242 844 3332. Elegant, marina-front dining, at comfy bamboo chairs pulled up to white-clothed tables, this Turkish/international upmarket restaurant does generous salads from ₺16, fajitas ₺23 and up and pizzas around the same. More sophisticated dishes such as fish start from over ₺30. Daily 8am–2am.

Cafe Del Mar Hasan Altan Cad ☎ 0242 844 1068. Just around the corner and up a steep flagged street from *Korsan*, this pretty café serves fresh coffees from ₺6, decent home-made cakes, and also has a small bistro-style menu. Daily 9am–1am.

★ **Iso's Kitchen** Süleyman Yılmaz Cad 39 ☎ 0242 844 2415. This characterful little restaurant is tucked away at the end of a backstreet running parallel to the harbour. Try to bag a table on the terrace for sea views before settling down to an array of *meze* (₺7 and up) washed down by a cold beer (₺5), and followed by a grill (₺15–30) or fish (₺20 and up). Daily 9am–2am.

★ **Korsan Meze/Korsan Balık** Atatürk Cad, 75m up

BEZIRGAN

★ **Owlsland** At the northwest edge of Bezirgan village ☎ 0242 837 5214 or 0535 940 1715, ⊛ owlsland.com. Turkish Erol and Scottish Pauline's well-signposted, excellent, 150-year-old village-house inn, *Owlsland*, is named after the scops and little owls resident in the nearby almond trees. It lies about 600m off the Lycian Way, making it a logical stop on the trek; Erol is a mean cook and you're well advised to have half board. At 720m elevation, you'll need the woodstoves in the minimally restored but en-suite rooms during spring or autumn. The B&B rate shown is for two; half board available for ₺45 extra per person. Closed Dec–Feb. ₺190

and in from the harbour ☎ 0242 844 3622. This long-established and elegant pair of restaurants offer arguably the best eating in Kalkan. The kitchen is in an attractive traditional building, the terrace of which specializes in fish, with sea bream costing ₺30. The *Meze* terrace, prettily decked out in blue and white, fronts the building and overlooks the harbour. Traditional Turkish starters from ₺9. Closed Nov to mid-April. Daily 10am–midnight.

Yalı Hasan Altan Cad. On a busy corner, with a big LCD TV out on the street, this bustling place is great for smoothies (₺12) in the day and reasonably priced drinks in the evening (beers ₺7, glass of wine ₺9). Daily 9am–2am.

İSLAMLAR

★ **Çiftlik** South of the village square ☎ 0242 838 6055. Budget favourite doing good *kızartma* vegetables and a garnish of olives, peppers and *yufka* with large trout for around ₺14 a portion. Daily 10am–11pm.

Değirmen South of the village square ☎ 0242 838 6295. Posh option that takes credit cards with a seasonally working mill in the basement grinding locally grown sesame seeds, which you can have served with *pekmez* or grape molasses. Daily 10am–11pm.

KAPUTAŞ BEACH

Ada Fish Restaurant Kalkan-Kaş yol uzeri 700m east of Kaputaş. Ali Taylı's welcoming restaurant, overlooking the Sidek peninsula and its Byzantine ruins, does a roaring trade thanks to the fresh and very reasonably priced fish bought in daily at 8am. Daily 11am–midnight.

Kaş and around

Until 1923, **KAŞ** was a small, Greek-populated shipping port, dwarfed by the cliffs, riddled with rock-cut tombs that tower behind it, and with views out to sea dominated by the nearby Greek island of **Kastellórizo** (Meis). Today, despite the fact that tourism has made inexorable inroads, with new development sprawling up every slope that's short of being totally precipitous, and the sleepy winter-time population of around eight thousand multiplying manyfold in summer, Kaş remains at heart a small town.

KAŞ

0   50
metres

N

ACCOMMODATION	
Aquarius	5
Arpia	6
Ateş	2
Begonvil	10
Gardenia	11
Gülşen	7
Hideaway	3
Kale	4
Kaş	8
Medusa	12
Nur	9
Oreo	1

SHOPS	
Merdiven	1
Old Curiosity Shop	2

RESTAURANTS	
Bahçe	4
Bahçe Balık	7
Enişte'nin Yeri	6
Hayta Meyhane	1
Kaşim	5
Köşk	3
Seçkin	3
Sultan Garden	8

CLUB	
Red Point Club	3

BARS AND CAFÉS	
Corner Cafe	1
Hideaway	4
Hi-Jazz	2
Mavi/Blue	5

MEDITERRANEAN SEA

Harbour

Küçük Çakıl Lidos

Büyük Çakıl Plajı & Path to Limanağzı

Lycian Rock Tombs

Stairs

Old Market Square

Harbour Mosque

Hellenistic Temple

WC & drinking water

Tour Boats

Swimming Platform

Lion Tomb

Hükümet Konağı

Jandarma

Taxi Rank

Doric Tomb

Theatre

Yeni Cami

Otogar

Friday Market, Fethiye & Kapıdağ beach

5

The tombs, cliffs and views out to sea remain as lovely as ever as well, though the Greek Christians who once admired them were replaced after the 1923 population exchanges by Muslim Turks.

The fact that the local beaches are hardly stellar, along with the lack of a really convenient airport, has spared Kaş the full impact of modern tourism. However, it gets lively at night, since shops stay open until 1am in season, and bars much later still. The modern town is built atop ancient **Antiphellos**, whose remaining ruins speckle the streets and cover the base of the Çukurbağ peninsula. A handy base from which to reach Kekova and nearby Patara, Kaş has also become the "adventure capital" of the southwest Turkish coast, offering all sorts of sea- and mountain-based **outdoor activities**.

Kaş being a major stop on "Blue Cruise" itineraries, **yacht and gulet culture** is as important here as at Kalkan. Day-trips are available for the less well-heeled, while there's a new yacht marina at **Bucak Limanı** (formerly Vathy), the long fjord west of town, wedged between Highway 400 and the Çukurbağ peninsula, which extends 5km southwest of Kaş.

Ancient Antiphellos

Ancient **Antiphellos** was the harbour of ancient Phellos, inland near modern Çukurbağ village and one of the few Lycian cities with a Greek name (*phellos* means "cork oak"). Excavations have dated the settlement to around the fourth century BC, although Antiphellos only gained importance in Hellenistic times, when increased seagoing commerce meant it thrived while Phellos withered. By the Roman era, it was famed particularly for its exceptionally soft sponges.

The remains of Antiphellos are few and scattered, but what's visible is quite impressive. A small, almost complete Hellenistic **theatre**, 500m west of the town centre along Necip Bey Caddesi, still holds 26 rows of seats, well used by those watching the sunset. Above and behind here, 100m northeast on a hilltop, a unique **Doric tomb**, the so-called *Kesme Mezar*, also remains almost completely intact. Its single chamber forms a slightly tapering cube cut from the rock on which it stands; inside, the bench at the back is decorated by a frieze of small female figures performing a dance.

The most interesting surviving sarcophagus is the **Lion Tomb**, towering at the top of the Uzun Çarşı. The lower of its two burial chambers forms a base for the Lycian sarcophagus above it. On the side of the lower chamber is an undeciphered Lycian inscription in the same poetic form as the Xanthian obelisk, possibly an epitaph. The tomb's name derives from the lifting bosses for the Gothic-style lid, in the shape of lions' heads resting their chins on their paws.

The beaches of Kaş

Considering that Kaş is a major Turkish resort, local natural beaches are surprisingly poor. In town itself, **Küçük Çakıl** has been pretty much taken over by the hotels above it, who have installed snackbar and sunbed concessions, and fitted the shoreline with flagstone or wooden-decked lidos – though the public is welcome to patronize the facilities. The only good pebble one on Bucak Limanı is **Akçagerme**, 3km west, where the tourism school runs an inexpensive snack bar.

Büyük Çakıl, just over 1km east of town, is a small (60m wide) and often crowded shingle-and-sand cove that holds a handful of snack bars. For more space, take a water dolmuş (hourly low season, every 20min peak times; ₺12.5 return) to **Limanağzı**, the next, large bay to the southeast, with three tavernas and sunbeds behind each of three swimming areas.

The **Çukurbağ peninsula**, west of town, enjoys good views of the Greek island of Kastellórizo, and is lapped by clear, aquamarine water, but again has no beaches other than two pebble coves either side of the isthmus. On the peninsula, there are only hotel-built lidos where you can reach the water unmenaced by ubiquitous sea urchins.

SCUBA DIVING AROUND KAŞ

The Mediterranean around Kaş offers arguably the best visibility (up to 30m) and greatest range of sea life along the entire Turkish coast. Fish you're likely to see – especially in spring or late summer – include grouper, barracuda, amberjack, garfish and ray; smaller common species include cardinal fish, damselfish, parrotfish, flying fish, ornate wrasse, breams and pandora.

Kaş notionally holds around ten **dive operators**, many operating out of Küçük Çakıl hotel basements, but in terms of boat comfort, safety standards, equipment condition and thorough instruction, only three stand out: **Sun Diving**, inside Kaş Camping (☎0242 836 2637, ⓦturkey-diving.com/divecenter-sundiving.html), **Anemone**, Uzun Çarşı Sok 16 (☎0242 836 3651, ⓦanemonedc-kas.com), and **BT Diving**, Çukurbağlı Cad 10 (☎0242 836 3737, ⓦbt-turkey.com).

It's quite common to dive only in the morning or afternoon, so prices are per dive rather than per day. The recommended operators advertise single dives at about €25, making Kaş the least expensive place to dive in Turkey. A PADI Open Water course costs €260, plus €42 for course materials, and advanced Open Water €200, plus €35 for course materials.

DIVE SITES

There are nearly sixty dive sites in the area, many along the Çukurbağ peninsula, with most others around the islets at the marine frontier with Kastellórizo. Beginners visit a tunnel at 15m and a shoreline cave fed by an icy freshwater spring in Bayındır Limanı, or "Stone Edge" or Güvercin Adası off the Çukurbağ peninsula. Moderately experienced divers are taken to "Canyon", where they drop through the namesake intact Greek cotton-carrying freighter that ran aground in the 1960s. This was later dynamited to remove the navigational hazard, so its stern lies in 35m of water. Next there's a traverse of a big-wall dropoff, and then a return north with prevailing currents via a tunnel system. Only advanced divers can visit a wrecked World War II bomber shot down between Kaş and Kastellórizo, resting nearly intact in 65m of water at "Flying Fish", just beyond "Canyon".

Kastellórizo

The picturesque island of **Kastellórizo**, known as Meis in Turkish after the Greek alternative name (Meyísti), lies just over three nautical miles off the Turkish coast. Among the smallest inhabited islands of the Greek Dodecanese archipelago, its harbourfront, lined with pastel-coloured Neoclassical houses, is a delight. You'll find complete coverage in *The Rough Guide to the Greek Islands*, but it's worth saying that there are at least two weekly onward boats to Rhodes most of the year, plus several inexpensive weekly flights on a small aircraft. If you just miss a departure, a day or two on Meis will be well spent, with affordable seafood, walking opportunities and adequate nightlife.

Kaş and Meis have since 2006 hosted an annual, late June, port-to-port **swimming and kayak race** in the interests of peace and friendship between Greece and Turkey, winked at thus far by both customs authorities as passport controls for all concerned are dispensed with.

ARRIVAL AND DEPARTURE KAŞ

By bus and dolmuş All buses and dolmuşes arrive at the *otogar* at the top inland end of Atatürk Bulvarı (alias Elmalı Caddesi). The schedules below are greatly enhanced in season by Batı Antalya Ko-op minibus, which shuttles almost constantly between Kaş and Antalya.
Destinations Antalya (10 daily; 3hr 30min); Bodrum (3 daily; 6hr); Fethiye (11 daily; 2hr); Gömbe (5 daily; 1hr 30min); İstanbul (2 daily; 14hr); Marmaris (4 daily; 5hr).
By ferry Boats to Kastellórizo sail from the harbour, just east

of Cumhüriyet Meydanı (Mon–Fri April–Oct, minimum 10am out 4pm back, extra departures by demand; winter usually Fri & Mon, depending on number of customers, 10.30am, returning 1.30pm; 20min; €20 one-way, €20 day return, €35 open return). The most reliable company is Meis Express (☎0242 836 1725, ⓦmeisexpress.com). You'll need to surrender your passport to customs the night before; returning to Kaş from Kastellórizo, no fresh visa fee is payable as long as time remains on your existing multiple-entry visa.

5

GETTING AROUND

By bus Minibuses labelled "Yarımada–Şehiriçi" operate a shuttle service around the Çukurbağ peninsula's loop road

(at least hourly, until midnight in summer).
Taxis Ranks in the old market square, and base of the jetty.

INFORMATION, TOURS AND ACTIVITIES

Tourist office Cumhuriyet Meyd 5, on the waterfront (May–Oct Mon–Fri 8.30am–noon & 1–7pm, Sat & Sun 10am–noon & 1–7pm; Nov–April Mon–Fri 9am–noon & 1–5pm; ☎0242 836 1238). Glossy brochures and hotel lists, but little other information.
Boat tours Boatmen at the harbour offer standard full-day tours (depart 10am, return 6pm) to either Kekova or Patara (from ₺60 per person, including lunch).
BT Adventure & Diving/Bougainville Travel Çukurbağlı (officially İbrahim Serin) Cad 10 ☎0242 836 3737, ☜bt-turkey.com. The foremost adventure-travel

agency in the area, British/Turkish-run, and offering diving, mountain treks, canyoning and sea-kayaking, as well as more conventional excursions.
Dragoman Uzun Çarşı 15 ☎0242 836 3614, ☜dragoman-turkey.com. This Francophone-orientated agency offers a wide range of high-quality outings, including yoga and wine tasting, and sea-level "coasteering".
Paragliding The cliffs above Kaş are beginning to rival Ölüdeniz as a paragliding venue, but you'll pay €100 a time here as well.

ACCOMMODATION

Kaş's nocturnal rhythms make it worth hunting away from the centre for calm, views and privacy. The highest concentration of desirable hotels and *pansiyons* within the town limits lies east of the centre, above **Küçük Çakıl**. There's also an enclave of budget lodgings west of Atatürk Bulvarı, along **Necip Bey Caddesi** (alias Hastane Caddesi) and around the hilltop **Yeni Cami**, formerly a Greek church. Few of the multi-starred hotels on the **Çukurbağ peninsula** deserve their ratings. Most in-town accommodation is open all year, while Çukurbağ establishments close Nov–April. All have a/c unless otherwise stated.

NECİP BEY CADDESİ AND AROUND YENİ CAMI

Ateş Pension Yeni Camii Cad 3 ☎0242 836 1393, ☜atespension.com. This backpackers' favourite is the only place in town with dorm rooms. Light, airy a/c rooms, some with sea views, and a rooftop terrace. Free wi-fi, and guests can use the pool at the nearby *Hideaway Hotel*. Dorm beds ₺25, doubles ₺90
Gülşen Pansiyon Necip Bey Cad 21 ☎0242 836 1171. Basic but right on the seafront, with access to the water from the very pleasant garden and breakfast area. Rooms are en-suite and a/c; lucky balconied rooms face the sea. ₺110
★ **Hideaway Hotel** Eski Kilise Arkası 7 ☎0242 836 1887, ☜hotelhideaway.com. Renovated in 2012, rooms have new tiled baths plus marble and wood trim; third-floor view rooms are white and airy. Common areas include a small plunge pool, internet corner, a TV-lounge-cum-library, and a stunning rooftop restaurant with home-style cooking and fair bar prices. Ahmet (Turkish) and Marie (Belgian) are your very engaging, multilingual hosts. ₺120
Kale Otel Kilise Mevkii ☎0242 836 4074. Four-building complex popular with German package tourists, though walk-ins welcome; pastel-hued rooms have marble, wood and white-tile decor. The sea view from the back garden is unobstructed, and there's an affiliated restaurant (*Leymona*) by the water. Rooms with sea views cost extra. €76
Kaş Otel Hastane Cad 20 ☎0242 836 1271, ☜myhotelkas.com. Spartan but superbly located, right on the seafront with its own sun loungers and a ladder into the sea. Try to get a balconied room near the water; the

ones behind have no views to speak of. ₺120
Oreo Hotel Yaka Mahallesi, north of the town centre ☎0242 836 2220 or ☎836 3737. This high-standard hotel is managed by BT Travel (see p.330), so it's often occupied by adventure sports groups. Over half the rooms have sea views, there's a big pool and adjacent shady garden for breakfast. €60

KÜÇÜK ÇAKIL

Begonvil Hotel Koza Sok, halfway along ☎0242 836 3079, ☜hotelbegonvil.com. Boutique hotel with old-photo decor, side-facing at the end of a terrace, with small-to medium-size, cheerful rooms with tile-mosaic and wrought-iron touches. All but three have sea views from small balconies, and some have double beds, though bathrooms could stand re-doing. Buffet breakfast taken in the courtyard. €65
★ **Gardenia** Küçük Çakıl shore road ☎0242 836 2368, ☜gardeniahotel-kas.com. Boutique hotel with just eleven quite different rooms and suites over four storeys (beware, no lift) with Philippe Starck decor and marble floors, and oriental art in the common areas. Proprietors Ömer and Nevin speak American English. No children under 12, sea-view rooms cost €30 extra. Closed Nov–April. €90
Medusa Hotel Küçük Çakıl shore road ☎0242 836 1440, ☜medusahotels.com. Well-equipped, well-run three-star hotel with a pool and lido, though standard rooms – some with double beds and island views – are rather small. Four-person family suites on the roof offer a bit more space. €70

Nur Hotel Küçük Çakıl shore road ☎ 0242 836 1203, ⊚ nurotel.com. The 18 rooms of this modish contemporary hotel are suitably white and bright, apart from the beige terracotta floors. All rooms have a/c and LCD TVs, and range from standard doubles to four-bed family suites that cost €35 extra. There's a good-sized pool out front and a bizarre parking area in the downstairs reception. €90

ÇUKURBAĞ PENINSULA

Aquarius South-shore loop road, 3.5km out ☎ 0242 836 1896, ⊚ aquariusotel.com. Discreet, Tardis-like hotel in lush landscaping, consisting of two wings of smallish but cheery rooms with veneer floors and average baths around a large kidney-shaped pool. But the main selling point is the best lido on the peninsula, right opposite Meis, with its own restaurant. Closed Nov–April. €105

Arpia North-shore loop road, 7km out of town ☎ 0242 836 2642, ⊜ arpia@bt-turkey.com. Rooms (including a deluxe grade) have been overhauled, but the place really scores for its sunset views, private lido and poolside restaurant (better-than-average breakfast and open buffet supper). Bookable direct or through the BT agency in town (see p.330). €60

CAMPING

Kaş Kamping Necip Bey Cad, 1km west of town, past the theatre ☎ 0242 836 1050. Well-located, quiet seafront campsite with a swimming platform, lively bar-restaurant and a popular caravan space. Also has its own diving school (see p.329). Tents €15, waterless A-frame cabins €30, en-suite chalets €70

EATING, DRINKING AND NIGHTLIFE

Kaş holds several excellent **restaurants**, but few actually face the waterfront, and some that do are prone to scams and rip-offs. The varied, crowded, sometimes high-decibel **nightlife and café society** is easily the best on the Turquoise Coast.

RESTAURANTS

★ **Bahçe** Uzun Çarşı ☎ 0242 836 2370. The broadest range of cold and hot *mezes* in town, served in the garden (*bahçe* in Turkish). Mains in comparison are almost incidental, though their *ayva tatlısı* makes a fitting finale. Nearby, their seafood annexe Bahçe Balık (booking needed in season on ☎ 0242 836 2779) serves *mezes* such as shrimp pie (₺12) and mains including swordfish fillet (₺25). Closed early Nov to April. Daily 10am–midnight.

★ **Enişte'nin Yeri** Necip Bey Cad ☎ 0242 836 3212. Unlicensed restaurant, nicely located on the waterfront just west of Cumhuriyet Meydan, which dishes up plenty of Turkish favourites including soups (₺5), *pide* (₺7) and kebabs (from ₺12). There's a nice a/c and covered garden room out back. Daily 9am–midnight.

★ **Hayta Meyhane** Zumrut Sok 5. This charming tavern, in an old Greek house, is a great place to try the Turkish aniseed spirit rakı with simple *meze* and grilled-fish mains (from ₺16). The place is named after the resident golden retriever Hayta, who greets guests with a friendly wag of his tail. Daily noon–10pm.

Kaşım Öztürk Sok 15. The best of several options on this inland pedestrian lane, with a mix of affordable *hazır yemek* (from ₺6 per portion), kebabs (from ₺12) and puddings. Unlicensed, but very popular at lunch. Daily 7am–midnight.

Köşk Gürsoy Sok 13 ☎ 0242 836 3857, ⊚ kask oskrestaurant.com. Well-regarded rustic-style restaurant with a dark-wood dining room warmed by an open fire for winter evenings, and tables out on the narrow street in summer. Starters from ₺6 include hummus; mains such as kebabs cost ₺16 and up, and they also offer

seafood. Wine is a reasonable ₺35–40 per bottle. Daily 10am–midnight.

Seçkin Atatürk Bul 2, behind Harbour Mosque ☎ 0242 836 1300. Cheap and cheerful place that tries to be all things to all people, with *döner* wraps (₺4), soups (₺5) and grills (from ₺12). It also serves great traditional desserts like *kabak tatlısı* topped with *kaymak* or *dondurma* at any hour. Daily 24hr.

Sultan Garden Hükümet Cad, opposite Coast Guard ☎ 0242 836 3762, ⊚ sultangarden.eu. The most romantic outdoor harbourfront venue, with unusual *mezes* like *paçanga böreği* and a good line in lamb dishes (from ₺22) and fish mains (from ₺16). Daily 10am–11pm.

BARS AND CAFÉS

Corner Cafe İbrahim Serin Cad 20 ☎ 0242 836 3661, ⊚ cafecornerkas.com. Popular café/bar serving shakes, crepes and ice creams by day, beers (₺8) and other alcoholic drinks in the evenings. It also does good pub grub including a mean home-made lasagne (₺19) or home-made *mantı* (₺17). Daily 10am–2am.

★ **Hideway** Cumhuriyet Cad 16/A, just off the square ☎ 0242 836 3369. Easily the coolest garden bar/café in town; vintage rock, reggae and blues soundtrack, divan and table seating, romantic lighting and ever-popular (if somewhat pricey) Sunday breakfast. Beers ₺9. Closed Dec–April. Daily 4pm–2am.

Hi-Jazz Zümrüt Sok 3 ☎ 0242 836 1165. This trendy L-shaped bar is at its best in winter, when the open fire is blazing and the mellow sounds of soul and jazz soothe the ear. A few tables outside in summer. Beer, and wine by the glass, ₺10. Daily 5pm–2am.

Mavi/Blue Cumhuriyet Meyd ☎ 0242 836 1834. The

5

CANYONING ABOVE KAŞ

Most **canyoning** outings from Kaş focus on one of two stream canyons: Hacıoğlan Çayı or Kıbrıs Çayı. The former traverse, starting near Hacıoğlan village east of Bezirgan, makes a good beginners' spring expedition of 6hr, finishing at Dereköy, with plenty of easy slides and long swims as well as one 6m abseil about two-thirds of the way along. In summer the action shifts to Kıbrıs Çayı, which retains water all year and, while shorter, takes the same time to emerge at Beldibi, with two abseils and two zip-wire transits. Days out typically cost €50 with the recommended agencies (see p.330).

oldest bar-café in town, right on the harbour. Three decades ago it was a coffee house where retired fishermen played backgammon, now it's favoured by Kaş's young moneyed locals who are happy to pay ₺9 for a beer. Less well-off locals and visitors buy beer from the off-licence and drink it on the harbour wall opposite. Daily 10am–2am.

CLUB

Red Point Club Süleyman Topçu Sok ☎ 0242 836 1165. Kaş's premier after-hours dance club in an old barn, packed solid after midnight despite a fairly spacious dancefloor for the sake of DJ-spun rock and soul. Tables out in the lane during summer. Daily 5pm–3am.

SHOPPING

The Uzun Çarşı (Long Market) is precisely that – an uninterrupted bazaar of antique and designer clothing shops with stock (and prices) matching European city-centre malls. Turkish towelling and bathrobes are currently big; besides overseas labels produced under licence, you can have garments custom-tailored from local hand-woven fabrics peddled at the shabby but lively Friday market, at the edge of town en route to Bucak Limanı. The antique shops are all of similar quality, with few worth singling out: carpets, jewellery, metal antiques and kitsch knick-knacks. Finally, Kaş has the only "supermarkets" between Fethiye and Kemer near Antalya, opposite the *otogar*: Gen-Pa and a mini-Migros.

Dem Müzik Evi Bahçe Sok, near the PTT ☎ 0242 836 4420. For the best traditional Turkish music CDs this is the place, with a good selection of Turkish folk, *özgun* and devotional music. Mon–Sat 9am–9pm.
Merdiven İlkokul Sok 4/B ☎ 0242 836 3022. Small

bookshop selling new and used paperbacks and a few new dictionaries and guidebooks. Daily 9am–10pm.
★**Old Curiosity Shop** Lise Sok, off Uzun Çarşı. Cornucopia of a place stocking a unique selection of objects in all sizes – and at a fair price. Mon–Sat 10am–9pm.

Gömbe and around

When sea-level pleasures at Kaş pall, especially in broiling weather, there's escape in the cool heights of the **Akdağ range**, which soars to over 3000m in the space of 20km. The standard starting point for excursions into the mountains, reachable by minibus, is **GÖMBE**, a small town 60km north of Kaş on the road to Elmalı. This provides access to **Yeşil Göl**, Lycia's only alpine lake, and also serves as a staging point for anyone intending to climb to the summit of Akdağ, a 3000m-plus peak.

The ninety-minute ride up to Gömbe from Kaş is graced by extensive pine forests, yielding to apple orchards as you grow closer. Few commercial maps show the huge **Çayboğazı reservoir**, which has re-routed any approach from the south – drivers can avoid the circuitous bypass road by going right over the dam-top road. Gömbe is famous for a June festival of the local Tahtacıs, and a farmers' fair in the latter half of August.

Yeşil Göl

Most people come to Gömbe to visit **Yeşil Göl** (Green Lake), a short way west and the only permanent body of water on generally arid, karstic Akdağ. Tucked into the mountain's east flank at about 1850m elevation, Yeşil Göl is a large, clean and fairly deep tarn that's at its best between April and June; the earlier in spring you show up, the finer the **wildflower** displays. The southern lakeshore has enough (slightly sloping) turf for a handful of tents, should you wish to **camp**.

To reach the lake, it's best to drive (2WD vehicles passable with care, but preferably 4WD), though the following directions apply equally to hikers. Leave the square heading north and turn left immediately after crossing the river bridge, then take the second paved right, and begin climbing in zigzags to the Çukurbağ Köyü mosque. Turn left here and keep parallel to an aqueduct, asking if necessary for the track to "Subaşı Yayla".

Exactly 6.2km above the bridge – half an hour's low-gear driving around ruts, boulders and tree falls – just above the highest gnarled junipers, the track widens beside a vigorous stream, near the start of the aqueduct. Some 500m past this widening is another parking place, flanked by a brick privy; immediately beyond, a landslide blocks the track. Down in the stream ravine a cement pedestrian bridge gives the only safe access to the far bank, where faint paths lead up to a non-vehicular track, blocked off by boulders at its turn-off from your original track. On foot, follow this rougher track past some rudimentary shepherds' huts and corrals; immediately after this, leave the track for proper paths over a gentle saddle that emerges abruptly at an overlook for the lake (maximum 30min from the privy).

The summit of Akdağ is some three hours or so above the lake, but unless you get hold of a good map (tricky) or manage to join Turkish climbers who know the route, the trek is not one to be undertaken lightly.

ACCOMMODATION AND EATING GÖMBE AND AROUND

Hotels are fairly basic but popular with Turks escaping the broiling heat, especially in July and August. The main Belediye square is ringed by several simple but adequate **restaurants**, all offering similar bean-soup and *köfte* menus.

Paşa Hotel On the central square ☎0242 831 5208. The simple rooms in this long-running favourite with Turkish visitors have tiled floors and white walls, and all are en-suite. The owner claims the roof terrace has the best view in Gömbe. There's no breakfast in the price so patrons use the attached kitchen. ₺50

Pınar Pansiyon Meltem Sok, by the PTT ☎0242 831 4109. Very friendly four-storey place with great views from the terrace, and 18 basic but en-suite rooms with 24hr hot water and a decent breakfast. Open all year. ₺60

Dereağzı

30km northeast of Kaş

The imposing ruins at **Dereağzı** – an enormous, half-intact Byzantine cathedral, and a strong Byzantine castle built atop earlier fortifications – make worthy destinations for anyone with transport. The latter guarded a strategic narrows (Dereağzı means "valley mouth") in the easiest route for shipping grain and cedar wood to Andriake (see p.341) from the rich uplands of Elmalı and Kasaba.

To get there, take the road to Gömbe and turn east at Kasaba village, following signs to Çatallar, and then proceed just over 8km to Dirgenler. At a crossroads here with a blue metal bus shelter, a sign points left to three villages; go right instead onto a gravel track. After 2.8km, you reach the head of a gorge, with some rock tombs visible, and a small pumping station in a concrete shed; here the Kasaba plateau begins draining towards the sea. The abrupt, roughly triangular hill on your right is in fact covered by the ruins of a castle, barely noticeable from afar.

The castle

The ancient Lycians first built a **castle** at Dereağzı during the sixth to fifth centuries BC, using polygonal, unmortared masonry, or occasionally even hewing into the rock. Following Arab raids in the eighth century AD, the Byzantines improved and enlarged it over two hundred years, using a mortared-rubble technique, and adding six triangular or rectangular **bastions and towers** still visible on the lowest, northwest wall, the castle's weakest side. American surveys from 1974 to 1981 revealed two

5

more inner layers of defence as one proceeds to the summit, complete with a **church**, plus dozens of **cisterns** and water-collecting channels.

The only way up to the castle is to follow the old Byzantine path, which you can reach by taking the faint goat paths that angle southwest from just before the pumping station. Within twenty minutes, you'll come to the overgrown **main gate** in the northwest-facing wall. Take care not to lose the path as you soon end up on steep, vegetated but dangerous crags.

Once up and in, you fully appreciate the amazing site, not unlike those of the Cathar castles of Languedoc. The southwest to northeast ridge is essentially a knife edge, and the entire fortified hill is lapped by two rivers, the Kasaba (Tokluca) and the Karadağ, which mingle at the hill's southeast base to form the Demre Çayı.

Byzantine church

Dereağzı's huge, knoll-top **cathedral** was erected at the same time as the castle was reconstructed. Given its size, and rich marble decoration – now in Antalya's archeological museum, leaving the brick-and-rubble core – this was clearly funded from Constantinople. It has two unusual, freestanding hexagonal structures, one at the apse end and one where the narthex presumably was. The cathedral served quite a large town, which disappeared within two centuries of its foundation; neither the Byzantine nor Lycian name for Dereağzı is known, since no identifying inscriptions or coins have been found.

To reach it from the water-pumping station, walk northwest on a riverbank track along the Karadağ (aka Boğluca) to a point facing the cathedral, where channels in the marsh are narrow enough for you to cross.

Lycian rock tombs

Down in the Karadağ gorge, most of the area's Lycian **rock tombs and sarcophagi** sit on the east bank of the stream, near the passage of an **ancient road** with numerous steps.

The Kekova region

Some of the most beautifully situated ruins on the Turquoise Coast are in the **Kekova** area, named for the eponymous offshore island. This stretch of rocky shore is littered with the remains of Lycian settlements, some now submerged under the translucent waters of the calm, shallow, almost landlocked gulf here. Land access – both by road and by the Lycian Way – has improved considerably, so the region is no longer the exclusive preserve of boat and yacht tours. Many monuments are easily visited by boat-tour from **Üçağız** on the inlet shore – the main activity at this beachless place – while inland lie the neglected remains of **Apollonia**, a dependency of coastal Aperlae, and the substantial ruins of **Cyaneae**.

Üçağız

The central village of the Kekova region, **ÜÇAĞIZ**, is 38km southeast of Kaş and connected to Highway 400 by a surfaced 20km road. Thus its quiet days are past: a bus park for coaches has been built right by the harbour; carpet, antique and jewellery shops have sprouted; and boat-trip touts swarm around you on arrival. However, the fact that most of the surroundings have been designated as an archeological site protects Üçağız from unseemly concrete expansion; indeed, some illegal buildings have been demolished. And its essential village identity has yet to be completely supplanted – out of season the place is still idyllic.

KEKOVA & AROUND

ARRIVAL AND DEPARTURE

ÜÇAĞIZ

By bus or dolmuş One daily dolmuş (₺5), geared towards villagers not tourists, heads from Demre to Üçağız at 5pm, and leaves Üçağız at 8am. To get here from Kaş, catch an Antalya-bound bus along the coastal highway and then hitch from the turning, or take a taxi all the way (around ₺70). One daily Batı Antalya dolmuş departs at 8am for Antalya, which is useful if you're heading to Çıralı/Olympos as well as Antalya itself.

ACCOMMODATION

Üçağız's *pansiyons* are simple, but often overpriced considering the remote location and lack of a beach. Note, however, that prices drop by up to half in winter. Although fresh water has been piped in from Gömbe, hot showers can still be erratic, but on the positive side all offer free boat trips to beaches on Kekova island. For something more upmarket it's worth considering staying in the hills to the northeast of Üçağız, in the village of Kapaklı köy.

Ekin Hotel Üçağız ☎ 0242 874 2064 or ☎ 0534 936 7783, ⓦ ekinpension.com. This waterfront place has a pleasant garden; clean, airy rooms in the original building; and a newer extension at the back housing suites, with insect screens plus a/c. It's well run by cultured brothers Ali and Yusuf. **₺70**

Kekova Pansiyon Üçağız ☎ 0242 874 2259, ⓦ kekovapansiyon.com. This attractive stone-clad building, located at the western end of the village and a few metres back from the water, has eight palatial a/c rooms and a shared wraparound balcony on the first floor with sea views. **₺140**

★ **Lykia Yolu Palas** Kapaklı Köyü 44 ☎ 0242 874 2222, ⓦ likyayolupalas.com. Wonderful five-room boutique hotel around 20km by road northeast of Üçağız, with sweeping views down to the sea and easterly tip of Kekova island, and its own pool. Owner Orhan is a keen walker and mountaineer – and cook –so expect some great food, perhaps while listening to his extensive collection of vinyl "classics". Good value for the individually decorated and furnished rooms. **€100**

★ **Theimussa Pension** Üçağız ☎ 0532 272 6407, ⓦ thiemussa.eu. Üçağız's smartest accommodation, in a great location at the very eastern edge of the village, abutting the necropolis. Rooms in this 80-year-old building are simple but immaculately presented, with tiled floors, white walls, comfy beds and a/c, and small bathrooms with new, quality fittings. A pleasantly landscaped area outside, complete with banana tree and breakfast room/bar, fronts the sea. **₺150**

Around Üçağız

Üçağız means "three mouths", in reference to the straits at each end of the island opposite, plus the entry to the lake-like gulf, at whose rear the village is situated. Several small islands, quarried in ancient times to near sea level, dot the bay.

5

Until the road was built, the **Lycian remains** around Üçağız were visited by few apart from hardy goats and archeologists. **Teimiussa** – and if you like walking, **Simena** and **Aperlae** – can be reached on foot from the village, though most visitors, especially in summer, opt for a boat excursion instead. The most popular combine both Kekova island and Kale for around ₺40 per person assuming a reasonable number of passengers, considerably more if you have to charter a boat specially.

Kekova island

The most romantically situated local ruins are submerged along the northern coast of **Kekova island**. Known locally as Batık Şehir (Sunken City), they have not yet been identified with any ancient city. The underwater remains of stairs, pavements, house walls and a long quay wall can all be seen; however, snorkelling or even just swimming are banned to prevent the removal of antiquities. Most boatmen won't approach the rocky shoreline, but you can get the best views from a kayak (see p.336).

Near the southwest tip of the island, at the spot called Tersane (Dockyard), looms the apse of a long-vanished church, in whose shadow bathers spread their towels on a fine-shingle beach; unhappily, much of the apse collapsed during a particularly violent storm in 1996.

Teimiussa

The acropolis and necropolis of ancient **Teimiussa** lie just east of Üçağız. While nothing is really known about its history, inscriptions indicate occupation in the fourth century BC. The site, apparently a settlement without walls and few or no public buildings, consists mainly of scattered rock tombs. Some have semicircular benches cut into their bases – convenient for pondering mortality as you stare out to sea, and used by the ancients when visiting their deceased relatives with *nekrodeipna* (food for the dead). On the hill above squats a house-sized fort or tower, while at sea level there's a tiny, rock-cut landing stage.

Kale

A ruined castle of the Knights of St John, visible on the horizon from Üçağız – and the village of **KALE** below it – can be reached via a ten-minute boat ride, or a longer kayak-paddle or walk. The secluded village is the haunt of Rahmi Koç, scion of a wealthy industrialist family, who donated a school while restoring an old house here as a holiday retreat. Even for lesser mortals, Kale makes a lovely place to stay – it's a protected archeological zone, with no new buildings permitted – though some rustic-looking **pansiyons**, overlooking the sea and a marooned sarcophagus, are pricey for what you get.

The acropolis of Simena

Daily: April–Oct 9am–7.30pm; Nov–March 8am–5pm • ₺8 when warden present

The steep but brief climb up to the **acropolis** of ancient Simena is worth it both for the views and for the medieval **castle** itself, whose ramparts are in good condition, partly

---

SEA KAYAKING AROUND KEKOVA

Kayaking day-tours in the Kekova area make a wonderful, low-impact way to appreciate the eerie seascapes. They have the further advantage of allowing you to approach the shoreline, and the Batık Şehir in particular, much closer than the glass-bottomed cruise boats, and also to use narrow, shallow channels off-limits to larger craft. So long as your head is covered and you bring enough water, you'll tolerate all but the hottest summer days, even wrapped inside a life vest. The principal operators are **BT Adventure** and **Dragoman** in Kaş (see p.330). Trips may begin with a motorized tow from Üçağız to the starting point of your choice, for example Tersane; outings can be as long or short as stamina allows. The typical cost, including a transfer from Kaş to Üçağız and a picnic lunch, is €30 per person.

WEST ALONG THE LYCIAN WAY: APERLAE AND APOLLONIA

Ancient **Aperlae** lies on the far side of a peninsula southwest of Üçağız, astride the Lycian Way. Access most comfortably involves a 40min boat ride to a landing stage that's home to a couple of restaurants, followed by a half-hour walk. It's a remote site, and practically deserted, though there's a cluster of modern houses at Sıçak İskelesi, beside the ruins. The **city walls** are fairly well preserved, enclosing a rectangular area with the sea lapping the southern side; the **necropolis**, typically, lies almost entirely outside the walls. As at Kekova, subsidence has submerged the harbour quarter, but swimming and snorkelling here are unrestricted. If you follow the line of the old **quay**, now in 1–2m of water and indented at 15m intervals for the mooring of ships, you'll see heaps of pottery shards, amphora necks, terracotta tiles and shell-middens from the ancient murex-dye industry, all encrusted together. There are also building foundations divided by narrow **streets**, with some intact pavement near the shore.

If Aperlae is neglected, unexcavated **Apollonia** is even more so. It can be reached on foot, either from Boğazcık, via a spur from the Lycian Way, or from Aperlae (2hr 15min), or partway by a 2km track from the modern village of **Kılınçlı** (alias Sıçak) on the Üçağız-bound road. You may share the path from Aperlae with a camel or two – road construction in this archeologically rich area has been forbidden, and working (as opposed to tourist-attraction) camels are the most efficient transport for shepherds on the Sıçak peninsula.

Apollonia is remarkable for its superb **necropolis**, which spikes the lower northeast slope of the hill on which the city is found, facing Kılınçlı. There is one conventional sarcophagus with extravagant Gothic-type details, but most distinctive are a half-dozen **pillar tombs**, considered the ur-burial method of the ancient Lycians, and proving Apollonia's antiquity. Isolated from the other tombs, at the west end of the hill facing Boğazcık, stands an unusual **carved tomb** on two levels. But there is more to see in the acropolis, at its east end effectively double: a much older stockade inside a Byzantine citadel. Particularly on the southwest flank, the **city walls** – made of unusually large quadrangular and pentagonal blocks – are pierced by windows and a gate. From atop the inner fort, you look west over a well-preserved **Byzantine church**, possibly of the sixth or seventh century; just west of this, overgrown but in a fair state of preservation, is a lovely little **theatre**. The views from the hill, whether inland to the Lycian mountains or out to sea, are the icing on the experience.

resting on ancient foundations. Inside the Knights' castle, a 15m-wide **theatre** is carved into the living rock, large enough for perhaps two hundred people. Some well-preserved **sarcophagi** stand on the eastern slopes of the hill, off the path. Brace yourself for being followed by children peddling printed headscarves, and village women pressing oregano into your hands or offering guiding services.

ACCOMMODATION AND EATING
KALE

Although accommodation is uniformly overpriced in high season (July & Aug), Kale is a special place, and a night or two here well worth the experience. Most of the half-dozen waterfront **restaurants**, which have had a long and jading acquaintance with the tour-boat trade, offer a set-price, fill-your-plate *meze* buffet.

Kale Pansiyon Kale ☎0242 874 2111, ⓦkalepansiyon .com. Simple but comfortable nine-room pension, in an old waterfront house. Plain whitewashed walls, *kilim*-decked wooden floors, and great island-view balconies. €80

Mehtap Pansiyon Kale ☎0242 874 2146, ⓦmehtappansiyon.com. Set back and up the hill from

the water, the *Mehtap* has eight plain but a/c wood-floored rooms in a lovely period house set in a sea of citrus, banana, carob, olive and palm trees. It also has camping space available, and good suppers served on the terrace. Friendly owner manager Saffet will collect/return you from/to Üçağız by boat. Open all year. Tents ₺20, rooms ₺180

Cyaneae

23km east of Kaş above the village of Yavu

The wild, inhospitable countryside east of Üçağız is amenable these days only to herds of sheep and goats. In antiquity, however, this region was scattered with small settlements, of which the most interesting now is **CYANEAE** (Kyaneai in Turkish signage). The name Cyaneae/Kyaneai derives from the ancient Greek for "dark blue" – also the origin of the word cyanide – but it's uncertain why the place was so named. The Lycian and Roman sarcophagi here are the most numerous of any local site, and the main reason to visit. Cyaneae was the most important Roman town between Myra and Antiphellos (modern Kaş), and linked by a direct road to Teimiussa port, 12km away.

A signposted 2km **path** leads to the site from Yavu village centre – 45 minutes of extremely steep hiking. Rather easier is an unmarked 4km **dirt road** that takes off from the north side of Highway 400, precisely 1km west of the side road to Yavu; the last stretch is rough, but negotiable with care in an ordinary car. It's possible to take a **local guide** along (from the so-called "tourist office" in the village, maximum €15 per party), but not strictly necessary. The only other facility, on Highway 400 500m towards Demre, is the seasonal *Çeşme* restaurant.

The site

Some of Cyaneae's oldest, most interesting **tombs** lie along the path up from Yavu, flanking what may have been part of the ancient road. The most impressive – a sarcophagus carved completely from the rock on which it stands – lies south of the road. Two lions' heads project from each side of the Gothic-arch "lid", cut from the same piece of rock. Near the top of the path, there's a subterranean shrine or tomb with six columns.

Below the city, fairly inaccessible on the south face of the hill, stands an impressive **temple-tomb** whose porch has a single freestanding column and, unusually, a recess above the pediment with a sarcophagus. An inscription states this was reserved for the heads of the household, while the rest of the family were buried in the tomb.

The **acropolis** is surrounded on three sides by a wall; the south side is too precipitous to need protection. The buildings inside are ruined and cloaked with vegetation, but a library, baths and two Byzantine churches (one with a lengthy inscription) have been identified. A tomb near the summit bears a relief of a charioteer driving a team of four horses. The city had no natural spring nearby, so vaulted cisterns and reservoirs square-cut into the rock are ubiquitous.

West of the summit beyond the parking area, a **theatre** retains 23 rows of seats. Those above the diazoma make ideal vantage points over the acropolis walls, Kekova inlet, and sarcophagi flanking an ancient path linking the theatre and the acropolis. Mainly Roman, these are mostly simple, with rounded lids and crests, but some have lion-head bosses.

Demre

East of Yavu, Highway 400 swoops down in a well-graded arc towards **DEMRE**, a rather scruffy, river-delta place, too far from the coast to be a beach resort. The main local businesses are citrus fruit and tomatoes, whose greenhouses – spread below as you descend the escarpment to the west – make Demre seem bigger than it really is. Unlike other nondescript towns along the coast, which juggle sun-and-wave motifs in their municipal logos, Demre is unequivocal about its self-image: a giant tomato occupies most of its coat of arms.

Father Christmas has also crept in, and the town centre is absolutely overrun with **Santa kitsch**, as well as considerable midday groups of Russian pilgrims, catered to by a huge number of icon stalls. As ancient Myra, Demre was the adult home of **Saint Nicholas**, a major Orthodox saint, and the **central church** honours him. In fact so many Russians visit the church that this is Antalya province's most visited site – incredible given the wealth of fabulous Graeco-Roman remains hereabouts. Nearby attractions include the

5

site of **Myra** just north, the ancient harbour of **Andriake**, and the Apollo oracle at **Sura**, a little way south (you pass both as you approach from the west), plus the beach at **Çayağzı**.

Brief history

An important member of the Lycian Federation, Myra remained important throughout the Byzantine area through its association with Bishop, later Saint, **Nicholas**, aka **Santa Claus** (see box, p.340). Some assocate the city's name with the Greek for myrrh, a plant resin used in the production of incense, but there's no evidence it was made here, and Myra is probably a corrupted Lycian place name. When the bishop's tomb was opened by eleventh-century grave robbers, however, they were supposedly overwhelmed by the smell of myrrh.

Despite its later fame, Myra wasn't heard from before 42 BC, when the city displayed typical Lycian defiance by refusing to pay tribute money to Brutus. Brutus's lieutenant had to break the chain closing off the mouth of Andriake harbour – Myra's port – and force his way in. Subsequently, Myra had an uneventful if prosperous history until abandonment in the fourteenth century, treated well by its imperial overlords and becoming capital of Byzantine Lycia in the fifth century.

Church of St Nicholas

Müze Cad • Daily: May–Oct 9am–7pm; Nov–April 8.30am–5pm • ₺10

The **Church of St Nicholas** dominates central Demre, on the right of the pedestrianized Müze Caddesi as you head west. Despite the unsightly synthetic protective canopy on one side, the building remains evocative of its patron saint. Nicholas was beatified after visitors to his purported tomb reported miracles, and Myra soon became a popular focus of pilgrimage; even after the Bari raiders stole his bones, the pilgrimages continued. Monks from a nearby monastery simply designated another tomb as the saint's, pouring oil through openings in the top and collecting it at the bottom, to sell to pilgrims as holy secretions.

The contemporary church – basically a three-aisled basilica, with a fourth added later – has little in common with the fourth-century original, having been rebuilt in 1043 after its destruction by occupying Saracens, and again in 1862 by Russian Tsar Nicholas I, who installed a vaulted ceiling instead of a cupola in the central nave, along with a belfry. Turkish archeologists have carried out more recent protective modifications, such as the extra small stone domes in the narthex.

The most typically Byzantine feature is the **synthronon** (bishop's throne) in the apse, rarely found *in situ* since most were removed when Anatolian churches were converted into mosques. Among the patchy interior **frescoes**, the best and clearest – in the dome

---

ST NICHOLAS – THE ORIGINAL SANTA CLAUS

Myra's prestige was greatly enhanced by the reputation of one of its citizens, namely **St Nicholas**, born in Patara in 270 AD and later appointed local bishop. The Orthodox patron saint of sailors, merchants, students, prisoners, virgins and children, his Western identity as a genial old present-giver is perhaps more familiar, based on the story of the three daughters of a poor man who were left without dowries. Nicholas is credited with throwing three purses of gold coins into the house by night, enabling them to find husbands instead of prostituting themselves. Many posthumous miracles were attributed to the saint, but little is actually known about the man. However, after his death he was probably buried in the church in Demre that's now dedicated to him, and it is also widely believed that in 1087 his bones were carried off to Italy by a group of devout raiders from Bari.

Demre still banks heavily on its connection with St Nicholas (**Noel Baba** or "Father Christmas" in Turkish); a special Mass is held here on his main feast day, December 6, attracting Orthodox and Catholic pilgrims, while others take place on random Sundays throughout the year.

of the north transept – is a *Communion of the Apostles*. **Mosaic floor-panels**, mainly geometric designs, adorn the nave and south aisle, while masonry fragments near the entrance include one carved with an anchor – either symbolic of Christian faith, or Nicholas as protector of sailors. His purported **sarcophagus**, in the southernmost aisle as you face the synthronon, is not considered genuine. The saint's bones were reputedly stolen from a tomb under a pavement – and, more significantly, on this one there's a relief representation of a married couple on the lid.

Myra

2km north of Demre's town centre • Daily: April–Oct 8.30am–7.30pm; Nov–March 8.30am–5pm • ₺15

As one of the most easily visited Lycian sites, ancient **Myra** is packed with tours even in the off season. In summer, it's best visited early or late in the day, though you'll still run a gauntlet of overwhelming tourist tat lining the approaches, plus kids selling oregano and unnecessary guide services.

Apart from a large theatre and some of the finest house-style rock tombs in Lycia, most of the city is still buried. The **theatre** was destroyed by an earthquake in 141 AD but rebuilt shortly afterwards; two concentric galleries cover the still-intact stairs by which spectators entered the auditorium. The substantial chunks of carving lying around the orchestra and just outside, which once decorated the stage building, include several theatrical masks, a bust of a woman and a Medusa head.

The main concentration of **tombs** (currently off-limits during ongoing archeological excavations) stands west of the theatre. Most are of the house type, in imitation of Lycian dwelling places, even down to the wooden roof-beams. Some are decorated with reliefs, including warriors at the climax of a battle, a naked page handing a helmet to a warrior, and a funerary scene.

A second group of tombs, called the **river necropolis**, is around the side of the second long ridge on the right as you stand with your back to the theatre stage. To get there, leave the main site, turn left off the final access drive onto the main approach road, and continue inland for 1.5km. Here the "**painted**" **tomb** (though it is no longer pigmented) features the reclining figure of a bearded man and his family in the porch, and outside on the rock face what's presumed to be the same family, in outdoor apparel.

Andriake

2.5 km southwest of Demre, almost 5km from Myra itself • No public transport; head west out of Demre towards Kaş. then bear left, and where the main highway starts to tackle the grade on the right bank of the stream leading down to the sea, turn left again at a black-on-yellow sign

Set astride the Androkos River, ancient Myra's port, **Andriake**, was the site of **Hadrian's granary**. This was vital to the whole Roman world, since its contents were sent to Rome to be distributed around the empire. The substantial remains of this building can still be seen south of today's river, which runs parallel to the road between Demre and the beach.

Built at Hadrian's behest in 119–139 AD, and very similar to the one at Patara, the granary consists of eight rooms constructed of well-fitting square blocks, the outer walls still standing to their original height. Above the main central gate are busts of Hadrian and possibly his wife, the empress Sabina. Another decorative relief on the front wall, near the second door from the west, depicts two deities of disputed identity, one flanked by a snake and a griffin, the other reclining on a couch.

Çayağzı

1km southwest of Andriake, 3.5 km southwest of Demre

Modern **Çayağzı** ("Rivermouth") anchorage, a possible launching point for boat trips to the Kekova region, consists of half a dozen snack-shacks opposite the main quay. Both these, and the lone full-service restaurant on the far side of the pedestrian bridge, operate fitfully. Çayağzı is still a working fishing port, with an active boatyard, and it's

5

possible to get a **boat** from here to the Kekova area, a 45-minute journey, followed by the standard tour of the underwater ruins at Kekova island. You'll need a group, as the three- to four-hour trips cost around ₺120 for the boat.

The only other reason to come here is for a swim. The adjacent beach is fairly short, if broad and duney – though also trash-strewn and prone to algae slicks, which, together with the Kaş–Demre highway passing just overhead and the area's status as an archeological zone, accounts for the minimal development here. However, the beauty of the skyline to the west cannot be underestimated, where parallel ridges – as in a Japanese print – march down to Kekova.

ARRIVAL AND DEPARTURE
DEMRE

By bus and dolmuş Buses and dolmuşes drop passengers at the *otogar*, close to the centre.
Destinations Antalya (at least 15 daily; 2hr 30min);

Fethiye (6 daily; 4hr); Finike (for Arykanda; hourly; 30min); Kaş (hourly; 1hr); Üçağız (1 daily; 45min).

ACCOMMODATION AND EATING

Camping & Cafe Andriake On the beach/river mouth at Çayağzı, 3.5km southwest of Demre ☎ 0242 871 3130, ⓦ andriake.com. In addition to tent camping, this green and attractive campsite holds a café that offers a wide range of food, including barbecued fish (₺20), served with salad and chips. ₺10
Derin Hotel Andriake Çayağız Yolu 99 ☎ 0242 871 3561, ⓦ hotelderin.com. A few hundred metres down from the turn off the main coastal highway, on the road to Andriake, the functional *Derin* ("deep" in Turkish) is nicer than any hotels in Demre itself, with comfy twins and doubles with a/c, simple but tasteful decor and tidy bathrooms. The setting is OK too, in a clump of trees

backing onto open fields. ₺100
Kent İlkokul Cad, Myra ☎ 0242 871 2042, ⓦ kentpansiyon.com. Very friendly and family run, and used mainly by trekkers on the Lycian Way, this is still the only accommodation opt on worth recommending. The rooms are simple but spacious and have a/c, and there's a basic bungalow in the leafy garden as well. Bungalow ₺50, doubles ₺70
Kismet Müze Cad. This faux-rustic pine barn of a restaurant dishes up the usual suspects, like *pide* (from ₺7), *kebap* (from ₺12) and soup (₺4). Probably the best bet in the town centre, it's usually busy with locals. Daily 8am–11pm.

Arykanda

60km northeast of Demre, 34km north of the Highway 400 town of Finike • Catch a frequent Antalya–Kaş bus to Finike's *otogar*, and catch an Elmalı-bound dolmuş as far as Arif, 1km signposted walk from the site

Set in a breathtaking location, high in the mountains on a steep, south-facing hillside that overlooks the main valley between the Akdağ and Bey mountain ranges, **Arykanda** is a fabulous ancient site that's comparable with Delphi in Greece. Its individual monuments are scattered, often only partly excavated and unlabelled, but there are good site plans by the entrance and the acropolis. While finds date to the fifth century BC, the typically Lycian "anda" suffix suggests that the city was founded a millennium earlier. Arykanda was a member of the Lycian Federation from the second century BC, and remained inhabited until the eleventh century.

The site

Daily: April–Oct 8am–7pm; Nov–March 8am–5pm • ₺10

A pronounced ravine and power pylons divide the site of Arykanda roughly in two. The function of the complex structure dubbed **Naltepesi**, entered by a right-angled stairway beside the parking area, is not yet completely understood, but you can make out a small bathhouse and presumed shops. North of the parking area, a large **basilica** holds extensive mosaic flooring under tin-roof shelters posed over each aisle, and a semicircular row of benches (probably a synthronon) in the outer apse; a more colourful mosaic just below features two birds. Another, smaller basilica just inside suggests eighth-century destruction and more modest rebuilding. The most impressive sight, however, looming on the east, is the 10m-high facade of the **main baths**, with numerous windows on two levels, and apsidal halls at each end. The westerly one holds a still-intact plunge pool, and the easterly one has stacked hypocausts.

Other constructions worth seeking out include a small **temple** or tomb above the baths complex (one of three "monumental tombs" on the site plan), adapted for Christian worship. There are more Roman or Byzantine mosaics in the tombs or temples immediately east of the Christianized one. West of the ravine and power lines, and above the **agora** – whose engaging odeion has been defaced by horrible new marble cladding – an impressive, six-aisled **theatre** retains twenty rows of seats plus a well-preserved stage building. Above this sprawls a short but attractive **stadium**, with several rows of seats exposed.

The coast to Olympos

East of Finike, which is noteworthy only for its yacht marina, Highway 400 runs dead straight before turning ninety degrees to enter the high-rise market town of Kumluca. Beyond that, it curls up through the **Beydağları National Park**, a spectacular sequence of densely pine-forested ridges and precipitous bare cliffs. Two relatively unspoiled beach resorts, **Adrasan** and **Olympos/Çıralı**, lie hidden at the mouths of canyons that plunge to the sea. If you're heading towards either by your own transport, leave the main highway for the narrow but paved side road that veers off east of Kumluca, signposted "Beykonak, Mavikent". This short cut rollercoasters through forested valleys and along dramatic coastline to **Gelidonya Burnu**, with its lighthouse and scenic sections of the Lycian Way, before emerging at Çavuş, the nearest proper village to Adrasan and Olympos. The only trick en route involves turning left (north) at a signposted junction near the outskirts of Karaöz, the last bay and village before Gelidonya Burnu.

Adrasan

Nestling in the shadow of pointy Musa Dağı (Mt Moses), **ADRASAN** is an attractive beach resort with a pretty curving beach bookended by pine-forested limestone spurs. It's more mainstream and less hip than nearby Çıralı (see p.346) and there's none of the backpacker scene so prevalent at Olympos (see p.344), a day's walk north along the Lycian Way. The resort is very popular with Turks, especially in July and August, while in spring and autumn it's an overnighting spot for trekkers following the Lycian Way. Though falling within national park boundaries, development (including second-home building) is proceeding slowly.

THE LYCIAN WAY AT GELIDONYA BURNU

From the small pebbly beach at Karaöz, an obvious dirt road heads south along the coast towards the cape. Roughly 6.5km along, leave the track in favour of the marked **Lycian Way**, now a steadily rising path through oaks and pines. From the trailhead, a round-trip of just under an hour (with a daypack) will take you to the photogenic **lighthouse** just above Taşlık Burnu (as **Gelidonya Burnu**, "Swallow Cape", has been officially renamed). Built by the French in 1936, the lighthouse is not currently inhabited, but a keeper cycles out from Karaöz at dusk to light the lamp. The treacherous **Beş Adalar** (Five Islands) that straggle beyond the cape are shipping hazards that have caused many a wreck, including an ancient one that yielded a huge amount of treasure to archeological divers during the 1960s.

North of the lighthouse, the Lycian Way threads deserted hillside between the sea and a high ridge on its 6hr course to Adrasan (path or cross-country except for the final hour). This dramatic stretch has become a popular organized group target, so you'll probably have company.

5

ARRIVAL AND DEPARTURE

By bus Adrasan is tricky to reach on public transport. Catch one of the very frequent coastal highway buses south and west from Antalya (₺10) or east and north from Kaş (₺15) as far as the turn-off, 13km north of the resort, and catch a minibus from there (every 2hr in season; ₺5). Most hotel/pension owners will collect guests – call ahead. If you're driving, look out for a steep road that descends right to Çavuş village and the bay of Adrasan, 12km beyond Kumluca on Highway 400. Whether you arrive from this direction, or from Mavikent, turn east in Çavuş village centre (bank ATM) onto the seaward road (marked "Sahil"), following hotel placards for 4km.

ACTIVITIES

Boat trips Ceneviz Limanı, a cliff-girt bay beyond Musa Dağı and inaccessible on foot, is the most popular outing, costing ₺30–40 including lunch.
Diving Center Adrasan Central beachfront (closed Feb to late March; beach dives €30; 10 dives €240; CMAS/PADI certification from €310; ☎0242 883 1353, ⓦ diving -adrasan.com). This German/Turkish outfit also offers accommodation/dive packages from €370 for seven nights.

ACCOMMODATION

Two dozen *pansiyons* and hotels are scattered inland from the long beach, or along the stream meeting the sea at its north end. The fancier **hotels** – though the term is only relative – overlook the south end of the bay, near the jetty.

★ **Aybars** Beside the river at the far north end of the beach ☎0242 883 1133 or ☎0532 314 1887, ⓦaybarshotel.com. The pick of the riverside accommodation. Large, a/c, balconied rooms, renovated in 2012, overlook lush grounds and an in-river restaurant. Aysın, on the mobile number given, speaks good English. Closed Dec–March. Rates include half board. ₺200

Ford At the very southern end of the beach ☎0242 883 1098, ⓦfordhotel.net. With a nicely landscaped pool and its own phalanx of beach sunbeds, this upmarket place has 29 rooms (including three family suites) in two wings, with hillside or sea views. Closed Nov–March, rates (for two) include breakfast. ₺210

EATING AND DRINKING

Several independent **restaurants** on the east bank of the watercourse, and also the *Aybars* hotel, are reached by wobbly suspension bridges. Diners are seated on platforms in the stream, where hundreds of ducks come to cadge your spare bread. The restaurants are very Anglicized in menu, clientele and price, and none is really worth singling out. In addition, several perfectly adequate, and more traditionally Turkish, restaurants back the beach; expect to pay ₺15 and up for kebabs, ₺20 and up for grilled fish.

Olympos

Around 60km northeast of Demre, a spectacular wooded cleft, the **Olympos valley**, runs down to a shingle beach and the sea. This valley is home to the atmospheric ruins of the ancient Lycian city of **Olympos**, virtually lost in thick scrub by a reed-fringed river, along with a veritable "village" of wooden huts and treehouses that has become a staple on Turkey's backpacking circuit. As well as backpackers, summer weekends see the place busy with young folk from Antalya escaping the heat; major holidays with groups of university students from elsewhere in the country; and the period around ANZAC day is often bristling with Australians and New Zealanders. Throw in an increasing number of Russian tourists seeking a break from the all-inclusive hotels down the coast, and it's easy to see why Olympos enjoys a reputation as the liveliest "alternative" resort on the Turkish coast.

Brief history

Although nothing is known about the origins of Olympos, the city presumably took its name from **Mount Olympos**, present-day Tahtalı Dağ, 16km north – one of over twenty mountains in the ancient world that bore the name Olympos. The city made its historical debut during the second century BC, minting its own coins; within a few decades Olympos was one of six cities in the Lycian Federation to possess three votes, confirming its importance.

The principal deity of Olympos – **Hephaestos** (the Roman Vulcan), god of fire and of blacksmiths – was considered native to this region, and traces of a temple dedicated to him exist near the Chimaera. During the first century BC, the importance of his cult diminished when pirates led by Zeniketes overran both Olympos and nearby Phaselis, and introduced the worship of the Indo-European god Mithras. Zeniketes made Olympos his headquarters, but in 78 BC he was defeated by the local Roman governor, and again in 67 BC by Pompey, after which Olympos became public property. The city's fortunes revived after it was absorbed into the Roman Empire in 43 AD, and Christianity became prominent. Olympos was later used as a trading base by the Venetians and Genoese – hence Ceneviz Limanı (Genoese Harbour) just south – but was abandoned after the Ottomans dominated the Mediterranean.

Olympos valley

The Olympos valley is quite beautiful in its own right; the vast majority of visitors are content to admire the scenery, chill in the treehouses, explore the ancient site that lies between the accommodation area and the beach, or swim.

More active pursuits include hikes along the Lycian Way, south over Musa Dağı to Adrassan (see p.343) or north to the flames of the Chimaera and, beyond, ancient Phaselis (see p.350). In addition, various agencies offer, usually through the pensions, activities such as jeep safaris, boat tours, sea-kayaking, diving and rock-climbing. The drawback to basing yourself in Olympos, as opposed to neighbouring Çıralı (see p.346), is that you're quite a way from the beach and have to negotiate the ancient site on each trip (see p.345). In winter, moreover, the secluded valley gets much less sun than its less confined neighbour and can be pretty cold.

The site of Olympos

Daily: April–Oct 8am–7pm; Nov–March 9am–5.30pm • ₺5; smart PlajKarts, valid for ten days, allow multiple entry to the site, for multiple users; 10 entries ₺7.5, 25 entries ₺15

Potentially, the site of **Olympos** should be idyllic, set on the banks of an oleander- and fig-shaded stream that runs between high cliffs. Alas, years of visitors littering and sleeping rough here, despite notices forbidding both, have seen the water muddied or worse, and the turtles, ducks and frogs that may still live here now make themselves scarce. The scanty ruins line the banks of the stream, which rarely dries up completely in summer, owing to three freshwater springs welling up on the north bank, close to the ocean.

The site has two entrances. One is inland, at the end of the southerly approach road; the other, which is often unmanned, and thus allows free access to the site, is fifteen minutes' walk south along the beach from Çıralı's river mouth. As at Patara, nocturnal "raids" of the ruins are expressly forbidden.

Extensive **Byzantine-Genoese fortifications** overlook the beach from each creek bank, just 25m up the crags. At the base of the north-bank fort are two "**harbour tombs**", with a touching epigraph on a ship captain translated for visitors. Further along the south bank stands part of a quay and an arcaded **warehouse**; to the east on the same side lies a Byzantine **church**; while in the river itself is a pillar from a vanished **bridge**. In the undergrowth there's a **theatre**, its seats mostly gone.

The most striking ruins are on the stream's north bank. East of the path to the beach looms a well-preserved marble **doorframe** built into a wall of ashlar masonry. An inscribed statue base at the foot of the carved doorway is dedicated to Marcus Aurelius, dated 172–175 AD. East of the portal, a Byzantine **aqueduct** that once carried water to the heart of the city overlaps the outflow of one of the aforementioned springs. Head upstream to reach a mausoleum-style **tomb**, and a Byzantine **villa** with mosaic floors.

5

ARRIVAL AND DEPARTURE

By bus and minibus Minibuses bound for Kumluca or Kaş from Antalya *otogar* pass the Olympos turn-off (every 20–30min; daily 6am–9pm; ₺10), where waiting minibuses ferry travellers the 9km down to Olympos (₺5).

Between November and April, you may have to wait a while before the driver deems he has sufficent customers. Minibuses leave Olympos for the main road every hour.

ACCOMMODATION

TREEHOUSE LODGES

Bayram's Olympos ☎0242 892 1243, ⊛bayrams.com. The closest option to the ruins, set in an orange grove, this well-run place has standard, a/c, all-wood treehouse-bungalows, with friendly and helpful staff. The youthful clientele lounge about the cushioned garden. Rates per person, including breakfast and evening meal: 6-bed dorms ₺30, treehouses ₺35, bungalows ₺50

Kadir's Top Tree Houses Olympos ☎0242 892 1250, ⊛kadirstreehouses.com. The original backpacker's lodge, furthest from the ruins. Quirky stilt-bungalows are its main appeal, but there's also a lively bar. In the summer heat the walk to the beach seems a whole lot longer. Rates per person, including breakfast and evening meal: dorms ₺30, treehouses (5-person) ₺35, bungalows ₺50, a/c bungalows ₺65

Türkmen Near the stream ford ☎0242 892 1249, ⊛olomposturkmentreehouses.com. The largest and most overtly commercial outfit, set between *Kadir's* and *Bayram's*, with "bloks" (sic) of standard hotel rooms as well as densely sown cabins. It attracts a substantial Turkish clientele and serves some of the best food in the valley. Rates per person, including breakfast and evening meal: treehouses (2–5 person) ₺35, a/c bungalows ₺45, luxury a/c bungalows ₺65

Şaban Near the stream ford ☎0242 892 1265, ⊛sabanpansion.com. One of the quieter establishments, opposite the *Türkmen*. It doesn't play constant music, but does have better-than-average food, lower-density treehouses (en-suite and not), and more personable management in Ali and Meral. Rates per person, including breakfast and evening meal: dorms ₺30, treehouses ₺35, bungalows ₺50

Çıralı

The laidback resort of **ÇIRALI**, shrouded in citrus groves, is situated on a narrow plain between the mountains and a long, curving, 3km-long shingle beach. Less oriented towards backpackers than neighbouring Olympos, and more family-friendly, it's located in a valley that runs parallel to Olympos on the south side of a mountain spur. Its major attraction is the natural phenomenon known as the **Chimaera**, an area of flames erupting from the ground on a pine-forested hillside. It's also possible to walk along the beach for around half an hour to the ruins of ancient Olympos (see p.344), and there are longer hikes on the Lycian Way, which blazes its way through the settlement. Apart from a surprising amount of accommodation tucked beneath the trees – six hotels and around a hundred *pansiyon*s – there's little here bar a beachfront strip of restaurants and, just over the river-bridge as you enter the settlement, a short parade of basic shops and cafés.

The fact that Çıralı is safeguarded by various Turkish bodies for its unique ecology, along with its designation as a protected area by the WWF, has enabled threatened loggerhead and green sea **turtles** to continue laying their eggs here. Don't dig up, litter or nocturnally illuminate the beach during the summer nesting season.

Locals and the government are currently in dispute over the future of Çıralı, as many of its pensions and other buildings have been built on what's either wholly or partly state forestry land. Some people claim that only ten to fifteen percent of its buildings are legal, and a few have been demolished as a result.

The Chimaera

Daily 24hr • ₺3.5 • The car park/ticket kiosk is 40min walk north of Çıralı along the road that skirts the mountains; to reach the flames themselves, walk another 20min, up steps

Named after a mythical fire-breathing monster supposed to have inhabited these mountains, the eternal flames of the **Chimaera** (alias Yanartaş) are fed by natural gases emanating from the ground. The climb up to the flames is most rewarding (and coolest) at dusk, since the fire is best seen after dark.

5

No one really knows what causes the phenomenon of clustered flames that sprout from cracks on the bare hillside. Analysis reveals traces of methane in the gas, but otherwise its make-up is unique. The flames can be extinguished temporarily if covered, when a gaseous smell is noticeable, but will spontaneously re-ignite. They have been burning since antiquity, and inspired local worship of Hephaestos (Vulcan), generally revered wherever fire or lava issued forth. The region was also home to a fire-breathing monster with a lion's head and forelegs, a goat's rear end, and a snake tail: the **Chimaera**. Close to the flames are a small Byzantine chapel and the tholos of Hephaestos.

ARRIVAL AND DEPARTURE
ÇIRALI

By bus and minibus Kumluca- or Kaş-bound minibuses from Antalya *otogar* pass the Çıralı turn-off, signed "Çıralı, Yanartaş, Chimaera" (every 20–30min; daily 6am–9pm; ₺10). From here waiting minibuses ferry travellers 7km down to Çıralı (₺5).

TOURS

Boat tours make a popular way to break up the beach routine, generally heading south to explore the dramatic cliffs and bays around Ceneviz Liman (Porto Genoese) or the opposite direction to Phaselis (see p.350).

Çıralı Beach Just behind the beach, where the main road in sweeps left ⓦciralibeach.com. Prices at this reliable boat-tour agency start at €25 per person. Cars and bikes are also available for rent.

ACCOMMODATION

Çıralı does not have a formal campsite, and rough camping is actively discouraged, so some *pansiyon*s offer space for tents. Following disputes that pitted the forestry and archeological services against local proprietors, beachfront **restaurants** have been moved back a token few metres from the sand, and seven survivors – in a line north of the river mouth – seem here to stay.

Barış Pansiyon Just behind the beach near the restaurants ☎0242 825 7080. A choice of spartan, older en-suite rooms, a new wing of part-balconied upper-floor units (₺20 extra) and three wooden chalets, plus ample parking. Doubles ₺110, chalets ₺150

★ **Cemil's Pansiyon** At the junction of the beach and Chimaera road ☎0242 825 7080. Cemil's place is run by a charming family. The six rooms, part of a long, low terrace, are simple but have a/c and good-quality stalled bathrooms. The buffet breakfast is eaten in the shade of spreading mulberry trees. There are also several more rooms in the family farmhouse, fronted by its own orange orchard, just down the road. ₺120

Emin Pansiyon On the beach road, 80m beyond Odile Hotel ☎0242 825 7320, ⓦeminpansiyon.com. A mix of stone- and wood-built chalets, with plenty of orchard and/or lawn between the rows. Popular with yoga and Lycian Way walking groups. Friendly family management, ample parking and superior breakfasts. ₺130

Güneş Pansiyon Start of beach road, inland from restaurants ☎0242 825 7161, ⓦgunespansiyon.com. Solid-built, nicely decorated units, set in lush premises edging onto the river, with good bathrooms, fridges and TVs, reflecting part-Turkish clientele. On-site restaurant, ample parking. ₺150

★ **Myland Nature Pansiyon** North end of beach strip, beyond the Odile ☎0242 825 7044, ⓦmylandnature.com. Better-than-average wooden chalets set in 15 acres of orchard. Pınar and Engin, refugees from the urban rat race, are your fluent English-speaking

BELLEROPHON AND PEGASUS

In legend, **Bellerophon** was ordered by Iobates, king of Xanthos, to kill the Chimaera in atonement for the supposed rape of his daughter Stheneboea. Astride the winged horse **Pegasus**, Bellerophon succeeded, dispatching the beast from the air by dropping lead into its mouth. Later, Bellerophon was found to have been falsely accused, and avenged himself on Stheneboea by persuading her to fly away with him on Pegasus and flinging her into the sea. Retribution came when he attempted to ascend to heaven on Pegasus, and was flung from the back of the magical horse. Lamed and blinded, Bellerophon wandered the earth as a beggar until his death.

hosts. The upscale restaurant, open to all, features organic food, evening slide shows (photo courses from Engin on demand). The good breakfasts are even more satisfying after one of Pinar's free 8am yoga sessions. Closed early Nov to late March. **₺225**

★ **Odile Hotel** Just past mid-beach ☎ 0242 825 7163, ⓦ hotelodile.com. Set in lush gardens around a large pool, this hotel has 36 large, decently equipped (fridges, top-drawer baths) rooms and suites. Keen management, a mixed clientele and yoga/massage teaching area complete the picture. Credit cards accepted; closed Nov–Feb. **€80**

Oleandro Pension On the road that runs from the village centre to the beach, opposite Güneş ☎ 0242 825 7213, ⓦ oleandropension.com. One of Çıralı's most stylish pensions. All the ten en-suite rooms in the main

building, and two lovely rustic/contemporary bungalow rooms, are elegantly decorated in plain wood, with white walls and white linen, and very tidy stalled bathrooms. A major plus is the shady garden and delightful attached restaurant. **€60**

Olympia Tree House Just north of the Ulupınar stream-mouth ☎ 0242 825 7351, ⓦ olympiatreehouse .freeservers.com. If you want the treehouse experience without the juvenalia prevalent in the Olympos canyon, come instead to this friendly spot. Of the twelve units-on-stilts, three (all year) are relatively luxurious, with sea-view balconies, the others basic (April–Nov); all lack plumbing. Tent space is available in summer only. Rates per person: tents **₺10**, basic stilt units **₺20**, balconied stilt units **₺30**

EATING AND DRINKING

There's very little to choose between the strip of restaurants backing the beach, all of which are reasonably good though a little overpriced, and offer free use of sun-loungers and umbrellas.

★ **Cemil's** At the junction of the beach and Chimaera road ☎ 0242 825 7080. Traditional Turkish home cooking at its best, with an ever-changing choice of starters such as stuffed vine leaves or runner beans (from ₺6) in olive oil, and mains like kebabs (from ₺12) or güveç (stews). Also great seafood, with generous portions of sea bream and sea bass for around ₺15. Decent wine is a very reasonable ₺30 a bottle. Eat at tables or sprawled on a cushioned platform beneath the mulberry trees. Daily 11am–11pm.

Oleandro On the road that runs from the village centre to the beach, opposite Güneş ☎ 0242 825 7213. Formerly the best restaurant on the beach strip, Oleandro has maintained its high standards now that it has moved to be a part of the eponymous pension. There's a small, stylish dining room looking out onto elegantly draped tables on wooden decking beneath the greenery. Food is Turkish/international. Lamb chops cost ₺18, lobster ₺30, and they also serve a decent latte. Daily 9am–11pm.

Beycik

The village of **BEYCİK** spreads out amid pleasant orchards, almost in the shadow of 2366m Mount Olympos (Tahtalı Dağı). At over 1000m above sea level, it has become something of a refuge for both Turks and foreigners to escape the humidity of the coastal belt in the summer months. Many have bought property here to enjoy the cool air and superb views over forest and mountain, though in truth there's not much to do bar relax or walk.

As the inland variant of the **Lycian Way** links Beycik with Çıralı, the village makes a logical staging point on the traverse to Yayla Kuzdere and Gedelme along the Lycian Way, crossing over the cedar-clad saddle of Mount Olympos at 1800m.

Keen walkers can enjoy a long hike from Beycik to the summit of **Mount Olympos**; allow ten hours for the full round trip. The peak itself is now crowned by a bunker-like restaurant, and can also be reached much more easily via a **cable car** that ascends via unsightly pylons from Tekirova. Known as Tahtalı 2365, the cable car runs through a supposedly protected national park, and can be reached via a side road that loops right from the main coastal highway 2km north of Phaselis (daily, every 30min: May–Sept 9am–7pm; Oct–March 10am–6pm; ₺50 return; ⓦ tahtali.com).

By car Beycik is a 45min drive southwest of Antalya, and some 17km above and northwest of Çıralı. To reach it, drive

7km inland from Highway 400, up a side road just east of the Ulupınar turning.

5

ACCOMMODATION AND EATING

Rivera Yukarı Beycik ☎0242 816 1005. Far better than the more famous places down on the coastal highway at Ulupınar, this quirky place dishes up sizzling trout oven-baked in clay dishes, accompanied by tender roasted onions and potatoes – all for ₺12. Just as big a draw is the setting, a series of wooden decks at different heights built into the spreading boughs of an ancient, monumental plane tree. Daily 11am–midnight.

★ **Villa il Castello** Beycik Köyü ☎0242 816 1013, ⓦvilla-castello.com. Extremely attractive Turkish-German-run place, set around a neat pool in immaculately landscaped grounds. The nine large, well-appointed suites hold two kids and two adults and, at 1000m elevation, are heated but not a/c. ₺190

Phaselis

Heading north from Olympos, there's scant pretext to stop before Antalya. The overdeveloped, overpriced package resorts along this coast – Tekirova, Kemer, Göynük and Beldibi – leave much to be desired. Only ancient **Phaselis**, with its superb swimming opportunities, will tempt you off the main road.

Brief history

Founded by Rhodian colonists in 690 BC, **Phaselis**, almost in Pamphylia, was not always Lycian. The Phaselitans were great traders, sailing as far as Egypt, and their coins were decorated with ships. Along with most of Asia Minor, Phaselis was overrun by the Persians in the sixth century, and not freed until 469 BC, when Athenian general Kimon "liberated" them with some difficulty, enrolling the reluctant city in the Athenian maritime confederacy along with Olympos. A century later, Phaselis helped Mausolus, satrap of Caria, attempt to subdue Lycia, while in 333 BC Phaselitan sycophancy continued: not content with merely surrendering to Alexander the Great, the city also proffered a golden crown.

Phaselis finally became part of the Lycian Federation during the second century BC, but was soon, like Olympos, occupied by Zeniketes' pirates. Although it rejoined the federation afterwards, the pirates had devastated the city. Under imperial Rome, Phaselis distinguished itself with yet more obsequiousness: when touring Emperor Hadrian visited in 129 AD, statues were erected, and a gateway dedicated to him.

The site

1km off Highway 400, 3km north of Tekirova • Daily: summer 8.30am–7pm; winter 9am–5.30pm • ₺8, plus parking fee

The **ruins** of Phaselis flank three small bays, providing ample opportunity to contemplate antique monuments while lying on the beach. While they can't compare with some sites east of Antalya, or nearby Arykanda, there's certainly enough to see at Phaselis, where *Jason and the Argonauts* was filmed in 1999. The natural beauty and clear sea make for a rewarding half-day outing – bring a picnic if you don't fancy the car-park snack-caravans.

The access road passes under a bluff that holds a **fortified settlement** enclosed by a Hellenistic wall, including a tower and three archery slits. The most obvious landmark, behind a helpful map placard and the first car park, is the substantial, elegant Roman **aqueduct**. Said to have been among the longest in the ancient world, it carried water from a spring inside the northern fortifications almost as far as the south harbour.

The harbours

Arrayed around the promontory behind which most of the fan-shaped city stood, Phaselis's three **harbours** are obvious, and ideal for orientation. The north harbour was too exposed to be used except in very favourable conditions, but traces of the ancient **south quay** remain. It made an easy landing point for aggressors, however, so was fortified with a 3m-wide wall – now submerged, but still intact. The middle harbour also had a strong sea wall, and its 18m-wide entrance could be closed off; today it's a shallow cove wonderful for swimming (and snorkelling out to explore the Roman breakwater), with a small beach.

The largest, **southwest port** (with its own parking and ticket booth for boat arrivals) was protected by a 180m-long breakwater, now mostly submerged. It sheltered the largest trading vessels, and now sees numerous pleasure craft calling for the sake of its fine, large beach.

The ancient city centre

Between the harbours, the promontory **acropolis** is covered with overgrown ruins of dwellings and round cisterns. The city's main axis is the **paved avenue** across the neck of the promontory, linking the south and middle harbours; a rectangular plaza partway along is thought to be the heart of the **agora**. At the southern-harbour end, only the foundations and tumbled marble masonry survive of the monumental **gateway** constructed to honour Hadrian's visit.

The well-preserved **theatre**, dating from the second century AD, looks towards Tahtalı Dağ from between the acropolis and the main street, and held around 1500 people. Three large doors above what's now ground level probably led to the stage; below these, five smaller doors would have opened into the orchestra, and may have been used to admit wild animals.

ARRIVAL AND DEPARTURE

PHASELIS

By bus Buses along the coastal highway from Antalya (frequent; 1hr; ₺5) drop passengers at the clearly marked turn, a pleasant pine-shaded walk from the site and beach.

ACCOMMODATION AND EATING

Sundance Nature Village Behind Phaselis's southwest beach ☎0242 821 4165, ⓦsundancecamp .com. The only reason to stay locally is this complex of bungalows and treehouses, set amid 120 partly forested acres on the coastal variant of the Lycian Way. It also offers a respected restaurant using home-grown produce, horseriding, and tent space. Tents (pp incl. breakfast) €12, treehouse €54, bungalows €72

The Mediterranean coast and the Hatay

KIZKALESI CASTLE

6

The Mediterranean coast and the Hatay

Turkey's Mediterranean coast, where the Toros (Taurus) mountain range sweeps down to meet the sea, broadly divides into three parts. The stretch from Antalya to Alanya is the most accessible tourist region, although intensive agriculture, particularly cotton growing, and package tourism have taken a toll on the environment. East of Alanya, the mountains meet the sea head-on, making for some of Turkey's most hair-raising roads, curving around jagged stretches of coastline. As a result, this is the least developed and unspoilt section of the Mediterranean shore. Further east the mountains finally recede, giving way to the flat, monotonous landscape of the Ceyhan river delta. South and east of here, turning the corner towards Syria, the landscape becomes more interesting, as the Amanus mountain range dominates the fertile coastal plain, with citrus crops and olives the mainstay of the economy.

The bustling, modern city of **Antalya** is the prime arrival and junction point. East of here, in the ancient region of Pamphylia, the ruins of three cities – **Perge**, **Aspendos** and **Side** – testify to the sophisticated civilization that flourished during the Hellenistic period, and are well-established day-trip destinations from Antalya. The more isolated **Termessos**, a Pisidian city north of Antalya, is the most spectacularly sited, with its rugged hilltop terrain peppered with stone ruins.

Seventy kilometres east along the coast from Side, the former pirate refuge of **Alanya** – now a bustling package-tour destination – is set on and around a dramatic headland topped by a Selçuk citadel. Continuing east, the best places to break your journey are **Anamur**, where a ruined Hellenistic city abuts some of this coast's finest beaches, and **Kızkalesi**, whose huge Byzantine castle sits 200m from the shore of a sandy bay. Kızkalesi also makes a good base from which to explore the ancient city of **Uzuncaburç**, a lonely ruin high in the Toros Mountains.

Beyond Kızkalesi, in the fertile alluvial delta known as the **Çukurova**, the Ceyhan River spills down from the mountains and meanders sluggishly into the eastern Mediterranean. This end of the coast – characterized by concentrations of industry and low-lying cotton plantations – has very little to recommend it. **Mersin** offers regular ferry connections to northern Cyprus; **Tarsus**, the birthplace of St Paul, holds a few surviving reminders of its long history; and **Adana**, one of the country's largest urban centres, is a hectic staging post for journeys further east.

From Adana, routes head north to the central Anatolian plateau, or east to the Euphrates and Tigris basins; this chapter turns its attention south, towards the area formed by the curve of the coast down towards Syria. This is the **Hatay**, a fertile, hilly region where different cultures have met – and often clashed – in their efforts

HADRIAN'S GATE, KALEİÇİ, ANTALYA

Highlights

❶ **Kaleİçi** Antalya's old quarter, clustered around a charming harbour, is great for nightlife and shopping. **See p.357**

❷ **Köprülü Kanyon** Spanned by a graceful Roman bridge, the Köprülü river gorge is ideal for novice whitewater rafters. **See p.365**

❸ **Termessos** Arguably the most dramatically situated of all Turkey's ancient sites, perched on the edge of a precipitous gorge. **See p.366**

❹ **Aspendos** Stunningly preserved Roman theatre, the impressive venue for an annual opera and ballet festival. **See p.370**

❺ **Uzuncaburç** Wander along the streets and through the temples of the ruined city, now a sleepy mountain village. **See p.385**

❻ **Kızkalesi** Recline on the sandy Mediterranean shore and ponder the serenity of the offshore Maiden's Castle. **See p.387**

❼ **Antakya's Archeological Museum** Don't miss the immaculately preserved collection of Roman mosaics. **See p.401**

❽ **Regional cuisine** For a taste of the Hatay try the unique fiery muhammara, served with flat bread and a chilled beer. **See p.404**

HIGHLIGHTS ARE MARKED ON THE MAP ON PP.356–357

to dominate the important Silk Route trade. **Antakya**, the Hatay's main centre, is the best starting point for explorations, though cosmopolitan **İskenderun** makes for a surprisingly agreeable base. Antakya has frequent dolmuş connections to **Harbiye**, site of the Roman resort of Daphne, and to the town of **Samandağ**, from where you can visit Armenian **Vakıflı**.

Antalya to Alanya

The stretch of coast between **Antalya and Alanya** is among the most developed in Turkey. With a four-lane highway running right behind many beaches, flanked by all-inclusive hotels and holiday-village complexes, it's hard to imagine this was once ancient **Pamphylia**, a loose federation of Hellenistic cities established by incomers from northern Anatolia. Home to a busy international airport, the booming city of **Antalya** is the gateway to the region. Now a fully-fledged resort, it is worth visiting for its restored old town and marvellous archeological museum. The nearest (and most fascinating) ruined city is **Termessos**, perched on the saddle of Mount Solymos overlooking the Antalya gulf. East of Antalya, the surviving ruined cities of Pamphylia also rival the beaches as tourist attractions, with **Perge** and **Aspendos** the best preserved and most evocative sites. Further along the coast, **Side** is a major resort, though the striking ruins of its ancient city are fast being overshadowed by package tourist facilities. **Alanya**, the next sizeable centre, has also seen an explosion of hotel building and tourism-related commerce over the last few years, but has retained an attractive old quarter.

Antalya

One of Turkey's fastest-growing cities, **ANTALYA** is blessed with an ideal climate (excluding the searing heat of July and August) and a stunning setting atop a limestone

THE MEDITERRANEAN COAST AND THE HATAY

plateau, with the formidable Beydağları looming to the west. In the heart of town, the pretty yacht harbour huddles below the Roman walls, while the crescent of Konyaaltı bay curves to the industrial harbour 10km west. Interest for tourists is largely confined to the relatively tiny and central old quarter within the Roman walls, known as the **Kaleiçi** (or "within the castle"). The city's renowned **Archeological Museum**, however, west of the old town, is home to one of the finest collections in the country.

Brief history

Antalya was founded as late as the second century BC by Attalus II of Pergamon, and named **Attaleia** in his honour. The Romans only consolidated their hold on the city and its hinterland during the imperial period, following successful campaigns against local pirates. Christianity and the Byzantines had a similarly slow start, though because of its strategic location and good anchorage Antalya was an important halt for the Crusaders. The Selçuks supplanted the Byzantines for good early in the thirteenth century, and to them are owed most of the medieval monuments visible today (albeit some built on Byzantine foundations). Ottoman Antalya figured little in world events until 1918, when the Italians made it the focus of their short-lived Turkish colony.

Kaleiçi

The best place to start exploring Antalya's old town, **Kaleiçi**, is from the old harbour, where the once-crumbling quays have been rebuilt, gardens laid out and the harbour walls restored. The redeveloped **old harbour**, now home to day-trip boats, some charter *gulets* and a few fishing boats, is popular with tourists and locals alike, who frequent the quayside restaurants, cafés and clubs.

From the harbour, head uphill along Uzun Çarşı Sokak, past the eighteenth-century **Mehmet Paşa Camii**, to **Kalekapısı** (Castle Gate), the main entrance to the old town. Nearby the **Saat Kulesi** (Clock tower), a Selçuk tower with inset Roman column drums, is built into a section of the old walls. Kalekapısı is overlooked by the **Yivli Minare** or

HIGHLIGHTS
1. Kaleiçi
2. Köprülü Kanyon
3. Termessos
4. Aspendos
5. Uzuncaburç
6. Kızkalesi
7. Antakya's Archeological Museum
8. Regional cuisine

6

"Fluted Minaret", erected during the thirteenth-century reign of the Selçuk sultan, Alâeddin Keykubad, and today something of a symbol of the city. Facing the Yivli Minare is an early, plain **Selçuk han** whose crumbling walls have been "restored", a rather grand term for encasing the ruins in glass and filling the interior with souvenir shops. Above this area, but accessed from Cumhuriyet Caddesi, is an old baths, and a pyramidal **mausoleum** from 1377.

Bearing right onto Atatürk Caddesi, you'll soon draw even with the triple-arched **Hadrian's Gate** (Üç Kapılar), recalling a visit by that emperor in 130 AD. Hesapçı Sokak, the quietest entry to Kaleiçi, begins here, a cobbled street of restored Ottoman houses that now holds assorted pensions, trinket shops, restaurants and bars. About halfway along, the tower and attendant buildings known collectively as the **Kesik Minare** (Broken Minaret) form an architectural anomaly that's done successive duty as temple, church and mosque.

Kaleiçi Museum

Kocatepe Sok 25, to the left off Hesapçı Sok • **Museum** Tues–Thurs 9am–noon & 1–6pm • ₺2 **Library** Tues–Thurs 9am–noon & 1–6pm • ₺3 • ⊛ kaleicimuzesi.org

Set in two restored Ottoman houses, the **Kaleiçi Museum** showcases traditional Turkish interiors and cultural heritage items. The first house depicts life in the nineteenth century, with costumed mannequins portraying scenes of daily life, but the second is arguably the most interesting, containing a marvellous library. Here, treasures include original editions of the engravings made by the archeologist-cum-explorer Texier when he investigated Asia Minor for the French government in the 1840s. Behind the two, the restored garden church of St George is used for exhibitions of items from the private collection of the Koç family, who sponsor the institute.

Mermerli beach

By the harbour • Day pass ₺10

The only city-centre beach, **Mermerli**, just by the harbour, and accessible via a private staircase from the *Mermerli* restaurant, is not surprisingly packed. Sunbeds and parasols are cramped along a mere sliver of sand; it's hardly idyllic, but this is the only place to catch some rays and take a dip without having to travel out of town.

Toy Museum

Iskele Cad 82, on the harbour • Tues–Sun 9.30am–12.30pm & 1.30–6.30pm • ₺5 • ☎ 0242 248 4933, ⊛ oyuncakmuzesi.antalya.bel.tr

Open since 2011, Antalya's quirky **Toy Museum** makes a fun change to the city's historical sights. The unique collection features toys dating back to the 1960s, with colourful displays sure to stir the imagination of even the most jaded of adults. The vast collection of international Ken and Barbie dolls is sure to prompt smiles, but the real interest is in admiring the well-loved antique toys, including some adorable wooden figurines carved by Anatolian children.

The bazaars

Antalya's **Pazar**, at the southeast corner of Şarampol, sells mainly gold, clothes and shoes. Of the daily bazaars throughout the city, the most interesting is the **Cuma Pazarı** (Friday Bazaar), with local produce stalls and clothing vendors packed into the streets west of Murat Paşa Camii.

Antalya Archeological Museum

At the far end of Konyaaltı Cad, on the western edge of town • Tues–Sun: April–Oct 9am–7.30pm; Nov–March 8.30am–5pm • ₺15 • Take any "Müze" or "Liman" dolmuş from the city centre – departing from one of the "D" signs along Cumhuriyet Cad – or catch the westbound tramway to its last stop, Müze (₺1.2)

The one must-see attraction in Antalya, well worth a few hours of your time, is the **Antalya Archeological Museum** (Arkeoloji Müzesi), which ranks among the top five

RESTAURANTS

Castle Restaurant	9
Club Arma	6
Dönerci Çarşısı	2
Gönlübol	4
Hasanağa	5
Kebapçı Topçu	1
Paşa Bey Kebapçı	10
Son Çare	3
St Paul's Place	8
Villa Perla	7

CLUBS & MUSIC VENUES

Akdeniz Çiçek Pasajı	1
Ally Club	4
Ayyaş	8

BARS & CAFÉS

The Bar	2
Dolma Meyhane	10
Filika	6
Gizli Bahçe	5
Rock Bull	7
Salman	11
Shaker Bar	3
Simurg Temple	9

ACCOMMODATION

Abad Otel	7
Alp Paşa Hotel	6
Atelya Pansiyon	2
Dantel Pansiyon	11
Özmen Pansiyon	10
Puding Marina	5
Sabah Pansiyon	8
Sabah Villas	9
Safran Sari	12
Tütav Türk Evi Otel	3
Tuvana Hotel	1
Villa Perla	4

ANTALYA

6

6

archeological collections in the country. The galleries are arranged both chronologically and thematically. Standing out among the early items is a cache of **Bronze Age** urn burials from near Elmalı. Dating from the seventh and sixth centuries BC, they include several silver and ivory Phrygian figurines sporting droll yet dignified expressions and silver *paterae* (plates for wine libations).

It's quite a jump in time to the next galleries, which contain second-century AD **statues from Perge**: a complete pantheon in unusually good condition has been assembled. Best exhibits of the adjoining sarcophagus wing are two almost undamaged coffers depicting the **labours of Hercules**. The corner hall leads into a gallery dedicated to **friezes** and statues from Perge's theatre. It's a marvellous display, including statues of gods and emperors and a frieze showing battles between heroes and giants.

The upstairs galleries are devoted to coinage and **icons** recovered after 1922 from various local churches, including a reliquary containing what are purported to be the bones of **St Nicholas of Myra** (see p.340). There's also a bookshop, a **café** and a pleasant shady garden scattered with fine overspill sculptures and tombs.

Konyaaltı beach

Free entry; loungers and umbrellas ₺5–10 • Catch a ₺25 taxi, or take the west-bound tram to the terminus and walk 5min down the steep hill

Antalya's lengthy western beach, **Konyaaltı**, now spruced up, is finally beginning to live up to its dramatic situation between Antalya's cliffs and the Beydağları mountains. Shingle rather than sand, it's clean and well maintained. Visitors with children should be aware that the beach shelves quite steeply, and there's a slight tow from west to east. A pleasant **promenade** lined with palm trees and cafés backs the beach.

Lara beach

10km southeast of Antalya • Catch buses or dolmuş along Atatürk Cad

Lara beach, with its long stretch of fine sand, runs east of Antalya's cliffs, just past the popular Lower Düden waterfall. It combines both free and pay areas, where you'll be charged ₺10 for the use of a parasol. The gentle waves make for some great swimming spots.

Adalar swimming area

₺7.5

Reached via steep steps from Karaalioğlu Park, the **Adalar** swimming area, with decking on the rocks and ladders running into the sea, makes a good alternative to the beach. The staff are friendly, drinks and snacks reasonably priced, and the views across the bay magnificent.

ARRIVAL AND DEPARTURE
ANTALYA

BY BUS OR DOLMUŞ

Otogar On the Ankara road, 7km north of town, and used by both buses and inter-town dolmuşes. To reach the town centre, catch either the bus companies' own *servis* buses, or the blue-and-white municipal bus marked "Terminal Otobusu" (₺2). Alight near the Atatürk statue on Cumhuriyet Cad for accommodation on the west of the old city, or at the *Belediye* (Town Hall) corner for the east side.

Tickets Pensions in the old town sell or book tickets for direct buses from Antalya *otogar* to almost all Turkey's provincial capitals. Major companies, such as Kamil Koç, Akdeniz and Metro, have ticket offices in town, mostly on Subaşı Cad.

Left luggage 24-hour office marked "Emanet" at the *otogar*.

Destinations from Antalya otogar Adana (13 daily; 12hr); Afyon (hourly, 5hr); Alanya (every 30min; 2hr); Ankara (every 30min; 10hr); Antakya (14 daily; 14hr); Denizli (5 daily; 5hr 30min); Diyarbakır (5 daily; 16hr); Eğirdir (8 daily; 3hr); Fethiye, by inland route (6 daily; 4hr); Isparta (hourly; 2hr 30min); İstanbul (every 30min; 12hr); İzmir (hourly; 9hr 30min); Konya (15 daily; 5hr 30min); Manavgat/Side (every 20min; 1hr 30min).

Destinations in the southwest Buses leave from *otogar* minibus terminal then stop at Devlet Hastane roundabout: Fethiye by coastal route (8 daily; 8hr); Finike (8 daily; 2hr); Kalkan (8 daily; 5hr); Kaş (8 daily; 4hr 30min); Kemer/Beldibi/Göynük (every 30min; 1hr).

BY FERRY

Ferry harbour The main ferry harbour and dock where fortnightly ferries arrive from Venice is west of Konyaaltı Beach, 10km from the centre of town. There is no dolmuş service, so you'll have to take a taxi to the centre.

Tickets Turkish Maritime Lines office, Konyaaltı Cad 40/19 (☎0242 241 1120).

BY PLANE

Airport Antalya's lushly landscaped airport is 12km east of the city, at the centre of a maze of motorways (general info ☎0242 330 3030, flight enquiries ☎0242 330 3600; ☦aytport.com). Official taxis (☎0242 330 3108; ☦antalyaairporttaxi.net), available outside the terminal, can be booked online. Expect to pay around €20 per car during the day, and €30 midnight–6am. If you flag a taxi, drivers may tell you that your chosen hotel has closed, and offer to take you to another. If this occurs, be insistent. Municipal bus #600 connects the airport with the *otogar* (every 30min), but check with your flight company, as some offer free shuttles to the city centre.

Airlines THY, Konyaaltı Cad 24, Antmarın İş Merkezi (☎0242 243 4383, reservations ☎0212 444 0849); Onur Air, Çağlayan Mah, 2055 Sok 20, Barınaklar (☎0242 324 1335, reservations ☎0212 444 6687); Atlas Jet, Antalya Airport (☎0242 330 3900, reservations ☎0242 444 3387). **Destinations** Ankara (3 daily; 1hr); Bodrum via İstanbul (5 weekly; 6hr); İstanbul (15 daily; 1hr–1hr 20min); İzmir via İstanbul (1 or 2 daily; 3hr 40min).

BY CAR

Car rental Kaleiçi holds numerous car rental agencies, and there are many more on Fevzi Çakmak Cad, near Antalyaspor's stadium. In July and August, book your car well in advance; at other times, bargain hard. Try the *Sabah Pansiyon* (see p.361), Mithra Travel (see p.361), or Hertz (☎0242 330 3848) out at the airport.

GETTING AROUND

By tram A tramway circles the old quarter and runs along the seafront, with departure times posted at the stops (every 30min; ₺1.70).

INFORMATION

Tourist office Cumhuriyet Cad, 100m north of the PTT (daily: summer 9am–6pm; winter 8.30am–5.30pm; ☎0242 241 1747). General information on Antalya and southern Turkey, as well as city maps.

TOURS AND ACTIVITIES

Boat tours Tours offered by the harbour in Kaleiçi range from 45min to a full day. The latter take in the best views of the Düden waterfalls, cascades that end at Lara Beach, plus a combination of local beaches, swimming, cruising the gulf and a barbecue lunch. Expect a two-hour trip to cost from ₺25 per person, an evening cruise with entertainment from ₺50.

Hiking Mithra Travel, Hesapçı Sok (☎0242 248 7747, ☦mithratravel.com), in the old city, organizes one- or two-day treks (from about €20 per person per day) in the limestone massifs overlooking Antalya, and can also arrange self-guided walks.

Scuba diving Assorted diving spots along Antalya's coastline include the possibility to try wreck diving or even diving to a sunken plane. The small, but extremely well equipped, Akdeniz Diving (at the harbour right next to the amphitheatre – look for the signs – ☦akdenizdiving.com, ☎0242 248 1257) is the best place to organize your trip, including PADI dive courses, try dives and more challenging excursions for experienced divers. A day's diving for beginners, including training and 2 full-length dives, will cost around €60, and the friendly, helpful staff will be happy to discuss different options and deals.

Waterparks Antalya's two waterparks offer a range of slides, chutes and wave pools. Aqualand, southwestern edge of the Kültür Parkı (May–Oct daily 10am–6pm; adults €20, kids €18; €60 to swim with dolphins; ☎0242 249 0908, ☦aqualandantalya.com). Aqua Park, behind the Dedeman Hotel, east of the centre (May–Oct daily 9am–dusk; adults ₺40, kids ₺30; ☎0242 316 4400, ☦aquaparkantalya.com).

6

Whitewater rafting A full-day excursion on the Köprülü river, with a day's rafting, plus transfers and meal, costs around €40 from Antalya. Book through Antalya travel agents – the most reliable is Medraft (☎0242 312 5770, ⓦmedraft.com), or one of the Kaleiçi *pansiyons*.

Yachting Some yachts are open to charter for groups of four to twelve. Ask around at the harbour during the slow spring season and you could get a bargain cruise for the same price as hotel bed and board.

ACCOMMODATION

Most travellers stay in the walled quarter of **Kaleiçi**, where many of the old houses have been restored as *pensions* or hotels, and there's accommodation to suit all budgets, with heavily discounted rates out of season.

Abad Otel Hesapçı Sok 65 ☎0242 248 9723, ⓦantalyahostel.com. Well-run *pansiyon* with simple, functional rooms that are impeccably clean, and in many cases newly refurbished. *Abad's* smiling housekeeper takes real pride in the presentation, with towels folded into hearts and crisp white linens to make this a great budget option. ₺70

Alp Paşa Hotel Hesapçı Sok 30 ☎0242 247 5676, ⓦalppasa.com. While this hotel's lush stylings score highly with the package tourist crowds, it's largely style over substance; the place lacks the homely vibe that's so endearing in nearby *pensions*. Staff are polite, but unwilling to go the extra mile, and while the cave-like dining area is undeniably atmospheric, many rooms lack the quality you'd expect from a hotel of this standing. Advance booking essential in high season. €60

Atelya Pansiyon Civelek Sok 21 ☎0242 241 6416, ⓦatelyahotel.com. Few places receive such rave reviews from guests as this delightfully restored Ottoman house, set around an attractive courtyard. The quirky design makes the most of the unusual nooks and crannies left by its former incarnation, making each room unique, complemented by upmarket bohemian decor. €50

Camping Bambus Lara Yolu, 3km southeast of central Antalya along the road to Lara ☎0242 321 5263. Oriented towards caravanners, this campsite does have its own beach and decent facilities. Make sure you negotiate a good deal if you're staying longer than a few nights. Tents ₺15

Dantel Pansiyon Zeytin Geçidi 4 ☎0242 247 3486, ⓦdantelpansiyon.net. A seafront location, charming staff and newly refurbished rooms combine to produce a good budget option. The cheerful rooms feature brightly coloured bedspreads and kitsch black chandeliers, livening up an otherwise clean and functional abode. ₺60

★ **Özmen Pansiyon** Zeytin Çıkmazı 5 ☎0242 241 6505, ⓦozmenpension.com. Surely the friendliest option in town, this sparkling-clean *pension* is run by bubbly couple Deniz and Aziz, who will go out of their way to make you feel at home. Tours, airport/*otogar* pickups, free parking and helpfully annotated maps are just some of the services, and their expansive buffet breakfast served on the sea-view rooftop terrace is a cut above the rest. €35

Puding Marina Mermerli Sok 15 ☎0242 244 0730, ⓦpudinghotels.net. Brand-new designer hotel that's quickly gaining fans among the young, hip and wealthy. Minimalist chic and so much white you feel like you're in heaven (even the staff are dressed head-to-toe in white), this has to be the trendiest hotel in town. Funky mirrored panels, marble floors and splashes of purple throughout the rooms liven it up, while the incredible pool bar and terrace (including a fully-equipped outdoor gym) are strewn with beautiful people. Rates include free use of the hamam and sauna, and a welcome massage. €90

★ **Sabah Pansiyon** Hesapçı Sok 60 ☎0242 247 5345, ⓦsabahpansiyon.com. Run by three friendly brothers who speak excellent English, this backpacker-oriented joint offers just about every service you can think of. Good-value car rental, tours, free luggage storage, cheap beer and satellite TV are all available, and there's even a small guest pool. Dorms ₺25, doubles ₺50

Sabah Villas Hesapçı Sok 60 ☎0242 247 5345, ⓦsabahpansiyon.com. Opposite the *Sabah Pansiyon* and operated by the same team, these brand-new two-storey villas offer great value, with large double and twin rooms, fully equipped kitchens, lounge and an enclosed courtyard area with a small pool. Deals for groups and longer stays. €100

Safran Sari Yenikapı Sok 10 ☎0242 247 4682, ⓦsafranantalya.info. An exceedingly friendly family run this newly refurbished *pension*, set in a restored *konak*. The family rooms are particularly good value, with 3–4 beds, a fully equipped kitchenette and plenty of space. €50

Tütav Türk Evi Otel (CH Hotels) Mermerli Sok 2 ☎0242 248 6591, ⓦchhotels.net. With prices starting high and only getting higher, this VIP place has set lofty aspirations for its impressive-sounding renovation; if all goes to plan it will be the plushest option in town. Best of all is the rooftop bar/restaurant, with seating nestled atop the ancient city walls and reachable by lamp-lit tunnels that burrow through the walls. Guests will be able to select their bedspreads, flowers and furnishings adorning their suites (each including its own hamam). €200

Tuvana Hotel Karanlık Sok 18 ☎0242 247 6015, ⓦtuvanahotel.com. All about timeless luxury and impeccable service, this hotel may lack the pizzazz of more modernist offerings, but there's little to complain about in the smart, spacious rooms. Built within a series of restored

Ottoman mansions, it's an impressive setting and the atmospheric restaurant and beautiful pool area make it a popular choice. **€105**

★ **Villa Perla** Hesapçı Sok 26 ☎ 0242 248 9793, ⓦ villaperla.com. 22 years of loving restoration have kept this 104-year-old Ottoman building in tip-top condition;

few places in town master homely luxury so perfectly. Each' of the boutique hotel's nine rooms resembles an exquisite boudoir, with glittering sequinned bedspreads, four-poster beds and deluxe Jacuzzi showers. A small pool, delightfully charismatic staff and an idyllic courtyard shaded by orange trees complete the package. **€90**

EATING

6

Antalya is full of cafés and **restaurants**, with excellent choices in Kaleiçi, Atatürk Parkı and along Atatürk and Işıklar caddesis. For the local speciality – *tandir kebap*, clay-roasted mutton – visit Eski Serbetçiler Içi Sokak, a narrow street down the side of the Dönerci Çarşısı (see p.363), crammed with restaurants.

KALEIÇI

Castle Restaurant Hıdırlık Kulesi Sok 48 ☎ 0242 248 6594, ⓦ kaleicicastel.com. Tucked beside the Hıdırlık Kulesi, this bar-bistro has some of the best views in Antalya with cooling updraughts from the ocean and candle-lit tables set right on the cliff edge. Much favoured by Antalya's young lovers, it serves a range of mezes, seafood (from ₺28) and steaks (from ₺40), alongside a sizeable cocktail menu. Daily 9am–1am.

Club Arma İskele Cad 75 48 ☎ 0242 244 9710, ⓦ clubarma.com. Formerly home to a waterside club, this glitzy oceanside joint, housed in a 600-year-old building, has turned its focus to its restaurant, serving up inventive Turkish-fusion food, albeit at a stiff price. Elaborate sushi plates (ranging from a reasonable ₺16 to a whopping ₺98), stone-oven pizzas (from ₺22), seafood (from ₺28) and an amazing range of salads (from ₺18) all grace the menu, but best of all is the indulgent dessert menu, spanning two long pages – try the *kizarmiş dondurma* (fried ice cream and tropical fruits). Daily 11am–11pm.

★ **Gönlübol** İmaret Sok 30 ☎ 0242 244 4334. Kaleiçi's best kebabs are grilled over charcoal at this alcohol-free *ocakbaşı*. The Urfa and Adana kebabs (from ₺12), served with a selection of salads, are especially good, and the friendly staff and well-shaded outdoor seating make it a pleasant place to refuel after scaling the cobbled hills. Daily 8am–11pm.

Hasanağa Mescit Sok 15, near Hadrian's Gate ☎ 0242 247 1313. With tables set out under a canopy of citrus trees in a charming courtyard garden, this is a great evening choice, especially for those on a budget, and also very popular with locals. The open buffet dinners (₺14 per plate) cook up Turkish specialities in front of you – try the spicy red-cabbage soup followed by fresh *hamsi* (sardines) – and there's live folk music at the weekends. Daily 6–11pm.

Son Çare Under the Saat Kulesi, at the entrance to Kaleiçi. Once a mobile stall owner, Mustafa has branched out to two proper locations (the other is on the south side of the Dönerci Çarşısı). The speciality here is *köfte*; help yourself to the array of tomatoes, onions, parsley, lettuce and rocket. With an *ayran* a full meal should set you back a mere ₺10. Daily 9am–10pm.

St Paul's Place Yenikapi Sok 24 ☎ 0242 247 6857. It may be attached to the American-run evangelical church, but this place is more arthouse café than church hall – there's an extensive library for guest use, slick cherry-wood furnishings and a pleasant courtyard out back. Sip a café latte (₺4) accompanied by your choice of delicious home-made cookies and cakes (₺3–5). Mon–Sat: winter 10am–5pm; summer 10am–10pm.

★ **Villa Perla Restaurant** Hesapçı Sok 26 ☎ 0242 248 9793, ⓦ villaperla.com. Kaleiçi's best restaurant, serving delicious *mezes* with a creative flair and hearty Ottoman mains (from ₺15) in the candle-lit garden of the *Villa Perla* hotel. If you can't make it for dinner, the breakfasts here are to die for, with European-style pancakes, Turkish breakfast *mezes* and the most delicious selection of home-made jams and marmalades mixed up by Madame Perla herself. Daily 7am–midnight.

ATATÜRK CADDESİAND IŞIKLAR CADDESİ

Dönerci Çarşısı Corner of Atatürk and Cumhuriyet cads. The cheapest place to hunt out some fast food, this *"Döner-sellers' market"* is devoted to food stalls hawking kebabs, *köfte* and *kokoreç*, as well as *midye* (mussels) in season. A meal here should cost less than ₺5, but select carefully; not all places are clean. Daily 8am–late.

Paşa Bey Kebapçı Işıklar Cad ☎ 0242 244 9690 ⓦ pasabeykebap.com. Crammed with locals, this stylish dinner spot offers delicious *güveç* (casseroles, from ₺12), a generous *meze* selection – the *kısır* (lightly spiced bulgar and peppers) and *baba ganush* (mashed aubergine) are scrumptious – and warm, freshly baked breads. No alcohol. Daily 8am–midnight.

Salman Işıklar Cad ☎ 0242 244 1455, ⓦ salman patisserie.com. Anyone with a sweet tooth will be spoilt for choice in this heavenly patisserie. Row upon row of home-made ornamental chocolates, bite-size biscuits, *baklava*, gooey pastries and *poğça* (plain and filled savoury breads) laid out in glass display cases, alongside a wide range of continental-style cakes and tarts. Smuggle a bag of treats (₺25 per kg) down to the nearby park for a sea view. Daily 7am–10pm.

Kebapçı Topçu Kazım Özalp Cad 21 ☎ 0242 241 1616. Packed with locals and featuring pleasant indoor and outdoor seating, this spotless kebab joint is a short stroll from the main shopping area. Soups (₺5) and kebabs (₺12) cooked up in front of you are the main speciality. Daily 8am–11pm.

DRINKING AND NIGHTLIFE

Much of Antalya's **nightlife** is concentrated around the harbour area, with its myriad bars, clubs and discos, and there are also plenty of places to listen to live **Turkish music**, particularly *halk*, *türkü* and *özgün*.

BARS

The Bar (*aka Rock Café*) Paşa Camii Sok ☎ 0242 243 7628. Favoured by students from the local university and Antalya's grunge contingent, this popular bar is tucked away down a side street; look out for the signs. Surprisingly passable live rock acts play in a crowded upstairs room most weekends, and the downstairs bar is set in a pleasant courtyard garden. Entry is typically free, and a beer will set you back ₺8. Daily 7am–10pm.

Dolma Meyhane Yenikapı Sok 11 ☎ 0242 247 4050. In this relaxed, modern bar, popular with expats and locals alike, you'll find plenty of cheap eats and well-priced drinks. There's live music a few times a week, and the impromptu dancing often spills out onto the streets. Daily 11am–midnight.

Filika Mescit Sok 46 ☎ 0242 244 8266. An atmospheric café-bar decorated with arty black-and-white photographs and painted silhouettes of jazz musicians, this place hosts rock, jazz and blues live acts on its small stage. There's some outdoor seating at the front and beers start at ₺7. Free live music nightly from 9pm. Daily 11am–1am.

Gizli Bahçe Karadayı Sok ☎ 0242 243 7628. An unassuming nameplate marks out this popular student bar, right opposite the *Rock Bull* – don't confuse it with the decidedly more upmarket *Gizli Bahçe Konakları*, advertised all over town. Grungey stylings with classic record covers adorning the walls, a shaded garden out the back and a chilled-out vibe make this place a hit – as does the choice selection of indie, rock and blues blasting from the stereo. Beers are ₺7 and come with a free helping of salted popcorn. Daily noon–midnight.

Rock Bull Karadayı Sok 4 ☎ 0242 243 8984, ⊛ rockbull .net. A dark, grimy rock pub filled with beer-guzzling rockers and blasting a mix of classic rock and metal throughout the afternoon and into the evening hours. If you like your music loud, it's a popular spot to grab a beer (₺6) and a bowl of chips (₺6). Daily 9am–1am.

Shaker Bar Hadrian's Gate ☎ 0541 403 7270. This modern café-bar sits in a prime location right next to Hadrian's Gate, serving up delicious cappuccinos by the day and a lengthy wine menu by night (from ₺6 a glass). The outside seating makes for great people-watching, and they sometimes host live music on a small stage. Daily 9am–1am.

CLUBS AND LIVE MUSIC

Ally Club Sur Sok 4/8 ☎ 0242 244 7704, ⊛ ally.com.tr. Pinging laser lights, nine bars, candle-lit seating over the harbour and DJs spinning Top 40 hits cranked to ear-splitting volumes, help make this mega-club a popular choice. The party really kicks off after midnight, and look out for guest pop stars appearing throughout the summer. Entry ₺30–65. Daily 10pm–5am.

Simurg Temple Hamam Sok 2 ☎ 0242 244 5105, ⊛ simurgtemple.com. Slick interiors and atmospheric garden seating nestled in a stonewalled courtyard. Come in the day to enjoy a nargile, or after hours to tackle one of the enormous beer kegs (₺40). Live pop and rock bands most nights, from 9pm. Daily 10am–4am.

TURKISH MUSIC VENUES

Akdeniz Çiçek Pasajı Uzun Çarşısı Sok 24–26 ☎ 0242 243 4303. The best place to catch live Turkish music, a couple of hundred metres down from the clock tower. Recently revamped, it has tiered seating areas surrounding a central well where the musicians play, and a small terrace with views over Kaleiçi and the bay. Daily 7pm–late.

Ayyaş Hamam Sok 16 ☎ 0542 783 6164. Music wafts into the small square in front of this chilled-out bar, where a bohemian mix of patrons sip beers (₺7 a bottle) at alfresco tables. Live music is provided by local classical Turkish musicians, with an open-air stage in summer. Daily 8.30pm–midnight.

GOLDEN ORANGE FILM FESTIVAL

Antalya's Altın Portakal or **Golden Orange film festival** runs for a week each autumn, usually at the start of October. It's a major international film event, screening around 150 films throughout the week. Events culminate with an award ceremony at the Atatürk Kültür Merkezi, where golden statuettes of Venus carrying an orange are handed out. All week, directors, screenwriters and producers of Turkish and Eurasian cinema hold panel discussions and workshops, and parties take place across the city. All films are subtitled in English as well as in Turkish. For the full festival programme, visit ⊛ altinportakal.org.tr.

DIRECTORY

Banks and exchange Banks with ATMs and *döviz* offices are scattered throughout the city. Most operate Mon–Sat 9am–7pm, but some *döviz* offices on Şarampol even open on Sundays. You can also exchange currency at the PTT.

Books The Owl Bookshop, Kocatepe Sok 9 in the old town, has an excellent selection of mainly English-language secondhand books. Ardic, in the Seleker shopping mall on Güllük Cad, is the best place to buy English-language guides and novels.

Cinemas The Plaza cinema, in the Antalya 2000 building, 100m northeast of Hadrian's Gate (☎0242 312 6296), is the most convenient cinema, or try Cine Bonus 8 (☎0242 230 1414), in the Migros centre.

Consulate UK, Gençlik Mahallesi, 1314 Sok, Elif apt 6/8 (☎0242 244 5313), to the right of and behind the *Talya Hotel*, off Fevzi Çakmak Cad.

Hamams In Kaleiçi, the Sefa Hamam (Kocatepe Sok 32, ☎0242 241 2321), restored in 1450, is a good choice with full bath, soap massage and oil massage packages for ₺45,

or try the slightly cheaper Tarihi Balik Pazarı Hamamı (Balik Pazarı Sok ☎0242 243 6175), at ₺15 for a bath and soap massage, and an additional ₺15 for an oil massage.

Hospital State Hospital (Devlet Hastane) and outpatients' clinic, Soğuksu Cad ☎0242 241 2010; University Teaching Hospital (Tip Fakultesi), Dumlupınar Bul ☎0242 227 4480.

Laundry Several places around the Kesik Minare offer laundry services, as do many *pansiyons*.

Police Tourist Police, Emniyet Müdürlüğü, Yat Limanı, Kaleiçi ☎0242 527 4503.

Post office The main PTT is at Güllük Cad 9 (daily 9am–5pm for exchange and letter service; 24hr for phones).

Shopping Although traditional take-home items are rugs, minerals and leather, you'll find that jeans, gold and designer-label clothes and shoes are a better bet these days. Check out the boutiques along Atatürk and Işıklar Cad and in the new Migros centre for the real thing; and Cumhuriyet Cad (past Güllük Cad) for fakes.

Köprülü Kanyon

90km northeast of Antalya • Little public transport apart from one afternoon dolmuş to nearby Selge; without your own transport, it's far easier to access as part of a tour

The **Köprülü Kanyon national park** (Köprülü Kanyon Milli Parkı) makes a good full-day outing from Antalya. Many companies operate half-day **rafting trips** down the Köprülü River, allowing time for a stop en route for a swim and lunch. Be warned that in peak season up to 45,000 rafters a day are bussed into this area, making both the road and river very crowded places – serious rafters should look elsewhere.

Selge

100km northeast of Antalya, 12km west of Köprülü Kanyon • Daily 24hr • ₺4 • One afternoon dolmuş runs to Selge/Zerk, returning early the next morning, but it's best reached by hiring a taxi and guide from Antalya (€100–150 for the day)

The ancient city of **Selge** lies at an altitude of 900m above sea level. As you climb up the steep road to reach it, the panoramas become more sweeping, the thickly wooded countryside more savage, and the 2500m Kuyucak range ahead more forbidding. The site itself is scattered around the hamlet of **ZERK** (also known as Altınkaya). Little is known for certain of the origins of Selge; it only entered history – and the Roman Empire – in the first century AD. The city was inhabited until early Byzantine times and must have been abandoned when the aqueduct supplying it with water collapsed.

The ten-thousand-spectator theatre that dominates **ancient Selge** is impressive, even though the stage building was pulverized by lightning some decades ago. Close by is the ancient **agora** with its part-visible paving, jumbled masonry and chunks of unexcavated inscriptions. The foundations of a **Byzantine church** sit up on a hill to the southeast and enjoy panoramic views down the valley and up to the snow-streaked peak of Bozburun, while the jumbled remains of a temple of Zeus and a large water cistern lie northwest along the ridge. From here you can catch views to the ruined temple of Artemis and old city wall to the northwest, and to the stoa in the valley below. Returning to the main track, you'll pass the **stadium**, of which only the western ranks of seats are left; the sporting area itself is now a wheat field.

Termessos

Situated more than 1000m above sea level, the ancient site of **Termessos**, 30km northwest of Antalya, is one of Turkey's prime attractions. Its dramatic setting and well-preserved ruins, tumbling from the summit of the mountain and enclosed within a national park – Güllük Dağ Milli Parkı – merit at least an afternoon of exploration.

Despite its close proximity to Lycia, Termessos was actually a Pisidian city, inhabited by the same warlike tribe who settled in the Anatolian Lakeland, around Isparta and Eğirdir, during the first millennium BC. The city's position, commanding the road from the Mediterranean to the Aegean, enabled Termessians to extract customs dues from traders; a wall across the valley is believed to be the site of their customs post. Later, in 70 BC, Termessos signed a treaty with Rome, under which their independence was preserved – a fact the Termessians proudly expressed by never including the face or name of a Roman emperor on their coinage. The city must have been abandoned quite early, probably after earthquake damage in 243 AD, and has only been surveyed, never excavated.

The site

Daily: April–Oct 9am–7pm; Nov–March 8.30am–5pm • ₺5

A thorough exploration of the **ancient site** can be quite strenuous; steep climbs are necessary to reach many of the key sights. Bring sturdy footwear and lots of water – there's nowhere to buy supplies beyond the park entrance – and time summer visits to avoid the midday sun. After checking the site map at the car park you'll need to climb a good fifteen minutes to reach the first remains of any interest. On the way, you pass a number of well-labelled, though mainly inaccessible, ruins, including the aqueduct and cistern high on the cliff face to the left of the path.

The King's Road and city walls

The second-century AD **King's Road** was the main road up to Termessos, close to which the massive lower and upper **city walls** testify to a substantial defence system. The central part of the city lies beyond the second wall, to the left of the path. Its surviving buildings, formed of square-cut grey stone, are in an excellent state of repair, their walls standing high and retaining their original mouldings. In part, this is due to the inaccessibility of the site; it's hard to imagine even the most desperate forager coming up here to pillage stone.

Gymnasium and theatre

While the first building you come to once you pass through Termessos' mighty walls is the well-preserved **gymnasium** and bath complex, this is far overshadowed by the nearby **theatre**. One of the most magnificently situated in Turkey, it's set on the edge of a steep gorge, with a backdrop of staggered mountains. Greek in style, it had seating space for 4200 spectators, and although some seats are missing, it's otherwise in an excellent state of preservation.

The agora, Corinthian temple and odeon

At the far end of the open grassy space of the **agora**, west of the theatre, a **Corinthian temple** is approached up a broad flight of steps, with a six-metre-square platform. The smaller theatre or **Odeon** on the far side of the agora was, according to inscriptions, used for horse and foot races, races in armour, and, more frequently, wrestling. The walls of the building rise to almost 10m, surrounded by four **temples**. Only one – that of Zeus Solymeus, god of war and guardian of the city of Termessos – is in a decent state of repair.

The necropolis

Uphill from the Odeon, Termessos' **necropolis** holds an incredible number of sarcophagi dating from the first to the third centuries AD. Most are simple structures

on a base, though some more elaborate ones were carved from the living rock, with inscriptions and reliefs.

Tomb of Alcatus

Set in a dramatic mountaintop location, the so-called **Tomb of Alcatus** is widely accepted as the mausoleum of the general, a pretender to the governorship of Pisidia. The tomb itself is cave-like and undistinguished, but the carvings on its facade are remarkable, particularly one depicting a mounted soldier, with a suit of armour, a helmet, a shield and a sword – the armour of a foot soldier – depicted lower down to the right of the figure.

ARRIVAL AND DEPARTURE · TERMESSOS

By car To drive to Termessos from Antalya, take the Burdur road, then turn left after 11km towards Korkuteli. From the left turning to Termessos, marked another 14km along, a track climbs 9km up through the forested national park to the site.

By bus and taxi Catch a Korkuteli-bound bus (hourly) from Antalya's *otogar* to the start of the forest track, where taxis tout for business (₺40–50, including waiting time and return to main road).

EATING

Yeşil Vadi Just off the main road near the park entrance ☎0242 423 7555, ⓦyesil-vadi.com. This perfectly located restaurant makes a popular stop-off for a cold beer (₺6) before the journey back to town. Simple but tasty food, with meat and vegetable *güveç* (casseroles, from ₺12) and assorted kebabs. Daily 8am–10pm.

The Pamphylian cities

The twelfth century BC saw a large wave of Greek migration from northern Anatolia to the Mediterranean coast. Many of the incomers moved into the area immediately east of Antalya, which became known as **Pamphylia**, meaning "the land of the tribes", reflecting the mixed origins of the new arrivals. Although Pamphylia was a remote area, cut off from the main Anatolian trade routes by mountains on all sides, three great cities grew up here – **Perge**, **Aspendos** and **Side**.

Most of Pamphylia fell to Alexander the Great in the fourth century BC. After his death the region became effectively independent, though nominally claimed by the various successor kingdoms that inherited Alexander's realm. During the first century BC, the Romans, annoyed by the Cilician pirates operating from further along the Mediterranean, took control of the coast. Their rule ushered in three centuries of stability and prosperity, during which the Pamphylian cities flourished as never before. In later years, Mark Antony was sent to take charge of the region, treating it as his personal domain until defeated by Octavius at the battle of Actium in 31 BC, after which Pamphylia was formally absorbed into the Roman Empire.

GETTING AROUND · THE PAMPHYLIAN CITIES

By taxi A guide and driver to visit the main Pamphylian sites in a single day should cost around €100 from most tour operators. Hiring a taxi for the trip may be marginally cheaper – check the wooden board at the rank at the southern end of Atatürk Bulvarı in Antalya, which lists prices for various destinations.

By bus tour Bus tours (from €25) organized by agents in Antalya's Kaleiçi district seldom include Selge, instead featuring tedious stops at out-of-town gold and carpet shops.

Perge

15km east of Antalya • Daily: April–Oct 9am–7pm; Nov–March 8.30am–5pm • ₺15 • Take a dolmuş (frequent) or *Belediye* bus (every 20min from the *otogar*) to the village of Aksu on the main eastbound road, then walk 15min to the site itself

Founded around 1000 BC, **Perge** ranked as one of the great Pamphylian trading cities, despite the fact that it's nearly 20km inland. Its defensive siting was deliberate, to avoid the unwanted attentions of the pirate bands that terrorized this stretch of the

Mediterranean. Later, when Alexander the Great arrived in 333 BC, the citizens of Perge sent out guides to lead his army into the city. Alexander was followed by the Seleucids, under whom Perge's most celebrated ancient inhabitant, the mathematician Apollonius, lived and worked. Most of the city's surviving buildings date from the period of Roman rule, which began in 188 BC. After the collapse of the Roman Empire, Perge remained inhabited until Selçuk times, before being gradually abandoned.

The site

Perge's **theatre**, just outside the site entrance, has been closed for excavation for several years. Originally constructed by the Greeks, it was substantially altered by the Romans in the second century AD. Capable of accommodating fourteen thousand people on 42 levels, it was the venue for theatrical entertainment, poetry contests and musical concerts. To the northeast, Perge's massive horseshoe-shaped **stadium** was at 234m by 34m the largest in Asia Minor, with a seating capacity of twelve thousand. It was used not only for chariot races, but also wild beast hunts, public executions and gladiator spectacles.

Beyond the site entrance, stretches of the Seleucid walls have survived, giving some indication of the extent and ground plan of the original city. Just in front of the outer gates stands the **Tomb of Plancia Magna**, a benefactress of the city. Passing through the first **city gate**, you'll see a ruined **Byzantine basilica** on the right, beyond which lies the fourth-century AD **agora**, centred on a ruined temple.

Southwest of the agora, in the excavated **Roman baths**, a couple of the pools have been exposed. Across the cracked surface of the inlaid marble floor, the original layout of frigidarium, tepidarium and caldarium can – with the help of a few signs – still be discerned. Also visible in places are the brick piles that once supported the hypocaust floor of the baths, enabling warm air to circulate underneath.

Perge's **Hellenistic Gate**, at the northwest corner of the agora, is with its two mighty circular towers the only building to survive from the Hellenistic period. Behind the horseshoe-shaped court and monumental archway were both erected at the behest of Plancia Magna. The former was once adorned with statues – the bases of which were found during mid-1950s excavations. Beyond is the start of a 300m-long **colonnaded street**, with a water channel running down the middle and the shells of shops to either side. Walking along it, you'll be able to pick out the ruts made by carts and chariots in the stone slabs of the roadway. Also visible are reliefs near the tops of the columns, just beneath the capitals. One depicts Apollo, while another shows a man in a toga, offering a libation at an altar.

From the **nymphaeum**, an ornamental water outlet at the end of the street, a stream splashes down into the water channel below. Above here is the **acropolis** – probably the site of the original defensive settlement, of which little has survived.

6

Aspendos

46km east of Antalya, 1km northeast of the village of Aspendos • Daily: April–Oct 9am–7pm; Nov–March 8.30am–5pm • ₺15 • Take a bus from Antalya's *otogar* to Serik, 6km southwest of Aspendos (every 2hr), then a *dolmuş* to Aspendos

Still used to stage the annual Aspendos Opera and Ballet Festival, the theatre of **Aspendos** is among the best preserved in Asia Minor. Aspendos changed hands regularly in ancient times between the Persians, Greeks and Spartans, before coming under the control of Alexander the Great around 333 BC. After his death, Aspendos became part of the Seleucid kingdom and was later absorbed by the kings of Pergamon. In 133 BC, the city became part of the Roman province of Asia. Roman rule consisted mainly of successive consuls and governors demanding protection money and carting off the city's treasures. Only with the establishment of the Roman Empire did the city prosper, growing into an important trade centre, its wealth based on salt from a nearby lake.

Aspendos remained important throughout the Byzantine era, although it suffered badly from the Arab raids of the seventh century. During the thirteenth century the Selçuks arrived, followed a couple of hundred years later by the Ottomans, who ruled here until the eighteenth century, when the settlement was abandoned.

The theatre

The Aspendos **theatre** was built in the second century AD by the architect Zeno. He used a Roman design, with an elaborate stage behind which the scenery could be lowered, instead of allowing the natural landscape behind the stage to act as a backdrop, as had been the custom in Hellenistic times.

The stage, auditorium and arcade above are all intact, as is the several-storey-high stage building. What you see today is pretty much what the spectators saw during the theatre's heyday. A dubious legend relates that the theatre was built after the king of Aspendos announced that he would give the hand of his beautiful daughter to a man who built some great work for the benefit of the city. Two men rose to the challenge, one building the theatre, the other an aqueduct. Both finished work simultaneously, so the king offered to cut his daughter in two, giving a half to each man. The builder of the theatre declared that he would rather renounce his claim than see the princess dismembered and was, of course, immediately rewarded with the hand of the girl for his unselfishness. Later, the theatre was used as a Selçuk *kervansaray*, and restoration work from that period – plasterwork decorated with red zigzags – is visible over the stage.

ASPENDOS OPERA AND BALLET FESTIVAL

The **Aspendos Opera and Ballet Festival** is staged in Aspendos's theatre every year, over a three- to four-week period starting in mid-June. Both Turkish and foreign companies perform, and the programme consists of popular and experimental opera, ballet and classical concerts (*Madame Butterfly* and *Swan Lake* feature regularly). With an inflow of choreographers and musicians from the ex-Soviet Union, Turkish opera and ballet companies have improved out of all recognition, and stage design and costumes match the standard of the performers.

Tickets (₺30–60 for foreigners, less for Turks) are available both in advance and on the night from the theatre, and you can also buy them in Antalya and Side, though the booking office seems to switch venues each year – ask at the tourist office and check ⓦaspendosfestival.gov.tr for programmes. Cheap city buses run here from Antalya and Side, and most festival-goers bring along supper to while away the time before the start of the 9.30pm performance, as well as cushions to sit on, and an umbrella or waterproof in case of a thunderstorm.

A number of year-round shows, including the popular **Fire of Anatolia** (ⓦaspendosfestival .gov.tr) dance troops, are performed at the Aspendos Arena, a nearby modern facility erected to help preserve the original arena. While many of these shows are excellent, if you are going in order to experience the ancient theatre, be sure your tickets are for the right place.

GOLF TOURISM IN BELEK

Turkey might not be your first thought as a golfing destination, but with its mild climate and vast acres of verdant countryside, the southern coastal region is fast gaining acclaim on the international golf scene. Belek, 30km east of Antalya, is the main hub of the sport, home to five golf courses. Designed by Ryder Cup player David Feherty, the 18-hole championship course at the impressive **National Golf Club** (☎0242 725 4625, ⓦnationalturkey.com) hosts the multi-million-dollar World Golf Final, which attracts eight of the planet's top golfers.

Luxury hotel resorts in the area offer inclusive golf packages (check out ⓦgolfinturkey.com for ideas). Even if your game isn't quite up to par, you'll be able to revel in the landscape of natural lakes, gently undulating lawns and eucalyptus forests, set to a backdrop of the snowcapped Taurus Mountains.

The acropolis

A path leads up from the right of the theatre entrance at Aspendos to the **acropolis**, built on a flat-topped hill. The site is a little overgrown, but some substantial buildings are still in place. Foremost among them are the **nymphaeum** and **basilica**, both 16m in height, while sections of the main street and a drainage system also remain in good condition.

The aqueduct

A Roman **aqueduct** stretches northwards across the plain below the acropolis. Originally 15km long, it brought water to Aspendos from the mountains above and incorporates an ingenious siphonic system that allowed the water to cross the plain at low level; you can still (with care) climb the towers. The aqueduct and towers can also be reached by taking a left turn down a paved path just outside Belkis, skirting around the western side of the hill.

Side

One-time trysting place of Antony and Cleopatra, **SİDE** was perhaps the foremost of the Pamphylian cities. Now, however, its impressive array of ruins forms the backdrop to a modern holiday resort, set within the boundaries of the old town. Despite the recent abundance of package tourists, Side remains one of the friendliest communities along the Mediterranean, home to a burgeoning number of expats and regular holidayers. Many of the old-fashioned charms beloved of past visitors are fast disappearing – the creaky tractors that once shunted arrivals from the *otogar* to the city walls have been replaced by air-conditioned shuttle buses, and the seafront is becoming overrun with hawkers. However, with many of the smaller, family-run pensions in the ancient city now competing for business with the big hotels on its outskirts, Side can make an affordable base for travels around the region. Wander down the dusty backstreets or strike up a conversation with one of the friendly pension owners and you'll catch a glimpse of the old Side that travellers still rave about.

Brief history

Side (meaning "pomegranate" in an ancient Anatolian dialect) was founded in the seventh century BC by colonists attracted by the defensive potential of the rocky cape. It grew into a rich port, home to an estimated sixty thousand inhabitants during its peak in the second century AD. Initially a significant proportion of Side's wealth stemmed from the slave trade; city authorities allowed pirates to run an illegal slave market inside the city walls. After the collapse of the Western Roman Empire, Side survived only until Arab invaders put the place to the torch during the seventh century AD, and drove out the last inhabitants. Side was abandoned until Muslim fishermen from Crete settled here early in the twentieth century. Despite later attempts by the Turkish government and

6

archeological agencies to evict them, these villagers stayed, and by the 1980s their descendants were starting to reap the rewards of Side's tourist boom.

Ancient Side

Ancient Side has been almost overwhelmed by the modern town, and becomes hideously crowded with tour groups in summer. Sadly, many areas, particularly the theatre and colonnaded street, have suffered serious damage from the sheer number of visitors. However, independent travellers who set out early in the day can still enjoy some corners of the city.

East of the badly preserved **city gate**, the old walls are in a reasonable state, with a number of towers still in place. Back at the gate, a colonnaded street runs down to the

SİDE

ACCOMMODATION
Beach House 5
Mine Motel 4
Onur Pansiyon 1
Villa Önemli 3
Yükser 2

RESTAURANTS
Antik Piknik Garden 3
Erol 1
Güneş Döner 2
Moonlight 5
Soundwaves 4

BAR
Stones Bar 3

CLUBS & MUSIC VENUES
Lighthouse 2
Pegasis 1

Kumköy

Manavgat, Alanya & Antalya

Western Beach

Car Rental Offices

Dolmuş Station

SORGUN YOLU

Ancient Walls

City Gate

MEDITERRANEAN SEA

Side Museum

Monumental Gate

Car Park

Theatre

Agora

Ancient Walls

Byzantine Basilica

Mosque

GÜL SOKAK

SUMBUL SOK

MENEKŞE SOK

TURGUTREİS SOK

LİMAN CAD

ZAMBAK

BARBAROS CAD

Antique Baths

@ SOK

Chips

Harbour

Temples of Apollo & Athena

Eastern Beach

N

0   200
metres

agora, the site of Side's second-century slave market, today fringed with the stumps of many of the agora's columns. The circular foundation visible at the centre of the agora is all that remains of a **Temple of Fortuna**, while in the northwest corner, next to the theatre, you can just about make out the outline of a semicircular building that once served as a public latrine, seating 24 people.

Side Museum and baths

Opposite the agora • Tues–Sun: April–Oct 9am–7pm; Nov–March 8am–5pm • ₺10 • ☎ 0242 753 1006, ⟨W⟩ sidemuseum.com

The site of Side's ancient Roman baths, restored in 1961, is now home to the small but well-executed **Side Museum**. It retains its original floor plan and contains a cross section of locally unearthed objects – mainly Roman statuary, reliefs and sarcophagi from local excavations made between 1947 and 1967.

   More of the city's **antique baths** lie just off Camii Sokak, where Cleopatra is supposed to have bathed. Here, the remains include several separate rooms, baths, a garden and even a marble seat with a dolphin armrest.

Monumental gate and theatre

Just south of the museum • Theatre Daily: April–Oct 9am–6.45pm; Nov–March 9am–noon & 1–5pm • ₺10

Side's still-intact **monumental gate** now serves as an entrance to the town's modern resort area. To the left of the gateway, an excavated monument to Vespasian, built in 74 AD, takes the form of a fountain with a couple of water basins in front. Inside the gate is the entrance to the stunning 20,000-seat **theatre**, a freestanding structure supported by massive arched vaults that was the largest in Pamphylia.

Temples of Apollo and Athena

Daily 24hr • Free

Modern Side's main street leads down from the monumental gate to the old harbour, and turns left toward the **temples of Apollo and Athena**. The Athena temple has been partly re-erected, and its white portico is becoming Side's trademark and a favourite place to take sunset photographs. Both temples were once partially enclosed in a huge Byzantine basilica, parts of which gradually disappeared under the shifting sand; the still-visible section now provides a home to birds and bats.

The beaches

Dolmuşes run in both directions along the coastline every 30min from Side's *otogar*

Given Side's fine sandy **beaches**, it's no surprise the resort has developed so rapidly. To the west, the 10km stretch of beach is lined with expensive hotels, beach clubs and watersports rental outfits, beyond which is the less crowded but equally developed **Kumköy beach**. **Sorgun Beach**, 3km east of Side, is well maintained by the local authority, but far quieter than its counterparts.

ARRIVAL AND DEPARTURE   SİDE

By bus or dolmuş From the *otogar* in Manavgat, where intercity buses drop passengers, regular dolmuşes run to Side's small dolmuş station (₺2), outside the old town entrance. From there it's a 10min walk into town, while regular buses run in season to the theatre (₺1).

By car Side is effectively pedestrianized. Cars can only enter the town 7–10am, 3–6pm, and after midnight (though attendants let through drivers heading to their hotels with luggage). There are a few car parks, including one just inside the monumental gate; fees range from ₺5 for a couple of hours to ₺15 for 24hr.

INFORMATION AND TOURS

Tourist office 10min walk from the *otogar*, on the main road out of town (Mon–Fri 8am–12.30pm & 1.30–5pm; ☎ 0242 753 1265). Good city maps and regional pamphlets.

Banks and PTT On the square at the southern tip of the promontory.

Bicycle & motorbike rental Dozens of outlets, mostly outside the city gates, rent bikes or motorbikes. Donetello, just before the gate (☎ 0242 753 2837), offers mountain

6

bikes or Yamaha mopeds for €10 per day.

Car rental Several outlets on the road approaching the main town entrance: Europcar (☎0242 753 1764, ⓦeuropcar.com) is next to the *Asteria Hotel*; Avis is on Atatürk Bulvarı (☎0242 753 1348, ⓦavis.com).

Internet Internet cafés include Chips near the *Pettino Otel* on Camii Sok.

Tours Outings from Side include trips to Manavgat (€15 boat tour), rafting on the Köprülü River (€20), the Pampylian cities (€25) and Alanya (€8). The most popular boat trip from Side goes to Manavgat waterfalls, 5km northeast of town (€15). You can also reach the falls (daily: summer 9am–8pm; winter 9am–5.30pm; ₺4) on the "Şelale" dolmuş from the central dolmuş station (₺2 each way). While the falls are small, and with the huge summer crowds you may not get a view anyway, it's a pleasant spot for a picnic.

ACCOMMODATION

Few towns can claim to have such genuinely friendly and generous hosts across the board, and Side's abundant family-run *pensions* form a huge part of the town's charm. For the most atmospheric options, in and around the ruins and never more than a few minutes' walk from the beach, give the package hotels on the outskirts a miss, and head inside the ancient city walls. Even in high season, when booking is strongly advised, you're still likely to stumble across available rooms in the smaller and slightly shabbier pensions.

★ **Beach House Hotel** Barbaros Cad ☎0242 753 1607, ⓦbeachhouse-hotel.com. Impeccably run by an Australian-Turkish couple, this bohemian-luxe hotel has excellent-value rooms right on the beachfront. The quiet, shaded rooftop terrace, private beach and clean, airy rooms, all with sea views, set this place apart, but best of all is the garden out back. Snaking around the remains of a Byzantine villa, the small courtyard is bursting with colourful flowers and home to an eclectic family of animals including fluffy white rabbits, an ever-increasing collection of birds and even a party of free-roaming tortoises. There's no place quite like it. Closed early Nov to late March. **₺100**

Mine Motel Gül Sok 61 ☎0242 753 2358, ⓔceyhunbaldan@hotmail.com. This homely pension offers cheap and cheerful rooms that are simple but spotless. The owner speaks only a little English but will win you over anyway with her cheery demeanour and delicious home cooking – breakfast (included) and dinner are served up in the pleasant courtyard shaded by orange, plum and pomegranate trees. **₺75**

★ **Onur Pansiyon** Karanfil Sok 2/A ☎0242 753 2328, ⓦonur-pansiyon.com. One of Side's most popular *pensions*, this place ticks all the boxes for backpackers and families alike. Rooms are bright and summery with pretty wooden shutters and tasteful pastel decor, and the outside eating area is a communal hub for guests to relax and escape the heat. Best of all is the owner, Onur, whose bubbly character and excellent English make you feel right at home – he even pulls together a pretty good English cuppa with milk! **₺80**

Villa Önemli Lale Sok ☎0242 247 6714, ⓦhotelvillaonemli.com. Swish hotel, set in a beautiful wood-and-stone manor house peering down on a flower-scattered courtyard below. Deluxe rooms have their own kitchenette with washing machine, fridge-freezer and stove, but you'll pay extra for a sea view. **€63**

Yükser Pansiyon Lale Sok 10 ☎0242 753 2010, ⓦyukser-pansiyon.com. Charming family abode, right next door to *Mine*, lent a quirky sense of fun by colourful paintings and brightly patterned rugs. Tasteful splashes of colour, laminate flooring and country wood interiors keep it on the smart side of boho, and the outside garden area is a big plus. **₺80**

EATING

Side holds plenty of places to **eat**; the main challenge is to walk past them without being dragged inside by the smooth-talking hustlers. For vastly cheaper and often tastier food, opt for the less pushy establishments or small local options, tucked away in the tumbledown backstreets.

Antik Piknik Garden Zambak Sok ☎0242 753 5033, ⓔside_piknikgarden@hotmail.com. With its ethnic-print cushions, ramshackle garden and rustic tipi-esque huts out the back (doubles €25 with breakfast), this campsite-cum-restaurant is the perfect place to while away the hours sipping tea and musing over a hard day's sightseeing. It's not just the peace-and-love vibe that's so appealing; the home-cooked food is also a hit – tuck into a clay pot casserole (from ₺17) and couple it with a cold beer (₺5). Daily in summer, 8am–midnight.

Erol Restaurant Sümbül Sok ☎0242 753 2826. All but opposite *Onur Pansiyon*, this basic restaurant serves up tasty Turkish staples and feeds a steady stream of locals throughout the day. Soups – typically, beans or vegetable – go for a mere ₺2.5, while ₺10 buys a mixed plate of whatever you want – the menu varies but always includes rice and a selection of meat and vegetable dishes. Daily 9am–11pm.

Güneş Döner Opposite the mosque entrance ☎0242 753 1315. Surely the cheapest place to get lunch in town, this unassuming local joint makes one of the best ₺2 *döner* in the region, packed with freshly cooked meat, loads of veggies and a deliciously spicy kick. There's a small but pleasant seating area out the back, or they'll wrap up your pita to go. Daily 9am–11pm.

Moonlight Barbaros Cad 49 ☎0242 753 1400. A romantic venue, with tables laid out on gravelled terraces overlooking the sea and a great choice for wine connoisseurs – waiters are full of excellent local recommendations, from ₺50 a bottle. A good range of *mezes*, fish dishes and a few traditional Turkish options pad the menu – the *Türk sofrası* (mixed grill plate, ₺31) or *et güveç* (meat casserole, ₺28.50) make good choices. Daily 9am–2am.

Soundwaves Restaurant Barbaros Cad ☎0242 753 1059. Run by the Turkish-Australian son of the *Beach Hotel* proprietors, this slick beachside restaurant ups the ante with its serene view over the Mediterranean and careful balance of swish decor, friendly service and laidback atmosphere. Thankfully, they put the same thought into the menu, with an excellent selection of fresh, local seafood on offer (including rarer local finds like kingfish and swordfish). Expect to pay ₺25–35 for mains, but there are some cheapies on the lunch menu too – burgers start from ₺6 – and guests can use the hotel's private beach. Daily 8am–midnight.

DRINKING AND NIGHTLIFE

For the best of Side's **nightlife**, head to the strip along the harbour, where bars and nightclubs open their doors in summer months, and penny-pinchers can cruise the staggered happy hours that run between 6pm and 9pm.

Lighthouse Just west of the harbour ☎0242 753 3588. One of the town's busiest nightclubs, where you can dance beside the fishing boats along the harbour and enjoy a blaring mix of house and techno music with Russian podium dancers as a diversion. Closed Dec–March. Daily 11pm–5am.

Pegasis Yasemin Sok 82 ☎0242 753 1400. One of the few places in the old city with live bands, this place comes alive in the evening, when rock, blues and country hits blast out from its small stage. The expansive and comparatively inexpensive cocktail menu (from ₺15) and

outside terrace right nearby the waterfront make this a pleasant evening haunt, but the venue itself takes the prize – set in the renovated remains of a 500-year-old church, it's nothing if not atmospheric. Daily 9pm– 2am.

Stones Bar Barbaros Cad 119 ☎0242 512 1498. If loud tunes, karaoke and video games against a backdrop of the moonlit Mediterranean sounds like your idea of a good night out, this bar is one of the best places in town to drink up and be merry. Look out for the weekly "ladies' nights", when the fairer sex are treated to cheap drinks and freebies. Daily noon–midnight.

Alanya

With vast swathes of golden sand hugging a ragged sea cliff, and the smooth waves of the Mediterranean lapping beneath a looming fortress, it's easy to explain **ALANYA's** booming popularity among tourists. The beachside sprawl of uninspiring yet all-encompassing restaurants, shops and nightclubs serves merely as a colourful fringe to the charismatic old city; peel yourself away from the watersports and overpriced cocktails and you'll find a city heaving with historical gems, atmospheric places to eat, and hiking possibilities.

Brief history

Little is known about Alanya's early **history**, but it's thought to have been founded by Greek colonists who named it Kalonoros, or "beautiful mountain". Things were pretty quiet until the second century BC, when Cilician pirates began using the town, known by now as Coracesium, as a base to terrorize the Pamphylian coast. Eventually, the Romans decided to put a stop to things and sent in Pompey, who destroyed the pirate fleet in a sea battle off Alanya in 67 BC. In 44 BC, Mark Antony gave the city to Cleopatra as a gift. Romantic as this might sound, there was a practical reason for his choice: this area was an important timber-producing centre, and Cleopatra needed its resources to build up her navy. In 1221, the Byzantine city fell to the Selçuk sultan Alâeddin Keykubad, who gave it its present name and made it his summer residence. Most buildings of historical importance date from that era.

Kızılkule

Tues–Sun 9am–7.30pm • ₺5

Guarding the harbour on the east side of the promontory, the **Kızılkule** – the "Red Tower" – is a 35m-high defensive tower of red stone. Built by Alâeddin Keykubad in 1226 and restored in 1951, it now houses a pedestrian **ethnographic museum**. Old wooden houses cling to the slopes above, and you can follow the old coastal defensive wall along the water's edge to the Tersane, an Ottoman shipyard, where five workshops are linked by an arched roof. Beyond here is a small defensive tower, the **Tophane**.

Alanya castle

Grounds open daily 24hr • Free • Tour buses head up almost every hour, while taxis are available behind the tourist office (₺10–15 per person)

No trip to Alanya would be complete without a visit to its crowning spectacle, reached by a winding, hour-long climb. The sprawling fortification system of its **castle** makes a fascinating alternative to the beach, with spectacular views to boot. The castle grounds are free and easy to explore on foot, but wear sturdy shoes if you plan to wander off-path. The castle walls are the best aid to navigation, snaking right around the upper reaches of the promontory and linked by a network of overgrown footpaths.

The main route is well waymarked, with plenty of restaurants and little cafés to stop off at. If you get lost, keep heading up and you'll eventually hit signs for the **İç Kale** (inner fortress), On the way, you'll pass the **Aksebe Türbesi**, a distinctive thirteenth-century tomb, half-restored but still with its original minaret (kids will enjoy clambering the stairwell inside, although there's no view) surrounded by clusters of wild thyme.

In among the foliage off the main road, in an area known as **Ehmediye**, lies a small village of a few old Ottoman houses. They're clustered around the dilapidated sixteenth-century **Süleymaniye Camii** – only open at prayer times – and a *kervansaray*.

Inner Fortress

Daily 9am–7pm • ₺10

The **İç Kale**, or **Inner Fortress**, of Alanya castle was built by Keykubad in 1226. Inside, the fortress is pretty much intact, with the shell of a **Byzantine church**, decorated with fading frescoes, in the centre and wooden-decking pathways making it easy to pick through the finds. Look out for the **cisterns** that supplied the fortress with water and to which it owed much of its apparent impregnability.

A platform in the northwest corner of the fortress gives fine views of the western beaches and the mountains. It originally served as a point from which prisoners were thrown to their deaths on the rocks below. These days tour guides assure their charges that it's customary to throw a rock from the platform, attempting to hit the sea rather than the rock below – an impossible challenge supposed to have been set for prisoners as a chance to save their necks.

Alanya Museum

On the western side of the promontory • Tues–Sun 8am–noon & 1–5pm • ₺5

The **Alanya Museum** is filled with local archeological and ethnological ephemera, including finds from (and photographs of) several small Pamphylian sites in the region. Most unusual is an inscription in sixth-century BC Phoenician, a sort of halfway house between cuneiform writing and the alphabet as the Greeks developed it. There's also a mock-up Ottoman living room complete with a beautiful carved ceiling, shutters and cupboards, and a model of a village wedding. The best thing about the museum, though, is the garden, a former Ottoman graveyard in which you can take refuge from the heat in summer; re-creations of grape presses and other farm implements share space with a gaggle of peacocks and chickens.

The beaches

Alanya's extensive **beaches** stretch from the town centre for a good 3km west and 8km east. They're lined with a multitude of bars, restaurants and souvenir shops as well as a surprising number of tattoo parlours and hamams.

Kleopatra Beach

Kleopatra Beach on Alanya's western side is arguably the most popular of the local beaches, and offers abundant activities in summer. Kids can visit the Go-Karting ring (€10) or **SeaLanya** seapark (☎0242 543 1139, ⓦsealanya.com), which puts on dolphin and sea-lion shows. Active types can sample a range of **watersports**: jet-ski rental (€30 for 15min), parasailing (Ulusky; €30 for 15min; ⓦulusky.com), waterskiing (€20 for 30min) and banana-boat rides (€8) are all available. The end nearest the castle holds mini golf (€10), beach volleyball nets, basketball courts and tennis courts.

6

COASTAL CAVE TOURS FROM ALANYA

Entrepreneurs in Alanya offer **boat tours** to several caves dotted along the waterline at the base of the promontory. Trips leave from the harbour, and cost from ₺20 per person for one hour, or from ₺30 for longer excursions that include dolphin watching. If you want to go inside the smaller caves, make sure you take a small boat tour; the bigger ships will simply pull up outside.

The first stop is usually the **Fosforlu** (Phosphorus Cave), where the water shimmers green; then it's on round the **Cilyarda Burnu**, a long spit of land that's home to a ruined monastery and former mint. It's not possible to go ashore.

On the other side of the skinny peninsula, according to a bizarre local story, a German woman and her Turkish boyfriend were stranded for three months in 1965 in the **Aşıklar Mağarası** (Lovers' Cave), while the police and army mounted searches for them.

More credibly, the **Korsanlar Mağarası** or pirate's cave, a little further around, is said to be where the pirates of yesteryear used to hide out. You will also be taken to **Cleopatra's Cave**, where legends claim the queen used to descend to bathe while staying here with Mark Antony.

People Beach

To the east, **People Beach** stretches out from the harbour, where boats leave for tours of the coastal caves and, come nightfall, lithe-limbed tourists pour out of the thumping bars and clubs. Here you can rent motorized stand-on scooters (€10/hr) to whizz along the promenade, or book a scuba-diving trip to local dive sites that include wrecks and caves.

Damlataş Mağarası

Not far from the Alanya Museum, accessible from behind the *Damlataş Restaurant* on Damlataş Beach • Daily 10am–sunset • ₺4.50

The aptly nicknamed "Cave of Dripping Stones", or **Damlataş Mağarası**, casts an eerie silhouette with its peculiar assemblage of stalagmites and stalactites drooping from the ceiling. Small, but easily accessible from the beach and undeniably dramatic, the underground cavern is believed to be around fifteen million years old, formed by crystallized limestones from the Permian era.

The cave's 95 percent humidity is supposedly beneficial for health, so it's dotted with benches. You'll probably see local asthma sufferers passing the time – and even sleeping.

Dim Mağrası

11km east of the town centre • Daily: summer 9am–7.30pm; winter 9am–5.30pm • ₺8 • Dolmuş #2 from the central dolmuş station runs hourly in season; shared taxis ₺10–15 per person

Dim Mağrası is a spectacular cavern set in the mountains high above the **Dimçay River**. To reach it by car, continue past the Dimçay bridge for a few hundred metres, make a U-turn through a gap in the central reservation, then head back to the bridge and take the right turn just before it. Follow this road for 3km, then turn right and follow a track for a further 5km through increasingly attractive scenery.

A 360m-long walkway leads through the well-lit cavern itself, with a series of limestone formations providing interest en route to the prime attraction, a lovely crystal-clear pool. A small café-cum-restaurant at the entrance offers great views over the heavily wooded mountains. Alternatively, stop beside the river itself, and either join in the riverside activities or eat out at one of the many trout restaurants scattered along the banks.

ARRIVAL AND DEPARTURE
ALANYA

By bus Alanya's *otogar* is a 30min walk north of the town centre; plenty of *servis* minibuses and municipal buses shuttle passengers to and fro. Most of the many buses to destinations east and west start their journeys elsewhere, so book your departure seat well in advance.
Destinations Adana (2 daily; 9hr); Ankara (7 daily; 9hr); Antalya (every 30min; 2hr); Diyarbakır (1 daily; 19hr);

İstanbul (4 daily; 18hr); Konya (6 daily; 5hr); Mersin (8 daily; 8hr); Samsun (3 daily; 15hr); Silifke via Taşucu (5 daily; 6hr).
By dolmuş Dolmuşes run to local beaches from the dolmuş terminal; the numbered route maps on display make it easy to plan your route.
By hydrofoil Fergün Denizcilik (ⓦfergün.net) and Akgunler (☎0242 512 8889, ⓦakgunler.com.tr) run

hydrofoils to and from Girne-Kyrenia in Turkish Cyprus in summer only; services leave Mon & Thurs at noon, returning from Girne on Sun & Wed at 11am (₺78 one way; 3hr 30min).

Car rental Alanya holds several outlets; prices are higher than in Antalya, so shop around, and bargain hard. Big names include Avis, just off the western end of Damlataş (☏0242 513 3513), and Europcar, Hasan Akcalioglu Cad 34 (☏0242 513 1929). Force Rental, Damlataş Cad 68/A (☏0242 511 4243), is cheaper.

INFORMATION, TOURS AND ACTIVITIES

Tourist office Opposite the Alanya museum on Damlataş Cad, and offering excellent booklets and maps on the region (summer Mon–Tues & Thurs–Sat 9am–2am, Wed & Sun 9am–6pm; winter Mon–Tues & Thurs–Sat 9am–9pm & Wed & Sun 9am–6pm; ☏0242 513 1240). There's also a Tourist Information booth, next to the Kuyularonü Camii on Bostancpınarı Cad 1, where you can pick up town maps and get information on the city sights.

Dive operators Dolphin Dive, overlooking the harbour at İskele Cad 23 (☏0242 512 3030, ⓦdolphin-dive.com), has PADI certified instructors and day-trips for beginners starting from €62 including lunch and two dives.

Magazine Published in English and Danish, *All About Alanya* features unbiased reviews, recommendations and off-the-beaten-track finds.

Tours and travel agents FAM Tour, Damlataş Cad 21 (☏0242 512 0539, ⓦfamtours.com), and Classical Tourism, Atatürk Cad 65/5 (☏0242 511 1100), offer trips to Cappadocia, Pamukkale or the Pamphylian cities (from €25 per person), as well as jeep safaris, boat tours and trips to the Manavgat waterfalls, including hotel pickup.

ACCOMMODATION

Despite the boom in package tourism, rooms are easy to find in Alanya, even in high season, and the competition has kept the prices manageable (although they can almost double come the end of June). Keykubat Caddesi, the extension of Atatürk Caddesi, leading off to Mersin and backing the eastern beach, is Alanya's out-of-town resort strip, lined with upmarket hotels and all-inclusive resorts.

AROUND İSKELE CADDESİ

Damlataş Otel Damlataş Cad 52 ☏0242 511 3224. A good-value cheapie in a great location for access to both parts of town, this place is mostly frequented by Turkish travellers. Its friendly atmosphere and sizeable balconies make it a welcoming choice for anyone on a budget. You get what you pay for though – there's no breakfast and the free wi-fi is available only in the lobby. ₺60

Hotel Kaptan İskele Cad 70 ☏0242 513 4900, ⓦkaptanhotels.com. Popular with European tourists, this offers good value for its location and the rooftop restaurant affords incredible views over the harbour. Inside, the carpeted rooms are clean and cosy, but the outdoor pool area could do with a re-vamp. B&B costs the same all year round – a nice change to the usual seasonal inflation. ₺150

★ **Seaport Hotel** İskele Cad 82 ☏0242 513 6487, ⓦhotelseaport.com. If you're looking for something swish combined with down-to-earth hospitality, look no further than this impeccably managed boutique hotel, where jovial service and sleek design go hand in hand. 65 rooms (including a specially designed disabled suite), with shimmering marble floors and charming anchor-print bedspreads, free parking and incredible balcony views. Rates include breakfast and dinner. ₺200

Temiz Otel İskele Cad ☏0242 513 1016, ⓦtemizotel .com.tr. Chic dark wood interiors, crisp linens and tastefully decorative wallpapers make this one of the best mid-range choices in town. The balcony views over the harbour are spectacular, but if you prefer peace and quiet, the helpful staff will happily assign you a room well padded against the thumping music from the bars below. ₺120

WEST BEACH

Cleo Mare Atatürk Cad 1 ☏0242 511 2224, ⓦcleomare .com. This homely hotel has clean, functional rooms with big balconies (many overlooking the beach) and all conveniences. All-inclusive packages are available in July and Aug, and they offer good deals on booking tours. ₺110

Hotel Hermes Meteoroloji Sok 4 ☏0242 513 7770, ⓦhermesotel.com. The shabby hallways do this hotel no favours, but the smiling staff, small on-site pool and bright, clean rooms make it a very reasonably priced alternative to the nearby resort hotels. The location is a plus too – one block from the beach and a 10min walk to the *otogar*. ₺80

EATING

While the overpriced and heavily westernized restaurants that clog the beachfront might make you doubt Alanya's culinary abilities, the city has a trove of quality options if you can tear yourself away from the main strip. Many restaurants offer free taxis to and from hotels, so it's worth calling ahead to book a table. A weekly **market**, with masses of fresh provisions, is held every Friday, next to the dolmuş station, north of İsım Tokuş Bulvarı.

6

★ **Josef's Platz** Demir Sok 5 ☎ 0242 513 9296. If you haven't experienced owner Josef's hilarious belly-dancing-cum-Irish-whiskey-making routine, then you've missed one of Alanya's most uniquely entertaining spectacles. There's no gimmicks when it comes to the food, though – the town's finest steakhouse holds true to its reputation by serving up some of the tastiest steaks in Turkey (best is Josef's Südsee special steak from ₺38), cooked right in front of you on an enormous stone grill and served with suitable aplomb. Daily 9am–midnight.

Marina Restaurant Along the harbour ☎ 0242 513 1034. Quietly sophisticated with a picturesque rooftop terrace overlooking the harbour and castle, this is one of the few waterfront restaurants that doesn't substitute substance for style, with an excellent menu of international and local cuisine (mains from ₺30) from a renowned chef. Multiple-language menus, waiters that are friendly without being pushy, and a vibrant array of fun sundaes for the kids (₺15) only add to the appeal – there's even a small play area to entertain the littl'uns. Daily 9am–1am.

★ **Ravza** Off Gazipaşa St, just before the park ☎ 0242 513 3983, ⓦ ravza.com.tr. For an authentic but unintimidating introduction to Turkish cuisine, this is the place, with delicious traditional foods for half the price of the beachside haunts, and outdoor seating that's constantly packed with locals and a smattering of in-the-know tourists. Tuck into a delicious, steaming clay-pot stew (₺16) – the osmanish and the karides güvec (shrimp pot) are particularly mouth-watering – and watch in awe as the baker kneads, moulds and bakes your bread in a deep stone oven in front of you – if you're lucky he'll make a special heart-shaped bread for your loved one. No alcohol. Daily: summer 9am–2am; winter 9am–11pm.

Red Tower Brewery & Restaurant İskele Cad, above the harbour ☎ 0242 513 6664, ⓦ redtowerbrewery .com. The brainchild of local entrepreneurs, this mega-restaurant not only houses its own unique microbrewery (try the refreshingly light homebrewed lager), but the city's first and foremost sushi bar (prices start at ₺20 for a six-roll plate), one of the best rooftop views in town, and live guitar music throughout the summer. If all that's a bit overwhelming, you can relax on the ground-floor terrace overlooking the harbour, and enjoy a café latte that puts the American coffee chains to shame. Daily 10am–midnight.

DRINKING AND NIGHTLIFE

A virtual circus of flashing neon and pop music pumping at ear-popping volumes, Alanya's coastal strip comes alive after dark with bars, discos and clubs, geared towards the package tourist masses. Several out-of-town mega-discos open their doors in summer (with free all-night buses to and from the city).

Cello Café & Bar İskele Cad 36 ☎ 0242 511 4290. With its rustic wooden panelling and walls hung with bongos and banjos, this dimly lit tavern has barrel-loads of character, and the varied set of live folk and ethnic music, from 9.30pm nightly, makes a refreshing change from the pumping beats that seep up from the waterfront. Daily 11am–11pm.

EV Bar & Restaurant Atatürk Cad 8, opposite Atatürk Statue ☎ 0242 511 1051. If you're looking for an alternative to the brash beach bars, sip your way through EV's expansive cocktail menu (from ₺16), to the sound of live guitar music sung in several languages (from 8pm). The relaxed crowd includes a good mix of locals, expats and foreigners, and the set list mixes traditional numbers with classic crowd-pleasers. Open all year. Daily 10am–1am.

James Dean Bar Rıhtm St (on the harbour) ☎ 0536 724 2992. James Dean might turn in his grave at the sight of the mini-skirted tourists knocking back cocktails (₺20) in his name, but while cheesy music and scantily clad Europeans reign here, the place itself has a quirky rock'n'roll vibe. Red and black interiors are reminiscent of a 1950s' diner, decorated with a collage of images and memorabilia of the man himself. Daily 9pm–3am.

Robin Hood Bar/Latin Garden Club & Restaurant Rıhtm St (on the harbour) ☎ 0242 511 2023. Popular waterfront bar, with a heaving summer-only rooftop terrace and a suitably loud blend of Latino grooves and international pop and dance. Friendly staff and good service lift this place a notch above the rest. The lower-floor Latin Garden restaurant runs until around midnight, serving up tasty Mexican cuisine with the usual favourites costing around ₺30. Daily 10pm–3am.

Summer Garden 10km west of town on Konakli Kasabasi ☎ 0242 565 0059, ⓦ summer-garden.com. All your balmy Mediterranean fantasies will come to life at this sprawling restaurant and nightclub where strobe-lit palm trees and man-made waterfalls circle the heaving dance-floors, and podium dancers parade a vibrant array of barely-there bikinis. Fill up your wallet though, as cocktails start from a pricey ₺28. Free buses whisk partygoers to and from the harbour, and event flyers dish out details daily along the beachfront. Daily: restaurant 7–11pm, club 7pm–5.30am.

DIRECTORY

Banks and exchange Several banks with ATMs on Atatürk and Hükümet cads, and plenty of stand-alone ATMs along the beachfront shops.

Bicycle, motorbike and car rental Available from several companies around town. Force Rental (Damlataş Cad 68 ☎ 0242 511 4243, ⓦ rentacar-alanya.com) is a good central outlet, with bike rental €5, mopeds €15 and car rental from €30 per day.

Bowling Universal Bowling (Yıldız Sok 1 ☎0242 514 1626, ⓦorneksinemalari.net) offers a modern ten-pin bowling experience with on-site café and bistro. Call for free hotel pick-up.

Cinema Örnek Sinemaları, on Damlataş Cad opposite the museum (☎0242 513 2671, ⓦorneksinemalari.net), shows some films in English with Turkish subtitles.

Hospital The State Hospital (Devlet Hastane) is on the bypass, east of the centre.

Internet Casper Internet Café, behind the Yeni Cami on the waterfront.

Post office The PTT, Atatürk Cad, opposite Kültür Cad (daily 24hr), sells phone cards. PTT caravans are scattered about town in summer.

Shopping Touristy silverware and carpets are sold in İskele Cad, and there are yet more shops on the side streets between Gazipaşa and Hükümet cads. Fake designer-label clothes are ubiquitous, while if you're looking to add to your collection of replica soccer shirts, Alanya is the place to do it.

East of Alanya

The region between Alanya and Adana formed ancient **Cilicia**, and was settled by refugees from Troy at the same time as Pamphylia further west. Its remoteness and rugged, densely wooded coastline made it a haven for pirates, which eventually spurred the Romans into absorbing Cilicia into the empire in the first century BC. Today, the region retains a wild appearance, and travel involves frighteningly daring drives along winding mountain roads that hug the craggy coastline. All this is to the good if you're trying to escape the crowds further west, as far fewer people make it here.

Immediately east of Alanya, roads scallop the coastal cliffs, occasionally dipping inland through verdant banana plantations and passing little wayside restaurants, sheltered but hard-to-reach sandy bays, and the odd camping ground. Decent stretches of beach around **Anamur** are overlooked by an Armenian castle and a partially excavated Greek site, while in the mountains above **Silifke** the abandoned city of **Uzuncaburç** is perhaps the most extensive of the region's ancient remains. The up-and-coming seaside resort of **Kızkalesi** is intent on earning its stripes as a summer holiday destination, with its impressive castles breaking up the shoreline and a mixed bag of historical sites and day hikes on its doorstep.

A miscellany of marginally interesting ruins and lesser-frequented beaches runs down the coast until the outskirts of **Mersin**, where ferries run to Northern Cyprus. A little further on, **Tarsus**, birthplace of St Paul, plays host to some significant Christian sites, although its modern aspect does little to betray its former historical importance. **Adana**, Turkey's fourth-largest city, contains few remains of any era despite its venerable history, but does have excellent market shopping.

Sapadere Kanyonu

40km east of Alanya • Daily: summer 9am–7.30pm; winter 9am–5.30pm • ₺4 • ⓦ sapaderekanyonu.com

If you're looking to escape Alanya's sweltering city heat for an afternoon, the sleepy village of **Sapadere** makes a popular picnic spot. The **Sapadere Kanyonu** itself, just outside the village, is a 750m canyon that reaches heights of 400m, winding through rocky coves, shallow rock pools and gushing waterfalls, before opening out into a sizeable pool, where the water remains cool even in summer. A network of wood and steel walkways has been erected, making it an easy stroll, and there's a café-restaurant on site.

If you have time, head back to the village to take a peek at the watermill, or visit the small **silk factory**, to watch the villagers raising silkworms and spinning silk threads.

Iotape

45km east of Alanya • Daily 24hr • Free

Oddly situated on a rocky peninsula between the road and the sea, the ancient site of **Iotape** was named after the wife of the Commagenian king Antiochus IV (38–72 AD), and struck its own coins from the reign of Emperor Trajan until that of Emperor Valerian. The ruins are mainly very tumbledown, apart from a fairly impressive triple-arched bathhouse that's clearly visible from the road. Closer inspection uncovers drainage and heating systems. The acropolis stands on the promontory out to sea, while a colonnaded street runs east–west to the mainland. The **beach** below Iotape is idyllic: with luck, you might get it to yourself.

İskele and around

Originally just a small harbour suburb of the unexciting town of **Anamur**, 4km northwest, **İSKELE**, which means "quay", has developed into a fully fledged, but unpretentious, resort. In summer, when holidaying Turks descend on the coastline, it's heaving with life. Its two beaches are sliced in half by a pier from which regular ferries run to Cyprus.

Mamure Kalesi

2.5km east of İskele • Daily: April–Oct 9am–7pm; Nov–March 8.30am–5pm • ₺3 • From İskele, either walk along the seashore, which involves a ₺4 ferry ride across the Dragon River, or catch a taxi for ₺10 per person

The forbidding castle known as the **Mamure Kalesi** was built by the rulers of the Cilician kingdom of Armenia, on the site of a Byzantine fort. It was later occupied by Crusaders, who had established a short-lived kingdom in Cyprus and used the castle as a kind of bridgehead in Asia. Used by successive local rulers to protect the coastal strip, it was most recently garrisoned by the Ottomans, who reinforced it after the British occupied Cyprus in 1878, and maintained a strong presence here during World War I. Constructed directly above the sea, its stark facade of crenellated outer walls and watchtowers is certainly impressive. The languorously decaying buildings in its interior have formed a backdrop to many Turkish films.

Anemurium

6km southwest of Anamur • Tues–Sun: April–Oct 9am–7pm; Nov–March 8.30am–5pm • ₺3 • No dolmuş service, but a taxi from İskele costs ₺10 per person; be sure to arrange a pick-up time

The ancient settlement of **Anemurium**, at its peak during the third century AD, stands on the eastern side of a headland where the Toros Mountains jut out into the sea. As you approach, you'll see two parallel **aqueducts** running north to south along the hillside to the right. Below these, a sun-baked **necropolis** contains numerous freestanding tombs whose cool interiors harbour murals of mythological scenes. To the right of the road, the hollow ruins of three **Byzantine churches** are starkly silhouetted against the blue backdrop of the Mediterranean.

Further down towards the beach, you'll see the crumbling remains of a **bath complex**, a desolate **palaestra** or parade ground, and a ruined but still identifiable **theatre** set into the hillside. Above the theatre, some of the ruined houses still have intact vaulted roofs, while to the east, the shell of a building holds sixteen curved rows of seating and a mosaic floor. It's thought to have been either a **council chamber** or a **concert hall**, or possibly both. With time, you might want to clamber up the scrubby slopes of the headland to what was once Anemurium's **acropolis**. The promontory is **Turkey's southernmost point**, and on a clear day gives views of the mountains of Cyprus, 80km south.

ARRIVAL AND DEPARTURE
İSKELE AND AROUND

By bus From Anamur's *otogar*, where the main street meets the coast road, dolmuşes and city buses run southeast to İskele (daily, every 30min; summer 7am–midnight, winter 7am–8pm). Taxis from the *otogar* to İskele cost around ₺10.

Destinations From Anamur: Alanya (6 daily, 3hr); Silifke (6 daily, 3hr), continuing to Antalya, Mersin and Adana.

ACCOMMODATION

Eser Pansiyon İnönü Cad 6 ☎0536 217 9878, ⓦeserpansiyon.com. Among the cheapest and most reliable options in town. Ongoing renovations will hopefully tidy up the slightly shabby interiors but in any case it's good value for money, with a vine-shaded rooftop restaurant and breakfast included. ₺40

Tayfun Hotel Yolu Yunuslu Kavşak 176 ☎0324 814 1161, ⓦtayfunotel.com. The enormous, springy beds in this newly refurbished offering from the manager of the

Eser Pansiyon could house a family – a huge plus for road-weary travellers. Rooms are sunny and spacious, but can be a bit smokey, so make sure they've been aired. ₺70

Yan Hotel Yalıevleri Mah ☎0324 814 2123, ⓦyanhotel.com. Built around an atrium, fringed with flowerbeds that blossom with colour come springtime, this place offers a relatively upmarket choice with its simple but stylish rooms. Opt for a balcony room with a sea view. ₺90

EATING AND DRINKING

İskele has several simple **restaurants**, all of which seem incredibly cheap after the overpricing so prevalent further west. Make sure you pick up some of the region's famed miniature bananas too, as featured on one of the town's principal statues. Market stalls abound with the yellow fruits, and restaurants offer creative banana-centred desserts.

Efsun İskele Köyü Yolu ☎0535 331 7740. A simple family establishment with cheap eats and good, friendly service; you can pick up a tasty fish sandwich for as little as ₺4, and tasty *gözleme* from ₺5. Daily 7.30am–10.30pm.

Tayfun Restaurant Yolu Yunuslu Kavşak 176

☎0324 814 1161, ⓦtayfunotel.com. A good option for cheap'n'hearty home-cooked food, with a daily menu of meat dishes and plenty of delicious salads and *mezes* on display. There's no menu but staples like an *adana kebap* will set you back around ₺10. Daily 8am–10pm.

Taşucu

Crammed with European birdwatchers in springtime, the small but charming port town of **TAŞUCU** makes a pleasant base from which to explore the nearby **Göksu Delta**. There are few attractions in the town itself, but its frequent ferry and hydrofoil services to Cyprus make it a popular transport hub. A stroll around the pretty marina makes a pleasant way to kill time, and there are some excellent fish restaurants along the main strip. You can take a dip in the water from the tiny pebble beach before the harbour, and the nearest sandy beaches are a 1km walk beyond the marina, heading south.

Amphora Museum

Cumhuriyet Meydanı • Mon & Fri–Sun 9am–5.30pm • ₺2

Despite its diminutive size – a mere three rooms – the **Amphora Museum** manages to cram in a trove of wacky curiosities. Its unassuming entrance, next door to the *Denizkizi Restaurant*, belies its quirky appeal. It holds a fascinating collection of Hellenistic, Roman and Byzantine amphorae, mostly from locally salvaged wrecks, while ladies can muse over the small but beautifully embellished assortment of antique dresses. A makeshift encampment is set up in one corner, with a Yörük tent, some traditional leather saddles hung with tribal tassels, and an old spinning wheel.

ARRIVAL AND DEPARTURE

TAŞUCU

By bus Frequent minibuses run to and from Silifke, 10km west (20min; ₺1.75).

FERRIES AND HYDROFOILS TO CYPRUS

By ferry For anyone travelling with a car, the quickest way to get to Girne, in the Turkish Republic of North Cyprus (TRNC), is by ferry (Sun–Thurs midnight; 5hr; ₺60 one way, from ₺150 for a car). These are packed with heavy lorries and their drivers, so solo women travellers may feel uncomfortable.

By hydrofoil On calm seas at least, hydrofoils (*deniz otobüsü*) to Girne make a quicker and more pleasant

alternative to the ferries (daily 10.30am; 2hr; ₺60 one way, ₺100 return).

Tickets Fergün, on the main road opposite the waterfront (☎0324 741 2323, ⓦFergün.net), and Akgungler (☎0324 741 4033, ⓦakgunler.com.tr) sell tickets for both ferries and hydrofoils.

Entry requirements To enter the TRNC, EU, US, Canadian and Australian citizens require only a valid passport, holding an unexpired Turkish entry visa. It's not possible to enter southern (Greek-speaking) Cyprus from the TRNC.

6

ACCOMMODATION

Hotel Fatih Atatürk Bul 199; follow signs from near the museum ☎ 0324 741 4125, ⓦ hotelfatih.net. A great budget option, with clean, functional rooms, livened up by impressive balcony views over the glittering Mediterranean. The owner, Abdullah, is a talented painter; his colourful creations are proudly displayed in the lobby. ₺80

Lades Motel İnönü Cad 45 ☎ 0324 741 4008,

ⓦ ladesmotel.com. The town's premium hotel, on the hill at the top of the waterfront. Enviable views of the waterfront from the terrace, and clean rooms in which the white-and-aqua colour palette and bowls of polished seashells on the bedside tables continue the ocean theme. There's also an enormous outdoor pool overlooking the Med. €54

EATING

The many small cafés lining the marina offer a scenic pit stop, but the real draw card in Taşucu is the seafood, with fresh local catches coming in daily.

Baba İnönü Cad 43 ☎ 0324 741 5991. A great choice to sample the local seafood, this terrace restaurant, next door to *Lades Motel*, offers stunning views over the marina. Besides fish sold by the kilo – expect to pay from ₺14 for a fish meal – *Baba*'s other speciality is its delicious home-made gelato, at ₺1 per scoop. The rich pistachio flavour is a popular choice, or opt for creamy banana. Daily 11am–midnight.

Denizkizi Restaurant İnönü Cad 62 ☎ 0324 741 4194.

The best place in town to get acquainted with the ocean's offspring, with everything from shrimp to eel gracing its extensive seafood menu. Try the popular *balik buğulama* (₺20), a fish stew made with onions, tomatoes and potatoes, or brave a platter of octopus tentacles (₺18), and pull up a chair on the delightful rooftop terrace, with its thatched roof, playful fish murals and dangling seashell mobiles. Daily 11.30am–midnight.

Silifke

SİLİFKE, 10km east of Taşucu, was once ancient Seleucia, founded by Seleucus, one of Alexander the Great's generals, in the third century BC. Nowadays, it's a quiet, fairly undistinguished town where only the occasional tourist, en route to the ruins at Uzuncaburç, passes through.

Silifke Kalesi, a Byzantine castle, dominates the local skyline. A twenty-minute walk southwest of town, it looks a lot less spectacular close up. On the way up you'll pass an old **cistern** – the so-called *tekir ambarı* or "striped depot" – that kept Byzantine Silifke supplied with water. Other sights include the second-century AD **Jupiter Tapınağı** (Temple of Jupiter) on İnönü Caddesi, which comprises little more than a pile of stones and one standing pillar topped by a stork's nest, and the early Christian site

---

WILDLIFE IN THE GÖKSU DELTA

The **Göksu delta** and its **Kuşcenneti bird reservation** are of outstanding environmental importance, boasting a tremendous variety of flora and fauna. The best place to start an exploration is Akgöl, the westerly lagoon, where pygmy cormorants, Dalmatian pelicans, marbled and white-headed ducks and even the practically extinct black francolin and purple gallinule feed. The sand spit is a nesting ground for loggerhead and green turtles as well as a home to sea daffodils and Audouin's gulls. East of this, reached by an access road halfway between Taşucu and Silifke, are extensive ditches where you'll see kingfishers (including the rare chestnut brown and white Smyrna variety), coots, wagtails, spoonbills, egrets and grey, purple and squacco herons. Still further east, the huge natural fishpond of Paradeniz lagoon and the flats beyond it harbour waders, ospreys and terns.

Nesting and migration seasons are in the spring (with a peak between late March and early April), and in October. Information leaflets and maps of the delta are available from **Lades Motel** (p.384) or Özel Çevre Koruma Kurumu (Special Environmental Areas Protection Agency; ☎ 0324 714 9508), 5km west of Silifke, who can also arrange an English-speaking guide for group trips. Alternatively, hire a taxi from your hotel to the **Göksu delta bird-watching tower** (daily 5am–9pm, free entry). Make sure you take your own water and supplies, as no cafés or facilities are available.

of **Aya Tekla**, 5km west of town off the road to Taşucu, where there's little to see except an underground chapel (take a torch).

Incidentally, it was near Silifke that **Frederick Barbarossa**, the Holy Roman Emperor, met his end: he drowned while fording the Calycadnus (now Göksu) River about 9km north of town, en route to Palestine with the Third Crusade. A plaque now marks the spot.

Archeological museum

On the main road to Taşucu and Antalya, 500m from the turn-off to Silifke • Tues–Sun 8am–noon & 1–5pm • ₺3

The **archeological museum** (Arkeoloji Müzesi) contains the finds from excavations at Meydancıkale, a fourth-century BC temple site in the mountains above the coast. Relics include two enormous caryatids; huge, shapeless stone blocks with human-looking feet carved into the bases; and a hoard of 5200 silver coins dating from the reigns of Alexander and his generals in Egypt, Syria and the province of Pergamon.

ARRIVAL AND DEPARTURE
SİLİFKE

By bus The *otogar* is 15min walk east, along İnönü Cad, from Menderes Cad in the town centre.
Destinations Adana (every 15–20min; 2hr); Alanya (8 daily; 7hr); Antalya (8 daily; 9hr); Konya (8 daily; 5hr); Mersin (every 20min; 2hr); Taşucu (minibuses every 30min; 20min).

INFORMATION

ATM Outside the *Göksu Hotel*.
Tourist office Veli Gürten Bozbey Cad 6, on the road opposite the *Göksu Hotel* (Mon–Fri 8am–noon & 1.30–5pm; ☎ 0324 714 1151). Look out for the yellow signs as you cross the bridge.

ACCOMMODATION AND EATING

Hotel possibilities are limited, but there are some great budget options close to the *otogar*. For eating, there are plenty of basic food stalls and teahouses, but most close after dark, leaving you with very few options for an evening meal – try to arrange dinner at your hotel if possible.

Arısan Otel İnönü Cad 81; turn left out of the otogar ☎ 0324 714 3331. The cheery proprietor doesn't speak a word of English, but don't be put off, this is one of the best budget options in the region. While it's certainly not luxury, it's spotless, with spacious rooms and enormous Western-style bathrooms. Many rooms have sizeable balconies from which you can see the Silifke Kalesi. The cheapest rooms lack showers; en-suites cost double. ₺50

Göksu Hotel Atatürk Bul 20 ☎ 0324 712 1021. The best-positioned hotel in town, on the northern riverbank, with great views over the river, bridge and castle. The large, well-furnished rooms are good value, and there's a decent restaurant too. ₺100

Otel Ayatekla Mirzabey Cad, next to the otogar ☎ 0324 715 1081. In a great location – turn left from the *otogar* and look for the signs – this two-star hotel offers great-value doubles. Basic but comfortable, it makes every effort to offer good service, with toiletries, a fridge in the room and free tea offered every time you walk through reception. Breakfast costs an additional ₺10. ₺60

Özkaymak Pastaneleri İnönü Cad 130, opposite the otogar ☎ 0324 714 8183. Although this diner is best for desserts – the ₺6 *şübiyet*, a kind of *baklava* with cream, is particularly good – it also serves a range of savouries, including decent ₺10 burgers. There's free wi-fi too. Daily 8am–9pm.

Uzuncaburç

30km north of Silifke • Daily 24hr • ₺3 when the site guardian is around • Uzuncaburç-bound dolmuşes leave from 50m west of Silifke's tourist office (Mon–Fri 9am–7pm, every 2hr, last departure from Uzuncaburç at 5pm; Sat & Sun only 3 departures daily)

The ancient city ruins at **Uzuncaburç** (Olba and Diocaesarea), a spectacular one-hour drive from Silifke through a jagged gorge, make a worthwhile day-trip. A small, rural village has sprung up in haphazard fashion around the ruins, with makeshift stalls flogging leather bags and handmade rugs (known as *çul*), and local teahouses where you can try local specialities like *kenger kahvesi* (coffee made from acanthus) and *pekmez* (grape molasses).

While the main **site of Uzuncaburç** lacks the size and scale of Perge and Aspendos, it's atmospheric enough in its own way, if only because of its relatively neglected state.

Although the area was first settled by the Hittites, they left little behind; the most impressive ruins that survive date from Hellenistic times.

Theatre and monumental gateway

The best place to start exploring Uzuncaburç is the overgrown Roman **theatre**, overlooked by a couple of beautiful houses whose walls are choc-a-bloc with Classical masonry. From here, pass through an enormous five-columned **monumental gateway** to reach a colonnaded street, once the city's main thoroughfare. Keep your eyes open for what look like small stone shelves on the columns, which once supported statues and busts.

Nymphaeum

A **nymphaeum**, now dried up, on the northern side of Uzuncaburç's colonnaded street once formed part of the city's water-supply system. This was part of a large network of pipes and tunnels, built by the Romans nearly two thousand years ago, that still supplies water to the modern village and others around.

Temple of Zeus Olbios

The columns of the **Temple of Zeus Olbios**, south of the nymphaeum, feature one of the earliest examples of the Corinthian order, erected during the third century BC by Seleucus I. Only the fluted columns now remain intact. Look out for the fine sarcophagus carved with three Medusa heads, and a sarcophagus lid depicting three reclining figures.

Temple of Tyche and city gate

The **Temple of Tyche** stands at the western end of Uzuncaburç's colonnaded street. Dedicated to the goddess of fortune, it's believed to date from the second half of the first century AD. Five Egyptian granite columns still stand proud, joined by an architrave bearing an inscription stating that the temple was the gift of a certain Oppius and his wife Kyria. From here a right turn leads to a large three-arched **city gate**, which dates from the fifth century AD and is home to nesting birds.

Tower

North of the main ruins; turn right at the Ak Parti office

The 22m-high, five-storey Hellenistic **tower** once formed part of the city wall and gives its name to the modern town (*Uzuncaburç* means "high tower"). In addition to playing a defensive role, it's believed that this tower also formed part of an ancient signalling network, whereby messages were relayed by flashing sunlight off polished shields.

Alahan

110km northwest of Silifke • Daily 8am–sunset • ₺3 • Buses along Hwy 715 between the coast and Konya drop passengers at a turning that's a steep 2km walk from the site; taxis are often available at the bottom; a taxi and driver from Silifke will cost around €100

Reached by a dramatic road that cuts through the Taurus mountains en route for Konya, the Byzantine site of **Alahan**, a well-preserved monastic complex, stands at a height of 1200m, overshadowing the idyllic Göksu Valley. Nominated as a UNESCO Cultural Heritage Site, it remains a little-visited treasure. That owes more to its isolated location and awkward transport links than any lack of impressive sights, and it's well worth a visit if you're passing through.

The monastery buildings, believed to date back to 440 AD, include two late fifth- and sixth-century basilicas (one sporting elaborate relief sculptures of the Evangelists and the two archangels), and a baptistry with a cross-shaped font. Christian tombs and some impressive owl and fish carvings and Bible inscriptions dotted around the three main structures.

Kızkalesi and around

Midway between Silifke and Mersin, **KIZKALESİ** ("Maiden's Castle") is the longest-established resort along the Eastern Mediterranean coastline, with its lively beaches burrowed between a pair of looming Byzantine castles. While Turkish families have been descending en masse for years, international tourists are still a relatively new phenomenon, and the genuine, unobtrusive hospitality of the locals makes a welcome relief from the tourist-packed haunts further up the coast. Fine sandy beaches, shallow waters and seaside camel rides make the resort an excellent choice for children, and there's everything from jet skiing to paragliding on hand to keep the rest of the family entertained.

With its improved transport links and tour possibilities, Kızkalesi also makes a great base for exploring the surrounding area, like the popular **Cennet ve Cehennem** (caves of heaven and hell), the dramatic chasm of **Kanlıdıvane**, or the mosaic-floored **Bath of Poimenius** in Narlıkuyu. If you have a special interest in exploring off-the-beaten-track ruins, buy Celal Taşkiran's *Silifke and Environs*, an exhaustive guide to all the sites between Anamur and Mersin, available for €10 from *Rain Tour & Travel Agency* (see p.389).

Brief history

Known as Corycus in ancient times, Kızkalesi changed hands frequently until the arrival of the **Romans** in 72 BC. It then prospered to become one of the most important ports along the coast. Roman-era relics still survive in the area, notably a series of mysterious rock reliefs north of town and the carvings at the chasm at Kanlıdıvane to the east. Kızkalesi continued to thrive during the Byzantine era despite occasional Arab attacks – against which its defences were strengthened by the construction of two **castles** during the twelfth and thirteenth centuries – before falling to the Ottomans in 1482.

Sea castle

On an island 300m offshore • Daily dawn–dusk • Boats run from the pier at the west end of the beach; ₺10 per person return

Kızkalesi's most compelling feature, the twelfth-century **sea castle** known as the *Kızkalesi* or Maiden's Castle, makes an imposing sight floating on the horizon out to sea. According to a story also found elsewhere in Turkey, a medieval Armenian king had a beautiful daughter. After it was prophesied that she would die from a snak ebite, the king had the castle built and moved the girl out to it for safety there. One day, however, an adviser sent a basket of fruit out to the island for the girl, out of which slid a snake that killed her. Locals say the snake still lives there, so the only people who venture out to the island are tourists, for whose benefit boat services operate; you can also hire a pedalo and go it alone. The unadorned walls and sturdy towers still stand, but apart from masonry fragments and weeds there's currently little to see within. Plans are currently under way, however, to develop the attraction into a museum (presumably with an entrance fee) and restaurant.

Land castle

At the eastern end of the beach, opposite the sea castle • Daily: April–Oct 8am–8pm; Nov–March 8.30am–5pm • ₺5

The overgrown ruins of Kızkalesi's mighty **land castle** (Korkyos Kalesi) are easily explored, while its battlements make a good venue for watching the sunset. The main gate, constructed from ancient stones, bears various Greek inscriptions, whereas the western gate was a third-century Roman structure that was later incorporated into the castle. The complete lack of restrictions on where you can walk means kids might need some supervision, but those happy to scramble a few rocky verges are rewarded with some wonderful lookout points.

Necropolis

Immediately northeast of Kızkalesi, across the main road from the land castle

Dating from the fourth century AD, Kızkalesi's **necropolis** contains hundreds of tombs and sarcophagi, some of them beautifully carved. Many of the epitaphs give the jobs of the

6

occupants – weavers, cobblers, goldsmiths, vintners, olive-oil manufacturers, ship-owners and midwives, who all had their last resting places here. Also scattered around this area are the remains of several Byzantine churches and cisterns. Explore these out-of-town areas at your own risk, as they are scattered throughout overgrown fields and farmers' plots.

Beaches

Kızkalesi's main **beach**, west of the land castle, is the most popular and equipped with sunbeds, parasols, children's playgrounds and plenty of options for eating and drinking. Between mid-June and mid-Sept (and on many weekends throughout the year), the main beachfront plays host to all sorts of watersports and activities – paragliding (around ₺100 for a 15min tandem flight), jet skiing (₺50 for 15min), and pedalos (₺15 per hour) are all available.

A smaller and less populated beach, to the east, offers quieter swimming areas but considerably fewer facilities.

Narlıkuyu
5km west of Kızkalesi

The village of **NARLIKUYU** lies on the fringes of a rapidly developing bay that's home to several renowned fish restaurants. Next to the small car park in the village centre, the remains of the Roman **Bath of Poimenius** hold a fine mosaic floor depicting the well-rounded nude forms of the Three Graces and the daughters of Zeus. Poimenius' bath was fed from the limestone caves above by an ancient Roman spring that supplied a celebrated fountain, drinking the waters of which was said to confer wisdom.

Cennet ve Cehennem
5km northwest of Kızkalesi • Daily dawn–dusk • ₺3

Cennet ve Cehennem, or the "Caves of Heaven and Hell", the most popular local sight, can be reached on a pleasant walk from Kızkalesi winding through the olive grove hills north of **Narlıkuyu**. Visitors could also come by taxi, or join a tour. The three main caves here, including the cave of Heaven and the menacing chasm of Hell, rank among the most impressive of the many limestone caverns scattered along this coast.

Cennet Deresi ("Heaven")

The large and impressive cave known as **Cennet Deresi** – the Cave of Heaven – is located at the end of a 70m-deep canyon, entered via 452 steps cut into the rock. The culmination of the descent is the **chapel of the Virgin Mary**, a well-preserved Byzantine church built over the former temple of Zeus and still containing a few frescoes. Next to the church and part of the Cave of Heaven is the entrance to a smaller cave, **Tayfun Mağrası** (Cave of Typhon), which is reputed to be one of the gateways to Hades. Typhon, an immense hundred-headed fire-breathing lizard, was the father of Cerberus – the three-headed guard dog to Hades. Down here you can also hear the start of the underground river, which flows downstream to meet the sea at Narlıkuyu.

Cehennem Deresi ("Hell")

The **Cehennem Deresi** or Cave of Hell, 100m north of "Heaven", is little more than a chasm, but considerably easier to reach than its counterpart. It's impossible to enter, as its sides are practically vertical, although you can teeter on the edge of a fenced platform and gaze, supposedly, into the depths of hell. Legend dictates that Typhon was once temporarily imprisoned here.

Dilek Mağarası

The opening of the third cave at Cennet ve Cehennem – the **Dilek Mağarası** or Wishing Cave, 500m west of "Heaven" – has been widened, and a spiral staircase provided for ease of access. Down below, solid pathways connect a number of subterranean halls, with a total length of about 200m. The main chamber is filled with stalactites and stalagmites, and the air is supposed to be beneficial for asthma sufferers.

Adamkayalar rock reliefs

6km north of Kızkalesi; the turning is near the PTT

An intriguing side trip from Kızkalesi leads to the **Adamkayalar rock reliefs**. These consist of a series of Roman men, women and children, carved into niches into the wall of a valley; seventeen human figures in total, plus a mountain goat. It's not clear who the figures are, or why they might have been constructed, and the fragmentary inscriptions below most of them offer few clues. Unfortunately, severe damage has been caused to one figure by treasure hunters, who blew up the statue in the hope of finding booty secreted inside.

Kanlıdivane

10km northeast of Kızkalesi • Daily 8am–7pm • ₺3 • Head 7km east, then follow a signposted turn-off 3km north

The village of **KANLIDIVANE**, which means "place of blood" or "place of bloody madness", owes its name to legends that describe condemned criminals being thrown into a huge gorge to be devoured by wild animals. That dramatic **chasm** stood at the core of the ancient city of **Kanytelis**, and remains terrifying to this day. Measuring 90m by 70m, the hole reaches a depth of 60m, while its red-rock walls lend it a menacing aura. From the car park and ticket-seller's hut that mark the entrance to the chasm, visitors can descend an eroded staircase to see several carvings set into niches. One, a portrait of a family of six, is known as the Armaronxas Family Relief.

Back at ground level, the impressive 17m-high **Tower of Zeus Olbios** bears an inscription on its southwest corner alongside a three-pronged triskele, a symbol that links the region to the nearby state of Olba. Various large Byzantine basilicas nearby survive in assorted states of collapse, while a cluster of tombs to the northeast includes numerous ancient sarcophagi, and a mausoleum dedicated by a woman to her husband and two sons, who probably fell victim to the plague.

ARRIVAL AND INFORMATION

KIZKALESİ AND AROUND

By bus Buses plying the coastal road between Mersin and Silifke drop passengers in the town centre, an easy walk from numerous hotels.

Tours Rain Tour & Travel Agency, Barbarossa Cad 15D, or ask next door at the adjoining restaurant (March–Nov daily 8am–6pm; ☎0324 523 2784,

ⓦoztoprain.com). The town's only travel agency doubles as a one-stop tourist information centre. Staff speak excellent English, and offer impartial advice, maps and transport information. They also organize day-trips to surrounding sights, and try to make up groups to keep costs low (around €35 per person in a group of ten).

ACCOMMODATION

While shabby cheaper options line the side streets near the main road, Kızkalesi's best hotels are at the western end, just over the bridge. Street names appear redundant in these parts so look out for the signs for your chosen hotel and book ahead for July and August. Check for discounts; considerable bargains can be had outside peak season.

Barbarossa Club & Hotel Çetin Özyaran Cad ☎0324 523 2364, ⓦbarbarossahotel.com. The marble floors and white stone mosaics of its expansive entrance hall lend this hotel a sense of Middle-Eastern luxury, with chic decor and top-end service. With several indoor and outdoor pools, a gym and spa, and great facilities for kids, there's little reason to leave, and the beachside gardens and bar out the back offer amazing views of the waterfront and castle. Rates include breakfast and dinner. ₺250

Lamos Hotel Üzeri Atatürk Cad 75, 10min drive east of Kızkalesi town ☎0324 522 2444, ⓦhotellamos.com. Set

atop the swooping coastal cliffs, this impressive cylindrical hotel is impossible to miss. The architectural prowess extends inside as well as out; the enormous rooms circle a central mezzanine and pendulum-like chandelier, while the outdoor pool and terrace restaurant offer incredible views of the Mediterranean. Buses cruising the main road will drop you on the road opposite the hotel. ₺220

★ **Rain Hotel** Ahmet Erol Cad ☎0324 523 2782, ⓦrainhotel.com. Just a short stroll to the beach, and offering sunny, peaceful rooms away from the noise of the beachside bars, it's hard to fault this relaxed yet modern guesthouse. Owner Şirin speaks English fluently and has great knowledge and enthusiasm for the region's sights – he'll happily show you around or help organize tours (including scuba-diving and spear-fishing trips). Call ahead in season, as it can get busy. ₺140

Yaka Hotel Avcılar Cad ☎0324 523 2444, Ⓦyakahotel.com.tr. A cheerful ambassador for Kızkalesi's outstanding hospitality, owner Yakup likes guests to feel like part of the family, entertaining them with his quick wit in any of four languages. The pride he takes in his hotel is obvious, and the clean, comfortable rooms and pleasant garden seating make this place a winner. ₺90

EATING, DRINKING AND NIGHTLIFE

Places to **eat and drink** line the beach, and the area is constantly undergoing new developments. Summer nights see many beachside venues converted into bars and clubs with booming music and lengthy cocktail lists, but the classiest place to drink is at the Barbarossa Hotel with its enormous garden, beachside bar and beanbags laid out for you to watch the tide coming in.

Albatross Beach Club & Restaurant On the pier, at the far western end of the beach ☎0536 676 3902, Ⓦalbatrossbeachclub.com. If you want to party with the locals this is the place to go; so long as you can stand the cheesy pop and dance music it's quite an experience. The party often spills over onto the waterfront. Closed Oct–May. Daily: restaurant 8am–10pm; club 10pm–4am.

Rain Restaurant Barbarossa Cad 15D ☎0324 523 2784, Ⓦoztoprain.com. Part of the extensive Rain family, this cosy restaurant serves tasty home-cooked delights, including some excellent vegetarian options. Dig into a hearty *tava* stew (₺16), slow-cooked in a traditional clay pot, or try the popular Rain Special (₺15), a mixed stir-fry of meat and vegetables. There's a good cocktail (₺17) selection too. March–Nov daily 8am–11pm.

Yaka Restaurant Avcılar Cad ☎0324 523 2444, Ⓦyakahotel.com.tr. As close as you'll get to your mother's cooking in this town, *Yaka*'s kitchen cooks up plenty of tasty Turkish and Western staples (think kebabs and burgers). Mains will set you back around ₺15, but the real draw is the picturesque gardens, blooming with flowers and shaded from the sun throughout the day. Daily 8am–11pm.

Mersin

From the flower-filled parks and palm-tree-lined walkways that stretch along its waterfront to the spirited bustle of its daily fish bazaar, **MERSİN** is a model example of contemporary Turkish urban planning, and living proof that modernization can flow alongside tradition. Turkey's largest Mediterranean port, home to 1.5 million people, Mersin has thanks to rapid industrial growth and its role as an international free-trade zone become an important trade and transport hub.

Despite being inhabited since Hittite times, however, the city retains little of historical interest, and aside from its regular ferries to Cyprus there's little to appeal to travellers. That said, the harbour city makes a pleasant stop-off along the coast, and the opening of an impressive new marina has opened up a new area of development, complete with hip bars and restaurants.

Mersin Müzesi

Atatürk Cad • Tues–Sun 8am–noon & 1–5pm • ₺3

The **Mersin Müzesi** (Mersin Museum), in the heart of town, is home to a small but well-presented collection of local archeological finds from Neolithic times to the Byzantine era. Its chief highlight is an assortment of Roman clay sarcophagi, some with lift-off lids, others with sliding ones.

Mersin Marina

8km west of the old city • Catch a westbound blue bus on İsmet İnönü Bulvarı (₺2)

Mersin's recently opened **Mersin Marina** is the largest on Turkey's Mediterranean shores. An impressive yacht harbour with berths for around five hundred boats now brightens up the coastline, while a number of trendy bars and restaurants make it the liveliest place to spend an evening. There's also a new sports centre with outdoor swimming pools and sunbeds, two shopping malls and a two-thousand-seat amphitheatre.

6

Bazaar

Between İstiklâl Cad and Uray Cad

While the goods on sale are nothing to rival İstanbul's bazaars, a few hours spent sidling through the cobbled streets of Mersin's old-town **bazaar** makes for a good introduction to the local medley of inhabitants. Most famous is the **fish bazaar**, a dimly lit street wriggling with live seafood and crammed with tiny, backstreet food stalls where you can tuck into a grilled fish sandwich fresh off the boat.

ARRIVAL AND INFORMATION

MERSİN

By bus From Mersin's *otogar*, just off Gazi Mustafa Kemal Bulvarı northeast of the centre, frequent minibuses run to İsmet İnönü Bulvarı in the centre, stopping outside the tourist office, and close to most of the bus companies' offices. Minibuses run to local destinations from here.
Destinations Adana (hourly; 1hr); Alanya (8 daily; 8hr); Silifke (every 20min; 3hr).
By train Mersin's train station is in walking distance of the tourist office.
Departures Adana (every 30min; 50min).
By ferry Ferries sail from Mersin to Mağosa (Famagusta) in Northern Cyprus (Mon, Wed & Fri 8pm; 12hr; ₺80 one

way, cars ₺205), and to Tripoli in Lebanon (2 wkly; 14hr; €105). To reach Cyprus, it's quicker to travel from Taşucu (see p.383). Buy tickets from Fergün, İsmet İnönü Bulvarı (☏0324 238 2881, ⊛fergun.net), or directly from the harbour, behind the tourist office.
Tourist office İsmet İnönü Bulvarı 5 (Mon–Fri 9am–5pm; ☏0324 238 3270, ⊛mersinkulturturizm.gov.tr). Helpful, English-speaking staff in the sizeable tourist office can give you an annotated city map and help book ferry tickets.
Car rental Companies include Hertz, at Adnan Menderes Bulvarı, in the *Hilton Hotel* (☏0322 458 5062).

ACCOMMODATION

As an important port, Mersin has plenty of accommodation, most of it concentrated on İstiklâl and Soğuksu caddesis, and all of it aimed at business travellers.

Mersin Hotel İsmet İnönü Bulvarı 62 ☏0324 238 1040, ⊛mersinoteli.com.tr. While the hallways of this popular stopover are dimly lit and glum, the incredible views of the marina and Atatürk Park below more than make up for it. Rooms are clean and airy, with spotless bathrooms and giant tubs. **€70**

Nobel Oteli İstiklâl Cad 73 ☏0324 237 7700, ⊛nobelotel.com. With its plush bedspreads, huge mirrors and spacious rooms, this place is decidedly more elegant than its peers, although the cramped bathrooms could do with a re-vamp. English-speaking staff are a plus too. **₺130**

EATING AND DRINKING

Mersin has no shortage of eating options, with plenty of fresh seafood on offer and some stylish new restaurants opening up along the new marina.

Deniz Yıldızı Restaurant Uray Cad ☏0324 237 9633. One of several fish restaurants nestled at the entrance to the Mersin Fish Bazaar. The friendly, English-speaking waiters can barely contain their enthusiasm as they talk you through the best catches of the day. *Levrek* (sea bass, ₺12) and sea bream (₺11) are always available, otherwise the menu depends on the fishermen's luck. Wash it down with raki (₺11 for a double) for the full experience. Daily 7am–9pm.
Gattini Bistro Adnan Menderes Bulvarı 160 ☏0324 326 9695 ⊛gattinibistro.com. Adding a touch of flamboyance to locally caught seafood, this stylish restaurant offers up a delicious stuffed sea bass, alongside international and Turkish mains (from ₺16). The decadent dessert menu has an international flavour, with fruit tarts, cheesecakes and profiteroles too tempting to pass over,

and the garden seating is particularly atmospheric in the evening. Daily 9.30am–late.
Gündoğdu İskender Silifke Cad ☏0324 231 9677. A thriving local establishment, easily spotted by the giant kebabs roasting in the windows and the mouthwatering scent of roasting meat wafting through the air. Traditional kebabs start at ₺9 and there's a selection of grills, including southeastern Turkish specialities such as *kuburga* (lamb ribs, ₺12). There's no menu, but staff will happily display examples for your selection. Daily 8am–9pm.
Nobel Cafe Silifke Cad ☏0324 237 7700. Adjoining its namesake hotel, this café serves up tasty sweets and pastries (from ₺4) in modern, a/c surrounds. There's a selection of light meals on offer too, and the glass fronting offers great opportunities for people-watching along the main street. Daily 7am–10pm.

Tarsus and around

TARSUS, the birthplace of St Paul and the city where Cleopatra met Mark Antony and turned him into a "strumpet's fool", lies about 30km east of Mersin, across the factory-dotted cotton fields of the Çukurova. St Paul was born as Saul in Tarsus about 46 years after the meeting between Cleopatra and Antony. He returned after his conversion on the road to Damascus, fleeing persecution in Palestine. Proud of his roots, he is described as having told the Roman commandant of Jerusalem "I am a Jew, a Tarsian from Cilicia, a citizen of no mean city."

Nowadays, the **Antik Şehir** or "old city" has been exposed by excavations, but although there remains a good section of black-basalt main street and some underground *stoas* and temples, only a few reminders of the town's illustrious past survive.

Kancık Kapısı

Near the main bus drop-off point

The **Kancık Kapısı** ("the gate of the bitch") is a Roman construction, also known as Cleopatra's Gate. Although it doesn't actually have any known connection with the Egyptian queen, she is thought to have come ashore for her first meeting with Mark Antony, back in 40BC, somewhere in the vicinity. At that time Tarsus was linked to the sea by a lagoon, which has since silted up.

Tarsus museum

From Cleopatra's Gate, head south to a roundabout flowing with fountains and turn right; the museum lies 100m west • Tues–Sat 9am–5pm • ₺3

The **Cultural Centre** (Kültür Merkezi) houses the **Tarsus museum**, an eclectic collection of objects uncovered in regional excavations with pieces from the Neolithic period onwards. The "Tarsus house corner" focuses on the lifestyles and culture of the Çukurovan nomads and there's a wide collection of stone works, coins and jewellery collections. Most inexplicably of all, you'll also see the mummified lower arm of an unnamed woman.

St Paul's well

Make your way through the backstreets to **St Paul's well**; you'll have to ask for "Sen Pol Kuyusu". It may be something of a disappointment, since it's just a borehole in the ground covered by a removable lid. However, as it's said to be on the site of St Paul's house, the steady stream of visitors gladly pay ₺2 for a sip of water from a bucket hauled up from the depths.

Roman road

15km north of Tarsus

The remains of a limestone paved **Roman road** run for around 2km along the hills above the village of Sağlıklı. Thought to have been constructed in the first century AD, and used until the middle of the fourth century, the road is mostly well preserved, featuring a monumental gate and vehicle entrance and exit points.

ARRIVAL AND DEPARTURE | TARSUS AND AROUND

By bus Tarsus's *otogar* is 2km east of town, but minibuses to and from Mersin and Adana stop near Cleopatra's Gate, right in the centre.

ACCOMMODATION

Cihan Palas Otel Mersin Cad 21 ☎0324 624 1623. The best budget option in town, handily located near the *otogar*, this place has recently redecorated its modern rooms; some have a/c and fridges. ₺100

Tarsus Şelale Otel Overlooking the Şelale waterfall just north of town ☎0324 614 0600, ⊛selalehotel .com. A monstrous hotel with its own pool and large a/c rooms. It's often virtually empty, so you may be able to negotiate a substantial discount. There's free parking too. ₺150

6

Adana

ADANA, Turkey's fifth-largest city, with more than 1.5 million inhabitants, sprawls 40km east of Tarsus. A modern place, which has grown rapidly since the 1990s, Adana continues to owe much of its wealth to the surrounding fertile countryside of the Çukurova. Its textile industry has grown up on the back of the local cotton fields.

The city itself is divided by the E5 highway into the swanky north, with its cinemas and designer malls, and the more traditional bustling south, with the markets, mosques and hotels of the old town. As there are few pedestrian bridges and underpasses, you have to negotiate mind-blowing traffic to reach many of the local sights.

Brief history

Despite its contemporary, metropolitan feel, Adana has historical roots going back to 1000 BC. The arrival of the Greeks precipitated an on-off power struggle with the powerful Persian Empire that was to last for a thousand years, ending only when the Romans arrived during the first century BC. Under the Romans, the city became an important trading centre, afterwards passing through various hands before falling to the Ottomans during the sixteenth century.

Archeological Museum

On the north side of the D-400 • Tues–Sun 8am–noon & 1–4.30pm • ₺5

Adana's small **Archeological Museum** (Arkeolji Müzesi) is in a prime location right next to the impressive **Sabancı Merkez Camii**. The small courtyard at the back enjoys beautiful views across the mosque gardens. Inside, two floors showcase predominantly Hellenistic and Roman statuary, plus some fine sarcophagi and Hittite statues. Unfortunately many of the upstairs exhibition rooms are now closed or empty, and aside from the Turkish nameplates there's very little information to guide visitors.

Sabancı Merkez Camii

On the north side of the D-400, next door to the Archeological Museum

With a capacity of 28,500 and the highest dome in Turkey, the **Sabancı Merkez Camii** is a testament to the continued strength of Islam in the southeast. A stunningly photogenic construction, it has gold trimmings, marble entrance arches, six towering minarets and beautiful İznik tile-work inside. It was built mainly by subscription, but finished with the aid of the Sabancı family – hence the name. These local boys made good and are now the second-richest family in Turkey.

Taş Köprü and around

100m southeast of the Sabancı Merkez Camii

Adana's most substantial ancient monument, the **Taş Köprü**, is an impressive sixteen-arched Roman bridge that was built by Hadrian to span the Seyhan River and still carries heavy traffic. Stretching along the west side of the river by the bridge, the **Zübeyde Harim Parkı** is a shaded park with pleasant tree-lined walkways and picnic areas that afford great views of the river and mosque.

Ulu Cami

Abidin Paşa Cad, not far from the bridge in the centre

The **Ulu Cami** was built in the Syrian style, using white-and-black marble, in 1507. It's the sole legacy of Halil Bey, Emir of the Ramazanoğlu Turks, who ruled Adana before the Ottoman conquest. His tomb features some fine tile-work and beautiful mosaics.

The bazaar area

South of Ulu Cami

A large clock tower, **Büyük Saat Kulesi**, marks the start of the **bazaar area**, where the narrow, barely paved streets and the echoing sound of metalworking makes many

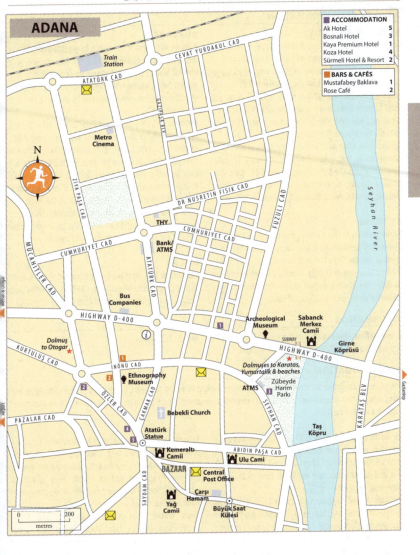

ADANA

6

visitors feel they've stepped back in time. A wander through the labyrinth of snaking pathways is a good way to uncover some of the intrigues of the old city. The **Çarşı Hamam** (see p.397) is reputed to date back to the time of Piri, son of Emir Halil Bey, and boasts a beautifully ornate doorway.

Yağ Cami

Just southeast of the central Atatürk statue

The **Yağ Cami**, on the west side of the bazaar, is accessed across a courtyard. Unusually, one bay of the mosque was a church until it was incorporated into the main structure in 1502. A peculiar square building in the courtyard has an interesting domed roof supported by a line of slabs with Selçuk decoration, although its original purpose is unknown.

6

ARRIVAL AND INFORMATION

ADANA

BY BUS OR DOLMUŞ

Frequent dolmuşes run from Adana's otogar, 5km west of town on the E5 (also known as Cemal Beriker Bulvarı), to the town centre. In addition, most bus companies lay on *servis* minibuses to and from their central offices, most of which are on Ziya Paşa Cad, just north of the E5. When you want to leave town, buy a ticket from one of these and a *servis* bus will take you to the *otogar*, connected with virtually every city in the country.

Destinations Adıyaman (10 daily; 6hr); Afyon (4 daily; 7hr); Alanya (2 daily; 9hr); Ankara (hourly; 10hr); Antalya (13 daily; 12hr); Diyarbakır (10 daily; 10hr); Gaziantep (12 daily; 4hr); İstanbul (hourly; 12 hr); Kayseri (14 daily; 7hr); Konya (5 daily; 7hr); Malatya (8 daily; 8hr); Şanlıurfa (4 daily; 6hr).

BY TRAIN

Train station At the northern end of Atatürk Caddesi, a 20min walk north of the centre. There are dolmuşes from town, or you can flag a taxi (less than ₺10).

Destinations Ankara (1 daily, overnight; 14hr); İskenderun (3 daily; 2hr 30min); Kayseri (daily; 6hr); Mersin (Every 30min between 6am–11.30pm; 50min).

BY PLANE

Airport 4km west of the centre. To get into town, it costs double to catch a taxi from outside the door; instead, walk another 50m to the street and either catch a dolmuş or a normal taxi. A shuttle bus leaves the city-centre THY office 1hr 30min before departure, and in theory a THY bus awaits arrivals.

Airlines THY, Prof Dr Nuşret Fişik Cad 22 (☎0322 457 0222), for flights to Ankara, İstanbul and İzmir; KTHY, Atatürk Cad 5 (☎0322 363 1224), near the tourist office, has five direct flights to Cyprus per week. For flights to İstanbul Onur Air's office is at the airport (☎0322 436 6766), while Atlas Jet tickets are sold at Adana Turizm at Toros Cad, Cemal Paşa Mah. Özlem apt 13/A, Seyhan (☎0322 458 7612).

Destinations Ankara (2 daily; 1hr); Antalya (daily; 1hr); Ercan (1 daily; 50min); İstanbul (9 daily; 1hr 20min); İzmir (2 daily; 1hr 30min); Munich (daily; 3hr 30min).

BY CAR

Car rental Avis, Ziyapaşa Bul, Nakipoglu Apt 9/A ☎0322 453 3045; Europcar, at the airport ☎0322 433 2957; and Talay Turizm, Resatpasa Mah Bul 46/B ☎0322 459 6448.

INFORMATION

Tourist office Atatürk Cad 7, on the south side of the E5 highway, next to the AKBank (Mon–Fri 8am–5pm; ☎0322 363 1448).

ACCOMMODATION

Adana's accommodation options have undergone some changes in the last few years. Boutique hotels have sprung up, and many new, swisher hotels have replaced their outdated predecessors. Plenty of budget options still survive on and around Saydam and Özler caddesis.

Ak Hotel Özler Cad 19 ☎0322 351 4208. As basic as it gets, but with bargain-basement prices and free wi-fi, there's little to complain about. The best rooms have a/c, sink and hot showers, but you'll still have to brave the communal squat toilet. ₺40

Bosnali Hotel Seyhan Cad 29 ☎0322 359 8000, ⓦhotelbosnali.com. Set in a 110-year-old wooden mansion, overlooking the river and the Sabanci mosque, this 4-star hotel is both smart and homely, with dark wood and cream decor, plus flat-screen TV, minibar, in-room safe and spacious bathrooms. ₺75

★ **Kaya Premium Hotel** Turhan Cemal Beriker Bul 16/A ☎0322 888 0336, ⓦkayapremium.com. Few boutique hotels could get away with such decadent interiors (think flamboyantly carved Ottoman furniture and tasteful lashings of gold) without appearing ostentatious, but this new establishment is comfortable and welcoming,

as well as visually stunning. 49 individually designed, colour-themed rooms, each more spectacular than the next, with engraved headboards, embossed wallpapers, glittering chandeliers and an eclectic array of antique telephones. Special offers for new guests make things even more enticing. ₺220

Koza Hotel Özler Cad 31 ☎0322 352 5857, ⓦhotelkoza.com. A comfortable, good-value 2-star option, with wi-fi and breakfast included. Slightly dated decor doesn't detract from the clean and cosy, carpeted rooms with TV and minibar. ₺100

Sürmeli Hotel & Resort Özler Cad 49 ☎0322 352 3600, ⓦsurmelihotels.com. It's all about stylish simplicity in this luxury dwelling, but the selling point is in the extras – an impressive rooftop swimming pool, traditional Turkish hamam and sauna, a snooker room and enormous flat-screen TVs in all the rooms. ₺149

EATING AND DRINKING

Although the local speciality is the spicy *Adana kebap* – minced lamb and pepper wrapped around a skewer and grilled – frankly, you can eat better ones elsewhere. Pavement **food stalls** selling sandwiches and pastries abound, as do hole-in-the-wall *börek* and kebab places near the bazaar and central PTT, although most local haunts can seem less than welcoming to foreigners, especially solo females.

Mustafabey Baklava Ziyapaşa Bul ☏ 0322 363 2737. With its glistening stacks of *halka tatlısı* (sweet fried pastries) and walnut *baklava* displayed out front on giant silver platters, anyone with a sweet tooth will have a tough job passing by this dessert house. Prices start from as little as ₺1, or you can enjoy a full dessert from ₺7 from the upstairs seating overlooking the street. Daily 8am–midnight.

Rose Café Ziyapaşa Bul ☏ 0322 363 3745. The least intimidating of the male-dominated local haunts, this cosy café is manned by a cheery, English-speaking proprietor. It's one of the few places you can get a beer (₺6) with your food. The cuisine is simple but tasty – the chicken *şiş* (₺10) is particularly good – and they do generous salad plates if you need a break from all that Turkish bread. Daily 8am–9pm.

DIRECTORY

Banks and exchange Most banks are near the tourist office. There are also several *döviz* offices around Saydam and Özler cads.

Cinema The Metro, a couple of blocks south of the train station.

Hamam Çarşı Hamam, Büyük Saat Civari (daily: women 9am–3pm, men 4–9.30pm; from ₺15 depending on level of service).

Hospital State Hospital (Adana Devlet Hastane), on Riza

Cad ☏ 0322 321 5752.

Post office The main PTT office (8.30am–9pm), on Ulu Cami, the street parallel to Abdin Paşa Cad, sells phonecards and *jetons*.

Shopping For foodstuffs, clothing, toiletries and the like, head for Çetinkaya shopping arcade at the roundabout at the western end of İnönü Cad. Also try the huge Galeria Shopping Mall, nearby on Fuzuli Cad.

East of Adana

A number of interesting ancient sites line the road that parallels the final eastern stretch of the Mediterranean coast, before it turns irrevocably southwards. Splendid castles watch over the towns of **Yakapinar** and **Toprakkale**, while the much older remains of a Hittite palace can still be seen at **Karatepe**, inland.

Yılan Kalesi

Follow signs from Yakapinar, 35km east of Adana, to Yılan Kalesi, 3km south of the main road • Daily 24hr • ₺2

From the first town along the road to İskenderun, **Yakapinar**, the **Yılan Kalesi**, or "Snake Castle", is clearly visible, peering down on the town from the top of a mountain. So called because of the legend that it belongs to the king of the snakes, it's actually an Armenian castle, dating from the eleventh century. There's still plenty left to see, including seven horseshoe-shaped towers, but it's worth the hike (or drive) just to admire the view of the meandering Ceyhan River below.

Toprakkale Kalesi

Toprakkale, 85km east of Adana, just off the main highway

The town of Toprakkale is dominated by a towering black basalt castle, **Toprakkale Kalesi**. Much fought over in medieval times by the Armenians and Crusaders, it has been abandoned since about 1337. If you do visit Toprakkale, be careful – much of it is unstable, with numerous concealed cisterns waiting for unwary people to fall into them.

Karatepe Aslantaş National Park

Head to Osmaniye, 95km east of Adana, then follow signs 30km north across the Ceyhan River, beyond the Hellenistic ruins of Hierapolis Castabala • Tues–Sun 8.30am–noon & 2–5.30pm • ₺3 • From the car park (₺2), walk up to the gatehouse to buy a ticket and join a tour

If you're heading down towards the Hatay and have your own transport you might want to consider a 70km detour to the **Karatepe Arslantaş National Park** (Karatepe Arslantaş Milli Parkı), where the wooded hillsides overlooking the **Arslantaş dam** provide the perfect picnic venue. **Karatepe** is thought to have been a frontier castle or summer palace of the ninth-century BC neo-Hittite king Asitawanda. Today, little of the building complex remains, but the eloquent stone carvings arranged around the two entrance gates of the former palace are exquisite.

The Hatay

Extending like a stumpy finger into Syria, the region known as the **Hatay** has closer cultural links with the Arab world than with the Turkish hinterland, and its multi-ethnic, multi-faith identity gives it an extra edge of interest. **Antakya** (ancient Antioch), a cosmopolitan city and gastronomic centre set in the valley of the Asi River, and **İskenderun**, a heavily industrialized port, are the two main destinations.

The region only became part of modern Turkey in 1939, having been apportioned to the French Protectorate of Syria following the dismemberment of the Ottoman Empire. Following the brief-lived independent **Hatay Republic** of 1938 it was handed over to Turkey after a plebiscite. This move, calculated to buy Turkish support, or at least neutrality, in the imminent world war, was successful. It was Atatürk, in a move to "Turkify" the region, who dreamt up the name "Hatay", supposedly based on that of a medieval Turkic tribe.

The majority of people here speak Arabic as well as Turkish, and there's some backing for union with Syria, though de facto Turkish sovereignty remains recognized. Although relations between the two countries improved dramatically during the "zero problems with neighbours policy" from 2002 onwards, the civil unrest in Syria in 2012, and President Assad's refusal to listen to Turkish calls for reform, meant that friction was, at the time of writing, once again escalating.

Arab influence in the Hatay goes back to the seventh century AD, when Arab raiders began hacking at the edges of the collapsing Byzantine Empire. Although they were never able to secure long-lasting political control over the region, the Arabs did establish themselves as permanent settlers, remaining even when the Hatay passed into Ottoman hands.

İskenderun

İSKENDERUN was founded by Alexander the Great to commemorate his victory over the Persians at the nearby battle of Issus, and, as Alexandria ad Issum, it became a major trade nexus during Roman times. Under the Ottomans, İskenderun became the main port for Halab (Aleppo), now in Syria, from where trade routes fanned out to Persia and the Arabian peninsula. Known as Alexandretta during the French-mandate era, the town is now an industrial, military and commercial centre. Although there is little of historical interest left to see, İskenderun's coastal strip is visually appealing, with its broad promenade and magnificent backdrop of the Amanus mountains and glistening ocean. İskenderun's numerous **churches** include the Catholic **St Mary's**, a sizeable nineteenth-century building, close to the tourist office; the pastel-coloured Greek Orthodox church of **St Nicholas**, built in 1876, on Şehit Paşa Cad; and the atmospheric **St George's** on Denizciler Cad, with its walled garden of palm and cypress trees.

Seafront park

Don't leave İskenderun without a stroll along its newly renovated **seafront park**, where kiosks, palm-tree-lined canals and gardens partially shield the industrial landscape across the bay and provide a lovely atmosphere for a picnic. **Boat trips** on the Mediterranean run from near the Atatürk monument area; a twenty-minute trip costs around ₺5 per person, a half-day tour with lunch around ₺50 per person.

ARRIVAL AND INFORMATION

By bus Buses from the *otogar*, a 15min walk north of the seafront, run to all major towns. Frequent minibuses to Antakya also leave from near the junction of Şehit Pamir and Prof Muammer Askoy Cad.

Destinations Adana (hourly; 2hr); Antakya (every 20min; 40min); Antalya (2 daily; 13hr).

By train İskenderun's station, 1km east of the centre, is reached by following 5 Temmuz Caddesi and then Bahçeli Sahil Evler Caddesi.

Destinations Adana (3 daily; 2hr 30min); Mersin (3 daily; 3hr 30min).

Tourist office On a side street off Şehit Pamir Caddesi (Mon–Fri 8.30am–noon & 1–5pm; ☎0326 614 1620). Follow yellow signs off Atatürk Bulvarı to a slightly ominous-looking building, and take the lift to the second floor, to pick some decent city maps and other information.

ACCOMMODATION

Hotel Açıkalan Şehit Pamir Cad 13 ☎0326 617 3732. With wi-fi, a/c and breakfast included, the simple rooms here might be at the lower end of the quality spectrum but are nonetheless very good value, and remain clean and comfortable. The cramped bathrooms have showers over the toilet, but the en-suite options definitely trump the dismal shared bathrooms. ₺50

Altındişler Oteli Şehit Pamir Cad 11 ☎0326 617 1011, ⓦaltindislerotel.net. Among the more chic budget options, this place offers spotless a/c rooms with dark wood furnishings and newly tiled bathrooms. Rooms facing Şehit Pamir Caddesi can be noisy, so ask for one around the back. ₺85

Sun Otel Muammer Aksoy Cad 31 ☎0326 613 5500, ⓦsuninnotel.com. This hotel's uninspiring rooms are rather worn, but great service and a friendly atmosphere make it a more inviting option. There's an American-style bar and a disco downstairs if you're looking to while away the evening. ₺130

EATING AND DRINKING

The promenade area is home to several *gazinos* where you can enjoy a beer overlooking the sea, but İskenderun's restaurants are mostly uninspiring.

Emirgan Bulvar Café Atatürk Bul 2 ☎0326 613 3131, ⓦemirgancafe.com. Well-positioned waterfront café, serving mainly western food including a pretty decent steak (₺20), with stunning views over the ocean. Nargiles (₺12) are available in various flavours, or try some freshly squeezed pomegranate juice (₺5). Daily 8am–midnight.

Petek Pastaneleri Mareşal Çakmak Cad 16 ☎0326 617 8888, ⓦpetekpastanesi.com.tr. Slightly off the main strip, this European-style restaurant boasts an idyllic location overlooking the water, with plenty of shaded outdoor seating. Dig into the impressive selection of ice creams (₺6), enjoy an ice-cold milkshake (₺7), or choose from Italian staples from pizza to pasta (mains from ₺12). Daily 7am–1am.

Belen and around

The road southeast from İskenderun climbs up into the mountains to reach the small hill town of **BELEN**, 13km southeast of İskenderun (and also accessible by dolmuş from Antakya). From here, the road strains and curves through the **Belen pass** (Belen Geçidi) – of great strategic importance during Roman times, when it was known as the *Pylae Syriae* or "Gates of Syria". For a week or two in early October (if the winds are right), Belen becomes the most important **migration route** on the western Palearctic corridor for birds of prey.

Bakras Kalesi

5km south of the Belen pass • From Bakras village, served by dolmuşes from Antakya and İskenderun, the castle is a 15min climb

Bakras Kalesi is an imposing medieval castle first erected by the Arabs during the seventh century and destroyed during the First Crusade. Later, the Knights Templar built a new fortress, which became an important link in their defensive system, and forms the basis of the impressive remains you see today. It was repeatedly fought over; in 1156, a bloody battle took place here between the Templars and the soldiers of Thoros, ruler of Cilician Armenia. The castle fell to Arabs in 1188, but possession was fiercely contested until the Ottomans took over during the sixteenth century.

Antakya and around

The city of **ANTAKYA**, 45km south of İskenderun, stands on the site of ancient Antioch. Its laidback pace, cosmopolitan outlook and subtly Arab atmosphere make it a unique destination. Flanked by mountains to the north and south, it sits in the bed of a broad river valley planted with olive trees; a welcome visual relief after travelling from the drab flatlands surrounding Adana.

Antakya is split in two by the **Asi River**, known in ancient times as the Orontes. Recent developments along the riverbank are slowly transforming the stretch into a fetching (if traffic-ridden) thoroughfare, bordered by flowerbeds, palm trees, fountains and cafés. The eastern bank is home to **old Antakya**, a maze of narrow streets that still offer glimpses of traditional Turkish life – clusters of men perched on low stools in their doorways sipping tea, and the odd scruffy horse dragging a dilapidated wooden cart laden with goods. Best of all is the **food**, which thanks to the city's Arab heritage is among the best, and most varied, in Turkey.

Brief history

Antakya was founded as **Antioch** in the fourth century BC by Seleucus Nicator, one of the four generals between whom the empire of Alexander the Great was divided. It soon grew, and by the second century BC it had developed into a multi-ethnic metropolis of half a million – one of the largest cities in the ancient world and a major staging post on the newly opened Silk Road. It also acquired a reputation as a centre for all kinds of moral excess, causing **St Peter** to choose it as the location of one of the world's first Christian communities, in the hope that the new religion would exercise a restraining influence. Indeed, the patriarchy of Antioch became one of the five senior official positions in the organization of the early Christian Church.

Despite being razed by earthquakes during the sixth century AD, Antioch maintained its prosperity after the Roman era. Only with the rise of Constantinople did it begin to decline. In 1098, after a vicious eight-month siege and a savage massacre of Turks, the Crusader kings Bohemond and Raymond took the city in the name of Christianity. They imposed a Christian rule that lasted until Antioch was sacked by the Mamluks of Egypt in 1268. By the time the Ottomans, under Selim the Grim, took over in 1516, Antioch had long since vanished from the main stage of world history. At the start of the twentieth century, the city was little more than a village, squatting amid the ruins of the ancient metropolis. After World War I, Antakya, along with most of the rest of the Hatay, passed into the hands of the French, who laid the foundations of the modern city.

Bazaar

North of Kemal Paşa Cad, running west–east just northeast of the main bridge, Ata Köprüsü

It's worth spending an hour or two wandering around Antakya's **bazaar** and market areas. Although many of the traditional stores have given way to clothing, household goods and cheap jewellery sellers, there are still plenty of ogling opportunities with colourful spice stalls, piles of home-made soaps and small wood workshops crammed alongside the obligatory Turkish-delight sellers.

Habibi Neccar Camii

At the junction of Kemal Paşa Cad and Kurtuluş Cad

The **Habibi Neccar Camii** is a mosque incorporated into the shell of a former Byzantine church, which was in turn built on the site of an ancient temple. Its distinctive pointed minaret, added during the seventeenth century, is not – as you might be tempted to imagine – a former church tower. From the southeast corner of the yard, a door leads downstairs to the tomb of the prophet Habibi Neccar. While very little is known about the prophet or exactly what became of him, he was allegedly violently done to death by

Christians, some time during the first century AD. If you believe the legends, only his head is buried here, while his body lies in the **Habibi Neccar cave** (Habibi Neccar Mağrası) on the hillside 1km east. A minor Muslim holy place, the cave was once home to the solitary prophet and exists now as a shrine.

Greek Orthodox Church

Hükümet Cad • 2 daily masses Mon–Sat, 1 on Sun

Numerous churches, synagogues and mosques dotted throughout Antakya bear witness to the Hatay's long history of toleration. Some four thousand Christians live in the region, 1500 of them in Antakya itself. The majority are Greek Orthodox, and their substantial nineteenth-century **church** is one of the more impressive of Antakya's remaining religious buildings, containing some beautiful Russian icons.

Archeological Museum

On the western side of the river • Tues–Sun: summer 9am–6pm; winter 8.30am–noon & 1.30–5pm • ₺8

The collection of locally unearthed Roman mosaics in Antakya's **Archeological Museum** (Arkeoloji Müzesi) ranks among the best of its kind in the world. Still in almost pristine condition, they make for an impressive display, laid out throughout the first four rooms of the museum.

6

Most of the **mosaics** were unearthed at the suburb of Daphne (now Harbiye), which was Antioch's main holiday resort in Roman times. That origin is reflected in the sense of leisured decadence that pervades many of the Greco-Roman mythology scenes. A good example is the so-called **Buffet Mosaic** (no. 4), a vivid depiction of the rape of Ganymede, abducted by Zeus in the form of an eagle, and a banquet scene showing different courses of fish, ham, eggs and artichokes. Memorable images in room 3 include a fine portrait of **Thetis and Oceanus** (no. 1), and a fascinating depiction of the **Evil Eye** (no. 6) – a superstition that still has remarkable resonance in modern Turkey. Room 4 continues with an inebriated Dionysos, too drunk to stand (no. 12), and Orpheus surrounded by animals entranced by the beauty of his music (no. 23). Climb the spiral staircase in the corner for a bird's-eye view of the floor mosaic.

After the mosaics, the rest of the museum seems a little mundane, though stand-out pieces include two stone lions, which served as column bases during the eighth century BC, and the Antakya sarcophagus, where the remains of two women and a man, as well as the fine gold jewellery with which they were buried, are displayed.

Sen Piyer Kilisesi

At the northeast edge of Antakya • Tues–Sun: summer 9am–6.30pm; winter 8.30am–12.30pm & 1.30–5.30pm • ₺8 • To drive, head 2km northeast on Kurtuluş Cad, then turn right and drive 5min to the church; or catch a dolmuş as far as the turn-off on Kurtuluş Cad

The **Sen Piyer Kilisesi**, a forty-minute walk from the centre, is the famous cave-church of St Peter, from which it's said that the apostle preached to the Christian population of Antioch. Whether the tale is true – and the exact dates of his stay in the city – remain open to question. Theologians do seem to agree that he spent some time in Antioch between 47 and 54 AD, founding one of the world's first Christian communities with Paul and Barnabas.

Inside the church, water drips down the cave walls and the cool atmosphere provides a welcome break from the heat of summer. Beneath your feet you'll be able to discern traces of fragmentary **mosaic** thought to date from the fifth century AD, while a kind of font set in the floor, to the right of the altar, is fed by a spring said to have curative properties.

Carved into the mountainside above the church (ask for directions at the ticket office), there's a relief thought by some to depict Charon, ferryman of the River Styx at the entrance to the underworld.

Harbiye

10km south of Antakya • Catch a minibus from Antakya's köy garajı, or flag down a dolmuş travelling southwest along Kurtuluş Cad

HARBİYE, a short way south of Antakya, is a beautiful gorge to which revellers and holidaymakers flocked in Roman times, drawn by shady cypress and laurel groves dotted with waterfalls and pools. The Romans built a temple to Apollo here, since it was held to be the setting for the god's pursuit of Daphne. According to the myth, Daphne, when seized by amorous Apollo, prayed for deliverance; in answer to her prayers, Peneus transformed her into a laurel tree. Another legend relates that Harbiye was where Paris gave the golden apple to Aphrodite, and indirectly precipitated the Trojan War. Later, and possibly with more basis in fact, Mark Antony and Cleopatra are said to have been married here.

Today, Harbiye makes for a pleasant day-trip from Antakya, especially for those with their own transport, and is famous for its Daphne (Defne) soap – a natural toiletry made from the scented fruit of the laurel tree, sold in regional bazaars.

Vakıflı

26km southwest of Antakya, or 6km north of Samandağ • Regular dolmuşes run from Antakya's köy garajı to Samandağ on the coast, where you can catch another dolmuş to Vakıflı

The tiny village of **VAKIFLI**, with its mix of dilapidated mudbrick and timber houses and modern concrete villas, may not look impressive but it possesses unique cultural significance. In fact, the unassuming community, set amid orange groves on the lush lower slopes of Musa Dağı, is Turkey's sole surviving **Armenian village**, founded almost two thousand years ago. The villagers held out against the Turkish forces during the 1915 Turkish deportations and massacres of the Armenians, until they were evacuated to Port Said by French and British warships. Most returned in 1919 when the Hatay became part of French-mandated Syria. When the Hatay joined the Turkish Republic in 1939, most of the region's Armenians fled, but the majority of Vakıflı's inhabitants chose to stay.

While the village holds few sights of interest, or many residents aged under sixty, its original architecture and traditional lifestyles provide a fascinating peek into community life. If you do choose to visit the village, be respectful – this is a living community, not a mere curiosity.

Saint Simeon monastery

29km southwest of Antakya • Daily 24hr • Free • No public transport; a day-trip by taxi from Antakya will cost around ₺130; to drive, turn south at Uzunbğ, just beyond Samandağ, continue uphill for 4km, then branch right along a dirt track for another 2km

One of the more bizarre aspects of early Christianity was the craze for sitting on pillars. Having emerged in Antioch during the fourth century, the art was perfected by **Simeon Stylites the Younger**, whose **monastery**, listed as a UNESCO World Heritage Site in 2011, perches on a high ridge southwest of Antakya.

Simeon the Younger first chained himself to a rock in the wilderness in an act of ascetic retreat, then ascended progressively higher pillars before reaching a final height of some thirteen metres. He lived chained to the top of this pillar for 25 years, meditating and sporadically castigating the citizens of Antioch for their moral turpitude. The base of the pillar still remains, surrounded by the complex octagonal layout of the monastery that grew up around Simeon as growing numbers of curious pilgrims flocked to share his enlightenment. It's possible to climb on top of the diminutive stump, which is just wide enough to lie down and reap the same views of the Orontes valley and of Mount Cassius looming out of the Mediterranean that Simeon must have enjoyed over fifteen centuries ago.

ARRIVAL AND INFORMATION

ANTAKYA AND AROUND

By plane Antakya's airport (often listed as Hatay airport), 19km north of the centre, is connected by the Havaş shuttle bus (timed to meet arrivals; ₺8) with İnönü and Atatürk caddesis in the town centre. Alternatively, a metered taxi from the airport will cost around ₺50 and takes around 25min, depending on traffic.
Destinations İstanbul (3 daily; 1hr 45min).

By bus Antakya's new *otogar*, 4km north of the town centre, is served by municipal buses from the centre (₺1.50). Many bus companies offer free service buses direct to central hotels, while if you buy tickets from the bus company offices at the old *otogar* on the northern edge of the town centre, they often include free shuttles to the new *otogar*. As well as domestic services, there are regular daily departures to towns in Syria (see p.404), and several weekly buses to Amman in Jordan. Regular minibuses run from the *köy garajı* (village garage) to İskenderun, Harbiye, Samandağ, Belen, Bakras and other destinations.
Destinations Adana (hourly; 3hr); Aleppo, Syria (3 daily; 3hr); Amman, Jordan (3 weekly; 12hr); Ankara (9 daily, 13hr); Antalya (14 daily; 14hr); Gaziantep (half-hourly; 4hr); İskenderun (every 20min; 1hr); İstanbul (5 daily; 22hr); Konya (5 daily; 15hr); Riyadh, Saudi Arabia (3 weekly; 24hr); Samandağ (hourly; 1hr).

Car rental Titus Turizm, under the *Büyük Antakya Oteli*, Atatürk Cad 8 (☎0326 213 9141), or several companies at the airport.

Tourist office Inconveniently located on a roundabout at the end of Atatürk Bulvarı, a 10min walk northwest of the museum (Mon–Fri 8am–noon & 1.30–5pm; ☎0326 216 6098).

ACCOMMODATION

Antik Grand Hürriyet Cad 10 ☎ 0326 215 7575, ⓦantikgrand.com. While the shabby facade with its blacked-out windows may not be particularly enticing, inside this boutique-style hotel is surprisingly stylish. Incredibly spacious rooms are furnished with chic dark wood, deep red linens and sparkling new en-suites, and a generous buffet breakfast of *mezes* and Turkish breads is included in the price. ₺120

6

Liwan Hotel Silahli Kuvvetler Cad 5 ☎0326 215 7777, ⊛theliwanhotel.com. This 1920s residence has everything you'd expect from a boutique hotel, with plush furnishings accented by French, Armenian and Italian antiques, and stylish, individually designed rooms. Spacious, pristine bathrooms and all conveniences make up for the slightly lacklustre views from the street-side balconies, while the shaded location ensures the rooms stay cool and airy, even in the blistering heat. **€95**

Mozaik Otel Silahli İstiklâl Cad 18 ☎0326 215 5020, ⊛mozaikotel.com. With its colourful mosaics inside and out, ornamental embossed wallpapers, sloping ceilings and sequinned embroidery adorning the bedspreads, this characterful option manages to land firmly on the stylish end of kitsch. Prices are open to negotiation during slow periods, so try your luck. **₺140**

Saray Hotel Hürriyet Cad 3 ☎0326 214 9001. Cheap and cheerful, if you can get over the drab furnishings and sickly peach-painted hallways, this friendly place is a great-value budget option, with free wi-fi, a/c and breakfast included. Call ahead if you're arriving late, and they'll meet you at the door. **₺70**

★ **Savon Hotel** Kurtuluş Cad 192 ☎0326 214 6355, ⊛savonhotel.com.tr. Every centimetre of this hotel – a former soap and olive oil factory – oozes elegance, from the pretty stone-paved courtyard flanked by wrought-iron gates to the striking entrance hall with its domed ceilings, ornate candlesticks and rich pink upholstery. The decadent double rooms, with marble bathrooms and balcony views over the mountains, offer far more than you'd expect for the price tag, making it an affordable splurge for those who typically travel on a budget. Welcoming staff complete the air of laidback luxury. **€100**

Şeker Palas Oteli İstiklâl Cad 79 ☎0326 215 1603. With all rooms costing a measly ₺20 per person, this is the place to go to if you're in need of a bargain bed. You get what you pay for, as the rooms are sparse and slightly claustrophobic, and the basic shared bathrooms are quite run-down. It's certainly good value though, and the friendly proprietor does his best to liven things up with his eclectic collection of knick-knacks on proud display around the hotel. **₺40**

EATING AND DRINKING

Antakya's renowned food shows its Arab influence in many regional specialities. Dishes to look out for include *Ispanak borani*, a soup-like stew of spinach, chickpeas, shredded meat, yoghurt and lemon juice; *serimsek börek*, a sort of chicken-filled samosa; and *kağıt kebap*, kebabs cooked in greased-paper packages.

Antakya Evi Silhali Kuvvetler Cad 3 ☎0326 214 1350. A pocket of tranquillity just off the busy central shopping streets, this well-turned-out Turkish restaurant has a good range of kebabs for around ₺10 and a pretty stone courtyard dominated by a tribe of free-roaming tortoises. Try the *Antioch kebap*, a *köfte* of minced lamb stuffed with cheese, walnuts and olives, washed down with a cold pint of *Efes* (₺7). Daily 9am–midnight.

★ **Antik Han** Hürriyet Cad ☎0326 215 8538, ⊛antikhan.com.tr. An underwhelming entrance stairwell opens out into an elegant stone courtyard and rooftop terrace reminiscent of an Italian villa. The varied menu features *ızgara* (grills) from ₺12, and an impressive array of *mezes* (₺7 each) including regional specialities *muhammara*, a fiery purée of walnuts, hot pepper and wheat, and *bakla*, a purée of broad beans, garlic, tahini and parsley. There's no alcohol licence, so sip an indulgent cup of buttermilk (₺3) instead. Daily 7am–midnight.

Cabaret Hürriyet Cad 26 ☎0326 215 5540. Climbing the crumbling staircase from the main street transports you into a dimly lit music grotto, with retro decor (old gramophones, amps and record covers adorning the walls), a well-stocked bar and twinkling sitars seeping from the stereo. Head to the courtyard around the back for cheap and tasty eats throughout the day (including a ₺9 kebab, salad and drink meal deal) or come in the evening to enjoy live performances by local rock bands. Daily 7am–2am.

Kral Künefe Kemal Paşa Cad ☎0326 214 7517. This long-established pudding shop is a great place to try the ubiquitous *künefe* (₺5), a regional favourite of shredded wheat and soft, mild cheese that's far sweeter and tastier than its ingredients suggest, or *haleb burması* (Aleppo roll, ₺2), a sweet confection stuffed with pistachios. The outdoor seating is crammed with locals come lunchtime, so

CROSSING INTO SYRIA

At the time of writing, Syria was in the midst of a civil war. Travel within the country remained theoretically possible – buses and taxis were still running between the two countries and the border to the east of Antakya at Cilvegözü/Baba al Hawa was open – but highly inadvisable. As of 2012, more than 25,000 Syrian refugees were housed in camps in the Hatay province. As and when Syria does reopen to travellers, the situation regarding visas and border crossings is very unlikely to be the same as it was before the war, so seek up-to-date advice from local tourist offices before heading out.

grab a takeaway bag and wander out to the benches on the street. Mon–Sat 8am–10pm.

Özsüt Cumhuriyet Alanı 2 ☎ 0326 213 5000. A recently opened dessert bar with plenty of balcony seating overlooking the river and the Ata Köprüsü bridge, the perfect place to tuck into some traditional Turkish desserts – try the *muhallebi* (₺5.50), a creamy rice-flour and milk pudding, or the *kadayıfı*, a sweet bread-based dessert (₺5). The real show-stopper though, is the location – the restaurant is housed in the Gündüz building, an impressive Art-Deco cinema with geometric friezes and porthole windows that once served as the parliament building for the Hatay Republic. Daily 8am–1am.

Sultan Sofrası İstiklâl Cad 20/A ☎ 0326 213 8469, ⊛ sultansofrasi.com A tour-group favourite for good reason, where a hearty array of regional specialities is laid out for your delectation; there's no menu, but the affable, English-speaking staff will happily talk you through the options. Expect to pay around ₺7 for a meat dish – *aşur*, a stringy stew of chickpeas, meat, walnuts and wheat, is a good choice, but even a side of rice and chickpeas (₺3) is delicious. Mon–Sat 11am–9.30pm.

DIRECTORY

Banks and exchange İstiklâl and Atatürk cads hold several banks, and you can change money at the weekends at the *döviz* on Kurtuluş Cad.

Hospital The Devlet Hastane (State Hospital) is a couple of kilometres southeast of the centre.

Internet Modanet, on Hürriyet Cad, and Shownet, between the PTT and the Konak Sineması, on the west bank of the river, both offer wi-fi.

Police Selçuk Cad; emergency number for foreigners ☎ 0326 213 5953.

Post office Northwest of the roundabout at the western end of the Ata Köprüs, across the square from the archeological museum (daily 9am–8pm).

Swimming The open-air pool on Gunduz Cad next to the municipal park (summer daily 10am–3pm; ₺8) has lockers where you can leave your gear if you're heading out on an evening bus.

South Central Anatolia

HOT-AIR BALLOONING

South Central Anatolia

At first sight, the central Anatolian plateau seems an unpromising prospect. A large area is virtual desert, while much of the central plateau is steppe, blitzed by cold and heavy snowfall in winter and suffering water shortages in summer. Yet this region holds two landscapes any traveller to the country should visit – the azure Lakeland, where the lakeside village of Eğirdir is a popular starting point for hikers following the St Paul Trail, and the unique rock formations of Cappadocia, one of Turkey's highest-profile tourist attractions. The cities too are well worth exploring. Kayseri holds a series of towering fortresses and venerated tombs, while Konya, once the capital of the Selçuk Empire, is the home of the Whirling Dervish sect, the Mevlevî, and the epicentre of Sufic mystical practice and teaching throughout the Middle East.

Further east, the area between the extinct volcanoes of Erciyes Dağı and the Melendiz range is **Cappadocia**. Here, water and wind have created a land of fantastical forms from the soft rock known as tuff, including forests of "fairy chimneys", table mountains, canyon-like valleys and castle-rocks. From the seventh to the eleventh centuries AD, this was a place of refuge for Christians during Arab and Turkish invasions into the steppe. Churches and dwellings carved into the rock, particularly by monastic communities, and unearthly landscapes make it an irresistible tourist draw. At its northwest fringes, the modern city of **Kayseri**, set below the imposing volcanic peak of Mount Erciyes, harbours a wealth of Islamic monuments.

Lakeland

After years of isolation, Turkish **Lakeland** has been discovered by birdwatchers, trekkers and skiers, and many tourists now stop off en route from Cappadocia and Konya to the south coast around Antalya or Fethiye. Facilities are quickly improving, especially in **Eğirdir**, but the area as a whole remains unspoiled by tourism, making it ideal for quiet unhurried holidays away from the seething coastal resorts. As well as the eye-catching **lakes** themselves, it holds the remains of Pisidian cities (notably at **Sagalassos** and **Antioch ad Pisidiam**), and the provincial town of **Afyon**, a popular winter destination with its acclaimed thermal spa hotels.

Brief history

Despite Lakeland's inhospitable nature, it has been populated as long as anywhere in Anatolia. In early Paleolithic times, the lakes provided a livelihood for primitive

WHIRLING DERVISHES, KONYA

Highlights

Sagalossos Perched high above the lakes region, these remote ruins are among the most beautifully sited in Central Anatolia. **See p.416**

Eğirdir Eat fillets of crisply fried lake fish as the sun sets over Lake Eğirdir. **See p.416**

St Paul Trail Follow in the footsteps of the apostle over the Toros Mountains, to reach stunning Lake Eğirdir. **See p.421**

Whirling dervishes, Konya Watch the dervishes whirl each December in their spiritual home. **See p.426**

Göreme Open-Air Museum The frescoes inside Göreme's cave churches are a vibrant reminder of the region's Christian past. **See p.437**

Hot-air ballooning An unforgettable experience – the interplay of light and shadow over Cappadocia's geological fairy-tale landscape, admired from the basket of a balloon. **See p.440**

Mustafapaşa One of Cappadocia's most attractive villages, sporting a wonderful concentration of old Greek houses. **See p.449**

Ihlara valley Don't miss the natural beauty of this fertile gorge, enhanced by its rock-cut Byzantine churches. **See p.454**

HIGHLIGHTS ARE MARKED ON THE MAP ON PP.410–411

hunters and fishermen, and during the Bronze Age, the **Hittites**, a race who once rivalled the Egyptians, chose the plateau as their homeland.

By the early historical period, northern Lakeland had been settled by the **Pisidians**, mountain people who sold their services as mercenaries throughout the eastern Mediterranean. Their strategically situated settlements were difficult to subdue, and Xenophon described them as perennially obstinate troublemakers, who succeeded in keeping their towns independent despite the continuing encroachments of the Persian Empire.

HIGHLIGHTS
1. Sagalossos
2. Eğirdir
3. St Paul Trail
4. Whirling dervishes, Konya
5. Göreme Open-Air Museum
6. Hot-air ballooning
7. Mustafapaşa
8. Ihlara valley

Afyon

Dominated by an ancient citadel that's built atop a tall, dark and imposing rock, **AFYON** certainly makes an impact, and it remains impressive on closer inspection. Clean and relaxed, it retains much interesting Ottoman architecture as well as some attractive mosques. Until recently, the city bore the resounding name of Afyon Karahisar, or "**Opium Black Fortress**". First fortified by the Hittites, the towering rock was later occupied by the Romans. The Byzantines built most of the present-day fortress, which served as an imperial treasury for both Selçuks and Ottomans.

SOUTH CENTRAL ANATOLIA

For three weeks leading up to August 26, 1922, Afyon was Atatürk's headquarters, prior to the last, decisive battle of the independence war, fought against the Greeks at nearby Dumlupınar.

The fortress

Afyon's **fortress** (220m), scaled via some 700 steps on the southern face of the rock – the 20min hike is best avoided in the heat of the day – is thought to stand on the site of the Hittite fortress of Khapanouwa, built by king Mursil II during the second millennium BC. The rock was subsequently fortified by the Phrygians, the Byzantines and the Turks, but all that remain are a few crenellated walls and towers. On the way up look out for hoopoes among the varied birdlife, and at the top for votive rags, representing wishes, tied to trees. At prayer time as many as eighty minarets resound and echo off the rock to dramatic effect.

The old town

7

A warren of tiny streets, the **old town** of Afyon surrounds the fortress rock. Several remarkably preserved mosques stand near here, complemented by many somewhat less distinguished ones in the bazaar area.

Ulu Cami

Opposite the base of the steps leading up the side of the rock • Outside of prayer time, wait for the caretaker to let you in

The **Ulu Cami**, a typically square Selçuk construction built between 1272 and 1277, has been restored. While its originally flat roof is now pitched, it retains forty original carved wooden columns with stalactite capitals and beams that support a fine geometric ceiling.

Mevlevî Camii

Slightly downhill from Ulu Cami • Open at prayer times

The **Mevlevî Camii** is a double-domed mosque notable for its pyramid-roofed *son cemaat yeri*, a porch in which latecomers pray – literally the "place of last congregation". The adjoining *semahane*, or ceremonial hall, has a walnut-wood floor on which Mevlevî dervishes once performed their whirling ceremony. This building has now been converted into the **Mevlevî Museum** (Mevlevî Müzesi), exhibiting musical instruments and the ceremonial costumes of the dervishes. After the son of the Mevlâna, Sultan Veled, introduced the branch of Islamic mysticism to the city from Konya, Afyon became the second-largest centre of the Mevlevî order.

Archeological Museum

Kurtuluş Cad, 1km east of the centre • Tues–Sun 8am–noon & 1.30–5.30pm • ₺3 • ☎ 0272 215 1191

Afyon's **Archeological Museum** (Arkeoloji Müzesi) is well worth visiting. Despite rather dimly lit display cabinets, the objects are attractively laid out and the explanatory signboards well written. The most interesting finds are Roman, excavated at nearby Çardalı and Kovalık Höyük, dating from the third and fourth centuries AD. This region was (and remains) the heart of the marble-quarrying industry in Anatolia, and the museum garden is full of noteworthy (but unlabelled) marble work and statuary from the Roman, Phrygian, Byzantine and Ottoman eras.

Gedik Ahmet Paşa Külliyesi

Kurtuluş Cad, near the centre in its own patch of parkland

The **Gedik Ahmet Paşa Külliyesi** was built for one of the viziers of Mehmet the Conqueror in 1477. Adjoining it are a stone *medrese* and a functioning hamam – the original marble floors are in good condition, but it's otherwise in a bad state of repair. The complex's mosque, identified as the **İmaret Camii**, has a fluted minaret dashed with zigzagging blue İznik tiles.

THE OPIUM POPPIES OF AFYON

A quarter of the world's legal production of **opium** is harvested from the poppy fields surrounding Afyon. While the authorities are reluctant to tout the city's eponymous enterprise as a tourist attraction, there are still tell-tale signs of civic pride in the traditional industry: a close look at the fountain in the town square reveals that it is a graceful bronze sculpture of poppy seed-pods.

If you want to take a look at the crop, in May/June head out of town for around 5km on the Sandıklı road, and the open fields of poppies are clearly visible from the road. Much more grows around Yalvaç and in the Toros mountains. The fields are regularly patrolled by officials, who check whether the seed heads have been illegally "bled" for heroin.

Zafer Müzesi

Next to tourist office, on Milli Egemenlik Cad • Daily 8.30am–noon & 1.30–5.30pm • ₺1

The **Zafer Müzesi** is a museum that commemorates Atatürk's brief stay in Afyon, housed in the building in which he planned his victory at Dumlupınar in the summer of 1922. His office has been preserved, and weapons and other paraphernalia from the war, as well as old photos of Atatürk and Afyon, are on show.

ARRIVAL AND DEPARTURE

AFYON

By train The station is at the far north end of Ordu Bulvarı, about 500m east of the centre.
Destinations Adana (1 daily; 11hr); İstanbul (1 daily; 8hr 30min); Konya (2 daily; 6hr).
By bus or dolmuş The otogar, 500m east of town on the çevre yolu (ring road), is linked to the middle of town by a dolmuş service marked "Sanayi/PTT". Free service buses run from the otogar to Hükümet Meydanı, the main square. To

reach the otogar from the town centre, take bus #9 from behind the post office.
Destinations Adana (10 daily; 7hr); Alanya (5 daily; 6hr 30min); Ankara (21 daily; 4hr); Antalya (hourly; 5hr); Aydın (4 daily; 5hr); Bursa (6 daily; 4hr); Fethiye (2 daily; 7hr); Isparta (6 daily; 2hr); İstanbul (20 daily; 8hr); İzmir (4 daily; 6hr); Konya (14 daily; 3hr); Kuşadası (2 daily; 7hr); Kütahya (6 daily; 1hr 30min); Marmaris (2 daily; 9hr).

INFORMATION

Tourist information A tourist booth in Hükümet Meyd (Mon–Fri 8.30am–noon & 1.30–5.30pm; ☏0272 215 7600) dishes out town maps and a brochure to the "Afyon

Tourism Route" (see p.414), north of the city.
Banks and money The major banks and ATMs are on Banklar Caddesi.

ACCOMMODATION

HOTELS

Cakmak Marble Hotel Süleyman Gonçer Cad 2, just east of Hükümet Meyd ☏0272 214 3300, ⓦcakmak marblehotel.com. The most upmarket central option, this 4-star hotel is in dire need of some TLC, with a shabby lobby area and grubby basement hamam. Centred around a garish tangerine-painted mezzanine, the rooms themselves are actually clean, stylish and well furnished, but hardly remarkable for the price. ₺160
Hotel Soydan Karagözoğlu Sok 2 ☏0272 215 6070, ⓦsoydantermal.com. If you need to stay in the centre, this place is easy to find, right near the tourist information booth, and run by friendly, German-speaking staff. Rooms are good value, but there's quite a difference between them, so ask to look before you check in. ₺90

SPA HOTELS

Hüdai Termal Otel 45km southwest of Afyon ☏0272 535 7300, ⓦhudai.sandikli.bel.tr. Comfortable rooms and an attached treatment centre, with mud baths that reach up to 50°C, a naturally heated thermal pool and spring water baths each with individual curative properties. ₺100
Termal Resort Oruçoğlu 14km north of Afyon, on the Kütahya road ☏0272 251 5050, ⓦorucoglu.com.tr. Part of the Ömer/Gecek Kaplıcıları hot springs complex, with accommodation ranging from simple chalets to half- and full-board luxurious rooms with air conditioning, balconies and thermal water on tap. Use of the hamam, sauna, indoor and outdoor pools is included, and massages and treatment packages are available. Rates include half board. €135

EATING AND DRINKING

İkbal Lokantası Close to Hükümet Meyd on Uzun Çarşı ☏0272 215 1205. Established in 1922, this old-fashioned

place is the most famous restaurant in town. It exudes a period charm rare in Turkey, with a snaking Art Deco

7

7

THERMAL TOURISM

Thanks to its natural thermal waters, the Afyon region has become synonymous with **thermal tourism**. Hot springs, whose waters bubble up to temperatures of 50–80°C and have a high content of fluoride, bromide and calcium salts, are located in four different districts of the city. Marketed for their curative properties, the natural springs have given rise to assorted spa hotels and treatment centres providing hydrotherapy exercise pools, whirlpool massage and therapeutic mud baths, used to treat muscular disorders, injuries and even neurological issues, as well as for pain relief and rehabilitation. Even drinking the water supposedly reaps health benefits, and mineral water from this region is bottled and sold all over Turkey.

If you don't fancy visiting one of the region's spa hotels (see p.413), the deep mineral **mud baths** at Hudai Kaplıcıları (48km south of Afyon, beyond Sandıklı off the Denizli road) are accessible for a ₺4 cover charge.

---

staircase leading up to the grand family dining area. The grills are excellent (₺15–20) and the famed puddings (₺7), all served with a generous slice of thick Afyon cream, delicious. Daily 8am–10pm.

İnyo Café Ordu Bul 10 ☎0272 213 0133. This surprisingly modern café, one of the few places you can grab a decent cappuccino (₺5), sticks out amid the drab city sprawl. A range of lunchtime eats is on offer and there's plenty of shady outdoor seating. Daily 8am–10pm.

Around Afyon

The most interesting side trip from Afyon is to a series of sixth-century **Phrygian sites** (Frig Vadisi) in the vicinity of İhsanıye. There are also several areas of rock formations similar to those in Cappadocia, and some rock-cut churches, promoted by the local tourism authorities as the *Afyon Turizm Kuşağı* (Afyon Tourism Route). As village roads are badly signed, and the locals unused to giving directions, the easiest way to make the trip is to form a group and hire a **taxi** for the day (around €80).

Ayazini

33km north of Afyon • Turn right off the minor Afyon–Eskişehir road at Kunduzlu

The modern village of **AYAZİNİ** is home to some remarkable Phrygian remains. As you approach the village, **cave houses** and a well-preserved ninth-century **Byzantine church** are visible across fields of opium poppies. Closer observation reveals lion reliefs and the scars from excavations by locals and archeologists, who have found coins and other objects in the rooms.

Kaya

32km north of Afyon • Turn left off the minor Afyon–Eskişehir road, north of the turn for Ayazini

The most noteworthy of several Phrygian ruins near the village of **Kaya** are the rock-cut tomb of **Arslantaş** (Lion Stone), flanked by another relief of lions, two enormous beasts snarling at each other with bared teeth, and the nearby cult monument called **Arslankaya** (Lion Rock), featuring a high relief of the goddess Cybele flanked by two more enormous lions. Close to Arslankaya is Lake Emre, set in the village of **DÖĞER**, where the remains of a fifteenth-century Ottoman *kervansaray* can also be found.

Isparta

The largely modern town of **ISPARTA** is set on a flat plain that's dominated by 2635m Mount Davraz to the south. Its only hint of romantic appeal lies in its chief industries: rosewater and oil, distilled here for over a century, and carpets, manufactured in industrial quantities. While the lakeside town of **Eğirdir**, 12km east, makes a more appealing base from which to explore the region, Isparta's surrounds blossom with colour come the annual rose harvest.

The Greek quarter

Until the 1923 exchange of populations many **Greeks** lived in Isparta, and their old residential quarter is a fifteen-minute walk southwest from the town centre, near the Devlet Hastanesi (State Hospital). The once handsome lath-and-plaster houses are now crumbling, but there are a couple of restored nineteenth-century churches to admire.

Archeological museum

Kenan Evren Cad, 500m northeast of the Belediye building • Tues–Sat 8.30am–5pm • ₺4 • ☎ 0246 218 3437

Isparta's **Archeological Museum** (Arkeoloji Müzesi) holds a reasonable collection of local finds, including some fine Roman grave stelae, plus assorted items from a nearby Bronze Age burial site. The ethnography section includes a wonderful felt-and-reed *yurt*, which, along with some fine old carpets and kilims, attests to the region's bygone nomadic culture.

ARRIVAL AND DEPARTURE
ISPARTA

7

By train No trains were running to Isparta when this book went to press.

By bus or dolmuş The *otogar* is a few kilometres northwest of town on Süleyman Demirel Bulvarı – free service buses run in to the centre and to the minibus terminal (*köy garajı*) in the middle of town, 500m southwest of Kaymakkapı Meydanı, from where you can take a dolmuş to Burdur, Eğirdir, Ağlasun or Atabey, all

around 40min away. There have been tales of travellers being ticketed to Eğirdir, but then left stranded in Isparta's *otogar*. If this happens to you, head for the *köy garajı* and onto Eğirdir by dolmuş (20min, last bus leaves around 7.30pm).

Destinations Afyon (6 daily; 2hr); Antalya (hourly; 2hr 30min); Beyşehir (6 daily; 2hr 30min); Kayseri (5 daily; 9hr); Konya (4 daily; 4hr).

INFORMATION

Tourist office On the fifth floor of the elaborate Valikonağı, or governor's building, next to the main square (Mon–Fri 8am–noon & 1.30–5pm; ☎ 0248 232 2210).

Largely unhelpful staff offer a town map and English-language brochure, but little else.

ACCOMMODATION

Hotel Artan Cengiz Topel Cad 12/B ☎ 0246 232 5700, ⊛ hotelartan.com. A good budget option, tucked away in a quiet side street off the main square, this place is clean

and well equipped, with polite, English-speaking staff. Rooms have a dated 1980s feel, but are nonetheless clean and functional. ₺8

ISPARTA: THE ROSE CITY

Endearingly nicknamed the **Rose City**, Isparta ranks among the world's biggest growers of the renowned Damascena rose, and exports rose oil all around the globe. Eco-friendly British brand Lush are buyers, and the rosewater is shipped out to the grand mosque at Mecca. With a 200-year history of rose oil distillation, **harvest time**, in May/June, in Isparta is more than just a boost to the economy (a mere 1kg of rose oil retails for around €8000, making it a profitable venture). It's also a time of celebration for the villagers' featuring a two-day **Isparta Rose Festival**, and a plethora of home-made rose marmalades, ice creams and cosmetics hit the markets.

Alia (⊛ essentialtravel.nl), a collective founded by Dutch rose specialist Joanne Klein Wolterink in conjunction with Isparta's Sebat Rose factory and Dutch eco-cosmetic brand, Natucos, run small-group **rose harvest tours** (from €20 for a half-day tour, with lunch; local homestays can also be arranged). The tours include the chance to help villagers with the morning rose harvest; explore the factory, including a demonstration of a traditional distillation kettle; sample organic rosewater cosmetics; and, most entertainingly, frolic on a 30cm-thick "bed" of roses.

Tours are also available for the lavender harvest (July/Aug) and the chamomile harvest (April/May). As this book went to press, a luxury wellness centre, set amid the factory's acres of plantations, was expected to open shortly.

Basmacıoğlu Hotel Süleyman Demirel Bul 81 ☎0246 223 2700, ⓦbasmacioglu.com.tr. A swanky boutique hotel offering standard, deluxe and suite rooms for very reasonable prices. The elegant entrance hall gives way to fancy furnishings and spotless bathtubs, making this the best of the city's limited options. ₺120

EATING AND DRINKING

Isparta's *fırın* kebabs (or *tandır* kebab), in which the meat – traditionally lamb or goat – is cooked in deep clay ovens throughout the summer, are delicious, while its largely alcohol-free restaurants serve huge jugs of Üzüm Hoşafi (sweet grape juice) with their meals.

★ **Ferah** Üzüm Pazarı 1, just next to the main square ☎0246 218 1270. One of the best local restaurants, this place is a dab hand at *fırın* kebabs (₺20), and they'll happily let you peek into their traditional clay oven, just by the entrance. Squeeze in between the regulars and sip some of the town's best *Üzüm hoşafi* (₺2.50), grape juice served in traditional copper jugs and swimming with sugary raisins. Mon–Sat 11am–8pm.

Hacı Benlioğlu Bedesten Civarı 4 ☎0246 218 1825. This stylish kebab house couples friendly service with great food and bustling outdoor seating. Try the oven-cooked *az yağlu* (lamb kebab, ₺20) served up with local speciality *kabune pilavı* (rice with shredded meat and chickpeas). Daily 8am–10pm.

Kebabçı Kadir Bedesten Civarı 8 ☎0246 218 2460. An atmospheric option for an evening meal, with garden seating right on the main square, this family-run place offers a wide range of *fırın* kebabs (₺10–20), and specializes in home-made *helva* (a traditional crumbly sweet made with tahini and various fillings; ₺5), which they also sell boxed to take away. Daily 10am–10pm.

Sagalassos

30km south of Isparta, 55km southwest of Eğirdir • Daily 7.30am–6pm • ₺5 • ⓦsagalassos.be • Dolmuşes run from Isparta to Ağlasun, from where taxis run 7km uphill to the site (₺15 return, including wait)

Identified as the first Pisidian city, the striking ruins of **SAGALASSOS** were first discovered in 1806. The population of Termessos (see p.366) likely moved here in 244 AD after an earthquake, but it was abandoned soon after, with the population moving downhill to the present town. Wear sturdy shoes if you visit, as the site is quite rugged and vertical.

The site

The **site** of Sagalassos is well labelled, with illustrations that show the buildings in their original state. The 96m-wide **theatre**, right of the entrance, remains much as the 244 AD earthquake left it, with seating mostly in place, but the stage building rather more wrecked. Two restored **nymphaea** (fountain-houses) here have retained their floor mosaic almost intact, along with the alcoves and a major inscription. Walking west you come to the **upper agora**, of which the second, huge nymphaeum formed one side. Two ceremonial arches opened off, and a pagoda-like monument stood in the centre.

Just above, north of the upper agora, a Doric **temple** of the second century BC is incorporated into the city walls. As you walk down from the upper agora, you'll see fragments of beautiful Roman friezes laid out like a giant jigsaw. Below the main track is the **lower agora** and adjacent baths; earthenware pipes and hypocausts reveal how water was distributed and heated. A temple with Corinthian columns dedicated to Antonius Pius stands beyond this area, while straight ahead down the steps are the **necropolis** and a hill that locals say is the site of an Alexander monument – they believe a gold statue dedicated to Alexander is waiting to be discovered.

Eğirdir

Few places can enjoy as idyllic a setting as **EĞİRDİR**, with its vast lake encircled by undulating mountains. Long heralded by locals as Anatolia's best-kept secret, this humble lakeside town has a reputation for enticing travellers to stay a lot longer than they'd intended. That's not surprising when you consider the plethora of hikes – Eğirdir

7

s a major stop on the acclaimed long-distance **St Paul Trail** (see box, p.421) – bike outes and watersports in close proximity.

A kilometre-long causeway divides the town, separating the mainland market town, with its historical sites and harbour filled with colourful fishing boats, from **Yeşilada**, tiny island reached by a sliver of land running out onto the lake, which is home to most of the local pensions and lakeside restaurants. Aside from its scenic vistas and outdoor activities, Eğirdir's real charm lies in its endearing indifference to modern tourism. You're more likely to find restaurant proprietors sipping tea on the terrace than rustling up business on the streets below, so take heed of the slower pace of life and relish lazy evenings relaxing by the lakeside. Just don't forget your insect repellent; summer nights are swarming with mosquitoes.

Brief history

Founded by the Hittites, Eğirdir was taken by the Phrygians in 1200 BC. Not until Lydian times, however, when it straddled the so-called King's Way from Ephesus to Babylon, did the town become famous for its recreational and accommodation facilities.

Early in the thirteenth century, the town came under the control of the Konya-based Selçuks, who refortified it in its role as a gateway to Pisidia. Shortly thereafter the city reached the height of its fortunes as capital of the **emirate of Felekeddin Dündar**, remaining prominent during the reign of the Hamidoğlu clan. The Byzantines knew the place as **Akrotiri** ("promontory" in Greek) after its obvious geographical feature. That name was originally corrupted in Ottoman times to **Eğridir** (meaning "it's bent"), but was changed again in the mid-1980s to **Eğirdir**, meaning "s/he's spinning", which officialdom thought more dignified.

Eğirdir Lake

Turkey's second-largest freshwater lake, spreading for a vast 488 square kilometres at around 900m above sea level, **Eğirdir Lake** is an expanse of glistening blue framed by dramatic mountain peaks. With its cool clear waters, the lake offers some ideal swimming spots. Come summer, it plays host to **watersports** such as kayaking, windsurfing and catamarans, all on offer for around ₺25 per hour at the Eğirdir Outdoor Centre (see p.418). Alternatively, local fishermen are more than happy to take you out in their boats (₺50 per half-day), and know all the best swimming, fishing and barbecue spots. There's even a growing trend for paragliding when the winds pick up, with tandem flights soaring up over the lake and affording some incredible views over the valley below.

Hızırbey Camii

Adjoining the Dündar Bey Medresi

Notable for its unique walkthrough minaret, the **Hızırbey Camii** has been tastefully restored, with its roof supported by Selçuk wooden pillars, an ornately carved door, wooden porch and İznik-tiled *mihrab*. The earliest building in the *medrese* complex, dating back to 1202, is Eğirdir's six-domed **bathhouse** (daily 8am–10pm), which retains its sixteen original washing basins.

Yeşilada

5min walk across the causeway from the citadel • 8 buses daily from the central *otogar*, the last at 9pm

The island of **Yeşilada** boasts the twelfth-century Byzantine church of **Ayios Stefanos**, now re-roofed but still awaiting internal restoration. The remaining Greek houses are mainly set in the centre of the island in walled gardens dominated by mulberries and grapes, accessed by tiny cobbled lanes. The small pebble **beaches** that border the island are hard on the feet, but the convenience of being able to take a dip from your pension before breakfast compensates.

7

THE MARKETS OF EĞİRDİR

Eğirdir's **weekly market** is held each Thursday. Locals from the surrounding areas pour into the mainland town centre, selling fresh produce, clothing, rosewater soaps from Isparta and just about everything else you can imagine. If they're in season make sure you pick a bag of deliciously sweet locally grown cherries.

Between the end of July and October, a special series of Sunday Pinar Pazars, or **Yörük Markets**, is held for the Yörük mountain tribes to trade produce and stock up for the winter. Single ladies should take care if they attend the women-only market that precedes the tenth and final market; legend has it that this is the negotiation ground for the mothers to discuss potential marriage matches for their sons or daughters.

Beaches

Belediye Plajı on the mainland, 750m northwest of the town centre in the Yazla district, is Eğirdir's least attractive beach. Sandy **Altınkum**, as you head towards the west shore of the lake, is much better, and great for children thanks to its shallow waters and offering umbrellas, pedal-boats and camping. However, its charm is diminished by a holiday-camp ambience and the modern housing development that backs it.

Sivri Dağı

The most popular hike close to Eğirdir scales the heights of **Sivri Dağı** (Needle Mountain), whose rugged peak dominates the skyline to the west of the lake. The nomadic village of **Akpinar**, 7km – or less than two hours' walk – south of town, makes a popular stopoff, part of the way uphill. It consists of just fifty houses clustered around a yurt (Yörük tent), selling *gözleme* and *ayran*, and a small apple orchard, peering down over the lake below.

ARRIVAL AND DEPARTURE

EĞİRDİR

By bus Eğirdir's very central *otogar* is south of the Hızırbey Camii. Eastbound buses stop opposite the Hızırbey Camii, not in front of the *otogar*. Many local pensions offer free pickups; call to let them know you're coming.

Destinations Ankara (4 daily; 7hr); Antalya (8 daily; 3hr); Beyşehir (12 daily; 1hr 30min); Denizli (4 daily; 3hr); Göreme (2 daily; 8hr); İstanbul (1 daily; 10hr); Konya (4 daily; 4hr).

INFORMATION AND TOURS

Tourist office The well-meaning but largely unhelpful office is at 2 Sahil Yolu 13, 5min walk west of town on the Isparta road (Mon–Fri 8.30am–noon & 1.30–5pm; ☏ 0246 311 4388).

Tours Eğirdir Outdoor Centre, opposite the harbour on the mainland (daily 7am–11pm; ☏ 0246 311 6688, ⓦ egidiroutdoorcenter.com). Run by İbrahim and the

team from *Lale/Charley's* pensions, this rental outlet offers everything from bikes, motorbikes, skis and windsurf to full trekking kits including backpacks, sleeping bags and tents. Doubling as a coffee house and travellers' meeting place, they also offer free information and maps on the local area and organize tours, drivers and pickups for hikers and day-trips.

ACCOMMODATION

THE KALE

★ **Charley's Pension** Kale ☏ 0246 311 4611, ⓦ charleyspension.com. Pension owner and all-round Lakeland expert İbrahim speaks excellent French and English, and is the go-to man for all your trekking needs. As such, *Charley's* has a great traveller vibe, with a relaxing terrace and chill-out area overlooking the lake and abundant information on local sights. Rooms are smart, clean and homely, but weekends and the summer season can get busy; call ahead to book, and secure a free pickup from the bus station. €35

★ **Lale Pension** Kale ☏ 0246 311 2406, ⓦ lalehostel .com/lalepension.net. Run by the same team as the nearby *Charley's Pension*, and set on the hillside with incredible views over the lake, *Lale* is a sanctuary for road-weary travellers. The best rooms in town; light and breezy with enormous modern bathrooms and comfy beds cocooned with pillows. Breakfast and lounge areas are available at *Charley's*. €40

YEŞILADA

★ **Ali's Pension** East side ☏ 0246 311 2547, ⓦ alispension.com. A popular and extremely friendl ension housed in a cheerful red building with a pleasant garden breakfast area. Rooms are clean and comfortable, but it's the English-speaking owners that make this place special, with their warm hospitality and genuine desire to help you enjoy your stay. The delicious home cooking is the icing on the cake. ₺85

Choo Choo Pension South side ☎ 0246 311 4926, ✉ huseyinp01@hotmail.com. New renovations have afforded this convivial family-run pension large sparkling bathrooms and spacious, light-filled rooms. Their restaurant, at the front, is the real selling point, with superb home cooking, and breakfast tables set up right on the lakeside. ₺95

Göl Pension South side ☎ 0246 311 2370, ✉ ahmetdavras@hotmail.com. The woman's touch is obvious at this exceedingly friendly, all-female pension run by a mother and her daughters. The simple rooms are pristine yet homely, the pretty terrace offers great lakefront

views and many of the bathrooms are brand new. Best of all are the delicious home-made Turkish breakfasts, included in the price. ₺70

Paris Pension South side ☎ 0246 311 5509. The cheapest option in town, right next door to *Choo Choo*. While this place could do with a revamp, its yellow-painted rooms are bright and cosy. It's good value for the price, and the gracious owners will make you feel right at home. ₺60

Sehsuvar Peace Pension Up the hill just behind *Ali's Pension* ☎ 0246 311 2433, ⊕ peacepension.com. Tucked away in a pretty mulberry-shaded courtyard surrounded by gardens of flowers, this serene pension more than lives up to its name. More akin to a home than a hotel, it has a country-cottage feel, with vanilla-scented bedrooms, floral bedspreads, bookshelves bursting with knick-knacks, and a lounge area where you can sip tea with the adorable landlady and muse over the regularly updated guest information board. ₺70

EATING AND DRINKING

Fresh-caught lake fish – especially carp (*sazan*), zander and crayfish – figure prominently on local restaurant menus, presented either as batter-fried fillets, grilled, or poached in tomato sauce (*buğulama*). Most restaurants serve alcohol.

Big Apple West side of the island ☎ 0246 311 4555, ⊕ bigapplerestoran.com. A sizeable restaurant with indoor and outdoor dining, this is a popular dinner option for visitors to the island. There's also a great all-morning buffet brunch at the weekends, a substantial wine list (₺10 glass), and some delicious home-made cakes and desserts – try the cherry or carrot cake (₺6.50 each). Daily 8am–midnight.

Big Fish West side of the island, next door to the *Big Apple* ☎ 0246 311 4413, ⊕ yesiladabigfish.com. This bright-white building is decked out with houseplants and an incongruous Swiss Alpine scene, and the family-run restaurant dates back to 1983. Both the food and service are good, with tender oven-baked trout (₺15) and tables set out on the lake's edge in summer. Daily 8am–midnight.

Felekabad Northeastern tip of the island ☎ 0246 311 5881, ⊕ felekabad.com. Set in a great location surrounded by the lake and a pretty park, this family-run establishment is one of the friendliest places in town and excellent value. A good lunch choice, with simple meals including delicious *gözleme* (₺5), a selection of fish dishes (from ₺10), and a decent range of desserts. No alcohol. Daily 7.30am–midnight.

Günaylar Opposite the Hızırbey Camii ☎ 0246 311 2899,

⊕ gunaylarestaurant.com. This bustling local joint serves tasty, good-value staples with a wide range of kebabs (₺8–15) and *pides* (₺3.50). The *menemen* (a breakfast dish of eggs, tomatoes, onions and peppers, ₺4) is especially delicious. Daily 6am–11pm.

Hakan Akinci Dondurmalari Cami Mahallesi 32 ☎ 0246 311 4888. This humble hole-in-the-wall serves up delicious ice creams (₺2.50 for a massive 3-scoop cone). There's plenty of flavours to dig into – chocolate, caramel, blackberry, lemon and mango are all on the menu – but if you're in town for the spring and summer months make sure you try the delicious home-made *gül* (rose) ice cream. May–Oct daily 10am–midnight.

Melodi Southeastern tip of the island ☎ 0246 311 2433. This deservedly popular establishment serves up better-than-average lake fish (₺15) plus a wide range of *mezes*. Don't be put off by the slightly shabby interiors; come nightfall, the candle-lit lakeshore tables are incredibly atmospheric. Daily 11am–midnight.

Meşir Köftecisi Uzun Çarşı. Local chef Güngör Gül serves up home-made tahini from a secret recipe and delicious grilled *köfte* (meatballs) at this Eğirdir institution. The food is served by weight (₺5 per 100g), and a full meal will set you back less than ₺15. Daily 8am–11pm.

DIRECTORY

Banks and money The town centre holds a couple of ATMs, plus several banks.

Car Parks Two car parks at the north and south of the mainland; many pensions offer limited parking spaces.

Police Next door to the tourist office.

Hamams Cumhuriyet Hamam Çay Boyu Sok 1 (daily 8am–10pm; ☎ 0246 242 4646).

7

EXCURSIONS FROM EĞİRDİR

Despite its comparatively small tourism industry, Eğirdir makes a great base from which to explore the region. The local pensions are now well organized, with tours, guides, maps and independent travel information all easily available.

HIKING TRAILS

While the **St Paul's Trail** (see p.421) is the region's most famous long-distance walking trail, numerous trekking routes have been mapped out, and independent hiking is easy. These range from half- or full-day walks to multi-day trips such as the hike to Barla (25km), and the overnight trips to the summits of Mount Dedegöl and Mount Davraz. The **Eğirdir Outdoor Centre** (ⓦ egirdiroutdoorcenter.com) can tailor routes to your requirements and arrange transport (costing around ₺1 per km), guides (around ₺100 per day), camping equipment and packed lunches.

CYCLING ROUTES

Potential bike routes vary from easier circuits around the region's many lakes, or the mostly flat terrain leading to Kovada National Park (54km round trip), to more challenging routes like the hilly climbs to Barla village (46km round trip) or the mountainous course to Zindan Cave (50km round trip).

KOVADA NATIONAL PARK

The lake, marshland and forests of **Kovada Gölü** form a carefully tended and hardly visited national park. Its animal population includes wolves, bears and wild boars, and the lake itself, teeming with fish, receives the outflow of Eğirdir Gölü. The limestone shore is harsh and the lake itself tinted green by its sediment, so it's not a particularly enticing swimming spot, but the largely untouched wildlife makes for some great walking and birdwatching opportunities.

ÇANDIR/CANYONS/KING'S WAY

Many tours of Kovada National Park continue 30km south on the main road through a gorge towards **Çandır** (signed Yazılı Kanyonu), passing a series of icy but scenic pools and waterfalls, crisscrossed by bridges, and best sampled in high summer. Well-preserved stretches still survive of the ancient **Kral Yolu**, or "King's Way", a road that threaded through Pisidia.

SKIING

Between December and the end of March, the northern slopes of the 2635m **Mount Davraz** (30min drive from Eğirdir) offer decent downhill skiing and snowboarding, and the views from the slopes down to Lake Eğirdir are superb. Conditions are fairly reliable, though the limited runs won't satisfy everyone. The **Eğirdir Outdoor Centre** (ⓦ egirdiroutdoorcenter.com) and the **Davraz Ski Centre** (ⓦ davraz.com) rent skis (from ₺30) and snowboards (from ₺35), and a weekday lift pass costs ₺30.

Antioch ad Pisidiam

75km northeast of Eğirdir, 2km from modern Yalvaç • Tues–Sun 8.30am–5.30pm • ₺3 • Catch a minibus from Isparta (via Eğirdir) to Yalvaç (12 daily in summer, 1hr 30min), then walk or take a taxi

The ancient city of **Antioch ad Pisidiam** is where the apostle **St Paul** first attempted to convert pagans to Christianity. Originally a Hellenistic foundation of the late third century BC, the city peaked as the capital of the Roman province of Pisidia, and remained important well into Byzantine times.

The most unusual surviving remains are of the sizeable **temple**, at the highest point of the city, built in a semicircular colonnaded precinct in honour of the Emperor Augustus. Below this is the toppled three-arched **propylon** (gateway) dedicated to Augustus, where the Tiberius and Augustus squares meet. Even more substantial are the remains of the **baths** fed by an **aqueduct** and surviving sections of a flagged Roman **street**.

At the lower end of the site, a few courses of monumental stone blocks belonging to the fourth-century **Church of St Paul** (on the site of the synagogue) still stand, but little else can be seen except for the ground plan and some small areas of mosaic floor.

Adada

Signposted off the Aksu road, 65km southeast of Eğirdir

Cut from grey stone, the ancient town of **Adada** lies along both sides of a minor road. Although there is a warden, no admission is charged, and it's permanently open to visitors. The site has never been excavated, and history books are strangely silent about it, but judging from coins found hereabouts, it was thriving during imperial Roman times. Visible remains include a particularly well-preserved Corinthian temple, plus two other small temples, a forum with unusual seating along one side, a badly preserved theatre, a church and various Hellenistic buildings.

If you follow the stream bed between the acropolis hill and the adjacent hill, heading southwest behind the forum, it's possible to trace the original Greco-Roman road from the south. This is almost certainly the original road that St Paul walked on his first missionary journey from Perge to Antioch in Pisidia.

Beyşehir

The town of **BEYŞEHIR**, on the eastern shore of the Beyşehir Gölü lake, sees a lot of through traffic, and its attractive lakeside position and historical legacy make it a good prospect for at least a day-trip.

Judging by Neolithic remains, there has been human settlement here since the sixth or seventh millennium BC, and evidence exists of Hittite settlement around the lake. The town itself was originally Byzantine, known as Karallia, and in Selçuk times acquired a citadel, mosques and hamams.

The most notable monument is the distinctive **Eşrefoğlu Camii**, dating back to the Eşrefoğlu dynasty (1277–1326), but there's also a lovely weir-bridge, built by German workers in 1902, from where you can watch locals throwing their nets out for the evening catch of *sazan* (carp).

THE ST PAUL TRAIL

Opened in 2004, the rugged **St Paul Trail** offers over 500km of trekking in the spectacularly beautiful Toros Mountains. Waymarked to international standards, with red and white flashes on rocks and trees, it allows relatively easy exploration of a remote, unspoiled area of Turkey. A detailed guidebook (which includes a map), written by Kate Clow, covers the trail.

The twin starting points of the route are the ancient cities of **Perge** (see p.368) and **Aspendos** (see p.370), on the Mediterranean coastal plain. It was from Perge that St Paul set out, in 46 AD, on his first proselytizing journey. His destination was the Roman colonial town of Antioch ad Pisidiam (see p.420), where he first preached Christ's message to non-Jews. En route from the Mediterranean to the Anatolian plateau, the trail crosses tumbling mountain rivers, climbs passes between limestone peaks that soar to almost 3000m, dips into deeply scored canyons, and weaves beneath shady pine and cedar forest. It even includes a boat ride across the glimmering expanse of Lake Eğirdir.

Hikers interested in archeology can discover remote, little-known Roman sites and walk along original sections of Roman road. The irrevocably active can raft the Köprülü River, scale 2635m Mount Davraz and 2799m Mount Barla (ascents of both appear in the trail guidebook; for more information check ⓦtrekkinginturkey.com), or even tackle the mighty Dedegül (2992m).

PRACTICALITIES

Eğirdir (see p.416) makes an ideal base for forays along the trail. The town's pension owners will be able to help you sort out the relevant dolmuşes, negotiate car rental or taxi hire and let you store unwanted gear until your return from the hills. **Guides**, camping equipment, pickups and luggage storage can be arranged by İbrahim at the Eğirdir Outdoor Centre (ⓦegirdiroutdoorcenter.com).

7

Eşrefoğlu Camii

Open at prayer times

The **Eşrefoğlu Camii**, Beyşehir's finest monument, was built by Eşrefoğlu Seyfeddin Süleyman between 1297 and 1299. A large, flat-roofed stone building, surmounted by a typical Selçuk flat-sided cone, it's an exceptional example of a medieval wooden *beylik* mosque. (The *beylik*s were the minor Turkish principalities that ruled Anatolia before the Ottomans gained supremacy.) Restoration carried out in the 1950s explains the ugly concrete blocks at the base of the minaret, but otherwise the mosque is in a remarkable state of preservation.

The effect inside is incredibly forest-like: not only are the columns and capitals wooden, but also the rafters, galleries, furniture and balustrades. Dappled light plays on the columns from a central aperture, now glassed over, and from high-set windows. Below this is a deep pit, which once held ice for preserving food and cooling the mosque. The *mihrab* is decorated in typical Selçuk style, its turquoise, black and white tiles being almost the last surviving of their type, and the *mimber* is also a lovely period piece of woodcarving, echoing the star motif apparent throughout the mosque.

The conically roofed building attached to the east side of the mosque, the **Eşrefoğlu Türbesi**, was built in 1302 to commemorate Eşrefoğlu Seyfeddin Süleyman who died in that year. Ask the *imam* if he'll open it up for a look at its beautifully tiled interior, one of the most ornate surviving examples of its type.

Beyşehir Gölü

Religious and civic architecture aside, the most obvious attraction near Beyşehir is the shallow, freshwater **Beyşehir Gölü**, Turkey's largest lake at 650 square kilometres. The number of its islands is a hotly disputed topic among the locals, hindered by the fact that smaller ones appear and disappear according to the water level (averaging a mere 10m in depth). Roughly twenty, however – mostly those that hold ruined Byzantine monasteries – have names.

Boat trips (₺10) take in several, including the formerly magnificent Selçuk island palace of **Kubadabad**, whose unique tiles can be seen in the Karatay museum in Konya (see p.426). Pedalos are also available for rent (₺5), while tiny cafés serve fish sandwiches by the lakeside; some offer seating on harboured boats.

The best **beach** on the lake is **Karaburnu**, signposted 500m off the Yeşildağ road, 18km west of Beyşehir.

Eflatun Pınar

On Beyşehir Gölü's east shore, on the main road towards Eğirdir • Turn right 15km northwest of Beyşehir, just before a petrol station; follow a paved side road for 5km, then bear left for another 2km, along a dirt track

The **Eflatun Pınar** (Violet Spring) is a Hittite shrine that dates from the thirteenth century BC. On its outskirts, a large, walled pond filling a natural depression receives the flow of vigorous springs. Huge carved blocks at one corner bear four relief figures with winged sun discs (symbols of royalty) carried by semi-human monsters, with statues of seated divinities to either side. Excavations by the Konya museum have revealed a row of mountain gods with holes in their skirts that once gushed water, and a large stone block with bull reliefs.

ARRIVAL AND DEPARTURE

BEYŞEHIR

By bus Service buses connect Beyşehir *otogar*, 2km north of town, with the centre (every 20min), dropping passengers near the weir-bridge.

Destinations Alanya (6 daily; 4hr); Ankara (4 daily; 5hr); Antalya (5 daily; 4hr); Eğirdir (12 daily; 1hr 30min); Isparta (6 daily; 2hr 30min); Konya (hourly; 1hr 30min).

ACCOMMODATION AND EATING

Adana Sofrasi Overlooking the weir at Çarşı Camii yanı ☎ 0332 512 4535. The best place to eat in Beyşehir, this

modern restaurant sprawls along the weir, with plenty of outdoor seating and a spotless open kitchen. A decent kebab or fish meal will set you back a very reasonable ₺10–12 but, like everywhere in town, they don't serve alcohol. Daily 8am–10pm.

Ali Bilir Bilir Sok 1, visible from the weir ☎ 0332 512 0455, ⓦ alibilirotel.com. Beyşehir's newest hotel is the best of the extremely limited options in town. New, modern furnishings, and a spotless terrace restaurant with wonderful views of the lake, make it a comfortable

choice. ₺110

Beyaz Park Overlooking the weir at Atatürk Cad 1 ☎ 0332 512 3865. If you're looking for the cheapest room in town, this is it. You should be able to haggle them down a bit too, but keep your expectations low. The interiors are just as shabby as the exterior, and the cleanliness is suspect – look around before you check in, as some rooms are more acceptable than others. ₺60

Konya

KONYA, the medieval Selçuk capital, is a place of pilgrimage for the whole Muslim world, and a city that holds pride of place in the hearts of all pious Turks. This was the adopted home of Celaleddin Rumi, better known as the Mevlâna (Our Master), the Sufic mystic who founded the **whirling dervish** sect, the Mevlevî; his writings helped reshape Islamic thought and modified the popular Islamic culture of Turkey.

Konya has a reputation as one of the country's most religious and thus conservative cities (while simultaneously holding the title as the single greatest consumer of raki in the nation). That said, most visitors are surprised by its modern and bustling city centre, with monumental landmarks sandwiched between trendy fashion stores and towering flat blocks.

Turkey's seventh-largest city is surrounded by some exceptionally fertile countryside; the region is known locally as "the breadbasket of Turkey". Its many parks – in particular, the central hillock of **Alâeddin Parkı** – add a splash of green to the ubiquitous light-coloured stone.

Brief history

Konya's history is as long and spectacular as that of any Turkish city. The earliest remains discovered date from the seventh millennium BC, and the acropolis was inhabited successively by Hittites, Phrygians, Romans and Greeks. **St Paul** and **St Barnabas** both delivered sermons here after they had been expelled from Antioch, and in 235 AD, one of the earliest Church councils was convened in the city – known then, under the Byzantines, as Iconium.

It also took a central role during the era of the western Selçuks, becoming the seat of the **Sultanate of Rum**. After they had defeated the Byzantine army at the Battle of Manzikert in 1071, the Selçuks attempted to set up a court in İznik, just across the Sea of Marmara from İstanbul. They were expelled from there by the combined Byzantine and Crusader armies, but still ruled most of eastern and central Asia Minor until the early fourteenth century.

While the concept of a fixed capital was initially somewhat alien to the Selçuks, Konya became the home of their sultans from the time of Süleyman Ibn Kutulmuz, successor to Alparslan, the victor at Manzikert. **Alâeddin Keykubad**, the most distinguished of all Selçuk sultans, established a court of artists and scholars in Konya early in the thirteenth century, and his patronage was highly beneficial to the development of the arts and philosophy. Many of the buildings constructed at this time are still standing, and examples of their highly distinctive tile-work, woodcarving, carpet making and masonry are on display in local museums.

Mevlâna Museum

Eastern end of Mevlâna Cad • Daily 9am–7pm; last admission 30min before closing • ₺3, audioguides ₺5

A visit to the **Mevlâna Museum** (Mevlâna Müzesi) is among Turkey's most rewarding experiences; the stunning manicured gardens and rainbow of rose bushes of the central courtyard are an attraction in themselves. Try to arrive early or late in the day, however, to avoid the usual crowds.

7

7

KONYA

0   200
metres

N

Koyunoğlu Museum & Mevlana Culture Centre

ACCOMMODATION
Balıkçılar   5
Mevlâna Sema   3
Rumi   2
Ulusan   4
Yeni Köşk Ezra   1

RESTAURANTS
Bolu   2
Damla   4
Halil İbrahim Sofrası 5
Mevlevi Sofrası   3
Şifa   1
Somatçı   6

BAR & CAFÉ
Nar-ı Aşk Art Café   1

Otogar

State
Hospital

Fairground

KONYA

İHSANİYE CAD

VATAN CAD

NALÇACI CAD

SULTAN CEM CAD

KAZIM KARABEKIR CAD

İstanbul Cad

SULTAN VELED CAD

ANKARA CAD

SULTANŞAH CAD

Karatay
Medresesi

Küçük
Karatay
Medresesi

Selçuk
Palace

Alâeddin
Camii

Alâeddin
Parkı

İnce Minare
Medresesi

Temuz @
Internet

KÖPRÜ BAŞI CAD

AZİZİYE CAD

İSTANBUL CAD

NAZİMBEY CAD

MEVLANA CAD

Dolmuş to Otogar

Selimiye
Camii

Mevlâna
Museum

Türbe Cad

Mevlâna
Çarşısı

Old Otogar

MENGEÇ CAD

MENÜÇ CAD

TOPRAKLIK CAD

Azizîye
Camii

KARAMAN CAD

Supermarket

BAZAAR

ATMS/
Banks

Şerafeddin
Camii

Buses
to Sille

İplikçi
Camii

HÜKÜMET
ALANI

TEVFIKIYE CAD

SELIMİYE CAD

SERAFEDDIN CAD

ALÂEDDIN CAD

ALÂEDDIN BUL

ALÂEDDIN BUL

SIRÇALI MEDRESE CAD

Sırçalı
Medrese

St Paul's
Catholic
Church

Öykü Net @

SAHIP ATA CAD

Sahip Ata
Külliyesi

Archeological
Museum

Ethnographic
Museum

ATAYURT CAD

SALİT PAŞA CAD

LAKENDE CAD
(MERAM ESKİYOL)

Atatürk
Monument

AMBERREIS CAD

THY

FERİT PAŞA CAD

Train Station

THE LIFE AND TEACHINGS OF THE MEVLÂNA

Celaleddin Rumi, later known as the **Mevlâna**, was born in the central Asian city of Balkh, in 1207. At the age of twenty, having received a warning vision, the young man convinced his father to flee with him for western Asia, which they did just in time to avoid being massacred with the rest of Balkh by marauding Mongols. They settled in Konya, where the reigning sultan Alâeddin Keykubad received them cordially. The city had a cosmopolitan population, whose beliefs were not lost on the young man, and it was here that he emerged as a leading heterodox mystic or **Sufi**.

During the 1250s, Rumi completed a masterpiece of Persian devotional poetry, the *Mathnawi*. A massive work covering several volumes, it concerns the soul's separation from God – characterized as the Friend – as a consequence of earthly existence, and the power of a mutual yearning to bring about a reunion, either before or after bodily death. The Mevlâna – as Rumi was by now widely known – himself died on December 17, 1273.

On a practical level, the Mevlâna instructed his disciples to pursue all manifestations of truth and beauty, while avoiding ostentation, and to practise infinite tolerance, love and charity. He condemned slavery, and advocated monogamy and a greater prominence for women in religious and public life. The Mevlâna did not advocate complete monastic seclusion – the Mevlevîs held jobs in normal society and could marry – but believed that the contemplative and mystical practices of the dervish would free them from worldly anxieties. Although his ideas have never been fully accepted as Islamic orthodoxy, they still attract Westerners and liberal Muslims alike.

Housed in a former *tekke*, the first lodge of the Mevlevî dervish sect, the museum is most easily found by locating the distinctive fluted turquoise spire that rises directly above Celaleddin Rumi's tomb. The *tekke* served as a place of mystical teaching, meditation and ceremonial dance (*sema*), from shortly after Rumi's death in 1273 until 1925, when Atatürk banned all Sufic orders. Over the centuries the various dervish orders had become highly influential in political life, and thus posed a potential threat to his secular reforms.

Most of the **buildings** in the compound, including the *tekke* and *semahane*, were built late in the fifteenth and early in the sixteenth centuries by sultans Beyazit II and Selim I. Along the south and east sides of the courtyard, the **cells** where the dervishes prayed and meditated now hold waxwork figures dressed in the costume worn during the whirling ceremony. Next to the quarters of the *şeyh* (head of the dervish order), today the museum office, a **library** preserves five thousand volumes on the Mevlevî and Sufic mysticism.

The mausoleum

The main building of the Mevlâna Museum is the **mausoleum** that contains the tombs of the Mevlâna, his father and other notables of the order. Slip the plastic bags provided at the entrance over your shoes and shuffle along in a queue of pilgrims, for whom this is the primary reason to visit. Women must cover their heads; regardless of gender, if you're wearing shorts you'll be given a skirt-like affair to cover your legs. The measure of devotion still felt toward the Mevlâna is evident in the weeping and impassioned prayer that takes place in front of his tomb, but non-Muslim visitors are treated with respect and even welcomed. This is in strict accordance with Rumi's own dictates on religious tolerance. If you're a lone *gavur* (infidel) in a centre of Islamic pilgrimage, this sentiment is surely to be cherished.

The semahane

The room that adjoins the mausoleum is the original **semahane** (the circular hall in which the *sema* was performed), considered the finest in Turkey. Exhibits include musical instruments belonging to the original dervishes, including the *ney* (reed flute), silk and woollen carpets and the original illuminated *Mathnawi* – the long devotional poem of the Mevlâna. One 500-year-old silk carpet from Selçuk Persia is said to be the finest ever woven, with 144 knots to the square centimetre; it took five years to complete.

7

KONYA'S DERVISH FESTIVAL AND DANCES

Since Konya is the spiritual and temporal home of the whirling dervishes, the city plays host to the annual **dervish festival**, held between December 7 and December 17, during the week prior to the anniversary of the Mevlâna's death. Unfortunately, with sub-zero temperatures, doubled hotel rates and shops full of whirling dervish kitsch, this is not the best time to witness a dervish rite. In fact the most authentic place to watch a ceremony is in the restored *semahane* in İstanbul, the Galata Mevlevîhane (see p.104). Unlike the dancers in Konya, its members are also practising dervishes who live according to the teachings of the Mevlâna. Alternatively, in July and August, official *sema* performances are staged in the gardens of Konya's Mevlâna complex, priced at ₺20, while free shows at the Mevlâna Culture Centre, 500m up the road from the Mevlâna Museum, take place every Sat night year-round, except during the festival period (May–Oct Sat 9pm, Nov–April Sat 8pm).

The **whirling ceremony** – the *sema* – for which the Mevlevî dervishes are renowned, is a means of freedom from earthly bondage and abandonment to God's love. The **clothes** worn by the Mevlevîs during the observance have symbolic significance. The camel-hair hat represents a tombstone, the black cloak is the tomb itself, and the white skirt the funerary shroud. During the ceremony the cloak is cast aside, denoting that the dervishes have escaped from their tombs and from all other earthly ties. The **music** reproduces that of the spheres, and the turning dervishes represent the heavenly bodies themselves. Every movement and sound made during the ceremony has an additional significance – for example, the right arms of the dancers extend up to heaven while their left arms point to the floor, denoting that grace is received from God and distributed to humanity.

The latticed gallery above the *semahane* was for women spectators, a modification introduced by the followers of the Mevlâna after his death. The heavy chain suspended from the ceiling, and the concentric balls that hang from it, were carved from a single piece of marble. In the adjoining room, a casket containing hairs from the beard of the Prophet is displayed alongside finely illuminated medieval Korans.

Alâeddin Parkı

Modern Konya stretches out from the **Alâeddin Parkı**, at the end of Mevlâna/Alâeddin Caddesi. Despite the encircling traffic, it's a lovely wooded place for a stroll, and holds many outdoor cafés to sit at. The site of the original acropolis, the *tepe*, has yielded finds dating back to 7000 BC, as well as evidence of Hittite, Phrygian, Roman and Greek settlers; most are now in the museum in Ankara. The scant remains of a **Selçuk palace** survive at the foot of the hill to the north.

Alâeddin Camii

Alâeddin Parkı • Daily 8.30am–5.30pm

Pride of place in Alâeddin Parkı belongs to the imposing **Alâeddin Camii**, started by Sultan Mesut I in 1130 and completed by Alâeddin Keykubad in 1221. Its typically plain Selçuk interior contains 42 ancient columns with Roman capitals supporting a flat roof, and there's a small domed area over the *mihrab*. Dated 1155, the beautiful carved ebony *mimber* is the oldest inscribed and dated Selçuk work of art in existence.

Karatay Medresesi

Ankara Cad • Tues–Sun 9am–noon & 1–5.30pm • ₺3

The recently restored **Karatay Medresesi** is a major Selçuk monument. Built in 1251, the *medrese*, or school of Islamic studies, now houses a museum of ceramics, but the building itself provides greater interest. Its main **portal** is a fine example of Islamic art at its most decorative, combining elements such as Arabic striped stonework and Greek Corinthian columns with a structure that is distinctly Selçuk: a tall doorway surmounted by a pointed, stalactite arch, resembling the entrance of a tent.

Inside the *medrese* the most attractive exhibit is again part of the building itself. Excavations beneath the floors reveal the building's terracotta hydraulic system, uncovered in 2008. The symmetrical tiling of the famed **dome of stars** is a stylized representation of the heavens in gold, blue and black monochrome tiles. Painted Ottoman tiles from İznik and Kütahya appear clumsy in contrast with those of this delicate mosaic.

Selçuk **ceramics** on display in the galleries bear witness to the fact that pious concerns were overruled by secular taste – not to mention the contributions of conquered Christian and pagan subjects – even in medieval times. The striking images of birds, animals and even angels would have been strictly forbidden in more orthodox Islamic societies.

İnce Minare Medresesi

West side of Alâeddin Parkı, by the tramway stop • Daily: May–Oct 8.30am–12.30pm & 1.30–5pm; Nov–April 8am–noon & 1–5pm; last entry 15min before closure • ₺3

Behind its fine Selçuk portal, the **İnce Minare Medresesi**, or "Academy of the Slender Minaret", is now a lapidary (stone) and woodcarving museum. The minaret from which it takes its name was severely truncated by lightning in 1901; its most exquisite feature is now the **portal**, even more ornate than that at the Karatay Medresesi.

Most of the museum's exhibits, like the ceramics in the Karatay Medresesi, came from the ruined Selçuk palace across the way. The finest individual items are Selçuk stone reliefs, explicitly showing the influence of Byzantium. Most prominent are winged angels, bestiary pediments and a two-headed eagle relief, said to be from the vanished walls of the medieval city and now the official logo of the modern town.

Sırcalı Medrese

A short walk southeast of Alâeddin Parkı, along Ressam Sami Sok • Daily: May–Oct 8.30am–12.30pm & 1.30–5.30pm; Nov–April 8am–noon & 1–5pm • Free

The thirteenth-century **Sırcalı Medrese** now houses government offices. Highlights of the building, mostly restored in harsh brick, are the fine blue-glazed tile-work in the rear porch, all that remains of what was once a completely ornamented interior, the handsome portal, and a collection of tombstones – all visible even when the gate is locked.

Archeological museum

Sahip Ata Cad 91 • Tues–Sun: May–Oct 8.30am–12.30pm & 1.30–5.30pm; Nov–April 8am–noon & 1–5pm • ₺3

Konya's small **Archeological Museum** (Arkeoloji Müzesi) contains the only pre-Selçuk remains in the city. These include the few Hittite artefacts from the nearby site of Çatal Höyük (see p.429) that have not been relocated to Ankara, and six well-preserved Roman sarcophagi from Pamphylia, one of which depicts Hercules at his twelve labours. Note how the hero's beard grows as his labours progress. Just northeast of the museum, the thirteenth-century **Sahip Ata Külliyesi** is semi-ruined, but retains its beautiful brick and stone entrance portal, plus a tiled minaret.

Around the bazaar

The north edge of Konya's weekday **bazaar**, on Hükümet Alanı, 100m from the Mevlâna Museum, is marked by the brick **İplikçi Camii**, Konya's oldest (1202) mosque to survive intact and still be in use; legend claims that the Mevlâna preached and meditated here. Look out, too, for the **Aziziye Camii** in the bazaar, an Ottoman mosque easily recognized by its unusual (for Turkey) Moghul-style minarets.

The bazaar, like the city itself, is very traditional and surprisingly relaxed, but keep an eye out for pickpockets. You'll probably also see alternative healing remedies on sale, from daisy water to leeches.

ARRIVAL AND DEPARTURE

KONYA

By plane Konya's airport, 17km northwest, is linked with the city centre by THY shuttle buses, which leave from Alâeddin Cad to connect with all departures. Check in advance at the THY office, Amberreis Cad ☎0332 239 1177. Destinations İstanbul (6 daily; 1hr 10min); Van via İstanbul (1 daily; 4hr 5min).

By bus To reach the city centre from Konya's *otogar*, inconveniently located 15km north, catch tram #2 to the end of the line, Alâeddin Parkı (buy tram passes from the ticket booth on the platform; they cost ₺3 for two fares, so hold on to your ticket). From there, either walk or take a dolmuş to the main street, Mevlâna Cad. Dolmuşes also connect the *otogar* with the Mevlâna Museum (₺1.75). Expect taxis to cost around ₺25.

Destinations Afyon (14 daily; 3hr); Alanya (6 daily; 5hr); Ankara (hourly; 3hr); Antalya (8 daily; 5hr); Beyşehir (hourly; 1hr 15min); Bursa (8 daily; 10hr); Göreme (6 daily; 3hr); Isparta (4 daily; 4hr); Kayseri (8 daily; 4hr); Silifke (8 daily; 5hr).

By train The station is at the far end of Ferit Paşa Cad, 4km from the centre and connected by dolmuş or by taxi (around ₺5).

Destinations Adana (3 weekly; 8hr); Afyon (1 daily; 6hr); Ankara (8 daily; 1.5hr).

By car Rental cars are available from Avis, Nalçacı Cad, Acentacılar Sitesi, B-Blok 87 (☎0332 237 3750); Rüya Turizm, Zafer Meydanı (☎0332 352 7228); and Selen, Aziziye Cad (☎0332 353 6745).

INFORMATION

Tourist office Aslanlıkışla Cad 5, just down from the Mevlâna Museum (Mon–Sat 8am–5pm, ☎0332 353 4021). Helpful English-speaking staff will weigh you down with brochures and up-to-date city plans. They also take bookings for the December dervish festival (see box, p.426) and weekly dervish concerts, and can help with local transport. Note that many old city maps still mark the

former tourist information centre on Mevlâna Cad, which no longer handles tourist information.

Tours Selene Travel Agency, Aziziye Cad 25/1, 2nd floor (☎0332 353 6745, ⓦselene.com.tr), offers private city tours and bespoke out-of-town excursions. A full-day tour for up to five people, with driver, English-speaking guide and lunch, costs €150.

ACCOMMODATION

Balıkçılar Mevlâna Karşısı 2 ☎0332 350 9470, ⓦbalikcilar.com. With 4 stars and a bucket load of style to its name, this slick hotel offers expansive views over the city from its sunny roof terrace, which you can marvel at over your buffet breakfast. Rooms are spotless and refined, with all the home comforts you'd expect, but it's the spiral stairwell with its stone mosaic walls and neon strip lighting that really ups the atmosphere. **€120**

Mevlâna Sema Mevlâna Cad 67 ☎0332 350 4623, ⓦsemaotel.com. A great-value option in the heart of the city, with a breezy terrace restaurant and a lobby decorated with cute whirling dervish stencils. The clean, smart rooms have spacious bathrooms and tasteful decor. **₺90**

Rumi Hotel Fakih Sok 3, behind the Mevlâna museum ☎0332 353 1121, ⓦrumihotel.com. With its aqua-blue facade looming from behind the walls of the Mevlâna Museum, this hotel is hard to miss, and it's just as attractive inside and out. Private parking, fitness centre, and great

views from the rooftop terrace. **₺140**

★**Ulusan Hotel** Çarşı PTT Arkası (on a sides treet behind the PTT building) ☎0332 351 5004. As budget accommodation goes, this humble, no-frills abode, dotted with homely trinkets, is near perfect. The spotless rooms (with sink and wi-fi) are both comfortable and quiet, despite being right off the main drag, and the shared bathrooms spacious and immaculate. The English-speaking owner takes great care of his guests, cooking up toasted sandwiches for breakfast, dishing out maps and offering tips on avoiding the latest tourist scams. **₺80**

Yeni Köşk Esra Otel Kadilar 2 Sok 7, off Aziziye Cad ☎0332 352 0671, ⓦyenikoskesraotel.com. This slightly shabby place looks like it's been decked out for a Turkish wedding, but it's constantly rammed with Turkish families so they must be doing something right. A maze of rooms sprawling over three properties – those in the newest section are considerably nicer – plus exceedingly friendly staff. **€45**

EATING AND DRINKING

Konya's innate religious conservatism has hampered the development of an "eating out" culture. That's begun to change recently, but restaurants serving alcohol are few and far between, and decor and service are usually strictly functional. For fast food, check out the numerous places on Atatürk Bulvarı.

Bolu İstanbul Cad, a few doors up from *Damla* ☎0332 352 4533. This Konya institution serves an excellent *etli ekmek* (the city's signature thin-crust *pide* topped with ground meat and finely diced peppers) and *ayran* for ₺6,

and is always packed with locals. Daily 7am–9pm.

★**Damla** Türbe Cad 59 ☎0332 352 0881, ⓦdamlakebap.com. This spotless kebab *salonu* is a cut above the rest, and one of the best (and most popular) places to try the city's staple foods – tuck into some delicious *bamya* (okra soup), tender *firin* kebabs (₺14) and crispy *etli ekmek* (₺7). No alcohol. Daily 7am–9pm.

Mevlevî Sofrası Amil Celebi Sok 1, north side of the Mevlâna complex ☎ 0332 353 3341. Contained within a series of beautifully restored houses, with a summer terrace that affords gorgeous views over the Mevlâna rose gardens, this well-priced restaurant is a popular tourist choice. A range of well-prepared Turkish *mezes*, grills and kebabs dominate the menu (mains from ₺12 up), alongside a few traditional dishes like okra soup (₺4) and the local semolina-based sweet, *hoşmeriim* (₺5). Daily 9am–10pm.

Nar-ı Aşk Art Café Mimar Sinan Sok 6 59 ☎ 0532 337 6070, ⓦ nar-iask.com. If cute, kitsch and colourful is your thing, you won't be able to resist this adorable art shop with its pretty stenciled walls and felt whirling dervish mobiles swinging from the doorframe. There's some exquisite, handmade souvenirs on sale here, but head downstairs to the cushioned courtyard area for a *Turk Kalvesi* (Turkish coffee, ₺3.50) and have your fortune read by the friendly hosts. Growing numbers of youngsters hang out here in the evenings, but come before lunch and you'll

have the place to yourself. Daily 10am–10pm.

Şifa Mevlâna Cad 29, opposite Şifa Otel ☎ 0332 352 0519. Conveniently located and well patronized by locals and pilgrims, with a wide variety of standard grills and a *pide* oven. Meat-based mains cost ₺10–13, and there's a wide selection of hot and cold *mezes* and desserts on display. Daily 6am–9pm.

★ **Somatçı** Mengüç Cad 36 ☎ 0332 351 6696, ⓦ somatci.com. Ducking through the maze of cove-like rooms, some with floor cushions, others with elegant furnishings and wooden-beam ceilings, is just the start of the journey at this recently opened restaurant. The atmospheric surroundings are matched by an inspired menu of time-honoured Ottoman, Sufi and Seljukian dishes (with a modern twist), whipped up with traditional ingredients. Apricot-stuffed chicken and veal and plum pottery kebabs grace the main menu (₺15–20), but save room for dessert – the *Badem Helvası* (almond helva, ₺7.50) and *Kremalı İncir* (stuffed figs with cream, ₺5) are divine. There's no alcohol, so wash it down with a glass of Sirkencübin (a sweet drink favoured by the dervishes, ₺3) instead. Daily 7.30am–10pm.

DIRECTORY

Banks and exchange Several *döviz* offices and ATMs on Hükümet Alanı.

Hamam Everything you could ask of a Turkish bath, behind Şerafeddin Camii on Hükümet Alanı: white stone and marble with traditional tiny round skylights striping the steam with rays of sunlight. Separate wings for men and women, and the masseurs are skilled and thorough.

₺16–20 for a scrub and massage.

Internet access Öykü Net, opposite the front entrance of the Catholic church, off Alâeddin Bul, and another couple near *McDonald's* on Alâeddin Bul.

Police Ferit Paşa Cad ☎ 0332 353 8141.

Post office PTT on Hükümet Alanı (daily 8.30am–midnight).

Around Konya

Konya's tourist office is well geared towards organizing day-trips to the area's more remote archeological and historical remnants. The highlights are **Çatal Höyük**, possibly Anatolia's earliest settlement; the ancient site of **Kilistra**; and the ruined Byzantine churches and monasteries of the **Binbir Kilise** region. Minor sites, like the beautiful crater lake of **Acı Göl** or the isolated ancient ruins of **İvriz**, make pleasant stopoffs en route to Cappadocia, but are hardly worth rerouting for.

Çatal Höyük

58km southeast of Konya • Daily 8.30am–5.30pm • Free • Catch the Karkin minibus from the old *otogar* on Fergandede Cad (Mon–Fri noon; ₺5; 70min); hire a taxi (₺130 return); or drive from Konya on the Karaman/Silifke road, Highway 715, then take a left to Çumra 2km before İçeri Çumra, and follow signs

Discovered by the British archeologist James Mellaart in 1958, and added to the UNESCO World Heritage list in 2012, the important Neolithic site of **Çatal Höyük** consists of twin, flattened hills that are supposed to resemble the shape of a fork. Hence the name, which means "Fork Tumulus". An international team, resident on site in summer, continues to excavate the prehistoric tumuli here. Summer is the best time to visit, but bear in mind that you'll need a lively imagination, as there's little to see.

Exciting discoveries at Çatal Höyük have provided significant clues about one of the world's oldest civilizations, dating from 6800 BC. Evidence pointed to entire complexes of houses, crammed together without streets to separate them, and entered through holes in the roof. Also found were murals of men being eaten by vultures, animal-head trophies stuffed with squeezed clay, and human bones wrapped in straw matting and placed under the seats in a burial chamber. There is also the world's first landscape painting, a mural depicting the eruption of a volcano, presumably nearby Hasan Dağa.

Most famous of all are the statuettes of the **mother goddess**, supposed to be related to the Phrygian goddess Cybele and her successor Artemis. The baked earthenware or stone figures are 5–10cm tall and show a large-breasted, broad-hipped woman crouching to give birth. While the most interesting pieces are now in Ankara's Museum of Anatolian Civilizations (see p.472), a small **museum** near the site entrance houses some less remarkable finds.

Binbir Kilise

Directly north of Karaman, 107km southeast of Konya • Take a paved road 21km north from Karaman via Kılbasan, then turn left (northwest) and follow a rougher dirt track for 10km towards the village of Maden Şehir

Scattered across the base of the extinct volcano Kara Dağ, the remote region known as **Binbir Kilise**, or "A Thousand and One Churches", does indeed hold close to that number of ruined churches and monasteries. Most date from the ninth to the eleventh centuries, when the area was a refuge for persecuted Christians.

The village of **MADEN ŞEHIR**, in the middle of one of the main concentrations of basalt-built chapels, is all that's left of a substantial, unidentified town that flourished from Hellenistic to Byzantine times.

Kilistra

45km southwest of Konya • No public transport

The ancient site of **Kilistra**, first established in Hellenistic and Roman times, remains something of an enigma. It's said to be one of a handful of "hidden cities" that were built by the first Christian settlers in Anatolia, and carved into the rocks in a similar architectural style to the cave dwellings of Cappadocia. The site lies on the famous King's Road, and St Paul supposedly stopped by here en route to nearby Lycia. That claim is loosely supported by an area of the city named **Paulönü**, and the **Sünbül church** (a possible translation of St Paul).

Today the site lies within the traditional farming village of **Gökyurt**, renowned for its so-called "black-hive honey". It contains the well-preserved remains of a meeting hall, antique tombs, numerous cave dwellings and the intriguing **Sandikkay chapel** carved from a single piece of rock.

Cappadocia

The unique landscape of **Cappadocia** has become one of the star attractions of Turkey. Despite being plastered across tour brochures, however, it still retains much of the mystique that makes it so enchanting. While the dryness and omnipresent dust give an impression of barrenness, the volcanic tuff that forms the land is exceedingly fertile, and the peculiar formations of soft, dusty rock have been populated for millennia. The area's major appeal has to be its startlingly dramatic vistas – light dancing over fields of **fairy chimneys** and still-inhabited **rock caves** dotted throughout modern villages. Both local **wine**, produced since Hittite times, and the renowned **pottery** works fashioned from the clay of the Kızılırmak River, are still key crafts. In addition, the **horses** from which the region takes its name – Cappadocia translates from Hittite as "land of the beautiful horses" – still play a big role in local life, and make a popular way for visitors to explore the region.

The most famous sites are located within a triangle delineated by the roads connecting Nevşehir, Avanos and Ürgüp. This region holds the greater part of the valleys of fairy chimneys; the **rock-cut churches** of the **Göreme Open-Air Museum**, with their beautiful frescoes; and the **Zelve Open-Air Museum**, a fascinating warren of

THE GEOLOGICAL FORMATION OF CAPPADOCIA

The peaks of three **volcanoes** – Erciyes, Hasan and Melendiz Dağları – dominate Cappadocia. It was their eruptions, which covered the former plateau of Ürgüp in ash and mud some thirty million years ago, that provided the region's raw material: **tuff**, formed by compressed volcanic ash. Erosion has worked on this soft stone ever since, to form the valleys and curious fairy chimney rock formations for which the region is so famous.

The original eruptions created a vast erosion basin, dipping slightly towards the Kızılırmak River, which marks an abrupt division between the fantasy landscapes of rocky Cappadocia and the green farmland around Kayseri. Where the tuff is mixed with rock, usually basalt, the erosion process can result in the famous cone-shape chimneys: the tuff surrounding the basalt is worn away, until it stands at the top of a large cone. Eventually the underpart is eaten away to such an extent that it can no longer hold its capital: the whole thing collapses and the process starts again.

In the **Cemil valley**, near Mustafapaşa, the cones give way to tabular formations – table mountains – caused by the deep grooves made by rivers in the harder geological layers. Another important region lies northwest of the Melendiz mountain range – the valley of the Melendiz Suyu, or **Ihlara valley**. The most individual feature of this region is the red canyon through which the river flows, probably the most beautiful of all the Cappadocian landscapes.

7

troglodyte dwellings and churches. **Nevşehir**, the largest town, is an important travel hub, while **Ürgüp** and its neighbouring villages, **Göreme**, **Çavuşin**, **Uçhisar** and **Ortahisar**, all make attractive bases for tours of the surrounding valleys. **Avanos**, beautifully situated on the Kızılırmak River, is the centre of the local pottery industry.

A little further out, the underground cities of **Derinkuyu** and **Kaymaklı** are astonishingly sophisticated labyrinths that attest to the ingenuity of the ancient inhabitants. The **Ihlara** valley near **Aksaray**, a red canyon riddled with churches cut into its sides, is perhaps the most spectacular sight not to have yet felt the full force of tourism. **Kayseri** has long been a quiet provincial capital, recommended for its Selçuk architecture and bazaars, and side-trips out to the ski resort on Erciyes Dağı and the Sultansazlığı bird sanctuary. To the south, attractions around the town of **Niğde** include the **Eski Gümüşler** monastery, whose frescoes rival the more famous examples in Göreme.

Brief history

The earliest known settlers in the Cappadocia region were the **Hatti**, whose capital, Hattuşaş, was located north of Nevşehir. The growth of the Hattic civilization was interrupted by the arrival of large groups of Indo-European immigrants from Western Europe, the **Hittites** (see p.493). After the fall of the Hittite Empire, around 1200 BC, the region was controlled to varying degrees and at different times by its neighbouring kingdoms, Lydia and Phrygia in the west, and Urartu in the east. This continued until the middle of the sixth century BC, when the Lydian king Croesus was defeated by the Persians under Cyrus the Great.

Saved from Persian rule by the arrival of **Alexander the Great** in 333 BC, Cappadocia subsequently enjoyed independence for 350 years, until it became a Roman province with Kayseri (Caesarea) as its capital. Despite this nominal annexation, effective **independence** was ensured in the following centuries by the relative lack of interest of the Roman and Byzantine rulers, whose only real concerns were to control the roads (and thereby keep open eastern trading routes), and to extort tributes. Meanwhile the locals existed in much the same way as they do now, living in rock-hewn dwellings or building houses out of local stone, and relying on agriculture, viniculture and livestock breeding.

This neglect, combined with the influence of an important east–west trading route, enabled various faiths, creeds and philosophies to flourish. **Christianity** was introduced in the first century by St Paul; suffering from increasingly frequent attacks by Arab raiders, the new Christian communities sought refuge in the hills, where they carved out dwelling places, churches and monasteries.

The **Selçuk Turks** arrived in the eleventh century, quickly establishing good relations with the local communities and channelling their energy into improving trade routes and building the *kervansaray*s that are strung along these roads to this day. After the Selçuk Empire was defeated by the **Mongols** in the middle of the thirteenth century, Cappadocia was controlled by the Karaman dynasty, based in Konya, until it was incorporated into the Ottoman Empire in the fourteenth century. The last Christian Greeks left the area in the 1920s, during the exchange of populations by the Greek and Turkish governments.

Nevşehir

Home to Cappadocia's main airport, **NEVŞEHIR** is an important transport hub, but hardly a place to linger. It consists of a couple of scruffy streets (**Atatürk Bulvarı** and **Lale Caddesi**) with no real centre or monumental architecture.

Since the *otogar* lies just 1km north of the town centre, it's easy to make a quick foray downtown, while if you do stay, dolmuş side-trips to the monastic complex at Açıksaray are also straightforward.

Although the long walk up to the remains of the Ottoman **kale** (castle) in the heart of the old city is pleasant enough, once you get there, there's little left apart from a few crenellated walls.

Damat İbrahim Paşa Camii
On the side of the citadel hill

Completed in 1726, the **Damat İbrahim Paşa Camii** is still the most imposing building in Nevşehir, with its *medrese* and library above it and a tea garden directly below. Its construction stone is an attractive, unadorned yellow, while its internal painting, especially under the sultan's loge and around the casements, is delightful.

Nevşehir Museum

Yeni Kayseri Cad • Tues–Sun 8am–5pm • ₺3

Nevşehir Museum (Nevşehir Müzesi) is well worth the fifteen-minute walk from the tourist office. Its comprehensively labelled exhibits include three terracotta sarcophagi, dating from the third to fourth centuries AD, which resemble abstract mummy cases with little doors inserted at face and knee level. Finds from the Phrygian and Byzantine periods include mirrors, pins, spoons, terracotta pots and the like; upstairs is an exhibition of Turkish carpets and kilims, and the looms on which they were made, as well as lovely, old, heavy silver Ottoman jewellery.

ARRIVAL AND DEPARTURE NEVŞEHİR

By plane The airport is 30km northwest of the town centre. You can arrange for an Argeus tour-agency minibus (☎0384 341 4688, ⓦ capadocciaexclusive.com) to meet Turkish Airlines flights and take you to the village of your choice in Cappadocia.
Destinations İstanbul (2 daily; 1hr 20min).
By bus or dolmuş Nevşehir otogar is 1km north – a short dolmuş or city-bus ride – from the town centre. Most

minibuses running to and from Göreme, Avanos and Ürgüp drop off and pick up on Hafız İnce Kara Cad in the centre. Destinations Adana (3 daily; 5hr); Ankara (7 daily; 4hr 30min); Antalya (3 daily; 11hr); Fethiye (1 daily; 11hr 30min); Göreme (every 30min; 15min); Hacıbektaş (4 daily; 1hr); İstanbul (3 daily; 10hr); Kayseri (8 daily; 2hr); Konya (6 daily; 3hr); Mersin (3 daily; 5hr); Ürgüp (every 30min; 30min).

INFORMATION

Tourist office Atatürk Bulvarı, on the right as you head downhill towards Ürgüp (daily 8am–5.30pm; ☎0384 213 3659).

PTT Lale Cad, near the top of Atatürk Bulvarı.

ACCOMMODATION

Hotel Şems Atatürk Bul 27 ☎0384 213 3597, ⓦ semshotel.com. A comfortable and friendly option if you find yourself stuck in town. Rooms have en-suite

bathrooms and guaranteed hot water, but are dingily furnished; ask for a quieter room at the back. ₺60

Açıksaray

19km north of Nevşehir • Served by half-hourly Gülşehir dolmuşes from Nevşehir's otogar

The **Açıksaray** is a sixth- to seventh-century monastic complex, carved out of fairy chimneys and tuff cliffs. The abandoned remains include living quarters, stables and some decorative church facades, stretching around a square kilometre.

Far more rewarding is the nearby **church of St John**, 2km north towards Gülşehir (daily 8.30am–5.30pm; ₺8), and home to some of the most vibrant **frescoes** in Cappadocia, rescued from beneath the soot in 1995. As it is so rarely visited, you have time and space to appreciate the poignant biblical scenes, including the *Last Supper* and the *Betrayal by Judas*.

Hacıbektaş

45km north of Nevşehir • Catch an Ankara-bound bus from Nevşehir, or a dolmuş from Gülşehir, 20km north of Nevşehir

The small town of **HACIBEKTAŞ** was chosen by one of the greatest medieval Sufic philosophers, Hacı Bektaş Veli, as the location of a centre of scientific study. It was renamed in his honour after his death, and his tomb is located within the **Hacı Bektaş monastery complex**. The main part of the complex, however, dates from the Ottoman period, when it was the headquarters of a large community of Bektaşi dervishes.

Hacıbektaş is also well known for its **onyx**, by far the cheapest in the region – the relevant shops are located in the street that leads up to the monastery.

THE LIFE AND TEACHINGS OF HACI BEKTAŞ VELİ

While little is known about the life of **Hacı Bektaş Veli**, he is believed to have lived from 1208 to 1270. Like other Turkish intellectuals of the time, he was educated in Khorasan, where he became well versed in religion and mysticism. After journeying with his brother, he returned to Anatolia and lived in Kayseri, Kırşehir and Sivas. Eventually he settled in a hamlet of seven houses, Suluca Karahöyük, the present location of the monastery.

Hacı Bektaş's **teachings**, on the other hand, are well known. His great work, the *Makalat*, gives an account of a four-stage path to enlightenment or *Marifet* – a level of constant contemplation and prayer. The faults that grieved him most were ostentation, hypocrisy and inconsistency: "It is of no avail to be clean outside if there is evil within your soul." This could be the origin of the unorthodox customs of later followers of the **Bektaşi sect**, which included drinking wine, smoking hashish, eating during Ramadan and – for women – uncovering the head outside the home. Hacı Bektaş's widely quoted dictum on women was unequivocal: "A nation which does not educate its women cannot progress."

The teachings reverberated throughout the Muslim world, and sects including the Bektaşi, the Alevî and the Tahtacı still follow traditions that originated in his doctrines. These now form the main counterbalancing force to Islamic fundamentalism in Turkey.

An annual festival, held in Hacıbektaş August 16–18, celebrates the philosopher's life.

The monastery complex

Tues–Sun 8am–5pm • ₺3

Construction of the **monastery complex** started during the reign of Sultan Orhan in the fourteenth century, and it reopened as a **museum** in 1964. It comprises three courtyards, the second of which contains the attractive Aslanlı Çeşmesi, the **lion fountain**, named after a lion statue brought from Egypt in 1853. The sacred *karakazan* or **black kettle** (actually a cauldron) can be seen in the kitchen to the right of the courtyard. Important to both the Bektaşi sect and the janissaries, the black kettle originally symbolized communality, with possible reference to the Last Supper of the Christian faith.

To the left of the courtyard, the **Meydan Evi**, where formal initiation ceremonies and acts of confession took place, bears the earliest inscription in the complex, dated 1367. Its beautifully restored timber roof shows an ancient construction technique that's still in use in rural houses in central and eastern Anatolia. It's now an exhibition hall containing objects of significance to the order, including musical instruments and a late portrait of Hacı Bektaş, apparently deep in mystical reverie.

The third courtyard holds a **rose garden** and a well-kept **graveyard**, where the tombs bear the distinctive headwear of the Bektaşi order. The **tomb of the sage** is also located in the third courtyard, entered through the Akkapı, a white-marble entranceway decorated with typical Selçuk motifs including a double-headed eagle. A small room off the corridor leading to the tomb is said to have been the cell of Hacı Bektaş himself.

Underground cities

Among the most extraordinary phenomena of the Cappadocia region are the remains of **underground settlements**, some of them large enough to have accommodated up to thirty thousand people. A total of forty such settlements, from villages to vast cities, has been discovered, but only a few have so far been opened to the public. The best known are **Derinkuyu** and **Kaymaklı**, on the road from Nevşehir to Niğde. There are no fairy chimneys here, but the ground consists of the same volcanic tuff, out of which the beleaguered, ever-resourceful Cappadocians created vast cities that are almost completely unnoticeable from ground level.

The cities are thought to date back to **Hittite** times at least (1900–1200 BC). Hittite-style seals have been found during excavations, and other Hittite remains, such as a lion statue, have turned up. The underground rooms may have served as shelters during the attacks of

1200 BC, when invaders from Thrace destroyed the Hittite Empire. Later the complexes were enlarged by other civilizations, and the presence of missionary schools, churches and wine cellars would seem to indicate that they were used by **Christian communities**.

Derinkuyu

29km south of Nevşehir • Daily: May & June 8am–6pm; July–Sept 8am–7pm; Oct–April 8am–5pm • ₺15 • Dolmuşes from Nevşehir *otogar*, every 30min

Derinkuyu, the most thoroughly excavated of the underground cities, is so popular with tour groups that it's advisable to get there before 10am. The city is well lit and the original ventilation system still functions remarkably well, but some of the passages are low, narrow and can feel claustrophobic. The lowest floor in particular is reached by a very low passageway, best avoided by anyone with back problems.

The area cleared to date occupies 1500 square metres, and consists of a total of eight floors reaching to a depth of 55m. What you'll see includes, on the first two floors, stables, winepresses and a dining hall or school with two long, rock-cut tables; living quarters, churches, armouries and tunnels on the third and fourth floors; and a crucifix-shaped church, a meeting hall with three supporting columns, a dungeon and a grave on the lower levels. A circular passageway in a room off the meeting hall is believed to have been a confessional.

The city takes its name, meaning "deep well", from the 52 large **ventilation shafts** and **deep wells** that drop between 70m and 85m, far below the lowest floor level. A number of escape routes connect different floors, while passages lead beyond the city; one is thought to have gone all the way to Kaymaklı, 9km away. The walls of the rooms are completely undecorated, but chisel marks are clearly visible and give some idea of the work that went into the creation of this extraordinary place. Most evocative are the huge **circular doors** that could be used to seal one level from another. Virtually impregnable from the outside, these doors would have been closed with a pole through the circular hole in their centre. Once the door was secure, arrows could have been shot through the hole.

Kaymaklı

On Nevşehir–Niğde highway, 9km north of Derinkuyu • Daily: March–Sept 8am–7pm; Oct–Feb 8am–5pm • ₺15 • Dolmuşes from Nevşehir's *otogar* (Mon–Fri every 15min, Sat & Sun every 30min)

The underground city of **Kaymaklı** is slightly smaller, and thus less popular, than Derinkuyu. While only five of its levels have been excavated to date, there's still plenty to marvel at. The layout is very similar to Derinkuyu, and showcases such ingenuities as the winery, with its 30m-deep winepress, and the 60m-deep ventilation shaft (peek inside to see the footholds along the wall). Small living spaces open into underground plazas with various functions, the more obvious of which are stables, smoke-blackened kitchens and storage spaces. Most adults have to duck to get through the low passageways.

Kaymaklı's small size means that the streets are easy to navigate without a guide, but the added information you get from a tour certainly helps to bring the place to life.

Uçhisar

Uçhisar, 7km east of Nevşehir, is the first truly Cappadocian village en route to the centre of the region from Nevşehir. Much quieter than neighbouring Göreme, Uçhisar is extremely popular with French visitors, who have been coming here for decades. Its stunning hillside residences are home to some of the region's most luxurious accommodation.

Castle

Daily 7am–8.15pm • ₺3

Uçhisar is dominated by an imposing, 60m-high **rock/castle**, riddled with abandoned caves and tunnels that once housed the entire village. It makes a striking introduction to Cappadocia's extraordinary geology. The best time for a visit is at sunset, when the views of the surrounding countryside, including Erciyes Dağı to the east and Melendiz and Hasan Dağları to the southwest, are particularly alluring.

ARRIVAL AND DEPARTURE
UÇHISAR

By bus or dolmuş Dolmuşes from Nevşehir, Göreme and Ürgüp drop visitors just west of the centre of the upper village. Regardless of what overzealous taxi drivers may say, you can also catch the bus from a layby in the main road to Göreme, below the village.

ACCOMMODATION

The old village on the hillside is home to an array of plush hotels and restaurants, many encompassed within the enormous Cappadocia Cave Resort (w ccr-hotels.com), which monopolizes much of the area. A number of reasonably priced pensions are tucked in between the luxury suites.

Binbir Gece (1001 Nuits) Orhan Gök, just off the main square in the upper village ☏ 0384 219 2293, w 1001gecehotel.com. With friendly staff and sunny, parquet-floored rooms, this is a good-value choice. Easy to find, just a short stroll from the bus stop, it boasts a magnificent hilltop view from its peaceful terrace. **€25**

Kaya Pension Below the rock/castle ☏ 0384 219 2441, w kayapension.com. A homely pension, quirkily decorated with traditional musical instruments hung up around the restaurant area, and hallways strewn with brightly patterned kilim. Rooms are recently refurbished with sparkling bathrooms, and the terrace area has a relaxed vibe. **₺90**

Lale Saray Tekelli Mah ☏ 0384 219 2333, w lalesaray .com. Housed in an attractive pale-stone building, with bands of carved black stonework framing the windows and flower-lined walkways, this hotel offers great views over the valley to Göreme. The spacious rooms are a mix of barrel-vaulted cellars and caves, all fitted with big comfy beds and immaculate bathrooms with hydro-massage showers. **€100**

★ **Les Terrasses D'Uçhisar** Eski Göreme Yolu ☏ 0384 219 2792, w terrassespension.com. While new management has taken over this previously French-owned cave hotel, the clientele, as with many of the village's hotels, remain largely French. There's a unique East-meets-West feel to the place, with multilingual staff and a French-inspired dinner menu, juxtaposed with authentic cave rooms hung with traditional paintings and embroidered bedspreads. **€45**

Taşkonaklar (Rocky Palace) On the cliffside road as you head down to the lower village ☏ 0384 219 3001, w taskonaklar.com. If self-effacing luxury is what you're after, this stunning boutique hotel ticks all the boxes. It's an architectural accomplishment in itself, the maze of rooms built around beautifully preserved rock dwellings with arched ceilings, uniquely shaped alcoves and original chimneys dating back 150 years. Antique furnishings, a lavish garden terrace bursting with roses, and perhaps the best views in town, make this a classy choice. **€120**

EATING AND DRINKING

Lil'a Museum Hotel, Tekelli Mah 1 ☏ 0384 219 2220, w lil-a.com.tr. Recommended for its magnificent views and creative, all-organic Turkish cuisine, you'll pay for the privilege of dining at this stylish establishment (expect a full meal to set you back around ₺60), but it's worth it for a treat. It's best to reserve a table in advance, and the dress code is strictly smart, with no shorts, trainers or even T-shirts allowed. The restaurant also runs cooking classes and cooking tours to those interested in learning about local cuisine. Daily 7–10pm.

Seki Restaurant Argos Hotel, ☏ 0384 219 3130, w argosincappadocia.com. Perched on the cliff edge with incredible views from its all-glass facade, this restaurant is hip without being pretentious and features live music in the evenings. The cuisine is suitably upmarket, with a range of dishes for those with a curious palette – try the trout pastrami (₺24) or the apricot and meat skewers (₺22). Daily 7.30am–midnight.

DIRECTORY

Banks and money ATMs are located in the main square, but there are no banks.

Internet The Uçhisar internet café is just off the main square.
PTT Just east of the main square.

Göreme

The village of **GÖREME**, just 3km northeast of Uçhisar, is one of few remaining Cappadocian settlements whose rock-cut houses and fairy chimneys are still inhabited. These, along with the village's celebrated open-air museum, make it a hugely popular tourist destination. The honeycomb of cave dwellings etched into the landscape not only provides visual intrigue, but is well equipped to provide for everyone from budget backpackers to luxury holiday-makers. and there are carpet shops, *pansiyon*s, tour companies and restaurants everywhere.

While the influx of visitors has enabled the local economy to boom, the fragile environment is under increasing pressure, and prolific construction has pushed out many local residents. Despite the commercialization, however, Göreme has held on to a degree of authentic charm, and a short stroll off the main street or into the nearby valleys will still take you up into tuff landscapes, vineyards that the locals cultivate for the production of *pekmez* (grape molasses), and the occasional rock-cut church, unknown to the crowds who frequent the nearby museum.

Churches of Göreme

Signposted off Uzundere Cad

Two ancient Christian **churches** are located in the hills above Göreme. Believed to date from the seventh century, **Kadir Durmuş Kilisesi** has a cave house with rock-cut steps next door to it, clearly visible from the path across a vineyard. It's not painted, but it has a fascinating and unusual upstairs gallery, and cradle-shaped tombs outside.

The eleventh-century **Yusuf Koç Kilisesi**, or "church with five pillars", boasts two domes, one of which has been damaged in the past to accommodate a pigeon coop, and frescoes in very good condition. Among them are the Annunciation, to the left; saints George and Theodore slaying the dragon, to the right; and Helena and Constantine depicted with the True Cross beside the door. The dome above the altar holds the Madonna and Child, while below, beside the altar, are the four Evangelists.

Göreme Open-Air Museum

1.5km southeast • Daily: summer 8am–7pm; winter 8am–5pm; last entry 45min before closing • ₺15, audioguide ₺10

The **Göreme Open-Air Museum** is the best known and most visited of all the monastic settlements in the Cappadocia region. It's also the largest of the religious complexes, and its **churches**, of which there are over thirty, contain some fascinating frescoes.

GÖREME

BARS & CAFÉS
Fat Boys	2
Mydonose	3
Panorama	1

RESTAURANTS
Cappadocian Cuisine	2
Dibek	4
Koy Evi	6
Meeting Point	3
Orient Restaurant	1
Top Deck	5

ACCOMMODATION
Anatolian Houses	6
Blue Moon	4
Dilek Camping	2
Dorm Cave	8
Göreme House	12
Kaya Camping	5
Kookaburra	7
Köse	1
Melek Cave Hotel	9
Rock Valley	11
SOS Cave Hotel	10
Walnut House	3

Virtually all date from the period after the Iconoclastic controversy, and mainly from the second half of the ninth to the end of the eleventh century.

The three columned churches

The best-known churches in the main complex of Göreme are the three eleventh-century columned churches: the **Elmalı Kilise** ("Church of the Apple"), the **Karanlık Kilise** ("Dark Church"; separate entrance fee of ₺8) and the **Çarıklı Kilise** ("Church of the Sandals"). All were heavily influenced by Byzantine forms: constructed to an inscribed cross plan, the central dome, supported on columns, contains the Pantocrator above head-and-shoulders depictions of the archangels and seraphim. The painting of the churches, particularly of Elmalı Kilise, is notable for the skill with which the form and movement of the figures correspond to the surfaces they cover, and their features are smoothly modelled. The intricately carved facade of the restored Karanlık Kilise is painted an expensive blue colour, obtained from the mineral azurite.

Barbara Kilise

The open-air museum holds various late eleventh-century single-aisle churches that are covered in crude geometric patterns and linear pictures, painted straight onto the rock. The **Barbara Kilise** ("Church of St Barbara") in this style is named after a depiction of the saint on the north wall. Christ is represented on a throne in the apse. The strange insect-figure for which the church is also known must have had a symbolic or magical significance that is now lost.

Yılanlı Kilise

The **Yılanlı Kilise** ("Church of the Snake") is most famous for the depiction of St Onophrius on the west wall of the nave. St Onophrius was a hermit who lived in the Egyptian desert, eating only dates, with a foliage loincloth for cover. Opposite him, Constantine the Great and his mother St Helena are depicted holding the True Cross. Between the Yılanlı and the Karanlık churches is a **refectory** with a rock-cut table designed to take about fifty diners.

Tokalı Kilise

50m before museum ticket office • Use museum ticket to gain entrance

The best preserved and most fascinating of the churches on the road back to Göreme village from the open-air museum is the **Tokalı Kilise** ("Church with the Buckle"). Different in plan to others in the area, it features a transverse nave and an atrium hewn out of an earlier church, known as the "Old Church". The **frescoes** here, dating from the second decade of the tenth century, are classic examples of the archaic period of Cappadocian painting: the style is linear, but like the mosaics of Aya Sofya in İstanbul, the faces are modelled by the use of different intensities of colour. The paintings in the New Church are magnificent examples of tenth-century Byzantine art, with scenes of the Passion and Resurrection: the Descent from the Cross, the Entombment, the Holy Women at the Sepulchre and the Resurrection.

Saklı Kilise

Halfway between museum and village

The **Saklı Kilise** ("Hidden Church") uses Cappadocian landscapes complete with fairy chimneys as a background for biblical scenes. It lives up to its name, so ask the church's keyholder to show you the way. You can find him in the shop Hikmet's Place.

Hiking to Uçhisar

The most rewarding **walk** in the Göreme region is the 4km, two-hour hike to the picturesque village of **Uçhisar**. Starting above the *Ataman Hotel*, the path heads through

7

OUTDOOR AND ADVENTURE TOURISM IN CAPPADOCIA

HOT-AIR BALLOONING

The region's canyons and fairy chimneys take on dazzling hues at sunrise and **hot-air balloon** trips have become ubiquitous. Hundreds of balloons take to the skies early each morning, so you won't be alone, but it's nevertheless an unmissable adventure. Be sure to pick a reputable company; very cheap prices may indicate that the company scrimps on safety.

Göreme Balloons ☎ 0384 341 5662, ⓦ goremeballoons.com. Reliable and safety-conscious, with daily flight departures; prices from €150 per hour, including transfer and breakfast.

Kapadokya Balloons Based in Göreme

☎ 0384 271 2442, ⓦ kapadokyaballoons.com. The original operator, with twenty years' experience and highly professional pilots. Standard flights (1hr) begin at dawn and cost €175 per person, including transfers, insurance and breakfast.

MOUNTAIN BIKING

Cappadocia is tailor-made for **mountain biking**. Amid its hilly terrain and plunging valleys, networks of dirt tracks connect villages to each other and to their fields. The annual Cappadocia Mountain Bike Festival attracts top bikers from around the world.

Argeus Istiklal Cad 7, Ürgüp ☎ 0384 341 4688, ⓦ capadocciaexclusive.com. The first local mountain-biking agency, offering guided tours and bike rental.

Kirkit Voyage Atatürk Cad 50, Avanos

☎ 0384 511 3259, ⓦ kirkit.com. Bike rental and tours.

Middle Earth Travel Göreme ☎ 0384 271 2559, ⓦ middleearthtravel.com. Mountain-bike rental and tours.

HORSERIDING

With its wide-open spaces, vast canyons and jutting mountain paths, Cappadocia evokes the Wild West, and **horseriding** makes a natural way to explore. Several ranches have opened up, but be wary of so-called "Turkish cowboys", with no track record of safety and horse welfare. Both companies below are long-standing and reputable, with excellent safety equipment.

Akhal-Teke Gesteriç Sok, Avanos ☎ 0384 511 5171, ⓦ akhal-tekehorsecenter.com. Modern stables housed in a beautiful garden and restaurant complex, with lessons also available in their arena. Rides start at ₺50 for an hour, but treks of up to 9 days are possible.

Kirkit Voyage Atatürk Cad 50, Avanos

☎ 0384 511 3259, ⓦ kirkit.com. A well-regarded stable with 45 well-groomed horses, tours to suit all abilities, and excellent, knowledgeable guides. This place featured on the US TV series *Equitrekking*, and has great options for more experienced riders too. 2-hour treks from €35.

HIKING

While there are plenty of **hiking trails** through the valleys, so far only basic sketch maps are widely available, and signposts sparse. The trail from Göreme to Uçhisar through Pigeon Valley (see p.437), and the Ihlara Gorge, are among the most popular routes with independent walkers.

Walking Mehmet Café Roma, Göreme ☎ 0532 382 2069, ⓦ walkingmehmet.com. Mehmet knows the area inside out, and leads group hikes for €50 per day.

Middle Earth Travel Göreme ☎ 0384 271 2559,

ⓦ middleearthtravel.com. From €40 per person for hikes in the Ihlara valley; from €175 for two-day climbs up Erciyes Dağı or Hasan Dağı; from €560 for a one-week trek, including accommodation.

SKIING AND SNOWSHOEING

Between Christmas and early March, winter snows give the Cappadocian landscape a hauntingly beautiful appearance, and **snowshoeing** is growing in popularity. Both Kirkit and Argeus can help organize **ski-touring/mountaineering** in the region, renting out equipment from €30/day as well as organizing all-inclusive guided tours. For downhill skiing the resort on the flank of Erciyes Dağı (see p.462) has reliable snow and reasonable facilities.

Argeus Istiklal Cad 7, Ürgüp ☎ 0384 341 4688, ⓦ capadocciaexclusive.com. This ski-touring and mountaineering operator organizes all-inclusive guided tours, and offers equipment rental from €30 per day.

Kirkit Voyage Atatürk Cad 50, Avanos ☎ 0384 511 3259, ⓦ kirkit.com. Experienced ski-touring and mountaineering company, offering a wide range of tours plus equipment rental.

the Uzundere valley, passing through rock-cut tunnels into the heart of the Cappadocian countryside. Good shoes are essential, and the final descent into Uçhisar is precipitous, with narrow stretches, but it's an easy route to follow. Minibuses run the route frequently, so you can easily catch a ride back to Göreme.

ARRIVAL AND DEPARTURE

GÖREME

By bus Göreme's *otogar* is in the town centre. Cappadocia Express (☎0384 271 3070, ⌨cappadociatransport.com) runs airport shuttle buses to Nevşehir (₺20) and Kayseri (₺25), with hotel pickup.

Destinations Alanya (2 daily; 12hr); Ankara (5 daily; 4hr); Antalya (2 daily; 10hr); Denizli (2 daily; 10hr); Eğirdir (2 daily; 3hr); İstanbul (3 daily; 11hr); İzmir (1 daily; 11hr 30min);

Kayseri (hourly; 1hr 30min); Konya (4 daily; 3hr); Marmaris (2 daily; 15hr); Nevşehir (hourly; 30min); Ürgüp (hourly; 20min).

Car and bike rental Several companies around the *otogar* rent out cars, mountain bikes and scooters, including Öz Cappadocia (cars from ₺90 per day; bikes from ₺20 for 8hr; mopeds from ₺40 for 8hr; ☎0384 271 2159, ⌨ozcappadocia.com).

INFORMATION AND TOURS

Tourist office Göreme's tourist office is right in the centre of the village, next to the *otogar* (daily 5am–8pm; ☎0384 271 2558).

Tours Reputable tour companies include Middle Earth

Travel, Cevizler Sok 20, Neşe (☎0384 271 2525, ⌨nesetour), and Matiana, Uzundere Sok (☎0384 271 2902, ⌨matiana .com). Both offer daily tours from €40 per person including the Ihlara valley, Soğanlı and the underground cities.

7

ACCOMMODATION

With tourism booming in Göreme, entrepreneurial locals are developing hotels on every available plot of land. While the desire for authentic cave dwellings is at least keeping the landscape attractive, many of the cheap and cheerful pensions beloved by backpackers are being transformed into luxury suites with price tags to match.

CAMPSITES

Dilek Camping Müzesi Yolu 11 ☎0384 271 2395. A short walk from the town centre, with basic but clean washing and cooking facilities, free wi-fi and power, and a pool, restaurant and tour company on site, this is a good budget option for campers. Weekly rates are possible and low-season rates can be bargained down. The rates shown here are for two people, per night. Tents ₺30, caravans ₺70

Kaya Camping 2.5km southeast on Ortahisar road ☎0384 343 3100. A spacious campsite with all facilities including a small shop selling necessities, shade provided by apricot and cherry trees, and a huge swimming pool. Weekly rates available. The rates shown here are for two people, per night. Tents ₺30, caravans ₺33

BACKPACKER/PENSIONS

Blue Moon Pension Müze Yolu 24 ☎0384 271 2433, ⌨bluemoonmotel.net. An easy stroll from the bus station, this hotel's sunny rooms are the light at the end of the eerily cool cave/lobby tunnel, with orange painted walls and patterned bedspreads. The huge flower-filled terrace with tables and floor cushions makes the place as inviting as it is cheery. ₺90

Dorm Cave Efendi Sok 4 ☎0384 271 2770, ⌨travellerscave.com. The latest addition to the ever-growing chain of Traveller's Cave hotels, this budget option makes a welcome alternative to Göreme's increasingly upmarket hotels, and is run by young, English-speaking staff. Newly refurbished cave rooms are clean, comfy and

well designed, and female-only dorms are available. Dorm beds ₺10

★**Kookaburra** Konak Sok 10 ☎0384 271 2549, ⌨kookaburramotel.com. Incredibly comfy beds, clean and roomy bathrooms, fast wi-fi and a nice quiet location make this the perfect place for budget travellers to indulge in some home comforts. Göreme-born owner İhsan will be happy to share his vast local knowledge as you share a beer on the idyllic rooftop terrace, and his eclectic collection of antique mementos lends the place a homely vibe. The cheapest rooms share bathrooms; en-suite doubles cost ₺20 extra. ₺60

Köse Pension Just off the Avanos road, near the post office ☎0384 271 2294, ⌨kosepension.com. Run by the hospitable Mehmet and Dawn, this travellers' favourite offers a pleasant garden with an excellent swimming pool and a choice of dorm beds, doubles with and without bathrooms, and simple singles, all clean and colourful. The food is well regarded, too, mixing local dishes with backpacker staples, but you'll pay extra for breakfast. Dorm beds ₺15, doubles ₺100

Rock Valley Pension Isali Mah, Iceri Dere Sok ☎0384 271 2831, ⌨rockvalleycappadocia.com. A deservedly popular option among budget visitors, adorned with colourful paintings, this friendly place also boasts a sizeable pool and communal lounge areas, making it a great place to meet other travellers. Rooms are clean, cheery and well furnished; the cheapest doubles share bathrooms, but en-suite rooms are available for ₺20 extra. Dorm beds ₺25, female-only dorms ₺30, doubles ₺70

7

Walnut House Uzundere Cad 6 ☎0384 271 2235, ⓦwalnuthousehotel.com. A delightful family-run pension right in the village centre, and flanked by beautiful rose gardens, this place instantly feels like home. The simple yet stylish rooms are the masterpiece of the architect owner, and feature modern furnishings, plenty of natural light and heated marble floors throughout. The backyard vegetable garden fuels the home-made breakfasts. **€40**

HOTELS

★ **Anatolian Houses** Garferli Mah ☎0384 271 2463, ⓦanatolianhouses.com.tr. While the steep asking price will put off mere mortals, if money's no object you'd be hard pushed to find a more stunningly beautiful hotel. Built around five natural fairy chimneys and sculpted from pristine white stone, not only are the cave rooms wonderfully preserved but each is individually designed to make the most of its unique features. A heavenly courtyard with a waterfall and wine fountain lead through to the underground spa, a work of art in glistening marble, with a large indoor pool and hamam. The spa and hamam are open to non-guests for a €15 cover charge. **€240**

Göreme House Eselli Mah 47 ☎0384 271 2060, ⓦgoremehouse.com. A smart, well-run hotel with chic dark-wood furnishings, modern bathrooms equipped with massage showers, and a mix of cave and non-cave rooms. The big breezy terrace offers wonderful views over the valleys, and the quiet cosy courtyard is perfect if you want a little privacy. **€65**

★ **Melek Cave Hotel** Cevizler Sok 28 ☎0384 271 2223, ⓦmelekcave.com. If you're looking for authentic cave dwellings coupled with an extremely friendly, family staff, this place is great value, with six of its ten rooms set in original cave surroundings. Stone stairwells and hobbit-hole doorways lead into the cosy rooms, with quirky cave features adding character to the relaxed decor. **₺80**

SOS Cave Hotel Just off Uzundere Cad ☎0384 271 2134, ⓦsoscavehotel.com. This humble and incredibly welcoming hotel has been open for 25 years and the genuinely friendly local staff will give you good, honest information about local sights. Excellent-value rooms (including nine authentic cave rooms) are clean, functional and comfortable, with a dorm for budget travellers and free pickup from the *otogar*. Dorm beds **₺15**, doubles **₺40**

EATING

★ **Cappadocian Cuisine** Yanı Uzundere Cad ☎0536 964 6225, ✉farmvillegoreme@hotmail.com. Delicious traditional foods are the order of the day in this humble family-run place, a great spot to tuck into good food at good prices. Owner Hatice also invites small groups into her traditional cave house nearby, where she'll cook up her most delicious dishes in her own kitchen for around ₺12–20 per person; advance bookings essential. Daily 6.30am–10.30pm.

★ **Dibek** On the main square ☎0384 271 2209, ⓦdibektraditionalcook.com. Set in a cool, vaulted cave room with traditional floor cushions and lantern-lit hallways, this place oozes atmosphere. Thankfully, it's not just a facade; the *testi* kebabs deserve their stellar reputation (a meat or vegetarian dish slow-cooked in a sealed clay pot, ₺28; pre-order, as they take 3hr to cook), and are best coupled with the excellent home-made wine and traditional village dessert *aside* (an oddly more-ish sweet made from flour, oil and grape molasses, ₺7). Daily 8am–late.

Koy Evi Aydınkırağı Sok 40 ☎0384 271 2008, ⓦcappadociakoyevi.com. Quickly gaining popularity with the masses for its traditional "village food", this friendly restaurant makes an interesting change from the many tourist haunts. While it's fascinating to watch the women cook your food in their traditional outdoor kitchen, and bake fresh bread in the *fırın* (stone oven), the food itself is rather bland. That said, there's plenty to go around and ₺25 buys you a dozen or so different dishes to share. Daily 8am–1am.

Meeting Point Müze Cad 34 ☎0535 894 9436. A lively café run by a bunch of friendly local ladies who serve up an extensive menu of delicious freshly squeezed fruit juices, smoothies and shakes (from ₺6). There's a good range of burgers, salads and *gözleme* on offer too, and a pleasant rooftop terrace to watch the world go by. Daily: summer 8.30am–11.30pm, winter 9am–9pm.

Orient Restaurant Adnan Menderes Cad ☎0384 271 2346, ⓦorientrestaurant.net. Favoured by locals and tourists alike, this sizeable restaurant has the ambience for a romantic evening, coupled with a good mix of Turkish and international cuisine, using ingredients sourced from their organic vegetable garden out the back. The lamb shank (₺40) are popular, but there are plenty of cheaper options, plus home-made desserts and an extensive wine list. Daily 9am–midnight.

★ **Top Deck** Efendi Sok 15 ☎0384 271 2474. Eating at *Top Deck* is more like an intimate dinner party, set in a cosy, windowless cave where guests sprawl on plump floor cushions and dine by the flicker of candlelight. Mustafa – Mr Top Deck himself – and his South African wife Zaida bring barrel-loads of personality and enthusiasm to the table, tailoring dishes to each individual and presenting a delicious array of soups, *mezes* (the *börek* are delicious) and tender lamb chops. Best of all is the very reasonable price – a mere ₺15 for a *meze* plate or main dish. Reservation only. Mon–Thurs 6pm–midnight, Sat & Sun 5pm–midnight.

DRINKING AND NIGHTLIFE

Göreme's once-thriving bar scene has been somewhat put to rest by the soaring popularity of hot-air ballooning. With many visitors heading to bed early in preparation for a 4am start, there's little market these days for partying.

Fat Boys ☎0536 936 3652, ✉yilmazsisman@hotmail .com. The best pub in town, run by Turkish-Australian couple Yilmaz and Angela, and serving local and imported beers (from ₺7.50), delicious fruit slushies (₺6), nargiles and cheap and tasty bar food. Board games, international football on TV, and a relaxed, varied crowd. Daily 9am–late.

Mydonose Müze Cad 18 ☎0384 271 2850. An atmospheric café and bar with excellent selection of international coffees (including decadent hot chocolates and frappuccinos, from ₺6), this is the place to get your after-dinner caffeine fix. The relaxed rooftop terrace has a good mix of people, great views, and comfy seating, and there's a cocktail menu if you prefer something a little stronger. Daily 8am–2am.

Panorama Uzundere Cad ☎0384 271 2494, ✉panoramacafe_cave@hotmail.com. Bohemian stylings and a rainbow of comfortable beanbag chairs lend this place a chilled-out vibe, and there's an extensive menu of reasonably priced drinks (beers ₺5) and waterpipes (₺8). Owner Demirci has been inviting guests to sign his extensive pottery collection for several years, and the results create an inspiring display across the walls. Daily 6am–2am.

DIRECTORY

Banks and money Several ATMs near the tourist office.
Cooking Classes Top Deck, Efendi Sok 15 ☎0384 271 2474, ✉topdeckcave@yahoo.com. English-speaking owner-chef Mustafa runs classes from his restaurant. For €40 per person, you spend the morning preparing a three-course menu, then sit down to enjoy the fruits of your labours.

Hamam Elis Kapadokya Hamamı in Göreme (☎0384 271 2975, ⊕elishamam.com) is an immaculate and unintimidating tourist-orientated hamam that offers excellent traditional services, perfect for those new to the experience. An all-in package costs ₺60 including soap massage/scrub, sauna and swimming pool, while an oil massage is ₺20 for 10min.

Çavuşin

A small village set beneath the abandoned cave dwellings of its old town, **ÇAVUŞIN** stands 6km north of Göreme, off the road to Avanos. While rock falls have rendered these caves uninhabitable, and villagers have gradually moved to the other side of town, the area is wonderful to explore – hire a local guide to make the most of it (and avoid crumbling pathways). Sadly, the original caves are being sold off to make way for developments, so the peaceful surrounds of the tiny village may not remain intact.

CHRISTIANITY IN CAPPADOCIA

Cappadocia today holds more than a thousand churches, dating from the earliest days of Christianity to the thirteenth century. For many centuries the religious authority of the capital of Cappadocia, Caesarea (present-day Kayseri), extended over the whole of southeast Anatolia, and it was where Gregory the Illuminator, the evangelizer of Armenia, was raised. The region also produced some of the greatest early ecclesiastical writers, including the fourth-century **Cappadocian Fathers**: Basil the Great, Gregory of Nazianzen and Gregory of Nyssa.

By the start of the eighth century, the political power of Cappadocia's increasing number of monks was beginning to cause concern, leading to the closure of monasteries and confiscation of their property. The worst period of repressive activity occurred during the reign of Constantine V, marked by the **Iconoclastic Council** of 754. All sacred images, except the cross, were forbidden, a ruling that had a profound effect on the creative life of the region's churches.

After the restoration of the cult of images in 843, the religious activity of Cappadocia saw a renewed vigour. The wealth of the Church increased to such an extent that in 964 monastery building was prohibited, an edict only withdrawn in 1003. Meanwhile, the religious communities were brought to heel, controlled to a greater extent by the ecclesiastical hierarchy. Even though Cappadocia continued to be a centre of religious activity well into the Ottoman period, it had lost the artistic momentum that had produced the extraordinary works of earlier centuries.

While Çavuşin is often overpowered by tour groups during the day, its unique landscape, great central location on hiking routes and quiet village feel make it a pleasant place to stay. Its shortage of eating options and facilities, however, means it's most suitable for travellers with their own transport.

The best approach to the village is to walk from Göreme through the fabulous tuff landscapes of the **Rose Valley**. Follow the path for about forty minutes, and where it takes a helter-skelter bend through a tuff tunnel to the left, follow the precipitous path to the right, heading down into the Kızılçukur valley: this will bring you to Çavuşin in another half-hour or so.

Church of St John the Baptist

Daily 8am–5pm, last entry 4.30pm • ₺8

A large basilica with a colonnaded and moulded facade set up on the cliff-face, the **church of St John the Baptist** was thought to have been a centre of pilgrimage, most probably constructed in the fifth century. Inside is a votive pit, the only one in Cappadocia, that is thought to have contained the hand of St Hieron, a local saint born a few kilometres away.

The Pigeon House

The church known as the **Pigeon House**, located in a tower of rock, is renowned for its frescoes, which commemorate the passage of the Byzantine emperor Nicephoras Phocas through Cappadocia in 964–965, during his military campaign in Cilicia. He's thought to have been making a pilgrimage to the church of St John the Baptist, nearby.

Paşabağı

The most picturesque of all the Cappadocian valleys, **Paşabağı**, between Zelve and Çavuşin, makes a pleasant hour's walk from the village. As a favourite place of retreat for stylite hermits who lodged in the abundant fairy chimneys, it was once known as "Valley of the Monks". One of the triple-coned chimneys contains a **chapel** dedicated to St Simeon Stylites, hollowed out at three levels, with a monk's cell at the top. A hundred metres east of the chapel, a **cell** bears the inscription "Receive me, O grave, as you received the Stylite."

ARRIVAL AND DEPARTURE   ÇAVUŞIN

By dolmuş The Avanos dolmuş drops visitors at the village.

ACCOMMODATION AND EATING

Panorama Pansiyon & Restaurant Set back from the road, towards the bottom of the village ☎ 0384 532 7002, ✉ panorama@cavusin.net. The basic, simply furnished rooms are clean, comfortable and good value, and the attached restaurant makes a pleasant lunchtime option, serving *gözleme* (₺6), traditional beef casseroles (₺13) and beers (₺6). **₺80**

Turbel Cave Hotel Behind the Panorama ☎ 0384 532 7084, ⓦ turbelcavehotel.com. This new hotel has only four rooms, featuring some original cave structures alongside wooden floors, big marble-floored bathrooms and clean, modern furnishings. **₺120**

Village Cave Hotel Nestled beneath a cliff at the head of a small valley ☎ 0384 532 7197, ⓦ thevillagecave .com. An intriguing building full of original cave features and eerie lantern-lit tunnels, this is a great option if you fancy a taste of authentic cave life. There's bags of atmosphere, but beware that these are traditional dwellings; while they're comfortable, rooms can be dark and a bit musty. **₺190**

Zelve Open-Air Museum

3km off the Avanos–Çavuşin road • Daily: May–Oct 8am–6.30pm; Nov–April 8am–4.30pm; last entry 15min before closing • ₺8 • Dolmuşes from Avanos, Göreme and Ürgüp (every 2hr)

A fascinating remnant of Cappadocia's troglodytic past, the deserted city that spreads across the three valleys of **Zelve** makes up the **Zelve Open-Air Museum**. The valley was inhabited by Turkish Muslims until 1952, when rock falls, which still occur, made it too dangerous to remain. Areas are frequently closed off due to unstable surrounds, and it's essential to heed the warning signs.

To explore the complex, bring a torch and old clothes, along with a considerable sense of adventure. At the top of the right-hand valley, on the right as you go up, a honeycomb of rooms is approached up metal staircases. Some are entered by means of precarious steps, others by swinging up through large holes in their floors (look for ancient hand- and foot-holes). Old stables, pigeon houses high up on the walls, an old mill, still with its wheel stone intact, and a large number of chapels and medieval oratories, many decorated with carved **crosses** and well-preserved altars, are scattered up and down the valleys. The few **painted images** found in Zelve are in the churches of the third valley, and nearby, the twin-aisled **Üzümlü Kilise** has grapevines painted in red and green on the walls, and a cross carved into the ceiling.

Ortahisar

The friendly little village of **ORTAHİSAR**, off the road between Göreme and Ürgüp, retains a degree of charm and innocence absent from many of Cappadocia's more touristed areas. Its chief attraction is the staggering, fortress-like 86m-high **rock** that once housed the entire village, which is now in precarious shape and should be explored only with extreme caution.

Pancarlık church and monastery complex

3km south of Ortahisar • Daily: summer 8am–7pm; winter 8am–5pm • ₺3 • Follow the road marked "Pancarlık Kilise" off the second square to reach the valley of the Üzenge Çay

Hardly visited due to the difficulty of access, the **Pancarlık church and monastery complex** holds some excellent frescoes in good condition – even their faces are intact. They include the Baptism of Christ and the Annunciation, and, to the left of the altar, the Nativity.

ARRIVAL AND DEPARTURE   ORTAHİSAR

By bus or dolmuş Regular *Belediye* buses run from Avanos direct to Ortahisar, or an Uçhisar–Ürgüp dolmuş will stop on the Nevşehir–Kayseri road, leaving you a 20min downhill walk to the village.

ACCOMMODATION AND EATING

Alkabris Ali Reis Sok 23 ☎0384 343 3433, ⓦalkabris .com. Tucked away in a peaceful warren of old dwellings behind the village rock, this elegant hotel is run by a friendly Turkish couple who speak some French and English. The immaculate white stone en-suite rooms are beautifully decorated, with colourful hand-made mosaics adorning walls, curtains and tabletops. There's parking outside, but the steep rocky roads can be quite difficult to navigate. **€100**

Culture Museum & Restaurant Cumhuriyet Meyd 15 ☎0384 343 3344, ⓦculturemuseum.com. Dinner by reservation only. Standing out amid Ortahisar's slim pickings, this stylish restaurant offers a wide range of local favourites, with mains starting from ₺15 and a pretty good wine list. Best of all is the quirky "culture museum" (free to guests, ₺2 otherwise), a series of installations showcasing traditional Cappadocian lifestyles – a fun, if limited, way to stir up your imagination and marvel at some of the traditional ways of cooking, building and socializing. Daily 9am–6.30pm.

★ **Hezen Cave Hotel** Tahir Bey Sok 87 ☎0384 343 3005, ⓦhezenhotel.com. One of Cappadocia's most distinctive and inspired boutique hotels, *Hezen* effectively meshes modern splashes of colour with beautifully preserved cave interiors, a *hezen* roof and creative furnishings. Each of the ten cave rooms is unique, with cosy alcoves, spotlit wall holes and quirky cave wardrobes, and one holds an original fresco. The roomy breakfast terrace enjoys incredible views across the valley. Best of all, with its friendly staff and welcoming, non-pretentious vibe, the place hasn't traded cordiality for style. **€150**

Ürgüp

With its clusters of stately cave hotels nuzzled in the tuff cliffs of the Esbelli district, and a burgeoning population of bijou bars and restaurants, **ÜRGÜP** makes a worthy rival to Göreme as the destination of choice for visitors to Cappadocia. Before 1923, Ürgüp had a largely Greek population, so many distinctive and beautiful houses of Greek (and Ottoman) origin are still scattered around the town.

The old village

Despite its rather incongruous modern central square, Ürgüp retains much of its rural village charm. Men and women in traditional working clothes, leading horse-drawn vehicles and donkeys out to the surrounding vineyards, orchards and vegetable gardens, are not an unusual early-morning sight. This is the time to explore the **old village**, whose buildings appear to be slowly emerging from the rocky hills into which they have been carved. Some feature stylish pillared and decorated facades of the same stone; others are simple caves with doors and windows cut into the cliffs themselves.

Temmeni

Daily 8.30am–6pm • Free

The walk up to the central park known as **Temmeni** ("Hill of Wishes") starts with a flight of steps opposite the thirteenth-century **Kebir Camii**, and includes a 700m-long tunnel, which leads to a "balcony", furnishing panoramic views of the town and surrounding countryside. Continuing uphill, past the former troglodyte town dwellings (now mainly used for storage or abandoned altogether), brings you to the park itself, where a Selçuk tomb, the **Kılıç Arslan Türbe**, dating from 1268, is open to visitors. A small, renovated *medrese* from the same period now serves as a café.

ÜRGÜP

CAPPADOCIAN WINE

With its cool mountain climate and fertile volcanic soils, Cappadocia is blessed with the ideal climate for growing grapes. Wine making here dates back four thousand years, and many vineyards remain small and family run. Their crops are used for both wine and grape juice, as well as being boiled to produce *pekmez*, a sweet grape syrup. Local wines are celebrated in Ürgüp's **International Wine Festival**, held each October, and can be sampled on vineyard tours.

Kocabağ Kav Butik Uçhisar ☎ 0384 219 2979, ⓦ kocabagurgup.com. A popular winehouse offering free samples of their award-winning wines (try the fruity white Narince) in an atmospheric traditional cave room. Kocabağ also offers guided tours by request of their wine production outlet, 45km out of town. Daily: summer 8am–8pm, winter 8am–6pm.

Turasan Yunak Mah, Tevrik Fikret Cad, Ürgüp ☎ 0384 341 4961, ⓦ turasan.com.tr. Cappadocia's oldest wine producer, established in 1943, produces some of the region's finest wines and has an annual output of 2,161,000 litres. The upmarket winery offers free tastings and guided tours (including additional tastings, ₺12.50). Friendly, English-speaking and extremely knowledgeable staff make this a great place to start your wine education – be sure to sample the crisp *Emir* and fruity, deep red *Öküzgözü*. Daily 8am–6pm.

Ürgüp Museum

Kayseri Cad • Tues–Sun 8am–12.30pm & 2.30–5.30pm • Free

Ürgüp's **museum** is tiny and not particularly well labelled, but the helpful staff are prepared to explain the exhibits. These include a selection of prehistoric ceramics, figurines, lamps, stelae, statues and ornaments found during excavations in the area.

ARRIVAL AND DEPARTURE ÜRGÜP

By bus or dolmuş The *otogar* is in the centre of town. Destinations Adana (4 daily; 5hr); Ankara (6 daily; 5hr); Antalya (2 daily; 10hr); Denizli (2 daily; 12hr); Göreme (hourly; 20min); İstanbul (3 daily; 13hr); Kayseri (hourly; 1hr 30min); Konya (8 daily; 3hr); Marmaris (2 daily; 15hr); Mersin (3 daily; 5hr); Nevşehir (hourly; 30min).

Car rental Avis, İstiklâl Cad 19, Belediye Pasajı ☎ 0384 341 2177; Alpin, Cumhuriyet Meyd 32 ☎ 0384 341 7522.
Bike rental Alpin, on Cumhuriyet Meyd, rents out scooters (€25 per day), while Argeus, Istiklal Cad 7 (☎ 0384 341 4688, ⓦ cappadociaexclusive.com), is good for mountain bikes (€20 per day).

INFORMATION AND TOURS

Tourist office Kayseri Cad 37, next to the museum in a park with tea garden (daily: May–Sept 8am–6pm, Oct–April 8am–5pm; ☎ 0384 341 4059).
Tours Euphrates Tours, İstiklâl Cad 59 (☎ 0384 341 7487, ⓦ cappadociatours.com). An excellent range of tailored cultural tours with the best local guides. A unique Culinary Village tour includes visits to local wineries and orchards, while cooking classes with a local family cost €70 per day.

ACCOMMODATION

CENTRAL ÜRGÜP

Elvan Hotel Barbaros Hayrettin Sok 11 ☎ 0384 341 4191, ⓦ hotelelvan.com. This old house is set around two characterful courtyards. Proprietors Fatma and Ahmet are extremely friendly and keep the place spotless. Some rooms have vaulted stone ceilings, and there's a cool, semi-underground lounge area. **₺100**
Hitit İstiklâl Cad 46 ☎ 0384 341 4481, ⓦ hitithotel .com. A 600-year-old house owned by a charming family and popular with Turkish travellers. The rooms, looking onto a pleasant courtyard, have attractive vaulted ceilings, *kayseri* rugs, minibars and TVs, but otherwise have everyday and practical fittings, which include central heating. Make sure you check out the cave bar, carved into the cliff face at the back. **₺120**

Sacred House Barbaros Hayrettin Sok 25 ☎ 0384 341 7102, ⓦ sacred-house.com. Twelve individually designed concept rooms in a beautifully restored mansion, featuring plush furnishings, and religious and medieval themes throughout. The flashy "King's Ego" room may be a bit grand for some tastes, but there's no doubting it's beautifully done. Genuine antiques make this place more of a museum than a hotel; candlelit dinner is available by reservation. **€200**
Ürgüp Inn Cave Hotel Mescit Sok 22 ☎ 0384 341 4147, ⓦ urgupinncavehotel.com. A good-value budget option in the town centre, run by the friendly and accommodating Ömer. Rooms are clean, quiet and comfortable, with free wi-fi and breakfast served beneath a flower-filled pergola. **€45**

7

7

ESBELLI AREA

4 Oda Esbelli Sok 46 Cad ☎ 0384 341 6080, ⓦ 4oda .com. The perfect blend of comfort and cool, with five – not four, despite the name – cave rooms, cosily decorated with traditional artworks and wooden flooring. The friendly owners also run the 68 restaurant, and lend their culinary wizardry to the breakfast menu with freshly baked pastries, home-made jams and a selection of cheeses keeping guests full through until dinner. <u>US$155</u>

Elkep Evi Esbelli Sok 26 ☎ 0384 341 6000, ⓦ elkepevi .com. The hypnotic rock-carved lobby swirling with orange stripes (thanks to iron ore deposits) is a nature-made gift to this hotel's modern stylings. Inside, tastefully restored cave and cellar rooms feature cool nooks and crannies for kids to sleep in; lounge cushions are positioned in cosy alcoves, and local handicrafts adorn the walls. <u>€115</u>

★ **Esbelli Evi** Esbelli Sok 8 ☎ 0384 341 3395, ⓦ esbelli .com. Owner Suhu has managed to create a tranquil space that's simultaneously luxurious, inviting and affordable. The spacious cave rooms offer unbeatable privacy, alongside some unique cave-design features, and the airy lounge areas, rose-filled gardens and delicious fruit-filled buffet breakfast lend themselves to a more communal vibe. Rooms range in size, and the impressive en-suite bathroom and kitchen facilities far surpass expectations for the price range. <u>US$150</u>

★ **Serinn House** Esbelli Sok 36 ☎ 0384 341 6076, ⓦ serinnhouse.com. Five ultra-modern rooms, decked out with sleek industrial design pieces whose clean lines create a beautiful contrast with the soft curves of the cave rooms, and resonate character. The delightfully welcoming owner Eren bakes delicious goodies for breakfast, served on the panoramic terrace. <u>US$150</u>

EATING AND DRINKING

68 İstiklâl Cad 68 ☎ 0384 341 6468. A bar-bistro serving creative food that's as hip as its surrounds, this place is popular among İstanbul transplants to Cappadocia. Head out to the shaded terrace, sip on some local wine and tuck into a varied meze plate (₺50). A 3-course set menu is particularly good value at ₺70 for two. Daily noon–midnight.

Angel Café Cumhuriyet Meyd 3 ☎ 0384 341 2566, ⓦ hanciragan.com. With its cool red beanbags strewn around the outside seating area, interiors decorated like a rock'n'roll hall of fame, and an eclectic mix of music on the stereo, this place makes an atmospheric choice for indulging in a cocktail or two (from ₺25). There's a good range of light bites and coffees too. Daily 9am–3am.

Han Çirağan Cumhuriyet Meyd ☎ 0384 341 6894, ⓦ angel-bistrobar.com. Set in a distinctive 150-year-old house, this restaurant started life as Ürgüp's very first teahouse, as depicted in the old black-and-white photos on the walls. An extensive menu features regional dishes like düğün çorbası (wedding soup), saç tava (wok-fried lamb in tomato sauce, ₺29) and mantı (Turkish ravioli), plus a good selection of local wines. Daily 9.30am–10pm.

İkinci Bahar Merkezi Karşisi 14 ☎ 0384 341 3133. This spotless kebab joint, catering mostly to local families, is great for cheap, good-value eats, with a wide range of grills (from ₺12), pides (₺5) and köfte. No alcohol. Daily 7am–11pm.

Merkez Pastaneleri Kayseri Cad 1 ☎ 0384 341 4281, ⓦ merkezpastaneleri.com. Small patisserie that receives a steady crowd of locals looking to satisfy their sugar cravings, via a mouthwatering selection of baklava, tulumba (sugary fried dough balls), pistachio-dusted éclairs and ice creams. Prices start at ₺2, or you can buy in bulk for around ₺20 per kg. Daily 7am–midnight.

Şömine Cumhuriyet Meyd ☎ 0384 341 8442, ⓦ sominerestaurant.com. Ürgüp's most popular restaurant is an elegant evening destination, with plenty of outdoor seating, a shaded rooftop terrace and an extensive wine list. Local specialities include osbar (haricot beans with pastrami, ₺20) and testi kebap (a slow-cooked lamb and vegetable clay-pot stew, ₺24). Daily noon–midnight.

★ **Ziggy's** Tevfik Fikret Cad 24 ☎ 0384 341 7107, ⓦ ziggycafe.com. This cutesy café-cum-restaurant is a living tribute to its namesake, the owner's dog (himself named after Ziggy Stardust), whose adorable logo adorns mugs, signs and lampshades. Jovial stylings aside, when it comes to food this place means business, serving up incredible mezes (the smoked aubergines and pastrami and cheese pastries are divine), and delicious cinnamon-laced desserts that have to be tasted to be believed. Opt for the ₺45 per person taster menu, which will take you on a 3-course journey through your tastebuds. Daily noon–11pm.

DIRECTORY

Banks and exchange Garanti Bank on Kazım Karabekir Cad 7 has an English-speaking manager, while the Ziraat Bankası on Atatürk Bul has a 24hr currency exchange machine.

Hamam Yeni Camii Mah 22, mixed men and women (daily 7am–11pm, ₺20 including massage).

Hospital Posthane Cad ☎ 0384 341 4031.

Pharmacy Elif Eczanesi, Kayseri Cad, across from the tourist office, is friendly, with some English spoken.

Police Opposite the PTT in the centre, on Posthane Cad.

Post office Posthane Cad (daily 8.30am–11pm for phone tokens and cards, 9am–5pm for ordinary business).

Mustafapaşa

The small village of **MUSTAFAPAŞA**, 6km south of Ürgüp, makes for a pleasant excursion or, with your own transport, a good base for explorations. Its charm lies in its concentration of attractive *konaks* with carved house facades, which date back a century or so to the era when it was known as Sinasos and home to a thriving Greek community.

Mustafapaşa is also central to a cluster of little-visited **churches**. Its main square holds the **Aios Konstantine Eleni Kilisesi** (daily: summer 8am–7pm, winter 8am–5pm; ₺3), dedicated to Constantine and his mother St Helena, while a monastery complex across the village, reached via streets of houses cut into the tuff cliffs, includes the churches of **Aya Nicolas** and **Aya Stefanos**.

Ayios Vasilios

1km north of Mustafapaşa; pick up key from tourist office • Daily: summer 8am–7pm; winter 8am–5pm • ₺3

The church of **Ayios Vasilios**, overlooking the Üzengı Dere ravine, holds some well-preserved frescoes, although the faces are damaged, as well as four rock-cut pillars. Below it, pre-Iconoclastic and tenth-century paintings in the partly rock-cut **Holy Cross** church include an attractive Christ of the Second Coming.

7

ARRIVAL AND INFORMATION

By dolmuş Regular dolmuşes connect Mustafapaşa with Ürgüp.

Tourist office On the main square (daily: summer 8am–7pm, winter 8am–5pm).

ACCOMMODATION AND EATING

Eleni In the town centre ☎0532 353 5005. Central Mustafapaşa holds few exciting eating options, but this local favourite is at least clean and friendly, serving up hearty kebabs (from ₺15), *pides* (₺8) and draught beers (₺6). Daily 8am–midnight.

Monastery Cave Hotel In the town centre ☎0384 353 5005, ⓦmonasteryhotel.com. Simple, slightly shabby rooms, but it's nonetheless clean, centrally located and comfortable. Wi-fi and breakfast are included, and a café downstairs serves smoothies and light bites. ₺45

★ **Perimasalı Cave Hotel** Sehit Aslan Yakar Sok 6 ☎0384 353 5090, ⓦperimasalihotel.com. With plush chaise-longues, spotlit jacuzzi baths and carved stone headboards, this stylish boutique hotel does its best to live up to its name, meaning "fairy tale". It's not all atmospheric lighting and designer furnishings, though – the old Anatolian cave rooms are full of incredibly preserved historical remnants, including stable fittings, chimneys and a carefully restored prayer room. Don't forget to ask the owner to make you a cup of his favourite *menengiç* coffee too – a delicious traditional drink made from roasted pistachio fruits. €120

Ukabeyn Up on the hillside at the top of the town ☎0384 353 5533, ⓦukabeyn.com. An atmospheric place with eight well-restored rooms, a peaceful rooftop terrace and a small pool – the only one in town – situated on the lip of a cliff overhanging the valley below. The small bathrooms are a letdown, but the rooms are spotless and welcoming. ₺120

South of Mustafapaşa

Along the Soğanlı road south from Mustafapaşa, the fairy chimneys give way to a table-mountain formation that is no less fantastic and surreal: the red canyon ridge that the road follows could be a backdrop for *Roadrunner*.

Keşlik Kilesi monastery complex

3km south of Mustafapaşa • April–Oct daily 9am–7.30pm; Nov–March by appointment only • ₺4 • ☎0536 8875517

The **Keşlik Kilesi monastery complex**, believed to be one of the earliest communal monastic establishments in Cappadocia, consists of three churches, a winepress and a refectory. The first church, named after a prominent picture of the archangel Gabriel, includes depictions of the Last Supper, the Annunciation and the Flight to Egypt, all badly damaged and soot-blackened (a torch is essential). The church of St Michael has a wine cellar downstairs, while the most beautiful of all, the church of St Stephen (seventh or eighth-century), is unusually decorated with stylized foliage and interlaced patterns reminiscent of Turkish *kilims*.

Ayvalı

With its jumble of largely unexplored caves and rock-cut churches, stunning topography, and daily market brimming with locally harvested fruits, the traditional Anatolian village of **AYVALI**, 12km south of Ürgüp, is irresistible.

Since being chosen as a "sample village" by the Ministry of Tourism in 2005, this humble harvest town has embarked upon a unique approach to tourism. Well-executed tours allow villagers to open their homes to tourists – guests can learn the art of cooking Cappadocian cuisine in a local home; witness the ritual of a wedding ceremony; help with the fruit harvest; or learn to cook up grape molasses, a local speciality. Even the premier boutique hotel not only employs many local workers, but funds community projects, creating as close to a sustainable tourism model as you'll find in Cappadocia.

Thankfully, tourism has done little to change the village. While it holds a cluster of attractions, and trekking routes circle the centre, the real delights are found in the simplicity of everyday life. Rooftops are blanketed with apricots drying in the sun; villagers collect water from the communal fountain; the local teahouses bustle with quickfire gossip; and the scent of bread wafts from the street-side stone ovens.

ARRIVAL AND DEPARTURE   AYVALI

By dolmuş While public transport to Ayvalı is scarce – dolmuşes only run as far as Mustafapaşa – the *Gamirasu Cave Hotel* offers free transfers for its guests.

Tours Euphrates Tours, İstiklâl Cad 59 in Ürgüp (☎ 0384 341 7487, ⓦ cappadociatours.com), offers tours to Ayvalı.

ACCOMMODATION

★ **Gamirasu Cave Hotel** Ayvalı Köyü Ürgüp ☎ 0384 354 5815, ⓦ gamirasu.com. The brainchild of local-boy-done-good İbrahim, *Gamirasu* offers the ultimate in guilt-free luxury, a deservedly popular boutique hotel at the heart and soul of Ayvalı village. A stone-cut honeycomb of homely cave rooms is overlooked by an exquisite terrace restaurant where stairwells lit by fairy lights glitter under the moonlight. Best of all are the vast king suites, with glistening marble floors punctuated by enormous stone pillars, and featuring beds that could sleep an army. **€165**

The Soğanlı valleys

40km south of Ürgüp • Daily: summer 8am–6pm; winter 8.30am–5pm • ₺3 entrance to the churches • No public transport

The little-visited **Soğanlı valleys** make a spectacular diversion as you head south of Ürgüp. **SOĞANLI** itself is an attractive village in two parts, Yukarı (upper) and Aşağı (lower) Soğanlı, set into the side of a table-top mountain. In winter, it's often completely cut off by snowdrifts.

As you face Yukarı Soğanlı, the most interesting local churches and monasteries are in the valley to the right. To reach the two-storey **Kubbeli Kilise** ("Church with the Dome"), follow the footpath across a stream bed from the village square, and proceed uphill through the village and along the side of the valley. This has perhaps the most striking exterior of all the Cappadocian rock churches, its form – a conical dome that's the tip of a fairy chimney, resting on a circular drum – being an imitation of a masonry structure. The **Saklı** (Hidden) **Kilise**, holding frescoes of the Apostles, stands 100m before the Kubbeli Kilise, its door facing into the valley.

Go down to the road, then head up the other side of the valley to reach the **Meryem Ana Kilisesi** ("Church of the Virgin"), which has four apsidal chapels with frescoes and Iconoclastic decoration. The **Yılanlı Kilise** ("Church of the Snake") is best seen using a torch, as it is blackened and damaged by Greek and Armenian graffiti. It derives its name from an eleventh-century painting of St George slaying the dragon, to the left of the entrance.

On the way back towards the village, the **Karabaş Kilise** ("Church of the Black Head") has two adjoining apsidal chapels. In the first, well-preserved tenth- and eleventh-century frescoes depict scenes from the life of Christ.

Avanos

The old city of **AVANOS** clambers up the hills overlooking the magnificent red Kızılırmak River, the longest in Turkey. After a good rainfall, the river appears to be on the verge of bursting its banks. Famous for its distinctive red-clay earthenware pottery, Avanos remains a characterful town that's delicately poised between the modern and the traditional. Cobbled backstreets and rustic, tumbledown Ottoman, Armenian and Greek buildings climb the hill north of Atatürk Caddesi, and pottery workers still employ techniques dating right back to Hittite times, yet there's no shortage of modern restaurants and activities. Exploration of the fields and hills around the town reveals further attractions: a tiny *kervansaray*, and even an underground city, 14km away at Özkonak.

Pottery shops

Most of Avanos's **pottery shops** are located just off the main street, a few minutes' walk east of the prominent **potter's monument**, sculpted from clay. The potters' square and the streets that surround it contain numerous tiny workshops, where local techniques can still be observed or even attempted.

Chez Galip Pottery and Hair Museum

In town centre, near Kirket Pension • Daily 8.30am–8.30pm • ☎ 0384 511 4577, ⓦ chezgalip.com

One of Avanos's most unusual pottery stores, **Chez Galip Pottery**, is famous for its bizarre **Hair Museum**. Inspired by the owner's French lover, who left behind only a lock of her hair, its incredible collection contains locks of hair from thousands of women around the world, each taped to a handwritten note from its benefactor and hung from every nook and cranny of the room. It's featured in the *Guinness Book of Records*, and fans of the eccentric will surely find it irresistible.

Despite its quirky claim to fame, the pottery store itself houses plenty of well-crafted and reasonably priced souvenirs (₺15 upwards for hand-painted crockery), alongside some incredible works of art with price tags to match. They'll happily showcase traditional pottery making and even let you have a go. And ladies – don't forget to snip off a lock of your hair for the museum!

Saruhan Kervansaray

On new Kayseri road, 6km east of Avanos

The Selçuk-era **Saruhan Kervansaray** is well worth a visit. Built in 1238, it features five naves, a courtyard and the remains of what was once a hamam. Beautifully restored, it offers evocative evening performances by a troupe of **whirling dervishes** (schedules vary; ask locally; ₺25).

Özkonak

Off Kayseri road, 14km north of Avanos • Daily: summer 8am–7pm; winter 8am–5pm, last entry 30min before closing • ₺8 • Hourly dolmuşes from outside Avanos PTT

The most interesting excursion near Avanos is to **Özkonak**, one of Cappadocia's least known and least excavated underground cities. While in its present state it's not as interesting as Derinkuyu or Kaymaklı, by the same token it's not as crowded.

The city was discovered in 1972 by a muezzin, Latif Acar, who was trying to find out where the water disappeared to when he watered his crops. He found a subterranean room, which, later excavation revealed, belonged to a city where sixty thousand people could exist underground for three months. Its ten floors descend to a depth of 40m, but at present only four are open, to 15m. The first two levels were used for food storage and wine fermentation, and a press and reservoir are labelled, as are mangers for stabled animals. Another typical feature is the stone doors, moved by wooden levers; above them was a small hole, through which boiling oil would have been poured on an enemy trying to break the soft sandstone door.

ARRIVAL AND DEPARTURE

AVANOS

By bus or dolmuş Avanos's *otogar* is 250m south of the river, across the bridge from the town centre.
Destinations Göreme (hourly; 30min); Nevşehir (hourly; 40min); Özkonak (half-hourly; 30min); Uçhisar (hourly; 35min); Ürgüp (every 2hr; 30min).

INFORMATION AND TOURS

Tourist office Atatürk Cad 55 (summer Mon–Fri 8.30am–noon & 1.30–7pm; winter Mon–Fri 8.30am–noon & 1.30–5pm; ☎ 0384 511 2298).

Tours Kirkit Voyage, Atatürk Cad 50 (☎ 0384 511 3259, ⓦ kirkit.com), is an excellent tour operator that runs horseback trips, as well as bike and snowshoe tours all over Cappadocia with English-speaking guides. A full day canoeing on the river will set you back around €70, with lunch, transfers and all equipment. Kapadokya Jet Boat & Gondola, on the riverbank (☎ 0384 511 3459, ⓦ kapadokyajet.com), run adrenaline-fuelled jet-boating tours (€90) and more peaceful gondola tours (€60) along the river; prices are far more reasonable if you book as part of a larger group.

ACCOMMODATION

Ada Camping On south bank of the Kızılırmak ☎ 0384 511 2429. This excellent campsite has good facilities, including a basic but clean kitchen, free wi-fi, a huge pool and plenty of lush grass to set up on. Friendly staff speak little English but are nonetheless very welcoming to international guests. Powered sites cost ₺5 extra. Rates are for tents and caravans, for two people. **₺30**

★ **Kirkit Pension** Off Atatürk Cad ☎ 0384 511 3148, ⓦ kirkitpension.com. Owned by the eponymous tour company, these great-value rooms are clean, comfortable and full of character, with beautiful *uzbek suzanne* embroidered bedsheets, sandstone interiors and antique curiosities dotted throughout. Guests eat around a communal table in the courtyard, where excellent traditional cuisine is served (dinner costs €10 extra) to the sounds of local folk musicians, with dancing and jamming by the owner and staff. It's a truly authentic experience that's not to be missed. **€50**

Sofa Hotel Orta Mahalle Gedik Sok 9 ☎ 0384 511 5186, ⓦ sofa-hotel.com. An imposing neo-Ottoman mansion, put together from fifteen redesigned Ottoman houses, this sprawling abode has plenty of style. Rooms are immaculate, well furnished and modern, with stunningly carved wooden furnishings, and there's a delightful terrace and garden courtyard. **€55**

Venessa Pansiyon Just off Atatürk Bul on Hafızağa Sok 20 ☎ 0384 511 3840, ⓦ katpatuka.org/venessa. A good budget option, with clean comfy rooms, albeit housed in slightly shabby surroundings. If you're interested in some little-known underground cave homes, this building has its very own network of tunnels and caves, open only to guests. Excavations are still taking place and it takes some squeezing and scrambling to make your way inside, but it's good fun to take a look. **₺100**

EATING, DRINKING AND NIGHTLIFE

Dayının Yeri Atatürk Cad, next to the bridge ☎ 0384 511 6840, ⓦ dayininyeri.com.tr. A bustling kebab house with a good mix of Turkish and international guests, and şiş kebabs cooking up on an open coal grill. Kebabs start at ₺13, but for a kebab with a twist, try the *dayu* special, an *Adana*-style kebab oven-baked with melted cheese (₺20). Daily 8am–midnight.

Kavi Restaurant Taş Köprü Yanı, on the riverfront ☎ 0384 511 6003, ⓦ kavi-restaurant.com. The best location in town, right on the waterfront overlooking the flocks of geese, this place is popular with tour groups for good reason. With friendly English-speaking staff and a well-translated menu, it's an ideal chance to get an introduction to the region's foods before heading to the local joints. The *şac tava* dishes (lamb or beef cooked on traditional iron plates, ₺18) are delicious. Daily 9am–11pm.

Sofra Çarşı içi 3 ☎ 0384 511 4687, ⓦ sofrarestaurant.com. A popular local haunt known for its delicious slow-cooked *testi* kebabs (₺45 for two people), and a wide range of kebab-based meals from around ₺15. Head out the back, where a large covered terrace area teems with local families, and the lively atmosphere makes you feel right at home. Daily 6.30am–10pm.

Tafana Pide Salonu Atatürk Cad 31 ☎ 0384 511 4862, ⓦ tafanarestoran. A colourful *pide* house, with elaborately decorated pottery and walls adorned with fascinating photographs and newspaper clippings of the elderly owner's extensive world travels, this place has so much character you'll be smiling all through dinner. Try the *firinda kuru fasulye* (white bean casserole cooked in a stone oven, ₺7) and wash it down with a glass of *şalgam suyu* (beetroot juice, ₺3). Daily 8am–midnight.

DIRECTORY

Hamams Alaaddin Turkish Bath, Orta Mahalle Peker Sok 6 (☎ 0384 511 5036, ⓦ alaaddinhamam.com). Clean, friendly and accustomed to tourists; a good option for first timers (from ₺30).

Southern Cappadocia

As most visitors to Cappadocia never get beyond the well-worn Nevşehir–Avanos–Ürgüp triangle, **southern Cappadocia** is far less charted and trampled. There's a reason for its obscurity – the two major towns, **Aksaray** and **Niğde**, leave a lot to be desired as tourist centres, and much of the scenery is a depressing mixture of scrub or barren steppe. That said, the area does have its fascinations – most notably, the **Ihlara valley**, between Aksaray and Niğde, where the Melendiz River has carved a spectacular narrow ravine with almost vertical walls. Also easily accessible from Niğde is a small enclave of beautifully painted rock-cut churches belonging to the **Eski Gümüşler** monastery. South and east of Niğde, the spectacular limestone spires of the **Aladağlar Mountains** rear from the plateau, affording excellent trekking and climbing.

Niğde

Despite a long history spent guarding the important mountain pass between Cappadocia and Cilicia, the small provincial town of **NIĞDE** holds few remaining monuments, aside from a Selçuk fortress perched above the main street. While Niğde feels as if it's been thrown together by people more interested in nomadic wandering than town planning, the nearby **Eski Gümüşler** monastery complex, with its remarkably preserved frescoes, makes it a popular stopover en route to the Aladağlar mountains.

Eski Gümüşler monastery

Off the Kayseri road, 9km east of Niğde • Daily: summer 9am–6pm; winter 9am–12.30pm & 1.30–5pm • ₺3 • Hourly Belediye buses from Niğde's *otogar*

Rediscovered in 1963, the **Eski Gümüşler monastery** has a deserved reputation for the excellent preservation of its paintings. The **main church**, with its tall, elegant pillars, is entered through an almost circular arched doorway opposite the entrance to the courtyard. Decorated with black-and-white geometric designs, it contains beautiful frescoes in the most delicate greens, browns and blues. These include a Nativity scene complete with tiny animal heads peering in at the swaddled Jesus and the Magi, off to the left, and a tall, serene Madonna, framed in a rock-cut niche. The upstairs **sleeping quarters** hold rock-cut beds, and the walls are decorated with hunters with bows and arrows and a Roman soldier. Outside in the central courtyard there's a skeleton in its grave, protected under glass, and a kitchen and underground baths reached down a set of steps, while below ground level are various chambers and a water reservoir.

ARRIVAL AND DEPARTURE — NIĞDE

By bus and dolmuş Niğde's *otogar* is on Emin Eşirgil Caddesi, off the Nevşehir–Adana highway, 1km north. Destinations Aksaray (8 daily; 1hr 30min); Alanya (1 daily; 7hr); Ankara (10 daily; 4hr 30min); Antalya (2 daily; 12hr); Çamardı (summer 4 daily; 1hr); Derinkuyu (hourly; 45min); İstanbul (3 daily; 12hr); Kayseri (hourly; 1hr 30min); Konya (8 daily; 3hr 30min); Mersin (5 daily; 4hr); Nevşehir (hourly; 1hr 30min); Sivas (1 daily; 6hr).

By train To reach the town centre from the station – right on the highway, within sight of the citadel's clocktower – cross the road and walk 10min along İstasyon Caddesi. Destinations Adana (2 daily, 4hr); Kayseri (2 daily; 3hr).

INFORMATION AND TOURS

Tourist office Atatürk Meyd 16, in the town centre (Mon–Sat 8.30am–noon & 1.30–5.30pm).

Trekking Sobek Travel, Bor Cad 70/16 (☎ 0388 232 1507, ⓦ sobekculture.com), a reputable company that deals mainly with package groups, can arrange treks in the Aladağlar mountains.

ACCOMMODATION

Hotel Şahiner Giray Sok 4 ☎ 0388 232 2121, ⓦ hotelsahiner.com. While the uninspiring decor is less than dazzling, the comfortable rooms here are well priced and spotless, and the staff welcoming. ₺90

Grand Hotel Niğde Hükümet Meyd ☎ 0388 232 7000, ⓦ grandhotelnigde.com. Clean, modern lines are the name of the game at this stylish hotel, and with a sauna, hamam, fitness centre and restaurant on the complex, it ticks all the boxes. ₺130

7

The Aladağlar Mountains

The **Aladağlar mountains** form part of the Toros range, at the point where it swings north of the Mesopotamian plain. The isolated gorges and lakes of the Aladağlar are a paradise for **birdwatchers**, at their best during the autumn migration, when the snow has melted and access is (relatively) easy. *Yaylas* (mountain pastures) are used after snowmelt by nomad families and their flocks, and black tents dot the upper valleys from June to September.

The best **trekking season** is May to June, followed by September, when the weather is at its most dependable – enquire at your *pansiyon* or the tourist office in Niğde for maps and a guide. By far the most popular way up to the peaks is via the **Emler valley**, where, in season, Sobek Travel (see p.453) run permanent base camps. From here you can take day-walks up many of the peaks, and also cross into the **Kokorot valley** on the east, or walk the north–south section of the range, emerging on the **Acıman plateau**.

ARRIVAL AND DEPARTURE THE ALADAĞLAR MOUNTAINS

By bus In summer, minibuses run from Niğde's *otogar* to Çamardı, 7km northwest of Aladağlar (4 daily; 1hr). Ask for the Demirkazık road, or the driver will automatically drop you at the Şafak Pansiyon.

ACCOMMODATION

Aladağlar Camping Çamardı 465 ☏ 0534 201 8995, ⓦ aladaglarcamping.com. A perfect base for hikers, there's a friendly, communal vibe at this homely campsite. Food is served on site, or else the kitchen is available for use; breakfast costs €7. The knowledgeable owner is full of advice on trekking in the region, and can even organize a private guide (€130 per day). Tents €6, cabins €22, bungalows €35

Demirkazik Just outside Çamardı ☏ 0536 464 5164, ⓦ demirkazik.net. This twenty-bed pension offers transfers to trekking routes, as well as organizing trekking groups and guides. Cool and comfortable, it's excellent value, with exceedingly friendly staff. ₺50

Aksaray

Huddled in a riverside oasis on the far side of the Melendiz mountain range from Niğde, **AKSARAY** is a market town with no real interest except as a base for reaching the Ihlara valley. It is perhaps best known for its namesake suburb in İstanbul, founded by people from here after the fall of Constantinople in 1453. Of marginal interest are the thirteenth-century **Eğri Minare**, the **Ulu Cami** on Banklar Caddesi, and the main square with its Atatürk statue and restored public buildings.

ARRIVAL AND DEPARTURE AKSARAY

By bus Aksaray's *otogar*, 6km west, is linked to the town centre by service buses and a blue *Belediye* bus. Destinations Konya (6 daily; 1hr 45min); Nevşehir (3 daily; 1hr 30min); Niğde (6 daily; 2hr).

INFORMATION

Tourist office Kadıoğlu Sok 1, in a restored Ottoman building a couple of minutes' walk from the main square (Mon–Fri 8am–noon & 1.30–5.30pm; ☏ 0382 213 2474).

ACCOMMODATION

Otel Yuvam Next to the Kurşunlu Camii at Eski Sanayi Cad ☏ 0382 212 0024. The best bet in town, occupying a renovated old townhouse; rooms are attractively furnished and clean, with modern bathrooms. ₺90

The Ihlara valley

Daily from 8am until 1hr before sunset • ₺5

A fertile gorge cut by a deep green river between red cliffs, the **Ihlara valley** is as beautiful a place as you could conceive. Add some of the most attractive and interesting churches and rock-carved villages in Cappadocia, and it's easy to see why the valley has become an increasingly popular destination.

Three villages offer ticketed entry points to the valley: **Selime**, **Belisırma** and **Ihlara village**. Most visitors come on day-trips from Ürgüp or Göreme. To appreciate the alley at its best, however, it's satisfying to do the trip independently, and to spend a ight in either Ihlara village or Selime.

The 6km **walk** from Selime to Belisırma takes around three hours, while you'll need urther three hours to complete the 10km walk to Ihlara village. There are places to eat n route, in Belisırma, and one or two river-pools to swim in if it's hot.

elime

he beautiful troglodyte village of **SELIME**, en route to Ihlara and the valley entrance, s often overlooked in favour of the busier Ihlara village area. Several of the massive, quat **fairy chimneys** that dot the valley here contain churches; there's even a rock-cut athedral, divided into three aisles by irregular pillars. The village takes its name from Selçuk **mausoleum** in its cemetery, with a pyramidal roof inscribed "Selime Sultan".

elisırma

he troglodyte village of **BELISIRMA**, three hours' walk from either Selime or Ihlara village, lends into the tawny rock face from which it was carved to such an extent that in a bad ght it can all but disappear from view. Its tranquil riverside location provides the pportunity to enjoy a meal at one of the simple tree-shaded restaurants on the west bank.

The eleventh-century **Direkli Kilise** ("Church with the Columns") holds some very ine Byzantine frescoes, including a beautiful long-fingered Madonna and Child on one f the columns from which the church takes its name, and a picture of St George ighting a three-headed dragon.

The **church of St George**, 50m up the cliffside, 500m south of Belisırma and 3km rom the stairs at the main entrance (see p.455), was dedicated to the saint by a hirteenth-century Christian emir, Basil Giagoupes, who was in the army of Mesut II. t bears an inscription expressing Christian gratitude for the religious tolerance of the elçuk Turks. St George is depicted in armour and cloak, holding a triangular shield nd flanked by the donor and his wife Tamara, who is handing a model of the church o the saint. To the right, St George can be seen in action, killing a three-headed erpent, with an inscription above that reads "Cleanse my soul of sins".

hlara Village

t the valley's southernmost point, the **Ihlara village** offers two separate entrance points o the valley. One is in the village itself, and the other at the **Ihlara Valley Visitor Centre**, car park and information point around halfway along the main road between Ihlara nd Belisırma. This latter entrance provides direct access to the area that holds most of he valley's churches, via a precipitous but manageable descent of several hundred **steps** hat plummet 150m to the valley floor. Walking from either village to this point offers tremendous sense of solitude; easy trails run in both directions, each taking about one nd a half hours.

hlara valley churches

he monastic occupation of the Ihlara valley, or **Peristrema** as it was originally known, eems to have been continuous from early medieval times until the fourteenth century. t would seem from the decoration of the churches, whose development can be traced hrough pre- and post-Iconoclastic periods, that the valley was little affected by the eligious disputes of the period; the paintings show both Eastern and Western influence.

The most interesting of the churches are located near the small wooden **bridge** at the ottom of the steps from the visitor centre. A plan down here shows all the accessible hurches, most of which are easy to find. To the right of the bridge, on the same side as the teps, is the **Ağaçaltı Kilise** ("Church under the Tree"). Cross-shaped with a central dome, he church originally had three levels, but two have collapsed, as has the entrance hall. The nagnificent frescoes inside depict the Magi presenting gifts at the Nativity, Daniel with the ons (opposite the entrance in the west arm) and, in the central dome, the Ascension.

7

THE IHLARA VALLEY

Aksaray
Selime
Yaprakhisar
Ziga Hamam
Melendiz River
Belishirma
Direkli Kilise
Bahattin Kilisesi
Church of St George
Karagedik Kilise
Bridge
Yılanlı Kilise
Sümbüllü Kilise
Steps
Ağaçaltı Kilise
Pürenli Seki Kilise
Kokar Kilise
Ihlara

N

0   1
kilometre

The **Pürenli Seki Kilise** – 500m beyond, 30m up the cliffside, also on the south bank – can be seen clearly from the river below, although its frescoes, mainly depicting scenes from the life of Christ, are badly damaged. Another 50m towards Ihlara, the **Kokar Kilise** is relatively easy to reach and showcases the Annunciation, the Nativity, the Flight into Egypt and the Last Supper in the main hall. In the centre of the dome, a picture of a hand represents the Trinity and the sanctification.

Perhaps the valley's most fascinating church is located across the wooden footbridge, 100m from the entrance. The **Yılanlı Kilise** ("Church of the Snakes") contains unusual depictions of sinners suffering in hell. Four women are being bitten by snakes, one of them on the nipples as a punishment for not breast-feeding her young. Another is covered in eight snakes, while the other two are being punished for slander and not heeding advice. At the centre of the scene, a three-headed snake is positioned behind one of the few Cappadocian depictions of Satan; each of its mouths holds a soul destined for hell.

Another church worth exploring is **Sümbüllü Kilise** ("Church of the Hyacinths"), just 200m from the entrance steps. Its attractive facade is decorated with horseshoe niches, while its badly damaged frescoes show Greek influence.

Güzelyurt

With its still-inhabited troglodyte dwellings, and old Greek houses with beautifully carved facades, **GÜZELYURT**, the nearest small town to the Ihlara valley, 13km northeast of Ihlara village, offers a chance to catch a glimpse of the old, untouched Cappadocia. The religious community was established by St Gregory of Nazianzen in the fourth century, and a newly renovated church (**Kilise Camii**) dedicated to him. The golden bell given to the church by a Russian Orthodox community in Odessa is now in Afyon museum, but other items of interior decor, such as a carved wooden iconostasis and chair, gifts from Tsar Nicholas I in the nineteenth century, can still be seen *in situ*.

The most breathtaking sight in the Güzelyurt area has to be **Monastery Valley** below the town, approached by taking a right turn out of the village after the Cami Kilise. The valley is riddled with over fifty rock-cut churches and monastery complexes, some dating from the Byzantine era. The most attractive, the nineteenth-century **Yüksek Kilise** ("High Church"), is dramatically located on a high rock. A walk along its entire 4.5km length takes about two and a half hours, and brings you to the village of Sivrihisar. From there, a signposted fifteen-minute walk south leads to a freestanding church of note, the sixth- or seventh-century **Kızıl Kilise** ("Red Church"), one of the few remaining churches containing masonry in the whole of Cappadocia.

ARRIVAL AND DEPARTURE {#ihlara-valley}

IHLARA VALLEY

By minibus Minibuses to Ihlara village leave Aksaray's otogar 3 times daily, passing Selime and the turn-off to Belisırma, and returning the same day. 6 dolmuşes run daily from Aksaray to Güzelyurt, and there are frequent dolmuş connections between Güzelyurt and Ihlara. Groups can rent a whole minibus from Aksaray or Ürgüp; you'll need about ten people to make it viable.

By taxi A taxi from Aksaray to Ihlara costs around €25.

ACCOMMODATION AND EATING

SELIME

⭐ **Çatlak Hotel** 1km from Selime entrance to the valley ☎0382 454 5006, ⓦcatlakturizm.com.tr. Proof that a little creativity can go a long way, this surprisingly charming hotel transforms its simple carpeted rooms into quirky havens decked out with varnished rough wood designs and stone mosaic walls. Crisp, white linens and modern bathrooms keep things modern, but there's no denying the rustic charm. Free transport is provided to the same-name restaurant at any time of day. **€40**

Çatlak Restaurant Directly opposite Selime entrance to the valley ☎0382 454 5006, ⓦcatlakturizm.com.tr. Resembling a castle flanked by giant plastic fairy chimneys, this fun restaurant is hard to miss, and the staff are exceedingly helpful without being overbearing. There's pleasant seating down by the river and a makeshift menu of all the usual suspects with healthy portion sizes. A set menu with soup, main and dessert costs ₺20, or else expect to pay upwards of ₺10 for a main course. Daily 9am–1am.

BELISIRMA

Anatolia Valley Restaurant & Camping Along riverfront ☎0382 457 3040. Lounge on *sofra* tables on the floating river platforms, and enjoy live music in the evenings at this conveniently located restaurant. Camping spots are good, with power supplies for caravans and clean shower blocks, and the restaurant (daily 8am–11pm) offers good casseroles (₺10–15), including vegetarian options. Rates are for two people. Camping **₺20**; caravans **₺30T**

Tandırcı Restaurant & Camping Along riverfront ☎0382 457 3110, ⓦtandircirestaurant.com. Friendly English-speaking staff help make this place a popular stop-off for trekkers, and the floating wooden huts along the river offer a unique resting point. Sip a beer (₺8) or enjoy fresh-caught trout, served with salad, *mezes* and bread from ₺15; the restaurant is open daily 7am–midnight. Camping facilities are basic (although wi-fi is available), but campers get a discount at the restaurant, and in the summer you can bed down on the floating platforms. Rates are for two people. Camping **₺20**

Vadi Pansiyon Up on the hill, signposted from riverfront ☎0382 457 3067. The only non-camping option in the village, if you prefer your sleeping arrangements to include four walls and a roof. Six good-value rooms housed in a Turkish family home; they're simple but very clean, and while the hosts speak almost no English they manage to make guests feel extremely welcome and cook up a good breakfast. **₺60**

IHLARA VILLAGE

Akar Pansiyon Atatürk Cad ☎0382 453 7018, ⓦihlara-akarmotel.com. The simple but clean rooms in this friendly *pansiyon* have laminate floors and slightly shabby bathrooms, but are nonetheless good value. New

7

rooms upstairs cost ₺10 more and come equipped with small but modern bathrooms and brand-new furnishings. Free shuttles to and from the valley entrance. ₺75

Star Restaurant Pansiyon Ihlara Çarşı ☎0382 453 7020. Set by the river in the centre of the village, with a relaxing garden full of ducks and some lovely views over the river from the balcony rooms. The ten rooms are a little run-down but clean enough and good value, and there's a decent restaurant (daily 8.30am–11pm). Tents (per person) ₺10, caravans ₺25, double rooms ₺60

GÜZELYURT

Güzelyurt Pide Salonu Just off main square ☎0382 451 2397. Don't be put off by the shabby exterior; this simple *pide* house is the best place to pick up some cheap grub, with freshly made *pides* from ₺5 and *köfte* portions starting from ₺3. Daily 7.30am–10pm.

Kalvari Restaurant On main square ☎0535 512 7448. A clean and inviting kebab house run by friendly locals, this humble restaurant offers cheap eats like tasty Adana kebabs (₺11) and *şaç tava* (₺13). Grab a beer and enjoy the shady outdoor seating on the main square. Da 9am–1am.

★ **Hotel Karballa** Just up from main square ☎03∄ 451 2103, �🌐 karballahotel.com. Run by the same crew the *Kirkit* pension in Avanos, this wonderfully inventive ho is housed in an arresting nineteenth-century Gre monastery. The nuns' quarters are now cosy bedrooms, wi spiral staircases leading to the top-floor rooms, and decor th pays homage to traditional handicrafts. Downstairs, th refectory retains much of its historical charm as a grand dinin hall where dinner is available by reservation, and the ba garden is home to a swimming pool overlooking the hills. €∎

Yilmaz Traditional Home Pension Ortaokul Sok signposted from main road ☎0382 451 269 ✉kadeh-68@hotmail.com. Three big, cheerfully decorate rooms in a genuine Turkish home, with home-made breakfa included and a glass of home-made wine on arrival. The sto floors covered with cheap DIY laminate are a little odd, but th place is nonetheless clean and comfy. The host family on speak a little English, but their friendly dispositions ar constant supply of tea will soon win you over. ₺70

Kayseri

Green fields, wooded hills and a snowcapped volcano surround the modern-looking concrete city that is today's **KAYSERİ**, encircling an old Selçuk settlement of black volcanic stone. While it has a reputation for religious conservatism and ultranationalism most visitors find the locals welcoming and accepting of foreigners. It's also a thriving business centre, where traditional commerce, particularly raw textiles and carpets, still flourishes in the medieval *han*s. Kayseri's long history and strategic importance have left it littered with striking monuments, while two nearby attractions, the bird sanctuary of **Sultansazlığı** and **Mount Erciyes**, are ideal for picnics in summer and skiing in winter.

Part of the delight of Kayseri is that its beautiful old buildings still play an important role in everyday life, their very existence witness to the social conscience of the Selçuks Koranic teaching forbade excessive concern with private houses, so public figures poured money into buildings for public welfare and communal activities.

Brief history

Originally called Mazaka, what's now Kayseri gained importance under the Phrygians. In 17–18 AD, renamed **Caesarea** in honour of Tiberius, it became the capital of Roman Cappadocia. As part of the Byzantine Empire, Caesarea was relocated 2km north of the ancient acropolis, allegedly around a church and monastery built by St Basil, the founder of eastern monasticism. Strategic in terms of both trade and defence, it soon became a cultural and artistic centre, though always vulnerable to attack from the east. The Arab invasions of the seventh and eighth centuries were particularly threatening, and in 1067 it finally fell to the great Selçuk leader Kılıç Arslan II. The Crusaders (from 1097) and the Mongols (from 1243) both briefly enjoyed possession before it became part of the Ottoman Empire in 1515, under Selim the Grim.

The citadel

Life in Kayseri centres around the towering crenellated walls of the **citadel** (*iç kale*), built from black volcanic rock. A sixth-century fortress erected in the reign of the Emperor Justinian once stood here, but the citadel you see today was built in 1224 by

OPPOSITE IHLARA VALLEY (P.454) >

KAYSERI

the Selçuk Sultan Keykubad. Naturally it has been much restored since, particularly by Mehmet II, who also built the **Fatih Camii**, the small mosque near the southwest gate.

Hunat Hatun külliye

Near the citadel

Construction of **Hunat Hatun** *külliye* began in 1239, making it the first mosque complex to be built by the Selçuks in Anatolia. It consists of a mosque and *medrese*, the latter ranking among the most beautiful examples of Selçuk architecture in Turkey. This former theological college has an open courtyard and two *eyvan*s (vaulted chambers open at the front). A wooden box containing a hair reputed to be from the Prophet Mohammed is located near the beautifully decorated *mihrab*.

Covered markets

Kayseri's three central **covered markets**, all dating from different periods, remain integral to the city. The **Bedesten**, built in 1497 and originally used by cloth-sellers, is now a carpet market, while in the **Vezir Hanı**, built by Damat İbrahim Paşa in 1727, raw cotton, wool and Kayseri carpets are sold, and leather is prepared for wholesale. The beautifully restored **covered bazaar**, built in 1859, holds five hundred individual shops.

Ulu Cami

Beyond the market area

The first of several ancient mosques in Kayseri, the **Ulu Cami**, or Great Mosque, was constructed under the Danişmend Turkish emirs in the first half of the thirteenth century. Still in remarkable condition, the mosque can be entered from three sides. Its roof is supported by four rows of stone pillars with assorted marble capitals, and it retains its original carved wooden *mimber*, although the central dome is modern.

Mausoleums

Thanks to its large number of tombs, Kayseri has been described as the **city of mausoleums**. Curious, squat, beautifully carved bits of masonry known as *kümbet*s, dating from the thirteenth to fifteenth centuries, can be found scattered in the most unlikely places – there are a couple on traffic islands on the main highway to Mount Erciyes.

The best-known mausoleum in Kayseri is the **Döner Kümbet**, "turning tomb", a typical example probably dating to the mid-thirteenth century, built for Shah Cihan Hatun. The tomb is decorated with arabesques and palmettes, and a tree of life with twin-headed eagles and lions beneath.

Gürgüpoğlu House

Off Turan Cad, just inside the city walls • Tues–Sun 8am–5pm • ₺3

The **Gürgüpoğlu House** (Gürgüpoğlu Konağı), a half-timbered fifteenth-century Ottoman family home, is now a museum of ethnography, complete with wax dummies. Its first room is a typical Turkish salon, the walls intricately painted using natural dyes, with models seated on low divans, holding musical instruments. Upstairs, the rooms have beautifully carved and painted wooden ceilings; displays include wedding objects such as headdresses, make-up applicators and masterfully crafted silver belts. One room holds Selçuk tiles from the Hunat Hatun and glass nargiles, while the landing has a *topak ev*, or nomad's tent.

Kayseri Museum

Kışla Cad • Tues–Sun 8am–5pm • ₺3

The **Kayseri Museum** (Kayseri Müzesi) contains important finds from Kültepe (see p.463), and is extremely well labelled in English. Its first room deals with the Hittites, their cuneiform writing and hieroglyphics, and includes a fascinating Hittite rock-relief from Develi and the head of a sphinx. Items from Kültepe include early Bronze Age depictions of the mother goddess, Assyrian bowls and jugs in the shape of animals, dating from the second millennium BC, and a collection of clay tablets in their clay envelopes – essentially small cheques – from the same period.

In the second room are finds from around Kayseri itself, including Hellenistic and Roman jewellery, and grave gifts from a Roman tumulus, among them highly worked pieces in gold and silver. In the garden, a pair of lovely seventh-century BC Hittite lions still have their teeth intact.

Surp Krikor Lusuvoriç

30min walk south of town on the Hacılar/Erciyes road

The domed Armenian church of **Surp Krikor Lusuvoriç** is a final architectural reminder of Kayseri's importance in the Byzantine Christian world. Dating from 700 AD, it's one of Turkey's largest consecrated churches, with room for a thousand worshippers. Surp Krikor (St Gregory), the first bishop and official founder of the Armenian Church, spent much of his early life here. To gain entry, ring the bell; the caretakers, a friendly Armenian family from İstanbul, will be happy to let you look around.

ARRIVAL AND DEPARTURE

KAYSERI

By plane Kayseri's airport, 10km north of the centre, is connected to the centre by municipal buses (every 20min). On request, minibuses run by the Argeus tour agency

(☎0384 341 4688, ⌨capadocciaexclusive.com) or the Göreme-based Neşe (☎0384 271 2525, ⌨nesetour.com) will meet Turkish Airlines flights and take you to any village in Cappadocia. Expect to pay around ₺20 per person to reach Ürgüp, for example. THY (Turkish Airlines) has an office at Istasyon Cad 48 (☎0352 222 3858).

Destinations İstanbul (6 daily; 1hr 30min); İzmir (1 daily; 1hr 35min).

By bus Kayseri's *otogar*, 2km west of the centre on Osman Kavuncu Cad, stands alongside a new minibus station used by minibuses to and from Ürgüp, Aksaray and Nevşehir. To reach the town centre, take the "Terminal" dolmuş from the minibus station, or from the opposite side of Osman Kavuncu Cad, to Cumhuriyet Meyd, 100m northwest of the Hunat Hatun complex.

Destinations Adana (22 daily; 7hr); Adiyaman (2 daily; 8hr); Afyon (6 daily; 9hr); Ankara (hourly; 4hr 30min); Antalya (8 daily; 11hr); Bursa (4 daily; 11hr); Isparta (5 daily; 9hr); İstanbul (12 daily; 12hr); İzmir (3 daily; 12hr); Konya (8 daily; 4hr); Niğde (hourly; 1hr 30min); Ürgüp (hourly; 1hr 30min).

By train The station is 1km north of town, at the end of Atatürk Bulvarı. "Terminal" dolmuşes into town – and to the *otogar* in the other direction – pass frequently.

Destinations Adana (2 daily; 7hr); Ankara (hourly; 9hr); Diyarbakır (4 weekly; 20hr); İstanbul (2 daily; 12hr); Kars (1 daily; 24hr); Malatya (2 daily; 6hr); Van (1 daily; 22hr).

INFORMATION

Tourist office Just north of Hunat Hatun complex on Sivas Cad (Mon–Sat: summer 8am–5.30pm, winter 8am–noon & 1–5pm; ☎0352 222 3903). Friendly, English-speaking

staff can provide all local timetables and information, including on the Mount Erciyes ski resort.
Internet Hollywood Internet Café, Sivas Cad 15.

ACCOMMODATION

Bent Hotel Atatürk Bul 40 ☎0352 221 2400, ⓦ benthotel.com. While this place might be a bit pricier than you'd expect from a three-star hotel, it's one of the city's few stylish abodes, decked out with cool artworks, fancy bedspreads and modern furnishings. The boutique-hotel feel is topped off by the atmospheric top-floor restaurant, offering great views over the city. ₺170
Hotel Meydan Osman Kavuncu Cad 12 ☎0352 336 5135. A good-value budget option in a convenient, easy-to-find location. Simple rooms are small, but clean and

well furnished, with clean, shared bathrooms – avoid the rooms overlooking the street if you want a quiet night. The same staff run the slightly more upmarket *Admiral* hotel up the road. ₺60
Hunat Otel Zengin Sok 5, behind the Hunat Hatun complex ☎0352 232 4319. It's a shame that this place couldn't fork out for a cleaner, as it's the best-located, friendliest and cheapest option in town – ask to see a couple of rooms before you decide, as some are notably more hygienic than others. ₺40

EATING AND DRINKING

While Kayseri is more famous for its spicy, garlicky *pastırma* (cured meat), *sucuk* (a kind of sausage-like salami) and *mantı* (Turkish ravioli) than its actual **restaurants**, it does hold a few decent places to eat.

Altıntabak et Lokantası Bankalar Cad 16 ☎0352 222 2522. A stylish local haunt with waiters kitted out in traditional uniforms, this is an atmospheric place to tuck into a generous bowl of *mantı* (₺10), served with a healthy dollop of fresh yoghurt. Daily 8am–10pm.
Elmacıoğlu Sivas Cad 14 ☎0352 231 9324, ⓦ elmacioglu iskender.com. A slick café-restaurant with pleasant outdoor seating and a prime location for people-watching, which

serves cheap eats from around ₺5. Daily 8am–9pm.
Lider Café & Restaurant Opposite tourist office at Sivas Cad 6 ☎0352 232 1530, ⓦ liderunmamulleri.com.tr. Immaculate and air-conditioned, this modern café serves up *pides* (₺5), reasonably priced kebabs (from ₺10), omelettes (₺3.50) and desserts, with pleasant views across to Mount Erciyes. Head to the open-air downstairs area to tuck into the wide range of ice-cream flavours. Daily 24hr.

Erciyes Dağı

25km south of Kayseri • Catch a Develi-bound dolmuş, near the Han Camii on Talas Cad (every 10min)

Visiting **Erciyes Dağı**, the 3916m-high extinct volcano that dominates Kayseri to the southwest, is one of the greatest pleasures that southern Cappadocia has to offer. If you have transport, take a packed lunch and head for its foothills, a twenty-minute drive from town. Otherwise, the city dolmuş will take you to Tekir Yaylası, at an altitude of 2150m. Hiking, mountain-biking and horseriding tours are also available in summer.

During the **ski season**, between December and May, five lifts provide access to some 12km of piste. It's a little barren, but snow conditions are often very good, and several winter sports are gaining popularity – snowrafting, snowshowing and snow tubing are all available. The tourist information centre has full information on mountain activities, and can help book tours and accommodation. Erciyes Ski Center offers **equipment rental** (☎0352 342 2020, ⊛erciyeskayak.com; skis cost around ₺30 per day).

Sultansazlığı

50km southwest of Kayseri • Catch a Yahyalı bus from the *otogar* to Ovaçiftlik (daily 8am–5pm, every 30min; 1hr), 1km walk from the water

You might assume that the flat, dull steppe that lies beyond Erciyes Daği, around the Kayseri–Niğde road, was barren of bird or plant life. Consequently, the oasis of the **Sultansazlığı** bird sanctuary is easy to miss, but it's worth the effort of hunting out.

The five thousand acres of freshwater marshes here, also known as **Kuş Cenneti** (Bird Paradise), stand at the crossroads of two migration routes, making it an extremely important wetland for breeding migrant and wintering birds. Visiting species include flamingos, pelicans, storks, golden eagles, herons, spoonbills and cranes. As the best time to spot birds is at dawn, it's worth staying overnight. A limited amount of accommodation is available nearby, but self-sufficent camping is also possible within the sanctuary.

7

ACCOMMODATION   SULTANSAZLIĞI

Sultan Pansion Sultansazlığı Kuş Cenneti ☎0352 658 5549, ⊛sultanbirding.com. The best choice for birdwatchers: eighteen clean, simple en-suite rooms, 200m from the marshes, and a restaurant serving tasty *saç tava* (wok-fried lamb). Boat trips in a flat-bottomed punt and jeep tours are also available. **€50**

Kültepe

22km northeast of Kayseri • Tues–Sun 8am–noon & 1–5pm • ₺3 • Catch a Bünyan-bound bus, from Sivas Caddesi in Kayseri; the site is signposted, near a petrol station, after 20km, but it's a 2km hike from the bus stop

The important archeological site of the ancient city of Kanesh is now known as **Kültepe**. Some 15,000 clay tablets and a well-preserved selection of household furnishings, including human and animal statuettes, were discovered here – the best are housed in Kayseri and Ankara museums. The site itself has been well excavated and gives some idea of building plans and street layouts, as well as construction techniques that are still prevalent in Anatolia.

Brief history

The city's golden age was in the second millennium BC. At that time, the nearby Karum of Kanesh – the most important of nine Assyrian *karum*s (trade centres) in Anatolia, importing tin and textiles in exchange for cattle, silver, copper and skins – was inhabited by the Assyrian trading colony and the lower classes, while Kanesh itself was reserved for royalty of Anatolian stock. The thin layer of ash covering the site dates from two massive conflagrations, the first in around 1850 BC, and the second around 1200 BC. The city lost its importance during the Hittite age, but was still occupied during the Hellenistic and Roman periods.

The sites

Excavations labelled "level II", from the second millennium BC, dominate the upper site of Kanesh, especially the Large Palace, which covered an area of 3000 square metres and included a paved central courtyard, and the **Palace of Warsana**, king of Kanesh. Walls were generally of large mud bricks with stone foundations, though the Large Palace held long storage rooms with stone walls.

The **Karum** is five minutes' walk further down the country lane that leads past the entrance to Kanesh. Here, excavations have revealed the foundations of shops, offices, archives and storerooms, all packed closely together inside a defensive wall. The dead were buried together with precious gifts under the floors of their own houses in stone cist graves, some of which can be seen on site.

North Central Anatolia

AMASYA

North Central Anatolia

When the first Turkish nomads arrived in Anatolia during the tenth and eleventh centuries, the landscape – rolling grassland dotted with rocky outcrops – must have been strongly reminiscent of their Central Asian homeland. Those who choose to trek through the region today are an equally hardy bunch, braving long journey times, occasionally tricky roads and seasonal temperature extremes to visit towns, cities and sights far less heralded than their counterparts in South Central Anatolia. However, visitors prepared to do a little digging will find it one of Turkey's most rewarding and undiscovered quarters. Ankara in particular, the provincial town that found itself suddenly elevated to become capital of the entire country, feels surprisingly untouristed despite being the political and social centre of modern Turkey.

Elsewhere, charming **Safranbolu**, north of Ankara towards the Black Sea coast, and **Amasya**, northeast of Ankara, boast some of Turkey's most beautiful ensembles of Ottoman buildings. Directly east of Ankara, the former Hittite capital of **Hattuşa**, with its temples and fortresses, is simply jaw-dropping, while there's some terrific Selçuk architecture in far-flung **Sivas** and **Divriği**.

Ankara

Few cities have changed so much, so quickly, as the Turkish capital of **ANKARA**. When Atatürk declared it capital of his nascent republic in 1923, it was little more than a small provincial town, known chiefly for its production of angora, soft goat's wool. Fast-forward to the present day, and it's a bustling, modern city of well over four million souls, its buildings spreading to the horizon in each direction across what, not too long ago, was unspoiled steppe. This was, of course, Atatürk's vision all along – a carefully planned attempt to create a seat of government worthy of a modern, Westernized state.

Many visitors to Turkey, of course, believe İstanbul to be the nation's capital, and comparisons between the two cities are almost inevitable. While Ankara is never going to be as attractive a destination, it certainly holds enough to keep you occupied for a few days – diverting sights, good restaurants and pumping nightlife. Most visitors' first taste of Ankara is **Ulus**, an area where a couple of **Roman monuments** lurk beneath the prevailing modernity. Heading east you'll pass the superb **Museum of Anatolian Civilizations** before heading up to **Hisar**, the oldest part of the city. Here, the walls of a Byzantine **citadel** enclose an Ottoman-era village of cobbled streets; climbing on up will buy you a jaw-dropping city view. Heading south of Ulus you'll soon come to

SİVAS

Highlights

❶ Museum of Anatolian Civilizations, Ankara
A treasure-hoard of artefacts contained in one of
Turkey's most prestigious museums. **See p.472**

❷ Kütahya Is Kütahya Turkey's most underrated
city? Fantastic little museums, an incredibly
appealing old town, superb food… and not a
tourist in sight. **See p.480**

❸ Stay the Ottoman way in Safranbolu This
small town's laidback nature is best appreciated
in its wonderfully restored Ottoman houses –
many are now hotels, featuring low-slung beds,
creaky floorboards and authentic antiques.
See p.487

❹ Hattuşa Former Hittite capital in a
magnificently bucolic setting – even more

reason for a 6km trek around the old city walls.
See p.492

❺ Rock tombs of Amasya The highlights of
this spellbinding city are the massive rock tombs
of the Pontic kings – carved into a cliff-face and
lit up at night to great effect. **See p.496**

❻ Tokat kebap Every Turkish city has its own
kebab, but Tokat's is truly unique – not least
because it's about twice the size of any other.
See p.502

❼ Selçuk monuments in Sivas At the centre
of this intriguing city you'll find superlative
examples of Mongol-inspired architecture, with
highly decorative facades and beautiful mosaic
work. **See p.502**

HIGHLIGHTS ARE MARKED ON THE MAP ON P.468

NORTH CENTRAL ANATOLIA

HIGHLIGHTS
1. Museum of Anatolian Civilizations, Ankara
2. Kütahya
3. Stay the Ottoman way in Safranbolu
4. Hattuşa
5. Rock tombs of Amasya
6. Tokat kebap
7. Selçuk monuments in Sivas

100
kilometres
0

High Speed Train

N

BLACK SEA

BLACK SEA

İstanbul
İstanbul
İstanbul

İsmit
Adapazarı
Zonguldak
Amasra
Bolu
Safranbolu
Karabük
Kastamonu
Sinop
Samsun
Ordu
Giresun
Gümüşhane

Eskişehir
Kütahya
Yoncalı
Aezani
Midas Şehri
Seyitgazi
Sivrihisar
Gordion
Polatlı
Afyonkarahisar

ANKARA
Esenboğa

Çorum
Sungurlu
Boğazkale
Alacahöyük
Alaca
Yazılıkaya
Hattuşa
Yozgat
Kırşehir

Amasya
Ezinepazarı
Pazar
Tokat
Turhal

Kayseri

Sivas
Zara
Suşehri
Koyulhisar
İmranlı
Refahiye
Kemah
Erzincan
Alpköy
Kelkit
Şiran
Alucra
Şebin Karahisar

Divriği
Kangal

Elazığ
Malatya

Kızılırmak
Yeşil
Kızılırmak
Kızılırmak
Tuz

E90
E90
E90

ANKARA ORIENTATION

Ankara is neatly bisected along its north–south axis by the 5km-long **Atatürk Bulvarı**, and everything you need is in easy reach of this broad and busy street. At the northern end is **Ulus Meydanı** – usually known simply as **Ulus** ("Nation") – a large square that has lent its name to the surrounding area. While it's not particularly attractive, it's where you'll probably gravitate on arrival as it holds cheap hotels and is well positioned for both sightseeing and city transportation.

Heading south down Atatürk Bulvarı from Ulus brings you to the main west–east rail line, and beyond that **Sıhhıye Meydanı**, an important junction that marks the start of **Yenişehir** ("New City"). A 10min walk south of Sıhhıye brings you to **Kızılay**, the busy square that's the main transport hub of the modern city. At the bottom of Atatürk Bulvarı, **Çankaya** is Ankara's most exclusive suburb and location of the **Presidential Palace**.

studenty **Kızılay**, filled with bars and cheap restaurants; real-estate values increase exponentially as you move south again towards **Kavaklıdere** and **Çankaya**, where the cafés and restaurants are somewhat more salubrious.

Brief history

After the **Hittites** founded Ankara around 1200 BC, naming it Ankuwash, the town prospered due to its position on the royal road running from Sardis to their capital at Hattuşa. Their successors, the **Phrygians**, called the city Ankyra, and left behind a huge necropolis that was uncovered near the train station in 1925. They, in turn, were followed by the **Lydians** and the **Persians**. Alexander the Great passed through on his way east, while in the third century BC invading **Galatians** (Gauls) held sway for a while.

By the start of the first century BC, the **Romans** had made substantial inroads into Asia Minor. In 24 BC Ankara was officially absorbed into the empire under Augustus and renamed Sebaste (Greek for Augustus). The city thrived under the Romans, but the later Byzantine era ushered in a period of decline. Arabs, Persians, Crusaders and Mongols stormed the city en route to greater prizes, but only the **Selçuks** were to settle, taking control in 1071. By 1361 Ankara had been incorporated into the burgeoning **Ottoman state** and went into another decline; only its famous wool stopped it disappearing altogether.

After Atatürk's final victory, and despite being little more than a backward provincial centre, Ankara was made the official **capital of the Turkish Republic**. Turkey's vociferous pro-İstanbul lobby was dismayed by the choice of capital, and many foreign governments also baulked at the idea of establishing embassies here. People were drawn to Ankara from the Anatolian countryside in search of work and a higher standard of living, and the city's **population** of 30,000 swiftly swelled.

Ulus

One of Ankara's busiest neighbourhoods, teeming **Ulus** neatly tells the story of the city – and served as the birthplace of modern Turkey itself. The area is home to an appealing smattering of sights dating back to **Roman** times: as well as an ancient temple, stone column and bathhouse, a small Roman theatre is presently undergoing excavation just off Hisarparkı Caddesi. **Ottoman** Ulus has largely been extinguished by the mania for concrete, but the intriguing new developments around the Hacı Bayram mosque give a Disney-fied impression of the era. Then, of course, there are the sights pertaining to the **Republic**: at Ulus Meydanı, a towering equestrian **statue of Atatürk** – flanked by threatening bronze soldiers in German-style coal-scuttle helmets – gazes out over the building that once housed his Grand National Assembly, and is now the **Museum of the War of Independence**. Lastly, attractive **Gençlik Parkı**, with its fairground rides and fancy tearooms, will bring you racing into the modern day.

ANKARA

RESTAURANTS

Bulvar	1
Büyükşehir Market	4
Günaydın	11
Kale Washington	5
Kınacızade Konağı	6
Komagane	8
Le Man Kültür	7
Sushico	12
Tapa Tapa Tapas	9
Tevhid	3
Urfalı	2
Yosun	10

ACCOMMODATION

Aldino	13
Angora House	8
And Boutique	6
Berlitz	4
Çevikoğlu	1
Deeps Hostel	11
Divan	9
Golden Boutique	17
Gordion	12
Gülpinar	2
Gülyeruz	7
Hilton International	15
Mostar	10
Radisson Blu	5
Sheraton	16
Tunalı	14
Ulus	3

BARS & CAFÉS

And Cafe	3
Bedesten	4
Copper Club	10
Eski Yeni	6
Hansaray	5
Hayyami	9
Kitchenette	11
Mado	2, 8
Up Lost Bar	7
Zerdali Konak	1

Temple of Augustus and Rome

Facing the Hacı Bayram Camii

The remains of the **Temple of Augustus and Rome** constitute Ankara's most important ancient monument. Built in honour of Augustus between 25 and 20 BC, after Ankara was made the provincial capital of Galatia, its main claim to fame is an inscription on the outer wall. Detailing the *Res Gestae Divi Augusti* (Deeds of the Divine Augustus), this was the emperor's political testament, carved on every temple of Augustus after his death. The Ankara version is the only one to survive in its entirety. The temple, whose walls alone have endured, was converted into a Christian church around the fifth century AD, and during the fifteenth century became the *medrese* of the Hacı Bayram mosque (see p.471).

Hacı Bayram Camii

Hacı Bayram Veli Cad

The hilltop **Hacı Bayram Camii** was named after **Bayram Veli**, Ankara's most celebrated Muslim saint, who founded the Bayrami order of dervishes at the start of the fifteenth century. His body is buried in the tomb in front of the building. Visit at prayer time and you'll hear some of Turkey's most distinctive **muezzins** at work; at other times you'll have to content yourself with superb views over the city.

At the time of writing, the whole area surrounding the mosque was being gentrified with a swathe of **mock-Ottoman buildings**, many of which are already functional shops. Those facing the mosque sell religious paraphernalia, while downhill you'll find a few cobblers, well over a dozen outlets selling chandeliers and other light fittings, a couple of **miniature mosques** with wooden minarets, and even a couple of mock-Ottoman guesthouses (see p.476).

8

Julian's Column

Hükümet Meyd

Julian's Column commemorates a visit to Ankara by the Byzantine emperor Julian the Apostate, chiefly remembered for his short-lived attempt to revive worship of the old Roman gods in the fourth century. The column's stonework is characterized by a strange, layered effect rather like a long, cylindrical kebab.

Roman baths

Off Çankırı Cad • Daily 8.30am–noon & 1–5.30pm • ₺3

Dating back to the third century AD, the **Roman baths** (Roma Hamamları) are set in a large *palaestra* (exercise field) that's scattered with overgrown truncated columns and fragments of cracked masonry. Of the baths themselves, the only extant features are the brick pillars that supported the floors, allowing warm air to circulate and heat the rooms above.

Museum of the War of Independence

Ulus Meyd • Tues–Sun 8.45am–12.15pm & 1.30–5pm • ₺1

The modest late-Ottoman schoolhouse building that's now home to the **Museum of the War of Independence** holds a special place in Turkish hearts. Atatürk and his Nationalist supporters convened their provisional parliament here on April 23, 1920, while three years later it was also the venue for the **declaration of the Turkish Republic**, serving as the parliament building until 1925.

Today's museum is devoted to the military struggle that preceded the foundation of the modern republic. An extensive collection of photographs, documents and ephemera covers every detail of the various campaigns. All the captions are in Turkish, but much of the material speaks for itself. Visitors can also view the chamber where delegates sat in small school desks, illuminated by candle- and oil-light, with Atatürk overseeing from the vantage point of a raised platform.

GECE KONDU

From the upper fortifications of Ankara's **citadel**, you'll see the city spread out in all its glory. Many of the nearby buildings look less than glorious, however – these are referred to by locals as **gece kondu**, which loosely translates as "built overnight". Though likely put together at sub-Amish speed, their hasty construction is all too apparent: after Ankara was declared national capital, Anatolians moved to the city in droves, and many erected their own houses around the citadel. Effectively **shanty towns**, these have remained the most impoverished parts of the city ever since; Ankara's present-day rulers would, of course, prefer to see the back of them, and bit by bit, the old buildings are being replaced with rows of ugly high-rises. Mercifully, the former residents of the *gece kondu* are being moved here, rather than flung to the outskirts of the city.

Gençlik Parkı

Filling most of the gap between Ulus Meydanı and the train station, **Gençlik Parkı** – "Youth Park" – was built on the orders of Atatürk to provide a worthy recreational spot for the hard-toiling citizens of his model metropolis. The park is often packed with families strolling around the artificial lake, and hosts occasional outdoor concerts. Its southern section features **fairground rides**, while near the eastern gate you'll find the **State Opera House** (Devlet Opera; see p.478). Looking like a dark pink, Art Deco underground station, this was built at Atatürk's behest – he developed a taste for opera as military attaché in Sofia in 1905.

Ethnographic Museum

Talat Paşa Cad • Tues–Sun 9am–noon & 1–5pm • ₺3

Just south of Ulus, the **Ethnographic Museum** is housed in a grandiose white-marble building that was the original resting place of Atatürk before the construction of the Anıt Kabir mausoleum (see p.474). It holds an extensive collection of folk costumes and artefacts from Selçuk times onwards, and some fine Selçuk woodcarving.

Museum of Anatolian Civilizations

Opposite southern end of İnönü Parkı • Daily 8.30am–5pm • ₺15, audioguides ₺5

Whenever you see a replica artefact at an archeological site in Turkey, you can bet the original lies under the protective wings of the unmissable **Museum of Anatolian Civilizations**. For most visitors, its outstanding archeological collection is the high point of a visit to Ankara, documenting the peoples and cultures of Anatolia from the late Stone Age through to Classical times.

The museum is housed in a restored fifteenth-century *bedesten*, which fell out of use after a catastrophic fire in 1881. Its vast cache of artefacts is laid out in chronological order, clockwise from the entrance, with large stone reliefs dating from the Hittite and Phrygian periods in the central chamber. Most exhibits are clearly labelled in English.

From the Paleolithic to the Bronze Age

The museum's first four sections move visitors through Turkey-time from the Old Stone Age to 2000 BC. The **Paleolithic** section features assorted bone fragments and primitive stone tools and weapons from a cave site at Karain, 30km northwest of Antalya, while objects found at Çatal Höyük, a settlement of New Stone Age mud-brick houses 52km north of Konya, have yielded significant evidence about the **Neolithic** period (7000–5500 BC). The importance of agriculture in this era may account for the abundant fertility-goddess figures – represented by baked-clay female forms of ample proportions – that reappear throughout the museum.

Most of the objects in the **Bronze Age** section (3000–2000 BC) come from Alacahöyük; among the most striking exhibits are the pieces of gold jewellery unearthed in the royal tombs. There then follows a small **Assyrian Trading Colony** section (1950–1750 BC), with the most notable exhibits being well-preserved cuneiform tablets that rank among Anatolia's earliest written records.

The Hittite sections

The Hittites (1700–700 BC) left spectacular sites at Boğazkale and nearby Yazılıkaya, east of Ankara (see p.495). Most of the objects here are from Boğazkale and Alacahöyük, with the most sophisticated example being a vase with a relief depicting a lively wedding procession. Stelae carved with hieroglyphs have proved a valuable source of information about the **Old Hittite kingdom** (1700–1450 BC).

There's even more to see from the **Hittite Empire** (1450–1200 BC) itself – elaborate reliefs from Alacahöyük indicate the sophistication of Hittite culture during this time, and if you're planning to visit Hattuşa, look out for the lion and sphinx figures from the city gates. The originals are here, replaced with replicas at the site itself.

Phrygian and Urartian sections

Most of the museum's **Phrygian** objects (1200–700 BC) were recovered from the royal tumulus at Gordion (see p.484), capital of Phrygian Anatolia after the fall of the Hittites. The timber-framed chamber at the heart of the tumulus has been re-created and objects from it are on display nearby. Most impressive are a wooden table of intricate design and skilfully wrought bronze vessels.

Modern knowledge of the **Urartians** largely derives from clay tablets listing military successes. On the evidence of such artefacts here, their culture was less sophisticated than that of the Phrygians, though the large bronze cauldron resting on a tripod with cloven bronze feet is austerely beautiful.

MUSEUM OF ANATOLIAN CIVILIZATIONS

Entrance

Palaeolithic Section

Neolithic Section

Phrygian Reliefs

Temporary Display

Chalcolithic Section

Late Hittite Reliefs & Statues

Urartian Section

Early Bronze Age

Hittite Empire Reliefs

Phrygian Section

Assyrian Trading Colony Section

Old Hittite Section

Ankara section

Downstairs, towards the exit, a section details finds from **Ankara** itself. While it can't really compete with the bounty upstairs, the collections of Roman coins are of interest – as are the remains of *Ankarapithecus*, a 9.8-million-year-old ape named after the city of its discovery.

The old town

A pathway leads up through İnönü Parkı between the inner and outer walls of the **Hisar**, the Byzantine **citadel** whose walls enclose the oldest part of the city. Of all Ankara's districts, this Ottoman-era village of cobbled streets and ramshackle wooden houses most fully rewards a relaxed and aimless stroll. Most of the area remains defiantly un-restored, but many grand Ottoman mansions have been renovated, decked out with carpets and antiques, and transformed into restaurants or carpet shops geared towards the tourist trade.

The citadel

Ankara's **city walls** were probably first constructed by the Hittites over three thousand years ago, when they recognized the defensive potential of the citadel outcrop. Today's walls are more recent, built on the orders of the Byzantine emperor Michael III (remembered as "Michael the Sot") in 859, who updated defences built by the Roman emperor Heraclius atop earlier Galatian fortifications.

At the northern end of the citadel, the **Ak Kale**, or "White Fortress", presents tremendous views. The northeast edge of the city, just about visible, is the approximate site of the battlefield where Pompey defeated the Pontic king Mithridates the Great in 74 BC. Rising from the eastern walls is **Şark Kulesi**, a ruined tower whose panoramic outlook makes it a favourite kite-flying spot for local children. Lastly, the **Güney Kapı** (South Gate) has two vast towers flanking a twin portal; embedded in the wall connecting the towers are various fragments of Roman masonry, including altars supported by recumbent statues of Priapus.

Alâeddin Camii

Just inside the citadel's western gate

Built in 1178, the **Alâeddin Camii** is the oldest mosque in Ankara, albeit much restored in later years. Its exterior is pretty, if unexceptional; duck inside and you'll find a painstakingly carved Selçuk *mimber* (a pulpit from which the imam delivers homilies).

Aslanhane Camii

Aslanhane Sok

An unadulterated example of Selçuk architecture lies a few streets southeast of the citadel, in the shape of the **Aslanhane Camii** or "Lion-House Mosque", whose interior is by far the most impressive in Ankara. It's known as a "forest mosque" on account of the 24 wooden columns that support the intricately carved wooden ceiling. The astonishingly detailed walnut *mimber* dates back to 1209 and is one of the last examples of Selçuk decorative carving.

Kocatepe Camii

Off Esat Cad

The minarets of the massive **Kocatepe Camii** loom a few blocks east of Kızılay's array of cheap restaurants. Ankara's largest mosque by far, and indeed one of the biggest in the world, this neo-Ottoman structure was completed in 1987, and has a shopping centre and car park underneath.

Anıt Kabir

Anıt Cad; rear entrance on Akdeniz Cad • Daily 9am–5pm • Free, though bring photo ID • Ankaray (LRT) train, or bus #265 from Ulus Meydanı, to Tandoğan; free shuttle buses every 5min from main entrance

The mausoleum of **Anıt Kabir** is a national shrine to **Mustafa Kemal Atatürk**, the man who shaped modern Turkey (see p.664). Both shrine and man are tremendously important to locals – the level of reverence inspired here is almost dictatorial, though nobody is forced to come, and you can be sure that the emotions are real. As with similar facilities in Pyongyang, Hanoi and Beijing, the complex has a larger-than-life air intended to convey a sense of power and majesty.

Approaching from the main (northern) entrance, you'll find yourself on **Lion Road**, a 260m-long pedestrian thoroughfare flanked with lion statues. At the end of this is a courtyard, with the **mausoleum** itself lying at its head – look for a squared-off Neoclassical temple with huge bronze doors. Visitors wearing hats must remove them as they enter; soldiers ensure that everyone shows the appropriate respect. The mausoleum interior is almost completely bare – the only decoration is some discreet mosaic work – so that all attention is focused on the plain sarcophagus. Atatürk's body was brought here in 1953 from its original resting place in what's now the Ethnographic Museum.

Three large halls are positioned around the courtyard. The largest houses the **Atatürk Museum** in which you'll find everything from Atatürk's evening dress to the rowing machine he used for exercise. Among the most eye-catching exhibits are a gun disguised as a walking stick, of which Ian Fleming would have been proud, and the gifts of a diamond-encrusted sword from the shah of Iran and an elegant toilet set from the king of Afghanistan. Lastly, note that a highly picturesque **changing of the guard** takes place hourly on the main courtyard.

ARRIVAL AND DEPARTURE   ANKARA

By plane Ankara's Esenboğa airport is 33km north of the city (ⓦesenbogaairport.com, ☎0312 398 0100). Havaş buses connect it with 19 Mayis Stadium in Ulus (every 30min; 35 min; ₺12). A taxi into the centre will cost around ₺65, or much more between midnight and 6am.
Destinations Adana (3–6 daily; 1hr); Antalya (4–5 daily; 1hr); Bodrum (2–5 daily; 1hr 20min); Dalaman (daily; 1hr 15min); Diyarbakır (4 daily; 1hr 20min); Elazığ (1–2 daily; 1hr 15min); Erzincan (daily; 1hr 20min); Erzurum (2–3 daily; 1hr 25min); Gaziantep (1–2 daily; 1hr 10min); İstanbul (hourly; 1hr); İzmir (8 daily; 1hr 20min); Kars (1–2 daily; 1hr 35min); Malatya (daily; 1hr 10min); Mardin (2 daily; 1hr 35min); Şanlıurfa (1–2 daily; 1hr 20min); Trabzon (3 daily; 1hr 20min); Van (3 daily; 1hr 35min).
Airline offices Mostly in Kavaklıdere or Çankaya. THY has offices at the airport (☎0312 398 0100), and at Atatürk Bul 211 (☎0312 465 6363).
By train The train station (☎0312 311 0602) is close to the heart of things at the bottom of Cumhuriyet Bul. Frequent buses head from the main entrance to Ulus and Kızılay, or you can walk through the tunnel under the railway line to Maltepe Ankaray (LRT) station.
Destinations Adana (daily; 7hr); Divriği (2 daily; 15hr); Diyarbakır (daily; 23hr); Erzurum (2 daily; 21hr); Eskişehir (10 daily; 1hr 30min); İstanbul (10 daily; 5–9hr); İzmir (2 daily; 14–15hr); Kars (daily; 26–28hr); Konya (7 daily;

2hr); Malatya (2 daily; 15–17hr); Sivas (2 daily; 11hr); Tatvan (weekly; 27hr); Tehran, Iran (Wed 10.25am; 60hr); Zonguldak (3 weekly; 10hr).
By bus The city *otogar* (known as Aşti) is in the western suburbs; free *servis* minibuses run to the centre from the car park out front. Some go to the plush hotels in Kavaklıdere, and others to Ulus station; alternatively, catch the Ankaray (LRT light railway).
Destinations Adana (10 daily; 7hr); Amasya (hourly; 6hr); Antalya (12 daily; 7hr); Bodrum (10 daily; 12hr); Bursa (hourly; 6hr); Diyarbakır (6 daily; 12hr); Erzurum (4 daily; 15hr); Eskişehir (6 daily; 3hr); Gaziantep (12 daily; 10hr); İstanbul (every 30min; 4hr 45min–6hr); İzmir (hourly; 8hr); Kayseri (14 daily; 5hr 30min); Konya (hourly; 3hr 30min); Kütahya (7 daily; 5hr); Mardin (3 daily; 16hr); Nevşehir (12 daily; 5hr); Safranbolu (16 daily; 3hr 30min); Samsun (10 daily; 6hr 30min); Şanlıurfa (4 daily; 12hr); Sivas (hourly; 7hr 30min); Sungurlu (hourly; 2hr 30min); Tokat (12 daily; 6hr 30min); Trabzon (5 daily; 13hr).
Car rental Avis, airport (☎0312 398 0315), and Tunus Cad 68, Kavaklıdere (☎0312 467 2313); Best, Büklüm Sok 89/9, Kavaklıdere (☎0312 467 0008); Budget, Tunus Cad 39, Kavaklıdere (☎0312 417 5952); Europcar, airport (☎0312 395 0506), and Koza Sok 154, Gaziosmanpaşa (☎0312 398 0503); Hertz, airport (☎0312 398 0535), and Atatürk Bul 138, Kavaklıdere (☎0312 468 1029).

GETTING AROUND

Tickets Ankara's public transport is pretty good, but tickets can be confusing for first-time arrivals. Basically, they come in blocks of two (₺3.5) to ten (₺17.5), and are valid on buses and both metro lines; buy them at metro stations or street kiosks.
By bus Buses run the length of Atatürk Bulvarı from Ulus to Kızılay, and then either branch off to Maltepe under a tunnel or continue to Çankaya via Kavaklıdere; check destinations on the front.

By metro Two modern metro lines with efficient, regular trainhhs until around 10.30pm. The line called the Ankaray or LRT (light railway) joins the other – simply called the metro – at Kızılay. This is also your best option for getting back out to the *otogar*.
By taxi Plentiful taxis can be flagged down just about anywhere (min fare ₺2.5, more midnight–6am). A trip from Ulus to Kavaklıdere, for example, costs around ₺12.

INFORMATION

Tourist office There's a small office in Gençlik Parkı, just downhill from the entrance opposite the Radisson Blu (Mon–Fri 8.30am–5pm; ☎0312 324 0101), and a helpful

one at the airport (daily 9.30am–6pm; ☎0312 398 0348).
Banks and exchange Banks and ATMs are all over the city, especially south of Ulus along Atatürk Bul. The airport

also has several places to change money.

Post office Ankara's main PTT is on Atatürk Bul in Ulus (open 24hr) for international calls and to buy stamps, phonecards etc. You can also place transfer-charge calls here. There's also a PTT at the train station (7am–11pm), and one on Gazi Mustafa Kemal Bul (8.30am–7pm) near the tourist office.

ACCOMMODATION

Finding a room in Ankara is rarely a problem, given the relative lack of tourists. Most of the cheaper hotels are in **Ulus**, though lone women may not feel comfortable in the very cheapest places. The few hotels in and around the **citadel** make by far the quietest after-dark options. Moving down into **Sıhhıye** and **Kızılay** takes you up another notch or two, and prices and standards steadily increase towards **Kavaklıdere**, further south.

AROUND ULUS

⭐ **Berlitz Hotel** Hükümet Cad 4 ☎ 0312 324 5316. One of the area's newest hotels, with surprisingly swish rooms decked out on a gold-maroon-brown colour scheme, featuring perfectly clean bathrooms. Those at the front have small, semicircular balconies. ₺140

⭐ **Otel Çevikoğlu** Çankırı Cad, Orta Sok 2 ☎ 0312 310 4535, 🖷 311 1940. Clean option whose backstreet setting cuts out a lot of noise. Curved furnishings provide retro chic in the clean, simple rooms, which also feature TVs and a minibar. Perhaps the cheapest safe option for lone females – single rooms can usually be haggled down to ₺40, including a tasty buffet breakfast. ₺70

Otel Gülpinar Hacı Bayram Cad 6 ☎ 0312 311 5998. As cheap as Ankara gets, especially for single travellers (₺26). Beyond its mock-Ottoman facade, it sports cell-like rooms and just-about-clean shared facilities; on the plus side it's so close to Hacı Bayram mosque that, unlike other places of this price, prostitutes shouldn't be a problem. ₺42

Otel Gülyeruz Sanayi Cad 37 ☎ 0312 310 4910, 🖷 gulyeruzotel.com. Great-value hotel featuring a curious, though appealing, mix of modern and retro fittings – the bright orange lift doors and yellow stained glass in the lobby seem lifted from another era, though this is offset with funky furniture and gold-painted picture frames. After all this, rooms are almost disappointingly plain. ₺100

Otel Mostar Opera Meyd, Tavus Sok 6 ☎ 0312 310 6242, 🖷 mostarhotelankara.com. Recently renovated, this hotel sports clean and bright rooms with spacious tiled bathrooms. There's a 24-hour restaurant on the premise. ₺150

Radisson Blu Istiklal Cad 20 ☎ 0312 310 4848, 🖷 radissonblu.com. The only "proper" hotel in the area, with well-appointed rooms, huge buffet breakfasts, and a largely business clientele. Try to get a park-facing room. ₺350

Otel Ulus Hacı Bayram Cad, Adliye Sok 1 ☎ 0312 310 5036. This mock-Ottoman option is far larger and measurably more comfortable than the *Gülpinar*. All the simple rooms are en suite. ₺70

THE CITADEL

⭐ **Angora House** Kalekapısı Sok 11 ☎ 0312 309 8380, 🖷 309 8381. It's well worth splashing out for a stay at this boutique hotel, set inside a 200-year-old house. The citadel location is perfect and the service first class, but best of all are the individually styled rooms – carved wooden ceilings, quality linen, large bathrooms and arty flourishes. Only six rooms, so book ahead. ₺160

⭐ **And Boutique** Opposite Alâeddin Camii ☎ 0312 310 2304. Modern, super-clean rooms with flat-screen TVs, in an excellent location just outside the citadel. Maybe the management got their sums wrong; the prices simply shouldn't be this cheap! Singles are ₺52, and you can lasso two rooms together to make an apartment for ₺110. Breakfast costs ₺15 per person. ₺82

⭐ **Divan** Depo Sok 3 ☎ 0312 306 6400, 🖷 divan.com .tr. Luxurious hotel set in a converted *han* – that's a bit of a trend across Turkey, but this is one of the better conversions, bar the ugly scaffolding that protects its large courtyard. Rooms are slick and charmingly decorated, and there are a couple of places to eat on the fringes of the complex. Best rates online. ₺300

KIZILAY AND KAVAKLIDERE

Otel Aldino Tunalı Hilmi Cad, Bülten Sok 22 ☎ 0312 468 6510, 🖷 hotelaldino.com. Prime location for dedicated shoppers, with a Turkish bath, two restaurant/bars, and garage parking. A/c rooms are bright and spacious with satellite TV, minibars and hairdryers. Friendly for a high-end place, and you should be able to score a small discount off the rack rates. ₺180

⭐ **Deeps Hostel** Atac Sok 2 ☎ 0312 213 6338, 🖷 deepshostelankara.com. Finally, Ankara has a decent hostel! It's a friendly, brightly painted affair with a wider range of rooms than the small lobby might suggest. Singles are good value at ₺45, and if there are enough willing participants, staff have been known to lead guests on bar-crawls. Dorms ₺27, doubles ₺80

Golden Boutique Boğaz Sok ☎ 0312 426 0111, 🖷 goldenboutiquehotel.com.tr. Golden? They're not kidding... from the sofas to the shower fittings, gold hues are absolutely all over the place in this hotel. On the plus side, staff are extremely friendly, the location nice and quiet, and the rates as cheap as the area gets. ₺130

Gordion Hotel Büklüm Sok 59 ☎ 0312 427 8080, 🖷 gordionhotel.com. Expensive and rather exclusive hotel with large, comfortable rooms all done in a tasteful, classical style. There's also a pool, and candelit massages on offer in the health club. ₺420

Hilton International Hotel Tahran Cad 12 ☎ 0312 468 2888, ⓦ hilton.com. Luxury rooms on sixteen floors, decorated in Anatolian stone and lots of plants, with individual a/c-cum-heating systems and laptop connections. For those on a generous expense account, though discounted weekend packages (Fri–Sun) can bring prices down to a very reasonable level. **€245**

Sheraton Noktalı Sok ☎ 0312 468 5454, ⓦ sheraton .com. Enjoy a pampered existence in this cylindrical concrete monolith. There's a friendly atmosphere for a five-star hotel, a great view of the city from the top, plus various restaurants, a pool and two cinemas. **€285**

Otel Tunalı Tunalı Hilmi Cad 119 ☎ 0312 467 4440, ⓦ hoteltunali.com.tr. A good upper-mid-range option, run by the same family for two generations; cheaper than most places in Kavaklıdere, it's close to all the nightlife. Rooms are ordinary but functional, with fridge, satellite TV and huge windows overlooking the busy street. Coffee shop and formal dining room attached. **₺210**

EATING

If you're looking for cheap eats, **Ulus** is your best bet. **Kızılay** has most of the mid-range places (particularly on and around Karanfil and Selanik *sokaks*), while classier restaurants can be found in **Kavaklıdere** and **Çankaya**. The exceptions to this general rule are the restaurants in the citadel's restored Ottoman houses.

AROUND ULUS

Bulvar İşkembecisi ve Lokantası Çankırı Cad 11. Simple restaurant serving good *İskender kebap*, *fırın sütlaç* (baked rice pudding) and other trusty favourites. Daily 24hr.

Büyükşehir Market Hal Sok. This excellent market (see p.479) is as good for budget dining as it is for self-catering. Though establishments change like the wind, you should be able to track down some *kokoreç* (something like Turkish haggis in a bun) or *cupra levrek* (fried fish and salad in a bun) for less than ₺5. Opening times vary.

Cevhid Anafartalar Cad 10. One of those restaurants that looks nothing out of the ordinary from the outside, but serves phenomenal food. Justly famed for its *İskender kebap* (₺12), which is up there with the best in the land – the slices of lamb are cut from the skewer with almost surgical precision. They also do good *pide* from ₺7. Daily 9am–10pm.

Urfalı Hacı Bayram Cad, Etizafer Sok 5a. Budget meals in one of the area's faux-Ottoman buildings. Inside, the atmosphere is pure canteen-style, and prices are incredibly cheap – take your pick from kebabs including *patlıcan* and *sarma beyti*, grab some salad and *ayran*, then have a tea for afters… and still get change from ₺10. Daily 8am–10pm.

AROUND THE CITADEL

Kale Washington Kale Sok 1. Atmospheric restaurant with a view-laden terrace perched on top of the old city walls. A good place for a cool beer, a dinner of the usual Turkish staples (kebabs ₺25 or so, starters ₺10), or something a little different, like beef stroganoff or chicken Kiev. Daily 10am–midnight.

★ **Kınacızade Konağı** Kalekapısı Sok 28. Set in a wonderful Ottoman house, this restaurant also has history to its credit – Atatürk himself swung by when it was still a home. The owners now whip up some great meals, though are proudest of their huge village breakfasts (₺25). Hot dishes such as clay-baked trout or sizzling lamb go for around ₺18, and the honey walnut *gözleme* just beg to be tried. Daily 8am–midnight.

KIZILAY, KAVAKLIDERE AND ÇANKAYA

Günaydın Arjentin Cad 18. A steak place on "Argentina Road"… you couldn't make it up. This classy restaurant has an almost religious following among expats and well-off locals alike, and the fact that meats are cured here lends it the air of an upscale butcher's – choose your table carefully. Daily 11am–11pm.

Komagane Konur Sok 13. A favourite with the backpackers staying at nearby *Deeps* hostel (see p.476), this small eatery serves *çiğ köfte dürüm* (spicy paste in a wrap) with *ayran* for just ₺3. Daily 8am–1am.

Le Man Kültür Konur Sok 8. A prime example of Ankara's recent swing towards the trendy and hip, with cartoon strips lining the tables and walls. Salads, sandwiches and pasta dishes go for around ₺9, Latino food for a little more. Daily 8am–1am.

Sushico Arjentin Cad, Attar Sok 10. Ankara's Asian restaurants are typically drab affairs serving food that can hardly be called authentic. What a pleasant change this highly attractive place is, serving well-prepared Japanese, Chinese and Thai dishes – try a bento set (from ₺29), crispy duck (₺26) or a green curry (₺20). Daily 11am–11pm.

Tapa Tapa Tapas Tunalı Hilmi Cad 87. Large, popular tapas restaurant (dishes from ₺6.5), complete with well-stocked horseshoe bar. Live music Tues, and frequent salsa nights held on the dancefloor at the back. Daily noon–midnight.

Yosun Iran Cad 27 ☎ 0312 467 5464. Customers return again and again for an authentic Turkish night out – start with *mezes*, then move on to fish (red mullet, sea bass or bream), while staff provide the entertainment by singing and playing the piano and accordion. Expect to pay around ₺45 with a half-bottle of wine or rakı thrown in. Daily noon–11pm.

8

DRINKING AND NIGHTLIFE

Cafés are strewn all over town, some of which segue into **bars** as the evening progresses. For alcohol you're best advised t avoid Ulus and head south instead – the studenty district of Kızılay is the obvious starting point. Ankara is prett progressive, so female visitors shouldn't attract too much unwelcome attention. For something more trendy head for th bars of Kavaklıdere. The **clubbing** scene is improving but don't expect too much; some studenty late-night venues ar hidden away in the backstreets of the university district, Cebeci, but you really need a local to guide you to them.

CAFÉS

And Cafe Just uphill from Alâeddin Camii, Hisar. Just inside the citadel, this open, elegant place serves Turkish coffee (₺5) or a slice of cake (₺6 and up), to enjoy over commanding views of the city. It's a restaurant too, but the food is overpriced. Tues–Sun 9am–11pm.

Bedesten Opposite Aslanhane Camii, Hisar. Rickety teahouse meets oversized treehouse: have a good clamber around before settling on a place to sit, squat, lie or lounge. The coffee's good too (₺3.5), but best of all you can buy anything you see hanging around the place, with the likely exception of other customers. Daily 9am–9pm.

Hansaray Gençlik Parkı, Ulus. The best of Ankara's many park-based tearooms, tucked into the area immediately behind the opera building. Despite the location, it's not too dear – ₺1.5 for tea, a little more for coffee, or ₺15 for a nargile. Try to bag one of their raised booths, set Ottoman-style around a metal table. Daily 8am–9pm.

Kitchenette Filistin Sok 22, Gaziosmanpaşa. The title of "Ankara's trendiest café" seems to change every month, but this is a terrific choice – three impeccably designed floors, the top two reached via an elegant spiral staircase. They make good brunch meals, including eggs Benedict (₺15) and granola yoghurt (₺11). Daily 9am–10pm.

Mado İşhani 1, Ulus. Part of a nationwide chain serving expensive (but delectable) traditional Turkish desserts, often with a contemporary twist. A round of baklava and ice cream will set you back around ₺10. There's another outlet at Ziya Gökalp 13, Kavaklıdere. Daily 8am–10pm.

Zerdali Konak Opposite Hacı Bayram Camii, Ulus. Small café-cum-tearoom, with a charming interior and some outdoor seats facing directly onto the Temple c Augustus and Rome. Augustus didn't specify which ice cream flavour he liked on the List of Achievements he le† there (see p.471), though there are well over a dozen t choose from, as well as good baklava. Daily 8am–9pm.

BARS AND CLUBS

Copper Club Sheraton Hotel, Noktali Sok, Kavaklıdere Large club frequented by expats and diplomats. One of th few places in Ankara where you can successfully order a gi & tonic, but expect to pay through the nose for it. Fri & Sa 10pm–4am.

★ **Eski Yeni** İnkılap Sok 6, Kızılay. With draught bee for ₺4 and a heaving dance floor, this is a great place t have a drink and throw some shapes on a weeken evening. The bar's name translates as "Old New", which i rather apt: the happy, easy-to-please crowd squeals i delight when the latest "Ankara house" hit comes on, the does exactly the same thing for Annie Lennox or Simpl Red. Daily 3pm–late.

Hayyami Bestekar Sok 82, Kavaklıdere. Cosy, laidba wine-bar-cum-restaurant. The Italian dishes play secon fiddle to an excellent selection of wines (₺30 and up for bottle, or ₺10 and up for a glass), with most peop popping by for live music in the evenings. Daily 11am late; music Wed–Sun.

Up Lost Bar Bayındır Sok 17, Kızılay. Grungy ye somehow homely, this sixth-floor bar is a friendly place wit live music and karaoke sessions on weekend evenings they'd be more than pleased to see a foreigner grabbing th mic. Mon–Sat 6pm–late.

ENTERTAINMENT

Once Ankara was made capital of the new republic, the city had to become the cultural capital of Turkey, supported by th opera-loving Atatürk. **Concerts**, and in particular **opera**, are well worth attending here if you can. A visit to Ankara **Opera House** is a unique experience, while classical music performances by the State Orchestra take place at the Stat Concert Hall and other venues. The atmosphere is refreshingly informal, and thanks to government subsidies tickets ar cheap. The main season starts in earnest in October and runs through to March, and monthly programmes are listed in th Sunday edition of the *Turkish Daily News*. Recent international **films** are usually shown in their original language wit Turkish subtitles; tickets cost around ₺15, with discounts before 6pm.

CLASSICAL MUSIC AND OPERA

State Opera (Devlet Opera) Atatürk Bul, just south of the entrance to Gençlik Parkı ☎ 0312 324 2210. Classics such as *Tosca*, *La Bohème* and *Madame Butterfly*, as well as occasional piano recitals and classical concerts. Tickets (₺25 and up) are available from the box office in season (9.30am–5.30pm, 8pm on performance days), up to month in advance and from the Dost bookshop in Kızıla (see "Directory", p.479).

State Orchestra (Devlet Orkestrasi) Talat Paşa Ca 38, just south of the Opera House and Gençlik Par ☎ 0312 309 1343. The Presidential Symphony Orchestr

---

FESTIVALS IN ANKARA

Ankara Film Festival ⓦ www.filmfestankara.org.tr. The city's main film festival, taking place over ten days each March.

Ankara Music Festival ⓦ www.ankarafestival.com. Now well over thirty years old, this major classical music festival takes place in the spring (usually April), and is spread across three weeks or so.

Büyük Ankara Festival A fun, family-friendly series of events taking place over one week each July – ask the tourist office (p.475) for the latest plans.

Flying Broom ⓦ festival.ucansupurge.org. Women's film festival hosted by a feminist organization, taking place each May.

International Cartoon Film Festival Cartoon festival aimed at children, but inevitably enjoyed by older folk too. Lasts for a few days each April – ask at the tourist office for info.

---

erforms here twice weekly, showcasing classical music by urkish and foreign composers. Tickets sold by the State pera box office, ₺15 and up. Thurs & Fri at 8pm, plus ccasionally Sat 11am.

ILM

egapol Konur Sok 33, Kızılay ☎ 0312 419 4493. More rty than the *Metropol*, which it backs onto, screening nything from Japanese to Eastern European films. Look

out for the occasional English-speaking classic.

Metropol Selanik Cad 76, Kızılay ☎ 0312 425 7479. Hugely popular multi-screen cinema showing new releases and special screenings of classic movies and foreign films. There's a coffee shop inside, a beer garden outside and any number of cafés and bars along this street.

Sheraton Cinema Noktalı Sok, Kavaklıdere ☎ 0312 468 5454. Two small, cosy cinemas, open to non-guests, with some of the comfiest seats you could find.

DIRECTORY

ooks Tuhran, corner of Konur Sok and Yüksel Cad, Kızılay, as a good selection of books. Dost, Karanfil Sok 11, Kızılay, as English novels and a good selection of pricier coffee-ble books.

mbassies Australia, Nenehatun Cad 83, Gaziosmanpaşa ☎ 0312 459 9500); Canada, Cinnah Cad 58 (☎ 0312 409 712); Iran, Tehran Cad 10, Kavaklıdere (☎ 0312 468 2820); ew Zealand, Iran Cad 13, Kavaklıdere (☎ 0312 467 9054); ussian Federation, Karyağdi Sok 5, Çankaya (☎ 0312 439 422); USA, Atatürk Bul 110, Kavaklıdere (☎ 0312 455 5555); K, Şehit Ersan Cad 46/A, Çankaya (☎ 0312 455 3344).

mergencies Ambulance ☎ 112; Fire ☎ 110; Police ☎ 155.

amams Karacabey Hamamı, Talat Paşa Cad 101, Ulus, is e oldest in town, built in 1445 (daily 10am–10pm; ₺20). little cheaper are the baths at the *Sürmeli Hotel*, Cihan ok 6, Sıhhıye (daily 10am–10pm; ₺15; ☎ 0312 231 560); and Eynebey Hamamı, Adnan Saygun Cad 11 (daily 4hr; ₺17; ☎ 0312 309 6865).

ospitals Hacettepe Hastanesi, just west of Hasırcılar Cad Sıhhıye (☎ 0312 466 5858 or 5859), should have an nglish-speaking doctor available at all times. You may be eated more quickly at one of Ankara's private hospitals:

Çankaya, Bülten Sok 44, Çankaya (☎ 0312 426 1450), is the most central.

Laundry All but the cheapest of hotels offer a reasonably priced laundry service, but if you get stuck try the Yimpaş department store on Sanayı Cad in Ulus – on the second floor is a laundry and dry cleaners.

Markets The Büyükşehir market in Ulus is a wonderfully atmospheric market, and heaven for self-caterers – fruit, veggies and honey from all over the country, including scrumptious olives from İzmir, and *beyaz* (yellow) cherries from Konya. The market's butchers sit uncomfortably close to a few pet shops outside, though mercifully these only trade in birds. Also worth a mention is the small fruit-and-nut market near the citadel – it's just down the road from the *Divan* hotel.

Pharmacies In each neighbourhood pharmacies take turns in providing a 24hr service called *Nöbetçi*, the information posted on the window of the other pharmacy shops. Most central is Ülkü, Meşrütiyet Cad 23, Kızılay.

Police The tourist police (☎ 0312 384 0606) are located in Ankara's main police station (Emniyet Sarayı) in the district of Akköprü, a short walk south of the Akköprü metro station.

West of Ankara

Vest of Ankara lie two cities which, though off the tourist radar, are immensely ppealing, and serve as perfect opportunities to take the true pulse of Turkey. First up is lt-of-the-earth **KÜTAHYA**, an initially scruffy-looking place where, if you look a little harder, you'll find some of Turkey's most delightfully located museums, as well as whole streets of buildings that are swathed with the city's famous glazed tiles. Then comes **ESKİŞEHİR**, a lively, student-filled city whose own crop of Ottoman buildings has been painted in surprisingly attractive pastel tones.

Kütahya

Tiles, tiles and more tiles. That's what you'll see when strolling around **KÜTAHYA**, a likeable, working-class city, halfway between İzmir and Ankara, in which a substantial number of buildings, including the old *otogar*, are swathed in decorative **glazed products**. Even the main square is distinguished by a fountain that centres on a huge ceramic vase. Kütahya tiles are used throughout Turkey, especially in restoration work on Ottoman mosques – İznik may be more famous (see box, p.164), but in reality much of the industry has moved here.

Most travellers whoosh straight past Kütahya, but those who choose to stay a night are usually glad: the town boasts an array of pleasing little **museums**, each housed in a superb piece of architecture, as well as Ottoman remains including a **fortress** and a crumbling swathe of old town. Throw in some value-for-money restaurants, a chance to visit the splendidly isolated Roman ruins of **Aezani** (see p.482) and a near-total absence of tourists, and you're onto an off-the-beaten-track winner. You'll also be able to take some of the famed tile-work home with you – ceramic shops on virtually every street sell tiles, dinner services and vases... not to mention toilets, of which Kütahya is the nation's largest producer.

All the city sights are within easy walking distance. Several well-preserved Ottoman-era houses lie near the main square, **Belediye Meydanı**, with the bulk of the museums and mosques at the end of **Cumhuriyet Bulvarı**, a pedestrianized road to the west. The action starts just past the little roundabout with a **rotating dervish** at its centre. (One can only hope that this feature takes hold across Turkey.) The fortress is a little further along, and visible from a distance.

Brief history

Kütahya enjoyed its golden age as a **tile-making centre** under the Ottomans, after Sultan Selim I forcibly resettled tile-workers from Tabriz here after defeating the Persians at Çaldıran in 1514. Contemporary Kütahya tiles look a little garish and crude in comparison with Ottoman-era examples – the secrets of the pigment blends that gave the original Kütahya tiles their subtle and delicate lustre have been lost with the centuries.

During the War of Independence, the Greek army were defeated twice in battles at the defile of İnönü, northeast of Kütahya, in January and April 1921. They managed to break out that same summer, capturing Eskişehir and Afyon and launching an offensive that took them to within striking distance of Ankara. The following year the Turkish offensive that was to throw the Greeks out of Anatolia once and for all began at Dumlupınar, midway between Kütahya and Afyon.

Ulu Cami

Cumhuriyet Cad, just past the dervish roundabout

The **Ulu Cami** is an attractive but unexceptional fifteenth-century mosque that stands in the middle of Kütahya's lively **bazaar** area, which extends over several streets. A couple of interesting **shops** opposite the entrance sell tiles and religious paraphernalia.

Archeological Museum

By the Ulu Camii • Tues–Sun 8.15am–noon & 1–5pm • ₺3

Kütahya's archeological museum houses finds from the area, including a beautiful **sarcophagus** from Aezani depicting a heroic battle between the Greeks and Amazons. The contents of the museum are considerably less interesting than the building itself, the

Vacidiye Medresesi, a fourteenth-century seminary built by the Germiyanid emir Bey Bin Savcı as an astronomical observatory and school of science and mathematics. The high point of the interior is the central marble pool, beneath a dome with glass skylights.

Tile Museum

Behind the Ulu Camii • Tues–Sun 8.15am–noon & 1–5pm • Free

Splendidly set inside an old mosque, a small museum just behind the Ulu Camii, focuses on **local tiles** from across the ages. The various plates, vases and wall-tiles are mostly local, though there are a few works from rival tile-city İznik too; they fill four small alcoves, surrounding a dome-covered fountain.

Kossuth Evi

Gediz Cad, signed "Macar Evi" • Tues–Sun 8.15am–noon & 1–4.45pm • ₺3

Tucked away in a side street, the charming Ottoman building known as the **Kossuth Evi** was once home to **Lajos Kossuth** (1802–94), a Hungarian patriot who fled to Turkey after the failure of the 1848 uprising against Habsburg rule. The immaculate house has been preserved much as it must have been when he lived there in 1850–51. It's the nineteenth-century Ottoman ambience of the rooms, rather than the Kossuth connection, which will be of interest to most visitors.

Kütahya fortress

Kütahya's hilltop **kale** towers above town; signposts point you in the right direction should you wish to wander up to the summit, which offers predictably impressive views of the city below. The fortress was originally built by the Byzantines and extended by their successors, but these days only the western walls survive in anything like their original state. It's a steep walk up (take a taxi for ₺10 or so), but there are a couple of places to eat and drink near the entrance.

8

ARRIVAL AND INFORMATION

KÜTAHYA

By bus Kütahya's new *otogar* is 3km northeast of the centre, along a road that eventually morphs into Atatürk Bulvarı; *servis* buses connect most arrivals to the centre. The old, tile-swathed *otogar*, on Atatürk Bulvarı just northeast of the centre, is now a fire station, but some local services start from outside.

Destinations Afyon (14 daily; 1hr 45min); Ankara (7 daily; 6hr); Antalya (5 daily; 5hr); Bursa (12 daily; 3hr); Eskişehir (11 daily; 1hr 20min); İstanbul (14 daily; 6hr); İzmir (12 daily; 6hr).

By train The small station, 1km east of the main square, is only really worth considering for the short hop to Eskişehir.

Destinations Eskişehir (6 daily, 1hr 20min).

Tourist office There's a booth on the main square (Mon–Fri 9am–noon & 1–5pm; ☏ 0274 223 6213).

Banks Every bank in Turkey has an ATM on Kütahya's main square, and there are plenty of banks up Cumhuriyet Cad.

ACCOMMODATION

Hotel Gül Palas Belediye Meyd ☏ 0274 216 1233, ✉ gulpalas@gulpalas.com. There are tiles all over the place at this mid-range option, which provides excellent value for money. Tiny lifts squeak up to rooms that, though carpetless, are comfortable enough, with cute shower areas. The hotel sign is actually above the decrepit *Kösk*; head next door to the tiled building. ₺100

★ **Hilton Garden Inn** Atatürk Bul ☏ 0274 229 5555, ⓦ hilton.com. If you can afford to stay here, do – three-star

prices for what, in essence, approximate five-star rooms. Such savings come because services here are pared down to a minimum, with little more than a fitness centre, bar and restaurant, though all these are excellent. ₺180

Hotel Yüksel Belediye Meyd 1 ☏ 0274 212 0111, ✉ otelyuksel@hotmail.com. The pick of the budget hotels, clean and about as central as you could hope for. Pastel-painted rooms feature colourful bedding straight from the local market. ₺50

EATING AND DRINKING

Kütahya holds some excellent places to eat. Its working-class nature, and lack of foreign tourists, keep prices to a minimum. Cheap snack-shacks do good trade around the main square; there are also a couple of **bars** on Atatürk Bul, and plenty of shops sell alcohol.

★**Acar Karavan** Cumhuriyet Cad. Occupying a charmingly gloomy old building, this café is hugely popular with local youth, who come for cheap eats – there are all sorts, from savouries (like *mantı* and *pide*, both ₺5) to sweets, as well as coffee, tea and nargiles (try the cappuccino one in which the smoke is drawn through milk, rather than water). There are also some Ottoman togs to try on, though staff will likely ask you to return them before you tuck into a gloopy chocolate *gözleme* (₺3.50). Daily 8am–11.30pm.

Kütahya Konağı Kurşunlu Sok 13. Set in an Ottoman house in the old town, tucked away on a side street signed from the Kossuth Evi, this charmer serves up simple traditional dishes; reckon on about ₺15 per head. Daily noon–3pm & 6–9pm.

Karavan Döner By the fortress entrance. Sister branch to *Acar Karavan*, focusing on grilled meats; prices are a little higher but still reasonable considering the views, which can be taken in while revolving if you ask the staff to turn on the machine. Daily 9am–11pm.

★**Mülayimoğulları** Atatürk Bul 11b. Attractive, inevitably tile-filled venue with the friendliest staff in the city, and meals that provide superb value for money. All the kebabs are great, but try the *yoğurtlu köfte* (₺8), a round of super-succulent (and therefore high-quality) meat rissoles served on yoghurt-cooked bread, served with *ayran* and a huge salad. Try to sit in the section with high ceilings, rather than that with uncomfortably low ones. Daily 9am–11pm.

Aezani

60km southwest of Kütahya • Daily 9am–6pm • Temple ₺5 • Buses from old *otogar* to village of Çavdarhisar, 1km southeast (every 30min; 1hr)

Roman **Aezani** is famed for its atmospheric **Temple of Zeus**, built by Hadrian in 125 AD, and one of Anatolia's best-preserved Roman buildings. The temple occupies a commanding position atop a large, rectangular terrace. On its north and west sides, double rows of columns topped by a pediment survive, but elsewhere the columns have largely collapsed, and broken fragments are scattered nearby.

At the heart of the temple, the **inner sanctum** was originally dominated by a magnificent statue of Zeus. Its walls, made of rectangular stone blocks, are largely intact, but the roof has long since caved in. A subterranean **sanctuary** beneath is dedicated to Cybele; the affable site attendant opens it on request. Back outside, just northeast, a fallen but well-preserved bust of Cybele – not, as locals will tell you, Medusa – surveys the landscape.

From the temple, you can walk north past the baths to the remains of the uniquely combined **stadium-theatre**. Paths lead from the fine inscriptions of the southern gate, up between ruined stadium seats, to the backdrop wall of the theatre and the fallen remains of its marble facade.

East of the temple stand the arches of the ruined **agora**. The old ceremonial road leads south from here, over a second Roman bridge, to the enigmatic **macellum** (marketplace), whose walls carry a fourth-century decree from Emperor Diocletian fixing market prices in an attempt to stop rampant inflation.

Complete your circular tour by heading back to the first Roman bridge, and ask the site guardian to open up the nearby second set of **baths**, with their satyr mosaic and statue of Hygeia, goddess of the baths.

Returning to Kütahya may involve a bit of a wait on the main road; this is within view most of the way from Aezani, so you may well see your bus scream past before you're within sprinting distance.

Eskişehir

Handily positioned on the new high-speed train line from Ankara, the modern university city of **ESKİŞEHİR** makes a potential stopover on the way from İstanbul, especially if you want to buy trinkets made from **meerschaum**, or are heading to the charming village of **Seyitgazi**.

Eskişehir's energetic mayor, Yılmaz Büyükerşen, has since 1999 implemented such reforms as pedestrianizing much of the centre, gentrifying the (now very attractive) **canal area**, and inaugurating a flashy new tram system. An appealing crop of **Ottoman houses** in the **Odunpazarı** district, just south of the centre, has also been restored –

MEERSCHAUM

Literally "sea foam" in German, **meerschaum** is a porous white stone, large deposits of which are mined in the villages that surround Eskişehir. While wet, the soft stone is carved into all manner of ornaments, but the smoke-cooling properties of a meerschaum pipe make that the most highly prized item. Several shops around Eskişehir, especially on İnönü Caddesi, work the mineral, and with a little haggling it's usually possible to pick up a bargain.

imagine a miniature, pastel-painted version of Amasya or Safranbolu. Nearby, the Kurşunlu Külliye complex includes a mosque and meerschaum museum.

ARRIVAL AND DEPARTURE ESKİŞEHİR

By train Eskişehir's train station is on the northwest edge of the centre, an easy walk along the nearby canal.
Destinations Ankara (10 daily; 1hr 30min); İstanbul (4 daily; 5hr); Kütahya (6 daily; 1hr 15min).
By bus The colossal *otogar* is 3km east of town, a distance usually spanned by *servis* minibus, though it's also linked to the centre by tram (₺1.60).
Destinations Ankara (6 daily; 3hr); Bursa (6 daily; 2hr 30min); İstanbul (4 daily; 5hr); Kütahya (11 daily; 1hr 20min).

ACCOMMODATION

Abacı Konak Türkmen Hoca Sok 29 ☎ 0222 333 0333, ⓦ abaciotel.com. The only option in the old town area is less than a hotel than a miniature village of faux Ottoman housing. Though comfy, it falls down a bit on the tradition front. ₺210
Ada Life Adalar Sok 2 ☎ 0222 233 7711, ⓦ adalifeotel .com. Decent business option, more or less overlooking the canal; if your room doesn't have a view, you'll be able to soak one up over a superb rooftop breakfast. ₺150
Olcaylar İstasyon Cad 43 ☎ 0222 231 1835. Ultra-budget place, pretty much facing the train station. Bare-bones rooms with shared facilities (squat toilets only). ₺35

EATING AND DRINKING

The canal banks are lined with places to eat and sup coffee – mostly cheap, since this is a university town. The local dish is *çi börek*, a kind of fried, half-moon dumpling with mincemeat and onions inside, always (oddly) bought in rounds of five. It's a Crimean Tatar delicacy – many locals, especially in the old town, are of similar stock. The city is quite conservative, so despite its huge student population, it's surprisingly hard to find a place to **drink**.

★ **Kasr-ı Nur** Kocamüftü Sok 7. The old town has few places to eat, and those that exist are disappointingly low on quality. Thank goodness for this little winner, a family-run place set in the area's most attractive square: at least eight different pastel hues on view, and not that many cars. All foods are organic and handmade – try the village-style breakfast (*köy kahvaltısı*; ₺15), a gigantic affair with loads of jams, olives and cheeses, mainly from İzmir (like the family); later in the day, a round of *çi börek* may be in order, and there's always good coffee and tea on offer. Daily 8am–10pm.
Travelers' Cafe Under *Ada Life* hotel. Fun restaurant-bar serving global food including pad thai, pasta, fajitas and burgers. In the evenings, most are here for the beer, sangrias and *caipirinhas*. Daily 9am–midnight.

Seyitgazi and around

45km south of Eskişehir • Direct buses from Eskişehir (hourly; 1hr; ₺5)

Little **SEYİTGAZİ** sits in a fertile valley set incongruously amid the rolling Anatolian steppe. Despite its beautiful location and a diverting historical attraction, visitors are rare and your arrival may take the tractor-driving locals by surprise – the ability to string a sentence together in Turkish will likely see you afforded hero status, and bought some tea.

The Türbe-tekke complex

On the valley slopes, above town • Daily 8am–6pm • Donations suggested for main hall

Seyitgazi takes its name from Şehit Battal Gazi, the commander of an Arab army that forayed into Anatolia during the eighth century. An unlikely legend relates that he was killed during the siege of Afyon and buried with a Byzantine princess who had pined away through love for him. The site of their resting place was revealed to the mother of the Selçuk sultan Alâeddin Keykubad, who promptly built a *türbe* (tomb) for the *gazi*. It became a popular place of pilgrimage, and during the thirteenth century Hacı Bektaş Veli, founder of the Bektaşi dervish order (see box, p.426), established a *tekke*, or monastery, here.

The **complex** itself is roughly horseshoe-shaped, open towards the slope with a Byzantine church and a Selçuk mosque by the entrance. The former is a reminder that a Christian convent originally stood on the site, while the latter contains the outsize sarcophagus of Şehit Battal, just under 7m in length. Next to it is the more modest sarcophagus of his princess.

Midas Şehri

30km south of Seyitgazi • No public transport

The wonderful valley that stretches between Seyitgazi and Afyon is filled with eerie rock formations, and dotted with **Phrygian tombs**, temples and fortifications. **MIDAS ŞEHRI** ("City of Midas" in Turkish, though there's no specific Midas connection) is by far the most accessible and substantial Phrygian sight, though you'll need your own transport to get here – it's on a lovely route used only by tractors. The cave-pocked site, too, is a beauty – it's as if Midas had touched Cappadocia and made it not gold, but green.

The **site** itself comprises the sketchy ruins of a Phrygian city atop a 30m-high plateau whose steep rock sides have been carved with elaborate decorative facades. The one on the northwest face of the plateau has come to be known as the **Midas tomb**; heading west from here leads to more niches carved in the rock, a number of rock tombs and an incomplete relief.

Access to the upper part of the plateau and the remains of the Phrygian **citadel** is via a flight of steps on the eastern side. Near the top of the steps, some of the many altars and tombs bear inscriptions and decorative reliefs.

In the southwestern part of the citadel is a **rock throne**, a kind of stepped altar on which the figure of a deity would have been placed. Its upper part holds a clear **inscription** and crude decorative scratchings. Elsewhere a few fragments of the citadel's defensive wall survive.

Gordion

18km northeast of Polatlı • Some high-speed trains between Eskişehir and Ankara stop at Polatlı, as do buses from Ankara's *otogar* (every 30min); onwards dolmuşes are very infrequent, so catch a taxi (at least ₺100 return, including waiting time)

After the collapse of the Hittite Empire the Phrygians briefly dominated Anatolia. Their capital, **GORDION**, is one of western Anatolia's most important archeological sites (albeit very hard to reach without your own transport). It's a name of much resonance, associated not only with the eponymous knot, but also with King Midas and his golden touch. The first things you'll see as you approach are the immense royal tumuli, scattered across the drab, steppe-like landscape. Inside these, archeologists found stunning artefacts that testified to the sophisticated nature of Phrygian culture. Nearby, the foundations of the Gordion acropolis have been uncovered.

Brief history

The original settlement at Gordion dates back to the Bronze Age, and the site was certainly occupied during the Hittite period. The Phrygians arrived during the ninth century BC, and a hundred years later the settlement became capital of the empire founded by the Phrygian king **Gordius**. Gordion, like the Phrygian Empire itself, experienced a brief flowering, followed by destruction and protracted decline.

FROM TOP OTTOMAN HOUSE, SAFRANBOLU (P.487); HATTUŞA (P.492) >

THE MYTHS AND LEGENDS OF GORDION

The name **Midas** is inextricably associated with Gordion. Several Phrygian kings bore this name, and over the centuries a kind of composite mythical figure has emerged. The best-known legend, of Midas and the **golden touch**, tells how Midas captured the water demon, Silenus, after making him drunk by pouring wine into his spring. As ransom, Midas demanded of Dionysos the ability to turn all he touched into gold. After Dionysos granted this wish, Midas was dismayed to find he had been taken literally, and his food and even his own daughter were transformed. He begged Dionysos for release from the curse, and was ordered to wash his hands in the River Pactolus. The cure worked, and thereafter the river ran with gold.

According to another tale, Midas was called upon to judge a musical contest between Apollo and the satyr Marsyas. Midas decided in favour of Marsyas and in revenge Apollo caused him to grow the ears of an ass. (Marsyas came off even worse – the god skinned him alive.) To hide his new appendages, Midas wore a special hat, revealing them only to his barber who was sworn to secrecy on pain of death. Desperate to tell someone the king's secret, the barber passed it on to the reeds of the river, which ever after whispered, "Midas has ass's ears."

Another story may have some basis in reality. During the reign of Gordius, an oracle foretold that a poor man who would enter Gordion by ox-cart would, one day, rule over the Phrygians. As the king and nobles were discussing this prediction, a farmer named Midas arrived at the city in his cart. Gordius, who had no heirs, saw this as the fulfilment of the prophecy and named Midas his successor. Subsequently, Midas had his cart placed in the temple of Cybele on the Gordion acropolis, where it was to stand for half a millennium. Somehow the belief arose that whoever untied the intricate knot that fixed the cart to its yoke would become master of Asia. During his stay in the city **Alexander the Great** decided not to untie the **Gordian Knot**, but to slice through it with his sword. The phrase "cutting the Gordian knot" is still used today, to describe solving any intractable problem in one swift move.

There's little left in the records, save for the myths and legends associated with the empire, though some concrete information survives about its final king, Mitas (Midas of Mushki, who is thought to have reigned from 725 BC to 696 BC.

It was invading **Cimmerians** who laid waste to the Phrygian Empire, destroying Gordion, and though the Phrygians made a comeback and rebuilt their capital, their power had been irreversibly reduced. The city was occupied in 650 BC by the **Lydians** fell in turn to the **Persians** just over a century later, and in 333 BC welcomed **Alexander the Great** for wintertime during his great march east. The arrival of the **Galatians** (Gauls) in Asia Minor in 278 BC was the final chapter in the long decline, precipitating the flight of Gordion's population.

The royal tombs and museum

Yassıhüyük • Tues–Sun 8am–5pm • Combined ticket ₺3

Of the main concentration of the huge and inscrutable tumulus tombs of the Phrygian kings, only the **Midas Tümülüsü** (Royal Tomb), conveniently located in the village of Yassıhüyük, just short of the site itself, is likely to attract your attention. Measuring 300m in diameter and over 50m high, it's thought to be the burial chamber of an unidentified Phrygian king, curiously buried without weapons or ornaments. The tumulus was excavated during the 1950s, when American archeologists bored a 60m **tunnel** through to its centre and discovered the intact wooden chamber. Inside they found the skeleton of a man in his sixties on a wooden couch surrounded by grave objects. Among these were three exquisitely crafted wooden tables, inlaid screens, large numbers of bronze clasps for garments and 178 bronze vessels, including three large cauldrons; now, the chamber is all you'll see.

The worthwhile **museum**, across the road, contains items recovered from the tombs, and some attractive mosaics. However, the best of the finds are, inevitably, in Ankara's Museum of Anatolian Civilizations (see p.472).

he acropolis

m south of Yassıhüyük

n easy-to-spot raised area, south of the village, is the site of an eighth-century BC cropolis. The heart of the city, this was the location of the royal palace, temples nd administrative buildings, the foundations of which have been revealed by xcavations.

Substantial remains of the huge Phrygian-era **town gate** survive on the utheastern side of the acropolis. This must have been a formidable structure: ven in its present truncated state it's over 10m high, making it one of the largest urviving pre-Classical buildings in Anatolia. The outer portal was flanked by twin wers, from which defenders would have been able to inflict heavy casualties on ttackers in front of the gate.

Fencing keeps visitors away from the central **palace**, which consisted of four megara, r large halls with vestibules, each featuring wonderful mosaics. The fourth megaron as probably a temple to Cybele, the Phrygian incarnation of the mother goddess. that's the case, then it was here that Alexander the Great cut the Gordian Knot.

Safranbolu and around

ittle **SAFRANBOLU** is, quite possibly, the one place in Turkey where you'll be glad our hotel room has a squeaky floor. Hundreds of the **whitewashed, half-timbered ouses** built here during **Ottoman** times have opened up as guesthouses. With few nodern buildings to speak of, it's essentially an entire village where architectural me seems to be standing still – an old-world feeling heightened by its setting in gorgeous rural valley. Such charm has endowed Safranbolu with a near-constant tream of "Ottomania"-seeking domestic tourists, and a growing number of foreign dventurers. Perhaps significantly, it's especially popular with visitors from China nd Korea, two countries where traditional wooden housing has largely gone the ay of the dodo.

Despite Safranbolu's popularity, its old way of life stays remarkably intact. Apart from bazaar of souvenir shops, few concessions have been made to the twenty-first century. Aost of the town remains slightly, and very pleasingly, run-down – heaven for the wallows that squeal and wheel their way from eave to wooden eave.

Many travellers, indeed, forget quite how small Safranbolu is. A short walk in either irection from the centre will soon see you in the countryside, while even in town the ackstreets – particularly those that head up to the park – are home to real people ving real lives, away from hotels and scented souvenirs.

8

OTTOMAN HOUSES

Whitewashed wooden houses are a distinctive and enduring legacy of **Ottoman** rule. Many Turkish towns feature a smattering of such buildings, while sizeable clutches can be found as far afield as Albania and Bosnia. The houses were often masterful pieces of design, exhibiting a flair for function and a use of space that prompts some to draw comparisons with Japanese design of the time – think built-in cupboards, carved ceilings and central heating, as well as plumbing systems able to draw cooking, cleansing and waste-disposal processes from a single stream of water.

Larger Ottoman mansions would have three or more levels and over a dozen rooms. The ground floor was often used as stable-space, though thanks to ingenious design the smell would not waft through to the upper floors, which were themselves split into male (*selâmlik*) and female (*haremlik*) quarters. Other features to look out for are interior courtyards, revolving cupboards and conical safe-rooms, as well as one innovation found in many Safranbolu hotels: tiny bathrooms located inside what appears to be a cupboard.

8

The mansions

All daily 9am–5.30pm • ₺3 each

Three mansions have been restored for visitors. Built in 1727, the **Kaymakamlar Evi**, or "Lieutenant Colonel's House", is the most popular. Its ground floor, devoid of external windows, served as a stable, while on the upper floors the *selâmlık*, overlookin the street, would have been divided from harem quarters, with a separate entrance and lattice windows looking onto interior courtyards. Each room has a distinctively carved wooden ceiling, and furniture would have been sparse, with personal items stored in decorative wall-niches, and bedding in cupboards doubling as bathrooms.

On the other side of town, **Mümtazlar Konağı** needs a little more love; its exhibits seem like modern-day cast-offs, and dusty rugs make it look like a house under construction. Coffee-coloured **Kileciler Paşa Evi** has been more attractively renovated and is more worthy of a visit; its various rooms are filled with Ottoman antiques, many of which are explained on the free information sheet you receive on entry.

Cinci Hamamı

Adjoining the town square • Daily 6am–10pm • ₺20 • Separate men's and women's sections

The seventeenth-century **Ottoman baths** known as the Cinci Hamamı stand right in the centre of Safranbolu, where the buses drop off. They've been fully restored so that you can relax in comfort, surrounded by their marble splendour – arguably they're up there with the best *hamams* in the land.

The bazaar and around

The courtyard of the unexceptional but easy to find seventeenth-century **Köprülü Mehme Paşa Camii** leads to a restored **arasta** (bazaar) where day-trippers are brought to browse at well-stocked souvenir and antique shops. The bazaar is completely covered by a magnificent vine, which in season dangles grapes so close to your head you'll be tempted to pick them – notices warn you not to. South of the *arasta*, in the old **bazaar district**, traditional stalls of blacksmiths, cobblers, leatherworkers, tanners and saddlemakers still work away – or, as is more common these days, sell items made elsewhere.

A short walk south, the **İzzet Mehmet Paşa Camii** is an elaborate, late eighteenth-
century mosque. Past here, the town slides into dilapidation, with a ravine now used as
a household dump and, further downstream, women washing clothes in the stream. If
you walk down here, though, there's a stunning view back towards the mosque, whose
domes and minarets seem to hover above the surrounding houses; the walk is also a real
beauty at night, just as Safranbolu is readying itself for sleep.

Hıdırlık Parkı

Superb views of Safranbolu can be had from **Hıdırlık Parkı**, a hilltop park that looks out
over town from the east. The Ottoman buildings appear at their best in the late afternoon
light, a prospect that can be enjoyed with tea or coffee from the small on-site café.

The museum and around

Hulealtı Sok • Tues–Sun 9am–5.30pm • Combined ticket with clock tower ₺3

The old Governor's House, a palatial-looking edifice that replaced what was once a
castle, now holds a so-so **museum**. Apart from the photos of "old Safranbolu" upstairs,
which show just how little things have changed since the 1920s, the general layout is
pretty slapdash. The modern mannequins, all too obviously lifted straight from some
high-street clothing store, may give you a laugh.
    Head around the back of the museum, and you'll find yourself in a curious park,
featuring miniature versions of famous buildings from all over Turkey. Here, surrounded
by mulberry trees, you'll find an Ottoman-era **clock tower** whose mechanism was
imported from London in the 1760s – clamber up for a grand view of town.

Around Safranbolu

A small clutch of sights in the vicinity make a good excuse to stay more than a night
in Safranbolu. Public transport is non-existent, but the tourist office can help with
tours (see p.492). Most visitors head east to **Yörük Köyü** village – the best of the sights –
before hitting the Byzantine-era **aqueduct** in **İncekaya**, and the cave network of
Bulak Mencilis Mağarası.

Bulak Mencilis Mağarası

Daily: summer 9am–6.30pm; winter 10am–4pm • ₺2.35

Set on a beautiful mountain slope, this small network of caves known as **Bulak Mencilis
Mağarası** is a joy to visit. Its location is quite spectacular, and the walk to the cave
mouth – a steep climb of over 150 steps – will give your calf muscles some definition.
You'll soon get the chance to cool down, since the temperature in the caves is 10–15°C
year-round; there's no real need for special clothing, since only 500m (out of a total of
around 4km) is open for viewing. As with cave systems across Asia, your guide will
compare some of the more distinctive formations to animals or religious figures.

Yörük Köyü

6km east of Safranbolu

Think of a smaller, more remote version of Safranbolu, minus the tourists and polished
Ottoman renovations, and you're already halfway to imagining the tiny village of **YÖRÜK
KÖYÜ**, not far east of its more illustrious brother. Most villagers here follow the moderate
Bektaşi sect of Islam, in which alcohol is allowed in moderation, and Ramadan only lasts
twelve days. Women also have greater equality and the right to choose whom they marry –
note the statue of Leyla Gencer, a noted intellectual born here.
    The village's one concession to the tourist trade is the **Sipahioğlu Evi**, an eighteenth-
century mansion that feels even more authentic than its counterparts in Safranbolu.

Owned by the same family for almost three centuries, it's now split in two by feuding sons. It's a bit of a slog to the *kule* on top, though the views are superb and you'll even find a handy stand on which to pop your fez.

ARRIVAL AND DEPARTURE

By bus From Safranbolu's *otogar*, up in the new town, most companies lay on a *servis* to the old town area, known as Eski Safranbolu. You can also take a dolmuş, bus (both ₺1) or taxi (₺10) down, or even enjoy a delightful 40min

SAFRANBOLU AND AROUND
walk down into the valley.

Destinations Ankara (16 daily; 3hr 30min); Görem (daily, 8hr); İstanbul (15 daily; 6hr 30min); İzm (daily; 12hr).

INFORMATION AND TOURS

Tourist office In the main square, next to the Kazdağlı Camii (daily 9am–5.30pm; ☎0370 712 3863). Helpful staff can book bus tickets up to 20min before departure.

Tours Touts just outside the tourist office offer golf-buggy tours of Safranbolu (₺10–20 per person), with taped

information delivered in squawky English. Of more interes are the half-day taxi-tours organized by the tourist office for ₺90 per carload – see p.489 for information on the sights visited.

ACCOMMODATION

Safranbolu's old **Ottoman houses** provide some of Turkey's most atmospheric accommodation. Prices may be a littl higher than you may be used to (and bathroom sizes necessarily smaller), but there are options to suit all budgets.

SAFRANBOLU

Bastoncu Hıdırlık Sok ☎0370 712 3411, ⓦbastoncu pension.com. Refurbished Ottoman-era house with affable, English-speaking owners and dormitory accommodation. The double and twin are huge, but there are only seven rooms – if you miss out on a berth, you'll be taken to an overflow building down the road. Dorms ₺25, doubles ₺90

Cinci Han ☎0370 712 0680, ⓦcincihan.com. Quality hotel, housed in a seventeenth-century *kervansaray* in the heart of town. Rooms are arranged around an open courtyard; the top-floor suites are nothing short of fantastic, but they could try harder with the standard doubles. Currently a bargain, though prices may well increase. ₺100

★ **Gül Evi** Hükümet Sok 46 ☎0370 725 4645, ⓦgulevisafranbolu.com.tr. Refurbished by an amiable local architect, this boutique hotel is the best in town. Rooms are traditionally styled but feature modern tweaks like large bathrooms – rare in Safranbolu's space-conscious old buildings – and comfy beds. Check out the old safe-room, now a tiny bar with a few primary-colour spotlights

poking up out of the darkness – highly atmospheric, an nightmarish in the best possible way. ₺180

Hatiçe Hanim Naiptarla Sok 4 ☎0370 712 7545. Large authentic Ottoman house with rooms named after the traditional functions; they're overpriced for sure, but com with creaking floorboards (don't jump around too much and closet bathrooms. The downstairs bar, once a stable, i a hoot. ₺180

Havuzlu Konak Çelik Gülersoy 18 ☎0370 725 2883 ⓦsafranbolukonak.com. Very appealing option, set in splendid 1820s building just outside the centre of the ol town. The four corner-rooms are best, but all ar immaculate and well laid out, with brass fittings and thi rugs. The eponymous indoor pool (*havuz*) provides superb setting for breakfast or coffee. ₺160

YÖRÜK KÖYÜ

Yörük Evi Yörük Köyü, 16km east of Safranbolu ☎037 737 2153. Anyone who fancies spending a night in isolate splendour should hunt down signs for this place, where th rooms are rustic but comfortable enough. ₺100

EATING AND DRINKING

While Safranbolu's old town holds several places to **eat**, prices are a little high, and quality a little low. **Cafés** are different matter entirely – many are quite superb, with interesting histories or excellent views.

RESTAURANTS

Berketet Sofrası Pazar Yeri. One of the cheapest places to eat in town, with *lokanta* dishes going for around ₺5. Ignore the saffron-flavoured items, made with no saffron whatsoever. Daily 8am–9pm.

Kazan Celal Bayar Cad. Tatar by name, Tatar by nature, this restaurant whips up tasty Turkish regulars, as well as

Crimean specialities – try the *peruhi* (dumplings; ₺6.5 Daily 8am–10pm.

Taşev Hıdırlık Sok 14. The only vaguely upmarket place t eat. Steaks cost around ₺20, and cheese plates, usuall enjoyed with a nice bottle of local wine, much the same Choose from a table in the garden, or a balcony seat with city view. Daily 9am–midnight.

PUTTING THE SAFRAN BACK INTO SAFRANBOLU

Safranbolu is famed for growing **saffron**, and even took its name from the precious herb. Although production fell to almost nothing before a recent **revival**, it's now quite possible to buy some to take home, or sample its taste in locally made sweets such as *safran lokum* and *helva*. You can purchase them – or munch free samples if you're feeling cheeky – in the ubiquitous **pastanes**. A number of local restaurants claim to serve meals made with saffron, but beware – many simply colour the food (and, in many cases, "saffron" tea) with Indian Yellow dye.

AFÉS AND TEAROOMS

rasta Arasta Bazar, beside the mosque. Café in the ‹onymous mosque-side bazaar, notable for its Turkish ›ffee (₺5) – the *cezve* is placed directly onto hot coals. ›ily 8am–10pm.

ines Saatli Dinlenme Bahçesi Köprülü Mehmet ›şa Camii. This pleasant outdoor courtyard, adjacent to ›e mosque, makes an ideal place to relax over tea (₺1) or ›argile (₺7.5). Daily 8am–10pm.

›ş Sefa Next to the clock tower. The town prison until ›94, this is now a café. The interior is, understandably, a ›ttle plain – all the more reason to head outside to drain a

tea (₺1) while drinking up great views. The place is surrounded by mulberry trees; if you're here in season there'll be a free selection of dried berries on your table. Daily 8am–8pm.

★ **Imren** Opposite Cinci Han entrance. There are plenty of sweetie shops in town, but locals will always point you here – they use powdered sugar rather than plain glucose. You can take free samples of saffron *lokum* with a clear conscience if buying tea, coffee or home-made *baklava*, all of which can be enjoyed under the vines outside. Alternatively, a box of 40 sweets is ₺10.5. Daily 8am–9pm.

East of Ankara

›ome of Turkey's finest sights lie in the tract of Anatolia that stretches **east of Ankara**; ›e fact that very few travellers go out of their way to see them simply enhances the ›llure for those who do. Coming from Ankara, the first sites of note are a clutch of ›uins from the ancient **Hittite** kingdom – those at **Hattuşa**, in particular, are up with ›he best in the land. Then come **Amasya**, a small city with a truly enchanting array of ›ttoman buildings; **Tokat**, home to the biggest **kebabs** in Turkey; and the Selçuk ›reasure-troves of **Sivas** and **Divriği**.

Hittite sites

›he **Hittite sites** centred on the village of **Boğazkale**, 150km east of Ankara, are the ›nost impressive and significant in the whole of Anatolia, and are appropriately located ›mid rolling countryside that has changed little through the centuries.

This area was once the heart of the Hittite Empire, with **Hattuşa**, spread south of the ›nodern village, as its capital. The temple site of **Yazılıkaya** is a few kilometres east, while ›emote **Alacahöyük**, 25km north, is worth the trip if you have your own transport.

Excavation on these sites began in earnest in 1905, and many of the objects unearthed ›re now housed in Ankara's Museum of Anatolian Civilizations. If you've already seen ›he museum, a visit to the original excavations is doubly interesting; if not, a quick visit ›o the new archeological museum in nearby **Çorum** is definitely worthwhile.

Boğazkale

BOĞAZKALE is a modern village, with the ancient Hittite capital of **Hattuşa** fanning out ›rom its southern rim. Finding your way around is fairly straightforward, as it basically ›onsists of one street, running up a hill to the main square.

The only attraction in the village itself is a small but very well laid-out **museum** on ›he way up to the village square (daily: summer 8am–7pm, winter 8am–5pm; ₺10, ›ncluding Hattuşa and Yazılıkaya), which has a small collection of cuneiform tablets, ›ottery and other objects from the former Hittite capital.

ARRIVAL AND DEPARTURE

By bus or dolmuş Public transport to Boğazkale is far from straightforward and can be incredibly frustrating. You'll first have to get to the small town of Sungurlu, just off the main Ankara–Samsun road. Buses leave Sungurlu's *otogar* for Boğazkale at 7.30am and 5.30pm (having left Boğazkale 30min earlier); otherwise, you'll have to catch a Boğazkale-bound dolmuş (weekdays only, no fixed

schedule; 30min; ₺5). You just might find one waiting the *otogar*, but you're more likely to have to head 1k north into Sungurlu itself (taxi ₺3–5), where dolmuş leave from alongside the park. If you get stuck in Sungur it holds plenty of cheap hotels.

By taxi A taxi from Sungurlu to Boğazkale costs ₺45–7 you'll almost certainly have to haggle.

ACCOMMODATION AND EATING

The hotels listed below are also the only options in the village for eating and drinking. If you're here in winter, note th heating and hot water is far from reliable in the village, so come prepared. Also note that curious stories come from gues staying at the *Aşıkoğlu Hotel*, which is best avoided.

★ **Hotel Baykal** Next to the PTT on the village square ☏ 0364 452 2013. Also known as the *Hattuşaş Pension*, this hotel offers two types of accommodation: clean and spacious pension rooms, mostly with showers (discounts for those without), and comfortable en-suite rooms in the hotel at the back. The restaurant serves up tasty and economical daily dishes. Pension ₺45, hotel ₺70

Kale Hotel Yazılıkaya Yolu Üzeri ☏ 0364 452 3126.

Family-run hotel in a pretty location, with simpl whitewashed rooms and adequate bathrooms, but lit atmosphere. ₺80

Otel Başkent Yazılıkaya Yolu Üzeri ☏ 0364 452 203 ⊛ baskenthattusa.com. The newest and mo presentable hotel in the area. All its large rooms hold or double and one single bed; try to get one facing field rather than the hotel car park. ₺80

8

BOĞAZKALE AND HATTUŞA

Sungurlu

Boğazkale

Yazıs Stream

MAIN SQUARE

Ticket Office

Büyük Mabet

Büyük Kale

Nişantepe

Sarıkale

N

Aslanlıkapı (Lion Gate)

Yenicekale

Kralkapı (King's Gate)

Tunnel

Yerkapı (Sphinx Gate)

Yazılıkaya

Yozgat

0   100
metres

■ ACCOMMODATION
Başkent   1
Baykal   3
Kale   2

——— Old City Walls
■■■ Restored City Walls

Hattuşa

Just southwest of modern Boğazkale • Daily: summer 8am–7pm; winter 8am–5pm • ₺10 joint ticket with Yazılıkaya • Accessible on foot from Boğazkale, though it's large enough that on a hot day yo might want to explore it by taxi

Enclosed by 6km walls, **Hattuşa** was, by the standards of its era, an immense city, and its scale is still awe-inspiring today. The site, on a steeply sloping expanse dotted with rocky outcrops, was originally occupied by the Hatti, who established a settlement here around 2500 BC. The Hittites moved in after their conquest of central Anatolia, and made it their capital from about 1375 BC onwards, as their empire was reaching its greatest extent.

Archeologists unearthed the Hittite city during the first half of the nineteenth century. Of the numerous buildings once scattered over a wide area, only the limestone foundation blocks survive. The vulnerable upper parts, originally consisting of timber frames supporting clay brick walls, have long since vanished.

The Büyük Mabet

The largest and best-preserved Hittite temple to survive at Hattuşa, the **Büyük Mabet**, or "Great Temple", stands immediately beyond the ticket office.

Built around the fourteenth or thirteenth century BC, and one of an original seventy on the site, it was dedicated to the storm god **Teshuba** and the sun goddess **Hebut**. It consisted of a central temple building, surrounded by 78 storage rooms laid out in an irregular plan.

You approach it between two large stone blocks, remnants of the **ceremonial gateway**. A stone lion nearby originally formed part of a cistern, while a large, green **cubic stone** a little further on was reputedly a wedding present from Ramses II of Egypt, who married a Hittite princess. In Hittite times the king and queen, in their roles as high priest and priestess, would have led processions through here on holy days. Most visitors now follow the same route, along a clearly defined processional way of uneven slabs.

The **temple** consisted of about twelve small chambers around a central courtyard, with the rooms that would have contained the cult statues of Teshuba and Hebut at the northeastern end – the god on the left and the goddess on the right.

THE HITTITES

The **Hittites** appear to have been an Indo-European people who moved into Anatolia around 2000 BC, and entered the territories of the indigenous Hatti. Where exactly the Hittites came from remains unclear; possibilities include the Caucasus and the Balkans. Neither do records survive of how the Hittites rose to dominance. Layers of burned material found in most Hatti settlements suggest at least some degree of violence was involved, but the Hittites also absorbed important elements of Hatti culture, so a more complex interaction may have taken place.

While Hattuşa is by far the most famous, the Hittites actually set up a number of **city-states**, drawn together during the mid-eighteenth century BC under King Anitta. He transferred his capital from the city of Kushara (possibly modern Alişar) to Nesha (Kültepe), and destroyed Hattuşa, cursing any Hittite king who might attempt to rebuild the place. A century or so later his successor Labarna returned to Hattuşa and did just that. The Hittites came to regard Labarna and his wife Tawannanna as founders of the Hittite kingdom, and their names were adopted as titles by subsequent monarchs.

In 1595 BC, Mursili I succeeded in capturing distant Babylon, but his successor (and assassin) Hantili lost many previous gains. Stability was restored when Tudhaliyas II re-established the Hittite state as an empire, around 1430 BC. An important period of expansion followed under King Suppiluliuma (1380–1315 BC), who secured the northern borders and conquered the Hurrian kingdom of Mitanni. This achievement raised the Hittites to superpower status, equal with Egypt, Assyria and Babylon. The Egyptians even asked Suppiluliuma to send one of his sons to marry the widow of Tutankhamun, but the boy was murdered en route, and the union never took place. Hittite expansion continued after Suppiluliuma's death. In 1286 BC, during the reign of Muwatalli II, a Hittite army defeated the Egyptians, commanded by Ramses II, at the **Battle of Kadesh**. Events from the battle can be seen carved into the columns at Luxor.

Following the conflict, peace between the two empires was established, cemented by the marriage of one of the daughters of Ramses II to Hattuşiliş III. However, the Hittite Empire had less than a century left. The arrival of the Sea Peoples in Anatolia ushered in a period of instability that was to erode Hittite power, culminating in the **destruction of Hattuşa** around 1200 BC, at much the same time as the fall of Troy. The Phrygians replaced the Hittites as the dominant power in central Anatolia, taking over the ruins of Hattuşa and other Hittite cities.

Hittite civilization was highly advanced, with a complex **social system**. While the Hittite kings were absolute rulers, an assembly called the *panku* appears at times to have wielded considerable influence. The major division in Hittite society was between free citizens – including farmers, artisans and bureaucrats – and slaves, who, while they could be bought and sold, were probably entitled to own property and to marry.

Hittite **religion** seems to have been adopted from the Hatti, with the weather god Teshuba and the sun goddess Hebut as the two most important deities. As the Hittites were in the habit of incorporating the gods of conquered peoples into their own pantheon, up to a thousand lesser gods also played a role in their beliefs.

8

Just below the Büyük Mabet, archeologists have identified an early Assyrian **merchant quarter**. This held the Hittite equivalent of the Rosetta Stone, a parallel Hittite hieroglyph and Akkadian inscription that was instrumental in the final cracking of the hieroglyphic code, and is now in Ankara's Museum of Anatolian Civilizations.

The Aslanlıkapı

The **Aslanlıkapı**, or "Lion Gate", takes its name from the two stone lions that flank the outer entrance (one an all-too-obvious replica), symbolically guarding Hattuşa from attackers and evil spirits. It also marks the start of a surviving section of dry-stone **city wall**, which runs along the top of a massive sloping embankment that's 10m in height and surfaced with irregular limestone slabs.

The Yerkapı

The **Yerkapı**, or "Earth Gate", along the embankment from the Aslanlıkapı, is more popularly known as the Sphinx Gate after the two huge sphinxes that once guarded its inner portal; one returned in 2011 to the museum in Boğazkale.

The most striking feature of the Sphinx Gate is the 70m **tunnel** that cuts through from the city side of the walls to the exterior. It was built using the corbel arch technique, a series of flat stones leaning towards each other creating its triangular profile. Some archeologists argue that it enabled the defenders of the city to make surprise attacks on besieging enemies. Others, citing the tunnel's obvious visibility from the outside – and the presence of two sets of monumental steps leading up the embankment – suggest that it had a more ceremonial function.

The Kralkapı

The **Kralkapı**, or "King's Gate", east of the Sphinx Gate, is named after the regal-looking figure carved in relief on the left-hand pillar of the inner gateway. This actually represents the god Teshuba, and shows him sporting a conical hat while raising his left fist in the air as though holding an invisible sword. What you see is a copy – the original is in Ankara's Museum of Anatolian Civilizations.

The Nişantepe and around

The **Nişantepe**, down the hill from the Kralkapı, is a rocky outcrop with a ten-line Hittite inscription carved into its eastern face, alternately reading right-to-left and left-to-right. Enough of the badly weathered, 30cm hieroglyphs have been deciphered to suggest that it's a memorial to Suppiluliuma II, last of the Hittite kings. Immediately southwest is the **Sarıkale**, the foundation of a Phrygian fort built on the site of an earlier Hittite structure.

The Büyük Kale

The **Büyük Kale**, or "Great Fortress", down the road from the Nişantepe, served the Hittite monarchs as a fortified palace during the fourteenth and thirteenth centuries BC. The palace consisted of three courtyards, each higher than the previous one, meaning that any attacker would have had to capture it piecemeal. The lower and middle courtyards are thought to have been given over to servants and aides of the royal family, while the upper courtyard was the palace proper. It's easy to see why they chose to reside at this wild and windswept location on the very eastern edge of Hattuşa. In effect, it was a citadel within the city, protected on all flanks by steep drops.

Only the lower parts of walls and some masonry fragments survive of the Büyük Kale, but it's worth coming up here to wander among the weather-battered remnants and take in the stunning view of the Great Temple.

Three thousand **cuneiform tablets** found on the site of a building near the southeast entrance have yielded important clues about Hittite society. Among them was the Treaty of Kadesh, signed in around 1270 BC by the Hittite king Hattuşiliş II and Ramses II of Egypt, the earliest surviving written treaty between two nations.

Yazılıkaya

3km northeast of Hattuşa • Daily: summer 8am–7pm; winter 8am–5pm • ₺10 joint ticket with Hattuşa

Although archeological evidence suggests that a temple of some sort existed on the site of Yazılıkaya as early as 1500 BC, not until the thirteenth century BC were the two small ravines that cut into a rocky outcrop here decorated with reliefs (hence Yazılıkaya, Turkish for "inscribed rock"). At roughly the same time a **gateway** and the **temple buildings** were constructed. Today, only a few sketchy foundations remain of these ancient structures, and attention is focused on the two "galleries" of reliefs that depict nearly a hundred figures, mostly gods from the vast array of Hittite deities.

The reliefs

The entrance to the **larger ravine** at Yazılıkaya is on the left behind the temple foundations. Its left-hand wall is lined with images of gods moving from left to right, and the right-hand one with goddesses wearing identical long, pleated dresses and conical headgear. Several figures on the male side stand out, in particular the group of twelve war gods bringing up the rear of the procession. Further along, two figures have human bodies and bulls' heads. The deities seem to rise in rank as the procession progresses, and towards the front are the conspicuous figures of the moon god Kusuh, with a crescent moon, and the sun god, seemingly balancing a winged sun symbol on his head. The two lines of deities meet on the far wall of the ravine, where a scene depicts Teshuba, astride a couple of mountain peaks, facing Hebut, who is standing on a panther.

The **smaller ravine**, over to the right, can be reached via a short flight of steps that leads up to a cleft in the rock. The entrance is guarded by two sphinx reliefs, which can be hard to spot, while a group of twelve figures armed with swords lines the left-hand wall. Similar to the warrior-god figures in the first ravine, these are much better preserved. Opposite this group are two separate reliefs. One shows an unusual figure that has come to be known as the "Sword God", a blade with a human torso and head where the handle should be. To add to the already strange effect, lions' heads, instead of arms, sprout from the torso shoulders. This vaguely disturbing image is thought to represent Neargal, the Hittite god of the underworld.

8

Alacahöyük

25km north of Boğazkale • **Site** Tues–Sun 8am–5pm **Museum** Tues–Sun 8am–noon & 1–5pm • ₺5 • ₺60 by taxi from Boğazkale including waiting time, or for around ₺120 a taxi from Sungurlu will show you around Hattuşa, Alacahöyük and Yazılıkaya, then drop you back in Sungurlu for an onward bus

After Hattuşa, **Alacahöyük** is the most important Hittite site in existence. Originally a major Hattic settlement, it was taken over by the Hittites during the early stages of the second millennium BC, and later, like Hattuşa, by the Phrygians as well. Most of the ruins that remain are Hittite, but archeologists have unearthed a vast array of Hattic artefacts, including standards featuring stags, bulls, sun-discs and statues of the earth goddess, from various tombs.

The site

The site of Alacahöyük is entered via the southern **Sphinx Gate**, named after the large sphinxes that guard it. These eerily impressive figures, stained ochre by lichen, have blunted faces with empty eye sockets, and sweeping headdresses. Either side of the gate are **reliefs** (copies of originals now in Ankara), depicting religious ceremonies. The left-hand section, the more lively of the two, shows a procession moving towards the god Teshuba – shown here as a slightly comical-looking bull with outsized sex organs. Approaching him are a king and queen, followed by sacrificial animals and priests, with a group of what look like acrobats bringing up the rear.

The Sphinx Gate opens onto a pathway with excavated areas on either side, all signed in English. Immediately behind the gate are vast irregular blocks, the remnants of the city walls, followed by the foundations of storage buildings. Beyond the storage areas, a few metres below ground level to the left of the path, are thirteen **tombs**. These date from the Hattic period and yielded much of the vast hoard that's now in the Bronze Age section of Ankara's Museum of Anatolian Civilizations. Judging by the opulence of the grave goods, these were the tombs of Hatti monarchs. The small on-site **museum** is well worth investigating. It includes some striking Hattic standards and pottery with elegant designs.

Amasya

Occupying the narrow valley of the **Yeşilırmak River**, and blessed with a super-abundant historical legacy, **AMASYA** is one of the high points of northern Anatolia. Most visitors come to see the **rock tombs** hewn into the cliffs above the town by the kings of Pontus, over two thousand years ago, but Amasya also harbours some truly beautiful Selçuk and Ottoman architecture, and a multitude of restored nineteenth-century **wooden houses**. Many of the latter are now authentic and atmospheric antique shops, *pansiyons* and restaurants, in keeping with the general Ottoman theme.

Brief history

Amasya was once part of **Pontus**, one of several small kingdoms to spring up following the death of Alexander the Great, which survived for two hundred years. Its downfall began when Mithridates VI Eupator reputedly ordered the massacre of eighty thousand Romans in a single day and plunged his kingdom into a series of wars, which culminated in its being absorbed by Pompey into the Roman sphere of influence around 70 BC.

Under the Romans, and through the succeeding centuries of Byzantine rule, the town prospered, and it continued to do so after falling to the **Selçuks** in 1071. In the late thirteenth century, Amasya became part of the burgeoning **Ottoman** state. It became a training ground for crown princes, who would serve as governors of the province to prepare them for the rigours of statesmanship at the Sublime Porte. Amasya then became a vital staging post en route to the creation of modern Turkey: it was here that, on June 21, 1919, Atatürk delivered a speech that was in effect a call to arms for the coming **War of Independence**.

North and west of the river

Amasya's finest sights, including the **rock tombs** and the vast majority of its **Ottoman buildings**, are on the north bank of the Yeşilırmak. The **kale** is further up again, though access is on the other side of the mountain.

The rock tombs

Daily 8am–7.30pm · ₺3

The massive **tombs** of the Pontic kings are carved into the cliff-face on the northern bank of the Yeşilırmak – there's little to see bar the holes, although the **city views** from here are absolutely spellbinding. Note that the paths can be a little **slippery**, and not all have fences to guard against falls; as well as bringing decent footwear, in summer you're advised to visit in the evening, when the cliffside is in welcome shadow.

There are **two main clusters** of tombs. Where the path splits above the entrance, bearing left will bring you to two large tombs; beside the entrance to one of them is the mouth of a tunnel, thought to lead to the river. Bearing right instead, then passing the **café**, will bring you to a less accessible group slightly sullied by graffitied love declarations. More tombs can be found with a bit of effort – there is a total of eighteen throughout the valley.

Hazeranlar Konağı

Tues–Sun 8am–7pm · ₺3

Amasya's half-timbered **Ottoman houses** make an enormous contribution to the atmosphere of the town. A good starting point for explorations is the nineteenth-century **Hazeranlar Konağı**, an imposing riverside mansion. Its heavily restored interior

ACCOMMODATION		RESTAURANTS	
Emin Efendi	6	Ali Kaya	6
Ezgi Butik	4	Bahçeli Ocakbaşı	5
Grand Pasha	2, 3	Grand Pasha	1, 3
Harşena Otel	5	Şehzade Balık Ekmek	4
İlk Pansiyon	1	Strabon	2
Konfor Palas	7		

AMASYA

- - - - Boardwalk

BARS AND CAFÉS	
Biyer Plus Pub	2
Kaymak Dondurma	3
Seyran Cafe	1

8

has been turned into a convincing re-creation of a nineteenth-century family home, liberally decked out with carpets, period furniture and domestic artefacts. It incorporates typical features of the time: wall niches for oil lamps, bathrooms secreted away behind cupboard doors, and *sedir*s or divan seating running along the walls.

Büyük Ağa Medresesi

Off Zübeyde Hanım Cad

Across the road from a small waterfall, the **Büyük Ağa Medresesi** is a **seminary** that was founded in 1488 by the chief white eunuch of Beyazit II. A roughly octagonal structure, it's now a Koranic school. It's not officially open to the public, but no one seems to mind if you take a look inside the courtyard.

The kale

2km uphill from Büyük Ağa Medresesi • ₺12 for a taxi up; around ₺25 return including waiting time

Amasya's sprawling citadel, or **kale**, dates back to Pontic times, though the surviving ruins are of Ottoman vintage. While it's difficult to reach, it's well worth the effort for the stupendous views of the town below.

At the top, the outer walls of the *kale* have been rebuilt in bright, modern stone, but beyond you'll find the crumbling remains of the Ottoman-era fortress. Nothing is signposted and there are no clear paths through the ruins, so much of the time you'll find yourself scrambling over rocks and rubble and through undergrowth.

The east bank

Amasya's relatively under-explored **east bank** holds a smattering of delightful mosques, a worthwhile museum, and the atmospheric **Sıhhı Mustafa Bey Hamamı** (see box, p.499). The northernmost mosque is the fifteenth-century **Beyazit Paşa Camii**, whose leafy riverbank location enhances the quiet beauty of its architecture. Further down, the sizeable **Mehmet Paşa Camii** was constructed in 1486, and boasts a *medrese* and finely decorated marble pulpit.

Sabuncuoğlu Museum of History of Medicine and Surgery

Daily 9am–noon & 1–6pm • ₺4

Phew, what a mouthful – but at least one is left with no illusions about the contents of the **Sabuncuoğlu Museum of History of Medicine and Surgery**. While its contents are not terribly interesting, the building itself is a stunner. It was built by the Mongols in 1308 as a **lunatic asylum**, and both its function and structural beauty go rather against the popular image of the Mongols as a brutal, destructive people. The Mongols used music therapy to pacify the lunatics; it was, in fact, used as a **music school** for centuries, and only opened as a museum in 2011.

Gümüşlü Camii

The creamy yellow **Gümüşlü Camii**, or "Silvery Mosque", was originally built in 1326 but has been reconstructed at various intervals since. Its almost pavilion-like oriental exterior and carved wooden porch overlook the river, and there's an unusual tall brick minaret.

Pir Mehmet Çelebi Camii

A real architectural oddity, the **Pir Mehmet Çelebi Camii** dates from 1507. It's an extremely small *mescit*, or mosque without a minaret, the Islamic equivalent of a Christian chapel. The carved facade of this particular example has been decorated with ochre paint, and it's improbably tiny, almost as though it were a play mosque built for children.

The south bank

At the centre of Amasya, the riverfront **Atatürk Meydanı** commemorates Atatürk's 1919 visit with an equestrian statue of the hero surrounded by admirers. A short way west, the **Kileri Süleyman Ağa Camii** is an imposing Ottoman mosque built in 1489. The south bank also has a **pedestrian promenade**, which is immensely popular with local youths.

Sultan Beyazit II Camii

Between Ziya Paşa Cad and Atatürk Cad

Set in a spacious rose garden, the **Sultan Beyazit II Camii**, Amasya's largest mosque, was built in 1486. It's laid out on a symmetrical plan, with two large central domes flanked by four smaller cupolas and two slightly mismatched minarets. Though some of Amasya's other mosques beat it for sheer whimsicality, none can quite match its structural harmony. It's best appreciated from the front, where it faces the river, flanked by two plane trees thought to be as old as the mosque itself.

Archeological and Ethnographic Museum

Tues–Sun 8.30am–noon & 1–5pm • ₺3

A real gem, Amasya's **Archeological and Ethnographic Museum** holds archeological finds dating back as far as the Bronze Age, which is represented by some practical-looking pottery and a case-full of rather unwieldy tools. Hittite relics include beak-spouted jugs, some with what look like built-in filters, and there's also a bronze statue of the storm god Teshuba. On the second floor you'll see the original door of

GETTING STEAMY IN AMASYA

Amasya boasts a couple of wonderfully atmospheric hamams, each of them centuries old – stay here a few days and you'll be able to take them in at your leisure.

Sıhhı Mustafa Bey Hamamı Mustafa Kehal Bul. Sandwiched between a mosque, a museum and the river, this hamam is very old but very much in use, as the wreaths of vapour emerging from its chimneys testify. Entry ₺12.5, same again for massage. Daily: men 7–10am & 5–11pm; women 10am–5pm.

Yıldız Hamamı On the north bank, next to the Hazeranlar Konağı. According to the plaque outside, this hamam was constructed "in the mid's of the 13th contray and rebult in the 16th countruy". Mercifully the interior beats the spelling hands down. Entry ₺12.5, ₺6 extra for a sponge-down or massage. Daily 6am–midnight.

the **Gök Medrese Camii** (a thirteenth-century mosque 5min walk west), a riot of arabesque geometrical patterns enclosing lattice reliefs.

Most visitors, however, head straight to the eight **mummies**, six of whom were family: the eldest, Cumudar, was a Selçuk minister apparently drowned in 1297. His son Izzettin Mehmet – a former governor of Amasya executed during a rebellion against the Mongols – is also here, together with four of his children and a concubine.

ARRIVAL AND INFORMATION
AMASYA

By train Amasya's train station (*very* slow services from Samsun and Sivas) is 1km west of the centre, and connected by regular dolmuşes.
Destinations Samsun (1 daily; 5hr); Sivas (1 daily; 7hr 30min).
By bus The *otogar* lies 3km east of the centre; *servis* minibuses and city buses (₺1.60) connect with bus company offices facing Atatürk's statue.

Destinations Ankara (hourly; 6hr); İstanbul (12 daily; 12hr); Kayseri (3 daily; 8hr); Malatya (5 daily; 9hr); Samsun (10 daily; 3hr); Sivas (10 daily; 3hr 30min); Tokat (10 daily; 1hr 30min).
Tourist office Inside the uninteresting Ottoman Selçuk museum, but don't expect too much (Tues–Sun 9am–5pm; ☎ 0358 212 4059).

8

ACCOMMODATION

Amasya's most appealing accommodation options are the clutch of antique-decorated, kilim-strewn *pansiyons* in restored Ottoman houses. Rates are reasonable so it's well worth splashing out, particularly given that the city's budget options are less than salubrious. Note that very few of the city's hotel staff speak English.

Emin Efendi Hazeranlar Sok 73 ☎ 0358 212 0852, �🌐 eminefendi.com. Friendly *pansiyon*, spread over a few buildings; opt for a room overlooking the river. If you're lucky, you may be treated to a little evening music in the attractive vine-shaded courtyard. ₺180
Ezgi Butik Hazeranlar Sok 56 ☎ 0358 218 7311, �🌐 ezgikonaklari.com. Rooms in this restored Ottoman house have pleasing modern flourishes, but it's otherwise a simple affair with a thoroughly relaxing air. It's also good for singles, for whom rooms can go for less than half the doubles price. ₺120
Grand Pasha Teyfik Hafız Sok 5 ☎ 0358 212 4158, �🌐 grandpashahotel.com. Beautiful Ottoman house on the river, arranged around a leafy courtyard. Small, with only eight vast, traditionally decorated rooms with cabinet bathrooms and river views. Rooms in the new building down the road are less appealing, but still perfectly comfortable. ₺180
Harşena Otel Across the Alçak footbridge, on the north bank ☎ 0358 218 3979, �🌐 harsenaotel.com.

Stunning former Ottoman residence with creaky floorboards and rooms furnished with period antiques, lace and linen curtains, and low-slung Ottoman beds. Some overlook the river, where you can breakfast on the balcony, but the best are at the back beneath the floodlit rock tombs where you can sleep to the sounds of gentle guitar music from the garden below. ₺100
İlk Pansiyon Hittit Sok 1 ☎ 0358 218 1689, ✉ ilkpansion @hotmail.com. Faultlessly restored eighteenth-century Armenian mansion, retaining much of the original decor and period antiques. Reservations advisable; there are just six rooms, some priced a category higher. Note there's a new place of the same name by the tourist office – best avoided. ₺100
Konfor Palas Ziyapşa Bul 2 ☎ 0358 218 1260, ⌐ www .konforpalas.com. Amasya's only decent budget option, nicely located south of the river; it's not too noisy despite the bustling square below. All rooms are en-suite, with TV but no breakfast, and it may be worth haggling. ₺80

EATING AND DRINKING

With a riverside setting and the rock tombs above lit up at night, dining out in Amasya provides unbeatable ambience Cheap eats can be found at *lokanta*-style joints around Atatürk Caddesi south of the river, or you can enjoy a traditional meal in the Ottoman-house **restaurants** on the north side. There aren't many **bars** around, and given the number of mosques in the centre it's even hard to find shops serving alcohol.

Ali Kaya On the hill on the south side of town; look up and you'll see the sign. Magnificent views, attentive service and tables under shady pine trees, with meals clocking in at around ₺50 including drinks. Best of all, they provide a free transport service from your hotel – just ask at reception. Daily 11am–11pm.

Bahçeli Ocakbaşı Ziyapaşa Bul 5. Popular place with outdoor seating. Inexpensive and piping-hot stews, soups, *pides* (from ₺5) and kebabs (from ₺13), including the famed Tokat variety (₺25) – see p.502. It's also *the* place to head for breakfast – laid out buffet style, and therefore all you can eat, for just ₺5. Daily 7am–11pm.

★ **Grand Pasha Restaurant** Teyfik Hafız Sok 5. Stylish venue with bare wooden floors, rustic furniture, exquisite antiques and kilims, a pretty walled garden with wishing well, and a riverside balcony. À la carte menu is typically Turkish, and there's an atmospheric basement bar, with tiny wooden tables and cushions set into stone walls, that stays open until 5am if the demand is there. Daily 10am–11pm.

Kaymak Dondurma Ziyapaşa Bul 35a. Is this place well located, or are its ice creams simply delicious? Either way, you'll see plenty of locals around town with one of their cones in hand. ₺2 and a smile for a few scoops. Daily 8am–10pm.

Şehzade Balık Ekmek Pedestrian promenade, off Ziyapaşa Bul. The only boat on the river (so far) has been converted into a sort of floating snack-shack serving yummy rounds of fried fish in bread for ₺5. Hours vary.

Seyran Cafe Just west of the Emin Efendi. The pick of Amasya's many cafés, a fun but relaxing place in which you can drain a coffee, suck on a nargile, swing on a hammock or simply enjoy a river view. Daily 9am–11pm.

Strabon By the Grand Pasha. Riverview restaurant that gets the basics right – good, cheap, filling meals, most of which are also in picture form on the menu. Try a *meze* platter (₺12), catfish (₺15) or some Albanian liver. Daily 9am–11pm.

Tokat

TOKAT clusters at the foot of a jagged crag, with a ruined Pontic fortress on top. Despite its undeniably dramatic setting – and richly colourful history – it lacks the appeal of Amasya or even Sivas, the two cities between which it's stuck, and most travellers whoosh straight past, seeing only the *otogar* en route.

However, there are certainly enough sights to justify at least a half-day stop – especially since the city's famed **kebab** (see box, p.502) is large enough to count as a sight. More conventional attractions include some excellent Ottoman buildings, a **Selçuk seminary** and a superb museum – more than enough to work off the kebab's calorific intake.

Brief history

Tokat first came to prominence as a staging post on the Persian trans-Anatolian royal road, running from Sardis to Persepolis. Later it fell to Alexander the Great and then to Mithridates and his successors. In 47 BC, **Julius Caesar** defeated Pharnaces, son of the Pontic king Mithridates VI, earlier Eupator, who had taken advantage of civil war in Rome to attempt to re-establish the Pontic kingdom as an independent state. Caesar's victory in a five-hour battle at Zile, just outside Tokat, prompted his immortal line "*Veni, vidi, vici*" (I came, I saw, I conquered).

Under **Byzantine** rule, Tokat became a frontline city in perpetual danger of Arab attack. That state of affairs continued until the Danişmend Turks took control of the city after the battle of Manzikert in 1071. Less than one hundred years later the İlhanid Mongols arrived, then Tokat was briefly transferred to the Ottoman Empire before a second great Mongol wave under **Tamerlane**.

With the departure of the Mongols and return of the **Ottomans**, life returned to normal, and prosperity ensued. In time, though, trade patterns shifted, the east–west routes to Persia lost their importance and Tokat became the backwater it remains today.

Gök Medrese

Gazi Osman Paşa Bul

Tokat's main tourist draw has long been the **Gök Medrese**, a squat, rectangular building built in 1275 by a Selçuk emir. It was named for the turquoise tiles that once covered its entire exterior; most have unfortunately vanished, but a few still tenaciously grip the walls of the inner courtyard. Until recently, the building was home to the town's **museum**, but this has moved elsewhere (see p.501), and the *medrese* is now off-limits.

Nearby, the **Taş Han**, originally called the Voyvoda Han, was built in 1631 by Armenian merchants. A large, rectangular building of two storeys, its courtyard houses some shabby shops, and makes a great place for tea (see p.502).

Tokat Museum

Sulusokak Sok; take the side road immediately south of the Taş Han, and zigzag left then right at the top • Tues–Sun 8am–noon & 1–5pm • ₺3

Set in the old **Arastalı Bedesten**, the **Tokat Museum** is a smart repository for local archeological finds. Its ethnographic section features examples of local *yazma*-making – printing with wooden blocks on cloth, to produce colourful patterned handkerchiefs, scarves and tablecloths – but perhaps of more note are the unusual relics collected from the churches that served the town's sizeable Greek and Armenian communities before World War I. Typical of these is a wax effigy of Christina, a Christian martyred during the rule of the Roman Emperor Diocletian.

Latifoğlu Konağı

Gazi Osman Paşa Bul, 660m south of the Taş Han • Tues–Sun 9am–noon & 1.30–5pm • ₺3

Assorted Ottoman-era half-timbered houses survive in the side streets of Tokat. While most are in states of advanced decrepitude, one exception is the heavily restored **Latifoğlu Konağı**. With its plain white walls, brown-stained woodwork and low-pitched roof, it stands out a mile from the surrounding modern buildings. The interior is opulent almost to the point of tastelessness, but gives a good impression of how a wealthy nineteenth-century family would have lived.

8

ARRIVAL AND INFORMATION   TOKAT

By bus The *otogar* is just north of the centre. Most bus companies run a *servis* into town, otherwise it's ₺5 by taxi, or an easy walk: head left down the main road, then turn left onto Gazi Osman Paşa Bul after 300m, and walk a further 10min south.

Destinations Amasya (12 daily; 2hr); Ankara (12 daily; 6hr 30min); Erzurum (2 daily; 9hr); Sivas (10 daily; 1hr 30min).
Tourist office You'll need a phrasebook to extract any information from the tiny office in Taş Han (daily 8am–6pm), and there are no maps or leaflets to collect.

ACCOMMODATION

Finding a place to stay should present few problems, with a clutch of establishments on Gazi Osman Paşa Bulvarı. If you're only making a day-trip, ask your bus company to keep your bags at the *otogar* while you see the sights.

Hotel Çağrı Gazi Osman Paşa Bul 92 ☎ 0356 212 1028. A pretty decent budget option: modern, clean and offering a spread of presentable en suites. ₺70

★ **Tower Otel** Gazi Osman Paşa Bul 172 ☎ 0356 212 3570. Tokat's newest and best option. Cheery youthful staff will proudly show you around the spa, terrace café and top-floor pool; the rooms themselves are large with funky

lighting, and have been nicely decorated along a monochrome colour scheme. Expect prices to rise. ₺150

Yücel Hotel Meydan Cad 22 ☎ 0356 212 5235, ⓦ yucelotel.com. Located on a pleasant side street, this welcoming hotel has fresh-looking rooms, some with mosque views (and, of course, the attendant noise). There's also a hamam in the basement. ₺80

EATING AND DRINKING

There are cheap **restaurants** on virtually every street in town, though you'll have to splurge a bit to sample the local speciality, *Tokat kebap* (see box, p.502). In addition, the courtyard of the Taş Han (p.502) is a nice setting for **tea**, as long as the music isn't on full blast (which it usually is).

> ## CONQUER A TOKAT KEBAB
>
> Julius Caesar uttered his famous "I came, I saw, I conquered" in Tokat, and unsubstantiated rumours suggest that he did so after sampling the huge local **kebab**. You can do the same on your visit to the city, though be warned that it's a beast – a mouthwatering (and *very* filling) combination of **roast lamb**, potatoes, **aubergine**, tomato and peppers, grilled beneath a whole bulb of garlic, whose juices permeate the meal. Amazingly, this style has yet to take hold anywhere further than Amasya, and almost faded out in Tokat itself before making a recent comeback. Prices are in the region of ₺20–25, and if it takes less than 20min to land on your table, it's not the real deal.

★ **Hanedan Kebap** Camii Yanı Meyd. The swishest restaurant in town, set in an elegantly restored *han*. It's the best place to head for *Tokat kebab*, and not too dear at ₺20 – when you see the size of the dish you'll know you've got yourself a deal, but the fact that they serve it with full rounds of salad and bread is almost torture. If you've any more room, order your *ayran "açık kapaldı"* and it'll arrive in a cute metal tankard. Daily 9am–11pm.

Karadeniz Gazi Osman Paşa Bul 142, just up the road from the Taş Han. Swish, two-level café-cum-*pastanesi* that's immensely popular with locals. Turkish coffee (₺3.50),

Turkish tea (₺1.5) and a fine range of Turkish sweets are available, as are simple pasta dishes. Daily 7am–9pm.

Şanlıurfa Plevne Modern İşhanı Altı, opposite the Ali Paşa Camii. It's quite unfortunate that the best kebab house in town does not dish out the famed local variety, but for all others, this friendly restaurant is the place to go. Daily 8am–10pm.

Sedirhan Meydan Camii Yanı. Attached to the *Hanedan*, and similarly attractive, this is a good place for coffee or snacks; they also have no fewer than 17 different nargile flavours. Daily 9am–11pm.

Sivas

An orderly city of around 200,000 people, **SİVAS** figures on few visitors' itineraries – a pity, since it's an immensely likeable place, with a concentration of **Selçuk monuments** that are up there with the finest in existence. Most were built during the Sultanate of Rum, and the period of Mongol sovereignty that followed under the İlhanids; with their highly decorative facades and elaborately carved portals, they epitomize architectural styles of the era. Most of these buildings are conveniently grouped together in the very centre of town, around a small area just off **Konak Meydanı**. The remainder are all within easy walking distance – as are all the good places to stay and eat.

Brief history

Sivas has been settled since Hittite times, and according to local sources was later a key centre of the Sivas Frig Empire (1200 BC), which seems to have been consigned to historical oblivion. The town's real flowering came during **Selçuk** times, after the Battle of Manzikert (1071). Sivas intermittently served as the Selçuk capital during the Sultanate of Rum in the mid-twelfth century, before passing into the hands of **İlhanid Mongols** during the late thirteenth century. The **Ottomans** took over in 1396, only to be ousted by the Mongols four years later under **Tamerlane**, who razed much of the city after an eighteen-day siege, and put its Christian inhabitants to the sword. The Ottomans returned in 1408 and Sivas pretty much faded out of history until a nineteenth-century reawakening.

Selçuk Parkı

Selçuk Parkı, right in the centre of the city, wouldn't fit most people's expectations of a "park", even if does sport a few odd patches of green, For visitors, its primary interest is that it holds three utterly superb examples of **Selçuk** architecture.

Bürüciye Medresesi

Selçuk Parkı • Daily 8am–11pm

Founded in 1271 by the İlhanid emir Muzaffer Bürücirdi, the **Bürüciye Medresesi** consists of a series of square rooms laid out to a symmetrical ground plan around a

SİVAS

ACCOMMODATION	
Büyük	4
Eray	2
Köşk	3
Sultan	1

KONAK
MEYDANI

Selçuk
Parkı

Kale Camii

Çifte Minare
Medrese

THY
Agent

Bürüciye
Medresesi

Şifaiye
Medresesi

Meydan
Hamamı

Ulu
Cami

Kale

Gök Medrese

RESTAURANTS	
Elif Kebap	1
Hakan Bistro	3
Sosyal Tesisleri	2

BARS AND CAFÉS	
Bürüciye Medresesi	2
Kahvemiz	3
Rain Bar	1

Erzurum

central courtyard. As you pass through the entrance, the *türbe* of the emir and his children is to the left. Most visitors, however, are here for a glass of tea, or a puff on a nargile (see p.47).

Directly opposite the entrance, the **Kale Camii** dates from 1580. As a straightforward Ottoman mosque, it's an oddity in this area.

Çifte Minare Medrese

The stunning **Çifte Minare Medrese**, the "Twin Minaret Seminary", dates (like the Bürüciye Medresesi) from 1271. Its facade alone still stands, adorned with tightly curled relief filigrees, topped by two brick **minarets**, speckled with pale blue tiles. Behind, only the well-defined foundations of student cells and lecture halls survive.

Şifaiye Medresesi

Built in 1217 on the orders of the Selçuk sultan Keykavus I, the **Şifaiye Medresesi** functioned as a **hospital** and **medical school**. At the time of writing it was the subject of heavy renovation, but it's likely to revert to its previous function as a bazaar.

Ulu Cami

Off Cumhuriyet Cad

The **Ulu Cami** is the oldest mosque in Sivas, built in 1197. Step inside its northern entrance, and you enter the subterranean cool of an interior supported by fifty wooden pillars. The peaceful silence is broken only by the murmur of boys reading from the Koran.

Gök Medrese

Off Cumhuriyet Cad

Famed for its ornate tile-studded minarets, the stunning **Gök Medrese Camii**, or "Blue Seminary", was undertaking substantial renovation at the time of writing. It was built in 1271 by the Selçuk grand vizier Sahip Ata Fahrettin Ali, who was also responsible for buildings in Kayseri and Konya.

THE SİVAS MASSACRE

Mention Sivas to any Turk, and you'll likely receive an abbreviated account of the events of **2 July, 1993** – a tragic massacre that has given the city an enduring notoriety, especially given the current friction between its secular and religious elements.

A group of **Alevi intellectuals** had gathered inside the *Madımak Hotel* for a small festival, celebrating the work of a sixteenth-century Alevi poet. One of their number, **Aziz Nasin**, had recently published translated extracts from Salman Rushdie's *The Satanic Verses*, and a vengeful mob of over a thousand Islamic fundamentalists gathered outside in protest after Friday prayers. The hotel was set alight; 37 perished, including hotel guests and employees. Aziz himself managed to escape.

ARRIVAL AND INFORMATION
SİVAS

By train The train station is 2.5km west of town, but municipal buses and dolmuşes run down İstasyon Caddesi (later İnönü Bulvarı) to Konak Meydanı.

Destinations Ankara (3 daily; 11hr); Divriği (2 daily; 4–7hr); Diyarbakır (4 weekly; 12hr); Erzurum (2 daily; 10hr); Kars (2 daily; 16hr).

By bus Buses from Ankara and beyond arrive at the *otogar*, 1.5km south of town. From here *servis* buses run to the centre, taking an indirect route along İnönü Bulvarı.

Destinations Amasya (10 daily; 3hr 30min); Ankara (hourly; 6hr 30min); Divriği (4 daily; 3hr); Diyarbakır (12 daily; 8hr); Erzurum (12 daily; 7hr 30min); Kayseri (10 daily; 3hr); Malatya (12 daily; 4hr 30min); Tokat (10 daily; 1hr 30min).

Hamam The Meydan Hamamı, up a side street off Atatürk Caddesi, has been hissing and steaming for over four centuries, and is still going strong (daily 7am–10.30pm; ₺12.5 for bath).

ACCOMMODATION

Büyük Otel İstasyon Cad ☏0346 225 4767, ⓦsivasbuyukotel.com. Monolith of a hotel trying desperately to cling onto its class. Bedrooms are large and soulless, but the dining room is one of the few places in town that serves alcohol. ₺260

Eray Pansiyon Eski Belediye Sok 12 ☏0346 223 1647. A few apartment rooms trying their best to function as a youth hostel. Dormitory beds are comfy enough; single travellers are likely to get the room to themselves for the same price. Dorms ₺30, doubles ₺60

Köşk Otel Atatürk Cad 7 ☏0346 255 1724, ⓦkoskotel.com. Beautifully decked-out contemporary hotel, complete with fitness centre. All rooms are spacious and spotless, with excellent showers, and breakfast is included in the price; no wonder they're almost always full. ₺130

Sultan Otel Eski Belediye Sok 18 ☏0346 221 2986, ⓦsultanotel.com.tr. Swish, very good value, contemporary hotel. While the rooms don't quite live up to the promise of a semi-opulent lobby, they're clean, cosy and quiet. ₺100

EATING AND DRINKING

Cheap **kebab places** line the road behind the PTT; keep an eye out for the flat *Sivas köfte*, which are essentially miniature burgers. Precious few places serve **alcohol**, even the shops; if you're desperate, try the *Rain Bar* on Atatürk Cad 26.

★ **Bürüciye Medresesi** Selçuk Parkı. Is this Anatolia's most atmospheric place for tea? Gulp one back (₺1) in the superb setting of this *medrese* courtyard (see p.503), which also functions as a swallow's playground of some sort. Also a great place to suck on a nargile (₺10). Daily 8am–11pm.

Elif Kebap Atatürk Cad 2. Clean, friendly and popular, this two-level restaurant doles out round after round of excellent kebab (including *Sivas köfte*, ₺8), and some very lengthy *pide* for a little less. Daily 9am–10pm.

Hakan Bistro Atatürk Cad 22. Presentable place whose upper floor is a great place for breakfast, if a little pricey – ₺12 for the regular, and ₺16.5 for the village feast with cheeses from all over Eastern Anatolia. International dishes include chow mein, quesadillas and salmon – just the

thing if you've been travelling a while – plus some of the best *baklava* and desserts in town. Daily 7.30am–10pm.

Kahvemiz Behind Büyük Otel. This café is popular with Sivas trendies: it's a relaxed, funkily designed place serving Turkish coffee (₺4) in a proper *cezve* – and usually throwing in some *lokum* and lemon-mint water for good measure. Also has wi-fi. Daily 11am–11pm.

Sosyal Tesisleri On the main square. This new venture is wildly popular with locals (especially the outdoor seats by the water feature), and makes a perfect stopoff while touring the sights. Try the *Sivas köfte* (₺9), or some tasty *içli köfte* (₺7), essentially meatball dumplings in a casing of cracked wheat. Daily 8am–midnight.

Divriği

Stuck in the middle of a mountainous nowhere, on a hill overlooking a tributary of the young Euphrates, sleepy **DIVRIĞI** merits a visit for the sake of a single monument – the whimsical and unique **Ulu Cami** and its dependency, the **Darüşşifa**. These date from the early thirteenth century, when the town was the seat of the tiny **Mengüçeh** emirate. The Mongols, who evicted the Mengüçehs in 1252, demolished the castle but left the religious foundations alone, and the place was not incorporated into the Ottoman Empire until 1516.

Divriği retains a ramshackle bazaar area, crisscrossed by cobbled lanes and grapevines. It also sports distinctive wooden **minarets** and old houses with inverted-keyhole windows, neither of which are seen elsewhere in Anatolia. The conspicuous **mosque** and **sanitorium**, joined in one complex at the top of a slope 250m east of town, command a fine view.

Ulu Cami

Dedicated in 1228 by a certain Ahmet Şah, the **Ulu Cami** is remarkable for its outrageous external **portals**, most un-Islamic with their wealth of floral and faunal detail. Far-fetched comparisons have been drawn to Indian Moghul art, but a simpler, more likely explanation is that Armenian or Selçuk craftsmen had a hand in the decoration.

The north door, festooned with vegetal designs, is the most celebrated, although the northwest one is more intricate – note the pair of double-headed eagles, not necessarily copied from the Byzantines since it's a very old Anatolian motif. Inside, sixteen columns and the ceiling they support are more suggestive of a Gothic cloister or Byzantine cistern. There's rope-vaulting in one dome, while the northeast one sports a peanut-brittle surface.

Darüşşifa

Theoretically open daily 8.30am–5pm, but you may have to find the caretaker to gain admission

The **Darüşşifa** like the Ulu Cami, was also built in 1228 by Adaletli Melike Turan Melek, Ahmet Şah's wife. Its portal is restrained in comparison to the mosque, but still bears medallions lifted almost free from their background.

The interior is asymmetrical in both ground plan and ornamentation, and even more eclectic than the mosque. The fan-reliefs on the wall behind this once formed an elaborate **sundial**, catching rays through the second-floor window of the facade.

ARRIVAL AND DEPARTURE
DIVRIĞI

By train Divriği's train station is down by the river, 20min walk from the bazaar; taxis meet most arrivals and won't cost more than a few lira. It also has to be said that the train rides into town are among the most beautiful in Turkey.

Destinations Erzurum (daily; 7hr); Sivas (2 daily; 4hr 30min–7hr).

By bus The *otogar* is 400m south of town on the road to Elazığ, but try to take the train instead.

ACCOMMODATION AND EATING

Divriği holds very few places to **stay**, though you'll see a clutch of simple guesthouses as you approach town from the train station. **Eating** options are certainly better, with cheap restaurants and snack bars concentrated around the bazaar area.

Konak On the way up to the mosque. Citadel views and the best *kahvaltı* for miles around (₺9), as well as succulent kebabs. Daily 7am–10pm.

Otel Ninni Sivas Divriği Yolu, no phone. Simple hotel that has renovated its lobby in recent years. They've still got a little way to go with the rooms, however. ₺50

Özkanlar Pansiyon Sivas Divriği Yolu ☏0346 418 1742. Consisting of a few rooms above an internet café; some are en-suite, meaning that they've a shower and urinal. ₺70

8

The Black Sea coast

SUMELA MONASTERY

9

The Black Sea coast

Extending from just east of İstanbul to the frontier with Georgia, the Black Sea region is a real anomaly, guaranteed to smash any stereotypes you may hold about Turkey. The combination of damp northerly and westerly winds, confronting an almost uninterrupted wall of mountains south of the shore, has created a relentlessly rainy and riotously green realm. It's not unlike the northwest coasts of North America or Spain. The peaks force the clouds to disgorge themselves on the seaward side of the watershed, leaving central Anatolia beyond the passes in a permanent rain shadow. With the short summer season ensuring the area sees few package tourists or backpackers, most foreign visitors are either archeology groups or trekkers.

That said, when the semi-tropical heat sets in, in July and August, you'll certainly want to swim. The sea here has its own peculiarities, just like the weather. Fed huge volumes of fresh water by the Don, Dnieper and Danube rivers to the north, it's diminished not by evaporation but by strong currents through the Bosphorus and the Dardanelles. The resulting upper layer is of such low salinity that you could almost drink it, were it not for the pollution.

Starting north of Ankara as mere humps, the coastal ranges attain world-class grandeur by the time they reach the Georgian border. Until recently they made land access all but impossible, and provided refuge for a complex quilt of tribes and ethnic subgroups that still exist among the **Hemşin valleys** and the **Kaçkar mountains**. Even so, travelling largely consists of soaking up the atmosphere, with little need to worry about missing important sights. Apart from the old mercantile towns of **Ünye** and **Giresun**, there are no major attractions outside the ancient port city of **Trabzon** (Trebizond) with its nearby **monastery of Sumela**.

Although the region's characterless central portion is dominated by the hulking port of **Samsun**, the coast west of the strikingly sited town of **Sinop**, towards the Byzantine/Genoese harbour of **Amasra**, is filled with attractive villages and deserted beaches. The lack of bus and dolmuş links spares the area from mass tourism.

Brief history

The ancient Greeks ventured onto the Black Sea, or as they called it, the Pontos Euxine, at the start of the first millennium BC. They fought with the local "barbarians" and occasionally, as in the semi-legendary tale of Jason and the Argonauts, got the better of them. Between the seventh and fourth centuries BC, the Aegean cities founded numerous colonies. These became the ancestors of virtually every modern Black Sea town, whose names as often as not are Turkifications of their ancient monikers. The region made its first brief appearance on the world stage when a local Pontic king, **Mithridates IV Eupator**, came close to expelling the Romans from Anatolia.

With the arrival of Christianity, relations between natives and imperial overlords hardly changed at all. Only the Byzantine urban centres by the sea became

UZUNGÖL

Highlights

Driving from Sinop to Amasra Cruise the ttle-used coast road from Sinop to Amasra, vhere sharp switchbacks lead to peaceful bays nd long beaches. **See pp.513–516**

Amasra Enjoy the smalltown charm and istorical pedigree of Amasra, with its old obbled streets, Byzantine gateways and Genoese castle walls. **See p.516**

Aya Sofya Thirteenth-century frescoes in this byzantine monastery at the edge of Trabzon are mong the most vivid sacred art in Anatolia. ee p.524

4 Sumela Cliff-clinging thirteenth-century monastery in a superb forested setting. **See p.529**

5 Uzungöl Large natural lake in the foothills of the Pontic range, the focus of a popular resort. **See p.531**

6 Hemşin valleys This lushly forested district is home to a colourful, outgoing people with their own tenaciously preserved culture. **See p.533**

7 Tea Learn the skills of making the nation's favourite drink and watch the leaves being picked from the hillsides surrounding Rize. **See p.537**

HIGHLIGHTS ARE MARKED ON THE MAP ON PP.510–511

thoroughly Hellenized. The Byzantine defeat at Manzikert in 1071 (see p.652) initially meant little to the Black Sea, safe behind its wall of mountains; the fall of Constantinople to the Fourth Crusade in 1204 had far greater immediate effects, prompting the Black Sea's second spell of historical prominence. For two and a half cultured (and ultimately decadent) centuries, the empire-in-exile of the Komnenos dynasty, centred on **Trebizond** (today's Trabzon), exercised influence grossly disproportionate to its size.

After Manzikert, Turkish chieftains had begun to encroach on the coast, especially at the gap in the barrier ranges near Sinop and Samsun. The Trapezuntine dynasty even concluded alliances with them, doubtless to act as a counter to the power of the Genoese and Venetians who also set up shop hereabouts. Most of this factionalism came to an end under the **Ottomans**, though even they entrusted semi-autonomous administration of the Pontic foothills to feudal *derebey*s ("valley lords") until early in the nineteenth century.

The equilibrium was upset when the Black Sea area entered the history books for the third time, as a theatre of war. Imperial Turkey and **Russia** clashed four times between 1828 and 1915, and the Tsarist regime gave aid and comfort to various regional separatist movements after 1877. Between 1918 and 1922, Greeks attempting to create a Pontic state fought with guerrillas loyal to Atatürk's Nationalists. Following the victory of the **Republic**, the Greek merchant class was expelled, and the Black Sea experienced temporary economic disarray, verging on famine during the 1930s.

Most of the credit for the last few decades of **recovery** must go to the *hamsi*s, as the locals are nicknamed (after the Black Sea anchovy formerly caught here in large numbers during winter). Enterprising, voluble and occasionally scandalous, they have set up mafias in the shipping, property and construction industries throughout the country, much of which is funded by industrious *hamsi*s overseas. The most visible sign of the post-Soviet era, since Turkey's eastern border opened up in the early 1990s, is a new coastal road and a further bout of urbanization.

The Black Sea region looks set to receive a further boost, with the state-run Turkish Petroleum Corporation joining with Shell in 2011 to develop vast beds of oil and gas reserves that apparently lie in waiting offshore.

THE BLACK SEA COAST

The western Black Sea

Thanks to its poor infrastructure, and lack of specific attractions, the coast from Samsun west to Amasra is perhaps the least visited part of the entire Turkish shoreline. Samsun makes a dreary and discouraging gateway to the region, but matters improve as you head northwest to **Sinop**, a more interesting place than any other Black Sea town except Trabzon. Beyond Sinop the coast road west is tortuous and slow, but spectacular scenery, unspoiled beaches and small ports offer some compensation. The only place that sees many tourists is **Amasra**, an old medieval stronghold at the western end of this beautiful stretch.

As a rule, the **beaches** are cleaner and the weather drier here than further east. Figs and olives attest to the mild climate, and if you simply want to laze on the sand without any other stimulation, you'll find plenty of opportunity. Sparse bus and dolmuş schedules are the only drawbacks; check frequencies to avoid getting stranded.

Samsun

Despite its long and turbulent history, **SAMSUN** has few remaining historical or scenic attractions, and even its tourist office now lies defunct. A thoroughly modern city with a population knocking on one million, it's laid out on a grid plan, with endless unruly suburbs stretching 30km along the east–west coast road. It's a busy port and centre for the processing of local agricultural produce and tobacco.

Because of its strategic location, Samsun changed hands frequently over the centuries. It was besieged, captured (and usually sacked) by the Pontic kings, Romans, Byzantines, several tribes of Turks and the Genoese, who had a major trading station here until 1425, when they torched the town rather than hand it over to Ottoman control. When the advent of the railway facilitated the transport of tobacco to Ankara and beyond, Samsun's flagging fortunes revived, and by 1910 it was a thriving city of 40,000 inhabitants. The port city gained a place in Turkish folklore when then Mustafa Kemal, under the guise of "Inspector General of the Ottoman forces in Anatolia",

HIGHLIGHTS
1. Driving from Sinop to Amasra
2. Amasra
3. Aya Sofya
4. Sumela
5. Uzungöl
6. Hemşin valleys
7. Tea

BLACK SEA

arrived in 1919 by steamship from İstanbul and quietly began to sow the seeds of independence among the local Turk population.

Nowadays, any spare time in Samsun may well weigh heavy on a traveller's hands, but it holds a couple of hours' worth of interesting sights, plus a fair amount to offer in terms of food and lodgings should you need to spend the night. The main square in the city centre, **Cumhuriyet Meydanı**, boasts a statue of Atatürk on horseback. Kazımpaşa Caddesi and Cumhuriyet Caddesi run north and south of the square respectively, while 19 Mayis Bulvarı, which runs both east and west, meets Fuar Caddesi, the main coastal road, at its far eastern end.

Archeological Museum

Fuar Cad • Tues–Sun 8.30am–noon & 1–5pm • ₺3

Samsun's **Archeological Museum** (Arkeoloji Müzesi) is poorly laid out, but worth visiting for its main exhibit, a Roman mosaic found in Karasamsun, site of an ancient acropolis that juts out to sea 3km west of town. The museum's grounds are also beautifully landscaped. A life-sized installation marks the spot where Atatürk arrived on May 19, 1919, to take control of the local anti-Greek forces.

Gazi Museum

Gazi Cad, off 19 Mayis Bul • Tues–Sun 8.30am–noon & 1–5pm • ₺3

Housed in the former *Mintika Hotel*, the **Gazi Museum** (Gazi Müzesi) commemorates Atatürk's 1919 visit to Samsun. He only stayed a week before moving on to Havza, 85km inland and away from the watchful eye of British warships. Scores of photos, letters and even clothing from the great man are on display.

ARRIVAL AND DEPARTURE SAMSUN

By plane Samsun-Çarşamba airport (☎0362 844 8830), 20km east of town on the coastal road towards Trabzon, is linked to the town centre by a service bus.
Destinations Ankara (1 daily; 1hr); Antalya (2 weekly; 1hr 30min); İstanbul (4–6 daily; 1hr 20min); İzmir (1–2 daily; 1hr 40min).
By bus Samsun's *otogar*, 4km south of the centre on the main Trabzon road, is connected by service buses and frequent dolmuşes to the bus companies' ticket offices on the east side of Cumhuriyet Meydanı.
Destinations Afyon (4 daily; 10hr); Amasya (hourly; 2hr 30min); Ankara (hourly; 7hr); Artvin (4 daily; 10hr); Balıkesir (2 daily; 14hr); Erzurum (2 daily; 10hr); Giresun (10 daily; 3hr 30min); İstanbul (15 daily; 11hr); Rize (every

30min; 8hr); Sinop (every 30min; 3hr); Sivas (5 daily; 6hr 30min); Tbilisi, Georgia (1 daily; 16hr); Trabzon (hourly; 7hr); Van (2 daily; 18hr).
By train The train station is halfway between the *otogar* and the centre, 2km south of Cumhuriyet Meydanı and connected by buses #2 and #10, and dolmuşes marked "Garaj".
Destinations Amasya (1 daily; 4hr 30min); Kayseri (4 weekly; 19hr); Sivas (1 daily; 12hr).
By ferry At the time of writing, the Russian shipping company AnRussTrans (☞anrusstrans.com) was scheduled to commence a weekly ferry service between Samsun and the Russian port of Novorossiysk. The ferry is expected to accommodate 70 trucks and 90 passengers on its 20hr voyage.

ACCOMMODATION

★ **Otel Necmi** Kale Mah 6, Bedesten Sok ☎0362 432 7164, ☞otelnecmi.com.tr. Super-friendly, well-located hotel – look out for signs on Kazımpaşa Caddesi – with compact, carpeted rooms accessed up a steep staircase. Slightly overpriced, the rooms have a/c; some will fit three beds at a squeeze, but the bathrooms are shared. Meals are served in a ground-floor living room. Doubles ₺65, triples ₺90
Otel Vidinli At junction of Cumhuriyet Meyd and Kazımpaşa Cad ☎0362 431 6050, ☞otelvidinli.com.tr. A short walk from the museums, this shiny business-class hotel offers modern if slightly bland rooms in neutral tones,

some with glimpses of the sea. The staff are generally friendly throughout, including the top-floor bar-restaurant which serves pricey drinks and an international menu. ₺165
Otel Yafeya Cumhuriyet Mey ☎0362 435 1131, ☞yafeyaotel.com. Housed in an imposing building on the corner of the square, the *Yafeya* boasts large, comfortable rooms with carpeted floors and large windows; some have a small sitting area with a couch. There's a bar and large restaurant, as well as a billiard room and a spacious lobby. ₺195

EATING AND DRINKING

Oskar Restaurant Şeyhhamza Sok 3, off Belediye Meyd. Friendly, family-run restaurant, recommended for its surroundings, service and food. The Turkish-only menu offers a good selection of *mezes*, plus meat and fish dishes, and traditional desserts such as *bafra nokul*, a flavoured sweet pastry. Mains ₺9–18. Daily noon–10pm.

★ **Samsun Balık Restaurant** Kazimpaşa Cad 20

☎ 0362 435 7550. Aptly named place in a welcoming brick house, halfway between *Otel Necmi* and *Otel Vidinli*, where diners select their fish downstairs and have it brought to them in the refined upstairs dining room. Non-fish eaters can ask for their vegetarian *meze* (₺7), and there's beer and wine available. Mains ₺15 upwards. Tues–Sun 7–11pm.

Bafra

West of Samsun, the coast road soon cuts inland through extensive tobacco fields to the market town of **BAFRA**, an ugly, grimy town of around 80,000 who mostly work in the tobacco industry. There's no reason to stop, though the surrounding countryside encompasses the **Kızılırmak delta**, also called Bafra Balık Gölleri ("Bafra fish lakes"), a 140,000-acre birdwatchers' paradise of wetlands, lakes, flooded forests, reed beds and sand dunes formed by the Kızılırmak River as it falls into the Black Sea.

Gerze

GERZE, 35km south of Sinop, is a pretty village that holds many handsome old buildings in a reasonable state of repair. A handful of hotels and restaurant are flanked by stony, not too crowded beaches. The past few years have seen the locals pitted against the Ankara government, which is pushing for the construction of a mega coal-fired power plant nearby, despite regular protests that have attracted crowds of up to ten thousand.

ARRIVAL AND DEPARTURE   **GERZE**

By bus Hourly buses along the coast stop at a small *otogar* towards Gerze's northern edge.

ACCOMMODATION

Otel Ermiş İskele Cad 50 ☎ 0368 718 1540. Basic but comfortable rooms, some accommodating three adults, overlooking the harbour. There's a pleasant beer garden shaded by large pine trees, and rates can usually be negotiated out of season. ₺125

North Star Hotel Kosk Burnu Mevkii 69 ☎ 0368 718 4747. The pick of Gerze's hotels, overlooking the sea on the north side of the village. Most of the light, airy rooms have balconies, and there's a selection of restaurants and bars, plus a pleasant garden with kids' playground. ₺145

Sinop

Straddling a beach-studded isthmus, and blessed with the finest natural harbour on the Black Sea, sleepy **SİNOP** is renowned as one of the prettiest towns along the coast. A fine clutch of monuments bestows a real authority on the place, even if most visitors are content to relax along the café-lined harbour-front, where bobbing boats supply the day's catch to the line of restaurants behind.

As the northernmost point of Anatolia, less than two hundred nautical miles from the Crimea, Sinop played a front-line role during the Cold War, when it was the location of a US-run listening post. These days fishing and tourism provide most of the income for its 35,000 inhabitants, who are currently fighting proposals to build a nuclear power station nearby.

Brief history

Sinop takes its name from the mythical Amazon queen **Sinope**. The daughter of a minor river-god, she attracted the attention of Zeus, who promised her anything she desired in return for her favours. Her request was for eternal virginity; Zeus played the gentleman and complied.

9

** SİNOP**

Map labels: Akliman Beach, BLACK SEA, Kumkapı, Alaiye (Pervane) Medresesi, Alâeddin Camii, Sinop Museum, Ethnographic Museum, Seyit Bilal Camii, RADAR YOLU, Samsun & Otogar, CUMHURİYET CAD, Sinop Kale Cezaevi, Kumsal Beach, SAKARYA CAD, Sinope Tours, KEMALETTIN SAMİ PAŞA CAD, ERGÜL SÖK, GELİNCİK MAHALLESİ YOLU, KURTULUŞ CAD, İSKELE CAD, ATATÜRK CAD, Balatlar Kilise, GAZİ CAD, Ferry Terminal, BLACK SEA, N

After a wealthy period of Roman rule, Sinop declined during the Byzantine era, while Persian and Arab raids thwarted sixth- and seventh-century attempts to revive its fortunes. The Selçuks took the town in 1214, converting churches into mosques and erecting a *medrese*, but after the Mongols smashed their short-lived state, Sinop passed into the hands of the İsfendiyaroğlu emirs of Kastamonu until Ottoman annexation in 1458. Thereafter the town was rarely heard of, except on November 30, 1853, when the Russians destroyed both Sinop and an Ottoman fleet anchored here, thus triggering the Crimean War, and again on May 18, 1919, when Atatürk passed through en route to Samsun.

The city walls

Although time has inevitably taken its toll, Sinop's prominent **city walls** remain by far its most compelling feature. Opposite the old fortress and prison, the bulky **Kumkapı** juts out bastion-like into the sea on the northern shore, while down near the harbour a hefty square tower offers good views out to sea, and strolls along the nearby sections of wall.

Sinop Kale Cezaevi

Gelincik Mahallesi Yolu • Tues–Sun 9am–noon & 1–5pm • ₺3 • ☎ 0368 260 4820

The first thing you'll notice on entering Sinop is its old **fortress**, **Sinop Kale Cezaevi**. Demarcating the area of the initial settlement, the fortress primarily served a defensive purpose. A citadel was added during the Selçuk era, which the Ottomans used as a shipyard. It was then converted into a prison in 1887, and housed prisoners for the next hundred years. Now open to visitors, it hosts the occasional cultural event.

Alâeddin Camii

Sinop's oldest **mosque** is the thirteenth-century Selçuk **Alâeddin Camii**, towards the town centre on Sakarya Caddesi. Five-domed, with a rectangular-plan mosque, it lies within a tree-shaded, high-walled courtyard with a central *şadırvan*, where a blue-painted porch lets onto a plain interior enlivened by a fine *mimber*.

Behind the mosque, the **Alaiye Medresesi** also dates from the 1260s, and is also known as the Pervane Medresesi after its founder, Mu'in al-Din Süleyman Pervane. Its most notable feature is a marble-decorated entrance portal, relatively restrained by Selçuk standards. The former pupils' rooms now house craft shops selling locally woven fabrics.

Sinop museum
Okullar Cad 2 • Tues–Sun 9am–noon & 1–5pm • ₺3 • ☎ 0368 261 1975

Sinop's modern **museum** has an array of objects (labelled in English) from the Bronze Age onwards, including the relatively recent Independence War. Many of its oldest exhibits were unearthed at Kocagöz, an archeological site a few kilometres southwest. The museum grounds hold the Aynalı Kadın Tomb, built in 1335, and the sparse remains of the Hellenistic **Temple of Serapis**, excavated in 1951.

Balatlar Kilise
Corner of Kaynak and Tarakçı Cads

The Byzantine **Balatlar Kilise** church is thought to have been built during the seventh century, atop the remnants of a Roman bath house. Only its northern and southern walls are still standing, while inside, traces of frescoes depicting Jesus and Mary are suffering from exposure to both the elements and graffiti taggers.

The town beaches
Twice-hourly dolmuşes connect Kumsal and Karakum, via the *otogar* and town centre; Akliman is a 20min dolmuş ride from town

Sinop's main beaches are **Kumsal**, less than 1km southwest of the bus station, and a pay beach at **Karakum**, 3km east of the harbour. Kumsal beach is smaller, but the sand is lighter and the sea rather more enticing than at Karakum, whose name, meaning "black sand", is a fairly honest description.

The best beach on the northern side of the peninsula is **Akliman**, where a fine stretch of white sand is backed by pine forests and picnic areas, but it's less frequented than the other beaches, as unpredictable currents make swimming here dangerous.

ARRIVAL AND INFORMATION SİNOP

By plane Sinop's small airport (☎ 0368 271 5609) is 5km west of the centre. An irregular airport bus leaves from beside the taxi rank outside the main PTT on Atatürk Cad; it should depart every 30min but seldom does. A taxi should cost around ₺20.
Destinations İstanbul (1 daily; 1hr 15min).
By bus or dolmuş Sinop's *otogar*, 3km southwest of town towards the airport, is connected with the centre by bus-company service buses, and dolmuşes that depart from just

west of the museum. Most dolmuşes from either the peninsula or around town arrive and depart from a stop behind the *Hotel Melia ve Kasım* on Gazi Caddesi.
Destinations Ankara (4 daily; 9hr); İstanbul (5 daily; 11hr); Kastamonu (hourly; 2hr); Samsun (every 30min; 3hr).
Tourist office Friendly office, just north of *Hotel Melia ve Kasım*, Gazi Cad (June–Aug daily 9am–11pm; ☎ 0368 261 5298). There are also irregularly manned booths at the prison and Alaiye Medresesi.

ACCOMMODATION

Sinop has a great selection of central **hotels**, mostly in the streets behind the harbour. Book ahead in summer, when they tend to fill up. Many small *pansiyons* have sprung up at Karakum beach near the large *Holiday Village*, a couple of kilometres east of the centre, but most are private homes that rent out spare bedrooms, so you'll have to look carefully for the signs.

Otel 57 Kurtuluş Cad 29 ☎ 0368 261 5462, ⓦ otel57 .com. Standard business-class place, within strolling distance of the water. Good value and comfortable, the rooms have wood-panelled floors, a/c and heating, modern bathrooms with walk-in showers, and balconies. There's a thumping nightclub at the rear, and a buffet breakfast. ₺90
Bossinop Uğurmumcu Meyd 37 ☎ 0368 260 5700, ⓦ bossinopotel.com. Overlooking the town's main

roundabout, with glimpses of the sea, the *Bossinop* offers spacious carpeted rooms – some hold three adults – with large windows and good-sized modern bathrooms. Breakfast is served on a roof terrace with views, and they'll usually find a parking spot for drivers. ₺180
Mola Kurtuluş Cad 34 ☎ 0368 261 1814, ⓦ sinopmolaotel.com.tr. In a great location across from the harbour, this modest hotel offers ageing but

comfortable rooms, some with balconies and (obviously) sea views. A very good buffet breakfast is included, there's a pleasant garden courtyard set into the fortress wall, and parking is close by. **₺140**

★ **Reis** Kurtuluş Cad 19 ☎0368 260 4020, ⓦsinopreisotel.com. Overlooking the harbour and surrounded by restaurants and cafés, the friendly and well-managed *Reis* has simple yet stylish rooms with smallish

bathrooms and large windows. A rooftop terrace serves a good breakfast and has great views. **₺170**

Yılmaz Aile Pansiyonu Tersane Çarşısı 11 ☎0368 261 5752. Family-owned and -run, this is the best-value budget option close to the water's edge. The small, clean rooms share basic but acceptable bathrooms and there's a kitchen for guest use. **₺80**

EATING AND DRINKING

Kale Burç Café Sinop Kalesi, İskele Cad ☎0368 260 0420. Enjoying glorious sea views, atop the massive stone tower by the waterfront, the mostly outdoor "Burç" is a popular place for both a cold beer (₺3) and live (and late) music, especially local folk bands. Daily 11am–late.

Liman İskele Cad 20 ☎0368 264 7821. This picturesque, much-loved wooden teahouse, one of many in Sinop, is set in a restored stone house, with chairs on the waterfront and a fine view of the boats in the harbour. Beer ₺2. Daily 11am–late.

Örnek Kahvaltı ve Börek İskele Cad 1/A ☎0368 261 7341. Friendly place with fast service, popular with locals for light and delicious breakfast pastries. You can ask for *paket servis* (take away) to enjoy in any of the local teahouses or while strolling along the harbour front. Daily 7am–6pm.

Saray İskele Cad 18 ☎0368 261 1729. One of the most popular fish restaurants along the harbour front, despite its sometimes-slow service. Located on a floating pier, the fish is often farmed rather than wild. Expect to pay ₺10–15 for fresh mackerel or sea bass. Daily noon–11pm.

Amasra

AMASRA brazenly flaunts its charms to new arrivals. Approached from any direction, the town suddenly appears below you, swarming up onto a rocky headland sheltering two bays. A narrow stone bridge links the main town to the island of **Boztepe** further out, while the headland shelters the east-facing **Büyük Liman** (Big Harbour) on one side and the west-facing **Küçük Liman** (Little Harbour) on the other. As the beaches at both are at best average, it's best to regard Amasra as a base for forays to better beaches further east.

Amasra's historical pedigree and colourful atmosphere make it worth at least an overnight stop. During the day it is a quiet place, full of shady corners to sit and contemplate. By night it's much livelier, and the old walls are lit up attractively, but it doesn't lose its small-town charm.

Brief history

Mentioned as Sesamus in the *Iliad*, Amasra was colonized by Miletus in the sixth century BC. The name derived from Queen Amastris, a lady of the court of Alexander the Great, who, after the death of her husband, acted as regent for her young son, only to be repaid with murder at his hands. Avid letter-writer Pliny the Younger was appointed Rome's special commissioner to this region in 110 AD. After the ninth century, following a barbarian attack, the town declined in importance, though the Byzantines maintained a garrison here. The Genoese took over when Byzantine strength declined, and held the city until the Ottomans assumed control in 1460.

Byzantine fortifications

Both Amasra itself and the island are scattered with stretches of ancient fortifications from two Byzantine/Genoese **castles** near the tip of the peninsula. One is situated in the modern town above Büyük Liman, where a short walk above the *Otel Timur* reveals old cobbled streets straddled by Byzantine gateways. The other castle is reached by following Küçük Liman Caddesi across the bridge to **Boztepe**, where a ruined watchtower on a piece of land jutting out into the harbour is still visible.

AMASRA

ACCOMMODATION	
Çarşı Butik Otel	1
Emin Apart Pansiyon	3
Otel Timur	2

RESTAURANTS	
Canlı Balık Restoran	1
Karadeniz Aile Pide Salonu	3
Martı Balık Restoran	2

BAR & CAFÉ	
Han Bar	1

Bus Terminal

Boztepe's heavy-duty **walls**, pierced by several gates, remain largely intact. The **inner citadel** is studded with towers and the Genoese coat of arms. Of the two **Byzantine churches** that you can hunt down in the maze of alleys on Boztepe, the larger was converted to a mosque after the Ottoman conquest, while the ruined smaller one was in use until 1923.

Amasra museum

amlik Sok 4, at the western inland extremity of Küçük Liman • Tues–Sun 8.30am–5.30pm • ₺5

Amasra's high-quality **museum** contains locally unearthed archeological finds, including a beautiful selection of Roman sculptures discovered in nearby Bartın. Pride of place is given to the torso of an emperor, with Romulus and Remus carved on his tunic, discovered in the citadel area in 1995.

ARRIVAL AND INFORMATION
AMASRA

By bus or dolmuş The dolmuş terminal is near the PTT on the small Atatürk Meydanı, near the middle of the main part of the headland. Long-distance buses use a new terminal on the southern end of town; irregular servis buses connect the two.

Destinations Ankara (5 daily; 7hr); Bartın (every 30min; 25min); İstanbul (8 daily; 11hr); İzmir (2 daily; 25hr); Sinop (6 daily; 6hr).

Tourist office A small information kiosk behind the museum is open irregularly in summer, and closed out of season (w amasra.net).

ACCOMMODATION

Çarşı Butik Otel Çekiciler Cad 23 ☏ 0378 315 1146 w carsibutikotel.com. Centrally located though surprisingly quiet, the wooden bungalow-style rooms here have individual entrances and patios, with spacious a/c interiors and small bathrooms with walk-in showers. Breakfast usually includes plenty of fruit, and the management is very friendly. ₺150

★ **Emin Apart Pansiyon** Çekiciler Cad 52

9

☎0378 315 1676. This tall, narrow *pansiyon* offers a surprisingly varied range of room sizes. All have wood-panelled floors and spacious modern bathrooms, one with its own kitchen. Breakfast and cold drinks are served by the friendly staff in a pleasant rear courtyard. **₺110**

Otel Timur Çekiciler Cad 53 ☎378 315 2589,

🖳timurotel.com. One block back from the seafront wit a can't-miss red facade, this popular budget hote offers simply furnished – mostly pink – rooms with thic windows and small bathrooms. A creaking lift climbs the top floor, where breakfast with a view is served. Som quad rooms available. **₺85**, quads **₺150**

EATING AND DRINKING

In addition to options listed here, the bridge to Boztepe houses a picturesque, unnamed café on its southwest corner – perfect place for a break with a cool drink and sea views while sightseeing. After dark the town takes to the streets alon both harbour fronts, especially along Küçük Liman, which holds a string of very good, licensed fish restaurants.

Canlı Balık Restoran Küçük Liman 8 ☎0378 315 2606. Also known as *Mustafa Amca'nin Lokantasi, Canlı*, this sixty-year-old fish restaurant has terraces on the water overlooking the Black Sea, and is popular with both locals and tour groups. A plate of *ıstavrit* (Black Sea mackerel) and a beer will set you back ₺20. Daily 11am–11pm.

Han Bar Küçük Liman Cad 17 ☎0378 315 6874. Amasra's late-night bar of choice, a typical low-lit smoky den with scattered loungers and bar stools. There's always plenty of drinking and dancing, and there's usually live music each night. Beer ₺10. Daily 7pm–late.

Karadeniz Aile Pide Salonu Eyiceoğlu Cad 25

☎0378 315 1543. Popular little place, just off the mai street, that's renowned for piping-hot *pide*, and also serve soup, grilled meats, fish and a few breakfast dishes. The are usually enough shaded tables to go round. *Pide* ₺ mains ₺7–11. Daily 9am–10pm.

★ **Martı Balık Restoran** Küçük Liman 15 ☎0378 31 3465, 🖳martibalik.com. This owner-managed restaurar offers tables by the water as well as on a small jetty. Th wonderful setting is matched by the cuisine, whic includes a varied breakfast menu until noon, followed b an *à la carte* option of fish and other seafood, accompanie by *meze* and salads. Mains ₺12–25. Daily 9am–11pm.

The eastern Black Sea

The **eastern coast** of the Black Sea sees far more visitors than the western half, partly because it holds more of interest, and partly because it's easier to get to. **Trabzon**, with its romantic associations and medieval monuments, is very much the main event. With good air and bus services, it makes a logical introduction to the region, and is the usua base for visits to **Sumela monastery**, the only place in this chapter that you could describe as being overwhelmed by tourists. Other forays inland, however, are just as rewarding – particularly the superlatively scenic **Hemşin valleys**, home to a welcoming, unusual people, and the northern gateway to the lofty Kaçkar Dağları.

Other than Trabzon, the coast itself between the Georgian frontier and Samsun offers little apart from fine scenery and swimming opportunities that become increasingly restricted. **Giresun** and **Ünye** are the most attractive and feasible towns. It's best appreciated with your own transport, but even without it you'll face few problems. The towns are close together, and served by endless relays of dolmuşes; just about every route is covered, so you can safely ask to be set down at an isolated beach in the near certainty that another minibus will pick you up when necessary.

East of Samsun: the coast to Trabzon

Just east of Samsun, the Black Sea coastal plain, watered by the **Yeşilırmak delta**, widens to its broadest extent. The area was once thought to be the land of the **Amazons**, a mythical tribe of women who cauterized their right breasts to facilitate spear-throwing and arrow-shooting, and who only coupled with men – their neighbours the Gagarians – during two months of the year, sending male babies to the Gagarians to rear. Nowadays the delta is home to rather more conventional Black Sea Muslims, who are welcoming enough to members of either sex.

Thanks to a new series of tunnels, the main highway heads well inland, through an especially fertile stretch of Turkey's interior, and thus bypasses the deathly slow coastal road.

Ünye

A small, friendly place, just over 100km east of Samsun, **ÜNYE**, the ancient Oinaion, makes a thoroughly pleasant overnight stay. It still holds a few grand buildings that date from Byzantine times and its eighteenth-century heyday as a regional port, including a former Byzantine church on the main square, Cumhuriyet Meydanı, that now serves as the Soysal Eski **Hamam** (daily 5am–midnight: women only Mon–Sat 11am–5pm; men only all other times).

The seafront is home to a leafy park, a pedalo hire station, and a pier that was built for leisure rather than commerce or fishing, a rarity in these climes. If possible, time your visit for the burgeoning **Wednesday market**, where gold-toothed farm women sell hazelnuts (harvested in August) and unusual edible plants (described under the catch-all term of *salata*), alongside churns full of milk and cheese.

Ünye beaches

Ünye profits from its reputation as a **beach resort**. The best strands lie to the west, where the highway is lined by ranks of motels and *pansiyon*s reminiscent of the Aegean or Marmara regions. The best of these give onto aptly named **Uzunkum** (Long Sand) beach, though signs warn you not to bathe when the sea is rough, and there's no consistent lifeguard presence.

Fortress of Çaleoğlu

Look for signs to "Ünye Kalesi" 5km inland, 2km off the D850 road to Niksar and Tokat; without your own vehicle, you'll have to hike the final 2km from there

Much the most important monument near Ünye is the medieval **fortress of Çaleoğlu**, which crowns a natural pinnacle inland from the coast. The Byzantine ramparts around the south-facing gateway have been restored, but the adjacent rock-cut tomb, of Roman or Pontic-kingdom vintage, suggests that one or other culture was originally responsible for fortifying the site. Beyond the gate little remains intact, though you can follow a slippery, usually damp path almost to the summit. The final approach to the very top of the fort is for competent climbers only. Near the summit, you're rewarded with views south over an exceptionally lush valley, and north to the coast.

Giresun

Founded in the second century BC by the Pontic king Pharnaces, **GİRESUN** is among the most pleasant stops between Samsun and Trabzon. With an imposing hillside location and a main street that strides straight upwards instead of shadowing the coastline, the town centre is narrower than others, and offers a welcome respite from the noise and pollution of the coastal highway.

Giresun Adası

2km offshore from Giresun • Travel agents in Giresun offer trips to the island

Giresun Adası is the only major island in the Black Sea. In pre-Christian times it was called Aretias, and was sacred to the Amazons who dedicated a temple to the war god Ares on it. Jason and his Argonauts supposedly stopped here to offer sacrifice, but were attacked by vicious birds. The island is also associated with ancient fertility rites, and still attracts women who wish to conceive during a festival each May.

Tirebolu and around

Curled above a bay enclosed by two headlands, and home to a Greek Orthodox community until 1923, **TİREBOLU**, 41km east of Giresun, is an attractive spot. The

9

intact **castle of St John**, built for a fourteenth-century Genoese garrison, stands on the easterly promontory. The only way to see its interior is by visiting the nocturnal tea garden that operates on its internal lawn – pleasant except for the blaring pop music. As well as Tırebolu's central *Belediye* **beach**, there's a much larger if more exposed sandy stretch to the east, plus more decent beaches towards Espıye, 12km west.

Tırebolu lies at the heart of a *fındık* (hazelnut) -growing area that extends from Samsun east to the Georgian frontier. During late July and August you'll see vast mats of them, still in their husks, raked out to dry. Impatient locals perversely insist on eating them slightly green, when they taste like acorns.

ARRIVAL AND DEPARTURE
EAST OF SAMSUN

ÜNYE

By bus Ünye's minuscule *otogar* is at the eastern edge of town, by the road to Niksar; some bus companies also operate from offices along the main seafront road.

GİRESUN

By bus Regular minibuses to Samsun and Trabzon run along the coastal highway; those for Tırebolu operate from the small *otogar*, east of the centre on the coast road.
Destinations Ordu (every 30–45min; 1hr); Tırebolu (every 30min; 45min); Trabzon (hourly; 2hr 15min).

ACCOMMODATION AND EATING

ÜNYE

Hotel Grand Kuşçalı Şehir Merkezi 42 ☎0452 324 5200, ⊛hotelgrandkuscali.com. Perhaps more comfortable than grand, this is one of the best central options. The carpeted rooms are very spacious and clean, with modern bathrooms; some have glorious seaviews. There's an on-site hamam and a good restaurant, as well as a free shuttle to a private beach. ₺135
Sebile Hanim Konağı Cubuku Arif Sok 10 ☎0452 323 7474, ⊛sebilehanimkonagi.com. This friendly restored Ottoman mansion has a range of en-suite rooms, including some attic-level singles. There's also a very good stone-and-wood restaurant at ground level, open to non-guests, and a lovely shaded courtyard. ₺130
Sofra Belediye Cad 25 ☎0452 323 6854. This stalwart of the local dining scene is often full, especially at lunchtime, with locals who come for the home-styled cooking. The limited but satisfying menu offers grills, *mezes*, *pide* and kebabs, as well as patisseries and some Western dishes. Mains ₺5–13. Daily 11am–3pm & 7–10.30pm.

GİRESUN

Damcilar Fatih Cad 16 ☎0454 201 2828, ⊛damcilarhotel.com. Giresun's newest hotel is located in the centre, near the seafront. The reasonably spacious, contemporary-styled rooms have earthy neutral tones, modern compact bathrooms, fridges and a/c. ₺180
Kit-tur Arif Bey Cad 2 ☎0454 212 0245, ⊛otelkittur .com. Beyond the bland, ageing exterior, just off the main coastal highway, lies a well-managed hotel, offering good-value rooms with a/c and clean bathrooms. There's a large top-floor restaurant as well as a rooftop terrace, perfect for a sunset beer. ₺110
Yetimoğulları Eski Yagcilar Sok ☎0454 218 5698. The pick of central Giresun's many *pide* and kebab houses, this friendly and well-managed restaurant boasts menus – a rarity hereabouts – detailing a range of soups, appetizers, pizzas and meats cooked over hot coals, as well as a few salads. Mains ₺4–12. Daily 9am–10pm.

Trabzon

No other Turkish city except İstanbul has exercised such a hold on the Western imagination as **TRABZON** (ancient Trebizond). Travel writers from Marco Polo to Rose Macaulay have been enthralled by the fabulous image of this quasi-mythical metropolis, long synonymous with intrigue, luxury, exotic customs and fairy-tale architecture. Today the celebrated gilded roofs and cosmopolitan texture of Trebizond are long gone, replaced by the blunt reality of a bustling, modern and initially disappointing Turkish provincial capital of over 400,000 people.

While modern Trabzon sprawls in all directions, its heart remains **Atatürk Alanı**. A plane- tree-shaded square ringed with tea gardens, restaurants and patisseries, it's now closed to traffic on two sides, which mercifully reduces the former necessity of making an Olympic-style sprint through traffic to reach it. To the west lie the two areas most worthy of exploration: the Bazaar and the Ortahisar district. A poke around their

9

cobbled alleyways will unearth tangible evidence of Trabzon's former splendour, as will a visit to the monastic church of **Aya Sofya**, home to some of Anatolia's most outstanding Byzantine frescoes.

Brief history

Trabzon was founded during the eighth century BC by colonists from Sinope and Miletus, attracted by the readily defensible high plateau or *trapeza* ("table" in ancient Greek) after which it was first named "Trapezus". Although the city prospered under both the Romans and Byzantines, Trabzon's romantic allure derives almost exclusively from its brief, though resplendent, golden age during the thirteenth and fourteenth centuries, when, after the sacking of Constantinople, it became the capital of the breakaway **Trapezuntine Empire**. Its wealth grew when the main Silk Route was diverted this way because Mongol raiders controlled territory further south.

Someone had to transport all the goods that accumulated at Trebizond's docks, and this turned out to be the **Genoese**, followed soon after by the Venetians as well. Each demanded and won the same maritime trading privileges from the Trapezuntine Empire as they received from the re-established empire at Constantinople. Western ideas and personalities arrived continually with the boats of the Latins, making Trebizond an unexpected island of art and erudition in a sea of Turkish nomadism, and a cultural rival to the Italian Renaissance city-states of the same era.

Unfortunately, the empire's factional politicking was excessive even by the standards of the age. One civil war in 1341 completely destroyed the city and sent the empire into its final decline. It was Mehmet the Conqueror, in a campaign along the Black Sea shore, who finally put paid to the self-styled empire; in 1461 the last emperor, David, true to Trapezuntine form, negotiated a more or less bloodless surrender to the sultan.

In late Ottoman times the population and influence of the city's Christian element enjoyed a resurgence. The presence of a rich merchant class ushered in a spate of sumptuous civic and domestic building. But it was a mere echo of a distant past, soon ended by a decade of world war, the foundation of the Republic, and the steady transference of trade from ship to rails.

Today the outlook for Trabzon remains uncertain. While both port and town have been overtaken by Samsun to the west, Trabzon now benefits from the transshipment of goods to the Caucasian republics and onwards to Russia.

The bazaar

Usually entered via the pedestrianized Kunduracılar Cad, northwest of Atatürk Alanı

Trabzon's crowded bazaar streets are perfect for aimless wandering, with an interesting mix of rickety wooden shops, air-conditioned Western-style shops, and the odd restored old building. Despite the name, just about everything *except* shoes can be found on "Shoemakers' Street", **Kunduracılar Caddesi**, with a special emphasis first on pharmacies and doctors, then gold jewellery. Once past Cumhuriyet Caddesi, Kunduracılar veers right to become **Semerciler Caddesi** (Saddlers' Street), devoted to a mix of factory-made clothing and the vibrantly coloured, striped *keşan*s (shawls) and *peştemal*s (waistbands) that are standard issue for the older generation of Trabzon-province women. Most young women now spurn the traditional dress for more contemporary fashion, and the *keşan* has been incorporated into items such as cushion covers, handbags and oven gloves. Copper merchants and tin-platers cluster on and just off Alacahan Sokak, which leads downhill from Semerciler to the water.

Sooner or later you'll stumble upon the monumental heart of the bazaar, and the **Çarşı Camii**, Trabzon's largest mosque, with a handsome exterior and late Ottoman interior. Just behind it, the sixteenth-century **Taş Han** is a rather standard tradesmen's hall that still holds retail outlets and (inside the courtyard) tailors' workshops.

The **Bedesten**, below the mosque, was built by the Genoese in the fourteenth century, and revamped by the Ottomans. After decades of dereliction, and use as a lumber mill, it has been restored as a somewhat touristy crafts bazaar, with a small café-restaurant on the top floor.

Trabzon Museum

Zeytinlik Cad 10, just south of Uzun Sok ☎ 0462 322 3822 • Tues–Sun 9.30am–noon & 1–5pm • ₺3

One of Trabzon's finest *belle époque* mansions, the Italian-designed (and originally Greek-owned) Kostaki Theophylaktos Konağı now houses the **Trabzon Museum** (Trabzon Müzesi). While crying out for a little maintenance and a lot of dusting, the ground- and first-floor rooms, with their parquet floors, painted ceilings, fancy drapes and plush armchairs, nonetheless give a wonderful idea of life among the Ottoman bourgeoisie with displays of glitzy furniture, silverware and antiques. Pride of place in the basement, which is devoted to a mildly interesting archeological collection, belongs to a complete but slightly crushed bronze, human-sized statue of Hermes unearthed in 1997.

Yeni Cuma Camii

Camii Sok, 300m south of Yavuz Selim Bul

The thirteenth-century mosque of **Yeni Cuma Camii** was formerly the church of St Eugenius, patron saint of Trabzon. Mehmet the Conqueror offered up his first Friday prayers here after capturing Trabzon in 1461, and immediately re-consecrated the church and added its minaret. Built of a faded white ashlar stone, it has a graceful cupola and a floor of exquisite mosaic tiling. Its high vantage point offers splendid views over Trabzon's old town.

The old town

West of the pedestrianized Uzun Sokak, the gorge known as the **Tabakhane Deresi** (Tannery Ravine) is spanned by a namesake bridge offering access to Trabzon's fortified old town. The best place to get a sense of the city's history, the heart of the old town is the Ortahisar (Middle Castle) Quarter. The birthplace of Suleyman the Magnificent, the neighbourhood is built over two tunnels that date back to Byzantine times, and is dotted with fine examples of Ottoman architecture. The city-backed Ortahisar Project aims to turn the district into an "island of culture", through the restoration of some 140 historic houses. The walls are in variable condition but at their crenellated and vine-shrouded best give some idea of Trabzon's skyline in its heyday.

Ortahisar Camii

Corner of Zağnos Cad and Kale Sok

Also referred to as the Fatih Camii, the golden-domed **Ortahisar Camii** was formerly the church of Panayia Khrysokefalos. As the main cathedral of the Trapezuntine Empire, this was the venue for most royal weddings, funerals and coronations. While a church almost certainly stood on this site from the third century, the present building dates mostly from the thirteenth, with major renovation after a fire during the 1341 civil war. Some fine Byzantine *opus sectile* stonework remains visible in the apse, but it's the sheer volume of the soaring basilica, with its massive interior columns, that impresses.

Zağnos bridge and tower

Built by a Greek convert who was one of Mehmet the Conqueror's chief generals, the **Zağnos bridge** leaves Ortahisar across the Kuzgun ravine, where dilapidated Greek mansions are steadily losing ground to contemporary tenements. Down below, the municipality pulled down some *gecekondus* (informal housing) and has laid out a park and amphitheatre. On the far side, the **Zağnos tower**, the southernmost dungeon in the outer boundary walls, sports the ornate, late Ottoman, Abdullah Paşa fountain at its base.

9

Gülbahar Hatun Camii

Junction of Şenul Güneş Cad, Soğuksu Cad and Yavuz Selim Bul

The **Gülbahar Hatun Camii**, the most important Ottoman monument in Trabzon, squats across a busy boulevard and a swathe of parkland from the Zağnos tower. Sultan Selim the Grim, father of Suleyman the Magnificent, who served as Trabzon's governor between 1490 and 1512, built this mosque in 1514 in honour of his mother, once a Byzantine princess. It was originally part of a greater complex that included a *medrese*, soup kitchen and hamam, but only the latter is easily distinguishable today, located under the largest of the building's five domes. Entered through a portico with marble columns, the prayer hall – still in use – includes a simple altar and pulpit made from marble, while a minaret outside has an unusual eight-sided base.

Next to the complex there's a huddle of teahouses and a lake filled with swans.

The Atatürk Köşkü

Soğuksu Cad, 6.5km southwest of Atatürk Alanı • Daily 8am–5pm • ₺3 • ☎ 0462 231 0028 • Catch a dolmuş marked "Köşk", or a red-and-white city bus marked "Park-Köşk", from a bus park on Sahil Yolu Cad

Set in immaculate gardens in the cooler, higher reaches above Trabzon, the **Atatürk Köşkü**, or Atatürk Villa, began life in 1903 as the property of the Greek banker Karayannidhis, who was obliged to abandon it two decades later. Atatürk stayed here on the first of three occasions in 1924, and the city formally presented it to him a year before his death. As an example of patrician Black Sea architecture, the whitewashed, wooden mansion is more compelling than the contents – which include a bevy of photos of Atatürk, plus a map bearing his strategic scribbles during the Kurdish Dersim revolt of 1937. A tea garden within the grounds offers splendid views.

Aya Sofya

D010 coastal highway, 3km west of Trabzon • March Tues–Sun 9am–5pm; April–Oct daily 9am–6pm; Nov–Feb Tues–Sun 9am–4pm • ₺ • Numerous dolmuşes from Atatürk Alanı, labelled "BLK Sigorta/Aya Sofya", drop passengers 300m south of Aya Sofya

The monastery **church of Aya Sofya** (Haghia Sophia) ranks among Turkey's most romantic clusters of Byzantine remains. It seems certain that there was a pagan temple here, and then an early Byzantine chapel, long before Manuel I Komnenos commissioned the present structure between 1238 and 1263. The ground plan and overall conception were revolutionary at the time, successfully assimilating most of the architectural trends, Christian and Muslim, prevalent in contemporary Anatolia. Converted to a mosque after 1461, Aya Sofya subsequently endured leaner and more ignominious times as an ammunition store and then as a hospital during the Russian occupation in World War I, before it was restored in the early 1960s.

The church

The **church** is laid out along a greatly modified cross-in-square scheme, with a dome supported by four columns and three apses at the east end of the triple nave. Before you rush inside to view the famous frescoes, take a moment to study the finely sculpted, albeit weatherworn, **frieze** illustrating *Adam and Eve in the Garden of Eden*, the only one of the three friezes that adorn the south portal that wasn't tampered with by the Ottomans when they re-consecrated the church.

In their fluidity, warmth and expressiveness, Aya Sofya's original **frescoes** represented a drastic break with the rigidity of earlier painting, and compare well with the best work of their century, and the next, in Serbia and Macedonia as well as in Constantinople itself. Of the frescoes in the central **apse**, a serene *Ascension* hovers over *The Virgin Enthroned* between the two Archangels; on the north wall of the same apse appears *The Miraculous Draught of Fishes*. The southeast apse is thought to have once held Manuel I's tomb. The Pantocrator in the **dome** was unhappily beyond repair, but a host of angels swirls around him, just above the Apostles.

FROM TOP AYA SOFYA, TRABZON (P.524); COASTAL DRIVE SİNOP (PP.513–516);

9

The **narthex**, whose ceiling is divided into three sections by stone ribs, is almost wholly devoted to scenes from the life of Christ. The central zone exploits its complicated quadruple vaulting by depicting each of the Tetramorphs, symbols of the Evangelists, accompanied by seraphim. Alongside, such miraculous episodes as *The Wedding at Cana*, a decidedly adolescent *Child Jesus Teaching in the Temple*, *Healing the Blind Man at Siloam* and *Healing the Canaanite's Daughter* (complete with vomited demon) fill the south vault, while *Feeding the Five Thousand* and *Calming the Storm on the Lake of Galilee* grace the north vault. The north portico is taken up mostly by Old Testament scenes, including *The Sufferings of Job* and *Jacob's Dream*. Between 1957 and 1964, technicians restored dozens of these frescoes to their former glory. Well lit – no flash photography is allowed – and accurately labelled in English, these are compulsory viewing even if you've only a passing interest in religious art.

Church grounds

An ensemble of sunken masonry just north of the church was once the baptismal font; the square belfry to the west is a 1443 afterthought, indicative of the strong Italianate flavour of the waning empire. If the tower is open – a rare event – you'll find that the frescoes within are not nearly of the same quality as those in the church proper.

The small **museum** consists of a village house built and furnished in typical Black Sea style, and a 1920s-vintage *serender* or grain crib on stilts, with wooden discs at the top of the stilts, to prevent mice attacking the stored grain. Adjacent to that is a gift shop and pleasant café, covered in wisteria and offering tea and snacks, including the popular local dish *muhlama*, a Black Sea-style cheese fondue.

The shoreline

An east–west walk along the seaward portion of Trabzon begins with the city's Genoese bastion, a tea garden and small park on the west flank of the castle. This seems to be Trabzon's sole acknowledgement of its seafront location, since – apart from the busy Russian market on Sahil Yolu – the shoreline in general is quiet, with the city introverted up on its plateau.

Sankta Maria

A few alleys south of the bastion • Open for Sunday masses, plus, for viewing, Tues–Sat 2–3pm

The **Catholic church of Sankta Maria** is the last surviving reminder of the Western powers' former pivotal role. It was built in 1854 by Italian Capuchin monks expelled from Russia by Czar Nicholas I, though the current building largely dates from an 1874 rebuild. The church has recently experienced bouts of intolerance; its sixty-year-old Italian priest was killed in an armed attack in 2006, while locals threatened to take down its cross in 2011. It still provides Sunday services for a small local congregation.

Boztepe

1.5km south of Atatürk Alanı, off Taksim Cad • Catch a dolmuş from Atatürk Alanı

Boztepe, the hill that dominates Trabzon to the southeast, has always been held in religious esteem. In ancient times, it was holy to the amalgamated cults of the Persian sun god Mithra and the Hellenic deity Apollo – ironic when you consider how little unfiltered sun this coast receives. That reverence persisted into the Christian era, when the hill was studded with churches and monasteries. Near the park's summit are an appealing **picnic park**, a **tea garden** and restaurant that share the view over the city with a military base, and the locked **mosque and tomb of Ahi Evren Dede**, a target of pilgrimage for Trabzon's faithful.

ARRIVAL AND DEPARTURE   **TRABZON**

BY PLANE

Trabzon Airport The airport (☎0462 325 9952), 7km

from the centre at the eastern edge of town, is served by taxis (₺25) and frequent dolmuşes. Airport dolmuşes operate from a rank on the coastal highway, 500m south of the terminal; in town they're in a small plaza one block north of Atatürk Alanı, just off Sıramağazalar Cad near the *Horon Oteli*. A Havas shuttle bus meets all incoming flights, departing 25min after each flight's arrival, and runs to several city stops (30min; ₺5; ⊛ havas.net). Heading to the airport, it picks up from the most central stop, the Migros Supermarket on Yavuz Selim Bul, at 5.40am, 7.40am, 9.25am, 11.40am, 6.10pm and 8.50pm.

Tickets Agencies selling tickets for all carriers include Onur Air, Gazipaş Cad 18 (☎ 0462 325 6292); Pegasus, Atatürk Alanı (☎ 0462 3257 713); and THY, in front of the *Usta Park Hotel*, İskenderpaşa Mah 6–8 (☎ 0462 325 7536).

Destinations Adana (2 daily; 1hr 30min); Ankara (4 daily; 1hr 20min); Antalya (3 weekly; 1hr 50min); İstanbul Atatürk (up to 10 daily; 1hr 50min); İstanbul Sabiha Gökçen (up to 5 daily; 1hr 50min); İzmir (2 daily; 2hr 10min).

BY BUS

Bus terminal Trabzon's *otogar*, 3km east of Atatürk Alanı, near the junction of Highway 010 with Route E97/885 (heading towards Sumela and Erzurum), is served by dolmuşes marked "Meydanı". All long-distance coaches use this terminal, while some local lines leave from a small terminal opposite the Russian bazaar (heading west towards Görele), or another opposite the port (heading east towards Rize).

Destinations Ankara (10 daily; 12hr); Artvin (5 daily, may have to change at Hopa; 4hr); Baku, Azerbaijan (1 daily via Georgia; 24hr); Batumi, Georgia (3 daily; 3hr); Bayburt

(3–5 daily; 4hr 30min); Erzurum (6 daily; 5hr); Giresun (every 30min; 2hr 15min); Hopa (every 30min; 2hr 30min); İstanbul (8–10 daily; 17hr); İzmir (5 daily; 22hr); Of (every 30min; 45min); Posof, Georgian border (2–4 daily); Rize (every 30min; 1hr); Samsun (hourly; 7hr); Tbilisi, Georgia (3 daily; 12hr).

BY CAR

Parking Parking is a trial anywhere in congested Trabzon – the closest legal car park to the centre is by the tourist office, next to the İskender Paşa Camii.

Car rental In summer, when Trabzon swarms with locals returned from northern Europe, you need to book rentals in advance. Companies include: Avis, Gazipaşa Cad 20/A (☎ 0462 322 3740) and airport (☎ 0462 325 5582); Cande, Maraş Cad 9 (☎ 0462 323 3727); and Europcar, Cikmaz Sok 38 (☎ 0462 444 1399) and airport (☎ 0462 325 3424).

BY FERRY

Ferry services A number of companies on Iskele Caddesi offer ferry services between Trabzon and Sochi, Russia, including Asya Shipping (☎ 0462 321 6035) and Sari Denizcilik Marine (☎ 0462 326 2667). Passenger-only "speed" ferries take 6hr, slower vehicle-carrying services 14hr. Competition between Russian and Turkish companies has seen ticket costs decrease in recent years; the schedules are erratic as ever, but there's currently at least one service daily, departing Trabzon late afternoon.

Destinations Sochi, Russia (daily ferries; 14hr; €40–60 one way for a reclining seat).

INFORMATION AND TOURS

Tourist office Camii Sok, a side street just east of Atatürk Alanı, opposite the İskender Paşa Camii (officially Mon–Fri 9am–5pm, actual hours erratic; ☎ 0462 326 4760). The excellent fold-up map of Trabzon – which contains the phone numbers of every travel agent, campsite and mountain hut in the region – is just as helpful as the mostly

English-speaking staff.

Travel agency Ey-Ce Tours, İskenderpaşa Cad 36, first floor, opposite *Sağıroğlu Hotel* (☎ 0462 326 7174, ⊛ eycetours .com). Volkan Kantarci and his team offer day tours to Sumela, Ayder and assorted caves in the mountains, plus air tickets, car rental and independent drivers.

ACCOMMODATION

Atatürk Alanı, at the heart of Trabzon, is home to many of its hotels, nightclubs, restaurants and tourist sights, and is also the main transport hub for attractions further afield. That said, if you have transport, you might consider more peaceful stopovers on the way to Sumela, at Uzungöl. Book ahead in midsummer, when the more comfortable lodgings tend to be packed with tour groups. Steer clear of the red-light district, along İskele Caddesi and the streets immediately off it, right down to the port along Çömlekçi Caddesi.

Anil Güzelhisar Cad 12 ☎ 0462 326 7282. Down in the cheapie area towards the port, this budget travellers' favourite has an attractive foyer and breakfast salon, to accompany clean, plain a/c rooms, most with port views. It's rarely full and makes a safe option for late-night arrivals. **₺70**

Karayel Iskenderpasa Mah 8 ☎ 0462 321 2528. Renovated mid-range hotel, down a surprisingly quiet side

street but still very close to the action. The spacious rooms – some with balconies – have modern decor and wood-panelled floors, and come with a/c and bathrooms with screened, walk-in showers. On-site parking, and a small bar-restaurant. **₺130**

Nur Cami Sok 15 ☎ 0462 323 0445. Popular with budget travellers, the *Nur* offers small but clean en-suite rooms with

9

a/c, TV and fridge; request one on the upper floors to miss the street noise. The friendly English-speaking management are a good source of information for onward travel. ₺80

★ **TS Park** Meydan Cad 5 ☎0462 323 3141, ⓦtspark otel.com. Opened in 2011 in a renovated eighteenth-century building, across from Atatürk Alanı, the spacious rooms here are plain but very comfortable, though the bathrooms are relatively small. Breakfast is served in a small, wood-panelled restaurant with an open balcony directly overlooking the square. Triples and 4-bed family rooms available. Doubles ₺120, triples ₺170, family rooms ₺210

Usta Park Hotel İskenderpaşa Mah 6–8 ☎0462 326 5700, ⓦustaparkhotel.com. Large, plush hotel with

impressive plasma-screened lobby and workmanlike, rather than friendly, staff. The luxurious rooms are pricey, but discounts of up to fifty percent are easily negotiable or available online. There's an impressive buffet breakfast, and free basement parking and wi-fi. ₺280

Zorlu Grand Hotel Maraş Cad 9 ☎0462 326 8400, ⓦzorlugrand.com. Suitably plush rooms, with marble-clad bathrooms, but you're really paying for the facilities – especially the opulent atrium, two restaurants, "English pub", nightclub, gym, a very small indoor pool, and valet parking. Rack rates are massively overpriced, but advance booking/bargaining may produce discounts. ₺480

EATING AND DRINKING

Central Trabzon holds plenty of places to eat. Most are good value, but few are really outstanding. Apart from the establishments listed, alcohol in this conservative town is hard to come by, as is – surprisingly for a port – fish. The almost uninterrupted line of **restaurants** on the north side of Atatürk Alanı gets most of the tourist custom; the original lokantas are gradually making way for smarter places that appeal to the younger generation. There are many more restaurants along Uzun Sokak and around. Most restaurants offer at least some **desserts** – the confectioners of Hemşin (see box, p.533) aren't far away – but some exclusively sweet-dedicated venues are worth seeking out.

RESTAURANTS

Kalabalık Siramangazalar Cad 14 ☎0462 321 9555. Opened since 2000 and still slightly trendy – for Trabzon – this large, busy (and licensed) restaurant specializes in fine fish *mezes* including pickled sea bass and *hamsi* (anchovy), along with grilled and fried local seafood for mains. Mains ₺12–20. Daily noon–4pm & 7–10.30pm.

★ **Körfez** Sahil Yolu Cad, Liman Mevki, Akçaabat ☎0462 228 0150, ⓦkorfezkofte.com.tr. This local legend, 16km west of Atatürk Alanı, serves up authentic "Akçaabat *kofte*" in classy, easy-to-find surroundings overlooking the sea. While they serve *kofte* by the kilo, accompanied by crispy salads and fresh bread, lots of other meat and fish dishes are available too. Plenty of tables and a small children's playground, and the service, location and cuisine are worth the effort to get here. Mains ₺8–23. Daily 11.30am–10pm.

Murat Balık Salonu Atatürk Alanı 11. On the square's northern edge, this tiny hole-in-the-wall fish restaurant displays the day's catch in a glass cabinet. The bright green interior houses a few tables, often busy with locals enjoying an inexpensive and quickly served meal. Mains ₺5–11. Daily 11am–9pm.

Üstad Lokantası Atatürk Alanı 18. One of a number of small *lokantas* that surround the square, always popular with locals looking for a quick meal of typical *lokanta* fare – meatballs, kebab, bean stew – from ₺2 per dish. Daily 10am–10pm.

CAFÉS AND SWEET SHOPS

Beton Helva Uzun Sok 21, next to Seyitoğlu Lahmacun ☎0462 321 2550. Huge blocks of *helva* on display – thus

the somewhat off-putting name, "Concrete Helva" – but also good *dondurma* (ice cream) and *sıra* (half-fermented grape must), in wonderfully retro-1950s surroundings, owner/managed by a local family. Daily 9am–9pm.

Koza Caffé Kunduracılar Cad, Sanat Sok 1 ☎0462 321 0225. A first-floor café with a small balcony, serving a surprising array of coffees and teas as well as tasty sandwiches and pizza. Despite the ersatz castle interior it's a warm and welcoming place to while away a few hours. Coffee ₺2, pizza ₺3. Daily 11am–10pm.

★ **Masal** Uzun Sok 89 ☎0462 322 3857. An artsy first-floor hangout serving Trabzon's best coffee in comfortable surroundings, with colourful feature walls, high-backed leather studded chairs and low-lying lounges. There's also a small balcony overlooking the busy pedestrian street below. Comfort food such as burgers and fries is also served, and backgammon and board games available. Coffee ₺2–3.50. Daily 9am–11pm.

Selim Gazipaşa Cad 11/A ☎0462 385 4698. This modern and airy *pastanesi* sports comfortable chairs and leather sofas, is family friendly, and is a pleasant place to stop for *dondurma*, milk-based sweets, pastries and *boza* (a millet-based drink). The menu also offers a few heartier options, such as grilled chicken. Desserts ₺1.50–4, mains ₺4–8. Daily 8am–11pm.

BARS

Café Paris Yavuz Selim Bul 151 ☎0462 321 1188. Popular with Trabzon's young intelligentsia, this classy bar-café's welcoming interior includes antique-and art-adorned walls, comfortable seats and large-screen TVs. Breakfasts and light meals are served, backgammon boards nd nargiles (sheesha pipe) are available, and live acoustic music is played most weekends. In summer, a smattering of pavement tables are shaded by umbrellas. Beer ₺3, mains ₺4–9. Daily 9am–1am.

fes Pub Maraş Cad 5 ☎0462 326 6083. A surprisingly accurate, not to mention pleasant, rendition of an English pub on a busy side street off Atatürk Alanı. Great for enjoying both a draught beer and classic people-watching, the music here also thankfully takes a back seat to conversation. If it's too smoky inside, head upstairs to the shaded balcony. Draught beer ₺3 glass, ₺16 for a two-litre "tower". Daily noon–midnight.

DIRECTORY

Consulates Georgia, Ortahisar Mah Pertev Paşa Sok 10 ☎0462 323 1343 or 326 2226, ❷trabzon.con@mfa.gov .e); Russia, opposite Ortahisar Camii, Refik Cesur Cad 6 ☎0462 326 2600, ⓦturkey.mid.ru/eng/trabzon.html).

Hamam Much the best is the eight-pillared Sekiz Direkli Hamam, Pazarkapı 8, Direkli Hamam Sok 1 (daily 7am–5pm; women-only Thurs, men-only all other days; ₺9).

Hospitals The Özel Karadeniz (private), Reşadiye Cad ☎0462 229 7070, ⓦkaradenizhastanesi.com.tr), and SSK (Social Security), Trabzonspr Bul (☎0462 230 2285), are both out near Aya Sofya. However, the biggest hospital in the region is the KTÜ's medical-school teaching hospital, or Tip Fakültesi Hastanesi, opposite the airport on Sahil Yolu Caddesi (☎0462 325 3011 or 377 5000) – buses and dolmuşes marked "KTÜ" run from the centre.

Police Tourism Police, by the harbour customs-zone gate, and on the east side of Atatürk Alanı (daily 9am–7pm; ☎0462 326 3077).

Post office PTT at Posthane Sok, corner of Kahraman Maraş Cad (post and exchange daily 8am–7pm); also a booth at southeast corner of Atatürk Alanı. Payphones and card sales on the south side of Atatürk Alanı.

The monastery of Sumela

At the start of the Byzantine era, a large number of **monasteries** sprang up in the mountains behind Trabzon. The most important and prestigious – and today the best preserved – was **Sumela** (increasingly signposted as Sümela), which clings to a cliff-face nearly a thousand feet above the Altındere valley, 46km south of Trabzon, in precisely the sort of setting that has always appealed to Greek Orthodox monasticism. Despite the usual crowds, often rainy or misty weather, and the rather battered condition of its frescoes, Sumela still rates as one of the mandatory excursions along the Black Sea.

If you don't have your own vehicle, you can make the hour-long journey to Sumela from Trabzon by taxi or on a tour. However you arrive, aim to spend at least three hours at the site, allowing for a good look around and a spot of lunch by the rapids which flow through the valley below. The monastery itself is linked to the valley floor

---

CROSSING TO RUSSIA, GEORGIA, ARMENIA AND AZERBAIJAN

At present, all non-Turkish travellers need to buy a **visa for Russia** in order to pass from Turkey into Russia. The Trabzon consulate (see p.529) currently issues visas to European Union passport holders, but no others (Australia, Canada, New Zealand and the US included). Visas cost US$70 (3-day wait) or US$120 (same day), and passport holders need to complete an application form (available at the consulate), invitation or proof of accommodation, and proof of medical insurance.

Trans-Black Sea services to Russia (Sochi) have increased in frequency over recent years; contact one of the ferry agencies in Trabzon (see p.527) for current information.

Citizens of most countries, including Australia, Canada, EU, New Zealand and the US, may enter **Georgia** visa-free for up to 360 days. From İstanbul, both Azerbaijan Airlines and Turkish Airlines offer regular **flights to Baku** in Azerbaijan.

Overland **bus services** have been less affected, with several services a day running over the border to Batumi. The Georgian frontier can be crossed either at **Sarp**, or at **Posof**, for onward connections to Armenia and Azerbaijan (see p.527). It's easy enough to do the trip to Georgia in smaller chunks, taking a dolmuş or taxi from Sarp to the border and then arranging local transport on to Batumi on the Georgian side, from where several daily buses run to Armenia.

9

by a newly paved road, as well as a commonly used, recently widened and often
slippery woodland trail (30min).

Brief history

The name "Sumela" is a Pontic Greek shortening and corruption of *Panayia tou Melas*
or "Virgin of the Black (Rock)". She has been venerated on this site since at least
385 AD, when the Athenian monk Barnabas, acting on a revelation from the Mother
of God, discovered an **icon** here said to have been painted by St Luke. He and his
nephew Sophronios found the holy relic on a site that matched the one in his vision –
a cave on a narrow ledge, partway up the all-but-sheer palisade – and installed it in a
shrine inside.

A **monastery** supposedly grew around the image as early as the sixth century, but
most of what's visible today dates from the thirteenth and fourteenth centuries. Over
the centuries the icon was held responsible for countless miracles, and the institution
that housed it shared its reputation, prompting even Turkish sultans to make
pilgrimages and leave offerings.

Six years after Sumela was hastily evacuated in 1923, along with all other Greek
Orthodox foundations in the Pontus, it was gutted by fire, possibly started by careless
squatters. In 1931 one of the monks returned secretly and exhumed various treasures,
including the revered icon of the Virgin, now housed in the new monastery of Sumela,
in northern Greece. Since 1996, the monastery has been undergoing **restoration**. The
work done thus far is in reasonable taste, extending to proper ceramic canal-tiles for the
roof. Most important of all, the surviving frescoes have been consolidated and cleaned.

The site

Daily: May–Sept 9am–6pm; Oct–April 9am–5pm • ₺8

However you reach Sumela, all paths converge at the **ticket booth** by the monastery
gate. The building itself actually occupies a far smaller patch of level ground than its
five-storey facade would suggest. A climb up the original entry stairs – lacking hand
rails and slightly hazardous after rain – followed by an equivalent drop on the far side
of the gate, deposits you in the central courtyard, with the monks' cells and guest hostel
on your right overlooking the brink, and the chapel and cave sanctuary to the left.
Reconstruction of most of the former living areas is complete, though there are still a
number of off-limits areas and unsightly scaffolding. The degree of vandalism and
decay is appalling: sophisticated art thieves were caught levering away large slabs of the
famous frescoes in 1983, and any within arm's reach have been obliterated by graffiti-
scrawlers. While much of the graffiti is pre-1923 vintage Greek, Turkish, European and
North American visitors have also left their marks.

The main grotto-shrine is closed off on the courtyard side by a wall, from which
protrudes the apse of a smaller chapel. A myriad of **frescoes** in varying styles covers
every surface, the earliest and best dating from the fourteenth or fifteenth centuries,
with progressively less worthwhile additions and retouchings done in 1710, 1740 and
1860. The highest cave paintings are in good condition – ceilings being harder to
vandalize – though the irregular surface makes for some odd departures from Orthodox
iconographic conventions. The Pantocrator, the Mother of God and various apostles
seem to float overhead in space; on the south (left) wall is an archangel and various
scenes from the Virgin's life (culminating in *The Virgin Enthroned*), while *Jonah in the
Whale* can be seen at the top right.

Outside on the divider wall, most of the scenes from the life of Christ are hopelessly
scarred. Among the more distinct is a fine *Transfiguration*, about 3m up on the right;
just above sits *Christ in Glory*, with two versions of the *Ascension* nearby. At the top
left is *Christ Redeeming Adam and Eve*. On the apse of the tiny chapel, the *Raising
of Lazarus* is the most intact image. Next to it is the *Entry into Jerusalem*, with the
Deposition from the Cross just right of this. On the natural rock face north of all this

ppears the *Communion of Saints in Paradise*. When craning your neck to ogle the surviving art gets too tiring, there is (mist permitting) always the spectacular view over the valley – and the process of imagining what monastic life, or a stay in the wayfarers' quarters, must have been like here in Sumela's prime.

Throughout the site, English-language signage is erratic and poorly translated, at best. No guides are available for hire at the site, but tours from Trabzon should include an English-speaking guide in the cost; check before you book.

ARRIVAL AND DEPARTURE

THE MONASTERY OF SUMELA

Taxis These leave from a rank signposted "Sumela Manastırı'na" on the south side of Atatürk Alanı, charging ₺120 return for a carload of four people.

Organized tours Ey-Ce Tours, İskenderpaşa Cad 36, first floor, opposite *Sağıroğlu Hotel* (**0**0462 326 7174, **w** eycetours.com), offer tours, run at 10am daily, bookable in person or through your hotel, and costing ₺25 per person for a return minibus seat (you pay the admission fee).

By car The main car park lot for Sumela, a 10min walk below the monastery itself, is 43km from the coastal junction of highways 010 and E97/885, 3.5km east of

central Trabzon. Turn off Highway E97/885 at Maçka, 26km along, and follow the Altındere valley upstream. This side road provides a stunning approach to the monastery; as you climb, the habitual cloud ceiling hereabouts drifts down from the equally dense fir forest to meet you. In exceptional circumstances you may catch an advance glimpse of the monastery's faded, whitewashed flank soaring above the trees at the top of the valley, at an altitude of 1200m. A few kilometres before you reach the site, a tollbooth signifies the start of the national park (₺20 per private car).

ACCOMMODATION AND EATING

Most overnight visitors stay in the village of Maçka, which holds a few decent hotels and restaurants. In addition, the road from Maçka up to Sumela is littered with trout farms and campsites, including the rustic *Verizana* and *Sumelas* campsite-cum-restaurants, 2km and 7km past Maçka respectively. A few hundred metres below the monastery, by the old car park, you'll find a shop, restaurant and picnic area, all scattered around the teeming rapids that mark the valley floor.

Büyük Sümela Attatürk Cad, Maçka **0**0462 512 3540, **w** sumelaotel.com. The main hotel offers over a

hundred spacious rooms with carpeted floors, heating, and large modern bathrooms. The faux-antique decor throughout borders on garish, however. They also have seven Swiss-style wooden chalets with cosy interiors and wood-burning stoves, a necessity almost year-round at these altitudes. Service in the licensed restaurant over the bridge can be abrupt, but the fish, *meze* and meat dishes (₺7–23) are reasonable and tasty, perhaps surprisingly so, given how many tour groups pass through. Chalet ₺195, room ₺225

Inland: the Eastern Kaçkar foothills

While Sumela is a hard act to follow, several other enticing destinations lie scattered in the **foothills** that stretch inland between Trabzon and Rize. The valleys that lead to and past them also make useful alternative routes toward Erzurum, avoiding some or all of the often congested E97/885 Highway.

Of

The coastal starting point for excursions up the valley of the Solaklı Çayı is the unprepossessing **OF** (pronounced "oaf", the ancient Ophis). Both Of and **Çaykara**, 27km south, the unexciting main town of the lower valley, are renowned for their devoutness, with the highest ratio of *kuran kursu*s (Koran schools for children) per capita in the country, and phalanxes of bearded and skull-capped *hoca*s and *hacı*s striding about in the shadow of huge, ever-multiplying mosques. It should come as no surprise, then, that you haven't a prayer of anything stronger than a fruit juice between Of and Uzungöl.

Uzungöl Lake

8km southeast of Çaykara

The trip to **Uzungöl** (Long Lake) is the second most popular excursion out of Trabzon, after Sumela. Were it not for the mosques, you could be in Switzerland. The scenic

9

lake, at just under 1100m, has a bazaar district around its outlet and is best seen by renting a mountain bike from one of the teashops.

Uzungöl makes an ideal base for rambles southeast up to the nearby peaks of **Ziyaret** (3111m) and **Halizden** (3376m), with a chain of glacier lakes at the base of the latter. It's a very long day's hike there and back – though you can go partway by car to save time – so take a tent and food for two days if at all possible.

The İkizdere Valley

While the **İkizdere Valley**, the next major valley east of Uzungöl, holds no specific attractions, the scenery along the way is memorable, and the road eventually winds up to the highest drivable pass in the Pontic ranges – one of the three loftiest in all Turkey. The place is mostly worth knowing about as an alternative route to Erzurum, or as an approach to the Kaçkar range (see p.556).

İKİZDERE, the main town in the valley, is the transfer point for the 27km trip up the Yetimhoca valley to **Başköy**, the westernmost trailhead for the Kaçkar Dağları. Watch out, though: at least three other Başköys or Başyaylas lie within a 30km radius, so don't let yourself or your driver get confused. A better alternative, if possible, is to arrange transfer to **Saler**, the highest village in the valley with road access.

Beyond İkizdere, the main road soon finds itself between jagged peaks and the *yaylas* gathered at the 2640m **Ovitdağı pass** (closed Nov–April), marking the edge of Rize province and far more alpine than the overrated Zigana Pass to the west. On the way up, you'll pass various grill and trout restaurants.

ARRIVAL AND DEPARTURE INLAND: THE EASTERN KAÇKAR FOOTHILLS

UZUNGÖL LAKE

By dolmuş Frequent dolmuşes make the trip up from Of (1hr 30min).

By tour bus Trabzon travel agencies (see p.527) organize daily tours, on demand (about ₺20 a head, transport only).

İKİZDERE

By bus A varying number of daily minibuses connect İkizdere with Rize; their frequency increases at weekends, especially in summer. Between May and October, the odd minibus travels from İspir on the southern side of the range.

ACCOMMODATION AND EATING

UZUNGÖL LAKE

In line with its mushrooming popularity both with Arabic-speaking tourists (most hotels don't serve alcohol) and with foreigners overnighting en route to or from Trabzon airport, Uzungöl Lake holds fifteen or so hotels, all similar in both style – easy-on-the-eye wooden exteriors – and value, as well as a handful of *pansiyons*. Weekends and school holidays are very busy, so book ahead.

Ensar Motel Fatih Cad 18, opposite İnan Kardeşler Tesisleri ☏ 0462 656 6321, ✍ ensarotel.com. One of the more upmarket hotels, with a welcoming feel, friendly management and good traditional cuisine. Choose from wooden bungalows with separate bathroom and living room, and en-suite doubles with (you guessed it) wooden interiors, arranged around small fountains. Rooms ₺180, bungalows ₺205

İnan Kardeşler Tesisleri Uzungöl Golbasi Cad, at the high south end of the lake ☏ 0462 656 6260, ✍ inankardeslerotel.com. The oldest hotel in town, a

pretty combination of trout farm/restaurant/hotel offering spacious all-wood rooms with balconies or chalet-style bungalows, and a canteen-like restaurant that serves excellent breakfasts, overlooking a gurgling stream. Rooms ₺185, bungalows ₺190

İKİZDERE

Hanci'nin Yeri At the northern entrance to town ☏ 0464 425 1295. This friendly, unlicensed restaurant with tables overlooking the often raging river, serves delicious and good-sized portions of *köfte* and grilled chicken cooked over glowing hazelnut shells. Mains ₺5–9. Daily 11am–10pm.

Ridos Beside the river, 800m above town ☏ 0464 41 2159, ✍ ridosotel.com.tr. This concrete hotel offers carpeted, well-appointed rooms with fantastic views, plus a string of newer villas, with more contemporary furnishings, across the river. Rooms ₺180, villas ₺270

THE HEMŞINLIS AND YAYLAS

With their fair skin and strong features, the people of the Hemşin valleys, known as the **Hemşinlis**, tend to look more Caucasian than Turkish. According to competing theories, these outgoing, gregarious people are either ethnic Armenians who arrived here at or before the time of the Georgian kingdoms, or natives descended from the Heptacomete tribesmen of old, who, through contact with "true" Armenians, adopted a dialect of Armenian and were nominally Christian or pagan until the early nineteenth century. Although most Hemşinlis are now Muslim, they wear their religion lightly: you're unlikely to be blasted out of bed at dawn by a muezzin around here, and, despite stern little signs in local shops warning that "alcohol is the mother of all ills", the men in fact are prodigious drinkers. This tendency is aggravated by the **environment**. This is by far the dampest and mistiest part of Turkey, with the sun in hiding two days out of three and up to 500cm annually of rain in some spots. The result is cloud-forest vegetation, with everything from moss-fringed fir and alders down to marsh species and creeping vines clinging to the slopes.

Hemşinlis are renowned for being intrepid and independent. They also have a special genius for the profession of pastry chef and pudding-maker: the top **sweet shops** (*pastanes*) of major Turkish cities are usually owned and/or staffed by natives of these valleys. But to fully understand the Hemşin mentality you need to visit at least one *yayla*, or summer pastoral hamlet.

Yaylas are found in the uplands throughout Turkey, but in the Kaçkar in general – and especially Hemşin – they're at their best. Tightly bunched groups of dwellings, usually stone-built to waist height, and chalet-style in timber thereafter, albeit with metal roofs, they begin just at the tree line and recur at intervals up to 2700m. They're inhabited only between late May and early September, when the snow recedes. Their tenants come from as far away as Holland or Germany to renew attachments to what they consider their true spiritual homeland. Traditional **summer activities** include making yoghurt, butter and cheese, and (increasingly) catering to trekkers' needs.

The Hemşin valleys

The most scenic and interesting of the foothill regions east of Trabzon are the valleys of the **Fırtına Çayı** and its tributaries, which tumble off the steepest slopes of the Pontic ranges, here known as the Kaçkar Dağları. Between the mountains and the sea lie a few hundred square kilometres of rugged, isolated territory known simply as **Hemşin**.

Çamlıhemşin

ÇAMLIHEMŞİN, 21km upstream from the mouth of the Fırtına Çayı, may at 300m be too low to give a real feel for the Hemşin country, but it offers a hint of what's to come. The last proper town before the mountains, it's utilitarian and busy. A constant chaos of minibuses and shoppers clogs its single high street, which holds a bank with an ATM, a PTT, and stores for last-minute hiking supplies.

To either side of Çamlıhemşin, along both the main stream and the tributary flowing down from Ayder, you begin to see some of the two dozen or so graceful humpbacked **bridges** that are a regional speciality.

The upper Fırtına valley

Above Şenyuva, along the main branch of the Fırtına Çayı, the road steadily worsens while the scenery just as relentlessly grows more spectacular. Below, the water roils in chasms and whirlpools that are irresistible to the lunatic fringe of the rubber-rafting fraternity – as well as the central government which, in the face of local opposition, plans to divert most of the river's flow into assorted hydroelectric projects.

The single-towered castle of **Zilkale**, improbably sited by either the Byzantines or the Genoese to control a decidedly minor trade route, appears at a bend in the track

9

A SHORT TREK: POKUT AND AMLAKIT

If your level of commitment isn't up to multi-day treks that require you to camp out in the high mountains, consider the track that heads southeast from **Şenyuva**, a typically dispersed community of occasionally impressive farmstead dwellings 6–8km above Çamlıhemşin. The best accommodation here is at *Fırtına Pansiyon* (see p.536).

Beyond Şenyuva, the route is blocked by snow for much of the year, so it's only advisable during high summer. **Pokut**, a 3hr walk from Şenyuva via Sal, is fairly representative of the more substantial Black Sea *yayla*s, with handsome woodwork capped by mixed tin-and-timber roofs rising from stone foundations. For the first night's lodging, try *Poket Yaylasi* (see p.536).

The following day you hike east to **Hazindag** (Hazıntak), a handsomely clustered settlement just above the tree line, then briefly follow a majestic river canyon on a corniche route south before veering up and southeast to the primitive rock-and-sod cottages of **Samistal**. Weather permitting, the ridge above Samistal offers spectacular views of the main Kaçkar summit ridge. You then double back west to **Amlakit**, with its *Pansiyon*, or drop in stiff zigzags from Samistal to Aşağı Kavron, which is linked by minibuses to Ayder (see p.535).

If you stay in Amlakit, a final day of walking would see you use a direct trail north to Hazindag and thence back to Pokut and Sal (there's a steep path northeast through cloud forest direct to Ayder, but it's presently in bad condition). Alternatively, keener trekkers can carry on south from Amlakit for 45min on a rough road to Palovit (2300m), and thence to Apevanak Yayla (2500m) en route to the true alpine zone.

12.5km beyond Çamlıhemşin. This tree-tufted ruin, more often than not garnished with wisps of mist, now dominates nothing more than one of the most evocative settings in the Pontus.

Çat

ÇAT, a classic base for rambles in the western Kaçkar, is located 1250m up, 16km worth of violent abuse to your vehicle's suspension beyond Zilkale. There's little to the village itself apart from a few scattered buildings and a final, exquisite bridge leading upstream, where the upper reaches of the Fırtına divide. One turning bears almost due east, to Elevit, while the road that runs parallel to the main fork of the river heads 30km due south to Ortayayla or Başhemşin. On the way is Zilkale's sister fort of **Varoş** (Kale-i-Bala) at Kaleköy, where yet another side road winds up to an alternative trailhead for the western Kaçkar mountains at Kale Yayla.

Elevit

The village of **ELEVIT**, 5km east of Çat, is a surprisingly substantial Laz *yayla* within Hemşin territory. It's high enough (1800m) to make a good trek from Çat, though there is only very basic food and lodgings available. The road surface from Çat is perennially poor, and Elevit marks the end of the road for ordinary cars. Only daily minibuses and 4WD vehicles continue east to Karunç, Tirovit and Palovit.

Yıldızlı Göl

The most rewarding of several possible day-hikes that start near Elevit is the three-hour walk up to **Yıldızlı Göl** (Starry Lake), at the top of the vale that opens south of Elevit. You won't appreciate the name unless you camp overnight there, for just after sunrise little scintillating points of light flash briefly – for perhaps twenty minutes – on the surface of the water. With more substantial equipment, you can continue along a superb **three-day traverse** southwest across the western Kaçkar, taking in Başyayla, Çiçekliyayla, the 2800m-high lakes at the base of Tatos and Verçenik peaks – all potential campsites – and finishing at Başhemşin at the head of the Fırtına valley. If necessary, you can "bail out" at Çiçekliyayla, where a road leads out.

Ayder

The busiest road above Çamlıhemşin ends after 17km at **AYDER**, the highest permanently inhabited settlement in the Hemşin valley system. All cars have to pay a toll of ₺8 at km13.

Having long since abandoned the struggle to be a genuine village or *yayla*, Ayder now revels in its role as a mountain-ringed **spa resort**, packed with river-terrace restaurants and charming wooden bungalows. Of its two small *mahalles* or districts, **Birinci** (Lower) Ayder, at about 1250m, holds the spas, dolmuş stop, a few restaurants and small supermarkets, a PTT booth – although there are no banking facilities, so get any money you need in Pazar or Çamlıhemşin – and most of the considerable high-season noise and congestion. İkinci (Upper), better known as **Yukarı Ambarlık**, at about 1350m elevation, is much calmer and has most (but not all) of the more desirable accommodation.

While the surrounding scenery – a narrow, sharply inclined valley with waterfalls pouring off the sides – has always been the main attraction, roads are being pushed ever higher, so Ayder no longer rates as a genuine trekking trailhead. Every walk necessitates a minibus transfer: the two most important are the day-jaunt to the Çengovit lakes above the Laz *yayla* of Yukarı Avusor, and the three lakes above Kavron.

Ayder is also a showcase for Hemşinli culture (see box, p.533); displays of ethnic pride during August feature spontaneous outbreaks of *horon* (dancing), both on the central meadow and in many of the restaurants.

The hot-spring complex

Ayder Kaplıcaları Cad • Daily 7am–7pm • ₺8; private family tub rooms ₺25

Ayder boasts an old *kaplıcalar* or sulphurous modern **hot-spring complex**, a big crowd-puller for the town. It's fed by a communal *havuz* (pool) from which scalding water (close to 60°C) is piped into rectangular tiled pools. Separate sections cater for men and women, and more expensive private family tub rooms are available, as well as safe-boxes for your valuables.

ARRIVAL AND DEPARTURE
THE HEMSİN VALLEYS

ÇAMLIHEMSİN

By minibus Minibuses to Çamlıhemşin depart daily all year, rising in frequency to hourly in summer, from the coastal towns of Ardeşen and Pazar, and in summer, a few times daily from Rize as well.

ÇAT

By dolmuş Despite the horrid road in, a fairly regular dolmuş service – at least daily – connects Çat with Çamlıhemşin; it's more comfortable, however, to come by mountain bike or 4WD.

AYDER

By bus Minibuses connect Ayder with Pazar in season; you may have to change vehicles in Çamlıhemşin, where out of season you'll more than likely have to pay around ₺60 for a taxi. If you're heading back down to the coast from Ayder, Çamlıhemşin offers much more frequent departures to Rize and onward to Trabzon. You can descend from Ayder to catch the single daily minibus that heads up the Fırtına valley toward Çat and Elevit without having to return all the way to Pazar, but you'll need to be in Çamlıhemşin by noon or so. Destinations Pazar (mid-June to mid-Sept, hourly, 10am–6pm; 1hr); Rize (2 daily; 2hr).

TOURS

ÇAMLIHEMSİN

Türkü Tourism İnönü Cad 47 ☎0464 651 7230, ⊕turkutour.com. Owner-managed since 1992 by Mehmet Demirci, the region's most genial and knowledgeable mountain guide. With a team of local guides, including daughter Güneyce, Mehmet offers assorted year-round multi-day treks, either tent-based (camping equipment provided), farmhouse-based or *pansiyon*-based, as well as day tours around Ayder and various themed tours, such as 4WD, photography and wildlife.

ACCOMMODATION AND EATING

ÇAMLIHEMSİN

★ **Ekodanitap** Asagi Camlica Mah, off the southern entrance to Çamlıhemşin ☎0464 651 7787, ⊕ekodanitap.com. Enviro-friendly, peaceful and

9

family-run setup in the hills below Çamlıhemşin, with a choice of solar-powered accommodation in traditional Hemşin houses, Kalif granaries or tree houses. Meals are provided fresh from the organic garden, served in a communal open-sided terrace with stunning views. ₺95

ŞENYUVA

Fırtına Pansiyon Şenyuva, northern end of the village ☎ 0464 653 3111 or ☎ 0532 783 2708, ⟨w⟩ firtinavadisi .com. Located on a bend of the gurgling river, this welcoming, family-run *pansiyon* is housed in the former schoolhouse. Various different-sized rooms and bungalows are spread around the property; all are simply furnished but exceptionally clean, as are the shared bathrooms. Home-cooked meals are offered, as is free wi-fi. Half board only. ₺150

POKUT

Poket Yaylası In the heart of the yayla ☎ 0464 651 7530 or ☎ 0530 228 6620. This two-storey wooden guesthouse holds four spacious rooms that can accommodate up to four adults each. The bathroom is shared, and there's a communal kitchen or meals provided. Half board only. ₺110

AMLAKIT

Ufuk Pansiyon Southern (upper) edge of the yayla ☎ 0464 213 0914. A friendly all-wood *pansiyon* run by a husband-and-wife team, with rooms of varying different sizes spread over three chalets, sharing bathrooms. The large, communal dining room has sweeping views over the valley. Half board only. ₺130

ÇAT

Cancık In the village centre ☎ 0464 654 4120. The most conspicuous building in the village is a surprisingly good combination hotel/restaurant (and general store/souvenir shop), with six clean wood-trimmed rooms upstairs, several bungalows and a simple trout and grilled meat restaurant. Half board only. ₺110

Toşi Pension 1km downstream from Çat ☎ 0464 654 4002 or ☎ 0535 621 5215. The best fallback if the *Cancık* is full, this concrete building has a riverside terrace and restaurant, though the double, triple, quads and bungalows can get packed out by organized trek groups. ₺120

AYDER

Most accommodation options in Ayder are open between April and October only, though a handful remain in operation all year round. Showing up on an August weekend without a reservation is not recommended. As for

food, most visitors arrange half-board with their *pansiyons*. Local cuisine tends to be repetitive, although that's no bad thing as it's based largely on trout, salad and *muhlama* (a fondue-like dish of cheese, butter and cornflour), the last scooped up with corn bread.

Ayder Sofrası Ayder Yaylası Yolu, between Birinci and Yukarı Ambarlık ☎ 0464 657 2974. This large, central restaurant is also one of the few to have a licence, and can get quite busy. There are plenty of tables inside, but it's the wooden tables on the outside stone-walled terrace where you want to be, overlooking the river and with sweeping mountain views. There's an open breakfast buffet, and an *à la carte* menu that includes the regional specialities of trout, *muhlama* and *labana sarması* (stuffed cabbage). Breakfast ₺6, mains ₺5–14. Daily 9am–10pm.

Haşimoğlu Otel Ayder Kaplıcaları Cad, Birinci Ayder ☎ 0464 657 2037, ⟨w⟩ hasimogluotel.com. A large and luxurious hotel with friendly staff and good management, the wood-lined rooms and bungalows come in assorted sizes and with balconies; some also boast their own living rooms and stone fireplaces. It also holds restaurants and cosy communal areas with fireplaces, as well as an in-house jacuzzi, and it's a short walk to the kaplıcalar. Half board only. ₺270

★ **Kalegon Butik Otel** Ayder Yaylası Yolu, near the top of Yukarı Ambarlık ☎ 0464 657 2135, ⟨w⟩ ayderkalegon.com. A notch up from most hotels in Ayder, the *Kalegon* offers slick, Swiss-style wooden-panelled rooms with central heating, flat-screen TV, and modern bathrooms. There's also a cosy communal area with an open fire in winter, and an outdoor summer dining terrace. The restaurant, open to non-guests, serves an impressive menu of trout, salads and lamb (daily noon–10pm; mains ₺6–17), while the small bar has cold beer and can get lively, especially when the friendly owner organizes live folk music. ₺230

Kuşpuni Ayder Yaylası Yolu, signposted before Yukarı Ambarlık ☎ 0464 657 2052, ⟨w⟩ ayderkuspuniotel.com. Ayder's cutest establishment, open all year, the family-run "bird's nest" is more of a *pansiyon* than a hotel, with basic low-ceilinged rooms that vary from doubles to family suites, all with central heating and ageing bathrooms. The kitchen serves up delicious regional food – river trout, salads, *muhlama* and home-made desserts – in the stove-heated lounge or outside on a very pleasant terrace. Half board only. ₺170

Serender Pansiyon Near top of Yukarı Ambarlık ☎ 0464 657 2201. A cosy, female owner-managed *pansiyon* with typical wooden trim rooms (with wooden cubicle bathrooms) in varying formats. Located in a peaceful corner of the village, with lots of common sitting areas and a modern, self-catering kitchen. ₺120

The coast east of Trabzon

The coast **east of Trabzon** gets progressively more extreme as you approach the Georgian border – if the Black Sea coast as a whole is wet, here it's positively soggy. The mountains, shaggy with tea plants and hazelnut trees, begin to drop directly into the ocean – imposing natural defences which have led to the development of distinct ethnic groups such as the **Laz**.

Sadly, the coast route has remarkably little to offer travellers. The first decent, unpolluted beaches east of Trabzon are found between **Arakli** and **Sürmene**, the towns which in themselves are nothing to write home about. The same goes for the boatyards with their colourful, top-heavy *taka* fishing boats at **Çamburnu**, 3km east. A much-touted pay beach is tucked at the base of the cliff just beyond the port, but equally good, or better, free beaches line the road to Of.

Rize

A modern Turkish city of almost eighty thousand inhabitants, in a grand setting, **RİZE** will at least be a familiar name to every traveller who's bought a souvenir box of "Rize Turist Çay" to brew back home. Of its ancient history as Rhizos nothing survives, and of its role as the easternmost outpost of the Trapezuntine Empire hardly more than a tiny, eighth-century castle. The local university is named after Prime Minister Recep Tayyip Erdoğan, who was born in the nearby village of Güneysu.

Rize has two main streets, Atatürk Caddesi (inland) and Cumhuriyet Caddesi which runs parallel to the sea; the town square, **Belediye Parkı**, lies between them. The PTT here has been smartened up with wooden trimmings, complementing the two nineteenth-century restored **wooden houses** on the hill behind, one now housing a mildly interesting museum. East of the square, Rize's major **tea garden** is, not surprisingly, the focus of the town's social whirl. Surrounding shops sell Rize tea in every conceivable packaging, plus the unlikely spin-off product of tea cologne.

Sarı Evi Museum

Hlubatlı Cad, uphill behind the tourist office • Tues–Sun 9am–noon & 1–4pm • ₺3 • ☏ 0464 214 0235

The "Yellow House", a restored Ottoman mansion known locally as the Tuzcuoğulları Konağı, now holds the **Sarı Evi Museum**, focusing on local life. The upstairs rooms are lavishly decorated in the opulent Western style of the later Ottoman bourgeoisie, and there's also some interesting displays of the traditional dress worn by the coastal Laz and the inland-dwelling Hemşin.

TEA

Thanks to a climate that's perfectly suited to its cultivation, **tea** is king east of Trabzon. The tightly trimmed bushes are planted everywhere between sea level and about 600m, to the exclusion of almost all other crops. As picking the tender leaves is considered women's work, during the six warmer months women can be seen humping enormous loads of leaves in back-strap baskets to the nearest consolidation station. Each year, nearly a million raw tonnes of tea is sent more or less immediately to the cutting, fermenting and drying plants whose stacks are recurring regional landmarks.

Oddly enough, tea is a very recent introduction to the Black Sea, the pet project of one Asim Zihni Derin, who imported the first plants just before World War II to a region left badly depressed following the departure of its substantial Christian population in 1923. Within a decade or so, tea became the mainstay of the local economy, overseen by Çaykur, the state tea monopoly. Despite the emergence of private competitors since 1985, and the Chernobyl accident, which spread radiation over the 1986 crop, Çaykur is still a major player in the domestic market. Export, however, seems unlikely, as supply can barely keep pace with domestic demand.

9

A *serander*, traditionally used to store grain safely out of reach of rats, stands alongside the museum. Beside that, another restored mansion houses an uninteresting display on the machinations of tea production.

Tea Research Institute

Narenciye Sok, Ziraat, 1km south, and uphill, from central Rize • Daily 9am–10pm • Free • Served by "Ziraat" buses from Sarı Evi Museum (Mon–Fri 7am–noon, hourly on the hour) • ☎ 0464 213 0241

If the sight of all the surrounding tea fields has you hankering for a cuppa, then the **Tea Research Institute** ("Çay Araştırma Enstitüsü") – part botanical garden, part tasting and sales outlet – is the best reason to pause in Rize. Beneath grand magnolia trees, all manner of tea can be tasted from heated *samovars* (₺2 per cup), while you take in sweeping views of Rize and the Black Sea.

ARRIVAL AND INFORMATION   RİZE

By bus Rize's *otogar* is 800m west of town; service buses connect with the centre. Minibuses heading east and west also leave from the main shorefront highway.
Destinations Ankara (6 daily; 14hr); Ayder (2 daily; 2hr); Batumi, Georgia (5 daily; 2hr); Bursa (5 daily; 18hr); Erzurum via İspir (5 daily; 7hr); Hopa (hourly; 1hr 15min); İkizdere (hourly; 1hr); İstanbul (7 daily; 18hr); Samsun

(every 30min; 8hr); Tbilisi, Georgia (1 daily; 11hr); Trabzon (every 30min; 1hr).
Tourist office The helpful office on the north side of the park, near the mosque, is usually staffed by eager local English students (daily in summer only, 9am–5pm; ☎ 0464 213 0408).

ACCOMMODATION

Milano Cumhuriyet Cad 115 ☎ 0464 213 0028, ⓦ hotelmilanorize.com. This well-established, central two-star hotel offers good-value, though ageing, rooms in shades of pink, green and orange, with a/c, fridges, TVs and clean bathrooms. Parking is usually available down the nearby side streets. **₺100**
Rize Dedeman Alipaşa Koyu, 5km west of Rize on the

coastal highway ☎ 0464 223 4444, ⓦ dedemanhotel .com. Head for this large, four-star chain hotel fo comfortable, contemporary-styled rooms with all mo cons; the suites have separate living areas and sea views. The restaurant serves decent buffets, but can get busy with tour groups. Room **₺230**, suite **₺350**

LAZLAND

When you pass what was once the eastern limit of the Trapezuntine Empire, around 35km east of Rize, you enter the territory of the **Laz**, the Black Sea's most celebrated minority group. While Turks often use the term "Laz" as a catch-all description of all residents of the country's eastern Black Sea coastline, strictly speaking the Laz themselves are a distinctively Caucasian people who speak a language related to Georgian, 150,000 of whom inhabit Pazar, Ardeşen, Fındıklı, Arhavi and Hopa, plus certain inland enclaves. The men, with their aquiline features and often reddish hair, particularly stand out; they also distinguish themselves by an extroversion unusual even for the Black Sea, and an extraordinary business acumen. Laz own and operate a sizeable chunk of Turkey's shipping, and the resultant worldly exposure has made them relatively modern in outlook; the women are out and about in Western garb from Fındıklı east, and the men, too, seem better dressed in the latest styles.

It seems likely that the Laz are descended from the ancient **Colchians** (from whom Jason supposedly stole the Golden Fleece). The Laz accepted Christianity in the sixth century and almost immediately got embroiled in protracted wars with the Byzantines, whose governors had managed to offend them. No power managed fully to subdue them until the Ottomans induced conversion to Islam early in the sixteenth century. Like their neighbours the Hemşinli (see box, p.533), they generally practise their faith without the dour piety of some of their countrymen, though they are now well integrated into the national fabric.

Perhaps too well integrated – **Lazuri**, the spoken language, is under threat, as until recently no systematic transcription system existed. The Turkish authorities have strongly discouraged any attempts to study the language *in situ*. Despite being declared *persona non grata*, German linguist Wolfgang Feurstein finally compiled the first Turkish–Lazuri dictionary, complete with a specially devised alphabet, in 1999.

THE BORDER WITH GEORGIA

The 540km Black Sea coastal highway continues for a final 20km beyond the industrial port of Hopa, which holds a limited selection of decent accommodation, to the **Turkish–Georgian frontier**. Set by the Turkish and Soviet revolutionary governments in 1921, the crossing was virtually inactive between 1935 and 1988, a casualty of Stalinist, then Cold War, paranoia. Since the gates have opened, and especially since a 2011 agreement that allows Georgian and Turkish citizens to cross passport-free, it has become a busy 24-hour way-station. The Turkish border post is in a modern building, with a bank, insurance counter and a small café-restaurant. Minibuses on either side transport passengers to Hopa and beyond (Turkey), or Batumi and Tbilisi (Georgia).

EATING AND DRINKING

Evval Zaaman Piri Çelebi Mahallesi, uphill behind the tourist office ☏ 0464 212 2188. Located within a restored Ottoman mansion, the "Past Times" is almost part-museum-part restaurant, with memorabilia scattered throughout its two floors and a leafy garden patio. The house speciality is a very tasty *muhlama* (cheese fondue), and it's a popular hangout for a slightly artsy university crowd. Mains ₺4.50–13. Tues–Sun noon–10.30pm.

Liman Lokantası Deniz Cad ☏ 0464 217 1568. Rize's best-known and most popular *lokantasi* won't disappoint, with waiters ready to help newcomers choose from a plethora of ready-made meat and vegetable dishes, including the regional *kuru fasuliye* (beans) dish. Mains ₺4–12. Daily 10am–10pm.

Northeastern Anatolia

KAÇKAR DAĞLARI

Northeastern Anatolia

10

Turkey's northeast is, quite simply, the most visually arresting part of the country: whitewater rivers bustle through valleys dotted with distinctive wooden housing, and there are muscular mountains every which way you look. In addition, an almost bewildering array of ruins showcases this area's heritage as part of the ancient kingdoms of Georgia and Armenia – eagle-eyed travellers will spy castle after castle crumbling away on inaccessible peaks. The region itself is easily accessible by bus, train or plane, though still maintains an air of remoteness – tell a big-city Turk you plan to visit the northeast, and you'll likely provoke astonishment, followed by a wistful admission that they'd love to visit. For the few foreign travellers who make it this far there's plenty to see and do, including tremendous skiing and hiking opportunities for active sorts.

Much of northeastern Anatolia is a high, windswept plateau segmented by ranks of eroded mountains. Four great rivers – the Çoruh, Kura, Aras and Euphrates – rise here, starting courses that take them to scattered ends in the Black, Caspian and Persian seas. Despite ambitious development projects, much of the area remains poor – horse-drawn ploughs are still a common sight, as are stacks of cow dung used for fuel; indeed, some of the more remote farm communities, and even whole villages, live partly underground in burrow-houses. In comparison, the relatively prosperous and forested valleys around Yusufeli and Artvin have a lighter atmosphere and quasi-Mediterranean climate, as a tangible Caucasian influence begins to be felt.

However you approach – from central Anatolia, the extreme southeast of Turkey, or the Black Sea – your first stop is likely to be **Erzurum**, long a goal of armies and merchants and the only real urban centre. Today it's the main jumping-off point to just about anywhere else, and also holds a clutch of post-Selçuk Turkish monuments. Nort of Erzurum, the **valleys of early medieval Georgia** hide dozens of little-visited churches and enchanting castles. The provincial capital of **Artvin** and smaller **Yusufeli** are logical overnight stops while in search of Georgian monuments. The latter also sits astride the most popular southern approach to the magnificent **Kaçkar Dağları**, a trekker's paradise that separates northeast Anatolia from the Black Sea.

East of Erzurum, **Kars** is the last major town before the Armenian frontier, and serves as the base for visits to the former Armenian capital of **Ani** and less heralded, isolated **Armenian churches** and **castles**. There's also good skiing, at **Palandöken** near Erzurum, and **Cibiltepe** near Kars.

Brief history

Thanks perhaps to its discouraging climate and meagre resources, this corner of the country was thinly settled until the second millennium BC. The **Urartians** had their northernmost city at today's Altıntepe, near Erzincan, between the ninth and sixth centuries, but the next imperial power to make an appearance was the **Roman** Empire,

Highlights

Palandöken Just south of the gritty city of Erzurum, Palandöken is Turkey's best ski resort by far, and also a great place for coffee in summer. **See p.550**

İşhan The most magnificent of the area's many ancient Georgian churches, and the most exciting to get to – it's a steep ride along a hair-raising mountain road, with spectacular views at every turn. **See p.551**

Yusufeli With its dramatic setting above a churning river and beneath craggy mountain tops, the village of Yusufeli makes an appealing base for hikers. **See p.553**

Kaçkar Dağları The glacially sculpted, wildflower-carpeted Kaçkar mountains rank as the most versatile and popular alpine trekking area of Turkey. **See p.556**

Kafkasör festival One of the most authentic folkloric expressions in the country, this picturesque event is celebrated outside Artvin in early summer. **See p.561**

Ani An absolute must for anyone visiting eastern Turkey, this ruined medieval capital boasts the region's densest concentration of Armenian ruins, plus a jaw-dropping location. **See p.568**

HIGHLIGHTS ARE MARKED ON THE MAP ON P.544

NORTHEASTERN ANATOLIA

BLACK SEA

GEORGIA

ARMENIA

ARARAT

HIGHLIGHTS

1 Palandöken
2 İşhan
3 Yusufeli
4 Kaçkar Dağları
5
6 Ani

Kaçkar Dağları (KAÇKAR DAĞLARI)
Mescit Dağları (MESCIT DAĞLARI)
Allahuekber Dağları (ALLAHUEKBER DAĞLARI)
Yalnızçam Dağları (YALNIZÇAM DAĞLARI)
Palandöken Dağları (PALANDÖKEN DAĞLARI)

Trabzon
Rize
Hopa
Arhavı
Sarp
Borçka
Artvin
Posof
Hanak
Çıldır
Çıldır Gölü
Göle
Ardahan
Şavşat
Çevizli
Tbeti
Dolishane
Porta
Hamamlı
Ardanuç
İşhan
Barhal
Hevek
Meretet
Yusufeli
Dörtkilise
Bayırkilise
Tekkale
Çamlıyamaç
Oşk Vank
Haho
Bağbaşı
Tortum Gölü
Tortum
Uzundere
Olur
Olttu
Narman
Bana (Armenian)
Haşköy
Gölbelen
Gülyüzü
Susuz
Kars
Kars Airport
Azıoğlu
Arazoğlu
Esenkent
Yalkesen
Karmir Vank
Ocaklı
Ani
Digor
Khtskonk
Kağızman
Kötek
Karabağ
Mren
Iğdır
Tuzluca
Arpa Çayı Dam
Frontier closed
Sarıkamış
Cibiltepe
Karakurt
Horasan
Pasinler
Erzurum
Erzurum Airport
Palandöken
Aşkale
Tercan
Erzincan
İspir
Çamlıkaya
Kelkit
Bayburt
Gümüşhane
Kura River
Çoruh River
Aras River
Kars Çayı
Doğrugol
Arpaçay
Çam Pass
Gülyurt Pass
Voadağı Pass
Namian

Sivas & Ankara
Sivas & Ankara
Tokat

E80/100

succeeded by the Byzantines and **Armenians**. The eleventh-century undermining of the Armenian state and the Byzantine defeat at Manzikert marked the start of a pattern of invasion and counterattack that continued until 1920. The **Selçuks**, their minor successor emirates and the newly ascendant **Georgian** kingdom jockeyed for position until swept aside by **Mongol** raids in the early thirteenth century and Tamerlane's juggernaut two hundred years later; the **Ottomans** finally reasserted some semblance of centralized control early in the sixteenth century.

Just as the northeast had been a remote frontier of the Byzantines, so it became the border of this new Anatolian empire, confronting an expansionist Tsarist Russia, which effectively ended what remained of Georgia's autonomy in 1783. As the Ottomans declined, **Russia** grew bolder, advancing out of its Caucasian fortresses to lop off slices of the region on several occasions during the nineteenth century, though they got to keep their conquests only in 1829 and 1878. Nearly half the sites described in this chapter were under Russian rule until 1914, with additional conquests up to 1917 nullified by the Bolshevik Revolution and the collapse of the Caucasian front. Between 1915 and 1921 the area was the scene of almost uninterrupted **warfare** between White Russian, Armenian Dashnakist and Turkish Nationalist armies, and of massacres among the mixed civilian population that had historically been over a third Armenian and Georgian-Christian.

By 1923 the northeast was all but prostrate, with ninety percent of its former population dead or dispersed. The present international boundaries between Turkey and Georgia or Armenia are the result of treaties between Atatürk and the **Soviet Union** in March and October 1921, and don't necessarily reflect historical divisions – indeed, as late as 1945 Stalin was still demanding that Kars and Ardahan be returned to the "Russian motherland".

The Georgian valleys and Kaçkar mountains

Despite centuries of Ottoman rule, evidence that Turkey's far northeast long lay under the command of the **Georgian kingdom** remains tangible. Ruined castles and churches abound, dotting a valley-chiselled landscape more redolent of modern Georgia than "regular" Turkey. The years of Georgian rule are also reflected in place names, most commonly in the form of the common prefix "Ar-" (as in Ardahan, Artvin, Ardanuç and so forth), equivalent to "-ville" or to "-burg".

Erzurum, the largest urban base, is the most common gateway for the few intrepid travellers who choose to pop by. To the north lie the southern valleys, home to the churches of **Haho** and **Öşk Vank**. Without your own transport, you'll find it easier to tour the western valleys, where the main town, **Yusufeli**, has reasonable transport links and accommodation, and also provides a good base from which to organize a tour of the stunning **Kaçkar Dağları** mountain range, or spectacular ruins such as **İşhan**. Heading north again, **Artvin** is the best base for a tour of the churches and castles of the northern valleys, or to continue on to Georgia proper. It's also possible to hit the border from Ardahan, the main base of the eastern valleys. Lastly, the town of **Bayburt**, astride the young Çoruh River, makes an acceptable stopover between Erzurum and the coast. Dwarfed by the largest fortress in Turkey, dating from the sixth century, it holds plenty of accommodation and dining options.

You'll need your own vehicle, or a lot of time for walking and hitching, to visit most of the sights. Bus services, where they exist, usually arrive near the sights in the afternoon and depart for the nearest town in the morning – exactly the opposite of tourist schedules. Some roads are bad, but if you can assemble a group and find a willing taxi driver, this can end up being far cheaper than renting a vehicle in Erzurum or Trabzon. Even with a car or taxi, you'll need at least three days to see all the monuments described below.

THE GEORGIANS

Georgians have lived in the valleys of the Çoruh, Tortum, Kura and Berta rivers, now in Turkey, since the Bronze Age. Like the neighbouring Armenians, they were among the first Near Eastern nations to be evangelized, and were converted rapidly to Christianity by St Nino of Cappadocia in the mid-fourth century. Unlike the Armenians, they never broke with the Orthodox Patriarchate in Constantinople, and maintained good relations with Byzantium.

THE GEORGIAN KINGDOMS

An effective Georgian state only entered the local stage early in the ninth century, under the auspices of the **Bagratid** dynasty. This clan contributed rulers to both the Georgian and Armenian lines – hence the partial overlap in the medieval history of the two kingdoms. They claimed direct descent from **David** and Bathsheba, which explains a preponderance of kings named David, a coat of arms laden with Old Testament symbols, and curiously Judaic stars of David embossed on many of their churches.

Ashot I Kuropalates began the first stages of territorial expansion and church-building in the area, under the guidance of the monk Gregory Khantzeli. Ashot's descendants included David "the Great" Magistros of Oltu (see p.549), as well as Bagrat III, who in 1008 succeeded in unifying the various Georgian principalities into one kingdom. The Selçuks arrived in 1064, ravaging Georgia and all of eastern Anatolia, but as soon as they turned to confront the Crusaders a Bagratid revival began. David the Restorer managed to expel the Selçuks by 1125, moved the Bagratid court to newly captured Tblisi, then reunited the various feuding principalities ruled by minor Bagratid warlords.

Under the rule of David's great-granddaughter **Tamara**, medieval Georgia acquired its greatest extent and prestige, controlling most of modern Georgia, Armenia and Azerbaijan, as well as the ancestral Georgian valleys. A formidable military strategist and shrewd diplomat, the queen displayed a humanity and tolerance unusual for the era. Many churches and monasteries were repaired or re-endowed under Tamara; despite being a woman and a non-Muslim, her name still elicits respect from local Turks.

After Tamara died, the Georgian kingdom began a slow but steady decline, effectively partitioned between the Ottoman and Persian empires. The rise of imperial Russia signalled the end of any viable Georgian state, and the last semi-independent king effectively surrendered to Catherine the Great in 1783.

GEORGIAN MONUMENTS

The Bagratids were a prolific bunch, who erected **castles** on just about every height; generally you'll have to be satisfied with a passing glance, since access to many of these eyries has long been impossible other than for technical climbers. The most remarkable examples are the early Bagratid monastic **churches**, all dating from before the move northeast to the Caucasus proper, and most sited amid oases at the heads of remote valleys. The Georgians borrowed many of the architectural features of Armenian churches. It takes a trained eye to distinguish the two styles, though in general the Georgians rarely attempted the rotundas or multi-lobed domed squares beloved of the Armenians.

There's not been nearly the degree of official stonewalling about Georgian Christians as there is concerning Armenians, and the churches have become recognized as tourist attractions. Almost all have suffered damage from dynamite- and pickaxe-wielding **treasure-hunters**: the locals have an unshakeable conviction that all the Christians who left the area in 1923 secreted precious items in or under their churches, in the mistaken belief that they'd eventually be able to return.

Erzurum

One of eastern Turkey's few large cities, **ERZURUM** sits almost 2000m above sea level on the slopes of a burly mountain range, some of whose peaks poke at least another kilometre higher. It's fair to say that the city's reputation fails to live up to these lofty heights – Turks from elsewhere deride Erzurum as too conservative and too prone to earthquakes, while travellers tend to use it as a place in which to break long journeys, or start mountaineering and rafting expeditions bound for the Kaçkar Dağları.

However, the city's devout nature is actually one of its highlights: mosques here are not only fancy but full of worshippers night after night, while many local women wear the black chador – a cultural import from nearby Iran – or the *çarşaf*, a full-length hooded robe tinted the same dun colour as the surrounding steppe. Add to this a compact group of very early Turkish monuments and a city centre recently beautified with fountains, small parks and the like, and you may even find yourself wanting to stay longer.

As the highest city in Turkey, Erzurum endures winters that are both long and hard – temperatures often plunge below -30°C. Keeping local homes warm at these times is a matter of survival, rather than comfort, and even some of the city's more modern apartment blocks sport wood-fire niches on their balconies. Despite the brutal wind and bone-chilling temperatures, however, winter is high season: tourists aplenty (mostly Turks and Russians) arrive to use the excellent skiing facilities at **Palandöken**, just south (see p.550).

10

Brief history

Because of a strategic location astride the main trade routes to Persia, the Caucausus and western Anatolia, Erzurum's sovereignty has always been contested. Although the site had been occupied for centuries before, a city only rose to prominence here towards the end of the fourth century AD, when the Byzantine emperor Theodosius II fortified the place and renamed it **Theodosiopolis**. Over the next five hundred years the town changed hands frequently between Constantinople and assorted Arab dynasties, with a short period of Armenian rule.

After the decisive battle of Manzikert in 1071, Erzurum – a corruption of Arz-er-Rum, or "Domain of the Byzantines" in Arabic – fell into the hands of first the Selçuks and then the Saltuk clan of Turks. These were in turn displaced by the İlhanid Mongols during the fourteenth century, forerunners of Tamerlane himself, who used the city as a springboard for his brief blitzkrieg into western Anatolia. Erzurum was incorporated into the Ottoman Empire by Selim I in 1515, where it remained securely until 1828, after which the Russians occupied it on three occasions. Finally, the 1970s saw Erzurum become a bit of a hippy hub, thanks to its location on the way east to Iran, Afghanistan and India – travellers of a certain vintage still remember it rather fondly.

Yakutiye Medresesi

Off Cumhuriyet Cad • **Museum** Tues–Sun 8am–5pm • ₺3

Work on the appealing **Yakutiye Medresesi** was started in 1310 by Cemaleddin Hoca Yakut, a local governor of the İlhanid Mongols. With its intricately worked portal, and truncated minaret featuring a knotted lattice of tile-work, it's easily the most fanciful building in town. The minaret in particular seems displaced from somewhere in Central Asia or Persia – not such a far-fetched notion when you learn that the İlhanids had their seat in Tabriz.

The beautiful interior of the *medrese* now holds an excellent **Museum of Islamic and Turkish Arts** (Türk-İslam Eserleri ve Etnografya Müzesi), nicely arranged around the students' cells. Exhibits include displays of local *oltu taşı* jewellery (see p.549), various dervish accessories, *ehram* (woven waistcoats for pilgrims to Mecca) and some interesting old prints of Erzurum.

Ulu Cami

Off Cumhuriyet Cad

The large, ornate **Ulu Cami** was erected in 1179 by Nasirüddin Muhammed, third in the line of Saltuk emirs. Like most mosques of that age, it's a big square hall, with dozens of columns supporting bare vaults; the one note of fancy is a wedding cake of stalactite vaulting, culminating in the central skylight.

Çifte Minareli Medrese

Off Cumhuriyet Cad, next to the Ulu Cami

The "double-minaretted" **Çifte Minareli Medrese** – the literal translation of the seminary's name – is Erzurum's most picturesque feature and main tourist attraction. Two ribbed, 30m-high minarets rise from its northern flank, each curiously devoid of a balcony for the *muezzin* to sound the call to prayer. There is some dispute about the structure's vintage, but majority opinion holds that Hüdavend Hatun, daughter of the Selçuk sultan Alâeddin Keykubad II, commissioned it in 1253. In conception the Çifte Minareli was the boldest and largest theological academy of its time, but was never finished.

At the time of writing the *medrese* was in the early stages of a major reconstruction, with completion scheduled for 2015. Following that, the courtyard is likely to revert to its previous function as an occasional marketplace.

Üç Kümbetler

250m south of Çifte Minareli Medrese

The cluster of mausoleums known collectively as **Üç Kümbetler** dates back to the early twelfth century. The oldest of the three tombs – and the most interesting by far – is that of the first Saltuk emir. Its octagonal base of alternating light and dark stone, breached by half-oval windows, demonstrates the mutual influence of Georgian, Armenian and early Turkish architecture.

The citadel

Just north of Cumhuriyet Cad • Tues–Sun 8am–5pm • ₺3

While Erzurum's **citadel** – or *kale* – is no longer the highest point in town, it still lends the best view over the city, and the great, intimidating vastness of the plateau beyond. Its vast rectangular bulk was originally laid out by Emperor Theodosius II.

The adjacent freestanding **Tepsi Minare** now doubles as a clock tower. Like the mosque it's mostly twelfth century, though the superstructure (which can be climbed) was added by the Russians during one of their occupations. Stairs on the east side lead up to the ramparts.

Rüstem Paşa Bedesteni

off Menderes Cad

Süleyman the Magnificent's grand vizier endowed Erzurum with the **Rüstem Paşa Bedesteni**, an enchanting covered bazaar, in the sixteenth century. The city owed much of its wealth to transcontinental trade routes; right up until the nineteenth century, some forty thousand laden camels passed through the city every year.

Trade in the bazaar today is almost totally monopolized by **oltu taşı**, an obsidian-like material mined near Oltu, 150km northeast, that's most frequently made into *tespih* (prayer beads), *kolye* (necklaces) and *küpe* (earrings).

10

ARRIVAL AND DEPARTURE

ERZURUM

By plane The airport, 10km northwest of town, is connected by hourly buses (₺3) with a stop opposite the train station; taxis charge ₺40 for the trip.

Destinations Ankara (5 daily; 1hr 30min); İstanbul (4 daily; 2hr).

By train The station is around 1km north of the centre, near a cluster of inexpensive accommodation.

Destinations Ankara (daily; 23hr); Divriği (daily; 7hr); İstanbul (daily; 32hr); Kars (daily; 5hr 30min); Sivas (daily; 1hr).

By bus The long-distance otogar is 3km northwest of the centre, and connected by several bus routes (₺1.5) as well as taxis (₺10). Some long-distance buses also pick up and drop off at the small Gölbaşı Semt Garajı, conveniently situated just over 1km northeast of downtown, which is also the starting point for some dolmuşes to Yusufeli and Artvin.

Destinations Ankara (8 daily; 13hr); Artvin (5 daily; 4hr); Bayburt (hourly; 2hr); Doğubeyazit (4 daily; 4hr); Kars (hourly; 3hr); Rize (2 daily; 6hr); Sivas (12 daily; 6hr 30min); Trabzon (3 daily; 6hr); Van (2 daily; 6hr); Yusufeli (3 daily; 3hr).

Car rental Avis, Terminal Cad, Blok 5 (☎ 0442 233 8088); National, Çaykara Cad Millet Bahçe Sok 45 and airport (☎ 0442 234 3025).

ACCOMMODATION

The supply of **accommodation** in Erzurum usually exceeds demand, and as long as you're not too fussy you should have no trouble finding a room in the area just uphill from the train station. Higher-end choices are all south of town at the base of **Palandöken** ski resort (see p.550), about 5km south. In summer, when the few hotels there cut their rates by up to seventy percent in summer, they can prove far better value than the motley hotels in the centre.

CITY CENTRE

Grand Hitit Kâzım Karabekir Cad 26 ☎ 0442 233 5001. Newer than most of the nearby competition, this little three-star has decent rooms with modern stylings. You may well be able to lop a fair chunk off the rack rates. ₺140

Kral Otel Erzincankapı 18 ☎ 0442 234 6400, ✉ kralhotel@gmail.com. This oddball hotel is a real love-it-or-hate-it affair. Some rooms have been intriguingly designed – the most striking feature mock İlhanid-Mongol decor in their mosaic-tiled baths – but the bedlinen can be tatty, while service standards are not always sky-high. ₺140

Polat Otel Kâzım Karabekir Cad 2 ☎ 0442 235 0364. Central hotel whose rooms are simple, but fair value for the price. Staff are amiable, and the rooftop breakfast room is a bonus – start your day with a buffet meal and a valley view. ₺100

Yeni Çınar Ayaşpaşa Cad 18 ☎ 0442 213 6690. Friendly, comfortable and cheap, this is about as far downmarket as you'll want to go in Erzurum. The establishment itself is fine for single females, though the dark alley on which it's located does not encourage wandering around at night. ₺35

Yeni Örnek Kâzım Karabekir Cad 25 ☎ 0442 233 0053, ⊛ www.ornekotel.com. Perfectly acceptable budget choice, especially for those travelling alone (single rooms ₺40). Friendly staff lead you from the pleasant, wood-panelled lobby to smart little rooms, some every bit as good as the nearby three-stars. ₺70

PALANDÖKEN

Dedeman 3km uphill from the resort entrance ☎ 0442 316 2414, ⊛ dedeman.com. Four-star hotel, in an alpine bowl 2450m above sea level, and aimed at doorstep skiers who want to be right at the heart of the action. Large (if spartan) rooms and wooden mock-chalet common areas. They also run the smaller *Ski Lodge* down the way, which some may find more likeable. Closed mid-May to Nov. ₺350

Palan Otel 1.5km uphill from the resort entrance ☎ 0442 317 0707, ⊛ www.palanotel.com. This decent

10

choice is set at about 2250m. Rooms are on the large side, with tubs in the bathrooms; try not to get one facing the car park. There's also an indoor pool, gym and sauna. ₺330

Polat Renaissance By the resort entrance ☎ 0442 232 0010, ⓦ polatrenaissance.com. This five-star is a bit remote from most of the ski slopes – a private chairlift bridges the gap – but compensates with cheerful, fair-sized rooms. Palatial common areas include a pleasant indoor pool, hamam and gym. ₺400

★ **Xanadu Snow White** By the resort entrance ☎ 0442 316 6851, ⓦ www.xanaduhotels.com.tr. Forge the cheesy name – this is by far the most luxurious accommodation in Palandöken, with highly classy rooms and common areas, ultra-efficient staff, and fantastic views over Erzurum – not to mention a café-bar with very fair prices. Rates drop to less than half in summer. ₺500

EATING AND DRINKING

Erzurum's **restaurants** tend to offer good value, with a concentration of sorts on or around Cumhuriyet Caddesi and the central park. Licensed places are rare in this devout town, as are shops selling alcohol, but there are a couple of bars including *Desibel* on Mumcu Cad.

Erzurum Evleri Yüzbaşı Sok 18, south of Cumhuriyet Cad. Eight old dwellings knocked together to make an institution that's equal parts funhouse maze, folklore museum and restaurant. Antique displays comprise everything from Ottoman houseware to 1950s portable gramophones. The food's merely OK – figure on ₺25 for a meal – but the cushion-seats in secluded alcoves are highly atmospheric. Daily 11am–11pm.

★ **Gel-Gör** İstasyon Cad 4. The best place to sample Erzurum's signature dish, *cağ kebap* (₺8), for which lamb meat is marinated with onions and black pepper, then grilled on a horizontal, rather than vertical, skewer. Doesn't sound all that different? Taste it for yourself – it's fantastic. Daily 11am–11pm.

Güzelyurt Restaurant Cumhuriyet Cad 54/C. Founded in 1928, this is one of the oldest restaurants in town, and one of the few licensed ones. Erzurum's *beau monde* retire behind curtained windows for a nip of rakı (in small measure pitchers), wine or beer to accompany good vegetable *mezes* and grilled mains (from ₺13). Daily 11am–11pm.

Kılıçoğlu Sütiş Cumhuriyet Cad 20. The main branch of three in town for this premier pudding-shop and nemesis of dieters: two dozen flavours of *dondurma*, plus profiteroles, biscuits and every imaginable sort of oriental sticky cake. Daily 11am–11pm.

Salon Asya Cumhuriyet Cad 27. Ace for kebabs and a full soup menu, with willing service, dazzling (read migraine-inducing) lighting and contemporary decor; you can fill up for under ₺10. Daily 11am–11pm.

DIRECTORY

Consulate Iran, Ülçer Apartments, Atatürk Bul, Yeni Şehir Girişi ☎ 0442 316 2285. If you plan to cross into Iran, it's important to know what you're doing before you leave Erzurum (see p.643).

Hamam Boyahane Hamamı (₺12.5), just across the road from the Rüstem Paşa Bedesteni, is both historic and salubrious.

Hospital Erzurum's best hospital is the research and teaching hospital, south of the Ağrı- and Kars-bound highway in Yenişehir itself.

Supermarket The Migros by the train station is good for stocking up with trek-suitable food.

SKIING AT PALANDÖKEN

Palandöken, the resort that stretches away 5km south of town, offers far and away the best **skiing** in Turkey – more than adequate compensation for being stuck in Erzurum during its habitually arctic winters. With largely north-facing slopes ranging from 2300m near the *Palan Hotel* up to Point 3140 on Mount Ejder, excellent conditions (essentially nice dry powder on a 2m base) are just about guaranteed. Pistes total 45km, with eight chairlifts, two drag-lifts and a tele-cabin giving access to eight easy, six intermediate and two advanced runs, as well as four recognized off-piste routes.

Palandöken is easily reached by taxi from Erzurum, for a fare, depending on your precise destination, of ₺15–20. Bus #5G (₺1.5) also heads this way from various points in the city centre, though since it stops a full 10min uphill walk short of the resort, it's not worth considering unless you're really strapped for cash. The handful of good hotels in the resort (see p.549) are your best bets for equipment rental, which costs around ₺70 per day.

Note that there's also good winter skiing at **Sarıkamış**, west of Kars – see box, p.567 for details.

Between Erzurum and Yusufeli

Between Erzurum and Yusufeli, a series of stupendously attractive valleys marks the southern extent of **medieval Georgia** (see box, p.546). The most atmospheric approach is from Erzurum – about 70km out, you'll spy a pair of **castles** crumbling away atop dramatic pinnacles, announcing the southern frontier of ancient Georgia more effectively than any signpost ever could. Pressing on, you'll find some superlative ruins – the churches of **Haho**, **Öşk Vank** and **İşhan** are simply gorgeous, though access is tricky without your own transport.

There are no real travellers' bases in this area; most visit the sights en route between Erzurum and Yusufeli. However, simple **accommodation** near Haho and right next to İşhan makes it tempting to stay the night in such rarified surroundings.

Haho

Tucked away in a small, wooded valley, just outside the large village of **Bağbaşı**, 8km west of Highway 950, the tenth-century church of **Haho** owes its excellent state of repair to its continuous use as a mosque since the eighteenth century. Entry is only possible around prayer time, or by tracking down the key-keeper in the village. Most of the monastery complex – the boundary wall and gate, and three satellite chapels – is in good condition, the effect spoiled only by aluminium corrugated sheets on the roof, though the conical-topped dome is still covered in multicoloured tiles.

Öşk Vank

7.2km west of Highway 950 • Occasional dolmuşes from Uzundere are of little use to travellers; to drive, turn west off the highway just south of Tortum Gölü, 15.4km north of the Haho turning, and follow a direct, mostly paved road up the valley to Çamlıyamaç

The most elaborate example of Georgian Gothic architecture in the western valleys, the monastery church of **Öşk Vank** (Oshki), is set in the pretty village of **Çamlıyamaç**, which holds a couple of shops and simple places to eat.

Founded by David Magistros in the late tenth century, Öşk Vank represents the culmination of Tao Georgian culture before the Bagratid dynasty's move northeast and the start of the Georgian "Golden Age" after 1125. The interior colonnade – with no two columns alike – exudes a European Gothic feel with its barrel-vaulted, coffered ceiling; halfway up the south transept wall, the vanished wooden floor of the mosque that once occupied the premises acted as protection for a stretch of **frescoes**, the best preserved in any of the Turkish Georgian churches.

Tortum Gölü

Tortum Gölü, beside the highway between Erzurum and Artvin, is a highly picturesque lake that's almost entirely surrounded by chunky, unspoiled mountains. The water is by turns muddy green, milky beige and dull slate even on a bright day, though views are magnificent from the road, forced up onto a corniche bypass above the western shore.

Created when a landslide blocked the north end of the valley a couple of centuries ago, the lake now measures roughly 10km long by 1km wide. The famous *şelale* or **falls of Tortum** are today its natural outlet, accessible by a signposted side road 12km north of the Öşk Vank turning. To get a good look at the 48m cascade, you'll have to scramble down a path; to be honest, though, it's only spectacular when the falls are at their fullest, in May and June. The road heading north to Yusufeli, on the other hand, is scenic in the extreme – corrugated walls of rock close in from both sides until you're spat out of a giant gate of rock.

İşhan

Far and away the most spectacular church in the western valley, **İşhan** enjoys a truly spectacular mountain setting. The road up – not recommended for vertigo sufferers – weaves a lonely course through a heavily eroded, lifeless moonscape, which makes it all the more surprising when you arrive at the church and its surrounding apple, mulberry and walnut groves. This is charming İşhan village, which despite its beauty seems to be in near-terminal decline – since the 1980s, when its one school had over 130 students, the number has dwindled to just eleven. Surprisingly, the village is served by occasional public transport, and even boasts a simple guesthouse.

The imposing **church** itself was originally dedicated to the Virgin, and constructed in stages between the eighth and eleventh centuries, ranking it among the oldest extant sacred Georgian architecture. The semicircular colonnade that lines the apse, with superb carved capitals, is the earliest surviving portion of the building, and was modelled consciously after the church at Bana (see p.563). Great chunks of the roof are now missing, so the 42m-high dome, constructed much like that at Öşk Vank, rests in isolation on four columns. The acoustics, however, remain superb, as you can hear for yourself if you stand directly beneath the dome, and some patches of fresco can be seen high up on the surviving walls of the south transept.

ARRIVAL AND DEPARTURE

HAHO

By bus Three of the four daily minibuses to Bağbaşı from Erzurum's Gölbaşı Semt Garajı leave by 9am (4 daily; 1hr; ₺9). There are no direct services to or from Yusufeli.

By car To drive to Haho from Erzurum, turn west from the highway over the Taş Köprü humpback bridge, then bear left, past a modern mosque, a few minutes after you pass through a large village. Finally, take a right towards Bağbaşı at the next, well-marked junction; Haho is listed here as "Taş Camii".

BETWEEN ERZURUM AND YUSUFELİ

İŞHAN

By bus One minibus each day makes the haul from Yusufeli to the church, setting off at 4pm and returning at 7am the next morning. Otherwise, the 9am bus from Kars to Rize will drop you at the turn-off on Highway 60, 6km east of the main Erzurum–Artvin highway, where the steep, part-paved 5.7km track to the church begins. If you're staying at the guesthouse (see p.552), they'll pick you up; if not, you'll have to hitch the remainder. Good luck – almost no vehicles make this journey.

ACCOMMODATION AND EATING

HAHO

Pehlivanlı 3km west of Highway 950 on the Haho road ☎ 0442 772 2054. A delightful little guesthouse on the way up to Haho, snuggled in between meaty cliff faces; you'll need your own transport to get here. The rooms are surprisingly well appointed given the location; the owners can also whip up small meals for guests and visitors alike, including trout from the on-site farm. ₺80

TORTUM GÖLÜ

İskele Alabalık Tesisleri 8km north of the Öşk Vank side road, Tortum Gölü. The best lunch option while touring the churches, at the far end of a little peninsula jutting into the lake. Simple but salubrious, it serves salad, trout and nothing else. Hours vary.

İŞHAN

Little House Next door to the church, in İşhan ☎ 0533 500 0128. This basic guesthouse, which feels more like a mountain-based youth hostel, has four simple twin rooms. Oddly, the only double beds sit happily in the dorm; toilets are shared, and a little far away from the bedrooms. Whichever bed you sleep in, the price is the same, and includes a delicious breakfast. Per person ₺35

Yusufeli and around

The **western Georgian valleys**, around the confluence of the Barhal and Çoruh rivers, are scenically and climatically some of the most favoured corners of the northeast. During the balmy summers, all sorts of fruits ripen, and you're treated to the incongruous spectacle of rice paddies (and further downstream, olive groves) by the Çoruh, within sight of parched cliffs overhead. The small, quirky town of **Yusufeli** is gateway to these river valleys, which in their lower reaches offer **Georgian churches** near **Tekkale** and **Barhal**, plus trekkers' trailheads not only at Barhal but also higher up at **Yaylalar** and **Olgunlar**. All these places have simple **accommodation**.

General tourism has never really taken off here, and the stark simplicity of local facilities will appeal mostly to hardier travellers. You'll need a steady hand at the wheel – or, if you're a minibus passenger, a strong stomach – for the steep, and often bumpy, rides out to the trailheads or Georgian churches.

THE DAMMING OF THE ÇORUH… AND THE END OF YUSUFELİ?

Anyone lucky enough to have visited Yusufeli in May or June will have seen, and certainly heard, the **Çoruh River** thumping along at a quite incredible speed, emitting a roar that's audible all along the valley – the result of the melting of winter snow in the Kaçkar mountains. The area's **hydroelectric** potential is enormous, and of major importance in a country accustomed to importing costly fossil fuels. The first schemes to **dam** the Çoruh were drawn up in the 1970s; thanks to poor planning, environmental lobbying and retracted investments, they have been torn up and put back together many times since.

Little **Yusufeli** has borne the brunt of this uncertainty – under the initial, and many subsequent, plans, the town would have been the largest of eighteen settlements swallowed, either in whole or in part, by the highest major dam. This lingering Sword of Damocles ensured that, for decades, nothing new was built in Yusufeli. In 2011, the pendulum swung back towards the creation of a series of smaller dams further up the river, and a small burst of new construction followed – at the time of writing, however, many local residents still expected to lose their homes. Should the upstream dams get the go-ahead, as seems likely, one casualty will be the local **rafting** industry – most operators were expecting to cease operations in 2013, though rest assured that they'll soon be back on whitewater elsewhere: check Ⓦ coruhrafting.com for news.

The gigantic **Deriner Dam** near Artvin was sealed in 2012, and it will slowly start to produce electricity as the waters rise. At the time of writing, the area behind the dam was a vast, post-apocalyptic mess – however, most of it will in due course be submerged, and the new roads linking Artvin with Yusufeli and Ardahan are likely to become incredibly scenic driving routes.

10

Yusufeli

Squeezed into a tight valley on the banks of the Çoruh, gritty little **YUSUFELİ** enjoys a truly spectacular location. Despite the Georgian ruins and Black Sea-style wooden dwellings on its periphery, the town itself is somewhat old-fashioned – no great surprise, given the fact that it has been on civic death row for several decades (see box, p.553).

The damming of the Çoruh River may soon drown the **rafting** possibilities that have brought Yusufeli so much of its custom over the years. Assuming the town itself remains above water, however, its small range of appealing places to eat and sleep will see it remain one of the best travel bases in northwest Turkey.

Tekkale and its churches

7km southwest of Yusufeli, on the same bank of the Çoruh

Although sleepy little **TEKKALE** only holds one simple guesthouse, a couple of shops, and no restaurants, some travellers prefer to stay here rather than busy Yusufeli. There are a couple of fantastic Georgian ruins along the way, but not much to see in the village itself. Do, however, keep your peepers peeled on the road in from Yusufeli – you'll pass two ruined chapels (one perched above the Çoruh in Yusufeli town, the second 2km upstream on the far side of the river) and a vertiginous castle guarding the valley road, before curving the last 2km into the village.

Dörtkilise

6.3km upstream from Tekkale • Follow a dirt road uphill from *Cemil's Pansiyon*; ignore the first two bridges that span the stream to the right – the church is on a grassy hillside to the left, just beyond the third bridge

Domeless, with a steep gabled roof and relatively plain exterior, **Dörtkilise** is a twin of the church at nearby Barhal, though built several decades earlier and later renovated by David Magistros (see box, p.546). Despite its name – meaning "Four Churches" – only one remains intact, but it's very fine and unlike most other Georgian places of worship.

As Dörtkilise is 3km from the nearest village, it was never reconsecrated as a mosque, and is now home only to bats, swallows and occasionally livestock. Inside, a double line of four columns supports the barrel ceiling hiding under the pitched roof; some fresco traces persist in the apse, while an unusual choir takes up much of the west end. The large half-ruined building to the northeast, arcaded and double-vaulted, was the monastery refectory, joined to the main body of the church by an equally decrepit gallery that served as a narthex.

Bayırkilise

5km walk beyond Dörtkilise • Follow the broad path from a jeep "ramp" and culvert beside a power pylon, 150m north of Dörtkilise; it dwindles as it climbs, changing banks of the adjacent stream, and fizzles out completely after 45min; the final 30min is a steep, trackless walk on an unstable surface; bring insect repellent

The remote church of **Bayırkilise** – outrageously perched on a seemingly inaccessible pinnacle rearing above the canyon – remains in distant view of Dörtkilise just long enough to give you bearings. In fair to middling condition, Bayırkilise has a gabled roof like its lower neighbour, with a single barrel vault and traces of frescoes inside; the views, and the sense of accomplishment in arriving, are the main rewards.

Barhal

29km north of Yusufeli

The most popular route out of Yusufeli follows the valley of the Barhal Çayı north through a landscape straight out of a Romantic engraving, complete with ruined Georgian castles on assorted crags overlooking the raging river. After 18km of one-lane asphalt, the road surface changes to dirt at river-straddling Sarıgöl; **BARHAL** (1300m), officially renamed Altıparmak after the mountains behind, is 11km beyond, ninety minutes' drive in total from Yusufeli. With its scattered wooden buildings peeking out from lush pre-alpine vegetation, Barhal conforms well to idealized notions of a mountain village, and makes a popular starting point for high-altitude treks (see p.556).

Church of Barhal

20min walk upstream from Barhal; follow signs to *Karahan Pansiyon*

The tenth-century **church of Barhal** (Parkhali) is the final legacy of David Magistros. Set in a hillside pasture next to the *mahalle*'s school, it's virtually identical to Dörtkilise (see p.553), except for being somewhat smaller – and in near-perfect condition owing to long use as the village mosque. It's now only used for Friday prayers, but it's worth securing admission to appreciate the sense of soaring height in the barrel-vaulted nave – and the debt European Gothic owed to Georgian and Armenian architects. You'll have to track down the imam for keys – the *Karahan Pansiyon* will be willing to give him a call.

Yaylalar

50km north of Yusufeli

Formerly known as Hevek, and still occasionally shown as such on maps, **YAYLALAR** lies 21km north of Barhal, along a scenic dirt road. At an elevation of over 2000m, you'd expect the setting to be spectacular, and it doesn't disappoint – jagged peaks muscle their way into the distance, and life dawdles by at a pedestrian pace. Architecturally the village varies from new concrete to century-old houses, and though the only specific sight is an Ottoman **bridge** just downstream at the mouth of the Körahmet valley, it's a pleasure simply to amble around.

Olgunlar

3km north of Yaylalar, 53km north of Yusufeli

The tiny road's-end village of **OLGUNLAR** is surrounded by gorgeous mountains on all sides. Once known as Meretet, this is the highest trailhead for the Kaçkar at 2200m (see p.556). While Barhal and Yaylalar are great places to stay, Olgunlar beats them hands down – it's smaller and more pastoral, the views are more spectacular, and there are some fine accommodation options. It's not a year-round settlement, and only really functions from April to October – other than the guesthouse owners, pretty much all villagers are farmers, many living in charming wooden houses at the top end of the settlement.

ARRIVAL AND DEPARTURE

YUSUFELİ

By bus and dolmuş If you can't get a direct bus from Erzurum or Artvin to Yusufeli, ask to be set down at Su Kavuşumu junction on the main highway, 10km below the centre; connecting taxis from there cost around ₺12. That same junction is also a good place to pick up transport to Ardahan and Kars. Yusufeli also marks the start of dolmuş routes to villages further upriver, including Barhal, Yaylalar and Olgunlar (see p.554), though services to these two high settlements adhere to a somewhat informal schedule. Vehicles leave to Barhal at 2pm, and also at 3pm if there's enough demand. Services to Yaylalar and Olgunlar leave at noon, and there may be one or two more later in the day. Destinations Artvin (hourly until 2pm; 1hr 20min); Barhal (1–2 daily; 1hr 30min); Erzurum (3 daily in the morning; 3hr); Yaylalar and Olgunlar (1–3 daily; 3hr); Tekkale (1–3 daily; 15min).

TEKKALE

By public transport Dolmuşes connect Tekkale to Yusufeli (1–3 daily; 15min), while taxis cost ₺10, or it's 1hr 30min on foot.

YAYLALAR

By dolmuş One dolmuş daily leaves Yusufeli for Yaylalar at noon, and Yaylalar for Yusufeli at 6am (90min; ₺25) – the price is steep, but so is the road. There may be occasional extra services in peak season.

OLGUNLAR

By dolmuş On request, the daily dolmuş to and from Yaylalar will continue to, or start from, Olgunlar.

INFORMATION

YUSUFELİ

Tourist office Just up the road from the *otogar* (☏ 0466 811 4008); staff often seem much keener to sell tours than give general travel advice.

Banks Several banks on Yusufeli's main drag have ATMs.

ACCOMMODATION

YUSUFELİ

★ **Almatur** Beside the river, in the town centre ☏ 0466 811 4056, ⊕ almatur.com.tr. By far the most appealing option in town, this three-star has excellent little rooms, though given its location on the road-bridge, surprisingly few have river views. They also offer superb breakfasts. **₺100**

Baraka Beside the river, in the town centre ☏ 0466 811 3403. On the main-road side of the pedestrian suspension bridge, this holds small, cleanish en-suite rooms that are deservedly popular with backpackers. Go for those that overlook the river. **₺40**

Barcelona Across the river, 500m upstream ☏ 0466 811 2627. Decent hotel a short walk upriver from town, though prices are a little steep for what you get; you can usually get them down to ₺120 for a double. Rooms are airy and bright, there's a swimming pool out front, and a passable on-site restaurant. **₺180**

Greenpeace Across the river, 500m upstream ☏ 0466 811 3620, ⊕ birolrafting.com. Ideally located just out of Yusufeli – easy to access, yet far away enough to foster a feeling of remoteness. Rooms are clean, if a bit small, and some are so close to the roaring river that you may have trouble sleeping. Camping is also available for ₺7.5 per person, and the in-house restaurant can knock up a tasty fish supper. **₺50**

TEKKALE

Cemil's Pansiyon By Dörtkilise turn-off, Tekkale ☏ 0466 811 2908, mobile 0536 988 5829. Tekkale's only accommodation is a ramshackle guesthouse that would be at home in Thailand. As well as basic doubles, there's sleeping-bag space on the wooden terrace, tent-space out back, a single communal hot shower, and a tank full of trout that you may well be eating come suppertime – meals are included in the price, which is just as well – there are no restaurants for miles around. Half board **₺100**

BARHAL

Barhal holds three good accommodation options, for which advance booking is strongly advisable in July and August. Village facilities are completed by a bakery, a few well-stocked shops, a restaurant and a well-attended teahouse.

Barhal Pansiyon At the entrance to Barhal village ☏ 0466 826 2031. This simple guesthouse is a perfectly acceptable choice, with a varied range of pleasant, pine-clad rooms and a homely atmosphere. You'll eat well here, too. **₺100**

Karahan Pansiyon 1.2km upstream from the village, next to the church ☏ 0466 826 2071, ⊕ karahanpension .com. The most characterful option, with treehouse-style chalets and views that get better as you climb up the various layers of rooms. Given the remote location, it may be wise to convert to half board for an extra ₺15 per person. **₺100**

Marsis Village House Just upstream from Barhal Pansiyon ☏ 0466 826 2026, ⊕ marsisotel.com. Three-storey building with clean double/triple/quad rooms (sharing bathrooms). A *teleferik* winch hoists your bags up the slope from the roadside. Suppers are large and strictly vegetarian, with beer available. You'll wake early here, as every footfall reverberates from the upper floors to the lower ones. ₺60

YAYLALAR

Yaylalar's two decent accommodation options, facing each other, belong to the same owner. You're likely to see him around quite a bit during your stay, since he also runs one of the town's few shops and the village bakery, hires out mules and arranges trekking expeditions – and occasionally drives the dolmuş in from Yusufeli.

Altunay Pansiyon Entrance to Yaylalar village ☎0466 832 2001, ⌨kackar3937.com. The cheaper of Yaylalar's two guesthouses, with 25 beds spread across a large, rambling building. Shared facilities. Half board ₺120

Çamyuva Pansiyon Entrance to Yaylalar village ☎0466 832 2001, ⌨kackar3937.com. Newer and slightly more luxurious than the neighbouring *Altunay*, with good, en-suite rooms, an open kitchen and a sitting room. The four-person chalets (₺90 per person) are great

value, and if demand is low you may be able to take the whole thing for the price of a single. ₺160

OLGUNLAR

Deniz Gölü Pansiyon The first large building you see in Olgunlar ☎0466 832 2105. This spartan but clean guesthouse offers a communal balcony, self-catering kitchen and reliable hot water. ₺120

★ **Kaçkar Pansiyon** Next door to the Deniz Gölü ☎0466 824 4432, ⌨kackar.net. Rambling affair with large en-suite rooms, a communal TV area and shared kitchen. It's the village's best option for food – try a trout straight from the farm. In addition, you can rent tents and other trekking equipment here for around €10 per day, and the owner is able to help with trekking plans. ₺140

Olgunlar Pansiyon Not far beyond the Kaçkar Pansiyon ☎0466 832 2105. Set in a rather garish pink building, this is by some stretch the most basic option in the village, though it has to be said that these are by far the cheapest rooms this side of Yusufeli. Breakfast costs a little extra. ₺40

EATING AND DRINKING

YUSUFELİ

★ **Almatur** Beside the river, in the town centre ☎0466 811 4056, ⌨almatur.com.tr. Breakfasts at this hotel's top-floor restaurant are gargantuan, and great value at just ₺10; pasta dishes and the like are served through out the day. Daily 7am–10pm.

Çınar Restoran Under the Barhal Hotel. This restaurant has the best location in town, with tables on a terrace

overhanging the river. The food's not bad either, with good *mezes* and grills, and very reasonable prices – you'll be able to eat for under ₺10. Daily 9am–9pm, sometimes later.

Çoruh Pide ve Lahmacun Salonu Just over the road-bridge from the town centre. The best spot to load up on its namesake flat breads (*pide* from ₺6), though it often closes earlier than its stipulated hours. Daily 10am–9pm.

The Kaçkar Dağları

A formidable barrier between the northeastern Anatolian plateau and the Black Sea, the **Kaçkar Dağları** are the high end of the Pontic coastal ranges – and Turkey's most rewarding and popular trekking area. Occupying a rough rectangle that measures 70km by 20km, the Kaçkars extend from the Rize–İspir road to the Hopa–Artvin highway. The more abrupt southeast flank is lapped by the Çoruh River, while the gentler northwest folds drop more gradually to misty foothills. At 3932m, their summit ranks only fourth highest in Turkey, but in scenic and human interest they fully earn their aliases "the Little Caucasus" and "the Pontic Alps".

Besides the principal summit area, several other major massifs are recognized: the Altıparmak and Marsis groups of about 3300m, at the north end of the Bulut ridge, which links them with Point 3932; and the adjacent Tatos and Verçenik systems of about 3700m, at the extreme southwest of the chain.

Partly due to intensive human habitation, the high Kaçkars support relatively few large **mammals**; bear and boar prefer the forested mid-altitude zones, while wolves and ibex are ruthlessly hunted in the treeless heights. **Birds** of prey and snow cocks are more easily seen and heard, while the summer months witness an explosion of **wildflowers**, butterflies – and vicious deer flies.

Trailhead villages

The six most popular trailhead villages are **Çat** and **Ayder** on the Black Sea slopes, and **Barhal**, **Yaylalar**, **Olgunlar** and **Tekkale** on the Çoruh side. The approach from the

Black Sea hills is gentler, with clearer trails, but the paths and villages can be crowded, and the almost daily mist rising up to 2900m is a problem. Hiking grades are tougher on the Çoruh flank, but the weather is more dependable. The main **season** is June to September, with the mists less of a hazard as autumn approaches; if you show up earlier than late July, you may need crampons and an ice axe to negotiate some of the higher passes. Note that it gets warm enough in midsummer for a quick swim in most of the lakes.

The northern Kaçkar: Barhal to Avusor

Starting from **Barhal** (1300m), most trekkers head west to the top of the valley walled off by the Altıparmak chain, finishing a tough first day either near **Karagöl** (2800m) or the nearby **Satibe** meadow (2450m). The following day usually involves a drop down to the Kışla/Önbolat valley just south, threading through the *yaylas* of Borivan, Binektaşı and Pişkankara before making camp higher up. If you pitch tent at **Libler Gölü** (2700m), near the top of the main valley, the next day will see you over the tricky Kırmızı Gedik saddle for an easy descent to **Avusor**, end of the road up from Ayder.

Alternatively, you can bear south from Pişkankara up to a camp in the Bulul valley, at the head of which is the wonderful **Öküz Gölü** (Ox Lake; 2800m) and an initially easy – but later steep – pass giving on to the **Körahmet valley**, still on the Çoruh side of the range. From an overnight next to **Satelev** *yayla*, you can choose between crossing the Bulul ridge via the Baber pass, dropping down to **Balakçur** just above Ayder; or rolling down-valley to **Yaylalar** via Körahmet (now served by a dirt road), with the option of ending your hike or stocking up to continue through the central Kaçkar.

10 Routes in the central Kaçkar

Above Yaylalar, two valleys lead up to the base of the highest Kaçkar peaks; the split occurs at 2200m, just above the small village of **Olgunlar**.

Olgunlar to Çaymakçur

Heading right – northwest – from Olgunlar brings you within 3hr 30min to camping spots near spectacular wildflowers high up in the Düpedüz valley. Leave early the next morning to complete the climb to the **Çaymakçur pass** (3230m), the easiest in the entire Kaçkar range, which will take around 1hr 30min further, then camp at **Kara Deniz Gölü** an hour beyond. That allows plenty of time for a day-hike south up to a group of three lakes at the top of the Cennakçur valley (see p.558) – and from a nearby overlook, your first, spectacular nose-to-nose view of Point 3932's north face. From Kara Deniz Gölü you can reach **Ayder** in another long walking day north, via the upper and lower **Çaymakçur** *yaylas*, which may have minibus service.

Olgunlar to Yukarı Kavron

The leftward path from Olgunlar follows the Büyük Çay southwest and upstream to the apparent cul-de-sac of the meadows at **Dilber Düzü** (3050m; 3hr from Meretet), a popular (and oversubscribed) camping venue at the formidable base of Point 3932 itself. Despite appearances there is a way up and out: first to the lake of **Deniz Gölü** (also known as Sevcov; 3400m; 1hr 45min more), with just two or three cramped sites for tents, and then over the low crest just south to **Peşevit Gölü** (Soğanlı; 3377m; 2hr 15min from Dilber Düzü), a lake with much better camping.

Try to get an early enough start out of Olgunlar to reach one of the lakes before dark, in preference to Dilber Düzü. Deniz Gölü, where ice floes last into August during many summers, is the veering-off point for the moderately difficult, five- to six-hour return climb north to the **summit**, where the climbers' register is hidden underneath a rubble cairn.

From Peşevit lake you've a pathless scree-scramble west up to a false pass, then an even more miserable scree descent, another climb and a final drop to some water meadows near the top of the **Davali valley**, where a faint cairned path takes you up to the **Kavron pass** (3310m; 2hr 45min from Peşevit). Because of the rough terrain, no organized expeditions or pack animals come this way, and you'll need walking poles to save your knees – and yourself, from a nasty fall.

Once on the Black Sea side of the pass, the most popular route follows the distinct path north an hour to another col (3200m) overlooking the **Kavron valley** – and allowing superb afternoon views of Point 3932's west flank. The trail, fainter now, drops within 45 minutes to **Derebaşı lake** (2885m), where it's advisable to camp. There are limited sites at the inflow, and a few better ones by the lake's exit, where you scout around for the easiest cross-country route down to the floor of the U-shaped, glacial Kavron Deresi. After two hours' walk along a clear, right-bank trail, you'll reach a roadhead at the busy, electrified *yayla* of **YUKARI KAVRON** (2350m), a substantial place with a central teahouse where you can get basic supplies, and also some simple accommodation.

From just past the *Şahin Pansiyon* on the access road, a sporadically cairned route leads west-southwest up the **Cennakçur valley** to the lakes at its head (2hr 30min; c.2900m). There are at least three lakes here – **Kavron Gölü**, right by the path with emergency camping, and **Büyük Deniz** and **Meterel** off to one side – Meterel is the highest and, in summer, often the driest. Another hour over a saddle behind Kavron Gölü will take you to Kara Deniz Gölü, and usually a lot of company. From here it's simple enough to reverse the directions given above for traversing the Düpedüz valley and Çaymakcur pass from Olgunlar, and complete a three-day, three-night circuit around Point 3932 – an excellent plan if you've left a vehicle or stored extra gear in Olgunlar or Yaylalar.

Another possibility from the ridge above Derebaşı lake is to veer west, initially cross-country, to Apevanak *yayla*, which is linked by path or track to the *yaylas* of Palovit and Tirovit; the latter gives access to the western Kaçkar.

The western Kaçkar: Elevit to Çat or İkizdere

Elevit *yayla* (see p.534), roughly halfway between Tirovit and Çat, is the starting point for the march up to **Yıldızlı Gölü** ("Star Lake"; a place with good camping), just across the top of the valley from Haçevanag *yayla*. The nearby, gentle Capug pass allows access to the headwaters of the Fırtına Çayı, though the onward route is briefly confused by the maze of bulldozer tracks around Başyayla (2600m) and Kaleyayla. At the latter, bear south up toward campsites by a lake at the foot of Tatos peak; the following day you'd cross a saddle to another lake, Adalı, at the base of 3711m Verçenik.

From this point you'd either descend to Çat via Ortaköy and Varoş, using a morning bus if possible part of the way, or continue walking west for another day, past other lakes just below the ridge joining Verçenik to Germaniman peak. A final 3100m pass just north of Germaniman leads to the valley containing Saler and Başköy *yaylas*, linked by daily bus to **İkizdere** (see p.532).

The southern Kaçkar: Tekkale to Yaylalar

Starting from Tekkale, the same dirt road that serves Dörtkilise (see p.553) continues another 3km to Bölükbaşı *yayla* and the start of a two- to three-day traverse finishing in the Yaylalar valley. The weather is more reliable (and also hotter) than elsewhere in the Kaçkar, but this route is thus far relatively unspoiled; sketch map and arrangements are available from Cemil at his *pansiyon* in Tekkale (see p.553).

From **Bölükbaşı** (1400m), a path heads west via the *yaylas* of **Kusana** (1630m) and **Salent** (2400m), before reaching a pair of **lakes** (imaginatively dubbed Küçük – "little" – and Büyük – "big"), below a 3300m pass. You'd prudently overnight east of the pass, possibly beside **Büyük Gölü** (2900m), before descending a valley northwest to **Modut** *yayla* (2300m) and then **Mikeles** (1700m), about 5km downstream from Yaylalar itself.

INFORMATION   THE KAÇKAR DAĞLARI

Itineraries In terms of potential itineraries, the Kaçkars are infinitely versatile. Manic or pressed-for-time hikers cross from Yaylalar to Ayder via certain passes in two gruelling days, but there's little pleasure in that. A more reasonable minimum time to switch sides of the mountains would be three or four days, and most visitors are happy to spend a week or even ten days trekking around.

Equipment Bring a full trekking kit appropriate to similar conditions in the Scottish Highlands, the Pacific Northwest or the Pyrenees: high-quality walking boots, wool socks, a waterproof jacket and trousers or gaiters, a backpack cover and a proper, freestanding tent. You'll need to bring it with you; there are few suppliers in the area. A camp stove and ample backpacking food are also essential – and carry ten to twenty percent more supplies than you think you'll need for the projected length of the

trek, in case you're stuck for an extra day by thick mist. Pure water, available everywhere from springs, is never scarce.

Maps The lack of good-quality, large-scale maps is a major drawback, but some thorough route descriptions are available in mountaineering books (see p.700). A GPS device will also come in handy: the integral altimeter function will be a godsend in the typically unstable weather conditions where conventional barometric altimeters are useless. Paths are not waymarked or signposted, but cairns may be present at ambiguous points.

Dangers Aside from unmarked paths, there are few specific dangers, apart from the absolute necessity of crossing all tricky passes early in the day – certainly by noon – before they're shrouded in mist or storm cloud. Territorial domestic bulls are also a nuisance, far more likely to charge a tent than any wild beast.

10

GUIDES

If you'd rather go with a guide, helpful individuals can be found in Ayder, Şenyuva, Yusufeli, Yaylalar and Olgunlar. Otherwise try one of the following adventure travel companies running Kaçkar group itineraries; a single-person supplement usually costs ₺100 extra on top of the standard tour prices.

Anatolian Adventures ☎0216 418 5222, Ⓦanatolianadventures.com. Week-long trips, between July and Sept, starting in Erzurum then heading out on the Olgunlar to Yukarı Kavron route, under the supervision of local mountaineers, for ₺300.

Arcadia Mountain Travel ☎0537 600 7835, Ⓦarcadiamountaintravel.com. Operator offering a choice of three eight-day-long trips, all starting in Trabzon and costing ₺1700 per person.

The Berta River valley

The northerly Georgian valleys form the heart of the province of **Artvin**, lying within a 50km radius of the town of the same name. While Artvin town itself is unappealing, the rest of the province is rather beautiful. Except for the Kaçkars, nowhere else in Turkey do you feel so close to the Caucasus: ornate wooden domestic and religious architecture, with lushly green slopes or naked crags for a backdrop, clinch the impression of exoticism. Here, too, you may actually encounter native **Georgian speakers**, though they're mostly confined to the remote valleys around the towns of Camili, Meydancık and Posof, and the immediate surroundings of Şavşat.

With its wet, alpine climate on the heights, the region once aspired to become a winter-sports playground, but global warming – and the fact that, in Turkey's current economic straits, existing ski resorts can barely cope – scotched such hopes. For the moment most tourists come in summer to see the local **Georgian churches** along the **Berta River valley**; individually these are not as impressive as their southern relatives, but their situations are almost always more picturesque.

Artvin

Few Turkish cities make you think "what on earth am I doing here?", but **ARTVİN** is certainly one such place. Arrayed in sweeping tiers across a steep, east-facing slope, it should possess one of the finest views in Turkey. Sadly, though, poorly planned development makes good views scarce, while the valley it calls home has in any case been turned into a quarry of sorts, in order to facilitate construction of the gigantic Deriner Dam down the road (see box, p.553).

Travellers usually stay in Artvin out of necessity rather than choice, since it's one of the few bases between Yusufeli and the Black Sea coast. However, like a bad joke you eventually come to love, there is a certain gritty appeal to walking the winding, heavily trafficked main road that wends its way through the city from bottom to top. In addition, Artvin becomes a destination in its own right when the **Kafkasör festival** comes to town (see box, p.561).

ARRIVAL AND INFORMATION ARTVİN

By bus Artvin's old *otogar* (now for local trips alone) sits high up on the approach to the town centre; a new one, at the bottom of the valley, now makes it far easier to head straight on if you're obliged to change buses here. All companies offer a *servis* between the new *otogar* and their ticket offices on İnönü Caddesi, the single main high street. Destinations Ardahan (10 daily; 2hr 30min); Erzurum (5 daily; 4hr 30min); Hopa (hourly from old *otogar* until 3pm; 1hr 30min); Kars (1 daily; 6hr); Rize (hourly until 3pm; 2hr 45min); Trabzon (8 daily; 4hr); Yusufeli (4 daily; 1hr 20min).

ACCOMMODATION

Things have improved slightly since the 1990s when nearly every hotel featured hot and cold running *natashas* as standard and Artvin ranked as the hooker capital of Turkey, but it still pays to be vigilant when selecting a place to stay.

Kafkasör Dağ Evleri Kafkasör ☎0466 212 6786. During the festival (see box, p.561) it may be more convenient to stay at this establishment, which offers en-suite bungalow rooms up on the Kafkasör meadow, well out of town – but you'll have to book months in advance to secure a vacancy. <u>₺100</u>

THE KAFKASÖR FESTIVAL

One of the best times to visit Artvin province is when the fantastic, multi-day **Kafkasör festival** takes place at an eponymous *yayla* (village) above town. The highlight has traditionally been the pitting of bulls in rut against each other, but since the opening of the nearby frontier the event has taken on a genuinely international character, with wrestlers, vendors, jugglers, musicians and dancers from both Turkey and Georgia appearing among crowds of over fifty thousand.

The festival is one of the last genuine folk fairs in the country so be there if you can. It usually takes place for several days over the third or fourth weekend in June, but in recent years has occasionally been brought forward as far as late May.

10

Karahan İnönü Cad 16, Artvin ☎ 0466 212 1800. Artvin's top-end choice – which is not saying very much at all. The rooms, mostly en-suite, are clean and comfortable, and in theory sport a/c – check that it's working before you pay. The restaurant is licensed to serve alcohol. ₺120

Otel Uğrak Hamam Sok, Artvin ☎ 0446 212 6505. Acceptable budget option with small, bare-bones rooms, all with shared facilities – try to nab one with a view. It's on a side street, just downhill from the post office. ₺20

Sadıkoğlu Oteli Cumhuriyet Cad, Artvin ☎ 0446 212 2162. One of the newer options in town, and certainly one of the few with an English-speaking owner. Rooms are fair value but can be a trifle stuffy, and don't quite live up to the promise of the small, spick-and-span lobby. ₺100

EATING AND DRINKING

Şakiroğlu Kebap 57 İnönü Cad 57. On the main road, this is your best bet for kebabs and *lokanta* fare – the *iskender kebap* (₺12) is particularly recommended. Daily 10am–10pm.

Sedir 50 İnönü Cad 50. Breakfast-time *börek* and the usual range of puddings are on offer at this cake shop. Daily 8am–10pm.

Georgian monuments in the Berta Valley

Georgian vernacular architecture reaches its apotheosis along the upper reaches of the **Berta River** (Imerhevi in Georgian) and its tributaries, most notably in the intricately carved chestnut-wood balustrades of the houses' wraparound balconies. The saturated greens of the lower hillsides rival those around Bulanık, while higher up dense forest cover evokes the alps of central Europe.

Public transport is both sparse and unreliable in this area, so having your own vehicle is a near necessity. Drawing a lazy parallel with the Berta, Highway 10 links Artvin (p.560) and Şavşat, though all three churches lie a significant distance away from the road.

Dolishane

28km east of Artvin • Regular dolmuş service

The dome of the tenth-century church of **Dolishane** looms above the lush vegetation of the oasis village of **Hamalı**. The interior was, for decades, used as an agricultural tool shed, but has now been cleared – a good job, since patches of fresco remain visible. The exterior is even more rewarding, the south facade window surrounded by such reliefs as the Bagratid builder-king Smbat I (954–958) offering the church to Christ; a Star of David; and an archangel.

Porta

Pırnallı village, 48km northeast of Artvin

The ninth-century monastery of Khantza is now known as **Porta** to the Turks. Its main church is still impressive despite gaping holes in the dome and walls, but the walk up is of greater reward: from the sign on Highway 10, it's an enjoyable but steep 45-minute climb up to the Bağcılar district of Pırnallı village. The slippery track makes good footwear an absolute necessity.

Tbeti

Cevizli village, 75km northeast of Artvin • Turn off the Artvin–Şavşat road at Söğütlü Kale, following signs for Veliköy, and follow the valley for 7km to Ciritdüzü, then another 3.5km

The tenth-century monastic **church of Tbeti** peeks out of the trees at the head of a beautiful valley. Its remains are visible at a distance to the sharp-eyed, though up close the building has suffered extensive damage from local treasure-hunters. The paved but one-lane side road up to it leaves the Artvin–Şavşat road at the compact fortress of **Söğütlü Kale**.

The eastern Georgian valleys

Bridging the overland trail between Artvin and Kars, the **eastern Georgian valleys** ripple their way across one of Turkey's most pristine and least visited corners. Here unspoiled countryside, rather than ancient ruins, is the main attraction. Some mountain passes edge towards 3000m in altitude, and you'll see patches of ice through to June.

All of the three principal routes between Artvin and Kars pass through the area's main base, **Ardahan**: first via **Çıldır Gölü**, second via Susuz, and third via Göle. The first, most northeasterly route is the scenically superior, though public transport is sparse; a couple of daily dolmuşes connect Kars and Posof via Çıldır town, handy if you're seeking an adventurous route into Georgia proper. Heading via Göle, you'll be able to make a small detour to see the fantastic Armenian ruins at **Bana**, though in this case access is even tricky *with* your own wheels.

Ardahan

120km east of Artvin, 90km northwest of Kars • Buses to and from Erzurum and Yusufeli use the *otogar* near the citadel, while dolmuşes for Kars, Artvin and Çıldır use the central depot

Faintly reminiscent of Kars with its Russian grid plan and *fin-de-siècle* architecture, **ARDAHAN** is one of the smallest Turkish provincial capitals. There's nothing in particular to see, except a fine old **bridge** over the Kura River, just opposite the massive **citadel**, originally Georgian but restored by Selim the Grim early in the sixteenth century. It's still an army camp, so no photography is allowed.

Ardahan is not somewhere you'd want to stay for long, and its few simple hotels, many of which are occupied by prostitutes, are less than inviting.

Çıldır Gölü

The slate-like expanse of **Çıldır Gölü**, nearly 2000m up, is the primary source of the Arpa Çayı/Ahuryan River, and the highest sizeable lake in Turkey. Only during the summer, when hay and grain grow by the shore, is there a hint of colour. Men on horseback, wielding scythes, rakes and other farming implements, canter splendidly across the steppe against the backdrop of 3197m-high Kısır Dağı, but their families live like moles, with houses burrowed even deeper than the norm for this province. Abundant birdlife, fishing boats and changeable weather give the shallow lake an air redolent of a Scottish highland loch. Frozen for six months of the year, it becomes an important **bird habitat** during the warmer months, when handsome falcons and hawks swoop over your vehicle, while migrating waterfowl include pelicans and more mundane gulls.

The unprepossessing town of **ÇİLDİR** is north of, and out of sight of, Çıldır Gölü. Its single commercial street is hard pressed to muster a proper restaurant, and the one grubby "hotel" is best left unpatronized. Çıldır serves as the theoretical jumping-off point for **Şeytan Kalesi** (Satan's Castle), a brooding medieval keep and watchtower perched on a gorge, but local taxis are pricey and it's best visited on a tour from Kars.

DOĞRUYOL, Djala in Georgian, is the only substantial town on the lake's eastern shore; its thirteenth-century hilltop church masqueraded until recently as a mosque. There are other eleventh- to thirteenth-century churches on the lake's southwest shore at the villages of **GÜLYÜZÜ** (Pekreşin; badly ruined) and **GÖLBELEN** (Urta; in a better state, still used as a mosque).

ON TO GEORGIA

While most travellers cross from Turkey to Georgia through the Black Sea ports of Sarp and Batumi (see p.529), the adventurous can make use of an inland border post linking Posof and Akhaltsikhe. At the time of writing, citizens of most countries could get a free visa on arrival, but double-check with your nearest Georgian embassy.

ARRIVAL AND DEPARTURE

Buses run from Kars and Ardahan to the cute Turkish border town of Posof; there's nothing to see there, but the lofty views may even entice you to stay the night. The border is 12km away and accessible by taxi (₺25); you'll pay just a little more for the remaining run to Akhaltsikhe (drivers will accept euros and Turkish lira), a pleasant Georgian town with banks, hotels and good links to Tbilisi and Batumi.

10

Bana

◀ 15km west of Kars • No public transport; leave Highway 60 at an unsigned, hard-to-spot turn-off 28km northeast of Oltu or 37km southwest of Göle, then continue through Penek and branch left 2.8km from the highway; depending on ruts and mud an ordinary car can drive with care almost all the way up

Perched on a knoll surveying water meadows, and dominated in turn by tawny crags, the seventh-century Armenian church of **Bana** enjoys a commanding position. A century after local Christians abandoned it, the Ottomans fortified Bana during the Crimean War, adding the crude bulwark still visible on the south side. The Russians blasted the upper levels off during the 1877–78 war, and later carted away much of the masonry to build a church in Oltu. Of an originally three-storeyed, vast rotunda, one floor remains, half-submerged in its own ruins. Even before you take into account the church's magnificent views of the surrounding countryside, its beauty fully justifies any trouble you may take to reach it.

The Armenian ruins

Centuries of **Armenian** rule have bequeathed eastern Turkey a series of superb ruins that pepper the modern-day border; most are made from a peach-coloured stone known as *duf*. Many visitors find this area even more scenic than the one that holds the Georgian ruins: think lofty, rolling fields instead of crinkle-cut valleys. You're almost certain to pass through **Kars**, the main city and transport hub, especially if you're heading to **Ani**, justifiably the best-known complex, and certainly up there with the best ruins in all Turkey. Once the Armenian capital, it now possesses an isolated, decaying grandeur carrying subtle echoes of former glories. Also in the area are the complexes of **Karmir Vank** and **Horomos**, though the latter is currently closed to tourists. Further afield, the churches at both Khtskonk and Mren are accessible from the small town of Digor.

Kars

Hidden in a natural basin on the banks of the Kars Çayı, **KARS** is an oddly attractive town, unusual in Turkey thanks to a few incongruous terraces of Russian *belle époque* buildings (see box, p.566). Although a couple of hundred metres lower than Erzurum, the climate is even more severe; winters are fierce, while when it rains, which it often does, the outskirts become a treacherous swamp. Most visitors have made the long trek out here for the sole purpose of visiting the former Armenian capital of **Ani** (see p.568), but a few sights are certainly worth dallying for, and the city makes a pleasant place in which to break up a tour of the northeast with a few days' rest. It has also found fame as the setting for the novel *Snow*, by Nobel Prize winner Orhan Pamuk (see p.695).

THE ARMENIAN ISSUE

The Turkish–Armenian border has been closed since 1993, when politicians in Ankara chose to side with their Turkic brethren in Azerbaijan over the conflict in Nagorno-Karabakh, a majority-Armenian area that lies in Azeri territory, and now forms a de facto independent state. Complicating matters were decades of ill feeling surrounding the fate of the Ottoman Empire's ethnic Armenians in the years following World War I: a hugely contentious issue on both sides of the border. The events are viewed by Armenia – and most international historians – as the world's first orchestrated genocide, a term that the Turkish government has repeatedly refused to accept (see p.682).

Turkish Prime Minister Recep Erdoğan's 2009 visit to Baku came during a political thaw, and at one stage the border seemed likely to reopen, but relations have since frosted over once again. The Kars–Yerevan rail line may one day reopen, but for now the fastest overland route from Turkey to Armenia is through Georgia, via the border crossing near Posof (see p.529).

Kars was once one of Turkey's ugliest cities, but things are improving. The central streets are clean, and have been repaved with cobbles or bricks, though watch out for some near-invisible steps on the pavements. The best area to stroll around, Ordu Caddesi, is lined with some fantastic **Russian architecture**, while the winding road to the citadel above town is dotted with appealing pre-Ottoman structures.

Brief history

Kars was originally founded by the Armenians, who knew it as Kari. It became the capital of their **Bagratid dynasty** early in the tenth century, when the citadel that still dominates the town was substantially improved. Later that century, the main seat of Armenian rule was transferred to nearby Ani, and Kars lost importance. The **Selçuks** took it along with almost everything else in the area during the mid-eleventh century, but devastating **Mongol** raids made a mockery of the new overlords' plans. In 1205 the **Georgians**, profiting from the waning of both Selçuk and Byzantine power, seized the town and held it for three centuries until displaced by the **Ottomans**.

The **Russians** tried repeatedly during the nineteenth century to capture what they saw as the key to Anatolia. Sieges in 1828 and 1855 – the latter during the Crimean War, when a British and Turkish garrison was starved out of the citadel after five months – were successful, but on both occasions Kars reverted to the Ottomans by terms of peace treaties. Not so in 1878, when, after a bloody eight-month war between the two powers, the city was finally awarded to the Tsar. It only returned to Turkish rule following the **Treaty of Kars** in 1920. In the immediate aftermath of World War II the Soviet Union made unsuccessful attempts to overturn the treaty and reclaim the city.

Church of the Holy Apostles

Just north of the Kars Çayı • Free

The **Church of the Holy Apostles** was erected between 930 and 937 by the Armenian king Abbas I. Crude reliefs of the twelve Apostles adorn the twelve arches of the dome, but otherwise it's a squat, functional bulk of dark basalt; the belfry and portico are relatively recent additions. A church when Christians held Kars, a mosque when Muslims ruled, it briefly housed the town museum before being reconsecrated in 1998 as the Kümbet Camii. Just before or after prayer times (the evening is most atmospheric), you can slip inside to view the elaborately carved altar-screen.

Kars Kalesi

Daily 9am–7pm • Free

Kars' lofty citadel, **Kars Kalesi**, is now open as a park, after decades spent off-limits as a military reserve. Locals come to enjoy the panoramic view, but there's little else to see other than the black-masonry military engineering. A fortress of some kind has

KARS

ACCOMMODATION
Büyük Kale   3
Güngören   1
Kar's   2
Kent   4

CAFÉS & BARS
Barış Türkü   3
Gaziantep   2
Kaya   4
Istikham   1

RESTAURANTS
Antep   1
Aspava   3
Ocak Başı   2

10

HUNTING THE BELLE ÉPOQUE IN KARS

Kars' period under Russian rule, between 1878 and 1920, explains both the unusual **grid layout** of the city centre, and its incongruous **belle époque buildings**. Most of these structures were made from basalt and sport elaborate street facades and iron roofs; rainwater is often channelled onto the ground with decorative (often animal-shaped) spouts.

The best place in which to hunt for these architectural treasures is the stretch of Ordu Caddesi north of Faikbey Caddesi, which is studded with several superb examples. Approaching from the north, the first building you'll come across is the old **Governor's Mansion**, a large, lemon-coloured structure built in 1883; this is where the Treaty of Kars was signed in 1921. Just southeast, the squat **Chamber of Industry and Commerce** sports decorative motifs on its front walls. Further south again is the peach-coloured **Revenue Office**, a large structure with false columns and some wonderfully elaborate balconies – you certainly wouldn't want to take tea on any of these, they all look set to drop off any second.

overlooked the river confluence from the hill for around two millennia. The Armeno-Byzantine structure was maintained by the Selçuks but levelled by the Mongols; the Ottomans rebuilt it as part of their late sixteenth-century urban overhaul, only to have the Russians blast it to bits, then put it back together again during the nineteenth century. On October 30, 1920, an Armenian Dashnakist army besieged in the castle surrendered to Turkish general Halitpaşa, and with that went any hopes of an Armenian state straddling both banks of the Ahuryan River.

Kars Museum

Daily 8.30am–5pm • Free

Kars' excellent **museum**, set over two levels in a quiet part of town, ranks among its finest attractions. The downstairs is given over to ancient pottery, and ecclesiastical artefacts of the departed Russians and Armenians, particularly a huge church bell inscribed "This Tolls for the Love of God". The upper floor hosts a less interesting collection of woven material and firearms.

ARRIVAL AND DEPARTURE   KARS

By plane Kars' airport is 6km south of town. Shuttle buses (₺5) meet Turkish Airlines flights; they can be picked up 90min before flight time in front of Sınır Turizm, Atatürk Cad 86 (❶0474 212 3838), or Atlas Jet on Faikbey Cad 66 (❶0474 212 4747). A taxi there or back costs around ₺25.
Destinations Ankara (1–2 daily; 1hr 50min); İstanbul (2–3 daily; 2hr 30min).

By train The train station lies 1km southeast of the centre, off Cumhuriyet Caddesi, on the way to the museum. A taxi to hotels in town should cost under ₺10.
Destinations Ankara (daily; 28hr); Erzurum (daily; 5hr 30min); İstanbul (daily; 37hr); Sivas (daily; 17hr).

By bus and dolmuş The long-distance *otogar* lies 5km east of the centre – *servis* buses link it with bus company ticket offices, most of which can be found on Faikbey Cad around the nexus with Atatürk Cad. The old *otogar*, or Küçük Kâzımbey Cad, now houses only dolmuşes to nearby Yusufeli, Ardahan, Posof (for Georgia) and Iğdır (change for Doğubeyazit).
Destinations Ankara (3 daily; 16hr); Ardahan (hourly; 1hr 30min); Artvin (daily; 6hr); Çıldır (2 daily; 1hr 30min); Digor (hourly; 45min); Erzurum (hourly; 3hr); Iğdır (hourly; 3hr); Trabzon (2 daily; 8hr).

INFORMATION

Tourist office On the corner of Faikbey Cad and Gazi Ahmet Muhtar Cad (daily 8.30am–5.30pm; ❶0474 212 6817); only worth visiting for its maps.

ACCOMMODATION

Accommodation options in Kars have improved immeasurably, thanks to the construction (or renovation) of a swathe of middle-end facilities. Some cheaper establishments remain beyond the pale – if you're really keen to save a few lira, you'll find the very cheapest in the grimy streets surrounding the market.

Büyük Kale Atatürk Cad 60 ☎0474 212 6444, ⓦ lbuyukkalehotel.com. Swish affair with large, well-appointed rooms that are excellent value. Breakfasts are prodigious, often featuring no fewer than twelve kinds of local cheese, and taken with a commanding view of the city. ₺190

Güngören Oteli Millet Sok 2, just off Halitpaşa Cad ☎0474 212 6767. Large, rambling hotel renovated to within an inch of its life in 2011. Rooms are large, with coffee-coloured carpets and trendy furniture. There's a decent restaurant on the ground floor, and a small hamam

on site. ₺120

Kar's Otel Halitpaşa Cad 79 ☎0474 212 1616, ⓦ karsotel.com. A boutique hotel in eastern Anatolia – wonders will never cease. It's a highly atmospheric place, if rather pricey; the eight muted-grey rooms feature flat-screen TVs, super-comfy beds and powerful showers. There's also an excellent restaurant downstairs. ₺280

Otel Kent Bakırcılar Cad 72 ☎0474 223 6666. Good budget choice by the market, with good, clean rooms and English-speaking management. Breakfast is served on a terrace that provides pleasant castle views. ₺50

10

EATING AND DRINKING

Fortunately the **restaurant** scene in Kars is excellent, and much better than its accommodation. One Russian legacy remains – despite the city's far-flung location, it's surprisingly easy to get **alcohol** with your meal, while most shops are also licensed.

RESTAURANTS

★ **Antep Pide ve Lahmacun** Atatürk Cad 7. Ordinary-looking restaurant doling out extraordinarily good *pide* for ₺7.5 and up. Simply delectable, and best savoured – if you're brave – over a glass of spicy turnip juice (₺1). Daily 10am–10pm.

Aspava Atatürk Cad 74. Never mind the lurid lighting and kitsch decor, this is the best of a handful of 24hr *lokantas* in town – a godsend if you've arrived on a late bus. You'll be able to fill up for ₺10 or so. Daily 24hr.

★ **Ocak Başı** Atatürk Cad 156. The more appealing of two identically named restaurants on Atatürk Cad, notable for its mock-troglodytic style. Prices are surprisingly reasonable, and portions large – try the superb *patlıcan kebap* for ₺13. Daily 10am–11pm.

BARS AND CAFÉS

Barış Türkü Bar Atatürk Cad 33. Set in a delightful colonial-era building, this (occasionally) lively bar pumps out freezing-cold beer, and often puts on traditional music in the evening (usually an extra ₺10 per table). Daily 3pm–late.

Gaziantep Baklava Salonu Atatürk Cad 39. The most appealing *pastane* in town, a tiny place serving small rounds of *baklava* and ice cream for just ₺3.5. Daily 8am–11pm.

Kaya Hapan Mevkii, opposite Otel Kent. Quite possibly the best *kahvaltı* in east Turkey. Filling breakfasts (₺6) feature plates of cream and local honey to dip your bread in – resistance is futile. Daily 7am–midnight.

Istihkam By the Kars Çayı. A terrific escape from Kars' often grimy streets, this relaxed, outdoor café allows you to drain a tea (₺1) or suck on a nargile (₺8) with a splendid view of the citadel. Snack food also available. Daily 8am–11pm.

DIRECTORY

Consulate Azerbaijan, Ordu Cad (Mon–Fri 9am–4pm; ☎0474 223 1361).

Hamams The *Güngören* hotel, Millet Sok 2, has an attached hamam, for men only. The newer Kızılay Hamamı (men 6.30am–11pm; women noon–5pm; ₺12.5) is 500m

northeast of the town centre on Faikbey Cad.

Post office The main PTT branch (open late into evenings) is on Ordu Cad; there's a useful, more central *çarşı* branch on Kâzımpaşa Cad.

Cibiltepe ski resort

Surrounded by conifers, 55km west of Kars, **Sarıkamış** is the coldest town in Turkey. Thick seasonal snow supports the very good **Cibiltepe ski resort**, 3km back east towards the main highway. Facilities comprise just two chairlifts from 2150m up to 2700m, serving two advanced runs, two intermediate ones and one novice piste threading the trees.

Equipment rental is cheap at around ₺35 per day – this, as well as the arrangement of lift passes and instruction, is cheapest at the lift offices rather than the resort's few hotels.

Çamkar At the foot of the lifts ☎0474 413 5259, ⓦcamkarotel.com. This ostensibly three-star hotel offers medium-sized standard units in a chalet-style structure with a sauna and licensed restaurant. Half board ₺250

Sarıkamış Turistik Otel Halk Cad 64, Sarıkamış ☎0474 413 4338. Though not in the resort itself, this simple hotel in Sarıkamış is the cheapest option if you intend to ski at Cibiltepe, with a funky rustic-style lobby and spacious rooms. ₺50

Toprak Hotel At the foot of the lifts ☎0474 413 4111, ⓦtoprakhotels.com. Relatively new hotel that's by far the most appealing option in the resort. It's dear but still good value, with attractive rooms exuding a sort of watered-down Alpine feel. ₺350

Ani

45km southeast of Kars, just beyond Ocaklı village • No buses; allowing 1hr driving each way, plus at least 2hr on site, expect to pay ₺100 for a 4hr round-trip by taxi, ₺120 for 5hr; minibus tours typically cost ₺50 per person; one guide, is particularly likely to hunt you down – don't give him your email address or you'll be getting spam until kingdom come

Once the capital of Bagratid Armenia, **ANI** is today a melancholy, almost vacant triangular plateau, divided from Armenia by the stunning **Arpa Çayı** (Ahuryan River) gorge and all but separated from the rest of Turkey by two deep tributaries.

While the site now consists of little more than an expanse of rubble, from it rise some of the finest examples of ecclesiastical and military architecture of its time. The Armenians were master stoneworkers, and the **fortifications** that defend the northern, exposed side of the plateau, and the handful of **churches** that lie behind, are exquisite compositions in a blend of ruddy sandstone and darker volcanic rock. Recent mining of the same materials has resulted in a few unsightly scars on the Armenian side of the border – which is surely the result of spite, given their positioning. However, the gently undulating landscape remains every bit as evocative as the ruins: it's inconceivable to venture east of Erzurum or Artvin without fitting Ani into your plans.

Be sure you're prepared for a trip to Ani. Midsummer is usually very hot, so you're advised to bring a hat, sun cream and water to tour the site, as well as snacks. Note also that the site itself nudges up against the highly sensitive **Armenian border**, and whole areas remain out of bounds. The *jandarma*, who patrol the site continuously, will let you know which areas to avoid.

Brief history

Ani first came to prominence after the local instalment of the Armenian Gamsarkan clan during the fifth century. Situated astride a major east–west caravan route, the city prospered, receiving fresh impetus when Ashot III, fifth in the line of the Bagratid kings of Armenia, transferred his capital here from Kars in 961. For three generations the kingdom and its capital enjoyed a golden age. Beautified and strengthened militarily, with a population exceeding one hundred thousand, Ani rivalled Baghdad and Constantinople themselves.

By the middle of the eleventh century, however, wars of succession took their toll. The Byzantine Empire annexed the city in 1045, but in the process dissolved an effective bulwark against the approaching Selçuks, who took Ani with little resistance in 1064. After the collapse of the Selçuks, the Armenians returned in less than a century. The Pahlavuni and Zakhariad clans ruled over a reduced but still semi-independent Armenia for two more centuries, continuing to endow Ani with churches and monasteries.

The Mongol raids of the thirteenth century, a devastating earthquake in 1319 and realigned trade routes proved mortal blows to both Ani and its hinterland; thereafter the city was gradually abandoned, and forgotten until noticed by European travellers of the nineteenth century.

OPPOSITE ANI (P.568)>

ANI

Kars

🅿

Aslan Kapısı
(Lion Gate)

Selçuk
Palace

Church of
St Gregory
(of Gagik)

Georgian Church
(ruined)

Path

Path

Stream

Church of the
Holy Apostles
(Arak Elots)

Oil or
Wine Press

Church of St Gregory
(Abighamrets)

Church of
the Redeemer
(Prkitch)

Shops

Cathedral

Church of
St Gregory
(Tigran Honents)

Alaca Çayı (dry)

Menüçehir
Camii

"Palace"

Convent of
the Virgins
(Kusanats)

Ruined
Bridge

Apra Çayı or Ahuryan River

Citadel or
İç Kale
(off limits)

ARMENIA

N

Alaca Çayı (dry)

Apra Çayı or Ahuryan River

Monastery
Kız Kilisesi
(off limits)

0   200
metres

The site

Daily 7am–8pm • ₺5

Ani's vast tenth-century walls, studded with towers, are visible from afar, as you
approach past villages teeming with sheep, buffalo, horses, donkeys and geese. **Aslan
Kapısı**, site of the **ticket office** and named for a sculpted Selçuk lion on the wall just
inside, is sole survivor of the four original gates. Once beyond the inner wall you're
confronted by the forlorn, weed-tufted plateau, dotted with only the sturdiest bits of
masonry that have outlasted the ages.

Signposted paths, many of them remnants of Ani's former streets, lead to or past all of the principal remains.

Church of the Redeemer

The **Church of the Redeemer** (Prkitch) was built between 1034 and 1036. In 1957, half the building was sheared away by lightning, so that the remainder, seen from the side, looks uncannily like a stage set, albeit one with carved filigree crosses and Armenian inscriptions. Three metres up on the exterior wall you can see a frieze of a cross on an ornate rectangular background; this is a fine example of the typically Armenian *khatchkar* (literally "cross-stone") carvings that gave their name to the Kaçkar mountains.

Church of St Gregory

The charming monastic **Church of St Gregory the Illuminator** (Tigran Honents), Ani's best-preserved monument, is somewhat confusingly one of three dedicated to the saint who brought Christianity to Armenia at the start of the fourth century. The pious foundation of a merchant nobleman in 1215, it's unusually laid out in a rectangle divided width-wise in three (though a colonnaded narthex and small baptistry have mostly collapsed). Its ground plan reflects the prominent Georgian influence in thirteenth-century Ani, and the fact that the Orthodox, not the Armenian Apostolic, rite was celebrated here. The church still sports delicate exterior relief-work, including extensive avian designs.

The church is most rewarding for its **frescoes**, the only ones to survive at Ani, which cover most of the interior and spill out around the current entrance onto what was once the narthex wall, giving the church its Turkish name *Resimli Kilise* or "Painted Church". They are remarkable both for their high degree of realism and fluidity – especially compared to the static iconography of the contemporaneous Byzantines – and for the subject matter, depicting episodes in early Armenian Christianity as well as the doings of ordinary people.

The Convent of the Virgins

The thirteenth-century **Convent of the Virgins** (Kusanats) perches on a ledge close to the river. A minuscule, rocket-like rotunda church, contemporary with Tigran Honents, is flanked by a smaller chapel or baptistry, and the whole enclosed by a perimeter wall. Just downstream are the evocative stubs of the ruined medieval **bridge** over the Arpa, though it's unwise (if not actually forbidden) to approach it – the Turkish bank of the river is stoutly fenced and probably mined as well.

The cathedral and around

Ani's elegantly proportioned **cathedral** was completed between 989 and 1010. The architect, one Trdat Mendet, could present rather impressive credentials, having very recently completed restoration of the earthquake-damaged dome of Aya Sofya in Constantinople. However, this is a surprisingly plain, rectangular building, with just the generic blind arcades of Armenian churches and no external apse; the dome, once supported by four massive pillars, has long since vanished. The main entrance was – unusually – not to the west, opposite the apse, but on the side of the nave, through the south wall.

A **replica** of this church was in the early stages of construction at the time of writing, across on the Armenian side of the river, and clearly visible (and audible) from Ani itself.

Menüçehir Camii

Just beyond an excavated area that's thought to have been a medieval street lined with shops, the **Menüçehir Camii** is billed as the earliest Selçuk mosque in Anatolia, though its lack of *mihrab*, alternating red and black stonework and inlaid mosaic ceiling invite suspicions of mixed antecedents. Certainly the view from the ornate gallery across the frontier river fits more with use as a small palace. Slightly southwest, the foundations of a purportedly verified "**palace**" have been exposed.

Beyond the mosque, you'll probably meet the friendly *jandarma*, who will prevent you from wandering any further.

The citadel and Kız Kilisesi

Although Ani's inner **citadel**, or İç Kale, has long languished in a forbidden zone and is likely to remain so, a few travellers – and occasionally entire groups – are lucky enough to sneak through.

Also off-limits is the fairy-tale monastery of **Kız Kilisesi**, spectacularly sited above a sharp curve in the river gorge and originally accessed by a tunnel carved into the rock that has long since eroded.

The second Church of St Gregory

The second **Church of St Gregory** (Abighamrets) was begun in 1040 by the same individual responsible for the Church of the Redeemer. This rotunda is like no other at Ani – instead of just merely blind arcades in a flat surface, the twelve-sided exterior is pierced by functional recessed vaults, which alternate with the six rounded interior niches to lend extra structural stability.

Church of the Holy Apostles

Ani's so-called "Kervansaray" began life as the eleventh-century **Church of the Holy Apostles** (Arak Elots). Despite ruinous first impressions, it proves a rewarding hybrid Selçuk–Christian monument. At first the church seems to have an odd south-to-north orientation, with a rounded apse at the north end. Then you realize that this is the *kervansaray* part, added at a later date, and that the western half of the church nave is three-quarters crumbled but still discernible. Copious Armenian inscriptions confirm the building's original use, while overhead in the nave, superb four-way ribbing arcs cross an intricate ceiling in a two-colour mosaic pattern, culminating in a stalactite-vaulted dome.

Church of St Gregory of Gagik

The sparse ruins of a third **Church of St Gregory of Gagik**, northwards on the main circuit beyond the Church of the Holy Apostles, was started in 998 by Trdat, architect of the cathedral. Intact, it would have been one of the largest rotundas in medieval Armenia proper, based on the three-storey, seventh-century rotunda at Zvartnots in Armenia. However, it collapsed almost immediately, and today only man-high outer walls, bases of the dome piers and giant column-stumps remain.

Selçuk Palace

Before completing your tour at the Aslan Kapısı, you can stop in at the **Selçuk Palace**, the only indisputably Islamic item at Ani, tucked into the northwest extremity of the ramparts. Since 1988, this has been meticulously rebuilt – the only structure to receive any degree of archeological investigation and maintenance, and a striking example of ultra-nationalist archeology in action.

Monuments around Ani

The region around Ani holds countless remote **churches and castles** – mostly Armenian besides those at Ani itself, a few of which can be visited with your own transport or a cooperative taxi. None of these sites holds any formal tourist facilities whatsoever – bring picnic fare or trust in village hospitality. It's also worth enquiring about the status of **Horomos**, a monastic complex rivalling Ani for beauty and location that's currently off-limits to tourists.

armir Vank

m east of Kars, towards Oğuzlu · Drive 4.5km east from the junction at Başgedikler, then loop to the right around the hamlet of ~aktar, fork left and continue another 3.2km to Yağkesen

he most fascinating sight in the vicinity of Ani, and remarkably intact for a thirteenth-ntury **church**, Karmir Vank (*Kızıl Kilise* in Turkish – both mean "Red Monastery") is a al beauty. It's stunningly located to boot, with hay and *tezek* patties stacked to one side d the land sloping gently down to a stream on the other.

lonuments around Digor

e churches at **Khtskonk** and **Mren** are even more architecturally and historically gnificant than those around Ani, but can only be reached via fairly long walks. To sit both, even with your own transport, you'll need to allow almost a full day. The arest large village – **Digor** (Tekor in Armenian), 40km southeast of Kars – is served fairly frequent dolmuşes, but holds few amenities.

tskonk

on foot up the gorge from Digor village, 40km southeast of Kars

he dramatically located church at **Khtskonk** is the closest monument to Digor, just few kilometres upstream along the Digor Çayı. There were originally five churches ence the Turkish name, *Beşkilise*) perched on the rim of the narrow canyon, but the tunda of **St Sergius**, founded in 1029, is the sole survivor. All five were restored in ⁊78, but at some time between 1920 and 1965 the other four were destroyed either rolling boulders onto them or with explosives. St Sergius's side walls are rent by sures, but the dome is still intact and the west wall is covered in intricate Armenian scriptions, making it the equal of any single monument at Ani.

ren

km southeast of Kars on Highway 70 · Around 21km southeast of Digor (itself 50km from Kars), look out for a dirt road heading east, ned for the village of Karabağ; park there, and walk another 50min (4.5km)

he seventh-century Cathedral of **Mren** (Mirini), atop a very slight rise near the nfluence of the Digor and Arpa streams, was once the focal point of a fair-sized wn. That town was abandoned at some point in the fourteenth century, amid İlhanid ongol raids, but its rubble still litters the immediate surroundings. The cathedral was mpleted in 640 by David Saharuni, Prince of Armenia, and is one of Turkey's earliest amples of Armenian architecture. Built of alternating red and dark basalt blocks, it eathered the centuries remarkably well before 1920, though the southwest corner and uth transept vault have collapsed since then.

The most outstanding **decorative features** include numerous, extravagant *hatchkar*s on the inner and outer south wall. The outer apse and north wall are by ontrast featureless, except for a somewhat defaced lintel relief over the north door, owing the *Restoration of the Cross* at Jerusalem in 630, following its removal by the ersians in 614.

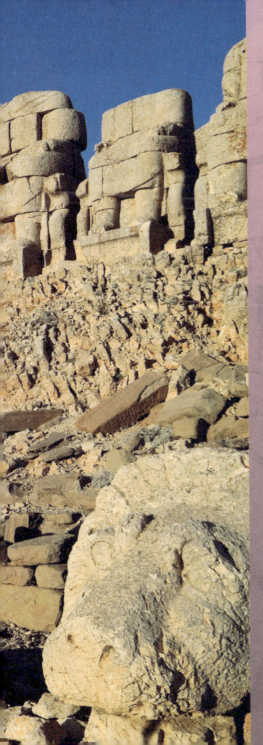

The Euphrates and Tigris basin

NEMRUT DAĞI

The Euphrates and Tigris basin

The mountain-rimmed basin of the Euphrates and Tigris rivers is perhaps the most exotic part of Turkey, offering travellers a heady mix of atmospheric ancient sites and bustling Middle-East-style towns. Forming the northern rim of ancient Mesopotamia (literally "between two rivers"), the region has been of importance since the Neolithic period. The eastern boundaries of the Roman and Byzantine empires lay here, and the two rivers were crossed by Arab Muslim invaders from the south and east after the birth of Islam in 632 AD. Thereafter, almost everybody of any import in Middle Eastern affairs seems to have passed through the region: Crusaders, Armenians, Selçuks, Turcomans, Mongols and finally the French, who invaded southeastern Turkey in World War I.

11

Traditionally, smallholding farmers and herdsmen scratched a living from this unrewarding land. Today, the new dams of the **Southeastern Anatolia Project** (see p.579 and p.616) have dramatically improved the fertility of the area, but population drift to the big cities continues. Close to the border with volatile Syria, Arab influence is strong, but even here **Kurds** predominate and ethnic Turks are in a distinct minority. The separatist sympathies of some Kurds mean there is often a security presence in the area – particularly around Diyarbakır and the frontier zone south and east of Mardin (see Security, p.57, for more information).

First stop coming from the west is the city of **Gaziantep**, booming on its new-found industrial wealth. East of here, the road shoots across the plain to cross the River Euphrates at bleached **Birecik** before cutting through rocky uplands to the pious town of **Şanlıurfa** – well worth a couple of days' sightseeing. It's also a good base for exploring **Harran**, an evocative village of beehive-shaped houses, the extraordinary Neolithic temple-complex of **Göbekli Tepe**, and the natural gateway to **Yuvacalı village** near Hilvan, where you can experience a genuine slice of rural life.

North of Gaziantep, the spectacular mountain-top funerary sanctuary of **Nemrut Dağı** fully justifies a pilgrimage, though the main base for reaching it from the south is small, scruffy **Kahta**. Malatya, to the north, makes for a more attractive gateway to Nemrut, and boasts the nearby attractions of **Eski Malatya** and **Aslantepe**.

From either Şanlıurfa or Malatya, it's a journey of half a day or less to **Diyarbakır**, Turkey's most militantly Kurdish city, on the banks of the River Tigris. Famed for its 6km black-basalt city walls, Diyarbakır is also peppered with fine mosques and churches. To the south lies the region's tourist "capital", **Mardin**, with its atmospheric collection of vernacular houses set on a crag overlooking the Syrian plain. East of here, the **Tür Abdin** plateau, scattered with monasteries and churches, is home to the remnants of Turkey's Syrian Orthodox Christian population. At its heart lies **Midyat**, a town of elegant mansions and working churches. The monastery of **Mar Gabriel** to the south, supported largely by émigrés, keeps the faith alive. Between Midyat and

ZEUGMA MOSAIC MUSEUM, GAZİANTEP

Highlights

❶ **Zeugma Mosaic Museum** A magnificent collection of Roman-era mosaics, rescued from the drowned site of Zeugma and displayed in a state-of-the-art museum in Gaziantep. **See p.580**

❷ **Göbekli Tepe** This unique hilltop Neolithic temple complex, still under excavation, challenges established views of human development. **See p.591**

❸ **Nemrut Dağı** One of the classic images of Turkey – massive stone heads of Hellenistic deities glare out from a remote mountain-top sanctuary. **See p.595**

❹ **Diyarbakır** Walk around the mighty basalt walls of this predominantly Kurdish city, high above medieval alleys teeming with street kids. See p.600

❺ **Syrian Orthodox Church** Catch a service in Diyarbakır, Mardin or Midyat, and experience a liturgy that has remained virtually unchanged for 1500 years. **See p.604, p.609 & p.613**

❻ **Mardin** A hilltop town of beautiful Arab-style houses interspersed with graceful mosques affording stunning views over the Mesopotamian plain. **See p.607**

❼ **Hasankeyf** A dam-threatened medieval city, spectacularly situated on a soaring cliff overlooking the green Tigris. **See p.615**

HIGHLIGHTS ARE MARKED ON THE MAP ON P.578

HIGHLIGHTS
1 Zeugma Mosaic Museum
2 Göbekli Tepe
3 Nemrut Dağı
4 Diyarbakır
5 Syrian Orthodox Church
6 Mardin
7 Hasankeyf

SYRIA

N

0   50
kilometres

Van

Cizre

İlısu
Dam
Dargeçit

Tür
Abdin
Churches

Mar
Gabriel

Hasankeyf

Midyat

Nusaybin

Batman

Deyr-az-Zaferan

Dara

Mardin

Diyarbakır

Dicle (Tigris) River

Hazar
Gölü

Harput

Pertek

Elazığ

Siverek

Yuvacalı

Ceylanpınar

Soğmatar

Şuayb

Göbekli
Tepe

Şanlıurfa

Harran

Akçakale

Kahta

Karadut

Nemrut Dağı

Eski Malatya

Aslantepe

Malatya

Keban Barajı

Adıyaman

Hilvan

Atatürk Barajı

Fırat (Euphrates) River

Halfeti

Birecik

Karkamış
Dam

E90

Gölbaşı

Belkıs/
Zeugma

Gaziantep

Kilis

K. Maraş

Tilmen Hüyük

Yesemek

İslahiye

Toprakkale

İskenderun

İskenderun
Körfezi

Antakya

Adana

THE SOUTHEASTERN ANATOLIA PROJECT (GAP)

The colossally expensive Güneydoğu Anadolu Projesi (GAP), or **Southeastern Anatolia Project**, was begun in 1974 with the aim of improving economic conditions in Turkey's impoverished southeast. Centred on the massive **Atatürk Dam**, the fourth largest in the world, the US$32 billion scheme has diverted waters from the Euphrates and Tigris to irrigate vast swathes of previously barren land and generate much-needed hydroelectric power.

In terms of the local benefits of GAP, the improvement to agriculture is apparent from the main road. Eastwards from Gaziantep, new pistachio and olive plantations flourish, and cotton is being grown around Harran. While this has benefited large landowners able to secure state bank loans to buy fertilizer and machinery, however, smaller farmers have seen few improvements. Many have given up agriculture altogether and migrated to the cities to work as unskilled labourers.

Environmentalists point out the scheme's other pitfalls, including local climate change caused by evaporation from the reservoirs; depletion of the soil from the overuse of artificial fertilizers; the lowering of the water table; and severe loss of habitat for wildlife.

The region's **archeological** heritage has been hit, too. While some artefacts have been painstakingly excavated and relocated – note especially the wonderful finds from Zeugma now on display in Gaziantep – much has vanished forever beneath the waters.

11

Diyarbakır are the evocative ruins of **Hasankeyf**, breathtakingly sited on the Tigris, but set to disappear beneath the waters of the İlisu Dam by 2019 (see p.616).

Getting around is easy, with good bus links between all the major towns and new motorways like the 0-52 and 54 to speed things up dramatically. Decent accommodation is available virtually everywhere, but bear in mind that summers are scorching.

Prior to the **civil war**, it was possible to **cross to Syria** from Akçakale and Kilis, although the usual crossing point used to be Antakya in the Hatay (see p.400).

Gaziantep

Rapidly expanding **GAZİANTEP**, with a population approaching a million and a half, is the wealthiest city in the region. A principal beneficiary of the GAP project, it derives its income largely from textile production and agriculture (and is especially famed for its **pistachio nuts**). Tourism is now a major industry as well, and many of the city's beautiful, pale-stone historic buildings – especially its *hans* and mosques – have been restored and made accessible to visitors, with explanatory display boards in English. The **Zeugma Mosaic Museum**, whose collection rivals the best in the world, is simply stunning; it alone would make a trip here worthwhile. Unfortunately, its role as a major trade entrepôt and tourist destination has been hit since 2012 by the civil war in nearby Syria – Aleppo, Syria's second city, is just 100km away. Cross-border trade has dried up, and visitors put off by a bomb that killed nine civilians in August 2012.

Gaziantep has been successively occupied by the Hittites, Assyrians, Persians, Hellenistic Greeks, Romans, Selçuks, Crusaders, Byzantines and Arabs. Locals still call it "Antep", a corruption of the Arab *ayn teb* ("good spring"); the prefix "Gazi" ("warrior for Islam") was added to honour the Turkish Nationalist forces who withstood a ten-month siege by the French in 1920. For centuries Gaziantep held a mixed Muslim and Christian Armenian population. The Armenians were expelled during the vicissitudes of World War 1, but their attractive old quarter remains on a hill above the prominent Atatürk statue in front of the *Adliye* (court) building. The traditional Muslim bazaar quarter, centred on the castle, lies a short walk northeast of the Atatürk statue.

Map legend:

RESTAURANTS
İmam Çağdaş	2
Kadir Usta	4
Kırkayak	1
Şahan	3

BARS AND CAFÉS
Papirus	2
Tahmiş Kahvesi	3
Yeşilsu	1

ACCOMMODATION
Anadolu Evleri	4
Belkız	2
Evin	6
Princess	1
Tudyalı	7
Tuğcan	3
Zeynep	5

GAZİANTEP

Zeugma Mosaic Museum

Haci Sani Konukloğlu Bul • Tues–Sun 9am –7pm • ₺8 • Catch a bus marked "Mezarlık" (Cemetery) from Hüriyet Caddesi (₺1.8)

The superb new **Zeugma Mosaic Museum**, slightly inconveniently located on the ring road north of the city centre, exhibits a superb collection of mosaics rescued from the once-luxurious Hellenistic/Roman border city of **Zeugma** (see p.584), now virtually submerged by the Birecik dam on the Euphrates.

On the ground floor, where visitors enter, arrows direct you along the best route around an incredible array of mosaic floor panels, taken from the houses of wealthy citizens at Zeugma. Particularly impressive are the re-creations of Roman peristyle villas, complete with their original mosaic flooring and wall frescoes. The mosaics themselves, most of which portray scenes from Classical Greek mythology, including Perseus and Andromeda, Eros and Psyche, and Pasiphae and Daedelus, are well labelled in English.

Below ground level, a section is devoted to the bathhouse of a gymnasium complex, including mosaics, water pipes, toilets and the under-floor heating system – and a magnificent bronze statue of the god of war, Mars. The first floor holds yet more wonderful mosaics, including a superb scene of Zeus kidnapping Europa. The mosaic panel that has become a symbol of today's city, the enigmatic face of a young female known as the "Gypsy Girl", gets a darkened room all to itself.

The free, 15-minute video on the history of Zeugma that's shown at regular intervals, to the left of the entry turnstiles, is well worth catching.

Archeological museum

İstasyon Cad, 10min walk northwest of the castle • Tues–Sun: summer 8.30am–noon & 1–6pm; winter 8.30–noon & 1–4.30pm • ₺3

Gaziantep's **archeological museum** (Arkeoloji Müzesi) remains well worth visiting, even though its former prize assets have been transplanted to the Zeugma Mosaic Museum. Out in the garden, don't miss the superb relief-carved slab depicting the Hittite storm-god Teisheba, and the bizarre human-headed lion from the Hittite stone quarry at Yesemek (see p.584). The interior holds over thirty cases of artefacts from regional sites. Case 33 is filled with exquisite bronze figurines of gods and animals, plus cylinder-seals from the Bronze, Hittite, Assyrian, Babylonian and Urartian periods.

The Kale

Castle closed at time of writing · **Panorama Museum** daily 8.30am–4.30pm · ₺1

An imposing **kale** (castle) dominates Gaziantep from the eastern hill, which is itself a partly artificial mound dating back to at least 3600 BC. The present structure, with its twelve bastions, probably started to take its present form during the Roman period, and was certainly enlarged by Justinian in the sixth century. What you see today, though, is largely Mamluk.

Although the castle itself was closed for renovation at the time of writing, the **Panorama Museum**, housed in an approach tunnel adjacent to the main gateway, remained open. It gives a vivid (if very one-sided) portrayal of the successful Turkish defence of the city against the French and Armenian irregulars who attempted to take Antep in 1920.

11

The bazaar quarter

Gaziantep's **bazaar** area, north of the *kale*, is home to several *hans*, including the attractive **Zincirli Han**, now given over to tourist-orientated shops. The over-restored **Şira Han** on the edge of the quarter houses the fine *Sahan* restaurant (see p.583). Between them lies a still touristy but much more interesting collection of lanes and alleys, lined with stalls piled high with pungent spices, the ubiquitous pistachio, decorative strings of the dried vegetables so crucial to Gaziantep's famous cuisine (peppers, aubergine and okra), and more unusual items such as *tarhana* (dried yoghurt used for soups) and *meyan* (liquorice root used in sherbet).

There are also some attractive mosques, with Syrian-style enclosed balconies atop the minarets. Look out in particular for the nineteenth-century **Alauddevle Camii**, with its bands of contrasting black and white stone, designed by an Armenian architect. The Ottoman-era **Tahtani** and **Şirvani** mosques, south and west of the *kale* respectively, are also worth seeking out. Many of these fine buildings have been restored over the last few years, with handy explanatory signboards in Turkish, Arabic and English. Craftsmen still manufacture furniture inlaid with *sedef* (mother-of-pearl) and beat copper in the bazaar.

Medusa Museum

Just west of the castle · Daily 9am–7pm · ₺4

Set in a pretty old courtyard house, the **Medusa Glass Artefacts and Archeology Museum** (Medusa Cam Eserler Arkeoloji Müzesi) displays a private collection of artefacts, spanning several millennia. Exquisite objects on show include a beautiful Islamic-period gold deer figurine; toy terracotta war chariots from the Hittite-era; and gorgeous Greek and Roman figurines. Among the more mundane items is a Roman bread-marking stamp, while there's plenty of Roman glass in the upstairs room. The courtyard holds a welcome café, where you can watch caged monkeys tumble and listen to the cooing of ornamental pigeons.

Emine Göğüş Culinary Museum

In the backstreets north of the *kale* · Daily 9am–6pm · ₺1

The **Emine Göğüş Culinary Museum** (Emine Göğüş Mutfağı Müzesi), housed in an old stone dwelling, gives a fascinating insight into Gaziantep's cuisine, with excellent display boards in English. Learn which ingredients give local food its distinctive flavours, and what implements are used to prepare the region's famous dishes.

The former Armenian quarter

Gaziantep's former **Armenian Christian quarter** stretches down a hill west of the Atatürk statue. It boasts a large number of old courtyard houses, each with its own well, food cellars and stabling. Many of the dwellings are now trendy cafés and boutique hotels, while a few former churches are sprinkled among them.

Hasan Süzer Ethnography Museum

Hanifioğlu Sok 64 • Daily 8am–noon & 1–5pm • ₺3

The **Hasan Süzer Ethnography Museum** (Hasan Süzer Etnografi Müzesi) freeze-frames the life of an upper-class Antep family in the 1930s. Successive rooms are laid out in traditional style, though the effect is somewhat spoiled by the incongruous mannequins. A basement below the courtyard was originally used to store food, while above it there's a German-made motorcycle that's said to have belonged to Lawrence of Arabia.

Kurtuluş Camii

The monumental **Kurtuluş Camii** (Independence Mosque), perched near the top of the hill, is claimed to be the largest Armenian church in the Middle East. Built in 1892 as the Church of the Virgin Mary, it features black-and-white stone trim, and restrained carvings around the windows.

Gaziantep City Museum

Atatürk Bul • Tues–Sun 9am–6.30pm • Free

In the state-of-the-art **Gaziantep City Museum** (Gaziantep Kent Müzesi), assorted exhibits, mock-ups and video presentations offer valuable background information on the city's recent history, culture and economy. Interesting, mannequin-filled tableaux depict bygone artisans at work. Headsets with English-language commentary are available.

ARRIVAL AND DEPARTURE

By plane From Sazgan airport, 20km southeast of Gaziantep, taxi (₺40) or Havaş buses (₺9) run (daily 2am–10pm) to a spot just west of the *Büyükşehir Belediyesi* (Municipality Building), 500m northwest of the city centre. The THY office is at the airport (☎0342 582 1045). Most travel agencies sell tickets for all domestic carriers – try Fırsat Turizm on Suburcu Cad 16/A (☎0342 232 8825).

Destinations Ankara (2 daily with Anadolujet; 1hr 10min); Antalya (2 weekly direct with Sunexpress; 1hr 15min); İstanbul (3 daily with Sunexpress; 1hr 35min, several daily with Pegasus and THY, 1 daily with Onurair); İzmir (4 weekly with Sunexpress; 1hr 50min).

By train The train station stands at the north end of İstasyon Caddesi, 2km from the centre. In theory, dolmuşes and trams run into town (both ₺1.8), but services were suspended at the time of writing due to major works.

By bus Gaziantep's *otogar*, 5km northwest of the centre, is served by free service buses, minibuses (₺1.8) and taxis (₺15) into town. Get off at Hükümet Konağı, near the junction of Suburcu and Hürriyet caddesi, close to most of the hotels and restaurants.

Destinations Adana via Mersin (10 daily; 4hr); Adiyaman (for Kahta/Mt Nemrut; 8 daily); Ankara (12 daily; 10hr); Antakya (8 daily; 4hr); Diyarbakır (5 daily; 5hr); Malatya (daily; 4hr); Mardin (5 daily; 6hr); Şanlıurfa (11 daily; 2.5hr).

Car rental Car rental outfits abound on Ordu Caddesi. One reliable outfit is Maksi Ay, Ordu Cad 18 (☎0342 338 5450), with rates from ₺70 per day, but you can shop around for other deals.

INFORMATION

Tourist office In a dark-glass block in Yüzüncü Yıl Parkı (Mon–Fri 8am–noon & 1–5pm; ☎0342 230 5969); good town maps plus lots of other literature. The main PTT is just west of the *Adliye* building.

ACCOMMODATION

Gaziantep holds a healthy mix of business-orientated and boutique-style hotels, but there's less choice at the budget end of the market. The **boutique hotels**, all housed in period Ottoman or Armenian dwellings, are either in the former Armenian quarter or the bazaar.

★ **Anadolu Evleri** Köröğlu Sok 6 ☎0342 220 9525, ⓦ anadoluevleri.com. The most authentic of the boutique hotel conversions, with high-ceilinged old rooms that are lined with period fitted cupboards. Bathrooms are cavernous and the collection of old phones, radios and carpets is a delight. There's a cosy bar off the courtyard, plus bags of atmosphere, and the castle is just a few minutes' walk. Single rooms cost little more than half doubles. ₺190

Belkiz Suburcu Cad, Çamurcu Sok 4 ☎0342 220 2020. Dowdy, with plain walls and tasteless brown-beige carpeting throughout, this is nonetheless a quiet and comfortable choice, with a/c rooms and free wi-fi, and a good location, just a short stroll from the bazaar and castle. Good value for a two-star establishment – try to get a north-facing room looking onto the castle. ₺65

Evin Kayacak Sok 11 ☎0342 231 3492. Small but passable rooms in an older building, handily situated between the modern centre and the former Armenian quarter. It's a friendly place, and a recent refurbishment has brought its bathrooms up to scratch. Great value. ₺45

Princess Çamurcu Sok 26 ☎0342 231 6565, ⓦ gaziantepprincesshotel.com. The best thing about this standard three-star place is its rooftop restaurant, part enclosed and part open terrace, with a great view across to the (very) nearby castle and city roofscape. The rooms are underwhelming but tick all the boxes in terms of comfort, making it good value for what it is. ₺90

Tuğcan Atatürk Bul 34 ☎0342 220 4323, ⓦ tugcanhotel .com.tr. Plush five-star establishment with spacious rooms tastefully furnished in contemporary style – and a pillow menu for the fussy sleeper. Perhaps the main reason to stay is the fancy spa and indoor pool – and the fact that standard rates are quite reasonable at slack periods. €75

Tudyalı Konak Tepebaşı Mah, Hastahane Cad 13 ☎0342 232 7060, ⓦ tudyalikonak.com. A fine boutique hotel, in an excellent location on a hill behind the former Armenian Church of St Mary's (Kurtuluş Camii). Tastefully furnished with period pieces, it boasts natural wood floors and exposed stone walls, as well as a/c and free wi-fi. The only letdown is its exposed courtyard. ₺160

★ **Zeynep Hanım Konağı** Eski Sinema Sok 17, off Atatürk Bul ☎0342 232 0207, ⓦ zeynephanimkonagi .com. Gaziantep needed a mid-range boutique hotel, and this place fits the bill admirably. Thirteen rooms set around the small courtyard of a former Armenian house provide compact and comfy accommodation in this atmospheric part of town. The composite stone cladding applied to many interior walls jars a little, but that's a small gripe, compensated for by the tea- and coffee-making facilities, flat-screen TV and free wi-fi. €45

EATING AND DRINKING

Gaziantep is unrivalled in Turkey for sweets, particularly pistachio-based pastries like *baklava* and *fıstık sarma*. Not surprisingly given the proximity of Syria, much of its cuisine is Arab-influenced, with many savoury dishes spicier and more sour than western Turkish dishes – the pizza-like *lahmacun* here is the best in the land.

★ **İmam Çağdaş** Kale Cıvarı Uzun Çarşısı 49 ☎0342 231 2678, ⓦ imamcagdas.com. This long-established traditional kebab-cum-*lahmacun* restaurant is best at lunchtimes, when it's thronging with local shopkeepers, craftsmen and shoppers. The *lahmacun* are spicy, huge and delicious (₺2.5), and the *ayran* is served up in a tinned copper bowl. Its *baklava* is famed even in Gaziantep, the home of the stuff. Daily 11am–10pm.

Kadir Usta Eyüpoğlu Mah Eblehan Cad 25 ☎0342 220 6839. Close to the Kurtuluş Camii, this cheap and cheerful place was established in 1966. Despite its humble origins, some of Turkey's top celebrities have eaten here, choosing from *lahmacun*, kebabs, or the local meaty soup, *beyran*. Daily 7am–10pm.

Kırkayak Kemal Köker Cad, Kırkayak Parkı İçi ☎0342 232 1500. Palatial, faux-Ottoman place, pleasantly set opposite a park. The emphasis is on families and local food (₺8–12 for a main course). Try the *yuvurlama* (bulgur-wheat *köfte* served in a yoghurt sauce) or the tender, piquantly spiced stuffed peppers, aubergines and vine leaves. Great value and you can linger, local-style, for tea long afterwards. Daily 9am–11pm.

Papirus Noter Sok 10 ☎0342 220 3279. Among the first of the rash of nargile cafés in the former Armenian quarter, this has a great vine-shaded courtyard that's always full with middle-class locals and students. The empty upstairs rooms hold some peeling, over-the-top nineteenth-century European-style murals. Be sure to try the *menengiç* (wild pistachio) coffee. Daily 10am–10pm.

Sahan Şirehan İcinde ☎0342 220 4246. This enormous restaurant, catering to weddings and tour groups alike, is a fine place to sample Gaziantep's famous cuisine. The ₺20 Sunday breakfast special offers a hundred different dishes to choose from. Daily noon–11pm.

Tahmiş Kahvesi Elmacı Pazarı Cıvarı. The city's oldest coffee house dates back to the seventeenth century. Dark wood ceilings and polished wood floors set the traditional tone of the place, as do the old boys playing *tavla* (backgammon) under the incongruously large TV. A range of traditional coffees and herbal teas, plus local delicacies such as *içli köfte* and *yuvarlama*. Daily 9am–10pm.

Yeşilsu Atatürk Bul. This superior tea garden, set beneath shady plane trees and overlooking the Kendirli Kilise, is the place to come for a break from the heat and/or from the local cuisine, with burgers, pizza, pasta dishes, shakes and brownies all on the menu – or just have *çay* and enjoy the relaxed ambience. Daily 8am–midnight.

11

DIRECTORY

Hamam The Ottoman-era Naib Hamam, tucked beneath the northern face of the *kale*, offers an atmospheric cleanse for ₺13; scrub and massage extra (daily: women 9.30am–5pm, men 6pm–midnight).

Hospital Housed in old American mission buildings, the Sev Amerikan Hastanesi on Yuksek Sok 3, Tepebaşı Mah (☎0342 220 0211), is the city's best hospital.

Southwest of Gaziantep

A couple of important archeological sites southwest of Gaziantep, **Tilmen Hüyük** and **Yesemek Open-Air Museum**, can only be visited by car. The best opportunity to do so comes if you are travelling to or from Antakya (see p.400).

Tilmen Hüyük

90km southwest of Gaziantep, 10km east of İslahiye • Daily dawn–dusk • Free

Situated not far from the Syrian border, **Tilmen Hüyük** – a *hüyük* is a settlement mound – is rich in material from the late Chalcolithic, Bronze and Iron ages. An important Hittite settlement between the eighteenth and fifteenth centuries BC, it's set beside a lazy, reed-fringed and frog-filled river in a broad valley that's actually a northern extension of the African Rift Valley.

Unlike so many of the settlement mounds that litter Turkey's Syrian borderlands, this one has been lovingly excavated and interpreted, with informative display boards to explain the surviving walls, steps and other features.

Yesemek Open-Air Museum

22km south of İslahiye, beyond Tilmen Hüyük • Daily dawn–dusk • ₺2

Between the fourteenth and seventh centuries BC, the remarkable **Yesemek Open-Air Museum** (Yesemek Açık Hava Müzesi) was a quarry-cum-workshop that churned out monumental statuary to be distributed around the Hittite world. Most common are sphinxes and lions (the latter of which often flanked temple doorways), but there are many other statue types as well.

The statues, which weigh many tonnes, were only quarried and roughly carved here before being transported to their destination to be finished off. Those left have been attractively lined up on a green hillside above a stream. The modern village of **Yesemek** lies beyond the café at the entrance.

East of Gaziantep: towards Şanlıurfa

The newly completed 0-52 toll motorway and the old D-400 link Gaziantep with the next destination for most travellers, **Şanlıurfa**. Either en route, or using Gaziantep as a base, it's worth also trying to see the site of **Zeugma**, where the magnificent mosaics on display in Gaziantep were found, and the relaxed village of **Halfeti**, on the banks of the Euphrates.

Zeugma

50km east of Gaziantep, 7km north of the village of Dutlu • Daily 8am–5pm • Free

For anyone intrigued by the incredible mosaics showcased in the Zeugma Mosaic Museum (see p.580), it's worth – assuming you have your own transport – visiting the waterside excavations at Hellenistic/Roman **ZEUGMA**, where they were found. In 2000, shortly before the Birecik Dam waters submerged most of the ancient villas here, an international archeological rescue mission recovered many of the mosaics that are now displayed in Gaziantep. A couple of villas left above the new waterline, named after the scenes depicted on their major mosaics – Dionysus and Danae – have been excavated, and are now housed under an impressive steel-and-mesh building. There's a café and toilets at the site entrance, pleasantly set above the reservoir.

Birecik

40km east of Gaziantep • Served by dolmuşes to and from Gaziantep's *otogar* (₺6), and Şanlıurfa (₺7)

The D-400 crosses the broad Euphrates River at **BIRECIK**. Set on a rise below the striking pale limestone bluffs backing the river, Birecik's **castle** was founded during the eleventh century, and served as a frontier outpost for the Crusader state of Edessa. Birecik is also the hub for onward transport to atmospheric **Halfeti**.

Halfeti

11

The spectacular old village of **HALFETI**, 110km east of Gaziantep, is now partially submerged beneath the waters of the Birecik dam, set in a gorge carved by the Euphrates. Most visitors now come to take one of the regular boat trips upstream (around ₺60 per boat-load), along the dramatic dam-flooded gorge, to see the impressive remains of the medieval castle of **Rumkale** (closed for restoration at the time of writing).

Pleasant restaurants line the palm-fringed waterfront in Halfeti itself. Most serve charcoal-grilled *şarbot*, a kind of catfish caught in the river. Behind the waterfront, lost in a canopy of mulberry, walnut, fig, olive and pomegranate trees, lie old honey-coloured houses once inhabited by Armenians.

ARRIVAL AND DEPARTURE   HALFETI

By dolmuş Halfeti is served by regular dolmuşes from Birecik (daily 7.30am–7pm; ₺6).

ACCOMMODATION

In addition to the *Şitamet Pansiyon*, another place was about to open at the time of writing, and there's also a municipal guesthouse.

Şitamet Pansiyon Halfeti ☎0535 706 6029. This rudimentary but charming pension, the main accommodation option hereabouts, essentially consists of a few simple rooms in the home of (basic) English-speaker Aydin. Find him at the municipally run local products store *Turizm Satış Noktaları*, opposite the Atatürk statue. **₺50**

Şanlıurfa and around

The name of **ŞANLIURFA**, or "Glorious Urfa" – most locals just say Urfa – commemorates resistance to the French invasion and occupation of 1918–20. A place of pilgrimage for many religions, and the reputed birthplace of the prophet Abraham, its chief attraction is a beautiful mosque complex, reflected in the limpid waters of a sacred pool. Just as compelling is the town's distinctly Middle Eastern atmosphere.

Much of the population is Kurdish, a significant minority Arab, and you'll find the bazaars full of veiled, henna-tattooed women, and men wearing baggy trousers and traditional headdresses. In Turkey this "city of the prophets" has gained a reputation as a focus for Islamic fundamentalism.

Although Urfa is one of Turkey's fastest-growing cities, thanks largely to the money generated by the GAP project, it still ranks very low (68 out of 81) in terms of socio-economic development. That fact is clear from a walk around its impoverished

ŞANLIURFA

ACCOMMODATION	
Aslan Konuk Evi	7
Hotel Arte	1
Beyzade Konak	5
Cevahir Konuk Evi	8
Güven	4
Harran	2
Manici	9
Hotel Rabis	6
Otel Uğur	3

RESTAURANTS	
Gülhan	1
Urfa Lezzet Kebap Salonu	3
Urfa Sofrası	2

BARS AND CAFÉS	
Altın Kupa	1
Türkü Konağı	2

LIVE MUSIC VENUES (SIRA GECELERI)	
Cevahir Konuk Evi	5
Gülizar Konak Evi	4
Yıldız Saray Konuk Evi	3

backstreets, and the number of occasionally annoying ragged urchins working them. Hotels, change-offices and ATMs are all found on the main street of Köprü Başı/Sarayonu Caddesi, which links, via Divan Caddesi, with the bazaar quarter and Pools of Abraham to the south and west.

Brief history

The **Hurri**, members of one of Anatolia's earliest civilizations, built a fortress on the site of Urfa's present citadel around 3500 BC. Later came the Hittites and Assyrians, but only after the city was re-founded as **Edessa** by Seleucus Nicator in 300 BC did it eclipse nearby Harran. It later became an important eastern outpost for the Romans against Persia.

From the second century AD, Edessa was a thriving centre of Christianity, and Abgar IV (176–213) made it the world's first Christian kingdom. The city changed hands between Byzantine and Arab several times; according to Syrian Orthodox legend it was once ransomed for the "*mandalyon*", a handkerchief bearing the imprint of Christ. As Byzantine control ebbed, the Arabs moved in, staying until the eleventh century. During the First Crusade, a French count, Baldwin of Boulogne, stopped off en route to Tripoli and the Holy Land to establish the county of Edessa, a short-lived Christian state. In 1144 the Arabs recaptured Edessa, giving the rulers of Europe a pretext to launch the Second Crusade. After being sacked by the Mongols in 1260, Edessa never recovered. The city declined into obscurity and was eventually absorbed as Urfa into the Ottoman Empire in 1637.

Old Urfa

Urfa's vibrant old core holds a number of fascinating sights. At the extreme south end of Sarayönü Caddesi the restored **Hacı Hafız Efendi** house is now a fine arts gallery. The adjoining **Kara Meydanı** boasts a venerable-looking nineteenth-century mosque, the Yusuf Paşa Camii. Beyond Kara Meydanı, Sarayönü Caddesi becomes Divan Caddesi, where you'll find the twelfth-century **Ulu Cami**, a typical Arab design based on the Grand Mosque in Aleppo in Syria. Its courtyard boasts a massive octagonal minaret (originally the belfry of the fifth-century Church of St Stephen) and graves, though the interior is unexceptional. Old stone-built houses, many of them once owned by the city's long-departed Armenian community, sprawl either side of the main drag.

The **Gümrük Hanı**, at the end of Divan Caddesi, is a magnificent late sixteenth-century *kervansaray*, whose shady courtyard is taken up by the tables of teahouses and watch repairers, and which makes a great place to watch old-timers enjoy a game of dominoes or backgammon. Surrounding it is a warren of narrow, covered streets – the **Kapalı Çarşı**, or covered bazaar. Stalls and hole-in-the-wall shops sell everything imaginable, from green Diyarbakır tobacco, sold by the kilo out of plastic sacks, to the lilac headscarves that are the favoured attire of traditional locals, male and female alike.

Turning right out of the Gümrük Hanı brings you to the *bedesten* next door, beyond which lies the **Hacı Kamil Hanı** and the coppersmiths' bazaar. Further west lie the **Sipahi** and **Hüseyniye** bazaars, both left over from the time when camel caravans moved regularly between Urfa and Aleppo, Palmyra, Mari and Baghdad.

İbrahim Halilullah Dergahı

West of the bazaar • Daily 8am–5.30pm • Donations welcomed

Named after the "Prophet Abraham and Friend of God", the colonnaded mosque and *medrese* complex that holds the **İbrahim Halilullah Dergahı** or "Cave of Abraham", set in the wall of its far courtyard, attracts numerous pilgrims. According to local legend, the prophet **Abraham** was born here, spending the first ten years of his life in hiding because a local Assyrian tyrant, Nemrut (Nimrod), had decreed that all newborn children be killed.

As Abraham is recognized as a prophet by Muslims, his birth-cave is a place of worship. The majority of visitors are pilgrims from all over the Muslim world. Inside is a pool where women throw a coin in the hope that their wish (often to become pregnant) will be granted. The atmosphere is reverential; there are separate entrances for men and women, dress must be respectful and shoes removed. There's another holy cave nearby, reputed to hold a hair plucked from Mohammed's head, as well as a modern, Ottoman-style mosque, the Yeni Cami.

Gölbaşı

Gölbaşı – literally "at the lakeside" – is a beautifully green and shady park at the foot of the *kale*, centred on a pair of mosques and two pools filled with fat carp. According to a continuation of the local legend, Abraham, after he emerged from his cave, became an implacable opponent of King Nemrut and tried to smash the idols in the local temple. The displeased tyrant had Abraham hurled from the citadel battlements into a fire below. Abraham was saved when God turned the flames into water and the firewood into carp. The carp are considered sacred, and local folklore has it that anyone who eats them will go blind.

Shady teahouses and cafés stand beside the first pool, the **Ayn-i-Zeliha** (named after the daughter of Nimrod). The elongated **Halil-ür Rahman** or Balıklı Göl is the pool that saved Abraham from a fiery end; it's surrounded by stone arches, its banks usually swarming with pilgrims and the water seething with fish (you can feed the carp with bait bought from poolside vendors).

The far western end of Balıklı Göl is closed off by the seventeenth-century **Abdürrahman Camii**. The present mosque replaced an older twelfth-century building whose square minaret, possibly once a church belfry, has survived. The north side of the pool is flanked by the **Rizvaniye Camii**, built by an Ottoman governor in 1716, with intricately carved wooden doors giving onto its peaceful courtyard.

The kale

Tues–Sun 8am–7pm • ₺3

Urfa's massive **kale**, looming above Gölbaşı, can be reached via a signed path between the new mosque and the first pool. Much of the castle's surviving structure is Mamluk. The interior has long since vanished, but it's worth clambering up the multitude of steps, and passing through the impressive gateway, to be rewarded with a bird's-eye view over Urfa. The two massive Corinthian columns at the top are thought to be the lone remnants of the palace of a second-century Christian king, Abgar. Look out for the crudely carved Syriac inscription near the bottom of one of the columns. You can descend via an old tunnel.

The Haleplibahçe Mosaics

Daily 8am–6pm • Free

The fabulous **Haleplibahçe Mosaics**, still *in situ*, were found at the rear of the Şanlıurfa Belediyesi Koruma Amaçlı İmar Müdürlüğü, itself behind the basic tea gardens opposite the prominent El-Ruha hotel just north of Abraham's pool.

Unearthed by accident during demolition work in 2008 and only excavated in 2010, the mosaics almost certainly formed part of a Roman-era palace and date to between the third and fifth centuries AD. Very different stylistically to those from Zeugma (see p.584), the scenes depicted are quite stunning, especially those that show a black African male leading a vibrantly executed zebra, and the centaur Chiron learning how to fight.

The archeological museum

Just north of the town centre • Tues–Sun 8am–noon & 1.30–5.30pm • ₺3

Urfa's excellent **archeological museum** (Arkeoloji Müzesi) holds jewellery and pottery from funerary tumuli on the Euphrates flood plain, but the pick of its exhibits is the stunning statues from the Neolithic site of Göbekli Tepe (see p.591). The so-called "totem-pole", a carving almost 2m tall, shows a composite animal/human figure apparently in the act of giving birth. In the museum display, it's flanked by wild animals such as boar. Also look out for the stunning phallic anthropomorphic statue, found in central Urfa and contemporary with the earliest finds at Göbekli Tepe, with obsidian eyes.

ARRIVAL AND DEPARTURE

ŞANLIURFA

By plane Urfa's airport, 40km north, is served by a Havaş bus (₺10) into the centre. The Turkish Airlines (and Sunexpress) ticketing office is in Kaliru Turizm, on the ground floor of the Özel Dünya hospital on Sarayönü Cad. Destinations Ankara (Anadolujet, at least 2 daily; 1hr 20min); Antalya (Anadolujet 2 daily via Ankara); İstanbul (Pegasus 1 daily; THY 3 daily; 1hr 55min).

By bus Urfa's *otogar* is 5km north of the centre. Underneath it is the provincial dolmuş garage for transport onto Hilvan (Yuvacalı village), Adiyaman/Kahta for Nemrut Dağı, or down to Harran. Buses into town are ₺1, taxis a steep ₺10. The usual eastern bus companies have offices all around town, especially on Sarayönü Cad, and provide service buses to the *otogar*. Harran Nemrut Tur at the *Aslan Konuk Evi* pension (see p.589), and some hotels, will book tickets. Destinations Adana (7 daily; 6hr); Adıyaman (6 daily; 2hr 30min); Ankara (5 daily; 13hr); Diyarbakır (8 daily; 3hr);

Gaziantep (8 daily; 2.5hr); Harran (hourly 7am–7pm; 1hr); Mardin (4 daily; 3hr).

Car rental Try Harran Nemrut Tur at the *Aslan Konuk Evi* pension (📞0414 215 1575; see p.589); Ruha, just off Sarayönü Cad on Bağdat Pasajı, rent cars for ₺70 and up daily.

INFORMATION AND TOURS

Tourist office In the *Vilayet* building, the Provincial Governor's headquarters, out of town on Atatürk Caddesi, but next to useless.

Tours Harran Nemrut Tur at the *Aslan Konuk Evi* pension (📞0414 215 1575; see p.589) runs full-day trips to Harran (₺125 full day including Şuayb and Soğmatar, min 3

people), as well as to Nemrut Dağı (₺125, min 3 people) and Göbekli Tepe (₺30 pp incl. guide). Mustafa at the *Uğur* hotel (see p.589) has his own a/c minibus and arranges one-day trips to Nemrut, including all subsidiary sites (₺130), and trips including Harran, Şuayb, Soğmatar and Göbekli Tepe for similar prices.

11

ACCOMMODATION

Accommodation at all levels is plentiful, from simple backpacker joints to plush chains. Be warned that the "boutique" hotels fashioned from some of Urfa's fine old stone houses vary in quality – always ask to see a room first – while others host noisy traditional music evenings (see p.590) until the early hours.

⭐ **Hotel Arte** Atatürk Bul/Sinema Sok 7 📞0414 314 7060, 🌐otel-arte.com. Good-value designer hotel with simple but stylish rooms boasting laminate parquet floors, a/c, flat-screen TVs et al, very well located in the central business/tourist area around Köprübaşı. There's wi-fi, and beer in the minibar. ₺90

Aslan Konuk Evi Demokrasi Cad, Sok 10 📞0414 215 1575, 🌐aslankonukevi.com. Run by the loquacious Özcan Aslan, a middle-school teacher and fluent English-speaker, this converted Armenian courtyard house is a backpackers' favourite. The breakfast is copious, there's free wi-fi and use of a washing machine, and the owner can (and will!) offer to sign you up for one of his tours (see p.589). Dorms ₺20–25, doubles ₺100

Beyazade Konak Sarayönü Cad, Yusufpaşa Camii Yanı 📞0414 216 3535, 🌐beyazadekonak.com. First of the new wave of budget boutique hotels, this authentic old mansion building is good value and, despite its disappointingly modern furnishings, has character. Particularly impressive are the vaulted-ceiling dining room and shady courtyard. Occasionally hosts *sira gecesi* (traditional music nights). ₺70

Cevahir Konuk Evi Selahhattin Eyyub Camii Karşısı 📞0414 215 9377. The best of the city's boutique hotels, arranged around a courtyard in a beautiful building (once part of an Armenian monastery), in a quiet street. It has been very expertly restored and oozes good taste and boasts all the requisite luxury features. The only potential drawback is the noise from the *sira gecesi*. ₺220

Güven Sarayönü Cad 133 📞0414 215 1700, 🌐hotelguven.com. Solid three-star hotel, recently made over. While rooms are a tad on the small side, the big, firm beds and crisp white linen compensate, as do the gleaming

bathrooms with their travertine floors and chrome fittings. Another plus is the top-floor breakfast room (a decent open-buffet spread) overlooking the Ulu Cami and the *kale*. ₺90

Harran Atatürk Cad 📞0414 313 2860, 🌐hotelharran .com. The best feature of the reasonable-value, four-star *Harran* is its large outdoor swimming pool, very welcome in Urfa's summer heat. The rooms are comfortable and bathrooms spotless – all have been recently refurbished, but ask for one in the newer B block, which is quieter. ₺150

Manici Hotel Şurkavi Alışveriş Merkezi 6 📞0414 215 9911, 🌐manici.com.tr. Successor to the now defunct *Edessa*, this opulent (some might say over-the-top) hotel is well located right opposite Balıklı Göl. Rooms feature elaborately hand-painted furniture and chintzy soft furnishings as well as standard features like a/c, wi-fi, TV and en-suite bathrooms with tubs. Cheaper accommodation can be found in the adjoining *Narlı Evi*, an old courtyard house run by the same company. ₺140

Hotel Rabis Sarayönü Cad, PTT Karşısı 📞0414 216 9595, 🌐hotelrabis.com. New and spotlessly clean, comfortable hotel, with a/c, flat-screen TVs, wi-fi and minibar. While not quite as stylish as the *Arte*, it's just as comfy, and boasts a breakfast terrace overlooking the old city. Recommended. ₺140

Otel Uğur Köprübaşı Cad 3 📞0414 313 1340, 📧musma63@yahoo.com. Behind the Özel Dünya Hospital, the distinctly old-school *Uğur*, linked in with Hostelworld, is Urfa's cheapest suitable option. Rooms are basic and garish, but are clean and have a/c and comfy beds. Waterless rooms are the cheapest, and the shared showers and loos are kept very clean; en-suite rooms cost ₺10 extra. The helpful owner Mustafa can arrange Harran Nemrut tours (see p.589). ₺40

SIRA GECELERİ – A NIGHT OUT IN URFA

Sira geceleri (literally "nights by turn") were originally informal gatherings of male friends at one of their homes, where a meal and conversation were accompanied by traditional live music. The idea was picked up by several Urfa restaurants (each invariably sited in an old courtyard house), and now "guests" pay for the experience, sitting cross-legged at a low *sofra* table and tucking into a banquet of speciality local dishes while being serenaded by a traditional band. Three of the best venues are listed below.

Cevahir Konak Evi Selahhattin Eyyub Camii Karşısı ☎0414 215 9377, ⓦ cevahirkonukevi.com. Probably the best, and certainly the dearest (₺50 for the set menu of eight different dishes). Wed, Fri & Sat from 8pm.

Gülizar Konak Evi Sarayönü Cad, İrfaniye Sok ☎0414 215 0505. Lovely old mansion set below the towering Ulu Cami minaret, with ₺35 set menu, and, usually, two *sira geceleri* each week. Wed & Sat from 8pm.

Yıldız Saray Konuk Evi Yorgancı Sok ☎0414 216 9494, ⓦ yildizsaraykonukevi.com. Courtyard mansion with a good reputation, ₺35 for the set menu. Performances usually Wed, Fri & Sun from 8pm.

EATING AND DRINKING

Urfa is the home of the Urfa *kebap* (spiced minced meat on a skewer), and *lahmacun* (a thin, chapati-like bread topped with spicy lamb). Numerous simple eateries offer other local specialities based on bulgur (cracked wheat), notably *çiğ köfte*) Ciğer (liver) kebabs are big business too, eaten accompanied by lashings of raw onion and hot pepper; *şıllık*, a local *baklava*, is made with walnuts and cream. Be warned that travellers seem to suffer more from stomach bugs and food poisoning in Urfa than elsewhere in Turkey; be extra careful, especially during the hottest months.

RESTAURANTS

★ **Gülhan** Atatürk Bul Akbank Bitişiği. Highly recommended, particularly for the lunchtime *sulu yemek* (vegetable dishes ₺7, meat-based ones ₺10) and the evening grills (₺13 for a delicious kebab). Well frequented by the local middle classes, its bustling nature ensures a fast turnover and fresh food. Daily 10am–10pm.

Urfa Lezzet Kebap Salonu Akarbaşı Göl Cad 31. What looks like a hole-in-the-wall kebab joint at street level actually boasts a dining room one floor up, and a pleasant roof terrace above that. Right on the edge of the bazaar, this is as local as it gets in Urfa, with cheap kebabs (₺9), *lahmacun* (₺2) and lentil soup. Daily 8am–10pm.

Urfa Sofrası Karakoyun ış Merkezi, Kat 1 No 226. Just off Köprübaşı Cad, this cool and pleasant roof-terrace restaurant is spotlessly clean (signs encourage you to wander around the kitchens to check). Tender kebabs from ₺12, *pide* and pizzas around ₺10. It's also a good place to try the local speciality dessert *şıllık* (₺6). No alcohol. Daily 10am–11pm.

BARS AND CAFÉS

Male-dominated bars dotted along a terrace on Atatürk Caddesi, opposite the *Harran* hotel, serve beer or rakı (but not during Ramadan), as well as snacks such as fruit and nuts. The only alternatives for alcoholic drinks are the upmarket bars at the *Harran* and the *Dedeman* hotels, or the *Türkü* bar (see p.590).

Altın Kupa Off Atatürk Cad. At the end of a short strip of bars opposite the Karakoyun İş Merkezi, the "Golden Cup" is set in an old stone building with a vaulted ceiling. Its big advantage over its competitors is the quiet adjoining beer-garden. Beers cost ₺5, and they'll send out for kebabs. Not recommended for female travellers without a male companion. Daily noon–2am.

Türkü Konağı Sarayönü Cad, Vatan Sok 7. Atmospheric bar with live *Türkü* music nightly. Set in the old camel stables of a *kervansaray*, it's very atmospheric on the right evening. Beers are a reasonable ₺6, wine ₺9 per glass – but watch out for the price of *çerez*. Daily noon–midnight.

DIRECTORY

Banks and exchange A couple of convenient *döviz* offices, and many ATMs on Sarayönü Cad.

Hospital Özel Dünya Hastanesi (Dünya private hospital), Köprübaşı Cad ☎0414 216 3616 or ☎215 4348; Devlet Hastane ve Polikliniği (State Hospital), Hastane Cad ☎0414 313 1928 or ☎313 1220.

Police station Sarayönü Cad.

Post office Sarayönü Cad (Mon–Sat 9am–noon & 1–5pm for money exchange and mail; 24hr for telephones).

A KURDISH VILLAGE EXPERIENCE – HOMESTAYS IN YUVACALI

The small village of **Yuvacalı**, set amid bleached fields of wheat, lentils and chickpeas, huddles at the foot of a prominent settlement mound as ancient as nearby Göbekli Tepe, not far from the market town of Hilvan. Here you can stay in a Kurdish village home (€35 per day full-board), eat with the family, sleep beneath the stars on the flat-roof of the family home, and try your hand at milking sheep and baking unleavened village bread. You'll also be introduced to Kurdish history and culture, taken on a 1hr 30min walk around the village and its ruins, and perhaps walk a part of the waymarked **Abraham Path** (w abrahamspathinturkey.org), which starts here.

The **homestay** is part of a responsible tourism project set up by village-born Omer Tanık and his English wife Alison. The host families keep all the money they receive from guests, as do the drivers on the couple's well-regarded **Nomad Tours** (☎ 0533 747 1850, w nomad toursturkey.com). Guests are asked to make a small donation to the project. The money goes straight into the local community and has, for example, helped to set up a pre-school in the village. Booking ahead is essential; accommodation can and does fill up.

To get to Yuvacalı, catch a bus from Urfa's *otogar* to Hilvan (₺5), where, if you call Nomad Tours in advance, someone from the village will meet you. With your own transport follow the D-885 to Hilvan (the Siverek/Diyarbakır road) and turn right (signed Gölcük) at the second set of lights. After a few kilometres, take the second left to Yuvacalı.

Göbekli Tepe

15km northeast of Urfa • Daily 24hr • Free, guarded by a *bekçi* (watchman) • Around ₺80 return by taxi from Urfa, including waiting time; to drive, follow the Mardin road (E-400) for 10km, then turn left (north) at a brown-on-white sign – Göbekli Tepe is another 11km

Set where the southern foothills of the Toros Mountains fade into the scorching flatlands of upper Mesopotamia, **Göbekli Tepe** (Hill of the Navel) ranks among Turkey's most intriguing archeological sites. Here, on a hilltop 870m above sea level, stands a man-made mound some 300m in diameter and 15m high, containing a series of circular enclosures, carbon-dated to between 9500 and 7500 BC.

The enclosures have burnt-lime floors and are lined with stone benches, but most remarkably contain a series of T-shaped monoliths, the tallest of which are 5m high. Clearly anthropomorphic, many of the monoliths are liberally covered with incredible relief carvings of wild animals, from scorpions and snakes to lions and wild boar. The enclosures were almost certainly used for cult purposes and the site is much hyped as the "world's first temple".

Göbekli Tepe also appears to disprove the theory that only settled societies were capable of producing monumental buildings and sophisticated art. Most of the work here was done when man was still in the hunter-gatherer stage of development – no evidence has been found of human settlement. An unsightly protective roof was removed in 2011 and a new wooden walkway added, allowing visitors to walk right around the main enclosures.

Harran

The beehive-style houses of **HARRAN** (Altınbaşak), 45km southeast of Urfa, are an established tourist attraction. The village has grown up within the crumbling remnants of the old, 4km circumference walls of a settlement once much more important than Urfa. Harran has strong biblical links, too: according to Genesis 11:31 and 12:4, the patriarch **Abraham** dwelt here before moving onto Canaan.

These days, Arabs and a few Kurds live amid the ruins of old Harran, surviving by farming the newly irrigated fields and smuggling goods across the Syrian border, 10km south. The stone-built, mud-covered beehive-shaped buildings owe their distinctive shape to the fact that no wood is used as support. Virtually all are now used for storage or animal – not human – habitation.

Brief history

Harran is thought to have been continuously inhabited for at least six thousand years. It became a prosperous trading town under the Assyrians, who turned it into a centre for the worship of Sin, god of the moon; there was a large temple here, later also used by the Sabians. Planet worshippers, they stand accused in some accounts of holding lurid orgies and carrying out human sacrifice, and with the arrival of the Arabs were given the choice of conversion to Islam or death. In 53 BC the Roman general Crassus was defeated here, crucified and had molten gold poured into his mouth by the Parthians. Despite this, the Romans later converted Harran into an important centre of learning, a role it continued to play under the Byzantines, then the Arabs, first under the Umayyad dynasty, then the Ayyubid. However, the arrival of the Mongols during the thirteenth century meant devastation.

The site

11

Harran's enigmatic ruins exude tragic grandeur, dwarfing the beehive dwellings of the ethnically Arab villagers. Near the *jandarma*, an artificial tumulus marks the site of the original settlement. Excavations currently under way here, by a team from Ankara University, have revealed the remains of an Umayyad palace. North of the mound, and most impressive of the ruins, is the **Ulu Cami**, the first mosque ever built on what is now Turkish soil. Its substantial square minaret, originally built in the eighth century, was mistaken for a cathedral belfry by T. E. Lawrence when he passed through in 1909. The layout of the mosque, much rebuilt under the Ayyubid dynasty in the twelfth century, can be made out clearly, though only fragments of its structure survive relatively intact.

The eleventh-century **citadel**, in the southeast corner of the old walled city, is possibly built on the site of the ancient temple of the moon god Sin. Three of its four polygonal towers have survived reasonably well, but take care scrambling around as there are several holes in the upper part of the structure.

ARRIVAL AND DEPARTURE   HARRAN

By dolmuş Dolmuşes run hourly from Şanlıurfa *otogar* to Harran (₺5); the last returning dolmuş leaves at 7pm.

By taxi A taxi for the trip to and from Şanlıurfa, with waiting time, should cost around ₺120.

ACCOMMODATION

Harran Kültür Evi ☎ 0414 441 2477. Staying in this atmospheric complex of restored beehive dwellings, right amid the ruin, you'll sleep on mattresses on the floor, but the place is scrupulously clean, the food good, and owner Reşat (the village headman) friendly and resplendent in his flowing Bedouin robes. Rates include half board (for two). €30

Kahta

Despite the fact it's drab and nondescript, the dusty town of **KAHTA**, as the most commonly used gateway to Nemrut Dağı and its spectacular mountain-top sanctuary, receives more than its fair share of visitors. Many travellers arrive from elsewhere in Turkey at the provincial capital of **Adıyaman**, 25km west, though several inter-city bus companies have services direct to Kahta. There is nothing of interest in the town, but it's only 1km from the Atatürk Barajı reservoir, where there are a few pleasant waterside restaurants and picnic spots.

ARRIVAL AND DEPARTURE   KAHTA

By plane Adıyaman airport, 20km west of Kahta, is served by Havaş bus (₺5) or taxi (₺25).
Destinations Ankara (Anadolujet, at least 2 daily; 1hr 20min);
By bus Services to and from Ankara (1 daily; 12hr);

İstanbul (2 daily; 20hr); Şanlıurfa (3 daily; 2hr 30min).
By dolmuş Adıyaman (every 10min, daily 6am–8pm; ₺3.5), Karadüt (hourly in season; 30min; ₺5); Siverek, for Diyarbkır (several daily; 2hr; ₺8).

ACCOMMODATION AND EATING

Hotel Kommagene Junction of main street and the road up to Nemrut ☎ 0416 725 9726, ✉ kommagenem @hotmail.com. Rebuilt in wood and now styling itself "boutique", the *Kommagene* is, despite its unpromising location on a major crossroads, not bad value, and travellers can use the kitchen and washing machine for free. It does have a bad reputation for hard-selling tours to Nemrut and misleading visitors about other accommodation options up the mountain, though, so be warned. ₺80

Neşetin Yeri 2km east of town, overlooking the Atatürk lake. Much better than the cheap and basic restaurants on Kahta's main street, this fish restaurant serves excellent-value lake fish, and grills on terraces with a view of the mountain and lake, but you'll need your own transport or a taxi to get here. Daily noon–11pm.

Zeus Hotel ☎ 0416 725 5694, 🌐 zeushotel.com.tr. Kahta's best hotel, with a prettily landscaped good-sized swimming pool, bar-restaurant, and spacious rooms with a/c, flat-screen TVs and wi-fi. ₺140

The road to Nemrut Dağı

The 75km paved road from Kahta to the sanctuary atop Nemrut Dağı (Mount Nemrut) is easily done with your own transport, but make sure you fill up with fuel in Kahta. Visitors intending to reach the summit sanctuary in time for dawn go up the quick way (via Narince), and return via the subsidiary site route, while those aiming for a sunset visit to the top usually take in the lesser sites en route. Nemrut's summit sanctuary, and the subsidiary site of Arsameia, both lie within the **Nemrut Dağı Milli Park** (Mt Nemrut National Park). The ₺8 entry to the park covers entry to both the summit and Arsameia. There are two gates to the park, one southwest of the summit, a couple of kilometres below Arsameia, the other a few kilometres above Karadut village, south of the summit.

Karakuş tumulus

9km north of Kahta

The huge **Karakuş tumulus**, said to be the funeral mound of Antiochus' wife, rises up dramatically by the roadside, just past a small oil-drilling field. It's adorned by three separate groups of three columns, each surmounted by either an animal statue or a relief carving. The best preserved is the eagle that gives the site its name – "black bird". There's a small café-cum-souvenir shop on site, plus toilets.

Cendere Köprüsü

18km north of Kahta, 9km beyond Karakuş tumulus

The **Cendere Köprüsü** is a monumental Roman bridge built between 193 and 211 AD, during the reign of Emperor Septimius Severus. It's closed to traffic; to reach its western end, take the signed but badly potholed stretch of road that branches left from shortly before the new bridge. Its graceful single arch spans the mouth of a spectacular gorge. Originally a pair of columns stood at either end of the bridge, but now only three of them survive. The fourth, dedicated to Severus' younger son Geta, was removed when his eldest son, Caracalla, had his brother put to death in a successful bid to become sole emperor.

Eski Kahta

25km north of Kahta; turning 6km beyond Cendere Köprüsü

The traditional hillside village of **ESKİ KAHTA** is dominated by the **Mamluk Yeni Kale**. The castle is spectacular when viewed from a distance, but few people have the time or nerve to explore its precipitous heights. Indeed the best place to view it is from the heights above the Hercules and Antiochus relief at Arsameia; see p.594.

11

Arsameia

25km north of Kahta; just off the main road 1km south of Eskı Kahta • Daily 8am–7pm • ₺8, includes summit entrance

The ancient site of **Arsameia**, the summer capital of the ancient Commagene kingdom, was excavated during the 1950s. From the shop/café/toilet block area at the site entrance, where it's also possible to camp, take the lower path to a truncated relief-stele of the god Mithras. Head up the steps to join the main path, then continue to reach a man-made cave, in which a tunnel runs down to what's thought to be a Mithraic cult chamber. A damaged stele below the cave entrance depicts Mithridates I Callinicus, and his son, Antiochus I, the founder of the complex at Nemrut Dağı.

Heading back a short distance then taking the path up the hillside will bring you to the highlight of the site: a fabulous, perfectly preserved **relief depicting Hercules and Antiochus I** shaking hands – as impressive, if not more so, than anything you'll see on the top of Nemrut Dağı itself. Above the entrance to a tunnel alongside, which leads down to another cult chamber, a huge, 25-line Greek inscription tells you that Mithridates I Callinicus, father of Antiochus, is buried in the vicinity, and that the site is consecrated to him.

A short way above and beyond the relief of Hercules and Antiochus, a plateau holds the remnants of a funerary/cult sanctuary complex that once must have rivalled that on Nemrut. Little remains, but the views across the mountains and down over Yeni Kale are spectacular. A road cuts across the mountains, via Kayadib village, to join the major summit road just above the Çeşme Pansiyon in upper Karadut.

Karadut

KARADUT village probably makes for the most relaxing approach to Nemrut. Some 800m above sea level, with grand views over terraced fields, a plunging valley and limestone peaks, it's a lovely cool place named after the black mulberry trees that grow here among the apricot groves.

ARRIVAL AND DEPARTURE   KARADUT

By bus Karadut is served by local dolmuşes from Kahta (hourly, 6am–6pm; 1hr).

ACCOMMODATION AND EATING

Çeşme Karadut's highest hotel ☎ 0416 737 2032, ⓦ cesmepansion.com. A couple of kilometres higher up the mountain than Karadut's other options, this laidback pension/restaurant offers tasty meals and expansive views. Rooms are plain and the plumbing temperamental, but it's cosy enough and there's a veranda where you can sit and watch the sun go down. Owner Mustafa will pick you up from lower Karadut and/or deposit you there to catch the dolmuş down to Kahta. Rates include half board for two. ₺80

Hotel Euphrat Just above the village ☎ 0416 737 2175, ⓦ hoteleuphratnemrut.com. Long-established hotel, just below the *Kervansaray Nemrut*, which has undergone a major face-lift. The rooms are ranged around a stone-built, L-shaped single-storey building (with outdoor pool), and there's a great terrace outside the restaurant with splendid mountain views. Rooms and bathrooms are on the small side, but fittings are new and

good quality so it's easily the most comfortable base in Karadut. €56

Karadut Motel Pansiyon Just above the village ☎ 0416 737 2169, ⓦ karadutpansiyon.net. This group-orientated place offers basic but comfortable en-suite rooms, a friendly atmosphere, good home-cooked food (₺8 extra for dinner) and wi-fi. The rooms on the first floor are cheerier than those on the dark ground floor. ₺70

Kervansaray Nemrut Just above the village ☎ 0416 737 2190, ⓦ nemrutkervansaray.con. This appealingly sited single-storey hotel was being upgraded at the time of writing, to compete with neighbouring rival the *Euphrat*, it's hard to say how things will turn out. It gets generally positive feedback, has a pool and great views, and the two local guys who run it are very charming. Rates include half board. Also offers hikes up to Nemrut (3hr). €62

Nemrut Dağı

The remote, grandiose mountain-top sanctuary at **Nemrut Dağı** is unforgettable, while the mighty stone heads that adorn the temple and tomb of King Antiochus have become one of the famous images of Eastern Turkey.

Most visitors want to get here **before dawn**, in order to watch the sunrise. The majority of the available minibus tours are therefore geared up to suit those timings, despite the drawback of making such an early start – between 2am and 4am, depending on season – and the crowded and chilly conditions at the summit, which is 2150m above sea level. Between late October and April, there's often snow on the ground. Minibus tours also target **sunset**, when it's not so cold, and the setting sun bathes the western terrace in a warm glow. A daytime visit means fewer visitors and the chance to explore the sanctuary at leisure and in the warmth.

Brief history

The result of one man's delusions of grandeur, the great tomb and temple complex of Nemrut Dağı was built by **Antiochus I Epiphanes** (64–38 BC), son of Mithridates I Callinicus, the founder of the Commagene kingdom. A breakaway from the Seleucid Empire, covering only a small territory from modern Adıyaman to Gaziantep, the Commagene dynasty wouldn't rate much more than a passing mention in histories of the region had Antiochus not chosen to build this colossal monument to himself. Having decided he was divine in nature, or at the very least an equal of the gods, he declared: "I, the great King Antiochus have ordered the construction of these temples…on a foundation which will never be demolished…to prove my faith in the gods. At the conclusion of my life I will enter my eternal repose here, and my spirit will ascend to join that of Zeus in heaven."

Antiochus's vanity knew no bounds – he claimed descent from Darius the Great of Persia and Alexander the Great – but eventually he went too far, siding with the Parthians against Rome, and was deposed. This was effectively the end of the Commagene kingdom, which afterwards passed into Roman hands.

The sanctuary lay undiscovered until 1881, when Karl Puchstein, a German engineer, located it while making a survey. Although he returned in 1883 with Karl Humann – the man who removed the Pergamon altar to Berlin – to carry out a more thorough

11

11

EXCURSIONS TO NEMRUT DAĞI

Organized **minibus trips to Nemrut Dağı** run in summer from Kahta, Malatya and Şanlıurfa. Given the distances involved, they are about the only way to get there if you don't have your own transport. Note that the summit road is usually only open from April 15 until the first snowfall of winter, but outside the peak summer months (July & Aug) there may well be insufficient demand to make up groups each day. For more on the best time of day to visit the site, see p.595.

FROM KAHTA AND KARADUT

In season, there are sunrise or sunset tours from **Kahta** (see p.592) – sunset trips leave around 2pm and return at 10pm; sunrise tours leave at around 2am, returning at 10am. Best arranged by the transport cooperative – see Bayram Çınar at the Karadut market, opposite the dolmuş garage – the trips cost ₺125 for the dolmuş, irrespective of numbers, with the entrance fee extra. They should include the subsidiary sites of the Karakuş tumulus, Cendere bridge and the ancient Commagene capital of Arsameia.

Don't be bludgeoned into booking a tour before you check various options – indeed, assuming you arrive in time to catch the last dolmuş (6pm), it's far better to head straight up to the lovely village of **Karadut** (see p.594). All the accommodation options here arrange summit tours – a taxi to the summit costs around ₺35, a minibus around ₺50 (regardless of numbers, entrance extra); tours including the subsidiary sites ₺100. Sunrise tours see the subsidiary sites on the return, sunrise tours en route.

FROM MALATYA

Tours from **Malatya** (p.597), on the north side of the range, may look more expensive, but if you count in the night's stay virtually at the summit, the difference is negligible. The main disadvantage is that you miss out on Nemrut's subsidiary sites, but on the other hand you view both sets of heads at sunrise and sunset, and you get to stay at the welcoming stone-built Guneş Hotel (☎0422 323 9378), which has clean and cheerful en-suite rooms and good food. A Kurdish yayla (summer tent encampment) lies a few minutes' walk away.

Bookings are best made the day before, either at the tourist office or the tea garden to one side. Departures are usually at noon, reaching the summit in good time for sunset; the return trip starts at about 7am, allowing time to admire the sunrise, and reaching Malatya at about 11am. The ₺100 fee per person includes transport, lodging and two meals, and trips run even if there's only one taker; the entrance fee is extra. If it suits your onward travel plans, after viewing the sanctuary at sunrise you could walk over to the south side of Nemrut and join one of the groups seeing the subsidiary sites on the way back to Kahta.

FROM ŞANLIURFA

Visiting Nemrut from **Şanlıurfa** (p.585) has the advantage of cutting out Adıyaman and Kahta, and can include a trip to see the Atatürk Dam, but the 420km (14hr) round trip takes in lots of uninteresting scenery – for details see p.589.

investigation, only in 1953 did a comprehensive American-led archeological survey of the site begin.

The site

A new visitors' centre was under construction at the time of writing, a couple of kilometres below the summit. How this will affect visiting is uncertain. At the time of research, the "original" car park/café/souvenir stall and toilet area stood twenty minutes' walk below the summit area.

The actual tomb of Antiochus has never been found, but is thought to lie buried beneath a 60m-high tumulus of small rocks that's rated by the *Guinness Book of Records* as the world's largest man-made mound, covering an area of 7.5 acres. The colossal heads for which the site is renowned are ranged in two groups, to the west and east of the tumulus.

he eastern temple

paved path along the south side of the central tumulus at Nemrut Dağı leads to the
rrace area, on which stands the **eastern temple** with six decapitated seated statues,
measuring several metres tall. Lined up in front of these truncated figures are the
much-photographed **detached heads**, each a couple of metres high. From left to right they
represent: Antiochus I, Fortuna (symbol of the Commagene kingdom), Zeus, Apollo and
Hercules. Scattered around them lie the remains of massive stone eagles and lions – one of
each creature originally stood, as symbolic guardian, at either end of the royal line-up.
The anthropomorphic statues were meant to incorporate several similar deities
drawn from different cultures, according to the principle of syncretism, which
Alexander the Great had promoted to try and foster a sense of unity among the
disparate peoples of his empire. On the date of Antiochus's birthday and the
anniversary of his coronation, the Commagene people would file up to the mountain
op to witness the dawn sacrifice and make offerings, carried out in strict accordance
with the Greek inscriptions carved onto the back of the royal statues. The stepped,
andstone sacrificial **altar** still stands in front of the statues.

he western terrace

ollow a path around the northern base of the tumulus to reach the **western terrace**,
ned by slabs that were once decorated with reliefs. None of the western statues is even
artially intact, but there are more of them – a complete set of five, plus two eagle-
eads to flank them – and the dispersed **heads** here are much less weathered than those
n the east.
The alignment of statues was originally the same as on the east side, but these heads
ave not been lined up in front of their "bodies". A well-paved path coils west then
outh from here back to the car park, so you don't have to retrace your steps around
he tumulus.

Malatya and around

he largest producer of apricots in the world, **MALATYA**, is a seldom-visited city of
early half a million people that's set in a broad green valley around 60km north of
Nemrut Dağı. Despite a long history going back over five thousand years, during
which the Assyrians, Hittites, Romans, Selçuk Turks and Ottomans all held sway,
here's little of any significant age left to see within the city. Nonetheless it makes a
leasant overnight stop before tackling Nemrut Dağı, while, very close at hand, the
ld town of **Eski Malatya** offers an interesting diversion, as does **Aslantepe** (Lion Hill),
millennia-old settlement mound that's been newly interpreted for visitors.
Scratch beneath the surface in Malatya, and an at-times uneasy mix of Turkish
ationalists, devout Sunni Muslims, Alevîs and Kurds soon becomes apparent. Always
political town, it's the home of two former presidents of the Republic, General İsmet
nönü and part-Kurdish Turgut Özal, and is also the birthplace of Armenian-Turk
Irant Dink, slain by an ultra-nationalist Turkish teenager in 2007 (see p.683).
The old **Şire Pazarı**, in the centre between Atatürk Bulvarı and the ring road, is
evoted to local agricultural produce, namely cherries, mulberries, apples, walnuts and,
specially, apricots. There's an **apricot festival** (second week in July) at Mişmiş Parkı,
km east of the centre.

Malatya museum

es–Sun 8am–noon & 1–4.45pm • ₺3

he excellent **Malatya museum** (Malatya Müzesi) is absolutely obligatory if you've any
nterest in the Bronze Age. Small but very well laid out, it concentrates on finds from

nearby **Aslantepe** (see p.599). The room to the left as you enter holds fine pottery and copper swords from 3000–3400 BC, plus reconstructions of graves from Aslantepe. Upstairs you'll find more artefacts from Aslantepe, plus a glass case devoted to decorative seals, used to guarantee the integrity of goods in containers; the most common motifs being deer and antelope. The pick of the exhibits is in the entry area downstairs, however, including three neo-Hittite relief-carved blocks depicting winged demons and an eagle-headed human.

Malatya Ethnographic Museum

Sinema Cad • Tues–Sun 8am–4.45pm • Free

Several traditional houses, of mainly mud-brick and timber construction, have been restored on Sinema Caddesi. One now holds the **Malatya Ethnographic Museum** (Malatya Beşkonaklar Müzesi). Labels are in English, and there's a series of upstairs rooms devoted to blocks for hand-printing cloth, muskets, pipes, hamam utensils and looms.

ARRIVAL AND DEPARTURE

MALATYA

By plane From Malatya's airport, 26km northwest of the city, a Havaş shuttle bus (₺9) meets THY flights and ferries passengers to the centre; get off on Atatürk Caddesi. Buy tickets for domestic flights from Bertaş, ☎0422 326 0037, Sivas Cad, Semercioğlu Apt Alt.

Destinations Ankara (1 daily with Anadolujet; 1hr 20min); Antalya (1 daily via Ankara with Anadolujet); İstanbul (1 daily with THY; 1hr 45min); İzmir (1 daily via Ankara with Anadolujet).

By train Malatya's train station, 2km west of the centre on

the Çevre Yolu (ring road), is served by the Maşti bus from opposite the *Vilayet*; buy ticket for ₺3 (two-use) from booth before boarding.

Destinations Adana (daily; 8hr 30min); Ankara (daily; 20hr); Diyarbakır (4 weekly; 6hr 30min); İstanbul (4 weekly; 26hr); Tatvan (3 weekly; 10hr 30min).

By bus The *otogar* is 7km west of the centre on the Çevre Yolu (ring road). It's served by the Maşti bus from opposite the *Vilayet*; you can only buy a two-use ticket (₺3) available from the booth before boarding.

estinations Adana (5 daily; 7hr 30min); Adıyaman ourly; 3hr); Ankara (8 daily; 10hr); Diyarbakır (7 daily; ır); Erzurum (1 daily; 7hr); Gaziantep (5 daily; 4hr);

İstanbul (5 daily; 14hr).

Car rental Bizim Rent a Car, Kanalboyu 30/1 (☎0533 282 1363).

NFORMATION

ourist office In the *Vilayet* (governor's office) building, hind the statue of İnönü in the main square, İnönü eydanı (Mon–Sat 9am–noon & 1–5pm; ☎0422 323 25). Its main function is to sign visitors up for a trip to

Nemrut Dağı (see p.596); ask the helpful Bülent for advice. There's also a small information office on Sinema Caddesi, next to the Ethnographic Museum (see p.598).

CCOMMODATION

ccommodation in Malatya is plentiful, but aimed squarely at businessmen rather than tourists. Most hotels and staurants are within walking distance of each other in the compact, tree-lined modern centre.

★ **Hanem** Fuzuli Cad 13 ☎0422 321 2839, hanemhotel.com.tr. Malatya's most stylish hotel atures floor-to-ceiling windows, trendy laminated floors, strained decor and big, comfy beds with crisp linen. Nice uches include free tea- and coffee-making facilities, free i-fi and a big-screen TV. **₺140**

lalatya Büyük Hotel Yeni Cami Karşısı ☎0422 321 00, ⓦmalatyabuyukotel.com. Offering good views of e pretty, early twentieth-century Yeni Camii, this friendly ɔtel was completely renovated in 2012. It's tastefully done ut with Scandinavian-style pale wood furniture and eam walls. Bathrooms gleam with chrome – and there

are flat-screen TVs and free wi-fi. Serves up an excellent buffet breakfast. **₺120**

Otel Park Atatürk Cad 17 ☎0422 321 1691, ⓔparkotelmalatya@mynet.com. A good budget option, with plain, pastel-hued rooms and tiled floors. Some rooms are fully en-suite, others just have showers and there are shared (squat) toilets down the hall. No breakfast. **₺60**

Yeni Otel Yeni Cami Karşısı ☎0422 323 1423, ⓦyenimalatyahotel.com. A good mid-range option, the two-star has all conveniences – a/c, TV, minibar, free wi-fi etc – and a decent buffet breakfast. The soft furnishings in the rooms are a little garish, though. **₺80**

ATING AND DRINKING

hile Malatya holds plenty of **cafés and restaurants**, none is outstanding. In Kanalboyu, on the south side of the city the end of Fuzuli Caddesi, a strip of pleasant cafés aimed at Malatya's middle classes line twin cobbled streets running ther side of a watercourse. Dozens of specialist city-centre stores sell apricots, plain, sun-dried or rolled in chocolate, or ocolate-covered marzipan goodies made from apricot kernels.

★ **Beşkonaklar Malatya Mutfağı** Sinema Cad 13 ☎0422 326 0051. The city's most atmospheric restaurant in a traditional house with a nice, green and shady arden out back. The specialities are *köfte* of various sorts, cluding some vegetarian options such as *patlıcan köftesi* alls of aubergine, chickpea and bulgur served in a quant tomato sauce). Unlicensed. Daily noon–10pm.

1angal Vadisi Turfanda Sok 1 ☎0422 326 2200. An *cakbaşı*-style restaurant where you can watch your meat eing grilled over charcoal. Kebabs or grills (from ₺10) are receded by free *lavaş* bread and accompanying *meze*. heese *pides* are available for veggies. Daily noon–10pm.

lostalji Mucelli Cad ☎0422 323 4209. The wooden ɔuse that holds this laidback café, more or less opposite

the five-screen Yeşil Sineması, dates back to 1840. It's a great place to sample local specialities such as *analı kızlı köfte*, laze over a Turkish coffee or ₺10 breakfast spread – or just puff on a nargile. Daily 9am–10pm.

Sevinç Kışla Cad 1. Established back in 1972, this spotless café-bakery just off Atatürk dishes up fresh *simit*, plain and stuffed *poğça* and cakes – ideal for breakfast with a glass of fresh tea. Daily 7am–10pm.

VIP Cafe Vilayet Parkı. Shady tea-garden/café, next to the Vilayet building and tourist office, that's an ideal place to hang out in the heat of the day. It has a surprisingly broad menu, with big salad bowls, *börek* (pies) and chicken wings etc, as well as the usual teas and coffees. You can also try a nargile (₺10) or rent a laptop for ₺3. Daily 8am–9pm.

Aslantepe

7km northeast of Malatya • Tues–Sun 8am–5pm • ₺3 • "Orduzu" buses, from the junction of Buharı and Sarıcıoğlu cads, stop 500m along signed street from the site

Following fifty years of meticulous excavations by Italian archeologists, the 6,000-square-metre settlement mound at **Aslantepe**, dating back to the fourth millennium BC, has recently opened as an open-air museum. At the entrance stand newly carved copies of some of the monumental neo-Hittite statuary found here, including the god Tarhunzas and a couple of fine grinning lions – after which the site was named when the originals were discovered in the nineteenth century. There's also the reconstruction of a typical mud-brick Bronze Age house.

A signed walkway leads visitors through the various layers of this complex but fascinating site, which has seen occupation in the Chalcolithic era (fourth millennium BC), the Bronze Age, the Hittite era, and finally the Roman and medieval periods. You can walk through the mud-brick remains of a palace dating from 3000 BC and a temple built circa 3500 BC. In the latter, archeologists found over a thousand pottery bowls – evidence of very early mass production. Everything is well explained by a series of informative display boards.

The top of the mound offers fine views, across a veritable sea of apricot trees, to the distant mountains.

Eski Malatya (Battalgazi)

12km north of Malatya • Catch a bus in front of Ziraat Bank on Atatürk Cad in Malatya, having bought a "smart" ticket from the booth on Fuzuli Caddesi, just east of the Vilayet building

The ruined Roman/Byzantine/Selçuk/Ottoman town of **Eski Malatya**, or "Old Malatya", north of modern Malatya, has now been engulfed by the modern settlement of **Battalgazi**.

From the main square where buses arrive, which holds plenty of shady *çay* places as well as a few basic restaurants, a 200m walk southwest brings you to a massive seventeenth-century *kervansaray*, the **Silahtar Mustafa Paşa**. The building has been so heavily restored it looks like new, and some of the former stables are now shops selling tacky souvenirs, but the *kışlık* (winter room), with its fine cross-vaulted ceiling and rows of fireplaces, is impressive.

The wonderful **Ulu Cami**, a huge mosque complex commissioned by Selçuk sultan, Alâeddin Keykubad, is a five-minute walk south. Built around a central courtyard, it comprises both summer and winter mosques. The latter consists of plain stonework with massive pillars, and the former of a central bay with a soaring domed roof flanked by two wings.

Diyarbakır

Superbly positioned on a bluff above a great loop in the Tigris, the old city of **DİYARBAKIR** shelters behind massive medieval walls of black basalt, enclosing a maze of cobbled streets and alleys. Many of its finest mosques and churches have been restored and renovation work is in progress on many more. There's plenty of decent accommodation right in the heart of the walled city, plus enough cafés and restaurants to keep the average visitor more than happy.

Diyarbakır struggled to cope with an influx of Kurdish refugees fleeing the state–PKK war in the 1990s, many of whom now occupy old houses in the very heart of the walled city. As a result, this is now the most proudly and most overtly Kurdish city in Turkey.

Be aware, however, that Diyarbakır still has a definite "edge". Violent street demonstrations break out from time to time, while other potential hazards include bag-snatchers, pickpockets and the odd stone-throwing youngster. Indeed an old Arab saying runs "Black the walls, black the dogs, and black the hearts in black Diyarbakır". That said, avoid the backstreets around and after dusk, and you'll have no problem – the vast majority of the population are justly proud of their fascinating city, and very welcoming to visitors.

DİYARBAKIR

Brief history

Diyarbakır dates back at least five thousand years, to the Hurrian period. Later subject to successive periods of Urartian, Assyrian and Persian hegemony, it fell to Alexander the Great and his successors, the Seleucids, in the late fourth century BC.

The Romans, who knew Diyarbakır as **Amida**, appeared on the scene in 115 AD. Over the next few centuries they and their successors, the Byzantines, struggled violently over the town with the Sassanid Persians. It was the Romans who built the first substantial walls around the city in 297 AD, though those visible today are the result of Byzantine and Arab rebuilds. The threatening basalt bulwarks gave the place its popular ancient name – Amid the Black – which is still used in the Kurdish language. The modern name comes from the Arabs: in 638 the Bakr tribe of Arabs arrived and renamed the city Diyar Bakr, or "Place of the Bakr". With the decline of Arab influence, Diyarbakır became a Selçuk, then an Artukid, and finally an Ottoman stronghold.

The city's position on the banks of the fertile Tigris encouraged fruit growing, particularly **watermelons** which are still cultivated here. In the old days they are said to have weighed 100kg, and had to be transported by camel and sliced with a sword.

The walls

Diyarbakır's 6km-long **city walls**, breached by four huge main gateways plus several smaller ones, are punctuated with 72 defensive towers. Much of what can be seen today dates from the eleventh-century Artukid kingdom of Malik Salih Şah. If you explore the walls in hot weather, be sure to bring water and a head covering. A torch is handy for the darkened interiors of the gate-towers.

Be warned that many sections of the walls lack either an external or internal parapet wall or rail, and can be just a couple of metres wide. The odd street urchin, especially if he is out of sight of adults, may find a visitor walking the walls a tempting target at which to throw stones, so be careful.

Exploring the walls – Mardin Kapısı to Urfa Kapısı

The best stretch of Diyarbakır's walls to walk lies between Mardin Kapısı and Urfa Kapısı. From **Mardin Kapısı**, turn right and follow the inside of the wall for 400m, at which point some steps lead up to the battlement walkway. Turn left and head back to Mardin Kapısı, threading through a vaulted passageway en route to an excellent viewpoint, then retrace your steps west along the ramparts. The first point of interest is the **Yedi Kardeş Burcu** (Seven Brothers Tower), a huge circular bastion decorated with Selçuk lions and a double-headed eagle. Not far beyond, the **Melikşah Burcu** (also known as the Ulu Badan) is also decorated with Selçuk motifs.

The views from the walls and towers over the Tigris are superb. Allow around thirty minutes to reach **Urfa Kapısı**. Follow the steps down into the gate-tower (hold your nose as there is a pungent stench of human excrement), and take care, as finding the next set of steps down to street level is not easy in the semi-darkness.

Keçi Burcu

The **Keçi Burcu** or "Goat's Tower" – the oldest, largest and best-preserved tower on the wall, just southeast of Mardin Kapısı – is by far the most popular location from which to admire the view down over the Tigris valley. It's especially busy around sunset on warm evenings, when locals and visitors alike come to drink tea purchased from a small

AROUND DAĞ KAPISI

Veni Vidi Hastanesi

ALI EMIRI CADDESI

BAR AND CAFÉ
Şeymus   1

Buses to İlçe Otogar & Yeni Otogar

Municipal Tourist office

Tower

KIBRIS CAD

YOĞURTÇU SOK

THY Office

İNÖNÜ CAD

Nebi Camil

Dağ Kapısı

State Tourist office

İZZET PAŞA CAD

Saray Kapısı

N

GAZİ CAD

Hasan Paşa Hanı

Ulu Cami

0   100
metres

ACCOMMODATION

Aslan Palas Oteli	2
Balkar Hotel	1
Hotel Birkent	5
New Tigris	3
SV Business	4
Hotel Surkent	6

RESTAURANTS

Aslan Yemek Salonu	1
Çarşı Konağı	3
Meşhur Kahvaltıcı Kadri	4
Şanlıurfa Kebab Evi	2

stall on the battlements. A cavernous, vaulted substructure beneath the tower now serves as a café-cum-exhibition space.

The Citadel (İç Kale)

To reach the **Citadel** or İç Kale (literally "inner fort"), in the northwest corner of Diyarbakır's walls, walk west along İzmet Paşa Caddesi and enter through the impressive Saray Kapı. Until recently a military zone, it is now open and under restoration. Inside, the substantial **Church of St George** probably dates back to the early Byzantine period. It once had twin domes, but structural changes suggest it was subsequently used as a palace by the Artukid rulers of the city.

The black stone **Hazreti Süleyman Camii**, built in 1160 by the Artukids and boasting a huge square minaret, comes alive on Thursdays, when hundreds of female pilgrims arrive to pray for their wishes to be granted. More recent buildings include stables, a prison and law courts.

The state tourism office is also here, while there are plans to relocate the city's long-closed **archeological museum** here too, though work had yet to start at the time of writing.

The old city

The **old city**, within the city walls, holds virtually all the sights worth seeing in Diyarbakır. Just inside Dağ Kapısı, the north gate piercing the walls, is the attractive **Nebi Camii**, or Mosque of the Prophet. Founded in the late fifteenth century by the Akkoyun Turcomans, it's attractively built of contrasting bands of black basalt and white limestone – a common look in Diyarbakır. Both stones are quarried locally, and their combination is considerably less threatening than the unrelenting black of the walls.

Further down Gazi Caddesi, on its eastern side, the late sixteenth-century **Hasan Paşa Hanı** is now home to a few decent café/restaurants (see p.697), as well as carpet, jewellery and souvenir shops. The city's **main bazaar** area occupies the narrow, twisting streets around it.

The Ulu Cami

The gatehouse of Diyarbakır's most important mosque, the **Ulu Cami**, stands opposite the *han*. The first of Anatolia's great Selçuk mosques, it's thought to have been built at the time of the Arab conquest in 639, on the site of, and using masonry from, the Byzantine church of St Thomas. It was probably extended in 1091 by Melik Şah, the Selçuk conqueror of the city, before being extensively refurbished after it was gutted by fire in 1155, since when it has remained little altered.

Beyond the entrance portal, decorated with bull and lion motifs, a large and singularly impressive **courtyard** holds two *şadırvan*s (ritual fountains). The north and south sides of the courtyard sport arcades, constructed using pillars salvaged from ornate late Roman and Byzantine buildings. The wing to the east and above the arch is a library, incorporating a much earlier stoa beneath it. At the northeast corner of the courtyard, you'll find the locked entrance to the **Mesudiye Medresesi**. Built in 1198 by the Artukids, this became the first university of Anatolia, and is still in use as a Koranic school.

The prayer hall is a triumph of Islamic restraint, its simple white interior and supporting arches enlivened by a superbly decorated carved-wood roof and a white *nimber*. The banded minaret is tall and angular, like many such structures in Diyarbakır. The mosque was under restoration at the time of writing, which meant that the prayer-hall was off-limits, but work should be completed by the time you read this.

Diyarbakır's subsidiary mosques

The stunning fifteenth-century **Safa Camii**, west of the Ziya Gökalp museum, is a mosque of notably graceful design and construction. Its tall, cylindrical minaret, a departure from the city norm, still bears traces of blue tile-work on its white, relief-worked surface.

Some way southeast across Melik Ahmet Caddesi, the **Behram Paşa Camii** is Diyarbakır's largest mosque. Built in 1572 by Behram Paşa, it's among the most important Ottoman-era mosques in southeastern Anatolia.

Also worth seeking out, east of Gazi Caddesi on Yenikapı Caddesi in the Balıkçılarbaşı bazaar, is the early sixteenth-century **Kasım Padişah Camii**, virtually the last Akkoyun monument built before the Ottomans took over. Its tall, square detached minaret, set on four 2m basalt pillars, is known colloquially as the Dört Ayaklı Minare or "Four-Legged Minaret". According to legend, if you walk around the minaret seven times and make a wish, it will be granted.

Diyarbakır's churches

Despite the fact that virtually the entire non-Muslim population of Diyarbakır – who formed around a third of the total early in the twentieth century – has gone, the city is now promoting itself as a multicultural, multi-faith destination, and several **churches** are now open to visitors.

Keldanı Kilisesi

Walk past the Kasım Padişah Camii and turn left down an alley, then immediately right

The **Keldanı Kilisesi** was founded by the Chaldeans, a schismatic Catholic group that broke away from the Nestorian church. The church and its bell tower date from 1602; the spacious, arched interior contains a rather garish altar with a crucifix and icons.

Surp Giragos Kilisesi

Turn right as you leave Keldani Kilisesi, then almost immediately left onto an alley, at the end of which you turn right, then first right and follow signs

Until the major renovation programme that enabled the **Surp Giragos Kilisesi** (Church of St George) to reopen in 2011, it was a roofless shell. The restorers have done a superb job, and what is reputed to be the largest church in the Middle East now has its traditional flat roof, supported by rows of black basalt arches decorated with white limestone trim, back in place. The Armenian population of Diyarbakır has shrunk from a quarter of the population in 1915 to just three individuals, but the Armenian community in İstanbul, as well those from the diaspora, use it on special days.

Meryamana Kilisesi

Southwest of the Behram Paşa Camii • Mon–Sat 9am–noon & 2–5pm, Sun 2–5pm

In Diyarbakır's Syrian Orthodox compound, the **Meryamana Kilisesi** (Church of the Virgin Mary), a small door leads onto a paved courtyard surrounded by buildings that were once part of a seventh-century monastery. The church itself dates from the third century, making it one of the oldest in the world. It was reconstructed after a fire a couple of centuries ago, and has been much renovated recently, the funding coming from the sizeable Syrian Orthodox diaspora. In addition to the official opening hours, visitors may be allowed to attend the services which are conducted in either Syriac (a form of Aramaic) or Turkish at 8am each Sunday morning. Contributions are welcome, as only five Syrian Orthodox families remain in the city.

FROM TOP MARDİN (P.607); HASANKEYF (P.615)

ARRIVAL AND DEPARTURE

By plane Kaplaner airport is 3km southwest of town; taxis to the centre cost ₺15.

Destinations Ankara (4 daily with Anadolujet; 1hr 30min); Antalya (6 weekly direct with Sunexpress; 1hr 40min or 3 daily via Ankara with Anadolujet); İstanbul (11 weekly direct with Sunexpress, 2 daily with Pegasus, 1 daily with Onurair, 2 daily with THY; 2hr); İzmir (2 daily with Sunexpress; 2hr 5min, several daily via Ankara with Anadolujet).

By train The train station is 1km west of town, at the end of İstasyon Caddesi.

Destinations Ankara (*Güney Kurtalan Ekspresi*, Mon, Wed, Fri, Sat & Sun; 26hr 15min); Kayseri (5 weekly; 18hr); Malatya (5 weekly; 6hr); Sivas (45 weekly; 13hr).

By bus Diyarbakır's new *otogar* (Yeni Otogar) is inconveniently located 10km west of the centre – the journey can take 45min at busy periods. Buses into town run 7am–11pm (₺2) and will drop you near Dağ Kapısı

(the northern gate to the old city), otherwise a taxi set you back ₺20. Dolmuşes from Mardin, Batman other provincial towns arrive at the dolmuş terminal (Otogar), from where it's a ₺1.5, 15min dolmuş ride i Dağ Kapısı. Eastern bus companies have booths near D Kapısı on Kıbrıs Cad. City buses and dolmuşes to both Yeni Otogar and İlçe Otogar run from a stop on Kibris C just west of the Büyükşehir Belediyesi Turizm Burosu.

Destinations Adana (6 daily; 8hr); Ankara (8 daily; 13h Batman (hourly; 1hr 30min); Bitlis (5 daily; 3hr 30m Doğubeyazıt (4 daily; 9hr); Gaziantep (5 daily; 5hr); Mala (6 daily; 4hr); Mardin (hourly; 1hr 45min); Şanlıurfa (8 da 3hr); Siirt (hourly, 3hr); Sivas (4 daily; 10hr); Siverek (hou 2hr); Tatvan (5 daily; 4hr); Van (8 daily; 7hr).

Car rental Many bus companies, with offices on Kıl Caddesi and dotted around the old centre, also arrange rental. Try Star Diyarbakır on Melikahmet Cad 20/B, or A Elazığ Cad (☎0412 229 0276), or at the airport.

INFORMATION

Tourist offices The state tourist office, in the İç Kale (Mon–Sat 9am–5pm; ☎0412 221 2173), has limited information. Far better is the Buyükşehir Belediyesi Turizm

Burosu (Tues–Sat 9am–noon & 1–6pm), run by the lo municipality and staffed by a charming and knowledgea Armenian woman, Dara.

ACCOMMODATION

AROUND DAĞ KAPISI

Aslan Palas Oteli Kıbrıs Cad 21 ☎0412 228 9224; map p.602. A good budget choice with small but newly renovated rooms (with a/c and flat-screen TVs), crisp white sheets and firm beds. The only down side is the tiny bathrooms, which, although clean, have no shower curtains. No breakfast. The very cheapest rooms lack running water, which costs ₺20 extra. **₺40**

Balkar Hotel İnönü Cad 26 ☎0412 228 7131; map p.602. Beautifully fitted out with nice textiles and paintwork, with a terrace restaurant for breakfast. Homelier than average but with all you'd expect in terms of wi-fi, a/c, fridge, TV etc. The attractive breakfast room overlooks a section of old city wall. **₺70**

Hotel Birkent İnönü Cad ☎0412 228 7131; map p.602. Good-value two-star place with very friendly staff. It's kept spotlessly clean, and TV, wi-fi and minibar are standard. With bright (and very blue) rooms, it's a good option and slightly quieter than similar establishments fronting Kibris Cad. **₺80**

New Tigris Hotel Kıbrıs Cad 3 ☎0412 224 9696, ⓦnewtigrishotel.com; map p.602. While the location, on the busy corner where Gazi and Kıbrıs Caddesis intersect, is not ideal from a noise point of view, this sixty-room place offers spotless rooms with laminated floors, tastefully muted contemporary decor, all the usual wi-fi, flat-screen TV, a/c et al, plus great views over the walls from the breakfast room. **₺120**

★ **Hotel Surkent** Hz Süleyman Cad 19, Sarayka ☎0412 228 1014, ⓦhotelsurkent.com; map p.6 Immaculately run hotel on a quiet (ish) street runn down to the İç Kale. All conveniences include wi-fi, fl screen TV, a/c – plus it's spotlessly clean, down to 1 cramped en-suite bathrooms. Excellent value. Breakf ₺5 extra. **₺45**

SV Business Hotel İnönü Cad 4 ☎0412 228 129 ⓦsvbusinesshotel.com; map p.602. You don't have to a businessman to stay in this smart new addition Diyarbakır's hotel scene. Its clean, bright ult contemporary lines make a refreshing change from standard eastern-Turkish hotel, as do the free tea- a coffee-making facilities. Single rooms have extra-wi beds. There's also a free fitness centre, sauna and hama **€85**

TOWARDS MARDİN KAPISI

★ **Büyük Kervansaray** Gazi Cad, Deliller Ha ☎0412 228 9606, ⓔkervansarayas@superonline.co map p.601. Smallish standard a/c rooms and bigger suit all nicely decorated and with new bathrooms, set in stunning converted *kervansaray* with a large swimmi pool and hamam. The central courtyard is a double-edg sword, wonderfully quiet and relaxing – unless there' wedding or other event on, in which case the volun pumps up and non-partying guests get irritable. **$100**

TING AND DRINKING

arbakır's **specialities** include lamb *kaburga* (ribs stuffed with fragrant *pilaf* rice), *bumbar* (stuffed intestines) and culent *içli köfte* (meatballs in a bulgur-wheat casing), available at various restaurants in town. Liver grilled at street lls is another local favourite, while sweet-toothed visitors should try the syrup-soaked shredded-wheat dessert, *kadayif*.

an Yemek Salonu Kıbrıs Cad; map p.601. Welcoming restaurant – try the *yufkalı incik*, lamb on the bone with ıs, pepper and tomato, wrapped in pastry. It also does a ent breakfast, with clotted cream, honey, bread and tea ₺10. Daily 6am–11pm.

yük Kervansaray Gazi Cad, Deliller Hanı ☎0412 ᴮ 9606; map p.601. The courtyard of this hotel hosts closest thing in the city centre to a nightclub; dinner is ed around the pool, and there's live music and dancing ne nights. Grills ₺15–20, and this is the only licensed ce in town, with (small) beers for ₺10. Daily ᴍ–midnight.

r Çarşı Konağı Gazi Cad, Çarşı Karakolu Çarşısı carsikonagi.com; map p.601. Set in an old Armenian rtyard house, this pleasant café/restaurant dishes up icious *menemen* and hearty grills (from ₺9) with plenty of ᵉ *meze* to begin and Kurdish coffee to finish. Also does quail d trout. Local middle-class women socialize here so it's ideal female travellers. Daily 11am–11pm.

ffee House Yeni Kapı Sok; map p.601. Right opposite ᵉ four-legged minaret, this small place serves standard kish and pistachio-enhanced Kurdish coffee, herbal teas d has street tables and a kitsch nargile room upstairs. ᵂner Barış speaks English, having worked in Marmaris for any years. Daily 8am–11pm.

eşhur Kahvaltıcı Kadri Hasan Paşa Hanı; map

p.601. Great late breakfast or early lunch spot, on a walkway around the courtyard of an atmospheric *han*. As much tea as you can drink with all the usual Turkish breakfast suspects plus clotted cream, eggs fried with tender lamb slices in a wok-like *tava*, and a fiery *acar* paste (walnuts, breadcrumbs and hot pepper). Good value for the ₺17.5 set price. Daily 7am–3pm.

★ **Selim Amca Sofra Salonu** Ali Emiri Cad ☎0412 224 4447; map p.601. A Diyarbakır institution, 5min walk west of Dağ Kapısı, serving both chicken and lamb *kaburga* mains, *içli köfte* starters and *İrmik helvası* desserts. A fixed menu will set you back ₺27.5, good value considering the opulence of the surroundings and the quality of the food. Daily 10.30am–10pm.

Şanlıurfa Kebap Evi İzzet Paşa Cad 4; map p.601. Very popular with the locals for its fast service, tasty food and keen prices. Watch your large *lahmacun* (₺2.5) or massive *pide* (₺10) being prepared in the wood-burning oven downstairs, or retire upstairs to the cooler *aile salonu*. Also serves a good range of kebabs. Daily 7am–10pm.

Şeymus Gazi Cad 25 ☎0412 229 4749; map p.602. This famous firm, which has many branches dotted around the city, specializes in the shredded-wheat dessert *kadayif*. Try it with *peynir* (cheese), *ceviz* (walnut) or *fıstık* (pistachio). ₺5 per portion, ₺7.5 with a generous dollop of (recommended) ice cream. Daily 7am–10pm.

IRECTORY

ınks and exchange Most of the banks and *döviz* offices ᵉ on Gazi Cad.

ospitals The Devlet Hastanesi (State Hospital) is north of ğ Kapısı, or try the private Özel Veni Vidi Hastanesi ᴼ 0412 229 2025) at Al Emiri Cad 1 (near Dağ Kapısı).

ılice Police station on Gazi Cad, just north of the main ᴼssroads.

ost office There is a small PTT on Yeni Kapı Cad, near the

junction with Gazi Cad (Mon–Sat 9am–noon and 1–5pm for mail; 24hr for telephones). For money exchange, go to the larger PTT on Ziya Gökalp Bul, 300m north of Dağ Kapısı (same hours).

Travel agencies Diyarbakır holds several reputable agencies, the best being Bat-Air, İnönü Cad 9 (☎0412 223 5373).

Mardin and around

een from the south, **MARDİN** looks spectacular, its tiered layers of vernacular houses, ᵐansions, mosques and churches clinging to a huge citadel-topped rock that rises out f the north Mesopotamian plain. Sunset is particularly striking, with locals flying ᵏites, a deep-blue sky filled with wheeling swifts, and shadows swallowing up the ᵖatchwork of fields on the endless plain.

Mardin's position has always made it a strategic military outpost – the higher of the ᵂo castellated bluffs today sports golf-ball radar domes. The population is a mix of ᴸurds, Arabs, Turks and Syrian Orthodox Christians, the latter of whom are known ᴺ Turkey as Süriyani (see p.614). Since the conflict between the state and the PKK

MARDİN

Kale (Forbidden Zone)

ACCOMMODATION					RESTAURANTS		BARS AND CAFÉS	
Antik Tatlı Dede	8	Maria Butik Otel	5	Cerciş Murat Konağı	4	Abbara	
Otel Başak	3	Reyhani Kasrı	6	Kamer	1	Attila Çay Bahçesi	
Otel Bilem	1	Şahmeran	2	Seyr-i Mardin	2	Cafe del Mar	
Erdoba Konakları	7	Zinciriye	4	Yusuf Üsta'nın Yeri	3	Leylan	

wound down in these parts, Mardin has boomed. Thanks largely to domestic visitors,
has become the centre of the region's tourism industry, a popular (and overpriced) spo
for well-off İstanbul Turks in search of the "quaint east". Many boutique hotels,
fashioned from the charming old buildings, have opened in recent years, along with a
few upmarket standard hotels. Handmade soaps are big business, as are silver jewellery
and, more prosaically, dried fruits and nuts. Mardin also boasts the small Sinemardin
film festival (⊛sinemardin.com.tr), held towards the end of June, with the accent on
Middle Eastern cinema.

The old town lies on the steep southern slopes below the citadel. The principal street
Birinci Caddesi, branches off the main road at the western end of town, and rejoins it a
the eastern end.

Brief history
Mardin's probable Roman origins are lost in a welter of war and conquest, while its
later history is tied up with the development of early Christianity. The first Christians
to settle here were Syrian Orthodox, who arrived during the third century AD. Having
survived the period of Arab occupation from 640 to 1104, the Christians were left
alone by the Selçuk and Turcoman rulers. Today, eleven churches remain hidden away
in the backstreets.

From the twelfth to the fourteenth centuries, the citadel was the capital of the
Artukid Turcoman tribe. They beat off Arab attacks and endured an eight-month siege
during the first Mongol onslaught, before falling to the second Mongol wave under
Tamerlane in 1394. The Mongols doled out death and misery in equal measures to
Christian and Muslim alike, before, in 1408, handing Mardin over to the Karakoyun
Turcoman tribe, who built the (now ruined) palace and mosque inside the citadel
walls. It became an Ottoman possession in 1517.

Before and during Turkey's War of Independence, Mardin's Christian population
was drastically reduced by massacre and emigration. Following renewed emigrations
in the early 1990s, only a few hundred practising Syrian Orthodox, Catholic and
Armenian Christians remain. Fortunately, local émigrés who made good in Europe
and the USA are now pouring money into the Syrian Orthodox communities in
Mardin and the Tür Abdin.

Islamic buildings in Mardin

Mardin boasts some superb **Islamic buildings**. Several hundred metres east of the Meydan, the easterly of two sets of stone steps leads up from Birinci Caddesi to the **Sultan İsa Medresesi** (daily 9am–6pm; free). Built in 1385, this striking structure features a magnificent doorway and fluted domes; the semi-translucent volcanic stones used in the *mihrab* glow when illuminated with a torch.

Above the Sultan İsa Medresesi, the **kale**, or citadel, was originally built by the Romans and extended by the Byzantines. The castle itself is a forbidden military zone, but it's possible to climb partway up the *kale* hill to a cemetery and get views down over the town and plain beyond.

Below Birinci Caddesi, the **Ulu Cami** is an eleventh-century Selçuk mosque with a minaret that's attractively carved with tear-drop motifs and geometric Arabic lettering. Prominent **Şehidiye Camii**, further east on Birinci Caddesi, also has a very ornate minaret. Further on, east of the Sakip Sabancı museum (see p.610), the **Sıttı Radviye Medresesi** is a newly restored theological school that dates back to the late twelfth century, and contains what's believed to be the Prophet Mohammed's footprint in stone.

The **Latifiye Camii**, south of Cumhuriyet Meydanı, dates from the fourteenth century. It has a carved Selçuk-style portal, and a courtyard with a shady garden. Around here lies a maze of streets, forming part of the **bazaar**. At the western end of town, 500m south of the main road, is the (over-restored) fifteenth-century **Kasım Paşa Medresesi**, similar in design to the Sultan İsa Medresesi.

The churches of Mardin

Mardin has a vibrant **Christian heritage**, and Christians and Muslims have always intermingled rather than living in separate quarters. The Syrian Orthodox **Kirklar Kilise** (Arbin Söhad in Syriac) or Church of the Forty Martyrs, which dates back, in part, to the sixth century, is the most welcoming church to visitors. The best time to attend is Sunday morning, at around 9am, when the local Süriyani population comes to pray, though you must dress respectfully and photography is forbidden.

Next door, **Mar Yusuf Kilisesi** (St Joseph's) serves the town's tiny Armenian Catholic population. Lacking a priest, it's usually locked, and the congregation attends services at the Kirklar Kilise.

Mardin's largest church, the **Süriyani Katolik Kilisesi** (Church of the Virgin Mary), is used by five families of Syrian Catholics, and adjoins the local museum (see p.610). The **Mar İşmuni Kilisesi**, which has a typical Syrian Orthodox walled courtyard, stands at the bottom of the hill in the southeastern part of the old town, while back on the main street the newly restored **Keldani Kilise** (Chaldean Church) is easily spotted but usually locked.

Mardin's domestic architecture

Mardin is famed for its **domestic architecture**. The soft, pale honey-coloured local stone is easy to work, allowing for the intricate carved reliefs that embellish most of its old houses.

Look out for the wonderfully ornate post office building on Birinci Caddesi (designed in the nineteenth century by the Armenian architect, Lole), which was being restored at the time of writing for use by the local Artuklu university. Also of note are the *abarra*, arched passageways covering the street, formed from the two houses either side. As well as providing much-needed shade, they act as cooling wind tunnels.

Mardin Museum

Immediately above the two car parks at Cumhuriyet Meydanı • Tues–Sun 8.30am–4.30pm • ₺3

Mardin Museum (Mardin Müzesi) is housed in a restored nineteenth-century mansion that was once the residence of the Syrian Catholic patriarch. It contains some impressive finds from nearby sites, from the Chalcolithic period onwards. Highlights include the burnished red Urartian pots, a large kneeling Assyrian figure carved from black basalt, and a five-thousand-year-old terracotta toy chariot, but most visitors feel that it holds too few exhibits to be all that satisfying.

Sakip Sabancı City Museum

On the continuation of Birinci Cad, beyond the post office • Tues–Sun 8am–5pm • ₺2

The state-of-the-art **Sakip Sabancı City Museum** (Sakip Sabancı Kent Müzesi) is far more exciting than Mardin Museum. Housed in a lovingly restored nineteenth-century barracks, it offers a bold and imaginative insight into the history, culture and arts of Mardin and its surroundings. There's information on everything from Christianity and Islam through to crafts and costumes, including artefacts, photographs and video presentations. Reached by steps from the main building, the adjoining **Dilek Sabancı Art Gallery** hosts top-notch temporary arts exhibitions.

ARRIVAL AND DEPARTURE   MARDİN

By plane Mardin's tiny airport is on the plain, 21km southwest. Catch a taxi for a hefty ₺50, or walk to the main road and hail a Kızıltepe-bound dolmuş.
Destinations Ankara (1 daily with Anadolujet; 1hr 35min); Antalya (1 daily with Anadolujet via Ankara); İstanbul (2 daily with THY, 3 weekly with Pegasus, 2 weekly with Sunexpress; 2hr 5min).

By bus Dolmuşes for Diyarbakır, Midyat and Nusaybin depart from the İlçe Otogar (dolmuş terminal) at the eastern end of town, on the main Syria-bound road. Reach the terminal by a blue *Şehir İçi* bus from Birinci Caddesi

(₺1.25). Buy inter-city coach tickets from a couple of companies on Birinci Caddesi (near the *meydan*), or from the offices close to the *Bilem Hotel* in Yenişehir (new town, reached from the old city by a blue *Şehir İçi* bus.
Destinations Cizre via Nusaybin (5 daily; 3hr, ₺25); Diyarbakır (25 daily; 1hr 45min, ₺10); Midyat (frequent on demand; 1hr); Savur (8 daily; 1hr, ₺7); Şanlıurfa (3 daily, 3hr, ₺25).

Car rental There are several rental places near the *Bilem Hotel* and bus agencies in New Mardin. Try Güven Vali Ozan Cad, Karataş Apt 5 ☎ 0482 212 5254.

INFORMATION

Tourist office The small tourist office, south of Birinci Caddesi near the *Tatlıdede Hotel*, should have good street maps.

ACCOMMODATION

A plethora of boutique hotels clusters either side of Birinci Caddesi, which cuts the old town in two. Accommodation often heavily booked during spring and autumn weekends, and during Turkish national holidays. Rooms vary markedly in size and location – some are large with great views, others dark and cramped, so look before agreeing to take a particular room. If you have your own vehicle, beware, none of the boutique hotels has parking spots.

Antik Tatlı Dede 104 Sok 27 ☎ 0482 213 2720, ⓦ tatlidede.com.tr. South of the main street, in a quiet backstreet – noise from the nearby Ulu Camii apart! – this is perhaps the most successful conversion from old house to boutique hotel in Mardin. Rooms are spacious with stone floors and barrel-vaulted ceilings, and there's a great terrace for sunset views. No a/c, fans only, as the owners reckon the stone walls keep out the summer heat. ₺180

Otel Başak Birinci Cad ☎ 0482 212 6246. Small rooms, cleanish squat toilets in the corridor and separate, grimy showers with no hot water. Despite the advent of the

Şahmaran guesthouse, this is still the cheapest spot in the old town, but is only really suitable for male travellers. ₺50

Otel Bilem Vali Özan Cad 72 ☎ 0482 212 5564, ⓦ bilemhotel.com. Roughly 1km northwest of, and below, the old town, the bland *Bilem*, despite a somewhat cramped bathrooms and decidedly average breakfast, still represents better value than most of the old-town hotels – particularly if you bargain. Bright and airy rooms with a/c and free wi-fi. Regular municipal buses to the old town run from a stop opposite the hotel. ₺100

doba Konakları Hotel Birinci Cad ☎ 0482 212 7677, erdoba.com.tr. Built in "period style" around a urtyard, the main building has an upmarket restaurant ached. A separate building lower down the hill offers oms in a converted merchant's mansion, and there are o further annexes to the east. All rooms have a/c and are ry comfortable, but the *Erdoba* has perhaps sat on its urels a little. **₺180**

aria Butik Otel Birinci Cad Üçyol Mevkii 255 ₺0482 212 5882, ⓦ mariabutikotel.com. Friendly male-run place, fashioned with discretion from a fine d mansion in 2012. The main drawback is that three of e six rooms are waterless but this is a very tastefully stored and decorated hotel and, by Mardin standards, presents good value. If it lives up to its early promise, is could well rank among Mardin's best boutique tels. **₺120**

eyhani Kasrı Birinci Cad 163 ☎0482 212 1333, reyhanikasri.com.tr. Blithely sitting on the fence tween boutique and conventional upmarket hotel, this ace might upset the purist but will tick a lot of boxes for

many visitors. Central old Mardin location, great views, good service and value, just enough character and all conveniences, including free tea- and coffee-making facilities. **₺150**

Şahmeran Butik Otel Birinci Cad, Sok 10 ☎0482 213 2300, ⓦ sahmeranpansiyon.com. Tucked up behind the main street opposite the *Erdoba Konakları Hotel*, this new venture looks set to be a backpackers' favourite. It's still overpriced, but has a friendly English-speaking manager, offers waterless and dark dorm beds, brighter pension beds, and doubles in the standard rooms. Have a good look before choosing. Free wi-fi but breakfasts **₺5** extra. Dorms **₺30**, pension beds **₺40**, doubles **₺100**

Zinciriye Medrese Mah 243, Sok 13 ☎0482 212 4866, ⓦ zinciriye.com. Well placed in the old town just below the Sultan İsa Medresesi, all fifteen rooms have exposed stone walls, vaulted ceilings, tasteful furnishings and views – and there's a splendid terrace with stunning panoramas. The owners also run the nearby *Kadım*, a useful backup in busy periods. **₺150**

11

ATING AND DRINKING

spite its popularity with well-off Turkish visitors from points west, and a fabulous local cuisine, Mardin does not hold as any good options for eating out as you might expect – particularly if you want alcohol with your meal.

bara Birinci Cad, Garanti Banası Karşısı. It's not eap, with a 70cl beer costing **₺10** – and watch you don't t overcharged for the bowls of *çerez* – but this is the best ghtspot in town. Great roof-terrace views, while inside ere's live music every Wed, Fri & Sat, with Turkish, rdish, Süriyani and Armenian styles all on offer. Daily oon–2am.

illa Çay Bahçesi. Mardin's oldest tea garden, opposite e PTT, affords shade and a terrace with sunset views over e Mesopotamian Plain to Syria. Daily 7am–10pm.

★ **Cercis Murat Konağı** Birinci Cad ☎0482 213 841, ⓦ cercismurat.com. The best restaurant in town, t in a restored Süriyani house west of the Meydan, with eat views from the terrace, and specializing in local shes such as *incassıye*, lamb flavoured with sweet kmez, plums, chilli and tomato. A fixed-menu meal 45) is a worthwhile treat; the *mezes*, which appear in a noply of silver ladles, are superb. Decent local red wine. ily noon–midnight.

fe del Mar Sanat Sok 17 ☎0482 212 7080. Located route to the Sakip Sabancı museum, this is the place come if you've a craving for a latte (**₺7**), chocolate ownie or other such decidedly un-Mardin-like

delicacy, but also does Turkish grills and *börek* (pie). Daily 8am–10pm.

Kamer Birinci Cad, 225 Sok 3 ☎0482 212 2545. Great place serving up home cooking, with a share of the profits going to victims of domestic abuse. Mains around **₺9**, soups **₺3**. The *dolma* (stuffed vine leaves) and *mantı* (Turkish ravioli) are recommended. Daily 11am–10pm.

Leylan Birinci Cad ☎0482 212 8575. Bookshop-cum-café/bar in a fine old house all decked out with ethnic artefacts, with a terrace overlooking the street. Good place for an early beer and toasted-sandwich snack, with tasteful local music playing in the background. Daily 10pm–midnight.

Seyr-i Mardin Birinci Cad ☎0482 213 4741. Great rooftop café above the noise and bustle of the main drag, with fabulous views to Syria. It's mostly standard Turkish dishes, with kebabs from **₺10**, but there are also hearty salad plates from **₺6** and burgers if you're fed up with local food. Daily 9am–11pm.

Yusuf Ustanın Yeri. This simple, family-oriented *ocakbaşı* (charcoal grill) garden restaurant, opposite the PTT, serves delicious kebabs and *köfte*, but no alcohol. Daily 10am–11pm.

RECTORY

amams The Emir Hamam on Birinci Caddesi is set in a lendid building, purpose-built in the thirteenth century. en 6.30am–noon & 6–10pm, women 6–10pm, **₺10**.

Hospital A good bet is the private Derman Tip Merkezi on Vali Ozan Caddesi, south of the *Bilem Hotel*.

Deyr-az-Zaferan

6km southeast of Mardin • Daily 9am–noon & 1–5pm • ₺5 • The walk takes 1hr 15min – follow the Nusaybin road southeast from the o
town centre until you see a white-on-brown sign pointing left (east) into the hills; a taxi from old Mardin costs around ₺40 for a return
trip, with waiting time

Founded in 493 AD, the Syrian Orthodox monastery of **Deyr-az-Zaferan** is known as
the "Saffron Monastery", on account of the yellowish rock from which it's built. From
1160 until the 1920s, this was the seat of the Syrian Orthodox patriarch, who has since
relocated to Damascus. Now the showpiece of the Syrian Orthodox Church in Turkey
it has been lovingly restored, largely with funds from the diaspora.

There's a posh gift shop and cafeteria at the entrance, and you'll be escorted around
the monastery complex by Süriyani men (who may look very bored indeed). First up
on the obligatory tour is an underground vault, topped by a stone ceiling constructed
without mortar, and believed to have been a sun-worshippers' temple in pagan times.
Next to it at ground level, the domed **Church of Beth Kadishe** boasts elaborately carved
Corinthian capitals and a late Roman-style frieze. The remains of several metropolitan
bishops and patriarchs are encased in niches lining the nave.

The domed **Church of Mor Hananyo**, immediately north, dates back to the sixth
century, but has been much rebuilt. It holds some gorgeous relief-carved friezes,
pretty faux-naif altar curtains, and a rather garish 1950s altar. The last room, a
chapel, contains a wooden altar from 1699, and an ancient wooden palaquin used
to carry patriarchs past. This remains a working church, with one of the four
metropolitan bishops of the Syrian Orthodox Church in Turkey, plus a few monks
and nuns, still in residence.

Savur

45km north of Mardin • Drive, or come by dolmuş from Mardin (8 daily; 1hr).

Set on twin hilltops in a dramatic confluence of valleys, **SAVUR** is often referred to as
"Little Mardin". It has the same beautifully carved, honey-hued stone houses, a fortress
atop one of its hills, and a number of the shady passages known as *abarra*. It's well
worth a visit if you'd like to see how Mardin used to look before it took off as the
southeast's tourist capital. While parts of the drive to Savur are stunningly beautiful,
however, it lacks the specific sights of Mardin, so the real reason to come is to stay at i
only accommodation, the fascinating *Haci Abdullah Konağı Evi*.

ACCOMMODATION   SAVU

★ **Haci Abdullah Konağı Evi** Devlet Mah, Savur
☎0482 571 2127 or ☎0533 239 7808. Fabulous
220-year-old mansion house, set on a hilltop overlooking
the town, valleys and surrounding plateau. The owner's
family trace their origins back to Hussein, grandson of the
Prophet Mohammed, and are very welcoming. Everythi
is original here, from the brass beds to the kilims a
elaborately carved wooden ceilings. Bathrooms are sim
and shared. Rates include breakfast and dinner. ₺160

Dara

Oğuz, 30km north of Mardin • Catch a dolmuş to Oğuz (3 daily), or take a Nusaybin-bound dolmuş as far as the turn for Oğuz, and hitch
remaining 9km east

The evocative ruins of Byzantine **Dara** (the ancient city of Anastopolis), dating from
the middle of the sixth century AD, and picturesquely set amid the houses of the
traditional Kurdish village of **Oğuz**, are difficult to access without your own vehicle.
As the most extensive remains in the region, however, they're well worth visiting,
testament to a time when this area formed the eastern bastion of the Byzantine
Christian world against the Persian Empire.

Assuming that you arrive from Mardin, the first area of interest lies to the left of the
road, just before the village. Excavations are ongoing at the massive **necropolis** (daily

3.30am–6pm; free), as well as what may well be a major temple. Excellent display boards explain the finds, while the on-site café holds a model of the whole site, and friendly guards will point you in the right direction.

To find the obvious remains of a large Byzantine cistern complex, head towards the village then turn left (north). To the south, a small, pleasant tea garden stands at the entrance to a monumental and totally unexpected piece of architecture – an underground (and well-lit) vaulted cistern, some 30m high. Beyond this, charmingly scattered amid olive orchards, lie other remains of the city, with stretches of paved road, bridges and parts of the city walls and towers.

The Tür Abdin plateau

The undulating plateau of the **Tür Abdin**, traditional heartland of the Syrian Orthodox Church (see p.685), starts just east of Mardin. It's still home to a few Christians, who co-exist uneasily with the local Muslim Kurds. The rocky plateau is more fertile than you might think if you only see it in the parched days of summer, dotted with what appear to be little more than masses of hardy scrub oak. Grape cultivation is a mainstay, as is lentil production, and walnut, almond, cherry, fig and pomegranate all flourish. Olives are few and far between, however, as the winters here are cold.

Midyat is the western gateway to the Tür Abdin proper, where several villages are still either wholly, or partially, inhabited by Syrian Orthodox Christians, and there are 46 **monasteries and churches**, some recently restored. Most are tricky to reach by public transport, so arrange either a taxi or rental car.

Midyat

The town of **MİDYAT**, an hour east of Mardin by road, consists of two distinct districts. The westerly portion is the modern business district of **Estel**, while the originally Christian portion of half-abandoned medieval mansions, known as **Eski** (Old) **Midyat**, lies 2km east. Inevitably, given Mardin's boom, tourism is growing in Midyat. A couple of posh new boutique hotels have opened their doors, and the multitude of silver (particularly *telkari* or filigree) shops for which the town is famous are bustling with domestic visitors in search of bargains.

Although nearly five thousand Syrian Orthodox Christians still lived here in 1974, the men mostly engaged in gold- or silversmithing, the population shrank to just eighty families and one priest after the conflict in the 1980s and 1990s between the PKK and Turkish security forces. However, thanks to the changed political climate as well as economic growth, some Syrian Orthodox families are starting to return.

The town's **churches**, dotted among the imposing mansions built in tiers along a low ridge, are easily spotted by virtue of their graceful belfries. **Mor Barsaumo**, close to the main road and reached by an alleyway opposite the *Cihan* restaurant, was built as early as the fifth century, destroyed in 1793 and rebuilt in 1910. As the most active of the churches, this is the best to visit. It holds a small schoolroom where the kids of the remaining Syrian Orthodox families come to learn Syriac, a language closely related to the Aramaic spoken by Christ.

ARRIVAL AND DEPARTURE   MİDYAT

By bus The dolmuş *garaj* in old Midyat is a couple of hundred metres south of town on the İdil/Mor Gabriel road.

Destinations Mardin (hourly; 1hr; ₺9); Hasankeyf (6 daily; 45min; ₺8); Nusaybin (5 daily; 1hr 15min; ₺9).

ACCOMMODATION

★ **Kasr-ı Nehroz Hotel** Işıklar Mah 219, Sok 14 ☎ 0452 464 0719, ⓦ hotelnehroz.com. Converted from

an old mansion house, this stunning hotel combines the very best of the old with contemporary flourishes. It's as

11

ASSYRISKA – A NATIONAL TEAM WITHOUT A NATION

While they lack a country of their own, Turkey's Süriyani or Assyrian population have found an unlikely rallying point – a football club in Sweden. **Assyriska**, a second-division team based near Stockholm, is made up entirely of immigrants, two-thirds of whom are Syrian Orthodox Christians who have emigrated from Turkey.

In 2006, Midyat-born journalist **Nuri Kino** brought their story to life in an award-winning documentary, *Assyriska*, charting the side's progress to a brief spell at the top of the Swedish premiership. The team are a symbol of pride for the Assyrian diaspora throughout the world, who have often been persecuted in their traditional heartlands (modern Turkey, Iraq, Iran and Syria). The documentary is controversial in Turkey, as it alleges that the massacres suffered by Assyrians at the hands of the Ottomans in World War I amount to genocide. See ⓦ nurikino .com for more information.

---

tasteful and comfortable a place as you'll stay in eastern Turkey, and far better value than Mardin's boutique hotels. It also holds a good restaurant, open to non-guests, where the menu is packed with local specialities. A sophisticated booking system means prices change according to demand; low-season rates can be half those in peak season. ₺220

Metro Just northeast of the central roundabout on the Hasankeyf–Batman road ☎ 0482 464 2317. The *Metro* hotel, on the fringes of old Midyat, offers basic rooms with metal-framed beds and shared bathrooms. Best fo impecunious male travellers only. ₺40

Shmayya Hotel Kışla Cad 126, Sok 12 ☎ 0452 464 0696, ⓦ shmayya.com. While slightly less appealing tha the rival *Nehroz*, this is still a beautifully appointe 21-room boutique hotel, crafted from the traditiona mansion house of a former Syrian Orthodox Patriarch Rooms are set around a courtyard, the Gilgamesh suite room a riot of elaborate relief carving vying for attentior with a massive flat-screen TV. ₺210

EATING AND DRINKING

★ **Cihan Lokantası** Cizre Yolu Üzeri, just south of the junction roundabout on the Mar Gabriel road. This spotlessly clean place is packed at lunchtimes for its superb *sulu yemek*, which includes tender *kaburga* (rib of lamb) and *perde pilaf* (delicately spiced rice with shredded chicken) ₺6. The creamy *yayık* (frothy) *ayran* is served in copper bowls. Daily 9am–10pm.

Tarihi Midyat Café & Restaurant Gelüşke Hanı. Thi touristy restaurant, set in the restored Gelüşke Hanı, a 2mir walk up into the old town from the silversmiths' quarter offers a (too) wide selection of Turkish and regional dishes Daily 11am–10pm.

Mar Gabriel

22km southeast of Midyat, 2km east of the İdil–Cizre road • Daily 9–11.30am & 1–4.30pm • İdil-bound dolmuşes (20min; ₺3) from old Midyat's dolmuş garage drop passengers at the signed Mar Gabriel junction, 2km walk on a surfaced road from the monastery; taxis from Midyat cost around ₺35, including waiting time

Founded in 397 AD, the monastery of **Mar Gabriel** (Deyrulumur) is the geographical and spiritual centre of the Tür Abdin plateau. The oldest and most vital surviving Syrian Orthodox monastery in Turkey, it's the seat of the metropolitan bishop of Tür Abdin. A working community, set among gardens and orchards, its primary purpose is to keep Syrian Orthodox Christianity alive in the land of its birth by providing schooling and ordination of native-born monks. There are thirteen resident nuns and three monks, as well as a fluctuating number of local lay workers, guests and students.

A lay person gives visitors guided tours of the monastery. The glittering, mosaic-covered ceiling of the apse of the main Anastasius (512 AD) church is particularly memorable, though Tamerlane stripped the gold ceiling of the nave. The tour also takes in the circular dining room, surmounted by a dome donated by the Byzantine empress Theodora early in the sixth century AD, and the Church of the Mother of God, dating back some fourteen hundred years.

Hah

3km northeast of Midyat • Follow the Hasankeyf road from Midyat for 3km; turn right for Dargeçit; after 17km turn right again (signed Meryemana/Hah); continue 6km to Hesterek village, then turn left and continue another 7km to Hah, also known as Anıtlı

Set in the fascinating village of **HAH** (Anıtlı in Turkish), the remote fifth-century **Church of the Mother of God** – İndath Aloho in Syriac, Meryemana in Turkish – is undoubtedly the most beautiful Syrian Orthodox building in Turkey. Local Süriyanis regard it as the jewel in the Tür Abdin crown. It sports a two-storey wedding-cake-like turret with blind arches topped by a pyramidal roof; the archways and lintels are also heavily ornamented. The church has a virtually square ground plan, with a transverse nave, but what's striking about the domed interior are the gorgeously ornate Corinthian capitals and an elaborate, relief-carved frieze.

Hah itself was once the centre of a community of several thousand, with over 44 churches in the vicinity, but just sixteen families now remain. At the heart of the village, atop a small rise, is a group of fortified houses where five thousand Christians held out for months against a vastly superior Ottoman force in 1915 – with no Christian lives lost. Downhill from here stand the remains of the church of **Mor Bacchus**, dating back to the second century, while en route back to the Church of the Mother of God, the ruined sixth-century church of **Mor Sovo** was destroyed by Tamerlane.

Other Syrian Orthodox churches worth seeing between Midyat and Hah include **Mor Dimet** at **Zaz**, and the important **Mar Yakoub** monastic church in Baraztepe (Salah) village.

Hasankeyf

The spectacular ruined settlement of **HASANKEYF**, an hour's dolmuş ride north of Midyat, is one of Turkey's most evocative historic sites. Poised on the very lip of a sheer cliff, carved from the mountainside by the swift-flowing waters of the Tigris, stands a remarkable series of remains of Selçuk, Arabic and Kurdish origin. Below the ruins, the Tigris is spanned by the arches of a vintage 1950s concrete bridge, itself overlooking the mighty piers of its medieval precursor. It's a photographer's dream, especially at sunset and sunrise, while a meal at one of the many simple fish restaurants lining the bank beneath the cliff is unforgettable.

While many of the four-thousand-plus caves in the surrounding hills were inhabited in prehistoric times, the original settlement was founded by the Romans as an eastern bastion of the empire, and later became the Byzantine bishopric of Cephe. In 640 AD, the conquering Arabs changed the town's name to Hisn Kayfa. During the twelfth century the Artukid Turcoman tribe decided to make Hasankeyf their capital, which it remained until the Mongols arrived in 1260. Hasankeyf then served as the stronghold of the Ayyubids, a clan of Kurdish chieftains supplanted by the Ottomans early in the fifteenth century.

The site

Daily 8.30am–6.30pm • ₺3

The modern town of **Hasankeyf** is strung out either side of the road leading to the concrete bridge across the river. To reach the **site**, head to the southern end of the modern bridge, then turn left. The 1km road is lined by rows of souvenir stalls, selling everything from tasteful, locally woven goat-hair blankets to garish wall-hangings. Its initial section, fronting the river, holds simple restaurants – some with platforms out in the water at the foot of the cliff.

The first sight of note is the **El Rizk Camii**, built under the Ayyubids in 1409 AD, which has a beautiful minaret decorated with *kufic* inscriptions and tear-drop patterns, and is topped by a stork's nest. It also holds useful toilets.

> ## THAT SINKING FEELING: THE DROWNING OF HASANKEYF
>
> The remarkable historic site of **Hasankeyf** was put on the World Monuments Fund Watch List in 2008, as one of the hundred most endangered heritage sites in the world. Despite this, and a domestic and international outcry, much of the ancient city is almost certain to be drowned by the waters of the **İlisu dam** across the Tigris, part of the GAP project (see p.579).
>
> Pledges to save key elements of the site, including for example the brick-built Zeyn El-Abdin Türbesi, and remove them to a reservoir-side open-air museum are decried by critics, who say the remains are far too delicate to move. The most vociferous critics of the scheme are the eighty thousand or so locals who stand to be displaced by the flood waters. Several other groups also oppose it, including those who live downstream in Iraq, who fear the dam will wipe out their already scant water resources; Kurdish nationalists, who view the dam as a deliberate attempt to wipe out their cultural heritage; and assorted national and international environmental groups.
>
> Meanwhile, work has started on the dam, 70km downstream of Hasankeyf, and a "new" concrete village of Hasankeyf can be seen emerging high on the slopes of the mountain across the river. Unhappy locals reckon the flood waters will subsume their homes by 2018 or 2019.

11

The ticket booth, beyond the mosque, marks the start of the ascent to the cliff-top ruins. Climbing the time-polished stone pathway is demanding in the heat of the day. The path cuts back from the cliff edge and weaves up to the **Ulu Camii**, an evocatively ruined, partially restored Ayyubid mosque, built in 1305, which holds a long, narrow prayer hall, finely carved *mihrab* and truncated minaret. Scattered all around are the remains of abandoned houses, exposed cisterns (take care), and Muslim cemeteries and mausoleums. Below it, the twelfth-century building conjectured to be the **palace of the Artukid kings** is perched right on the cliff edge above the Tigris. At the time of writing, it was under excavation and off-limits.

Head back down the cobbled steps to the cliff top, now guarded by a rail, next to the so-called Küçük Sarayı or "Small Palace", which is off-limits for safety reasons. The grill to the left guards the entrance to the stepped tunnel, which once gave secret access to the river below but has now been deemed unsafe. Look right to see the four massive pillars of the old **Artukid bridge**, once the largest in Anatolia. Its central span is thought to have been constructed from wood.

From the cliff top, you can also see the conspicuous fifteenth-century **Zeyn El-Abdin Türbesi**, a beautiful, onion-domed cylindrical building clad in glazed turquoise tiles and red brick, across the river to the left (northwest). To explore, head back down to the modern bridge, cross it and walk west for ten or fifteen minutes either along the main road or the river banks. Constructed in 1475, it was made for Zeynel Bey, the son of an Akkoyunlu sultan, Uzun (Tall) Hasan. Recent excavations around the tomb have revealed an extensive complex of buildings including a couple of *medreses* (theological schools).

ARRIVAL AND DEPARTURE   HASANKEYF

By bus Regular dolmuşes run to Hasankeyf from Midyat; leaving Hasankeyf, the first Midyat-bound dolmuş passes through at 8am. Heading to Hasankeyf from Diyarbakır, you need first to catch a dolmuş from the İlçe Otogar to Batman (frequent; 1hr 30min), and catch another dolmuş to Hasankeyf from Batman; the last dolmuş of the day leaves Batman around 6pm.

Destinations Batman (every 30min; 1hr); Cizre (1 daily; 2hr); Midyat (8 daily; 1hr).

ACCOMMODATION AND EATING

An **overnight stay** is recommended to fully appreciate the wonderful setting and subtle early-morning and sunset light and, especially if you arrive on a warm weekend, to avoid the picnicking hordes from Batman and domestic tourists from Mardin. Food options are pretty standard but it's a good place to try Tigris-caught catfish. Note also that there's a small PTT, ATM and internet café on the main drag south of the bridge.

Eski Köprü Çardak Kale Yolu. On the right of the road to the old city, this restaurant actually has three levels. Below the average street-level dining area, there's a kilim- and cushion-bedecked raised dais, while lower down and projecting right into the river there's a platform with yet more tables. *Gözleme* (₺5), meat grills and fish from ₺10. Daily 10am–11pm.

Has Bahçe 500m right of the bridge on the town side ☎ 0488 381 2624, ⊛ hasankeyfhasbahce.com. Set in a peaceful riverside garden area, this low-key place has 15 bright, clean rooms with a/c and free wi-fi. Owner Fırat (ironically, the Turkish name for the Euphrates River) is a laidback host. There's also a decent trout restaurant (₺15 including salad). Rates including breakfast. Dorms ₺30, doubles ₺80

Hasankeyf Motel At the entrance to the south end of the bridge ☎ 0488 381 2005. In this basic accommodation option, the waterless rooms do at least have small balconies backing over the cliff and great views of the Tigris and cave-pocked cliffs in the far bank. They share clean (squat) toilets down the hall. ₺60

Nehir Et Lokantası On the main street that leads down to the bridge. A standard but spotless Anatolian working-men's restaurant, good and cheap for soup, assorted kebabs and *lahmacun*. Daily 8am–10pm.

11

Lake Van
and the
southeast

İSHAK PAŞA SARAYI

Lake Van and the southeast

Bordered by Iran to the east and Iraq to the south, Turkey's remote southeast is a land dominated by soaring peaks, rugged plateaux and plunging valleys. Its austere natural beauty makes the perfect backdrop for some impressive and intriguing sights, while the predominantly ethnically Kurdish population gives the region a distinctively different feel to the rest of the country. At its heart lies Lake Van, a vast inland sea ringed by snowcapped peaks. The Armenians who once lived around the lake were so enamoured with its beauty and fertility they had a saying "Van in this life, paradise in the next". North of the lake is the graceful 5137m volcanic cone of Ağrı Dağ – better known as Mount Ararat – the highest peak in Turkey, while the wild alpine range south of the lake contains mighty Reşko (4135m), the nation's second-highest peak.

Winters, starting in early November, are severe, with roads often blocked by heavy snow, but in July and August, while much of the rest of Turkey is sweltering, these highlands are relatively cool and humidity free. The once-poor road system has been improved significantly, often due to military requirements during the **PKK troubles** (see box, p.638), but ongoing roadworks are a minor nuisance.

Food out here is plainer than in the west of Turkey, but it's worth trying some of the local Kurdish specialities such as the matured herb cheese, *otlu peynir*. Until quite recently the economy of the region was largely based on nomadic pastoralism, but the lure of the big cities and the forced evacuation of hundreds of villages during the struggle with the PKK has decimated the rural population. This population decline was exacerbated in October 2011 when a massive **earthquake** struck the eastern part of the lake, causing devastation in Van city and the surrounding towns and villages (see box, p.630).

Various cities in western Turkey offers daily flights to the regional capital, **Van** (1642km from İstanbul), on the eastern shore of the lake. Van has an ancient citadel set atop a dramatic limestone outcrop, overlooking the atmospheric but scant remains of the tragically destroyed old town. Rapidly expanding and modernizing, Van is a remarkably civilized and welcoming centre for exploration. Overland, the conventional approach is by bus from Diyarbakır (see p.600), via the old trade route through the stark hill town of **Bitlis** and dull **Tatvan**, itself a base for exploring the northwest shore of Lake Van. Alternatively, from Erzurum (see p.546), travellers can head due east to **Doğubeyazıt** and its fanciful palace below the impressive bulk of Mount Ararat. From Van, a four-hour journey leads through spectacular mountains to **Hakkari**, from where the truly adventurous can exit the region by following the road along the Iraqi Kurdish border to **Şırnak**.

Lake Van

Virtually an inland sea, covering almost 4000 square kilometres at an elevation of 1750m, **Lake Van** is one of eastern Turkey's most unusual features. Along with Lake Sevan in Armenia and Lake Urumiya in Iran, it is one of a trio of huge upland lakes

Van in the wake of the quake p.530
A forgotten kingdom– Urartu p.636

Travel in the mountains south of Lake Van: a warning p.638
Nestorian Christians p.639

AHLAT CEMETERY

Highlights

❶ **Nemrut Dağı** The massive crater of this towering volcano shelters migrating birds in May and September, and in between offers the possibility of a dip in the crater lakes. **See p.626**

❷ **Ahlat** The eerie cemeteries of lakeshore Ahlat are home to beautifully carved, improbably angled tombstones and striking cylindrical mausoleums. **See p.626**

❸ **Van Kalesi** The lakeside "Rock of Van", fortified by the ancient Urartians and covered in their cuneiform inscriptions, rises above the poignant old town of Van. **See p.629**

❹ **Akdamar Kilisesi** Superbly restored tenth-century Armenian church, liberally decorated with relief-carved biblical scenes, picturesquely set on a tiny island in Lake Van. **See p.634**

❺ **İshak Paşa Sarayı** An architectural folly of richly carved golden limestone, nestling beneath a dramatic rocky spur above the Silk Road to Iran. **See p.642**

❻ **Mount Ararat** This iconic biblical peak, at 5137m the highest mountain in Turkey, rises in Mount Fuji-like volcanic magnificence above the bustling frontier town of Doğubeyazit. **See p.644**

HIGHLIGHTS ARE MARKED ON THE MAP ON P.622

LAKE VAN AND THE SOUTHEAST

HIGHLIGHTS
1 Nemrut Dağı
2 Ahlat
3 Van Kalesi
4 Akdamar Kilisesi
5 Ishak Paşa Sarayı
6 Mount Ararat

ARMENIA

NAKHCHIVAN AZERBAIJAN

IRAN

→ Tehran

Gürbulak

6 Ağrı Dağı (Mount Ararat 5165m)

5 Ishak Paşa Sarayı

Doğubeyazıt

→ Iğdır

Çaldıran

Muradiye

Diyadin

Muradiye Şelalesi

Balık Gölü

Ulu Pamir

Ercis

Ağrı

Patnos

Süphan Dağı (4050m)

Kefkalesi

Adilcevaz

Malazgirt

Lake Van

Ayanis

Çarpanak

3 Yedi Kilise

Akköy

Van

Akdamar 4

St Thomas

Altınsaç

2 Ahlat

1 Nemrut Dağı (3050m)

Tatvan

Por

El-Aman Kervansarayı

Bitlis

Muş

Bingöl

Murat River

Silvan

Malabadi Köprüsü

Kapıköy

Soradir

Surb Bertolomeos

Hoşap

Güzelsu

Başkale

Albayrak

Yeni Köprü

Esendere

Yüksekova

Reşko (4135m)

Hakkari

Koçhanes

Karadağ (3752m)

CİLO-SAT DAĞLARI

Çukurca

Şemdinli

IRAQ

Edremit

Gevaş

Aşağı Narlıca

Gürpınar

Çavustepe

Çatak

Görüdü

Bahçesaray

Andzghonts

Beytüşşebap

Uludere

Şırnak

Cudi Dağı (2114m)

Tyre

Siirt

Kurtalan

Batman

Midyat

Diyarbakır

Erzurum

HWY E-23

0 50 kilometres

N

Sivas

Malatya & Istanbul

Şanlıurfa

hereabouts that lack outlets. Surrounded on all sides by a narrow but fertile plain, and then mountains, the lake – nearly 200m deep in spots – occupies what was once a lowland basin that was later dammed by lava flowing from Nemrut Dağı. Owing to rapid evaporation in this desert climate, the lake water is highly alkaline.

Although venerable **Bitlis** is a twenty-minute drive from the western shores of the lake, and set 200m below it in a narrow valley, the vast majority of visitors pass through the town en route to or from Lake Van and its immediate environs. On the west shore of the lake, workaday **Tatvan** makes a handy base for forays up impressive **Nemrut Dağı** and its crater lakes. Of interest on the austerely volcanic north shore of the lake are **Ahlat** and its incredible medieval Muslim cemeteries, while to the northwest pastoral **Adılcevaz** nestles in the shadow of 4058m Mt Süphan Dağı. The major draw on the south shore of the lake is the beautiful Akdamar island and its **Church of the Holy Cross**, while the east shore holds the regional capital, **Van**.

Although you can **swim** from the stony beaches on and opposite Akdamar Island, and along the more sparsely populated stretches of shoreline, **pollution** makes it inadvisable to bathe near Tatvan or Van. In places the shoreline is littered with plastic detritus washed up from the lake – it's a major eyesore and a public awareness campaign has had little appreciable effect.

Set on a major **bird** migration route between Africa and Russia/Central Asia, Lake Van is a magnet for serious birdwatchers. Pelican and flamingo can be seen, as well as the rare white-headed duck, velvet scoter and paddyfield warbler.

Two species of **fish** – one called *dareka* – live in the lake, but only where fresh water enters. They are caught for food during spring when, salmon-like, they migrate up incoming streams to spawn.

The **Van cat**, a fluffy white beast endowed naturally with one blue and one gold eye, is now rare, but a few specimens are still kept at local carpet shops as tourist bait, and there is a breeding station (open to visitors) on the campus of Van's Yüzüncü Yıl university.

12

Bitlis

The historic town of **BİTLİS** (1545m altitude) is reached along an attractive winding gorge dotted with *kervansaray*s and old bridges. Its lifeblood used to be its location on the main west–east transit road linking the Tigris and Euphrates basins with that of Lake Van, but Bitlis has recently been bypassed by a 4km-long tunnel. The plus side for visitors is that the once very noisy, polluted main drag is much more pleasant.

Bitlis is a fascinating and atmospheric town, ignored by most travellers in the headlong rush to Lake Van. Assuming you arrive early enough in the day, it's easy to alight here and explore before you catch one of the very frequent dolmuşes on to Tatvan. The most important monuments lie west of the road, in narrow streets busy with people rather than vehicles.

With its dark stone houses and steep valley setting, Bitlis has the feel of an isolated nineteenth-century English mill town, though it once controlled the pass from Syria to the Van region and Persia and Armenia beyond. Before World War I it was a prosperous place, and about half the inhabitants were Armenian. Today this predominantly Kurdish town is impoverished, and its last major employer, a factory that processes the famous local tobacco, closed down in 2008.

Şerefiye Külliyesi

In the town centre, just south of the castle

The most notable monument in Bitlis, the sixteenth-century **Şerefiye Külliyesi** is a fine mosque/*medrese*/hamam complex. It was built in the Ottoman period, but in a distinctly Selçuk style, especially the finely carved stalactite-style portal of the mosque, enlivened by a band of black and white stone. The tombs of several dignitaries are located on the grounds. At the time of writing the interior was undergoing restoration, but entry was possible.

İhlasiye Medresesi

North of the castle • Mon–Fri 8am–5pm • Free

Reached by a steep flight of steps that climbs up from the main street opposite the *Dideban* hotel, the turreted **İhlasiye Medresesi** was built in 1569 by the Kurdish emir Şerefxan. This fine theological school complex is today home to the Directory of Tourism, and boasts a beautiful minaret as well as fine views across the town to the surrounding hills.

Ulu Cami

Just west of, and below, the castle

The unusual-looking **Ulu Cami** mosque was built from the local dark stone in 1126 by the Artukids. Even by Bitlis' severe standards it's an austere structure, enlivened by zigzag motifs on the cylindrical minaret and an unusual dome on the part of the *mihrab* extending to the outside of the building.

Küfrevi Türbesi

East of the main drag

A walled complex, accessible via steps above the Tatvan dolmuş stop on the main street holds both the **Küfrevi Türbesi**, dating from 1316, and a much more modern *türbe* buil by Greek craftsmen under the orders of Sultan Abdülhamid in 1898. Together these house the tombs of six Sunni saints, who draw pilgrims from all over the Muslim world. To gain entry, you'll need to find the caretaker.

The citadel

Bitlis' huge **citadel**, originally built by one of Alexander the Great's generals (though the walls now visible date back only to 1530 AD), is built on a rock outcrop looming over the town. Reach it by following a road that snakes around its base to the far side, from where steps continue to the top, with great views over Bitlis.

Por

9km northeast of Bitlis • Turn right, signed towards Değirmenaltı, 3km north of Bitlis on the road to Tatvan; a taxi will cost around ₺40 return, including waiting time

Although little remains of Bitlis' Armenian past, the beautifully situated Kurdish village of **Por** (Değirmenaltı in Turkish) holds Turkey's best collection of surviving **Armenian khatchkars**. One of these beautifully inscribed memorial stones is over 3m high. The adjoining **church of St Anania**, now used as a barn, dates back to the seventh century, and is in surprisingly good condition.

ARRIVAL AND DEPARTURE

BİTLİS

By bus and dolmuş Tatvan dolmuşes depart from the foot of the steps below the Küfrevi Türbesi, on the main road just south of the *Dideban* hotel. Intercity buses heading west from Van pass through Bitlis, but may be full **Destinations** Tatvan (daily 8am–6pm; journey time; ₺4).

ACCOMMODATION AND EATING

Büryancı Vahit Usta Yeri Balıkçılar Sok 20 ☏0434 226 1892. One of numerous simple restaurants, tucked beneath the *kale*, devoted to the local speciality, *büryan kebap*, leg of goat steamed in a *tandır* oven for four hours, and served on the bone atop a pile of fresh *pide*. Note that food can run out early at busy times. Daily 5am–3pm.

Çağlayan Nur Cad ☏0434 226 4057. If you don't fancy leg of goat, standard Turkish cuisine is dished up at this functional but spotless place at bargain prices, with a couple of *lahmacun* and an *ayran* for ₺4. They also serve soups, *pide* and kebab. Daily 6am–10pm.

Dideban Nur Cad 1 ☏0434 226 2821, ✉ didebanotel @hotmail.com. Functional, clean en-suite rooms boasting wi-fi, hairdryers and a fridge. Owner Muşfik is friendly and always pleased to see foreigners visiting his home town. ₺80

Tatvan

TATVAN, a functional town lodged between the mountains and lakeshore 25km northeast of Bitlis, makes a good base for exploring the surrounding sights. It has smartened up considerably in the last few years, with a couple of new shopping centres, one of which holds a cinema and bowling, and a newly constructed promenade along the lakeshore. To the north is the massif of **Nemrut Dağı** with its crater lakes; further east around the lake are the impressive medieval remains at Ahlat (see p.626).

Tatvan's streets follow the grid layout common in new developments in Turkey, with the main street, **Cumhuriyet Caddesi**, running east to west 100m south of the lake.

ARRIVAL AND DEPARTURE
TATVAN

By bus and dolmuş Tatvan's *otogar* is 1km along the Bitlis road, but buses invariably drop passengers near the PTT at Cumhüriyet Meydan (Square) on Cumhuriyet Caddesi. Buses to Van usually depart from in front of the various bus company offices on Cumhüriyet Caddesi, following the main road along the beautiful south shore of the lake; Ahlat dolmuşes leave from the corner of the PTT, near Cumhuriyet Caddesi, and run along the north shore of the lake; and Bitlis dolmuşes depart from Cumhüriyet Caddesi, 400m north of the square.
Destinations Ahlat (every 45min; 45min); Bitlis (hourly; 30min); Diyarbakır (5 daily; 4hr); Van (hourly; 3hr).

By train The train station is 1km northwest of the centre. The *Transasya Ekspresi* arrives from Ankara at 2.50pm on Fridays. International, Iran-bound passengers only can stay with the carriages as they're shipped by ferry across the lake to Van.

By ferry Ferries between Tatvan and Van usually make at least two daily crossings (morning and afternoon). The ₺8 foot passenger fee makes for a bargain cruise, but timings are unpredictable and you may wait hours to depart.
Destinations Van (up to 3 daily; 5hr).

INFORMATION AND TOURS

Tourist office Inconveniently located in the new Kültür Merkezi, 1km southwest of town on the Bitlis road.

Tours Nimetullah Özkan at the *Kardelen* hotel

(☎0532 798 2441) charges around ₺140 for a dolmuş excursion to Nemrut Dağı.

ACCOMMODATION

Hotel Karaman Yeni Çarşısı 11 ☎0434 827 1104, ⚐ hotelkaraman.com. A reliable addition to the town's accommodation scene, this central 36-room hotel has all the facilities you'd expect of a three-star, plus nice touches like free juice and cakes in the minibar. **₺100**

Hotel Kardelen Belediye Yanı, Cumhuriyet Cad ☎0434 827 9500, ✉otelkardelen@turkei.net. Tatvan's oldest quality hotel was closed for major renovation at the time of writing, but has always been well managed, so it will be worth checking out their prices and rooms before going elsewhere. They also run the *Nemrut Kardelen* at the ski resort on Mt Nemrut, well worth considering if you have your own transport. Bright, clean and superb lake views. **₺160**

★ **Sahra Hotel** Cumhuriyet Cad, Sahil Yolu Üzeri ☎0434 827 6969, ⚐sahrahotel.com. The best value of Tatvan's new tranche of classier hotels, 600m south of Cumhuriyet Meydan. Singles have wide beds, all rooms are light and contemporary in style, with rug-bedecked tiled floors, white/pastel decor and crisp white bedlinen. A few rooms have views down to the lake. **₺90**

Üstün Otel Hal Cad 23 ☎0434 827 9014. A couple of blocks east of Cumhuriyet Cad, the *Üstün* is a basic family-run pension-style hotel that offers the cheapest suitable accommodation in town. Some of the simple but adequate rooms have their own shower, but toilets are communal; rates include a simple breakfast. **₺50**

EATING AND DRINKING

Altın Kup/Deniz Kızı Just off Cumhuriyet Cad, behind the Hotel Dilek. This small, kitschy male-oriented bar plays *Türkü* music and doles out cheap beer (₺5). It also serves decent grills, with *pirzola* (lamb chops) and grilled fish dishes for a reasonable ₺15. Daily 11am–midnight.

Çınar Kebab Cumhuriyet Cad, Özel İdare Pasajı ☎0434 827 1051. Locals swear Çınar has the best kebabs in town,

and they're probably right. Adana kebab ₺10, but also more unusual versions like liver for a fraction more. Daily 5am–midnight.

Eyvan Cumhuriyet Cad, Sok 7 ☎0432 827 6579. Tucked away on a side street behind the Bestvantur bus office on the main drag, this basic but clean restaurant provides tasty *pide* (₺7) and different types of the egg dish *menemen* (₺5) served up sizzling hot in a small

12

wok-style pan – try the one dripping with *kaşar* cheese. Daily 7am–11pm.

Gökte Ada Yaşam İş Merkezi (Carrefour), Cumhuriyet Cad ☏0434 827 6282. This shiny, spacious place, on the third floor of the shopping centre, dishes up a wide range of kebabs, *lahmacun* and *pide*. Much favoured by the local middle classes, it's a little dearer than most, with kebabs

from ₺11.5. Also serves good *sulu yemek* for lunch. Dail 10am–10pm.

Per 10 Near the Ahlat dolmuş stop, Cumhuriye Cad. This small café serves a decent breakfast with fla bread, butter, honey and a large tea for ₺8, and offe Tatvan's best selection of cakes and *baklava*. Dail 6am–11pm.

Nemrut Dağı

Dolmuşes charge around ₺140 for a 3–4hr excursion from Tatvan; driving your own vehicle, join the main road to Bitlis from Tatvan, then turn right after 500m

Immediately north of Tatvan, the extinct volcano of **Nemrut Dağı** – no relation to the mountain with the statues – rises to 3050m. Six thousand years ago Nemrut is believed to have stood 4450m tall; as a result of a huge volcanic explosion, the whole upper section of the peak was deposited in the Van basin, thus blocking the natural outlet and creating the lake. The present-day volcanic cone, which is accessible after snowmel from May or June through to November, contains two crater lakes, one of which is pleasantly warm.

From the rim, an asphalt road drops down and right towards the crater floor. To reac crescent-shaped **Soğukgöl** (cold lake), bear left on a dirt track. The lake occupies the western half of the crater, and on its east shore there are some swimmable hot springs. Better for a dip, however, is smaller **Sıcakgöl** (warm lake), connected to its partner by a narrow path leading east or a left branch off the asphalt road and heated to 60°C by ongoing volcanic activity. The 7km-diameter **crater** is lushly vegetated (beech, aspen and juniper), contrasting sharply with the bare landscape outside. In summer Kurds graze their flocks on the slopes.

A small **ski resort** on the mountain, 8km from Tatvan at an altitude of 2200m, holds a smart new hotel, the *Nemrut Kardelen* (see p.625). A chairlift ride takes visitors to the summit for ₺10, but only runs in summer for groups of ten or more. The lift goes righ to the crater rim, and the views are spectacular.

Ahlat

The shabby town of **AHLAT**, which lies a picturesque drive 42km northeast of Tatvan along the north shore of Lake Van, is known chiefly for its medieval **Muslim cemetery**, holding hundreds of beautifully carved gravestones, and for its monumental **tombs**, known as *türbe* in Turkish.

The cemetery and tombs are by far the most substantial remains of a settlement that can boast a very long history. The Urartians are known to have been here in the first millennium BC, and were followed in turn by the Armenians. Ahlat fell to the Arabs during the seventh century, was retaken by the Byzantines two hundred years later, and subsequently passed to the victorious Selçuks after the nearby Battle of Manzikert in 1071. The Mongols, who arrived in 1244, were succeeded by the İlhanids a century later; by the fifteenth century Ahlat had become the main base of the Akkoyunlu Turcomans. Even after the local Ottoman conquest of 1548, real power in this remote region remained in the hands of the Kurdish emirs of Bitlis. Ahlat continued to be a populous, polyglot city until World War I.

Old Ahlat is a sprawling site, centred on a small museum, with the most visited of the monumental tombs, the Ulu Kümbet, some 300m south. The Meydan cemetery, peppered with intricately carved tombstones, is immediately north of the museum, while the Bayındır tomb lies 600m north of the museum across the cemetery. The city ruins nestle in a valley around 400m west of the Bayındır tomb.

Ahlat Museum

km southwest of central Ahlat • Tues–Sat 8am–noon & 1–5pm • Free • Arriving from Tatvan by dolmuş, ask to be dropped here, or you'll continue to Ahlat and have to catch a town dolmuş back again

Interesting artefacts in the small **Ahlat Museum** range from the Urartian era (first millennium BC) to the medieval period, but everything is labelled in Turkish. To get an idea of the extent of medieval Ahlat, take a look at the museum's well-plotted ground plan. Otherwise, it's best to concentrate on the Urartian bronze-work, and the pottery that was mass-produced here in medieval times.

Ulu Kümbet (Great Tomb)

km southwest of central Ahlat, just south of the main road opposite the museum

Ahlat's famous *kümbet* **tombs** lie scattered southwest of the town centre. The largest and most beautifully decorated of all, the **Ulu Kümbet** or "Great Tomb", built for a late thirteenth-century Mongol chieftain, now stands isolated in a field.

As is typical of local *kümbets*, which could accommodate one to four persons, it was constructed of deep brown basalt; most of the stonemasons were Armenian. The deceased was interred in an underground chamber, beneath a prayer room reached by steps from the outside. The distinctive conical style may have been inspired by the traditional nomadic tent or yurt, or by the drum and conical roof of Armenian church architecture.

Meydan cemetery

adjacent to, and north of, the museum, 2km southwest of central Ahlat

The reason most visitors make the trek out to Ahlat is to see the **Meydan cemetery**, a wonderful collection of tilted, lichen-encrusted headstones that dates from the eleventh to the sixteenth centuries and covers almost two square kilometres. Most are covered with floral, geometric and calligraphic (Persian and Arabic scripts) decoration. Some restoration work was under way at the time of writing, with wooden props being placed to support those grave markers that were most in danger of toppling over.

Bayındır Türbesi

adjoining the northern rim of the Meydan cemetery

With its colonnaded upper storey, domed rather than conical roof, and small, still much-used *mescit* (prayer room), the **Bayındır Türbesi** is the most distinctive of Ahlat's *kümbets*. It was built in 1492 to house the remains of the Turcoman chief Bayındır.

Harabe Şehir

around 400m west of the Bayındır Türbesi

The idyllic valley known as **Harabe Şehir** ("City Ruins") holds the remains of a huge mosque, a castle, rock-cut houses and the pretty fifteenth-century humpbacked bridge of Emir Bayındır. It's also alive with colourful birds such as hoopoes and bee-eaters as well as the odd tortoise. Set on a bluff above, the prominent **Hasan Padişah Türbesi**, built in 1275, stands almost 20m high, its cylindrical body topped by a pyramidal roof.

ARRIVAL AND DEPARTURE AHLAT

By bus and dolmuş The first daily dolmuş from Tatvan to Ahlat leaves at 7.30am. Ask to be dropped by the museum. Regular dolmuşes run from there to the town centre (₺1.25), where you can catch a dolmuş back to Tatvan (last departure 6pm) or on to Adilcevaz, or a bus on to Van. The last of the five daily buses from Adilcevaz to Van departs at 2pm (₺15).

Destinations Adilcevaz (6 daily, 30min; ₺5); Tatvan (frequent; 45min; ₺5).

ACCOMMODATION AND EATING

Büyük Selçuklu Zübeyde Hanım Cad ☎0434 412 5695. Dark-stone place right on the shore at the extreme east end of town. At the time of writing it was undergoing a major overhaul and should be of three-star standard when complete.

Doğu Sahil Cad, just east of the Selçuklu ☎0535 484 6036. For the impecunious male traveller, this basic accommodation above a decent restaurant is really a truckers' stop, with two twin bunks in each waterless room.

But it's clean and pleasant enough. Per person ₺20

Vangölü Aşağı Çarşı PTT Yanı ☎0434 412 5500. I spanking new premises on Ahlat's main street, th excellent, scrupulously clean first-floor restaurant is alway full of local teachers, women and families. Döner keba and *sulu yemek* take precedence in the day, grills and pia in the evenings. There's a terrace with (partial) lake view for warm days. Daily 9am–10pm.

Adilcevaz

The charming modern village of **ADILCEVAZ**, a smaller but more pleasant place to stay than either Tatvan or Ahlat, huddles 25km north of Ahlat in a fertile valley that's surrounded by poplars, walnut and apricot trees. It's dominated by the shattered shell of a Selçuk fortress, which is in turn overshadowed by the 4058m volcanic peak of **Süphan Dağı**, Turkey's fourth highest. Although not technically difficult to climb, the mountain's remoteness and unreliable water supply make the trek a serious undertaking (temperatures can drop to -50°C in winter).

Below Adilcevaz, near the shore and constructed using the dark brown volcanic stone typical of the area, the distinctive, multi-domed sixteenth-century **Tuğrul Bey Camii** is ascribed to the ubiquitous Sinan. The lakefront near here has an attractive promenade area and a pleasant café.

A startlingly evocative shattered shell, the Armenian monastery church of **Skantselorgivank** stands high on the bare mountainside, above a small dam on the town's upper slopes. Reached via a rocky trail, it features bands of red and black stonework, *khatchkar*s (stones inscribed with crosses) and a black basalt font. Above it is the Urartian citadel of **Kefkalesi**, separated from the church by a steep, scree-strewn valley that can only be negotiated with difficulty (taxi ₺30).

ARRIVAL AND DEPARTURE   ADILCEVAZ

By bus and dolmuş Adilcevaz offers connections to Ahlat and on to Van (last daily departure 2pm).

Destinations Ahlat (6 daily, 30min; ₺5); Van (5 daily; 2h 30min; ₺15).

ACCOMMODATION AND EATING

Cevizlibağ Otel Recep Tayip Erdoğan Cad 31 ☎0434 311 3151, ⓦcevizlibagotel.com. The best hotel in Adilcevaz is bright, new and clean, with lake views from

some rooms and important features like free wi-fi, LCD TV and central heating. It also has a decent restaurar downstairs. ₺80

Van

Just as it was transforming itself into a modern, buzzing city, **VAN** was rocked by a major quake in 2011 (see box, p.630). At the time of writing, reconstruction was under way, and many hotels, restaurants and bars were open for business. The region is well used to earthquakes, and despite the initial trauma there's an air of steely determination to recover. Van itself, set 4km from Lake Van against the backdrop of the volcanic, 3200m Erek Dağı, continues to make a great base to explore the lake's numerous attractions. Its highlight, ancient **Van Kalesi**, is spectacularly situated 3km west by the lake, where it overlooks the poignant remains of the old city destroyed during World War I.

Most visitors reach Van by road, along the scenic **southern-shore route** from Tatvan, which initially follows a pretty willow-fringed valley to the pass of Kuskunkıran (2234m), then descends through a checkpoint and along the lakeshore,

th vistas of Akdamar and Süphan Dağı reflected in the still waters. The lake and
ountain views are similarly spectacular if you approach Van by air, or on the erratic
rries from Tatvan.

Although Van is basically a conservative town, that's mitigated by the presence of the
rge student population attending Yüzüncü Yıl university. Numerous bars litter the
ntre, where it's possible to drink in mixed company, and listen to Turkish and
urdish folk and rock music. Van is also a good place to shop, with a wide selection
local (Kurdish) tribal rugs, as well as often cheaper ones from nearby Iran, though
u need to bargain hard to get a good price.

Following the winding down of the war with the PKK, the locals are increasingly
serting their **Kurdish identity**. In 2009 the pro-Kurdish DTP party won sixty percent
the vote in local elections, and the city's central tea garden on Cumhüriyet Caddesi
s been given a Kurdish name.

an museum

giz Cad • Closed by earthquake, but likely to reopen

ter **Van museum** (Van Müzesi) was hit by the quake, all its artefacts were put into
orage. This is a shame, as the **Urartian** exhibits really made an excellent primer for
siting sites such as Çavuştepe or Ayanis. The museum is almost certain to reopen in
new location close to Van Kalesi – though how long this will take to materialize is
yone's guess.

The **garden**, however, remains open. Pride of place here belongs to the black basalt
lief-carving of an Urartian god, possibly Shivini, astride a bull, but it also holds a
mber of fine stelae, liberally covered in cuneiform Urartian inscriptions.

an Kalesi: the Rock of Van

n west of central Van • Daily 8.30am–7.30pm • ₺3 • Frequent dolmuşes from Beş Yol junction drop passengers at the eastern end of the
ck; to reach the entrance, follow the road 500m towards the lake

he narrow outcrop known as **Van Kalesi** – 1.5km long, over 100m tall and perhaps
0m wide at the base – holds the nearest visitable Urartian fortification to Van.
quipped with its own spring, it was an eminently suitable stronghold. As you pass
e northern face, note the arched niches, which originally belonged to an **Urartian**
mple, set in the base of the cliff, behind an Ottoman-era mosque and *türbe*. These
ce held stelae; cuneiform inscriptions on the base of one document the life and
orks of a powerful Urartian king.

VAN IN THE WAKE OF THE QUAKE

The Van region was struck by a magnitude 7.1 **earthquake** in October 2011, followed by a second, less powerful quake in early November. Over six hundred people lost their lives and tens of thousands spent a miserable winter in tents as their homes had either collapsed or were declared unsafe. Fortunately the initial quake happened during the day, or casualties would have been far higher.

By the spring of 2012, tens of thousands of people were still living in temporary accommodation, mainly in the form of container (*konteyner* in Turkish) dwellings, and Van city centre held several empty plots where unsafe buildings had been demolished, while many more stood empty and awaiting demolition. At least fifteen thousand buildings are likely to be pulled down in total. That said, many hotels, offices and homes had been checked and declared safe – some after quake-proofing – and life on the streets of Van was pretty much back to normal.

Villages in the region were also badly affected. Some, like Yukarı Bakraçlı, will be completely rebuilt. Over four hundred thousand people fled the quake zone to escape unsafe buildings and the harsh winter, but by spring 2012 many had returned. The government, initially criticized for refusing outside help, is providing housing and interest-free loans for those affected by the disaster.

Entry is from the car park and **ticket booth** on the northwest side, where there's also decent restaurant/café and a replica of an old Van house, built of mud brick and home to one of the famous Van cats. Just west of the tea gardens is a large stone platform (possibly a jetty) made of limestone blocks, some over 5m long. Two inscriptions adorn the structure, both in the Assyrian, rather than the Urartian, language, praising the Urartian king Sarduri I (844–838 BC).

From the "jetty" or ticket booth, a path ascends the gentler north face of the Rock and leads, eventually, to the citadel on top. A slight diversion south from the route leads to the single most impressive part of Van Kalesi, the rock **tomb of Argishti 1** (785–760 BC), which is set in the sheer cliff face on the south side of the Rock, west of the summit area. As the door is gated and locked, you'll need to be guided by one of the security officials who hang out near the ticket booth – expect to give a small tip. The tomb is reached by a set of worn steps, fortunately protected by metal railings. The carved rock face above the stairs is covered in well-preserved cuneiform inscriptio relating Argishti's conquests. Take a torch to explore the interior, where the fixing hole for votive plaques can still be seen. Several more anonymous rock-cut tombs are scattered on the south face of the Rock, east of the summit area, but take care – the path is badly worn, and the drops deadly.

The most prominent building on the top today is a restored **Ottoman-era mosque**. The arch-roofed building next to that is a *medrese*, while the former barracks of the Ottoman garrisons stand close by. The curious steps cut into the limestone are actually the foundation bases for cyclopean Urartian walls; the mud-brick ones visible today are much later. The new-looking sections of crenellated wall on the eastern part of the Rock are just that, but probably follow the line of ancient walling.

Old Van

The destruction of **Old Van** in 1915 was so thorough that today only four mosques and fragments of an Armenian church remain. The rest is a sea of overgrown, rubble-strewn mounds where once an attractive settlement was home to eighty thousand people. Within the walls lay bazaars, churches, mosques and government offices. Nearby orchards give an indication of the once-extensive "garden suburbs" of **Aygestan**, where the bulk of the population lived in the nineteenth and early twentieth centuries. To walk through Old Van, head around the western (lake) end of the Rock to skirt the southern face of the Rock. You can exit through a gap in the

nce at the southeast end of the Rock and catch a dolmuş back into Van.
ternatively, enter the ruins here and make your way through the old city to the
ficial entrance to Van Kalesi.

The first structure as you approach from the west is the badly ruined **Topçuloğlu**
mii. The fifteenth-century **Ulu Cami** is of more interest, with an attractive brick
inaret still bearing traces of faience tiles. Look due north from the mosque to see the
assive fifth-century BC **cuneiform inscription** of Xerxes. Inscribed in Persian, Medean
d Babylonian, and celebrating the might of the famous Persian king, it was first

CENTRAL VAN

Ferry Docks, Otogar & Train Station — İlçe Otogar

Dolmuşes to the Rock of Van

Buses to İskele

Hastane Hospital

İSKELE CADDESİ

BEŞ YOL

HASTANE CADDESİ

Yeni Cami

ŞIKKE CADDESİ

Dabakoğlu Parkı

ŞEYİT MEHMET E. CADDESİ

Şehir Hamamı

Dolmuşes to Edremit & Gevaş (Akdamar)

ZÜBEYDE HANIM CADDESİ

N

12

CUMHURİYET CADDESİ

PTT CADDESİ

ORDU CADDESİ

Dolmuş to Bahçesaray

Cami

Cami

HACI OSMAN SOKAK

Akdamar Travel

YUZBAŞIOĞLU SOKAK

Feqiye Teyran Parkı

MÜZE SOKAK

Star 2000

Belediye

Van Museum

CENGİZ ZİGDEŞ CADDESİ

POSTA CADDESİ

THY Office

MARAŞ CADDESİ

FEVZİ ÇAKMAK CADDESİ

Bus Companies

Urartu Turizm

Artoş İş Merkezi & cinema

Dolmuş to Hoşap

Dolmuş to Başkale/Albayrak

0 — 100 metres

BARS AND CAFÉS	
Frida	2
Halay Türkü	3
Ilanya	1
Niçhe	4

RESTAURANTS	
Aişe Ev	2
Firavin	1
Halil İbrahim Sofrası	4
Şafak	5
Sütçü Kenan Evren Kahvaltı Salonu	3

SHOPS	
Atsoy Gumuş	3
Galeri Kirman	1
Star 2000	2

ACCOMMODATION	
Ada Palas	4
Büyük Asur	6
Büyük Urartu	1
Şahin	3
Side	2
Tamara	5

recorded in 1827 by the traveller/archeologist Friedrich Schulz (later murdered by Kurdish tribesmen), dangling on a rope from the summit.

The remains of an Armenian church, still bearing traces of frescoes, huddled right under the Rock towards its southeast corner; behind it are some *khatchkar*s inscribed onto the rock face. A pair of sixteenth-century Ottoman-era mosques near the crumbled south town wall were undergoing restoration at the time of writing. The easterly one is the **Kaya Çelebi Camii** (1586), while the western mosque, rather more intact, with attractive banded stonework and an attached tomb, is the **Hüsrev Paşa Camii** (1567), a work of the great Ottoman imperial architect Sinan (see p.93). The south gate that once pierced the medieval wall nearby was being rebuilt (as opposed to restored) at the time of writing. Picnicking families descend on the grassed-over ruins on warm weekends, leaving nothing behind but their litter.

ARRIVAL AND DEPARTURE

By plane Van's airport, 6km south of town, is linked to the centre by dolmuş (₺1.25), though you have to walk 500m to the main road to get one, and taxis (₺20).

Destinations Ankara (3 daily direct with Anadolujet; 1hr 35min); Antalya (1 daily, direct with Sunexpress; 2hr 5min, or 3 daily via Ankara with Anadolujet); İstanbul (1 daily direct with Sunexpress; 2hr 15min, 2 daily direct with THY, 3 daily via Ankara with Anadolujet); İzmir (1 or 2 daily direct with Sunexpress; 2hr 20min), or via Ankara with Anadolujet, 3 daily).

By bus and dolmuş From the *otogar*, a little way northwest of the centre, dolmuşes and *servis* buses run to the busy junction of Beş Yol, at the northern end of Cumhuriyet Caddesi. Dolmuşes to Douğbeyazit (₺15) run from the İlçe *otogar*, 400m north of the Beş Yol junction, at 7.30am, 9am, noon, 2pm & 3.30pm. The major companies have offices clustered around the junction of Cumhuriyet/Kazım Karabekir/Fevzi Çakmak cads.

Destinations Ankara (8 daily; 22hr); Bahçesaray (3 da 2hr 30min); Diyarbakır (5 daily; 7hr); Doğubeyazıt (5 da 3hr); Erzurum (4 daily; 7hr); Hakkari (hourly in daylig hours; 3–4hr); Şanlıurfa (5 daily; 9hr); Tatvan (5 daily; 3h Trabzon (2 daily; 15hr).

Travel to Iran Regular buses run to the Iranian border Esendere-Sero, southeast of Van (daily 8am–5pm; 4 30min; ₺30), while it's also theoretically possible to cro the border at Kapıköy, reachable by dolmuş from the İ *otogar* (1hr).

By train Trains arrive at the station 3km northwest of centre, where you can find a dolmuş or taxi into town.

Destinations Tehran (Fri at 6.25pm; 25hr).

By ferry The ferry port, 5km west of town, is connect with the centre by dolmuş (₺1.30).

Car rental Reliable cars are available from Europ agents Akdamar, just off Cumhuriyet Cad behind the Ya Kredi bank (☎0432 215 8990).

INFORMATION AND TOURS

Tourist office Cumhuriyet Cad 127 (☎0432 216 2018); city street maps and glossy brochures.

Travel agencies Central Van is liberally dotted with travel

agencies. For daily tours try Urartu Turism, Cumhuriyet C (☎0432 214 2020), who are agents for Avis a Sunexpress, Pegasus and THY.

ACCOMMODATION

Van has plenty of **hotels**, in all price ranges; and for women travelling alone staying here is safer and more comfortab than at other towns in the area. Many hotels were damaged in the quake and remain closed at the time of writing; tho that are open and listed here have been inspected by various authorities and given the all clear. If in doubt, check w tourist office as to whether individual hotels have been sanctioned before you book.

★ **Ada Palas** Cumhuriyet Cad ☎0432 216 2716. Gleaming contemporary-styled hotel with top-notch beds and bathroom fittings, plus a very cheerful breakfast room. Spotlessly clean (and with female staff on reception), this is a great choice for women travellers. Wi-fi and foreign-channel TV too. ₺120

Büyük Asur Cumhuriyet Cad, Turizm Sok 5 ☎0432 216 8792, ⊛buyukasur.com. Rooms, refurbished post-quake, are painted a plain cream and are pleasantly simple and well kept. The real bonus is part-owner Remzi,

who speaks good English and offers day-trips taking Hoşap, Çavuştepe and Akdamar, or simply dishes out go advice for making the best of the area. There's a we stocked bar, free wi-fi and LCD TVs, but the breakfast only average. ₺150

Büyük Urartu Hastane Cad 60 ☎0432 212 066 ⊛buyukurartuotel.com. Well-run, safe choice with indoor pool, sauna, wi-fi access and rooftop breakf room. At the time of writing twelve of the old-style roo had been tastefully overhauled, with king-siz rthopaedic beds, LCD TVs and tidy glass and chrome athrooms. The ebullient manager, Celal, knows his usiness well. ₺180

Merit Şahmaran Edremit Yolu ☎0432 312 3060, ᴡmeritsahmaranotel.com. If you're looking for peace nd quiet, try this friendly group-oriented place on the akeshore 12km southwest of town, beyond the airport. he spacious rooms are tastefully decorated and the n-suites all have large baths. The buffet breakfast is xcellent, there's an outdoor pool, and the views from the rrace at sunset are lovely. Make sure you get a room with lake view. €130

ahin İrfan Baştuğ Cad ☎0432 216 3062, ᴡotelsahin om. Reliable choice. Single rooms are claustrophobically ose to the next building and offer little natural light, but ont rooms are spacious and, together with the rooftop eakfast room, offer views over the city. Firm beds, clean

and well kept. ₺80

Side Sikhe Cad 1 ☎0432 216 6265. One advantage of staying at this budget-mid-range option is the presence of English-speaking Harun Toprak (☎0536 5772 026, ᴡararat-trek.com), who can help sort out reasonably priced tours, rental cars etc. Rooms were undergoing renovation following the quake at the time of writing but should feature all facilities, including free wi-fi. ₺90

Tamara Otel Yüzbaşıoğlu Sok 1 ☎0432 214 3296, ᴡtamaraotel.com. Van's first attempt at a boutique hotel works pretty well, and has received a tasteful makeover since the quake. Crisp white linen on firm beds, light-wood furniture, muted tones and sparkling bathrooms complete with spacious tubs, wi-fi access and a/c. There's an in-house grill-your-own-meat restaurant and the *North Shield* pub. ₺215

ATING AND DRINKING

an's famous **breakfast salons**, most on or just off Cumhuriyet Caddesi, serve a selection of cheeses (including the ature, herb-studded *otlu peynir*), olives, honey and cream (*kaymak*) with fresh hot bread and gallons of tea. A scattering f new *ev yemekleri* (home-cooking) places has livened up a culinary scene once totally dominated by kebab and *pide* tablishments.

12

AFÉS AND RESTAURANTS

işe Ev Yemekleri Hastane 2 Cad, Özkok İş Merkezi arşısı 5 ☎0432 216 1515. Traditional Turkish and urdish dishes served up in a spotless emporium, all oked by a hard-working female team led by Aişe. Mains om ₺6. Daily 8.30–10pm.

ravin Hastane Cad, Nedim Odabaşı Ticaret Merkezi ☎0432 216 6686. Female-run home-made food joint ecializing in local Kurdish dishes – try the *Çukurca köfte*, eatballs in a rice and mincemeat shell served in a yoghurt uce, though they also serve standard Turkish dishes like ru fasuliye (haricot beans in tomato sauce). Mains 7–10. Mon–Sat 8am–8pm.

alil İbrahim Sofrası Cumhuriyet Cad, Ziraat Bankası nı 62 ☎0432 210 0070. Spotlessly clean, prettily corated but cavernous place, with a pleasant rear terrace. the standard grills, *sulu yemek* dishes, *pides* etc, plus ore unusual offerings (for this type of restaurant) like illed trout and *hamsi* (anchovies). Mains from ₺7. Daily m–11pm.

afak Et Lokantası Yuzbaşıoğlu Sok, off Kazım rabekir Cad ☎0432 216 1444. Highly recommended the fresh *döner*, tender lamb slices served up with shings of hot *pide* and a bowl of sumac-smothered sliced ions (₺10). Best washed down with a bowl of fresh, thy *yayık ayran*. Daily 9am–11pm.

★ **Sutçu Kenan Evren Kahvaltı Salonu** Kahvaltıcılar k 7/A ☎0432 216 8499. On a small street devoted to eakfast places, this is the bustling best. It serves all the

usual standards, with tables out on the street in the warmer months. A (very) hearty breakfast will set you back ₺15 – as an extra, try the *yumurtalı kavurma* (eggs and tender lamb served in a small wok-like dish). Daily 5am–3pm.

BARS

Frida Bar Sanat Sokağı ☎0507 923 0343. Popular first-floor bar/music venue, with beers a reasonable ₺7 and bar snacks available. There's live music on Fri & Sat evenings, with surprisingly good acts. Everything from Rammstein sung in Kurdish to traditional folk and Turkish pop. Daily noon–2am.

★ **HalayTürkü Bar** Maraş Cad, Artoş İş Merkezi Karşısı ☎0432 214 8283. Trendy top-floor *Türkü* bar with live music 8pm–2am nightly, an open-air terrace and *ocakbaşı* (charcoal grill) restaurant. Beers are ₺7, grills ₺12 and up. British film director Ben Hopkins shot some of his 2008 film *Pazar* here. Daily noon–2am.

Janya Bar ve Şarap Evi Cumhüriyet Cad. Promising new fifth-floor venue with live music every night – Kurdish, Turkish, Armenian and rock. Watch the action down on Van's main street from a window table. Beers ₺6, a glass of decent wine ₺8. Daily noon–2am.

Niçhe (Nietzsche) Bar Maraş Cad ☎0505 903 3570. If the philosopher's main tenet had been that everyone should drink and smoke themselves to death, he would be delighted by the number of (mainly young) people doing just that at Van's hippest bar. Beers ₺6, other customers' cigarette smoke free. Daily 1pm–2am.

SHOPPING

Atsoy Gumuş Maraş Cad 8/b ☎ 0432 216 1234. This jewellery shop isn't cheap but there are some beautiful silver bracelets, earrings and necklaces to be had, some based on original Urartian pieces. They have another outlet beside the ticket entrance to Van Kalesi. Mon–Sat 9am–8pm.

Galeri Kirman Müze Çarşısı, opposite the museum

☎ 0432 215 3789. A wide range of carpets and kilims decent prices. Mon–Sat 10am–6pm.

Star 2000 Sanat Sok 2 ☎ 0432 214 0032. Stude orientated book and music store, with a trendy inter café downstairs and decent pizza/café place upstairs. Da 9am–10pm.

DIRECTORY

Hospitals Devlet Hastanesi is on Hastane Cad, just east of Beş Yol (☎ 0432 216 4740), or Güven Hastanesi on İpek Yolu, near the Van cat statue (☎ 0432 217 5900).

Police West of town on İpek Yolu.
Post office Behind the tourist office, just off Cumhüri Cad.

Around Van

While the main attraction near Van is the Armenian island church of **Akdamar**, nearb **St Thomas** and the splendidly isolated church on the island of **Çarpanak** are almost equally worthwhile. The ancient Urartian settlements at **Çavuştepe** to the south and **Ayanis** to the north also make excellent day-trips from Van. The rocky foothills to the east hold more church remains, at **Yedi Kilise**, while the landscape south of Van is the most physically impressive in Turkey, featuring rugged mountains dotted with isolate settlements such as **Bahçesaray**. The imposing castle at **Hoşap** lies en route for the wile mountain town of Hakkari.

Although it's possible to visit some of these sights by public transport, to really make the most of one of Turkey's most fascinating regions, it's worth considering **renting a car** for a couple of days.

Yedi Kilise

10km southeast of Van • Around ₺50 by taxi, with waiting time

Beautifully situated in the foothills of Erek Dağı, the village of Yukarı Bakraçlı is home to the remains of the once-grand monastery of the Holy Cross, founded in th seventh century.

The locals know the village as **Yedi Kilise** (Seven Churches), or "Varaga Vank" in Armenian, as seven Armenian churches and the monastery once stood here. The thirteenth-century Church of St George has survived, but was much damaged in the 2011 earthquake. Access to the interior, with its frescoes and crosses carved into the walls, is unlikely to be possible in the near future. Despite this, the village is worth a trip for a slice of rural Kurdish life and the great mountain location, with grand vistas down onto Lake Van.

Akdamar island

50km southwest of Van • Daily 8.30am–7.30pm • ₺3 • 20min by boat (₺7.5) from the roadside quay, which is served by dolmuşes from Van's İlçe *otogar* (daily in summer 6am–7pm; ₺5); if they're not full of island visitors, these stop at the town of Gevaş, 5km short (taxi ₺20)

The tiny island of **Akdamar**, just off Lake Van's southern shore, is home to the exquisit tenth-century Armenian **Surb Khach** or Church of the Holy Cross. Recently restored t the tune of US$1.5 million by the Turkish government, it stands as a glimmer of hope of reconciliation between Turks and Armenians. A metal cross has been erected on the conical dome of the church, and there's now an altar inside; services are held at irregular intervals.

The church was erected between 915 and 921 AD, at the behest of Gagik Artsruni, ruler of the Armenian kingdom of Vaspurakan. The small building is gracefully proportioned, but what makes it so special are the **relief carvings** that run in a series

OPPOSITE AKDAMAR KİLİSESİ (P.634)

of five bands around the exterior. As well as animal scenes there are several depictions of Bible stories, including Jonah appearing to dive from a boat into the jaws of a most unlikely-looking whale (south facade), and David taking on Goliath, sling in hand (south facade). King Gagik himself is carved in bold relief on the west facade, presenting a model of Surb Khach to Jesus. A number of **khatchkars** – the Celtic-looking, obsessively detailed carved crosses that the Armenians used both as celebratory or commemorative offerings and as grave markers – are also set into the facade and scattered beneath the almond trees to the east of the church.

The **frescoes** inside, formerly in a shocking state, have been sensitively restored. It's possible to make out New Testament scenes such as the Baptism of Christ, the raising of Lazarus and the Crucifixion. Outside, to the south, are the partially excavated remains of the monastery complex of which the church was once a part.

Clamber up the steep hillside behind the church for spectacular views down over the church to the lake and, beyond, to the magnificent peaks that ring the lakeshore and run all the way down to the Iraqi border. Be wary, though, of plodding tortoises, and gull-infested cliffs that drop sheer into the azure waters below.

The church of St Thomas

76km southwest of Van • 12km west of the Akdamar island quay, turn right at the first petrol station to Göründü village, 3km from the main road; continue 15km on a windy coast road to Altınsaç; 2km after that you'll see the church on a spur to your left, a 20–30min walk from where you park

The stunningly situated monastic **church of St Thomas** (Kamrak Vank), on an isolated promontory overlooking Lake Van, is best reached with your own vehicle. The final 18km of shoreline road here is extremely picturesque.

Built to a cruciform plan, the fourteenth-century church overlooks the bay of Varış from a plateau 2km from the modern village of **Altınsaç** (formerly Ganjak). Its sparsely decorated walls uphold a twelve-sided, capped drum; the extensive covered courtyard on the west was added late in the seventeenth century.

Çavuştepe

28km southeast of Van, on the Hakkari road • Daily 24hr • ₺3 • On Başkale and Gürpınar dolmuş routes (₺5)

The **Urartian royal palace** of **ÇAVUŞTEPE** was built between 764 and 735 BC by King Sardur II in classic Urartian style, at the end of a rocky spur running down onto a plain. The quality of the masonry is incredible, with expertly cut and sited blocks that join so perfectly no mortar was necessary. Among the pick of the hilltop remains are some massive sunken *pithoi* (storage urns), a temple with a remarkably well-preserved cuneiform inscription, some sunken cisterns and what is quite clearly a squat toilet. Below the ridge the line of the so-called Semiramis Canal can be seen, an Urartian irrigation channel that was used to take water to Van, and which still functions.

A FORGOTTEN KINGDOM – URARTU

Between the ninth and seventh centuries BC, the **Urartian Kingdom**, centred on Van (then known as Tushpa), encompassed most of the territory described in this chapter, plus parts of present-day Iran, Iraq and Syria.

Around a dozen Urartian **citadels** have been unearthed in modern Turkey and Armenia, always sited on naturally defensible rocky spurs or outcrops. More than a castle, they incorporated a palace, workshops, storage depots and temples.

Great engineers, the Urartians built numerous dams and irrigation channels, and their bronze-work was legendary – examples have been found in the Etruscan cities of Italy. They also planted many vineyards, and have been credited with the discovery of **wine**; curiously their biggest rivals, the Assyrians from the flatlands of Mesopotamia to the south, were beer drinkers. Eventually centuries of fighting with the Assyrians and later the Scythians took their toll, and the Urartian Empire went into decline at the start of the seventh century.

Former warden Mehmet Kuşman is one of the few people in the world who can read, write and speak Urartian, and lectures in the language at Van University. Despite his retirement, Mehmet is often on site, ready to read out the temple inscription for you and sell you attractive, if pricey, Urartian-style carvings made from basalt.

Hoşap Kalesi

55km southeast of Van, on the Hakkari road • Daily 8.30am–noon & 1.30–5pm • ₺3 • Dolmuşes to and from Başkale's dolmuş garage, on Cumhuriyet Cad, drop passengers at Hoşap/Güzelsu (₺10); the last dolmuş leaves the site around 6pm

The photogenic medieval Kurdish fortress of **Hoşap Kalesi** is an extraordinary flight of fancy, constructed in the 1640s at the behest of Sarı Süleyman Mahmudi, a local Kurdish strongman. Take a look at the pretty bridge, dating to 1671, at the foot of the castle before wending your way up. The main entrance boasts lion **reliefs**, a symbolic chain of power and a Persian inscription. Little is left of the mosques, three hamams and *medrese* inside. Best preserved is the **keep** – reached by a path from the outer fortress. Looking east from the fortress you can see a skeletal line of mud defensive walls that once encircled the village.

Çarpanak Island

25km northwest of Van • 1hr 30min by boat from the docks at Van İskelesi or 2hr from the jetty opposite Akdamar island; bargaining with the help of a Turkish-speaker, you should be able to rent a boat for upwards of ₺400; or simply chance your luck on a Sunday morning, when locals cross by boat to picnic

The well-preserved remains of the **monastery church of St John** are set on the pear-shaped island of **Çarpanak** (Ktuts in Armenian), just offshore from a promontory. The island also holds a huge Armenian gull colony.

After Akdamar's Surb Khach, this is the best-preserved Armenian church near Van. A monastery grew up here around a twelfth-century church at least as early as 1414, but a disaster befell it during the next century and the present church was heavily restored early in the eighteenth century. Despite this late date it's a handsome, rectangular compound, with a shallow dome sporting a pyramidal roof, though graffiti mars some of the walls.

Ayanis Kalesi

29km northwest of Van • Come by private car or taxi (₺80 with waiting time); turn left off the main road 20km north of Van, and then turn right in the village of Alaköy 8km further on, to follow an unsurfaced road over hills to the site itself

Ayanis Kalesi, the most beautifully located Urartian site, perches dramatically above the beautiful lakeside north of Çarpanak. Dating to the reign of Rusa II (685–645 BC), this hilltop fortification is still under excavation; digs have so far revealed the perimeter walls and an impressive central **temple** compound, whose doorway bears a long cuneiform inscription.

Remarkably, the interior of the temple (only visitable when archeologists are on site, in July and early August) is decorated with stone-inlay (intaglio) designs including lion and griffin, unique in the Urartian world. Unfortunately it was damaged in the 2009 quake. The **beaches** below the site are great for a dip.

Bahçesaray

Reaching the rural town of **BAHÇESARAY**, 110km southwest of Van, involves cresting the 2985m Karabel Geçiti, the highest road pass in Turkey and usually the last to open after the winter snow, in May or June. Bahçesaray was once far more important than its present size would suggest, with a population of twelve thousand over a century ago (three times today's size). While the recent asphalting of the road has reduced journey times, you'll still need to overnight to make the trip worthwhile. The scenery is breathtaking, even better than the trip to Hakkari for the variety of scenery, vegetation and birdlife on display. Seasonally scattered **encampments** (*zoma*) of Kurdish shepherds and their flocks on the east slopes of the pass form a colourful complement to the spectacular mountain views.

In the town itself, attractive tea gardens mark the start of the single main street, which ends at a mosque and a welcoming restaurant by the stream. Still known to mo locals by the Armenian name of Müküs, Bahçesaray holds the remains of a small Armenian church, called **Andzghonts**. Much damaged by fire in 1805, it still has *khatchkars* (stones inscribed with crosses) visible in the exterior walls.

Other pleasant diversions include an upstream walk to the underground source of th **Botan Çay**, a tributary of the Tigris, and, a few kilometres downstream, a single-arched poorly restored Selçuk bridge, the **Kızıl Köprü**.

ARRIVAL AND DEPARTURE	AROUND VA
BAHÇESARAY	east of the prominent Küçük Cami mosque.
By dolmuş Dolmuşes to Bahçesaray leave from outside a small teahouse on Ordu Cad in Van, a few hundred metres	Destinations Van (3 daily, at 10am, noon & 3pm; 2 30min; ₺15).

ACCOMMODATION	
BAHÇESARAY	accommodation, which contains a couple of rooms wi
Öğretmen Evi (Teacher's House) Main street; no phone. Overnight in this basic and informal	beds and blankets, and a small washroom. Per person ₺1

EATING AND DRINKING	
AKDAMAR ISLAND	camping, but will probably waive the fee providing you e
Akdamar Camping Restaurant Akdamar İskelesi Yanı ☎0432 216 1515. The friendly İbrahim also offers	at the (reasonable) restaurant, which serves fish from th lake for ₺15. Camping per person ₺2

Hakkari

Most of the few travellers who reach the wild, impoverished mountain town of **HAKKARİ**, 200km south of Van along the gorge of the Zab River, do so after a three- to four-hour bu trip through some spectacular mountain scenery. The town itself is dramatically situated high above the surging river, backed to the east by the Cilo range, which incorporates Turkey's second-highest peak, Reşko (4135m). Locals wear their Kurdish identity more openly than anywhere else in Turkey, apart from Diyarbakır. The handful of visitors who get this far tend to spend one night here and return to Van, though a few adventurous souls take the checkpoint-littered road along the mountainous Iraqi border to Şırnak.

Koçhanes

20km north of Hakkari • Best found with the help of a taxi driver from Hakkari

The church of **Koçhanes**, marked as Quodshanes on some maps, was once the patriarchal seat of the Nestorian Christians. Small and plain, save for some inscribed

---

TRAVEL IN THE MOUNTAINS SOUTH OF LAKE VAN: A WARNING

Although we visited the mountains that lie south of Lake Van in 2012, it's important to note that the British Foreign Office among others advises against all but essential travel to both **Hakkari** and **Şırnak**.

This remote area is sensitively located next to the proto-Kurdish state in northern Iraq, part of which is used as a base by PKK (Kurdish Workers Party) rebels to launch cross-border raids. For more information on the security situation in the southeast see p.57 and check the latest travel advice from your home government – and keep an ear to the ground while you're travelling in Turkey.

NESTORIAN CHRISTIANS

The **Nestorian Church** traces its existence back to Nestorius, fifth-century bishop of Constantinople, who formulated a doctrine that Christ was predominantly human in nature. Although this was declared a **heresy** by the Council of Ephesus in 431, the faith flourished, and Edessa (Şanlıurfa), Antioch (Antakya) and Nusaybin near Mardin became important Nestorian centres. After Mongol attacks, the Nestorians fled to the Zagros mountains of western Iran and the wild mountains around present-day Hakkari. Isolated in the inaccessible mountains, they developed their own ethnic as well as religious identity, with half the population organized into tribes little different from their Kurdish neighbours.

Serious rivalries developed during the nineteenth century between the Nestorians and the Kurds, exacerbated by the British and American missionaries who were proselytizing in the region. Local Kurdish leaders massacred many Nestorian men around Hakkari, and sold the women and children into slavery. In 1915 the Nestorian patriarch sided with the World War I Allies. After the war the Nestorians, now seen as traitors, fled to Iran and then Iraq, though half their number perished in the exodus. A short-lived attempt to resettle their mountain fastnesses was crushed by Atatürk in the early years of the Turkish Republic. Today just a few tens of thousands survive in Iraq, Iran and Syria, with the patriarchate now in Chicago.

geometric designs around the doorway, it's beautifully situated on a grassy spur high above the Zab valley. While it's not officially off-limits, the security forces may discourage you from visiting. The village around the church was ruined when the army forcibly evacuated it during the 1990s, but a couple of elderly watchmen and former residents still tend vegetable plots here in the summer.

A few kilometres north, the lovely, lush highland pasture of **Berçelan** is home to transhumant Kurds in summer – when they have been given permission to use it.

12

ARRIVAL AND DEPARTURE   HAKKARİ

By bus and dolmuş Most buses and dolmuşes arrive outside the bus offices on the main street, though the Şırnak dolmuş departs from near the Atatürk statue on the same street; book the night before.
Destinations Şırnak (1 daily; 6hr, ₺25); Van (hourly in daylight hours; 3–4hr).

ACCOMMODATION AND EATING

Kedamak Ocakbaşı Et Lokantası Bulvar Cad. This lovely first-floor place is the best restaurant in town, serving up grills (including trout) from ₺8, and *pide* from ₺5. Daily 8am–10pm.

Şenler Hotel Bulvar Cad ☎0544 211 3808. Decidedly average but still the best hotel in Hakkari, with spacious, mainly decorated rooms with wi-fi, TVs and (alcohol-free) minibars. Bathrooms have mosaic tiles and small tubs. There's a hamam, sauna and rooftop terrace with stunning views over Mount Sümbül. **₺110**

Sibar Hotel Altay Cad 15 ☎0438 211 2505. Offers a similar standard of comfort to the *Şenler* but has flock-wallpapered rooms and garish bedspreads offset by the delights of free wi-fi and a sauna. **₺90**

Valilik Parkı At the end of Bulvar Cad. A very pleasant chill-out spot, set on a steep, terraced hillside above the bustle of the main street, with sweeping views across the Zap valley to the Cilo range, and serving snacks such as toasted sandwiches and (soft) drinks. Daily 10am–8pm.

West of Hakkari

From Hakkari a road heads southwest to **Çukurca**, along the valley of the rapid-strewn Zab River, for about 50km. At a major checkpoint the bus turns right and west instead of continuing to Çukurca, along a road that runs parallel to the border with Iraqi Kurdistan, to Şırnak.

As the road runs close to the Kurdish enclave in northern Iraq and was built in order to patrol the frontier with it, you can expect a heavy military presence and up to ten checkpoints, where your bags may be searched. You may be refused permission to make this journey if there have been any recent incidents involving the PKK, who cross the border here from their bases in the Kandil mountains, in what now amounts to an autonomous Iraqi Kurdistan. The journey is beautiful, especially where the road crosses a 2350m pass in the Konaklı range, near to the turn for the mountain town of Beytüşşebap.

Şırnak

ŞIRNAK, an hour beyond Uludere, is perched on a hillside with views across a broad river valley to the peak of **Cudi Dağı** (2114m). Many believe the mountain to be the true resting place of Noah's Ark, while the tomb of Noah himself can be found in nearby Cizre (see p.640). One semi-collapsed stone house apart, nothing is left of old Şırnak; while the mountain scenery hereabouts is certainly spectacular, it serves only as a stepping stone to other destinations.

Cizre

The hot, scruffy but bustling border town of **CİZRE**, on the Tigris near the point where the modern Turkish, Syrian and Iraqi frontiers meet, has at least half a day's worth of sightseeing if you are waiting for a bus or get stuck overnight. From here it's possible to catch a bus to westward destinations such as Mardin and Diyarbakır, eastwards to Şırnak (for the border road to Hakkari), or to cross the Habur border-gate into the Kurdish enclave in northern Iraq.

Ulu Cami

Ulu Cami, Cizre's impressive chief mosque, is tucked away in the backstreets behind the citadel. Converted from a Byzantine church during the seventh century, it is very much in the Arab style, with a long, narrow, flat-roofed prayer hall. Most interesting, though, is the tapering brick-built minaret, reminiscent of a ziggurat.

Kırmızı Medrese

The **Kırmızı Medrese**, or Red Medrasah, is a superb sixteenth-century theological school, just a short walk from the main drag. Recently restored, in part with EU funding, and constructed entirely from red brick, it attests to Cizre's former importance as a seat of Islamic learning. Very Persian in style, the single-storey structure rings a pretty courtyard, with a fine *mescit* (small mosque) at one end and the cells of the students around the other sides.

Noah's Tomb
A little beyond the Kırmızı Medrese

Displayed inside a *türbe* that's garishly decorated with modern İznik tiles, an enormously long sarcophagus is believed by local Kurds (and many others) to hold the body of Noah. **Noah's Tomb** has become a shrine, so expect to see pilgrims praying and kissing the glass screen surrounding the sarcophagus.

The citadel

Only recently vacated by the Turkish military, Cizre's **citadel**, pleasantly set beside by the Tigris a few hundred metres south of the bridge, is about to undergo major restoration. Inside are the base of a tower prettily constructed of alternate bands of black and white stone, and the HQ of the notorious Hamidiye regiment of Kurdish irregulars. Raised in the late nineteenth century to help maintain Ottoman control of eastern Anatolia, they actually spend much of their time terrorizing the local Armenian population.

ARRIVAL AND DEPARTURE

ŞIRNAK

By dolmuş Dolmuşes bound west to Cizre leave from the square near the Atatürk tea gardens, as do dolmuşes for the spectacular journey to Siirt (for onward travel to Bitlis/Tatvan and Van); the Hakkari dolmuş leaves from 200m east of the *Hotel Murat*.

Destinations Hakkari (1 daily, around 8am; 6hr; ₺25); Cizre (hourly; 45min; ₺5); Siirt (several daily; 2hr; ₺10).

CIZRE

By dolmuş Dolmuşes from Şırnak drop passengers in the centre, 300m west of the bridge across the Tigris. The *otogar* is 2km south of here, reached by a *şehir içi* dolmuş

ACCOMMODATION AND EATING

ŞIRNAK

Murat Uludere Cad 16 ☎0486 216 2857. The central *Murat*, with its mock-classical facade, is a modest place but probably Cizre's best budget choice, with a/c, wi-fi and ensuite bathrooms. ₺70

Menekşe Uludere Cad ☎0486 216 1901. A little cheaper than the *Murat* and with great views from the rear rooms across to Mount Cudi, it does have some advantages over its nearby rival. That's without mentioning the pretty lovebirds resident in the lobby, but it's not so well maintained or run. ₺60

Berivan 2 Kafeterya Cumhuriyet Cad 5. The pick of several restaurants hereabouts, serving some local dishes including *perde pilaf*. Daily 7am–11pm.

Aydo Pastanesi Vakıf Bank Yanı 12. Decent cake-and-pastry place, ideal for breakfast, with a couple of tables

WEST OF HAKKARI

(₺125). Buses also run to Mediterranean destinations and İstanbul, as well as south into northern Iraq.

Destinations Şırnak (hourly; 45min; ₺5); Diyarbakir (5 daily, 7.30am–6.30pm; 4hr), via Nusaybin (1hr 30min) and Mardin (2hr 30min).

Travel to northern Iraq Visiting the Kurdish enclave in northern Iraq is surprisingly straightforward; for the latest information on whether you need a visa, check ⓦkrg.org, the Kurdistan Regional Government's website. Luxury Cizre–Nuh buses run to Erbil from Cizre's *otogar* at 7.30am, 2pm and 10.30pm daily for ₺50. Buses to the proto-Kurdish state also run from Mardin, Diyarbakir and several other Turkish cities, including İstanbul.

outside overlooking the central square, Atatürk tea garden and across the valley to Mount Cudi. Daily 7am–10pm.

CIZRE

Mem u Zin Yafes Cad ☎0486 616 9433, ⓦhotelmemuzin.com.tr. This cavernous, overpriced place takes advantage of Cizre's strategic location on the road to oil-rich northern Iraq. It's tired but clean and inoffensive, however, and adequate to overnight if you get stuck here. ₺120

Teras Aksoy Plaza, Orhan Doğan Cad. An unlikely find in dusty Cizre, this posh café-cum-restaurant, on the top floor of a small shopping centre, serves a decent Turkish breakfast for ₺10, grilled fish mains for ₺15 and *pide* for ₺8. Much favoured by the local middle classes, it even puts on live *saz* (lute) music most evenings. Daily 8am–11pm.

12

Lake Van to Doğubeyazıt

Northeast of Van, the road skirts the lake before heading up into the volcanic peaks bordering Iran. The drive, over a bizarrely contorted lava landscape, is spectacular in places, especially on the 2644m Tendurek Pass. In clear weather, the views of Mount Ararat from the far side of the pass are stunning. Huddled on the plain south of Ararat, the unkempt border/garrison town of **Doğubeyazıt** is a functional base from which to visit the spectacular palace of **İshak Paşa** or, more adventurously, ascend the peak or cross into neighbouring Iran.

Muradiye waterfalls

On the west side of the main Van–Doğubeyazıt road, 20km north of the junction with the road from Tatvan/Erciş • Dolmuşes (₺20) depart hourly from the İlçe dolmuş garage, 400m north of Beş Yol in Van, and from the northbound side of the main road in Tatvan (₺25); it's possible to take a dolmuş as far as Muradiye and break the journey there, but as dolmuşes direct to Doğubeyazıt are often full you may have to take a dolmuş (regular) from Muradiye to Çaldıran, a major bus garage 26km northeast, and then onto Doğubeyazıt

The roadside **Muradiye waterfalls**, particularly spectacular in the late spring and early summer snow melt, make a welcome break en route to or from Doğubeyazıt. A rickety wooden suspension bridge crosses the Bendihmah River in front of the falls, which cascade prettily over a 15–20m-high drop. Across the bridge, you can stop for a break at a couple of cafés; *Yaşarlar Alabalık*, furthest from the falls, is best and dishes up delicious trout.

A white-on-brown sign on the main road, 1km south of the falls, points towards an old bridge known as **Şeytan Köprüsü** (Devil's Bridge) that spans the deep gorge. Further down on the far side of the river, a lovely but ruined Armenian church looks down over the village of Muradiye itself.

Doğubeyazıt

Impoverished **DOĞUBEYAZIT**, 130km northeast of Van and just half an hour from Iran, is, thanks to its border position and largely Kurdish population, heavily militarized, with a huge army camp just outside town on the road to a spectacular ridge-top fortified place, **İshak Paşa Sarayı**. In response to the blatant Turkish army presence, the truculent locals boldly elected a (female) Kurdish mayor from the now banned DTP party in 2009, and have named the main street after dissident pro-Kurdish intellectual İsmail Beşikçi.

İshak Paşa Sarayı

6km southeast of Doğubeyazıt • Tues–Sun 8am–7pm • ₺5 • Especially at weekends, dolmuşes ply the route from the main road outside the *otogar* (₺3); a taxi from Doğubeyazıt's Atatürk statue costs around ₺35 return, including waiting time

Overlooking Doğubeyazıt from atop a rocky promontory, the iconic **İshak Paşa Sarayı** is an overblown, impossibly romantic palace. This was once the site of a Urartian fortress; both the Selçuks and Ottomans later built castles to control traffic along the Silk Route.

The palace itself was begun in 1685 by Çolak Abdı Paşa, a local chieftain, and completed by his son, İshak Paşa, in 1784. By 1877, the complex was already in decline, being used by the Turkish army as a barracks; subsequent periods of Russian

■ ACCOMMODATION	
Ararat Hotel	4
Grand Derya	2
Isfahan	6
Lalezar Camping	3
Sim-Er	1
Tahran	5

■ BAR AND CAFÉ	
Can Yaprak Pastanesi	1

● RESTAURANTS	
Saray	1
Şark Sofrası	2

DOĞUBEYAZIT

occupation set the seal on its decay. A controversial new glass and steel roof, added to preserve the walls of the crumbling palace, has spoilt the classic photograph of the palace taken from above.

The palace

The grandiose **gateway** of İshak Paşa Sarayı once boasted gold-plated doors; removed by the Russians in 1917, during their retreat from Anatolia, they're now on show at the Hermitage Museum in St Petersburg. From the outer courtyard, an ornately carved portal leads to a smaller, inner courtyard. Straight ahead is the harem entrance, while to the right is the entrance to the *selâmlık* or men's quarters. The **tombs** of İshak Paşa and his favourite wife stand in a *türbe* in one corner of the inner court.

The **harem** contains fourteen fireplace-equipped bedrooms (in which four hundred soldiers were quartered in 1877), overlooking the valley below, a kitchen and two circular bathrooms. At its centre is a colonnaded dining hall. The *selâmlık* also holds a library, bedrooms and a fine **mosque**, retaining much of its original relief decoration and ceiling painting.

Behind the palace is the picturesque, recently restored Ottoman mosque. It's possible to scramble up behind the mosque to a rock-cut **Urartian tomb** flanked by two carved relief figures. Above this, reachable only by a scramble, there's a narrow niche in the dramatic ridge-top fortress wall. Squeeze through this and you can descend to the much-visited tomb of the Kurdish poet and philosopher Ehmede Xani. His **Mem u Zin** (1692), a tale of star-crossed lovers, is *the* epic work of Kurdish literature. Drinks and souvenir stalls here cater to pilgrims.

The foundations on the plain below the palace are all that's left of **Eski Beyazıt** (Old Beyazıt), a city founded by the Urartians. It was inhabited until 1930, when – in the wake of an unsuccessful local Kurdish rebellion – it was forcibly depopulated and the new Doğu (East) Beyazıt founded in its present location.

12

ARRIVAL AND DEPARTURE   DOĞUBEYAZIT

By bus and dolmuş Dolmuşes from Van drop passengers on Küçük Ağrı Caddesi on the eastern side of town, while buses stop at the small *otogar* in the town centre.

Destinations Ankara (1 daily; 16hr); Erzurum (10 daily; 7hr); Gaziantep (1 daily; 6hr); Iğdır (for Kars; every 45min; ₺7); İstanbul (3 daily; 22hr); Kayseri (1 daily; 10hr); Van (5 daily, at 6.30am, 8am, 9am, noon & 2pm; 3hr; ₺20).

Travel to Iran If you are considering visiting Iran, it's generally better to apply for a tourist visa in your home country. If you decide to try while you're in Turkey, the best bet is Trabzon, followed by Ankara, İstanbul and finally

Erzurum – all have Iranian consulates. Ask Bilal at the *Hotel Tahran* (see p.644) for the latest information and possible visa procurement.

Transport The nearest Iranian border crossing to Doğubeyazit is at Gürbulak, 34km southeast, accessible by dolmuş from Ağrı Caddesi (regular departures until 5pm; ₺6). Iranian currency is best obtained over the border at Bazargan. From there, you can take a taxi to Maku and then an onward bus to Tabriz. Alternatively, you can cross at Esendere-Sero, southeast of Van; see p.632.

INFORMATION AND TOURS

Tourist office There's no official tourist office, but the various travel agents and bus companies – mainly on Belediye Caddesi (south of the Atatürk statue) – will be able to help.

Tours Tamzara Travel, Belediye Cad 16 (☎0472 312 2189,

⊕ mtararattour.com), run by the genuine and friendly Mustafa Arsin, is the most reliable operator for Ararat ascents and daily tours to Diaydin hot springs, the supposed "Ark" and a meteor crater near the Iranian border for €45; half-day tours €25.

ACCOMMODATION

Ararat Hotel Belediye Cad 16 ☎0472 312 4988, ⊕ hotelararatturkey.com. Well run by the owners of Tamzara Travel, the blue-themed rooms are spacious and all have balconies – some with partial Ararat views. A big plus in summer is the roof terrace where you can lounge on

cushions and drink beers brought in from outside. Good value despite the average bathrooms. **₺65**

Grand Derya Çarşı Cad ☎0472 312 7531. Central, friendly place, almost next door to the mosque, popular with trekking groups. Rooms are cheerful, and there's a bar and wi-fi. Bargain if there are no groups in. ₺120

Isfahan Hotel İsageçit Cad 26 ☎0472 312 4363, ⓦhotelisfahan.com. Rooms are spacious, though a little dingy, with garish bedlinen to compensate. A decent backup if the *Ararat* is full with groups. ₺60

Lalazer Camping İshak Paşa Saray Yolu Üzeri ☎0544 269 1960, ⓔlalazercamping@hotmail.com. A couple of kilometres from town on the road to the palace, this curious place is run by Kurdish Mecit and Dutchman Bertil. Very popular with the camper-van contingent, it has clean loos and showers and decent tent pitches. Rates per person ₺10

Sim-Er Hotel Iran Yolu ☎0472 312 0061, ⓔdbeyazit @simerhotel.com. Catering predominantly to coach groups, this place is really only of use if you have your own vehicle. Rooms are a little gloomy and the buffet meals very average, but the location, amid greenery a few kilometres east of town, is excellent, with the kind of unobstructed views of Mt Ararat you pray – unsuccessfully – for in the town centre. Half board only. ₺160

★ **Hotel Tahran** Büyük Ağrı Cad 124 ☎0472 312 0195, ⓦhoteltahran.com. Despite the cramped toilets and scruffy carpets, this is a good-value budget option, with free internet (or wi-fi) access and comfortable beds. Some rear rooms have Ararat views, as does the breakfast terrace. Friendly, fluent English-speaking manager Bilal is a fount of knowledge about the local area and getting to Iran. ₺50

EATING AND DRINKING

Can Yaprak Pastanesi Dr İsmail Beşikçi Cad 47 ☎0472 312 6897. The best-value place for breakfasts and desserts, with everything from *simit* and *poğaça* (stuffed bread rolls) to *baklava* with glutinous ice cream. Daily 6am–10pm.

Saray Dr İsmail Beşikçi Cad. This long-established place on the busy main street serves a mean İskender kebab as well as tender *pide*. Daily 8am–11pm.

★ **Şark Sofrası** Dr İsmail Beşikçi Cad 85 ☎0472 312 3455. A cut above the average kebab joint, the *Şark Sofrası* offers excellent-value *lahmacun* (₺1.5), *pide* (from ₺6) and kebabs from ₺6. Try the pistachio-studded *fıstıklı* kebap for a couple of lira more. It even has a roof terrace for the summer months. Daily 8am–11pm.

DIRECTORY

Banks Doğubeyazıt is well supplied with banks and *döviz*.
Hamam Yeni Hamam, near the *İsfahan Hotel* on İsageçit Cad (men and women; from ₺10).

PTT On the main İsmail Beşikçi (Çarşı) Cad (Mon–Sat 8.30am–12.30pm & 1–5.30pm).

Mount Ararat

Few mountains west of the Himalayas have as compelling a hold on Western imagination as **Mount Ararat** (Ağrı Dağı in Turkish). Traditionally, Armenian monks considered this volcanic mountain holy, and nobody was allowed to climb it; it was not until 1829 that Dr Johann Jacob Parrot, a German academic, conquered the peak. Numerous other ascents have followed, though it was forbidden by Turkish officialdom until the 1950s.

Despite the efforts of American astronaut James Irwin and others, no reliable trace of **Noah's Ark** has been found. Locals, however, insist that the oval mound of earth spotted by a Turkish air-force pilot on a routine flight is the "Ark", which now boasts a visitor centre and is included in tours of the area. Genesis 8:4 reports the Ark as coming to rest on the "mountains of Ararat", but this is prone to misinterpretation, as Ararat was the Assyrian rendition of Urartu, the ancient kingdom centred on Lake Van, meaning the Ark could have come to rest anywhere within the bounds of the kingdom. According to the Koran, the Ark was deposited on Mount Cudi, hundreds of kilometres away near Cizre (see p.640).

The ascent

Treks up Mount Ararat are normally five-day affairs, supported as far as Camp 2 by mules. From the starting point at **Eli** (2150m), 10km north of Doğubeyazıt, it's a half-day walk to **Camp 1** (3200m).

Camp 2, at 4200m, is a strenuous six-hour march higher. From Camp 2, a 1am start is needed to reach the summit (5hr) before cloud cover becomes too thick. At around 4900m the stones give way to permanent snowpack and then glacier. The views on a clear day are stupendous, compensating for the hard slog of the ascent. Winter climbs followed by ski-descents have become increasingly popular for experienced mountaineers.

INFORMATION   MOUNT ARARAT

When to visit The main climbing season is June to September.

Equipment Ararat is a serious mountain (two Italians died in a blizzard descending the peak in 2006), and you will need proper equipment, including an ice axe and crampons.

Access The mountain lies in a sensitive military zone, adjoining both the Armenian and Iranian frontiers, and was also a focal point for PKK activity – the group kidnapped three German climbers in 2008, who were later released unharmed. While access has been eased recently, permits are essential, and best obtained through a reputable,

registered travel/trekking agency (see p.30). They require a photocopy of your passport well in advance of the mooted climb. Permits are then processed by the authorities in the provincial capital of Ağrı, usually taking around two weeks. Qualified guides are mandatory. Trips cost around €450 per head, ski expeditions around €680. Applicants with Armenian surnames will be denied permission to climb.

Touts Local touts in Doğubeyazit may offer to obtain a permit for you immediately, or even take you up the peak without one. If you take their advice, you risk loss of your deposit at best, and arrest at worst. That said, quite a few visitors take the chance.

12

TEMPLE OF HADRIAN, EPHESUS

Contexts

History

The present Turkish Republic is all that remains of a vast medieval empire, which at its zenith extended from the Indian Ocean almost to the Atlantic – and all of its territories contributed personalities and events. The following history covers the key events of a complex saga.

The earliest cultures

Discoveries in the heart of modern Turkey – the region known historically as Anatolia or Asia Minor – indicate settled habitation since the Paleolithic age in the eighth millennium BC, which makes it among the oldest on earth. Excavations at Göbekli Tepe, on the northern rim of the fertile crescent, have brought to light a remarkable temple complex built by hunter-gatherer communities as early as 9500 BC, while extensive Neolithic discoveries include entire farming communities, notably Çatal Höyük near Konya (c.6500–5650 BC), demonstrating that early settlers lived in sizeable villages. Their tools were made from local obsidian and flint; pottery included stylized figures representing the Mother Goddess.

Influence from Upper Mesopotamia and northern Syria brought southeast Anatolia into the **Chalcolithic Age**. Sites of this period were more like fortified towns, and evidence of violent destruction suggests that they regularly waged war. More independent cultures of central Anatolia and the west Anatolian lakeland produced burnished pottery and idols of local deities.

The third-millennium BC **Bronze Age** witnessed the emergence of local dynasties ruling from fortified settlements. Sophisticated equipment found in Alacahöyük's royal cemetery suggests early Anatolian kings benefited from metallurgy. Religious art included standards with stylized deer and bulls; hoards of gold jewellery plus musical instruments.

Meanwhile, trade was expanding along the south and west coasts. **Troy** had links with Aegean islands, mainland Greece, and other Anatolian populations in the southeast. Anatolian metals, jewellery, weapons and tableware were exchanged for lapis lazuli, rock crystal and ivory. Great wealth was amassed, as epitomized by the "Treasure of Priam", a third-millennium hoard rediscovered in the nineteenth century.

The Middle and Late Bronze Ages, during the second millennium BC, began with violent destruction and turbulence, out of which the **Hatti** emerged in central Anatolia, whose culture was later assimilated by the Hittites. Commerce took place along fixed trade routes, and many Anatolian cities were colonized by Assyrian merchants. Their meticulous records show that textiles and tin were traded for copper and ornamental pottery.

The Hittites

The first truly major civilization to emerge in Anatolia was that of the **Hittites**. They first appeared around 2000 BC, though their so-called "Old Kingdom" was founded around 1650 BC. The capital at Hattuşaş, created by Hattusilis I, was a huge city for its

9500 BC	2900 BC	1650 BC
Hunter-gatherers build the temple complex at Göbekli Tepe in southeast Anatolia	Foundation of Troy at the mouth of the Dardanelles, northwest Anatolia	The Hittites establish an imperial capital at Hattuşaş, in central Anatolia

time, with a citadel overlooking a gorge. Hittite artistic style was a direct outgrowth of Anatolian predecessors and, unlike Syrian art, was never overwhelmed by Mesopotamian and Egyptian conventions. The principal examples are enormous rock-cut reliefs of warrior gods and stylized sphinx-like beings.

Besides their imperialist nature, the Hittite kingdoms are known for their relatively humane constitution and religion, and highly developed sense of ethics. Diplomacy was preferred to warfare, and often cemented by royal marriages. Libraries, archives and bureaucracy were central to Hittite society, and rulers were not despotic but tied to a constitution like their subjects. The Old Kingdom dynasty lasted several generations before being riven by succession struggles; the empire was re-established by Tudhaliyas II around 1430 BC, just as a rival power arose in Upper Mesopotamia. These Mitanni or Hurrians, ruled by an Indo-European dynasty, were defeated in battle by Hittite king Suppiluliumas (1385–1345 BC).

Under Muwatallis, the Hittites confirmed their military strength by defeating the Egyptians under Ramses II at the battle of **Kadesh** (1290 BC). Subsequently the two dynasties became allied through the division of Syria and the marriage of Ramses II to a daughter of another Hittite ruler. The Hittites' landlocked empire was not completely secure, however, and in the southeast Mediterranean, the Kizzuwadna region, later Cilicia, was taken by the Hurrians, who also married into the Hittite royal line.

While, he west coast was not well documented in Hittite records, excavations show that Troy was rebuilt by a new dynasty, and vast supplies were amassed inside its citadel. The second-millennium Trojans were rivals to the Greeks, who eventually sacked Troy in the **Trojan War** around 1200 BC, when the Hittite Empire also collapsed.

The post-Hittite era

As more Indo-European tribes, especially the "Sea Peoples" – early Iron Age migrants from the Aegean and Balkan mainland – invaded, Hittite cities were destroyed, and Anatolia entered a long cultural Dark Age. Surviving Hittites and their Anatolian allies founded small city-states in the southeast, preserving elements of the old culture and forming a bridge between the Bronze and **Iron** ages. At these lively Neo-Hittite entrepôts, early Greek art encountered Hittite reliefs and statuary, and knowledge of oriental mythology and religion passed to Greece. They finally fell to the Arameans and the Assyrians in the eighth century BC.

To the east, the kingdom of **Urartu** was founded by descendants of the Hurrians. Their cities, including Tushpa near Lake Van, were elaborately engineered, with citadels and tunnel systems for escape or survival under attack. The Urartians expanded into central Anatolia and northern Syria before being checked, in the latter eighth century BC, by the Assyrians. The Urartians specialized in metalwork, and bronzeware was traded as far away as Greece.

To the west, a new immigrant tribe, the **Phrygians**, attained prominence; their capital was Gordion, on a strategic trading route by the River Sangarius (today Sakarya). This kingdom peaked around 725 BC under King Midas, but he committed suicide in despair when Cimmerian horsemen sacked Gordion. The

1200 BC	900 BC	725 BC
Troy sacked by the Greeks at the end of the Trojan War	Sometime around this date, the Urartian kingdom emerges in the Lake Van basin	Under King Midas, the western Anatolian kingdom of Phrygia reaches its peak

outhwest coast was settled during the Iron Age by Lycians, possibly the "Lukka" of
Bronze Age records.

The **Lydians** occupied the Hermus valley, with their capital at Sardis. They survived
the Bronze Age with an indigenous Anatolian language, emerging from the eighth
century BC to dominate western Anatolia, including former Phrygian zones. Lydian
luxury goods were widely exported, and their elegant art forms influenced those of
Greek Ionia and even Persia.

The Persians and Alexander

Lydian power endured until 546 BC, when their king, **Croesus**, was defeated by
Cyrus's ascendant **Persian Empire**. Over the next half-century, the Persians subdued
the Greek coastal cities and the interior, ending Anatolian self-rule. Satraps
(compliant local puppets) were enthroned but obliged to pay tribute to the Persian
"Great King"; Persian allies like the Phoenicians were favoured at the expense of
Greek cities as commercial intermediaries with the West. In 499 BC, western
Anatolia, led by Miletus, revolted, but lacking massive aid from mainland Greece,
the rebellion failed.

Enraged by even token Athenian support for the rebels, **Darius** I and his successor
Xerxes crossed into Greece and were soundly beaten at the land battles of Marathon
and Plataea, and the sea engagements of Salamis and Mykale, the latter in the straits
between Samos and Anatolia. This thwarting of Persia initially availed the cities of Asia
Minor little, though they soon exploited growing rivalry between Athens and Sparta to
negotiate more autonomy. By the mid-fourth century BC, some quasi-independent
dynasties had arisen in western Anatolia, the most notable being the Hecatomnids at
Halikarnassos, whose illustrious rulers included **Mausolus** (377–353 BC), and his wife
and successor Artemisia II.

In spring 334 BC, a new power swept out of Macedonia: **Alexander**, later "the
Great", equipped merely with a guiding vision and some Corinthian volunteers to
supplement his small Macedonian army. Having crossed the Dardanelles, he defeated
the Persians and proceeded down the Asia Minor coast via the major cities, treating
them with lenience or harshness depending on whether or not they rallied to his
standard. Having wintered in Lycia, Alexander and his juggernaut rolled on across
Pamphylia, inland to Gordion, then over the Toros range into coastal Cilicia, intent
on attacking the Persian heartland beyond Syria. **Darius III** awaited Alexander at Issos
(modern Dörtyol), but was crushed by the Macedonians, despite outnumbering them
two to one. This rapid conquest of Anatolia was as much indicative of Persian dynastic
rottenness as of Alexander's military genius.

The prodigy swept through Persia proper as far as the Indus valley, but died of
malaria – or possibly poisoning – on the return trip, in 323 BC. Following his death,
Alexander's generals **divided Anatolia**: Lysimakhos took the west, while Seleukos –
succeeded by Antiokhos – received most of the southeast; much of the centre and
north remained independent. Lysimakhos's successor Philetaros made **Pergamon** the
greatest Hellenistic city of Asia Minor; by the late second century BC, however, his heir
Attalos III bequeathed it to the Romans.

546 BC	334 BC	89 BC
Lydian King Croesus defeated by the Persians	Alexander the Great defeats the Persians at the battle of Granicus, northwest Anatolia	Mithridates of Pontus rebels against the Romans for the first time

Roman rule

Roman power in Asia Minor was almost immediately challenged by **Mithridates** of
Pontus (ruled 110–63 BC), a brilliant, resourceful polymath; from 89 BC on, his
rebellious campaigns kept assorted Roman generals occupied. In 72 BC, Mithridates
sought refuge at the court of Tigranes the Great in regional power Armenia. The
Romans promptly invaded, but it suited them to maintain Armenia as a buffer
principality between themselves and the Parthians on the east, successors to the Persians.

First Emperor Augustus's reign marked the start of fairly durable peace and prosperity
in Anatolia, as witness the numerous ruined cities dating from Roman imperial rule,
many endowed by **Hadrian** (117–138 AD). Politically, however, it remained a
backwater, with only the texts of Strabo and Pliny to flesh out life here – as well as the
first-century AD biblical writings of St Paul during his evangelical tours of Asia Minor.

In 284 AD, **Diocletian** divided the empire into two administrative units, each ruled
by an emperor (Augustus) cooperating with a designated successor (Caesar) – the
so-called tetrarchy. Within forty years, however, this system collapsed into civil war.
The victor, **Constantine**, moved the headquarters of the eastern portion from Salonica
to the minor, but strategically located, town of Byzantium, on the western shores of
the Bosphorus straits linking the Black Sea and the Sea of Marmara. This new capital,
renamed **Constantinople**, was a conscious imitation of Rome. Soon afterwards
Constantine began to favour Christianity, which by the end of the fourth century
became the state religion of an empire that had long persecuted Christians.

A unified empire, too unwieldy to be governed from a single centre, did not survive
much beyond Constantine's forceful reign. Theodosius the Great (ruled 379–395), who
officially proscribed paganism in 391, was the last sovereign of a united empire, which
upon his death formally split into two realms: the western one Latin-speaking and
Rome-based, the eastern part Greek-speaking and focused on Constantinople.

The Byzantine Empire

The western provinces had always depended financially on the east, and the badly
governed west could not easily survive this revenue loss – or "barbarian" invasions from
the north. The wealthier, more densely populated eastern **Byzantine Empire** had abler
rulers and more defensible frontiers, but was severely weakened by religious tensions.
Constantinople's writ was resented in the southeastern provinces of Egypt, Palestine,
Syria and Armenia with their non-Classical indigenous cultures; moreover, their
churches embraced the **Monophysite doctrine**, which maintained that Christ had a
single divine nature. Until the thirteenth century clerics in the capital persecuted the
provincial "heretics", at the same time resenting claims to papal supremacy and
quarrelling over dogma with Rome. This culminated in the formal separation of the
eastern **Orthodox** and western **Roman Catholic** churches in 1054.

Following the death of Justinian in 565, the empire's character changed radically. All
his peripheral conquests were lost: the western realms to the Lombards and Goths, the
southeastern provinces to Persians and Arabs. By 711, the Byzantine Empire consisted
only of the Balkan coasts, parts of Italy, and Asia Minor. Equally significantly, it had
acquired a strongly Greek character, both linguistically and philosophically, and Latin
influence faded as relations with Rome worsened.

330 AD	**391**	**1054**
The inauguration of Constantinople as the new capital of the Roman Empire	The Christian Byzantine emperor Theodosius the Great officially proscribes paganism	Separation of the eastern Orthodox and western Roman Catholic churches

EMPEROR JUSTINIAN

Byzantium's response to the collapse of the West after the fifth century was expansionist – or rather, nostalgic. Energetic emperor **Justinian** (527–565) attempted to recapture the glory and territory of ancient Rome in campaigns across the Mediterranean. Imperial generals Belisarius and Narses re-absorbed Italy, North Africa and southern Spain into the empire, though the Byzantines were unable to stem the flow of Slavs into the Balkans, and concluded an uneasy truce with the Persians after a long, inconclusive war.

Justinian also pursued an ambitious domestic agenda. He inaugurated a programme of public works, resulting in such masterpieces as **Aya Sofya** in Constantinople and San Vitale in Ravenna. Justinian's streamlining of the huge, often contradictory, body of Roman **law** was perhaps his most enduring achievement: the new code became the basis for the medieval legal systems of France, Germany and Italy.

Justinian's reign marked the definitive emergence of a strictly **Byzantine** – as opposed to Roman – identity, with institutions that sustained the empire for the rest of its life. Having widened its boundaries to their maximum extent and established the theocratic nature of Byzantium, he can be reckoned among the greatest Byzantine emperors. Ultimately, though, many of his achievements proved ephemeral, and so exhausted the empire that it had difficulty withstanding subsequent attacks.

After 867, the **Macedonian dynasty**, founded by Basil I, a former stable boy who rendered Justinian's law code into Greek, reversed Byzantium's fortunes. Under Basil II (976–1025), nicknamed "Bulgar-Slayer" for his ruthless campaigns against the Slavs, the empire again extended its frontiers into eastern Anatolia and up the Balkan peninsula, while Constantinople enjoyed unparalleled prosperity at the crossroads of new Eurasian trade routes. Literature and the arts flourished; missionaries converted Balkan Slavs to Orthodoxy.

After Basil II, however, the empire began its final decline, slow but relentless over four centuries. For much of the eleventh century, Anatolia was wracked by civil war, with bureaucrats in Constantinople pitted against landed generals in the countryside. Each promoted their own candidates for the throne, resulting in successive nonentities as emperors. Simultaneously the patriarchate renewed its vendetta against the Monophysite churches, whose members were concentrated in the critical eastern borderlands. The warlords reduced the free peasantry to serfdom; the bureaucrats, usually in control at Constantinople, matched their own extravagance with stinginess toward the army, increasingly staffed by unreliable mercenaries.

The first major threats came from the West. The **Normans**, greedy for Byzantine craftsmanship and splendour, invaded the Balkans late in the eleventh century, and were only repulsed with Venetian help, who in return demanded trading concessions – as did the **Genoese**. Government tolls and taxes plummeted as imperial monopolies were broken by the new Latin maritime powers, and western covetousness – which culminated in the sacking of Constantinople by the Fourth Crusade in 1204 – knew no bounds. Though able emperors emerged from the twelfth-century Komnenos dynasty and the later Paleologos clan, without consistent western aid the Byzantines were doomed to fight a long, rearguard action against enemies from the east and

527–565	1204	1000
The reign of Justinian, the greatest Byzantine emperor after Constantine	Decline of the Byzantine Empire is hastened by the sacking of Constantinople during the Fourth Crusade	Around this period, the first Turks begin to appear in Anatolia

north. Imperial twilight was marked by a final flourishing of sacred art and architecture, as Anatolia and the Balkans were adorned with beautiful churches – this period's main legacy.

The arrival of the Turks

Early in the eleventh century, a new people began to raid Byzantium from the east. They had first appeared in seventh-century Mongolia, a shamanistic, nomadic bunch whom the Chinese called "Tu-kueh" or Dürkö – **Turks** to the west. These tribes began migrating westward, encountering the Arabs by the ninth century. The latter, recognizing their martial virtues, recruited them and set about converting them to **Islam**, a process completed by the late tenth century.

One branch of the Turkish tribes, followers of the chieftain **Selçuk**, adopted **Sunni** Islam and a settled life in Baghdad. The majority, however, the so-called Turcomans, remained nomadic and heterodox, drawing on **Shi'ite** and pagan beliefs, and unamenable to state control. Selçuk rulers took advantage of their warrior zeal by diverting them into Byzantine territory.

These raiders penetrated Byzantine Armenia, and it was more to restrain them than to confront the Byzantines that Selçuk ruler Alparslan marched north from Baghdad in 1071. Meeting, almost accidentally, the demoralized armies of Byzantine emperor Romanus IV Diogenes, he defeated them easily at Manzikert. The Selçuks didn't follow up this victory, but it led to redoubled rampages by the Turcomans. The Byzantines, alternately menaced and assisted by Latin crusaders, managed to re-occupy western Anatolia, plus the Black Sea and Mediterranean coasts, by the mid-twelfth century. The Selçuk **Sultanate of Rum**, based at Konya (Iconium), consolidated the Turcoman-ravaged areas; after winning the battle of Myriokephalo in 1176, the Selçuks came to terms with the Byzantines.

Following the occupation of Constantinople by the Fourth Crusade in 1204, the Selçuks continued their good relations with the provisional Byzantine Empire of Nicaea; with peace assured, the Sultanate of Rum evolved into a highly cultured mini-empire, reaching its zenith in the first half of the thirteenth century as imposing *kervansarays*, *medreses* and other monuments adorned central Anatolia. The Selçuks also excelled in tile- and relief-work, and in the spiritual field the sultanate, despite Sunni orientation, gave refuge to many heterodox religious figures, including Celaleddin Rumi, founder of the Mevlevî dervish order.

The **Mongols** crushed the Selçuks at the battle of Köse Dağ in 1243, and although the sultanate lingered on until about 1300, the Turcoman tribes, never fully pacified, swarmed over the lands of both Selçuks and the Byzantines, who had abandoned Asia Minor after returning to Constantinople in 1261. For two centuries there was no single authority in Anatolia, but the process of Turkification and Islamization, begun in 1071, continued apace.

The rise of the Ottomans

Following the Selçuk collapse, Anatolia fragmented into mostly Turcoman **emirates**. That centred on Söğüt was not initially important; its chieftain Ertuğrul was a typical

1071	1243	1290
Battle of Manzikert, in which the Byzantines lose disastrously to the Selçuk Turks	The Mongols crush the Selçuk Turks at the battle of Köse Dağ in central Anatolia	Around this time, Osman assumes control of a tribal dynasty that will become the Ottoman Empire

azi, a convert to Islam, and carried the faith ever westward. His son Osman, however, ead of the clan from the 1290s, gave his name to a dynasty: Osmanlı in Turkish, **Ottoman**" to the West. This emirate began to expand under Osman's son Orhan, vho by the 1330s captured Byzantine Bursa and İznik.

Anatolian culture had long been hybrid, with frequent intermarriage between Muslims and Christians, and descendants or converts bilingual in Greek and Turkish. The Bektaşi dervish order effected a synthesis between Islam and numerically windling Christianity. As Byzantine authority diminished, the assets and facilities of Christian monasteries were appropriated by the **vakıfs**, or Islamic pious foundations; the demoralized Christian priesthood and population often converted to Islam simultaneously.

Complementing this was the *devşirme*, a fourteenth-century innovation whereby boys from conquered Christian districts were levied by the Ottomans to serve as an elite force, the janissaries. Slaves of the sultan, they were admitted to the eclectic Bektaşi order, and trained meticulously to become not only warriors but administrators. As free-born Muslims were ineligible for this corps, and promotion was by merit, the Ottoman state, up to the office of grand vizier, was run by converts. The only chance of advancement for free-born Muslims lay within the *ulema*, the Koranic sages who decreed on religious matters, or as a member of the *defterdar* (accountant) bureaucracy overseeing the empire's revenues.

While the janissaries formed a powerful praetorian guard, they were supplemented by a standing army, paid indirectly by *timar* (land grant), an adopted Byzantine practice. Conquered territory remained the sultan's property, with such grants dispensed on the understanding that the man's "salary" was the proceeds of his estate – and that he remained liable for armed service at any time. *Timar*s reverted to the crown upon the holder's death, with his sons having to re-earn their portion by service.

Despite tolerance shown to Christians, Ottoman society was hierarchical. Distinctions between Muslims and infidels were preserved in every particular from dress code to unequal status before the law. Christians were not conscripted for campaigns, and hence could not qualify for *timar*s; instead they paid a tax in lieu of military service, and congregated in towns as tradesmen.

To continue the *timar* system, more land had to be seized, and the *gazi* ethos continued. By the mid-fourteenth century the Ottomans had entered Thrace, and in 1362 **Sultan Murat** I took Adrianopolis (Edirne). Constantinople was surrounded, and the almost-vanished Byzantine Empire existed on Ottoman sufferance. With Latin and Orthodox Christians at each other's throats, Ottoman ascendancy was assured, and Murat further isolated Constantinople with new acquisitions in the lower Balkans, routing a Serbian-led coalition at Kosovo in 1389. After Murat was murdered on the battlefield by a Serbian infiltrator, his elder son and successor **Beyazit** I established an unfortunate precedent by promptly strangling his brother Yakub to assure untroubled rule. Beyazit, nicknamed Yıldırım (Lightning) for his swift battle deployments, defeated a Hungarian/Crusader army at Bulgarian Nicopolis in 1396, and the fall of Constantinople seemed imminent.

However, in expanding eastwards, Beyazit – more impulsive and less methodical than Murat – provoked the great Mongol warrior **Tamerlane**. Tamerlane routed Beyazit's

1362	**1402**	**1453**
Ottoman Sultan Murat I takes Adrianople (today's Edirne), which becomes the new capital	Tamerlane's Mongols defeat Beyazit I at the Battle of Ankara – a major setback for the Ottomans	Sultan Mehmet II takes Constaninople, to mark the end of the Byzantine world

armies at the **Battle of Ankara** in 1402, trundling the captive sultan about in a cage for a year before his demise, while laying waste to much of Anatolia. Even though the Mongols soon vanished, the remnant Byzantine Empire was granted a fifty-year reprieve, and for a decade the fate of the Ottoman line hung in the balance as Beyazit's four sons fought it out. The victor, Mehmet I, and his successor the mystically inclined Murat II, restored Ottoman fortunes.

The fall of Constantinople

The greatest prize – **Constantinople** – still eluded the Ottomans. Both symbolically, as the seat of two previous empires, and practically – as the throttle between the Black Sea and the Mediterranean – its capture was imperative. **Mehmet II**, who became sultan in 1451, immediately began preparations, studding the sea approaches to the severely depopulated capital with fortresses, engaging artillery experts from Europe with an eye to breaching the city walls, and for the first time outfitting a substantial Ottoman fleet. The final siege of Constantinople, during spring 1453, lasted seven weeks, ending on May 29 when the sultan's armies finally entered the city while the last Byzantine emperor died unnoticed in the melee. Mehmet's epithet was henceforth Fatih, "the Conqueror", and no doubt remained that the Ottoman Empire was the legitimate successor of the Roman and Byzantine ones.

The Ottoman Golden Age

Mehmet refurbished the city, renamed İstanbul, as a worthy imperial capital, repopulating it with Muslims and Christians from rural areas, establishing public amenities and constructing a fine palace at Topkapı. The non-Muslim communities were organized into *millets* (nations), headed by a patriarch or rabbi, answerable for his flock's good behaviour (plus tax remittances) and under whom Greek or Slavic Orthodox, Armenian and Jew were subject to their own communal laws. This system, which guaranteed more freedom of worship than in contemporary Europe, lasted until 1926.

Mop-up campaigns during 1458–60 in the Peloponnese and along the Black Sea eliminated satellite Byzantine and Genoese states. Mehmet then returned to the upper Balkans, adding Wallachia, most of Greece, Bosnia-Herzegovina and part of Albania to his domains, while expanding his navy to counter the Venetians.

Mehmet was succeeded in 1481 by **Beyazit II**, "the Pious", who despite that disposition relegated Venice to secondary maritime status by enlisting pirates into the Ottoman navy. The skills of Greek renegades and Italian mercenaries were supplemented in 1493 by those of Iberian Jews, the ancestors of most contemporary Turkish Jewry, fetched by "mercy ships" sent by Beyazit upon their expulsion from Spain and Portugal.

In 1512 Beyazit was forced to abdicate by his son **Selim I**, vigorous like his grandfather but with an added streak of cruelty and bigotry, hence his moniker Yavuz ("the Fierce" – "the Grim" to the West). Both of Selim's predecessors had entertained Sufic and heterodox doctrines, but now religious orthodoxy was seen as vital, since neighbour Shah İsmail of Persia was promoting Shi'ism both within and without his frontiers. Selim massacred forty thousand Shi'ites in Anatolia, and then defeated the

1481	1514	1516
Jews expelled from Spain are given sanctuary by the Muslim Ottoman Turks	Selim I (the Grim) defeats the Persians at the battle of Çaldıran on the Ottoman–Persian frontier	Selim I captures Cairo and Mesopotamia and the Ottomans are seen as upholders of the Islamic Caliphate

SÜLEYMAN THE MAGNIFICENT AND ROXELANA

Domestically Süleyman distinguished himself as an administrator, builder and patron of the arts; in Turkey he is known as *Kanunî*, "the Lawgiver". In his personal life, however, his judgement had enduringly harmful consequences. He became so enamoured of his favourite concubine **Roxelana** that he broke with Ottoman precedent and married her.

Scheming and ambitious, Roxelana used her influence to incite the sultan to murder his capable son and heir (by a previous liaison), Mustafa, and later her own son Beyazit – as well as his grand vizier İbrahim. Süleyman died a lonely, morose man on his last campaign on the Danube in 1566; with the two ablest princes gone, no obstacles blocked the succession of Roxelana's first-born son, the useless **Selim**.

Shah at Çaldıran in 1514. Rather than continue into Persia, however, Selim turned his armies south against the Mamluks, overrunning Mesopotamia and Egypt by 1516, and occupying most of the holy cities of Islam. By capturing the caliph in Cairo and transporting him back to İstanbul, Selim became Defender of the (Sunni) Faith – and the caliphate was identified with the Ottoman sultanate.

Although the empire would reach its greatest extent after his death, **Süleyman the Magnificent** laid the foundations for this expansion during a long reign (1520–1566). The strongholds of the Knights of St John at Rhodes and Bodrum – which controlled the sea lanes to Egypt – were taken early on, as was Belgrade, leaving lands further up the Danube unguarded; by 1526 Budapest was in Ottoman hands. Campaigns in Persia and the Arabian peninsula were successful, but the **siege of Vienna** in 1529 was not – nor was an attempt to drive the Portuguese from the Indian Ocean. Süleyman was better able to control the Mediterranean, with such admirals as Greek-born Barbaros Hayrettin (**Barbarossa**) and Turgut Reis besting Venetian/Habsburg fleets. But in 1565 the siege of Malta, where the Knights of St John had retreated, failed, marking the end of the Mediterranean as an "Ottoman lake". Nonetheless, the Ottoman Empire, however unwieldy and heterogeneous, was the leading world power of the sixteenth century.

It was accordingly regarded with both terror and fascination by Europe. Only the **French**, under Francis I, saw possibilities of alliance and manipulation, concluding a treaty with Süleyman in 1536. In addition to granting France trading advantages in the empire, the treaty's clauses stipulated various privileges for French nationals, the so-called **Capitulations**: exemption from most Ottoman taxes and the right to be judged by their own consuls under foreign law. What began as a stimulus to commerce became, over time, a pernicious erosion of Ottoman sovereignty, as many European nations and overseas companies secured their own capitulations, extending immunity to local employees (usually Christian) provided with appropriate passports.

Centuries of Ottoman decline

The reign of bibulous **Selim II** ("the Sot" to the West) is the best marker as the start of Ottoman decline. He was succeeded by sixteen other, generally ineffectual, sultans, of whom only bloodthirsty but resolute **Murat IV** and peace-loving aesthete **Ahmet II** did

1529	1536	1566
The unsuccessful Siege of Vienna is a rare setback for the Ottoman war machine	European influence in Ottoman affairs, which will ultimately prove disastrous, begins with a treaty between the Ottomans and the French	Ottoman decline is symbolized by the accession of Selim II "the Sot"

much to prevent the gradual deterioration. From Roxelana's time onwards, the **harem** occupied Topkapı palace, so the scheming of its tenants impinged directly on day-to-day government. Early in the seventeenth century the grisly custom of fratricide upon the enthronement of a new sultan was abandoned in favour of the debilitating confinement of other heirs-apparent to the so-called Kafes (Cage). Few sultans campaigned overseas any longer, or presided personally over councils of state, instead delegating authority to their grand viziers.

Able and honest viziers halted or reversed the downward slide of the empire, but usually nepotism and corruption flourished in the decadent palace atmosphere. The early Ottoman principle of meritocracy was replaced by **hereditary aristocracy**; the *devşirme* was all but abandoned by the late seventeenth century, and the janissary corps was no longer celibate or religiously exclusive. Sinecure passed from father to son, and the corps expanded as free Muslims enrolled. Many were artisans who only appeared to collect pay, desire for more of which often prompted the janissaries to rebel, extorting money from hapless villagers and sultans alike, and on occasion deposing and murdering the sovereign. Similarly, land grants became hereditary, and their holders evolved into local warlords (the *derebeys*, "lords of the valley"). Revolts of idle, underpaid troops devastated Anatolia, already wracked by overpopulation and land shortage; thus began a steady rural depopulation that continues today.

More problems came from abroad. The influx into the Mediterranean of gold and silver from the New World set off a spiral of inflation, while the Age of Exploration forged new sea lanes around Africa to the East Indies, reducing the importance of overland caravan routes through Ottoman territories. Most importantly, Europe underwent the **Renaissance**, while the Ottomans remained stagnant. New, centralized nation-states in the West began to acquire well-trained standing armies and navies, equipped with new armaments, ships and navigation devices. To these manifestations of European superiority the Ottomans reacted disdainfully, seeing no reason to learn from the infidels.

External evidence of the rot took nearly a century to show: although the defeat of an Ottoman fleet at **Lepanto** (today Náfpaktos) in 1571 shattered the myth of Turkish invincibility, that victory was neutralized by their taking Cyprus from Venice the same year, and the reconquest of North Africa by 1578. The seventeenth century proceeded well, with the seizure of Crete and parts of Poland, but already the Ottomans were drafting treaties with adversaries as equals rather than, as before, condescending to suppliant Christian kings. Towards the end of the century, the most notorious of several defeats at the hands of the Austrians and allies was the bungled second siege of Vienna in 1683. Most of Hungary and other central European lands were ceded before the treaties of Carlowitz (1699) and Passarowitz (1718) stabilized the Balkan frontier for two centuries.

During the eighteenth century most Ottoman territorial loss was to **Russia**; Russo-Turkish enmity remained a constant thereafter until the 1920s. Catherine the Great humiliated the Turks with the treaties of Küçük Kaynarca (1774) and Jassy (1792), which ceded extensive territory to the tsarina and gave Russia long-coveted access to the Black Sea – as well as the right to interfere, anywhere in the Ottoman Empire, to protect Orthodox Christians.

1571	1683	1830
Ottoman military might is questioned, following the naval defeat at the Battle of Lepanto	The second siege of Vienna fails – a humiliating reverse for the Ottomans	Greece wins independence from the Ottoman Empire

Reforms and Young Ottomans

The start of **Selim III**'s rule in 1789 coincided with new revolutionary regimes in France and the US – hence the name of his proposed reforms, the Nizam-i-Cedid (**New Order**). With the Napoleonic wars as a background, he hired foreign experts to set up a Western-style army. This aroused the hostility of the janissaries and the *ulema*; Selim was deposed, then murdered, in 1808, despite having dissolved the new army as a sop to the conservatives.

The new sultan, **Mahmut II**, innovated more cautiously, before being confronted by the major crisis of his reign: full-scale **Greek rebellion** in 1821. This proved impossible to crush even after the army of Mehmet Ali, semi-autonomous ruler of Egypt, was sent to the scene. The destruction of an Ottoman fleet at Navarino by French, Russian and English ships in 1827, an 1829 overland attack by Russia on İstanbul, and a treaty in 1830 created an independent Greece – the first major Ottoman loss in the south Balkans. The French simultaneously invaded Algeria, and Mehmet Ali attacked Anatolia, which went unchecked until the Russians, now supporting Mahmut, landed on the Bosphorus. In consideration for services rendered they imposed the Treaty of Hunkâr İskelesi, giving the tsar unimpeded access to the Bosphorus straits.

Mahmut had notably more success at home. In 1826 the janissaries mutinied again, but the sultan liquidated them with loyal forces in the so-called "**Auspicious Incident**". The Bektaşi sect, the janissary "house religion", was suppressed until the 1860s, and a proper army created. Prussian and Austrian advisers arrived to train it during the 1830s, starting a tradition of Teutonic involvement in Turkey's military that endured for almost a century. A formal foreign service and civil service were also established. A version of Western dress became mandatory for all except clerics – including the replacement of the turban by the more "progressive" **fez**. These centralizing reforms widened the gap between the Ottoman masses and the new elite.

Mahmut's efforts bore more fruit when his son Sultan Abdülmecid and vizier Mustafa Reşid proclaimed the **Tanzimat** (Reorganization) in 1839, an Ottoman Magna Carta that delegated some sultanic authority to advisers, ended taxation irregularities, and stipulated equal legal treatment of Muslims and non-Muslims. While this permitted the founding of newspapers and secular schools, the proposal of infidel equality deeply offended many.

Foreign economic penetration of the Ottoman Empire increased sharply, with growing commerce in port cities, and massive imports of European products; the Greeks, Armenians and foreign-Christian merchants benefited disproportionately. Inland centres and traditional bazaar crafts declined sharply, unable to compete with industrial products.

By mid-century the empire was thoroughly enmeshed in European power struggles, since England and France had determined that the Ottomans must be propped up as a counter to Russian expansionism. Thus the empire found itself among the winners of the 1853–56 **Crimean War**, which began as a dispute between Russia and France over the protection extended by each to Christians in Ottoman Palestine. The war ended with little significant territorial adjustment, but did bring twenty years of peace for the Ottomans.

Abdülmecid, well-meaning but weak and extravagant, was succeeded in 1861 by **Abdülaziz**, who combined his predecessor's defects with a despotic manner. From

1839	1853–56	1877
The Ottoman Empire attempts to modernize with the Tanzimat reforms	The Ottomans and their allies, France and Britain, prevail against Russia in the Crimean War	The Ottomans lose a great deal of territory in the Caucasus and Balkans to imperial Russia

among the first graduates of the empire's secular schools arose the Society of **Young Ottomans**, which advocated a constitutional monarchy; its stellar figure, poet and essayist Namık Kemal, was exiled (like others) by the sultan. Young Ottomans oversea penned reams of seditious literature, smuggled into the empire to good effect.

Faced with Abdülaziz's financial irresponsibility and his growing mental instability, together with new Russian mischief in İstanbul and brutally suppressed revolts in the Balkans, Young Ottomans among the bureaucratic elite deposed him on May 30, 1876. The sultanate was passed to his promising nephew Murat, but he too suffered a nervous breakdown and was declared unfit to rule. The next heir-apparent was his brother **Abdülhamid**, an unknown quantity, offered the throne on condition that he accept various Young Ottomans as advisers and rule constitutionally.

Abdülhamid and the Young Turks

The new sultan duly presided over the first Ottoman parliament and retained – briefly – his hapless brother's advisers. But implementation of reforms was interpreted by outsiders as a sign of weakness. Accordingly **Russia attacked** in 1877, in the Caucasus and in the Balkans, with an explicitly pan-Slavic agenda. The war went badly for the Ottomans, with extensive territorial losses confirmed by the harsh peace treaty of San Stefano (at the ceasefire line near İstanbul), later mitigated by the 1878 Conference of Berlin. This provided for an independent Romania, Montenegro and Serbia; an autonomous if truncated Bulgaria; the cession of Kars and Ardahan districts to Russia; and the occupation of Bosnia and Herzegovina by Austria.

THE YOUNG TURK REVOLUTION

In 1889 the Ottoman Society for Union and Progress – later the **Committee for Union and Progress** (CUP) – arose among army doctors and the huge exile community in Europe. It took strong root in **Macedonia**, the most polyglot Ottoman province, completely infiltrating the Third Army at Salonica. Threats of intervention by European powers in Macedonia – where disorderly Greek and Bulgarian guerrilla bands rampaged – coincided with arrears in army pay, sparking the revolt of the so-called "**Young Turks**". Macedonian army units demanded by telegraph that Abdülhamid restore the 1876 constitution, or face unpleasant consequences; on **July 24, 1908**, the sultan assented. There was rejoicing in major imperial cities as mullahs fraternized with bishops, and Bulgarians walked arm in arm with Greeks.

Euphoria subsided as the **revolutionary government** fumbled for coherent policy. The coup had had as immediate goals the curbing of Abdülhamid's despotism and the physical preservation of the empire – but even these limited aims proved beyond it. By October Bulgaria declared full independence and absorbed eastern Rumelia, while Austria formally annexed Bosnia-Herzegovina. **Elections** for the reconvened parliament were reasonably fair, and the CUP, organized as a party, gained a majority. Opposition to its Westernization and autocracy simmered, however, and in spring 1909 a **counter-revolt** of low-ranking soldiers, anti-CUP politicians and religious elements seized İstanbul. Abdülhamid, overestimating the rebels' strength, unwisely supported them. The "Young Turks" fought back from Salonica, sending Third Army general Mahmut Şevket to crush the insurrection, and then **banished the sultan** to house arrest in Salonica. His younger brother ascended the throne as Mehmet V, promising to respect the "will of the nation".

1878	1889	1895–96
Sultan Abdülhamid embarks upon a period of repressive, despotic rule	The formation of the Committee of Union and Progress (CUP) marks the start of Turkish nationalism	Massive pogroms against the Ottoman Empire's Armenian minority

ationalism had been unleashed – and rewarded – in the Balkans, and would be a
eme for the next forty years. Britain, as compensation for fending off further
ussian advances, was given Cyprus.

During all this the new **parliament** displayed too much independence for the sultan's
king, criticizing policy and summoning ministers to answer for their conduct. In early
878, between the San Stefano and Berlin negotiations, Abdülhamid dropped any
etence of consultative government and dissolved the Chamber of Deputies; with all
straining influences gone, he ruled despotically and directly. Numerous spies and
gorous press censorship attended a police state and a new telegraph network helped
irveillance.

After his disastrous early wars, Abdülhamid's foreign policy was xenophobic and
sia-oriented, espousing Islam as a unifying force and emphasizing his role as caliph.
his didn't prevent the loss of Tunis and Egypt, along with worsening treatment of
e Armenians of eastern Anatolia, who began to show the same nationalist sentiments
 Balkan Christians. Abuses culminated in organized **pogroms** of 1895–96, during
hich nearly 150,000 Armenians died. In 1897, war with Greece and a revolt on Crete
incided; although the Prussian-trained army defeated the Greeks, the Ottomans were
rced to grant Crete autonomy.

Despite opposing political reform, Abdülhamid promoted technological
'esternization – most famously German-built railways across Anatolia. Investment
edits were extended, and a Public Debt Administration gathered revenues of state
onopolies to service the enormous debt run up since the 1850s. Secular schooling
d technical training were encouraged, as long as they remained apolitical – but the
eation of an educated elite inevitably resulted in change.

Nationalism and the Balkan wars

lthough the Young Turks managed to save the CUP revolution in 1909, there was still
o agreed programme as three notions contended for supremacy. **Ottomanism** asserted
at a Eurasian federal empire, in which all ethnic and religious minorities had equal
ghts – in return for loyalty to the sultan – was both viable and desirable.
an-Islamism, Abdülhamid's pet creed, stressed the Islamic nature of the Ottoman
mpire and the ties between Muslim Albanians, Caucasians, Kurds, Arabs and Turks.
an-Turanism, mainly promoted by Caucasian Muslims exiled by the Russians, was
nore blatantly racial, dwelling on the affinities of all Turkic peoples between central
sia and the Balkans; over time it morphed into a more realistic **Turkism**, protecting
ne interests of Anatolia's Turkish-speaking Muslims. Although that eventually carried
ne day, uninhibited discussion of these alternatives – and cultural life in general
 briefly flourished. Between 1908 and 1912 the CUP was hardly monolithic, and
arliamentary opposition was not completely quashed until 1912.

The CUP's growing authoritarianism coincided with renewed external threats.
taly invaded Tripolitania (Libya) in 1911, and the next year took all of the
Dodecanese islands. In late 1912, Bulgaria, Serbia, Montenegro and Greece united,
riving Turkey out of Europe in the **First Balkan War**, even approaching İstanbul by
arly 1913. Enraged at attempts to limit the army's, and the CUP's, involvement in
overnment, and the poor terms of a pending peace treaty, key CUP officers staged

1908	1912	1914
he Young Turk revolution eads to the restoration of he 1876 constitution	Balkan War is a setback for the Ottomans, who lose out to Bulgaria, Montenegro and Serbia	The CUP triumvirate that now effectively rules the Ottoman Empire decides to ally with Germany in World War I

a coup, murdering the minister of war; new grand vizier Mahmut Şevket's assassination soon after allowed the CUP to suppress all dissent and establish a **military junta**.

The unlikely Balkan alliance fell apart, with Bulgaria turning on Serbia and Greece in the **Second Balkan War**, and the Ottomans regaining eastern Thrace up to Edirne. This made temporary heroes of the triumvirate junta: **Enver Paşa**, dashing, courageous, abstemious, as well as vain, ambitious and megalomaniac; **Talat Paşa**, a brutal Thracian civilian who later ordered the 1915 deportation of the Armenians (see pp.681–684); and **Cemal Paşa**, a ruthless but competent professional soldier from an old family. They avenged the ethnic cleansing of Balkan Muslims by deporting or killing nearly half a million Greek Orthodox from Aegean Turkey in early 1914.

World War I

CUP ideology was now overtly Turkish-nationalist and secular, as well as anti-democratic – and increasingly pro-German. Public opinion, and sager CUP members, hoped that the Ottoman Empire would remain neutral in the pending conflict, but Germanophile Enver signed a secret agreement with the Kaiser on August 2, 1914. Britain committed a major blunder the same day, impounding two battleships paid for by public subscription in Turkey. In response the Germans sailed two replacement ships through an Allied blockade to İstanbul in October, presenting them to the Turkish navy – whose German commander promptly sent them to bombard Russian Black Sea ports. By November the Ottomans were at war with the Allies, though some CUP ministers resigned in protest.

The **Turkish war effort**, fought on five fronts simultaneously, was an almost unmitigated disaster. Within four years, the empire lost all its Middle Eastern domains as Arabs backed the British on the promise of subsequent autonomy, thus proving pan-Islamism as dead as Ottomanism. Enver Paşa lost an entire army on the Russian front during winter 1914–15; the subsequent Tsarist advance deep into Anatolia was only reversed after 1917. The sole Ottoman successes were bloodily defeating the British at Mesopotamian Kut, and the successful defence of **Gallipoli**, guarding the Dardanelles and the sea approaches to İstanbul. Credit for the seven-month Turkish resistance there belonged largely to a hitherto unknown Colonel **Mustafa Kemal**, later **Atatürk**. He had come of age just before the Young Turk agitation and, while an early CUP member, had opposed its autocratic tendencies and entry into the war with Germany. The Turkish public craved a hero, but jealous Enver denied them this satisfaction by shuttling Kemal between various backwoods commands, until war's end saw him overseeing a strategic retreat near Syria.

On October 30, 1918, Ottoman and British officers signed an **armistice** at Greek Límnos. Two weeks later an Allied fleet sailed into İstanbul, and occupied strategic points around the Sea of Marmara, though Turkish civil administration continued, providing no "disturbances" took place. Meanwhile, the CUP triumvirate had fled on German ships, and all soon met violent deaths: Talat killed in revenge by an Armenian in Berlin; Cemal assassinated in Caucasian Georgia; and Enver dying flamboyantly as a self-styled emir fighting the Bolsheviks in central Asia.

1918	1919	1919
The Allies occupy İstanbul after the Ottoman defeat in World War I	French troops occupy southeast Anatolia, Italians the western Mediterranean region, and Greek troops land at İzmir	Atatürk lands at Samsun on the Black Sea, marking the "official" start of Turkey's War of Independence.

he struggle for independence

e Allies could now carry out long-deferred designs on the Ottoman heartland. By
rly 1919 French troops occupied southeast Anatolia, the Italians landed on the coast
tween Bodrum and Antalya, and the Greeks disembarked at İzmir, where Greek
rthodox formed much of the population. The British concentrated their strength in
tanbul and Thrace, and along with the other victors garrisoned in the capital dictated
olicy to the defeated. New sultan **Mehmet VI** was interested mainly in retaining his
rone, and ready to make any necessary territorial or administrative concessions
including dissolving the Ottoman parliament.

In Thrace and Anatolia, however, various Committees for the Defence of Rights
patriotic guerrilla bands often led by ex-CUP personnel – had arisen, and a
bstantial Ottoman army survived at Erzurum, under Kâzım Karabekir. Together
ese would form the nucleus of resistance. Only visionary leadership, and further
llied provocations, were lacking; neither was long in coming.

Mustafa Kemal was the only undefeated Ottoman commander at war's end, and was
ot compromised by association with the CUP leadership. Popular and outspoken,
emal itched to cross over to Anatolia and begin organizing **resistance**, but not
ithout a suitable pretext. In spring 1919, he wrangled a post as a military inspector
npowered to wind up the CDRs. His first destination was the Black Sea, where
urkish guerrillas were battling local Greeks intent on setting up a Pontic republic. On
lay 19, 1919, he landed at Samsun, four days after the Greek landing at İzmir – the
st straw for many hitherto apathetic Turks. Contrary to his brief, Kemal promptly
egan organizing and strengthening the Turkish guerrillas. The İstanbul government,
ealizing what he was up to, dismissed him, then ordered his arrest; he responded by
signing his commission. Kemal and Karabekir, plus other high-ranking Ottoman
fficers, planned resistance with support from Anatolian religious authorities. Two
leological congresses (at Erzurum in July, in Sivas in September) elected Kemal
airman, and ratified the so-called **National Pact**, which demanded Turkish borders
pproximating those of today, an end to the Capitulations and a guarantee of rights to
l minorities. The pact also reaffirmed its loyalty to the institution of the caliphate, if
ot the sultan himself, deemed an Allied puppet.

The **Nationalists**, as they were soon called, began to joust with the İstanbul regime.
y late 1919, they forced the resignation of the grand vizier and elections for a new
arliament dominated by Nationalists, which proclaimed the National Pact. Thefts
om Allied arms depots, with the connivance of the French and Italians who opposed
reek aims, became common. At the instigation of the outraged Ottoman court,
e British placed İstanbul under formal occupation on March 16, 1920, raiding
arliament and bundling many deputies into exile on Malta. Luckier MPs escaped to
nkara, where on April 23 the Nationalists opened the first Grand National Assembly.
he sultanate secured a **fetva** from Islamic authorities sanctioning holy war against the
rebels" and condemning Nationalist leaders to death in absentia. Kemal and friends
ecured a counter-*fetva* from sympathetic religious figures in Ankara, and shortly after
he Bektaşi dervish *şeyh* ordered his followers to help the Nationalists.

Such moral support was vital to the beleaguered guerrillas, now fighting a war on
ultiple fronts: against the French in the southeast, the Italians in the southwest,

920	1920	1921
he British formally ccupy İstanbul in larch	May sees the signing of the controversial Treaty of Sèvres, which, had it been implemented, would have stripped Turkey of virtually all its territory	An invading Greek army is turned back by Atatürk's right-hand man, İsmet İnönü

Armenians in the northeast, irregulars supporting the sultan in various locations, and – most dangerously – the Greeks in western Anatolia. The only consistent aid came from the young Soviet Union, which sent gold and weapons, then partitioned the short-lived Armenian republic between itself and Turkey, thus closing that theatre of war by late 1920.

The Allied governments, oblivious to all this, presented the humiliating **Treaty of Sèvres** to the Ottoman government in May 1920. By its terms, an independent Armenia and an autonomous Kurdistan were created; the Dardanelles and Bosphorus straits were internationalized; Thrace plus İzmir and its hinterland were given to Greece; France and Italy were assigned spheres of influence in Anatolia; and Turkish finances were placed under Allied supervision, with a revival of the Capitulations. By signing this document, the demoralized sultanate sacrificed its last shred of credibility, convinced waverers to back the Nationalist movement – and sparked a predictable Greek response.

The Greco-Turkish War

Greek forces, authorized by British prime minister Lloyd George, pressed inland from İzmir to capture Edirne, İzmit and Bursa, seeking to realize a "Greater Greece" on both shores of the Aegean. Only French and Italian objections halted them short of the strategic Afyon–Eskişehir railway. In early 1921 the Greeks were on the move again, but Nationalist general İsmet Paşa stopped them twice at the **İnönü** gorge, from which he later took his surname. Since the replacement of the republican Venizelos government in Greece by royalists, the Greek armies had become more corrupt, incompetently led and brutal in their treatment of Muslim civilians. Kemal's forces, on the other hand, had gotten more cohesive and professional, with irregular bands suppressed or absorbed.

But when the Greeks advanced east once more in July 1921, they swiftly captured Afyon, Eskişehir and its vital linking railway; the Nationalists strategically retreated east of the Sakarya River, less than 100km from Ankara, to buy time and extend enemy lines. Panic and gloom reigned in Ankara, with Kemal appointed to command the defending army, and share its fate. The Greeks went for the bait, sensing an easy chance to finish off the Nationalists. But in the ferocious, three-week **Sakarya** battle that started on August 13, they failed to make further headway. Although most of the Greek army survived, anything but the capture of Ankara was a defeat. The jubilant GNA conferred on Kemal the title *Gazi*, or "Warrior for the Faith".

Sakarya greatly enhanced the Nationalists' position: both the French and Italians soon concluded peace treaties, and contributions from Muslims abroad poured in to finance the "holy war". With support for the Greek adventure evaporating, the British tried unsuccessfully to arrange an armistice. Both sides dug in until, on August 26, 1922, Kemal launched a **final offensive** to drive the Greeks out of Anatolia, at Dumlupınar near Afyon. The Greek lines crumbled, and those not taken prisoner or killed fled in a disorderly rout towards waiting boats in İzmir, committing atrocities against the Turkish population, destroying the harvest and abandoning Greek civilians to the inevitable Turkish reprisals. The latter included the **sacking and burning of İzmir** within four days of the triumphant entry of the Nationalists.

Despite this resounding triumph, ongoing conflict beckoned. A large Greek army remained in Thrace, disposed to fight on, and British contingents guarding the

1922	1922	1923
The Turks win a decisive victory over Greek troops at the battle of Dumlupınar in August	An armistice is signed at Mudanya, on the Sea of Marmara south of İstanbul	The Treaty of Lausanne recognizes the boundaries won by the Turkish Nationalists in the War of Independence

ardanelles faced off against the Nationalist army sent to cross the straits. Some
ationalists even advocated re-taking western Thrace and Greek Macedonia, a sure
ath to renewed world war. Cooler heads prevailed, however, and at Mudanya on
ctober 11, 1922, an armistice was signed, obliging the last Greek troops to quit
astern Thrace. A week later British premier Lloyd George, utterly discredited, resigned.

he fall of the sultanate and the population exchanges

here remained just one obstacle to full Nationalist control: Sultan Mehmet VI still
resided over İstanbul. Few in Ankara had much time for the man himself, but many
xpressed reluctance to abolish his office, favouring a constitutional monarchy. The
llies helped decide the matter by extending a clumsy double invitation to a final peace
onference – one to the sultanate, the other to the Grand National Assembly. The
utrage this provoked in the GNA made it easy for Kemal to persuade them to **abolish
he sultanate**, which took place on November 1. Within two weeks Mehmet VI, last
f the House of Osman, sneaked ignominiously out of the old imperial capital on a
ritish warship, bound for Italian exile; his cousin Abdülmecid became caliph, but
ith no temporal powers.

At the 1923 Lausanne peace conference, İsmet Paşa was the sole Turkish
epresentative. The Allies, hoping to dictate terms as at Sèvres, were quickly
isappointed; the dogged İsmet reduced seasoned diplomats to despair by feigning
eafness and repetitive insistence on the tenets of the National Pact. The **Treaty of
ausanne**, signed on July 24, recognized the National Pact frontiers; abolished the
apitulations; demilitarized the Dardanelles; and postponed a decision on the status
f oil-rich Mosul (now in Iraq).

More drastically, Greece and Turkey agreed to **exchange minority populations** to
liminate future communal conflict (see p.684). Lausanne marked the true end of
World War I, and saw Turkey, alone of the defeated, emerge in dignity, with modest
emands made of her. Compared to the old empire, this was a compact state – 97
ercent Anatolian and Muslim. A new political party, the **Republican People's Party**,
as formed, as was a new GNA, its members drawn from RPP ranks.

he young republic

n October 1923 the GNA officially moved the capital to **Ankara** and proclaimed
he **Republic of Turkey**; Kemal was designated head of state and İsmet prime minister.
Although the sultan was gone, Caliph Abdülmecid was still around and a conspicuous
ublic personality. That was an intolerable situation for Kemal and other Westernizers;
vith the war over, they no longer needed the legitimizing function of Islam. In March
924 the caliphate was abolished and all royal Osmalıs exiled, the *medreses* and
eligious courts closed, dervish orders dissolved, and **vakıf** assets assigned to a new
Ministry of Religious Affairs.

Many Turks, including some of his followers, were dismayed by Kemal's increasing
utocracy, and some – including Kâzım Karabekir – resigned from the RPP in October
o form the opposition **Progressive Republican Party** (PRP). At first Kemal tolerated it
s a safety valve, but he became alarmed when PRP speakers attracted large crowds and
he less supervised İstanbul press sided with them. In February 1925 the first of several

1923	1924	1925
n October, Ankara becomes he capital of the new urkish Republic	The caliphate is abolished and all Ottoman royalty are sent into exile	The first of the Kurdish revolts that still bedevil Turkey begins

KEMAL ATATÜRK'S REFORMS

Anxious to turn his revolutionary, westernizing principles into reality, Kemal introduced a series of far-reaching and controversial **reforms**. Traditional **headgear**, such as women's veils, the turban and the fez, were seen as reactionary; new sartorial laws outlawed them, and required the use of hated European hats. Ottoman dress had been a vital indicator of social rank, and the new regulations met with stiff resistance. Not a few recidivists were hanged by the Independence Tribunals, but secularists have to this day not eliminated the cloaking of women in rural areas.

In 1926, the **Gregorian calendar** supplanted the Muslim lunar one for official use, and the *şeriat* (Islamic **law code**) was replaced by adaptations of European versions. The Jewish, Armenian and Greek minorities relinquished their communal laws; henceforth all citizens were judged by a uniform legal system. Along with a secular law code came relative **emancipation of women**: marriage and divorce became civil rather than religious or customary, polygamy was abolished, and by 1930 women were voting in local elections.

Kemal's next agenda item was **alphabet reform**. A special commission prepared a Roman script within six weeks in 1928, and by 1929 its universal use was law. The entire language was targeted over the next few years, with a language commission purging Turkish of Arabic and Persian accretions and reviving old Turkish words, coining new ones or adopting French words. Scholars now reckon the process was carried too far, as the language soon became as top-heavy with borrowed Western terms as it had been with oriental ones, but with the script change the measures substantially increased literacy and comprehension. (A deliberate side effect of language reform was to isolate Turks from their imperial past by becoming unable to read Ottoman Turkish.)

Less successful, and ultimately embarrassing, were historical "revision" programmes, variously asserting that all other languages derived from Turkish; that the Turks were Aryan (and other racial nonsense mimicking Nazi theories), or that they descended from Hittites or Sumerians. Such hypotheses, springing from feelings of inferiority and a need for political legitimacy, remained in Turkish schoolbooks until the 1970s. A more constructive 1934 move was full **suffrage for women** in national elections and the mandatory adoption of **surnames**; previously this had been discretionary. Kemal chose for himself **Atatürk**, "Father-Turk", dropping his first name Mustafa.

twentieth-century **Kurdish revolts** – both fundamentalist Muslim and separatist-nationalist in nature – erupted; it took Ankara two months to suppress. Kemal, demanding unity in crisis, secured the PRP's closure and established draconian Independence Tribunals; the revolt's leaders plus a few PRP members found themselve on the wrong end of a rope. By that autumn all **dervish orders** had been prohibited (though they were never completely suppressed), and pilgrimage to Sufi saints' tombs was forbidden.

Kemal's reforms re-inflamed opposition, and in mid-1926 a plot to assassinate him was uncovered. Most of the former PRR leadership, including Karabekir, were charged and tried, plus the entire surviving CUP leadership, who were hanged; even those acquitted were barred henceforth from public life. This was the last purge, however, and the feared Independence Tribunals were disbanded, having served their purpose.

Belatedly Atatürk addressed the economy. Already weakened by ten years of constant warfare and the loss of Greek and Armenian industrial know-how, its problems were exacerbated by the 1929 crash. "**Kemalism**" stressed state-funded heavy industry with a

1929	1934	1938
Turkey's change from the Arabic to the Roman alphabet is made law	Turkey joins the League of Nations	Atatürk dies of liver failure in Dolmabahçe Palace in İstanb…

oal of complete import substitution (except for factory equipment). Development anks had been set up in 1925, and the rail network extended, with mining, steel, ement and paper mills heavily subsidized in imitation of Italian fascism. This rogramme was, however, grossly inefficient, and relegated agriculture to penury ntil the 1950s. The east was condemned to a subsistence existence – aggravating urdish feelings of punitive neglect – a situation that remained unchanged until assive irrigation and hydroelectric projects during the 1970s and 1980s.

Foreign policy espoused non-interventionism and isolationism, though Turkey joined the League of Nations in 1934. Atatürk's slogan "Peace at home, peace in the world" ight now seem unfortunately similar to Neville Chamberlain's utterances after Munich, but secured for Turkey years of badly needed calm. Though the RPP imitated spects of contemporary totalitarian systems, Turkey had no wish to follow Germany, aly and the USSR over a cliff. Atatürk removed the last irritant to Anglo-Turkish elations by renouncing claims to Mosul, but started a campaign in 1936 to annex the Hatay, part of French Syria with a large Turkish population.

Fortunately for Turkey, Atatürk had accomplished most of his intended life's work by 938, since his health, after decades of heavy drinking, was steadily worsening. He died om liver cirrhosis in İstanbul's Dolmabahçe palace at 9.05am on November 10, 1938. housands of mourners bearing torches lined the route of his funeral cortege-train etween İstanbul and Ankara. Fifteen years later he was interred in a mausoleum, the nıt Kabir – designed by an Italian and a German, in monumental 1930s fascist style.

Atatürk's legacy is considerable: unlike his totalitarian peers, he refrained from xpansionism and overt racial/ethnic hatred, leaving behind a compact state and a uiding ideology, however uneven, which was expressly intended to outlive him. ersonally he was a complex, even tragic, figure: his charisma, energy and quick grasp f situations and people were unparalleled, but he had little inclination for methodical lanning or systematic study. While revered, he was not particularly lovable – despite ponsoring women's rights, he was a compulsive womanizer, with one brief, unhappy arriage. He nursed grudges that bore deadly consequences for those who might herwise have lived to extricate Turkey from later dilemmas. Like a huge tree that lows nothing to grow underneath, Atatürk deprived Turkey of its next generation of adership. His personality cult, obvious from the silhouettes and quotations on every llside, is symptomatic of an inability to conceive of alternative ideologies or heroes, ough since 1983 Kemalist economics has vanished completely.

World War II and after

atürk was succeeded as president by **İsmet İnönü**, and his Hatay policy was osthumously vindicated in 1939 with the region's annexation. France, eager for urkish support in the imminent war with Germany, acquiesced in return for Turkey gning a vaguely worded treaty of alliance with France and Britain in 1939. But France as swiftly defeated, while German propaganda convinced Turkey that Britain was robably doomed too, and that the Axis would also dispatch Russia, the hereditary urkish enemy. Accordingly a "Treaty of Friendship" was signed with Nazi Germany in 941, guaranteeing at least Turkish non-belligerence. Entry into the war on either side as always doubtful, since Turkey's armed forces had become desperately antiquated;

938	1942	1945
e former French-mandated ovince of Hatay becomes rt of Turkey	Turkey introduces the Wealth Tax, unfairly targeting its minorities	Neutral for most of World War II, Turkey finally declares war on Germany

memories of World War I defeat were strong as well. Turkey remained **neutral**, but despite this fence-sitting, the country was on a war footing with mobilization, and the economy stressed by black markets and huge budget deficits.

All these, and the infiltration of Nazi ideology, provoked the 1942 imposition of the **Varlık Vergisi** (Wealth Levy), a crippling, discriminatory tax applied against businessmen of Armenian, Greek, Jewish and Dönme descent. Non-payers had their property confiscated and/or were deported to labour camps in the interior, where many died. The measure, having raised very little money, was rescinded in 1944, but not before urban commerce had been set back a decade, and the Republic's reputation with non-Muslim minorities severely dented.

Even after the collapse of Italy, Turkey still declined to enter the war, despite assurances of Allied support. Turkey only declared war on Germany early in 1945 to qualify for UN membership – not soon enough to prevent the USSR from demanding the return of Kars and Ardahan, and joint control of the Sea of Marmara straits. While demurring, Turkey badly needed a protective ally, and found one in the **United States**. The 1946 arrival in İstanbul of the American warship USS *Missouri* was greeted with such euphoria that the city fathers opened the local bordellos for free to the sailors.

The first results of this mutual wooing were Turkey's participation in the Korean War and admission to **NATO**. This new pro-Western stance had as other consequences the expulsion from Warsaw Pact Bulgaria into Turkey of numerous ethnic Turks, harbinger of an identical act four decades later, and consistently bad relations with neighbouring Arab states, particularly after Turkey recognized Israel.

At home, discontent with one-party rule, secularization and the stagnant, centralized economy coalesced when four MPs expelled from the RPP formed the **Democrat Party** in early 1946. Despite snap elections that summer and widespread balloting irregularities, the new opposition won fifteen percent of parliamentary seats. Amazingly, this result was not reversed by force or chicanery, but a definitive showdown could not be long postponed, and campaigning for May 14, 1950 polls was unimpeded. The DP promised an end to anti-business strictures, freer religious observance, and attention to neglected farmers. Although the Democrats were sure to win, the scale of their victory – 55 percent of votes, and over eighty percent of parliamentary seats – proved a surprise. **Celal Bayar** replaced İnönü as president, while **Adnan Menderes** became prime minister.

Populist government

Among the first acts of the new government was to permit, after a seventeen-year gap, calls to prayer in Arabic; simultaneously, outbreaks of fez- or turban-wearing, polygamy and the use of Arabic script erupted in the provinces (where Atatürk's reforms had barely penetrated). With sweeping **economic reforms** Menderes effectively opened up a country where for three decades little in the way of people, ideas, capital or goods had moved in or out. However, much of this relied on unsound investment in state enterprises or patronage to supporters. Farmer-lawyer Menderes had his colossal vanity aggravated by adoring peasants who sacrificed livestock in his honour and named boy-children after him.

1950	1955	1960
Turkey's first truly free elections see the Atatürk-founded Republican Peoples Party replaced by the Democrat Party	Anti-Greek minority riots in İstanbul leave thousands of shops and businesses in ruins	The elected government is toppled in the country's first military coup

Bumper harvests helped keep the electorate sweet through the mid-1950s, though by
954 enormous **national debt** and trade deficits helped put the black-market value of
e Turkish lira at one-fourth the official exchange rate. But the increasingly sensitive
P would not tolerate criticism: in 1953 both the RPP and the right-wing/religious
ational Party, with their handful of seats, were dissolved, while repressive press laws
ok effect just before May 1954 elections. These the Democrats won even more easily,
ut instead of giving them confidence, they took this as a mandate to continue
rushing dissent and run the country even more shamelessly for their clientele's benefit.
he economy kept deteriorating with rampant **inflation**, thereafter a constant of
urkish life. During 1955 the government gave tacit support to pogroms aimed at
inority groups, and in particular the Greeks (see p.684).
In the wake of all this, the government lost support and, although they won the 1957
lections these were heavily rigged, with the tally never being announced. Turkey thus
pproached 1960 in a parlous state, with a huge gulf between the pro-DP peasantry
nd the urban elite – and, more dangerously, an alienated, antagonized military.

irst military coup and the 1960s

Nowhere had dismay over DP policies been keener than in the military, who
onsidered themselves the guardians of Atatürk's heritage. On May 27, 1960, middle-
anking officers, barred from voting and fed up with the inflation that was eroding the
alue of their fixed salaries, staged a **coup**, announced on the radio by Colonel
lparslan Türkeş.
The putsch was bloodless, swift and complete; DP MPs and ministers were jailed as
he larger cities celebrated. For the next sixteen months, a **National Unity Committee**
NUC) under Cemal Gürsel governed Turkey, while preparing a new constitution to
upersede the 1924 one. The NUC, however, was a marriage of convenience between
dealistic top brass, who expected the resumption of civilian rule, and junior officers
ho desired an indefinite period of authoritarian military government. The new
onstitution was submitted to public referendum in July, with elections set for October.
The **referendum**, essentially a vote of confidence on the NUC, clocked just 62
ercent in favour – evidence of lingering support for the Democrat Party. Leading DP
nembers, including Menderes and Bayar, were found guilty of undermining the 1924
onstitution, corruption and planning the 1955 riots. Upon the return of guilty
erdicts and fifteen death sentences, the NUC hastily carried out three – against
Menderes, foreign minister Zorlu and finance minister Polatkan. The three hangings
ust before the elections backfired badly, making Menderes a martyr and ensuring a
ong life for the **Justice Party** (JP), the Democrat Party reincarnated.
The elections again disappointed the NUC; neither the Justice Party nor a revitalized
RPP gained a majority. The two front-runners formed a coalition, with Gürsel as
resident and İnönü prime minister for the first time since 1938. All this annoyed
isaffected junior officers who mounted two subsequent coup attempts, one in
ebruary 1962 and another fourteen months later.
Unstable coalitions continued as NUC reforms faltered; import-substitution policies
vere revived, while land reform and rural development were deferred. The first wave
f **emigration to Europe** acted as a social safety valve, and "guest workers" returned on

1963	1964	1969
urkish workers win the ght to strike	Sectarian strife between Greeks and Turks on Cyprus almost leads to war between Greece and Turkey	Right- and left-wing extremists clash with depressing frequency across the nation

holidays with consumer goods and some European notions. Independent labour unions organized, with the right to strike conferred in 1963. The urban proletariat flocked to the Turkish Workers' Party (TWP), whose very existence nudged the RPP, now led by Bülent Ecevit, leftward. **Süleyman Demirel**, among the main political figures of the next three decades, became JP leader in 1964, pushing free enterprise and foreign investment. In 1965 elections, Demirel's JP got a solid majority.

Cyprus, independent since 1960 with extensive constitutional concessions to its Turkish Cypriot minority, again intruded as the rickety setup there collapsed in December 1963. This cued civil strife on the island throughout 1964, abetted by smuggled-in Greek and Turkish troops; a full-scale Greco-Turkish war was only avoide by US pressure. The Turkish government had to confine itself to retaliations against th Greeks of Turkey's Aegean islands and İstanbul (including the expulsion of 12,000 resident Greek nationals).

The spirit of 1968 was manifest in increased **anti-Americanism** and leftist sentiment particularly at universities. Many Turks felt betrayed by the lack of US support on Cyprus, having studiously followed its foreign-policy lead since 1946. Even the government found obvious American tutelage offensive, and soon most US military installations passed to Turkish or NATO control. Demirel was returned to office in 1969 amid increased political violence. Extreme left-wing groups like Dev Sol (Revolutionary Youth) clashed with right-wing and/or Islamist activists like the Grey Wolves, their paramilitary training camps set up by Alparslan Türkeş, founder of the fascist **Nationalist Action Party** (MHP).

"Memorandum coup" and the 1970s

Faced with domestic unrest and sterile parliamentary manoeuvres, the generals acted again. Their March 12, 1971 proclamation forced Demirel out in favour of an "above-party" technocratic government. This "**memorandum coup**" kept parliament ir session, but martial law was imposed, thousands were arrested and tried for inciting violence or class conflict, and much of the 1961 constitution was curtailed. The new government, stymied by JP MPs, resigned. The army, mindful of the hash the colonel: junta had made of neighbouring Greece since 1967, decided to let politicians take the blame for any adverse outcome here. October 1973 elections produced a coalition of Ecevit's RPP with Necmettin Erbakan's Islamist National Salvation Party.

In July 1974, the Greek junta ousted Cypriot president Makarios, replacing him wit extremists supporting union with Greece. Ecevit felt compelled to order an **invasion of Cyprus** on July 20 that ended, in August, with the Turkish army occupying the northern third of the island, which has since become the self-proclaimed Turkish Republic of Northern Cyprus. Ecevit resigned in September to seek early elections but Demirel clung to power until 1977.

All this further polarized Turkey, which by 1980 saw escalating political violence ratchet annual death tolls up to three thousand. While extremists initially confined activities to each other, deteriorated parliamentary decorum and politicized workplaces meant that incidents became widespread. İstanbul neighbourhoods were controlled by factions – having the wrong newspaper or the wrong attire and moustache ensured trouble.

1971	1974	1978
The so-called "memorandum coup" brings martial law to the country	Turkey invades Cyprus, to protect the Turkish minority on the island	Civil unrest across Turkey continues with right-wing extremists and left wing Alevis clashing in Maraş

Ecevit regained power in late 1977, but proved unequal to a dire situation. In December 1978, Türkeş's MHP orchestrated bloody street battles in Maraş between fundamentalist Sunnis and left-wing Alevis; in Fatsa, an Alevi commune was smashed by army tanks. Demirel took office again in 1979, but he too failed to halt the maelstrom despite declaring martial law.

The 1980 coup and after

The army soon decided that the Republic was facing its gravest crisis yet. Plans for a coup existed earlier, but public rumblings first surfaced as an open letter to civilian politicians at New Year is 1980. Economist-engineer **Turgut Özal** was appointed head of the State Planning Organization; he jettisoned import-substitution policies in favour of an export-orientated economy.

Turkey's importance had been underlined by the Iranian revolution and Soviet invasion of Afghanistan, and the US, keen to secure a stable Middle Eastern base, gave tacit consent to martial law and a coup. This occurred bloodlessly on September 12, 1980, to the initial relief of most Turks. The frenzied killing ceased; all political parties were disbanded, their leaders detained; all trade unions and NGOs were closed down. Turgut Özal was, however, left in charge of the economy, since his reforms were seen as both effective and essential for Western support.

It was soon obvious that this coup would not resemble the previous two. A junta of generals, not junior officers – the **National Security Council** (NSC) – controlled matters, and return to civilian rule would be long delayed. Bannings, indictments and purges proceeded apace, and while the radical Right was not immune, the Left bore the brunt of prosecutions. Nationalist right-wing beliefs, if not violent or fascist, were compatible with the NSC agenda – as were mildly Islamic views, as long as fundamentalists stayed out of the military.

The NSC's principal targets, relatively untouched in prior putsches, were labour unions, internationalist or separatist groups and the left-leaning intelligentsia, all crippled by show trials that dragged on so long that many defendants walked free based on time served on remand. NSP leader Necmettin Erbakan was acquitted on charges of attempting to create an Islamic state. The MHP was decimated by eight capital verdicts and dozens of prison terms – though leader Türkeş was acquitted. The military purged university staff, and all campuses were supervised by a Higher Education Council (YÖK). A committee of carefully vetted applicants drew up a new, highly restrictive constitution in 1982, countermanding most of its 1960 predecessor. This was ratified by ninety percent of the electorate in a coercive referendum, also an election for the presidency. No campaigning against was allowed; the only candidate was NSC chief **General Kenan Evren**, and it was an all-or-nothing package.

Return to civilian rule: ANAP

Pre-coup parties and personalities remained banned at heavily supervised November 1983 elections, but the generals' centrist slate came last, as Turgut Özal's centre-right Motherland Party (ANAP) won just under half the votes and just over half of parliamentary seats.

1980	1982	1983
Fed up with years of unrest, the Turkish public watch with relief as the military take power again	A new constitution is overwhelmingly approved by an undemocratic vote that also sees General Kenan Evran become president	The charismatic Turgut Özal and his moderate Motherland Party wins the first elections since the coup

ANAP was a party of uneasy alliance incorporating a wide range of opinion from economic liberals to Islamists. Half-Kurdish Özal embodied these contradictions in h
person: a devout Muslim, ex-member of the NSP and adherent of the still-clandestin
Nakşibendi order, he had strong appetites for booze, tobacco, food and *arabesk* tunes,
while his charismatic speaking manner belied a Texan engineering degree. He juggled
ANAP's technocratic and traditionalist factions while introducing sweeping economi
reforms, with record export levels and six percent growth rates. Inflation and foreign
debt, however, soared, as budgets were swollen.

While ANAP (and Özal) can be credited with ushering Turkey into the world
economy, an ostentatious display of wealth created an ethical climate conducive to
corruption. A provincial elite, sharing Özal's small-town, lower-middle-class
background, earned an initial reputation of "getting things done". While trained
abroad, they hadn't necessarily absorbed Western values, and when they had, their
model was Texas, not Europe. English became their lingua franca, and that of many
universities, which under YÖK's watchful eye became apolitical polytechnics.

Pre-coup politicians were un-banned by referendum in 1987; November
parliamentary elections gave just 36 percent to ANAP but, thanks to a skewed
system, nearly two-thirds of the seats. Özal's two prime-ministerial terms
saw a dramatic, deliberate increase in Islamic activity, to offset Iranian-style
fundamentalism and leftist ideology. The Department of Religious Affairs expande
mandatory teaching of Islam in schools increased and *vakıfs* swelled with Saudi
donations. **Kurdish separatism** resurfaced violently in the southeast, courtesy of
the Kurdish Workers' Party (PKK), strengthened by overzealous reaction of the
authorities (see p.679).

Ties with Greece were strained by Cyprus, disputes over Aegean airspace and
territorial waters and the Greek government's harassment of ethnic Turks in Greek
Thrace. Bulgarian-Turkish relations made headlines during summer 1989, as the
Communist Bulgarian regime's policy of forced Slavification ultimately escalated into
the largest European **mass emigration** since World War II. Over 300,000 ethnic Turks
fled Bulgaria for Turkey, which initially welcomed them and tried to capitalize
politically on the exodus. The numbers soon hit home, however, the border was shut
by August, and in 1990 Sofia's new post-Communist government renounced the
heavy-handed assimilationist campaign, while many new arrivals returned to Bulgaria
or emigrated to western Europe.

In contrast to Turkey's concern for Turkish minorities abroad, **human rights violatio**
continued at home with inhumane prison conditions, torture of suspects and increase
prosecutions of journalists and publishers testing the limits of censorship. Özal in
particular reacted to even mild criticism with dozens of libel suits.

Özal as president

ANAP's influence was waning due to hyperinflation and blatant nepotism benefiting
Özal's cronies and extended family – including his flamboyant, cigar-smoking wife
Semra. Only the second civilian president, and officially "above-party", Özal still acted
as the ANAP chief. He chose the next prime minister, Yıldırım Akbulut, a lacklustre
yes-man, then repeatedly undermined him.

1989	1990	1991
Turkey welcomes 300,000 Bulgarian Muslim Turks forced out of Communist Bulgaria	Özal's Turkey offers support to the US against Saddam Hussein's Iraq following its invasion of Kuwait	Turkey's first openly Islamist party, REFAH, comes fourth in the elections

raq's 1990 **invasion of Kuwait** reinforced Özal's position, and reiterated Turkey's
ategic importance. Özal invited the US to use İncirlik and Diyarbakır airbases,
curred considerable financial loss by closing the pipeline shipping Iraqi oil through
rkey, and permitted coalition troops near the Iraqi Kurdish "safe haven". In return he
on Bush the Elder's promise that an independent Kurdistan would not emerge from a
smembered Iraq.

1991 polls, the fairest ever, surprisingly had DYP finishing first, ANAP a strong
cond, İnönü's Social Democratic Peoples Party (SHP) third, and Erbakan's Islamist
elfare Party (Refah Partisi) a close fourth. A DYP–SHP coalition, with Demirel
ime minister and İnönü deputy prime minister, began with both parties pledging to
ill together in rescuing the economy.

There were also promises to make Turkey a *konuşan* (talking) society, where opinions
ere freely aired without fear of retribution. This ideal ran aground immediately when

UNCIVIL LIBERTIES: HUMAN RIGHTS IN TURKEY

Turkey's **human rights record** has been a perennial irritant in foreign relations.
Notwithstanding Demirel's 1991 pledge that police stations would have "walls of glass", there
was little significant change for years, with torture and suspicious deaths in custody frequent,
and Turkish jails holding over a hundred nonviolent political prisoners well into the new
millennium. Civilian governments deferred to the internal security forces, which, together with
elements of the State Security Tribunals, the police and the gendarmerie, formed a para-state
– the so-called "**deep state**" (*derin devlet*) – accountable to no one.

Urban terrorism re-emerged in the 1990s, with political assassinations perpetrated by
Islamists, far-leftists and rogue operatives of the Special Warfare Department, and police
mysteriously unable to identify suspects. Targets included army officers; secularist professors;
prominent lawyers; and the Jewish community. The murder of prominent journalist **Uğur
Mumcu** in a 1993 Ankara car-bombing caused widespread revulsion. His funeral, attended
by hundreds of thousands, included mass demonstrations of support for his secularist,
democratic ideals. As ever, nobody significant was apprehended, prompting allegations of a
cover-up and/or involvement of the "deep state". Another feature of the era was numerous
"**disappeared**" **persons** – usually left-wing or Kurdish activists who vanished after being
detained by police or unidentified civilians.

Following his 1995 article in *Der Spiegel* describing the Turkish state as a "system of unbearable
repression and atrocity" and deeming the Kurdish rebellion a justifiable response to official
repression, prominent novelist **Yaşar Kemal** (see p.694) was charged with promulgating
"separatist propaganda" and fomenting "hatred between races". With the European customs-
union ratification at stake, he was given a suspended sentence in 1996 after a year-long trial, but
not before 99 other prosecutions against artists and intellectuals who supported him. Similar
court cases and violent incidents (including the attempted assassination of the İHD – Turkey's
Human Rights Association chief) continued until the unprecedented liberalization laws of 2002.

But there was another upsurge in 2005, occasioned by penal code Article 301's making it a
crime to "denigrate Turkishness" and by **Orhan Pamuk**'s (see p.695) attempted prosecution
under it for comments to a Swiss newspaper asserting the killing of a million Armenians and
40,000 Kurds. Worse was to come, when – after also being prosecuted under Article 301 –
Hrant Dink (see p.683), proprietor of Armenian-Turkish newspaper *Agos*, was assassinated on
January 19, 2007 by a young nationalist acting at the behest of Trabzon "deep state"-ers. Dink's
funeral, attended by 100,000, became a protest with chants of "We are all Armenians!"

993	1993	1995
zal, now president, dies of a heart attack, ough conspiracy theorists cry foul	Respected journalist Uğur Mumcu dies in a car bombing	Turkey enters into a customs union with the EU

some of the 22 Kurdish HEP MPs – compelled to run on the SHP national ticket – refused to recite the standard loyalty oath upon being sworn in. An un-banning of pre-1980 parties revived the Republican People's Party (CHP).

During 1992 Özal played an increasingly negative role, goaded by a hatred of Demirel; Özal also feuded with new ANAP premier Mesut Yılmaz, attempting to unseat his protégé. As president, Özal delayed signing many bills, prompting discussion of impeaching him. Özal died suddenly of a heart attack on April 17, 1993, and conspiracy theories still rage as to whether he was bumped off by the "deep state".

Özal, despite his many faults, was the most eloquent and influential head of state since Atatürk. Respected by many for his energy, courage and vision, despised by an equal number for his overbearing manner and shameless self-aggrandizement, he remains an ambiguous figure who sometimes did the right thing (eg, advocating concessions to the Kurds) for opportunistic reasons.

After Özal, chaos

Demirel eventually emerged as president, while US-educated technocrat **Tansu Çiller** became prime minister in June 1993. With her assertive style and telegenic manner, her rise to power was initially viewed positively, though she soon proved woefully inadequate. Hopes of a fresh take on Kurdish issues vanished as Çiller deferred to military hardliners, the death toll in east Anatolia rocketed. and the latest Kurdish-interests party (DEP) was proscribed. Inflation shot up to a staggering 120 percent, before dipping to "only" 80 percent. Major **corruption scandals** erupted regularly; no party escaped guilt, as all had governed recently. In 1996 an Associated Press article listed Tansu Çiller among the world's ten most corrupt politicians.

The only significant – if controversial – foreign-policy success was the 1995 customs union with the EU. Overseas, there was stiff opposition because of Turkey's poor human rights record; domestic opponents noted that considerable import duties were being forfeited, while Turks would still not have freedom of movement in Europe. Though falling well short of EU membership, the agreement, applied incrementally between 1996 and 2000, was brandished as a triumph by the beleaguered coalition.

Even before Çiller's term, the coalition was becoming unpopular. Racked by dissension, the SHP dissolved in February 1995, the remnants merging with the CHP. In September CHP leader Baykal and Çiller dissolved the coalition; elections were set for December.

THE SOURCE OF ISLAMIST POLITICS

In post-1923 Turkey, "secularism" means the state controlling religious affairs and suppressing public expressions of Islam. An official ban on **traditional Islamic dress** in state facilities effectively bars many young people of conservative social background from a public career, or even admittance to university. But for most Turks, Islam remains a much stronger source of values than assertive Westernizing, and a more homespun expression of national spirit than the quasi-colonial arrogance associated with the Kemalist elite, which offers little spiritual succour.

1995	**1995**	**1998**
Well-known left-wing novelist Yaşar Kemal is prosecuted for expressing pro-Kurdish sentiments	The pro-Islamist REFAH government is forced from power in the so-called "soft coup"	Tayip Erdoğan, arguably Turkey's most successful politician since Atatürk, is elected mayor of İstanbul

The rise and fall of Refah

Islamist **Refah** shocked the establishment by garnering the most votes in the December 1995 elections, with support coming from the urban underclass, devout Kurds and disparate individuals fed up with the discredited mainstream parties. DYP leader Çiller, under investigation for corruption, negotiated a coalition with Refah provided all proceedings against her ceased. Erbakan became prime minister, with Çiller as his deputy; the NSC, at this point with mixed civilian-military membership, geared up to safeguard secularism. In June 1997, Erbakan was forced out in the so-called "**soft coup**", replaced by an unlikely ANAP–DSP coalition.

Seven months later, Refah was closed down (for "acting against the principles of the secular Republic"); the Islamists regrouped as the Fazilet party, but in September 1998 the popular Fazilet mayor of İstanbul (and future prime minister), **Recep Tayyip Erdoğan**, was jailed for four months for a speech the prosecution claimed "incited armed fundamentalist rebellion". He had in fact quoted from a poem by Ziya Gökalp, main architect of secular Turkish nationalism. Erdoğan was respected for both literally and figuratively cleaning up İstanbul, and his imprisonment was widely regarded as a hollow victory by a suspect establishment over an honest (if "Islamist") politician. In November, the coalition collapsed as Prime Minister Yılmaz was accused of corruption. April 1999 elections saw the DSP at the head of a weak coalition.

Earthquake – and meltdown

On August 17, 1999 a catastrophic **earthquake** struck the eastern Marmara region, killing almost 40,000. Many died trapped in shoddily built tower blocks, exposing the corruption of local authorities who had allowed building and zoning codes to be flouted. Both the shambolic emergency response and the army were criticized, with soldiers tending to their own rather than joining the rescue effort. Ironically, the earthquake had lasting positive consequences. Substantial material aid and sympathy from Greece – whose aid teams were first on the scene – heralded a sustained thaw in bilateral relations. In December 1999 Greece dropped its objections to Turkish accession and Turkey became an official candidate for eventual **EU membership**.

A wave of private bank failures preceded a definitive economic crash in February 2001. The Turkish lira – formerly tied to the dollar in an IMF-backed plan – was free-floated; the exchange rate (and domestic inflation) soared as the value of lira investments and wages plummeted. The crisis forced sweeping monetary reforms under the aegis of veteran World Bank supremo Kemal Derviş.

In June, Fazilet was banned for "anti-secular activities", specifically inciting protests against the prohibition of headscarf-donning by women in schools and government offices. The closure proved futile as the **AKP** (*Adalet ve Kalkınma Partisi*, Justice and Development Party), led by former İstanbul mayor Erdoğan, replaced it immediately. By mid-2002, PM Ecevit was an invalid, the DSP had imploded, the economy had contracted eight percent and Turkey had become the IMF's single biggest debtor. More positively, despite the imminent end of the coalition, legislators passed several **EU-required reforms** touching on human rights and freedom of expression. The death penalty was abolished, press freedom increased and education and broadcasting in several minority languages was now theoretically permissible.

1999	2002	2003
A catastrophic earthquake near İstanbul claims the lives of more than 20,000 people	The pro-Islamic AKP sweeps to power in the national elections, with 34 percent of the vote	Al-Qaeda terrorists bomb İstanbul synagogues, the HSBC bank and the British Consulate

Start of the AKP era

Given the preceding stasis, the **AKP swept to power** on November 3, 2002, with 34 percent of the vote. For the first time since 1987 Turkey had a majority government. The only other parliamentary party was the CHP; all others failed to clear the ten percent nationwide minimum. By European standards, this is exceptionally high, but other parties, having benefited handsomely from this bar (introduced by the 1982 constitution to exclude "minority or regional" – ie Kurdish – parties), weren't in a position to complain.

Turkey's secularist establishment suspected that the AKP would soon drag the nation into an **Islamic theocracy**; instead, given stable government, Turkey's economy revived. More remarkable was the new government's commitment to compliance with EU directives by introducing 36 reforms meeting the "Copenhagen criteria" of acceptable civic practice. Both foreign and domestic observers appreciated the irony of Turkey's EU membership quest – and meaningful reform – being pursued more fervently by an "Islamic" government than by any of the country's previous secularist governments.

In early 2003, Turkey declined to be used as a springboard for the **US-led invasion of Iraq**. By the time Parliament voted (on March 20, invasion day) to allow US planes to overfly Turkish airspace, Turkish–American relations had already hit an all-time low. Turkey's reluctance to be involved stemmed from fears that the war would lead to a Kurdish state, and that the country might suffer a terrorist backlash. On November 15 2003, car bombs exploded outside İstanbul synagogues, killing 25 and injuring three hundred. Five days later, suicide car-bombers targeted the British consulate and the HSBC bank, killing thirty and injuring 450. Although the perpetrators were linked to al-Qaeda, they proved to be ethnic Kurds from the southeast.

The long-running **Cyprus problem** continued to bedevil foreign affairs and Turkey's EU quest. A UN-devised reunification scheme backed by Turkey seemed to offer hope that the long-divided island would unify under the EU umbrella. In 2004, however, despite a solid majority (65 percent) of Turkish Cypriots voting in favour, 75 percent of Greek Cypriots rejected it in the necessary referendum. A week later southern (Greek) Cyprus joined the EU on behalf of the whole island. Turks – unaccustomed to occupying the moral high ground on Cyprus – were understandably annoyed.

On October 3, 2005, **accession talks** for Turkey's joining the EU formally began. A November EU report criticized human rights issues, military–civilian relations and inequality but, more positively, praised the "functioning market economy." The AKP government had proven a competent manager under IMF guidelines, with inflation down to single figures for the first time in decades.

AKP's second term

After a relatively quiet 2006, 2007 began tumultuously with the **assassination of Hrant Dink** (see p.671, p.683). In spring 2007, AKP nominated foreign minister **Abdullah Gül** as president over military objections, particularly as Gül's wife publicly wore a headscarf. In what became known as the "**e-coup**", the military posted an online warning, hinting they might act if Gül were appointed. Millions of secular Turks took to the streets in orchestrated rallies against Gül's candidacy and what they saw as creeping Islamicization. The threat of a coup forced an early election in July 2007, in which the AKP captured

2004	2005	2007
After a referendum dashes hopes of reunification, southern Cyprus alone joins the EU	Formal accession talks for Turkey's long-awaited EU membership finally begin	Leading Turkish-Armenian activist Hrant Dink is shot dead by an ultra-nationalist teenager in İstanbul

THE ERGENEKON CONSPIRACY

The alleged **Ergenekon conspiracy** was revealed in June 2007, with defendants finally sent to trial in late 2008. The plot, a variation on the usual methods of the "deep state", had long been hinted at in the media. But the sight of high-ranking generals (albeit retired ones), a *jandarma* commander, a lawyer, a nationalist politician, journalists, academics and mafiosi charged with membership in an armed terrorist group, attempted overthrow of the (AKP) government, and treason, was one the Turkish public never thought they'd witness. The group is accused of carrying out high-profile provocateur assassinations, including that of Armenian-Turkish activist Hrant Dink (see p.671, p.683), and bombings of secularist entities such as the *Cumhuriyet* newspaper, to create the impression that Kemalism was under threat from Islamic extremists and thus justify a coup. The case drags on as of writing, with ever more suspects being arrested and arms and explosives caches uncovered in unlikely places. By 2012 over one hundred top military officers were on trial in either the Ergenekon or associated **Balyoz** (Sledgehammer) cases, including former Chief of General Staff İlker Başbuğ. Advocates say that the "deep state" is finally being decisively confronted; detractors dismiss the proceedings as a frame-up concocted by a vindictive AKP regime. These contadictory views continued to pervade Turkish political opinion even after the conclusion of the Sledgehammer trial in September 2012, which saw 326 people, most of them mid- to high-ranking military officers, given long prison sentences for plotting to overthrow the government.

7 percent of the vote, the first time in fifty years that a party had won a second term office with an increased majority. Ominously the CHP lost seats to the MHP, now ack in parliament along with Kurdish independents. Gül was duly elected president nd attention focused on the **headscarf issue** once again, as the AKP attempted to repeal 1998 law forbidding its wearing in universities. In response the state prosecutor filed case against the party early in 2008 for "anti-secular activities" and the AKP narrowly voided being closed down. Legislation introduced by the party allowing the headscarf be worn in universities was overturned, the guardians of the state having deemed it an expression of Islamic sympathies in a state institution".

With France and Germany openly hostile to Turkish EU membership, and Erdoğan ailing to implement more reforms, the **accession process** stalled. The 2008 global ump hit the economy badly; despite a banking system annealed by the 2001 crisis, he TL tumbled against other currencies, and by mid-2009 unemployment stood at ver 16 percent. Erdoğan's feistiness won him admirers and critics in equal measure hen he stormed out of a February Davos summit after an altercation with Israeli resident Shimon Peres over Gaza.

STREET-FIGHTING MAN – RECEP TAYIP ERDOĞAN

The founder of the AKP and Turkish prime minister for a record three times, **Tayip Erdoğan** has caught the imagination of huge swathes of the Turkish public like no politician since Turgut Özal. A pugnacious but charismatic firebrand of a leader, he was brought up in the mean streets of the gritty İstanbul dockland neighbourhood of Kasımpaşa, on the northern shores of the Golden Horn. He famously sold *simits* (sesame-coated bread-rings) on the streets as a child to supplement his family's meagre income and later, a sure-fire winner in this soccer-obsessed nation, he was a semi-professional player with his local team, Kasımpaşa.

007	2009	2010
e AKP increase their majority national elections in July	PM Erdoğan storms off stage in Davos after a row with Israel's Shimon Peres	Nine Turkish citizens die when Israeli commandos attack the *Mavi Marmara*.

Although March 2009 local elections saw support for the AKP dip, in February 2010 they managed to pass crucial legislation enabling military figures to be tried in civilian courts, thus reducing the chances of a future coup. Europe approved, while the supposedly progressive CHP objected, referring the measure to the Constitutional Court. In September the AKP went even further in challenging the military/secularist establishment by organizing a national referendum on the constitution that had been in place since the 1980 military coup, and timed to coincide with its thirtieth anniversary. A massive 58 percent voted in favour of the government package, which included changes to the judicial system. Crucially, it permitted generals involved in past coups to be put on trial, retrospectively, for their actions. Opponents claimed the AKP were simply attempting to fill the judiciary with pro-Islamists and pave the way for Islamic rule; the vast majority of "no" votes were cast in the traditionally secularist Aegean and Mediterranean coastal belts.

Relations with Israel, already at an all-time low following Erdoğan's altercation with Peres at Davos in 2009, plummeted even further in May 2010 after Israeli commandos stormed the *Mavi Marmara*, a Turkish ship taking aid to Gaza, killing nine Turkish citizens, and Turkey's once buoyant Israeli tourism trade slumped dramatically. The understanding between these two countries, once at least nominally allies, was hardly helped by AKP support of Hamas.

The rise and rise of the AKP

In June 2011, for the first time in the history of the Turkish Republic, a party was elected for a **third consecutive term**. This time, although the AKP actually garnered a slightly higher number of votes (almost fifty percent), the number of seats they had in parliament dropped slightly, making it more difficult for the party to push through reforms without consulting the opposition.

A major reason for the AKP's repeated electoral success was not its Islamic conservatism but the fact that the country began a period of sustained economic growth. In part this was because the AKP were prepared to do business with everyone, from pariah regimes such as Syria and Libya through to Saudi Arabia, Russia and China. Foreign capital flowed into the country, not least from the oil-rich Gulf states. Tourism incomes were booming too, with over thirty million visitors in 2011.

Turkey, under the urbane Foreign Minister Ahmet Davutoğlu, also introduced a grandiose "zero problems with neighbours" policy. This was primarily aimed at increasing trade and influence in the former Ottoman lands, from the mainly Arab Middle East and North Africa to the Balkans. The "Arab Spring" that began in early 2011 placed Turkey in a new role in the region, as a beacon of democracy (and global capitalism) amid a sea of dictatorial and protectionist regimes – or that's how some in the West wanted to see the country. Indeed, many of the poor majority in countries like Egypt saw Turkey, with its booming economy and democratic-secular system being steered by a conservative Muslim government, as the ideal alternative to their own despotic regimes.

In late 2011, with Israel still refusing to apologize for the *Mavi Marmara* deaths, Turkey downgraded its relations with Israel, expelling high-ranking diplomats and cutting military ties. Such actions made the tough, hard-talking and pious Erdoğan a

2010	2011	2011
The Turkish economy is ranked as the 17th largest in the world	The AKP wins a record third general election	So-called "Arab Spring" casts Turkey as icon of democratic stability in a region swept by turmoil

well-known and popular figure to the Arab man in the street, although cynics at home saw his moves as cheap populism at best, dangerous neo-Ottomanism (that is, a bid to regain influence in lands once under Ottoman control) at worst. Turkey's "zero problems" policy was soon sorely tested, however, when Erdoğan was forced to condemn Syria's leader Assad, as ten thousand refugees flooded over the border into Turkey, and evacuate thousands of Turks from Libya, where they were working in the drilling and construction industries.

In 2012 Turkish relations with Syria, fostered so carefully over the previous decade and a half (border minefields were cleared, Syrian and Turkish citizens could travel visa-free to each other's countries), collapsed as Assad refused to heed Erdoğan's calls for the Syrian leader to institute massive reforms. With the opposition Syrian National Council setting up a government in exile in İstanbul and Turkey overtly supporting Syrian rebels, relations between the two countries foundered. In June 2012, the Syrians shot down a Turkish military jet just south of the Turkish province of Hatay, escalating tensions yet further. By October, with Syria in the throes of a devastating civil war and almost 100,000 refugees finding safe haven in Turkey, and a de-facto Kurdish enclave (see p.680) emerging on the Syrian side of the 900km-plus border, the situation in Turkey's southeast was becoming very tense.

Trends for the future

Thus far the AKP has successfully challenged the so-called "**White Turks**" – mostly of Balkan descent – comprising the army, academia, civil service, big business and much of the media, who have run the republic since 1923. Despite being mostly devout and lower-middle-class, the AKP and its supporters ostensibly view EU entry as the best way to raise their voters' standard of living and promote reform. The burning question is whether the AKP is genuinely liberal, or merely introducing Islamic theocracy by the back door, as their opponents assert. The fact that EU accession reforms had petered out completely by 2010 suggest that Turkey and its current government do not value membership as highly as it once appeared to do – hardly surprising, given the economic and other crises affecting the union in 2012.

Paradoxically, a secular elite of strange bedfellows apparently opposes EU accession of a truly democratic Turkey: nationalists loathing the prospect of increased minority rights, military brass who'd be denied the role of national guardians, old-style leftists who brand the EU as an imperialist plot. The conclusion of the **Ergenekon case** (see p.675) may be a litmus test of whether the country will turn out to be a truly democratic state with a conservative, Muslim majority, or one that's still dominated from behind the scenes by a military/bureaucratic elite intent on preserving its privileges at all costs. The position of the Turkish military remains very powerful and lacking in transparency, while a solution to the interrelated **Kurdish problem** is even more crucial.

A substantial body of European opinion views Turkey as a developing Muslim country inherently unsuitable for membership in a "white, Christian" club that would be overwhelmed by Turkey's geographically lopsided development and demographic profile. One excuse used to block Turkey's accession is its refusal to recognize Greek Cyprus, thus blocking Turkey from fulfilling 14 of 35 accession criteria. This in turn has sparked a resentful attitude among many Turks, and support for accession has dropped noticeably.

2011	2012	2012
Turkey is now attracting more than thirty million foreign tourists per year.	Turkish and Syrian relations are in tatters after Syria downs a Turkish military jet close to the border	With refugees streaming into southeast Turkey, the Kurdish community across the border in Syria approaches effective autonomy

Turkey's **economy** is far more resilient than formerly, with consumer spending steady and foreign investment flooding in – especially since 2002 – from the Gulf states (but also through the purchase of second homes by Europeans). Particularly important is the country's role as an oil and natural gas conduit, with pipelines from Russia, Azerbaijan and Kazakhstan all crossing Turkish territory. In 2009 a deal was signed to pipe gas from Iran to Western Europe. **Tourism** is also crucial, with annual visitor numbers topping 31 million in 2011. Unemployment, exacerbated by rural depopulation, remains stubbornly high, especially among the young people who constitute such a large part of the population (the median age in 2011 was 28.5). The over-centralized educational system, undergoing constant tinkering, cannot produce sufficient well-trained workers. Despite lip service to the Islamic tenet of alms-giving, the AKP has done little to reduce the massive gap between rich and poor.

Turkey is rapidly becoming a major regional power, with its moderate Islamist government viewed as a bulwark against Islamic extremism. Initially anxious about the emergence of an independent Kurdish entity in northern Iraq, Turkey is now happy to do business with the oil-rich enclave. Despite the "Arab Spring", links with the Arab world have improved. Egypt and Libya in particular look to Turkey as a role model, and many wealthy Arabs from the Gulf states now holiday and invest in the country. On the downside, the civil war in Syria, and Turkey's poor relations with the Shia-dominated government in Iraq, have led to very strained ties with these two important neighbours. What could make things even worse is a "water war": the Euphrates and Tigris rivers have their headwaters in Turkey, and the dams (some complete, others still projected) of the gigantic GAP project (see p.579) threaten water supplies in both Syria and Iraq.

In the Caucasus, Turkey assiduously cultivates **Azerbaijan**, a nation not only ethnically Turkish (albeit Shi'ite rather than Sunni), but also petroleum-rich. This precludes meaningful links with **Armenia** following its occupation of the ethnically Armenian Azerbaijani enclave of Nagorno-Karabagh in 1992 (see p.683). Turkey has also shown increased interest in its former Balkan territories, especially those retaining Muslim populations. Albania has received military training and civilian advisers, and Turkey was among the first countries to recognize Macedonia. Perhaps the biggest surprise is strong links with **Greece** in trade, banking and tourism, offset by the total inability to come to a solution over Cyprus.

There is no doubt, however, that Turkey has been transformed economically under the AKP. Major new highways lace the mountainous Anatolian interior, high-speed train links are being forged between major cities, and cheap domestic air travel is booming. Along with Brazil, Russia, India and China, Turkey has become a major emerging economy, ranking seventeenth in the world in 2010. As a result of this new-found wealth, stable government and (albeit stalled) EU-accession-orientated reforms, Turkey stands in 2012 as a major regional player in a part of the world that has enormous geo-political importance.

The peoples of Turkey

Thanks to its long history, and repeated waves of migration over many millennia, modern Turkey is home to many distinct population groups. The roots of the Turks themselves are described on p.12, while you'll find accounts of two distinctive peoples who live on the Black Sea coast, the Hemşinli and the Laz, on pages 533 and 538 respectively. This section details some of the country's most obvious minority groups, from the Muslim Kurds to the Syrian Orthodox Christians.

The Kurds

Although the **Kurds** inhabit several Middle Eastern countries, including Iran, Iraq and Syria, the largest population is in southeast Turkey. Present in Anatolia long before the Turks, they are of Indo-European origin and language, and until the twentieth century were largely a tribal, nomadic people. Their dominant faiths are the same as the Turks – Sunni Islam, with significant numbers of Alevi (see box, p.684). As Kurds are not recognized as a minority by Turkey, accurate figures are debatable, but at least twelve million (and up to twenty) of the country's seventy-million-plus population are ethnically Kurdish.

A history of rebellion

Relations between the Ottomans and the Kurds were generally good. Successive sultans allowed the Kurds, split into semi-autonomous federations, to act as a buffer between the Ottoman Empire and Russia or Persia. After the collapse of the Ottoman Empire, most Kurds supported Kemal's Nationalists in the independence struggle; following the Republican victory, however, relations began to sour. Many Kurds had backed the Turkish nationalists as co-religionists, but they were outraged when Atatürk abolished the caliphate in 1924, especially as all institutions of a specifically Kurdish nature were also closed down.

The initial response was a revolt under Nakşibendi dervish *şeyh* Said; then a more overtly nationalist insurrection broke out near Mount Ararat, which wasn't quelled until 1929. A 1936 rebellion further west in the Alevi Kurdish heartland of Dersim, modern Tunceli, lasted two years. The Turkish state crushed each uprising with executions, expulsions to western Anatolia, and the suppression of all expressions of ethnic identity. The entire southeast became a military zone, closed to foreigners until the 1960s, with a backward, stagnant economy.

The PKK and its guerrilla war

Inevitably, an extremist organization – the **PKK** (Kurdish Workers' Party) – emerged in 1978 in reaction to forced-assimilation policies. Its founder, political-science student **Abdullah Öcalan**, set up a nominally Marxist guerrilla group intent on independence for Turkey's Kurds. The PKK's appeal cut across traditional tribal loyalties, offering something to those at the very bottom of the clan hierarchies, and it thrived in the repressive atmosphere after the 1980 coup. In 1984, from Syrian bases, the PKK started to launch attacks against the *jandarma* and army; later it targeted civil servants, especially teachers.

PKK power peaked in the mid-1990s, with over 15,000 guerrillas in the field. The state barely controlled some parts of the southeast as the PKK encouraged mass civil disobedience; schools closed as teachers refused to operate in the danger zone; and the army forcibly evacuated thousands of settlements to stop villagers (willingly or unwillingly) aiding the PKK. Successive pro-Kurdish political parties, accused by the state (sometimes correctly) of being fronts for the PKK, were closed down, and their leaders imprisoned. By 1998, the army's superior tactics and weaponry began to tell; after being expelled from his base in Damascus, Öcalan was captured in Kenya with CIA and Mossad aid in 1999. Convicted of treason and murder, he was imprisoned on İmrali island in the Sea of Marmara, where he still languishes.

Despite these setbacks, the PKK had succeeded in placing Turkey's Kurdish issue on both the domestic and world stages. In 2005, PM Erdoğan departed from the official doctrine that there were no Kurds in Turkey – "mountain Turks" were historically the code words – by referring, in a speech in Diyarbakır, the unofficial "capital" of Turkish Kurdistan, to the "Kurdish problem". Prohibitions on the public use of Kurdish were lifted, private courses in the language permitted, and in 2008 a state-broadcast Kurdish channel opened to great fanfare (and controversy).

In 2009 the AKP government announced the "**Kurdish Initiative**", aimed at solving the long-standing problem. Universities were permitted to teach Kurdish-language courses, human rights laws were changed, and settlements in the southeast were allowed to use Kurdish names. There was even an attempt to "bring home" PKK fighters from northern Iraq, by offering amnesties to those who had not been involved in attacks resulting in the deaths of Turkish soldiers or civilians. The latter policy backfired, however, when scenes of flag-waving supporters greeting the returning PKK members as homecoming heroes were aired on Turkish news channels – a sight the Turkish public and government alike found totally unacceptable.

Behind the scenes, the government at least tried to make progress, almost certainly carrying on secret talks with jailed PKK leader Öcalan. Then, in 2011, news leaked that Turkish and PKK representatives had engaged in secret talks in Oslo. Unfortunately for the initiative, however, the pro-Kurdish DTP (Democratic Society Party) was closed down by the courts in December 2011; it quickly morphed into the BDP (Peace and Democracy Party), but the damage was done.

Meanwhile, the cycle of PKK attacks and Turkish military reprisals continued; a particularly bloody PKK attack resulted in the deaths of 13 Turkish soldiers near Diyarbakır in June 2011, and mutual mistrust was reinforced later that year when a Turkish military aircraft struck a convoy of what they thought were PKK terrorists near Uludere, and killed what turned out to be 34 smugglers. PKK attacks escalated in 2012, and violence flared to levels not seen since the 1990s, with over 400 PKK and in excess of 100 Turkish security forces killed in the first nine months of the year. The arrest and detention of thousands of members of the KCK (Kurdish Communities Union, an organization seen by the Turkish state as the urban wing of the outlawed PKK), who included prominent academics as well as many members of the pro-Kurdish BDP, only exacerbated ill feeling.

Relations with Iraqi Kurdistan and Syria

Ironically, Turkey now enjoys far better relations with virtually autonomous Iraqi **Kurdistan** than with its own Kurds. High-level visits between leaders of Turkey and the booming, oil-rich proto-state are common, and Turkish companies are doing big business in the region. While relations are of course bedevilled by the PKK's continued incursions from Iraqi Kurdish soil, Turkey appears to have accepted the de facto Kurdish state in northern Iraq.

What's more worrying for Turkey is the situation in **Syria**, which also holds a very sizeable Kurdish minority. The PKK has tentacles within the Syrian-Kurdish community, and launches occasional attacks into Hatay province from Syria, and as of 2012 there's no telling whether some kind of proto-Kurdish state could also emerge from the Syrian quagmire. Many Turkish analysts have linked the upsurge in PKK attacks with the situation in Syria, accusing Assad of renewing his support for the outlawed organization to punish Ankara for its support of anti-Assad rebel groups.

Prospects for the future

The bloody struggle between Turkish forces and the PKK has indisputably polarized Turkish society. Many Turkish families have lost sons, and the sight of weeping crowds as the flag-draped coffin of the latest loved one is borne through the streets of his home town has become depressingly familiar on TV. The less scrupulous media exploit this to stoke nationalist feelings, and most processions are accompanied by chants of "Martyrs don't die, the homeland can't be divided". In fact, however, most of the 45,000-plus estimated casualties of the conflict are of Kurdish origin – and the Kurds too mark the deaths of their "martyrs" with flamboyant funerals.

Now down to perhaps five thousand combatants based on Mount Kandil in Iraqi Kurdistan, the PKK continue to strike across remote stretches of the Turkish–Iraqi frontier, usually using remote-controlled mines to blow up military vehicles, but sometimes, as at Dağlıca, launching full-scale attacks. Turkish Kurds have since 1986 been divided by the village-guard system, which exploits local rivalries with around 65,000 gun-toting, state-paid militiamen "protecting" their villages against PKK attack. With the economy of the southeast otherwise ruined, millions of Kurds have migrated westwards in search of work. This has led to tension in some cities, as the often poorly educated new arrivals bring a different way of life (and language), and compete on the local job and housing markets. Many Kurds are in turn resentful about having to leave their homes to face discrimination in the west. Indeed, a 2012 survey found that over half of all Turks would not want a Kurdish neighbour, while a quarter of all Kurds would not want a Turkish neighbour or in-law.

Firmly entrenched in power after its third successive electoral success in 2011, the once-progressive AKP government appears today to be following a more conservative, Turkish nationalist course. There's little doubt that Prime Minister Erdoğan is perfectly happy to accept the Kurds as a distinct, yet fellow, Muslim people, but, like the vast majority of Turks, he's adamant that they accept "Turkishness" as a supra-identity. His assertion at a party congress in 2012 that "We have four red lines: one state, one nation, one flag and one religion" left Turkish Kurds with any aspirations towards autonomy in little doubt as to where they stood.

There are grounds for cautious optimism, however. The ethnic genie is now out of the bottle, which at least means the Kurdish question can be openly discussed. Turkey is slowly removing provocative Turkish nationalist slogans (such as "How happy is he who can say 'I am a Turk'") from the hillsides of the southeast, and investigations are probing an illegal branch of the *jandarma* responsible for thousands of extra-judicial killings of Kurds during the 1980s and 1990s. Although the EU accession process is stalled, Turkey continues to implement EU-mandated reforms, thus improving civil liberties (at least in theory), and the AKP government has promised a new, more democratic constitution in the near future. Some hope remains that, in time, Turks and Kurds can heal the wounds of the past few decades and co-exist peaceably in a more inclusive, fully democratic Turkey.

Let's hope so, as with more than half of Turkey's ethnically Kurdish population living outside the southeast – over three million of them in İstanbul, far more than in any other single city worldwide, including all those in their "homeland" – any attempt to separate the country into Turkish and Kurdish zones would probably result in a bloodbath.

The Armenians

The **Armenians** (Ermeni in Turkish) have been present in and around eastern Anatolia since the Urartian empire collapsed, in around 600 BC. Attempts to form their own state have, however, invariably been short-lived – at least until an independent Armenian state emerged in the southern Caucasus after World War I. Under the Ottoman Turks, the Armenians generally prospered as a loyal and favoured Christian

millet (nation), but during the early twentieth century they fell victim to the competin
nationalisms that tore the Ottoman world asunder.

Armenian history and Christianity

The Armenians gradually developed their own identity after their arrival in Anatolia
in the seventh century BC. That process crystallized with the advent of Christianity,
which they fervently embraced. Towards the end of the third century, Armenia becam
the first nation to officially adopt the new faith, thanks mainly to the efforts of
St Gregory "the Illuminator". The invention of the Armenian alphabet in 404, by
Mesrop Mashtots, furthered the Armenians' view of themselves as a distinct race.

This separate identity was further strengthened when the Armenian Apostolic
Church refused to accept the ruling of the Byzantine Council of Chalcedon in 451,
which declared that Christ had two equal and co-existent natures. By retaining their
monophysite views – that is, believing that Christ had a single, divine nature – the
Armenians cut themselves off from the mainstream Byzantine Orthodox Christian
world, which held that Christ combined both human and divine natures.

During the ninth and tenth centuries, Armenian culture flowered, especially in the
Van basin under the Artsruni dynasty, and under the Bagratid dynasty around Ani.
The arrival of the Selçuk Turks and other Turcoman groups in the eleventh century,
however, heralded a decline in their fortunes.

The Ottomans finally took control of Armenia during the fifteenth and sixteenth
centuries. Ottoman rule benefited the Armenians who, like the other non-Muslim
minorities, were conceded substantial control over education and family law, and even
earned for themselves the epithet of *sadık millet* (loyal nation). During the nineteenth
century, however, as the Ottoman Empire declined, some Armenians (along with othe
Christian groups in Anatolia) developed nationalist aspirations – often encouraged by
the Russians, bent on fragmenting the Ottoman Empire.

The Armenian deportations

For the Armenians of the Ottoman Empire, **April 24, 1915** was a fateful day. Acting on
plans finalized in March, the CUP authorities disarmed all Armenians serving in the
Turkish army, and rounded up Armenian civilians from Anatolian cities, towns and
villages; only İstanbul and İzmir were exempted, for economic and public-relations
reasons. During ten months of deportations, Armenian men were usually shot
immediately by gendarmes, Kurdish irregulars or bands of recruited thugs, while
women and children were forced to march hundreds of kilometres towards
concentration camps in the Mesopotamian desert. Estimating total casualties is
controversial, but Ottoman and foreign censuses around 1900 counted nearly
1.5 million Armenians living in Anatolia. Allowing for about half a million refugees
who managed to hide in Turkey or escape abroad, most of the remainder can be
assumed to have perished, making it the first deliberate, large-scale **genocide** of the
twentieth century. In 1919 the Ottomans themselves admitted 800,000 killed.

The Genocide issue

The above scenario has been hotly disputed by more recent Turkish governments,
which have consistently denied that any officially approved, systematic expulsion or
killing occurred. They have conceded a maximum of 300,000 Armenian fatalities,
while implying that most were combatants in treasonous alliance with Russia or
France. While it is true that many Armenians, particularly in Van, Kars and Adana,
sided with those two powers in the hope of securing a postwar state for themselves,
this happened after the deportation and massacre orders were issued, and could be
construed as legitimate self-defence.

The "so-called genocide" issue, as the Turkish press describes it, continues to poison
relations between modern Turkey and the tiny Armenian state – soon subsumed by

oviet Russia – that emerged in the aftermath of World War I, and also with the large nd powerful Armenian diaspora. It bedevils relations between two peoples who, though they may have different religions, share much in common culturally, socially nd historically. The issue is a PR nightmare for Turkey, which constantly lobbies other ountries not to officially acknowledge the "genocide".

The Armenian lobby in the USA continually presses the administration to recognize he massacres of World War I as genocide. The pressure has been resisted, largely ecause Turkey remains a vital US ally in the Middle East. While running for the residency, Barack Obama confirmed his support for the Congressional passage of he Armenian Genocide Resolution, but once elected he failed to fulfil his promise. rance, however, which holds an Armenian community of some 300,000, passed a ill recognizing the genocide in 1998, while in Switzerland it is a criminal offence to eny it. Relations between Turks and Armenians deteriorated even further following two-year war between Caucasus rivals Armenia and Azerbaijan (1992–94) when rmenia occupied Nagorno-Karabagh, Azeri territory but with an overwhelmingly rmenian population. Turkey, in support of its co-Turkic brethren in Azerbaijan, broke ff diplomatic relations with Armenia, and the land border between the two countries emains closed.

The Armenians in Turkey today

t's estimated that up to two million "Turks" today have Armenian blood. During the leportations and massacres of 1915 and later, many local Kurdish and Turkish families nd individuals took in Armenian children, who were raised as Muslim Turkish itizens. Later generations were usually completely unaware of their origins – read *My Grandmother* by Fethiye Çetin (see p.699).

Only in İstanbul, however, did a sizeable Christian Armenian community survive. Under the 1923 Treaty of Lausanne, they were protected as an official minority, like ome other non-Muslim groups, by international law. Now estimated at between forty nd seventy thousand, İstanbul's Armenians have their own spiritual leader and a patriarchal church at Kumkapı on the Sea of Marmara below Sultanahmet, as well as many others scattered across the city, plus their own schools, newspapers and business organizations. Unfortunately, they are all too often misunderstood and viewed with uspicion by the majority Muslim Turks, who see them as potential fifth-columnists for outside powers, unfairly prosperous and simply not "real" Turks. The strenuous and unflagging efforts of the Armenian diaspora and their brethren in Armenia itself to have the "genocide" recognized internationally (including by Turkey) put them in a very difficult position, and they are often the target of discrimination, both from officialdom and the Turkish public. In 2011, for example, an Armenian-Turk conscripted into the Turkish army was shot in suspicious circumstances by a fellow soldier on the day Armenians commemorate the "genocide" (April 24). The mistrust is

---

HRANT DINK – "WE ARE ALL ARMENIANS"

In January 2007, 100,000 Turkish citizens marched down İstanbul's İstiklal Caddesi to protest their solidarity with slain Armenian-Turkish journalist and human rights campaigner **Hrant Dink**, chanting "We are all Armenians". While some of the protesters were İstanbul Armenians, the majority were Turks marching in sympathy.

Dink had been shot dead earlier that month in the street in broad daylight in the prosperous İstanbul business district of Sisli, close to the offices of the Armenian-Turkish newspaper *Agos*, which he co-founded and worked for as editor-in-chief. His killer was a Turkish ultra-nationalist teenager, but many believe the assassin was part of a broader, ultra-nationalist "deep state" conspiracy designed to foment unrest. To put the sympathy shown for Dink in the march in perspective, the assassin, following his capture, was photographed posing beneath a picture of Atatürk, holding a Turkish flag and flanked by smiling security officials.

THE ALEVİS

Cutting awkwardly across Turkey's ethno-religious divisions, the **Alevis** form up to twenty percent of the total population. Although they're officially classed as Muslims, their faith, a curious hybrid of shamanism and Shi'ism, is viewed with suspicion by many of the country's mainstream Sunni Muslim majority – not least because men and women worship together and alcohol is tolerated. Whereas Sunni Islam is the state religion, and imams are government employees whose sermons are centrally checked, Alevis are neither recognized by, nor receive funding from, the state, and worship semi-clandestinely in prayer halls known as *cemevis*. To complicate matters further for this little-understood group, they can be drawn from either the ethnically Turkish or ethnically Kurdish population, and, to avoid Sunni Muslim bigotry, virtually all are staunch supporters of the secularist/Kemalist regime.

not all one way, however; in 2010 a Christian İstanbul Armenian shot his sister and he new Muslim Turkish husband for marrying across the religious and ethnic frontier.

Some attempts at rapprochement have been made – the Turkish government's restoration of the long-neglected Armenian church on Akdamar island (see p.634) at least represents a start. Even if no Turkish government, fearful of demands for reparations, is likely to accept the events of 1915 as genocide, an increasing number of Turkish journalists, academics and ordinary citizens are prepared to acknowledge the events as ethnic cleansing. With the Armenian community worldwide gearing up to mark 2015's centenary of the "genocide", however, atop a hundred years of mutual suspicion and Armenia's refusal to withdraw from Nagorno-Karabagh, things are unlikely to get easier for Turkey's remaining Armenian community any time soon.

The Greeks

Mycenaean **Greeks** started to colonize Anatolia's Aegean coast as early as 1500 BC, so they can probably claim to be the oldest of the ethnic groups who have survived to the present day on modern Turkish soil. During the Byzantine Christian era, the Greeks were the dominant grouping in what's now Turkey. Now, referred to by Turks as **Rum**, they number under three thousand – a precipitous decline.

Greek history in Anatolia

From 1500 BC onwards, Greek-speaking peoples colonized first the Aegean coastline of Anatolia, and, later, parts of the Mediterranean and Black Sea coasts as well. Greek domination of the Aegean coastal belt was curbed by the Persians during the sixth century BC, but in the fourth century BC the victories of Alexander the Great helped to spread Greek culture throughout Anatolia and beyond. While Rome progressively annexed the region from the second century BC onwards, Greek language and culture remained dominant in the Greek city-states that the Romans absorbed into their empire. The Byzantine Empire subsequently developed as a Christian, Greek-speaking entity, with its capital in Constantinople.

It is to these Byzantine, eastern Orthodox Christian roots that today's tiny minority Greek Orthodox population – most of whom live either in İstanbul or on the Aegean islands of İmroz (Imbros) and Bozcaada (Tenedos) – look back. The inexorable Byzantine decline started as early as the seventh century, but the balance of power truly tilted with the arrival of the Muslim Turks in Anatolia following their crushing victory at Manzikert in 1071. As the Turks gradually brought Anatolia under their control, more and more Orthodox, Greek-speaking Christians converted to Islam and intermarried with their conquerors. The Ottoman Turkish capture of Constantinople in 1453 finally extinguished Christian power in Anatolia, but the Christians – Orthodox Greeks, Armenian and Syrian Orthodox among others – were allowed to run their own affairs through the *millet* (nation) system.

From the Capitulations to the population exchange

Following the introduction of the Capitulations in the sixteenth century (see p.655), the European traders who became increasingly influential in the Ottoman economy tended to favour their Christian brethren – and especially the Greeks. Although this arguably marked the start of Muslim-Turkish resentment, Turks and Greeks continued to get along, even after Greece itself won independence from the Ottoman Empire in 1830.

During World War I and its aftermath, the Greek presence in Anatolia was fatally compromised by the idea of a **Greater Greece**, to include not only the Greek state that had emerged in 1830, but also much of the Aegean and Black Sea coastline of Anatolia, where millions of Greeks still lived. A British-backed invasion by a Greek army ended in disaster for the Greeks from both Greece and Anatolia following a decisive victory for Turkish nationalists at Dumlupınar in 1923. The Treaty of Lausanne, signed on July 24, 1923, recognized the frontiers won by the Turks in the War of Independence.

There was no place for the Greeks in the new Turkish Republic. Some Pontic Greeks from the Black Sea had rebelled, other Greeks had agitated for independence from Ottoman Turkey. Now all were deemed treacherous and untrustworthy. In the internationally mediated **population exchange** of 1923, nearly all the Greek Orthodox Christians left in Turkey (some 1.3 million) were sent to Greece, while the Muslim Turkish population of Greece was sent to Turkey. Only the Greek Orthodox population of İstanbul was exempted, due to the importance of the Greek Orthodox Patriarchate in İstanbul.

The Greeks today

İstanbul held an estimated 297,000 Greeks in 1924. Many left after the Wealth Tax of 1942 unfairly targeted Turkey's minorities, while in 1955, looking for a distraction from the country's economic woes and with tensions high over Cyprus, Turkish PM Menderes deemed İstanbul's Greek minority a suitable scapegoat. Government-sponsored demonstrations soon got out of hand, and mobs ransacked Greek property. The police, apparently under orders not to intervene, stood and watched the mayhem. The riots were the beginning of the end for the city's Greek Orthodox Christian minority, many of whom left in the immediate aftermath. A further major exodus followed in 1964, again against the backdrop of nationalism inflamed by events in Cyprus, and by 1965 the Greek population was down to 48,000.

Today the 2500 or so Greek Orthodox Turkish citizens left in İstanbul are elderly, and the churches that still dot areas like Fener, the Princes' Islands and Beyoğlu virtually empty. Like the Armenians, under the Treaty of Lausanne they are recognized as an official minority and have their own schools, a newspaper (granted some funds by the Turkish government in 2011) and other organizations, but all are in severe decline. One remaining source of pride is the Greek Orthodox Patriarchate. Set on the banks of the Golden Horn in the İstanbul district of Fener, it's still, by tradition at least, the spiritual centre of the entire Eastern Orthodox Christian world.

The Syrian Orthodox

Adherents of the **Syrian Orthodox** Church (Süriyani in Turkish), who form a distinct, if much reduced, ethno-religious group of their own, are found mostly in the Syrian borderlands of southeast Turkey. Their origins lie with Jacobus Baradaeus, appointed bishop of Edessa in AD 543. A native of Mesopotamia, he was locked in a century-old theological dispute with the patriarchate in Constantinople about the divine nature of Christ. The ecclesiastical Council of Chalcedon (451 AD) ruled that Christ had both a human and a divine nature, but dissenting bishops throughout the Middle East held that Christ had only a divine nature – a creed known as monophysitism, whose adherents risked condemnation as heretics and excommunication.

An energetic proselytizer throughout what is now the Hatay and Syria, Baradaeus helped to revive his church as it suffered determined attack by the agents of Constantinopolitan orthodoxy. Under Arab dominion in the seventh century, Syrian Orthodox Christians enjoyed considerable religious freedom. By the time of the First Crusade, at the end of the eleventh century, the Tür Abdin in particular encompassed four bishoprics and eighty monasteries, the ruins of which remain dotted across the plateau. Ironically, the Christian Crusaders persecuted the "heretical" Syrian Orthodox Church, while the Mongols later massacred its adherents and pillaged its properties.

The Syrian Orthodox community enjoyed a long period of tolerance and stability under Ottoman rule. During World War I, though, tainted by association with Allied plans to dismember the Ottoman Empire, they suffered widespread persecution and massacre, a fate they shared with the Armenian and Greek minorities. Of today's global population of seven million Syrian Christians, only a few thousand are now left in Turkey, served by the bishoprics of Tür Abdin (Midyat/Mor Gabriel), Mardin (Deyr-az-Zaferan), Adiyaman and İstanbul. Many have emigrated to Europe (notably Sweden) and North America, but the seat of the patriarchy is in Damascus.

The Jews

There have been **Jews** in Anatolia since the fifth century BC. By and large they were tolerated by the Greeks, the Romans and, later, the Christian Byzantine Empire. Following the capture of Constantinople by the Ottoman Turks in 1453, many Jews from elsewhere in the Ottoman Empire were compelled to move to, and help regenerate, the new Ottoman capital. The Ottomans were incredibly tolerant in comparison to standards then prevalent in Western Europe; during the late fifteenth century, they gave sanctuary to over 150,000 Jews escaping persecution in Spain, most of whom settled in Salonika and Constantinople.

Like other non-Muslim minority groups within the Empire, the Jews prospered in their own partly self-governing *millet* (nation). By the eighteenth and nineteenth centuries, however, their wealth decreased, as the Greeks especially made the most of their Christian links with the European powers. During the early period of the Turkish Republic, the Jews did reasonably well, while Atatürk gave sanctuary (and employment) to Jewish academics expelled from Nazi Germany in the 1930s. Like all non-Muslim minority groups, the Jews fell victim to the unfair Wealth Tax of 1942, and many left following the creation of the state of Israel in 1948. The recent rift between an AKP-led Turkey and Israel in the wake of the *Mavi Marmara* (Gaza Flotilla) incident, and Turkish support for the Palestinians, has already resulted in increased emigration of Turkish Jews to Israel. The population has dropped from 23,000 to 17,000, the vast majority of whom live in İstanbul.

Turkish cinema

Turkey has had a moderately successful film industry since the 1950s, when corny rural-boy-meets-rural-girl melodramas provided escapism for Anatolian villagers. The outside world took little notice until the 1970s, when a few maverick filmmakers took Turkish cinema in a more radical direction.

1971–99: early successes

Although imprisoned for his leftist leanings several times during the 1970s and 1980s, popular actor-turned-director **Yılmaz Güney** produced a series of hard-hitting films in the years around the coups of 1971 and 1980. The best were *Sürü* ("The Herd"), which follows a Kurdish shepherd and his family taking their flock to sell in distant Ankara, and *Yol* ("The Road"). Written from the confines of his prison cell, with the outside directorial assistance of **Derif Gören**, *Yol* takes an allegorical look at the state of the nation (then still under martial law) by following the fortunes of five prisoners who have been allowed a week's parole. That the film was banned in Turkey only served to bring it to the notice of the international community, and in 1981 *Yol* was joint winner of the Palme d'Or. The film finally made it onto the country's cinema screens in 1999, when it played to packed houses. Güney died of cancer in 1984, aged 46, the year after the release of his last film, *Duvar* ("Wall"), an unrelentingly gloomy critique of the country's overcrowded and brutal prison system.

With the exception of 1983's visually stunning *Hakkâri'de Bir Mevsim* ("A Season in Hakkâri"), examining the experiences of a young teacher sent to staff the local school in a remote Kurdish village, Turkish films in the 1980s made little impact on the outside world. Despite a lack of financial backing, the 1990s proved kinder, and in 1994 **Erden Kıral**'s *Mavi Sürgün* ("The Blue Exile") was nominated for an Academy Award. In 1995, **Mustafa Altıoklar**'s *İstanbul Kanatlarımın Altında* ("İstanbul Beneath my Wings"), set in the seventeenth century during the reign of tyrant **Murat IV**, drew critical acclaim and was a box-office hit. **Hamam**, made in 1998 by **Ferzan Özpetek**,

---

BOX OFFICE SUCCESS

As in every country, what the critics adore, the vast majority of the public ignore. Ceylan's arty **Uzak** attracted some 20,000 cinema-goers within Turkey, whereas 2008's **Recep İvedik**, director Şahan Gökbakar's tale of an uneducated burping, farting and spitting taxi driver let loose in a five-star hotel, grossed $24 million domestically. Equally successful was 2006's ultra-nationalistic **Kurtlar Vadisi – Irak** ("Valley of the Wolves – Iraq"), a huge box-office action-thriller hit, in which the Turks get their fictional revenge for the real-life arrest of some of their military boys by the Americans in northern Iraq in 2003. Both films have spawned equally popular formulaic sequels.

Production in Turkey has boomed in recent years, with more and more films hitting the country's big screens (invariably today in shopping malls), and Turkish cinema is by far the most profitable in the Muslim world. Home-produced films are proving extraordinarily popular, taking a 55 percent slice of the domestic market. All the top five films in 2011 were Turkish productions, including glossy thriller *New York'ta Beş Minare* (Five Minarets in New York), which co-starred several Hollywood actors. Budgets are growing ever bigger as well, culminating in 2012's *Fetih 1453*, a CGI-filled sword-and-turban blockbuster about the siege and conquest of Constantinople by the Ottoman Turks in 1453. Its $17 million budget was huge by Turkish standards, but by April 2012 it had already repaid the investors' faith by grossing over $34 domestically – making it the most watched Turkish movie ever.

sees an Italian star inherit a run-down Turkish baths in İstanbul. Through his efforts to restore it, he discovers his own sexuality, making this one of the few Turkish films dealing with gay relationships to have gone on general release.

2000–2010: a worthy decade

The new millennium has seen Turkish cinema hit new heights. Leading the way is **Nuri Bilgi Ceylan**, who won the prestigious Best Director Award at Cannes in 2008 for *Üç Maymun* ("Three Monkeys"), which tells a familiar story of how power corrupts. In it a powerful politician involved in a hit-and-run incident escapes justice by sending his driver to prison in his place – and then sexually abuses the driver's wife. Ceylan had come to prominence with *Uzak* ("Distant"), a beautifully crafted, İstanbul-set film of urban alienation that won the Grand Prix award at Cannes. In between these two classics was the critically acclaimed but rather self-indulgent *Bklimler* ("Climates"), an existentialist tale of a failing relationship starring Ceylan and his wife, Ebru.

Fatih Akın, a German-born and -bred Turk, had both Turkey and Germany claiming his 2004 Golden Bear winner, *Duvar Karsısı* ("Head On"), as their own. Personalities and cultures clash in this sometimes brutal tale of ill-matched Turkish–German lovers. Akın's 2005 documentary *Crossing the Bridge: The Sound of Istanbul*, made with **Alexander Hacke**, has won many recent plaudits, and makes an unparalleled introduction to this great city's music scene (see p.692). 2007's *Yadamın Kıyısında* ("Edge of Heaven") won the best screenplay award at Cannes, and five awards at Turkey's equivalent of the Oscars, Antalya's Golden Orange festival. Shot in Germany, İstanbul and the eastern Black Sea city of Trabzon, it traces the interconnecting lives of four Turks and two Germans, touching on issues of cultural estrangement, family relationships, lesbianism and political activism.

Other Turkish films to have achieved critical accolades during the first decade of the twenty-first century include **Reha Erdem**'s 2006 *Bed Vakıt* ("Times and Winds"), which portrays the often-grim reality of growing up in an idyllic-looking Turkish village. It makes moving use of both the village's breathtaking location, overlooking the Mediterranean from a cliff-edge eyrie, and the fresh-faced innocence of its child actors. 2007's *Yumurta* ("Egg"), the first part of a trilogy directed by **Semih Kaplanoulu**, won a fistful of awards at the Golden Orange. A typically Turkish tale, it traces the life of Yusuf, a struggling poet running a secondhand bookshop in İstanbul who returns to his home town when his mother dies. The second part of the trilogy, *Süt* ("Milk"), winds back the clock to Yusuf's youth in his hometown, where he struggles financially trying to balance the family's milk business with writing poetry. 2010's *Bal* ("Honey"), the final part of the trilogy, won a Golden Bear at the Berlin International Film Festival and is set in the wild mountains of the eastern Black Sea. Based on a true story, 2008's *Gitmek* ("My Marlon, My Brando"), the first feature from respected documentary filmmaker **Hüseyin Karabey**, is the gripping story of a Turkish woman's search for her Kurdish lover, trapped in northern Iraq following the American invasion of 2003. The emotionally candid theatre actress Ayça leaves a rather grim-looking Beyoğlu, crosses snowy Anatolia and enters Iran, hoping to meet her B-movie actor lover, Hamal Ali, on the Iran–Iraq border.

Recent releases: more critical accolades

Of recent acclaimed releases, *Iki Dil Bir Bavul* ("On the Way to School"), a heart-warming documentary about the trials and tribulations of a Turkish teacher from the affluent west trying to teach in a dirt-poor village school in the ethnically Kurdish southeast, won directors **Orhan Eskiköy** and **Özgür Doğan** the best first film award at Antalya's Golden Orange Film Festival. *Çoğunluk* ("Majority"), a 2011 offering from director **Seren Yüce**, showed a side of İstanbul that few visitors are likely (or indeed want) to see. Set in unremittingly dull concrete suburbs, it tells the grubby but all-too-believable tale of a middle-class Turk, still living at home in his late twenties, attempting to subvert the brutal authority of his manipulative father by getting involved with the most "unsuitable" of women, an impoverished Kurdish waitress.

2011 also saw a return to top form for **Nuri Bilge Ceylan**, whose *Bir Zamanlar Anadolu'da* ("Once Upon a Time in Anatolia") was co-winner of the Grand Prix at Cannes. Set in small-town Anatolia, it's a murder story of sorts but, as you would expect from Ceylan, is far stronger on atmosphere and mood than plot. 2011's *Zenne* ("Zenne Dancer"), directed by Caner Alpay, won a host of domestic and international awards for its gripping tale of the murder of a male belly dancer – all the more powerful for being based on true events. The same year's *Yürüyüş* ("Walking") by **Shiar Abdi** and **Selamo**, set in the dusty, ethnically Kurdish Syrian border town of Nusaybin during the lead-up to the 1980 military coup, vividly evokes – through the eyes of a disturbed old man and a young boy – the horrors of the period.

Turkish music

Overseas, Turkish music was long considered mere accompaniment to belly dancing or, more recently, to Mevlevi ("Whirling") dervish ritual. But beyond these stereotypes there's far more, from refined classical to camp Arabesk by way of rural bards and fiery Gypsy ensembles. Turkish music is at best the millennial legacy of the many Anatolian civilizations, at worst globally marketed pop music with a bit of exotic colour. Thankfully, it has managed to maintain both its creativity and popularity – even with the younger generation – though this has not prevented the rise of a lively, Western-influenced rock, pop and even hip-hop scene.

Traditional Turkish music

Traditional sounds have more than held their own in this fast-changing country. Channel-surf Turkish TV any evening, and you're bound to hit upon a show or two devoted to native Turkish music, with a moustached bard coaxing melancholic Anatolian folk songs from his *saz* or *bağlama* (types of lute), or an orchestra of tuxedo-ed men and sombrely clad women solemnly accompanying a warbling *sanatçi* (singer of Turkish classical music). **Arabesk**, an Arab/Egyptian-influenced style of music invariably charting the singers' wretched lot in life, remains extremely popular, especially among the poor and dispossessed. Its most famous proponent, **İbrahim Tatlıses**, is a national institution, and until a drive-by shooting in İstanbul in 2010 left him paralyzed, hosted his own enormously popular TV show. *Türkü* bars (see p.127) are devoted to the various lovelorn strands of **halk muziği** – best translated as people's or folk music – and are very popular with the younger generation.

Played mainly by Roma (Gypsy) bands, **fasil**, a curious but lively hybrid of Ottoman classical and folk, with violins, clarinets, *darbuka* drums and powerful, emotive vocals to the fore, is the genre of İstanbul's vibrant **meyhane** scene (see p.127). The hypnotic, spiritual strains of **Sufi** music, most often associated with the Mevlevi or "whirling" dervish order, and popular among world-music aficionados, is very much a minority interest in its home country, though it can be heard in various places across the country wherever the dervishes "whirl" for visitors – for example at the Mevlevihanesi in İstanbul's Galata district (see p.101), in Konya (see p.423), or in Cappadocia (see p.430).

Turkish classical or **sanat** music is the most inaccessible home-grown style to foreign ears – and, despite the undoubted virtuosity of its leading musicians, the least popular domestically. Originating in the Ottoman court, this subtle, partly improvisational but often gloomy-sounding music is performed by chamber orchestras using a combination of traditional Turkish wind and string instruments backed by drums.

Many popular singers in Turkey are of Kurdish origin, though they usually perform in Turkish. Now that restrictions on singing (and speaking) Kurdish have been lifted, it's easy to obtain CDs by Kurdish artists singing in their native tongue. The doyen of Kurdish performers is **Şivan Perwer**, who chronicles the plight of his people with his powerful voice and stunning *saz* playing. Some of his CDs are still banned in Turkey because of their politics, and he lives in exile in Sweden. Other well-regarded Kurdish artists include Aynur Doğan, Ciwan Haco and Rojin.

SELECTED DISCOGRAPHY

ARABESK

İbrahim Tatlıses *Fosforlu Cevriyem* (Emre). This live recording offers a rare chance to hear what *Arabesk* sounds like in the flesh, and gives a sense of Tatlıses' phenomenal vocal presence. Includes some of his all-time favourites, plus superb *uzun hava* semi-improvisations.

FOLK

Belkis Akkale *Türkü Türkü Türkiyem* (Sembol Plak). One of the greatest female *türkü* singers at her earthiest, carried along by driving *saz* rhythms – plus almost all of the traditional instruments of Turkey.

FASIL

Karşılama *Karşılama* (Green Goat, Canada/Kalan). İstanbul Gypsy musicians led by Selim Sesler on G-clarinet, with locally trained Canadian vocalist Brenna MacCrimmon, interpret Roma music from western Turkey and the Balkans. Played with real panache, and it's good to have some of the vocal repertoire – gleaned from archival recordings and manuscripts – expertly showcased.

SUFI

Mevlana *Dede Efendi Saba Ayini* (Kalan). A benchmark recording of a complete Mevlevi suite (*ayin*) composed by Dede Efendi. The performers read like a who's-who of early twentieth-century Turkish *sanat*, with Mesut Cemil on cello, Akagündüz Kutbay, Ulvi Erguner and Niyazi Sayın on the wind instrument known as a *ney*, Cüneyt Orhan on *kemençe* (a kind of violin) and Saadettin Heper on *küdüm* (kettle drum).

SANAT

Mesut Cemil *Early Recordings (Vol 1)* and *Instrumental and Vocal recordings (Vols 2–3)* (Golden Horn Records/US). Virtuoso musicianship and compositions from the man who ran the classical music section of TRT-İstanbul for decades.

KURDISH

Şivan Perwer *Zembilfroş* (Ses Plak 1992). One of Perwer's most varied albums, partly because he is accompanied by his wife Gülistan. The vocals by the talented pair are outstanding, soaring above Perwer's insistent *saz* playing and some lush orchestration.

Music documentaries

Nezih Ezen's 2008 documentary, **Lost Songs of Anatolia** (Ⓦlostsongsofanatolia.com), provides the best introduction to a whole range of traditional Turkish music. A talented musician himself, Ezen's unsentimental but sensitive film was a labour of love some five years in the making. Travelling across Turkey's vast landscape, recording and filming in obscure towns and remote villages, he vividly captures the musical heritage of modern Turkey, deeply rooted in the many ethnic and cultural identities that make up the nation.

In the rain-soaked mountains of the eastern Black Sea, Laz (a Caucasian people who speak a language related to Georgian) dance the *horon* (a line dance) to the sound of the *kemençe* (upright fiddle) and *tulum* (bagpipe), while in the mountains of Bingöl a *dengbey* (Kurdish bard) uses only his voice to chart the history of his people. In an İstanbul apartment, a couple of elderly Armenian ladies sing a moving lament to an Anatolia long lost to them, while in the same city an ethnically Greek ensemble play a "Greek blues" *rebétika* number. A couple of rake-thin elderly bards in a smoky teahouse in the Armenian border-town of Kars play the *saz* and battle out an instrument- and lyric-based duel; in the cotton fields of the Çukurova near Adana a group of young women from Diyarbakir, poorly paid seasonal workers, find solace from their back-breaking labour in song. The DVD is reasonably easy to obtain in Turkey but you will have to rely on the power of the songs and fabulous scenery, as there are no English subtitles.

Although much of Fatih Akın's documentary **Crossing the Bridge** concentrates on contemporary music in İstanbul, there is plenty to keep traditional music buffs happy. It features the superb vocals and even better *saz* playing of Orhan Gençbay, a legend rivalled only by İbrahim Tatlıses in Arabesk music, and the heart-rending voice of the young Kurdish singer Aynur Dogan. The haunting sounds of Mercan Dede, a fusion of Sufi and modern electronica and big on the world music scene, get an airing, as do the Balkan sounds of Selim Sesler, playing with an unlikely (but very talented) singer of traditional Turkish songs, Canadian Brenna MacCrimmon. Difficult to buy for a sensible price in the UK, it's far cheaper in the US. The DVD is also widely available in İstanbul, but you'll struggle to find a copy with English subtitles.

Contemporary music

Pop has a surprisingly long history in Turkey, from the Tango stars of the 1930s through to Elvis imitators in the 1950s. Not until the 1970s, though, did **rock** really take root, with the rise of the Anadolu (Anatolian) rock movement. Western-style contemporary music now forms part and parcel of the diverse Turkish music scene, especially in cosmopolitan İstanbul. The vast majority of these bands and singers perform in Turkish, which undermines their chances of achieving international success. But the best of them are worth a listen – and if you venture out into the city's labyrinthine **nightlife** scene you are bound, at some point, to have your ears assailed by familiar pop or hip-hop beats, accompanied by unfamiliar Turkish vocals.

Rock

Duman are among the most accessible of the current crop of rock bands. Erroneously labelled punk in their early days (itself indicative of the relatively conservative nature of the scene here), the İstanbul-based group are in fact a straightforward rock band, mixing up-tempo anthems with lighter-waving ballads and traditional Turkish folk songs. *Bu akşam* ("This evening") and *Belki alışmam lazım* ("Maybe I'd better get used to it") are great songs by any standards.

   Pinhani shot to fame when some of their songs were used in the popular TV soap *Kavak Yelleri* ("Young and Carefree"), but don't let this put you off. Despite the number of disparate influences in their music – everything from Radiohead and the late, great Alevi troubadour Aşık Veysel to Greek *bouzouki* and Bach – their album *İnandığım Masallar* ("Fairy tales you can believe in") is a wonderfully laidback, melodic and cohesive debut. Both bands have written paeans to their hometown, Duman's *İstanbul* an angry, punky thrash, while Pinhani's *In İstanbul* drips with urban melancholia.

   Fellow "Stamboul" boys **Mor ve Ötesi** formed in 1995 and have built up a huge following in Turkey – in 2003 the indie four-piece played in front of 100,000 anti-Iraq war demonstrators in Ankara. Surprisingly, given their reputation for protest, they were chosen to represent Turkey in the 2008 **Eurovision Song Contest**, with *Deli* ("Crazy") coming in seventh. Bear in mind that in Turkey the Eurovision Song Contest is not seen as the laughably kitsch endeavour it is across much of Europe – in this most patriotic of nations it's taken very seriously indeed.

   Sertab Erener, the İstanbul-born belly-dancing diva who won the contest for Turkey in 2003 was, like Mor ve Ötesi, already a major star before the competition. She has recorded an album in English, and appeared in **Fatih Akın's** *Crossing the Bridge* documentary singing an orientalized version of Madonna's *Music*.

   Another couple of bands who feature in Akın's *Crossing the Bridge* are **Baba Zula** and **Replikas**. Prog-rockers Replikas take extended, experimental soloing to extremes but are talented musicians with a loyal following. Baba Zula may be wacky, but their self-styled "oriental-dub" or "psyche-belly" is mesmeric live, and with their 1960s hippie-throwback looks (big beards, long straggly hair, cowboy hats) and very un-PC belly dancer they're entertaining performers.

Far more popular is **Şebnem Ferah**. Born in Yalova, near Bursa, she is of Balkan (Macedonian) ancestry. Her goth-metal looks, powerful voice and the helping hand of that doyenne of the Turkish music scene, **Sezen Aksu**, have helped secure her fame – though her brand of soft rock and power ballads will not be to everyone's taste. **Hayko Çepkin**, of Armenian origin, mixes Anatolian rock with scream metal and a lively stage act. Long-established punks **Rashit** have played with the likes of the Dead Kennedys and the Offspring; their 2005 album *Herşeyin Bir Bedeli Var* was released on Sony.

Hip-hop

The roots of the **rap** scene in Turkey lie among the Turkish community in Germany. Invariably urban, often poor, disenfranchised and discriminated against, hip-hop provided a natural outlet for their anger and frustration. The movement was kick-started by the suitably controversial **Cartel** in the mid-1990s. Their debut album was banned in Turkey and the group split soon after. The scene in İstanbul really got going with another star of *Crossing the Bridge* (see p.688), the city's very own Eminem – **Ceza**. Worshipped by multitudes of the city's disaffected youth, he was born on the Asian side of the Bosphorus in Üsküdar, taking his stage name (*ceza* means punishment) from one of his early jobs – handing out fines to people who failed to pay their electricity bills. Ceza's success has bred envy, and in 2007 he was accused of lifting his beats straight from Eminem by rival İstanbul rapper **Ege Çubukçu**. Other names to look out for are **Sagopa Kajmer** and Ceza's sister, **Ayben**. Turkish vocals apart, what marks this home-grown hip-hop out from its US inspiration is the sampling of *Arabesk* and other forms of traditional Turkish music rather than Western pop.

Pop

Pop music is huge in Turkey. It's also incredibly varied – though you might not think so on a first listen. Once a teen idol, now a housewives' favourite, **Tarkan** swivels his hips and belts out dance-oriented pop with apparent abandon. A big star in Germany as well as Turkey, he has produced one album in English.

Pop rockers/balladeers **Mustafa Sandal** and **Teoman** are firm fixtures on the TV music channels (see box, p.50), as is the chanteuse **Yıldız Tilbe**. The multi-talented queen of the Turkish pop scene, **Sezen Aksu**, has helped to preserve and build upon the best of traditional Turkish urban music, both through skilfully updated covers of old songs and with new material incorporating their best elements. Nor is she afraid of controversy, tackling feminism, human rights and ethnic cleansing in Bosnia and singing in Ladino (the language of Turkey's Jewish population) and Kurdish as well as her native Turkish. Her albums vary enormously in style, but 1995's *Işık Doğudan Yükselir* ("The Light Rises from the East") makes a good starting point. Another queen of the scene is the incredibly well-preserved, İstanbul-schooled **Ajda Pekkan**. Born in 1946 and still touring, she has sold some thirty million albums worldwide and is a national icon.

Books

There are numerous books about every aspect of Turkey in English, many recently published or reissued. Books with Turkish publishers are rarely available outside Turkey. In the recommendations below, "o/p" means out of print, but almost all such books can be easily found through websites such as ⓦabe.com/.co.uk or ⓦbookfinder.com.

Turkish writers

Given that Atatürk's language and alphabet reforms in the early years of the Turkish Republic effectively cut off the vast majority of its citizens from the language of their Ottoman imperial past – and therefore of its literature – it's hardly surprising that it took some time for new generations of Turkish writers to establish themselves in what was a very different world.

Equally, relatively few Turkish writers have had their works translated into other languages, and today the works of only two novelists are widely available in English, Orhan Pamuk and Elif Shafak. A limited number of books by two earlier writers of note, Orhan Kemal and Yaşar Kemal, are available in English, and several Turkish publishing houses produce English-language versions of novels by Turkish authors that are generally only easily available within the country.

Orhan Kemal

Born in the then-Ottoman Turkish city of Adana in 1914, **Orhan Kemal** is sometime viewed as a Turkish Dickens. His simply told tales, many based around his own experiences, invariably deal with the lot of the poor, the dispossessed and political dissidents. His family were affluent until his father's political opinions put him at odds with the ruling Kemalist regime, and they were forced to flee the country. An impoverished Kemal eventually returned to his beloved Turkey, where he started at the bottom of the ladder as a weaver in a cotton factory, then as a clerk. His imprisonment in 1938 for his leftist beliefs was the turning point in his life, as there he met the famous communist poet Nazim Hikmet, who encouraged his literary aspirations. Kemal struggled to make ends meet for the rest of his life, combining relatively menial office work with his writing, leaving a legacy of 38 touching stories before he died, in Sofia, in 1970.

The best introduction to Orhan Kemal's work is **The Idle Years**, which in the English version combines two semi-autobiographical tales, **My Father's House** and **The Idle Years**. The two stories recount, in deceptively simple prose, the story of the author's life from his youth in Adana, through his family's Beirut exile, to his marriage to a factory girl in Adana. Also worth reading is his account of his years of incarceration, **In Jail With Nazim Hikmet**.

Yaşar Kemal

Until the advent of Orhan Pamuk and Elif Shafak, **Yaşar Kemal** was by far Turkey's best-known novelist, in part thanks to English translations by his wife Thilda of seventeen of his titles. Indeed, so widely known was Kemal that one of his early works, **Mehmed My Hawk**, was turned into a film (1984) of the same name starring Peter Ustinov.

Although of Kurdish origins, Kemal was born (in 1923) and raised close to the cotton-growing Çukurova plain, in the shadow of the Toros mountains, in southern Turkey. Here he witnessed first-hand the exploitation of the rural peasantry by wealthy landowners. Championing the oppressed has been a *leitmotif* of Kemal's works ever since,

espite the fact he himself escaped his family's rural origins and, following a stint at
niversity in İstanbul, became a petition writer, journalist and, finally, author. Although
e was nominated for the Nobel Prize in Literature in 1973, his nonconformist views
onetheless brought him into conflict with the state, and in 1995 he was prosecuted for
is support for Turkey's Kurdish minority following an interview he gave to *Der Spiegel*.
Kemal's older books are powerful epics set in southern Anatolia and include the
loving *Mehmed My Hawk* and its sequel **They Burn the Thistles** (o/p). The **Wind from
ie Plain** trilogy deals with similar themes and is equally hard-hitting. Later novels
iclude **The Sea-Crossed Fishermen** (o/p), contrasting an old man's struggle to save the
olphins in the Sea of Marmara with the fortunes of a desperate hoodlum in the city,
nd **The Birds Have Also Gone** (o/p), a symbolic, gentle story about bird-catchers. In the
iore recent **Salman the Solitary**, Kemal returns to his native Çukurova with a tale of a
isplaced Kurdish family.

rhan Pamuk

1ost Turks just don't know what to make of their nation's first Nobel Prize-winning
ovelist, **Orhan Pamuk**, who was born into a wealthy family in the posh İstanbul
ıburb of Nişantaşı. To the liberal left, he's a talented writer who dares to challenge the
Lemalist, nationalist-orientated establishment – who in turn accuse him of betraying
is country. Moderates are happy to bask in the success of one of their nation's sons
rithout questioning his beliefs too closely; many others are quick to condemn him
vhilst studiously avoiding reading any of his output.

The controversy surrounding Pamuk began in 2004, when the previously cautious
ovelist granted an interview to a Swiss newspaper and was reported as saying "I am
he only one willing to say that one million Armenians and thirty thousand Kurds were
iurdered in Turkey". He was accused of "insulting Turkishness", a crime under article
01 of the Turkish Constitution. Although the accusation was subsequently dropped,
n 2008 it emerged that Pamuk may have been the assassination target of an ultra-
iationalist "deep-state" gang working within the establishment. As a result, he now
pends most of his time abroad.

What's surprising is that such a storm has broken over the head of this benign-
looking, fifty-something intellectual. An urbane, cerebral author, his early works dealt
vith cultural and philosophical rather than political issues, and not until 2004's *Snow*
lid he engage in any kind of political discourse. Many Turkish cynics, however, believe
hat by bringing up two of the nation's "sacred cows" – the so-called Armenian
Genocide and the "Kurdish problem" – he was deliberately courting what they saw as
he anti-Turkish West in the hope of winning the Nobel Prize. Such machinations are
inlikely, although his open rejection of nationalism in a country still in nation-
iuilding mode makes him an object of suspicion.

Pamuk's enduring concerns are Turkey's often-corrosive encounter with the West, and
he irrepressibility of its Islamic heritage. His debut, **The White Castle**, was an excellent
iistorical meditation about a seventeenth-century Italian scholar enslaved by an
)ttoman astronomer, but he arrived on the world literature scene with 1998's **The New
ife**, which despite its unappealing narrator and slight tale had foreign critics hailing the
ieir-apparent of Calvino and Borges. **Snow**, Pamuk's most controversial and political
iovel, is arguably his best. Set in bleak, northeastern Kars, it examines once-taboo topics
uch as political Islam and Kurdish nationalism. His latest novel, the mammoth **The
Iuseum of Innocence**, is a fictional memoir of *amour fou* set in late 1970s İstanbul.
>stanbul: Memories of a City is a moving reflection on the author's troubled relationship
vith himself, his parents, and the city in which he was born and raised.

Elif Shafak

3orn of Turkish parents in Strasbourg in 1971, brought up from the age of one by her
ingle mother, raised in Spain and Jordan and now, following several years in the USA,

residing in London, **Elif Shafak** is very much a product of the new, fast-changing, more international Turkey. Several of her books have been bestsellers domestically, challenging the traditional male domination of Turkey's literary scene. All this from a woman who is a political science rather than a literature graduate, and who writes in English first, then has the work translated into Turkish before re-working it. The photogenic Shafak found herself, like Pamuk, a target of establishment ire for her 200?, *The Bastard of Istanbul*, and was prosecuted under article 301 for "insulting Turkishness", though the charges were eventually dropped.

The Flea Palace interweaves tragic-comic lives in a once-grand İstanbul apartment block built atop an old cemetery. **The Bastard of Istanbul** tells the tale of an exuberant, if dysfunctional, Turkish family hosting an Armenian-American girl in search of her identity. Well-drawn, strong female characters drive a narrative that inevitably delves into Ottoman Turkey's treatment of its Armenians. Shafak's critically acclaimed 2011 follow-up, **The Forty Rules of Love**, centres less controversially on a woman's search for spiritual awareness through the teachings of the thirteenth-century Islamic mysticism of the Mevlana (Rumi) – a subject dear to the Sufi-influenced author's heart. Even better i; **Honour** (2012), set in southeast Turkey, İstanbul and London, which brings to life a ver real socio-cultural problem in contemporary Turkey – honour killings, the murder by a male family member of a woman deemed to have brought shame on the family.

THE CLASSICS

Herodotus *The Histories*. A fifth-century BC citizen of Halikarnassos (Bodrum), Herodotus – the first systematic historian/anthropologist – described the Persian Wars and assorted nations of Anatolia.

Strabo *Geography*. A native of the Pontus, Strabo travelled widely across the Mediterranean; our best (multi-volume) document of Roman Anatolia.

Xenophon *Anabasis*, or *The March Up-Country* (best as th abridged *The Persian Expedition*). The Athenian leader the Ten Thousand, mercenaries for Persian king Cyrus th Younger, led the long retreat from Cunaxa to the Black Se. An ancient travel classic that's still mined for titbits ethnology, archeology and geography.

ANCIENT HISTORY AND ARCHEOLOGY

Ian Hodder *Çatalhöyük: The Leopard's Tale*. Neolithic Çatal Höyük is one of the world's earliest cities, and thus crucial to the origins of Western civilization. This reasonably accessible book, written by the principal excavator, brings it to life.

Seton Lloyd *Ancient Turkey – A Traveller's History of Anatolia*. Accessibly written by a former head of Ankara's British Archeological Institut, without sacrificing detail and research results.

J.G. Macqueen *The Hittites and Their Contemporaries in*

Asia Minor. Well-illustrated general history of the first grea Anatolian civilization (c.1800–1200 BC).

Anthony Sagona and Paul Zamansky *Ancient Turke* Comprehensive coverage of the archeology of Turkey, fro early prehistory up to the Classical era. A textbook, but worthy and very readable one.

David Traill *Schliemann of Troy: Treasure and Deceit* (o/p The man versus his self-promulgated myth. This portray of the crumbling edifice of Schliemann's reputation als helps bring the old walls of Troy to life.

BYZANTINE HISTORY

★ **Roger Crowley** *Constantinople*. Former İstanbul resident Crowley's 2005 account of the 1453 siege is more detailed than Runciman's (see p.697), but the pace never flags.

Jonathan Harris *Constantinople: Capital of Byzantium*. Although this very accessible book concentrates on Constantinople circa 1200, its scope is inevitably much wider, making it a great introduction to the Byzantine city for the uninitiated.

Cyril Mango *Byzantium: The Empire of the New Rome*. Survey of daily life, economic policy and taxation, scholarship, cosmology and superstition, among other

topics. The newer, more lavishly illustrated *Oxford History* Byzantium, edited by Mango, will also appeal.

★ **John Julius Norwich** *Byzantium: The Early Centuries Byzantium: The Apogee* and *Byzantium: The Decline* Astonishingly detailed trilogy, a well-informed and wittil readable account (there's a single-volume abridgement, *Short History of Byzantium*).

Procopius *The Secret History*. Often raunchy demolitio job of Justinian and his sluttish empress, Theodora, fron the imperial general Belisarius's official chronicle Belisarius, one of the greatest Byzantine generals, is (lik Justinian) portrayed as spinelessly uxorious.

teven Runciman *Byzantine Style and Civilisation* (o/p). even centuries of Byzantine art, culture and monuments one small paperback; still unsurpassed. His *The Fall of nstantinople, 1453* remains the classic account of the ent, while *The Great Church in Captivity*, about Orthodoxy

under the Ottomans, is readable if partisan.
Speros Vryonis *The Decline of Medieval Hellenism in Asia Minor and the Process of Islamization from the Eleventh through the Fifteenth Century*. The definitive study of how the Byzantine Empire culturally became the Ottoman Empire.

TTOMAN HISTORY

★ **Caroline Finkel** *Osman's Dream*. Meticulously searched yet engaging history of the Ottoman Empire, om twelfth-century origins to collapse.

alil İnalcık *The Ottoman Empire 1300–1600*. Ever since appeared in 1973, this has been the standard work.

atrick Balfour Kinross *The Ottoman Centuries*. omprehensive, balanced summary of Ottoman history om the fourteenth to the twentieth century.

etin Kunt and Christine Woodhead *Süleyman the agnificent and His Age*. Concise summary of the greatest

Ottoman sultan's reign and its cultural renaissance.

★ **Philip Mansel** *Constantinople: City of the World's Desire, 1453–1924*. Nostalgic, faintly anti-Republican popular history, organized topically as well as chronologically. Obscure, intriguing factoids abound – Boğaziçi University began life as a hotbed of Bulgarian nationalism; Russian floozies have previously (1920–22) held Turkish men in thrall. The highlights of his *Sultans in Splendour – Monarchs of the Middle East, 1869–1945* are rare photos of characters from the late Ottoman Empire.

MODERN HISTORIES

eroz Ahmad *The Making of Modern Turkey*. Not the most rthodox history: lively, partisan and full of wonderful necdotes and quotes you'll find nowhere else. His more cent *Turkey: The Quest for Identity* updates matters to 2003.

Marjorie Housepian Dobkin *Smyrna 1922: The estruction of a City*. Partisan (ie rabidly anti-Turkish) but holarly and harrowingly graphic account of the sack of mir, when about 150,000 of the 400,000 Armenians and reeks trapped in the city were killed. Focuses on why the lied powers failed to act and subsequently covered up the cident.

Michael Hickey *Gallipoli: A Study in Failure*. Currently the est history of the campaign.

ean McMeekin *The Berlin–Baghdad Express*. In this veting cautionary tale, McMeekin shows how German ttempts to expand their influence into Turkey and the iddle East, by building a railway and raising Islamic Jihad mong the British Empire's Muslim subjects, have had far-aching consequences.

★ **Giles Milton** *Paradise Lost: Smyrna 1922*. Wonderful, ultimately heartbreaking, picture of Smyrna (İzmir) at he time of its destruction, towards the end of the Turkish Var of Independence.

★ **Barry Rubin** *Istanbul Intrigues: A True-Life Casablanca* (o/p). Unputdownable account of Allied/Axis activities in neutral Turkey during World War II, and their attempts to drag it into the conflict. Surprising revelations about the extent of Turkish aid for Britain, the US and the Greek resistance.

Antonio Sagona *The Heritage of Eastern Turkey*. Copiously illustrated guide to the archeology and history of neglected eastern Turkey, covering everything from the Neolithic to the Selçuk periods.

Richard Stoneman *A Traveller's History of Turkey*. Easy-reading volume, updated to 2009, which touches all bases from Paleolithic times to the AK government.

Speros Vryonis *The Mechanism of Catastrophe: The Turkish Pogrom Of September 6–7, 1955, And The Destruction Of The Greek Community Of Istanbul*. Remarkably impartial considering the author's Greek background; shows how the Menderes government and police actively aided the rampaging mobs.

★ **Erik J. Zürcher** *Turkey, A Modern History*. If you have time for only one book covering the post-1800 period, make it this one (revised up to 2004), which breathes revisionist fresh air over the received truths of the era.

BIOGRAPHIES

aime Göksu and Edward Timms *Romantic ommunist: The Life and Work of Nazım Hikmet*. The efinitive biography of Turkey's most controversial modern oet, who rubbed shoulders with Pablo Neruda, Jean-Paul artre and Paul Robeson. Banned and imprisoned for eventeen years at home, Hikmet spent much of his life in xile, dying in 1963 in Moscow.

hea Halo *Not Even My Name*. Remarkable, moving story f a Pontic-Greek girl, caught up in the 1920s ethnic leansing, who managed to escape to America. Aged 79

she returns, in the company of her daughter, the author, to her birthplace in the Black Sea mountains.

M. Şükrü Hanioğlu *Atatürk, an intellectual biography*. Intelligently written account focusing on the ideological development of Turkey's founder. If you want to know why modern Turkey is full of such paradoxes, you'll find out by reading this masterful book by a Princeton professor.

Patrick Balfour Kinross *Atatürk, the Rebirth of a Nation*. Long considered the definitive English biography – as opposed to hagiography – of the father of the

Republic, and still preferred by some to the newer Mango text (see p.698).

Andrew Mango *Atatürk*. Does not supersede Kinross's more readable tome, but complements it. Authoritative,

but also steeped in military and conspiratorial minutia. Sympathetic to its subject, and the Turkish national proje overall; the post-1922 population exchanges and th Armenian episodes rate hardly a mention.

ETHNIC MINORITIES AND RELIGION

★ **Taner Akçam** *From Empire to Republic: Turkish Nationalism and the Armenian Genocide*. Brilliant study by a Turkish academic resident in the US, which shows how the ethnic cleansing of the Armenian population from 1895 to 1923, and subsequent suppression of any memory of these events, was essential for Turkish nationalism – and remains at the root of the Republic's modern problems. His more recent *A Shameful Act: The Armenian Genocide and the Question of Turkish Responsibility*, focuses more closely on how CUP nationalist ideology bred the massacres.

Peter Balakian *The Burning Tigris: the Armenian Genocide and America's Response*. As partisan as you'd expect from an Armenian-American, but nonetheless a compelling analysis of the background to, and execution of, the massacres. Strong evidence from American and European missionaries in the region; harrowing photographs.

Donald Bloxham *The Great Game of Genocide*. This scholarly and coherent historical inquiry doesn't question whether there was a genocide, but rather concentrates on explaining – in the most dispassionate way – why and how it happened.

★ **Bruce Clark** *Twice a Stranger: How Mass Expulsion Forged Modern Greece and Turkey*. The build-up to and execution of the 1923 population exchanges, and how both countries are still digesting the experience nine decades on. Readable and compassionate, especially encounters with surviving elderly refugees.

William Dalrymple *From the Holy Mountain: A Journey in the Shadow of Byzantium*. Retraces a classic sixth-century monkish journey through the Near East. Section II is devoted to Turkey, and Dalrymple takes a suitably dim view

of the sorry history and current poor treatment of Christia and their monuments in eastern Turkey.

John Freely *The Lost Messiah: In Search of the Mystic Rabbi Sabbatai Sevi*. Story of the millennial, Kabbalist seventeenth-century movement in İzmir and Saloni that engendered the Dönme, a crypto-Judaic se disproportionately prominent in modern Turkish histor

F.W. Hasluck *Christianity and Islam under the Sultan* Ample documentation of shrines and festivals, the veneration and attendance by different sects at the turn the last century, plus Christian and pagan contributions Bektaşi and Alevî rites. Great for dipping into, though a b repetitive since edited posthumously.

Aliza Marcus *Blood and Belief: The PKK and the Kurdis Fight for Independence*. Definitive, if controversial, study c the organization; neither the Turkish state nor the PK (especially its leader, Abdullah Ocalan) get an easy ride.

★ **David McDowall** *A Modern History of the Kurd* About a third of this book is devoted to Turkey's Kurds, th balance to those in Iran and Iraq – few states get hig marks here for their treatment of Kurds, up to 2003.

Jonathan Rugman and Roger Hutchings *Atatürk Children: Turkey and the Kurds*. Excellent, even-hande handling of the topic up to 2001 by (in part) the *Guardian* former Turkey correspondent.

Gordon Taylor *Fever and Thirst: An American Doct Amongst the Tribes of Kurdistan 1835–1844*. The war-tor but stunningly beautiful mountains of Hakkari in southea Turkey were once home to a remote Christian group wh caught the imagination of the West. This account of a American doctor-cum-missionary working among th Nestorians is compelling reading.

VIEWS OF CONTEMPORARY TURKEY

Tim Kelsey *Dervish: The Invention of Modern Turkey*. The troubled soul of the 1990s country, sought among minority communities, faith healers, bulging prisons, brothels and the transsexual underground, plus the mystics of the title; pitiless analysis of Turkish angst, with little optimism for the future.

Stephen Kinzer *Crescent and Star: Turkey Between Two Worlds*. Entertaining account from a former *New York Times* bureau chief in İstanbul. Whether rakı-drinking or nargile-toking with ordinary Turks, interviewing politicos, swimming across the Bosphorus or DJ-ing his own Turkish radio show, Kinzer brings the country to life.

Chris Morris *The New Turkey: The Quiet Revolution on the Edge of Europe*. Long Turkey's BBC correspondent, Morris writes accessibly on the usual topics: political Islam, Greeks

and Armenians, the Kurdish question, Turkey's EU quest. A ideal introduction to contemporary Turkey.

★ **Nicole and Hugh Pope** *Turkey Unveiled*. Interlinke essays, arranged topically and chronologically, by tw foreign correspondents who over two decades got understand Turkey pretty well. Good grasp of Kurdish- an Europe-related issues. Despite their affection for th country, unflinching description of its shortcoming Updated in 2011.

Fred Reed *Ionia – Anatolia Junction*. A mazy meande through modern Turkey by journalist Reed. Particular enlightening on Sait Nursi, a religious figure wh challenged Atatürk and his reforms and whose follower the Nurcu, are so controversial in today's Turkey.

RAVEL AND IMPRESSIONS

★ **John Ash** *A Byzantine Journey*. Historically inclined reflections of a poet taking in all the major, and some minor, Byzantine sites in Anatolia; a lot better than it sounds.

Anastasia Ashman and Jennifer Eaton Gökmen *Tales from the Expat Harem: Foreign Women in Modern Turkey*. Collected short memoirs of female experiences; light but insightful.

Frederick Burnaby *On Horseback through Asia Minor*. Victorian officer's thousand-mile ride to spy on the Russians in the run-up to the 1877 war. Prophetically observant and inadvertently humorous; anti-Armenian, condescendingly Turkophilic.

★ **Geert Mak** *The Bridge*. Quite brilliant travelogue weaving the compelling tales of the petty street-traders, hustlers, pickpockets, shoe-shiners, fishermen and other characters who frequent İstanbul's landmark Galata bridge with a marvellously succinct, yet evocative, history of one of the world's great cities.

Mary Wortley Montagu *Turkish Embassy Letters*. Impressions of an eccentric but perceptive traveller, resident in İstanbul during 1716–18, whose open-mindedness gave her the edge over contemporary historians.

Jeremy Seal *Meander: East to West Along a Turkish River*. Seal is a witty yet perceptive writer, and this account of a journey along the famously winding course of the River Meander is every bit as engaging as *A Fez of the Heart*, in which Seal meanders around Turkey tracing the origins of that distinctive headwear.

Brian Sewell *South from Ephesus: An Escape from the Tyranny of Western Art*. Pre-touristic coastal Turkey and its ruins during the 1970s and 1980s, when vile hotels, domineering guides, patchy transport and amorous, bisexual villagers were all negotiated.

Freya Stark *Alexander's Path, Ionia – a Quest, The Lycian Shore* and *Riding to the Tigris*. All Stark's work makes great reading even today – especially if you're visiting Aegean/Mediterranean Turkey.

MEMOIRS

Fethiye Çetin *My Grandmother* A Turkish woman discovers her secret past – a Christian Armenian grandmother. Up to two million "Turks" today share the same origins. Slim, very readable memoir by a female lawyer who represented Hrant Dink.

★ **Dmetri Kakmi** *Mother Land*. Moving coming-of-age memoir of the last (1969–71) days of the Greek Orthodox community on the remote Aegean Turkish island of Bozcaada (Greek Tenedos).

★ **İrfan Orga** *Portrait of a Turkish Family*. This heartbreaking story follows Orga's family from idyllic

existence in late Ottoman İstanbul through grim survival in the early Republican era. His *The Caravan Moves On: Three Weeks among Turkish Nomads* is a fine snapshot of the Menderes era – and a clear-eyed portrayal of a Toros *yörük* community, about whom reams of rose-tinted nonsense have otherwise been written.

★ **Daniel de Souza** *Under a Crescent Moon* (o/p but available on Kindle). Turkish society seen from the bottom looking up: prison vignettes by a jailed foreigner, and in its compassion and black humour the antithesis of *Midnight Express*. Compellingly written.

ARCHITECTURE, ART AND MONUMENTS

Metin And *Turkish Miniature Painting – the Ottoman Period* (Dost Yayınları, İstanbul; o/p). Attractive coverage of the most important Ottoman art form, with well-produced colour plates.

Diana Barillari and Ezio Godoli *Istanbul 1900: Art Nouveau Architecture and Interiors*. Superbly researched and illustrated account of İstanbul's neglected Art Nouveau legacy, in particular works by Italian architect and resident Raimondo D'Aronco. A nice corrective to the axiom that the city consists only of palaces, concrete tower blocks and wooden terrace-houses.

★ **Godfrey Goodwin** *A History of Ottoman Architecture*. Definitive guide covering the whole country and providing a sound historical and ethno-geographical context for every important Ottoman construction. His *Sinan: Ottoman Architecture and Its Values Today* is also eminently readable.

Richard Krautheimer *Early Christian and Byzantine Architecture* (o/p). Excellent survey from Pelican's "History of Art" series.

Cyril Mango *Byzantine Architecture* (o/p). A complete survey of the most significant Byzantine structures, around a quarter of which fall within modern Turkey.

Gülru Necipoğlu *The Age of Sinan: Architectural Culture in the Ottoman Empire*. As it says: the master in his social context, and the best, newest of several studies on the man.

★ **David Talbot Rice** *Islamic Art* (o/p). Vast geographical and chronological span gives useful perspectives on Ottoman and Selçuk art forms. His *Art of the Byzantine Era* (o/p), a lavishly illustrated study in the same "World of Art" series, is unlikely ever to be superseded. For specialists *The Church of Hagia Sophia in Trebizond* (o/p) remains the last word, from the Talbot Rice-headed team that restored its frescoes.

Stephane Yerasimos *Constantinople: Istanbul's Historical Heritage*. Good colour photos, with attention to mosaics and icons, plus coverage of Edirne and Bursa. The English translation of the French original via a German edition is stilted, though.

Stephane Yerasimos, Ara Güler and Samih Rifat *Living in Turkey* (Overseas, and by Dünya in Turkey). Views and interiors to drool over – a bit prettified and nouvea riche, but still an alluring ideal.

CARPETS

★ **Alastair Hull and José Luczyc-Wykowska** *Kilim: The Complete Guide: History – Pattern – Technique – Identification*. Comprehensive and thoroughly illustrated survey of Turkish kilims. Hull's *Living with Kilims* (with Nicholas Barnard) is an excellent use-and-care manual.
James Opie *Tribal Rugs: A Complete Guide to Nomadic and*

Village Carpets. Contains examples of Turcoman ar Kurdish rugs as part of a general Central Asian survey.
Kurt Zipper and Claudia Fritzsche *Oriental Rug* Turkish Volume 4 of this series. Coverage of weavin techniques, symbols and rug categories, plus region surveys of distinctive patterns.

SPECIALIST GUIDEBOOKS

Arın Bayraktaroğlu *Turkey: Culture Shock! A Survival Guide to Customs and Etiquette*. Useful, especially for a prolonged stay or business trip.
George E. Bean *Turkey's Southern Shore, Turkey Beyond the Maeander, Lycian Turkey, Aegean Turkey* (all o/p). Scholarly guides to coastal archeological sites based on Professor Bean's original research, much of it never superseded.
Everett Blake and Anna Edmonds *Biblical Sites in Turkey*. If it's mentioned in the New Testament, it's fully

described here. Edmonds' *Turkey's Religious Sites* (o/p) better produced and includes Jewish and Muslim sites.
★ **Hilary Sumner-Boyd and John Freely** *Strollin Through Istanbul*. First published in 1972 and indispensable The authors' knowledge of, and love for, the city shin through; sketch-maps and monument plans complemer informative text.
Jane Taylor *Imperial Istanbul*. Excellent, stone-by-ston guide, complete with site plans, of the major Ottoma monuments in Bursa and Edirne as well as the old capital.

HIKING AND MOUNTAINEERING

Kate Clow *The Lycian Way*. Hour-by-hour, west-to-east route guide for Turkey's first officially marked long-distance trail (see p.304); supplied with folding map.
Kate Clow and Terry Richardson *St Paul Trail*. Illustrated guide to Turkey's second long-distance, waymarked trail (see p.421), loosely following in the footsteps of St Paul from Perge to Antioch in Pisidia, taking in wonderful mountain and lakeland scenery en route. GPS data and map included.
★ **Kate Clow** *The Kaçkar: Trekking in Turkey's Black Sea Mountains*. Meticulously described routes in the centre of

Turkey's most popular alpine range, both multi-day trek and waymarked day-walks.
Caroline Finkel and Kate Clow: *The Eliviya Çelebi Way* Guide to this long-distance cultural route in northwes Turkey, suitable for walkers, horseriders and cyclists following in the steps of Ottoman traveller Çelebi.
Ömer B. Tözel *The Ala Dağ: Climbs and Treks in Turkey* Crimson Mountains. More technical and less hike orientated than the title implies, but the only volume i English.

TURKISH FICTION IN TRANSLATION

Faik *A Dot on the Map* (o/p). Short-story collection, translated by various scholars, from the acknowledged Turkish master of the genre; most are set around İstanbul during the early Republican years.
Moris Farhi *Young Turk*. Ankara-born Farhi conjures thirteen interwoven short stories in this delightful evocation of İstanbul either side of World War II. Characters, whether

Armenian, Greek, Gypsy, Levantine or Turkish, are lovingl sketched; the "coming of age" tales are the most convincing
Latife Tekin *Berji Kristin: Tales from the Garbage Hills*. Th hard underbelly of Turkish life, in this surreal allegory set in shantytown built on an İstanbul rubbish dump. By the same author, and similar in tone, *Dear Shameless Death* examine how rural families cope with the move to the big city.

TURKISH POETRY IN TRANSLATION

Coleman Barks (trans) *Like This*; *Open Secret*; *We Are Three*. Three of various volumes of Rumi's poetry, in lively if not literal translations.
Yunus Emre (tr. Süha Faiz) *The City of the Heart: Verses of Wisdom and Love* (o/p). After Rumi, the most esteemed Turkish medieval Sufi poet. *The Drop That Became the Sea*, rendered by Kebir Helminski, will also appeal.

Talat S. Halman *Living Poets of Turkey* (Milet, İstanbul). A wide selection of modern Turkish poetry, with an introduction
★ **Nazım Hikmet** *Poems of Nazım Hikmet* and *Beyond the Walls*. The most easily available, reasonably pricec anthologies by the internationally renowned Turkish communist poet. An earlier collection, *A Sad State o Freedom* (o/p), is also worth looking for.

FOREIGN LITERATURE SET IN TURKEY

Louis de Bernières *Birds Without Wings*. This repeats, with mixed results, the formula of his blockbuster *Captain Corelli's Mandolin*, applied to Asia Minor of the 1910s and 20s. Most of the action occurs in "Eskibahçe", a fictionalized version of Kaya Köyü near Fethiye, though the Gallipoli set-pieces are the best bits. Take it as epic entertainment, not gospel – his grip on Turkish language, ethnography and history can be shaky.

Jason Goodwin *The Janissary Tree*. Racy historical thriller with all kinds of skulduggery being uncovered by Yashin, a eunuch detective. A very palatable entry into a nineteenth-century İstanbul on the verge of the Tanzimat reforms, and a successful formula that has spawned three sequels, *The Snake Stone*, *The Bellini Card* and 2011's *An Evil Eye*.

Pierre Loti *Aziyade*. For what's essentially romantic twaddle set in nineteenth-century İstanbul, this is surprisingly racy, with good insights into Ottoman life and Western attitudes to the Orient.

Rose Macaulay *The Towers of Trebizond*. Classic send-up of Low and High Church conflict, British eccentricity and naïvety among a group travelling from İstanbul to Trebizond in the 1950s.

Barbara Nadel *A Chemical Prison*; *Arabesque*; *Harem*. Some love Nadel's İstanbul-set thrillers, where doughty, chain-smoking Inspector İkrem and associates trawl the city's underworld; others find them a tad unconvincing. But they do evoke a side of the city barely imaginable to the average visitor.

★ **Edouard Roditi** *The Delights of Turkey*. Twenty short stories, by turns touching or bawdy, of rural Turkey and İstanbul, by a Sephardic Jew of Turkish descent long resident in Paris and America.

Turkish

It's worth learning as much Turkish as you can; if you travel far from the tourist centres you may well need it, and Turks always appreciate foreigners who show enough interest and courtesy to learn at least basic greetings. The main advantages of the language for learners are that it's phonetically spelled and (98 percent of the time) grammatically regular. The disadvantages are that the vocabulary is unrelated to any language you're likely to have encountered – unless you know Arabic or Persian – while the grammar, relying heavily on suffixes, gets thornier the further you delve into it. Concepts like vowel harmony further complicate matters.

Pronunciation

Mastering pronunciation in Turkish is important; once you've got it, the phonetic spelling and regularity helps you progress fast. The following letters differ significantly from English pronunciation.

Aa	short a, similar to that in far	Çç	like ch in **ch**at
		Gg	hard g as in **g**et
Ee	as in b**e**t	Ğğ	generally silent, but lengthens the preceding vowel, and between two vowels approximates a y sound
İi	as in p**i**n		
Iı	vowel resembling the vestigial sound between the b and the l of probable		
Oo	as in n**o**te	Hh	as in **h**en, never silent
Öö	like ur in b**ur**n	Jj	like the s in plea**s**ure
Uu	as in bl**u**e	Şş	like sh in **sh**ape
Üü	like ew in f**ew**	Vv	soft sound, somewhere between a v and a w
Cc	like j in **j**elly		

Vowel harmony and loan words

Turkish usually exhibits **vowel harmony**, whereby words contain either so-called "back" vowels a, ı, o and u, or "front" vowels e, i, ö and ü, but rarely mix the two types. Back and front vowels are further subdivided into "unrounded" (a and ı, e and i) and "rounded" (o and u, ö and ü), and again rounded and unrounded vowels tend to keep exclusive company. A small number of native Turkish words (eg, *anne*, mother; *kardeş*, brother) violate the rules of vowel harmony, as do compound words, eg *bugün*, "today" formed from *bu* (this) and *gün* (day).

PHRASEBOOKS AND DICTIONARIES

For a straightforward **phrasebook**, look no further than *Turkish: A Rough Guide Phrasebook*, which has useful two-way glossaries and a brief and simple grammar section. For an **at-home course**, Geoffrey L. Lewis's *Teach Yourself Turkish* is best.

Among widely available Turkish **dictionaries**, the best are probably the Langenscheidt/ Lilliput in miniature or coat-pocket sizes, or the *Concise Oxford Turkish Dictionary* (o/p but sold online), a hardback suitable for serious students. The Redhouse dictionaries, produced in Turkey but marketed by Milet in the UK, are the best value, despite eye-straining fine print.

The main exceptions to vowel harmony, however, are foreign **loan words** from Arabic
Persian (plus Greek). Despite Atatürk's best efforts to substitute Turkish or French
pressions (the latter again violating vowel harmony), these still make up a good third
modern Turkish vocabulary. Most words that start with f, h, l, m, n, r, v and z are
erived from Arabic and Persian.

ORDS AND PHRASES

ASICS

ood morning	Günaydın
ood afternoon	İyi günler
od evening	İyi akşamlar
oodnight	İyi geceler
ello	Merhaba
oodbye	Allahaısmarladık
s	Evet
o	Hayır
o (there isn't any)	Yok
ease	Lütfen
ank you	Teşekkür ederim/ Mersi/Sağol
ou're welcome	Bir şey değil
ow are you?	Nasılsınız? Nasılsın? Ne haber?
n fine	İyiyim/İyilik
o you speak English?	İngilizce biliyormusunuz?
on't understand (Turkish)	Anlamadım/Türkçe anlamıyorum
on't know	Bilmiyorum
eg your pardon	Affedersiniz
xcuse me (in a crowd)	Pardon
n sightseeing	Geziyorum or Dolaşıyorum
n English/Scottish Irish/ American/ Austalian	İngilizim/İskoçyalıyım/ İrlandalıyım/ Amerikalı/ Avustralyalıyım
ive in…	…'de/da oturuyorum
oday	Bugün
omorrow	Yarın
ay after tomorrow	Öbür gün/Ertesi gün
esterday	Dün
ow	Şimdi
ater	Sonra
/ait a minute!	Bir dakika bekle!
n the morning	Sabahleyin
n the afternoon	Öğle'den sonra
n the evening	Akşamleyin
ere/there/over there	Bur(a)da/Şur(a)da/ Or(a) da
ood/bad	İyi/Kötü, Fena
ig/small	Büyük/Küçük
heap/expensive	Ucuz/Pahalı
arly/late	Erken/Geç
ot/cold	Sıcak/Soğuk
ear/far	Yakın/Uzak

Vacant/occupied	Boş/Dolu
Quickly/slowly	Hızlı/Yavaş
Enough	Yeter
Mr	Bey (follows first name)
Miss	Bayan (precedes first name)
Mrs	Hanım (polite Ottoman title follows first name)
Master craftsman	Usta (honorific title bestowed on any tradesman; follows first name)

DRIVING

Left	Sol
Right	Sağ
Straight ahead	Doğru, direk
Turn left/right	Sola dön/Sağ'ta dön
No parking	Parkyapılmaz
Your car will be towed	Aracınız Çekilir
One-way street	Tek yön
No entry	Araç giremez
No through road	Çıkmaz sokak
Abrupt verge	Düşük banket
Slow down	Yavaşla
Road closed	Yol kapalı
Crossroads	Dörtyol, kavşak
Pedestrian crossing	Yaya geçidi

SOME COMMON SIGNS

Entrance/exit	Giriş/Çıkış
Free/paid entrance	Giriş ücretsiz/Ücretlidir
Gentlemen	Baylar
Ladies	Bayanlar
WC	WC/Tuvalet
Open/closed	Açık/Kapalı
Arrivals/departures	Varış/Kalkış
Pull/push	Çekiniz/İtiniz
Out of order	Arızalı
Drinking water	İçilebilir su
To let/for hire	Kiralık
Foreign exchange	Kambiyo
Beware	Dikkat
First aid	İlk yardım
No smoking	Sigara içilmez
Keep off the grass	Çimenlere basmayını
Stop, halt	Dur
Military area	Askeri bölge

Entry forbidden	Girmek yasaktır
No entry without a ticket	Biletsiz girmek yasaktır
No entry without a woman	Damsız girilmez
Please take off your shoes	Lütfen ayakkabılarınızı çıkartınız
No entry on foot	Yaya giremez

ACCOMMODATION

Is there a hotel nearby?	Bir yakında otel var mı?
Pension, inn	Pansiyon
Campsite	Kamping
Tent	Çadır
Do you have a room?	Boş odanız var mı?
Single/double/triple	Tek/çift/üç kişilik
Do you have a double room for one/two/ three nights?	Bir/iki/üç gecelik çift yataklı odanız var mı?
For one/two weeks	Bir/iki haftalık
With an extra bed	İlâve yataklı
With a double bed	Fransız yataklı
With a shower	Duşlu
Hot water	Sıcak su
Cold water	Soğuk su
Can I see it?	Bakabilirmiyim?
I have a booking	Reservasyonum var
Is there wi-fi?	Kablosuz var?
What's the password?	Şifre nedir?

QUESTIONS AND DIRECTIONS

Where is the…?	…nerede?
When?	Ne zaman?
What/What is it?	Ne/Ne dir?
How much (does it cost?)	Ne kadar/Kaça?
How many?	Kaç tane?
Why?	Niye?
What time is it?	(polite) Saatınız var mı? (informal) Saat kaç?
How do I get to…?	…'a/e nasıl giderim?
How far is it to…?	…'a/e ne kadar uzak?
Can you give me a lift to…?	Beni…'a/e götürebilirmisiniz?
When does it open?	Kaçta açılıcak?
When does it close?	Kaçta kapanacak?
What's it called in Turkish?	Türkcesi ne dir? or, Türkçe nasıl söylersiniz?

TRAVELLING

Aeroplane	Uçak
Bus	Otobüs
Train	Tren
Car	Araba
Taxi	Taksi
Bicycle	Bisiklet
Ferry	Feribot, vapur
Catamaran, sea-bus	Deniz otobüsü
Hitch-hiking	Otostop
On foot	Yaya
Bus station	Otogar
Railway station	Gar, tren ıstasyonu
Ferry terminal/jetty	İskele
Harbour	Liman
A ticket to…	…'a bir bilet
One-way	Gidiş sadece
Return	Gidiş-dönüş
What time does it leave?	Saat kaçta kalkıyor?
Can I book a seat?	Reservasyon yapabilirmiyim?
When is the next bus/train/ferry?	Bir sonraki otobus/ tren/vapur kaçta kalkıyor?
Where does it leave from?	Nereden kalkıyor?
Must I change?	Aktarma var mı?
What platform does it leave from?	Hangi perondan kalkıyor?
How many kilometres is it?	Kaç kilometredir?
How long does it take?	Ne kadar sürer?
Which bus goes to…?	Hangi otobus…'a gider?
Which road leads to…?	Hangi yol…'a çıkar?
Can I get out at a convenient place?	Müsait bir yerde inebilirmiyim?

DAYS OF THE WEEK, MONTHS AND SEASONS

Sunday	Pazar
Monday	Pazartesi
Tuesday	Salı
Wednesday	Çarşamba
Thursday	Perşembe
Friday	Cuma
Saturday	Cumartesi
January	Ocak
February	Subat
March	Mart
April	Nisan
May	Mayıs
June	Haziran
July	Temmuz
August	Ağustos
September	Eylül
October	Ekim
November	Kasım
December	Aralk
Spring	İlkbahar
Summer	Yaz
Autumn	Sonbahar
Winter	Kış

UMBERS AND ORDINALS

	Bir	140	Yüz kırk
	İki	200	İki yüz
	Üç	700	Yedi yüz
	Dört	1000	Bin
	Beş	100,000	Yüz bin
	Altı	500,000	Beşyüz bin
	Yedi	1,000,000	Bir milyon
	Sekiz	Compound numbers tend to be run together in
	Dokuz	spelling: 50,784 Ellibinyediyüzseksendört	
	On	**First**	Birinci
	On bir	**Second**	İkinci
	On iki	**Third**	Üçüncü
	On üç		
	Yirmi	**TIME CONVENTIONS**	
	Otuz	(At) 3 o'clock	Saat üç(ta)
	Kırk	2 hours (duration)	İki saat
	Elli	Half hour (duration)	Yarım saat
	Altmış	5.30	Beş büçük
	Yetmiş	It's 8.10	Sekizi on geçiyor
	Seksen	It's 10.45	On bire çeyrek var
	Doksan	At 8.10	Sekizi on geçe
	Yüz	At 10.45	On bire çeyrek kala

ood and drink

ASICS

	Honey	Tabak	Plate
lgur	Cracked wheat	Bıçak	Knife
z	Ice	Çatal	Fork
mek	Bread, as:	Kaşık	Spoon
avdar	Rye	Peçete	Napkin
epekli	Wholegrain	Hesap	Bill, check
ısır	Corn	Servis ücreti	Service charge
rabiber	Black pepper	Garsoniye	"Waiter's" charge
kik	Oregano		
karna	Pasta (noodles)	**COOKING TERMS**	
ne	Mint	Acı	Hot, spicy
av, pirinç	Rice	Buğlama	Steamed
ker	Sugar	Çevirme	Spit-roasted
ke	Vinegar	Etli	Containing meat
	Water	Etli mi?	Does it contain meat?
t	Milk	Etsiz yemek	Do you have any
eyağı	Butter	var mı?	meatless food?
z	Salt	Ezme	Puréed/mashed dip
ytin) Yağ(ı)	(Olive) Oil	Fırında(n)	Baked
ğurt	Yoghurt	Haşlama	Meat stew without oil,
murta	Eggs		sometimes with
)li/(Et)siz	With/without (meat)		vegetables
		İyi pişmiş	Well-cooked
		Izgarada(n), Izgarası	Grilled
SEFUL WORDS		Kızartma	Fried then chilled
karmısınız!	Polite way of getting	Kıymalı	With minced meat
	waiter's attention	Peynirli, kaşarlı	With cheese
rdak	Glass	Pilaki	Vinaigrette, marinated
şka bir…	Another…	Pişmemiş	Raw

Sıcak/soğuk	Hot/cold (*meze*)
Soslu, salçalı	In red sauce
Sucuklu	With sausage
Tava, sahanda	Deep-fried, fried
Yoğurtlu	In yoghurt sauce
Yumurtalı	With egg (eg *pide*)
Zeytinyağlılar	Vegetables cooked in their own juices, spices and olive oil (*zeytin yağı*), then allowed to cool

SOUP (ÇORBA)

Düğün	Egg-lemon
Ezo gelin	Rice/vegetable broth
İşkembe	Tripe
Mercimek	Lentil
Paça	Trotters
Tarhana	Yoghurt, grain and spice
Tavuk	Chicken
Yayla	Similar to *tarhana*, with mint
Yoğurt	Yoghurt, rice and celery greens

APPETIZERS (MEZE OR ZEYTINYAĞLI)

Antep or acılı ezmesi	Hot chilli mash with garlic, parsley, onion
Barbunya	Red kidney beans
Börülce	Black-eyed peas, in the pod
Cacık	Yoghurt, cucumber and herb dip
Çerkez tavuğu	Chicken in walnut sauce
Çoban salatası	Tomato, cucumber, parsley, pepper and onion salad
Deniz börülcesi	Glasswort, marsh samphire
Deniz otu	Rock samphire
Haydarı	Dense garlic dip
Hibeş	Spicy sesame paste
İçli köfte	Bulgur, nuts, vegetables and meat in a spicy crust
İmam bayıldı	Cold baked aubergine, onion and tomato
Mantar sote	Sautéed mushrooms
Mücver	Courgette frittata
Paçanga böreği	*Pastırma* containing, tomato and cheese
Patlıcan ezmesi	Aubergine pâté
Piyaz	White haricots, onions and parsley vinaigrette
Rus salatası	"Russian" salad – potatoes, peas, gherkins in mayonnaise
Semizotu	Purslane, usually mixed into yoghurt

Sigara böreği	Cheese-filled pastry "cigarettes"
Tarama	Pink fish-roe
Tere	Rocket greens
Turşu	Pickled vegetables
Yaprak dolması	Stuffed vine leaves, with mince
Yeşil salata	Green salad
Zeytin	Olives

MEAT (ET) AND POULTRY (BEYAZ ET)

Adana kebap	Spicy Arab-style kebab
Beyti	Minced kebab wrapped in pitta
Bıldırcın	Quail
Böbrek	Kidney
Bonfile	Small steak
Ciğ köfte	Spicy bulgur patties
Ciğer	Liver
Çöp kebap	Tiny chunks of offal
Dana eti	Veal
Dil	Tongue
Döner kebap	Rotisseried cone of fatty lamb slabs
İnegöl köftesi	Mince rissoles laced with cheese
İskender or Bursa kebap	Döner drenched in yogurt and sauce
Kaburga	Spare ribs
Kağıt kebap	Meat and vegetables baked in wax paper
Kanat	Chicken wing
Karışık ızgara	Mixed grill
Kiremit'te kebap	Meat served on a hot ceramic tray
Köfte	Meatballs
Koyun	Mutton
Kuzu	Lamb
Keçi	Goat
Orman kebap	Roast lamb refried with vegetables
Pastırma	Cured beef
Piliç	Roasting chicken
Pirzola	Chop, cutlet
Saray kebap	Rissoles baked with vegetables
Sığır	Beef
Şiş kebap	Shish kebab
Tandır kebap	Tender, boneless lamb baked in outdoor oven
Tavuk	Boiling chicken
Tekirdağ köftesi	Finger-shaped rissoles with cumin, onion, mint
Yürek	Heart

SH (*BALIK*) AND SEAFOOD (*DENIZ ?RÜNLERI*)

?tapod	Octopus
?abalık	Trout
?rbunya/tekir	Red mullet, small/large
?akop	Baby lüfer
?pura	Gilt-head bream
?msi	Anchovy (Black Sea)
?karoz	Parrotfish
?aroz	Annular bream
?akoz	Aegean lobster
?avrit	Horse mackerel
?lamar	Squid
?lkan	Turbot
?aragöz	Two-banded bream
?rides	Prawns
?fal	Grey mullet (Aegean)
?ıç	Swordfish
?lyoz	Club mackerel
?vrek	Bass; usually farmed
?fer	Bluefish
?endik	Type of bream
?ercan	Pandora or red bream
?ezgit	Whitebait
?dye	Mussel
?foz	Giant grouper
?kinos	Tuna
?lamut/torik	Small/large bonito
?rıgöz	Black bream
?rıkanat	Young *lüfer*
?rdalya	Sardine
?kumru	Atlantic mackerel
?yın	Catfish
?ngeç	Crab

?EGETABLES (*SEBZE*)

?ı biber	Hot chillis
?kla	Broad beans
?mya	Okra, lady's fingers
?zelye	Peas
?mates	Tomato
?ginar	Artichoke
?ardal	Mustard greens
?avuç	Carrot
?anak	Spinach
?tifno	Boiled wild greens
?bak	Courgette, zucchini
?rnabahar	Cauliflower
?ru fasulye	White haricots
?antar	Mushrooms
?arul	Lettuce
?aydanoz	Parsley
?hut	Chickpeas
?tates	Potato

Patlıcan	Aubergine, eggplant
Roka, tere	Rocket greens
Salatalık	Cucumber
Sarımsak, sarmısak	Garlic
Sivri biber	Thin peppers, hot or mild
Soğan	Onion
Taze fasulye	French beans
Turp	Radish

SNACKS

Antep fıstığı	Pistachios
Badem	Almonds
Börek	Rich layered pastry with varied fillings
Çerez	Nibbles, usually nuts
Cezer(i)ye	Carrot, honey-nut bar
Çiğ börek	Hollow turnovers
Dürüm	Pitta-like dough roll used to wrap meat for takeaway
Fındık	Hazelnuts
Gözleme	Village crêpe with various fillings
Kestane	Chestnuts
Kokoreç	Mixed innard roulade
Kuru üzüm	Raisins
Lahmacun	Round Arabic-Armenian "pizza"
Leblebi	Roasted chickpeas
Midye dolması	Mussels stuffed with rice and pine nuts
Pestil	Sheet-pressed dried fruit
Pide	Turkish "pizza"
Poğaça	Soft, often filled, bread roll
Simit	Bread rings studded with sesame seeds
Su börek	"Water börek" – runny cheese between filo
Yer fıstığı	Peanuts

TYPICAL DISHES

Civil	Variant of *mihlama*, served on Çoruh side of Kaçkar
Güveç	Meat and vegetable clay-pot casserole
İç pilav	Spicy rice
Karnıyarık	Aubergine and meat dish, firmer than mussaka
Lahana sarma	Black Sea *dolma*, with baby cabbage leaves
Laz böreği	Meat-filled crêpes, topped with yoghurt
Mantı	Mince-stuffed "ravioli" topped with yoghurt and chilli oil

Menemen	Stir-fried omelette with tomatoes and peppers
Mıhlama, muhlama	Fondue-like Hemşin dish of cheese, butter and corn flour
Otlu peynir	Herb-flavoured cheese, common around Van
Saç kavurma	"Wok"-fried medley
Sebze turlu	Vegetable stew
Şakşuka	Aubergine, tomato, pepper and other vegetable fry-up
Tas kebap	Meat and vegetable stew especially in eastern Anatolia
Tatar böreği	Similar to *mantı* but served with cheese and mint
Testi kebap	Stew in a sealed Avanos (Cappadocia) pot, broken at serration to serve
Türlü sebze	Alias of *tas kebap*

CHEESE (*PEYNIR*)

Beyaz	White; like Greek feta
Çerkez	Like Edam
Dil	Like mozzarella
Lor	Like ricotta
Kaşar	Kasseri, variably aged
Tulum	Dry, crumbly, parmesan-like cheese

FRUIT (*MEYVE*)

Ahududu	Raspberry
Armut	Pear
Ayva	Quince
Böğürtlen	Blackberry
Çilek	Strawberry
Elma	Apple
Erik	Plum
Hurma	Persimmon or date
İncir	Figs
(Kara)dut	(Red) mulberry
Karpuz	Watermelon
Kavun	Persian melon
Kayısı	Apricot
Kiraz	Sweet cherry
Limon	Lemon

Mandalin	Tangerine
Muşmula	Medlar
Muz	Banana
Nar	Pomegranate
Papaz/hoca eriği	Green plum
Portakal	Orange
Şeftali	Peach (June)
Üzüm	Grape
Vişne	Sour cherry
Yarma	August Bursa peach

SWEETS (*TATLILAR*) AND PASTRIES (*PASTALAR*)

Acı badem	Giant almond biscuit
Aşure	Pulse, wheat, fruit and nut "soup"
Baklava	Layered honey and nut pie
Dondurma	Ice cream
Kaymak	Clotted cream
Fırın sütlaç	Baked rice pudding
İrmik helvası	Semolina and nut *helva*
Kabak tatlısı	Baked orange-fleshed squash topped with nuts and *kaymak*
Kadayıf	"Shredded wheat" in syrup
Kadın göbeği	Doughnut in syrup
Kaymak	Clotted cream
Kazandibi	Browned version of *tavukgöğsü*
Keşkül	Vanilla-almond custard
Komposto	Stewed fruit
Krem karamel	Crème caramel
Kurabiye	Almond-nut biscuit dusted with powdered sugar
Lokum	Turkish Delight
Muhallebi	Milk pudding with rice flour and rosewater
Mustafakemalpaşa	Syrup-soaked dumpling
Sakızlı	Anything mastic-flavoured
Süpangile	Ultra-rich chocolate pudding, with sponge or a biscuit embedded
Sütlaç	Rice pudding
Tahin helvası	Sesame paste *helva*
Tavuk göğsü	Chicken-breast, milk, sugar and rice taffy

COMMON TOASTS

The closest equivalents to "Cheers" are: **Şeref'e, şerefiniz'e** "to your honour" and **Neşe'ye** "to joy". Otherwise there's the more formal **Sağlığınız'a** "to your health" or **Mutluluğ'a** "to happiness".

To a good cook one says: **Eliniz'e sağlık** "health to your hands". For a short grace after meals: **Allah bereket versin** ("may Allah bring blessings").

Zerde	Saffron-laced jelly	Meyva suyu	Fruit juice
		Papatya çayı	Camomile tea
DRINKS		Rakı	Aniseed-flavoured
Ada çayı	Sage tea		spirit distilled from
Ayran	Drinking yoghurt		grape pressings
Bira	Beer	Sahlep	Orchid-root-powder
Boza	Lightly fermented		drink
	millet or wheat drink	Şarap	Wine
Çay	Tea	Şıra	Grape must, lightly
Kahve	Coffee		fermented
Maden suyu	Mineral water (fizzy)	Sütlü/Sütsüz	With/without milk

Glossary

Many of the Turkish terms below will change their form according to their grammatical declension (eg *ada*, island, but *Eşek Adası*, Donkey Island); the genitive suffix is appended in brackets, or the form written separately when appropriate.

GENERAL TURKISH TERMS

Ada(sı) Island.

Ağa A minor rank of nobility in the Ottoman Empire, still a term of respect; follows the name (eg Ismail Ağa).

Ahi Medieval Turkish apprentice craftsmen's guild and religious brotherhood, predecessor of the more conventional dervish orders.

Ayazma Sacred spring.

Bahçe(si) Garden.

Bekçi Caretaker or warden at an archeological site or monument.

Belediye(si) Municipality – both the corporation and the actual town hall, for a community of over 2000 inhabitants.

Bey Another minor Ottoman title like *ağa*, still in use; follows the first name.

Cami(i) Mosque.

Çarşaf "Sheet" – the full-length, baggy dress-with-hood worn by religious Turkish women.

Çarşı(sı) Bazaar, market.

Çay(ı) 1) Tea, the national drink; 2) a stream or small river.

Çeşme(si) Street-corner fountain.

Çıkmaz(ı) Dead-end alley.

Dağ(ı) Mount.

Dağlar(ı) Mountains.

Dolmuş Shared taxi system operating in larger towns.

Eski Old (frequent modifier of place names).

Ezan The Muslim call to prayer; these days often taped or at the very least transmitted up to an elevated loudspeaker.

Ferace Similar to a *çarşaf*, but less all-enveloping.

Gazi Warrior for the (Islamic) faith; also a common epithet of Atatürk.

Gazino Open-air nightclub, usually featuring live or taped music.

Gecekondu A house built quickly without proper permission. Translates as "founded-by-night" – a reference to the Ottoman law whereby houses begun in darkness that had acquired a roof and four walls by dawn were inviolable.

Gişe Ticket window or booth.

Göl(ü) Lake.

Hamam(ı) Turkish bath.

Hamsi The Black Sea anchovy; by extension, nickname for any native of this area.

Han(ı) Traditionally a tradesmen's hall, or an urban inn; now also means an office block.

Harabe Ruin; *harabeler* in the plural, abbreviated "Hb" on old maps.

Harem Women's quarters in Ottoman houses.

Hastane(si) Hospital.

Hicrî The Muslim dating system, beginning with Mohammed's flight to Medina in 622 AD, and based on the thirteen-month lunar calendar; approximately six centuries behind the *Miladî* calendar. Abbreviated "H." on monuments and inscriptions.

Hisar Same as *kale*.

Hoca Teacher in charge of religious instruction.

Ilıca Hot spring.

İl(i) Province, subdivided into *ilçes* (counties or districts).

İmam Usually just the prayer leader at a mosque, though it can mean a more important spiritual authority.

Irmak River, eg Yeşilırmak (Green River).

İskele(si) Jetty, dock.

Janissary One of the sultan's elite corps during the fourteenth to eighteenth centuries; *yeniceri* in Turkish. Famous for their devotion to the Bektaşi order, outlandish headgear and marching music.

Kaplıca Developed hot springs, spa.

Kervansaray(ı) Strategically located "hotel", often Selçuk, for pack animals and men on Anatolian trade routes; some overlap with *han*.

Kilim Flat-weave rug without a pile.

Kilise(si) Church.

Konak Large private residence, also the main government building of a province or city; genitive form *konağı*.

Lokanta Restaurant; from Italian locanda.

Mağara(sı) Cave.

Mahalle(si) District or neighbourhood of a larger municipality, village or postal area.

Meydan(ı) Public square or plaza.

Meyhane Tavern where alcohol and *meze*-type food are served together.

eze Often vegetable-based appetizer, typically fried, puréed and/or marinated.

iladı The Christian year-numbering system; abbreviated "M." on inscriptions.

uezzin Man who pronounces call to prayer (*ezan*) from the minaret of a mosque.

uhtar Village headman.

uhtarlık The office of the *muhtar*; also designates the status of any community of under 2000.

amaz The Muslim rite of prayer, performed five times daily.

ehir (Nehri) River.

togar Bus station.

va(sı) Plain, plateau.

ren Alternative term for *harabe*, "ruin"; common village name.

ansiyon Typical budget to mid-priced accommodation in Turkish resorts.

amadan The Muslim month of fasting and prayer; spelt *Ramazan* in Turkish.

az Long-necked, fretted stringed instrument central to Turkish folk ballads and Alevî/Bektaşi devotional music.

elçuk Pertaining to the first Muslim Turkish state based in Anatolia, which lasted from the eleventh to the thirteenth centuries.

Sema A dervish ceremony; thus *semahane*, a hall where such ceremonies are conducted.

Şehzade Prince, heir apparent.

Şeyh Head of a Sufi order.

Sufi or dervish An adherent of one of the heterodox mystical branches of Islam. In Turkey the most important sects were the Bektaşi, Mevlevî, Helveti, Nakşibendi, Cerrahi and Kadiri orders.

Sultan valide The Sultan's mother.

Tatil köyü or site(si) Holiday development, usually for Turkish civil servants – not meant for foreign tourists.

Tuğra Monogram or seal of a sultan.

Ulema The corps of Islamic scholars and authorities in Ottoman times.

Vakıf Islamic religious trust or foundation, responsible for social welfare and upkeep of religious buildings.

Vezir The principal Ottoman minister of state, responsible for managing the empire.

Vilayet(i) Formal word for province; also a common term for the provincial headquarters building itself.

Yalı Ornate wooden mansion on the Bosphorus.

Yayla(sı) Pastoral mountain hamlet occupied only in summer; in the Black Sea region, may have rustic accommodation.

Yeni New (common component of Turkish place names).

ARCHITECTURAL/ARTISTIC TERMS

cropolis Ancient fortified hilltop.

gora Marketplace and meeting area of an ancient Lycian, Greek or Roman city.

pse Curved or polygonal recess at the altar end of a church.

rasta Marketplace built into the foundations of a mosque, a portion of whose revenues goes to the upkeep of the latter.

edesten(i) Covered market hall for valuable goods, often lockable.

ouleuterion Council hall of a Hellenistic or Roman city.

amekan Changing rooms in a hamam.

apital Top, often ornamented, of a column.

avea Seating curve of an ancient theatre.

eesis or Deisis Portrayal of Christ between the Virgin and John the Baptist.

iazoma A horizontal walkway dividing the two blocks of seats in an ancient theatre.

xedra Semicircular niche.

yvan Domed side-chamber of an Ottoman religious building; also applies to three-sided alcoves in secular mansions.

öbek taşı Literally "navel stone" – the hot central platform of a hamam.

alvet Corner room in a hamam.

Hararet The hottest room of a hamam.

İmaret(i) Soup kitchen and hostel for dervishes and wayfarers, usually attached to a *medrese*.

Kale(si) Castle, fort.

Kapı(sı) Gate, door.

Katholikon Central shrine of a monastery.

Kemer Aqueduct, or a series of vaults/arches.

Khatchkar An ornate relief-carving centred around stylized crosses, on the walls of Armenian churches; also a freestanding cruciform gravestone so carved.

Köşk(ü) Kiosk, pavilion, gazebo, folly.

Kubbe Dome, cupola – as in *Kubbeli Kilise* (the Domed Church).

Kule(si) Tower, turret.

Kurna Hewn stone basin in a hamam.

Külliye(si) A mosque and its dependent buildings.

Kümbet Vault, dome; by analogy the cylindrical "hatted" Selçuk tombs of central Anatolia.

Medrese(si) Islamic theological academy.

Mescit Small mosque with no *mimber*; Islamic equivalent of a chapel; genitive *mescidi*.

Mezar(i) Grave, tomb; thus *mezarlık*, cemetery.

Mihrab Niche in a mosque indicating the direction of Mecca, and prayer.

Mimber Pulpit in a mosque, from where the *imam* delivers homilies; often beautifully carved in wood or stone.

Minare(si) Turkish for "minaret", the tower from which the call to prayer is delivered.

Naos The inner sanctum of an ancient temple.

Narthex Vestibule or entrance hall of a church; also *exonarthex*, the outer vestibule when there is more than one.

Nave Principal lengthwise aisle of a church.

Necropolis Place of burial in an ancient Greek or Roman city.

Nymphaeum Ornate, multistoreyed facade, often with statue niches, surrounding a public fountain in an ancient city.

Odeion Small ancient theatre used for musical performances, minor dramatic productions or civic councils.

Pendentive Curved, triangular surface, by means of which a dome can be supported over a square ground plan.

Pier A mass of supportive masonry.

Porphyry Hard purplish-red volcanic rock containing crystals.

Revetment Facing of stone, marble or tile.

Saray(ı) Palace.

Sebil Public drinking fountain, freestanding or built into the wall of an Ottoman structure.

Selamlık Area where men receive guests in any sort of dwelling.

Serender Wooden, enclosed corn-crib on stilts, particular to the Black Sea; sometimes spelt *serander*.

Son cemaat yeri Literally "Place of the last congregation" – a mosque porch where latecomers pray.

Stoa Colonnaded walkway in an ancient Greek agora.

Synthronon Semicircular seating for clergy, usually in the apse of a Byzantine church.

Şadırvan Ritual ablutions fountain of a mosque.

Şerefe Balcony of a minaret.

Tabhane Hospice for travelling dervishes or *ahi*s, often housed in an *eyvan*.

Tapınak Alternative term for "temple" at archeological sites; genitive *tapınağı*.

Tekke(si) Gathering place of a Sufi order.

Tersane(si) Shipyard, dry-dock.

Transept The "wings" of a church, extending north and south perpendicular to the nave.

Tuff Soft rock formed from volcanic ash.

Türbe(si) Freestanding, usually domed, tomb.

Tympanum The surface, often adorned, enclosed by the top of an arch; found in churches or more ancient ruins.

Verd(e) antique Mottled or veined green serpentine.

Voussoir Stripes of wedge-shaped blocks at the edge of an arch.

Zaviye Mosque built specifically as a hospice for dervishes, usually along a T-plan.

Zhamatoun Chapter (council) hall of an Armenian church.

ACRONYMS AND ABBREVIATIONS

AKP *Adalet ve Kalkınma Partisi* or Justice and Development Party; the Islamist movement headed by Recep Tayyip Erdoğan, which has governed with a large majority from 2002 until the present.

Bul Standard abbreviation for *bulvar(ı)* (boulevard).

Cad Standard abbreviation for *cadde(si)* (avenue).

CHP *Cumhuriyetçi Halk Partisi* or Republican People's Party (RPP) – founded by Atatürk, disbanded in 1980, revived in 1992. The main opposition party at present, it also controls many municipalities.

KDV Acronym of the Turkish VAT.

MHP *Milliyet Hareket Paritisi* (National Action Party); originally quasi-fascist group, later rebranded by new leader Devlet Bahçeli; now third party in parliament.

NSC National Security Council (*Milli Güvenlik Kurulu*); mixed military-civilian council established after the 1980 coup.

PKK *Partia Karkaris Kurdistan* or Kurdish Workers' Party; actually an armed guerrilla movement, formed in 1978 and still present in the southeast.

PTT *Post Telefon ve Telegraf*, the joint postal, telegraph and (formerly) phone service in Turkey, and by extension its offices.

Sok Abbreviation for *sokak* (*sokağı*) or street.

THY Türk *Hava Yolları*, Turkish Airways.

TIR (pronounced "turr" locally) *Transport International Routière* – large, slow trucks, your greatest road hazard.

TL Standard abbreviation for the Turkish lira, these days increasingly replaced by the typographic symbol ₺.

TRT Acronym of *Türk Radyo ve Televizyon*, the Turkish public broadcasting corporation.

Small print and index

A ROUGH GUIDE TO ROUGH GUIDES

Published in 1982, the first Rough Guide – to Greece – was a student scheme that became a publishing phenomenon. Mark Ellingham, a recent graduate in English from Bristol University, had been travelling in Greece the previous summer and couldn't find the right guidebook. With a small group of friends he wrote his own guide, combining a highly contemporary, journalistic style with a thoroughly practical approach to travellers' needs.

The immediate success of the book spawned a series that rapidly covered dozens of destinations. And, in addition to impecunious backpackers, Rough Guides soon acquired a much broader readership that relished the guides' wit and inquisitiveness as much as their enthusiastic, critical approach and value-for-money ethos.

These days, Rough Guides include recommendations from budget to luxury and cover more than 200 destinations around the globe, as well as producing an ever-growing range of eBooks and apps.

Visit **roughguides.com** to see our latest publications.

Rough Guide credits

Editor: Greg Ward
Layout: Jessica Subramanian and Umesh Aggarwal
Cartography: Ashutosh Bharti
Picture editor: Mark Thomas
Proofreader: Jan McCann
Managing editor: Keith Drew
Assistant editor: Prema Dutta
Production: Charlotte Cade
Cover design: Nicole Newman, Jessica Subramanian

Editorial assistant: Olivia Rawes
Senior pre-press designer: Dan May
Design director: Scott Stickland
Travel publisher: Joanna Kirby
Digital travel publisher: Peter Buckley
Operations coordinator: Helen Blount
Publishing director (Travel): Clare Currie
Commercial manager: Gino Magnotta
Managing director: John Duhigg

Publishing information

This eighth edition published June 2013 by
Rough Guides Ltd,
80 Strand, London WC2R 0RL
11, Community Centre, Panchsheel Park,
New Delhi 110017, India
Distributed by the Penguin Group
Penguin Books Ltd,
80 Strand, London WC2R 0RL
Penguin Group (USA)
375 Hudson Street, NY 10014, USA
Penguin Group (Australia)
250 Camberwell Road, Camberwell,
Victoria 3124, Australia
Penguin Group (NZ)
67 Apollo Drive, Mairangi Bay, Auckland 1310,
New Zealand
Penguin Group (South Africa)
Block D, Rosebank Office Park, 181 Jan Smuts Avenue,
Parktown North, Gauteng, South Africa 2193
Rough Guides is represented in Canada by Tourmaline
Editions Inc. 662 King Street West, Suite 304, Toronto,
Ontario M5V 1M7
Printed in Malaysia by Vivar Printing Sdn Bhd

MIX
Paper from
responsible sources
FSC   www.fsc.org   FSC™ C018179

Help us update

We've gone to a lot of effort to ensure that the eighth edition of **The Rough Guide to Turkey** is accurate and up-to-date. However, things change – places get "discovered", opening hours are notoriously fickle, restaurants and rooms raise prices or lower standards. If you feel we've got it wrong or left something out, we'd like to know, and if you can remember the address, the price, the hours, the phone number, so much the better.

Please send your comments with the subject line "**Rough Guide Turkey Update**" to ✉ mail@uk.roughguide .com. We'll credit all contributions and send a copy of the next edition (or any other Rough Guide if you prefer) for the very best emails.

Find more travel information, connect with fellow travellers and plan your trip on ⓦ roughguides.com

ABOUT THE AUTHOR

Terry Richardson is based in southwest Turkey, a country he first visited in 1978. Terry has crisscrossed this endlessly fascinating country on numerous occasions, and wrote both the Rough Guide and the Pocket Guide to İstanbul.

Acknowledgements

Terry Richardson: I'd like to thank, in no particular order: Yasemin at Antalya Press Office for help obtaining a Turkish press card; Turkish tour guide Seyhun Aktoprak for his boundless knowledge of his native land; Erkan at Talisman Travel for his support and organisational skills; Remzi of the Büyük Asur hotel for his hospitality and knowledge of Van; Leyla, daughter of an old friend, for the low-down on Van's nightlife; Harun for information on his hometown of Van; İsmail, Zehra and family who, though forced to leave Van because of the earthquake, still provided valuable support; the theology students who put me up in Şırnak; Muşfik of the Dideban hotel in Bitlis for showing me the khatchkars in Por; Mustafa of Tamzara Travel in Doğubeyazit for the lift; Andante Travels in the UK for giving me the opportunity to visit a wonderful array of ancient sites across Turkey; Phil Buckley and Ufuk of Bougainville Travel in Kaş; Prof. Trevor Watkins, inspirational archeologist and mentor; Anne Louise and Muzaffer in Patara and Marion Tuohy and Halil in Kalkan; Doug, my eldest offspring for company on the road and more than a little assistance, my youngest offspring Jake for roadtrip company, step-son James for some valuable help and his sis Rhiannon for alternative 'yoof' views on Turkey; my co-author Marc for invaluable support; Greg Ward for his thorough and supportive editing; and finally Lem, my companion on the road and in all else.

Zoe Smith: Thanks to Jan from All About Alanya magazine for insider tips on Alanya; Şirin at Rain Hotel, Kızkalesi, for going above and beyond; İbrahim at Lale Hostel, Eğirdir, for hospitality and unparalleled local knowledge; Joanne and Özgür from Alia for their spirited introduction to Isparta's roses; Turan Kıraç for unrivalled guide services, skilled driving and aside dessert in Cappadocia; Middle Earth Travel and guide Gokhan; İhsan at Kookaburra, Göreme; Euphrates Travel; Kirkit Voyage; Deniz, Aziz & Şehmus at Özmen Pension for providing a home away from home in Antalya; and Terry Richardson for his ever-encouraging mentorship.

Martin Zatko: First and foremost, thanks to Ali and Asim for their assistance through Anatolia – great travel companions whose insights, humour and patience were sincerely appreciated. Thanks also to Seda for some wonderful Ottoman hospitality in Şirince, as well as Hasan in Kuşadası, Robert Lorimer in Selçuk, Zeynep in Alaçatı, Idris and Gizem in Bodrum, Solenne in Selimiye, Ogun in Datça, Mehmet in Pamukkale, and sister Nicole for flying out to join me in Kars (of all places). Lastly, thanks to the staff at each and every restaurant that I covered... gaining weight has never been so pleasurable.

Readers' updates

Thanks to all the readers who have taken the time to write in with comments and suggestions (and apologies if we've inadvertently omitted or misspelt anyone's name):

Mark Abbott, Archie Bowman, Jean-Luc Bretton, Barry Carmody, Antonia Cevizli, Clive Collins, Andy Conner, Alexander Goldsmith, Joan Grainger, Miriam Hare, Melanie and David Hook, June Johnson, Meline Koruk, Fabiani Milani, Alan Sheppard and Wendy Vale.

Photo credits

All photos © Rough Guides except the following:
(Key: a-above; b-below/bottom; c-centre; f-far; l-left; r-right; t-top)

p.1 Getty Images: Jon Arnold
p.2 Getty Images: Gavin Hellier
p.4 Getty Images: Flickr RM
p.7 Axiom Photographic Agency: Bertrand Gardel (t); Getty Images: Steve Outram (br, bl)
p.8 Getty Images: Scott R Barbour
p.9 Alamy: Dennis Cox (b); Images & Stories (c); Getty Images: Andrea Pistolesi (t)
p.10 Alamy: Hemis
p.11 4Corners: Simeone Giovanni (b); Axiom Photographic Agency: Ellen Rooney (t)
p.12 Alamy: Funkyfood London – Paul Williams
p.14 Getty Images: Christopher Pillitz

p.15 Alamy: Frans Sellies (t); Getty Images: Jane Sweeney (c)
p.16 Axiom Photographic Agency: R Valterza (t)
p.17 Alamy: Ivan Vdovin (bl); Rawdon Wyatt (tl); Corbis: Bob Krist (br); Robert Landau (tr)
p.18 Alamy: Peter Horree (tl); Getty Images: Ken Gillham (tr); Mary Sward (c); Jane Sweeney (b)
p.19 Alamy: funkyfood London – Paul Williams (b); Getty Images: Salvator Barki (t)
p.20 Alamy: blickwinkel (b); Jan Csernoch (t)
p.21 Alamy: Imagebroker (b); Ali Kabas (t); Getty Images: Gavin Hellier (c)
p.22 Alamy: Michele Burgess (t); Getty Images: Demetrio Carrasco (b); Ahmet Gul (cr)

ndex

Maps are marked in grey

Y

Z

Map symbols

The symbols below are used on maps throughout the book

✈	Airport	♜	Castle	💦	Waterfall	♟	Church (regional maps)
★	Bus/taxi stop	⊠	Gate	⛷	Skiing	⇨	Church (town maps)
P	Parking	〽	Mountain range	⛪	Monastery	✡	Synagogue
M	Metro stop	▲	Mountain peak	⊙	Statue	🕌	Mosque
T	Tram stop		Cliff	🗼	Lighthouse	⬭	Stadium
🚢	Boat		Gorge	🏛	Monument		Building
♦	Point of interest		Hill Shading	🏛	Museum		Park
@	Internet access	〰	Spa	⛺	Campsite		Beach
ⓘ	Tourist office	🏔	Cave	🚻	Toilet		Christian cemetery
✉	Post office	∴	Ruins	🍇	Winery		Muslim cemetery
✚	Hospital		Marshland		Wall		
🏊	Swimming pool	✕	Mountain pass		Ferry route		

Listings key

■	Accommodation
●	Restaurant
■	Bar/café/club/nightlife/music venue
●	Shop

CANYONING

MOUNTAIN BIKE

PARAGLIDING

SEAKAYAK

DIVING

TREKKING

The Adventure Capital of the Med

info@bougainville-turkey.com

www.bougainville-turkey.com